ORDER FORM

Prices are for current editions only.
Call 1-800-FILMBKS or 213/471-8066 for more information.

YES! PLEASE SEND THE FOLLOWING BOOKS:

QTY.	ANNUAL DIRECTORIES	PRICE	CA. TAX	TOTAL
_____	FILM DIRECTORS—8th Ed.	$59.95	$4.05	$_____
_____	PRODS/STUDIOS/ AGENTS & CASTING DIRECTORS—2nd Ed.	29.95	2.02	$_____
_____	CINEMATOGRAPHERS PRODUCTION DESIGNERS COSTUME DESIGNERS & FILM EDITORS—2nd Ed.	29.95	2.02	$_____
_____	FILM WRITERS—2nd Ed.	29.95	2.02	$_____
_____	FILM COMPOSERS—1st Ed.	29.95	2.02	$_____
_____	TV WRITERS—2nd Ed.	39.95	2.70	$_____
_____	TV DIRECTORS - 1st Ed.	29.95	2.02	$_____
_____	FILM ACTORS GUIDE—1st Ed.	29.95	2.02	$_____
_____	SPECIAL EFFECTS & STUNTS—1st Ed.	24.95	1.68	$_____

SUBTOTAL $________
ADD IN SHIPPING $________
TOTAL ORDER $________

UPS SHIPPING CHARGES CONT. USA/CANADA		
First Directory	$5.50	$10.00
Add'l. Directory	$3.00	$ 5.00

SHIPPING CHARGES (Overseas)	AIRMAIL	SURFACE
Film Directors	$45.00	$12.50
Other Directories	$30.00	$10.00

For Faster Service
Call 213/471-8066 (CA) or
1/800-FILMBKS

FAX ORDERS ACCEPTED: 213/471-4969

PAYMENT IS BY:

Check _____ Money Order_____ Visa_____ MC ____ AMEX________
Card No.________________________________Exp. Date________
Signature____
(exactly as it appears on your card)

SHIP BOOKS TO:

NAME____
COMPANY______________________ PHONE (very imp't.!)______________
ADDRESS ____
CITY/STATE/ZIP____

ORDER FORM

Prices are for current editions only.
Call 1-800-FILMBKS or 213/471-8066 for more information.

YES! PLEASE SEND THE FOLLOWING BOOKS:

QTY.	ANNUAL DIRECTORIES	PRICE	CA. TAX	TOTAL
_____	FILM DIRECTORS—8th Ed.	$59.95	$4.05	$_____
_____	PRODS/STUDIOS/ AGENTS & CASTING DIRECTORS—2nd Ed.	29.95	2.02	$_____
_____	CINEMATOGRAPHERS PRODUCTION DESIGNERS COSTUME DESIGNERS & FILM EDITORS—2nd Ed.	29.95	2.02	$_____
_____	FILM WRITERS—2nd Ed.	29.95	2.02	$_____
_____	FILM COMPOSERS—1st Ed.	29.95	2.02	$_____
_____	TV WRITERS—2nd Ed.	39.95	2.70	$_____
_____	TV DIRECTORS - 1st Ed.	29.95	2.02	$_____
_____	FILM ACTORS GUIDE—1st Ed.	29.95	2.02	$_____
_____	SPECIAL EFFECTS & STUNTS—1st Ed.	24.95	1.68	$_____

SUBTOTAL $________
ADD IN SHIPPING $________
TOTAL ORDER $________

UPS SHIPPING CHARGES CONT. USA/CANADA		
First Directory	$5.50	$10.00
Add'l. Directory	$3.00	$ 5.00

SHIPPING CHARGES (Overseas)	AIRMAIL	SURFACE
Film Directors	$45.00	$12.50
Other Directories	$30.00	$10.00

For Faster Service
Call 213/471-8066 (CA) or
1/800-FILMBKS

FAX ORDERS ACCEPTED: 213/471-4969

PAYMENT IS BY:

Check _____ Money Order_____ Visa_____ MC ____ AMEX________
Card No.________________________________Exp. Date________
Signature____
(exactly as it appears on your card)

SHIP BOOKS TO:

NAME____
COMPANY______________________ PHONE (very imp't.!)______________
ADDRESS ____
CITY/STATE/ZIP____

ORDER FORM

Prices are for current editions only.
Call 1-800-FILMBKS or 213/471-8066 for more information.

YES! PLEASE SEND THE FOLLOWING BOOKS:

QTY.	ANNUAL DIRECTORIES	PRICE	CA. TAX	TOTAL
_____	FILM DIRECTORS—8th Ed.	$59.95	$4.05	$_____
_____	PRODS/STUDIOS/ AGENTS & CASTING DIRECTORS—2nd Ed.	29.95	2.02	$_____
_____	CINEMATOGRAPHERS PRODUCTION DESIGNERS COSTUME DESIGNERS & FILM EDITORS—2nd Ed.	29.95	2.02	$_____
_____	FILM WRITERS—2nd Ed.	29.95	2.02	$_____
_____	FILM COMPOSERS—1st Ed.	29.95	2.02	$_____
_____	TV WRITERS—2nd Ed.	39.95	2.70	$_____
_____	TV DIRECTORS - 1st Ed.	29.95	2.02	$_____
_____	FILM ACTORS GUIDE—1st Ed.	29.95	2.02	$_____
_____	SPECIAL EFFECTS & STUNTS—1st Ed.	24.95	1.68	$_____

SUBTOTAL $________
ADD IN SHIPPING $________
TOTAL ORDER $________

UPS SHIPPING CHARGES CONT. USA/CANADA		
First Directory	$5.50	$10.00
Add'l. Directory	$3.00	$ 5.00

SHIPPING CHARGES (Overseas)	AIRMAIL	SURFACE
Film Directors	$45.00	$12.50
Other Directories	$30.00	$10.00

For Faster Service
Call 213/471-8066 (CA) or
1/800-FILMBKS

FAX ORDERS ACCEPTED: 213/471-4969

PAYMENT IS BY:

Check _____ Money Order_____ Visa_____ MC ____ AMEX________
Card No.________________________________Exp. Date________
Signature____
(exactly as it appears on your card)

SHIP BOOKS TO:

NAME____
COMPANY______________________ PHONE (very imp't.!)______________
ADDRESS ____
CITY/STATE/ZIP____

ORDER FORM

Prices are for current editions only.
Call 1-800-FILMBKS or 213/471-8066 for more information.

YES! PLEASE SEND THE FOLLOWING BOOKS:

QTY.	ANNUAL DIRECTORIES	PRICE	CA. TAX	TOTAL
_____	FILM DIRECTORS—8th Ed.	$59.95	$4.05	$_____
_____	PRODS/STUDIOS/ AGENTS & CASTING DIRECTORS—2nd Ed.	29.95	2.02	$_____
_____	CINEMATOGRAPHERS PRODUCTION DESIGNERS COSTUME DESIGNERS & FILM EDITORS—2nd Ed.	29.95	2.02	$_____
_____	FILM WRITERS—2nd Ed.	29.95	2.02	$_____
_____	FILM COMPOSERS—1st Ed.	29.95	2.02	$_____
_____	TV WRITERS—2nd Ed.	39.95	2.70	$_____
_____	TV DIRECTORS - 1st Ed.	29.95	2.02	$_____
_____	FILM ACTORS GUIDE—1st Ed.	29.95	2.02	$_____
_____	SPECIAL EFFECTS & STUNTS—1st Ed.	24.95	1.68	$_____

SUBTOTAL $________
ADD IN SHIPPING $________
TOTAL ORDER $________

UPS SHIPPING CHARGES CONT. USA/CANADA		
First Directory	$5.50	$10.00
Add'l. Directory	$3.00	$ 5.00

SHIPPING CHARGES (Overseas)	AIRMAIL	SURFACE
Film Directors	$45.00	$12.50
Other Directories	$30.00	$10.00

For Faster Service
Call 213/471-8066 (CA) or
1/800-FILMBKS

FAX ORDERS ACCEPTED: 213/471-4969

PAYMENT IS BY:

Check _____ Money Order_____ Visa_____ MC ____ AMEX________
Card No.________________________________Exp. Date________
Signature____
(exactly as it appears on your card)

SHIP BOOKS TO:

NAME____
COMPANY______________________ PHONE (very imp't.!)______________
ADDRESS ____
CITY/STATE/ZIP____

NO POSTAGE
NECESSARY IF
MAILED IN THE
UNITED STATES

BUSINESS REPLY CARD

FIRST CLASS PERMIT NO. 4842, BEVERLY HILLS, CA.

POSTAGE WILL BE PAID BY:

LONE EAGLE PUBLISHING CO.
9903 Santa Monica Blvd. #204
Beverly Hills, CA 90212-9942

NO POSTAGE
NECESSARY IF
MAILED IN THE
UNITED STATES

BUSINESS REPLY CARD

FIRST CLASS PERMIT NO. 4842, BEVERLY HILLS, CA.

POSTAGE WILL BE PAID BY:

LONE EAGLE PUBLISHING CO.
9903 Santa Monica Blvd. #204
Beverly Hills, CA 90212-9942

NO POSTAGE
NECESSARY IF
MAILED IN THE
UNITED STATES

BUSINESS REPLY CARD

FIRST CLASS PERMIT NO. 4842, BEVERLY HILLS, CA.

POSTAGE WILL BE PAID BY:

LONE EAGLE PUBLISHING CO.
9903 Santa Monica Blvd. #204
Beverly Hills, CA 90212-9942

NO POSTAGE
NECESSARY IF
MAILED IN THE
UNITED STATES

BUSINESS REPLY CARD

FIRST CLASS PERMIT NO. 4842, BEVERLY HILLS, CA.

POSTAGE WILL BE PAID BY:

LONE EAGLE PUBLISHING CO.
9903 Santa Monica Blvd. #204
Beverly Hills, CA 90212-9942

FILM COMPOSERS

GUIDE

First Edition

FILM COMPOSERS

GUIDE

First Edition

Compiled and Edited by Steven C. Smith

LONE EAGLE

FILM COMPOSERS GUIDE
First Edition

LONE EAGLE PUBLISHING CO.
9903 Santa Monica Blvd.
Beverly Hills, CA 90212
213/471-8066

Printed in the United States of America

Book designed by Liz Ridenour and Heidi Frieder

This book was entirely typeset using an Apple Macintosh Plus, Apple Macintosh Two, LaserwriterPlus, Microsoft Word and Aldus Pagemaker.

Printed by McNaughton & Gunn, Saline, Michigan 48176

ISBN: 0-943728-36-3

NOTE: We have made every reasonable effort to ensure that the information contained herein is as accurate as possible. However, errors and omissions are sure to occur. We would appreciate your notifying us of any which you may find.

* Lone Eagle Publishing is a division of Lone Eagle Productions, Inc.

LONE EAGLE PUBLISHING STAFF
Publishers .... Joan V. Singleton
Ralph S. Singleton
Editorial Director .... Bethann Wetzel
Advertising Director .... Lori Copeland
Customer Service .... Alain Bismut
Computer Consultant .... Glenn Osako
Art Director .... Heidi Frieder

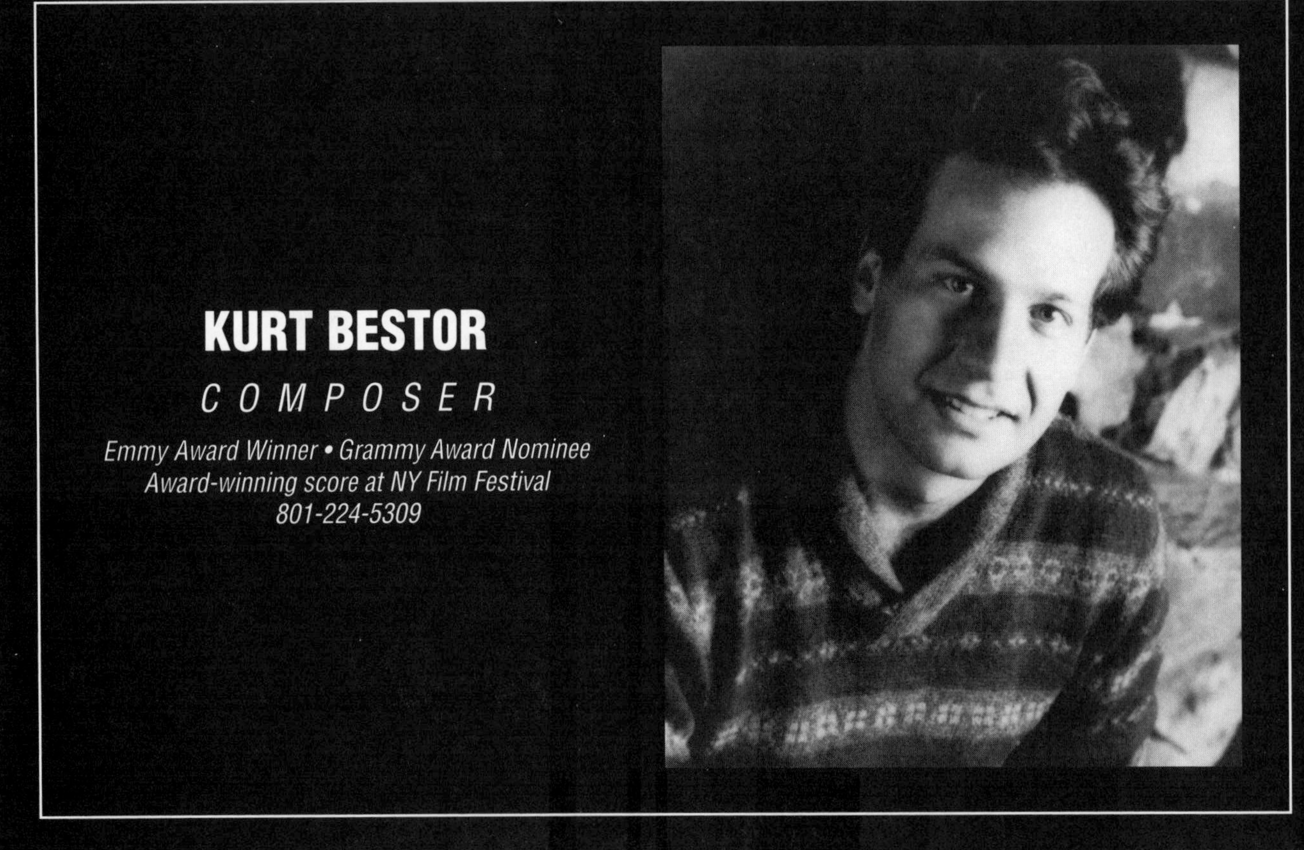

KURT BESTOR
COMPOSER
Emmy Award Winner • Grammy Award Nominee
Award-winning score at NY Film Festival
801-224-5309

LETTER FROM THE PUBLISHERS

It is with great pride and pleasure that we bring this first edition of the newest member of Lone Eagle's line of annual directories: **FILM COMPOSERS GUIDE**. We have been expanding our interests into the various areas of film and television-making—both above- and below-the-line, and have now created a directory which we feel will cross over into the areas of the theatre and the music industry.

Having spent a summer working on a film, we both gained an enormous respect for the part of a film which many people take for granted: the music. The right music can truly be as important as the right actor, the right script, the right location. It can make us jump out of our seats when the "scary" parts are coming, get teary-eyed when the lovers have to part, or help us laugh till the tears are rolling down our cheeks. If you have any doubts about this, try watching a few of your favorite movies with the sound turned off during a chase scene—doesn't it seem a little boring without the music?

Steve Smith is a true aficionado of film compositions and we truly feel he would have compiled all this information even if we hadn't published it! We know you will appreciate all the hard work he has put into this, but, as always, we welcome your comments—pro or con. For those of you listed in this directory, please help us keep your listings current by including us on your mailing (or fax) lists with credits and changes of addresses, agents, vital information, etc.

We thank you for your support and patronage.

Joan V. Singleton Ralph S. Singleton

Joan V. Singleton and Ralph S. Singleton
Publishers

The Biggest Films Of 1990 Have One Thing In Common

BACK TO THE FUTURE PART II	Alan Silvestri (BMI)
BACK TO THE FUTURE PART III	Alan Silvestri (BMI)
BIRD ON A WIRE	Hans Zimmer (PRS/BMI)
BONFIRE OF THE VANITIES	Dave Grusin (BMI)
DANCES WITH WOLVES	John Barry (BMI)
DAYS OF THUNDER	Hans Zimmer (PRS/BMI)
DICK TRACY	Danny Elfman (BMI)
DIE HARD 2	Michael Kamen (BMI)
DRIVING MISS DAISY	Hans Zimmer (PRS/BMI)
EDWARD SCISSORHANDS	Danny Elfman (BMI)
FLATLINERS	James Newton Howard (BMI)
HAVANA	Dave Grusin (BMI)
HOME ALONE	John Williams (BMI)
HUNT FOR RED OCTOBER	Basil Poledouris (BMI)
KINDERGARTEN COP	Randy Edelman (BMI)
LOOK WHO'S TALKING TOO	David Kitay (BMI)
PREDATOR II	Alan Silvestri (BMI)
PRESUMED INNOCENT	John Williams (BMI)
PRETTY WOMAN	James Newton Howard (BMI)
TEENAGE MUTANT NINJA TURTLES	John DuPrez (PRS/BMI)
THE RUSSIA HOUSE	Jerry Goldsmith (BMI)
THE SHELTERING SKY	Ryuichi Sakamoto (JASRA/BMI)
THREE MEN AND A LITTLE LADY	James Newton Howard (BMI)
TOTAL RECALL	Jerry Goldsmith (BMI)

Congratulations to our composers whose scores contributed to a record-breaking season

TABLE OF CONTENTS

INTRODUCTION

"We must use the music of Johannes Brahms in this film," insisted the producer (his name, alas, lost to history). "Bring Brahms himself to Hollywood to conduct it."

A tall order, even for Hollywood; but the producer's demand raises a good point. In the days of the silents, Brahms, Wagner and other pre-ASCAP masters were the world's most popular "film composers," their music used by improvising keyboardists everywhere. Gradually, living composers turned their hands to film music with increasing sophistication, and an exciting new genre was created.

Film scoring has always been, to some degree, a collaborative enterprise; but today it is perhaps more difficult than ever to determine who wrote a film's score. Sharing screen time with the composer(s) you'll find orchestrators, music supervisors, songwriters and music producers. In the shadows are uncredited men and women who, rumor has it, "actually" did the work. Consequently, the editing of this book involved a number of choices.

I have attempted to provide accurate, concise listings for the work of film composers—the individuals most responsible for what is commonly (if not always accurately) called "background music." An example or two may be helpful:

Despite the number of films based on his musicals, Richard Rodgers is credited in these pages with exactly one film score: 1932's *LOVE ME TONIGHT* the only film for which he actually *composed* the underscoring. (It was Irwin Kostal, for example, who scored the film of *THE SOUND OF MUSIC* using Rodgers' melodies.) And although you may leave *CASABLANCA* humming *As Time Goes By*, it was Max Steiner who wrote the film's original score, which incorporated the 1931 tune. Steiner receives sole credit here.

Generally I have followed a film's official credits in my listings...with a few exceptions. (For example: considering composer John Barry's long association with the James Bond series, it seemed inaccurate to ignore his contribution—albeit uncredited—to the first Bond film, *DR. NO.*) Similarly I have avoided listing film scores that were never used...with a few important exceptions, always noted (e.g., Bernard Herrmann's discarded score for *TORN CURTAIN*—the film that ended that composer's long relationship with Hitchcock.)

Winners and nominees of Academy and Emmy awards are noted in both the principal section, Composers Listings, and in Notable Composers of the Past. Indexes of film titles and their composers follow both sections; but since a film may have multiple composers, please consult the actual entry for a complete listing.

In addition to their scoring duties, composers have occasionally shown up onscreen as well—not just typecast as intense conductors (Max Steiner in *THE HALF-NAKED TRUITH*, Bernard Herrmann in *THE MAN WHO KNEW TOO MUCH*) but also in more challenging roles (Jerry Goldsmith as the angry yoghurt shop customer in *GREMLINS II*). As tacit encouragement of this nontraditional casting, I note these appearances wherever possible.

This book's format and criteria are based on its reference predecessors at Lone Eagle, chiefly **Michael Singer's FILM DIRECTORS: A Complete Guide**. A brief summary:

FILM CRITERIA:
FEATURES: A running time of 60 minutes or longer (with some exceptions for older films).

TELEFEATURES: On commercial television, an air time of 90 minutes to 4-1/2 hours. (Without commercials, a 90-minute television program runs approximately 72 minutes—the length of a short feature—and a 4-1/2 hour "mini-series" is about 3 hours and 45 minutes, the length of such long features as *GONE WITH THE WIND* and *HEAVEN'S GATE*.)

TELEVISION MINI-SERIES: On commercial television, an air time of 4-1/2 hours or longer; 4 hours or more on non-commercial television. Videotaped (as opposed to filmed) television dramas are not included.

TITLES: American release titles are used with alternate titles following in italics. In case of films from English-speaking foreign countries, a title in italics usually represents the original title in that country if different from its American release title. For foreign films distributed in the U.S., the American title is listed first, followed by the foreign-language title.

DISTRIBUTORS AND PRODUCTION COMPANIES: Original American distributors of feature films are listed. For foreign films that received no U.S. distribution, the original distributors or production companies are included wherever possible. Telefeatures and mini-series are identified with the names of their production companies. In a few cases, I was unable to find releasing companies for certain (usually less than mainstream) films. Any information on these from readers is welcomed.

YEAR OF RELEASE: In the case of foreign films, the original year of release is provided wherever possible.

Thanks are due to the many composers and agencies that cooperated in the preparation of this book; Doreen Ringer, Michael McGehee and Scott Willingham at BMI; Nick Redman; and the staff at the Academy of Motion Picture Arts and Sciences Margaret Herrick Library. Special thanks to David Kraft and Richard Kraft whose knowledge and love of the subject helped keep me on course; and to the excellent staff at Lone Eagle, especially Joan Singleton, Bethann Wetzel, Steve LuKanic and Lori Copeland. A grateful nod also to my predecessors in documenting this subject, Clifford McCarty and James L. Limbacher.

Let us know what you think of the **FILM COMPOSERS GUIDE**. And to anyone out there who's thinking of compiling an Ennio Morricone filmography: kids...don't try this at home.

Steven C. Smith

COMPOSERS

LISTINGS

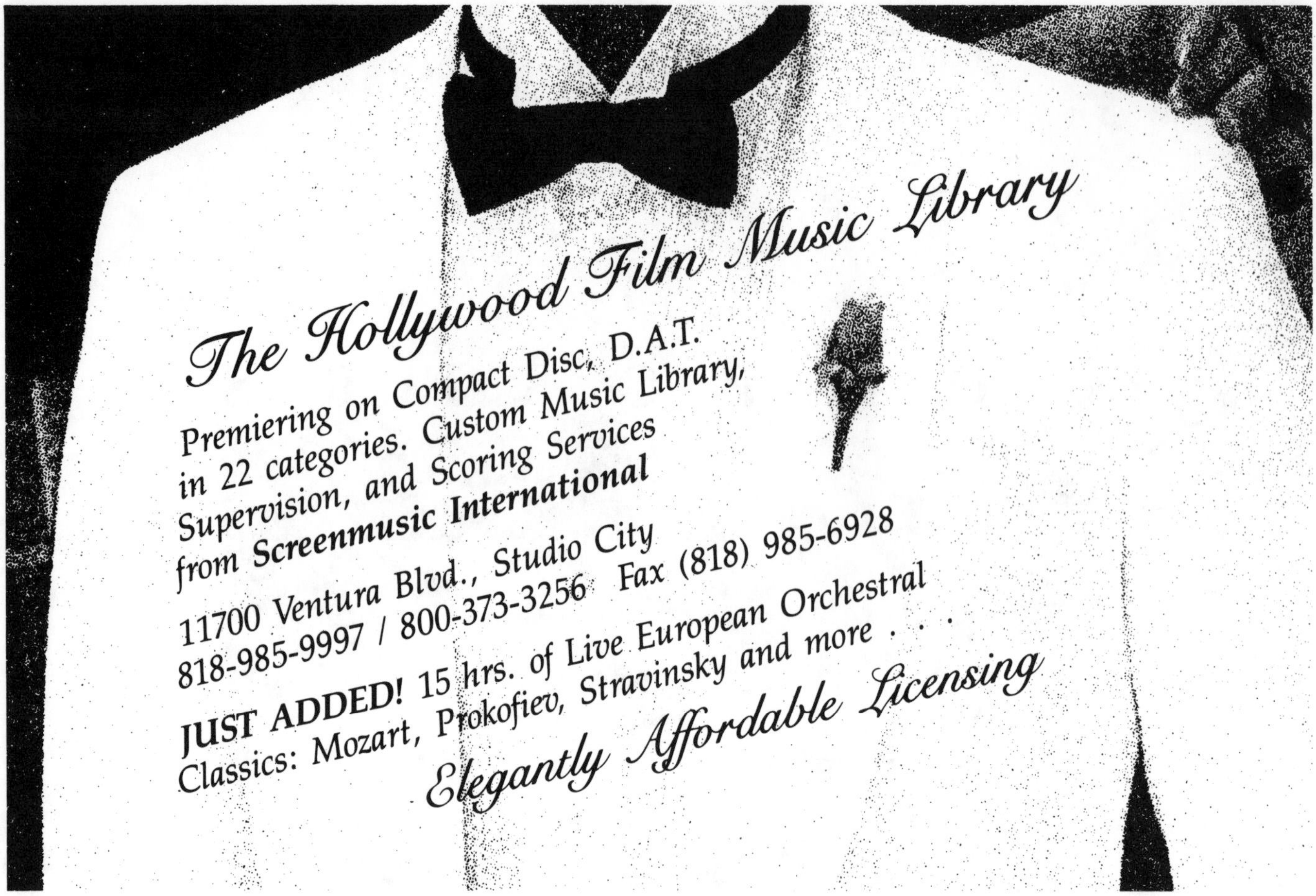
The Hollywood Film Music Library
Premiering on Compact Disc, D.A.T.
in 22 categories. Custom Music Library,
Supervision, and Scoring Services
from Screenmusic International
11700 Ventura Blvd., Studio City
818-985-9997 / 800-373-3256 Fax (818) 985-6928
JUST ADDED! 15 hrs. of Live European Orchestral
Classics: Mozart, Prokofiev, Stravinsky and more . . .
Elegantly Affordable Licensing

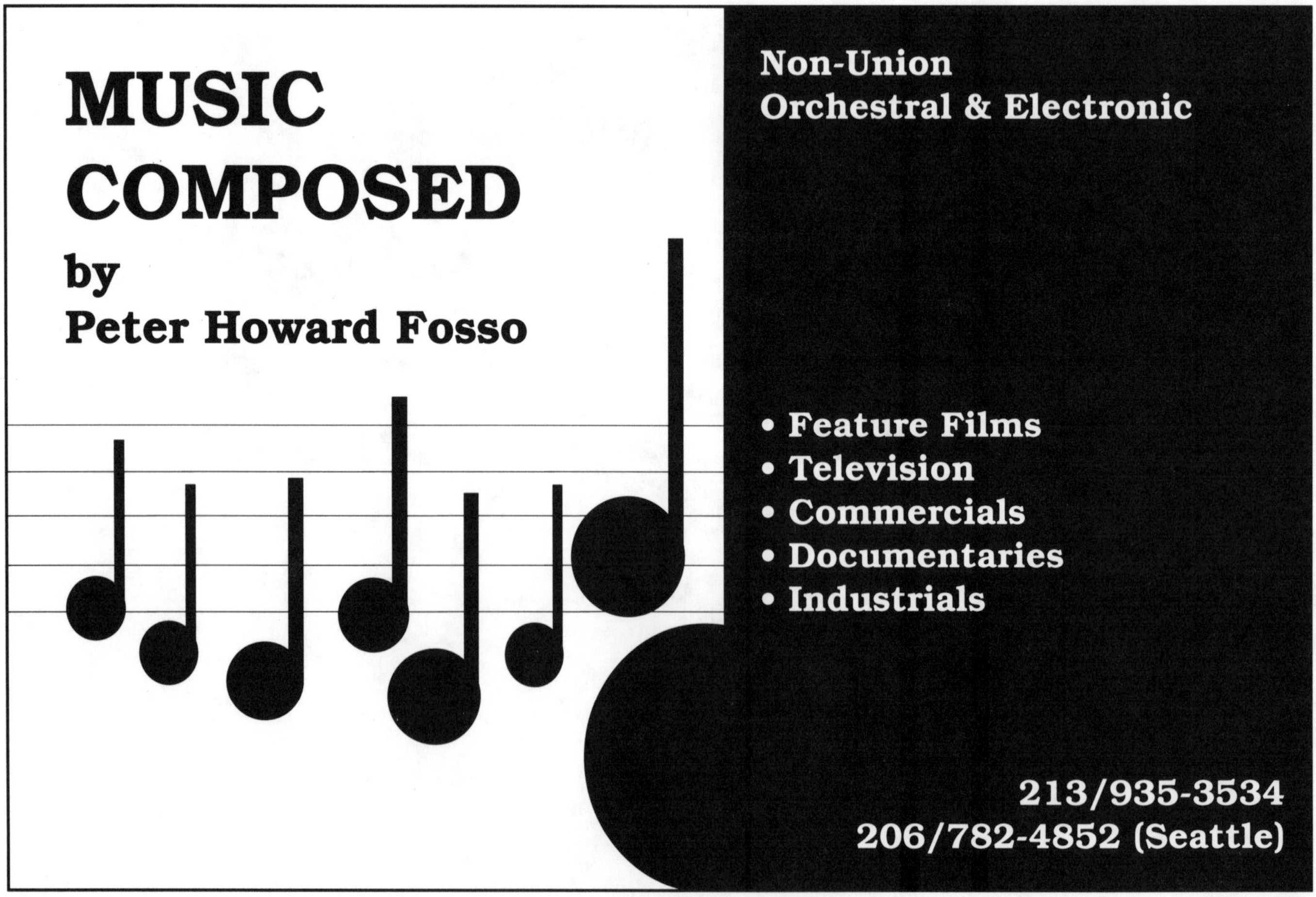
MUSIC
COMPOSED
by
Peter Howard Fosso
Non-Union
Orchestral & Electronic
• Feature Films
• Television
• Commercials
• Documentaries
• Industrials
213/935-3534
206/782-4852 (Seattle)

KEY TO ABBREVIATIONS

(TF) = TELEFEATURE
Motion pictures made for television with an on-air running time of 1-1/2 hours to 4-1/2 hours on commercial television; or 1 hour to 4 hours on non-commercial television.

(CTF) = CABLE TELEFEATURE
Motion pictures made for cable television with an on-air running time of 1 hour to 4 hours.

(MS) = MINISERIES
Motion pictures made for television with an on-air running time of 4-1/2 hours and more on commercial television; or 4 hours or more on non-commercial television.

(CMS) = CABLE MINISERIES
Motion pictures made for cable television with an on-air running time of 4 hours or more.

(FD) = FEATURE DOCUMENTARY
Documentary films made for theatrical distribution or feature length (1 or more hours.)

(TD) = TELEVISION DOCUMENTARY
Documentary films made for television of feature length (1-1/2 hours or more on commercial television, 1 or more hours on non-commercial television.)

(CTD) = CABLE TELEVISION DOCUMENTARY
Documentary films made for cable television of feature length (1 or more hours.)

(AF) = ANIMATED FEATURE

(ATF) = ANIMATED TELEFEATURE

KEY TO SYMBOLS

★ after a film title denotes a directorial Academy Award nomination.

★★ after a film title denotes a directorial Academy Award win.

☆ after a film title denotes a directorial Emmy Award nomination.

☆☆ after a film title denotes a directorial Emmy Award win.

ORIGINAL SCORE
ACADEMY AWARDS AND NOMINATIONS
1977-1989

★★ = WINNER IN CATEGORY

1977
CLOSE ENCOUNTERS OF THE THIRD KIND .... John Williams
JULIA .... Georges Delerue
MOHAMMAD - MESSENGER OF GOD .... Maurice Jarre
THE SPY WHO LOVED ME .... Marvin Hamlisch
STAR WARS .... John Williams★★

1978
THE BOYS FROM BRAZIL .... Jerry Goldsmith
DAYS OF HEAVEN .... Ennio Morricone
HEAVEN CAN WAIT .... Dave Grusin
MIDNIGHT EXPRESS .... Giorgio Moroder ★★
SUPERMAN .... John Williams

1979
THE AMITYVILLE HORROR .... Lalo Schifrin
THE CHAMP .... Dave Grusin
A LITTLE ROMANCE .... Georges Delerue ★★
STAR TREK - THE MOTION PICTURE .... Jerry Goldsmith
10 .... Henry Mancini

1980
ALTERED STATES .... Jogn Corigliani
THE ELEPHANT MAN .... John Morris
THE EMPIRE STRIKES BACK .... John Williams
FAME .... Michael Gore ★★
TESS .... Philippe Sarde

1981
CHARIOTS OF FIRE .... Vangelis ★★
DRAGONSLAYER .... Alex North
ON GOLDEN POND .... Dave Grusin
RAGTIME .... Randy Newman
RAIDERS OF THE LOST ARK .... John Williams

1982
E.T. THE EXTRA-TERRESTRIAL .... John Williams ★★
GANDHI .... Ravi Shankar and George Fenton
AN OFFICER AND A GENTLEMAN .... Jack Nitzsche
POLTERGEIST .... Jerry Goldsmith
SOPHIE'S CHOICE .... Marvin Hamlisch

1983
CROSS CREEK .... Leonard Rosenman
RETURN OF THE JEDI .... John Williams
THE RIGHT STUFF .... Bill Conti ★★
TERMS OF ENDEARMENT .... Michael Gore
UNDER FIRE .... Jerry Goldsmith

1984
INDIANA JONES AND THE TEMPLE OF DOOM .... John Williams
THE NATURAL .... Randy Newman
A PASSAGE TO INDIA .... Maurice Jarre ★★
THE RIVER .... John Williams
UNDER THE VOLCANO .... Alex North

1985
AGNES OF GOD .... Georges Delerue
THE COLOR PURPLE .... Quincy Jones, Jeremy Lubbock, Rod Temperton, Caiphus Semenya, Andrae Crouch, Chris Boardman, Jorge Calandrelli, Joel Rosenbaum, Fred Steiner, Jack Hayes, Jerry Hey and Randy Kerber
OUT OF AFRICA .... John Barry ★★
SILVERADO .... Bruce Boughton
WITNESS .... Maurice Jarre

1986
ALIENS .... James Horner
HOOSIERS .... Jerry Goldsmith
THE MISSION .... Ennio Morricone
'ROUND MIDNIGHT .... Herbie Hancock ★★
STAR TREK IV: THE VOYAGE HOME .... Leonard Rosenman

1987
CRY FREEDOM .... George Fenton and Jonas Gwangwa
EMPIRE OF THE SUN .... John Williams
THE LAST EMPEROR .... Ryuichi Sakamoto, Dave Byrne and Cong Su ★★
THE WITCHES OF EASTWICK .... John Williams
THE UNTOUCHABLES .... Ennio Morricone

1988
THE ACCIDENTAL TOURIST .... John Williams
DANGEROUS LIASONS .... George Fenton
GORILLAS IN THE MIST .... Maurice Jarre
THE MILAGRO BEANFIELD WAR .... Dave Grusin ★★
RAIN MAN .... Hans Zimmer

1989
BORN ON THE FOURTH OF JULY .... John Williams
THE FABULOUS BAKER BOYS .... Dave Grusin
FIELD OF DREAMS .... James Horner
INDIANA JONES AND THE LAST CRUSADE .... John Williams
THE LITTLE MERMAID .... Alan Menken ★★

★★★★

MICHAEL ABENE
Contact: BMI - Los Angeles, 213/659-9109

GOODBYE NEW YORK Castle Hill Productions, 1985, U.S.-Israeli

AC/DC
Contact: APRA - Australia, 011-61-2-922-6422

MAXIMUM OVERDRIVE DEG, 1986

JACK ACKERMAN
Contact: ASCAP - Los Angeles, 213/466-7681

FACES Continental, 1968

STUART ADAMSON
Contact: PRS - London, England, 011-44-1-580-5544

RESTLESS NATIVES Thorn/EMI, 1985, British

JOHN ADDISON
b. March 16, 1920 - Surrey, England
Agent: Gorfaine-Schwartz - Burbank, 818/954-9500

THE OUTSIDER *THE GUINEA PIG* Pathe, 1948, British
SEVEN DAYS TO NOON Mayer-Kingsley, 1950, British
POOL OF LONDON Universal, 1951, British
THE LIGHT TOUCH MGM, 1951
HIGH TREASON Rank, 1952, British
THE HOUR OF 13 MGM, 1952, British
THE MAN BETWEEN United Artists, 1953, British
THE BLACK KNIGHT Columbia, 1954, British
TOUCH AND GO Rank, 1954, British
THAT LADY 20th Century Fox, 1954, British
THE COCKLESHELL HEROES Columbia, 1956, British
REACH FOR THE SKY Rank, 1956, British
PRIVATE'S PROGRESS DCA, 1956, British
THE SHIRALEE MGM, 1957, British
LUCKY JIM Kingsley International, 1957, British
THREE MEN IN A BOAT DCA, 1958, British
LOOK BACK IN ANGER Warner Bros., 1958, British
I WAS MONTY'S DOUBLE NTA Pictures, 1958, British
MAN IN A COCKED HAT *CARLTON BROWN OF THE F.O.* Show Corporation, 1960, British
SCHOOL FOR SCOUNDRELS Warner Bros., 1960, British
THE ENTERTAINER Continental, 1960, British
A TASTE OF HONEY Continental, 1962, British
THE LONELINESS OF THE LONG DISTANCE RUNNER Continental, 1962, British
TOM JONES ★★ Lopert, 1963, British
THE GIRL WITH GREEN EYES United Artists, 1964, British
THE LOVED ONE MGM, 1965
THE UNCLE Lennart, 1966, British
GUNS AT BATASI 20th Century Fox, 1964, British-U.S.
THE AMOROUS ADVENTURES OF MOLL FLANDERS Paramount, 1965, British
A FINE MADNESS Warner Bros., 1966
TIME LOST AND TIME REMEMBERED *I WAS HAPPY HERE* Continental, 1966, British
TORN CURTAIN Universal, 1966
THE HONEY POT United Artists, 1967, British-U.S.-Italian
SMASHING TIME Paramount, 1967, British
THE CHARGE OF THE LIGHT BRIGADE United Artists, 1968, British
BROTHERLY LOVE COUNTRY DANCE MGM, 1970, British
START THE REVOLUTION WITHOUT ME Warner Bros., 1970, British
CRY OF THE PENGUINS *MR. FORBUSH AND THE PENGUINS* EMI, 1971, British
SLEUTH ★ 20th Century Fox, 1972, British
DEAD CERT United Artists, 1973, British
LUTHER American Film Theatre, 1974
THE SEVEN PER CENT SOLUTION Universal, 1976
SWASHBUCKLER Universal, 1976
RIDE A WILD PONY Walt Disney Productions, 1976
A BRIDGE TOO FAR United Artists, 1977, British
JOSEPH ANDREWS Paramount, 1977, British
PEARL (TF) Silliphant-Konigsberg Productions/Warner Bros. TV, 1978
BLACK BEAUTY (MS) Universal TV, 1978
THE BASTARD (TF) Universal TV, 1978
LIKE NORMAL PEOPLE (TF) Christiana Productions, 20th Century Fox TV, 1979
REX STOUT'S NERO WOLFE (TF) Emmett Lavery, Jr. Productions/Paramount TV, 1979
CENTENNIAL (MS) Universal TV, 1980
HIGH POINT 1980, Canadian
MISTRESS OF PARADISE (TF) Lorimar Productions, 1981
THE PILOT Summit Features, 1981
I WAS A MAIL ORDER BRIDE (TF) Jaffe Productions/ Tuxedo Limited Productions/MGM TV, 1982
CHARLES AND DIANA: A ROYAL LOVE STORY (TF) St. Lorraine Productions, 1982
ELEANOR, FIRST LADY OF THE WORLD (TF) Murbill Productions/Embassy TV, 1982
GRACE QUIGLEY Cannon, 1984
AGATHA CHRISTIE'S 'THIRTEEN AT DINNER' (TF) Warner Bros. TV, 1985
CODE NAME: EMERALD MGM/UA, 1985
SOMETHING IN COMMON (TF) New World TV/Freyda Rothstein Productions/Littke-Grossbart Productions, 1986
AGATHA CHRISTIE'S 'DEAD MAN'S FOLLY' (TF) Warner Bros. TV, 1986, U.S.-British
BRIDE OF BOOGEDY (TF) Walt Disney TV, 1987
STRANGE VOICES (TF) Forrest Hills Productions/ Dacks-Geller Productions/TLC, 1987
BERYL MARKHAM: A SHADOW ON THE SUN (TF) Tamara Asseyev Productions/New World TV, 1988
THE PHANTOM OF THE OPERA (TF) ☆ Saban/Scherick Productions, 1990

LARRY ADLER
Contact: BMI - Los Angeles, 213/659-9109

GENEVIEVE ★ Universal, 1954, British
A CRY FROM THE STREETS Tudor, 1959, British
THE HELLIONS Columbia, 1962, British
THE HOOK MGM, 1963
THE GREAT CHASE Continental, 1963
A HIGH WIND IN JAMAICA 20th Century-Fox, 1965, British
KING AND COUNTRY Allied Artists, 1965, British

MARK ADLER
Contact: BMI - Los Angeles, 213/659-9109

BREAK OF DAWN Cinewest, 1988
EAT A BOWL OF TEA Columbia, 1989
LIFE IS CHEAP Far East Stars, 1989
SUPER CHIEF (FD) Direct Cinema Limited, 1990

ALFONSO AGULLO
Contact: Luis Mas, SGAE - New York, 212/752-7230

MONSTER ISLAND Fort Films, 1981, U.S.-Spanish

JEFFREY AINIS
DANGER USA Double-Helix

ROBERT ALCIVAR
Contact: BMI - Los Angeles, 213/659-9109

BUTTERFLIES ARE FREE Columbia, 1972
THE CRAZY WORLD OF JULUIS VROODER 20th Century-Fox, 1974
OLLY, OLLY, OXEN FREE Sanrio, 1978
ONE FROM THE HEART Columbia, 1982
HYSTERICAL co-composer with Robert O. Ragland, Embassy, 1983
THAT SECRET SUNDAY (TF) CBS Entertainment, 1986
NAKED LIE (TF) Shadowplay Films/Phoenix Entertainment Group, 1989
ROXANNE: THE PRIZE PULITZER (TF) Qintex Entertainment, 1989
BLIND WITNESS (TF) King-Phoenix Entertainment/ Victoria Principal Productions, 1989
SPARKS: THE PRICE OF PASSION (TF) Shadowplay Films/Victoria Principal Productions/King Phoenix Entertainment, 1990

VAN ALEXANDER
Contact: ASCAP - Los Angeles, 213/466-7681

THE ATOMIC KID Republic, 1954
THE TWINKLE IN GOD'S EYE Republic, 1955
JAGUAR Republic, 1956
WHEN GANGLAND STRIKES Republic, 1956
BABY FACE NELSON Allied Artists, 1957
ANDY HARDY COMES HOME MGM, 1958
THE BIG OPERATOR MGM, 1959
GIRLS TOWN *INNOCENT AND THE DAMNED* MGM, 1959
PLATINUM HIGH SCHOOL *TROUBLE AT 16* MGM, 1960
THE PRIVATE LIVES OF ADAM AND EVE Universal, 1960
SAFE AT HOME! Columbia, 1962
13 FRIGHTENED GIRLS Columbia, 1963
STRAIT-JACKET Columbia, 1964
I SAW WHAT YOU DID Universal, 1965
A TIME FOR KILLING Columbia, 1967

ERIC ALLAMAN
Agent: MCEG Management - Santa Monica, 213/315-7800

THE BATTLESHIP POTEMKIN composer of new score for 1925 silent film, Deutche Kinemathek
DOWN TWISTED Cannon, 1987
ANGEL III: THE FINAL CHAPTER New World, 1988

CAMERON ALLAN
Agent: CAA - Los Angeles, 213/288-4545

STIR Hoyts Distribution, 1980, Australian
MIDNITE SPARES Roadshow Australia, 1983, Australian
GOING SANE Sea Change Films, 1986, Australian
THE GOOD WIFE Atlantic Releasing Corporation, 1986, Australian
THE CLEAN MACHINE (TF) Kennedy-Miller, 1988, Australian
KOJAK (TF) Universal TV, 1989

WOODY ALLEN
(Allen Stewart Konigsberg)
b. December 1, 1935 - Brooklyn, New York
Agent: Sam Cohn, ICM - New York City, 212/556-6810
Personal Manager: Jack Rollins/Charles Joffe, 130 West 57th Street, New York, NY, 212/582-1940

SLEEPER United Artists, 1973

BYRON ALLRED
Contact: ASCAP - Los Angeles, 213/466-7681

DON'T ANSWER THE PHONE! Crown International, 1980

GERALD ALTERS
Contact: ASCAP - Los Angeles, 213/466-7681

YOUR PLACE OR MINE (TF) Finnegan Associates/ Poolhouse Productions, 1983

MINETTE ALTON
CHILDREN OF DIVORCE (TF) co-composer with Raoul Kraushaar, Christiana Productions/Marble Arch Productions, 1980

ALLAN ALPER
Contact: BMI - Los Angeles, 213/659-9109 or 818/348-8032

SUPERCHICK Crown, 1974
ON ANY SUNDAY II (FD) International Film Marketing, 1981

RON ALTBACH
Contact: ASCAP - Los Angeles, 213/466-7681

ALMOST SUMMER co-composer with Charles Lloyd, Universal, 1978

ED ALTON
b. May 29, 1955 - Hartford, Connecticut
Home: 5752 Murietta Ave., Van Nuys, CA 91401, 818/994-4809

MY DEMON LOVER additional music, New Line Cinema, 1987

DAVE ALVIN
Contact: BMI - Los Angeles, 213/659-9109

BORDER RADIO co-composer, Coyote Films, 1987

DAVID AMRAM
b. 1933
Contact: BMI - Los Angeles, 213/659-9109

ECHO OF AN ERA 1957
PULL MY DAISY G-String Productions, 1959
SPLENDOR IN THE GRASS Warner Bros., 1961
THE YOUNG SAVAGES United Artists, 1961
THE MANCHURIAN CANDIDATE United Artists, 1962
WE ARE YOUNG 1967
THE ARRANGEMENT Warner Bros., 1969

BENNY ANDERSEN
b. Sweden
Contact: STIM - Sweden, 011-46-8-783-8800

WHEN SVANTE DISAPPEARED Dagmar Distribution, 1976, Danish

LAURIE ANDERSON
Contact: BMI - Los Angeles, 213/659-9109

SOMETHING WILD co-composer with John Cale, Orion, 1986
SWIMMING TO CAMBODIA Cinecom, 1987

GERARD ANFOSSO
Contact: SACEM - France, 011-33-14-747-5650

VOYAGE TO GRAND TARTARIE *LE VOYAGE EN GRANDE TARTARIE* New Line Cinema, 1973, French
COUSIN, COUSINE Libra, 1975, French
THE BLUE COUNTRY *LE PAYS BLEU* Quartet, 1977, French
IT'S A LONG TIME THAT I'VE LOVED YOU *SOUPCON* Durham/Pike, 1979, French

PAUL F. ANTONELLI
Contact: MusiCum Laude - Los Angeles, 800/776-8932 or 213/660-5444

PRINCESS ACADEMY co-composer with David Wheatley, Weintraub Productions, 1987, U.S.-French-Yugoslav
THE WOMEN'S CLUB co-composer with David Wheatley, Weintraub-Cloverleaf/Scorsese Productions, 1987
CHINA O'BRIEN co-composer with David Wheatley, Golden Harvest, 1989, U.S.-Hong Kong
OUT OF THE DARK co-composer with David Wheatley, New Line Cinema, 1989

SEBASTIAN ARGOL
YOL Triumph/Columbia, 1982, Turkish-Swiss-West German

EDDIE ARKIN
Contact: BMI - Los Angeles, 213/659-9109

HARDBODIES 2 co-composer with Jay Levy, CineTel Films, 1986
MODERN GIRLS co-composer with Jay Levy, Atlantic Releasing Corporation, 1986
PRETTY SMART co-composer with Jay Levy, New World, 1987

MARTIN ARMIGER
Contact: APRA - Australia, 011-61-2-922-6422

SWEETIE Avenue Pictures, 1990, Australian

MICHAEL ARMSTRONG
SILENT NIGHT, DEADLY NIGHT PART II Silent Night Releasing Corp./Ascot Entertainment Group, 1987

MALCOLM ARNOLD
b. October 21, 1921 - Northampton, England
Contact: PRS - London, England, 011-44-1-580-5544

AVALANCHE PATROL (FD) 1947, British
CHARTING THE SEAS (FD) 1948, British
BADGER'S GREEN 1948, British
EVW'S (FD) 1949, British
THE FORBIDDEN STREET *BRITTANIA MEWS* 20th Century-Fox, 1949
EYE WITNESS YOUR WITNESS Eagle Lion, 1950, British
HOME TO DANGER Eros, 1951, British
NO HIGHWAY IN THE SKY *NO HIGHWAY* 20th Century-Fox, 1951, British
BREAKING THE SOUND BARRIER *THE SOUND BARRIER* United Artists, 1952, British
STOLEN FACE Exclusive Films, 1952, U.S.-British
WINGS OF DANGER *DEAD ON COURSE* Exclusive Films, 1952, British
THE RINGER British Lion, 1952, British
IT STARTED IN PARADISE Astor, 1952, British
CURTAIN UP General Film Distributors, 1952, British
HOME AT SEVEN *MURDER ON MONDAY* 1952, British
FOUR-SIDED TRIANGLE Exclusive Films, 1953, British
THE HOLLY AND THE IVY British Lion, 1953, British
THE CAPTAIN'S PARADISE British Lion, 1953, British
BREAK TO FREEDOM *ALBERT R.N.* United Artists, 1953, British
DEVIL ON HORSEBACK British Lion, 1953, British
TWIST OF FATE *THE BEAUTIFUL STRANGER* United Artists, 1954, British
YOU KNOW WHAT SAILORS ARE United Artists, 1954, British
THE SEA SHALL NOT HAVE THEM United Artists, 1954, British
THE SLEEPING TIGER Astor, 1954, British
HOBSON'S CHOICE United Artists, 1954, British
A PRIZE OF GOLD Columbia, 1954
THE CONSTANT HUSBAND British Lion, 1955, British
THE DEEP, BLUE SEA 20th Century-Fox, 1955, British
A WOMAN FOR JOE Rank Film Distributors, 1955, British
THE NIGHT MY NUMBER CAME UP General Film Distributors, 1955, British
I AM A CAMERA British Lion, 1955, British
MAN OF AFRICA Group 3/Eden, 1956
PORT AFRIQUE Columbia, 1956, British
HELL IN KOREA *A HILL IN KOREA* British Lion, 1956, British
TRAPEZE United Artists, 1956
1984 Columbia, 1956, British
PORTRAIT IN SMOKE Columbia, 1956
VALUE FOR MONEY Rank, 1957, British
BELLES OF ST. TRINIAN'S British Lion, 1957, British
THE BRIDGE ON THE RIVER KWAI ★★ Columbia, 1957, British
ISLAND IN THE SUN 20th Century-Fox, 1957
WICKED AS THEY COME Columbia, 1957, British
BLUE MURDER AT ST. TRINIAN'S British Lion, 1958, British

DUNKIRK MGM, 1958, British
THE INN OF THE SIXTH HAPPINESS 20th Century-Fox, 1958, British
THE KEY Columbia, 1958, British
THE ROOTS OF HEAVEN 20th Century-Fox, 1958
SOLOMON AND SHEBA United Artists, 1959
BOY AND THE BRIDGE Columbia, 1959
SUDDENLY LAST SUMMER co-composer with Buxton Orr, Columbia, 1960
THE ANGRY SILENCE Valiant, 1960, British
TUNES OF GLORY Lopert, 1960, British
PURE HELL OF ST. TRINIANS British Lion/Continental, 1961, British
OPERATION SNAFU American International, 1961, British
NO LOVE FOR JOHNNIE Embassy, 1961, British
WHISTLE DOWN THE WIND Pathe-America, 1962, British
LISA THE INSPECTOR 20th Century-Fox, 1962
THE LION 20th Century-Fox, 1962, British
NINE HOURS TO RAMA 20th Century-Fox, 1963, British-U.S.
TAMAHINE MGM, 1964, British
THE CHALK GARDEN Universal, 1964, British
THE THIN RED LINE Allied Artists, 1964
THE HEROES OF TELEMARK Columbia, 1965, British
THE GREAT ST. TRINIAN'S TRAIN ROBBERY British Lion, 1966, British
GYPSY GIRL *SKY WEST AND CROOKED* Rank/ Continental, 1966, British
AFRICA - TEXAS STYLE! Paramount, 1967, British-U.S.
THE RECKONING Columbia, 1969, British
DAVID COPPERFIELD (TF) Omnibus Productions/ Sagittarius Productions, 1970, British-U.S.

PETER ARNOW
Contact: ASCAP - Los Angeles, 213/466-7681

TORN APART Castle Hill, 1990

LEON ARONSON
EDDIE AND THE CRUISERS II: EDDIE LIVES co-composer with Marty Simon, Scotti Bros. Pictures/ Aurora Film Partners, 1989

BRUCE ARNSTSON
Contact: BMI - Los Angeles, 213/659-9109

ERNEST GOES TO JAIL co-composer with Kirby Shelstad, Buena Vista, 1990

EDUARD ARTEMYEV
Contact: VAAP - U.S.S.R., Telex: 871-411327

AT HOME AMONG STRANGERS 1974, Soviet
A SLAVE OF LOVE Cinema 5, 1976, Soviet
PLATANOV 1977, Soviet
SOLARIS Mosfilm, 1972, Soviet
STALKER New Yorker/Media Transactions Corporation, 1979, Soviet
SIBERIADE IFEX Film, 1979, Soviet
HOMER AND EDDIE King's Road Entertainment, 1989

GIL ASKEY
Contact: BMI - Los Angeles, 213/659-9109

DUMMY (TF) The Konigsberg Company/Warner Bros. TV, 1979

EDWIN ASTLEY
Contact: PRS - London, England, 011-44-1-580-5544

TO PARIS, WITH LOVE General Film Distributors, 1955, British
THE CASE OF THE MUKKINESE BATTLEHORN 1956, British
KILL HER GENTLY 1957, British
WISHING WELL INN 1958, British
IN THE WAKE OF A STRANGER 1958, British
THE GIANT BEHEMOTH 1959, British
THE MOUSE THAT ROARED Columbia, 1959, British
WOMAN EATER 1959, British
THE DAY THEY ROBBED THE BANK OF ENGLAND MGM, 1960, British
PASSPORT TO CHINA *VISA TO CANTON* Columbia, 1961, British
A MATTER OF WHO Herts Lion, 1962, British
THE PHANTOM OF THE OPERA Universal, 1962, British
DIGBY, THE BIGGEST DOG IN THE WORLD Cinerama Releasing Corporation, 1974, British

CHET ATKINS
Contact: BMI - Los Angeles, 213/659-9109

STROSZEK co-composer with Sonny Terry, New Yorker, 1977, West German

DAVID A. AXELROD
Contact: BMI - Los Angeles, 213/659-9109

CANNONBALL New World, 1976

ROY AYERS
Contact: ASCAP - Los Angeles, 213/466-7681

COFFY American International, 1973

PEDRO AZNAR
Contact: BMI - Los Angeles, 213/659-9109

MAN FACING SOUTHEAST FilmDallas, 1987, Argentine
LAST IMAGES OF THE SHIPWRECK Enrique Marti, Films Cinequanon SRL, 1989, Argentine-Spanish

B

LUIS BACALOV

b. Spain
Contact: SIAE - Rome, Italy, 011-39-6-59-90-1

LA BANDA DEL BUCO 1960, Italian
VINO, WHISKY E ACQUA SALATA co-composer, 1962, Italian
I DUE DELLA LEGIONE Ultra Film, 1962, Italian
THE EMPTY CANVAS *LA NOIA* Embassy, 1964, Italian
DONDE TU ESTES 1964, Spanish-Italian
THE GOSPEL ACCORDING TO ST. MATTHEW ★ Continental, 1965, Italian
LA CONGIUNTURA Fair Film/Les Films Concordia, 1965, Italian-French
EXTRA CONJUGALE composer of "La Roccia" segment, 1965, Italian
LET'S TALK ABOUT MEN *QUESTA VOLTA PARLIAMO DI UOMINI* Allied Artists, 1965, Italian
ALTISSIMA PRESSIONE co-composer with Ennio Morricone, 1965, Italian
THRILLING co-composer with Ennio Morricone, 1965, Italian
DJANGO BRC, 1966, Italian
BALLATA DA UN MILIARDO 1966, Italian
A MATTER OF HONOR 1966, Italian
MI VEDRAI TORNARE co-composer, 1966, Italian
SE NON AVESSI PIU TE co-composer, 1966, Italian
LA STREGA IN AMORE Arco Film, 1966, Italian
SUGAR COLT 1966, Italian
PER AMORE...PER MAGIA 1967, Italian
A CIASCUNO IL SUO *WE STILL KILL THE OLD WAY* 1967, Italian
THE GREATEST KIDNAPPING IN THE WEST 1967, Italian
LO SCATENATO *CATCH AS CATCH CAN* 1967, Italian
QUESTI FANTASMI *GHOSTS ITALIAN STYLE* 1967, Italian
A QUALISIASI PREZZO *VATICAN STORY* 1968, Italian
LA BAMBOLONA *BABY DOLL* 1968, Italian
LA PECORA NERA *THE BLACK SHEEP* 1968, Italian
I PROTAGONISTI 1968, Italian
REBUS 1968, Italian
BULLET FOR THE GENERAL *QUIEN SABE?* Avco Embassy, 1968, Italian-Spanish
TUTTO PER TUTTO co-composer with Marcello Giombini, 1968, Italian
LA MORTE SULL' ALTA COLLINA 1969, Italian
I QUATTRO DEL PATER NOSTER 1969, Italian
IL PREZZO DEL POTERE *THE PRICE OF POWER* 1969, Italian
L'AMICA Fair Film, 1969, Italian
CUORI SOLITARI *LONELY HEARTS* 1970, Italian
L'ORO DEI BRAVADOS 1970, Italian
LA VITTIMA DESIGNATA 1971, Italian
LA SUPERTESTIMONE 1971, Italian
LA GRANDE SCROFA NERA 1971, Italian
LO CHIAMAVANO KING 1971, Italian
ROMA BENE 1971, Italian
THE SUMMERTIME KILLER co-composer with Sergio Bardotti, 1971, Italian
BEATI E RICCHI 1972, Italian
SI PUO FARE, AMIGO *CAN BE DONE, AMIGO* 1972, Italian
IL GRANDE DUELLO *THE GRAND DUEL* 1972, Italian
MILANO CALIBRO 9 1972, Italian
MONTA IN SELLA, FIGLIO DI! 1972, Italian
LO CHIAMAVANO MEZZOGIORNO *THE MAN CALLED NOON* 1972, Italian
L'ULTIMA CHANCE 1973, Italian
LA ROSA ROSSA *THE RED ROSE* 1973, Italian
PARTIRONO PRETI, TORNARONO...CURATI 1973, Italian
IL BOSS 1973, Italian
LA SEDUZIONE *SEDUCTION* Gemini, 1973, Italian
IN LOVE WITH SEX EFC, 1973, French-Italian-Canadian
LA POLIZIA E AL SERVIZIO DEL CITTADINO? 1073, Italian
IL POLIZIOTTO E MARCIO 1974, Italian
SISTEMO L'AMERICA E TORNO *I FIX AMERICA AND RETURN* 1974, Italian
L'UOMO CHE SFIDO L'ORGANIZZAZIONE 1975, Italian
GLI ESECUTORI *STREET PEOPLE* 1975, Italian
IL LUNGO VIAGGIO (TF) 1975, Italian
COLPO IN CANNA 1975, Italian
COLPITA DA IMPROVVISO BENESSERE 1975, Italian
LA CITTA SCONVOLTA: CACCIA SPIETATA AI RAPITORI 1975, Italian
GRAZIE TANTE E ARRIVEDERCI 1976, Italian
GLI AMICI DI NICK HEZARD 1976, Italian
IL CONTO E CHIUSO *THE LAST ROUND* 1976, Italian
I PADRONI DELLA CITTA 1976, Italian
I PROSSENETI 1976, Italian
UN ANNO DI SCUOLA 1976, Italian
DIAMANTI SPORCHI DI SANGUE 1977, Italian
IL BALORDO (TF) 1978, Italian
IMPROVVISO 1979, Italian
LE MAESTRO (TF) 1979, Italian
THE GREEN JACKET CEP, 1979, Italian
LE ROSE DI DANZICA 1979, Italian
VACANZE PER UN MASSACRO 1979, Italian
TEN TO SURVIVE (AF) co-composer, 1979, Italian
LA RAGAZZA DI VIA MILLE LIRE 1980, Italian
CITY OF WOMEN New Yorker, 1980, Italian-French
LE JEUNE MARIE AMLF, 1982, French-Italian
ENTRE NOUS *COUP DE FOUDRE* United Artists Classics, 1983, French
L'ART D'AIMER Parafrance, 1983, French-Italian
LE JUGE 1983, French
UN AMOUR INTERDIT 1983, French
UN CASO DI INCOSCIENZA (TF) 1983, Italian
UNA STRANA PASSIONE 1984, Italian-French
LE TRANSFUGE 1985, French-Italian

BURT BACHARACH

b. May 12, 1929 - Kansas City, Missouri
Contact: ASCAP - Los Angeles, 213/466-7681

WHAT'S NEW PUSSYCAT? United Artists, 1965, British
AFTER THE FOX United Artists, 1966, Italian-U.S.-British
CASINO ROYALE Columbia, 1967, British
BUTCH CASSIDY AND THE SUNDANCE KID ★★ 20th Century-Fox, 1969
LOST HORIZON Columbia, 1972
TOGETHER? 1979, Italian
ARTHUR Warner Bros., 1981
NIGHT SHIFT The Ladd Company/Warner Bros., 1982
ARTHUR 2 - ON THE ROCKS Warner Bros., 1988

PIERRE BACHELET
b. France
Contact: SACEM - France, 011-33-14-747-5650

EMMANUELLE Columbia, 1974, French
COUP D'ETAT French
BLACK AND WHITE IN COLOR *LA VICTOIRE EN CHANTANT* Allied Artists, 1978, French-Ivory Coast-Swiss
UN HOMME A MA TAILLE 1983, French
GWENDOLINE Samuel Goldwyn Company, 1984, French
EMMANUELLE 5 AAA, 1987, French

ANGELO BADALAMENTI
Agent: Bart-Milander - North Hollywood, 818/761-4040

GORDON'S WAR 20th Century Fox, 1973
LAW AND DISORDER Columbia, 1974
ACROSS THE GREAT DIVIDE Pacific International, 1976
BLUE VELVET DEG, 1986
NIGHTMARE ON ELM STREET III New Line Cinema, 1987
TOUGH GUYS DON'T DANCE Cannon, 1987
WEEDS DEG, 1987
COUSINS Paramount, 1989
NATIONAL LAMPOON'S CHRISTMAS VACATION Warner Bros., 1989
TWIN PEAKS (TF) Lynch-Frost Productions/ Propoganda Films, 1990
THE COMFORT OF STRANGERS Elle Productions, 1990
WILD AT HEART Samuel Goldwyn Co., 1990

WALLY BADAROU
Agent: CAA - Los Angeles, 213/288-4545

COUNTRY MAN 1982
GOOD TO GO Island Pictures, 1986

DON BAGLEY
Contact: ASCAP - Los Angeles, 213/466-7681

MAMA'S DIRTY GIRLS 1974
THE STUDENT BODY 1975
YOUNG LADY CHATTERLEY adaptation, PRO International, 1977

TOM BAHLER
Agent: BMI - Los Angeles, 213/659-9109

MARY, MARY, BLOODY MARY 1975
FAST FORWARD Columbia, 1985
U.S. MARSHALS: WACO & RHINEHART (TF) co-composer, Touchstone Films, 1987
COLD FEET Avenue, 1989

BUDDY BAKER
(Norman Dale Baker)
b. January 1, 1918 - Springfield, Missouri
Contact: ASCAP - Los Angeles, 213/466-7681

SUMMER MAGIC Buena Vista, 1963
THE MISADVENTURES OF MERLIN JONES Buena Vista, 1964
A TIGER WALKS Buena Vista, 1964
THE MONKEY'S UNCLE Buena Vista, 1964
THE GNOME-MOBILE Buena Vista, 1967
MILLION DOLLAR DUCK Buena Vista, 1971
NAPOLEON AND SAMANTHA ★ Buena Vista, 1972
SUPERDAD Buena Vista, 1974
THE BEARS AND I Buena Vista, 1974
THE APPLE DUMPLING GANG Buena Vista, 1975
NO DEPOSIT, NO RETURN Buena Vista, 1976
THE SHAGGY D.A. Buena Vista, 1976
TREASURE OF MATECUMBE Buena Vista, 1976
HOT LEAD AND COLD FEET Buena Vista, 1978
THE APPLE DUMPLING GANG RIDES AGAIN Buena Vista, 1979
THE DEVIL AND MAX DEVLIN co-composer with Marvin Hamlisch, Buena Vista, 1981
THE FOX AND THE HOUND (AF) Buena Vista, 1981
THE PUPPETOON MOVIE (FD) Expanded Entertainment, 1987

MICHAEL CONWAY BAKER
b. Canada
Agent: Bart-Milander - North Hollywood, 818/761-4040

SILENCE OF THE NORTH Universal, 1981, Canadian
DESERTERS Exile Productions, 1983, Canadian
THE GREY FOX United Artists Classics, 1983, Canadian
ONE MAGIC CHRISTMAS Buena Vista, 1985, U.S.-Canadian
LOYALTIES Norstar Releasing, 1986, Canadian-British
OVERNIGHT Lauron Productions, 1986, Canadian
ANYTHING TO SURVIVE (TF) ATL Productions/B.C. Films, 1990

RICHARD H. BAND
Agent: BMI - Los Angeles, 213/659-9109

LASERBLAST co-composer with Joel Goldsmith, Irwin Yablans, 1978
THE DAY TIME ENDED Compass International, 1979
DR. HECKLE AND MR. HYPE Cannon, 1980
PARASITE Embassy, 1982
THE HOUSE ON SORORITY ROW Artists Releasing Corporation/Film Ventures International, 1983
TIME WALKER New World, 1983
METALSTORM: THE DESTRUCTION OF JARED SYN Universal, 1983
NIGHT SHADOWS *MUTANT* Artists Releasing Corporation/Film Ventures International, 1984
GHOULIES co-composer with Shirley Walker, Empire Pictures, 1985
THE DUNGEONMASTER co-composer with Shirley Walker, Empire Pictures, 1985
THE ALCHEMIST Empire Pictures, 1985
H.P. LOVECRAFT'S REANIMATOR *REANIMATOR* Empire Pictures, 1985
ELIMINATORS Empire Pictures, 1986
TERRORVISION Empire Pictures, 1986
GHOST WARRIOR *SWORDKILL* Empire Pictures, 1986
FROM BEYOND Empire Pictures, 1986
TROLL Empire Pictures, 1986
ZONE TROOPERS Empire Pictures, 1986
THE CALLER Empire Pictures, 1987
DOLLS Empire Pictures, 1987
PRISON Empire Pictures, 1988
PUPPET MASTER Full Moon, 1989
BRIDE OF RE-ANIMATOR Empire Pictures, 1990

ANTHONY BANKS

Contact: PRS - London, England, 011-44-1-580-5544

THE SHOUT co-composer with Rupert Hine and Michael Rutherford, Films Inc., 1979, British
THE WICKED LADY MGM/UA/Cannon, 1983, British
QUICKSILVER Columbia, 1986

BRIAN BANKS

Agent: William Morris Agency - Beverly Hills, 213/274-7451

EPILOGUE OF DOOM co-composer with Anthony Marinelli, Odette Productions, 1984
RIGGED co-composer with Anthony Marinelli, CineStar, 1985
NICE GIRLS DON'T EXPLODE co-composer with Anthony Marinelli, New World, 1987
PINOCCHIO AND THE EMPEROR OF THE NIGHT (AF) co-composer with Anthony Marinelli, New World, 1987
YOUNG GUNS co-composer with Anthony Marinelli, 20th Century Fox, 1988
SPOONER (TF) co-composer with Anthony Marinelli, Walt Disney Productions, 1989
INTERNAL AFFAIRS co-composer with Mike Figgis and Anthony Marinelli, Paramount, 1990
STEPHEN KING'S GRAVEYARD SHIFT co-composer with Anthony Marinelli, Paramount, 1990

DON BANKS

b. 1923 - Australia
Contact: PRS - London, England, 011-44-1-580-5544

NIGHT CREATURES *CAPTAIN CLEGG* 1962, British
NIGHTMARE Universal, 1964, British
THE EVIL OF FRANKENSTEIN Universal, 1964, British
HYSTERIA MGM, 1965, British
DIE, MONSTER, DIE! American International, 1965, U.S.-British
RASPUTIN - THE MAD MONK *I KILLED RASPUTIN* 20th Century-Fox, 1966, British-French-Italian
THE REPTILE 1966, British
THE MUMMY'S SHROUD 20th Century-Fox, 1967, British
THE FROZEN DEAD Warner Bros., 1967, British
TORTURE GARDEN co-composer with James Bernard, Columbia, 1968, British

JOHN BARBER

THE INCREDIBLE TWO-HEADED TRANSPLANT American International, 1971
PINOCCHIO EUE, 1971

GATO BARBIERI

Contact: BMI - Los Angeles, 213/659-9109

BEFORE THE REVOLUTION New Yorker, 1964, Italian
NOTES FOR AN AFRICAN ORESTES 1970, Italian
LAST TANGO IN PARIS United Artists, 1973, Italian-French
THE PIG'S WAR 1975, Argentine
FIREPOWER AFD, 1979, British
STRANGER'S KISS Orion Classics, 1983

CHARLES P. BARNETT

HELL SQUAD Cannon, 1986
BUSTED UP Shapiro Entertainment, 1987

GEORGE BARRIE

Contact: ASCAP - Los Angeles, 213/466-7681

FINGERS Brut Productions, 1978

BEBE BARRON

FORBIDDEN PLANET co-composer with Louis Barron, MGM, 1956
THE VERY EDGE OF THE NIGHT co-composer with Louis Barron, 1959
SPACEBOY co-composer with Louis Barron, 1972

JEFF BARRY

Contact: Richard Emler - Los Angeles, 213/651-0222

THE IDOLMAKER United Artists, 1980
SPIKER Seymour Borde & Associates, 1986
YOUR MOTHER WEARS COMBAT BOOTS (TF) co-composer with Barry Fasman, NBC Productions, 1989

JOHN BARRY

b. 1933 - York, England
Contact: CAA - Los Angeles, 213/288-4545

WILD FOR KICKS *BEAT GIRL* Renown, 1959, British
NEVER LET GO Rank, 1960, British
DR. NO uncredited co-composer with Monty Norman, United Artists, 1962, British
MIX ME A PERSON 1962, British
THEY ALL DIED LAUGHING *A JOLLY BAD FELLOW* Continental, 1963, British
THE L-SHAPED ROOM Columbia, 1963, British
FROM RUSSIA WITH LOVE United Artists, 1963, British
THE AMOROUS MR. PRAWN British Lion, 1964, British
MAN IN THE MIDDLE 20th Century-Fox, 1964, British-U.S.
ZULU Embassy, 1964, British
SEANCE ON A WET AFTERNOON Artixo, 1964, British
GOLDFINGER United Artists, 1964, British
FOUR IN THE MORNING West One, 1965, British
THE IPCRESS FILE Universal, 1965, British
KING RAT Columbia, 1965, British
THE KNACK...AND HOW TO GET IT Lopert, 1965, British
MISTER MOSES United Artists, 1965, British
THUNDERBALL United Artists, 1965, British
BORN FREE ★★ Columbia, 1966, British
THE QUILLER MEMORANDUM Paramount, 1966, British
THE CHASE Columbia, 1966
THE WRONG BOX Columbia, 1966, British
DUTCHMAN Continental, 1967, British
THE WHISPERERS United Artists, 1967, British
YOU ONLY LIVE TWICE United Artists, 1967, British
PETULIA Warner Bros., 1968, U.S.-British
BOOM! Universal, 1968, British-U.S.
DEADFALL also appears as conductor, 20th Century-Fox, 1968, British
THE LION IN WINTER ★★ Avco Embassy, 1968, British
THE APPOINTMENT MGM, 1969
ON HER MAJESTY'S SECRET SERVICE United Artists, 1969, British
MIDNIGHT COWBOY United Artists, 1969
MONTE WALSH National General, 1970
WALKABOUT 20th Century Fox, 1971, British-Australian
THE LAST VALLEY Cinerama Releasing Corporation, 1971, British
MURPHY'S WAR Universal, 1971
DIAMONDS ARE FOREVER United Artists, 1971
MARY, QUEEN OF SCOTS ★ Universal, 1971, British
THEY MIGHT BE GIANTS Universal, 1971
ALICE'S ADVENTURES IN WONDERLAND American National Enterprises, 1972, British
THE PUBLIC EYE Universal, 1972
A DOLL'S HOUSE Tomorrow Entertainment, 1973, British-French
THE GLASS MENAGERIE (TF) Talent Associates, 1973

THE MAN WITH THE GOLDEN GUN United Artists, 1974, British
THE DOVE Paramount, 1974
THE TAMARIND SEED Avco Embassy, 1974
LOVE AMONG THE RUINS (TF) ABC Circle Films, 1975
THE DAY OF THE LOCUST Paramount, 1975
ELEANOR AND FRANKLIN (TF) Talent Associates, 1976
ROBIN AND MARIAN Columbia, 1976, British
KING KONG Paramount, 1976
ELEANOR AND FRANKLIN: THE WHITE HOUSE YEARS (TF) ☆ Talent Associates, 1977
THE WAR BETWEEN THE TATES (TF) Talent Associates, 1977
THE GATHERING (TF) Hanna-Barbera Productions, 1977
YOUNG JOE, THE FORGOTTEN KENNEDY (TF) ABC Circle Films, 1977
THE DEEP Columbia, 1977
THE WHITE BUFFALO United Artists, 1977
FIRST LOVE Paramount, 1977
THE BETSY Allied Artists, 1978
THE CORN IS GREEN (TF) Warner Bros. TV, 1979
GAME OF DEATH Columbia, 1979, U.S.-Hong Kong
HANOVER STREET Columbia, 1979
STARCRASH New World, 1979, Italian
MOONRAKER United Artists, 1979, British-French
WILLA (TF) GJL Productions/Dove, Inc., 1979
THE BLACK HOLE Buena Vista, 1979
RAISE THE TITANIC AFD, 1980, British-U.S.
NIGHT GAMES Avco Embassy, 1980
TOUCHED BY LOVE Columbia, 1980
SOMEWHERE IN TIME Universal, 1980
INSIDE MOVES AFD, 1980
MURDER BY PHONE *BELLS* New World, 1980, Canadian
THE LEGEND OF THE LONE RANGER Universal/AFD, 1981
BODY HEAT The Ladd Company/Warner Bros., 1981
FRANCES Universal, 1982
HAMMETT Orion/Warner Bros., 1982
SVENGALI (TF) Robert Halmi Productions, 1983
THE GOLDEN SEAL co-composer with Dana Kaproff, Samuel Goldwyn Company, 1983
HIGH ROAD TO CHINA Warner Bros., 1983, U.S.-Yugoslavian
OCTOPUSSY MGM/UA, 1983, British
MIKE'S MURDER Universal, 1984
UNTIL SEPTEMBER MGM/UA, 1984
THE COTTON CLUB Orion, 1984
A VIEW TO A KILL MGM/UA, 1985, British
THE JAGGED EDGE Columbia, 1985
OUT OF AFRICA ★★ Universal, 1985
HOWARD THE DUCK co-composer with Sylvester Levay, Universal, 1986
PEGGY SUE GOT MARRIED Tri-Star, 1986
HEARTS OF FIRE Lorimar, 1987, U.S.-British
THE LIVING DAYLIGHTS MGM/UA, 1987, British
A KILLING AFFAIR Hemdale, 1988
MASQUERADE MGM/UA, 1988
DANCES WITH WOLVES Orion, 1990

LIONEL BART

b. 1930
Contact: PRS - London, England, 011-44-1-580-5544

BLACK BEAUTY Paramount, 1971, British-West German-Spanish

DEE BARTON

Contact: ASCAP - Los Angeles, 213/466-7681

PLAY MISTY FOR ME Universal, 1971
HIGH PLAINS DRIFTER Universal, 1972
THUNDERBOLT AND LIGHTFOOT United Artists, 1974

RICHARD BASKIN

Contact: ASCAP - Los Angeles, 213/466-7681

CONGRATULATIONS, IT'S A BOY! (TF) co-composer with Basil Poledouris, Aaron Spelling Productions, 1971
NASHVILLE Paramount, 1976
BUFFALO BILL AND THE INDIANS or SITTING BULL'S HISTORY LESSON United Artists, 1976
WELCOME TO L.A. United Artists/Lions Gate, 1976
JAMES AT 15 (TF) 20th Century-Fox TV, 1977
HONEYSUCKLE ROSE co-composer with Willie Nelson, Warner Bros., 1980
UFORIA Universal, 1984

KEVIN BASSINSON

Contact: ASCAP - Los Angeles, 213/466-7681

CYBORG Cannon, 1989

GEORGE BASSMAN

b. 1914
Contact: ASCAP - Los Angeles, 213/466-7681

A DAMNSEL IN DISTRESS adaptation, RKO Radio, 1937
A DAY AT THE RACES MGM, 1937
EVERYBODY SING MGM, 1938
BABES IN ARMS MGM, 1939
TOO MANY GIRLS adaptation, RKO Radio, 1940
TWO GIRLS ON BROADWAY MGM, 1940
GO WEST MGM, 1940
LADY BE GOOD MGM, 1941
THE BIG STORE MGM, 1941
BABES ON BROADWAY MGM, 1941
PANAMA HATTIE MGM, 1942
FOR ME AND MY GAL MGM, 1942
CABIN IN THE SKY adaptation, MGM, 1943
BEST FOOT FORWARD adaptation, MGM, 1943
YOUNG IDEAS MGM, 1943
WHISTLING IN BROOKLYN MGM, 1943
THE CANTERVILLE GHOST MGM, 1944
MAIN STREET AFTER DARK MGM, 1945
THE CLOCK MGM, 1945
ABBOTT & COSTELLO IN HOLLYWOOD MGM, 1945
A LETTER FOR EVIE MGM, 1946
THE POSTMAN ALWAYS RINGS TWICE MGM, 1946
TWO SMART PEOPLE MGM, 1946
LITTLE MISTER JIM MGM, 1947
THE ROMANCE OF ROSY RIDGE MGM, 1947
THE ARNELO AFFAIR MGM, 1947
JAPAN AND THE WORLD TODAY (D) U.S. Government, 1950
THE JOE LOUIS STORY United Artists, 1953
LOUISIANA TERRITORY RKO Radio, 1953
CANYON CROSSROADS United Artists, 1955
MIDDLE OF THE NIGHT Columbia, 1959
RIDE THE HIGH COUNTRY MGM, 1962
MAIL ORDER BRIDE MGM, 1963

MIKE BATT

Contact: PRS - London, England, 011-44-1-580-5544

CARAVANS Universal, 1979, U.S.-Iranian
DIGITAL DREAMS Ripple Productions Ltd., 1983

FRANCO BATTIATO

Contact: SIAE - Rome, Italy, 011-39-6-59-90-1

AN INFAMOUS LIFE Artisti Associati International, 1990, Italian-French-West German

LES BAXTER

b. March 14, 1922 - Mexia, Texas
Contact: ASCAP - Los Angeles, 213/466-7681

TANGA TIKA 1953
THE YELLOW TOMAHAWK United Artists, 1954
THE KEY MAN United Artists, 1955
WETBACKS 1955
THE BLACK SLEEP United Artists, 1956
HOT BLOOD Columbia, 1956
HOT CARS United Artists, 1956
QUINCANNON, FRONTIER SCOUT United Artists, 1956
REBEL IN TOWN United Artists, 1956
A WOMAN'S DEVOTION Republic, 1956
BOP GIRL *BOP GIRL GOES CALYPSO* United Artists, 1957
THE VICIOUS BREED 1957
VOODOO ISLAND United Artists, 1957
PHARAOH'S CURSE United Artists, 1957
HELL BOUND United Artists, 1957
THE DALTON GIRLS United Artists, 1957
THE INVISIBLE BOY MGM, 1957
JUNGLE HEAT United Artists, 1957
OUTLAW'S SON United Artists, 1957
THE STORM RIDER 20th Century-Fox, 1957
TOMAHAWK TRAIL United Artists, 1957
UNTAMED YOUTH United Artists, 1957
WAR DRUMS United Artists, 1957
REVOLT AT FORT LARAMIE United Artists, 1957
THE GIRL IN BLACK STOCKINGS United Artists, 1958
THE BRIDE AND THE BEAST *QUEEN OF THE GORILLAS* Allied Artists, 1958
ESCAPE FROM RED ROCK 20th Century-Fox, 1958
FORT BOWIE United Artists, 1958
THE LONE RANGER AND THE LOST CITY OF GOLD United Artists, 1958
MACABRE Allied Artists, 1958
MONIKA re-scoring of 1953 Ingmar Bergman film, 1959
GOLIATH AND THE BARBARIANS composer of U.S. version only, American International, 1959
LA CIUDAD SAGRADA 1959, Mexican
GOLIATH AND THE DRAGON composer of U.S. version only, American International, 1960
ALAKAZAM THE GREAT composer of U.S. version only, American International, 1960
HOUSE OF USHER *FALL OF THE HOUSE OF USHER* American International, 1960
BLACK SUNDAY composer of U.S. version only, American International, 1960, Italian
MASTER OF THE WORLD American International, 1961
LISETTE 1961
GUNS OF THE BLACK WITCH American International, 1961
THE PIT AND THE PENDULUM American International, 1961
SAMSON AND THE 7 MIRACLES OF THE WORLD composer of U.S. version only, American International, 1961
REPTILICUS composer of U.S. version only, American International, 1961
ERIC THE CONQUEROR *GLI INVASORI/FURY OF THE VIKINGS* American International, 1961, Italian-French
MARCO POLO American International, 1961, Italian-French
WARRIORS FIVE American International, 1962, Italian
TALES OF TERROR American International, 1962
DAUGHTER OF THE SUN GOD American International, 1962
LOST BATTALION American International, 1962, Filipino-U.S.
SAMSON AND THE SEVEN MIRACLES OF THE WORLD American International, 1962
A HOUSE OF SAND American International, 1962
GOLIATH AND THE VAMPIRES *VAMPIRES* composer of title music for U.S. release, American International, 1962
SAMSON AND THE SLAVE QUEEN American International, 1962
WHITE SLAVE SHIP American International, 1962, Italian
PANIC IN THE YEAR ZERO American International, 1962
THE RAVEN American International, 1963
EVIL EYE *LA RAGAZZA CHE SAPEVE TROPPO* American International, 1963, Italian
BEACH PARTY American International, 1963
THE COMEDY OF TERRORS American International, 1963
OPERATION BIKINI American International, 1963
BATTLE BEYOND THE SUN American International, 1963
"X" - THE MAN WITH X-RAY EYES American International, 1963
THE YOUNG RACERS American International, 1963
MUSCLE BEACH PARTY American International, 1963
BLACK SABBATH *I TRE VOLTI DELLA PAURA* composer of U.S. version only, American International, 1963, U.S.-French-Italian
PAJAMA PARTY American International, 1964
BEACH BLANKET BINGO American International, 1965
A BOY TEN FEET TALL Paramount, 1965
DR. GOLDFOOT AND THE BIKINI MACHINE American International, 1965
HOW TO STUFF A WILD BIKINI American International, 1965
SERGEANT DEADHEAD *SERGEANT DEADHEAD, THE ASTRONAUT* American International, 1965
DR. GOLDFOOT AND THE GIRL BOMBS *LE SPIE VENGONO DAL SEMIFREDDO* American International, 1966, U.S.-Italian
GHOST IN THE INVISIBLE BIKINI American International, 1966
FIREBALL 500 American International, 1966
SADISMO American International, 1967
TERROR IN THE JUNGLE co-composer with Stan Hoffman, 1967
THE GLASS SPHINX composer of U.S. version only, 1967, American International, Italian-Spanish
THE YOUNG REBEL *CERVANTES* American International, 1968, Italian-Spanish-French
THE MINI-SKIRT MOB American International, 1968
THE YOUNG ANIMALS American International, 1968
ALL THE LOVING COUPLES U-M, 1968
BORA BORA 1968, French-Italian
TARGET: HARRY *HOW TO MAKE IT* ABC Pictures International, 1968
WILD IN THE STREETS American International, 1968
FLAREUP MGM, 1969
HELL'S BELLES American International, 1969
THE DUNWICH HORROR American International, 1970
EL OGRO *THE OGRE* 1970
CRY OF THE BANSHEE American International, 1970, British
THE BIG DOLL HOUSE New World, 1971
FROGS American International, 1972
THE DEVIL AND LEROY BASSETT 1972
BARON BLOOD *GLI ORRORI DEL CASTELLO DE NORIMBERGA* composer of U.S. version only, American International, 1972, Italian-West German

BLOOD SABBATH *YGALAH* 1972
I ESCAPED FROM DEVIL'S ISLAND United Artists, 1973
SAVAGE SISTERS American International, 1974, U.S.-Filipino
SWITCHBLADE SISTERS *THE JEZEBELS/PLAYGIRL GANG* Centaur, 1975
BORN AGAIN Avco Embassy, 1978
THE BEAST WITHIN United Artists, 1982

IRWIN BAZELON
Contact: ASCAP - Los Angeles, 213/466-7681

WILMA (TF) Cappy Productions, 1977

DAVID BEAL
Contact: ASCAP - Los Angeles, 213/466-7681

THE TAKE (CTF) co-composer with Michael Shrieve, Cine-Nevada Inc./MCA TV, 1990

JOHN BEAL
Contact: ASCAP - Los Angeles, 213/466-7681

THE FUNHOUSE Universal, 1981
TERROR IN THE AISLES Universal, 1984
KILLER PARTY MGM/UA, 1986

JOE BECK
GOODBYE, NORMA JEAN Filmways, 1976, U.S.-Australian

DANNY BECKERMAN
Contact: PRS - London, England, 011-44-1-580-5544

FORTRESS (CTF) Crawford Productions/HBO Premiere Films, 1985, Australian

DANIEL BELL
Contact: STIM - Sweden, 011-41-1-482-6666

FANNY AND ALEXANDER Embassy, 1983, Swedish-French-West German

DAVID BELL
Agent: Gorfaine-Schwartz - Burbank, 818/954-9500

KILLING AT HELL'S GATE (TF) CBS Entertainment, 1981
FINAL JUSTICE Arista, 1985
THE RETURN OF THE SHAGGY DOG (TF) Walt Disney TV, 1987
EQUAL JUSTICE (TF) co-composer with Susan Marder, The Thomas Carter Co./Orion TV, 1990

THOM BELL
Contact: BMI - Los Angeles, 213/659-9109

THE FISH THAT SAVED PITTSBURGH United Artists, 1979

WAYNE BELL
THE TEXAS CHAINSAW MASSACRE co-composer with Tobe Hooper, Bryanston, 1974
EATEN ALIVE *DEATH TRAP* Virgo International, 1977
LAST NIGHT AT THE ALAMO co-composer with Chuck Pinnell, Alamo Films, 1983

ANDREW BELLING
Agent: Richard Emler - Los Angeles, 213/651-0222

DELIVER US FROM EVIL (TF) Playboy Productions, 1973
A SUMMER WITHOUT BOYS (TF) Playboy Productions, 1973
THE KILLING KIND Media Trend, 1974
WIZARDS (AF) 20th Century Fox, 1977
END OF THE WORLD Yablans Films, 1977
CRASH! AKAZA, GOD OF VENGEANCE Group 1, 1977
CINDERELLA Group 1, 1977
DRACULA'S DOG *ZOLTAN, HOUND OF DRACULA* Crown International, 1978
FAIRY TALES Yablans Films, 1978
THE DEERSLAYER (TF) co-composer with Bob Summers, Schick Sunn Classics Productions, 1978
THIRTY DANGEROUS SECONDS Independent Productions
STARCHASER: THE LEGEND OF ORIN (AF) Atlantic Releasing Corporation, 1985

RICHARD BELLIS
Agent: Carol Faith - Beverly Hills, 213/274-0776

BLACK MARKET BABY (TF) co-composer with George Wilkins, Brut Productions, 1977
BREAKING UP IS HARD TO DO (TF) Green-Epstein Productions/Columbia TV, 1979
A SHINING SEASON (TF) Green-Epstein Productions/ T-M Productions/Columbia TV, 1979
FALLEN ANGEL (TF) Green-Epstein Productions/ Columbia TV, 1981
THE OTHER VICTIM (TF) Shpetner Company, 1981
MONEY ON THE SIDE (TF) Green-Epstein Productions/ Hal Landers Productions/Columbia TV, 1982
SHATTERED INNOCENCE (TF) Green-Epstein Productions/Lorimar TV, 1988
ADDICTED TO HIS LOVE (TF) Green-Epstein Productions/ Columbia TV, 1988

ROGER BELLON
Contact: ASCAP - Los Angeles, 213/466-7681

THE SHIEK new score for 1926 silent film
THE PRINCESS ACADEMY Empire Pictures, 1987
THE UNHOLY Vestron, 1988
WAXWORK Vestron, 1988

RICHARD RODNEY BENNETT
b. March 29, 1936 - Broadstairs, England
Contact: PRS - London, England, 011-44-1-580-5544

INTERPOL *PICKUP ALLEY* Columbia, 1957, British
INDISCREET Warner Bros., 1958, British
THE MAN INSIDE Columbia, 1958, British
MENACE IN THE NIGHT United Artists, 1958, British
THE SAFECRACKER MGM, 1958, British
CHANCE MEETING *BLIND DATE* Paramount, 1959, British
THE ANGRY HILLS MGM, 1959
THE DEVIL'S DISCIPLE United Artists, 1959, British
THE MAN WHO COULD CHEAT DEATH Paramount, 1959, British
THE MARK Continental, 1961, British
SATAN NEVER SLEEPS 20th Century Fox, 1962, U.S.-British
ONLY TWO CAN PLAY British Lion, 1961, British
THE WRONG ARM OF THE LAW Continental, 1963, British

HEAVENS ABOVE British Lion, 1963, British
BILLY LIAR Continental, 1963, British
ONE WAY PENDULUM United Artists, 1964
THE NANNY 20th Century Fox, 1965, British
THE DEVIL'S OWN *THE WITCHES* 1966, British
FAR FROM THE MADDING CROWD ★ MGM, 1967, British
BILLION DOLLAR BRAIN United Artists, 1967, British
SECRET CEREMONY Universal, 1968, British-U.S.
THE BUTTERCUP CHAIN Warner Bros., 1970, British
FIGURES IN A LANDSCAPE National General, 1971, British
NICHOLAS AND ALEXANDRA ★ Columbia, 1971, British
LADY CAROLINE LAMB United Artists, 1973, British
VOICES Hemdale, 1973, British
OF JEWELS AND GOLD 1973
MURDER ON THE ORIENT EXPRESS ★ Paramount, 1974, British
PERMISSION TO KILL Warner Bros., 1975, British
SHERLOCK HOLMES IN NEW YORK (TF) 20th Century-Fox TV, 1976
L'IMPRECATEUR THE ACCUSER Parafrance, 1977, French
EQUUS United Artists, 1977, British
THE BRINK'S JOB Universal, 1978
YANKS Universal, 1979, British
RETURN OF THE SOLDIER European Classics, 1982, British
AGATHA CHRISTIE'S 'MURDER WITH MIRRORS' ☆ Hajeno Productions/Warner Bros. TV, 1985
TENDER IS THE NIGHT (MS) Showtime/BBC/Seven Network, 1985, U.S.-British-Australian
THE EBONY TOWER (TF) Granada TV, 1987, British
POOR LITTLE RICH GIRL: THE BARBARA HUTTON STORY (MS) Lester Persky Productions/ITC Productions, 1987
THE ATTIC: THE HIDING OF ANN FRANK (TF) Telecom Entertainment, 1987

DAVID BENOIT
Contact: BMI - Los Angeles, 213/659-9109

CAPTIVE HEARTS MGM/UA, 1987, Canadian

ROBBY BENSON
(Robby Segal)
b. January 21, 1956 - Dallas, Texas
Contact: Directors Guild of America - Los Angeles, 213/289-2000

WALK PROUD Universal, 1979
DIE LAUGHING co-composer with Craig Safan and Jerry Segal, Orion, 1980

TONY BERG
Agent: CAA - Los Angeles, 213/288-4545

HIGH SCHOOL U.S.A. (TF) co-composer with Miles Goodman, Hill-Mandelker Productions, 1983
ATTACK ON FEAR (TF) Tomorrow Entertainment, 1984
SPACE (MS) co-composer with Miles Goodman, Stonehenge Productions/Paramount TV, 1985
AMERICA 3000 Cannon, 1986
WELCOME TO 18 American Distribution Group, 1986

DAVID BERGEAUD
Contact: ASCAP - Los Angeles, 213/466-7681

TWICE DEAD Concorde, 1989

BERLIN GAME
DOWN TWISTED Cannon, 1987
ANGEL III: THE FINAL CHAPTER New World, 1988

JAMES BERNARD
b. September 20, 1925 - London, England
Agent: PRS - London, England, 011-44-1-580-5544

THE CREEPING UNKNOWN *THE QUARTERMASS EXPERIMENT* United Artists, 1955, British
X THE UNKNOWN Warner Bros., 1956, British
THE CURSE OF FRANKENSTEIN Warner Bros., 1957, British
THE DOOR IN THE WALL 1957, British
ENEMY FROM SPACE *QUARTERMASS II* United Artists, 1957, British
ACROSS THE BRIDGE Rank, 1958, British
HORROR OF DRACULA *DRACULA* Universal, 1958, British
THE HOUND OF THE BASKERVILLES United Artists, 1959, British
THE STRANGLERS OF BOMBAY Columbia, 1959, British
THESE ARE THE DAMNED *THE DAMNED* Columbia, 1961, British
THE TERROR OF THE TONGS Columbia, 1961, British
THE KISS OF THE VAMPIRE Universal, 1963, British
THE GORGON Columbia, 1964, British
SHE MGM, 1965, British
DRACULA - PRINCE OF DARKNESS 20th Century-Fox, 1967, British
THE PLAGUE OF THE ZOMBIES Warner/Pathe, 1966, British
FRANKENSTEIN CREATED WOMAN 20th Century-Fox, 1967, British
TORTURE GARDEN co-composer with Don Banks, Columbia, 1968, British
THE DEVIL'S BRIDE *THE DEVIL RIDES OUT* 20th Century-Fox, 1968, British
DRACULA HAS RISEN FROM THE GRAVE Warner Bros., 1969, British
FRANKENSTEIN MUST BE DESTROYED! Warner Bros., 1970, British
TASTE THE BLOOD OF DRACULA Warner Bros., 1970, British
THE SCARS OF DRACULA American Continental, 1971, British
FRANKENSTEIN AND THE MONSTER FROM HELL Paramount, 1974, British
THE 7 BROTHERS MEET DRACULA *THE LEGEND OF THE SEVEN GOLDEN VAMPIRES* Dynamite Entertainment, 1979, British

CHARLES BERNSTEIN
b. February 28, 1943 - New York, New York
Agent: ICM - Los Angeles, 213/550-4000
Contact: P.O. Box 11413, Beverly Hills, CA 90213, 213/467-0154

HEX 20th Century-Fox, 1973
INVASION OF THE BEE GIRLS Centaur, 1973
WHITE LIGHTNING United Artists, 1973
THAT MAN BOLT Universal, 1973
MR. MAJESTYK United Artists, 1974
A SHADOW IN THE STREETS (TF) Playboy Productions, 1975
TRACKDOWN United Artists, 1976
GATOR United Artists, 1976
A SMALL TOWN IN TEXAS American International, 1976
LOOK WHAT'S HAPPENED TO ROSEMARY'S BABY (TF) Paramount TV, 1976

NIGHTMARE IN BADHAM COUNTY (TF) ABC Circle Films, 1976
OUTLAW BLUES co-composer with Bruce Langhorne, Warner Bros., 1977
ESCAPE FROM BOGEN COUNTY (TF) Paramount TV, 1977
VIVA KNIEVEL! Warner Bros., 1977
FOOLIN' AROUND Columbia, 1978
WILD AND WOOLY (TF) Aaron Spelling Productions, 1978
THADDEUS ROSE AND EDDIE (TF) CBS, Inc., 1978
KATIE: PORTRAIT OF A CENTERFOLD (TF) Moonlight Productions/Warner Bros. TV, 1978
ARE YOU IN THE HOUSE ALONE? (TF) Charles Fries Productions, 1978
STEEL COWBOY (TF) Roger Gimbel Productions/ EMI TV, 1978
THE WINDS OF KITTY HAWK (TF) Charles Fries Productions, 1978
LOVE AT FIRST BITE American International, 1979
WOMEN AT WEST POINT (TF) Green-Epstein Productions/Alan Sacks Productions, 1979
THE HOUSE ON GARIBALDI STREET (TF) Charles Fries Productions, 1979
FOOLIN' AROUND Columbia, 1980
COAST TO COAST Paramount, 1980
THE HUNTER composer of foreign version, Paramount, 1980
BOGIE: THE LAST HERO (TF) Charles Fries Productions, 1980
SCRUPLES (TF) Lou-Step Productions/Warner Bros. TV, 1981
THE ENTITY 20th Century Fox, 1982
INDEPENDENCE DAY Warner Bros., 1983
SADAT (TF) Blatt-Singer Productions/Columbia TV, 1983
CUJO Warner Bros., 1983
DADDY'S DEADLY DARLING *THE PIGS/DADDY'S GIRL* Aquarius, 1984
A NIGHTMARE ON ELM STREET (The Original) New Line Cinema, 1984
SECRET WEAPONS (TF) Goodman-Rosen Productions/ ITC Productions, 1985
MALICE IN WONDERLAND (TF) ITC Productions, 1985
GENERATION (TF) Embassy TV, 1985
COVENANT (TF) Michael Filerman Productions/20th Century Fox TV, 1985
THE LONG HOT SUMMER (TF) Leonard Hill Productions, 1985
CHASE (TF) CBS Entertainment, 1985
APRIL FOOL'S DAY Paramount, 1986
DEADLY FRIEND Warner Bros., 1986
ROCKABYE (TF) Roger Gimbel Productions/Peregrine Entertainment/Bertinelli Poructions, 1986
THE LAST FLING (TF) Leonard Hill Films, 1987
THE ALLNIGHTER Universal, 1987
GHOST OF A CHANCE (TF) Stuart-Phoenix Productions/ Thunder Bird Road Productions/Lorimar-Telepictures Productions, 1987
THE MAN WHO BROKE 1,000 CHAINS (CTF) HBO Pictures/Journey Entertainment, 1987
DUDES Cineworld, 1987
A WHISPER KILLS (TF) Sandy Hook Productions/Steve Tisch Company/Phoenix Entertainment Group, 1988
DESPERATE FOR LOVE (TF) Vishudda Productions/ Lorimar TV, 1989
LOVE AND BETRAYAL (TF) Gross-Weston Productions/ ITC, 1989
TOO YOUNG TO DIE? (TF) Von Zerneck/Sertner Films, 1990
CAROLINE? (TF) ☆ Barry and Enright Productions, 1990
FALL FROM GRACE (TF) NBC Productions, 1990
DRUG WARS (TF) *THE CAMARENA STORY* Michael Mann Productions, 1990
THE LAST ELEPHANT (CTF) Robert Halmi/TNT, 1990
SHE SAID NO (TF) Steve White Productions, 1990
THE LOVE SHE SOUGHT Orion Television/Andrew Fenedy, 1990

ELMER BERNSTEIN

b. April 4, 1922 - New York, New York
Agent: Gorfaine-Schwartz - Burbank, 818/954-9500

SATURDAY'S HERO Columbia, 1951
BOOTS MALONE Columbia, 1952
BATTLES OF CHIEF PONTIAC Realart, 1952
SUDDEN FEAR RKO Radio, 1952
NEVER WAVE AT A WAC RKO Radio, 1953
ROBOT MONSTER Astor, 1953
CAT WOMEN OF THE MOON Astor, 1954
MISS ROBIN CRUSOE 20th Century Fox, 1954
MAKE HASTE TO LIVE Republic, 1954
SILENT RAIDERS Lippert, 1954
THE ETERNAL SEA Republic, 1955
IT'S A DOG'S LIFE MGM, 1955
THE VIEW FROM POMPEY'S HEAD 20th Century Fox, 1955
THE MAN WITH THE GOLDEN ARM ★ United Artists, 1955
THE TEN COMMANDMENTS Paramount, 1956
STORM FEAR United Artists, 1956
DRANGO United Artists, 1957
MEN IN WAR United Artists, 1957
FEAR STRIKES OUT Paramount, 1957
SWEET SMELL OF SUCCESS United Artists, 1957
THE TIN STAR Paramount, 1957
SADDLE THE WIND MGM, 1957
DESIRE UNDER THE ELMS Paramount, 1958
ANNA LUCASTA United Artists, 1958
GOD'S LITTLE ACRE United Artists, 1958
KINGS GO FORTH United Artists, 1958
THE BUCCANEER Paramount, 1959
THE RACE FOR SPACE (FD) U.S. Government, 1959
THE STORY ON PAGE ONE 20th Century Fox, 1959
SOME CAME RUNNING MGM, 1959
THE MIRACLE Warner Bros., 1959
THE RAT RACE Paramount, 1960
FROM THE TERRACE 20th Century Fox, 1960
THE MAGNIFICENT SEVEN United Artists, 1960
THE MAKING OF THE PRESIDENT (TD) ☆☆ David Wolper Productions, 1960
BY LOVE POSSESSED United Artists, 1961
THE YOUNG DOCTORS United Artists, 1961
THE COMANCHEROS 20th Century-Fox, 1961
SUMMER AND SMOKE ★ Paramount, 1961
WALK ON THE WILD SIDE Columbia, 1962
BIRDMAN OF ALCATRAZ United Artists, 1962
TO KILL A MOCKINGBIRD ★ Universal, 1962
A GIRL NAMED TAMIKO Paramount, 1962
THE GREAT ESCAPE United Artists, 1963
HUD Paramount, 1963
RAMPAGE Warner Bros., 1963
THE CARETAKERS United Artists, 1963
KINGS OF THE SUN United Artists, 1963
THE CARPETBAGGERS Paramount, 1964
LOVE WITH THE PROPER STRANGER Paramount, 1964
THE WORLD OF HENRY ORIENT United Artists, 1964
BABY, THE RAIN MUST FALL Columbia, 1965
THE HALLELUJAH TRAIL United Artists, 1965
SEVEN WOMEN MGM, 1965

THE SONS OF KATIE ELDER Paramount, 1965
THE REWARD 20th Century-Fox, 1965
FOUR DAYS IN NOVEMBER (FD) United Artists, 1965
THE SILENCERS Columbia, 1966
RETURN OF THE SEVEN ★ United Artists, 1966
HAWAII ★ United Artists, 1966
CAST A GIANT SHADOW United Artists, 1966
THOROUGHLY MODERN MILLIE ★★ Universal, 1967
THE SCALPHUNTERS United Artists, 1968
I LOVE YOU, ALICE B. TOKLAS Warner Bros., 1968
WHERE'S JACK? Paramount, 1969, British
TRUE GRIT Paramount, 1969
THE GYPSY MOTHS MGM, 1969
MIDAS RUN Cinerama Releasing Corporation, 1969
GUNS OF THE MAGNIFICENT SEVEN United Artists, 1969
THE BRIDGE AT REMAGEN United Artists, 1969
WALK IN THE SPRING RAIN Columbia, 1970
THE LIBERATION OF L.B. JONES Columbia, 1970
CANNON FOR CORDOBA United Artists, 1970
BIG JAKE National General, 1971
SEE NO EVIL Columbia, 1971, British
DOCTORS' WIVES Columbia, 1971
OWEN MARSHALL, COUNSELOR AT LAW (TF) Universal TV, 1971
THE AMAZING MR. BLUNDEN Goldstone, 1972, British
THE ROOKIES (TF) Aaron Spelling Productions/ABC Circle Films, 1972
THE MAGNIFICENT SEVEN RIDE! United Artists, 1972
CAHILL, U.S. MARSHALL Warner Bros., 1973
DEADLY HONEYMOON *NIGHTMARE HONEYMOON* MGM, 1974
McQ Warner Bros., 1974
GOLD Allied Artists, 1974, British
MEN OF THE DRAGON (TF) Wolper Productions, 1974
THE TRIAL OF BILLY JACK Taylor-Laughlin, 1974
MR. QUILP Avco Embassy, 1975, British
ELLERY QUEEN (TF) Universal TV, 1975
REPORT TO THE COMMISSIONER United Artists, 1975
THE INCREDIBLE SARAH Reader's Digest, 1976, British
FROM NOON TILL THREE also cameo as piano player, United Artists, 1976
THE SHOOTIST Paramount, 1976
CAPTAINS AND THE KINGS (MS) ☆ Universal TV, 1976
SERPICO: THE DEADLY GAME (TF) Dino De Laurentiis Productions/Paramount TV, 1976
THE 3,000 MILE CHASE Public Arts Productions/ Universal TV, 1977
SLAP SHOT Universal, 1977
BILLY JACK GOES TO WASHINGTON Taylor-Laughlin, 1978
NATIONAL LAMPOON'S ANIMAL HOUSE Universal, 1978
LITTLE WOMEN (TF) Universal TV, 1978
CHARLESTON (TF) Robert Stigwood Productions/RSO, Inc., 1979
BLOODBROTHERS Warner Bros., 1979
MEATBALLS Paramount, 1979
ZULU DAWN American Cinema, 1979, British
THE CHISHOLMS (MS) adaptation, Alan Landsburg Productions, 1979
THE GREAT SANTINI THE ACE Orion/Warner Bros., 1980
SATURN 3 AFD, 1980
AIRPLANE! Paramount, 1980
GUYANA TRAGEDY: THE STORY OF JIM JONES (TF) The Konigsberg Company, 1980
MOVIOLA: THIS YEAR'S BLONDE (MS) David S. Wolper-Stan Margulies Productions/Warner Bros. TV, 1980
TODAY'S F.B.I. (TF) David Gerber Company, 1981
STRIPES Columbia, 1981
GOING APE! Paramount, 1981
HEAVY METAL (AF) Columbia, 1981, Canadian
AN AMERICAN WEREWOLF IN LONDON Universal, 1981
HONKY TONK FREEWAY co-composer with George Martin, Universal/AFD, 1981
GENOCIDE (FD) Simon Wiesenthal Center, 1982
THE CHOSEN 20th Century Fox International Classics, 1982
FIVE DAYS ONE SUMMER The Ladd Company/Warner Bros., 1982, British
AIRPLANE II: THE SEQUEL Paramount, 1982
SPACEHUNTER: ADVENTURES IN THE FORBIDDEN ZONE Columbia, 1983, Canadian-U.S.
TRADING PLACES ★ adaptation, Paramount, 1983
CLASS Orion, 1983
PRINCE JACK Castle Hill Productions, 1984
GHOSTBUSTERS Columbia, 1984
THE BLACK CAULDRON (AF) Buena Vista, 1985
SPIES LIKE US Warner Bros., 1985
GULAG (CTF) Lorimar Productions/HBO Premiere Films, 1985
LEGAL EAGLES Universal, 1986
THREE AMIGOS! Orion, 1986
AMAZING GRACE AND CHUCK Tri-Star, 1987
LEONARD PART 6 Columbia, 1987
A NIGHT IN THE LIFE OF JIMMY REARDON foreign version only, 20th Century Fox, 1988
FUNNY FARM Warner Bros., 1988
THE GOOD MOTHER Buena Vista, 1988
DA FilmDallas, 1988
SLIPSTREAM Entertainment Film, 1989, British
MY LEFT FOOT Miramax, 1989, British-Irish
THE GRIFTERS 1990

PETER BERNSTEIN

Agent: Bart-Milander - North Hollywood, 818/761-4040

THE HOUSE THAT CRIED MURDER *THE BRIDE* Golden Gate/Unisphere, 1974, Canadian
SILENT RAGE Columbia, 1982
NATIONAL LAMPOON'S CLASS REUNION 20th Century Fox, 1983
SURF II Arista, 1983
HOT DOG...THE MOVIE MGM/UA, 1984
BOLERO Cannon, 1984
SUMMER FANTASIES (TF) Moonlight Productions II, 1984
THE EWOK ADVENTURE (TF) Lucasfilm Ltd./Korty Films, 1984
MY SCIENCE PROJECT Buena Vista, 1985
THE RAPE OF RICHARD BECK (TF) Robert Papazian Productions/Henerson-Hirsch Productions, 1985
KICKS 1985
EWOKS: THE BATTLE FOR ENDOR (TF) Lucas film Ltd., 1985
ALFRED HITCHCOCK PRESENTS (TF) Universal TV, 1985
HAMBURGER...THE MOTION PICTURE FM Entertainment, 1986
MIRACLES Orion, 1986
CLUB MED (TF) Lorimar Productions, 1986
THE RICHEST CAT IN THE WORLD (TF) Les Alexander Productions/Walt Disney TV, 1986
LITTLE SPIES (TF) Walt Disney TV, 1986
MORGAN STEWART'S COMING HOME New Century/ Vista, 1987

THE ALAMO: 13 DAYS TO GLORY (TF) Briggle, Hennessy, Carrothers Productions/The Finnegan Company/Fries Entertainment, 1987
REMOTE CONTROL Vista Organization, 1988
HEARTBEAT (TF) Aaron Spelling Productions, 1988
NIGHTBREAKER (CTF) Turner Network TV, 1989
DREAM DATE (TF) Robert Kosberg Productions/Saban International, 1989

STEVE BERNSTEIN

BEFORE & AFTER Little Deer, 1985

SANH BERTI

Contact: BMI - Los Angeles, 213/659-9109

CATTLE ANNIE AND LITTLE BRITCHES co-composer with Tom Slocum, Universal, 1981

PETER BEST

Contact: APRA - Australia, 011-61-2-922-6422

THE MORE THINGS CHANGE Hoyts, 1986, Australian
"CROCODILE" DUNDEE Paramount, 1986, Australian
THE HARP IN THE SOUTH (MS) Quantum Films, 1987, Australian
HIGH TIDE Tri-Star, 1987, Australian
CROCODILE DUNDEE II Paramount, 1988, Australian

HARRY BETTS

Contact: BMI - Los Angeles, 213/659-9109

WINTER A-GO-GO Columbia, 1965
THE BIG MOUTH Columbia, 1967
THE FANTASTIC PLASTIC MACHINE 1969
A TIME FOR DYING Etoile, 1971
HOT, HARD AND MEAN American International, 1972
GOODNIGHT MY LOVE (TF) ABC Circle Films, 1972
BLACK MAMA, WHITE MAMA American International, 1973, U.S.-Filipino
LITTLE CIGARS American International, 1973
CHEECH & CHONG'S NICE DREAMS Columbia, 1981
RICHARD PRYOR LIVE ON THE SUNSET STRIP Columbia, 1982

AMIN BHATIA

Agent: MCEG Management - Santa Monica, 213/315-7800

STORM Cannon, 1986
IRON EAGLE II Tri-Star, 1988, Canadian-Israeli

NICK BICAT

Contact: PRS - London, England, 011-44-1-580-5544

OLIVER TWIST (TF) Claridge Group Ltd./Grafton, 1982, British
THE SCARLET PIMPERNEL (TF) London Films, 1982, British
TO CATCH A KING (CTF) Entertainment Partners/ Gaylord Production Co./HBO Premiere Films, 1984
LACE (MS) Lorimar Productions, 1984
A CHRISTMAS CAROL (TF) Entertainment Partners, 1984
LACE II (TF) Lorimar Productions, 1985
WETHERBY MGM/UA Classics, 1985, British
IF TOMORROW COMES (TF) CBS Entertainment Productions, 1986
STEALING HEAVEN FilmDallas, 1988, British-Yugoslavian
STRAPLESS Granada Film, 1989, British

JOHNNY BISHOP

Contact: BMI - Los Angeles, 213/659-9109

THE GODS MUST BE CRAZY TLC Films/20th Century Fox, 1979, Botswana

CASARE BIXIO

b. Italy
Contact: SIAE - Rome, Italy, 011-39-6-59-90-1

THE DIVINE NYMPH 1979, Italian

KAREN BLACK

b. July 1, 1942 - Park Ridge, Illinois

CAN SHE BAKE A CHERRY PIE? Castle Hill Productions/ Quartet Films, 1983

STANLEY BLACK

b. 1913 - London, England
Contact: PRS - London, England, 011-44-1-580-5544

THE FATAL NIGHT 1948, British
SHADOW OF THE PAST 1950, British
TONIGHT'S THE NIGHT Allied Artists, 1954
THE CRAWLING EYE 1958, British
JACK THE RIPPER British version only, Paramount, 1960
MANIA THE FIENDISH GHOULS 1960, British
HOUSE OF MYSTERY 1961, British
MANIAC Columbia, 1963, British
WAR GODS OF THE DEEP *THE CITY UNDER THE SEA* American International, 1965, British-U.S.

WENDY BLACKSTONE

Agent: CAA - Los Angeles, 213/288-4545

EL SALVADOR: ANOTHER VIETNAM (FD) Catalyst Productions, 1982
EDDIE MACON'S RUN Universal, 1983
THE GOOD FIGHT (FD) 1983
FIVE A.M. *N.* Tanis Company, 1985
ARE WE WINNING, MOMMY? *AMERICA & THE COLD WAR* (FD) CineInformation/Canadian Film Board, 1985
A STITCH FOR TIME (FD) 1987
KING JAMES VERSION Joseph E. Taylor/ Vitascope Inc., 1988
THE LODZ GHETTO (FD) 1989
DANCE OF HOPE (FD) 1989
BLOWBACK 1989

RUBEN BLADES

Contact: ASCAP - Los Angeles, 213/466-7681

Q&A Tri-Star, 1990

HOWARD BLAKE

Agent: PRS - London, England, 011-44-1-580-5544

AN ELEPHANT CALLED SLOWLY American Continental, 1971, British
THE RAINBOW BOYS 1973, Canadian
STRONGER THAN THE SUN (TF) BBC, 1977, British
THE ODD JOB Columbia, 1978, British
THE RIDDLE OF THE SANDS Satori, 1979, British
S.O.S. TITANIC (TF) Roger Gimbel Productions/EMI TV/ Argonaut Films Ltd., 1979, U.S.-British
FLASH GORDON co-composer with Queen, Universal, 1980, British

AMITYVILLE II: THE POSSESSION Orion, 1982
AMITYVILLE 3-D Orion, 1983
THE LORDS OF DISCIPLINE Paramount, 1983
THE CANTERVILLE GHOST (TF) Pound Ridge Productions/Inter- Hemisphere Productions/HTV/ Columbia TV, 1986, U.S.-British
A MONTH IN THE COUNTRY Orion Classics, 1987, British

RONNIE BLAKLEY

b. 1946 - Caldwell, Idaho
Agent: The Lantz Office - Los Angeles, 213/858-1144

LIGHTNING OVER WATER *NICK'S MOVIE* Pari Films, 1980, West German-Swiss-U.S.
I PLAYED IT FOR YOU (FD) Ronee Blakley Productions, 1985

CHRIS BOARDMAN

THE COLOR PURPLE ★ co-composer, Warner Bros., 1985
THE HIJACKING OF THE ACHILLE LAURO (TF) ☆ Tamara Asseyev Productions/New World TV/ Spectacor Films, 1989
JOHNNY RYAN (TF) Dan Curtis TV Productions/ MGM/UA/NBC Productions, 1990

ROLAND BOCQUET

b. France
Contact: SACEM - France, 011-33-14-747-5650

LA BALANCE 1982, Spectrafilm, French

MICHAEL BODDICKER

Agent: Bart-Milander - North Hollywood, 818/761-4040

GET CRAZY Embassy, 1983
THE ADVENTURES OF BUCKAROO BANZAI: ACROSS THE 8TH DIMENSION 20th Century Fox, 1984
WHITE WATER SUMMER Columbia, 1987
THE ADVENTURES OF MILO & OTIS *THE ADVENTURES OF CHATRAN* composer of U.S. version, Columbia, 1989, Japanese

TODD BOEKELHEIDE

Contact: ASCAP - Los Angeles, 213/466-7681

DIM SUM: A LITTLE BIT OF HEART Orion Classics, 1985
CONTRARY WARRIORS (FD) Rattlesnake Prods., 1985
DEAR AMERICA: LETTERS HOME FROM VIETNAM (FD) Taurus Entertainment, 1987
THE BLOOD OF HEROES New Line Cinema, 1990
WALDO SALT

ED BOGAS

Contact: BMI - Los Angeles, 213/659-9109

BLACK GIRL Cinerama Releasing Corporation, 1972
FRITZ THE CAT (AF) American International, 1972
HEAVY TRAFFIC (AF) American International, 1973
RACE FOR YOUR LIFE, CHARLIE BROWN (AF) Paramount, 1977
WHO ARE THE DE BOLTS? ...AND WHERE DID THEY GET 19 KIDS? (FD) Pyramid Films, 1977
LOVE AND THE MIDNIGHT AUTO SUPPLY Producers Capitol Corporation, 1978
BON VOYAGE, CHARLIE BROWN (AND DON'T COME BACK) Paramount, 1980
A CHRISTMAS WITHOUT SNOW (TF) Korty Films/Frank Konigsberg Productions, 1980
STREET MUSIC co-composer, Specialty Films, 1983

WILLIAM BOLCOM

b. 1938 - Seattle, Washington
Contact: BMI - Los Angeles, 213/659-9109

HESTER STREET Midwest Film Productions, 1975

CLAUDE BOLLING

b. April 10, 1930 - Cannes, France
Contact: SACEM - France, 011-33-14-747-5650

AUTOUR D'UNE TROMPETTE (FD) 1952, French
BONJOUR CINEMA co-composer with Sidney Bechet and Christian Chevallier, 1955, French
CETTE NUIT-LA 1958, French
L'HOMME A FEMMES *MEN AND WOMEN* 1960, French
ON FRIDAY AT ELEVEN British Lion, 1961, West German-British
THE HANDS OF ORLAC Columbia, 1962, British-French
THE DAY AND THE HOUR MGM, 1962, French-Italian
VIVRE LA NUIT 1967, French
CADET L'EAU DOUCE 1969, French
LE MUR DE L'ATLANTIQUE 1969, French
LA CROISIERE DU NAVIGATOR 1969, French
BORSALINO Paramount, 1970, French-Italian
QUI? 1970, French
LA MANDARINE 1971, French
CATCH ME A SPY Rank, 1971, British
DOUCEMENT LES BASSES! CIC, 1971, French
LUCKY LUKE 1971, French
LE SOLITAIRE *THE LONER* 1973, French
LE MAGNIFIQUE *THE MAGNIFICENT ONE* Cine III, 1973, French
J'AI MON VOYAGE 1973, French
BORSALINO AND CO. Medusa, 1974, French-Italian
DEUX GRANDES FILLES DANS UN PYJAMA 1974, French
DIS-MOI QUE TU M'AIMES *TELL ME YOU LOVE ME* 1974, French
DITES-LE AVEC DES FLEURS *SAY IT WITH FLOWERS* 1974, French
FLIC STORY Adel Productions/Lira Films/Mondial, 1975, French
LE GITAN 1975, French
IL FAUT VIVRE DANGEREUSEMENT *ONE MUST LIVE DANGEROUSLY* 1975, French
L'ORDINATEUR DES POMPES FUNEBRES 1976, French
LES PASSAGERS *THE PASSENGERS* 1976, French
L'ANNEE SAINTE *SAINT ANNE* 1976, French
LE MILLE-PATTES FAIT DES CLAQUETTES 1977, French
SILVER BEARS Columbia, 1978
UN PAPILLON SUR L'EPAULE Action Films, 1978, French
L'HOROSCOPE 1978, French
LA BALLADE DES DALTON *THE BALLAD OF THE DALTONS* 1978, French
CALIFORNIA SUITE Columbia, 1978
THE ANGRY MAN 1979, French
THE AWAKENING Orion/Warner Bros., 1980
WILLIE & PHIL 20th Century-Fox, 1980
JIGSAW 1980, French
LOUISIANA (CTF) ICC/Antenne-2/Superchannel/CTV/ Societe de Development de L'Industrie Cinematographique Canadienne, 1983, Canadian-French
LE LEOPARD 1983, French

LE BRACONNIER DE DIEU Les Artistes Associes, 1983, French
BAY BOY Orion, 1984, Canadian
ON NE MEURT QUE DEUX FOIS UGC, 1985, French
LA RUMBA Hachette Premiere/UIP, 1987, French

BERNARDO BONAZZI
Contact: Luis Mas, SGAE - New York, 212/752-7230

WOMEN ON THE VERGE OF A NERVOUS BREAKDOWN Orion Classics, 1988, Spanish

JOHN BOSHOFF
THE GODS MUST BE CRAZY TLC Films/20th Century-Fox, 1979, Botswana

SIMON BOSWELL
Agent: CAA - Los Angeles, 213/288-4545

DANGEROUS OBSESSION Curb Esquire Films, 1990
SANTA SANGRE Expanded Entertainment, 1990
HARDWARE Miramax, 1990

PERRY BOTKIN
Agent: Robert Light - Los Angeles, 213/651-1777

R.P.M. Columbia, 1970
BLESS THE BEASTS AND CHILDREN Columbia, 1971
THEY ONLY KILL THEIR MASTERS MGM, 1972
SKYJACKED MGM, 1972
LADY ICE National General, 1973
YOUR THREE MINUTES ARE UP Cinerama Releasing Corporation, 1973
LADY ICE National General, 1973
GOIN' SOUTH co-composer with Van Dyke Parks, Paramount, 1978
PLEASURE COVE (TF) Lou Shaw Productions/David Gerber Productions/Columbia Pictures TV, 1979
THE GOLDEN MOMENT: AN OLYMPIC LOVE STORY (TF) Don Ohlmeyer Productions/ Telepictures Corporation, 1980
TARZAN THE APE MAN MGM/United Artists, 1981
DANCE OF THE DWARFS Dove Inc., 1983
SILENT NIGHT, DEADLY NIGHT Tri-Star, 1984
WEEKEND WARRIORS The Movie Store, 1986
ORDINARY HEROES Crow Productions/Ira Barmak Productions, 1986
SIDNEY SHELDON'S WINDMILL OF THE GODS *WINDMILL OF THE GODS* (TF) Dove Productions/ ITC Productions, 1988

LILI BOULANGER
Contact: SACEM - France, 011-33-14-747-5650

BEATRICE *LA PASSION BEATRICE* co-composer with Ron Carter, Samuel Goldwyn Company, 1987, French-Italian

JEAN BOUCHETY
Contact: SACEM - France, 011-33-14-747-5650

THE GAME IS OVER *LA CUREE* Royal Films International, 1966, French-Italian

HUBERT BOUGIS
Contact: SACEM - France, 011-33-14-747-5650

SWEET REVENGE The Movie Group, 1990, U.S.-French

ROGER BOURLAND
Agent: Robert Light - Los Angeles, 213/651-1777

THE WOLF AT THE DOOR *OVIRI* International Film Marketing, 1986, Danish-French
THE TROUBLE WITH DICK FilmDallas, 1987
NIGHT LIFE Wild Night Productions, 1989

DENNIS BOVELL
Contact: PRS - London, England, 011-44-1-580-5544

BABYLON National Film, 1980, British

RICHARD BOWDEN
Contact: ASCAP - Los Angeles, 213/466-7681

THE SWEET CREEK COUNTY WAR Key International, 1979

PAUL BOWLES
b. 1910 - New York

SIVA Central Films, 1933
INNOCENT ISLAND Harry Durham, 1934
VENUS AND ADONIS Harry Durham, 1934
145 WEST 21 Rudolph Burckhardt, 1936
SEEING THE WORLD: A VISIT TO NEW YORK Rudolph Burckhardt, 1936
AMERICA'S DISINHERITED Sharecropper Committee, 1937
HOW TO BECOME A CITIZEN OF THE UNITED STATES Rudlph Burckhardt, 1938
CHELSEA THROUGH THE MAGNIFYING GLASS Rudolph Burckhardt, 1938
THE SEX LIFE OF THE COMMON FILM Rudolph Burckhardt, 1938
FILM MADE TO MUSIC WRITTEN BY PAUL BOWLES Rudolph Burckhardt, 1939
ROOTS IN THE EARTH (D) Department of Agriculture, 1940
THE CONGO (D) Belgian Government, 1944
DREAMS THAT MONEY CAN BUY co-composer, Films International of America, 1948

EUEL BOX
Contact: ASCAP - Los Angeles, 213/466-7681

BENJI Mulberry Square, 1974
HAWMPS Mulberry Square, 1976
FOR THE LOVE OF BENJI Mulberry Square, 1978
THE DOUBLE McGUFFIN Mulberry Square, 1979
BENJI, THE HUNTED Buena Vista, 1987

MICHAEL BOYD
BREAKIN' co-composer with Gary Remal, MGM/UA/ Cannon, 1984

ROBERT BOYLE
ANNE DEVLIN Aeon Films, 1984, Irish

OWEN BRADLEY
Contact: BMI - Los Angeles, 213/659-9109

COAL MINER'S DAUGHTER Universal, 1980

ERNST BRADNER
BLOOD AND HONOR: YOUTH UNDER HITLER (MS) Daniel Wilson Productions/SWF/Taurus Films, 1982

CARL BRANDT
Contact: ASCAP - Los Angeles, 213/466-7681

LITTLE MO (TF) co-composer with Billy May, Mark VII Ltd./Worldvision Enterprises, 1978

FRED BRATHWAITE
WILD STYLE co-composer with Chris Stein, Wild Style, 1983

CREED BRATTON
Contact: BMI - Los Angeles, 213/659-9109

DANGEROUS COMPANY (TF) The Dangerous Company/Finnegan Associates, 1982

ALAN BREWER
Contact: BMI - Los Angeles, 213/659-9109

TOKYO POP Skouras, 1988

PETER BREWIS
Contact: PRS - London, England, 011-44-1-580-5544

MORONS FROM OUTER SPACE Thorn/EMI, 1985, British
THE TALL GUY Vestron, 1989, British

LESLIE BRICCUSE
b. January 29, 1931 - London, England
Contact: BMI - Los Angeles, 213/659-9109

DR. DOOLITTLE ★ 20th Century Fox, 1967
GOODBYE, MR. CHIPS ★ adaptation, MGM, 1969, British
SCROOGE ★ National General, 1970, British
WILLIE WONKA AND THE CHOCOLATE FACTORY ★ Paramount, 1971, British
BABES IN TOYLAND (TF) The Finnegan/Pinchuk Company/Orion TV/Bavaria Atelier GMBH, 1986

TONY BRITTEN
Contact: PRS - London, England, 011-44-1-580-5544

JOYRIDERS Granada Film Prods., 1989, British

JOSEPH BROOKS
Business: Chancery Lane Films, Inc., 41-A East 74th St., New York, NY 10021, 212/759-8720

THE LORDS OF FLATBUSH Columbia, 1974
YOU LIGHT UP MY LIFE Columbia, 1977
IF EVER I SEE YOU AGAIN Columbia, 1978
HEADIN' FOR BROADWAY 20th Century-Fox, 1980
INVITATION TO THE WEDDING New Realm, 1983, British

BRUCE BROUGHTON
b. 1945 - Los Angeles, California
Agent: Gorfaine-Schwartz - Burbank, 818/954-9500

PARADISE CONNECTION (TF) Woodruff Productions/QM Productions, 1979
THE RETURN OF FRANK CANNON (TF) QM Productions, 1980
DESPERATE VOYAGE (TF) Barry Weitz Films/Jack Wizan TV Productions, 1980
THE GIRL, THE GOLD WATCH AND DYNAMITE (TF) Fellows-Keegan Company/Paramount TV, 1981
KILLJOY (TF) ☆ Lorimar Productions, 1981
DESPERATE LIVES (TF) Fellows-Keegan Company/Lorimar Pictures, 1982
ONE SHOE MAKES IT MURDER (TF) Fellows-Keegan Company/Lorimar Productions, 1982
THE BLUE AND THE GRAY (MS) ☆ Larry White-Lou Reda Productions/Columbia TV, 1982
TWO MARRIAGES (TF) Lorimar Productions/Raven's Claw Productions, 1983
COWBOY (TF) Bercovici-St. Johns Productions/MGM TV, 1983
M.A.D.D.: MOTHERS AGAINST DRUNK DRIVERS (TF) Universal TV, 1983
THE ICE PIRATES MGM/UA, 1983
THIS GIRL FOR HIRE (TF) Barney Rosenzweig Productions/Orion TV, 1983
THE MASTER OF BALLANTRAE (TF) Larry White-Hugh Benson Productions/HTV/Columbia TV, 1984, U.S.-British
THE PRODIGAL World Wide, 1984
THE COWBOY AND THE BALLERINA (TF) Cowboy Productions, 1984
PASSIONS (TF) Carson Production Group/Wizan TV Enterprises, 1984
THE FIRST OLYMPICS - ATHENS 1896 (MS) ☆☆ Larry White-Gary Allison Productions/Columbia TV, 1984
SILVERADO ★ Columbia, 1985
STORMIN' HOME (TF) CBS Entertainment, 1985
YOUNG SHERLOCK HOLMES Paramount, 1985
SWEET LIBERTY Universal, 1986
THE BOY WHO COULD FLY 20th Century Fox, 1986
SQUARE DANCE Island Pictures, 1986
THE THANKSGIVING PROMISE (TF) Mark H. Ovitz Productions/Walt Disney TV, 1986
GEORGE WASHINGTON: THE FORGING OF A NATION (TF) David Gerber Company/MGM TV, 1986
HARRY AND THE HENDERSONS Universal, 1987
THE MONSTER SQUAD Tri-Star, 1987
BIG SHOTS 20th Century Fox, 1987
CROSS MY HEART Universal, 1987
THE PRESIDIO Paramount, 1988
THE RESCUE Buena Vista, 1988
MOONWALKER Warner Bros., 1988
LAST RITES MGM/UA, 1988
JACKNIFE Kings Road, 1989
SORRY, WRONG NUMBER (CTF) 1989
ERNEST HEMINGWAY'S THE OLD MAN AND THE SEA (TF) ☆ Stroke Enterprises/Green Pond Productions/Yorkshire TV, 1990
BETSY'S WEDDING Buena Vista, 1990

EARL BROWN, JR.
AMERICATHON United Artists, 1979

GREG BROWN
ZADAR! COW FROM HELL Stone Peach, 1989

TOM BRUNER
Contact: ASCAP - Los Angeles, 213/466-7681

SCHOOL SPIRIT Concorde/Cinema Group, 1985

ROBERT F. BRUNNER
Contact: ASCAP - Los Angeles, 213/466-7681

THAT DARN CAT Buena Vista, 1965
LT. ROBIN CRUSOE, U.S.N. Buena Vista, 1966

MONKEYS, GO HOME! Buena Vista, 1967
BLACKBEARD'S GHOST Buena Vista, 1968
NEVER A DULL MOMENT Buena Vista, 1968
THE COMPUTER WORE TENNIS SHOES Buena Vista, 1969
SMITH! Buena Vista, 1969
THE BOATNIKS Buena Vista, 1970
THE BAREFOOT EXECUTIVE Buena Vista, 1971
THE WILD COUNTRY Buena Vista, 1971
THE BISCUIT EATER Buena Vista, 1972
NOW YOU SEE HIM, NOW YOU DON'T Buena Vista, 1972
THE SNOWBALL EXPRESS Buena Vista, 1972
THE CASTAWAY COWBOY Buena Vista, 1974
THE STRONGEST MAN IN THE WORLD Buena Vista, 1975
GUS Buena Vista, 1976
THE NORTH AVENUE IRREGULARS Buena Vista, 1979
AMY Buena Vista, 1981

GEORGE BRUNS

b. July 3, 1914 - Sandy, Oregon

DAVY CROCKETT, KING OF THE WILD FRONTIER Buena Vista, 1955
DAVY CROCKETT AND THE RIVER PIRATES Buena Vista, 1956
WESTWARD HO, THE WAGONS Buena Vista, 1956
JOHNNY TREMAIN Buena Vista, 1957
SLEEPING BEAUTY (AF) ★ adaptation, Buena Vista, 1959
ONE HUNDRED AND ONE DALMATIONS (AF) Buena Vista, 1960
THE ABSENT-MINDED PROFESSOR Buena Vista, 1960
BABES IN TOYLAND ★ adaptation, Buena Vista, 1961
SON OF FLUBBER Buena Vista, 1963
THE SWORD IN THE STONE (AF) ★ Buena Vista, 1963
THE MAN FROM BUTTON WILLOW (AF) co-composer with Dale Robertson and Mel Hank, 1965
THE FIGHTING PRINCE OF DONEGAL Buena Vista, 1966
FOLLOW ME, BOYS! Buena Vista, 1966
THE ADVENTURES OF BULLWHIP GRIFFIN Buena Vista, 1967
THE JUNGLE BOOK (AF) Buena Vista, 1967
ISLAND OF THE LOST 1967
DARING GAME Paramount, 1968
THE HORSE IN THE GRAY FLANNEL SUIT Buena Vista, 1968
THE LOVE BUG Buena Vista, 1969
THE ARISTOCATS (AF) Buena Vista, 1970
ROBIN HOOD (AF) Buena Vista, 1973
HERBIE RIDES AGAIN Buena Vista, 1974

CHICO BUARQUE

Contact: SACEM - France, 011-33-14-747-5650

DONA FLOR AND HER TWO HUSBANDS New Yorker, 1977, Brazilian

ROY BUDD

Contact: PRS - London, England, 011-44-1-580-5544

SOLDIER BLUE Avco Embassy, 1970
FLIGHT OF THE DOVES Columbia, 1971, British
ZEPPELIN 1971
GET CARTER MGM, 1971, British
KIDNAPPED American International, 1971, British
CATLOW MGM, 1971, U.S.-Spanish
THE MAGNIFICENT SEVEN DEADLY SINS 1971, British
SOMETHING TO HIDE *SHATTERED* 1972, British
EXTREMES (FD) co-composer, 1972, British
THE CAREY TREATMENT MGM, 1972
FEAR IS A KEY Paramount, 1972, British
THE STONE KILLER Columbia, 1973
THE DESTRUCTORS *THE MARSEILLES CONTRACT* American International, 1974, British-French
THE INTERNECINE PROJECT Allied Artists, 1974, British
THE BLACK WINDMILL Universal, 1974, British
DIAMONDS Avco Embassy, 1975, U.S.-Israeli-Swiss
PAPER TIGER Joseph E. Levine Presents, 1976, British
SINBAD AND THE EYE OF THE TIGER Columbia, 1977, British
WELCOME TO BLOOD CITY EMI, 1977, British
TOMORROW NEVER COMES 1977, British
FOXBAT 1978
THE WILD GEESE Allied Artists, 1979, British
THE MISSING LINK 1980, French
MAMMA DRACULA 1980, French-Belgian
THE SEA WOLVES Paramount, 1981, British
THE FINAL OPTION *WHO DARES WINS* MGM/UA, 1982, British
WILD GEESE II Universal, 1985, British
FIELD OF HONOR Cannon, 1986, U.S.-Dutch
THE BIG BANG (AF) 20th Century Fox, 1987, Belgian-French

JIMMY BUFFETT

Contact: BMI - Los Angeles, 213/659-9109

RANCHO DELUXE United Artists, 1975

ERIC BURDON

Contact: BMI - Los Angeles, 213/659-9109

COMEBACK Rocco Film, 1982, West German

GEOFFREY BURGON

Agent: PRS - London, England, 011-44-1-580-5544

LIFE OF BRIAN Orion, 1979, British
THE DOGS OF WAR United Artists, 1980
BRIDESHEAD REVISITED (MS) Granada TV/WNET-13/ NDR Hamburg, 1982, British-U.S.-West German
TURTLE DIARY Samuel Goldwyn Company, 1985, British
BLEAK HOUSE (MS) BBC, 1985, British

CHRIS BURKE

SPLATTER UNIVERSITY Troma, 1984

RALPH BURNS

b. June 29, 1922 - Newton, Massachusetts
Agent: Gorfaine-Schwartz - Burbank, 818/954-9500

CABARET ★★ Allied Artists, 1972
LENNY United Artists, 1974
PIAF AMLF, 1974
LUCKY LADY 20th Century Fox, 1977
NEW YORK, NEW YORK United Artists, 1977

MOVIE MOVIE Warner Brothers, 1978
ALL THAT JAZZ ★★ adaptation, 20th Century Fox, 1979
MAKE ME AN OFFER (TF) ABC Circle Films, 1980
URBAN COWBOY Paramount, 1980
FIRST FAMILY adaptation, Warner Bros., 1980
GOLDEN GATE (TF) Lin Bolen Productions/Warner Bros. TV, 1981
SIDE SHOW (TF) Krofft Entertainment, 1981
PENNIES FROM HEAVEN co-composer with Marvin Hamlisch, MGM/United Artists, 1981
ANNIE ★ adaptation, Columbia, 1982
KISS ME GOODBYE 20th Century Fox, 1982
MY FAVORITE YEAR MGM/UA, 1982
STAR 80 The Ladd Company/Warner Bros., 1983
NATIONAL LAMPOON'S VACATION Warner Bros., 1983
PHANTOM OF THE OPERA (TF) Robert Halmi Inc., 1983
THE MUPPETS TAKE MANHATTAN Tri-Star, 1984
ERNIE KOVACS - BETWEEN THE LAUGHTER (TF) ABC Circle Films, 1984
PERFECT Columbia, 1985
A CHORUS LINE Columbia, 1985
MOVING VIOLATIONS 20th Century-Fox, 1985
PENALTY PHASE (TF) Tamara Asseyev Productions/ New World TV, 1986
THE CHRISTMAS STAR (TF) Lake Walloon Productions/Catalina Productions. Group/ Walt Disney TV, 1986
IN THE MOOD Lorimar, 1987
AFTER THE PROMISE (TF) Tamara Asseyev Productions/New World TV, 1987
BERT RIGBY, YOU'RE A FOOL Warner Bros., 1989
SWEET BIRD OF YOUTH (TF) 1989
ALL DOGS GO TO HEAVEN (AF) MGM/UA, 1989, British
THE JOSEPHINE BAKER STORY (CTF) HBO Pictures/ Anglia TV/John Kemeny/RH Entertainment, 1991

GEORGE BURT
Contact: ASCAP - Los Angeles, 213/466-7681

SECRET HONOR Sandcastle 5, 1984
FOOL FOR LOVE Cannon, 1985

CARTER BURWELL
Agent: CAA - Los Angeles, 213/288-4545

BLOOD SIMPLE Circle Releasing Corporation, 1984
PSYCHO III Universal, 1986
RAISING ARIZONA 20th Century Fox, 1987
PASS THE AMMO New Century/Vista, 1988
IT TAKES TWO MGM/UA, 1988
BEAT Vestron, 1988
CHECKING OUT Warner Bros., 1989

GERALD BUSBY
THREE WOMEN 20th Century-Fox, 1977

ARTIE BUTLER
Contact: Bart-Milander - North Hollywood, 818/761-4040

THE LOVE MACHINE Columbia, 1971
WHAT'S UP, DOC? Warner Bros., 1972
THE HARRAD EXPERIMENT Cinerama Releasing Corporation, 1973
WONDER WOMAN (TF) Warner Bros. TV, 1974
FOR PETE'S SAKE Columbia, 1974
AT LONG LAST LOVE adaptation, 20th Century Fox, 1975
RAFFERTY AND THE GOLD DUST TWINS Warner Bros., 1975
IT'S SHOWTIME United Artists, 1976
OPERATION PETTICOAT (TF) Heyday Productions/ Universal TV, 1977
THE RESCUERS (AF) Buena Vista, 1978
SEXTETTE Crown International, 1978
SULTAN AND THE ROCK STAR (TF) Walt Disney Productions, 1978
ANGEL ON MY SHOULDER (TF) Mace Neufeld Productions/Barney Rosenzweig Productions/Beowulf Productions, 1980
SIZZLE (TF) Aaron Spelling Productions, 1981
AMERICAN DREAM (TF) Mace Neufeld Productions/ Viacom, 1981
SHE'S IN THE ARMY NOW (TF) ABC Circle Films, 1981
GREASE 2 Paramount, 1982
O'HARA'S WIFE Davis-Panzer Productions, 1982
THE MAKING OF A MALE MODEL (TF) Aaron Spelling Productions, 1983
THE OTHER WOMAN (TF) CBS Entertainment, 1983
LAST OF THE GREAT SURVIVORS (TF) CBS Entertainment, 1984
COPACABANA (TF) Dick Clark Cinema Productions/ Stiletto Ltd., 1985
CLASSIFIED LOVE (TF) CBS Entertainment, 1986

BILLY BYERS
HAUSER'S MEMORY (TF) Universal TV, 1970
THE BORROWERS (TF) co-composer with Rod McKuen, Walt DeFaria Productions/20th Century-Fox TV, 1973

DONALD BYRD
Contact: BMI - Los Angeles, 213/659-9109

CORNBREAD, EARL AND ME American International, 1975

JOSEPH BYRD
HEALTH 20th Century-Fox, 1980

DAVID BYRNE
b. Dumbarton, Scotland
Contact: ASCAP - Los Angeles, 213/466-7681

TRUE STORIES Warner Bros., 1986
DEAD END KIDS (FD) co-composer with Philip Glass, Mabou Mines, 1986
THE LAST EMPEROR ★★ co-composer with Cong Su and Ryuichi Sakamoto, Columbia, 1987, British-Chinese

C

JOHN CACAVAS

b. South Dakota
Agent: Bart-Milander - North Hollywood, 818/761-4040

PANCHO VILLA Scotia, 1972, Spanish
HORROR EXPRESS 1972, Spanish-British
BLADE Green/Pintoff, 1973
COUNT DRACULA AND HIS VAMPIRE BRIDE *SATANIC RITES OF DRACULA* Warner Bros., 1973
REDNECK International Amusements, 1975, British-Italian
SHE CRIED "MURDER" (TF) Universal TV, 1973
LINDA (TF) Universal TV, 1973
THE ELEVATOR (TF) Universal TV, 1974
AIRPORT 1975 Universal, 1974
FRIENDLY PERSUASION (TF) International TV Productions/Allied Artists, 1975
KATE McSHANE (TF) Paramount TV, 1975
MURDER AT THE WORLD SERIES (TF) ABC Circle Films, 1977
SST - DEATH FLIGHT (TF) ABC Circle Films, 1977
AIRPORT '77 Universal, 1977
RELENTLESS (TF) CBS, Inc., 1977
SUPERDOME (TF) ABC Circle Films, 1978
BJ & THE BEAR Universal TV, 1978
THE TIME MACHINE (TF) Sunn Classic Productions, 1978
HUMAN FEELINGS (TF) Crestview Productions/ Worldvision, 1978
HANGAR 18 Sunn Classic, 1980
ONCE UPON A SPY (TF) David Gerber Company/ Columbia TV, 1980
HANGAR 18 Sunn Classic, 1980
SEPARATE WAYS Crown International, 1981
HELLINGER'S LAW (TF) Universal TV, 1981
NO PLACE TO HIDE (TF) Metromedia Producers Corporation, 1981
THE GANGSTER CHRONICLES (TF) Universal TV, 1981
TODAY'S FBI (TF) David Gerber Company, 1981
CHILD BRIDE OF SHORT CREEK (TF) Lawrence Schiller-Paul Monash Productions, 1981
THE NEIGHBORHOOD (TF) David Gerber Company/ Columbia TV, 1982
THE EXECUTIONER'S SONG (TF) Film Communications Inc., 1982
CRY FOR THE STRANGERS (TF) David Gerber Company/MGM TV, 1982
MORTUARY Artists Releasing Corporation/Film Ventures International, 1983
A TIME TO DIE Almi Films, 1983
STILL THE BEAVER Bud Austin Productions/ Universal TV, 1983
WOMEN OF SAN QUENTIN (TF) David Gerber Company/MGM-UA TV, 1983
THEY'RE PLAYING WITH FIRE New World, 1984
JESSIE (TF) Lindsay Wagner Productions/ MGM-UA TV. 1984
LADY BLUE (TF) David Gerber Productions Productions/ MGM-UA TV, 1985
A DEATH IN CALIFORNIA (TF) Mace Neufeld Productions/Lorimar Productions, 1985
JENNY'S WAR (TF) Louis Rudolph Productions/HTV/ Columbia TV, 1985, U.S.-British
A TIME TO TRIUMPH (TF) Billos-Kauffman Productions/ Phoenix Entertainment Group, 1986
THE DIRTY DOZEN: THE DEADLY MISSION (TF) MGM-UA TV/Jadran Film, 1987, U.S.-Yugoslavian
POLICE STORY II: THE FREEWAY KILLINGS (TF) David Gerber Productions/MGM-UA TV/Columbia TV, 1987
THE DIRTY DOZEN: THE FATAL MISSION (TF) MGM-UA TV, 1988
BODY OF EVIDENCE (TF) CBS Entertainment, 1988
MARGARET-BOURKE WHITE (CTF) TNT Inc./Project VII/ Central TV, 1989
COLOMBO GOES TO THE GUILLOTINE (TF) Universal TV, 1989
MURDER IN PARADISE (TF) Bill McCutchen Productions/ Columbia Pictures TV, 1990

JOHN CAFFERTY

Contact: BMI - Los Angeles, 213/659-9109

EDDIE AND THE CRUISERS Embassy, 1983

STEVEN CAGAN

THE CAT AND THE CANARY Quartet, 1978, British

JOHN CAGE

b. 1912 - Los Angeles, California
Contact: ASCAP - Los Angeles, 213/466-7681

HORROR DREAM Peterson
DREAMS THAT MONEY CAN BUY co-composer, Films International of America, 1948
WORKS OF CALDER Herbert Matter, 1950

JORGE CALANDRELLI

b. Argentina
Agent: Richard Emler - Los Angeles, 213/651-0222

SOLA 1976, Argentinian
THE COLOR PURPLE ★ co-composer, Warner Bros., 1985
THE TOWN BULLY (TF) Dick Clark Productions, 1988
I'LL BE HOME FOR CHRISTMAS (TF) NBC Productions, 1988

JOHN CALE

Contact: ASCAP - Los Angeles, 213/466-7681

SOMETHING WILD co-composer with Laurie Anderson, Orion, 1986

CHARLES CALELLO

THE LONELY LADY Universal, 1983

PAUL CALLUM

DEATH WISH 4: THE CRACKDOWN Cannon, 1988

CHRISTOPHER CAMERON

GOD'S WILL Power and Light Production, 1989

JOHN CAMERON

Contact: PRS - London, England, 011-44-1-580-5544

THINK DIRTY *EVERY HOME SHOULD HAVE ONE* 1970, British
KES United Artists, 1970, British

THE RISE AND RISE OF MICHAEL RIMMER Warner Bros., 1970, British
THE RULING CLASS Avco Embassy, 1972, British
CHARLEY-ONE-EYE Paramount, 1973, British
NIGHT WATCH Avco Embassy, 1973, British
A TOUCH OF CLASS ★ Avco Embassy, 1973, British
SCALAWAG Paramount, 1973, U.S.-Italian
SEX PLAY 1974
MOMENTS Warner/Columbia, 1974, British
MADE International Co-Productions, 1975, British
OUT OF SEASON *WINTER RATES* Athenaeum, 1975, British
WHIFFS 20th Century-Fox, 1975
THE GREAT SCOUT AND CATHOUSE THURSDAY American International, 1976
I WILL, I WILL...FOR NOW 20th Century-Fox, 1976
SPECTRE (TF) Norway Productions/20th Century-Fox TV, 1977
NASTY HABITS Brut Productions, 1977, British
THE THIEF OF BAGHDAD (TF) Palm Productions, 1978
THE BERMUDA TRIANGLE Sunn Classic, 1979
LOST AND FOUND Columbia, 1979
SUNBURN Paramount, 1979, U.S.-British
THE MIRROR CRACK'D AFD, 1980, British
WHO? Lorimar, 1982, British-West German
WITNESS FOR THE PROSECUTION (TF) Norman Rosemont Productions/United Artists TV, 1982
THE JIGSAW MAN United Film Distribution, 1984, British
THE SECRET GARDEN (TF) Norman Rosemont Productions, 1987
JACK THE RIPPER (TF) Euston Films/Thames TV/Hill-O'Connor Entertainment/Lorimar TV, 1988, British-U.S.
JEKYLL & HYDE (TF) David Wickes TV/LWT/King Phoenix Entertainment, 1990

DAVID CAMPBELL

Contact: ASCAP - Los Angeles, 213/466-7681

ALL THE RIGHT MOVES 20th Century Fox, 1983
NIGHT OF THE COMET Atlantic Releasing Corporation, 1984

JAMES CAMPBELL

b. October 15, 1946 - Laguna Beach, California
Agent: Lawrence B. Marks - 818/831-1830

DRACULA'S WIDOW DEG, 1988
ELVIRA, MISTRESS OF THE DARK New World, 1988

TOM CANNING

Agent: The Artists Group - Los Angeles, 213/552-1100

FALLING WATER 1986
THE HENRY SOLUTION 1988
THE KISS Tri-Star, 1988, U.S.-Canadian

MICHAEL CANNON

Contact: BMI - Los Angeles, 213/659-9109

TORCHLIGHT Film Ventures, 1984

LARRY CANSLER

Contact: ASCAP - Los Angeles, 213/466-7681

KENNY ROGERS AS THE GAMBLER (TF) Kragen & Co., 1980
COWARD OF THE COUNTY (TF) Kraco Productions, 1981
KENNY ROGERS AS THE GAMBLER - THE ADVENTURE CONTINUES (TF) Lion Share Productions, 1983
SEPTEMBER GUN (TF) QM Productions, 1983
SMOKEY & THE BANDIT - PART 3 Universal, 1983
SONGWRITER Tri-Star, 1984
KENNY ROGERS AS THE GAMBLER III: THE LEGEND CONTINUES (TF) Lion Share Productions, 1987

AL CAPPS

Contact: BMI - Los Angeles, 213/659-9109

TRIBES (TF) 20th Century-Fox TV/Marvin Schwartz Productions, 1970
TWICE IN A LIFETIME (TF) Martin Rackin Productions, 1974
STROKER ACE Universal, 1983
RUNNING HOT New Line Cinema, 1984
CANNONBALL RUN II Warner Bros., 1984

MICHAEL CARLOS

Contact: APRA - 011-61-2-922-6422

STORM BOY South Australian Film Corp., 1976, Australian
BLUE FIN Roadshow Distributors, 1978, Australian
LONG WEEKEND 1978, Australian

WALTER CARLOS

(See Wendy Carlos)

WENDY CARLOS

(Walter Carlos)
Contact: BMI - Los Angeles, 213/659-9109

A CLOCKWORK ORANGE Warner Bros., 1971, British
THE SHINING Warner Bros., 1980, British
TRON Buena Vista, 1982

LARRY CARLTON

Contact: Bart-Milander - North Hollywood, 818/761-4040

AGAINST ALL ODDS co-composer with Michel Colombier, Columbia, 1984
DEADLINE (TF) 1989

RALPH CARMICHAEL

Contact: ASCAP - Los Angeles, 213/466-7681

JONI World Wide Pictures, 1980

JOHN CARPENTER

b. January 16, 1948 - Carthage, New York
Agent: Jim Wiatt, ICM - Los Angeles, 213/550-4000

DARK STAR Jack H. Harris Enterprises, 1974
ASSAULT ON PRECINCT 13 Turtle Releasing Corporation, 1976
HALLOWEEN Compass International, 1978
THE FOG Avco Embassy, 1981
ESCAPE FROM NEW YORK co-composer with Alan Howarth, Avco Embassy, 1981
HALLOWEEN II co-composer with Alan Howarth, Universal, 1981
HALLOWEEN III: SEASON OF THE WITCH co-composer with Alan Howarth, Universal, 1982
CHRISTINE co-composer with Alan Howarth, Columbia, 1983
BIG TROUBLE IN LITTLE CHINA 20th Century Fox, 1986

PRINCE OF DARKNESS co-composer with Alan Howarth, Universal, 1987
THEY LIVE co-composer with Alan Howarth, Universal, 1988

FIORENZO CARPI

b. 1918 - Milan, Italy
Contact: SIAE - Rome, Italy, 011-39-6-592-3351

ZAZIE *ZAZIE DANS LE METRO* Astor, 1960, French
LEONI AL SOLE 1961, Italian
PARIGI O CARA 1962, Italian
A VERY PRIVATE AFFAIR MGM, 1962, French-Italian
INCOMPRESO 1966, Italian
ITALIAN SECRET SERVICE 1968, Italian
INFANZIA, VOCAZIONE E PRIME ESPERIENZE DI GIACOMO CASANOVA - VENEZIANO 1969, Italian
I BAMBINI E NOI (TF) 1970, Italian
EQUINOZIO San Diego, 1971, Italian
LA VACANZA Lion Film, 1972, Italian
LE AVVENTURE DI PINNOCHIO RAI/ORTF/Bavaria Film, 1972, Italian-French-West German
MIO DIO, COME SONO CADUTA IN BASSO! Dean Film, 1974, Italian
LA CHAIR DE L'ORCHIDEE 1974, French
NON SI SCRIVE SUI MURI A MILANO 1975, Italian
VIETNAM SCENE DEL DOPOGUERRA 1975, Italian
SALON KITTY American International, 1976, Italian

DAVID CARRADINE

b. December 8, 1936 - Hollywood, California
Agent: Peter Rawley, ICM - Los Angeles, 213/550-4000

AMERICANA co-composer with Craig Hundley, Crown International, 1981

NICHOLAS CARRAS

Contact: ASCAP - Los Angeles, 213/466-7681

THE DOLL SQUAD *SEDUCE AND DESTROY* 1973
10 VIOLENT WOMEN New American Films, 1984
OMEGA SYNDROME co-composer with Jack Cookerly, New World, 1987

BERTHOLD CARRIERE

LITTLE GLORIA...HAPPY AT LAST (TF) Edgar J. Scherick Associates/Metromedia Producers Corporation, 1982, U.S.-Canadian-British

BENNY CARTER

b. August 7, 1907 - New York, New York
Contact: ASCAP - Los Angeles, 213/466-7681

THE HANGED MAN (TF) Universal TV, 1964
A MAN CALLED ADAM Embassy, 1966
FAME IS THE NAME OF THE GAME (TF) Universal TV, 1966
BUCK AND THE PREACHER Columbia, 1972
MANHUNTER (TF) QM Productions, 1974
LOUIS ARMSTRONG - CHICAGO STYLE (TF) Charles Fries Productions/Stonehenge Productions, 1976

RON CARTER

A GATHERING OF OLD MEN (TF) Consolidated Productions/Jennie & Company/Zenith Productions, 1987
BEATRICE *LA PASSION BEATRICE* co-composer with Lili Boulanger, Samuel Goldwyn Co., 1987, French-Italian

TRISTRAM CARY

Contact: PRS - London, England, 011-44-1-580-5544

THE LADYKILLERS Continental, 1956, British
TIME WITHOUT PITY Astor, 1956, British
TOWN ON TRIAL Columbia, 1957, British
THE BOY WHO STOLE A MILLION Paramount, 1960, British
A LECTURE ON MAN 1962, British
A BOY TEN FEET TALL *SAMMY GOING SOUTH* Paramount, 1963, British
FIVE MILLION YEARS TO EARTH *QUARTERMASS AND THE PIT* 20th Century-Fox, 1968, British
A TWIST OF SAND United Artists, 1968, British
BLOOD FROM THE MUMMY'S TOMB American International, 1971, British

JOHNNY CASH

b. February 26, 1932 - Kingsland, Arizona
Contact: ASCAP - Los Angeles, 213/466-7681

THE PRIDE OF JESSE HALLAM (TF) The Konigsberg Company, 1981

MATHIEU CHABROL

Contact: SACEM - France, 011-33-14-747-5650

LES FANTOMES DU CHAPELIER Gaumont, 1982, French
POULET AU VINAIGRE MK2 Diffusion, 1985, French
INSPECTOR LAVARDIN MK Diffusion, 1986, French
UNE AFFAIRE DE FEMMES MK2, 1988, French
QUIET DAYS IN CLICKY Pathe-Europa, 1990, French

GARY CHANG

Agent: Bart-Milander - North Hollywood, 818/761-4040

THE BREAKFAST CLUB Universal, 1985
3:15 Cannon, 1986
52 PICK-UP Cannon, 1986
FIREWALKER Cannon, 1986
STICKY FINGERS Spectrafilm, 1988
DEAD-BANG co-composer with Michael Kamen Warner Bros., 1989
MIAMI BLUES Orion, 1989
SHOCK TO THE SYSTEM 1990

JOHN CHARLES

Contact: APRA - Australia, 011-61-2-922-6422

THE QUIET EARTH Skouras Pictures, 1985, New Zealand
A SOLDIER'S TALE Atlantic Releasing Corporation, 1988, New Zealand

TOM CHASE

Contact: ASCAP - Los Angeles, 213/466-7681

SCARED TO DEATH co-composer with Ardell Hake, Lone Star Pictures, 1982
CREATURE *TITAN FIND* co-composer with Steve Rucker, Cardinal Releasing, 1985
FEEL THE HEAT co-composer with Steve Rucker, Trans World Entertainment, 1987
ALIEN PREDATOR co-composer with Steve Rucker, Trans World Entertainment, 1987
AND GOD CREATED WOMAN co-composer with Steve Rucker, Vestron, 1988
976-EVIL co-composer with Steve Rucker, New Line Cinema, 1988

LITTLE NEMO (AF) co-composer with Steve Rucker, 1990
SYNGENOR co-composer with Steve Rucker, Syngenor Production Co., 1990

JAY CHATTAWAY

Agent: Carol Faith - Beverly Hills, 213/274-0776

MANIAC Analysis, 1981
VIGILANTE *STREET GANG* Artists Releasing Corporation/Film Ventures International, 1983
THE LAST FIGHT Marvin Films, 1983
THE BIG SCORE Almi Distribution, 1983
HOME FREE ALL Almi Classics, 1984
VIGILANTE Artists Releasing Corporation/Film Ventures International, 1983
MISSING IN ACTION Cannon, 1984
WALKING THE EDGE Empire Pictures, 1985
THE ROSEBUD BEACH HOTEL Almi Pictures, 1985
INVASION, U.S.A. Cannon, 1985
STEPHEN KING'S SILVER BULLET Paramount, 1985
HARD CHOICES Lorimar, 1986
VERY CLOSE QUARTERS Cable Star Ltd., 1986
MANIAC COP Shapiro Entertainment, 1987
BRADDOCK: MISSING IN ACTION III Cannon, 1988
JAKARTA! Troma, 1988, U.S.-Indonesian
RED SCORPION Shapiro Glinkenhaus Entertainment, 1989
RELENTLESS New Line Cinema, 1989
FAR OUT MAN CineTel Films, 1989
BARR SINISTER Intermedia, 1990
MANIAC COP 2 The Movie House, 1990

VLADIMIR CHEKASSINE

Contact: VAAP - U.S.S.R., Telex: 871-411327

TAXI BLUES MK2 Diffusion, 1990, Soviet-French

PAUL CHIHARA

b. July 9, 1938 - Seattle, Washington
Agent: Gorfaine-Schwartz - Burbank, 818/954-9500

DEATH RACE 2000 New World, 1975
FAREWELL TO MANZANAR (TF) Korty Films/ Universal TV, 1976
SWEET REVENGE *DANDY, THE ALL AMERICAN GIRL* MGM/United Artists, 1976
THE KEEGANS (TF) Universal TV, 1976
I NEVER PROMISED YOU A ROSE GARDEN New World, 1977
THE BAD NEWS BEARS GO TO JAPAN Paramount, 1978
NIGHT CRIES (TF) Charles Fries Productions, 1978
DEATH MOON (TF) Roger Gimbel Productions/ EMI TV, 1978
A FIRE IN THE SKY (TF) Bill Driskell Productions, 1978
DR. STRANGE (TF) Universal TV, 1978
BETRAYAL (TF) Roger Gimbel Productions/ EMI TV, 1978
THE DARKER SIDE OF TERROR (TF) Shaner-Ramrus Productions/Bob Banner Associates, 1979
MIND OVER MURDER (TF) Paramount TV, 1979
ACT OF VIOLENCE (TF) Emmet Lavery, Jr. Productions/Paramount TV, 1979
BRAVE NEW WORLD (TF) Universal TV, 1980
THE CHILDREN OF AN LAC (TF) Charles Fries Productions, 1980
THE PROMISE OF LOVE (TF) Pierre Cossette Productions, 1980
PRINCE OF THE CITY Orion/Warner Bros., 1981
THE LEGEND OF WALKS FAR WOMAN (TF) Roger Gimbel Productions/EMI TV/Racquel Welch Productions/ Lee Levinson Productions, 1982
THE RULES OF MARRIAGE (TF) Entheos Unlimited Productions/Brownstone Productions/20th Century Fox TV, 1982
MISS ALL-AMERICAN BEAUTY (TF) Marian Rees Associates, 1982
DIVORCE WARS: A LOVE STORY (TF) Wrye-Kenigsberg Films/Warner Bros. TV, 1982
THE SURVIVORS Columbia, 1983
JANE DOE (TF) ITC, 1983
THE HAUNTING PASSION (TF) BSR Productions/ ITC, 1983
MANIMAL (TF) Glen A. Larson Productions/20th Century-Fox TV, 1983
COVER UP (TF) Glen A. Larson Productions/20th Century Fox TV, 1984
CRACKERS Universal, 1984
IMPULSE 20th Century Fox, 1984
WITH INTENT TO KILL (TF) London Productions, 1984
VICTIMS FOR VICTIMS (TF) Daniel L. Paulson-Loehr Spivey Productions/Orion TV, 1984
MACGRUDER AND LOUD (TF) Aaron Spelling Productions, 1985
NOON WINE (TF) Noon Wine Company, 1985
THE BAD SEED (TF) Hajeno Productions/Warner Bros. TV, 1985
A BUNNY'S TALE (TF) Stan Margulies Company/ABC Circle Films, 1985
PICKING UP THE PIECES (TF) CBS Entertainment, 1985
RIGHT TO KILL? (TV) Wrye-Konigsberg Productions/Taper Media Enterprises/Telepictu res Productions, 1985
TOUGHLOVE (TF) Fries Entertainment, 1985
CRIME OF INNOCENCE (TF) Ohlmeyer Communications Company, 1985
THE MORNING AFTER 20th Century Fox, 1986
A DEADLY BUSINESS (TF) Thebaut-Frey Productions/Taft Entertainment TV, 1986
JACKALS *AMERICAN JUSTICE* The Movie Store, 1986
THE LAST DAYS OF FRANK AND JESSE JAMES (TF) Joseph Cates Productions, 1986
RESTING PLACE (TF) Marian Rees Associates, 1986
A CASE OF DEADLY FORCE (TF) Telecom Entertainment, 1986
WHEN THE BOUGH BREAKS (TF) Taft Entertainment TV/ TDF Productions, 1986
ROANOAK (TF) South Carolina ETV Network/First Contact Films/National Video Corporation, 1986
A WALK ON THE MOON Skouras Productions, 1987
THE KILLING TIME New World, 1987
THE KING OF LOVE (TF) Sarabande Productions/ MGM-UA TV, 1987
WE ARE THE CHILDREN (TF) Paulist Pictures/Dan Fauci-Ted Danson Productions/The Furia Organization, 1987
BABY GIRL SCOTT (TF) Poison Company Productions/The Finnegan-Pinchuk Company, 1987
DOTTIE (TF) Dottie Films Inc., 1987
ALMOST PARTNERS (TF) South Carolina Educational TV Network, 1987
HAUNTED BY HER PAST (TF) Norton Wright Productions/ ITC Productions, 1987
CROSSING DELANCEY Warner Bros., 1988
CHINA BEACH (TF) Sacret Inc. Productions/Warner Bros. TV, 1988
JAMES CLAVELL'S NOBLE HOUSE *NOBLE HOUSE* (MS) Noble House Productions Ltd./De Laurentiis Entertainment Group, 1988
SHOOTER (TF) UBU Productions/Paramount TV, 1988

KING OF THE OLYPMICS (TF) Harmony Gold/Rete Europa/SFP Productions, 1988, U.S.-Italian
KILLER INSTINCT (TF) Millar-Bromberg Productions/ITC, 1988
BRIDESMAIDS (TF) Motown Productions/Qintex Entertainment/Deaune Productions, 1989
DARK HOLIDAY (TF) Peter Nelson/Lou Antonio Productions/The Finnegan-Pinchuk Co./Orion TV, 1989
PENN AND TELLER GET KILLED Warner Bros., 1989
ROCK HUDSON (TF) Konigsberg/Sanitsky Co., 1990
FAMILY OF SPIES (MS) King Phoenix Entertainment, 1990

JACK CHIPMAN

BEHIND ENEMY LINES (TF) co-composer with Steve Lindsey, MTM Enterprises/TVS, 1985

ELLIOT CHIPRUT

Contact: ASCAP - Los Angeles, 213/466-7681

THE G.I. EXECUTIONER *WIT'S END* co-composer with Jason Garfield, Troma, 1985

CHRIS CHRISTIAN

Contact: ASCAP - Los Angeles, 213/466-7681

DAKOTA Miramax, 1988

SUZANNE E. CIANI

Agent: MCEG Management - Santa Monica, 213/315-7800

THE INCREDIBLE SHRINKING WOMAN Universal, 1981
MOTHER TERESA (FD) Petrie Productions, 1986

CINEMASCORE

RAW DEAL DEG, 1986

STELVIO CIPRIANI

b. Italy
Contact: SIAE - Rome, Italy, 011-39-6-59-90-1

EL PRECIO DE UN HOMBRE *THE STRANGER RETURNS* 1966, Italian
OPERAZIONE SAN PIETRO Ultra Film, 1967, Italian
LUANA LA FIGLIA DELLA FORESTA VERGINE 1968, Italian
WOMAN LAUGHS LAST 1969, Italian
THE ANONYMOUS VENETIAN 1970, Italian
INTIMITA PROIBITA DI UNA GIOVANE SPOSA 1970, Italian
LA BELVA 1970, Italian
A CUORE FREDDO 1971, Italian
IL DIAVOLO A SETTE FACCIE 1971, Italian
L'IGUANA DALLA LINGUA DI FUOCO 1971, Italian
SE TI INCONTRO TI AMMAZZO 1971, Italian
LA MORTE CAMMINA CON I TACCHI ALTI 1971, Italian
TESTA T'AMMAZZO, CROCE...SEI MORTO...MI CHIAMANO ALLELUJA 1971, Italian
ESTRATTO DAGLI ARCHIVI SEGRETI DELLA POLIZIA DI UNA CAPITALE EUROPA *FROM THE POLICE, WITH THANKS* 1972, Italian
IL WEST TI VA STRETTO AMICO...E ARRIVATO ALLEJUA 1972, Italian
ECOLOGIA DEL DELITTO 1972, Italian
LA POLIZIA RINGRAZIA 1972, Italian
L'ASSASSINO E AL TELEFONO 1972, Italian
EL MAS FABULOSO GOLF DEL FAR WEST 1972, Italian
METTI LO DIAVOLO TUO NE LO MIO INFERNO 1972, Italian
RACCONTI PROIBITI...DI NIENTE VESTITI 1972, Italian
UCCIDERE IN SILENZIO 1972, Italian
IL MIO CORPO CON RABBIA 1972, Italian
LA NOTTE DELL'ULTIMO GIORNO 1973, Italian
CONTINUAVAMO A METTERE LO DIAVOLO NE LO INFERNO 1973, Italian
LEVA LO DIAVOLO TUO DAL CONVENTO 1973, Italian
TRE PER UNA GRANDE RAPINA 1974, Italian
LA MANO SPIETATA DELLA LEGGE 1974, Italian
DUE CUORI, UNA CAPPELLA 1974, Italian
PROCESSO PER DIRETTISSIMA 1974, Italian
BLONDY 1975, Italian
MARK IL POLIZIOTTO 1975, Italian
IL MEDAGLIONE INSANGUINATO 1975, Italian
PECCATO SENZA MALIZIA 1975, Italian
FRANKENSTEIN—ITALIAN STYLE 1976, Italian
MARK COLPISCE ANCORA 1976, Italian
GLI ANGELI DALLE MANI BENDATE 1976, Italian
TENTACLES American International, 1977, Italian
TAKE ALL OF ME Group 1, 1978
SOLAMENTE NERO 1978, Italian
SCORTICATELI VIVI 1978, Italian
UN POLIZIOTTO SCOMODO *CONVOY BUSTERS* 1978, Italian
PICCOLE LABBRA 1978, Italian
PROVINZIA VIOLENTA 1978, Italian
DISCRETAMENTE UNA SERA D'ESTATE 1978, Italian
IL FIUME DEL GRANDE CAIMANO *THE GREAT ALLIGATOR* 1979, Italian
MATERNALE Rai-Radiotelvision Italiana, 1978, Italian
LIBIDINE 1979, Italian
UN OMBRA NELL'OMBRA 1979, Italian
PENSIONE AMORE SERVIZIO COMPLETE *DER SEXBOMBER* 1979, Italian
SBIRRO, LA TUA LEGGE E LENTA...LA MIA NO! 1979, Italian
LA VEDOVA DEL TRULLO 1979, Italian
VUDU BABY 1979, Italian-Spanish
BERSAGLIO ALTEZZA UOMO 1979, Italian
DE CRIADA A SIGNORA 1979, Italian
CONCORDE AFFAIR '79 1979, French-Italian
LA SUPPLENTE VA IN CITTA 1979, Italian
TWO IN THE STARS 1980, Italian
CITY OF THE WALKING DEAD *NIGHTMARE CITY* 21st Century, 1980, Italian
AVVOLTOI SULLA CITTA 1980, Italian
TRES MUJERES DE NOW 1980, Spanish-Italian
POLIZIOTTO SOLITUDINE E RABBIA 1980, Italian
VERTIGO EN LA PISTA 1980, Italian-Spanish
JOURNAL D'UNE MAISON DE CORRECTION 1980, French-Italian
EL PODEROSO INFLUJO DE LA LUNA 1980, Spanish-Italian
PORNO, SITUACION LIMITE 1980, Spanish-Italian
IL GIARDINO DELL'EDEN 1980, Italian
TIMIDO Y SALVAJE 1980, Italian
UN LENTESIMO DI SECONDO 1980, Italian
L'ULTIMA VOLTA INSIEME 1981, Italian
MAFIA, UNA LEGGE CHE NON PERDONA 1981, Italian
IL FALCO E LA COLOMBA 1981, Italian
L'ULTIMO HAREM 1981, Italian
SWEET SINS *BONA COME IL PANO* 1981, Italian
LA MAESTRA DI SCI 1981, Italian
PIERINO IL FICHISSIMO 1981, Italian
ANGKOR-CAMBODIA EXPRESS Monarex Hollywood, 1981, Thai-Italian
LA VOCE 1982, Italian

LOS LIOS DE STEFANIA 1982, Italian
PIRANHA II - THE SPAWNING Saturn International, 1983, Italian-U.S.
IL SOMMERGIBILE PIU PAZZO DEL MONDO 1983, Italian
UN POVERE RICCO 1983, Italian
LA CASA DEL TAPPETO GIALLO Gaumont, 1983, Italian
UN TENERO TRAMONTO 1984, Italian
LA CLASSE 1984, Italian
RAGE Tiber International, 1984, Italian-Spanish
RAGE OF HONOR Trans World Entertainment, 1987

CHUCK CIRINO
Contact: BMI - Los Angeles, 213/659-9109

DEATHSTALKER New World, 1983, U.S.-Argentine
CHOPPING MALL Concorde/Cinema Group, 1986
BIG BAD MAMA II Concorde, 1987
NOT OF THIS EARTH Concorde, 1988
THE RETURN OF SWAMP THING Lightyear Entertainment, 1989

ERIC CLAPTON
b. March 30, 1945 - Surrey, England
Contact: PRS - London, England, 011-44-1-580-5544

EDGE OF DARKNESS (MS) co-composer with Michael Kamen, BBC/Lionheart Television International, 1986, British
LETHAL WEAPON co-composer with Michael Kamen, Warner Bros., 1987
HOMEBOY co-composer with Michael Kamen, Redbury Ltd./Elliott Kastner Productions, 1988
LETHAL WEAPON II co-composer with Michael Kamen and David Sanborn, Warner Bros., 1989
COMMUNION co-composer with Allan Zavod, New Line Cinema, 1989

STANLEY CLARKE
Agent: Bart-Milander - North Hollywood, 818/761-4040

OUT ON THE EDGE (TF) Rick Dawn Enterprises/The Steve Tisch Co./King Phoenix Entertainmen, 1989

ALF CLAUSEN
Agent: Bart-Milander - North Hollywood, 818/761-4040

STRANDED (TF) Tim Flack Productions/ Columbia TV, 1986
AGATHA CHRISTIE'S 'MURDER IN THREE ACTS' (TF) Warner Bros. TV, 1986
NUMBER ONE WITH A BULLET Cannon, 1987
DOUBLE AGENT (TF) Walt Disney TV, 1987
MY FIRST LOVE (TF) The Avnet-Kerner Company, 1988
SHE KNOWS TOO MUCH (TF) The Fred Silverman Company/Finnegan-Pinchuk Productions/ MGM TV, 1989

PAUL CLEMENTE
CALIGULA Analysis Film Releasing, 1979, Italian-U.S.

RICHARD CLEMENTS
Contact: ASCAP - Los Angeles, 213/466-7681

YOU'LL NEVER SEE ME AGAIN (TF) Universal TV, 1973
HOUSTON, WE'VE GOT A PROBLEM (TF) Universal TV, 1974
THE INVISIBLE MAN (TF) Universal TV, 1975
PEEPER 20th Century-Fox, 1975
STRANGE NEW WORLD (TF) co-composer with Elliot Kaplan, Warner Bros. TV, 1975

JIMMY CLIFF
Contact: BMI - Los Angeles, 213/659-9109

THE HARDER THEY COME New World, 1973, Jamaican
BONGO MAN Arsenal Kino Tubingen, 1982, Jamaican

MATT CLIFFORD
THE RETURN OF THE LIVING DEAD Orion, 1985

GEORGE S. CLINTON
Contact: ASCAP - Los Angeles, 213/466-7681

CHEECH & CHONG STILL SMOKIN' Paramount, 1983
THE BOYS NEXT DOOR New World, 1985
AMERICAN NINJA Cannon, 1985
THE CORSICAN BROTHERS (TF) Rosemont Productions, 1985, British-U.S.
AVENGING FORCE Cannon, 1986
WILD THING Atlantic Releasing Corp., 1987
TOO MUCH Cannon, 1987
THE LION OF AFRICA (CTF) HBO Pictures/Lois Luger Productions, 1987
PLATOON LEADER Cannon, 1988
GOTHAM (CTF) Phoenix Entertainment/Keith Addis and Associates Productions, 1988
AMERICAN NINJA 3: BLOOD HUNT Cannon, 1989

ELIA CMIRAL
Contact: PRS - London, England, 011-44-1-580-5544

APARTMENT ZERO Summit Company Ltd., 1988, British-Argentine

COATI MUNDI
SPIKE OF BENSONHURST FilmDallas, 1988

BOB COBERT
b. 1926
Agent: Robert Light - Los Angeles, 213/651-1777

LADYBUG, LADYBUG United Artists, 1963
HOUSE OF DARK SHADOWS MGM, 1970
NIGHT OF DARK SHADOWS MGM, 1971
FRANKENSTEIN (TF) Dan Curtis Productions, 1973
THE PICTURE OF DORIAN GRAY (TF) Dan Curtis Productions, 1973
THE NIGHT STRANGLER (TF) ABC Circle Films, 1973
THE NORLISS TAPES (TF) Metromedia Producers Corporation, 1973
SCREAM OF THE WOLF (TF) Metromedia Producers Corporation, 1974
DRACULA (TF) Universal TV/Dan Curtis Productions, 1974
MELVIN PURVIS: G-MAN (TF) American International TV, 1974
THE GREAT ICE RIP-OFF (TF) ABC Circle Films, 1974
TURN OF THE SCREW (TF) Dan Curtis Productions, 1974
TRILOGY OF TERROR (TF) ABC Circle Films, 1975
THE KANSAS CITY MASSACRE (TF) ABC Circle Films, 1975
BURNT OFFERINGS United Artists, 1976
SCALPEL *FALSE FACE* United International, 1976
CURSE OF THE BLACK WIDOW (TF) Dan Curtis Productions/ABC Circle Films, 1977

THE LAST RIDE OF THE DALTON GANG (TF) NBC Productions/Dan Curtis Productions, 1979
MRS. R'S DAUGHTER (TF) NBC Productions/Dan Curtis Productions, 1979
THE SCARLET PIMPERNEL (TF) London Films Ltd., 1982, British
THE LAST NINJA (TF) Paramount TV, 1983
THE WINDS OF WAR (MS) Paramount TV/Dan Curtis Productions, 1983
BONANZA: THE NEXT GENERATION (TF) Gaylord Production Company/LBS Communications/Bonanza Ventures, 1988
WAR AND REMEMBRANCE (MS) ☆ Dan Curtis Productions/ABC Circle Films, 1989

TED COCHRAN

CAT CHASER Vestron, 1989

DAVID ALLAN COE

Contact: BMI - Los Angeles, 213/659-9109

STAGECOACH (TF) co-composer with Willie Nelson, Raymond Katz Productions/Heritage Entertainment, 1986

HARVEY R. COHEN

Contact: BMI - Los Angeles, 213/659-9109

GHOST TOWN Trans World Entertainment, 1988

JOHN COLBY

HUEY LONG (FD) RKB/Florentine Films, 1985

RAY COLCORD

Contact: ASCAP - Los Angeles, 213/466-7681

THE DEVONSHIRE TERROR MPM, 1983
JURY DUTY (TF) Steve White Productions/Spectacor, 1990

CY COLEMAN

b. June 14, 1929 - New York, New York
Contact: ASCAP - Los Angeles, 213/466-7681

FATHER GOOSE Universal, 1964
THE TROUBLEMAKER Janus, 1964
THE ART OF LOVE Universal, 1965
SWEET CHARITY ★ adaptation, Universal, 1969
GARBO TALKS MGM/UA, 1984
POWER 20th Century Fox, 1986
FAMILY BUSINESS Tri-Star, 1989

JIM COLEMAN

THE UNBELIEVABLE TRUTH Action Features, 1989

PATRICK COLEMAN

Contact: PRO-Canada - Canada, 1-416-445-8700

BLUE MONKEY co-composer with Paul Novotny, Spectrafilm, 1987, Canadian

MICHAEL COLINA

FINNEGAN BEGIN AGAIN (CTF) co-composer with David Sanborn, HBO Premiere Films/Zenith Productions/Jennie & Co. Film Productions, 1985, U.S.-British

BUDDY COLLETTE

Contact: ASCAP - Los Angeles, 213/466-7681

TRAUMA Parade, 1962
TODAY IS FOR THE CHAMPIONSHIP (FD) Breakthrough Racing, 1980

MICHEL COLOMBIER

b. 1939 - France
Agent: CAA - Los Angeles, 213/288-4545

L'ARME A GAUCHE 1965, French
UN MONDE NOUVEAU *A NEW WORLD* 1966, French-Italian
COLOSSUS: THE FORBIN PROJECT Universal, 1970
THE OTHER MAN (TF) Universal TV, 1970
LES ASSASSINS DE L'ORDE 1971, French
UN FLIC *DIRTY MONEY* Warner Bros., 1972, French-Italian
L'HERITIER *THE INHERITOR* EMI, 1973, French-Italian
LE HASARD ET LA VIOLENCE *CHANCE AND VIOLENCE* 1974, French
PAUL AND MICHELLE Paramount, 1974, British-French
L'ALPAGUEUR 1975, French
LES 11,000 VERGES 1975, French
THE PREDATOR 1976, French
THE GUINEA PIG COUPLE 1977, French
TESTIMONY OF TWO MEN (TF) composer of parts 1 and 3, Universal TV/Operation Prime Time, 1977
THE RHINEMANN EXCHANGE (MS) Universal TV, 1977
11TH VICTIM (TF) Marty Katz Productions/Paramount Pictures TV, 1979
STEEL *LOOK DOWN AND DIE* World Northal, 1980
AGAINST ALL ODDS co-composer with Larry Carlton, Columbia, 1984
PURPLE RAIN Warner Bros., 1984
WHITE NIGHTS Columbia, 1985
THE MONEY PIT Universal, 1986
RUTHLESS PEOPLE Buena Vista, 1986
THE GOLDEN CHILD Paramount, 1986
FLORIDA STRAITS (CTF) HBO Premiere Films/Robert Cooper Productions, 1986
DOUBLE SWITCH (TF) Walt Disney TV, 1987
DESPERADO (TF) Walter Mirisch Productions/Universal TV, 1987
SURRENDER Warner Bros., 1987
MIDNIGHT CABARET 1987
THE RETURN OF DESPERADO (TF) Walter Mirisch Productions/Universal TV, 1988
THE COUCH TRIP Orion, 1988
COP Atlantic Releasing Corporation, 1988
DESPERADO: AVALANCHE AT DEVIL'S RIDGE (TF) Walter Mirisch Productions/Universal TV, 1988
SATISFACTION 20th Century Fox, 1988
THE WIZARD OF LONELINESS Skouras, 1988
OUT COLD Hemdale, 1989
LOVERBOY Tri-Star, 1989
WHO'S HARRY CRUMB? Tri-Star, 1989
BACKTRACK Vestron, 1990
IMPULSE Warner Bros., 1990
BURIED ALIVE (CTF) Niki Marvin Productions/MCA Entertainment, 1990

FRANK COMSTOCK

Contact: ASCAP - Los Angeles, 213/466-7681

THE LAST TIME I SAW ARCHIE United Artists, 1961
THE D.A.: MURDER ONE (TF) Mark VII Ltd./Universal TV/Jack Webb Productions, 1969

THE D.A.: CONSPIRACY TO KILL (TF) Mark VII Ltd./ Universal TV/Jack Webb Productions, 1971
THE NIGHT THAT PANICKED AMERICA (TF) The Culzean Corporation/Paramount Pictures TV, 1975

JOSEPH CONLAN

Contact: BMI - Los Angeles, 213/659-9109

KILL SQUAD Summa Vista Pictures, 1982
THE CONCRETE JUNGLE Pentagon, 1982
THE RENEGADES (TF) co-composer with Barry De Vorzon, Lawrence Gordon Productions/Paramount Pictures TV, 1982
CHAINED HEAT Jensen Farley Pictures, 1983
SCREAM *THE OUTING* Cal-Com Releasing, 1983
V: THE FINAL BATTLE (TF) co-composer of part one with Barry De Vorzon, Blatt-Singer Productions/ Warner Bros. TV, 1984
KOJAK: THE BELARUS FILE (TF) co-composer with Barry DeVorzon, Universal TV, 1985
STICK Universal, 1985
THE HIGH PRICE OF PASSION (TF) Edgar J. Scherick Associates/Taft Entertainment, 1986
THE WRONG GUYS New World, 1988
NICK KNIGHT (TF) Barry Weitz Films/Robirdle Pictures/ New World TV, 1989
MEMORIES OF MURDER (CTF) Lifetime Television/ Houston Lady Co./Viacom, 1990

CONG SU

b. China
Agent: Bart-Milander, North Hollywood, 818/761-4040

THE LAST EMPEROR ★★ co-composer with David Byrne and Ryuichi Sakamoto, Columbia, 1987, British-Chinese

BILL CONNOR

Contact: PRS - London, England, 011-44-1-580-5544

THE VISION (TF) BBC-TV, 1988, British

RICK CONRAD

Contact: BMI - Los Angeles, 213/659-9109

THE DRIFTER Concorde, 1988
CRIME ZONE Concorde, 1989
THE TERROR WITHIN Concorde, 1989
AMITYVILLE: THE EVIL ESCAPES (TF) Steve White Productions/Spectacor, 1989
WATCHERS II Concorde, 1990

PAOLO CONTE

Contact: SIAE - Rome, Italy, 011-39-6-59-90-1

SOTTO...SOTTO Triumph/Columbia, 1984, Italian

BILL CONTI

b. April 13, 1942 - Providence, Rhode Island
Agent: Bart-Milander - North Hollywood, 818/761-4040

JULIETTE DE SADE *MADEMOISELLE DE SADE E I SUOVI VIZI* 1967, Italian
CANDIDATE PER UN ASSASSINO 1969, Italian-Spanish
LIQUID SUBWAY 1972, Italian
BLUME IN LOVE Warner Bros., 1973
HARRY AND TONTO 20th Century Fox, 1974
PACIFIC CHALLENGE (FD) Concord Films, 1975
NEXT STOP, GREENWICH VILLAGE 20th Century Fox, 1976
ROCKY United Artists, 1976
SMASH-UP ON INTERSTATE 5 (TF) Filmways, 1976
CITIZENS BAND *HANDLE WITH CARE* Paramount, 1977
IN THE MATTER OF KAREN ANN QUINLAN (TF) Warren V. Bush Productions, 1977
A SENSITIVE, PASSIONATE MAN (TF) Factor-Newland Production Corporation, 1977
KILL ME IF YOU CAN (TF) Columbia TV, 1977
AN UNMARRIED WOMAN 20th Century Fox, 1978
SLOW DANCING IN THE BIG CITY United Artists, 1978
F.I.S.T. United Artists, 1978
FIVE DAYS FROM HOME Universal, 1978
THE BIG FIX Universal, 1978
PARADISE ALLEY Universal, 1978
HAROLD ROBBINS' THE PIRATE (TF) Howard W. Koch Productions/Warner Bros. TV, 1978
RING OF PASSION (TF) 20th Century Fox, 1978
UNCLE JOE SHANNON United Artists, 1979
ROCKY II United Artists, 1979
DREAMER 20th Century Fox, 1979
A MAN, A WOMAN, AND A BANK Avco Embassy, 1979, Canadian
STUNT SEVEN (TF) Martin Poll Productions, 1979
GOLDENGIRL Avco Embassy, 1979
THE SEDUCTION OF JOE TYNAN Universal, 1979
THE FORMULA MGM/United Artists, 1980
GLORIA Columbia, 1980
PRIVATE BENJAMIN Warner Bros., 1980
CARBON COPY Avco Embassy, 1981
VICTORY Paramount, 1981
FOR YOUR EYES ONLY United Artists, 1981, British
I, THE JURY 20th Century Fox, 1982
ROCKY III MGM/UA, 1982
NEIGHBORS Columbia, 1982
SPLIT IMAGE Orion, 1982
FARRELL FOR THE PEOPLE (TF) InterMedia Entertainment/TAL Productions/MGM-UA TV, 1982
THAT CHAMPIONSHIP SEASON Cannon, 1982
BAD BOYS Universal/AFD, 1983
THE RIGHT STUFF ★★ The Ladd Company/Warner Bros., 1983
THE TERRY FOX STORY (CTF) HBO Premiere Films/ Robert Cooper Films II, 1983, Canadian
UNFAITHFULLY YOURS 20th Century Fox, 1984
MASS APPEAL Universal, 1984
THE KARATE KID Columbia, 1984
THE BEAR Embassy, 1984
THE COOLANGATTA GOLD Film Gallery, 1984, Australian
NOMADS Atlantic Releasing Corporation, 1985
GOTCHA! Universal, 1985
BEER Orion, 1985
NORTH AND SOUTH (MS) ☆ Wolper Productions/Warner Bros. TV, 1985
BIG TROUBLE Columbia, 1986
F/X Orion, 1986
THE KARATE KID II Columbia, 1986
NORTH AND SOUTH, BOOK II (MS) Wolper Productions/ Robert A. Papazian Productions/Warner Bros. TV, 1986
HAPPY NEW YEAR Columbia, 1987
THE BOSS'S WIFE Tri-Star, 1987
MASTERS OF THE UNIVERSE Cannon, 1987
BABY BOOM MGM/UA, 1987
A PRAYER FOR THE DYING Samuel Goldwyn Company, 1987, British

NAPOLEON & JOSEPHINE: A LOVE STORY (MS) David L. Wolper Productions/Warner Bros. TV, 1987
BROADCAST NEWS 20th Century Fox, 1987
I LOVE N.Y. Manhattan Films, 1988
FOR KEEPS Tri-Star, 1988
A NIGHT IN THE LIFE OF JIMMY REARDON composer of U.S. version, Island Pictures/20th Century Fox, 1988
BETRAYED MGM/UA, 1988
COHEN & TATE Hemdale, 1988
THE BIG BLUE composer of U.S. version, Columbia/WEG, 1988, French
LEAN ON ME Warner Bros., 1989
MURDERERS AMONG US: THE SIMON WISENTHAL STORY (CTF) HBO Pictures/Robert Cooper Productions/TVS Films, 1989, U.S.-Canadian-British
KARATE KID III Columbia, 1989
LOCK UP Tri-Star, 1989
BACKSTREET STRAYS 1990
THE FOURTH WAR Cannon, 1990
ROCKY V MGM/UA, 1990

MICHAEL CONVERTINO

Contact: BMI - Los Angeles, 213/659-9109
Agent: Denise Shaw, Flick East-West Talents, Inc. - Los Angeles, 213/463-6333

HOLLYWOOD VICE co-composer with Keith Levine, Concorde/Cinema Group, 1986
CHILDREN OF A LESSER GOD Paramount, 1986
THE HIDDEN New Line Cinema, 1987
MISTRESS (TF) Jaffe/Lansing Productions/Republic, 1987
BULL DURHAM Orion, 1988
QUEEN OF HEARTS Cinecom, 1989, British
SHATTERED DREAMS (TF) Roger Gimbel Productions/Carolco TV, 1990
THE END OF INNOCENCE Skouras, 1990

RY COODER

Contact: BMI - Los Angeles, 213/659-9109

THE LONG RIDERS United Artists, 1980
SOUTHERN COMFORT 20th Century Fox, 1981
THE BORDER Universal, 1983
PARIS, TEXAS TLC Films/20th Century Fox, 1984, West German-French
STREETS OF FIRE Universal, 1984
ALAMO BAY Tri-Star, 1985
BREWSTER'S MILLIONS Universal, 1985
BLUE CITY Paramount, 1986
CROSSROADS Columbia, 1986
TALES FROM THE CRYPT (CTF) co-composer, Tales from the Crypt Holdings, 1989
JOHNNY HANDSOME Tri-Star, 1989

ERIC COOK

Contact: APRA - Australia, 011-61-2-922-6422

BREAKER MORANT New World/Quartet, 1980, Australian

JACK COOKERLY

Contact: BMI - Los Angeles, 213/659-9109

OMEGA SYNDROME co-composer with Nicholas Carras, New World, 1987

RAY COOPER

Contact: PRS - London, England, 011-44-1-580-5544

SCRUBBERS co-composer with Michael Hurd, Orion Classics, 1983, British
SHOOT FOR THE SUN (TF) co-composer with Michael Kamen, BBC-TV, 1986, British

STEWART COPELAND

Agent: ICM - Los Angeles, 213/550-4000

RUMBLE FISH Universal, 1983
OUT OF BOUNDS Columbia, 1986
WALL STREET 20th Century Fox, 1987
TALK RADIO Universal, 1988
SHE'S HAVING A BABY Paramount, 1988
SEE NO EVIL, HEAR NO EVIL Tri-Star, 1989
HIDDEN AGENDA Hemdale, 1990, British
THE FIRST POWER Orion, 1990

AARON COPLAND

b. November 14, 1900 - Brooklyn, N.Y.

THE CITY (D) Civic Films, 1939
OF MICE AND MEN ★ United Artists, 1939
OUR TOWN ★ United Artists, 1940
THE NORTH STAR ★ *ARMORED ATTACK* RKO Radio, 1943
THE CUMMINGTON STORY (D) U.S. Government, 1945
THE RED PONY Republic, 1949
THE HEIRESS ★★ Paramount, 1949
SOMETHING WILD United Artists, 1961

(Note: "Love and Money" [Paramount, 1982] uses existing Copland music, utilized with input from the composer.)

CARMINE COPPOLA

Contact: ASCAP - Los Angeles, 213/466-7681

TONIGHT FOR SURE Premier Pictures, 1961
THE PEOPLE (TF) Metromedia Productions/American Zoetrope, 1972
THE GODFATHER, PART II ★★ co-composer with Nino Rota, Paramount, 1974
THE LAST DAY (TF) C Lyles Productions/Paramount Pictures TV, 1975
APOCALYPSE NOW United Artists, 1979
THE BLACK STALLION United Artists, 1979
NAPOLEON composer of new score for 1927 silent film, Zoetrope, 1980
THE OUTSIDERS Warner Bros., 1983
GARDENS OF STONE Tri-Star, 1987
TUCKER additional music only, Paramount, 1988
NEW YORK STORIES composer of "Life with Zoe" segment, also cameo as street flutist, Buena Vista, 1989
THE GODFATHER PART III Paramount, 1990

MARIA CORDIO

ATOR Comworld Pictures, 1983

JOHN CORIGLIANO

b. February 16, 1938
Agent: Gorfaine-Schwartz - Burbank, 818/954-9500

ALTERED STATES Warner Bros., 1980
REVOLUTION Warner Bros., 1985, British-Norwegian

VLADIMIR COSMA

b. 1940 - Bucharest, Romania
Agent: Bart-Milander - North Hollywood, 818/761-4040

VERY HAPPY ALEXANDER *ALEXANDER* Cinema 5, 1968, French
LES PRISONNIERS DE LA LIBERTE 1968, French
ILS ALLAIENT DANS LES CHAMPS 1968, French
MALDONNE 1968, French
CLEREMBARD 1969, French
LE DISTRAIT *THE DAYDREAMER* 1970, French
CAFEN DE NULLE PART 1970, French
TERESA 1970, French
CHALEURS 1971, French
LES MALHEURS d'ALFRED 1971, French
LES ZOZOS 1972, French
THE TALL BLOND MAN WITH ONE BLACK SHOE Cinema 5, 1972, French
LA RAISON DU PLUS FOU 1972, French
LE DINGUE 1972, French
NEITHER BY DAY NOR BY NIGHT 1972, Israeli
LES EXPERIENCES EROTIQUES DE FRANKENSTEIN 1972, French
LA VIEREE SUPERBE 1973, French
LA DERNIERE BOURREE A PARIS 1973, French
PLEURE PAS LA BOUCHE PLEINE *DON'T CRY WITH YOUR MOUTH FULL* 1973, French
LES GRANDS SENTIMENTS FONT LES BONS GUEULETONS *BIG SENTIMENTS MAKE FOR GOOD SPORTS* 1973, French
SALUT L'ARTISTE Exxel, 1973, French
L'AFFAIRE CRAZY CAPO 1973, French
LA GUEULE DE L'EMPLOI 1973, French
THE MAD ADVENTURES OF 'RABBI' JACOB 20th Century-Fox, 1974, French-Italian
LUCKY PIERRE *LA MOUTARDE ME MONTE AU NEZ* 1974, French
LE JOURNAL INTIME D'UNE NYMPHOMANE co-composer, 1974, French
LA RIVALE *MY HUSBAND, HIS MISTRESS AND I* 1974, French
RETURN OF THE TALL BLONDE MAN WITH ONE BLACK SHOE Lanir Releasing, 1974, French
DUPONT-LAJOIE *RAPE OF INNOCENCE* 1974, French
LE CHAUD LAPIN 1974, French
HUGHES LE LOUP (TF) 1974, French
CATHERINE ET CIE 1975, French
THE PINK TELEPHONE *LE TELEPHONE ROSE* SJ International, 1975, French
LA COURSE A L'ECHALOTE *WILD GOOSE CHASE* 1975, French
LA SURPRISE DU CHEF 1975, French
LES OEUFS BROUILLES 1975, French
DRACULA AND SON 1976, French
PARDON MON AFFAIRE *AN ELEPHANT CA TROMPE ENORMEMENT* First Artists, 1976, French
L'AILE OU LA CUISSE 1976, French
THE TOY *LE JOUET* Show Biz Company, 1976, French
A CHACUN SON ENFER 1976, French
L'ENFER DES AUTRES 1976, French
LES FELINES Key Films, 1976, French
PARDON MON AFFAIRE, TOO! *NOUS IRONS TOUS AU PARADIS* First Artists, 1977, French
L'ANIMAL *THE ANIMAL* 1977, French
LA ZIZANIE 1978, French
LA RAISON D'ETAT *STATE REASONS* 1978, French
ANNE (TF) 1978, French
JE SUIS TIMIDE...MAIS JE ME SOIGNE 1978, French
CONFIDENCES POUR CONFIDENCES 1978, French
LE CONNETABLE DE BOURBON (TF) 1978, French
ILS SONT GRANDS CES PETITS! 1978, French
LA SERVANTE (TF) 1978, French
HISTOIRE DE VOYOUS: LES MARLOUPINS (TF) 1978, French
LE BAISER AU LEPREUX (TF) 1978, French
CAUSE TOUJOURS, TU M'INTERESSES 1978, French
COURAGE FUYONS *COURAGE - LET'S RUN!* Gaumont, 1979, French
LA DEROBADE *THE GETAWAY* 1979, French
C'EST PAS MOI, C'EST LUI! 1979, French
MEDECINS DE NUIT: HENRI GILLOT, RETRAITE (TF) 1979, French
MEDECINS DE NUIT: LEGITIME DEFENSE (TF) 1979, French
LA BELLE VIE (TF) 1979, French
LES MAITRES SONNEURS (TF) 1979, French
HISTOIRES INSOLITES: LA STRATEGIE DU SERPENT (TF) 1979, French
LE BAR DU TELEPHONE 1980, French
LA FEMME-ENFANT 1980, French
LE COUP DU PARAPLUIE 1980, French
LAAT DE DOCKTER MAAR SCHUIVEN! 1980, Dutch
INSPECTEUR LA BAVURE 1980, French
LA BOUM 1980, French
CELLES QU'ON N'A PAS EUES 1980, French
MEDECINS DE NUIT: L'USINE CA STEL (TF) 1980, French
MEDECINS DE NUIT: LA DECAPOTABLE (TF) 1980, French
PURQUOI PAS NOUS? 1980, French
STUMME LIEBE MUTE LOVE 1980, French-West German
MEDECINS DE NUIT: UN PLAT CUISINE (TF) 1980, French
MEDECINS DE NUIT: AMALGINE (TF) 1980, French
MEDECINS DE NUIT: LA PENSION MICHEL (TF) 1980, French
MEDECINS DE NUIT: L'ENTREPOT (TF) 1980, French
L'ANNEE PROCHAINE, SI TOUT VA BIEN 1981, French
LA DOUBLE VIE DE THEOPHRASTE LONGUET (TF) 1981, French
UNE AFFAIRE D'HOMMES 1981, French
DIVA United Artists Classics, 1982, French
LA CHEVRE 1982, French
L'AS DES AS *ACE OF ACES* Gaumont/Cerito Rene Chateau, 1982, French-West German
LA BOUM II Gaumont, 1983, French
LE BAL Almi Classics, 1983, French-Italian-Algerian
LES COMPRES AAA, 1983, French
L'ETINCELLE 1983, French
LE PRIX DU DANGER UGC, 1983, French
TOUT LE MONDE PEUT SE TROMPER S.N. Prodis, 1983, French
BANZAI AMLF, 1983, French
RETENEZ MOIL...OU JE FAIS UN MALHEUR *TO CATCH A COP* Gaumont, 1984, French
P'TIT CON *LITTLE JERK* Gaumont, 1984, French
MISTRAL'S DAUGHTER (MS) Steve Krantz Productions/ R.T.L. Productions/Antenne-2, 1984, U.S.-French
JUST THE WAY YOU ARE MGM/UA, 1984
LE JUMEAU *THE TWIN* AAA, 1984, French
ASTERIX VS. CAESAR (AF) Gaumont, 1985, French
LES FUGITIFS Gaumont, 1986, French
THE NIGHTMARE YEARS (CMS) Consolidated Productions, 1989
JUDITH KRANTZ'S TILL WE MEET AGAIN (MS) Steve Krantz Productions/Yorkshire TV, 1989

DON COSTA
Contact: ASCAP - Los Angeles, 213/466-7681

ROUGH NIGHT IN JERICHO Universal, 1967
THE IMPOSSIBLE YEARS MGM, 1968
MADIGAN Universal, 1968
THE SOUL OF NIGGER CHARLEY Paramount, 1973
LOOSE CHANGE (MS) Universal TV, 1978
THE GREAT BRAIN Osmond Distribution Company, 1978

PHIL COULTER
Contact: PRS - London, England, 011-44-1-580-5544

THE WATER BABIES Pethurst International/Film Polski, 1978, British-Polish

ALEXANDER COURAGE
Contact: BMI - Los Angeles, 213/659-9109

HOT ROD RUMBLE Allied Artists, 1957
SIERRA STRANGER Allied Artists, 1957
UNDERSEA GIRL Allied Artists, 1957
HANDLE WITH CARE MGM, 1958
THE LEFT-HANDED GUN Warner Bros., 1958
DAY OF THE OUTLAW United Artists, 1959
TOKYO AFTER DARK Paramount, 1959
A WEDDING ON WALTONS MOUNTAIN (TF) Amanda Productions/Lorimar Productions, 1982
A DAY FOR THANKS ON WALTONS MOUNTAIN (TF) Amanda Productions/Lorimar Productions, 1982
SUPERMAN IV: THE QUEST FOR PEACE adaptation, Warner Bros., 1987

JEAN COUSINEAU
Contact: CAPAC - Ontario, Canada, 1-416-924-4427

LES BEAUX SOUVENIRS *FOND MEMORIES* National Film Board of Canada, 1982, Canadian

ANDY COX
TIN MEN co-composer with David Steele, Buena Vista, 1987

RICHARD COX
Contact: Unlimited Groove Music - Los Angeles, 213/559-4134

SLUMBER PARTY MASSACRE II Concorde/New Horizons, 1987
THE AMERICAN SCREAM Genesis Home Video, 1988
BACK TO BACK Motion Picture Corporation of America, 1989

BOB CREWE
Contact: BMI - Los Angeles, 213/659-9109

BARBARELLA co-composer with Charles Fox, Paramount, 1968, Italian-French

CARLO CRIVELLI
Contact: SIAE - Rome, Italy, 011-39-6-59-90-1

DEVIL IN THE FLESH Istuto Luce/Italnoleggio, 1986, Italian-French

ANDRAE CROUCH
THE COLOR PURPLE ★ co-composer, Warner Bros., 1985

MICHAEL CRUZ
BASIC TRAINING The Movie Store, 1985

XAVIER CUGAT
b. January 1, 1900 - Barcelona, Spain
d. 1990

WHITE ZOMBIE co-composer with Guy Bevier Williams, RKO, 1932

PATRICIA CULLEN
Agent: Robert Light - Los Angeles, 213/651-1777

AFTER THE AXE (FD) Canadian
ROME-O AND JULIE 8 IN OUTER SPACE (ATF) Canadian
ROCK & RULE (AF) MGM/UA, 1983, Canadian
UPS AND DOWNS co-composer, JAD International, 1983, Canadian
UNFINISHED BUSINESS Zebra Films/National Film Board of Canada/CBC, 1984, Canadian
THE CARE BEARS MOVIE (AF) Samuel Goldwyn Company, 1985, Canadian
CARE BEARS MOVIE II: A NEW GENERATION (AF) Columbia, 1986, Canadian

DAVID CUNNINGHAM
END OF THE LINE TERMINUS Hemdale, 1987, French-West German

BILL CUOMO
Contact: BMI - Los Angeles, 213/659-9109

THAT WAS THEN...THIS IS NOW co-composer with Keith Olsen, Paramount, 1985

MIKE CURB
b. December 24, 1944 - Savannah, Georgia
Contact: BMI - Los Angeles, 213/659-9109

THE WILD ANGELS American International, 1966
THE GLORY STOMPERS American International, 1967
DEVIL'S ANGELS American International, 1967
BORN LOSERS American International, 1967
THE BIG BOUNCE Warner Bros., 1969
BLACK WATER GOLD (TF) co-composer with Jerry Steiner, Metromedia Producers Corporation/CTV, 1970

LEE CURRERI
Contact: ASCAP - Los Angeles, 213/466-7681

BILL: ON HIS OWN (TF) Alan Landsburg Productions, 1983

HOYT CURTIN
b. Los Angeles, California
Contact: Anihanbar Publishing - Los Angeles, 213/851-5000

THE MESA OF LOST WOMEN 1952
SHOOTOUT IN A ONE-DOG TOWN (TF) Hanna-Barbera Productions, 1974
KISS MEETS THE PHANTOM OF THE PARK (TF) Hanna-Barbera Productions/KISS Productions, 1978
C.H.O.M.P.S. American International, 1979
HEIDI'S SONG (AF) Paramount, 1982
GOBOTS: BATTLE OF THE ROCK LORDS (AF) Clubhouse/Atlantic Releasing Corporation, 1986

MIRIAM CUTLER
Contact: BMI - Los Angeles, 213/659-9109

WITCHCRAFT PART II: THE TEMPTRESS Vista Street Entertainment, 1990

LUCIO DALLA
b. Italy
Contact: SIAE - Rome, Italy, 011-39-6-59-90-1

MARIO PUZO'S THE FORTUNE PILGRIM (MS) co-composer with Mauro Malavasi, Carlo & Alex Ponti Productions/Reteitalia S.P.A., 1988, Italian

JOHN D'ANDREA
Contact: ASCAP - Los Angeles, 213/466-7681

LOVE'S DARK RIDE (TF) co-composer with Michael Lloyd, Mark VII/Worldvision Enterprises, 1978
STRANGER IN OUR HOUSE (TF) co-composer with Michael Lloyd, InterPlanetary Pictures Productions/ Finnegan Associates, 1978
GRAMBLING'S WHITE TIGER (TF) co-composer with Michael Lloyd, Inter Planetary Productions/Jenner/ Wallach Productions, 1981
SAVAGE STREETS co-composer with Michael Lloyd, MPM, 1984
BODY SLAM co-composer with Michael Lloyd, DEG, 1987
SWIMSUIT (TF) co-composer with Michael Lloyd, Musifilm Productions/American First Run Studios, 1989

OSWALD D'ANDREA
Contact: SACEM - France, 011-33-14-747-5650

LA VIE ET RIEN D'AUTRE UGC, 1989, French

JOHN DANKWORTH
b. 1927 - London, England
Agent: Triad Artists - Los Angeles, 213/556-2727

WE ARE THE LAMBETH BOYS Rank, 1958, British
THE CONCRETE JUNGLE *THE CRIMINAL* Fanfare, 1960, British
SATURDAY NIGHT AND SUNDAY MORNING Continental, 1961, British
THE SERVANT Landau, 1964, British
MORGAN! *MORGAN: A SUITABLE CASE FOR TREATMENT* Cinema 5, 1966, British
MODESTY BLAISE 20th Century-Fox, 1966, British
SANDS OF THE KALAHARI Paramount, 1965, British
DARLING Embassy, 1965, British
THE IDOL Embassy, 1966, British
FATHOM 20th Century-Fox, 1967
ACCIDENT Cinema 5, 1967, British
THE LAST SAFARI Paramount, 1967, British
RETURN FROM THE ASHES United Artists, 1965, British-U.S.
SALT AND PEPPER United Artists, 1968, British
THE MAGUS 20th Century-Fox, 1968, British
THE LAST GRENADE Cinerama Releasing Corporation, 1970, British
PERFECT FRIDAY Chevron, 1970, British
10 RILLINGTON PLACE Columbia, 1971, British
LOSER TAKE ALL Miramax Films, 1989, British

CARL DANTE
b. July 15, 1950 - Detroit, Michigan
Agent: Jeff Black, Triad Artists - Los Angeles, 213/556-2727
Home: 818/901-0030
In Europe: 011/49-40 66 88 5411

KIEZ United Artists, 1983
IMPRESSIONS OF MONET Zeitlos Films, 1983, West German
THE FREE RETURN NDR Fernsehen, 1984, West German
2006 Filminvest, 1986
MIDNIGHT DREAMS Filminvest, 1986
SUMMER CAMP Filminvest, 1986
THE DANGEROUS TYPE Sony Corp., 1987
SLAVE GIRLS FROM BEYOND INFINITY Urban Classics, 1987
STORIES FROM LOBOS CREEK Home Vision, 1988
CELLAR DWELLER Empire Pictures, 1988
CANNIBAL WOMEN IN THE AVOCADO JUNGLE OF DEATH Paramount, 1989
901: AFTER 45 YEARS OF WORKING Home Vision, 1990

KEN DARBY
b. May 13, 1909 - Hebron, Nebraska

THE CANADIANS 20th Century-Fox, 1961

MASON DARING
Agent: Bart-Milander - North Hollywood, 818/761-4040

RETURN OF THE SECAUCUS SEVEN Libra/Specialty Films, 1980
LIANNA United Artists Classics, 1983
THE BROTHER FROM ANOTHER PLANET Cinecom, 1984
KEY EXCHANGE TLC Films/20th Century Fox, 1985
OSA 1985
MATEWAN Cinecom, 1987
JENNY'S SONG (TF) Westinghouse Broadcasting, 1988
DAY ONE (TF) Aaron Spelling Productions/Paragon Motion Pictures, 1988
EIGHT MEN OUT Orion, 1988
THE LASERMAN Peter Wang Films/Hong Kong Film Workshop, 1988
MURDER IN MISSISSIPPI (TF) David L. Wolper Productions, 1990

OLIVER DASSAULT
b. France
Contact: SACEM - France, 011-33-14-747-5650

UNE FILLE COUSUE DE FIL BLANC *A STRAITLACED GIRL* Parafrance, 1977, French
LOVE IN QUESTION 1978, French
THE HEROINES OF EVIL 1979, French

PETER MAXWELL DAVIES
b. 1934 - Salford, England
Contact: PRS - London, England, 011-44-1-580-5544

THE DEVILS Warner Bros., 1971, British

RAY DAVIES

b. England
Contact: PRS - London, England, 011-44-1-580-5544

PERCY MGM, 1971, British

AARON DAVIS

STREETS Concorde, 1990

CARL DAVIS

b. 1936 - Brooklyn, New York
Agent: Bart-Milander - North Hollywood, 818/761-4040

THE OTHER WORLD OF WINSTON CHURCHILL 1967, British
THE BOFORS GUN Universal, 1968, British
THE ONLY WAY *OKTOBER DAGE* 1970, Dutch-Panamanian-U.S.
PRAISE MARX AND PASS THE AMMUNITION 1970, British
UP POMPEII MGM, 1971, British
THE SNOW GOOSE (TF) ☆ NBC, 1971
UP THE CHASTITY BELT 1971
I MONSTER Cannon, 1972, British
WHAT BECAME OF JACK AND JILL? co-composer, 1972, British
RENTADICK 1972, British
THE LOVERS British Lion, 1972, British
THE NATIONAL HEALTH 1972, British
CATHOLICS (TF) Sidney Glazier Productions, 1973
WHAT'S NEXT? Kingsgate Films, 1974, British
MAN FRIDAY Avco Embassy, 1975, British
THE NAKED CIVIL SERVANT (TF) Thames TV, 1976, British
THE SAILOR'S RETURN Euston Films Ltd., 1978
BIRTH OF THE BEATLES (TF) Dick Clark Productions, 1979, British-U.S.
NAPOLEON new score for 1927 silent film, 1980
THE FRENCH LIEUTENANT'S WOMAN United Artists, 1981, British
THE CROWD new score for 1928 silent film, 1981
OPPENHEIMER (MS) BBC-TV/WGBH-Boston, 1982, British-U.S.
PRAYING MANTIS Portman Productions/Channel Four, 1982, British
SHOW PEOPLE new score for 1928 silent film, 1982
FLESH AND THE DEVIL new score for 1927 silent film, 1982
CHAMPIONS Embassy, 1983, British
THE AEODROME (TF) BBC, 1983, British
THE WEATHER IN THE STREETS (TF) Rediffusion Films/BBC/Britannia TV, 1983, British
WINSTON CHURCHILL: THE WILDERNESS YEARS (MS) Southern Pictures Productions, 1983, British
GEORGE STEVENS: A FILMMAKER'S JOURNEY (FD) Castle Hill Productions, 1984
SAKHAROV (CTF) HBO Premiere Films/Titus Productions, 1984, U.S.-British
THE FAR PAVILLIONS (CMS) Geoff Reeve & Associates/Goldcrest, 1984, British
THE THIEF OF BAGHDAD new score for 1924 silent film, 1985
KING DAVID Paramount, 1985, U.S.-British
SILAS MARNER (TF) BBC, 1985, British
MURROW (CTF) HBO Premiere Films/Titus Productions/TVS Ltd. Productions, 1986, U.S.-British
HOTEL DULAC (TF) Channel Four, 1986, British
THE BIG PARADE new score for silent film
INTOLERANCE new score for silent film
GREED new score for silent film
THE GENERAL new score for silent film
THE WIND new score for silent film
BEN HUR new score for silent film
SCANDAL Miramax Films, 1989, British
THE RAINBOW Vestron, 1989, British
THE GIRL IN THE SWING Millimeter Films, 1989, British-U.S.
THE SECRET LIFE OF IAN FLEMING (CTF) Saban/Scherick Productions, 1990
CROSSING TO FREEDOM (TF) Procter & Gamble Productions/Stan Margulies Productions/Granada TV, 1990, U.S.-British
FRANKENSTEIN UNBOUND 1990

DAVID DAVIS

H.O.T.S. Derio Productions, 1979

DON DAVIS

Agent: Bart-Milander - North Hollywood, 818/761-4040

HYPERSPACE Regency Entertainment, 1986
A STONING AT FULHAM COUNTY (TF) The Landsburg Company, 1988
BLUEGRASS (TF) co-composer with Mark Snow, The Landsburg Company, 1988
HOME FIRES BURNING (TF) Marian Rees Associates, 1989
BLACKOUT Magnum Entertainment, 1989
BEAUTY AND THE BEAST (TF) Witt-Thomas Productions/Ron Koslow Films/Republic, 1989

JOHN DAVIS

Agent: Bart-Milander - North Hollywood, 818/761-4040

BREACH OF CONTRACT Atlantic Releasing Corporation, 1984
BLOOD SPORT (TF) Spelling-Goldberg Productions/Columbia TV, 1986

MARK DAVIS

Contact: BMI - Los Angeles, 213/659-9109

WHICH WAY IS UP? co-composer with Paul Riser, Universal, 1977
CHEECH AND CHONG'S NEXT MOVIE Universal, 1980
BUSTIN' LOOSE Universal, 1980
CRASH COURSE (TF) Fries Entertainment, 1988
CLASS CRUISE (TF) Portoangelo Productions, 1989

MILES DAVIS

b. 1926 - Alton, Illinois
Contact: BMI - Los Angeles, 213/659-9109

FRANTIC *ASCENSEUR POUR L'ECHAFAUD* Times, 1957, French
STREET SMART Cannon, 1987
SIESTA Lorimar, 1987, British

GUIDO De ANGELIS

Contact: SIAE - Rome, Italy, 011-39-6-59-90-1

RUN RUN JOE co-composer with Maurizio De Angelis, 1974, Italian-French-Spanish-West German
KILLER FISH co-composer with Maurizio De Angelis, Associated Film Distribution, 1979
GREAT WHITE co-composer with Morton Stevens, Film Ventures International, 1982

MAURIZIO De ANGELIS
Contact: SIAE - Rome, Italy, 011-39-6-59-90-1

RUN RUN JOE co-composer with Guido De Angelis, 1974, Italian-French-Spanish-West German
KILLER FISH co-composer with Guido De Angelis, Associated Film Distribution, 1979
GREAT WHITE co-composer with Guido & Maurizio De Angelis, Film Ventures International, 1982

LEX DE AZEVEDO
WHERE THE RED FERN GROWS Doty-Dayton, 1974

GREG DE BELLES
Agent: Triad Artists - Los Angeles, 213/556-2727

SAVAGE STREETS 1984
KINJITE *FORBBIDEN GAMES* Cannon, 1989
LAMBADA Warner Bros., 1990

RICHARD DeBENEDICTIS
b. 1937
Agent: Robert Light - Los Angeles, 213/651-1777

THE COUPLE TAKES A WIFE Universal TV, 1972
THE GREATEST GIFT (TF) Universal TV, 1974
THIS IS THE WEST THAT WAS (TF) Public Arts Productions/Universal TV, 1974
THE BIG RIPOFF (TF) Universal TV, 1975
THE MANCHU EAGLE MURDER CAPER MYSTERY United Artists, 1975
DEADLY TRIANGLE (TF) Barry Weitz Productions/ Columbia Pictures TV, 1975
THE RETURN OF THE WORLD'S GREATEST DETECTIVE (TF) Universal TV, 1976
HOW THE WEST WAS WON (MS) MGM TV, 1977
CRISIS IN SUN VALLEY (TF) Barry Weitz Films/ Columbia Pictures TV, 1978
ZIGFELD: THE MAN AND HIS WOMEN (TF) ☆ Frankovich Productions/Columbia TV, 1978
DESPERATE WOMEN (TF) Lorimar Productions, 1978
MURDER BY NATURAL CAUSES (TF) Levinson-Link Productions, 1979
THE EARTHLING 1980, Australian
PERRY MASON RETURNS (TF) Intermedia Productions/ Strathmore Productions/Viacom Productions, 1985
PERRY MASON: THE CASE OF THE NOTORIOUS NUN (TF) Intermedia Productions/Viacom Productions, 1985
DIARY OF A PERFECT MURDER (TF) Viacom Productions/InterMedia Entertainment/Strathmore Productions, 1986
PERRY MASON: THE CASE OF THE SHOOTING STAR (TF) Intermedia Entertainment Company/ Strathmore Productions/Viacom, 1986
PERRY MASON: THE CASE OF THE MURDERED MADAM (TF) The Fred Silverman Company/ Strathmore Productions/Viacom, 1987
PERRY MASON: THE CASE OF THE LOST LOVE (TF) The Fred Silverman Company/Strathmore Productions/ Viacom Productions, 1987
PERRY MASON: THE CASE OF THE SCANDALOUS SECRETS (TF) The Fred Silverman Company/ Strathmore Productions/Viacom, 1987
PERRY MASON: THE CASE OF THE SINISTER SPIRIT (TF) The Fred Silverman Company/ Strathmore Productions/Viacom Productions, 1987
FATAL CONFESSION: A FATHER DOWLING MYSTERY (TF) co-composer with Dick DeBenedictis, Fred Silverman Company/Strathmore Productions/Viacom Productions, 1987
IN THE HEAT OF THE NIGHT (TF) The Fred Silverman Company/Jadda Productions/MGM/UA TV, 1988
PERRY MASON: THE CASE OF THE LADY OF THE LAKE (TF) The Fred Silverman Company/Strathmore Productions/Viacom, 1988
PERRY MASON: THE CASE OF THE AVENGING ACE (TF) ☆ The Fred Silverman Company/Strathmore Productions/Viacom, 1988
PERRY MASON: THE CASE OF THE LETHAL LESSON (TF) The Fred Silverman Company/Dean Hargrove Productions/Viacom, 1989
PERRY MASON: THE CASE OF THE MUSICAL MURDERER (TF) The Fred Silverman Company/Dean Hargrove Productions/Viacom, 1989
JAKE AND THE FATMAN (TF) The Fred Silverman Company/Dean Hargrove Productions/Viacom, 1989
PERRY MASON: THE CASE OF THE ALL-STAR ASSASSIN (TF) The Fred Silverman Company/Dean Hargrove Productions/Viacom, 1989
PERRY MASON: THE CASE OF THE FINAL CURTAIN (TF) The Fred Silverman Company/Dean Hargrove Productions/Viacom, 1990
PERRY MASON: THE CASE OF THE DESPERATE DECEPTION (TF) The Fred Silverman Company/Dean Gargrove Productions/Viacom, 1990

JOHN DEBNEY
Agent: Bart-Milander - North Hollywood, 818/761-4040

THE WILD PAIR *DEVIL'S ODDS* Trans World Entertainment, 1987
NOT SINCE CASANOVA 1988
SEVEN HOURS TO JUDGMENT Trans World Entertainment, 1988
THE FURTHER ADVENTURES OF TENNESSEE BUCK Trans World Entertainment, 1988
TRENCHCOAT IN PARADISE (TF) Ogiens/Kate Co., 1989
JETSONS: THE MOVIE (AF) Universal, 1990

DARRELL DECK
RETURN TO BOGGY CREEK 777 Distributors, 1977

CHRISTOPHER DEDRICK
GLORY! GLORY! (CTF) Atlantis Films Ltd./Orion TV, 1989

LUCHI DeJESUS
Contact: ASCAP - Los Angeles, 213/466-7681

THE CALIFORNIA KID (TF) Universal TV, 1974
SWEET HOSTAGE (TF) Brut Productions, 1975

GEORGES DELERUE
b. March 12, 1925 - Roubaix, France
Agent: ICM - Los Angeles, 213/550-4000

LE CHAPEAU DE PAILLE D'ITALIE new score for 1927 silent film, 1952, French
LES DEUX TIMIDES new score for 1928 silent film, 1952, French
MARCHE FRANCAISE 1956, French
DES HOMMES...UNE DOCTRINE 1959, French
LE BEL AGE co-composer with Alain Goraguer, 1959, French
HIROSHIMA, MON AMOUR co-composer with Giovanni Fusco, Zenith, 1959, French

MERCI NATERCIA 1959, French
MARCHE OU CREVE 1959, French
THE BIG RISK United Artists, 1960, French-Italian
UNE FILLE POUR L'ETE 1960, French
LES JEUX DE L'AMOUR 1960, French
LE VILLAGE AU MILIEU DES BRUMES 1960, French
PAR-DESSUS LE MUR 1960, French
LA MORTE SAISON DES AMOUR 1960, French
SHOOT THE PIANO PLAYER Astor, 1960, French
UNE AUSSI LONGUE ABSENCE 1960, French
LA FRANCAISE ET L'AMOUR composer of "La Femme Seule" segment, 1960, French
ARRETEZ LES TAMBOURS 1960, French
LE RECREATION *PLAYTIME* 1960, French
THE PASSION OF SLOW FIRE *LA MORT DE BELLE* Trans-Lux, 1961, French
THE JOKER Lopert, 1961, French
THE FIVE DAY LOVER Kingsley International, 1961, French- Italian
JULES AND JIM Janus, 1961, French
EN PLEIN CIRAGE 1961, French
LE PETIT GARCON DE L'ASCENSEUR 1961, French
LE DENONCIATION 1961, French
UN COEUR GROS COMME CA (FD) co-composer with Michel Legrand, 1961, French
RIFIFI IN TOKYO MGM, 1961, French-Italian
L'AFFAIRE NINA B 1962, French-West German
CRIME DOES NOT PAY Embassy, 1962, French-Italian
CARTOUCHE Embassy, 1962, French-Italian
LE BONHEUR EST POUR DEMAIN 1962, French
L'ABOMINABLE GOMME DES DOUANES 1962, French
JUSQU'AU BOUT DU MONDE 1962, French
L'IMMORTELLE co-composer with Tashim Kavacioglu, 1962, French
LE MONTE-CHARGE 1962, French
LOVE AT TWENTY co-composer, Embassy, 1962, French-Italian-Japanese-Polish-West German
L'AINE DES FERCHAUX 1962, French
VACANCES PORTUGAISES 1963, French
MURIEL additional music, Lopert, 1963, French-Italian
L'HONORABLE STANISLAS, AGENT SECRET 1963, French
DES PISSENLITS PAR LA RACINE 1963, French
DU GRABUGE CHEZ LES VEUVES 1963, French
CHAIR DE POULE *HIGHWAY PICKUP* 1963, French-Italian
LE JOURNAL D'UN FOU 1963, French
NUNCA PASA NADA 1963, Spanish
HITLER...CONNAIS PAS 1963, French
L'AUTRE FEMME 1963, French
GREED IN THE SUN 1963
FRENCH DRESSING Warner-Pathe, 1963, British
CONTEMPT *LE MEPRIS* Embassy, 1964, French-Italian
THE SOFT SKIN Cinema 5, 1964, French
THAT MAN FROM RIO Lopert, 1964, French-Italian
L'INSOUMIS 1964, French
LE GROS COUP 1964, French
L'AMOUR A LA CHAINE 1964, French
LUCKY JO 1964
THE PUMPKIN EATER Royal International, 1964, British
L'AGE INGRAT 1964, French
LOS PIANOS MECANICOS *THE UNINHIBITED* 1964, Spanish
MATA-HARI AGENT H21 1964, French
KILLER SPY 1965
LE BESTIAIRE D'AMOUR (FD) 1965, French
VIVA MARIA! United Artists, 1965, French-Italian
PLEINS FEUX SUR STANISLAS 1965, French
RAPTURE International Classics, 1965, British-French
MONA, L'ETOILE SANS NOM 1965, French
THE SUCKER Royal Films International, 1966, French-Italian
UN MONSIEUR DE COMPAGNIE *MALE COMPANION* International Classics, 1966, French-Italian
UP TO HIS EARS *LES TRIBULATIONS D'UN CHINOIS EN CHINE* Lopert, 1966, French-Italian
LOUIS DECOIN 1966, French
IT BEGAN IN BRIGHTON 1966, British
DERRIERE LA FENETRE 1966, French
UNE ALCHIMIE 1966, French
LE TEMPS REDONNE 1966, French
A MAN FOR ALL SEASONS Columbia, 1966, British
JEUDI ON CHANTERA COMME DIMANCHE 1966, French
MONSIEUR ROBERT HOUDIN (TF) 1966, French
LE DIMANCHE DE LA VIE 1967, French
THE KING OF HEARTS Lopert, 1967, French-Italian
THE 25TH HOUR MGM, 1967, French-Italian-Yugoslavian
OUR MOTHER'S HOUSE MGM, 1967, British
LES CRACKS 1967, French
LA PETITE VERTU 1967, French
LE SECRET DE WILHELM STORITZ (TF) 1967, French
UN COEUR QUI SE BRISE (TF) 1967, French
OSCAR co-composer with Jean Marion, 1968, French
THE TWO OF US *LE VIEL HOMME ET L'ENFANT* Cinema 5, 1968, French
INTERLUDE Columbia, 1968, British
THE HIGH COMMISSIONER *NOBODY RUNS FOREVER* Cinerama Releasing Corporation, 1968, British
THE DEVIL BY THE TAIL Lopert, 1969, French-Italian
THE BRAIN Paramount, 1969, French-Italian
LES GOMMES 1969, French
LE JEU DE LA PUCE 1969, French
HEUREUX QUI COMME ULYSSE 1969, French
HIBERNATUS 1969, French
A WALK WITH LOVE AND DEATH 20th Century-Fox, 1969, British
ANNE OF A THOUSAND DAYS ★ Universal, 1969, British
PROMISE AT DAWN Avco Embassy, 1970, French-U.S.
GIVE HER THE MOON *LES CAPRICES DE MARIE* United Artists, 1970, French-Italian
WOMEN IN LOVE United Artists, 1970, British
COUNTDOWN *COMPTES A REBOURS* 1970, French
YVETTE 1970, French
SULTAN A VENDRE (TF) 1970, French
UN OTAGE (TF) Also cameo as "Alfred," 1970, French
MIRA 1971, Dutch
THE CONFORMIST Paramount, 1971, Italian-French-West German
THE HORSEMEN Columbia, 1971
LES AVEUX LES PLUS DOUX MGM, 1971, French
L'INGENU 1971, French
MALPERTUIS: HISTOIRE D'UNE MAISON MAUDITE 1971, French
SOMEWHERE, SOMEONE *QUELQUE PART, QUELQU'UN* 1971, French
CHERE LOUISE Warner-Columbia, 1972, French-Italian
TWO ENGLISH GIRLS *LES DEUX ANGLAISES ET LE CONTINENT* also cameo as a businessman, Janus, 1972, French
SUCH A GORGEOUS KID LIKE ME Columbia, 1973, French
THE DAY OF THE JACKAL Universal, 1973, British-French
ANGELA *LOVE COMES QUIETLY* 1973, Dutch
DAY FOR NIGHT *LA NUIT AMERICAINE* Warner Bros., 1973, French-Italian
THE DAY OF THE DOLPHIN ★ Avco Embassy, 1973
LA FEMME DE JEAN *JOHN'S WIFE* 1973, French

DAN CANDY'S LAW *ALIEN THUNDER* 1973, Canadian
THE SLAP *LA GIFLE* 1974, French
PLUS AMER QUE LA MORT (TF) 1974, French
L'IMPORTANT C'EST D'AIMER 1974, French
OUBLIE-MOI MANDOLINE 1975, French
INCORRIGIBLE EDP, 1975, French
JAMAIS PLUS TOUJOURS 1975, French
MILADY (TF) 1975, French
COMME UN BOOMERANG 1976, French
LE GRAND ESCOGRIFFE 1976, French
LE JEU DU SOLITAIRE 1976, French
THE CASE AGAINST FERRO *POLICE PYTHON 357* 1976, French
FEMMES FATALES *CALMOS* New Line Cinema, 1976, French
JULIE-POT-DE-COLLE Prodis, 1977, French
JULIA ★ 20th Century-Fox, 1977
LE POINT DE MIRE Warner-Columbia, 1977, French
TENDRE POULET 1977, French
VA VOIR MAMAN...PAPA TRAVAILLE 1977, French
LA PETITE FILLE EN VELOURS BLEU 1977, French
LE NAUFRAGE DE MONTE CRISTO (TF) 1977, French
GET OUT YOUR HANDKERCHIEFS New Line Cinema, 1978, French
DEAR DETECTIVE 1978, French
LE CAVALEUR 1978, French
PIERROT MON AMI (TF) 1978, French
POURQUOI PATRICIA (TF) 1978, French
LES JEUDIS D'ADRIENNE (TF) 1978, French
LE MECREANT (TF) 1979, French
LUNDI (TF) 1979, French
LOVE ON THE RUN New World, 1979, French
A LITTLE ROMANCE ★★ Orion/Warner Bros., 1979, U.S.-French
AN ALMOST PERFECT AFFAIR Paramount, 1979
MIJN VRIENDE 1979, Dutch
LE CADRAN SOLAIRE (TF) 1979, French
SIMONE DE BEAUVOIR 1979, French
PREMIER VOYAGE 1979, French
MESSIEURS DE VOUOUS: LE CONCIERGE REVIENT DE SUITE (TF) 1980, French
LA FOLLE DE CHAILLOT (TF) 1980, French
THE LAST METRO United Artists Classics, 1980, French
RICHARD'S THINGS New World, 1981, British
RICH AND FAMOUS MGM/United Artists, 1981
LA PASSANTE 1981, French
GARDE A VUE *UNDER SUSPICION* 1981, French
BROKEN ENGLISH Lorimar, 1981
TRUE CONFESSIONS United Artists, 1981
THE WOMAN NEXT DOOR United Artists Classics, 1981
DOCUMENTEUR: AN EMOTION PICTURE (FD) Cine-Tamaris, 1981
LA VIE CONTINUE Triumph/Columbia, 1982, French
L'AFRICAIN Renn Productions, 1982, French
A LITTLE SEX Universal, 1982
PARTNERS Paramount, 1982
THE ESCAPE ARTIST Orion/Warner Bros., 1982
LIBERTY BELLE Gaumont, 1983, French
EXPOSED MGM/UA, 1983
MAN, WOMAN AND CHILD Paramount, 1983
THE BLACK STALLION RETURNS MGM/UA, 1983
CONFIDENTIALLY YOURS *VIVEMENT DIMANCHE* Spectrafilm, 1983, French
SILKWOOD 20th Century-Fox, 1983
L'ETE MEURTRIER *ONE DEADLY SUMMER* SNV, 1983, French
FEMMES DE PERSONNE 1983, French
LES MORFALOUS AAA, 1984, French
LE BON PLAISIR MK2, 1984, French
LOVE THY NEIGHBOR (TF) Patricia Nardo Productions/ 20th Century Fox TV, 1984
SILENCE OF THE HEART (TF) David A. Simons Productions/Tisch-Avnet Productions, 1984
AURORA (TF) Roger Gimbel Productions/The Peregrine Producers Group/Sacis, 1984, U.S.-Italian
AGNES OF GOD ★ Columbia, 1985
ARCH OF TRIUMPH (TF) Newland-Raynor Productions/ HTV, 1985, U.S.-British
THE EXECUTION (TF) Newland-Raynor Productions/ Comworld Productions, 1985
AMOS (TF) The Bryna Company/Vincent Pictures, 1985
DEADLY INTENTIONS (TF) Green-Epstein Productions, 1985
STONE PILLOW (TF) Schaefer-Karpf Productions/Gaylord Productions, 1985
A TIME TO LIVE (TF) Blue Andre Productions/ITC Productions, 1985
MAXIE Orion, 1985
CASANOVA new score for silent film, Cinema '89, 1985
SIN OF INNOCENCE (TF) Renee Valente Productions/ Jeremac Productions/20th Century Fox TV, 1986
CONSEIL DE FAMILLE European Classics, 1986, French
SALVADOR Hemdale, 1986
LA DESCENTE AUX ENFERS 1986, French
SWORD OF GIDEON (CTF) Alliance Entertainment/ Les Films Ariane/HBO Premiere Films/CTV/Telefilm Canada/Rogers Cablesystems/Radio-Canada, 1986, Canadian-French
CRIMES OF THE HEART DEG, 1986
PLATOON Hemdale, 1986
WOMEN OF VALOR (TF) Inter Planetary Productions/Jeni Productions, 1986
MAID TO ORDER New Century/Vista, 1987
THE PICK-UP ARTIST 20th Century-Fox, 1987
HER SECRET LIFE (TF) Phoenix Entertainment Group, 1987
THE LONELY PASSION OF JUDITH HEARNE Island Films, 1987, British
ESCAPE FROM SOBIBOR (TF) Rule-Starger Productions/ Zenith Productions, 1987, U.S.-British
QUEENIE (MS) von Zerneck-Samuels Productions/ Highgate Pictures, 1987
A MAN IN LOVE Cinecom, 1987, French
CHOUANS UGC, 1988, French
A SUMMER STORY Atlantic Releasing Corporation, 1988, British
THE HOUSE ON CARROLL STREET Orion, 1988
BILOXI BLUES Universal, 1988
MEMORIES OF ME MGM/UA, 1988
TO KILL A PRIEST Columbia, 1988, U.S.-French
HEARTBREAK HOTEL Buena Vista, 1988
TWINS co-composer with Randy Edelman, Universal, 1988
BEACHES Buena Vista, 1988
PARIS BY NIGHT Cineplex Odeon, 1988, British
HER ALIBI Warner Bros., 1989
STEEL MAGNOLIAS Columbia/Tri-Star, 1989
THE FRENCH REVOLUTION Films Ariane/Films A2/ Laura Films/Antea, 1989, French
JOE VS. THE VOLCANO Warner Bros., 1990
SHOW OF FORCE Paramount, 1990

JOSEPH DELIA

Contact: BMI - Los Angeles, 213/659-9109

DRILLER KILLER Rochelle Films, 1979
CHINA GIRL Vestron, 1987
FREEWAY New World, 1988
KING OF NEW YORK Reteitalia/Scena Films, 1990, Italian-U.S.

GAYE DELORME

THINGS ARE TOUGH ALL OVER Columbia, 1982

AL DeLORY

Contact: BMI - Los Angeles, 213/659-9109

PIONEER WOMAN (TF) Filmways, 1973
THE DEVIL'S RAIN Bryanston, 1975, U.S.-Mexican
MAD BULL (TF) Steckler Productions/Filmways, 1977
RODEO GIRL (TF) Steckler Productions/Marble Arch Productions, 1980

PACO DE LUCIA

CARMEN Orion Classics, 1983, Spanish
THE HIT Island Alive, 1984, British

MILTON DeLUGG

SANTA CLAUS CONQUERS THE MARTIANS Embassy, 1964
GULLIVER'S TRAVELS BEYOND THE MOON (AF) co-composer with Anne DeLugg, U.S. version only, 1966, Japanese
THE GONG SHOW MOVIE Universal, 1980

CHRISTOPHER DE MARCO

TROMA'S WAR Troma, 1988

FRANCESCO DE MASI

b. 1930 - Rome, Italy
Contact: SIAE - Rome, Italy, 011-39-6-59-90-1

TI-KOYO E IL SUO PESCECANE 1962, Italian
MACISTE IL GLADIATORE PIU FORTE DEL MONDO 1962, Italian
LO SCEICCO ROSSO 1962, Italian
MACISTE L'EROE PIU GRANDE DEL MONDO 1963, Italian
GLI SCHIAVI PIU FORTI DEL MONDO 1964, Italian
IL LEONE DI TEBE 1964, Italian
ARIZONA COLT 1966, Italian
F.B.I. OPERAZIONE VIPERA GIALLA 1966, Italian
LA MORTE VIENE DA MANILA 1966, Italian
LA LAMA NEL CORPO 1966, Italian
RINGO IL VOLTO DELLA VENDETTA 1966, Italian
SETTE DOLLARI SUL ROSSO 1966, Italian
SETTE CONTRO TUTTI 1966, Italian
KOMMISSAR X, DREI GRUNE HUNDE 1967, Italian
087 MISION APOCALIPSIS 1967, Italian
QUINDICI FORCHE PER UN ASSASSINO 1968, Italian
AMMAZZALI TUTTI E TORNA SOLO 1968, Italian
QUELLA SPORCA STORIA DEL WEST 1968, Italian
OSTIA 1969, Italian
EL LARGO DIA DEL AGUILA 1969, Italian
CONCERTO PER PISTOLA SOLISTA 1970, Italian
QUEL MALEDETTO GIORNO DELLA RESA DEI CONTI 1971, Italian
LA ORGIA DE LOS MUERTOS 1971, Italian
F.B.I. OPERAZIONE PAKISTAN 1972, Italian
BAWDY TALES United Artists, 1973, Italian-French
THE ARENA New World, 1974
LA TECNICA E IL RITO 1975, Italian
PRIVATE VICES, PUBLIC VIRTUES 1976, Italian
COUNTERFEIT COMMANDOS *INGLORIOUS BASTARDS* Aquarius, 1978, Italian
LONE WOLF McQUADE Orion, 1983
THUNDER WARRIOR *THUNDER* Trans World Entertainment, 1983
RUSH Cinema Shares International, 1984, Italian
THE MANHUNT Samuel Goldwyn Company, 1985, Italian
ESCAPE FROM THE BRONX New Line Cinema, 1985, Italian
FORMULA FOR MURDER Fulvia International, 1986, Italian

FRANK DENSON

Agent: Robert Light - Los Angeles, 213/651-1777

BAKER'S HAWK Doty-Dayton, 1976
RABBIT TEST Avco Embassy, 1978
OH HEAVENLY DOG 20th Century Fox, 1980
SUNSET LIMOUSINE (TF) Witzend Productions/ITC Productions, 1983

LUIS De PABLO

b. Spain
Contact: Luis Mas, SGAE - New York, 212/752-7230

THE CHALLENGES 1970, Spanish
GOYA 1971, Spanish
ANNA AND THE WOLVES 1973, Spanish
THE SPIRIT OF THE BEEHIVE Janus, 1973, Spanish
DON RAMIRO 1973, Spanish
PASCUAL DUARTE 1976, Spanish
TO AN UNKNOWN GOD 1977, Spanish
THE CARROT QUEEN 1978, Spanish
WHAT MAX SAID 1978, Spanish

DELIA DERBYSHIRE

Contact: PRS - London, England, 011-44-1-580-5544

THE LEGEND OF HELL HOUSE co-composer with Brian Hodgson, 20th Century-Fox, 1973, British

PAUL De SENNEVILLE

b. France
Contact: SACEM - France, 011-33-14-747-5650

CELESTINE, MAID AT YOUR SERVICE co-composer with Oliver Touissaint, 1974, French
IRRECONCILABLE DIFFERENCES co-composer with Oliver Touissaint, Warner Bros., 1984

MANUEL DE SICA

b. Italy
Agent: Bart-Milander - North Hollywood, 818/761-4040

A PLACE FOR LOVERS *AMANTI* MGM, 1968, Italian-French
IO E DIO 1970, Italian
LE COPPIE "Il Leone" segment, 1971, Italian
THE GARDEN OF THE FINZI-CONTINIS Cinema 5, 1971, Italian-West German
COSE DI COSA NOSTRA 1971, Italian
IO NON VEDO, TU NON PARLI, LUI NON SENTE Italian, 1971
CAMORRA 1972, Italian
LO CHIAMEREMO ANDREA 1972, Italian
L'ETA DI COSIMO (TF) 1973, Italian T.V.

A BRIEF VACATION Allied Artists, 1973, Italian
IL VIAGGIO *THE VOYAGE* United Artists, 1974, Italian
IL CASO RAOUL Iskra Cinematografica, 1975, Italian
LA MADAMA 1975, Italian
OCCHIO ALLA VEDOVA! 1975, Italian
QUEL MOVIMENTO CHE MI PACE 1975, Italian
CAGLIOSTRO 1975, Italian
FOLIES BOURGEOISES FFCM, 1976, French-Italian-West German
SETTE SCIALLI DI SETA GIALLA Italian
VADO A VIVERE DA SOLO Italian
LUI E PEGGIO DI ME Italian
CARO PAPA Dean Film/AMLF/Prospect Film, 1979, Italian-French-Canadian
SONO FOTOGENICO Dean Film/Marceau Cocinor, 1980, Italian-French
SUNDAY LOVERS MGM/United Artists, 1980, U.S.-British-French-Italian
IL MATRIMONIO DI CATERINA (TF) 1982, Italian
IL MOMENTO DELL'AVVENTURA SACIS, 1983, Italian
VACANZE IN AMERICA C.G. Silver Film, 1984, Italian
BYE BYE BABY Seymour Borde & Associates, 1989, Italian-U.S.

ROBERTO DE SIMONE

Contact: SIAE - Rome, Italy, 011-39-6-59-90-1

HOW WONDERFUL TO DIE ASSASSINATED 1975, Italian
THE END OF THE WORLD IN OUR USUAL BED IN A NIGHT FULL OF RAIN Warner Bros., 1978, Italian-U.S.

DEVO

Contact: BMI - Los Angeles, 213/659-9109

HUMAN HIGHWAY co-composer with Neil Young, Shakey Pictures, 1982

FRANK DE VOL

b. 1925
Contact: ASCAP - Los Angeles, 213/466-7681

WORLD FOR RANSOM Allied Artists, 1954
KISS ME DEADLY United Artists, 1955
THE BIG KNIFE United Artists, 1955
PARIS FOLLIES OF 1956 *FRESH FROM PARIS* Allied Artists, 1955
ATTACK! United Artists, 1956
PARDNERS Paramount, 1956
JOHNNY TROUBLE Warner Bros., 1957
THE RIDE BACK United Artists, 1957
PILLOW TALK ★ Universal, 1959
MURDER, INC. 20th Century-Fox, 1960
LOVER, COME BACKUniversal, 1962
BOY'S NIGHT OU MGM, 1962
WHATEVER HAPPENED TO BABY JANE? Warner Bros., 1962
FOR LOVE OR MONEY Universal, 1963
McLINTOCK! United Artists, 1963
THE THRILL OF IT ALL Universal, 1963
UNDER THE YUM-YUM TREE Columbia, 1963
THE WHEELER DEALERS MGM, 1963
GOOD NEIGHBOR SAM Columbia, 1964
SEND ME NO FLOWERS Universal, 1964
HUSH...HUSH SWEET CHARLOTTE ★ 20th Century-Fox, 1964
CAT BALLOU Columbia, 1965
THE FLIGHT OF THE PHOENIX 20th Century-Fox, 1966
THE GLASS BOTTOM BOAT MGM, 1966
TEXAS ACROSS THE RIVER Universal, 1966
CAPRICE 20th Century-Fox, 1967
THE DIRTY DOZEN MGM, 1967
GUESS WHO'S COMING TO DINNER ★ Columbia, 1967
THE HAPPENING Columbia, 1967
THE LEGEND OF LYLAH CLARE MGM, 1968
WHAT'S SO BAD ABOUT FEELING GOOD? Universal, 1968
KRAKATOA, EAST OF JAVA Cinerama Releasing Corporation, 1969
THE RELUCTANT HEROES (TF) Aaron Spelling Productions, 1971
ULZANA'S RAID Universal, 1972
FEMALE ARTILLERY (TF) Universal TV, 1973
EMPEROR OF THE NORTH POLE *EMPEROR OF THE NORTH* 20th Century-Fox, 1973
KEY WEST (TF) Warner Bros. TV, 1973
THE LONGEST YARD Paramount, 1974
DOC SAVAGE, THE MAN OF BRONZE Warner Bros., 1975
HUSTLE Paramount, 1975
HEY, I'M ALIVE! (TF) Charles Fries Productions/ Worldvision Enterprises, 1975
PANACHE (TF) Warner Bros. TV, 1976
HERBIE GOES TO MONTE CARLO Buena Vista, 1977
THE CHOIRBOYS Universal, 1977
THE MILLIONAIRE (TF) Don Fedderson Productions, 1978
THE FRISCO KID Warner Bros., 1979
THE GHOSTS OF BUXLEY HALL (TF) Walt Disney Productions, 1980
...ALL THE MARBLES MGM/United Artists, 1981
THE WILD WOMEN OF CHASTITY GULCH (TF) co-composer with Tom Worrall, Aaron Spelling Productions, 1982

BARRY DE VORZON

Contact: BMI - Los Angeles, 213/659-9109

DILLINGER American International, 1973
HARD TIMES Columbia, 1975
BOBBIE JO AND THE OUTLAW American International, 1976
DOG AND CAT (TF) Largo Productions, 1977
ROLLING THUNDER American International, 1977
SKI LIFT TO DEATH (TF) The Jozak Company/Paramount Pictures TV, 1978
LACY AND THE MISSISSIPPI QUEEN (TF) Lawrence Gordon Productions/Paramount Pictures TV, 1978
THE WARRIORS Paramount, 1979
STUNTS UNLIMITED (TF) Lawrence Gordon Productions/ Paramount Pictures TV, 1980
THE NINTH CONFIGURATION Warner Bros., 1980
REWARD (TF) Jerry Adler Productions/Espirit Enterprises/ Lorimar Productions, 1980
THE COMEBACK KID (TF) ABC Circle Films, 1980
XANADU Universal, 1980
LOOKER The Ladd Company/Warner Bros., 1981
TATTOO 20th Century-Fox, 1981
THE CHILDREN NOBODY WANTED (TF) Blatt-Singer Productions/Warner Bros. TV, 1981
TARZAN, THE APE MAN MGM/UA, 1982
THE RENEGADES (TF) co-composer with Joseph Conlan, Lawrence Gordon Productions/Paramount Pictures TV, 1982
JEKYLL AND HYDE...TOGETHER AGAIN Paramount, 1982
INTIMATE STRANGERS (TF) Nederlander TV and Film Productions/Telepictures Productions, 1983

V: THE FINAL BATTLE (TF) co-composer of part one with Joseph Conlan, Blatt-Singer Productions/Warner Bros. TV, 1984
KOJAK: THE BELARUS FILE (TF) co-composer with Joseph Conlan, Universal TV, 1985
STICK Universal, 1985
NIGHT OF THE CREEPS Tri-Star, 1986
EXORCIST III 20th Century-Fox, 1990

FREDERIC DEVREESE

Contact: SABAM - Brussels, Belgium, 011-32-2-230-2660

L'HOMME AU CRANE RASE 1966, French
UN SOIR UN TRAIN 1969, French
RENDEZ-VOUS A BRAY 1971, French
BELLE 1973, French
DU BOUT DES LEVRES *ON THE TIP OF THE TONGUE* Elan Films, 1976, Belgian
BENVENUTA UGC, 1983, Belgian-French

DE WOLFE

Contact: PRS - London, England, 011-44-1-580-5544

ON THE GAME Eagle, 1973, British
THE HOT GIRLS New Realm, 1974, British
MONTY PYTHON AND THE HOLY GRAIL co-composer with Neil Innes, Cinema 5, 1974, British
JABBERWOCKY Cinema 5, 1977, British

JOHN WILLIAM DEXTER

DREAM A LITTLE DREAM Vestron, 1989

VON DEXTER

THE TINGLER Columbia, 1959
HOUSE ON HAUNTED HILL Allied Artists, 1959
13 GHOSTS Columbia, 1960
MR. SARDONICUS Columbia, 1961

A.S. DIAMOND

THE GODDESS OF LOVE (TF) co-composer with Mitch Margo and Dennis Dreith, Phil Margo Enterprises/New World TV/Phoenix Entertainment Group, 1988

DAVID DIAMOND

b. 1915 - Rochester, New York
Contact: ASCAP - Los Angeles, 213/466-7681

A PLACE TO LIVE (D) Philadelphia Housing Association, 1941
DREAMS THAT MONEY CAN BUY co-composer, Films International of America, 1948
STRANGE VICTORY (D) Target, 1948
ANNA LUCASTA Columbia, 1949

MANU DIBANGO

Contact: SACEM - France, 011-33-14-747-5650

FORTY DEUCE Island, 1982

VINCE DiCOLA

Agent: Richard Emler - Los Angeles, 213/651-0222

STAYIN' ALIVE Paramount, 1983
ROCKY IV MGM/UA, 1985
THE TRANSFORMERS - THE MOVIE (AF) DEG, 1986

JAMES DIETRICH

b. 1894 - Missouri

THE MUMMY Universal, 1932

LOEK DIKKER

b. 1944 - Amsterdam, Holland
Contact: BUMA - Holland, 011-31-20-540-7911

THE 4TH MAN Spectrafilm, 1983, Dutch
SLOW BURN (CTF) Joel Schumacher Productions/ Universal Pay TV, 1986
PASCALI'S ISLAND Avenue Pictures, 1988, British-U.S.

DANNY DI PAOLO

JACK'S BACK Palisades Entertainment, 1988

JAMES DI PASQUALE

Agent: Gorfaine-Schwartz - Burbank, 818/954-9500

SHOWDOWN Universal, 1973
SENIOR YEAR (TF) Universal TV, 1974
FORCE FIVE (TF) Universal TV, 1975
THE JERICHO MILE (TF) composer of theatrical version, ABC Circle Films, 1976
FAST BREAK Columbia, 1976
SARAH T. - PORTRAIT OF A TEENAGE ALCOHOLIC (TF) Universal TV, 1975
MALLORY: CIRCUMSTANTIAL EVIDENCE (TF) Universal TV/Crescendo Productions/R.B. Productions, 1976
THE CRITICAL LIST (TF) MTM Productions, 1978
THE CONTENDER (TF) Universal TV, 1980
ESCAPE (TF) Henry Jaffe Enterprises, 1980
ADVICE TO THE LOVELORN (TF) Universal TV, 1981
FANTASIES (TF) Mandy Productions, 1982
TWO OF A KIND (TF) Lorimar Productions, 1982
LISTEN TO YOUR HEART (TF) CBS Entertainment, 1983
TRAUMA CENTER (TF) Glen A. Larson Productions/ Jeremac Productions/20th Century-Fox TV, 1983
AGATHA CHRISTIE'S 'SPARKLING CYANIDE' (TF) Stan Margulies Productions/Warner Bros. TV, 1983
QUARTERBACK PRINCESS (TF) CBS Entertainment, 1983
THE RED-LIGHT STING (TF) J.E. Productions/Universal TV, 1984
LOVE LIVES ON (TF) Script-Song Productions/ABC Circle Films, 1985
YOUNG AGAIN (TF) Sharmhill Productions/Walt Disney Productions, 1986, U.S.-Canadian
ONE CRAZY SUMMER Warner Bros., 1986
RAD Tri-Star, 1986
A STRANGER WAITS (TF) Bruce Lansbury Productions/ Edgar Lansbury Productions/Lewisfilm Ltd./New Century TV Productions, 1987
BROKEN ANGEL (TF) The Stan Margulies Company/ MGM-UA TV, 1988
THE SHELL SEEKERS (TF) ☆☆ Marian Rees Associates/ Central TV, 1989
STOLEN: ONE HUSBAND (TF) King Phoenix Entertainment, 1990

ANDREW DIXON

Contact: PRS - London, England, 011-44-1-580-5544

MEANTIME 1983, British
HIGH HOPES Skouras Pictures, 1988, British

WILLIE DIXON
Contact: BMI - Los Angeles, 213/659-9109

GINGER ALE AFTERNOON NeoPictures Ltd., 1989

NANA DJANELIDZ
b. U.S.S.R.
Contact: VAAP - U.S.S.R. Telex: 871-411327

REPENTANCE Cannon, 1984, Soviet, originally made for television

CRAIG DOERGE
Contact: ASCAP - Los Angeles, 213/466-7681

RICH KIDS United Artists, 1979

THOMAS DOLBY
Contact: PRS - London, England, 011-44-1-580-5544

FEVER PITCH MGM/UA, 1985
GOTHIC Vestron, 1987

KLAUS DOLDINGER
Agent: Bart-Milander - North Hollywood, 818/761-4040

DAS BOOT *THE BOAT* Triumph/Columbia, 1981, West German
DIE WILDEN FUENZIGER 1983, West German
LOVE IS FOREVER *COMEBACK* (TF) Michael Landon-Hall Bartlett Films/NBC-TV/20th Century-Fox TV, 1983
THE NEVERENDING STORY co-composer with Giorgio Moroder, Warner Bros., 1984, West German
A FATHER'S REVENGE (TF) Shadowplay/Rosco Productions/Phoenix Entertainment Group, 1987
ME AND HIM Columbia, 1989, West German

FRANCOIS DOMPIERRE
b. France
Contact: SACEM - France, 011-33-14-747-5650

THE BLOOD OF OTHERS (CTF) HBO Premiere Films/ICC/Filmex Productions, 1984, Canadian-French

PINO DONAGGIO
(Giuseppe Donaggio)
b. November 24, 1941 - Burano, Italy
Agent: ICM - Los Angeles, 213/550-4000

DON'T LOOK NOW Paramount, 1974, British-Italian
CORRUPTION IN THE HALLS OF JUSTICE Italnoleggio, 1975, Italian
UN SUSURRO NEL BUIO 1976, Italian
CARRIE United Artists, 1976
HAUNTS *THE VEIL* Intercontinental, 1977
NERO VENEZIANO *DAMNED IN VENICE/VENETIAN BLACK* 1978, Italian
CHINA 9, LIBERTY 37 Titanus, 1978, Italian
PIRANHA New World, 1978
TOURIST TRAP Compass International, 1979
SENZA BUCCIA *WITHOUT SKIN* 1979, Italian
HOME MOVIES United Artists Classics, 1980
BEYOND EVIL IFI-Scope III, 1980
DRESSED TO KILL Filmways, 1980
LA VITA INTERIORE 1980, Italian
THE BLACK CAT Selenia Cinematografica, 1980, Italian
THE HOWLING Avco Embassy, 1981
THE FAN Paramount, 1981
BLOW OUT Filmways, 1981
A VENEZIA, CARNEVALE, UN AMORE 1981, Italian
MORTE IN VATICANO 1982, Italian
THE SECRET BEYOND THE DOOR Gaumont, 1982, Italian
TEX Buena Vista, 1982
DON CAMILLO 1983, Italian
VIA DEGLI SPECCHI *STREET OF MIRRORS* 1983, Italian
HERCULES Cannon, 1983
HERCULES II Cannon, 1983, Italian
OVER THE BROOKLYN BRIDGE *MY DARLING SHIKSA* MGM/UA/Cannon, 1984
BODY DOUBLE Columbia, 1984
ORDEAL BY INNOCENCE Cannon, 1984, British
DEJA VU Cannon, 1985, British
THE ASSISI UNDERGROUND Cannon, 1985
THE BERLIN AFFAIR Cannon, 1985, Italian-West German
THE FIFTH MISSILE (TF) Bercovici-St. Johns Productions/MGM-UA TV, 1986
CRAWLSPACE Empire Pictures, 1986
HOTEL COLONIAL Orion, 1987, U.S.-Italian
DANCERS Cannon, 1987
THE BARBARIANS Cannon, 1987
CATACOMBS Empire Pictures, 1988
APPOINTMENT WITH DEATH Cannon, 1988
ZELLY AND ME Columbia, 1988
KANSAS Trans World Entertainment, 1988
PHANTOM OF DEATH Globe Films, 1989, Italian
NIGHT GAME Trans World Entertainment, 1989
MERIDIAN Full Moon Entertainment, 1990

MARC DONAHUE
Contact: BMI - Los Angeles, 213/659-9109

OPPOSING FORCE *HELL CAMP* Orion, 1986
MURPHY'S LAW Cannon, 1986

DONOVAN
THE PIED PIPER Paramount, 1972, British-West German

STEVE DORFF
Agent: Gorfaine-Schwartz - Burbank, 818/954-9500

EVERY WHICH WAY BUT LOOSE Warner Bros., 1978
BRONCO BILLY Warner Bros., 1980
HONKY TONK FREEWAY Universal/AFD, 1981
HONKYTONK MAN Warner Bros., 1982
WALTZ ACROSS TEXAS Atlantic Releasing Corporation, 1983
CANNONBALL RUN II Warner Bros., 1984
STICK Universal, 1985
RUSTLERS' RHAPSODY Paramount, 1985
RATBOY Warner Bros., 1986
THE DEFIANT ONES (TF) MGM-UA TV, 1986
CONVICTED (TF) Larry A. Thompson Productions, 1986
MANHUNT FOR CLAUDE DALLAS (TF) London Films, Inc., 1986
BACK TO THE BEACH Paramount, 1987
THE QUICK AND THE DEAD (CTF) HBO Pictures/Joseph Cates Company, 1987
INFIDELITY (TF) Mark-Jett Productions/ABC Circle Films, 1987
MY BEST FRIEND IS A VAMPIRE Kings Road, 1988
TOO YOUNG THE HERO (TF) Rick-Dawn Productions/Pierre Cossette Productions/The Landsburg Company, 1988

KISS SHOT (TF) Lonson Productions/Whoop Inc., 1989
THE RETURN OF SAM McCLOUD (TF) Michael Sloan Productions/Universal TV, 1989
PINK CADILLAC Warner Bros., 1989
B.L. STRYKER (TF) Blue Period Productions/TWS Productions/Universal TV, 1989

JOEL DORN

BOARDWALK Atlantic Releasing Corporation, 1979

MICHAEL DOUCET

Contact: BMI - Los Angeles, 213/659-9109

BELIZAIRE THE CAJUN Skouras Pictures, 1986
I WENT TO THE DANCE (FD) Brazos Films/Flower Films, 1989

TERRY DOUGHERTY

Contact: PRS - London, England, 011-44-1-580-5544

LONG SHOT Mithras Films, 1978, British

JOHNNY DOUGLAS

Contact: PRS - London, England, 011-44-1-580-5544

CRACK IN THE WORLD Paramount, 1965, British
THE BRIDES OF FU MANCHU 7 Arts, 1966, British

JULIA DOWNES

A MAN FOR ALL SEASONS (CTF) Agamemnon Films, 1988

PATRICK DOYLE

b. Scotland
Contact: PRS - London, England, 011-44-1-580-5544

HENRY V Samuel Goldwyn Company, 1989, British

DARRYL DRAGON

Contact: BMI - Los Angeles, 13/659-9109

SANDSTONE co-composer with Dennis Dragon, Henderson Films, 1977

DENNIS DRAGON

Contact: BMI - Los Angeles, 213/659-9109

GO FOR IT World Entertainment, 1976
SANDSTONE co-composer with Darryl Dragon, Henderson Films, 1977

ROBERT DRASNIN

Agent: Carol Faith - Beverly Hills, 213/274-0776

PICTURE MOMMY DEAD Embassy, 1966
RIDE IN THE WHIRLWIND American International, 1966
DAUGHTER OF THE MIND (TF) 20th Century-Fox, 1969
THE KREMLIN LETTER 20th Century-Fox, 1970
CROWHAVEN FARM (TF) Aaron Spelling Productions, 1970
THE OLD MAN WHO CRIED WOLF (TF) Aaron Spelling Productions, 1970
DR. COOK'S GARDEN (TF) Paramount TV, 1970
DESPERATE MISSION (TF) 20 Century-Fox TV, 1971
A TATTERED WEB (TF) Metromedia Productions, 1971
CANNON (TF) QM Productions, 1971
MURDER ONCE REMOVED (TF) Metromedia Productions, 1971
LONGSTREET (TF) Paramount TV, 1971
A TASTE OF EVIL (TF) Aaron Spelling Productions, 1971
THEY CALL IT MURDER (TF) 20th Century-Fox TV, 1971
NIGHT OF TERROR (TF) Paramount TV, 1972
JIGSAW *MAN ON THE MOVE* (TF) Universal TV, 1972
THE HEIST (TF) Paramount TV, 1972
CRISIS IN MID-AIR (TF) CBS Entertainment, 1979
ILLUSIONS (TF) CBS Entertainment, 1983
HOBSON'S CHOICE (TF) CBS Entertainment, 1983
BURNING RAGE (TF) Gilbert Cates Productions, 1984
LOVE, MARY (TF) CBS Entertainment, 1985
WHO IS JULIA? (TF) CBS Entertainment, 1986
SECRET WITNESS (TF) Just Greene Productions/CBS Entertainment Productions, 1988

DENNIS DREITH

THE GODDESS OF LOVE (TF) co-composer with Mitch Margo and A.S. Diamond, Phil Margo Enterprises/New World TV/Phoenix Entertainment Group, 1988
THE PUNISHER New World International, 1990

MICHAEL DRESS

Contact: PRS - London, England, 011-44-1-580-5544

THE MIND OF MR. SOAMES Columbia, 1970, British
THE HOUSE THAT DRIPPED BLOOD Cinerama Releasing Corporation, 1971, British

GEORGE DREYFUS

TENDER MERCIES Universal/AFD, 1983

ANNE DUDLEY

Agent: ICM - Los Angeles, 213/550-4000

DISORDERLIES co-composer with Art of Noise Warner Bros., 1987
HIDING OUT DEG, 1987
BUSTER Hemdale, 1988, British
SILENCE LIKE GLASS Bavaria/Lisa/Roxy, 1989, West German
THE MIGHTY QUINN MGM/UA, 1989
SAY ANYTHING 20th Century-Fox, 1989
THE MISADVENTURES OF MR. WILT Samuel Goldwyn, 1990, British

ANTOINE DUHAMEL

b. July 30, 1925 - France
Contact: SACEM - France, 011-33-14-747-5650

GALA 1962, French
LIBERTE DE LA NUIT 1962, French
MEDITERRANEE 1963, French
LE PUITS ET LE PENDULE 1963, French
UN AMOUR DE GUERRE 1964, French
EVARISTE GALOIS 1964, French
LE GRAIN DE SABLE 1964, French
LE VOLEUR DE TIBIDABO 1964, French
TINTIN ET LES ORANGES BLEUES 1964, French
BELPHEGOR (TF) 1965, French
PIERROT LE FOU Pathe Contemporary, 1965, French
LES MIETTES 1965, French
FUGUE 1966, French
LA LONGUE MARCHE 1966, French
ROGER LA HONTE 1966, French
POUR LE MISTRAL 1966, French
LE GRAND DADAIS 1967, French
UN HOMME A ABATTRE 1967, French

LE FRANCISCAIN DE BOURGES 1967, French
WEEKEND Grove Press, 1968, French-Italian
STOLEN KISSES Lopert, 1969, French
MISSISSIPPI MERMAID United Artists, 1970, French-Italian
THE WILD CHILD United Artists, 1970, French-Italian
BED AND BOARD *DOMICILE CONJUGAL* Columbia, 1971, French
LE MISTRAL 1972, French
M. COMME MATHIEU 1973, French
LA COUPE A DIX FRANCS *THE TWO DOLLAR HAIRCUT* co-composer with Anthony Braxton, 1974, French
LET JOY REIGN SUPREME *QUE LA FETE COMMENCE.* adaptation, SJ International, 1975, French
L'ACROBATE 1975, French
LA QUESTION 1977, French
AU PLAISIR DE DIEU (TF) 1977, French
LA BARRICADE DU POINT DU JOUR 1977, French
LA CHANSON DE ROLAND 1978, French
BIT BETWEEN THE TEETH 1979, French
FELICITE 1979, French
MAIS OU ET DONC ORNICAR 1979, French
RETURN TO THE BELOVED 1979, French
TWISTED OBSESSION Iberoamericana, 1990
DADDY NOSTALGIE Clea Productions, 1990, French

DAVID DUNDAS

Contact: PRS - London, England, 011-44-1-580-5544

WITHNAIL AND I Cineplex Odeon, 1987, British
HOW TO GET AHEAD IN ADVERTISING co-composer with Rick Wentworth, Warner Bros., 1989, British

GEORGE DUNING

b. 1919 - Richmond, Virginia
Contact: ASCAP - Los Angeles, 213/466-7681

THE DEVIL'S MASK co-composer with Irving Gertz, Columbia, 1946
MYSTERIOUS INTRUDER Columbia, 1946
JOHNNY O'CLOCK Columbia, 1947
THE GUILT OF JANET AMES Columbia, 1947
THE CORPSE CAME C.O.D. Columbia, 1947
DOWN TO EARTH co-composer with Heinz Roemheld, Columbia, 1947
HER HUSBAND'S AFFAIRS Columbia, 1947
I LOVE TROUBLE Columbia, 1948
TO THE ENDS OF THE EARTH Columbia, 1948
THE UNTAMED BREED Columbia, 1948
THE RETURN OF OCTOBER Columbia, 1948
THE GALLANT BLADE Columbia, 1948
THE MAN FROM COLORADO Columbia, 1948
SHOCKPROOF Columbia, 1949
THE DARK PAST Columbia, 1949
SLIGHTLY FRENCH Columbia, 1949
THE UNDERCOVER MAN Columbia, 1949
LUST FOR GOLD Columbia, 1949
JOHNNY ALLEGRO Columbia, 1949
THE DOOLINS OF OKLAHOMA co-composer with Paul Sawtell, Columbia, 1949
JOLSON SINGS AGAIN ★ Columbia, 1949
AND BABY MAKES THREE Columbia, 1949
CARGO TO CAPETOWN Columbia, 1950
NO SAD SONGS FOR ME ★ Columbia, 1950
CONVICTED Columbia, 1950
THE PETTY GIRL Columbia, 1950
BETWEEN MIDNIGHT AND DAWN Columbia, 1950
HARRIET CRAIG Columbia, 1950
THE FLYING MISSILE Columbia, 1951
LORNA DOONE Columbia, 1951
TWO OF A KIND Columbia, 1951
THE LADY AND THE BANDIT Columbia, 1951
THE MOB Columbia, 1951
THE BAREFOOT MAILMAN Columbia, 1951
THE FAMILY SECRET Columbia, 1951
MAN IN THE SADDLE Columbia, 1951
SCANDAL SHEET Columbia, 1952
SOUND OFF Columbia, 1952
PAULA Columbia, 1952
CAPTAIN PIRATE Columbia, 1952
ASSIGNMENT—PARIS Columbia, 1952
LAST OF THE COMMANCES Columbia, 1953
ALL ASHORE Columbia, 1953
SALOME Columbia, 1953
FROM HERE TO ETERNITY ★ Columbia, 1953
PICNIC ★ Columbia, 1955
THE EDDY DUCHIN STORY ★ Columbia, 1956
HOUSEBOAT Paramount, 1958
BELL, BOOK AND CANDLE Columbia, 1958
COWBOY Columbia, 1958
1001 ARABIAN NIGHTS (AF) Columbia, 1959
THE DEVIL AT 4 O'CLOCK Columbia, 1961
MY BLOOD RUNS COLD Warner Bros., 1965
ANY WEDNESDAY Warner Bros., 1966
THEN CAME BRONSON (TF) MGM TV, 1969
QUARANTINED (TF) Paramount Pictures TV, 1970
BUT I DON'T WANT TO GET MARRIED! (TF) Aaron Spelling Productions, 1970
YUMA (TF) Aaron Spelling Productions, 1971
BLACK NOON (TF) Fenady Associates/Screen Gems, 1971
CLIMB AN ANGRY MOUNTAIN (TF) Herbert F. Solow Productions/Warner Bros. TV, 1972
A GREAT AMERICAN TRAGEDY (TF) Metromedia Producers Corporation/J. Lee Thompson/Ronald Shedlo Productions, 1972
THE WOMAN HUNTER (TF) Bing Crosby Productions/ Jerome L. Epstein Productions, 1972
HONOR THY FATHER (TF) Metromedia Producers Corporation/Halcyon Productions, 1973
ARNOLD Cinerama Releasing Corporation, 1973
TERROR IN THE WAX MUSEUM Cinerama Releasing Corporation, 1974
THE ABDUCTION OF SAINT ANNE (TF) QM Productions, 1975
THE TOP OF THE HILL (TF) Fellows-Keegan Co./ Paramount Pictures TV, 1980
THE DREAM MERCHANTS (TF) Columbia TV, 1980
THE MAN WITH BOGART'S FACE 20th Century-Fox, 1980
GOLIATH AWAITS (TF) Larry White Productions/Hugh Benson Productions/Columbia TV, 1981

PAUL DUNLAP

Contact: ASCAP - Los Angeles, 213/466-7681

THE BARON OF ARIZONA Lippert, 1950
HI-JACKED Lippert, 1950
THE STEEL HELMET Lippert, 1950
CRY DANGER RKO Radio, 1951
LITTLE BIG HORN Lippert, 1951
JOURNEY INTO LIGHT 20th Century-Fox, 1951
THE LOST CONTINENT Lippert, 1951
BREAKDOWN Realart, 1952
PARK ROW United Artists, 1952
HELLGATE Lippert, 1952
BIG JIM McLAIN Warner Bros., 1952
THE SAN FRANCISCO STORY Warner Bros., 1952

COMBAT SQUAD Columbia, 1953
FORT VENGEANCE Allied Artists, 1953
JACK SLADE Allied Artists, 1953
THE ROYAL AFRICAN RIFLES Allied Artists, 1953
DUFFY OF SAN QUENTIN Warner Bros., 1953
DRAGONFLY SQUADRON Allied Artists, 1954
FANGS OF THE WILD Lippert, 1954
LOOPHOLE Allied Artists, 1954
RETURN FROM THE SEA Allied Artists, 1954
SHIELD FOR MURDER United Artists, 1954
TARGET EARTH! Allied Artists, 1954
BLACK TUESDAY United Artists, 1955
BIG HOUSE, U.S.A. United Artists, 1955
DESERT SANDS United Artists, 1955
FINGERMAN Allied Artists, 1955
FORT YUMA United Artists, 1955
GHOST TOWN United Artists, 1955
THE RETURN OF JACK SLADE Allied Artists, 1955
ROBBER'S ROOST United Artists, 1955
SHACK OUT ON 101 Allied Artists, 1955
STRANGER ON HORSEBACK United Artists, 1955
THE BRASS LEGEND United Artists, 1956
THE BROKEN STAR United Artists, 1956
THE COME-ON Allied Artists, 1956
CRIME AGAINST JOE United Artists, 1956
THE CRUEL TOWER Allied Artists, 1956
DANCE WITH ME, HENRY United Artists, 1956
EMERGENCY HOSPITAL United Artists, 1956
MAGNIFICENT ROUGHNECKS Allied Artists, 1956
STAGECOACH TO FURY 20th Century-Fox, 1956
STRANGE INTRUDER Allied Artists, 1956
THREE BAD SISTERS United Artists, 1956
WALK THE DARK STREET Associated Artists, 1956
APACHE WARRIOR 20th Century-Fox, 1957
CRIME OF PASSION United Artists, 1957
DRAGON WELLS MASSACRE Allied Artists, 1957
I WAS A TEENAGE WEREWOLF American International, 1957
I WAS A TEENAGE FRANKENSTEIN American International, 1957
THE QUIET GUN 20th Century-Fox, 1957
BLOOD OF DRACULA American International, 1957
LURE OF THE SWAMP 20th Century-Fox, 1957
YOUNG AND DANGEROUS 20th Century-Fox, 1957
OREGON PASSAGE Allied Artists, 1957
PORTLAND EXPOSE Allied Artists, 1957
ROCKABILLY BABY 20th Century-Fox, 1957
UNDER FIRE 20th Century-Fox, 1957
GOD IS MY PARTNER 20th Century-Fox, 1957
FRANKENSTEIN - 1970 Allied Artists, 1958
FRONTIER GUN 20th Century-Fox, 1958
GANG WAR 20th Century-Fox, 1958
GUN FEVER United Artists, 1958
TOUGHEST GUN IN TOMBSTONE United Artists, 1958
WOLF LARSEN Allied Artists, 1958
HOW TO MAKE A MONSTER American International, 1958
THE FOUR SKULLS OF JONATHAN DRAKE United Artists, 1959
HERE COME THE JETS 20th Century-Fox, 1959
LONE TEXAN 20th Century-Fox, 1959
THE OREGON TRAIL 20th Century-Fox, 1959
THE REBEL SET Allied Artists, 1959
THE ROOKIE 20th Century-Fox, 1959
GUNFIGHTERS OF ABILENE United Artists, 1960
THE PURPLE GANG Allied Artists, 1960
TWELVE HOURS TO KILL 20th Century-Fox, 1960
WALK LIKE A DRAGON Paramount, 1960
THE ANGRY RED PLANET American International, 1960
SEVEN WOMEN FROM HELL 20th Century-Fox, 1961
THE THREE STOOGES MEET HERCULES Columbia, 1962
THE THREE STOOGES IN ORBIT Columbia, 1962
BLACK ZOO Allied Artists, 1963
SHOCK CORRIDOR Allied Artists, 1963
THE THREE STOOGES GO ROUND THE WORLD IN A DAZE Columbia, 1963
THE NAKED KISS Allied Artists, 1964
STAGE TO THUNDER ROCK Paramount, 1964
VOICE OF THE HURRICANE RAM, 1964
THE OUTLAWS IS COMING! Columbia, 1965
YOUNG FURY Paramount, 1965
CASTLE OF EVIL United Pictures, 1966
CYBORG 2087 Features, 1966
DESTINATION INNER SPACE Magna, 1966
PANIC IN THE CITY United Pictures, 1967
THE DESTRUCTORS United Pictures, 1968
THE MONEY JUNGLE United Pictures, 1968

MURPHY DUNNE

Contact: BMI - Los Angeles, 213/659-9109

OUTSIDE CHANCE (TF) co-composer with Lou Levy, New World Productions/Miller-Begun Productions, 1978
LOOSE SHOES *COMING ATTRACTIONS* Atlantic Films, 1981

JOHN DU PREZ

Agent: Bart-Milander - North Hollywood, 818/761-4040

MONTY PYTHON AT THE HOLLYWOOD BOWL Columbia, 1982, British
BULLSHOT! Island Alive, 1983, British
MONTY PYTHON'S THE MEANING OF LIFE Universal, 1983, British
A PRIVATE FUNCTION Island Alive, 1984, British
OXFORD BLUES MGM/UA, 1984, British
SHE'LL BE WEARING PINK PAJAMAS Film Four International, 1985, British
ONCE BITTEN Samuel Goldwyn Company, 1985
LOVE WITH A PERFECT STRANGER (CTF) Yorkshire Television/Atlantic Video Ventures, 1986, British
PERSONAL SERVICES Vestron, 1987, British
A FISH CALLED WANDA MGM/UA, 1988
U.H.F. Orion, 1989
A CHORUS OF DISAPPROVAL Orion, 1989, British
TEENAGE MUTANT NINJA TURTLES New Line Cinema, 1990

BOB DYLAN

(Robert Zimmerman)

b. May 24, 1941
Agent: Joan Hyler, William Morris Agency - Beverly Hills, 213/274-7451

PAT GARRETT AND BILLY THE KID MGM, 1973

DAVID EARL
Contact: PRS - London, England, 011-44-1-580-5544

KIPPERBANG *P'TANG YANG, KIPPERBANG* MGM/UA Classics, 1983, British

BRIAN EASDALE
b. 1909 - Manchester, England
Contact: PRS - London, England, 011-44-1-580-5544

MEN IN DANGER 1939, British
SPRING OFFENSIVE 1940, British
BLACK NARCISSUS Universal, 1947, British
THE RED SHOES ★★ Eagle-Lion, 1948, British
THE SMALL BACK ROOM *HOUR OF GLORY* Snader Productions, 1948, British
THE WILD HEART *GONE TO EARTH* RKO Radio, 1950, British
OUTCAST OF THE ISLANDS United Artists, 1951, British
THE GREEN SCARF 1955, British
PURSUIT OF THE GRAF SPEE *THE BATTLE OF THE RIVER PLATE* Rank, 1956, British
PEEPING TOM Astor, 1960, British

BERNARD EBBINGHOUSE
Contact: PRS - London, England, 011-44-1-580-5544

PRUDENCE AND THE PILL 20th Century-Fox, 1968, British
MUMSY, NANNY, SONNY AND GIRLY *GIRLY* Cinerama Releasing Corporation, 1970, British
TALES THAT WITNESS MADNESS Paramount, 1973, British

NICOLAS ECONOMOU
Contact: GEMA - Munich, West Germany, 011-49-89621400

ROSA LUXEMBOURG New Yorker, 1986, West German

BRIAN EDDOLLS
THE FEUD Castle Hill, 1990

RANDY EDELMAN
Agent: ICM - Los Angeles, 213/550-4000

OUTSIDE IN Harold Robbins International, 1972
SNATCHED (TF) Spelling-Goldberg Productions/ABC Circle Films, 1973
EXECUTIVE ACTION National General, 1973
BLOOD SPORT (TF) Danny Thomas Productions, 1973
RYAN'S FOUR (TF) Fair Dinkum Inc./Groverton Productions/Paramount TV, 1983
WHEN YOUR LOVER LEAVES (TF) Major H Productions, 1983
A DOCTOR'S STORY (TF) Embassy TV, 1984
SCANDAL SHEET (TF) Fair Dinkum Productions, 1985
THE CHIPMUNK ADVENTURE (AF) Samuel Goldwyn Company, 1987
DENNIS THE MENACE (TF) DIC Enterprises Productions, 1987
FEDS Warner Bros., 1988
TWINS co-composer with Georges Delerue, Universal, 1988
TROOP BEVERLY HILLS Columbia, 1989
GHOSTBUSTERS II Columbia, 1989
QUICK CHANGE Warner Bros., 1990
COME SEE THE PARADISE 20th Century-Fox, 1990

DAVE EDMONDS
Contact: PRS - London, England, 011-44-1-580-5544

PORKY'S REVENGE 20th Century Fox, 1985

BERNARD EDWARDS
Contact: ASCAP - Los Angeles, 213/466-7681

SOUP FOR ONE co-composer with Nile Rodgers, Warner Bros., 1982

CLIFF EIDELMAN
Agent: Bart-Milander - North Hollywood, 818/761-4040

SILENT NIGHT TAT, 1988, West German
DEAD MAN OUT (CTF) HBO Showcase/Robert Cooper Entertainment/Granada TV, 1988, U.S.-Canadian-British
TO DIE FOR Skouras Pictures, 1989
THE FINAL DAYS (TF) The Samuels Film Co., 1989
ANIMAL BEHAVIOR Millimeter Films, 1989
TRIUMPH OF THE SPIRIT Triumph Releasing Corporation, 1989
STRIKE IT RICH co-composer with Shirley Walker, Millimeter Films, 1990
CRAZY PEOPLE Paramount, 1990

RICHARD EINHORN
Contact: ASCAP - Los Angeles, 213/466-7681

SHOCK WAVES *DEATH CORPS.* Joseph Brenner Associates, 1977
DON'T GO IN THE HOUSE Film Ventures International, 1980
EYES OF A STRANGER Warner Bros., 1981
THE PROWLER Sandhurst Corporation, 1981
NIGHTMARE AT SHADOW WOODS FCG, 1987
DEAD OF WINTER MGM/UA, 1987
SISTER, SISTER New World, 1987

DANNY ELFMAN
Agent: ICM - Los Angeles, 213/550-4000

FORBIDDEN ZONE Samuel Goldwyn Co., 1980
PEE WEE'S BIG ADVENTURE Warner Bros., 1985
BACK TO SCHOOL Orion, 1986
WISDOM 20th Century Fox, 1987
SUMMER SCHOOL Paramount, 1987
HOT TO TROT Warner Bros., 1988
BIG TOP PEE WEE Paramount, 1988
BEETLEJUICE The Geffen Company/Warner Bros., 1988
MIDNIGHT RUN Universal, 1988
SCROOGED Paramount, 1988
BATMAN Warner Bros., 1989
NIGHTBREED 20th Century Fox, 1990
DARKMAN Universal, 1990
DICK TRACY Buena Vista, 1990
EDWARD SCISSORHANDS 20th Century-Fox, 1990

JONATHAN ELIAS

Contact: ASCAP - Los Angeles, 213/466-7681

CHILDREN OF THE CORN New World, 1984
ALMOST YOU 20th Century-Fox, 1984
TUFF TURF New World, 1985
KEY EXCHANGE TLC Films/20th Century Fox, 1985
VAMP New World, 1986
TWO MOON JUNCTION Lorimar, 1988
SHAKEDOWN Universal, 1988
PARENTS Vestron, 1989
FAR FROM HOME Vestron, 1989
RUDE AWAKENING Orion, 1989
HOWARD BEACH: MAKING THE CASE FOR MURDER (TF) Patchett-Kaufman Entertainment Productions/WIN, 1989

JOHN ELIZALDE

THE CITY (TF) QM Productions, 1977
DEATH RAY 2000 (TF) Woodruff Productions/QM Productions, 1981

JACK ELLIOTT

Agent: Gorfaine-Schwartz - Burbank, 818/954-9500

THE COMIC Columbia, 1969
WHERE'S POPPA? United Artists, 1970
THE FEMINIST AND THE FUZZ (TF) co-composer with Allyn Ferguson, Screen Gems/Columbia Pictures TV, 1971
T.R. BASKIN Paramount, 1971
GET TO KNOW YOUR RABBIT Warner Bros., 1972
EVERY MAN NEEDS ONE (TF) co-composer with Allyn Ferguson, Spelling-Goldberg Productions/ ABC Circle Films, 1972
PLAYMATES (TF) co-composer with Allyn Ferguson, ABC Circle Films, 1972
THE BAIT (TF) co-composer with Allyn Ferguson, Spelling-Goldberg Productions/ABC Circle Films, 1973
THE MAN WITHOUT A COUNTRY (TF) co-composer with Allyn Ferguson, Norman Rosemont Productions, 1973
JARRETT (TF) co-composer with Allyn Ferguson, Screen Gems/Columbia Pictures TV, 1973
BIRDS OF PREY (TF) co-composer with Allyn Ferguson, Tomorrow Entertainment Inc., 1973
HIJACK! (TF) co-composer with Allyn Ferguson, Spelling-Goldberg Productions, 1973
WHAT ARE BEST FRIENDS FOR? (TF) co-composer with Allyn Ferguson, ABC Circle Films, 1973
GET CHRISTIE LOVE! (TF) co-composer with Allyn Ferguson, David L. Wolper Productions, 1974
THE GIRL WHO CAME GIFT-WRAPPED (TF) co-composer with Allyn Ferguson, Spelling-Goldberg Productions, 1974
ONLY WITH MARRIED MEN (TF) co-composer with Allyn Ferguson, Spelling-Goldberg Productions, 1974
THE RED BADGE OF COURAGE (TF) Norman Rosemont Productions/20th Century-Fox TV, 1974
ROLL, FREDDY, ROLL! (TF) co-composer with Allyn Ferguson, ABC Circle Films, 1974
CHARLIE'S ANGELS (TF) co-composer with Allyn Ferguson, Spelling-Goldberg Productions, 1976
DANGER IN PARADISE (TF) co-composer with Allyn Ferguson, Filmways, 1977
THE MAGNIFICENT MAGICAL MAGNET OF SANTA MESA (TF) co-composer with Allyn Ferguson, David Gerber Productions/Columbia Pictures TV, 1977
DELTA COUNTY U.S.A. (TF) co-composer with Allyn Ferguson, Leonard Goldberg Company/Paramount Pictures TV, 1977
OH, GOD! Warner Bros., 1978
A GUIDE FOR THE MARRIED WOMAN (TF) co-composer with Allyn Ferguson, 20th Century-Fox TV, 1978
SANCTUARY OF FEAR (TF) co-composer with Allyn Ferguson, Marble Arch Productions, 1979
JUST YOU AND ME, KID Columbia, 1979
THE JERK Universal, 1979
THE SOLITARY MAN (TF) John Conboy Productions, 1979
DON'T LOOK BACK (TF) TBA Productions/Satie Productions/TRISEME, 1981
THE DAY THE BUBBLE BURST (TF) Tamara Productions/ 20th Century-Fox TV/The Production Company, 1982
COMPUTERSIDE (TF) co-composer with Allyn Ferguson, The Culzean Corporation/Paramount Pictures TV, 1982
FOUND MONEY (TF) Cypress Point Productions/Warner Bros. TV, 1983
SENTIMENTAL JOURNEY (TF) Lucille Ball Productions/ Smith-Richmond Productions/20th Century Fox TV, 1984
SPIES, LIES AND NAKED THIES (TF) Robert Halmi Productions, 1988

DON ELLIOTT

THE HAPPY HOOKER Cannon, 1975

RICHARD ELLIOTT

Contact: BMI - Los Angeles, 213/659-9109

COVERUP: BEHIND THE IRAN CONTRA AFFAIR (FD) Empowerment Project, 1988
TEEN WITCH Trans World Entertainment, 1989

KEITH EMERSON

Agent: MCEG - Santa Monica, 213/315-7800

INFERNO 20th Century Fox, 1980
NIGHTHAWKS Universal, 1981
BEST REVENGE Lorimar Distribution International, 1983, Canadian
MURDEROCK, UCCIDE A PASSO DI DANZA Scena Film, 1984, Italian

MATTHEW ENDER

Contact: ASCAP - Los Angeles, 213/466-7681

STREETWALKIN' co-composer with Doug Timm, Concorde, 1985

CHARLES ENGSTROM

A FLASH OF GREEN Spectrafilm, 1984

BRIAN ENO

b. 1948
Agent: CAA - Los Angeles, 213/288-4545

LAND OF THE MINOTAUR *THE DEVIL'S MEN* co-composer with Harold Budd, 1976, U.S.-British
EGON SCHIELE - EXCESS AND PUNISHMENT Gamma Film, 1981, West German
DUNE co-composer with Toto, Universal, 1984
FOR ALL MANKIND (FD) Apollo Associates, 1989

ROGER ENO

Agent: CAA - Los Angeles, 213/288-4545

WARM SUMMER RAIN Trans World Entertainment, 1989

JACK ESKEW
Contact: ASCAP - Los Angeles, 213/466-7681

SUPERCARRIER (TF) co-composer with Bill Conti, Real Tinsel Productions/Fries Entertainment, 1987

DAVID ESSEX
Contact: PRS - London, England, 011-44-1-580-5544

SILVER DREAM RACER Rank, 1980, British

BOB ESTY
Contact: BMI - Los Angeles, 213/659-9109

ROLLER BOOGIE United Artists, 1980
YOU CAN'T HURRY LOVE Lightning Pictures, 1988

ALAN ETT
Contact: BMI - Los Angeles, 213/659-9109

ANGEL III: THE FINAL CHAPTER additional music, New World, 1988

EURYTHMICS
1984 co-composers with Dominic Muldowney, Atlantic Releasing Corporation, 1984, British

GREG EVIGAN
Agent: MCEG - Santa Monica, 213/315-7800

PRIVATE ROAD *NO TRESPASSING* Trans World Entertainment, 1987

DONALD FAGEN
Contact: ASCAP - Los Angeles, 213/466-7681

BRIGHT LIGHTS, BIG CITY MGM/UA, 1988

GARY FALCONE
NINJA TURF co-composer with Charles Pavlosky and Chris Stone, Ascot Entertainment Group, 1986

HAROLD FALTERMEYER
Agent: CAA - Los Angeles, 213/288-4545

THIEF OF HEARTS Paramount, 1984
BEVERLY HILLS COP Paramount, 1984
FLETCH Universal, 1985
TOP GUN Paramount, 1986
FIRE AND ICE co-composer, Concorde, 1987
FATAL BEAUTY MGM/UA, 1987
BEVERLY HILLS COP II Paramount, 1987
THE RUNNING MAN Tri-Star, 1987
FLETCH LIVES Universal, 1989
TANGO & CASH Warner Bros., 1989

DAVID FANSHAWE
Contact: PRS - London, England, 011-44-1-580-5544

THREE MEN IN A BOAT (TF) BBC, 1975, British
REQUIEM FOR A VILLAGE (FD) British Film Institute, 1976
HERE ARE LADIES (FD) Arthur Cantor Films, 1983, Irish

DENNIS FARNON
ARRIVEDERCI, BABY! *DROP DEAD, DARLING* Paramount, 1966, British

ROBERT FARNON
Contact: PRS - London, England, 011-44-1-580-5544

JUST WILLIAM'S LUCK United Artists, 1947, British
CAPTAIN HORATIO HORNBLOWER Warner Bros., 1951, British
GENTLEMEN MARRY BRUNETTES United Artists, 1955
LET'S MAKE UP *LILACS IN THE SPRING* Republic, 1954, British
THE LITTLE HUT MGM, 1957, British
THE SHERIFF OF FRACTURED JAW 20th Century-Fox, 1959, British
EXPRESSO BONGO co-composer with Norrie Paramor, Continental, 1960, British
THE ROAD TO HONG KONG United Artists, 1962
THE TRUTH ABOUT SPRING Universal, 1965, British-U.S.
A MAN CALLED INTREPID (MS) Lorimar Productions/ Astral Bellevue Pathe/CTV Network, 1979, British-Canadian
MARY AND JOSEPH: A STORY OF FAITH (TF) Astral Films/Lorimar Productions, 1979

ROBERT FARRAR
DON'T LOOK IN THE BASEMENT Hallmark, 1973

BARRY FASMAN
Agent: Robert Light - Los Angeles, 213/651-1777

DEAD RINGER co-composer with Dana Walden, Stock Grange Productions, 1988
MY MOM'S A WEREWOLF co-composer with Dana Walden, Crown International, 1988
THE IMMORTALIZER co-composer with Dana Walden, Filmwest Productions, 1989
WHISPERS co-composer with Dana Walden, Distant Horizon, 1989
YOUR MOTHER WEARS COMBAT BOOTS (TF) co-composer with Jeff Barry, NBC Productions, 1989
HELLGATE co-composer with Dana Walden, New World, 1989
RICH GIRL co-composer with Dana Walden, Filmwest Productions, 1989
STREET HUNTER co-composer with Dana Walden, 21st Century, 1989
NIGHT CLUB co-composer with Dana Walden, Crown International, 1990

LARRY FAST
Contact: ASCAP - Los Angeles, 213/466-7681

JUPITER MENACE 1982

RICKY FATAAR
Contact: APRA - Australia, 011-61-2-922-6422

HIGH TIDE co-composer with Mark Moffiatt, Hemdale, 1987, Australian

JESSE FEDERICK
Contact: ASCAP - Los Angeles, 213/466-7681

ALOHA SUMMER Spectrafilm, 1988

DON FELDER
Contact: ASCAP - Los Angeles, 213/466-7681

FLESHBURN additional music, Crown International, 1984
BLUE De VILLE (TF) B & E Enterprises Ltd./NBC Productions, 1986

ERIC FENBY
b. 1906 - Scarborough, England

JAMAICA INN Paramount, 1939, British

RICK FENN
Contact: PRS - London, England, 011-44-1-580-5544

WHITE OF THE EYE co-composer with Nick Mason, Palisades Entertainment, 1988

GEORGE FENTON
Agent: ICM - Los Angeles, 213/550-4000

HUSSY Watchgrove Ltd., 1980, British
GANDHI ★ co-composer with Ravi Shankar, Columbia, 1982, British-Indian
RUNNERS Goldcrest Films & TV, 1983, British
AN ENGLISHMAN ABROAD (TF) BBC, 1983, British
SAIGON - YEAR OF THE CAT (TF) Thames TV, 1983, British
THE COMPANY OF WOLVES Cannon, 1984, British
THE JEWEL IN THE CROWN (MS) Granada TV, 1984, British
CLOCKWISE Universal, 1986, British
LOVING WALTER (TF) Central TV Productions, 1986, British
EAST OF IPSWITCH (TF) BBC, 1986, British
WHITE OF THE EYE Palisades Entertainment, 1987, British
84 CHARING CROSS ROAD Columbia, 1987, British
CRY FREEDOM ★ co-composer with Jonas Gwangwa, Universal, 1987, British-U.S.
HIGH SPIRITS Tri-Star, 1988, British
THE DRESSMAKER Euro-American, 1988, British
A HANDFUL OF DUST New Line Cinema, 1988, British
WHITE MISCHIEF Columbia, 1987, British
DANGEROUS LIASONS ★ Warner Bros., 1988
WE'RE NO ANGELS Paramount, 1989
MEMPHIS BELLE Warner Bros., 1990
WHITE PALACE Universal, 1990

ALLYN FERGUSON
b. October 18, 1924 - San Jose, California
Agent: Carol Faith - Beverly Hills, 213/274-0776

THE FEMINIST AND THE FUZZ (TF) co-composer with Jack Elliot, Screen Gems/Columbia TV, 1971
SUPPORT YOUR LOCAL GUNFIGHTER United Artists, 1971
EVERY MAN NEEDS ONE (TF) co-composer with Jack Elliot, Spelling-Goldberg Productions/ABC Circle Films, 1972
PLAYMATES (TF) co-composer with Jack Elliot, ABC Circle Films, 1972
JARRETT (TF) co-composer with Jack Elliot, Screen Gems/Columbia TV, 1973
THE BAIT (TF) co-composer with Jack Elliot, Spelling-Goldberg Productions/ABC Circle Films, 1973
THE MAN WITHOUT A COUNTRY (TF) co-composer with Jack Elliot, Norman Rosemont Productions, 1973
BIRDS OF PREY (TF) co-composer with Jack Elliot, Tomorrow Entertainment Inc., 1973
HIJACK! (TF) co-composer with Jack Elliot, Spelling-Goldberg Productions, 1973
WHAT ARE BEST FRIENDS FOR? (TF) co-composer with Jack Elliot, ABC Circle Films, 1973
GET CHRISTIE LOVE! (TF) co-composer with Jack Elliot, David L. Wolper Productions, 1974
THE GIRL WHO CAME GIFT-WRAPPED (TF) co-composer with Jack Elliot, Spelling-Goldberg Productions, 1974
ONLY WITH MARRIED MEN (TF) co-composer with Jack Elliot, Spelling-Goldberg Productions, 1974
RED FLAG: THE ULTIMATE GAME (TF) Marble Arch Productions, 1974
ROLL,FREDDY,ROLL! (TF) co-composer with Jack Elliot, ABC Circle Films, 1974
THE COUNT OF MONTE CRISTO (TF) Norman Rosemont Productions/ITC, 1975, U.S.-British
CHARLIE'S ANGELS (TF) co-composer with Jack Elliot, Spelling-Goldberg Productions, 1976
CAPTAINS COURAGEOUS (TF) Norman Rosemont Productions, 1977
DANGER IN PARADISE (TF) co-composer with Jack Elliot, Filmways, 1977
THE MAGNIFICENT MAGICAL MAGNET OF SANTA MESA (TF) co-composer with Jack Elliot, David Gerber Productions/Columbia Pictures TV, 1977
DELTA COUNTY U.S.A. (TF) co-composer with Jack Elliot, Leonard Goldberg Productions/Paramount Pictures TV, 1977
THE MAN IN THE IRON MASK (TF) Norman Rosemont Productions/ITC, 1977, U.S.-British
THE FOUR FEATHERS (TF) Norman Rosemont Productions/Trident Films Ltd., 1978, U.S.-British
LES MISERABLES (TF) Norman Rosemont Productions/ITV Entertainment, 1978
A GUIDE FOR THE MARRIED WOMAN (TF) co-composer with Jack Elliot, 20th Century-Fox TV, 1978
SANCTUARY OF FEAR (TF) co-composer with Jack Elliot, Marble Arch Productions, 1979
AVALANCHE EXPRESS 20th Century-Fox, 1979
ALL QUIET ON THE WESTERN FRONT (TF) Norman Rosemont Productions/Marble Arch Productions, 1979
LITTLE LORD FAUNTLEROY (TF) Norman Rosemont Productions, 1980, U.S.-British
A TALE OF TWO CITIES (TF) Norman Rosemont Productions/Marble Arch Productions, 1980, U.S.-British
THE GOSSIP COLUMNIST (TF) Universal TV, 1980
CRY OF THE INNOCENT (TF) Tara Productions, 1980
BEULAH LAND (TF) David Gerber Company/Columbia TV, 1980
PLEASURE PALACE (TF) Norman Rosemont Productions/Marble Arch Productions, 1980
TERROR AMONG US (TF) David Gerber Productions, 1981
THE RED FLAG: THE ULTIMATE GAME (TF) Marble Arch Productions, 1981
PETER AND PAUL (TF) Universal TV/Procter & Gamble Productions, 1981

ELVIS AND THE BEAUTY QUEEN (TF) David Gerber Company/Columbia TV, 1981
IVANHOE (TF) ☆ Rosemont Productions, 1982, British-U.S.
COMPUTERSIDE (TF) co-composer with Jack Elliot, The Culzean Corporation/Paramount Pictures TV, 1982
MASTER OF THE GAME (TF) ☆ Rosemont Productions, 1984
CAMILLE (TF) ☆☆ Rosemont Productions, 1984, U.S.-British
ROMANCE ON THE ORIENT EXPRESS (TF) Frank von Zerneck Productions/Yorkshire TV, 1985, U.S.-British
THE CORSICAN BROTHERS (TF) Rosemont Productions, 1985, British-U.S.
THE LAST DAYS OF PATTON (TF) ☆ Entertainment Partners, 1986
THE CHRISTMAS GIFT (TF) Rosemont Productions/ Sunn Classic Pictures, 1986
ANGEL IN GREEN (TF) Aligre Productions/Taft Hardy Group, 1987, U.S.-New Zealand
STONE FOX (TF) co-composer with Peter Matz, Hanna-Barbera Productions/Allarcom Ltd./Taft Entertainment TV, 1987, U.S.-Canadian
THE WOMAN HE LOVED (TF) The Larry Thompson Organization/HTV/New World TV, 1988, U.S.-British
APRIL MORNING (TF) ☆ Robert Halmi, Inc./Samuel Goldwyn TV, 1988
PANCHO BARNES (TF) ☆ Blue Andre Productions/ Orion TV, 1988

DAVID FERGUSON

TAILSPIN: BEHIND THE KOREAN AIRLINE TRAGEDY (CTF) Darlow Smithson Productions/ HBO, 1989

JAY FERGUSON

Agent: ICM - Los Angeles, 213/550-4000

DEATH OF AN ANGEL 20th Century-Fox, 1985
THE PATRIOT Crown International, 1986
QUIET COOL New Line Cinema, 1986
BEST SELLER Orion, 1987
PULSE Columbia, 1988
JOHNNY BE GOOD Orion, 1988
BAD DREAMS 20th Century Fox, 1988
LICENSE TO DRIVE 20th Century Fox, 1988
AMERICAN BUILT Midwood Productions, 1989
GLEAMING THE CUBE 20th Century Fox, 1989
A NIGHTMARE ON ELM STREET 5: THE DREAM CHILD New Line Cinema, 1989
RACE FOR GLORY New Century/Vista, 1989

RUSSELL FERRANTE

Contact: BMI - Los Angeles, 213/659-9109

WIRED TO KILL American Distribution Group, 1986

PAUL FERRIS

Contact: PRS - London, England, 011-44-1-580-5544

THE SORCERERS 1967, British
THE CONQUEROR WORM *THE WITCHFINDER GENERAL* American International, 1968, British
THE VAMPIRE BEAST CRAVES BLOOD 1969, British
THE CREEPING FLESH Columbia, 1973, British
THE TERROR OF SHEBA *PERSECUTION* Blueberry Hill, 1974, British

BRAD FIEDEL

Agent: Gorfaine-Schwartz - Burbank, 818/954-9500

APPLE PIE Aumont Productions, 1975
DEADLY HERO co-composer with Tommy Mandel, Avco Embassy, 1976
LOOKING UP Levitt-Pickman, 1977
MAYFLOWER: THE PILGRIM'S ADVENTURE (TF) Syzygy Productions, 1979
HARDHAT AND LEGS (TF) Syzygy Productions, 1980
THE DAY THE WOMEN GOT EVEN (TF) Otto Salamon Productions/PKO Television Ltd., 1980
PLAYING FOR TIME (TF) Syzygy Productions, 1980
THE BUNKER (TF) Time-Life Productions/SFP France/ Antenne-2, 1981, U.S.-French
PEOPLE VS. JEAN HARRIS (TF) PKO TV Ltd., 1981
JUST BEFORE DAWN Picturmedia Limited, 1981
NIGHT SCHOOL *TERROR EYES* Paramount, 1981
DREAM HOUSE (TF) Hill-Mandelker Productions/Time-Life Productions, 1981
HIT AND RUN Comworld, 1982
MAE WEST (TF) Hill-Mandelker Productions, 1982
DREAMS DON'T DIE (TF) Hill-Mandelker Productions, 1982
BORN BEAUTIFUL (TF) Procter & Gamble Productions/ Telecom Entertainment, 1982
MURDER IN COWETA COUNTY (TF) Telecom Entertainment/International Picture Show Company, 1983
COCAINE: ONE MAN'S SEDUCTION (TF) Charles Fries Productions/David Goldsmith Productions, 1983
RIGHT OF WAY (CTF) HBO Premiere Films, Schaefer-Karpf Productions/Post-Newsweek Video, 1983
JACOBO TIMERMAN: PRISONER WITHOUT A NAME, CELL WITHOUT A NUMBER Chrysalis-Yellen Productions, 1983
GIRLS OF THE WHITE ORCHID *DEATH RIDE TO OSAKA* (TF) Hill-Mandelker Productions, 1983
HEART OF STEEL (TF) Beowulf Productions, 1983
WHEN SHE SAYS NO (TF) I&C Productions, 1984
MY MOTHER'S SECRET LIFE (TF) Furia-Oringer Productions/ABC Circle Films, 1984
ANATOMY OF AN ILLNESS (TF) Hamner Productions/ Jerry Gershwin Productions/CBS Entertainment, 1984
CALENDAR GIRL MURDERS (TF) Tisch-Avnet Productions, 1984
EYES OF FIRE Elysian Pictures, 1984
THE TERMINATOR Orion, 1984
THE BARON AND THE KID (TF) Telecom Entertainment, 1984
THE THREE WISHES OF BILLY GRIER (TF) I&C Productions, 1984
CHILDREN IN THE CROSSFIRE (TF) Schaefer-Karpf Productions/Prendergast-Brittcadia Productions, 1984
DEADLY MESSAGES (TF) Columbia Pictures TV, 1985
FRATERNITY VACATION New World, 1985
COMPROMISING POSITIONS Paramount, 1985
BRAKER (TF) Blatt-Singer Productions/Centerpoint Productions/MGM/UA TV, 1985
FRIGHT NIGHT Columbia, 1985
INTO THIN AIR (TF) Major H Productions/Tony Ganz Productions, 1985
THE MIDNIGHT HOUR (TF) ABC Circle Films, 1985
UNDER SIEGE (TF) Ohlmeyer Communications Co./ Telepictures Productions, 1986
SECOND SERVE (TF) Linda Yellen Productions/ Lorimar-Telepictures, 1986
DESERT BLOOM Columbia, 1986
A FIGHTING CHOICE (TF) Walt Disney Pictures, 1986

BROTHERHOOD OF JUSTICE (TF) Guber-Peters Entertainment Co. Productions/Phoenix Entertainment Group, 1986
NORTHSTAR (TF) Daniel Grodnick Productions/Warner Bros. TV, 1986
POPEYE DOYLE (TF) December 3rd Productions/ 20th Century-Fox TV, 1986
LET'S GET HARRY Tri-Star, 1986
OF PURE BLOOD (TF) K-M Productions/Joseph Sargent Productions/Warner Bros. TV, 1986
SUNDAY DRIVE (TF) Wizan TV Enterprises/Walt Disney TV, 1986
THE BIG EASY Columbia, 1987
THE LAST INNOCENT MAN (CTF) HBO Pictures/ Maurice Singer Productions, 1987
BLUFFING IT (TF) Don Ohlmeyer Productions, 1987
NOWHERE TO HIDE New Century/Vista, 1987, U.S.-Canadian
RIGHT TO DIE (TF) Ohlmeyer Communications, 1987
WEEKEND WAR (TF) Pompian/Columbia Pictures TV, 1988
HOSTAGE (TF) CBS Entertainment, 1988
THE SERPENT AND THE RAINBOW Universal, 1988
HOT PAINT (TF) Catalina Production Group, 1988
THE ACCUSED Paramount, 1988
FRIGHT NIGHT PART 2 New Century/Vista, 1989
TRUE BELIEVER Columbia, 1989
COLD SASSY TREE (CTF) Faye Dunaway Productions/Ohlmeyer Productions, 1989
PERFECT WITNESS (CTF) HBO Pictures/Granger Productions, 1989
IMMEDIATE FAMILY Columbia, 1989
BLUE STEEL MGM/UA, 1990

ERNIE FIELDS
Contact: BMI - Los Angeles, 213/659-9109

DISCO GODFATHER 1980

MIKE FIGGIS
Agent: William Morris - Beverly Hills, 213/274-7451

STORMY MONDAY Atlantic Releasing Corporation, 1988, British
INTERNAL AFFAIRS co-composer with Anthony Marinelli and Brian Banks, Paramount, 1990

IRWIN FISCH
Contact: BMI - Los Angeles, 213/659-9109

SPEARFIELD'S DAUGHTER (MS) Robert Halmi, Inc/ Channel Seven, 1986, U.S.-Australian

GUENTHER FISCHER
Contact: GEMA - Munich, West Germany, 011-49-89621400

THE FLIGHT 1978, East German
OTTOKAR, THE WORLD REFORMER 1978, East German
JUST A GIGOLO United Artists Classics, 1979, West German
DER AUFENTHALT DEFA, East German
MAERKISCHE FORSCHUNGEN DEFA, 1983, East German
DER STEINERNE FLUSS *THE STONE RIVER* 1983, West German

FISHBONE
TAPEHEADS DEG, 1988

CLARE FISHER
UNDER THE CHERRY MOON Warner Bros., 1986

VIC FLICK
Contact: PRS - London, England, 011-44-1-580-5544

HULLABALOO OVER GEORGIE AND BONNIE'S PICTURES Corinth, 1979

BOB FLOKE
STITCHES International Film Marketing, 1985

DAN FOLIART
Agent: Bart-Milander - North Hollywood, 818/761-4040

THE ONLY WAY HOME Regional, 1972
RETURN TO GREEN ACRES (TF) Jaygoe Productions/ Orion TV, 1990

ROBERT FOLK
Agent: Lawrence Marks - Northridge, 818/831-1830

SAVAGE HARVEST 20th Century-Fox, 1981
THE SLAYER 21st Century Distribution, 1982
PURPLE HEARTS The Ladd Company/Warner Bros., 1984
BACHELOR PARTY 20th Century Fox, 1984
POLICE ACADEMY The Ladd Company/Warner Bros., 1984
THUNDER ALLEY Cannon, 1985
POLICE ACADEMY 2: THEIR FIRST ASSIGNMENT Warner Bros., 1985
PRINCE OF BEL-AIR (TF) Leonard Hill Films, 1986
STEWARDESS SCHOOL Columbia, 1986
POLICE ACADEMY 3: BACK IN TRAINING Warner Bros., 1986
ODD JOBS Tri-Star, 1986
COMBAT HIGH (TF) Frank & Julie Films/Frank Von Zerneck Productions/Lynch-Biller Productions, 1986
THE ROOM UPSTAIRS (TF) Marian Rees Associates/The Alexander Group Productions, 1987
CAN'T BUY ME LOVE Buena Vista, 1987
POLICE ACADEMY 4: CITIZENS ON PATROL Warner Bros., 1987
HIGH MOUNTAIN RANGERS (TF) Shane Productions, 1987
MILES FROM HOME Cinecom, 1988
POLICE ACADEMY 5: ASSIGNMENT MIAMI BEACH Warner Bros., 1988
GLORY DAYS (TF) A. Shane Company/Sibling Rivalries, 1988
POLICE ACADEMY 6: CITY UNDER SIEGE Warner Bros., 1989
WICKED STEPMOTHER MGM/UA, 1989
JESSE HAWKS (TF) A. Shane Co., 1989
HONEYMOON ACADEMY Triumph, 1990
HAPPY TOGETHER Borde Releasing Corporation, 1990
THE NEVERENDING STORY 2 Warner Bros., 1990

RUSSELL FORANTE
WIRED TO KILL American Distribution Group, 1986

MITCHEL FORMAN
Contact: ASCAP - Los Angeles, 213/466-7681

JEZEBEL'S KISS Shapiro-Glickenhaus, 1990

GREG FORREST

Contact: BMI - Los Angeles, 213/659-9109

CRYSTAL EYES 1981

DAVID FOSTER

Contact: BMI - Los Angeles, 213/659-9109

ST. ELMO'S FIRE Columbia, 1985
THE SECRET OF MY SUCCESS Universal, 1987
STEALING HOME Warner Bros., 1988
FRESH HORSES co-composer with Patrick Williams, Columbia/WEG, 1988
LISTEN TO ME Columbia, 1989

CHARLES FOX

Agent: William Morris - Beverly Hills, 213/274-7451

THE INCIDENT 20th Century Fox, 1967
BARBARELLA co-composer with Bob Crewe, Paramount, 1968, Italian-French
GOODBYE COLUMBUS Paramount, 1969
PUFNSTUFF Universal, 1970
STAR-SPANGLED GIRL Paramount, 1971
A SEPARATE PEACE Paramount, 1972
THE LAST AMERICAN HERO 20th Century Fox, 1973
DYING ROOM ONLY (TF) Lorimar Productions, 1973
THE LAUGHING POLICEMAN 20th Century Fox, 1973
ALOHA MEANS GOODBYE (TF) Universal TV, 1974
THE STRANGER WITHIN (TF) Lorimar Productions, 1974
THE DROWNING POOL co-composer with Michael Small, Warner Bros., 1975
THE OTHER SIDE OF THE MOUNTAIN Universal, 1975
BUG Paramount, 1975
THE DUCHESS AND THE DIRTWATER FOX 20th Century Fox, 1976
TWO-MINUTE WARNING Universal, 1976
ONE ON ONE Warner Bros., 1977
FOUL PLAY Paramount, 1978
RAINBOW (TF) Ten-Four Productions, 1978
OUR WINNING SEASON American International, 1978
BETTER LATE THAN NEVER (TF) Ten-Four Productions, 1979
THE LAST MARRIED COUPLE IN AMERICA Universal, 1980
LITTLE DARLINGS Paramount, 1980
WHY WOULD I LIE? MGM/United Artists, 1980
OH GOD! BOOK II Warner Bros., 1980
NINE TO FIVE 20th Century Fox, 1980
ZAPPED! Embassy, 1982
SIX PACK 20th Century Fox, 1982
LOVE CHILD The Ladd Company/Warner Bros., 1982
TRENCHCOAT Buena Vista, 1983
STRANGE BREW MGM/UA, 1983, Canadian
DOIN' TIME The Ladd Company/Warner Bros., 1984
NATIONAL LAMPOON'S EUROPEAN VACATION Warner Bros., 1985
A SUMMER TO REMEMBER (TF) Inter Planetary Productions, 1985
BETRAYED BY INNOCENCE (TF) Inter Planetary Pictures/CBS Entertainment, 1986
THE LONGSHOT Orion, 1986
UNNATURAL CAUSES (TF) Blue Andre Productions/ ITC Productions, 1986
PARENT TRAP II (TF) The Landsburg Company/ Walt Disney TV, 1987
CHRISTMAS COMES TO WILLOW CREEK (TF) Blue Andre Productions/ITC Productions, 1987
IT HAD TO BE YOU Panther Filmworks, 1988
BABY M (TF) ABC Circle Films, 1988
LOVE AT STAKE *BURNIN' LOVE* Tri-Star, 1988
SHORT CIRCUIT II Tri-Star, 1988
GOING TO THE CHAPEL (TF) Furia Organization/ Finnegan-Pinchuk Company, 1988
THE GODS MUST BE CRAZY II WEG/Columbia, 1989, South African
IT HAD TO BE YOU Limelite Studios, 1989
TARZAN IN MANHATTAN (TF) American First Run Productions, 1989
RICH MEN, SINGLE WOMEN (TF) Aaron Spelling Productions, 1990
A FAMILY FOR JOE (TF) Gross-Jacobson Productions/ NBC Productions, 1990
VOICES WITHIN: THE LIVES OF TRUDDI CHASE (TF) Itzbinzo Long Productions/P.A. Productions/New World TV, 1990

R. DONOVAN FOX

THE GEORGIA PEACHES (TF) New World Pictures, 1980

ALUN FRANCIS

Contact: PRS - London, England, 011-44-1-580-5544

GIRO CITY Silvarealm, 1982, British

DAVID FRANK

Contact: BMI - Los Angeles, 213/659-9109

A DIFFERENT STORY Avco Embassy, 1978
THE KID FROM LEFT FIELD (TF) Gary Coleman Productions/Deena Silver-Kramer's Movie Company, 1979
AN INNOCENT LOVE (TF) Steve Binder Productions, 1982
MAID IN AMERICA (TF) Georgian Bay Productions/CBS Entertainment, 1982
CODE OF SILENCE Orion, 1985
GLADIATOR (TF) Walker Brothers Productions/New World TV, 1986
THE CHECK IS IN THE MAIL Ascot Entertainment Group, 1986
OFF THE MARK Fries Entertainment, 1987
ABOVE THE LAW Warner Bros., 1988
HERO AND THE TERROR Cannon, 1988
CALL ME Vestron, 1988

DAVID MICHAEL FRANK

Contact: BMI - Los Angeles, 213/659-9109

I'M GONNA GET YOU SUCKA MGM/UA, 1988
ONE MAN FORCE Shaprio Glickenhaus, 1989
FALSE WITNESS (TF) Valente-Kritzer-EPI Productions/ New World TV, 1989
DIVE Warner Bros., 1990
HARD TO KILL Warner Bros., 1990

SERGE FRANKLIN

Contact: SACEM - France, 011-33-14-747-5650

THE SIROCCO BLOW 1979, French
LE GRAND CARNIVAL Gaumont, 1983, French
HOLD-UP AMLF-Cerito, 1985, French
THE SAINT: THE BRAZILIAN CONNECTION (TF) Saint Productions/London Weekend Television, 1989, British
A TALE OF TWO CITIES (TF) Granada TV/Antenne 2, 1989, British-French

MICHAEL FRANKS

ZANDY'S BRIDE Warner Bros., 1974
BORN TO KILL New World, 1975

DAVE FRASER

Contact: APRA - Australia, 011-61-2-922-6422

WILD HORSES Endeavour, 1983, Australian
THE LOST TRIBE Meridian Films/Film Investment Corporation of New Zealand/New Zealand Film Commission, 1983, New Zealand

IAN FRASER

TORN BETWEEN TWO LOVERS (TF) Alan Landsburg Productions, 1979
HOPSCOTCH Avco Embassy, 1980
ZORRO, THE GAY BLADE 20th Century-Fox, 1981
FIRST MONDAY IN OCTOBER adaptation, Paramount, 1981
LIFE OF THE PARTY: THE STORY OF BEATRICE (TF) Welch-Welch Productions/Columbia Pictures TV, 1982

JILL FRASER

Agent: Robert Light - Los Angeles, 213/651-1777

PERSONAL BEST co-composer with Jack Nitzsche, The Geffen Company/Warner Bros., 1982
CUTTING CLASS Republic, 1989

JESSE FREDERICK

Contact: ASCAP - Los Angeles, 213/466-7681

ALOHA SUMMER co-composer with Bennett Salvay, Spectrafilm, 1988

MARC FREDERICKS

THE RED MANTLE 1973, Finnish
SEEDS OF EVIL *THE GARDENER* KKI Films, 1981

IAN FREEBAIRN-SMITH

DEADLY LESSONS (TF) Leonard Goldberg Company, 1983

GERALD FRIED

b. February 13, 1928 - New York, New York
Agent: Bart-Milander - North Hollywood, 818/761-4040

FEAR AND DESIRE Joseph Burstyn, Inc., 1954
BLOOD MONEY 1954
KILLER'S KISS United Artists, 1955
THE KILLING United Artists, 1956
BAYOU United Artists, 1957
THE VAMPIRE *MARK OF THE VAMPIRE* United Artists, 1957
PATHS OF GLORY United Artists, 1957
TROOPER HOOK United Artists, 1957
DINO Allied Artists, 1957
I BURY THE LIVING United Artists, 1958
CRY BABY KILLER Allied Artists, 1958
THE RETURN OF DRACULA *THE CURSE OF DRACULA* United Artists, 1958
THE FLAME BARRIER United Artists, 1958
CURSE OF THE FACELESS MAN United Artists, 1958
THE LOST MISSILE United Artists, 1958
TERROR IN A TEXAS TOWN United Artists, 1958
MACHINE GUN KELLY American International, 1958
TIMBUKTU United Artists, 1959
I, MOBSTER 20th Century Fox, 1959
CAST A LONG SHADOW United Artists, 1959
A COLD WIND IN AUGUST Lopert, 1961
TWENTY PLUS TWO Allied Artists, 1961
THE SECOND TIME AROUND 20th Century Fox, 1961
THE CABINET OF DR. CALIGARI 20th Century Fox, 1962
ONE POTATO, TWO POTATO Cinema 5, 1964
ONE SPY TOO MANY MGM, 1966
THE KILLING OF SISTER GEORGE Cinerama Releasing Corporation, 1968
WHAT EVER HAPPENED TO AUNT ALICE? Cinerama Releasing Corporation, 1968
TOO LATE THE HERO Cinerama Releasing Corporation, 1970
THE GRISSOM GANG Cinerama Releasing Corporation, 1971
SOYLENT GREEN co-composer with Frank Myrow, MGM, 1972
THE BABY Scotia International, 1973, British
BIRDS DO IT, BEES DO IT ★ Columbia, 1975
I WILL FIGHT NO MORE FOREVER (FD) Wolper Productions, 1975
SURVIVE! Paramount, 1975
VIGILANTE FORCE United Artists, 1976
FRANCIS GARY POWERS: THE TRUE STORY OF THE U-2 SPY INCIDENT (TF) Charles Fries Productions, 1976
ROOTS (MS) ☆☆ co-composer with Quincy Jones, Wolper Productions, 1977
SEX AND THE MARRIED WOMAN (TF) Universal TV, 1977
THE SPELL (TF) Charles Fries Productions, 1977
TESTIMONY OF TWO MEN (MS) Universal TV, 1977
CRUISE INTO TERROR (TF) Aaron Spelling Productions, 1978
MANEATERS ARE LOOSE! (TF) Mona Productions/ Finnegan Associates, 1978
THE BEASTS ARE ON THE STREETS (TF) Hanna-Barbera Productions, 1978
RESCUE FROM GILLIGAN'S ISLAND (TF) Sherwood Schwartz, 1978
THE IMMIGRANTS (TF) Universal TV, 1978
THE TWO-FIVE (TF) Universal TV, 1978
THE SEEKERS (TF) Universal TV, 1978
ROOTS: THE NEXT GENERATION (MS) Wolper Productions, 1979
THE INCREDIBLE JOURNEY OF DOCTOR MEG LAUREL (TF) Columbia TV, 1979
THE BELL JAR Avco Embassy, 1979
SON RISE: A MIRACLE OF LOVE (TF) Rothman-Wohl Productions/Filmways, 1979
THE REBELS (MS) Universal TV, 1979
BREAKING UP IS HARD TO DO (TF) Green-Epstein Productions/Columbia TV, 1979
THE CASTAWAYS OF GILLIGAN'S ISLAND (TF) Sherwood Schwartz Productions, 1979
DISASTER ON THE COASTLINER (TF) Moonlight Productions/Filmways, 1979
THE CHISHOLMS (MS) Alan Landsburg Productions, 1979
ROOTS: THE NEXT GENERATIONS (MS) Wolper Productions, 1979
THE ORDEAL OF DR. MUDD (TF) BSR Productions/ Marble Arch Productions, 1980
MOVIOLA: THE SILENT LOVERS (MS) ☆ David L. Wolper-Stan Margulies Productions/Warner Bros. TV, 1980
FLAMINGO ROAD (TF) MF Productions/Lorimar Productions, 1980
THE WILD AND THE FREE (TF) BSR Productions/Marble Arch Productions, 1980
CONDOMINIUM (TF) Universal TV, 1980

THE HARLEM GLOBETROTTERS ON GILLIGAN'S ISLAND (TF) Sherwood Schwartz Productions, 1981
MURDER IS EASY (TF) David L. Wolper-Stan Margulies Productions/Warner Bros. TV, 1982
FOR US, THE LIVING (TF) Charles Fries Productions, 1983
THE RETURN OF THE MAN FROM U.N.C.L.E. (TF) Martin Sloan Productions/Viacom Productions, 1983
KILLER IN THE FAMILY (TF) Stan Margulies Productions/Sunn Classic Pictures, 1983
THE MYSTIC WARRIOR (MS) ☆ David S. Wolper-Stan Margulies Productions/Warner Bros. TV, 1984
EMBASSY (TF) Stan Margulies Company/ABC Circle Films, 1985
NAPOLEON AND JOSEPHINE: A LOVE STORY (TF) ☆ David L. Wolper Productions/Warner Bros. TV, 1987
ROOTS: THE GIFT (TF) Wolper Productions/Warner Bros. TV, 1988
DROP-OUT MOTHER (TF) Fries Entertainment/Comco Productions, 1988

GARY WILLIAM FRIEDMAN

Agent: Richard Emler - Los Angeles, 213/651-0222

FORE PLAY Cinema National, 1975
SURVIVAL RUN Spiegel-Bergman, 1980
FULL MOON HIGH Filmways, 1981
MY TWO LOVES (TF) Alvin Cooperman Productions/Taft Entertainment TV, 1986
NIGHT OF COURAGE (TF) Titus Productions/The Eugene O'Neill Memorial Theater Center, 1987
WHO GETS THE FRIENDS? (TF) CBS Entertainment, 1988
LIBERACE (TF) The Liberace Foundation for the Performing and Creative Arts/Dick Clark Productions/Republic Pictures, 1988

FABIO FRIZZI

b. Italy
Contact: SIAE - Rome, Italy, 011-39-6-59-90-1

HOT DREAMS *AMORE LIBERO* 1974, Italian
DRACULA IN THE PROVINCES co-composer, 1975
ZOMBI 2 *ZOMBIE FLESH EATERS* co-composer with Giorgio Tucci, Variety Film, 1979, Italian
PAURA NELLA CITTA' DEI MORTI VIVENTI Dania Film/Medusa Distribuzione/National Cinematografica, 1980, Italian
...E TU VIVRAI NEL TERRORE! L'ALDILA' Fulvia Film, 1980, Italian
MANHATTAN BABY Fulvia Film, 1982, Italian
THE GATES OF HELL MPM, 1983, Italian
SUPERFANTAGENIO *ALADDIN* Cannon, 1987, Italian

EDGAR FROESE

Contact: GEMA - Munich, West Germany, 011-49-89621400

KAMIKAZE 1989 1982

DOMINIC FRONTIERE

b. June 17, 1931 - New Haven, Connecticut
Agent: Gorfaine-Schwartz - Burbank, 818/954-9500

ONE FOOT IN HELL 20th Century-Fox, 1960
SEVEN THIEVES 20th Century-Fox, 1960
INCUBUS 1961
HERO'S ISLAND United Artists, 1962
BILLIE United Artists, 1965
HANG 'EM HIGH United Artists, 1968
LOST FLIGHT (TF) Universal TV, 1969
NUMBER ONE United Artists, 1969
POPI United Artists, 1969
THE LOVE WAR (TF) Aaron Spelling Productions, 1970
BARQUERO United Artists, 1970
CHISUM Warner Bros., 1970
THE SHERIFF (TF) Screen Gems/Columbia Pictures TV, 1971
ON ANY SUNDAY Tigon, 1971
REVENGE (TF) Mark Carliner Productions, 1972
HAUNTS OF THE VERY RICH (TF) ABC Circle Films, 1972
HAMMERSMITH IS OUT Cinerama Releasing Corporation, 1972
THE TRAIN ROBBERS Warner Bros., 1973
CLEOPATRA JONES Warner Bros., 1973
FREEBIE AND THE BEAN Warner Bros., 1974
FER DE LANCE (TF) Leslie Stevens Productions, 1974
THE MARK OF ZORRO (TF) Thompson-Paul Productions/20th Century-Fox TV, 1974
VELVET (TF) Aaron Spelling Productions, 1974
WHO IS THE BLACK DAHLIA? (TF) Douglas S. Cramer Productions, 1975
BRANNIGAN United Artists, 1975, British
CLEOPATRA JONES AND THE CASINO OF GOLD Warner Bros., 1975
GUMBALL RALLY Warner Bros., 1976
PIPE DREAMS Avco Embassy, 1976
YESTERDAY'S CHILD (TF) Paramount TV, 1977
WASHINGTON: BEHIND CLOSED DOORS (TF) Paramount TV, 1977
PERFECT GENTLEMEN (TF) Paramount TV, 1978
VEGAS (TF) Aaron Spelling Productions, 1978
MY OLD MAN (TF) Zeitman-McNichol-Halmi Productions, 1979
DEFIANCE American International, 1980
THE STUNT MAN 20th Century-Fox, 1980
ROAR Filmways Australasian, 1981
MODERN PROBLEMS 20th Century-Fox, 1981
DON'T GO TO SLEEP (TF) Aaron Spelling Productions/Warner Bros. TV, 1982
SHOOTING STARS (TF) Aaron Spelling Productions, 1983
DARK MIRROR (TF) Aaron Spelling Productions, 1984
VELVET (TF) Aaron Spelling Productions, 1984
THE AVIATOR MGM/UA, 1985
HARRY'S HONG KONG (TF) Aaron Spelling Productions, 1987

MITCHELL FROOM

Contact: ASCAP - Los Angeles, 213/466-7681

CAFE FLESH 1983
SLAM DANCE Island Pictures, 1987

GARY FRY

CEASE FIRE Cineworld, 1985

JUN FUKAMACHI

b. Japan
Contact: JASRAC - Tokyo, Japan, 011-81-3-502-6551

HINOTORI co-composer with Michel Legrand, Toho, 1980, Japanese

PARMER FULLER

b. 1949 - San Francisco, California
Agent: Robert Light - Los Angeles, 213/651-1777

SATURDAY THE 14TH New World, 1981
SPIRIT OF THE EAGLE Queen's Cross Productions
WHITE GHOST Trans World Entertainment, 1988
SATURDAY THE 14TH STRIKES BACK Concorde, 1988
TIMETRACKERS Concorde, 1989
MORTAL PASSIONS Gibraltar Releasing Organization, 1989
NIGHT VISITOR MGM/UA, 1989

LEWIS FUREY

Contact: SACEM - France, 011-33-14-747-5650

FANTASTICA Les Productions du Verseau/El Productions, 1980, Canadian-French
AGENCY Taft International, 1980, Canadian
AMERICAN DREAMER Warner Bros., 1984
THE PEANUT BUTTER SOLUTION New World, 1985, Canadian

PETER GABRIEL

b. 1950
Contact: BMI - Los Angeles, 213/659-9109

BIRDY Tri-Star, 1984
THE LAST TEMPTATION OF CHRIST Universal, 1988

TEDRA GABRIEL

REFORM SCHOOL GIRLS New World, 1986

HENRY GAFFNEY

Contact: BMI - Los Angeles, 213/659-9109

SIDEWALK STORIES Island Pictures, 1989

ANDRE GAGNON

Contact: Pro-Canada - Canada, 1-416-445-8700

RUNNING Columbia, 1979, Canadian-U.S.
PHOBIA Paramount, 1980, Canadian

SERGE GAINSBOURG

b. Paris, France
Contact: SACEM - France, 011-33-14-747-5650

L'EAU A LA BOUCHE 1960, French
COMMENT TROUVEZ-VOUS MA SOEUR? 1964, French
SI J'ETAIS UN ESPION 1966, French
MANON 70 1966, French
L'HORIZON 1967, French
LE JARDINIER D'ARGENTEUIL 1967, French
L'INCONNU DE SHANDIGOR 1967, French
LA PACHA 1968, French
PARIS N'EXISTE PAS 1968, French
MISTER FREEDOM 1969, French
LES CHEMINS DE KATMANDOU 1969, French
LA HORSE 1969, French
CANNABIS 1970, French
TROP JOLIES POUR ETRE HONNETES 1972, French
PROJECTION PRIVEE 1972, French
LE SEX SHOP Peppercorn-Wormser, 1973, French
JE T'AIME MOI NON PLUS 1975, French
GOODBYE EMMANUELLE 1977, French
THE FRENCH WOMAN *MADAME CLAUDE* Monarch, 1979, French
EQUATOR Gaumont, 1983, French
MENAGE *TENUE DE SOIREE* Cinecom, 1986, French

JACK GALE

Contact: BMI - Los Angeles, 213/659-9109

THE LUCKIEST MAN IN THE WORLD co-composer with Warren Vache, Co-Star Entertainment, 1989

JOHN GALE

Contact: PRS - London, England, 011-44-1-580-5544

DR. PHIBES RISES AGAIN American International, 1972, British

PHILO GALLO

THE REDEEMER...SON OF SATAN! co-composer with Clem Vicari, 1978
MOTHER'S DAY co-composer with Clem Vicari, United Film Distribution, 1980

PHIL GALSTON

Contact: ASCAP - Los Angeles, 213/466-7681

THE JERK, TOO (TF) co-composer with John Sebastian, Share Productions/Universal TV, 1984

DOUGLAS GAMLEY

b. 1924
Contact: PRS - London, England, 011-44-1-580-5544

ONE WISH TOO MANY 1956, British
THE ADMIRABLE CRICHTON *PARADISE LAGOON* Columbia, 1957, British
ANOTHER TIME, ANOTHER PLACE Paramount, 1958
tom thumb co-composer with Ken Jones, MGM, 1958
GIDEON OF SCOTLAND YARD *GIDEON'S DAY* Columbia, 1958, British
TARZAN'S GREATEST ADVENTURE Paramount, 1959, British-U.S.
WEB OF EVIDENCE *BEYOND THIS PLACE* Allied Artists, 1959, British
HORROR HOTEL *CITY OF THE DEAD* Trans-World, 1960, British
THE HORROR OF IT ALL 20th Century-Fox, 1964, British
THE RETURN OF MR. MOTO 20th Century-Fox, 1965
SPRING AND PORT WINE EMI, 1970, British
TALES FROM THE CRYPT Cinerama Releasing Corporation, 1972, British
ASYLUM Cinerama Releasing Corporation, 1972, British
THE VAULT OF HORROR *TALES FROM THE CRYPT II* Cinerama Releasing Corporation, 1973, British
AND NOW THE SCREAMING STARTS Cinerama Releasing Corporation, 1973, British
FROM BEYOND THE GRAVE *THE CREATURES* Howard Mahler Films, 1973, British
MADHOUSE American International, 1974, British

THE BEAST MUST DIE Cinerama Releasing Corporation, 1974, British
THE LAND THAT TIME FORGOT American International, 1975, British
THE MONSTER CLUB ITC, 1981, British

RUSSELL GARCIA

b. 1916

RADAR SECRET SERVICE co-composer with Richard Hazard, 1949
THE TIME MACHINE MGM, 1960, British
ATLANTIS, THE LOST CONTINENT MGM, 1961
THE PAD (AND HOW TO USE IT) Universal, 1966
THREE GUNS FOR TEXAS Universal, 1968

STU GARDNER

Contact: BMI - Los Angeles, 213/659-9109

THE KLANSMAN co-composer with Dale O. Warren, Paramount, 1974
TOP SECRET (TF) co-composer with Teo Macero, Jemmin, Inc./Sheldon Leonard Productions, 1978

JASON GARFIELD

THE G.I. EXECUTIONER *WIT'S END* co-composer with Elliot Chiprut, Troma, 1985

SNUFF GARRETT

Contact: BMI - Los Angeles, 213/659-9109

BRONCO BILLY Warner Bros., 1980
SMOKEY AND THE BANDIT II Universal, 1980
THE CANNONBALL RUN 20th Century-Fox, 1981
ANY WHICH WAY YOU CAN Warner Bros., 1981

MIKE GARSON

Agent: Andi Howard - Los Angeles, 213/278-6483

A YEAR IN THE LIFE (MS) Universal TV, 1986
TIME FLIES WHEN YOU'RE ALIVE (CTF) HBO Showcase/Kings Road Entertainment, 1989

MORT GARSON

Contact: ASCAP - Los Angeles, 213/466-7681

BEWARE! THE BLOB *SON OF BLOB* Jack H. Harris Enterprises, 1972
BLACK EYE Warner Bros., 1974

GEORGES GARVARENTZ

b. France
Contact: SACEM - France, 011-33-14-747-5650

UN TAXI POUR TOBROUK 1961, French
LES BONNES CAUSES 1963, French
COMMENT REUSSIR EN AMOUR 1963, French
LE RAT D'AMERIQUE 1964, French
PARIS AU MOIS D'AOUT 1966, French
LE GRAND DADAIS 1966, French
L'HOMME QUI VALAIT DES MILLIARDS 1967, French
UN MILLIARD DANS UN BILLARD 1967, French
THEY CAME TO ROB LAS VEGAS *SUDARIO DI SABBIA* 1968, Spanish-French-Italian
THE SOUTHERN STAR Columbia, 1969, French-British
LE TATOUE 1969, French
L'INVITEE 1969, French
LE TEMPS DES LOUPS 1969, French
UN BEAU MONSTRE *A LOVELY MONSTER* 1970, French
L'INTRUS 1971, French
LES GALETS D'ETRETAT *PEBBLES OF ETRETAT* 1972, French
CAROLINE CHERIE 1973, French
KILLER FORCE American International, 1975
THE KILLER WHO WOULDN'T DIE (TF) Paramount Pictures TV, 1976
THE GOLDEN LADY Target International, 1979, British
LA LUMIERE DES JUSTES 1979, French
TRIUMPHS OF A MAN CALLED HORSE Jensen Farley Pictures, 1984
TOO SCARED TO SCREAM The Movie Store, 1985
A STATE OF EMERGENCY Norkat Co., 1986
QUICKER THAN THE EYE Condor, 1989, Swiss

BRIAN GASCOIGNE

Contact: PRS - London, England, 011-44-1-580-5544

UNDER MILK WOOD Altura, 1973, British
PHASE IV Paramount, 1974

CHRISTIAN GAUBERT

Contact: SACEM - France, 011-33-14-747-5650

THE LITTLE GIRL WHO LIVES DOWN THE LANE American International, 1977, U.S.-Canadian-French
THE DEMON OF THE ISLE AMLF, 1983, French

FRANKIE GAYE

PENITENTIARY Jerry Gross Organization, 1979

RALPH GEDDES

THE LAND OF NO RETURN International Picture Show, 1981

RON GEESIN

Contact: PRS - London, England, 011-44-1-580-5544

SWORD OF THE VALIANT Cannon, 1984, British

HARRY GELLER

Contact: BMI - Los Angeles, 213/659-9109

LET'S SWITCH (TF) Universal TV, 1975
DEAD MAN ON THE RUN (TF) Sweeney-Finnegan Productions, 1975

HAROLD GELMAN

SWEET BIRD OF YOUTH MGM, 1962

IRVING GERTZ

b. May 19, 1915 - Providence, Rhode Island

THE DEVIL'S MASK co-composer with George Duning, Columbia, 1946
DRAGNET Screen Guild, 1947
BLONDE ICE Film Classics, 1948
THE COUNTERFEITERS 20th Century-Fox, 1948
THE ADVENTURES OF GALLANT BESS Eagle Lion, 1948
JUNGLE GODDESS Screen Guild, 1948
PREJUDICE New World/MPSC, 1949
DESTINATION MURDER RKO Radio, 1950
EXPERIMENT ALCATRAZ RKO Radio, 1950
SKIPALONG ROSENBLOOM United Artists, 1951
TWO DOLLAR BETTOR Realart, 1951

THE BANDITS OF CORSICA United Artists, 1953
IT CAME FROM OUTER SPACE co-composer, Universal, 1953
THE CREATURE WALKS AMONG US co-composer, Universal, 1956
THE INCREDIBLE SHRINKING MAN co-composer, Universal, 1957
LOVE SLAVES OF THE AMAZON co-composer, Universal, 1957
THE MONOLITH MONSTER co-composer, Universal, 1957
THE ALLIGATOR PEOPLE 20th Century-Fox, 1959
CURSE OF THE UNDEAD Universal, 1959
THE LEECH WOMAN Universal, 1960
THE WIZARD OF BAGHDAD 20th Century-Fox, 1960

BARRY GIBB

Contact: BMI - Los Angeles, 213/659-9109

HAWKS Skouras Pictures, 1989

MAURICE GIBB

Contact: BMI - Los Angeles, 213/659-9109

A BREED APART Orion, 1984

MICHAEL GIBBS

b. Sept. 25, 1937 - Salisbury, S. Rhodesia
Agent: Bart-Milander - North Hollywood, 818/761-4040

SECRETS Lone Star, 1971, British
MADAME SIN (TF) ITC, 1972, British
SECRETS Lone Star, 1978
RIDING THE EDGE Kodiak Films
HEAT New Century/Vista, 1987
HOUSEKEEPING Columbia, 1987
AMERICAN ROULETTE Film Four International/British Screen/Mandemar Group, 1988, British
RIDING THE EDGE Trans World Entertainment, 1989
BREAKING IN Samuel Goldwyn Company, 1989

RICHARD GIBBS

Agent: ICM - Los Angeles, 213/550-4000

SWEET HEART'S DANCE Tri-Star, 1988
A DEADLY SILENCE (TF) Robert Greenwald Productions, 1989
SAY ANYTHING 20th Century-Fox, 1989
UPWORLD Vestron, 1989
KILLING IN A SMALL TOWN (TF) The IndieProd Co./ Hearst Entertainment Productions, 1990
HOW TO MURDER A MILLIONAIRE (TF) Robert Greenwald Films, 1990

DAVID GIBNEY

Contact: BMI - Los Angeles, 213/659-9109

SUPERSTITION *THE WITCH* Almi Pictures, 1985

ALEX GIBSON

Contact: BMI - Los Angeles, 213/659-9109

THE WILD SIDE New World, 1983
FROM HOLLYWOOD TO DEADWOOD Island Pictures, 1989

DAVID GIBSON

SCHLOCK Jack H. Harris Enterprises, 1973

MICHAEL GIBSON

ROSELAND Cinema Shares, 1977

HERSCHEL BURKE GILBERT

b. 1918 - Milwaukee, Wisconsin
Contact: ASCAP - Los Angeles, 213/466-7681

MR. DISTRICT ATTORNEY Columbia, 1947
OPEN SECRET Eagle Lion, 1948
AN OLD-FASHIONED GIRL Eagle Lion, 1948
SHAMROCK HILL Eagle Lion, 1949
THERE'S A GIRL IN MY HEART Allied Artists, 1949
THE JACKIE ROBINSON STORY Eagle Lion, 1950
THREE HUSBANDS United Artists, 1950
THE SCARF United Artists, 1951
THE MAGIC FACE Columbia, 1951
THE HIGHWAYMAN Allied Artists, 1951
WITHOUT WARNING United Artists, 1952
KID MONK BARONI Realart, 1952
MODELS, INC. Mutual, 1952
THE RING United Artists, 1952
THE THIEF ★ United Artists, 1952
NO TIME FOR FLOWERS RKO Radio, 1952
THE MOON IS BLUE United Artists, 1953
SABRE JET United Artists, 1953
VICE SQUAD United Artists, 1953
RIOT IN CELL BLOCK 11 Allied Artists, 1954
CARMEN JONES ★ adaptation, 20th Century-Fox, 1954
WITNESS TO MURDER United Artists, 1954
THE NAKED DAWN Universal, 1955
WHILE THE CITY SLEEPS RKO Radio, 1956
THE BOLD AND THE BRAVE RKO Radio, 1956
BEYOND A REASONABLE DOUBT RKO Radio, 1956
COMANCHE Universal, 1956
THE NAKED HILLS Allied Artists, 1956
NIGHTMARE United Artists, 1956
NO PLACE TO HIDE Allied Artists, 1956
SLAUGHTER ON TENTH AVENUE Universal, 1957
CRIME AND PUNISHMENT, USA Allied Artists, 1959
SAM WHISKEY United Artists, 1969
I DISMEMBER MAMA *POOR ALBERT AND LITTLE ANNIE* Valiant International, 1972

RICHARD GILLIS

DEMONOID American Panorama, 1981

IRIS GILLON

FAST FOOD Fries Entertainment, 1989

PAUL GILMAN

Contact: BMI - Los Angeles, 213/659-9109

BEST OF THE BEST Taurus Entertainment, 1989

PAUL GILREATH

Contact: ASCAP - Los Angeles, 213/466-7681

NO RETREAT NO SURRENDER New World, 1986

CLAUDIO GIZZI

Contact: SIAE - Rome, Italy, 011-39-6-59-90-1

WHAT? Avco Embassy, 1973, Italian-French-West German
ANDY WARHOL'S FRANKENSTEIN *FLESH FOR FRANKENSTEIN* Bryanston, 1974, Italian-French
ANDY WARHOL'S DRACULA *BLOOD FOR DRACULA* Bryanston, 1974, Italian-French

PAUL GLASS
b. 1910

THE ABDUCTORS 20th Century-Fox, 1957
LADY IN A CAGE United Artists, 1964
BUNNY LAKE IS MISSING Columbia, 1965, British
SOLE SURVIVOR (TF) Cinema Center 100, 1970
FIVE DESPERATE WOMEN (TF) Aaron Spelling Productions, 1971
SANDCASTLES (TF) Metromedia Productions, 1972
OVERLORD 1975, British
TO THE DEVIL A DAUGHTER EMI, 1976, British

PHILIP GLASS
b. 1937 - Baltimore, Maryland
Agent: CAA - Los Angeles, 213/288-4545

MARK DI SUVERO, SCULPTOR (FD) 1977
KOYAANISQATSI Island Alive/New Cinema, 1983
MISHIMA: A LIFE IN FOUR CHAPTERS Warner Bros., 1985, Japanese-U.S.
DEAD END KIDS (FD) co-composer with David Byrne, Mabou Mines, 1986
HAMBURGER HILL Paramount, 1987
POWAQQATSI Cannon, 1988
THE THIN BLUE LINE (FD) Miramax Films, 1988

ALBERT GLASSER
b. January 25, 1916 - Chicago, Illinois
Contact: ASCAP - Los Angeles, 213/466-7681

CALL OF THE JUNGLE Monogram, 1944
THE CONTENDER Producers Releasing Corp., 1944
THE MONSTER MAKER Producers Releasing Corp., 1944
THE CISCO KID IN OLD NEW MEXICO Producers Releasing Corp., 1945
THE CISCO KID RETURNS Producers Releasing Corp., 1945
THE KID SISTER Producers Releasing Corp., 1945
ABILENE TOWN United Artists, 1946
GAS HOUSE KIDS IN HOLLYWOOD Producers Releasing Corp., 1947
BORDER FEUD Producers Releasing Corp., 1947
KILLER AT LARGE co-composer with Alvin Levin, Producers Releasing Corp., 1947
GAS HOUSE KIDS GO WEST Producers Releasing Corp., 1947
LAW OF THE LASH Producers Releasing Corp., 1947
PHILO VANCE RETURNS Producers Releasing Corp., 1947
WHERE THE NORTH BEGINS Screen Guild, 1947
HE TRAIL OF THE MOUNTIES Screen Guild, 1948
ASSIGNED TO DANGER Eagle Lion, 1948
BEHIND LOCKED DOORS Eagle Lion, 1948
THE COBRA STRIKES Eagle Lion, 1948
IN THIS CORNER Eagle Lion, 1948
LAST OF THE WILD HORSES Lippert, 1948
THE RETURN OF WILDFIRE Lippert, 1948
THE WHITE PHANTOM 1948
URUBU United Artists, 1948
THE VALIANT HOMBRE United Artists, 1948
THE GAY AMIGO United Artists, 1949
THE DARING CABALLERO United Artists, 1949
APACHE CHIEF Lippert, 1949
I SHOT JESSE JAMES Lippert, 1949
OMOO-OMOO, THE SHARK GOD Screen Guild, 1949
GRAND CANYON Lippert, 1949
SATAN'S CRADLE United Artists, 1949
THE TREASURE OF MONTE CRISTO Lippert, 1949
TOUGH ASSIGNMENT Lippert, 1949
HOLLYWOOD VARIETIES Lippert, 1950
THE GIRL FROM SAN LORENZO United Artists, 1950
WESTERN PACIFIC AGENT Lippert, 1950
EVERYBODY'S DANCIN' Lippert, 1950
GUNFIRE Lippert, 1950
TRAIN TO TOMBSTONE Lippert, 1950
I SHOT BILLY THE KID Lippert, 1950
THE RETURN OF JESSE JAMES Lippert, 1950
BORDER RANGERS Lippert, 1950
BANDIT QUEEN Lippert, 1950
TRAIN TO TOMBSTONE Lippert, 1950
THREE DESPERATE MEN Lippert, 1951
TOKYO FILE 212 RKO Radio, 1951
THE BUSHWACKERS Realart, 1951
OKLAHOMA TERRITORY United Artists, 1951
GEISHA GIRL Realart, 1952
INVASION U.S.A. Columbia, 1952
THE NEANDERTHAL MAN United Artists, 1952
PORT SINISTER RKO Radio, 1953
CAPTAIN JOHN SMITH AND POCAHONTAS United Artists, 1953
PARIS MODEL Columbia, 1953
PROBLEM GIRLS Columbia, 1953
MAN OF CONFLICT Atlas, 1953
DRAGON'S GOLD United Artists, 1954
TOP BANANA United Artists, 1954
THE GIANT OF DEVIL'S CRAG *GIANT FROM THE UNKNOWN* Astor, 1955
MURDER IS MY BEAT Allied Artists, 1955
TOP OF THE WORLD United Artists, 1955
THE BOSS United Artists, 1956
HUK United Artists, 1956
PLEASE MURDER ME DCA, 1956
THE INDESTRUCTIBLE MAN Allied Artists, 1956
BEGINNING OF THE END Republic, 1957
BAILOUT AT 43,000 United Artists, 1957
THE BIG CAPER United Artists, 1957
CYCLOPS American International, 1957
THE BUCKSKIN LADY United Artists, 1957
THE SAGA OF THE VIKING WOMEN AND THEIR VOYAGE TO THE WATERS OF THE GREAT SEA SERPENT American International, 1957
THE AMAZING COLOSSAL MAN American International, 1957
DESTINATION 60,000 Allied Artists, 1957
FOUR BOYS AND A GUN United Artists, 1957
THE HIRED GUN MGM, 1957
MOTORCYCLE GANG American International, 1957
STREET OF SINNERS United Artists, 1957
VALERIE United Artists, 1957
TEENAGE BAD-GIRL DCA, 1957
MONSTER FROM GREEN HELL DCA, 1957
GIRL IN THE WOODS Republic, 1958
HIGH SCHOOL CONFIDENTIAL *YOUNG HELLIONS* MGM, 1958
THE MUGGER United Artists, 1958
SNOWFIRE Allied Artists, 1958
WHEN HELL BROKE LOOSE Paramount, 1958
ATTACK OF THE PUPPET PEOPLE American International, 1958
THE SPIDER American International, 1958
TEENAGE CAVEMAN American International, 1958
WAR OF THE COLOSSAL BEAST American International, 1958
THE BEAT GENERATION *THIS REBEL AGE* MGM, 1959
NIGHT OF THE QUARTER MOON *FLESH AND FLAME* MGM, 1959

OKLAHOMA TERRITORY United Artists, 1960
TORMENTED Allied Artists, 1960
THE HIGH POWERED-RIFLE 20th Century-Fox, 1960
THE BOY AND THE PIRATES United Artists, 1960
20,000 EYES 20th Century-Fox, 1961
AIR PATROL 20th Century-Fox, 1962
CONFESSIONS OF AN OPIUM EATER *SOULS FOR SALE/EVILS OF CHINATOWN* Allied Artists, 1962
THE UNBELIEVABLE 1966
THE CREMATORS New World, 1972

PATRICK GLEESON

Agent: Robert Light - Los Angeles, 213/651-1777

THE PLAGUE DOGS (AF) Nepenthe Productions, 1982, British
THE ZOO GANG New World, 1985
THE CHILDREN OF TIMES SQUARE (TF) Gross-Weston Productions/Fries Entertainment, 1986
STACKING Spectrafilm, 1987
IN SELF DEFENSE (TF) Leonard Hill Films, 1987
THE BEDROOM WINDOW co-composer with Michael Shrieve, DEG, 1987
DEADLY ILLUSION CineTel Films, 1987
PERFECT PEOPLE (TF) Robert Greenwald Productions, 1988

GOBLIN

Contact: SIAE - Rome, Italy, 011-39-6-59-90-1

PROFUNDO ROSSO Howard Mahler Films, 1976, Italian
SUSPIRIA International Classics, 1977, Italian
DAWN OF THE DEAD United Film Distribution, 1979
PATRICK composers of Italian version only, Cinema Shares International, 1979, Australian
ALIEN CONTAMINATION Cannon, 1980, Italian
NIGHT OF THE ZOMBIES Motion Picture Marketing, 1980, Spanish-Italian
BURIED ALIVE Aquarius Releasing, 1981, Italian
CREEPERS *PHENOMENA* New Line Cinema, 1985, Italian

ERNEST GOLD

b. July 13, 1921 - Vienna, Austria
Agent: Robert Light - Los Angeles, 213/651-1777

THE GIRL OF THE LIMBERLOST Columbia, 1945
SMOOTH AS SILK Universal, 1946
THE FALCON'S ALIBI RKO Radio, 1946
G.I. WAR BRIDES Republic, 1947
LIGHTHOUSE Producers Releasing Corp., 1947
WYOMING co-composer with Nathan Scott, Republic, 1947
EXPOSED Republic, 1947
OLD LOS ANGELES Republic, 1948
UNKNOWN WORLD Lippert, 1951
JENNIFER Allied Artists, 1953
MAN CRAZY 20th Century-Fox, 1953
KARAMOJA (FD) Hallmark, 1954
THE OTHER WOMAN 20th Century-Fox, 1954
THE NAKED STREET United Artists, 1955
UNIDENTIFIED FLYING OBJECTS (FD) United Artists, 1956
EDGE OF HELL Universal, 1956
RUNNING TARGET United Artists, 1956
AFFAIR IN HAVANA Allied Artists, 1957
MAN ON THE PROWL United Artists, 1957
TOO MUCH TOO SOON Warner Bros., 1958
WINK OF AN EYE United Artists, 1958
TARZAN'S FIGHT FOR LIFE MGM, 1958
THE DEFIANT ONES United Artists, 1958
THE SCREAMING SKULL American International, 1958
THE YOUNG PHILADELPHIANS Warner Bros., 1959
THE BATTLE OF THE CORAL SEA Columbia, 1959
ON THE BEACH ★ United Artists, 1959
INHERIT THE WIND United Artists, 1960
EXODUS ★★ United Artists, 1960
A FEVER IN THE BLOOD Warner Bros., 1961
THE LAST SUNSET Universal, 1961
JUDGMENT AT NUREMBERG United Artists, 1961
PRESSURE POINT United Artists, 1962
A CHILD IS WAITING United Artists, 1963
IT'S A MAD, MAD, MAD, MAD WORLD ★ United Artists, 1963
SHIP OF FOOLS Columbia, 1965
THE SECRET OF SANTA VITTORIA ★ United Artists, 1969
FOOTSTEPS (TF) Metromedia Producers Corporation/ Stonehenge Productions, 1972
THE SMALL MIRACLE (TF) FCB Productions/Alan Landsburg Productions, 1973
BETRAYAL (TF) Metromedia Producers Corporation, 1974
THE WILD McCULLOCHS American International, 1975
FUN WITH DICK AND JANE Columbia, 1977
CROSS OF IRON Avco Embassy, 1977, British-West German
GOOD LUCK, MISS WYCKOFF Bel Air/Gradison, 1979
THE RUNNER STUMBLES 20th Century-Fox, 1979
LETTERS FROM FRANK (TF) Paramount Pictures Television, 1979
MARCIANO (TF) ABC Circle Films, 1979
TOM HORN Warner Bros., 1980
SAFARI 3000 United Artists, 1982
WALLENBERG: A HERO'S STORY (TF) Dick Berg-Stonehenge Productions/Paramount TV, 1985
DREAMS OF GOLD: THE MEL FISHER STORY (TF) Inter Planetary Productions, 1986
GORE VIDAL'S LINCOLN (MS) Chris-Rose Productions/ Finnegan-Pinchuk Company, 1988

BARRY GOLDBERG

Agent: Bart-Milander - North Hollywood, 818/761-4040

THE TRIP American International, 1967
THRASHIN' Fries Entertainment, 1986
THE SPIRIT (TF) von Zerneck-Samuels Productions/ Warner Bros. TV, 1987
THREE FOR THE ROAD New Century/Vista, 1987
POWWOW HIGHWAY Warner Bros., 1989, U.S.-British
BEVERLY HILLS BRATS Taurus Entertainment, 1989
FLASHBACK Paramount, 1990
HOMETOWN BOY MAKES GOOD (CTF) HBO, 1990

BILLY GOLDENBERG

b. February 10, 1936 - New York, New York
Agent: Gorfaine-Schwartz - Burbank, 818/954-9500

CHANGE OF HABIT Universal, 1968
THE GRASSHOPPER National General, 1969
SILENT NIGHT, LONELY NIGHT (TF) Universal TV, 1969
RED SKY AT MORNING Universal, 1971
THE HARNESS (TF) Universal TV, 1971
THE NEON CEILING (TF) Universal TV, 1971
DUEL (TF) Universal TV, 1971
UP THE SANDBOX National General, 1972
PLAY IT AGAIN, SAM Paramount, 1972
TRUMAN CAPOTE'S THE GLASS HOUSE *THE GLASS HOUSE* (TF) Tomorrow Entertainment, 1972

THE LAST OF SHEILA Warner Bros., 1973
A BRAND NEW LIFE (TF) ☆ Tomorrow Entertainment, 1973
BUSTING United Artists, 1974
THE MIGRANTS (TF) ☆ CBS, Inc., 1974
REFLECTIONS OF MURDER (TF) ABC Circle Films, 1974
THE LEGEND OF LIZZIE BORDEN (TF) Paramount TV, 1975
QUEEN OF THE STARDUST BALLROOM (TF) ☆ Tomorrow Entertainment, 1975
DARK VICTORY (TF) ☆ Universal TV, 1976
THE LINDBERGH KIDNAPPING CASE (TF) Columbia TV, 1976
HELTER SKELTER (TF) ☆ Lorimar Productions, 1976
JAMES DEAN (TF) The Jozak Company, 1976
THE DOMINO PRINCIPLE Avco Embassy, 1977
MARY JANE HARPER CRIED LAST NIGHT (TF) Paramount TV, 1977
KING (MS) ☆☆ Abby Mann Productions/Filmways, 1978
A QUESTION OF LOVE (TF) Viacom, 1978
SCAVENGER HUNT 20th Century-Fox, 1979
FLESH AND BLOOD (TF) The Jozak Company/Cypress Point Productions/Paramount TV, 1979
THE FAMILY MAN (TF) Time-Life Productions, 1979
THE CRACKER FACTORY (TF) Roger Gimbel Productions/EMI TV, 1979
THE MIRACLE WORKER (TF) Katz-Gallin Productions/ Half-Pint Productions, 1979
THE LOVE TAPES (TF) Christiana Productions/ MGM TV, 1980
ALL GOD'S CHILDREN (TF) Blinn-Thorpe Productions/ Viacom, 1980
THE DIARY OF ANNE FRANK (TF) Katz-Gallin/ Half-Pint Productions/20th Century-Fox TV, 1980
A PERFECT MATCH (TF) Lorimar Productions, 1980
FATHER FIGURE (TF) Finnegan Associates/Time-Life Productions, 1980
THE WOMEN'S ROOM (TF) Philip Mandelker Productions/Warner Bros. TV, 1980
HAYWIRE (TF) Pando Productions/Warner Bros. TV, 1980
SIDNEY SCHORR (TF) Hajeno Productions/Warner Bros. TV, 1981
DIAL M FOR MURDER (TF) Freyda Rothstein Productions/Time Life TV, 1981
CRISIS AT CENTRAL HIGH (TF) Time-Life Productions, 1981
CALLIE & SON (TF) Rosilyn Heller Productions/Hemdale Presentations/City Films/Motown Pictures Co., 1981
THE BEST LITTLE GIRL IN THE WORLD (TF) Aaron Spelling Productions, 1981
THE ORDEAL OF BILL CARNEY (TF) Belle Company/ Comworld Productions, 1981
JACQUELINE BOUVIER KENNEDY (TF) ☆ ABC Circle Films, 1981
REHEARSAL FOR MURDER (TF) Levinson-Link Productions/Robert Papazian Productions, 1982
MASSARATI AND THE BRAIN (TF) Aaron Spelling Productions, 1982
THE GIFT OF LIFE (TF) CBS Entertainment, 1982
MARION ROSE WHITE (TF) Gerald Abram Productions/Cypress Point Productions, 1982
COUNTRY GOLD (TF) CBS Entertainment, 1982
BARE ESSENCE (TF) Warner Bros. TV, 1982
REUBEN, REUBEN 20th Century-Fox International Classics, 1983
SIDNEY SHELDON'S RAGE OF ANGELS *RAGE OF ANGELS* (TF) ☆☆ Furia-Oringer Productions/NBC Productions, 1983
INTIMATE AGONY (TF) Hennerson-Hirsch Productions/ Robert Papazian Productions, 1983
WILL THERE REALLY BE A MORNING? (TF) Jaffe-Blakely Films/Sama Productions/Orion TV, 1983
DEMPSEY (TF) Charles Fries Productions, 1983
PROTOTYPE (TF) Levinson-Link Productions/Robert Papazian Productions, 1983
HAPPY (TF) Bacchus Films Inc., 1983
MEMORIAL DAY (TF) Charles Fries Productions, 1983
THE AWAKENING OF CANADA (TF) Michael Klein Productions, 1983
WHY ME? (TF) Lorimar Productions, 1984
SENTIMENTAL JOURNEY (TF) Lucille Ball Productions/ Smith-Richmond Productions/20th Century Fox TV, 1984
SCORNED AND SWINDLED (TF) Cypress Point Productions, 1984
HIS MISTRESS (TF) David L. Wolper Productions/Warner Bros. TV, 1984
THE SUN ALSO RISES (TF) Furia-Oringer Productions/20th Century Fox TV, 1984
FOR LOVE OR MONEY (TF) Robert Papazian Productions/ Henerson-Hirsch Productions, 1984
THE ATLANTA CHILD MURDERS (TF) Mann-Rafshoon Productions/Finnegan Associates, 1985
KANE & ABEL (MS) Schrekinger Communications/ Embassy TV, 1985
OBSESSED WITH A MARRIED WOMAN (TF) Sidaris-Camhe Productions/The Feldman-Meeker Company, 1985
LOVE ON THE RUN (TF) NBC Productions, 1985
LOVE IS NEVER SILENT (TF) Marian Rees Associates, 1985
THE RIGHT OF THE PEOPLE (TF) Big Name Films/Fries Entertainment, 1986
DRESS GRAY (TS) Frank von Zerneck Productions/Warner Bros. TV, 1986
RAGE OF ANGELS: THE STORY CONTINUES (MS) NBC Productions, 1986
JOHNNIE MAE GIBSON: FBI (TF) Fool's Cap Productions, 1986
THERE MUST BE A PONY (TF) R.J. Productions/ Columbia TV, 1986
SADIE AND SON (TF) Norton Wright Productions/Kenny Rogers Organization/ITC Productions, 1987
NUTCRACKER: MONEY, MADNESS AND MURDER (MS) ☆ Green Arrow Productions/Warner Bros. TV, 1987
LITTLE GIRL LOST (TF) Marian Rees Associates, 1988
THE RICHEST MAN IN THE WORLD: THE ARISTOTLE ONASSIS STORY (TF) The Kongsberg-Sanitsky Company, 1988
18 AGAIN New World, 1988
AROUND THE WORLD IN 80 DAYS (MS) Harmony Gold/ ReteEuropa/Valente-Baerwald Productions, 1989
PEOPLE LIKE US (TF) ☆ CM Two Productions/ITC, 1990

MARK GOLDENBERG

Contact: BMI - Los Angeles, 213/659-9109

SILENT RAGE additional music, Columbia, 1982
NATIONAL LAMPOON'S CLASS REUNION additional music, 20th Century Fox, 1983
TEEN WOLF TOO Atlantic Releasing Corporation, 1987

ELLIOT GOLDENTHAL

Agent: Gorfaine-Schwartz - Burbank, 818/954-9500

PET SEMETARY Paramount, 1989
DRUGSTORE COWBOY Avenue Pictures, 1989

PETER GOLDFOOT

JUDGMENT IN BERLIN New Line Cinema, 1988

JERRY GOLDSMITH

b. 1930 - Los Angeles, California
Agent: ICM - Los Angeles, 213/550-4000

BLACK PATCH Warner Bros., 1957
CITY OF FEAR Columbia, 1959
FACE OF A FUGITIVE Columbia, 1959
STUDS LONIGAN United Artists, 1960
THE CRIMEBUSTER MGM, 1961
LONELY ARE THE BRAVE Universal, 1962
THE SPIRAL ROAD Universal, 1962
THE STRIPPER 20th Century-Fox, 1962
FREUD ★ Universal, 1963
THE LIST OF ADRIAN MESSENGER Universal, 1963
A GATHERING OF EAGLES Universal, 1963
LILLIES OF THE FIELD United Artists, 1963
TAKE HER, SHE'S MINE 20th Century-Fox, 1963
THE PRIZE MGM, 1963
SEVEN DAYS IN MAY Paramount, 1964
SHOCK TREATMENT 20th Century-Fox, 1964
FATE IS THE HUNTER 20th Century-Fox, 1964
RIO CONCHOS 20th Century-Fox, 1964
IN HARM'S WAY Paramount, 1964
THE SATAN BUG United Artists, 1965
VON RYAN'S EXPRESS 20th Century-Fox, 1965
MORITURI *THE SABOTEUR, CODE NAME "MORITURI"* 20th Century-Fox, 1965
A PATCH OF BLUE★ MGM, 1965
THE AGONY AND THE ECSTASY composer of prologue music, 20th Century-Fox, 1965
OUR MAN FLINT 20th Century-Fox, 1966
TO TRAP A SPY MGM, 1966
THE TROUBLE WITH ANGELS Columbia, 1966
STAGECOACH 20th Century-Fox, 1966
THE BLUE MAX 20th Century-Fox, 1966, British-U.S.
SECONDS Paramount, 1966
THE SAND PEBBLES★ 20th Century-Fox, 1966
IN LIKE FLINT 20th Century-Fox, 1967
THE FLIM FLAM MAN 20th Century-Fox, 1967
HOUR OF THE GUN United Artists, 1967
WARNING SHOT Paramount, 1967
SEBASTIAN Paramount, 1968, British
PLANET OF THE APES ★ 20th Century-Fox, 1968
THE DETECTIVE 20th Century-Fox, 1968
BANDOLERO! 20th Century-Fox, 1968
THE ILLUSTRATED MAN Warner Bros., 1969
100 RIFLES 20th Century-Fox, 1969
THE CHAIRMAN 20th Century-Fox, 1969, British
JUSTINE 20th Century-Fox, 1969
PATTON ★ 20th Century-Fox, 1970
THE BALLAD OF CABLE HOGUE Warner Bros., 1970
TORA! TORA! TORA! 20th Century-Fox, 1970, U.S.-Japanese
THE TRAVELING EXECUTIONER MGM, 1970
BROTHERHOOD OF THE BELL (TF) Cinema Center 100, 1970
RIO LOBO National General, 1970
THE MEPHISTO WALTZ 20th Century-Fox, 1971
DO NOT FOLD, SPINDLE OR MUTILATE (TF) Lee Rich Productions, 1971
ESCAPE FROM THE PLANET OF THE APES 20th Century-Fox, 1971
THE LAST RUN MGM, 1971
THE CABLE CAR MURDER (TF) Warner Bros. TV, 1971
WILD ROVERS MGM, 1971
THE HOMECOMING (TF) Lorimar Productions, 1971
THE CULPEPPER CATTLE CO. 20th Century-Fox, 1972
THE MAN Paramount, 1972
CRAWLSPACE (TF) Titus Productions, 1972
THE OTHER 20th Century-Fox, 1972
PURSUIT (TF) ABC Circle Films, 1972
SHAMUS Columbia, 1973
ACE ELI AND RODGER OF THE SKIES 20th Century-Fox, 1973
ONE LITTLE INDIAN Buena Vista, 1973
HAWKINS ON MURDER (TF) Arena-Leda Productions/MGM TV, 1973
THE DON IS DEAD Universal, 1973
THE RED PONY (TF) ☆ Universal TV/Omnibus Productions, 1973
POLICE STORY (TF) Screen Gems/Columbia TV, 1973
PAPILLION ★ Allied Artists, 1973
TAKE A HARD RIDE 20th Century-Fox, 1974
A TREE GROWS IN BROOKYLN (TF) Norman Rosemont Productions/20th Century-Fox TV, 1974
S.P.Y.S. U.S. version only, 20th Century-Fox, 1974, British-U.S.
WINTER KILL (TF) Andy Griffith Enterprises/MGM Television, 1974
CHINATOWN ★ Paramount, 1974
QB VII (MS) ☆☆ Screen Gems/Columbia TV/The Douglas Cramer Company, 1974
THE REINCARNATION OF PETER PROUD American International, 1975
BREAKOUT Columbia, 1975
THE WIND AND THE LION ★ MGM/United Artists, 1975
A GIRL NAMED SOONER (TF) Frederick Brogger Associates/20th Century-Fox TV, 1975
THE TERRORISTS *RANSOM* 20th Century-Fox, 1975, British
BABE (TF) ☆☆ MGM TV, 1975
LOGAN'S RUN MGM/United Artists, 1976
THE LAST HARD MEN 20th Century-Fox, 1976
BREAKHEART PASS United Artists, 1976
THE OMEN ★★ 20th Century-Fox, 1976
THE CASSANDRA CROSSING Avco Embassy, 1977, British-Italian-West German
HIGH VELOCITY 1977
TWILIGHT'S LAST GLEAMING Allied Artists, 1977, U.S.-West German
ISLANDS IN THE STREAM Paramount, 1977
MacARTHUR Universal, 1977
CONTRACT ON CHERRY STREET (TF) Columbia TV, 1977
DAMNATION ALLEY 20th Century-Fox, 1977
COMA MGM/United Artists, 1978
CAPRICORN ONE 20th Century-Fox, 1978
DAMIEN: OMEN II 20th Century-Fox, 1978
THE SWARM Warner Bros., 1978
MAGIC 20th Century-Fox, 1978
THE BOYS FROM BRAZIL ★ 20th Century-Fox, 1978
THE GREAT TRAIN ROBBERY United Artists, 1979, British
ALIEN 20th Century-Fox, 1979, U.S.-British
PLAYERS Paramount, 1979
STAR TREK: THE MOTION PICTURE ★ Paramount, 1979
CABOBLANCO Avco Embassy, 1981
THE SALAMANDER ITC, 1981, British-Italian-U.S.
THE FINAL CONFLICT 20th Century-Fox, 1981
OUTLAND The Ladd Company/Warner Bros., 1981
MASADA (MS) ☆☆ composer of Parts 1 and 2, Arnon Milchan Productions/Universal TV, 1981
RAGGEDY MAN Universal, 1981
INCHON MGM/UA, 1982, South Korean-U.S.
THE CHALLENGE Embassy, 1982
THE SECRET OF NIMH (AF) MGM/UA, 1982
NIGHT CROSSING Buena Vista, 1982
POLTERGEIST ★ MGM/UA, 1982

FIRST BLOOD Orion, 1982, Canadian
TWILIGHT ZONE: THE MOVIE Warner Bros., 1983
PSYCHO II Universal, 1983
UNDER FIRE ★ Orion, 1983
GREMLINS Warner Bros., 1984
SUPERGIRL Warner Bros., 1984, British
BABY - SECRET OF THE LOST LEGEND Buena Vista, 1985
RUNAWAY Tri-Star, 1984
LEGEND composer of European version, Universal, 1986, British
EXPLORERS Paramount, 1985
RAMBO: FIRST BLOOD PART II Tri-Star, 1985
KING SOLOMON'S MINES Cannon, 1985
LINK Thorn EMI/Cannon, 1986, U.S.-British
POLTERGEIST II: THE OTHER SIDE MGM/UA, 1986
HOOSIERS ★ Orion, 1986
EXTREME PREJUDICE Tri-Star, 1987
INNERSPACE Warner Bros., 1987
LIONHEART Orion, 1987
RENT-A-COP Kings Road Productions, 1988
RAMBO III Tri-Star, 1988
CRIMINAL LAW Hemdale, 1988
WARLOCK New World, 1989
THE 'BURBS Universal, 1989
LEVIATHAN MGM/UA, 1989, U.S.-Italian
STAR TREK V: THE FINAL FRONTIER Paramount, 1989
TOTAL RECALL Tri-Star, 1990
GREMLINS II also cameo as yoghurt shop customer, Warner Bros., 1990
THE RUSSIA HOUSE Pathe, 1990

JOEL GOLDSMITH

Contact: BMI - Los Angeles, 213/659-9109

LASERBLAST co-composer with Richard Band, Irwin Yablans, 1978
A TASTE OF SIN *FACES OF FEAR* Ambassador Pictures, 1981
THE MAN WITH TWO BRAINS Warner Bros., 1983
CRYSTAL HEART New World, 1987
BANZAI RUNNER Montage Films, 1987
WATCHERS Universal, 1988
RICKY I Tapeworm, 1988
NO SAFE HAVEN Overseas Filmgroup, 1989
JOBMAN Blue Rock Films, 1990

JONATHON GOLDSMITH

Contact: Pro-Canada - Canada, 1-416-445-8700

VISITING HOURS 20th Century-Fox, 1982, Canadian
PALAIS ROYALE Spectrafilm, 1988, Canadian

GIL GOLDSTEIN

Contact: ASCAP - Los Angeles, 213/466-7681

RECKLESS DISREGARD (CTF) Telecom Entertainment/Polar Film Corporation/ Fremantle of Canada Ltd., 1985, U.S.-Canadian

WILLIAM GOLDSTEIN

Agent: Bart-Milander - North Hollywood, 818/761-4040

THE STOOLIE Jama, 1972
THE BINGO LONG TRAVELING ALL STARS AND MOTOR KINGS Universal, 1976
NORMAN...IS THAT YOU? MGM/United Artists, 1976
DOOMSDAY 2000 Savadove Productions, 1977
TERROR OUT OF THE SKY (TF) Alan Landsburg Productions, 1978
THE WHITE LIONS Alan Landsburg Productions, 1979
JENNIFER: A WOMAN'S STORY (TF) Marble Arch Productions, 1979
THE ALIENS ARE COMING (TF) Woodruff Productions/ QM Productions, 1980
MARILYN: THE UNTOLD STORY (TF) Lawrence Schiller Productions, 1980
MANBEAST (TF) Alan Landsburg Productions, 1981
FORCE: FIVE American Cinema, 1981
AN EYE FOR AN EYE Avco Embassy, 1981
A LONG WAY HOME (TF) Alan Landsburg Productions, 1981
FORCED VENGEANCE MGM/United Artists, 1982
REMEMBRANCE OF LOVE (TF) Doris Quinlan Productions/Comworld Productions, 1982
HAPPY ENDINGS (TF) Motown Productions, 1983
UP THE CREEK Orion, 1983
GETTING PHYSICAL (TF) CBS Entertainment, 1984
THE TOUGHEST MAN IN THE WORLD (TF) Guber-Peters Productions/Centerpoint Productions, 1984
REARVIEW MIRROR (TF) Simon-Asher Entertainment/ Sunn Classic Pictures, 1984
LOTS OF LUCK (CTF) Tomorrow Entertainment, 1985
BAD GUYS Interpictures, 1986
SAVING GRACE Columbia, 1986
LIBERTY (TF) Robert Greenwald Productions, 1986
HERO IN THE FAMILY (TF) Barry & Enright Productions/ Alexander Productions/Walt Disney Productions, 1986
ON FIRE (TF) Robert Greenwald Productions, 1987
BLOOD VOWS: THE STORY OF A MAFIA WIFE (TF) Louis Rudolph Films/Fries Entertianment, 1987
SIX AGAINST THE ROCK (TF) Schaefer-Karpf-Epstein Productions/Gaylord Production Company, 1987
HELLO AGAIN Buena Vista, 1987
THE THREE KINGS (TF) Aaron Spelling Productions, 1987
THE FAVORITE Kings Road, 1989, U.S.-French
SHOCKER Universal, 1989
CROSS OF FIRE (TF) Leonard Hill Films, 1989

BENNY GOLSON

Contact: BMI - Los Angeles, 213/659-9109

THE SOPHISTICATED GENTS (TF) Daniel Wilson Productions, 1981

MILES GOODMAN

Agent: CAA - Los Angeles, 213/288-4545

SLUMBER PARTY '57 Cannon, 1976
A LAST CRY FOR HELP (TF) Myrt-Hal Productions/Viacom Productions, 1979
SKATETOWN, U.S.A. Columbia, 1979
LOOKIN' TO GET OUT Paramount, 1982
JINXED co-composer with Bruce Roberts, MGM/UA, 1982
HAVING IT ALL (TF) Hill-Mandelker Productions, 1982
THE FACE OF RAGE (TF) Hal Sitowitz Productions/ Viacom, 1983
THE MAN WHO WASN'T THERE Paramount, 1983
HIGH SCHOOL U.S.A. (TF) co-composer with Tony Berg, Hill-Mandelker Productions, 1983
TABLE FOR FIVE co-composer with John Morris, Warner Bros., 1983
AN UNCOMMON LOVE (TF) Beechwood Productions/ Lorimar, 1983
FOOTLOOSE Paramount, 1984
A REASON TO LIVE (TF) Rastar Productions/Robert Papazian Productions, 1985
POISON IVY (TF) NBC Entertainment, 1985

SPACE (MS) co-composer with Tony Berg, Stonehenge Productions/Paramount Pictures TV, 1985
TEEN WOLF Atlantic Releasing Corporation, 1985
CHILDREN OF THE NIGHT (TF) Robert Guenette Productions, 1985
THOMPSON'S LAST RUN (TF) Cypress Point Productions, 1986
PASSION FLOWER (TF) Doris Keating Productions/ Columbia Pictures TV, 1986
BLIND JUSTICE (TF) CBS Entertainment Productions, 1986
ABOUT LAST NIGHT... Tri-Star, 1986
AMERICAN GEISHA (TF) Interscope Communications/ Stonehenge Productions, 1986
LITTLE SHOP OF HORRORS The Geffen Company/ Warner Bros., 1986
LA BAMBA co-composer with Carlos Santana, Columbia, 1987
REAL MEN MGM/UA, 1987
THE SQUEEZE Tri-Star, 1987
LIKE FATHER LIKE SON Tri-Star, 1987
DIRTY ROTTEN SCOUNDRELS Orion, 1988
OUTBACK BOUND (TF) Andrew Gottlieb Productions/ CBS Entertainment, 1988
K-9 Universal, 1989
THE TRAVELLING MAN (CTF) Irvin Kershner Films, 1989
STAYING TOGETHER Hemdale, 1989
MONEY, POWER, MURDER (TF) Skids Productions/ CBS Entertainment, 1989
OPPORTUNITY KNOCKS Universal, 1990
VITAL SIGNS 20th Century-Fox, 1990
PROBLEM CHILD Universal, 1990

TOMMY GOODMAN

MY LITTLE PONY - THE MOVIE (AF) DEG, 1986

GORDON GOODWIN

Contact: ASCAP - Los Angeles, 213/466-7681

ATTACK OF THE KILLER TOMATOES co-composer with Paul Sundfor, NAI Entertainment, 1979

RON GOODWIN

b. 1929 - Plymouth, England
Agent: Robert Light - Los Angeles, 213/651-1777

WHIRLPOOL Continental, 1959, British
THE WITNESS Anglo-Amalgam, 1959, British
I'M ALL RIGHT JACK Columbia, 1960, British
IN THE NICK Columbia, 1960, British
VILLAGE OF THE DAMNED MGM, 1960, British
THE TRIALS OF OSCAR WILDE Kingsley International, 1960, British
THE MAN WITH THE GREEN CARNATION Warwick-Viceroy/Kingsley, 1960
THE MAN AT THE CARLTON TOWER Anglo-Amalgam, 1961, British
THE CLUE OF THE NEW PIN Merton Park, 1961, British
PARTNERS IN CRIME Allied Artists, 1961, British
INVASION QUARTET MGM, 1961, British
MURDER, SHE SAID MGM, 1962, British
POSTMAN'S KNOCK MGM, 1962, British
VILLAGE OF DAUGHTERS MGM, 1962
THE DAY OF THE TRIFFIDS Allied Artists, 1963, British
I THANK A FOOL MGM, 1962
KILL OR CURE MGM, 1962, British
FOLLOW THE BOYS MGM, 1963
SWORD OF LANCELOT *LANCELOT AND GUINEVERE* Universal, 1963, British
MURDER AT THE GALLOP MGM, 1963, British
THE CRACKSMAN Warner Bros./Pathe, 1963, British
LADIES WHO DO Fanfare/Continental, 1963, British
OF HUMAN BONDAGE MGM, 1964, British
CHILDREN OF THE DAMNED MGM, 1964, British
633 SQUADRON United Artists, 1964, British
MURDER AHOY! MGM, 1964, British
GO KART GO! Fanfare/CFF, 1964
JOHNNY NOBODY Victory-Medallion, 1965, British
MURDER MOST FOUL MGM, 1965, British
A HOME OF YOUR OWN Dormer/British Lion, 1965, British
THOSE MAGNIFICENT MEN IN THEIR FLYING MACHINES 20th Century-Fox, 1965, British
OPERATION CROSSBOW MGM, 1965, British-Italian
THE ALPHABET MURDERS *THE A.B.C. MURDERS* MGM, 1966, British
THE EARLY BIRD Rank, 1966, British
THAT RIVIERA TOUCH Continental, 1966, British
THE TRAP Rank, 1966, British
MISTER TEN PERCENT Associated British, 1966
WHAT HAPPENED AT CAMPO GRANDE? *THE MAGNIFICENT TWO* Alan Enterprises, 1967, British
MRS. BROWN, YOU'VE GOT A LOVELY DAUGHTER MGM, 1968, British
SUBMARINE X-1 United Artists, 1969, British
DECLINE AND FALL OF A BIRD WATCHER 20th Century-Fox, 1969, British
WHERE EAGLES DARE MGM, 1969, British
THOSE DARING YOUNG MEN IN THEIR JAUNTY JALOPIES Paramount, 1969, British-Italian-French
BATTLE OF BRITAIN United Artists, 1969, British
THE EXECUTIONER Columbia, 1970, British
THE SELFISH GIANT (AF) Readers Digest, 1971
GAWAIN AND THE GREEN KNIGHT United Artists, 1972, British
FRENZY Universal, 1972, British
DIAMOND ON WHEELS Buena Vista, 1972, U.S.-British
THE LITTLE MERMAID (AF) Readers Digest, 1973
THE HAPPY PRINCE (AF) Readers Digest, 1974
DEADLY STRANGERS Fox-Rank, 1974, British
ONE OF OUR DINOSAURS IS MISSING Buena Vista, 1975, U.S.-British
SPANISH FLY EMI, 1975, British
RIDE A WILD PONY *BORN TO RUN* Buena Vista, 1976, U.S.-Australian
BEAUTY AND THE BEAST (TF) Palms Films Ltd., 1976, British
THE LITTLEST HORSE THIEVES *ESCAPE FROM THE DARK* Buena Vista, 1977, U.S.-British
CANDLESHOE Buena Vista, 1977, U.S.-British
FORCE 10 FROM NAVARONE American International, 1978
UNIDENTIFIED FLYING ODDBALL Buena Vista, 1979
CLASH OF LOYALTIES Jorephani, 1983
VALHALLA (AF) Swan Productions, 1985, Danish

MICHAEL GORE

FAME ★★ MGM/United Artists, 1980
TERMS OF ENDEARMENT ★ Paramount, 1983
PRETTY IN PINK Paramount, 1986
BROADCAST NEWS additional music, 20th Century Fox, 1987
BOYFRIEND SCHOOL Hemdale, 1990

AL GORGONI
Contact: BMI - Los Angeles, 213/659-9109

I NEVER SANG FOR MY FATHER co-composer with Barry Mann, Columbia, 1970

ALAIN GORRAGUER
b. France
Contact: SACEM - France, 011-33-14-747-5650

LE CORBUSIER 1956, French
LE PIEGE co-composer with Maurice Le Roux, 1957, French
LE BEL AGE 1958, French
J'IRAI CRACHER SUR VOS TOMBES 1959, French
BLAGUE DANS LE COIN 1963, French
PARIS-SECRET 1965, French
THAT MAN GEORGE! *L'HOMME DE MARRAKECH* Allied Artists, 1966, French-Italian-Spanish
UN CHOIX D'ASSASSINS 1967, French
SUR UN ARBRE PERCHE 1971, French
L'AFFAIRE DOMINICI 1972, French
LA PLANETE SAUVAGE 1972, French
THE FANTASTIC PLANET (AF) Hemdale, 1973, French
THE SILENT ONE co-composer with Jacques Datin, 1973, French-Italian
URSULE ET GRELU 1973, French
AU-DELA DE LA PEUR 1975, French

MORTON GOULD
b. 1913 - Richmond Hill, New York
Contact: ASCAP - Los Angeles, 213/466-7681

DELIGHTFULLY DANGEROUS United Artists, 1945
WINDJAMMER 1958
F. SCOTT FIZTGERALD IN HOLLYWOOD (TF) Titus Productions, 1976
HOLOCAUST (MS) ☆ Titus Productions, 1978

GERALD GOURIET
Agent: ICM - Los Angeles, 213/550-4000

MADAME SOUSATZKA Universal, 1988, British
NUNS ON THE RUN composer of British version, 1989, British

JOHN GOUX
Contact: BMI - Los Angeles, 213/659-9109

ALFRED HITCHCOCK PRESENTS (TF) co-composer, Universal TV, 1985

MARK GOVERNOR
Contact: ASCAP - Los Angeles, 213/466-7681

MASQUE OF THE RED DEATH Concorde, 1989
OVEREXPOSED Concorde, 1990

PATRICK GOWERS
b. May 5, 1936 - London, England
Agent: Nigel Britton, Lemon Unna & Durbridge Ltd., 24 Pottery Lane, Holland Park, London W11 4LZ, 01/727-1346 or 01/229-9216

GIVE GOD A CHANCE ON SUNDAYS Asafilms, 1970, British
THE VIRGIN AND THE GYPSY Chevron, 1970, British
A BIGGER SPLASH Lagoon Associates, 1975, British
CHILDREN OF RAGE LSF, 1975, U.S.-Israeli
STEVIE First Artists, 1978, British
SMILEY'S PEOPLE (MS) BBC/Paramount TV, 1982, British
MY COUSIN RACHEL (TF) BBC, 1983, British
ANNA KARENINA (TF) Rastar Productions/Colgems Productions, 1985
SORRELL AND SON (TF) Yorkshire Television, 1986, British
WHOOPS APOCALYPSE ITC Entertainment, 1986, British
THE SIGN OF FOUR (TF) Grenada, 1988, British
THE HOUND OF THE BASKERVILLES (TF) Grenada, 1988, British

DAVID GRAHAM
Contact: PRS - London, England, 011-44-1-580-5544

COMRADES co-composer with Hans Werner Henze, British Film Institute, 1986, British

RON GRAINER
Contact: BMI - Los Angeles, 213/659-9109

A KIND OF LOVING Continental, 1962, British
THE MOUSE ON THE MOON United Artists, 1963, British
STATION SIX-SAHARA Allied Artists, 1963, British-West German
THE GUEST *THE CARETAKER* Janus, 1963, British
THE FINEST HOURS 1964, British
THE MOONSPINNERS Buena Vista, 1964
NIGHT MUST FALL Embassy, 1964, British
NOTHING BUT THE BEST Royal Films International, 1964, British
THE TIGER MAKES OUT Columbia, 1967
TO SIR WITH LOVE Columbia, 1967, British
ONLY WHEN I LARF Paramount, 1968, British
THE ASSASSINATION BUREAU Paramount, 1969, British
BEFORE WINTER COMES Columbia, 1969, British
DESTINY OF A SPY (TF) Universal TV, 1969
IN SEARCH OF GREGORY Universal, 1970, British
HOFFMAN Levitt-Pickman, 1971, British
THE OMEGA MAN Warner Bros., 1971
THIEF (TF) Stonehenge Productions/Metromedia Producers Corporation, 1971
AND NO ONE COULD SAVE HER (TF) Associated London Films, 1973
MOUSEY *CAT AND MOUSE* (TF) Universal TV/ Associated British Films, 1974, U.S.-British
THE BAWDY ADVENTURES OF TOM JONES Universal, 1976, British
THE DEVIL WITHIN HER *I DON'T WANT TO BE BORN* American International, 1976, British

RON GRANT
Agent: Gorfaine-Schwartz - Burbank, 818/954-9500

THE KID FROM NOT-SO-BIG William Crain Productions, 1982
"SAY YES" Cinetel, 1986

STEPHANE GRAPPELLI
b. 1908 - Paris, France

MAY FOOLS Orion, 1990, French

BARRY GRAY

Contact: PRS - London, England, 011-44-1-580-5544

THUNDERBIRDS ARE GO 1966
THUNDERBIRDS SIX 1968
JOURNEY TO THE FAR SIDE OF THE SUN
DOPPLEGANGER Universal, 1969, British
THUNDERBIRDS TO THE RESCUE 1980
REVENGE OF THE MYSTERIONS FROM MARS 1981

DON GREAT

Contact: BMI - Los Angeles, 213/659-9109

ANGEL III: THE FINAL CHAPTER additional music, New World, 1988

BERNARD GREEN

BLIND GODDESS 1948
THE FAT MAN Universal, 1951
EVERYTHING'S DUCKY Columbia, 1961
ZOTZ! Columbia, 1962
ALL THE WAY HOME Paramount, 1963
MGM'S BIG PARADE OF COMEDY MGM, 1964
THE BRASS BOTTLE Universal, 1964
HARVEY MIDDLEMAN, FIREMAN Columbia, 1965

RICHARD GREENE

Contact: BMI - Los Angeles, 213/659-9109

GETTING EVEN Quantum Films, 1981

RALPH GRIERSON

TO FIND MY SON (TF) Green-Epstein Productions/ Columbia Pictures TV, 1980
RED EARTH, WHITE EARTH (TF) Chris/Rose Productions, 1989

DAVID GRISMAN

Contact: BMI - Los Angeles, 213/659-9109

BIG MAD MAMA New World, 1974
CAPONE 20th Century-Fox, 1975
EAT MY DUST New World, 1976
KING OF THE GYPSIES Paramount, 1978

CHARLES GROSS

Agent: Gorfaine-Schwartz - Burbank, 818/954-9500

THE GROUP United Artists, 1965
TEACHER, TEACHER NBC, 1969
VALDEZ IS COMING United Artists, 1971
BROCK'S LAST CASE (TF) Talent Associates/ Universal TV, 1973
NICKY'S WORLD (TF) Tomorrow Entertainment, 1974
THE TENTH LEVEL (TF) CBS, Inc., 1976
THE GARDENER'S SON (TF) RIP/Filmhaus, 1977
THE DAIN CURSE (MS) Martin Poll Productions, 1978
SIEGE (TF) Titus Productions, 1978
HEARTLAND Levitt-Pickman, 1979
YOU CAN'T GO HOME AGAIN (TF) CBS Entertainment, 1979
NO OTHER LOVE (TF) Tisch-Avnet Productions, 1979
A PRIVATE BATTLE (TF) Procter & Gamble Productions/ Robert Halmi, Inc., 1980
A RUMOR OF WAR (TF) Charles Fries Productions, 1980
WHEN THE CIRCUS CAME TO TOWN (TF) Entheos Unlimited Productions/Meteor Films, 1981
PRIME SUSPECT (TF) Tisch-Avnet Television, 1982
SOMETHING SO RIGHT (TF) List-Estrin Productions/ Tisch-Avnet Television, 1982
CHINA ROSE (TF) Robert Halmi, Inc., 1983
SESSIONS (TF) Roger Gimbel Productions/EMI TV/ Sarabande Productions, 1983
COOK & PEARY: THE RACE TO THE POLE (TF) Robert Halmi Productions/ITT Productions, 1983
COUNTRY Buena Vista, 1984
BRADY'S ESCAPE Satori Entertainment, 1984, U.S.-Hungarian
TERRIBLE JOE MORAN (TF) Robert Halmi, Inc., 1984
THE BURNING BED (TF) Tisch-Avnet Productions, 1984
NAIROBI AFFAIR (TF) Robert Halmi, Inc., 1984
THE NIGHT THEY SAVED CHRISTMAS (TF) Robert Halmi, Inc., 1984
SWEET DREAMS Tri-Star, 1985
ARTHUR THE KING (TF) Martin Poll Productions/Comworld Productions/Jadran Film, 1985, U.S.-Yugoslavian
IZZY AND MOE (TF) Robert Halmi, Inc., 1985
THREE SOVEREIGNS FOR SARAH (TF) Night Owl Productions, 1985
CHOICES (TF) Robert Halmi, Inc., 1986
BETWEEN TWO WOMEN (TF) The Jon Avnet Company, 1986
VENGEANCE: THE STORY OF TONY CIMO (TF) Nederlander TV and Film Productions/Robirdie Pictures, 1986
BARNUM (TF) Robert Halmi, Inc./Filmline International, 1986, U.S.-Canadian
TRAPPED IN SILENCE (TF) Reader's Digest Productions, 1986
THE MURDERS IN THE RUE MORGUE (TF) Robert Halmi, Inc./International Film Productions, 1986
BROKEN VOWS (TF) Brademan-Self Productions/Robert Halmi, Inc., 1987
AT MOTHER'S REQUEST (TF) Vista Organization Ltd., 1987
IN LOVE AND WAR (TF) Carol Schreder Productions/ Tisch-Avnet Productions, 1987
APPRENTICE TO MURDER New World, 1988, Canadian
PUNCHLINE Columbia, 1988
OPEN ADMISSIONS (TF) The Mount Company/Viacom Productions, 1988
SIDE BY SIDE (TF) Avnet-Kerner Productions, 1988
LEAP OF FAITH (TF) Hart, Thomas & Berlin Productions, 1988
THIRD DEGREE BURN (CTF) HBO Pictures/MTM Enterprises/Paramount Pictures, 1989
TURNER AND HOOCH Buena Vista, 1989
NO PLACE LIKE HOME (TF) Feury-Grant Productions/ Orion TV, 1989
AIR AMERICA 1990

JIM GROSS

A DIFFERENT AFFAIR (TF) Rogers/Samuels Productions, 1987

LARRY GROSSMAN

Contact: BMI - Los Angeles, 213/659-9109

SUSPICION (TF) Hemisphere Productions/HTV, 1988

DAVE GRUSIN

b. June 26, 1934 - Denver, Colorado
Agent: Gorfaine-Schwartz - Burbank, 818/954-9500

THE SCORPIO LETTERS (TF) MGM TV, 1967
DIVORCE AMERICAN STYLE Columbia, 1967
WATERHOLE #3 Paramount, 1967

THE GRADUATE Avco Embassy, 1967
CANDY Cinerama Releasing Corporation, 1968, U.S.-Italian-French
THE HEART IS A LONELY HUNTER Warner Bros., 1968
TELL THEM WILLIE BOY WAS HERE Universal, 1969
GENERATION Avco Embassy, 1969
WINNING Universal, 1969
THE MAD ROOM Columbia, 1969
HALLS OF ANGER United Artists, 1970
THE INTRUDERS (TF) Universal TV, 1970
SARGE: THE BADGE OR THE CROSS (TF) Universal TV, 1971
THE DEADLY DREAM (TF) Universal TV, 1971
A HOWLING IN THE WOODS (TF) Universal TV, 1971
THE FORGOTTEN MAN (TF) Grauman Productions, 1971
FUZZ United Artists, 1972
THE GREAT NORTHFIELD, MINNESOTA RAID Universal, 1972
THE FAMILY RICO (TF) CBS Entertainment, 1972
THE FRIENDS OF EDDIE COYLE Paramount, 1973
THE MIDNIGHT MAN Universal, 1974
THE NICKEL RIDE 20th Century-Fox, 1974
THE TRIAL OF CHAPLAIN JENSEN (TF) Monash-Preissman Productions/20th Century-Fox TV, 1975
W.W. AND THE DIXIE DANCEKINGS 20th Century-Fox, 1975
THE YAKUZA Warner Bros., 1975
3 DAYS OF THE CONDOR Paramount, 1975
ERIC (TF) Lorimar Productions, 1975
MURDER BY DEATH Columbia, 1976
THE FRONT Columbia, 1976
MR. BILLION 20th Century-Fox, 1976
BOBBY DEERFIELD Columbia, 1977
FIRE SALE 20th Century-Fox, 1977
THE GOODBYE GIRL Warner Bros., 1977
HEAVEN CAN WAIT ★ Paramount, 1978
THE CHAMP ★ MGM/United Artists, 1979
...AND JUSTICE FOR ALL Columbia, 1979
THE ELECTRIC HORSEMAN Columbia, 1979
MY BODYGUARD 20th Century-Fox, 1980
ABSENCE OF MALICE Columbia, 1981
REDS Paramount, 1981
ON GOLDEN POND ★ Universal/AFD, 1981
AUTHOR! AUTHOR! 20th Century-Fox, 1982
TOOTSIE Columbia, 1982
RACING WITH THE MOON Paramount, 1984
SCANDALOUS Orion, 1984
THE POPE OF GREENWICH VILLAGE MGM/UA, 1984
THE LITTLE DRUMMER GIRL Warner Bros., 1984
FALLING IN LOVE Paramount, 1984
GOONIES Warner Bros., 1985
LUCAS 20th Century Fox, 1986
ISHTAR Columbia, 1987
THE MILAGRO BEANFIELD WAR ★★ Universal, 1988
CLARA'S HEART Warner Bros., 1988
TEQUILA SUNRISE Warner Bros., 1988
A DRY WHITE SEASON MGM/UA, 1989, U.S.-British
THE FABULOUS BAKER BOYS ★ 20th Century Fox, 1989
BONFIRE OF THE VANITIES Warner Bros., 1990
HAVANA Universal, 1990

JAY GRUSKA
b. April 23, 1952
Agent: Gorfaine-Schwartz - Burbank, 818/954-9500

THE PRINCIPAL Tri-Star, 1987
THERE WERE TIMES, DEAR (TF) Lilac Productions, 1987
SHADOW DANCING Shapiro Glickenhaus Entertainment, 1988, Canadian
TRAXX DEG, 1988
SING Tri-Star, 1989
WHEELS OF TERROR (CTF) Once Upon a Time Productions/Wilshire Court Productions, 1990

BARRIE GUARD
Contact: PRS - London, England, 011-44-1-580-5544

THE TOXIC AVENGER, PART II Troma, 1989

ANTHONY GUEFEN
Contact: ASCAP - Los Angeles, 213/466-7681

DEADLY EYES *THE RATS* Warner Bros., 1983, Canadian
ASSASSIN (TF) Sankan Productions, 1986

CHRISTOPHER GUNNING
Contact: PRS - London, England, 011-44-1-580-5544

GOODBYE GEMINI Cinerama Releasing Corporation, 1970, British
HANDS OF THE RIPPER Universal, 1972, British
MAN ABOUT THE HOUSE EMI, 1974, British
GET CHARLIE TULLY TBS Distributing Corporation, 1976, British
WHEN THE WHALES CAME 20th Century Fox, 1989, British

JONAS GWANGWA
Contact: BMI - Los Angeles, 213/659-9109

CRY FREEDOM ★ additional music, Universal, 1987, British-U.S.

MANOS HADJIDAKIS
b. 1925 - Athens, Greece
Contact: SACEM - France, 011-33-14-747-5650

STELLA Milas Films, 1955, Greek
BED OF GRASS 1957, Greek
NEVER ON SUNDAY Lopert, 1960, Greek
IT HAPPENED IN ATHENS 20th Century-Fox, 1962
THE 300 SPARTANS 20th Century-Fox, 1962
ALIKI Funos-Aquarius, 1963, West German-U.S.
AMERICA, AMERICA Warner Bros., 1963
TOPKAPI United Artists, 1964
GREECE, LAND OF DREAMS 1965
BLUE Paramount, 1968, British
THE MARLET'S TALE 1970
THE PEDESTRIAN Cinerama Releasing Corporation, 1974, West German-Swiss-Israeli
SWEET MOVIE Biograph, 1975, French-Canadian-West German
HONEYMOON 1979

EARLE HAGEN
Contact: BMI - Los Angeles, 213/659-9109

THE MONK (TF) Thomas-Spelling Productions, 1969
HAVING BABIES (TF) The Jozak Company, 1976
KILLER ON BOARD (TF) Lorimar Productions, 1977
TRUE GRIT (A FURTHER ADVENTURE) (TF) Parmaount Pictures TV, 1978
MURDER IN MUSIC CITY (TF) Frankel Films/ Gank Inc., 1979
EBONY, IVORY AND JADE (TF) Frankel Films, 1979
THE HUSTLER OF MUSCLE BEACH (TF) Furia-Oringer Productions, 1980
STAND BY YOUR MAN (TF) Robert Papazian Productions/Guber-Peters Productions, 1981
MUGGABLE MARY: STREET COP (TF) CBS Entertainment, 1982
MICKEY SPILLANE'S MIKE HAMMER: MURDER ME, MURDER YOU (TF) Jay Bernstein Productions/ Columbia Pictures Television, 1983
I TAKE THESE MEN (TF) Lillian Gallo Productions/ United Artists TV, 1983
MICKEY SPILLANE'S MIKE HAMMER: MORE THAN MURDER (TF) Jay Bernstein/Columbia, 1984
NORTH BEACH AND RAWHIDE (TF) CBS Entertainment Productions, 1985
RETURN TO MAYBERRY (TF) Viacom Productions/ Strathmore Productions, 1986
THE RETURN OF MICKEY SPILLANE'S MIKE HAMMER (TF) Columbia Pictures TV/Jay Bernstein Productions, 1986

STEPHEN HAGUE
SOME KIND OF WONDERFUL co-composer with John Musser, Paramount, 1987

RONALD HALICKI
Contact: BMI - Los Angeles, 213/659-9109

GONE IN 60 SECONDS H.B. Halicki International, 1974

TOM T. HALL
Contact: BMI - Los Angeles, 213/659-9109

DEADHEAD MILES Paramount, 1971

DICK HALLIGAN
Contact: BMI - Los Angeles, 213/659-9109

THE OWL AND THE PUSSYCAT Columbia, 1970
GO TELL THE SPARTANS Avco Embassy, 1978
ZUMA BEACH (TF) Edgar J. Scherick Associates/ Bruce Cohn Curtis Films/Warner Bros. TV, 1978
DIRT American Cinema Releasing, 1979
A FORCE OF ONE American Cinema Releasing, 1979
THE OCTAGON American Cinema, 1980
CHEAPER TO KEEP HER American Cinema, 1980
FEAR CITY Chevy Chase Distribution, 1985

CHICO HAMILTON
b. 1921
Contact: BMI - Los Angeles, 213/659-9109

REPULSION Royal Films International, 1965, British
THE CONFESSOR 1973
MR. RICCO United Artists, 1975
COONSKIN Bryanston Pictures, 1975

MARVIN HAMLISCH
b. June 2, 1944 - New York, New York
Agent: Carol Faith - Beverly Hills, 213/274-0776

THE SWIMMER Columbia, 1968
TAKE THE MONEY AND RUN Cinerama Releasing Corporation, 1969
THE APRIL FOOLS National General, 1969
MOVE 20th Century-Fox, 1970
FLAP *THE LAST WARRIOR* Warner Bros., 1970
BANANAS United Artists, 1971
SOMETHING BIG National General, 1971
KOTCH Cinerama Releasing Corporation, 1971
FAT CITY Columbia, 1972
THE WAR BETWEEN MEN AND WOMEN National General, 1972
THE WORLD'S GREATEST ATHLETE Buena Vista, 1973
SAVE THE TIGER Paramount, 1973
THE WAY WE WERE ★★ Columbia, 1973
THE STING ★★ partial adaptation, Universal, 1973
THE PRISONER OF SECOND AVENUE Warner Bros., 1975
THE ENTERTAINER (TF) RSO Films, 1976
THE SPY WHO LOVED ME ★ United Artists, 1977, British-U.S.
SAME TIME NEXT YEAR Universal, 1979
ICE CASTLES Columbia, 1979
STARTING OVER Paramount, 1979
ORDINARY PEOPLE adaptation, Paramount, 1980
NEIL SIMON'S SEEMS LIKE OLD TIMES *SEEMS LIKE OLD TIMES* Columbia, 1980
THE DEVIL AND MAX DEVLIN co-composer with Buddy Baker, Buena Vista, 1981
PENNIES FROM HEAVEN MGM/UA, 1981
I OUGHT TO BE IN PICTURES 20th Century-Fox, 1982
SOPHIE'S CHOICE ★ Universal/AFD, 1982
ROMANTIC COMEDY MGM/UA, 1983
A STREETCAR NAMED DESIRE (TF) Keith Barish Productions, 1984
D.A.R.Y.L. Paramount, 1985
THE TWO MRS. GRENVILLES (TF) Lorimar-Telepictures, 1987
RETURN OF THE SIX MILLION DOLLAR MAN & THE BIONIC WOMAN (TF) Michael Sloan Productions/ Universal TV, 1987
WHEN THE TIME COMES (TF) Jaffe-Lansing Productions/ Republic Pictures, 1987
THREE MEN AND A BABY Buena Vista, 1987
LITTLE NIKITA Columbia, 1988
DAVID (TF) Tough Boys Inc./Donald March Productions/ITC Entertainment Group, 1988
THE JANUARY MAN MGM/UA, 1989
THE EXPERTS Paramount, 1989

JAN HAMMER
Agent: Gorfaine-Schwartz - Burbank, 818/954-9500

A NIGHT IN HEAVEN 20th Century-Fox, 1983
GIMME AN F 20th Century Fox, 1984
TWO FATHER'S JUSTICE (TF) Shane Co. Productions, 1985
SECRET ADMIRER Orion, 1985
CHARLEY HANNAH (TF) Shane Company Productions/ Telepictures Productions, 1986
CLINTON AND NADINE (CTF) HBO Pictures/ITC, 1988
CAPITAL NEWS (TF) MTM, 1990
CURIOSITY KILLS (CTF) Dutch Productions, 1990

HERBIE HANCOCK

b. 1940
Agent: CAA - Los Angeles, 213/288-4545

BLOWUP Premier, 1966, British-Italian
THE SPOOK WHO SAT BY THE DOOR United Artists, 1973
DEATH WISH Paramount, 1974
A SOLDIER'S STORY Columbia, 1984
JO JO DANCER, YOUR LIFE IS CALLING Columbia, 1986
ROUND MIDNIGHT ★★ Warner Bros., 1986, U.S.-French
THE GEORGE McKENNA STORY (TF) The Landsburg Company, 1986
ACTION JACKSON co-composer with Michael Kamen, Lorimar, 1988
COLORS Orion, 1988
HARLEM NIGHTS Paramount, 1989

KENTARO HANEDA

b. Japanese
Contact: JASRAC - Tokyo, Japan, 011-81-3-502-6551

SENGOKU JIEITAL *TIME SLIP* Toei, 1981, Japanese

JONATHAN HANNAH

ROOMMATES Platinum Pictures, 1982

PETR HAPKA

Contact: OSA - Tr. Cs. Armady 20, 160-56 Prague 6-Bubene, Czechoslovakia

THE NINTH HEART Ceskoslovensky Filmexport, 1980, Czech

HAGOOD HARDY

b. Canada
Agent: Robert Light - Los Angeles, 213/651-1777

SECOND WIND Health and Entertainment Corporation of America, 1976, Canadian
TELL ME MY NAME (TF) co-composer with Mickey Erbe, Talent Associates Ltd., 1977
HOME TO STAY (TF) Time-Life Productions, 1978
ANATOMY OF A SEDUCTION (TF) Moonlight Productions/Filmways, 1979
AN AMERICAN CHRISTMAS CAROL (TF) Scherick/Chase/Slan Productions/Smith-Hemion Productions/Scrooge Productions, 1979
PORTRAIT OF AN ESCORT (TF) Moonlight Productions/Filmways, 1980
KLONDIKE FEVER 1980
DIRTY TRICKS Avco Embassy, 1981, Canadian
FORBIDDEN LOVE (TF) Gross-Weston Productions, 1982
THE WILD PONY (TF) Sullivan Films, Inc., 1982, Canadian
RONA JAFFE'S MAZES AND MONSTERS (TF) McDermott Productions/Procter & Gamble Productions, 1982
THIS CHILD IS MINE (TF) Beth Polson Productions/Finnegan Associates/Telepictures Productions, 1985
THE CANADIANS (MS) Cineworld, Canadian
ANNE OF GREEN GABLES (MS) Anne of Green Gables Productions/PBS WonderWorks/CBS/60 Film Productions/ZDF/City TV/Telefilm Canada, 1985, Canadian-U.S.-West German
ANNE OF AVONLEA: THE CONTINUING STORY OF ANNE OF GREEN GABLES (MS) Sullivan Films/CBC/The Disney Channel/PBS WonderWorks/Telefilm Canada, 1987, Canadian-U.S.
LIBERACE: BEHIND THE MUSIC (TF) Canadian International Studios/Kushner-Locke Productions, 1988, U.S.-Canadian
PASSION AND PARADISE (TF) Picturebase International/Primedia Productions/Leonard Hill Films, 1989, U.S.-Canadian
AVONLEA (CTF) The Disney Channel/Sullivan Films, 1990

JOE HARNELL

b. August 2, 1924 - New York, New York
Agent: Richard Emler - Los Angeles, 213/651-0222

THE INCREDIBLE HULK (TF) Universal TV, 1977
THE RETURN OF THE INCREDIBLE HULK (TF) Universal TV, 1977
THE MURDER THAT WOULDN'T DIE (TF) co-composer with Glen A. Larson, Glen A. Larson Productions/Universal TV, 1980
SENIOR TRIP (TF) Kenneth Johnson Productions, 1981
V (TF) ☆ Kenneth Johnson Productions/Warner Bros. TV, 1983
HOT PURSUIT (TF) Kenneth Johnson Productions/NBC Productions, 1984
THE LIBERATORS (TF) Kenneth Johnson Productions/Walt Disney TV, 1987

UDI HARPAZ

Agent: Bart-Milander - North Hollywood, 818/761-4040

THE LAST HORROR FILM *FANATIC* Twin Continental, 1982
NINJA III: THE DOMINATION Cannon, 1984
THE ANNIHILATOR (TF) Universal TV, 1986
RUNNING SCARED co-composer with Rod Temperton, 1986
THE WHOOPEE BOYS co-composer with Jack Nietzche, 1986
HOLLYWOOD SHUFFLE co-composer with Patrice Rushen, Samuel Goldwyn Company, 1987

ANTHONY HARRIS

Contact: ASCAP - Los Angeles, 213/466-7681

THE KILLING OF A CHINESE BOOKIE Faces Distribution, 1976
COACH Crown International, 1978

ARTHUR HARRIS

Contact: BMI - Los Angeles, 213/659-9109

BRONTE Charlotte Ltd. Partnership/Radio Telefis Eireann, 1983, U.S.-Irish

JOHNNY HARRIS

Contact: BMI - Los Angeles, 213/659-9109

MAN IN THE WILDERNESS Warner Bros., 1971
THE INITIATION OF SARAH (TF) Charles Fries Productions/Stonehenge Productions, 1978
THE EVIL New World, 1978
THE LAST SONG (TF) Ron Samuels Productions/Motown Productions, 1980
BORN TO BE SOLD (TF) Ron Samuels Productions, 1981
HOTLINE (TF) Ron Samuels Productions/Wrather Entertainment International, 1982

CAN YOU FEEL ME DANCING? (TF) Robert Greenwald Productions, 1986
NECESSITY (TF) Barry-Enright Productions/Alexander Productions, 1988

MAX HARRIS

Contact: PRS - London, England, 011-44-1-580-5544

DREAMCHILD additional music, Universal, 1985, British

GEORGE HARRISON

b. February 25, 1943 - Wavertree, England
Contact: PRS - London, England, 011-44-1-580-5544

SHANGHAI SURPRISE co-composer with Michael Kamen, MGM/UA, 1986, British-U.S.

JOHN HARRISON

CREEPSHOW Warner Bros., 1982
DAY OF THE DEAD United Film Distribution, 1985
TALES OF THE DARKSIDE: THE MOVIE co-composer, Paramount, 1990

KEN HARRISON

Agent: Bart-Milander - North Hollywood, 818/761-4040

WAIT TILL YOUR MOTHER GETS HOME (TF) Blue-Greene Productions/NBC Productions, 1983
MEATBALLS PART II Tri-Star, 1984
HOLLYWOOD BEAT (TF) Aaron Spelling Productions, 1985
DARK MANSIONS (TF) Aaron Spelling Productions, 1986
HEARTBEAT (TF) Aaron Spelling Productions, 1988

JAMES HART

Contact: BMI - Los Angeles, 213/659-9109

GHOST FEVER Miramax, 1987

RICHARD HARTLEY

Agent: Bart-Milander - North Hollywood, 818/761-4040

GALILEO co-composer with Hanns Eisler, American Film Theatre, 1975
THE ROMANTIC ENGLISHWOMAN New World, 1975, British
THE ROCKY HORROR PICTURE SHOW 20th Century-Fox, 1975, British
ACES HIGH Cinema Shares International, 1977, British
THE LADY VANISHES Rank, 1979, British
BAD TIMING/A SENSUAL OBSESSION World Northal, 1980, British
SHOCK TREATMENT 20th Century-Fox, 1981, British
LA TRUITE *THE TROUT* Gaumont, 1982, French
BAD BLOOD Southern Pictures/New Zealand Film Commission, 1983, New Zealand
KENNEDY (MS) Central Independent Television Productions/Alan Landsburg Productions, 1983, British-U.S.
SHEENA Columbia, 1984
HITLER'S S.S.: PORTRAIT IN EVIL (TF) Colason Limited Productions/Edgar J. Scherick Associates, 1985, British-U.S.
BLUE MONEY (TF) London Weekend Television, 1985, British
PARKER Virgin Films, 1985, British
THE McGUFFIN (TF) BBC, 1985, British
DANCE WITH A STRANGER Samuel Goldwyn Company, 1985, British
THE GOOD FATHER Skouras Pictures, 1986, British
NAZI HUNTER: THE BEATE KLARSFELD STORY (TF) William Kayden Productions/Orion TV/Silver Chalice/Revcom/George Walker TV/TF1/SFP, 1986, U.S.-British-French
THE IMPOSSIBLE SPY (CTF) HBO Showcase/BBC/Quartet International/IMGC, 1987, British-Israeli
MANDELA (CTF) Titus Productions/Polymuse Inc./TVS Ltd., 1987, U.S.-British
TUMBLEDOWN (TF) BBC, 1988, British
SOURSWEET Skouras Pictures, 1988, British
CONSUMING PASSIONS Samuel Goldwyn Company, 1988, British
THE FOUR MINUTE MILE (TF) Oscar-Sullivan Productions/Centre Films, 1988, Australian
THE TREE OF HANDS Greenpoint/Granada/British Screen, 1989, British
DEALERS Samuel Goldwyn Company, 1989, British
SHE'S BEEN AWAY BBC Films, 1989, British

PAUL HARTZOP

KICKBOXER Pathe Entertainment, 1989

RICHARD HARVEY

Agent: Bart-Milander - North Hollywood, 818/761-4040

THE MARTIAN CHRONICLES (TF) Charles Fries Productions/Stonehenge Productions, 1980
DEATH OF AN EXPERT WITNESS (MS) Anglia TV, 1982, British
BEYOND THE LIMIT *THE HONORARY CONSUL* additional music, Paramount, 1983, British
HOUSE OF THE LONG SHADOWS MGM/UA/Cannon, 1983, British
STEAMING New World, 1984, British
WINTER FLIGHT Cinecom, 1984, British, originally made for television
THE ASSAM GARDEN The Moving Picture Company, 1985, British
PING PONG Samuel Goldwyn Company, 1985, British
DEFENSE OF THE REALM Hemdale, 1985, British
DIRTY DOZEN: THE NEXT MISSION (TF) MGM-UA TV, 1985
HALF MOON STREET 20th Century Fox, 1986, British
FIRST AMONG EQUALS (MS) Grenada, 1987, British
INSIDE STORY (MS) Anglia International, 1988, British
GAME, SET AND MATCH (MS) Grenada, 1989, British

BO HARWOOD

A WOMAN UNDER THE INFLUENCE Faces International, 1974
THE KILLING OF A CHINESE BOOKIE Faces International, 1976
OPENING NIGHT Faces International, 1978
HAPPY BIRTHDAY TO ME co-composer with Lance Rubin, Columbia, 1981
UPS & DOWNS Astral Films, 1983, Canadian
LOVE STREAMS Cannon, 1984

JIMMIE HASKELL

b. Brooklyn, New York
Agent: Andi Howard - 213/278-6483

LOVE IN A GOLDFISH BOWL Paramount, 1961
THE GUN HAWK Allied Artists, 1963
BLACK SPURS Paramount, 1965
I'LL TAKE SWEDEN United Artists, 1965

LOVE AND KISSES co-composer with William Loose, Universal, 1965
TOWN TAMER Paramount, 1965
WILD ON THE BEACH 20th Century-Fox, 1965
WACO Paramount, 1966
APACHE UPRISING Paramount, 1966
JOHNNY RENO Paramount, 1966
RED TOMAHAWK Paramount, 1967
FORT UTAH Paramount, 1967
HOSTILE GUNS Paramount, 1967
BUCKSKIN Paramount, 1967
ARIZONA BUSHWACKERS Paramount, 1967
THE WICKED DREAMS OF PAULA SCHULTZ United Artists, 1968
DAGMAR'S HOT PANTS, INC. 1971
WALLS OF FIRE 1971, U.S.-Mexican
ZACHARIAH Cinerama Releasing Corporation, 1971
THE HONKERS United Artists, 1972
NIGHT OF THE LEPUS MGM, 1972
OUTRAGE! (TF) ABC Circle Films, 1973
DIRTY MARY CRAZY LARRY 20th Century-Fox, 1974
LIPSTICK co-composer with Michel Polnareff, Paramount, 1976
DEATH GAME Levitt-Pickman, 1977
JOYRIDE American International, 1977
JUST A LITTLE INCONVENIENCE (TF) Universal TV, 1977
SEE HOW SHE RUNS (TF) ☆☆ CLN Productions, 1978
A CHRISTMAS TO REMEMBER (TF) George Englund Enterprises, 1978
DALLAS COWBOY CHEERLEADERS (TF) Aubrey-Hamner Productions, 1979
SILENT VICTORY: THE KITTY O'NEIL STORY (TF) The Channing-Debin-Locke Company, 1979
THE SEEDING OF SARAH BURNS (TF) Michael Klein Productions/Papazian Productions, 1979
THE JERICHO MILE (TF) ABC Circle Films, 1979
THE CHILD STEALER (TF) The Production Company/ Columbia TV, 1979
BEFORE AND AFTER (TF) The Konigsberg Company, 1979
MIRROR, MIRROR (TF) Christiana Productions, 1979
GOLDIE AND THE BOXER (TF) Orenthal Productions/ Columbia Pictures TV, 1979
WHEN HELL WAS IN SESSION (TF) Aubrey-Hamner Productions, 1979
THE STREETS OF L.A. (TF) George Englund Productions, 1979
THE $5.20 AN HOUR DREAM (TF) Thomas-Sagal Productions/Finnegan Associates/Big Deal, 1980
DALLAS COWBOY CHEERLEADERS II (TF) Aubrey-Hamner Productions, 1980
A CRY FOR LOVE (TF) Charles Fries Productions/ Alan Sacks Productions, 1980
FOR THE LOVE OF IT (TF) Charles Fries Productions/ Neila Productions, 1980
THE JAYNE MANSFIELD STORY (TF) Alan Landsburg Productions, 1980
MARK, I LOVE YOU (TF) The Aubrey Company, 1980
GOLDIE AND THE BOXER GO HOLLYWOOD (TF) Orenthal Productions/Columbia Pictures TV, 1981
A GUN IN THE HOUSE (TF) The Channing-Debin-Locke Company, 1981
THE STAR MAKER (TF) The Channing-Debin-Locke Company/Carson Productions, 1981
LEAVE 'EM LAUGHING (TF) Julian Fowles Productions/ Charles Fries Productions, 1981
HARD COUNTRY co-composer with Michael Martin Murphey, Universal/AFD, 1981
TWIRL (TF) Charles Fries Productions/Atrium Productions, 1981
PORTRAIT OF A SHOWGIRL (TF) Hamner Productions, 1982
DIXIE: CHANGING HABITS (TF) George Englund Productions, 1983
CARPOOL (TF) Charles Fries Productions, 1983
JEALOUSY (TF) co-composer with Gil Melle, Charles Fries Productions/Alan Sacks Productions, 1984
THE VEGAS STRIP WARS (TF) George Englund Productions, 1984
TERRORIST ON TRIAL: THE UNITED STATES VS. SALIM AJAMI (TF) George Englund Productions/Robert Papazian Productions, 1988
BRING ME THE HEAD OF DOBIE GILLIS (TF) 20th Century Fox TV, 1988
SHE'S BACK Vestron, 1989
JAKE SPANNER, PRIVATE EYE (TF) Andrew J. Fenady Productions/Scotti-Vinnedge TV, 1989

GEORGE HATZINASSIOS

b. Greece
Contact: SACEM - France, 011-33-14-747-5650

JUPITER'S THIGH *ON A VOLE LA CRUISSE DE JUPITER* Quartet/Films Inc., 1980, French
SWEET BUNCH *GLYKIA SYMMORIA* 1983, Greek
SHIRLEY VALENTINE co-composer with Willy Russell, Paramount, 1989

GREG HAWKES

Contact: ASCAP - Los Angeles, 213/466-7681

ANNA Vestron, 1987

ALAN HAWKSHAW

Contact: PRS - London, England, 011-44-1-580-5544

MAGIC MOMENTS (CTF) Arena Films/Atlantic Videoventures/Yorkshire TV, 1989, U.S.-British

TODD M. HAYDEN

Contact: LH-81 Entertainment

A SINFUL LIFE New Line Cinema, 1989

ISAAC HAYES

b. August 20, 1942 - Covington, Kentucky

SHAFT ★ MGM, 1971
SHAFT'S BIG SCORE co-composer with Gordon Parks, MGM, 1972
THREE TOUGH GUYS Paramount, 1974, Italian-U.S.
TRUCK TURNER American International, 1974

JACK HAYES

FAST FORWARD co-composer with Tom Scott, Columbia, 1985
THE COLOR PURPLE ★ co-composer, Warner Bros., 1985

RICHARD HAZARD

b. 1921
Contact: BMI - Los Angeles, 213/659-9109

SOME CALL IT LOVING Cine Globe, 1973
THE UNDERGROUND MAN (TF) Aries Films/Paramount Pictures TV, 1974
LAW AND ORDER (TF) P A Productions/Paramount Pictures TV, 1976

NICKELODEON Columbia, 1976
HEROES co-composer with Jack Nitzsche, Universal, 1977
WITH THIS RING (TF) co-composer with George Aliceson Tipton, The Jozak Company/Paramount Pictures TV, 1978
ALL NIGHT LONG co-composer with Ira Newborn, Universal, 1981
BETWEEN TWO BROTHERS (TF) Turman-Foster Company Productions/Finnegan Associates, 1982
AIRPLANE II Paramount, 1982

NEAL HEFTI

b. October 29, 1922 - Hastings, Nebraska
Contact: ASCAP - Los Angeles, 213/466-7681

SEX AND THE SINGLE GIRL Warner Bros., 1965
HOW TO MURDER YOUR WIFE United Artists, 1965
BOEING BOEING Paramount, 1965
HARLOW Paramount, 1965
SYNANON Columbia, 1965
LORD LOVE A DUCK United Artists, 1966
DUEL AT DIABLO United Artists, 1966
BAREFOOT IN THE PARK Paramount, 1966
OH DAD, POOR DAD, MAMA'S HUNG YOU IN THE CLOSET AND I'M FEELIN' SO SAD Paramount, 1967
THE ODD COUPLE Paramount, 1968
P.J. Universal, 1968
LAST OF THE RED HOT LOVERS Paramount, 1972
THE 500-POUND JERK (TF) David L. Wolper Productions, 1973
CONSPIRACY OF TERROR (TF) Lorimar Productions, 1975
WON TON TON, THE DOG WHO SAVED HOLLYWOOD Paramount, 1976

FRED HELLERMAN

Contact: ASCAP - Los Angeles, 213/466-7681

LOVIN' MOLLY Columbia, 1974

JIM HELMS

Contact: ASCAP - Los Angeles, 213/466-7681

KUNG FU (TF) Warner Bros. TV, 1972
DEATH AMONG FRIENDS (TF) The Douglas Cramer Company/Warner Bros. TV, 1975
NIGHT CREATURE Dimension Pictures, 1979

DAVID HENTSCHEL

Contact: PRS - London, England, 011-44-1-580-5544

OPERATION DAYBREAK Warner Bros., 1976
SEVEN NIGHTS IN JAPAN Paramount, 1976, British-French
THE SQUEEZE Warner Bros., 1977
EDUCATING RITA Columbia, 1983, British

HANS WERNER HENZE

Contact: GEMA - West Germany, 011-49-89621400

MURIEL Lopert, 1963, French-Italian
YOUNG TORLESS Kanawha, 1966, West German-French
THE LOST HONOR OF KATHARINA BLUM New World, 1975, West German
GOOD FOR NOTHING 1978, French
SWANN IN LOVE Orion Classics, 1984, French-West German

L'AMOUR A MORT Roissy Film, 1984, French
COMRADES co-composer with David Graham, British Film Institute, 1986, British

ANDY HERNANDEZ

Contact: ASCAP - Los Angeles, 213/466-7681

MIXED BLOOD Sara Films, 1984, U.S.-French

PAUL HERTZOG

Contact: The Artists Group - Los Angeles, 213/552-1100

MY CHAUFFEUR Crown International, 1985
BLOODSPORT Cannon, 1988
DANGEROUS LOVE Concorde, 1988
KICKBOXER Kings Road, 1989
STREET JUSTICE co-composer with Jamii Szmadzinski, Street Justice Productions, 1989

DAVID ALEX HESS

LAST HOUSE ON THE LEFT Hallmark Releasing Corporation, 1973

NIGEL HESS

Contact: PRS - London, England, 011-44-1-580-5544

A WOMAN OF SUBSTANCE (MS) Artemis Productions/Portman Productions, 1984
REUNION AT FAIRBOROUGH (CTF) HBO Premiere Films/Alan Wagner Productions/Alan King Productions/Columbia TV, 1985
DECEPTIONS (TF) Louis Rudolph Productions/Consolidated Productions/Columbia TV, 1985, U.S.-British
THE DOG IT WAS THAT DIED (TF) Granada TV, 1988, British

JERRY HEY

THE COLOR PURPLE ★ co-composer, Warner Bros., 1985

RICHARD HIERONYMOUS

Contact: ASCAP - Los Angeles, 213/466-7681

THE FOREST *TERROR IN THE FOREST* co-composer with Alan Oldfield, Fury Film Distribution Ltd., 1983
INVISIBLE STRANGLER co-composer with Alan Oldfield, Seymour Borde & Associates, 1984

RICHARD HILL

BAFFLED! (TF) Arena Productions/ITC, 1973

FRANCES HIME

Contact: UBC - Brazil, 011-55-21-223-3233

DONA FLOR AND HER TWO HUSBANDS New Yorker, 1977, Brazilian
LOVE LESSON Embra, 1978, Brazilian

RUPERT HINE

Contact: PRS - London, England, 011-44-1-580-5544

THE SHOUT co-composer with Anthony Banks and Michael Rutherford, Films Inc., 1979, British
BETTER OFF DEAD Warner Bros., 1985

JOEL HIRSCHHORN

Agent: Robert Light - Los Angeles, 213/651-1777

WHO KILLED TEDDY BEAR? Magna, 1965
FAT SPY Magna, 1966
TRAPPED BENEATH THE SEA (TF) co-composer with Al Kasha, ABC Circle Films, 1974

GENE HOBSON

Contact: ASCAP - Los Angeles, 213/466-7681

STUDENT BODIES Paramount, 1981

BRIAN HODGSON

Contact: PRS - London, England, 011-44-1-580-5544

THE LEGEND OF HELL HOUSE co-composer with Delia Derbyshire, 20th Century-Fox, 1973, British

MICHAEL HOENIG

Agent: Triad Artists - Los Angeles, 213/556-2727

DEADLY ENCOUNTER (TF) co-composer with Fred Karlin, Roger Gimbel Productions/EMI TV/Promises Productions, 1982
SILENT WITNESS (TF) Robert Greenwald Productions, 1985
SHATTERED SPIRITS (TF) Sheen-Greenblatt Productions/Robert Greenwald Productions, 1986
THE WRAITH New Century/Vista, 1986
THE GATE co-composer with J. Peter Robinson, New Century/Vista, 1987, Canadian
THE BLOB Tri-Star, 1988
CLASS OF 1999 Vestron, 1989
I, MADMAN Trans World Entertainment, 1989

BERNARD HOFFER

Contact: ASCAP - Los Angeles, 213/466-7681

THE IVORY APE (TF) co-composer with Maury Laws, Rankin-Bass Productions, 1980
THE SINS OF DORIAN GRAY (TF) Rankin-Bass Productions, 1983

PAUL HOFFERT

Contact: Pro-Canada - Canada, 1-416-445-8700

FLICK 1970, Canadian
DR. FRANKENSTEIN ON CAMPUS co-composer with Skip Prokop, 1970
THE GROUNDSTAR CONSPIRACY Universal, 1972, U.S.-Canadian
SUNDAY IN THE COUNTRY American International, 1973, British
OUTRAGEOUS! Cinema 5, 1977, Canadian
HIGH-BALLIN' American International, 1978
THE THIRD WALKER 1978
THE SHAPE OF THINGS TO COME Film Ventures International, 1979, Canadian
WILD HORSE HANK Film Consortium of Canada, 1979, Canadian
DOUBLE NEGATIVE Quadrant Films, 1980
MR. PATMAN Film Consortium, 1980, Canadian
CIRCLE OF TWO World Northal, 1981, Canadian
PARADISE Embassy, 1982
HOOVER VS. THE KENNEDYS: THE SECOND CIVIL WAR (MS) Sunrise Films/Selznick-Glickman Productions, 1987

LEE HOLDRIDGE

b. 1944
Agent: Bart-Milander - North Hollywood, 818/761-4040

JONATHAN LIVINGSTON SEAGULL co-composer with Neil Diamond, Paramount, 1973
JEREMY United Artists, 1973
SKYWAY TO DEATH (TF) Universal TV, 1974
NOTHING BY CHANCE Hugh Downs/Richard Bach, 1974
MAHOGANY co-composer with Michael Masser and Gil Askey, Paramount, 1975
WINTERHAWK Howco International, 1976
MUSTANG COUNTRY Universal, 1976
GOIN' HOME Chris Prentiss, 1976
FOREVER YOUNG, FOREVER FREE *E'LOLLIPOP* Universal, 1976, British
PINE CANYON IS BURNING (TF) Universal TV, 1977
THE GREATEST co-composer with Michael Masser, Columbia, 1977
ALASKA: AN AMERICAN CHILD (FD) 1977
SUNSHINE CHRISTMAS (TF) Universal TV, 1977
THE PACK Warner Bros., 1977
TO KILL A COP (TF) David Gerber Company/ Columbia TV, 1978
HAVING BABIES III (TF) The Jozak Company/ Paramount TV, 1978
LIKE MOM, LIKE ME (TF) CBS Entertainment, 1978
THE OTHER SIDE OF THE MOUNTAIN - PART 2 Universal, 1978
MOMENT BY MOMENT Universal, 1978
FRENCH POSTCARDS Paramount, 1978
VALENTINE (TF) Malloy-Philips Productions/Edward S. Feldman Company, 1979
TILT Warner Bros., 1979
OLIVER'S STORY co-composer with Frances Lai, Paramount, 1979
IF THINGS WERE DIFFERENT (TF) Bob Banner Associates, 1980
MOTHER AND DAUGHTER - THE LOVING WAR (TF) Edgar J. Scherick Associates, 1980
SKYWARD (TF) Major H-Anson Productions, 1980
AMERICAN POP (AF) Paramount, 1981
JOHN STEINBECK'S EAST OF EDEN *EAST OF EDEN* (MS) Mace Neufeld Productions, 1981
300 MILES FOR STEPHANIE (TF) Edward S. Feldman Company/Yellow Ribbon Productions/PKO, 1981
FREEDOM (TF) Hill-Mandelker Films, 1981
THE DAY THE LOVING STOPPED (TF) Monash-Zeitman Productions, 1981
FLY AWAY HOME (TF) An Lac Productions/Warner Bros. TV, 1981
FOR LADIES ONLY (TF) The Catalina Production Group/ Viacom, 1981
THE BEASTMASTER MGM/UA, 1982
THOU SHALT NOT KILL (TF) Edgar J. Scherick Associates/Warner Bros. TV, 1982
THIS IS KATE BENNETT (TF) Lorimar, 1982
IN LOVE WITH AN OLDER WOMAN (TF) Pound Ridge Productions/Charles Fries Productions, 1982
MR. MOM 20th Century-Fox, 1983
AGATHA CHRISTIE'S 'A CARIBBEAN MYSTERY' (TF) Stan Margulies Productions/Warner Bros. TV, 1983
THURSDAY'S CHILD (TF) The Catalina Production Group/ Viacom, 1983
LEGS (TF) The Catalina Production Group/Radio City Music Hall Productions/Comworld Productions, 1983
RUNNING OUT (TF) CBS Entertainment, 1983
I WANT TO LIVE (TF) United Artists Corporation, 1983
FIRST AFFAIR (TF) CBS Entertainment, 1983
SPLASH Buena Vista, 1984

MICKI & MAUDE Columbia, 1984
HE'S FIRED, SHE'S HIRED (TF) CBS, 1984
SHATTERED VOWS (TF) Bertinelli-Pequod Productions, 1984
MOONLIGHTING (TF) Picturemaker Productions/ ABC Circle Films, 1985
LETTING GO (TF) Adam Productions/ITC Productions, 1985
SYLVESTER Columbia, 1985
16 DAYS TO GLORY (FD) Paramount, 1985
TRANSYLVANIA 6-5000 New World, 1985
THE OTHER LOVER (TF) Larry Thompson Productions/ Columbia TV, 1985
MAFIA PRINCESS (TF) Jack Farren Productions/ Group W Productions, 1985
THE MEN'S CLUB Atlantic Releasing Corporation, 1986
MIRACLE OF THE HEART: A BOY'S TOWN STORY (TF) Larry White Productions/Columbia TV, 1986
PLEASURES (TF) Catalina Productions Group/ Columbia TV, 1986
WALK LIKE A MAN MGM/UA, 1987
I'LL TAKE MANHATTAN (MS) Steve Krantz Productions, 1987
YOUNG HARRY HOUDINI (TF) Walt Disney TV, 1987
A TIGER'S TALE Atlantic Releasing Corporation, 1987
BORN IN EAST L.A. Universal, 1987
DESPERATE (TF) Toots Productions/Warner Bros. TV, 1987
EIGHT IS ENOUGH: A FAMILY REUNION (TF) Lorimar TV, 1987
HIGHER GROUND (TF) Green-Epstein Productions/ Columbia TV, 1988
FATAL JUDGMENT (TF) Jack Farren Productions/ Group W Productions, 1988
BIG BUSINESS Buena Vista, 1988
A FRIENDSHIP IN VIENNA (CTF) Finnegan-Pinchuk Productions, 1988
THE TENTH MAN (TF) Rosemont Productions/ William Self Productions, 1988, U.S.-British
A MOTHER'S COURAGE: THE MARY THOMAS STORY (TF) Interscope Communications/Chet Walker Enterprises/Walt Disney TV, 1989
DO YOU KNOW THE MUFFIN MAN? (TF) ☆ Avnet-Kerner Co., 1989
OLD GRINGO Columbia, 1989
CHRISTINE CROMWELL (TF) Wolf Film Productions/ Universal TV, 1989
INCIDENT AT DARK RIVER (TF) Farrell-Minoff Productions/Turner Network TV, 1989
DAUGHTER OF THE STREETS (TF) Adam Productions/20th Century Fox Film Corp., 1990

NICKY HOLLAND

Agent: ICM - Los Angeles, 213/550-4000

THE GREAT OUTDOORS Universal, 1988
SHE'S HAVING A BABY Paramount, 1988

RUPERT HOLMES

b. 1947
Contact: ASCAP - Los Angeles, 213/466-7681

THE ANIMALS 1971
A.W.O.L. BFB, 1972
MEMORIES WITHIN MISS AGGIE 1974
DEATH PLAY New Line Cinema, 1976
A STAR IS BORN co-composer, Warner Bros., 1976
NO SMALL AFFAIR Columbia, 1984

NIGEL HOLTON

Contact: The Artists Group - Los Angeles, 213/552-1100

GEMINI, THE TWIN STARS 1988, Swiss-U.S.
SOUTH OF RENO co-composer with Clive Wright, Open Road Productions/Pendulum Productions, 1987
GRANDMOTHER'S HOUSE Omega Pictures, 1988

JUNIOR HOMRICH

Agent: ICM - Los Angeles, 213/550-4000

THE EMERALD FOREST Embassy, 1985, British
STREETS OF JUSTICE (TF) Universal TV, 1985
GHOSTS CAN'T DO IT Trans World Entertainment, 1989

TOSHIYUKI HONDA

b. Japan
Contact: JASRAC - Tokyo, Japan, 011-81-3-502-6551

A TAXING WOMAN Toho, 1987, Japanese

TOBE HOOPER

b. 1943 - Austin, Texas

THE TEXAS CHAINSAW MASSACRE co-composer with Wayne Bell, Bryanston, 1974
THE TEXAS CHAINSAW MASSACRE PART 2 co-composer with Jerry Lambert, Cannon, 1986

ANTONY HOPKINS

b. 1921 - London, England
Contact: PRS - London, England, 011-44-1-580-5544

IT'S HARD TO BE GOOD 1946, British
VICE VERSA General Film Distributors, 1948, British
VOTE FOR HUGGETT General Film Distributors, 1949, British
DECAMERON NIGHTS RKO Radio, 1953, British-U.S.
JOHNNY ON THE RUN Associated British Film Distributors/ Children's Film Foundation, 1953, British
THE PICKWICK PAPERS 1954, British
THE ANGEL WHO PAWNED HER HARP 1954, British
CHILD'S PLAY 1954, British
BILLY BUDD Allied Artists, 1962, British

KENYON HOPKINS

b. 1932
Contact: BMI - Los Angeles, 213/659-9109

BABY DOLL Warner Bros., 1956
THE STRANGE ONE *END AS A MAN* Columbia, 1957
TWELVE ANGRY MEN United Artists, 1957
THE FUGITIVE KIND United Artists, 1957
WILD RIVER 20th Century-Fox, 1960
WILD IN THE COUNTRY 20th Century-Fox, 1961
THE YELLOW CANARY 20th Century-Fox, 1963
LILITH Columbia, 1964
MISTER BUDDWING MGM, 1966
THIS PROPERTY IS CONDEMNED Paramount, 1966
DOCTOR, YOU'VE GOT TO BE KIDDING MGM, 1967
THE BORGIA STICK (TF) Universal TV, 1967
A LOVELY WAY TO DIE Universal, 1968
DOWNHILL RACER Paramount, 1969
THE FIRST TIME United Artists, 1969
THE TREE Guenette, 1969

MICHAEL HOPPE
Contact: BMI - Los Angeles, 213/659-9109

MISUNDERSTOOD MGM/UA, 1984

STEPHEN HORELICK
Contact: ASCAP - Los Angeles, 213/466-7681

MADMAN Jensen Farley Pictures, 1982

JAMES HORNER
b. 1953 - Los Angeles, California
Agent: Gorfaine-Schwartz - Burbank, 818/954-9500

UP FROM THE DEPTHS New World, 1979
THE LADY IN RED New World, 1979
BATTLE BEYOND THE STARS New World, 1979
ANGEL DUSTED (TF) NRW Features, 1980
HUMANOIDS FROM THE DEEP New World, 1980
A FEW DAYS IN WEASEL CREEK (TF) Hummingbird Productions/Warner Bros., 1981
DEADLY BLESSING United Artists, 1981
THE HAND Orion/Warner Bros., 1981
WOLFEN Orion/Warner Bros., 1981
THE PURSUIT OF D.B. COOPER Universal, 1981
RASCALS AND ROBBERS—THE SECRET ADVENTURES OF TOM SAWYER AND HUCK FINN (TF) CBS Entertainment, 1982
A PIANO FOR MRS. CIMINO (TF) Roger Gimbel Productions/EMI TV, 1982
STAR TREK II: THE WRATH OF KHAN Paramount, 1982
48 HOURS Paramount, 1982
BETWEEN FRIENDS (CTF) HBO Premiere Films/Marian Rees Associates/Robert Cooper Films III/List-Estrin Productions, 1983, U.S.-Canadian
BRAINSTORM MGM/UA, 1983
SOMETHING WICKED THIS WAY COMES Buena Vista, 1983
KRULL Columbia, 1983, U.S.-British
UNCOMMON VALOR Paramount, 1983
TESTAMENT Paramount, 1983
THE DRESSER Columbia, 1983, British
GORKY PARK Orion, 1983
THE STONE BOY TLC Films/20th Century Fox, 1984
STAR TREK III: THE SEARCH FOR SPOCK Paramount, 1984
SURVIVING (TF) Telepictures Corporation, 1985
HEAVEN HELP US Tri-Star, 1985
VOLUNTEERS Tri-Star, 1985
COCOON 20th Century Fox, 1985
THE JOURNEY OF NATTY GANN Buena Vista, 1985
COMMANDO 20th Century Fox, 1985
OFF BEAT Buena Vista, 1986
ALIENS ★ 20th Century Fox, 1986
THE NAME OF THE ROSE 20th Century Fox, 1986, West German-Italian-French
WHERE THE RIVER RUNS BLACK MGM/UA, 1986
AN AMERICAN TAIL (AF) Universal, 1986
P.K. AND THE KID Castle Hill Productions, 1987, made in 1982
PROJECT X 20th Century Fox, 1987
BATTERIES NOT INCLUDED Universal, 1987
WILLOW MGM/UA, 1988
RED HEAT Tri-Star, 1988
VIBES Columbia, 1988
THE LAND BEFORE TIME (AF) Universal, 1988
COCOON: THE RETURN 20th Century Fox, 1988
FIELD OF DREAMS ★ Universal, 1989
HONEY, I SHRUNK THE KIDS Buena Vista, 1989
IN COUNTRY Warner Bros., 1989
DAD Universal, 1989
GLORY Tri-Star, 1989
I LOVE YOU TO DEATH Warner Bros., 1990
ANOTHER 48 HOURS Paramount, 1990
CLASS ACTION 1990

JOSEPH HOROVITZ
b. 1926 - Vienna, Austria
Contact: PRS - London, England, 011-44-1-580-5544

TARZAN'S THREE CHALLENGES MGM, 1963, British

VLADIMIR HORUNZHY
b. September 19, 1949 - Kirovgrad, U.S.S.R.
Contact: Los Angeles, 213/876-2949

FUNNY COMPANY (AF) Kiev Studio, 1972, Soviet
ANOTHER LIFE DocuStudio, Kiev, 1974, Soviet
ROYAL REGATTA Dovzsenco Films, 1976, Soviet
UNSUNG SONG Dovzsenco Films, 1977, Soviet
ROAD TO VICTORY Mosfilm, 1978, Soviet
SILENT KILLER (TD) CBS, 1984
FINE GOLD Overseas Film Group, 1988
A MAN OF PASSION Noble Entertainment, 1988
ELVES Windstar Studios, 1989
THE FORBIDDEN DANCE 21st Century, 1990

JAMES NEWTON HOWARD
Agent: Gorfaine-Schwartz - Burbank, 818/954-9500

HEAD OFFICE Tri-Star, 1986
WILDCATS co-composer with Hawk Wolinski, Warner Bros., 1986
NEVER TOO YOUNG TO DIE Paul Releasing, 1986
8 MILLION WAYS TO DIE Tri-Star, 1986
NOBODY'S FOOL Island Pictures, 1986
TOUGH GUYS Buena Vista, 1986
CAMPUS MAN Paramount, 1987
FIVE CORNERS Cineplex Odeon, 1987
RUSSKIES New Century/Vista, 1987
PROMISED LAND Vestron, 1987
OFF LIMITS 20th Century Fox, 1988
SOME GIRLS MGM/UA, 1988
EVERYBODY'S ALL AMERICAN Warner Bros., 1988
GO TOWARD THE LIGHT (TF) Corapeake Productions, 1988
TAP Tri-Star, 1989
MAJOR LEAGUE Paramount, 1989
THE PACKAGE Orion, 1989
THE IMAGE (CTF) Citadel Entertainment/HBO, 1990
COUPE DE VILLE Universal, 1990
PRETTY WOMAN Buena Vista, 1990
REVEALING EVIDENCE (TF) T.W.S. Productions/Universal, 1990
FLATLINERS Columbia, 1990
KING RALPH Universal, 1990

KEN HOWARD
FOREIGN BODY Orion, 1986

RIK HOWARD
Contact: Andi Howard - Los Angeles, 213/278-6483

BOYS WILL BE BOYS (TF) co-composer with Bob Wirth
SECOND CHANCE (TF) co-composer with Bob Wirth

ALAN HOWARTH
Agent: Carol Faith - Beverly Hills, 213/274-0776

ESCAPE FROM NEW YORK co-composer with John Carpenter, Avco Embassy, 1981
HALLOWEEN II co-composer with John Carpenter, Universal, 1981
HALLOWEEN III: SEASON OF THE WITCH co-composer with John Carpenter, Universal, 1982
CHRISTINE co-composer with John Carpenter, Columbia, 1983
THE LOST EMPIRE JGM Enterprises, 1984
RETRIBUTION United Film Distribution, 1987
PRINCE OF DARKNESS co-composer with John Carpenter, Universal, 1987
HALLOWEEN 4: THE RETURN OF MICHAEL MYERS Galaxy International, 1988
THEY LIVE co-composer with John Carpenter, Universal, 1988
HALLOWEEN 5: THE REVENGE OF MICHAEL MYERS Galaxy International, 1989

PETER HOWELL
Contact: PRS - London, England, 011-44-1-580-5544

YURI NOSENKO, KGB (CTF) BBC TV/Primetime TV Ltd., 1986, British

JACK HUES
Contact: PRS - London, England, 011-44-1-580-5544

THE GUARDIAN Universal, 1990

STEVEN HUFSTETER
Contact: BMI - Los Angeles, 213/659-9109

REPO MAN co-composer with Tito Larriva, Universal, 1984

COOPER HUGHES
C.H.U.D. New World, 1984

CRAIG HUNDLEY
Contact: ASCAP - Los Angeles, 213/466-7681

DISAPPEARANCE 1977, Canadian
ALLIGATOR Group 1, 1980
ROADIE United Artists, 1980
SCHIZOID *MURDER BY MAIL* Cannon, 1980
THE ACORN PEOPLE (TF) Rollins-Joffe-Morra-Breszner Productions/NBC Entertainment, 1981
AMERICANA co-composer with David Carradine, Crown International, 1981
BOOGEYMAN II New West Films, 1983
PROGRAMMED TO KILL Trans World Entertainment, 1987

ALBERTA HUNTER
REMEMBER MY NAME Columbia/Lagoon Associates, 1979

STEVE HUNTER
Contact: BMI - Los Angeles, 213/659-9109

THE INVISIBLE KID Taurus Entertainment, 1988

MICHAEL HURD
Contact: PRS - London, England, 011-44-1-580-5544

SCRUBBERS co-composer with Ray Cooper, Orion Classics, 1983, British

BRENDA HUTCHINSON
LIQUID SKY co-composer with Slava Tsukerman and Clive Smith, Cinevista, 1982

LUCIA HWONG
FORBIDDEN NIGHTS (TF) Tristine Rainer Productions/ Warner Bros., 1990

CHRISTOPHER HYANS-HART
HELL HIGH co-composer with Rich Macar, MGM Enterprises, 1989

DICK HYMAN
b. 1927
Agent: Bart-Milander - North Hollywood, 818/761-4040

SCOTT JOPLIN adaptation, Universal, 1977
THE DEADLIEST SEASON (TF) Titus Productions, 1977
THE LAST TENANT (TF) Titus Productions, 1978
THE HENDERSON MONSTER (TF) Titus Productions, 1980
KING CRAB (TF) Titus Productions, 1980
ZELIG Orion/Warner Bros., 1983
BROADWAY DANNY ROSE Orion, 1983
THE PURPLE ROSE OF CAIRO Orion, 1985
JOHNNY BULL (TF) Titus Productions/Eugene O'Neill Memorial Theatre Center, 1986
RADIO DAYS Orion, 1987
LEADER OF THE BAND New Century/Vista, 1987
MOONSTRUCK MGM/UA, 1987
ASK ME AGAIN (TF) DBR Films Ltd./American Playhouse, 1989

AKIRA IFUKUBE
b. 1914 - Hokkaido, Japan
Contact: JASRAC - Tokyo, Japan, 011-81-3-502-6551

THE QUIET DUEL Daiei, 1949, Japanese
CHILDREN OF HIROSHIMA *CHILDREN OF THE ATOM BOMB* 1952, Japanese
THE SAGA OF ANATAHAN *ANA-TA-HAN* 1953, Japanese
GODZILLA, KING OF THE MONSTERS *GOJIRA* Embassy, 1954, Japanese-U.S.
DOWNTOWN 1955, Japanese
HIROSHIMA 1955, Japanese
THE BURMESE HARP *HARP OF BURMA* Brandon, 1956, Japanese
RODAN DCA, 1957, Japanese
SECRET SCROLLS Toho, 1957, Japanese
VARAN THE UNBELIEVABLE Crown International, 1958, Japanese-U.S.
THE MYSTERIANS Columbia, 1959, Japanese
THE THREE TREASURES 1960, Japanese

BATTLE IN OUTER SPACE Columbia, 1960, Japanese
DAREDEVIL IN THE CASTLE 1961, Japanese
CHUSHINGURA Toho, 1962, Japanese
THE WHALE GOD 1962, Japanese
BUDDHA 1963, Japanese
KING KONG VS. GODZILLA composer of Japanese version only, Universal, 1963, Japanese
THE LITTLE PRINCE AND THE EIGHT-HEADED DRAGON (AF) 1963, Japanese
GODZILLA VS. THE THING *GODZILLA VS. MOTHRA* American International, 1964, Japanese
FRANKENSTEIN CONQUERS THE WORLD American International, 1964, Japanese
ATTRAGON American International, 1965, Japanese
DAGORA, THE SPACE MONSTER Toho, 1965, Japanese
KIGANJO NO BOKEN *ADVENTURES OF TAKLA MAKAN* 1965, Japanese
GHIDRAH, THE THREE-HEADED MONSTER Continental, 1966, Japanese
MAJIN, THE HIDEOUS IDOL 1966, Japanese
WAR OF THE GARGANTUAS 1966, U.S.-Japanese
MONSTER ZERO 1966, Japanese
RETURN OF GIANT MAJIN 1967, Japanese
MAJIN STRIKES AGAIN 1967, Japanese
KAIDEN YUKUJORO *SNOW GHOST* 1968, Japanese
KING KONG ESCAPES Universal, 1968, Japanese
DESTROY ALL MONSTERS American International, 1969, Japanese
LATITUDE ZERO National General, 1970, Japanese
YOG - MONSTER FROM SPACE American International, 1971, Japanese
THE HUMAN REVOLUTION 1974
BOKYO Toho, 1975, Japanese
REVENGE OF MECHA-GODZILLA *TERROR OF MECHA-GODZILLA/TERROR OF GODZILLA* 1977, Japanese
LOVE AND FAITH: LADY OGIN 1979, Japanese

SHINCHIRO IKEBE

b. Japan
Contact: JASRAC - Tokyo, Japan, 011-81-3-502-6551

KAGEMUSHA: THE SHADOW WARRIOR 20th Century-Fox, 1980, Japanese
VENGEANCE IS MINE Shochiku Co. Ltd., 1980, Japanese
OKINAWAN BOYS 1983, Japanese
THE BALLAD OF NARAYAMA Kino International/ Janus, 1983, Japanese
MacARTHUR'S CHILDREN (FD) Orion Classics, 1985, Japanese
ZEGEN Toei, 1987, Japanese
AKIRA KUROSAWA'S DREAMS Warner Bros., 1990, Japanese

JERROLD IMMEL

Contact: ASCAP - Los Angeles, 213/466-7681

THE HOUSE ON SKULL MOUNTAIN 20th Century-Fox, 1974
THE MACAHANS (TF) Albert S. Ruddy Productions/ MGM TV, 1976
REVENGE FOR A RAPE (TF) Albert S. Ruddy Productions, 1976
SOURDOUGH Film Saturation Inc., 1977
NOWHERE TO HIDE (TF) MTM Enterprises, 1978
GO WEST, YOUNG GIRL! (TF) Bennett-Katleman Productions/Columbia Pictures TV, 1978
MATILDA American International, 1978
THE SACKETTS (TF) Douglas Netter Enterprises/ M.B. Scott Productions/Shalako Enterprises, 1979
THE LEGEND OF THE GOLDEN GUN (TF) Bennett-Katleman Productions/Columbia Pictures TV, 1979
WILD TIMES (TF) Metromedia Producers Corporation/ Rattlesnake Productions, 1980
POWER (TF) David Gerber Productions/Columbia Pictures TV, 1980
ROUGHNECKS (TF) Metromedia Producers Corporation/ Rattlesnake Productions, 1980
ALCATRAZ: THE WHOLE SHOCKING STORY (TF) Pierre Cossette Enterprises, 1980
THE OKLAHOMA CITY DOLLS (TF) IKE Productions/ Columbia Pictures TV, 1981
DEATH HUNT 20th Century-Fox, 1981
SILENCE OF THE NORTH adaptation, Universal, 1981, Canadian
MEGAFORCE 20th Century-Fox, 1982
THE SHADOW RIDERS (TF) Pegasus Group Ltd./Columbia Pictures TV, 1982
TRAVIS McGEE (TF) Hajeno Productions/Warner Bros. TV, 1983
THE OUTLAWS (TF) Limekiln and Templar Productions/ Universal TV, 1984
PEYTON PLACE: THE NEXT GENERATION (TF) Michael Filerman Productions/20th Century-Fox TV, 1985
MIDAS VALLEY (TF) Edward S. Feldman Productions/ Warner Bros. TV, 1985
DALLAS: THE EARLY YEARS (TF) Roundelay Productions/Lorimar-Telepictures, 1986
PROGRAMMED TO KILL co-composer with Craig Huxley, Trans World Entertainment, 1987
GUNSMOKE: RETURN TO DODGE (TF) CBS Entertainment, 1987
NORMAN ROCKWELL'S BREAKING HOME TIES (TF) John Wilder Productions/Telecom Entertainment, 1987
PARADISE (TF) Roundelay Productions/Lorimar TV, 1988

NEIL INNES

Contact: PRS - London, England, 011-44-1-580-5544

MONTY PYTHON AND THE HOLY GRAIL co-composer with De Wolfe, Cinema 5, 1974, British
ERIC THE VIKING Orion, 1989, British

ROBERT IRVING III

STREET SMART Cannon, 1987

MARK ISHAM

Agent: CAA - Los Angeles, 213/288-4545

NEVER CRY WOLF Buena Vista, 1983
MRS. SOFFEL MGM/UA, 1984
THE LIFE AND TIMES OF HARVEY MILK (FD) Teleculture, 1984
TROUBLE IN MIND Alive Films, 1985
THE HITCHER Tri-Star, 1986
MADE IN HEAVEN Lorimar, 1987
THE MODERNS Alive Films, 1988
THE BEAST Columbia, 1988
EVERYBODY WINS Orion, 1990
LOVE AT LARGE Orion, 1990
REVERSAL OF FORTUNE Warner Bros., 1990

PETER IVERS

Contact: BMI - Los Angeles, 213/659-9109

GRAND THEFT AUTO New World, 1977
ERASERHEAD Libra, 1977

PAUL JABARA
Contact: BMI - Los Angeles, 213/659-9109

CHANEL SOLITAIRE United Film Distribution, 1981, French-British

DAVID A. JACKSON
Contact: ASCAP - Los Angeles, 213/466-7681

COLD STEEL Cinetel, 1987
CYCLONE Cinetel, 1987

JOE JACKSON
Contact: CAA - Los Angeles, 213/288-4545

MIKE'S MURDER additional music, The Ladd Company/Warner Bros., 1984
PRIVATE EYE (TF) Yerkovich Productions/ Universal TV, 1987
TUCKER Paramount, 1988

JULIAN JACOBSON
Contact: PRS - London, England, 011-44-1-580-5544

WE THINK THE WORLD OF YOU Cinecom, 1988, British

DENNY JAEGER
Contact: BMI - Los Angeles, 213/659-9109

THE HUNGER co-composer with Michel Rubin, MGM/UA, 1983, British

ETHAN JAMES
Contact: BMI - Los Angeles, 213/659-9109

THE BLUE IGUANA Paramount, 1988
DEADLY INTENT Fries Entertainment, 1988

TERRENCE JAMES
FREDDOM ROAD (TF) co-composer with Coleridge-Taylor Perkinson, Zev Braun TV/ Freedom Road Films, 1979

CHAZ JANKEL
Agent: ICM - Los Angeles, 213/550-4000

MAKING MR. RIGHT Orion, 1987
D.O.A. Buena Vista, 1988
KILLING DAD (TF) 1989
THE RACHEL PAPERS MGM/UA, 1989, U.S.-British
WAR PARTY Hemdale, 1989
TALES FROM THE DARKSIDE: THE MOVIE co-composer, Paramount, 1990

ENZO JANNACCI
b. Italy
Contact: SIAE - Rome, Italy, 011-39-6-59-90-1

COME HOME AND MEET MY WIFE 1974, Italian
SEVEN BEAUTIES *PASQUALINO SETTEBELLEZZE* Cinema 5, 1976, Italian
STORMTROOPERS 1977, Italian
SAXAPHONE 1978, Italian

ALARIC JANS
Contact: ASCAP - Los Angeles, 213/466-7681

HOUSE OF GAMES Orion, 1987
THINGS CHANGE Columbia, 1988

PIERRE JANSEN
b. February 28, 1930 - Roubaix, France
Contact: SACEM - France, 011-33-14-747-5650

LES BONNES FEMMES Robert Hakim, 1960, French-Italian
LES GODELUREAUX Cocinor-Marceau, 1961, French-Italian
SEVEN DEADLY SINS composer of Chabrol segment, Embassy, 1962, French-Italian
OPHELIA New Line Cinema, 1962, French-Italian
LANDRU Embassy, 1963, French-Italian
LES PLUS BELLES ESCROQUERIES DU MONDE composer of Chabrol segment, 1964, French-Italian-Japanese
LE TIGRE AIME LA CHAIR FRAICHE Gaumont, 1964, French-Italian
MARIE-CHANTAL CONTRE LE DOCTEUR KHA SNC, 1965, French-Italian-Moroccan
LA 317 SECTION 1965, French
LA LIGNE DE DEMARCATION CCFC, 1966, French
THE CHAMPAGNE MURDERS *LE SCANDALE* Universal, 1967, French
LA ROUTE DE CORINTHE CCFC, 1967, French-Italian-West German
OBJECTIF 500 MILLIONS 1967, French
LES BICHES VGC, 1968, French-Italian
LA FEMME INFIDELE Allied Artists, 1968, French-Italian
LE SAUVEUR 1969, French
THIS MAN MUST DIE *QUE LA BETE MEURE* Allied Artists, 1969, French-Italian
LE BOUCHER Cinerama Releasing Corporation, 1969, French-Italian
LA RUPTURE New Line Cinema, 1970, French-Italian-Belgian
JUST BEFORE NIGHTFALL *JUSTE AVANT LA NUIT* Libra, 1971, French-Italian
TEN DAYS' WONDER *LA DECADE PRODIGIEUSE* Levitt-Pickman, 1971, French
HIGH HEELS *DOCTEUR POPAUL* Les Films La Boetie, 1972, French-Italian
WEDDING IN BLOOD *LES NOCES ROUGES* New Line Cinema, 1973, French-Italian
THE NADA GANG *NADA* New Line Cinema, 1974, French-Italian
DIRTY HANDS *LES INNOCENTS AUX MAIN SALES* New Line Cinema, 1975, French-Italian-West German
NUIT D'OR *GOLDEN NIGHTS* 1976, French
ALICE OU LA DERNIERE FUGUE *ALICE OR THE LAST ESCAPADE* Filmel/PHPG, 1977, French
LA DENTELLIERE *THE LACEMAKER* New Yorker, 1977, Swiss-French

LES LIENS DE SANG Filmcorp, 1978, Canadian-French
VIOLETTE *VIOLETTE NOZIERE* New Yorker, 1978, French
L'ETAT SAUVAGE 1978, French
LE CHEVAL D'ORGEUIL Planfilm, 1980, French

WERNER JANSSEN

b. June 1, 1900 - New York, New York

THE GENERAL DIED AT DAWN Paramount, 1936
BLOCKADE ★ Warner Bros., 1938
ETERNALLY YOURS ★ United Artists, 1939
WINTER CARNIVAL Warner Bros., 1939
LIGHTS OUT IN EUROPE (FD) 1939
THE HOUSE ACROSS THE BAY United Artists, 1940
SLIGHTLY HONORABLE United Artists, 1940
GUEST IN THE HOUSE ★ United Artists, 1944
CAPTAIN KIDD ★ United Artists, 1945
THE SOUTHERNER ★ United Artists, 1945
A NIGHT IN CASABLANCA United Artists, 1946
RUTHLESS Eagle Lion, 1948
UNCLE VANYA 1958

MAURICE JARRE

b. September 13, 1924 - Lyons, France
Contact: SACEM - France, 011-33-14-747-5650

BRAVO ALFA 1956, French
LE GRAND SILENCE 1956, French
LA GENERATION DU DESERT 1957, French
LE GRAND OUEVRE 1958, French
VOUS N'AVEZ RIEN A DECLARER? 1958, French
CHRONIQUE PROVINCIALE 1958, French
LA BETE A L'AFFUT 1958, French
LES DRAGUEURS 1958, French
LA TETE CONTRE LES MURS 1958, French
RECOURS EN GRACE 1959, French
LES ETOILES DU MIDI 1959, French
LE TAPIS VOLANT 1959, French
LA CORDE RAIDE 1959, French
MALRIF, AIGLE ROYAL 1959, French
LE MAIN CHAUDE 1959, French
THE HORROR CHAMBER OF DR. FAUSTUS *LES YEUX SANS VISAGE* Lopert, 1960, French-Italian
CRACK IN THE MIRROR 20th Century-Fox, 1960
LE PRESIDENT 1960, French
PLEINS FEUX SUR L'ASSASSIN 1960, French
THE BIG GAMBLE 20th Century-Fox, 1961
THE WITNESSES *LE TEMPS DU GHETTO* 1961, French
THE OLIVE TREES OF JUSTICE *LES OLIVIERS DE LA JUSTICE* 1961, French
LES AMOURS CELEBRES 1961, French
LE PUITS AUX TROIS VERITES 1961, French
LA BRIDE SUR LE COU 1961, French
THERESE DESQUEYROUX 1962, French
SUNDAYS AND CYBELE ★ *CYBELE OU LES DIMANCHES DE VILLE d'AVRAY* Davis-Royal, 1962, French
THE LONGEST DAY 20th Century-Fox, 1962
LES TRAVESTIS DU DIABLE 1962, French
TON OMBRE EST LA MIENNE 1962, French
L'OISEAU DE PARADIS 1962, French
MOURIR A MADRID 1962, French
LAWRENCE OF ARABIA ★★ Columbia, 1962, British
MORT, OU EST TA VICTOIRE? 1962, French
LES ANIMAUX (FD) 1963, French
UN ROI SANS DIVERTISSEMENT 1963, French
POUR L'ESPAGNE 1963, French
JUDEX 1964, French
BEHOLD A PALE HORSE Columbia, 1964
WEEKEND A ZUYDCOOTE 1964, French
THE TRAIN United Artists, 1965, U.S.-French-Italian
TO DIE IN MADRID (FD) 1965, French
THE COLLECTOR Columbia, 1965, U.S.-British
DOCTOR ZHIVAGO ★★ MGM, 1965, British
IS PARIS BURNING? Paramount, 1966, French-U.S.
THE PROFESSIONALS Columbia, 1966
GRAND PRIX MGM, 1966
GAMBIT Universal, 1966
THE NIGHT OF THE GENERALS Columbia, 1967, British-French
VILLA RIDES! Paramount, 1968
5 CARD STUD Paramount, 1968
THE FIXER MGM, 1968, British
ISADORA *THE LOVES OF ISADORA* Universal, 1969, British
THE EXTRAORDINARY SEAMAN MGM, 1969
THE DAMNED *LA CADUTA DEGLI DEI/ GOTTERDAMERUNG* Warner Bros., 1969, Italian-West German
TOPAZ Universal, 1969
THE ONLY GAME IN TOWN 20th Century-Fox, 1970
EL CONDOR National General, 1970
RYAN'S DAUGHTER MGM, 1970, British
PLAZA SUITE Paramount, 1971
A SEASON IN HELL 1971, Italian
RED SUN National General, 1972, French-Italian-Spanish
POPE JOAN Columbia, 1972, British
THE EFFECT OF GAMMA RAYS ON MAN-IN-THE-MOON MARIGOLDS 20th Century-Fox, 1973
THE LIFE AND TIMES OF JUDGE ROY BEAN National General, 1973
THE MACKINTOSH MAN Warner Bros., 1973, U.S.-British
ASH WEDNESDAY Paramount, 1973
LIFE SIZE *GRANDEUR NATURE* 1974, French
THE ISLAND AT THE TOP OF THE WORLD Buena Vista, 1974
GREAT EXPECTATIONS Transcontinental Film Productions, 1974, British
MANDINGO Paramount, 1975
POSSE Paramount, 1975
MR. SYCAMORE Film Venture, 1975
THE MAN WHO WOULD BE KING Allied Artists, 1975, British
THE SILENCE (TF) Palomar Productions, 1975
SHOUT AT THE DEVIL American International, 1976, British
THE LAST TYCOON Paramount, 1976
MOHAMMED, MESSENGER OF GOD ★ *THE MESSAGE* Tarik, 1977, Lebanese-British
MARCH OR DIE Columbia, 1977, British
JESUS OF NAZARETH (MS) Sir Lew Grade Productions/ ITC, 1978, British-Italian
CROSSED SWORDS *THE PRINCE AND THE PAUPER* Warner Bros., 1978, British
TWO SOLITUDES New World-Mutual, 1978, Canadian
ISHI: THE LAST OF HIS TRIBE (TF) Edward & Mildred Lewis Productions, 1978
THE USERS (TF) Aaron Spelling Productions, 1978
THE MAGICIAN OF LUBLIN Cannon, 1979, Israeli-West German-U.S.
WINTER KILLS Avco Embassy, 1979
THE TIN DRUM Argos Films, 1979, West German-French
THE AMERICAN SUCCESS COMPANY *SUCCESS* Columbia, 1979, West German-U.S.
THE BLACK MARBLE Avco Embassy, 1980
THE LAST FLIGHT OF NOAH'S ARK Buena Vista, 1980

SHOGUN (MS) Paramount TV/NBC Entertainment, 1980, U.S.-Japanese
RESURRECTION Universal, 1980
ENOLA GAY (TF) The Productions Company/ Viacom, 1980
LION OF THE DESERT United Film Distribution, 1981, Libyan-British
TAPS 20th Century-Fox, 1981
DON'T CRY, IT'S ONLY THUNDER Sanrio, 1982, U.S.-Japanese
CIRCLE OF DECEIT *DIE FALSCHUNG* United Artists Classics, 1982, West German-French
COMING OUT OF THE ICE (TF) The Konigsberg Company, 1982
FIREFOX Warner Bros., 1982
YOUNG DOCTORS IN LOVE 20th Century-Fox, 1982
THE YEAR OF LIVING DANGEROUSLY MGM/UA, 1983, Australian
FOR THOSE I LOVED 20th Century-Fox, 1983, Canadian-French
THE SKY'S NO LIMIT (TF) Palance-Levy Productions, 1984
SAMSON AND DELILAH (TF) Catalina Production Group/Comworld Productions, 1984
TOP SECRET! Paramount, 1984
DREAMSCAPE 20th Century Fox, 1984
A PASSAGE TO INDIA ★★ Columbia, 1984, British
WITNESS ★ Paramount, 1985
THE BRIDE Columbia, 1985, British
MAD MAX BEYOND THUNDERDOME Warner Bros., 1985, Australian
ENEMY MINE 20th Century Fox, 1985
SOLARBABIES MGM/UA, 1986
TAI-PAN DEG, 1986
APOLOGY (CTF) Roger Gimbel Productions/ Peregrine Entertainment Ltd./ASAP Productions/ HBO Pictures, 1986
THE MOSQUITO COAST Warner Bros., 1986
GABY - A TRUE STORY Tri-Star, 1987, U.S.-Mexican
NO WAY OUT Orion, 1987
JULIA AND JULIA Cinecom, 1987, Italian
FATAL ATTRACTION Paramount, 1987
WILDFIRE Zupnick Enterprises/Jody Ann Productions, 1987
THE MURDER OF MARY PHAGAN (MS) George Stevens Jr. Productions/Century Tower Productions, 1988
DISTANT THUNDER Paramount, 1988
HOTEL TERMINUS: THE LIFE AND TIMES OF KLAUS BARBIE (FD) Samuel Goldwyn Company, 1988, French
GORILLAS IN THE MIST ★ Universal, 1988
MOON OVER PARADOR Universal, 1988, U.S.-Brazilian
CHANCES ARE Tri-Star, 1989
DEAD POETS SOCIETY Buena Vista, 1989
PRANCER Orion, 1989
ENEMIES, A LOVE STORY 20th Century Fox, 1989
GHOST Paramount, 1990
AFTER DARK, MY SWEET Avenue Pictures, 1990

KEITH JARRETT

b. 1945
Contact: BMI - Los Angeles, 213/659-9109

SORCERER additional music, Universal/ Paramount, 1977
MY HEART IS RED 1977, French
THE EIGHTH DAY 1979, Swedish

HERMAN JEFFREYS

KILLPOINT co-composer with Daryl Stevenett, Crown International, 1984

TOM JENKINS

GOOD-BYE, CRUEL WORLD Sharp Features, 1982

WAYLON JENNINGS

b. June 15, 1937 - Littlefield, Texas
Contact: BMI - Los Angeles, 213/659-9109

MACKINTOSH & T.J. Penland Productions, 1975

MERRILL B. JENSEN

TAKE DOWN Buena Vista, 1979
WINDWALKER Pacific International, 1980
HARRY'S WAR Taft International, 1981

PETER JERMYN

b. Canada
Contact: Pro-Canada - Canada, 1-416-445-8700

ESCAPE FROM IRAN: THE CANADIAN CAPER (TF) Canamedia Productions, 1981, Canadian

J.J. JOHNSON

Contact: BMI - Los Angeles, 213/659-9109

ACROSS 110TH STREET United Artists, 1972
MAN AND BOY Levitt-Pickman, 1972
TOP OF THE HEAP Fanfare, 1972
CLEOPATRA JONES Warner Bros., 1973
WILLIE DYNAMITE Universal, 1974
STREET KILLING (TF) ABC Circle Films, 1976

LAURIE JOHNSON

b. 1927 - Hampstead, England
Contact: PRS - London, England, 011-44-1-580-5544

I AIM AT THE STARS Columbia, 1960, U.S.-West German
DR. STRANGELOVE OR: HOW I LEARNED TO STOP WORRYING AND LOVE THE BOMB Columbia, 1964, British
FIRST MEN IN THE MOON Columbia, 1964, British
YOU MUST BE JOKING! Columbia, 1965, British
HOT MILLIONS MGM, 1968, British
MR. JERICHO (TF) ITC, 1970, British
THE BELSTONE FOX *FREE SPIRIT* Cine III, 1973, British
CAPTAIN KRONOS: VAMPIRE HUNTER Paramount, 1974, British
THE MAIDS American Film Theatre, 1975, British
HEDDA Brut Productions, 1975, British
IT SHOULDN'T HAPPEN TO A VET EMI, 1976, British
IT LIVES AGAIN *IT'S ALIVE II* adaptation of Bernard Herrmann score for "It's Alive," Warner Bros., 1978
A HAZARD OF HEARTS (TF) The Grade Company/ Gainsborough Pictures, 1987, British
THE LADY AND THE HIGHWAYMAN (TF) Lord Grade Productions/Gainsborough Pictures, 1989, British
A GHOST IN MONTE CARLO (CTF) TNT/The Grade Co., 1990, U.S.-British

SCOTT JOHNSON

PATTY HEARST Zenith Group/Atlantic Entertainment, 1988

JIM JOHNSTON

NO HOLDS BARRED New Line Cinema, 1989

RICHARD JOHNSTON

Contact: Pro-Canada - Canada, 1-416-445-8700

TERROR IN THE AISLES additional music, Universal, 1984

ALAIN JOMY

b. France
Contact: SACEM - France, 011-33-14-747-5650

LA MEILLEURE FACON DE MARCHER 1975, French
DITES-LUI QUE JE L'AIME 1977, French
L'EFFRONTEE *THE HUSSY* UGC, 1985, French
THE LITTLE THIEF AMLF, 1989, French

JOHN PAUL JONES

Contact: PRS - London, England, 011-44-1-580-5544

SCREAM FOR HELP Lorimar, 1984

KENNETH V. JONES

Contact: PRS - London, England, 011-44-1-580-5544

HOW TO MURDER A RICH UNCLE Columbia, 1957, British
TANK FORCE Columbia, 1958, British
INTENT TO KILL 20th Century-Fox, 1958, British
INDISCREET Warner Bros., 1958, British
ROOM 43 1958, British
TOM THUMB co-composer with David Gamley, MGM, 1958
THE HORSE'S MOUTH adaptation, United Artists, 1958, British
TEN SECONDS TO HELL United Artists, 1959, British
TARZAN THE MAGNIFICENT Paramount, 1960, British
OSCAR WILDE Films Around the World, 1960, British
JAZZ BOAT Columbia, 1960, British
TWO-WAY STRETCH Showcorporation, 1960, British
HORROR HOTEL *THE CITY OF THE DEAD* Trans-World, 1960, British
THE GREEN HELMET MGM, 1961, British
NEARLY A NASTY ACCIDENT Universal, 1961, British
TARZAN GOES TO INDIA MGM, 1962, British-U.S.-Swiss
OPERATION SNATCH Continental, 1962, British
THE BRAIN *VENGEANCE* Garrick, 1962, British-West German
DR. CRIPPEN Warner Bros., 1964, British
THE TOMB OF LIGEIA American International, 1965
MAROC 7
THE PROJECTED MAN 1967, British
BATTLE BENEATH THE EARTH 1968, British
TOWER OF HELL 1971, British
WHO SLEW AUNTIE ROO? American International, 1971, British
HORROR ON SNAPE ISLAND *BEYOND THE FOG* Fanfare, 1972, British
PROFESSOR POPPER'S PROBLEMS 1974

MICK JONES

Contact: PRS - London, England, 011-44-1-580-5544

RUDE BOY co-composer with Joe Strummer, Atlantic Releasing Corporation, 1980

QUINCY JONES

b. March 14, 1933 - Chicago, Illinois
Contact: ASCAP - Los Angeles, 213/466-7681

BOY IN THE TREE 1961
THE PAWNBROKER Landau/Allied Artists, 1965
THE SLENDER THREAD Paramount, 1965
WALK, DON'T RUN Columbia, 1966
ENTER LAUGHING Columbia, 1967
IRONSIDE (TF) Harbour Productions/Universal TV, 1967
IN COLD BLOOD Columbia, 1967
IN THE HEAT OF THE NIGHT ★ United Artists, 1967
THE DEADLY AFFAIR Columbia, 1967, British
THE COUNTERFEIT KILLER Universal, 1968
A DANDY IN ASPIC Columbia, 1968, British
FOR LOVE OF IVY Cinerama Releasing Corporation, 1968
THE HELL WITH HEROES Universal, 1968
SPLIT SECOND TO AN EPITAPH (TF) Universal TV, 1968
THE SPLIT MGM, 1968
THE ITALIAN JOB Paramount, 1969, British
BOB & CAROL & TED & ALICE Columbia, 1969
CACTUS FLOWER Columbia, 1969
JOHN AND MARY 20th Century-Fox, 1969
MACKENNA'S GOLD Columbia, 1969
THE LOST MAN Universal, 1969
LAST OF THE MOBILE HOT-SHOTS Warner Bros., 1970
THEY CALL ME MISTER TIBBS! United Artists, 1970
THE ANDERSON TAPES Columbia, 1971
$ *DOLLARS* Columbia, 1971
BROTHER JOHN Columbia, 1971
HONKY Jack H. Harris Enterprises, 1971
KILLER BY NIGHT (TF) Cinema Center 100, 1972
MAN AND BOY Levitt-Pickman, 1972
THE GETAWAY National General, 1972
THE HOT ROCK 20th Century-Fox, 1972
THE NEW CENTURIONS Columbia, 1972
ROOTS (MS) ☆☆ co-composer with Gerald Fried, Wolper Productions, 1977
THE WIZ ★ adaptation, Universal, 1978
THE COLOR PURPLE ★ co-composer, Warner Bros., 1985

RALPH JONES

THE SLUMBER PARTY MASSACRE Santa Fe, 1982
MY LOVE LETTERS New World, 1983

RON JONES

Contact: Robert Light - Los Angeles, 213/651-1777

NAKED VENGEANCE Concorde/Cinema Group, 1986
KIDNAPPED Virgin Vision, 1987

TONY JONES

HOMEWORK co-composer Jim Wetzel, Jensen Farley Pictures, 1982

TREVOR JONES

b. South Africa
Agent: ICM - Los Angeles, 213/550-4000

THE BENEFICIARY National Film School, 1980, British
BROTHERS AND SISTERS British Film Institute, 1980, British
EXCALIBUR Orion/Warner Bros., 1981, British-Irish
THE SENDER Paramount, 1982, U.S.-British
THE DARK CRYSTAL Universal/AFD, 1982, British
THOSE GLORY, GLORY DAYS Cinecom, 1983, British, originally made for television

NATE AND HAYES *SAVAGE ISLANDS* Paramount, 1983, New Zealand
AND PIGS MUST FLY (TF) S4C, 1984, Welsh
THE LAST DAYS OF POMPEII (MS) David Gerber Company/Columbia TV/Centerpoint Films/RAI, 1984, U.S.-British-Italian
DOCTOR FISCHER OF GENEVA (TF) Consolidated Productions/BBC, 1985, British
THE LAST PLACE ON EARTH (MS) Central Productions/Renegade Films, 1985, British
RUNAWAY TRAIN Cannon, 1985
LABYRINTH Tri-Star, 1986, British
ANGEL HEART Tri-Star, 1987
DOMINICK AND EUGENE Orion, 1988
JUST ASK FOR DIAMOND Kings Road, 1988, British
SWEET LIES Island Pictures, 1988, U.S.-French
MISSISSIPPI BURNING Orion, 1988
SEA OF LOVE Universal, 1989
MURDER BY MOONLIGHT (TF) Tamara Asseyev Productions/London Weekend TV/Viacom, 1989, U.S.-British
DEFENSELESS New Visions, 1990
BAD INFLUENCE Triumph Releasing Corporation, 1990
BY DAWN'S EARLY LIGHT (CTF) HBO/Paravision International, 1990
ARACHNOPHOBIA Buena Vista, 1990

GLENN JORDAN
Agent: Robert Light - Los Angeles, 213/651-1777

MEET THE HOLLOWHEADS Moviestore Entertainment, 1989

WILFRED JOSEPHS
Contact: PRS - London, England, 011-44-1-580-5544

CASH ON DEMAND Columbia, 1962, British
DIE! DIE! MY DARLING *FANATIC* Columbia, 1965, British
THE DEADLY BEES Paramount, 1967, British
MY SIDE OF THE MOUNTAIN Paramount, 1969
DARK PLACES Cinerama Releasing Corporation, 1974, British
SWALLOWS AND AMAZONS LDS, 1974, British
ROBINSON CRUSOE (TF) BBC/NBC TV, 1974, British
ALL CREATURES GREAT AND SMALL (TF) Talent Associates Ltd./EMI, 1975
CALLAN Cinema National, 1975, British
THE UNCANNY 1977, British-Canadian
POPE JOHN PAUL II (TF) Cooperman-DePaul Productions/Taft International Pictures, 1984
MARTIN'S DAY MGM/UA, 1985
MATA HARI Cannon, 1985

PAUL JOST
LAST RITES *DRACULA'S LAST RITES* co-composer with George Small, Cannon, 1980

LAURENCE JUBER
Contact: ASCAP - Los Angeles, 213/466-7681

WORLD GONE WILD Lorimar, 1988
A VERY BRADY CHRISTMAS (TF) The Sherwood Schwartz Co./Paramount Network TV, 1988
THE BRADYS (TF) Brady Productions, Paramount TV, 1990

PHIL JUDD
Contact: APRA - Australia, 011-61-2-922-6422

RIKKY AND PETE co-composer with Eddie Raynor, MGM/UA, 1988, Australian

LARRY JURIS
THE REJUVENATOR SVS Films, 1988

BILL JUSTIS
Contact: ASCAP - Los Angeles, 213/466-7681

SMOKEY AND THE BANDIT co-composer with Jerry Reed and Dick Feller, Universal, 1977
HOOPER Warner Bros., 1978
THE VILLAIN Columbia, 1979

SUSAN JUSTIN
FORBIDDEN WORLD New World, 1982
THE FINAL TERROR Aquarius, 1984
GRUNT! THE WRESTLING MOVIE New World, 1985

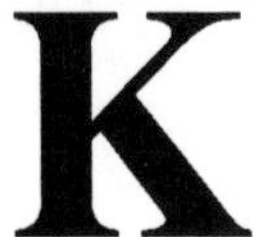

ALFI KABILJO
b. Yugoslavia
Agent: Robert Light - Los Angeles, 213/651-1777

FALL OF ITALY Yugoslavian
THE MISS Yugoslavian
DEPS 1974, Yugoslavian
GET IT MAN Yugoslavian
ACCUSED Yugoslavian
THE DREAM ROSE Yugoslavian
ANNO DOMINI 1573 1976, Yugoslavian
FLYERS OF THE OPEN SKIES 1977, Yugoslavian
OCCUPATION IN 26 PICTURES 1978, Yugoslavian
THE JOURNALIST 1979, Yugoslavian
SLOW MOTION 1979, Yugoslavian
THE PEASANT UPRISING Yugoslavian
CHRONICLE OF A CRIME Yugoslavian
THE AFTERNOON OF A PEASANT Yugoslavian
TRAVEL TO THE PLACE OF THE ACCIDENT Yugoslavian
PROMISED LAND Yugoslavian
HONEYMOON 1983, Yugoslavian
NIGHT AFTER DEATH 1983, Yugoslavian
THE AMBASSADOR MGM/UA/Cannon, 1984
GYMKATA MGM/UA, 1985
THE GIRL IN THE PICTURE Samuel Goldwyn Company, 1986, British
SKY BANDITS Galaxy International, 1986, British
SLEEP WELL, MY LOVE Planbourg Films, 1987
FEAR CineTel Films, 1988

MICHAEL KAMEN
b. 1948 - New York, New York
Agent: Gorfaine-Schwartz - Burbank, 818/954-9500

THE NEXT MAN Allied Artists, 1976
LIZA'S PIONEER DIARY (TF) Nell Cox Films, 1976
BETWEEN THE LINES Midwest Film Productions, 1977

STUNTS New Line Cinema, 1977
S*H*E (TF) Martin Bregman Productions, 1980
POLYESTER co-composer with Chris Stein, New Line Cinema, 1981
VENOM Paramount, 1982, British
PINK FLOYD - THE WALL MGM/UA, 1982, British
ANGELO, MY LOVE Cinecom, 1983
THE DEAD ZONE Paramount, 1983, Canadian
BRAZIL Universal, 1985, British
LIFEFORCE additional music, Tri-Star, 1985
EDGE OF DARKNESS (MS) co-composer with Eric Clapton, BBC/Lionheart Television International, 1986, British
HIGHLANDER 20th Century Fox, 1986, British-U.S.
MONA LISA Island Pictures, 1986, British
SHANGHAI SURPRISE co-composer with George Harrison, MGM/UA, 1986, British-U.S.
SHOOT FOR THE SUN (TF) co-composer with Ray Cooper, BBC-TV, 1986, British
RITA, SUE AND BOB, TOO Orion Classics, 1987, British
LETHAL WEAPON co-composer with Eric Clapton, Warner Bros., 1987
ADVENTURES IN BABYSITTING Buena Vista, 1987
SOMEONE TO WATCH OVER ME Columbia, 1987
SUSPECT Tri-Star, 1987
ACTION JACKSON Lorimar, 1988
DIE HARD 20th Century Fox, 1988
THE RAGGEDY RAWNEY HandMade Films, 1988, British
CRUSOE Island Pictures, 1988, U.S.-British
FOR QUEEN AND COUNTRY Atlantic Releasing, 1988, British
HOMEBOY co-composer with Eric Clapton, Redbury Ltd./Elliott Kastner Productions, 1988
THE ADVENTURES OF BARON MUNCHAUSEN Columbia, 1989, British
ROOFTOPS co-composer with Dave A. Stewart, New Century/Vista, 1989
DEAD-BANG co-composer with Gary Chang, Warner Bros., 1989
ROADHOUSE MGM/UA, 1989
RENEGADES Universal, 1989
LICENSE TO KILL MGM/UA, 1989, British
LETHAL WEAPON 2 co-composer with Eric Clapton and David Sanborn, Warner Bros., 1989
THE KRAYS Rank, 1990, British
DIE HARD II 20th Century Fox, 1990

JOHN KANDER

b. March 18, 1927 - Kansas City, Missouri
Contact: ICM - Los Angeles, 213/550-4000

SOMETHING FOR EVERYONE National General, 1970, British
KRAMER VS. KRAMER Columbia, 1979
STILL OF THE NIGHT MGM/UA, 1982
BLUE SKIES AGAIN Warner Bros., 1983
AN EARLY FROST (TF) ☆ NBC Productions, 1985
I WANT TO GO HOME MK2, 1989, French

ARTIE KANE

Agent: Carol Faith - Beverly Hills, 213/274-0776

THE BAT PEOPLE *IT LIVES BY NIGHT* American International, 1974
THE NEW LOVE BOAT (TF) additional music, Aaron Spelling Productions, 1977
LOOKING FOR MR. GOODBAR Paramount, 1977
EYES OF LAURA MARS Columbia, 1978
DEVIL DOG: THE HOUND OF HELL (TF) Zeitman-Landers-Roberts Productions, 1978
A QUESTION OF GUILT (TF) Lorimar Productions, 1978
YOUNG LOVE, FIRST LOVE (TF) Lorimar Productions, 1979
MURDER CAN HURT YOU! (TF) Aaron Spelling Productions, 1980
NIGHT OF THE JUGGLER Columbia, 1980
WRONG IS RIGHT Columbia, 1982
MILLION DOLLAR INFIELD (TF) CBS Entertainment, 1982
CONCRETE BEAT (TF) Picturemaker Productions/ Viacom, 1984
LONG TIME GONE (TF) Picturemaker Productions/ABC Circle Films, 1986
FATAL CONFESSION: A FATHER DOWLING MYSTERY (TF) co-composer with Dick DeBenedictis, Fred Silverman Company/Strathmore Productions/ Viacom, 1987
THE RED SPIDER (TF) CBS Entertainment, 1988
TERROR ON HIGHWAY 91 (TF) Katy Film Productions, 1989
MAN AGAINST THE MOB: THE CHINATOWN MURDERS (TF) von Zerneck-Sertner Productions, 1989

IGO KANTOR

Contact: BMI - Los Angeles, 213/659-9109

GOOD MORNING...AND GOODBYE Eve, 1967
RUSS MEYER'S VIXEN Eve, 1968
CHERRY, HARRY AND RACQUEL Eve, 1969
THE PROJECTIONIST Maron Films Limited, 1971
THE COMEBACK TRAIL Dynamite Entertainment/ Rearguard Productions, 1971
SCORCHY American International, 1976

ELLIOTT KAPLAN

b. Boston, Massachusetts
Agent: Robert Light - Los Angeles, 213/651-1777

THE PLAYGROUND General, 1965
THE SQUARE ROOT OF ZERO 1965
FINNEGANS WAKE Evergreen Films, 1965
CRY BLOOD, APACHE Golden Eagle International, 1970
STRANGE NEW WORLD (TF) co-composer with Richard Clements, Warner Bros. TV, 1975
MAN ON THE OUTSIDE (TF) Universal TV, 1975
YOU LIE SO DEEP, MY LOVE (TF) Universal TV, 1975
BRIDGER (TF) Universal TV, 1976
THE FOOD OF THE GODS American International, 1976
A MARRIED MAN (TF) London Weekend TV Productions/ Lionhearted Productions, 1984

SOL KAPLAN

b. 1913 - New York

TALES OF MANHATTAN 20th Century-Fox, 1942
UNEXPECTED RICHES MGM, 1942
APACHE TRAIL MGM, 1943
HOLLOW TRIUMPH Eagle Lion, 1948
REIGN OF TERROR Eagle Lion, 1949
DOWN MEMORY LANE Eagle Lion, 1949
TRAPPED Eagle Lion, 1949
PORT OF NEW YORK Eagle Lion, 1949
711 OCEAN DRIVE Columbia, 1950
MISTER 880 20th Century-Fox, 1951
HALLS OF MONTEZUMA 20th Century-Fox, 1951
I'D CLIMB THE HIGHEST MOUNTAIN 20th Century-Fox, 1951

I CAN GET IT FOR YOU WHOLESALE 20th Century-Fox, 1951
RAWHIDE 20th Century-Fox, 1951
HOUSE ON TELEGRAPH HILL 20th Century-Fox, 1951
THE SECRET OF CONVICT LAKE 20th Century-Fox, 1951
ALICE IN WONDERLAND 1951
RED SKIES OF MONTANA 20th Century-Fox, 1952
RETURN OF THE TEXAN 20th Century-Fox, 1952
KANGAROO 20th Century-Fox, 1952
DIPLOMATIC COURIER 20th Century-Fox, 1952
WAY OF A GAUCHO 20th Century-Fox, 1952
SOMETHING FOR THE BIRDS 20th Century-Fox, 1952
NIAGRA 20th Century-Fox, 1953
TREASURE OF THE GOLDEN CONDOR 20th Century-Fox, 1953
SALT OF THE EARTH Independent Productions, 1954
THE BURGLAR Columbia, 1956
HAPPY ANNIVERSARY United Artists, 1959
GIRL OF THE NIGHT Warner Bros., 1960
THE VICTORS Columbia, 1963
THE GUNS OF AUGUST (FD) Universal, 1964
THE YOUNG LOVERS MGM, 1964
THE SPY WHO CAME IN FROM THE COLD Paramount, 1965, British
JUDITH Paramount, 1965, U.S.-British-Israeli
WINCHESTER '73 (TF) Universal TV, 1967
NEW YORK CITY—THE MOST 1968
SHADOW ON THE LAND (TF) Screen Gems/ Columbia Pictures TV, 1968
EXPLOSION 1969, Canadian
LIVING FREE Columbia, 1972, British
LIES MY FATHER TOLD ME Columbia, 1975, Canadian
OVER THE EDGE Orion/Warner Bros., 1979
THE GOLDEN GATE MURDERS (TF) Universal TV, 1979

DANA KAPROFF

b. April 24, 1954 - Los Angeles, California
Agent: Bart-Milander - North Hollywood, 818/761-4040

ONCE AN EAGLE (MS) Universal TV, 1976
EMPIRE OF THE ANTS American International, 1977
EXO-MAN (TF) Universal TV, 1977
SPIDER-MAN (TF) Charles Fries Productions, 1977
THE LAST OF THE GOOD GUYS (TF) Columbia TV, 1978
THE LATE GREAT PLANET EARTH (FD) Robert Amram Productions, 1979
WHEN A STRANGER CALLS Columbia, 1979
THE ULTIMATE IMPOSTER (TF) Universal TV, 1979
BELLE STARR (TF) Entheos Unlimited Productions/ Hanna-Barbera Productions, 1980
THE BIG RED ONE United Artists, 1980
SCARED STRAIGHT! ANOTHER STORY (TF) Golden West TV, 1980
INMATES: A LOVE STORY (TF) Henerson-Hirsch Productions/Finnegan Associates, 1981
BERLIN TUNNEL 21 (TF) Cypress Point Productions/ Filmways, 1981
DEATH VALLEY Universal, 1982
PANDEMONIUM MGM/UA, 1982
THE GOLDEN SEAL co-composer with John Barry, Samuel Goldwyn Company, 1983
SECOND SIGHT: A LOVE STORY (TF) Entheos Unlimited Productions/T.T.C. Enterprises, 1984
CHILLER (TF) Polar Film Corporation/J.D. Feigleson Productions, 1985
BETWEEN THE DARKNESS AND THE DAWN (TF) Doris Quinlan Productions/Warner Bros. TV, 1985
A WINNER NEVER QUITS (TF) Blatt-Singer Productions/ Columbia TV, 1985
A SMOKY MOUNTAIN CHRISTMAS (TF) Sandollar Productions, 1986
FIREFIGHTER (TF) Forest Hills Productions/ Embassy TV, 1986
DOCTORS WILDE (TF) Columbia TV, 1987
THE STICK Distant Horizon International, 1987, South African
DOIN' TIME ON PLANET EARTH Cannon, 1988
I SAW WHAT YOU DID (TF) Universal TV, 1988
GLITZ (TF) Robert Cooper Films, 1988
THE PEOPLE ACROSS THE LAKE (TF) Bill McCutchen Productions/Columbia TV, 1988
FULL EXPOSURE: THE SEX TAPES SCANDAL (TF) Von Zemeck-Sertner Films, 1989
THE CHINA LAKE MURDERS (CTF) Papazian-Hirsch Entertainment/MCA TV, 1990

EDDIE KARAM

Contact: CAPAC - Ontario, Canada, 1-416-924-4427

TULIPS Avco-Embassy, 1981, Canadian

FRED KARGER

Contact: ASCAP - Los Angeles, 213/466-7681

NECROMANCY American International, 1972
CHATTER-BOX American International, 1977

FRED KARLIN

b. June 16, 1936 - Chicago, Illinois
Agent: Robert Light - Los Angeles, 213/651-1777

UP THE DOWN STAIRCASE Warner Bros., Warner Bros., 1967
YOURS, MINE AND OURS United Artists, 1968
THE STALKING MOON National General, 1969
THE STERILE CUCKOO Paramount, 1969
LOVERS AND OTHER STRANGERS Cinerama Releasing Corporation, 1970
THE BABY MAKER National General, 1970
MARRIAGE OF A YOUNG STOCKBROKER 20th Century-Fox, 1971
MR. & MRS. BO JO JONES (TF) 20th Century-Fox TV, 1971
BELIEVE IN ME MGM, 1971
THE LITTLE ARK National General, 1972
EVERY LITTLE CROOK AND NANNY MGM, 1972
WESTWORLD MGM, 1973
THE MAN WHO COULD TALK TO KIDS (TF) Tomorrow Entertainment, 1973
CHOSEN SURVIVORS Columbia, 1974
MIXED COMPANY United Artists, 1974
IT COULDN'T HAPPEN TO A NICER GUY (TF) The Jozak Company, 1974
BAD RONALD (TF) Lorimar Productions, 1974
THE GRAVY TRAIN *THE DION BROTHERS* Columbia, 1974
BORN INNOCENT (TF) Tomorrow Entertainment, 1974
THE AUTOBIOGRAPHY OF MISS JANE PITTMAN (TF) ☆☆ Tomorrow Entertainment, 1974
PUNCH AND JODY (TF) Metromedia Producers Corporation/Stonehenge Productions, 1974
THE SPIKES GANG United Artists, 1974
THE TAKE Columbia, 1974
DEATH BE NOT PROUD (TF) Good Housekeeping Productions/Westfall Productions, 1975

BABY BLUE MARINE Columbia, 1976
LEADBELLY Paramount, 1976
WOMAN OF THE YEAR (TF) MGM TV, 1976
DAWN: PORTRAIT OF A TEENAGE RUNAWAY (TF) Douglas S. Cramer Productions, 1976
WANTED: THE SUNDANCE WOMAN (TF) 20th Century-Fox TV, 1976
FUTUREWORLD American International, 1976
JOE PANTHER Artists Creation & Associates, 1976
THE DEATH OF RICHIE (TF) Henry Jaffe Enterprises/NBC TV, 1977
ALEXANDER: THE OTHER SIDE OF DAWN (TF) Douglas Cramer Productions, 1977
LUCAN (TF) MGM TV, 1977
THE TRIAL OF LEE HARVEY OSWALD (TF) Charles Fries Productions, 1977
BILLY: PORTRAIT OF A STREET KID (TF) Mark Carliner Productions, 1977
THE HOSTAGE HEART (TF) Andrew J. Fenady Associates/MGM TV, 1977
HAVING BABIES II (TF) The Jozak Company, 1977
THE MAN FROM ATLANTIS (TF) Solow Production Company, 1977
GREASED LIGHTNING Warner Bros., 1977
MINSTREL MAN (TF) ☆ Roger Gimbel Productions/EMI TV, 1977
GREEN EYES (TF) ABC TV, 1977
DEADMAN'S CURVE (TF) Roger Gimbel Productions/EMI TV, 1978
KISS MEETS THE PHANTOM OF THE PARK (TF) Hanna-Barbera Productions/KISS Productions, 1978
FOREVER (TF) Roger Gimbel Productions/EMI TV, 1978
ROLL OF THUNDER, HEAR MY CRY (TF) Tomorrow Entertainment, 1978
LEAVE YESTERDAY BEHIND (TF) ABC Circle Films, 1978
JUST ME & YOU (TF) Roger Gimbel Productions/EMI, 1978
BUD AND LOU (TF) Bob Banner Associates, 1978
MORE THAN FRIENDS (TF) Reiner-Mishkin Productions/Columbia TV, 1978
LADY OF THE HOUSE (TF) Metromedia Productions, 1978
WHO'LL SAVE OUR CHILDREN? (TF) Time-Life Productions, 1978
LONG JOURNEY BACK (TF) Lorimar Productions, 1978
MEAN DOG BLUES American International, 1978
THE AWAKENING LAND (MS) ☆ Bensen-Kuhn-Sagal Productions/Warner Bros. TV, 1978
THIS MAN STANDS ALONE (TF) Roger Gimbel Productions/EMI TV/Abby Mann Productions, 1979
SAMURAI (TF) Danny Thomas Productions/Universal TV, 1979
RAVAGERS Columbia, 1979
VAMPIRE (TF) MTM Enterprises, 1979
...AND YOUR NAME IS JONAH (TF) Charles Fries Productions, 1979
TRANSPLANT (TF) Time-Life Productions, 1979
AND BABY MAKES SIX (TF) Alan Landsburg Productions, 1979
STRANGERS: THE STORY OF A MOTHER AND A DAUGHTER (TF) Chris-Rose Productions, 1979
WALKING THROUGH THE FIRE (TF) Time-Life Films, 1979
SEX AND THE SINGLE PARENT (TF) Time-Life Productions, 1979
TOPPER (TF) Cosmo Productions/Robert A. Papazian Productions, 1979
CALIFORNIA DREAMING American International, 1979
RAVAGERS Columbia, 1979
BLIND AMBITION (MS) Parts 3 and 4, Time-Life Productions, 1979
IKE (MS) ABC Circle Films, 1979
ONCE UPON A FAMILY (TF) Universal TV, 1980
THE SECRET WAR OF JACKIE'S GIRLS (TF) Public Arts Productions/Penthouse Productions/Universal TV, 1980
MARRIAGE IS ALIVE AND WELL (TF) Lorimar Productions, 1980
A TIME FOR MIRACLES (TF) ABC Circle Films, 1980
LOVING COUPLES 20th Century-Fox, 1980
THE PLUTONIUM INCIDENT (TF) Time-Life Productions, 1980
FIGHTING BACK (TF) MTM Enterprises, 1980
HOMEWORD BOUND (TF) ☆ Tisch-Avnet Productions, 1980
CLOUD DANCER Blossom, 1980
MY KIDNAPPER, MY LOVE (TF) Roger Gimbel Productions/EMI TV, 1980
MOM, THE WOLFMAN AND ME (TF) Time-Life Productions, 1981
THORNWELL (TF) MTM Enterprises, 1981
JACQUELINE SUSANN'S VALLEY OF THE DOLLS 1981 (MS) 20th Century-Fox TV, 1981
WE'RE FIGHTING BACK (TF) Highgate Pictures, 1981
BROKEN PROMISE (TF) EMI TV, 1981
THE FIVE OF ME (TF) Jack Farren Productions/Factor-Newland Production Corporation, 1981
BITTER HARVEST (TF) Charles Fries Productions, 1981
NOT IN FRONT OF THE CHILDREN (TF) Tamtco Productions/The Edward S. Feldman Company, 1982
MISSING CHILDREN: A MOTHER'S STORY (TF) Kayden-Gleason Productions, 1982
INSIDE THE THIRD REICH (TF) ABC Circle Films, 1982
DEADLY ENCOUNTER (TF) co-composer with Michael Hoenig, Roger Gimbel Productions/EMI TV/Promises Productions, 1982
IN DEFENSE OF KIDS (TF) MTM Enterprises, 1983
ONE COOKS, THE OTHER DOESN'T (TF) Kaleidoscope Films Ltd./Lorimar Productions, 1983
BABY SISTER (TF) Moonlight Productions II, 1983
NIGHT PARTNERS (TF) Moonlight Productions II, 1983
THE GIFT OF LOVE: A CHRISTMAS STORY (TF) Telecom Entertainment/Amanda Productions, 1983
CALAMITY JANE (TF) CBS Entertainment, 1983
KIDS DON'T TELL (TF) Chris-Rose Productions/Viacom Productions, 1985
ROBERT KENNEDY AND HIS TIMES (TF) Chris-Rose Productions/Columbia TV, 1985
HOSTAGE FLIGHT (TF) Frank von Zerneck Films, 1985
DREAM WEST (MS) Sunn Classic Pictures, 1986
INTIMATE STRANGERS (TF) Nederlander TV & Film Productions/Telepictures Productions, 1986
VASECTOMY: A DELICATE MATTER Seymour Borde & Associates, 1986
A PLACE TO CALL HOME (TF) Big Deal Productions/Crawford Productions/Embassy TV, 1987, U.S.-Australian
CELEBRATION FAMILY (TF) Frank von Zerneck Films, 1987
LADY MOBSTER (TF) Danjul Films/Frank von Zerneck Productions, 1988
WHAT PRICE VICTORY (TF) Wolper Productions/Warner Bros. TV, 1988
MOVING TARGET (TF) Lewis B. Chesler Productions/Bateman Company Productions/Finnegan-Pinchuk Company/MGM-UA TV, 1988
DADAH IS DEATH (TF) Steve Krantz Productions/Roadshow, Coote & Carroll Productions/Samuel Goldwyn TV, 1988, U.S.-Australian
BRIDGE TO SILENCE (TF) ☆ Fries Entertainment, 1989
FEAR STALK (TF) Donald March Productions/ITC, 1989

FRED KARNS

Contact: BMI - Los Angeles, 213/659-9109

FAMILY BUSINESS (TF) Screenscope Inc./South Carolina Educational TV Network, 1983
THE IMAGEMAKER Castle Hill Prods., 1986

LAURA KARPMAN

Agent: Bart-Milander - North Hollywood, 818/761-4040

MY BROTHER'S WIFE (TF) Adam Productions/Robert Greenwald Productions, 1989

AL KASHA

b. January 22, 1937 - New York, New York
Agent: Robert Light - Los Angeles, 213/651-1777

WHO KILLED TEDDY BEAR? Magna, 1965
FAT SPY Magna, 1966
TRAPPED BENEATH THE SEA (TF) co-composer with Joel Hirschhorn, ABC Circle Films, 1974
SOMEONE I TOUCHED (TF) Charles Fries Productions/Stonehenge Productions, 1975

FRED KATZ

b. 1919 - Brooklyn, New York
Contact: ASCAP - Los Angeles, 213/466-7681

A BUCKET OF BLOOD American International, 1959
THE WASP WOMAN American International, 1959

STEVE KATZ

Contact: BMI - Los Angeles, 213/659-9109

HOME REMEDY Kino International, 1988

EMILIO KAUDERER

Agent: Robert Light - Los Angeles, 213/651-1777

LOPEZ'S SONS Aries, Argentine
LA DISCOTECA DEL AMOR Aries Films, 1980, Argentine
HOLIDAY LOVE Aries Films/Microfon, Argentine
TIEMPO DE REVANCHA Aries Films, 1981, Argentine
SWEET MONEY Aries Films, Argentine
ULTIMOS DIAS DE LA VICTIMA Aries Films, 1982, Argentine
SEARCH FOR THE LOST DIAMOND Microfon, Argentine
GRAY OF ABSENCE Argencine, Argentine
IN DANGEROUS COMPANY Manson International, 1988
FISTFIGHTER Taurus Entertainment, 1989
SLASH DANCE Glencoe Entertainment, 1989

GENE KAUER

Contact: ASCAP - Los Angeles, 213/466-7681

THE ADVENTURES OF THE WILDERNESS FAMILY co-composer with Douglas Lackey, Pacific International, 1976
ACROSS THE GREAT DIVIDE co-composer with Douglas Lackey, Pacific International, 1976
FURTHER ADVENTURES OF THE WILDERNESS FAMILY co-composer with Douglas Lackey, Pacific International, 1978

FRED KAZ

Contact: BMI - Los Angeles, 213/659-9109

THE MONITORS Commonwealth United, 1969
LITTLE MURDERS 20th Century-Fox, 1970

JOHN KEANE

Contact: BMI - Los Angeles, 213/659-9109

NANOU Umbrella Films/Arion, 1986, British-French
THE KITCHEN TOTO Cannon, 1988
A VERY BRITISH COUP (TF) Skreba Films, 1988, British
CHATTAHOOCHEE Hemdale, 1989, British

SHANE KEISTER

Contact: BMI - Los Angeles, 213/659-9109

ERNEST GOES TO CAMP Buena Vista, 1987

ROGER KELLAWAY

Contact: BMI - Los Angeles, 213/659-9109

PAPER LION United Artists, 1968
THE PSYCHIATRIST: GOD BLESS THE CHILDREN (TF) Universal TV/Arena Productions, 1970
WHO FEARS THE DEVIL *THE LEGEND OF HILLBILLY JOHN* Jack H. Harris Enterprises, 1974
LEGACY Kino International, 1976
THE MOUSE AND HIS CHILD (AF) Sanrio, 1977
SHARON: PORTRAIT OF A MISTRESS (TF) Moonlight Productions/Paramount Pictures TV, 1977
THE MAFU CAGE Clouds Production, 1979
THE DARK Film Ventures, 1979
SILENT SCREAM American Cinema, 1980
SATAN'S MISTRESS MPM, 1982

RICKEY KELLER

Contact: BMI - Los Angeles, 213/659-9109

GETTING IT ON Comworld, 1983

ARTHUR KEMPEL

Agent: Robert Light - Los Angeles, 213/651-1777
Contact: Underscore Associates - Burbank, 818/845-4000

GRADUATION DAY IFI-Scope III, 1981
IT'S CALLED MURDER Lima Productions, 1982
THE LAST HORROR SHOW *WACKO* Jensen Farley, 1983
FLESHBURN Crown International, 1984
THE COMING Alan Landsburg Productions
FATHER DOWLING: THE MISSING BODY MYSTERY (TF) Viacom Productions/NBC TV, 1989
A CRY IN THE WILD Concorde/New Horizons Corp., 1990
HIT MAN (TF) MGM-UA, 1990

RANDY KERBER

Contact: BMI - Los Angeles, 213/659-9109

THE COLOR PURPLE ★ co-composer, Warner Bros., 1985
DATE WITH AN ANGEL DEG, 1987

ROBERT KESSLER

Contact: BMI - Los Angeles, 213/659-9109

BUM RAP co-composer with Ethan Neuburg, Millenium, 1988

ROBERT KIKUCHI-YNGOJO
CHAN IS MISSING New Yorker, 1982

WOJCIECH KILAR
b. Poland
Contact: ZAIKS - Warsaw, Poland, 011-48-2-277-577

VAMPIRE *UPIOR* 1968, Polish
LOKIS 1970, Polish
THE BEAR 1970, Polish
THE TASTE OF THE BLACK EARTH 1970, Polish
THE STAR OF THE SEASON 1971, Polish
PEARL IN THE CROWN 1972, Polish
THE WICKET GATE 1974, Polish
LAND OF PROMISE 1975, Polish
QUARTERLY BALANCE-TAKING 1975
CAMOUFLAGE Libra, 1977, Polish
LEPER 1977, Polish
THE SPIRAL 1978, Polish
DAVID Kino International, 1979, 1979, West German
THE KING AND THE MOCKINGBIRD Gaumont, 1980, French
FROM A FAR COUNTRY *POPE JOHN PAUL II (TF)* Trans World Film/ITC/RAI/Film Polski, 1981, British-Italian-Polish
IMPERATIV Telefilm Saar, 1982, West German
LE POUVOIR DU MAL Films Moliere, 1985, French-Italian
WHEREVER YOU ARE Mark Forstater Productions/ Gerhard Schmidt Filmproduktion/Film Polski, 1988, British-West German-Polish
THE TURNING TABLE (AF) Neuf de Coeur, 1988, French
KORCZAK Filmstudio Perspektywa, 1990, Polish

BRUCE KIMMEL
b. December 8, 1947 - Los Angeles, California
Office: The Culver Studios, 9336 Washington Blvd., Culver City 90230, 213/559-0346

THE ALL-AMERICAN WOMAN Conde Enterprises, 1974
THE FIRST NUDIE MUSICAL Paramount, 1976
THE RATINGS GAME (CTF) additional music, Imagination-New Street Productions, 1984
PRIME SUSPECT S.V.S., 1989

CAROL KING
Contact: BMI - Los Angeles, 213/659-9109

MURPHY'S ROMANCE Columbia, 1985

DENIS KING
Contact: PRS - London, England, 011-44-1-580-5544

PRIVATES ON PARADE Orion Classics, 1983, British

GERSHON KINGSLEY
SILENT NIGHT, BLOODY NIGHT Cannon, 1974
DEATHHOUSE Cannon, 1981

BASIL KIRCHIN
Contact: PRS - London, England, 011-44-1-580-5544

THE SHUTTERED ROOM Warner Bros., 1966, British
ASSIGNMENT K Columbia, 1968, British
NEGATIVES Continental, 1968, British
THE STRANGE AFFAIR Paramount, 1968, British
I START COUNTING United Artists, 1969, British
THE ABOMINABLE DR. PHIBES American International, 1971, British
THE MUTATIONS Columbia, 1974, British

OSAMU KITAJIMA
Contact: BMI - Los Angeles, 213/659-9109

CAPTIVE HEARTS MGM/UA, 1987

KITARO
Agent: MCEG - Santa Monica, 213/315-7800

QUEEN MILLENIA (AF) 1982
CATCH YOUR DREAMS 1983, West German
SAMUEL LOUNT Moonshine Prods., 1985, Canadian

DAVID KITAY
Contact: ICM - Los Angeles, 213/550-4000

UNDER THE BOARDWALK New World, 1988
LOOK WHO'S TALKING Tri-Star, 1989
SKETCHES MCEG, 1990
BORIS AND NATASHA MCEG, 1990

KEVIN KLINGER
Contact: Richard Emler - Los Angeles, 213/651-0222
Contact: 15135 Burbank Blvd., Suite 107, Van Nuys, CA 91411, 818/901-0877

HARD TICKET TO HAWAII Malibu Bay Films, 1987
ARIZONA HEAT Spectrum Entertainment, 1988
PICASSO TRIGGER Malibu Bay Films, 1988
AFTERSHOCK Bonaire Films, 1989
NECROMANCER co-composer with Gary Stockdale and Bob Mamet, Bonnaire Films, 1989
DYING TIME Overseas Film Group, 1990
WELCOME TO OBLIVION Concorde Pictures, 1990
CHECKERED FLAG New World Entertainment, 1990

JURGEN KNIEPER
Contact: GEMA - West Germany, 011-49-89621400

THE SCARLET LETTER Bauer International, 1973, West German-Spanish
THE WRONG MOVE New Yorker, 1975, West German
DIE ANGST DES TORMAN West German
AUF BIEGEN UND BRECH West German
OUTPUT West German
EIEDRIEBE West German
LIEB VATTERLAND MAGS West German
THE AMERICAN FRIEND New Yorker, 1977, West German-French
DERBY FIEBER USA West German
KALTE HEIMAT *COLD HOMELAND* Triangel Film, 1979, West German
ARABISCHE NACHTE West German
DEUTSCHLAND, BLEICHE West German
ALLES IN EIMER West German
CHRISTIANE F. additional music, 20th Century-Fox, 1981, West German
KAUBERGERG West German
DABBEL TRABBEL West German
MENSCHEN AUS GLASS West German
THE STATE OF THINGS Gray City, 1982, U.S.-West German-Portugese
EDITH'S DIARY 1983, West German
DER KLEINE BRUDER *THE LITTLE BROTHER* 1983, West German

FLUGEL UND FESSELN West German
EINMAL KU'DAMM UND Z West German
THE RIVER'S EDGE Island Pictures, 1986
DES TEUFELS PARADIES West German
WINGS OF DESIRE *DER HIMMEL UBER BERLIN* Orion Classics, 1987, West German-French
GETEILTE LIEBE *MANEUVERS* Helma Sanders-Brahms/Metropolis Films, 1988, West German
END OF THE NIGHT In Absentia, 1990

MARK KNOPFLER
Contact: PRS - London, England, 011-44-1-580-5544

LOCAL HERO Warner Bros., 1983, British-Scottish
CAL Warner Bros., 1984, Irish
COMFORT AND JOY Universal, 1984, British-Scottish
THE PRINCESS BRIDE 20th Century Fox, 1987
LAST EXIT TO BROOKLYN Cinecom, 1990

BUZ KOHAN
Contact: ASCAP - Los Angeles, 213/466-7681

THE NEW ADVENTURES OF HEIDI (TF) Pierre Cossette Enterprises, 1978

DAVID KOLE
Agent: Robert Light - Los Angeles, 213/651-1777

THE KAREN CARPENTER STORY (TF) Weintraub Entertainment Group, 1989
CHALLENGER (TF) The Indie Production Company/King Phoenix Entertainment/George Englund Productions, 1990

REIJIRO KOROKU
b. Japan
Contact: JASRAC - Tokyo, Japan, 011-81-3-502-6551

GODZILLA 1985 New World, 1985

MARK KORVEN
Contact: Pro-Canada - Canada, 1-416-445-8700

I'VE HEARD THE MERMAIDS SINGING Miramax, 1987

ANDRZEJ KORZYNSKI
b. Poland
Contact: ZAIKS - Warsaw, Poland, 011-48-2-277-577

THE THIRD PART OF THE NIGHT 1971, Polish
SALVATION 1973, Polish
TAKE IT EASY 1974, Polish
DOCTOR JUDYM 1976, Polish
MAN OF MARBLE New Yorker, 1977, Polish
JOERG RATGEB, PAINTER 1978, Polish
MAN OF IRON United Artists Classics, 1981, Polish
POSSESSION Gaumont, 1981, French-West German

IRWIN KOSTAL
b. October 1, 1911 - Chicago, Illinois
Contact: ASCAP - Los Angeles, 213/466-7681

WEST SIDE STORY ★★ adaptation, United Artists, 1961
MARY POPPINS ★ adaptation, Buena Vista, 1964
THE SOUND OF MUSIC ★★ adaptation, 20th Century-Fox, 1965
BEDKNOBS AND BROOMSTICKS ★ adaptation, Buena Vista, 1971
THE BLUE BIRD 20th Century-Fox, 1976, U.S.-Soviet
PETE'S DRAGON ★ adaptation, Buena Vista, 1977

LEO KOTTKE
Contact: ASCAP - Los Angeles, 213/466-7681

DAYS OF HEAVEN additional music, Paramount, 1978
LITTLE TREASURE Tri-Star, 1985
FAT GUY GOES NUTZOID Troma, 1987

ROBERT KRAFT
Agent: Bart-Milander - North Hollywood, 818/761-4040

SEVEN MINUTES IN HEAVEN Warner Bros., 1986

WILLIAM KRAFT
b. Chicago, Illinois
Agent: Richard Emler - Los Angeles, 213/651-0222

PSYCHIC KILLER Avco Embassy, 1975
AVALANCHE New World, 1978
BILL (TF) Alan Landsburg Productions, 1981
FIRE AND ICE (AF) 20th Century Fox, 1983

BERNARD KRAUSE
Contact: BMI - Los Angeles, 213/659-9109

DARK CIRCLE (FD) co-composer with Gary Remal, Independent Documentary Group, 1983

RAOUL KRAUSHAAR
b. 1908 - Paris

(The following is an incomplete list of Mr. Kraushaar's credits.)

PREHISTORIC WOMEN co-composer with Mort Glickman, United Artists, 1950
BRIDE OF THE GORILLA co-composer with Mort Glickman, Realart, 1951
UNTAMED WOMEN co-composer with Mort Glickman, United Artists, 1952
INVADERS FROM MARS co-composer with Mort Glickman, 20th Century-Fox, 1953
THE GOLDEN MISTRESS United Artists, 1954
BACK FROM THE DEAD co-composer with Dave Kahn, 20th Century-Fox, 1957
THE UNKNOWN TERROR co-composer with Dave Kahn, 20th Century-Fox, 1957
THE 30-FOOT BRIDE OF CANDY ROCK Columbia, 1959
JESSE JAMES MEETS FRANKENSTEIN'S DAUGHTER 1966
CHILDREN OF DIVORCE (TF) co-composer with Minette Alton, Christiana Productions/Marble Arch Productions, 1980

TIM KROG
Contact: BMI - Los Angeles, 213/659-9109

THE BOOGEY MAN Jerry Gross Organization, 1980
BOOGEYMAN II 1983

ZANE KRONJE
SCHWEITZER Sugar Entertainment, 1990

DAVID KRYSTAL
Contact: CAPAC - Ontario, Canada, 1-416-924-4427

BUYING TIME MGM/UA, 1989

CHRISTIAN KUNERT
Contact: SACEM - France, 011-33-14-747-5650

SINGING THE BLUES IN RED *FATHERLAND* co-composer with Gerulf Pannach, Angelika Films, 1986, British-West German-French

RUSS KUNKEL
CERTAIN FURY co-composer with Bill Payne and George Massenburg, New World, 1985, Canadian
SMOOTH TALK co-composer with Bill Payne and George Massenburg, Spectrafilm, 1985

DAVID KURTZ
Contact: ASCAP - Los Angeles, 213/466-7681

BLADE IN HONG KONG (TF) Becker Enterprises Productions, 1985
THE LAST ELECTRIC KNIGHT (TF) Walt Disney Productions, 1986
IMPURE THOUGHTS ASA Communications, 1986
HUNK Crown International, 1987

MILAN KYMLICKA
Contact: CAPAC - Ontario, Canada, 1-416-924-4427

BABAR: THE MOVIE New Line Cinema, 1989

DOUGLAS LACKEY
Contact: ASCAP - Los Angeles, 213/466-7681

THE ADVENTURES OF THE WILDERNESS FAMILY co-composer with Gene Kauer, Pacific International, 1976
ACROSS THE GREAT DIVIDE co-composer with Gene Kauer, Pacific International, 1976
FURTHER ADVENTURES OF THE WILDERNESS FAMILY co-composer with Gene Kauer, Pacific International, 1978

YVES LAFERRIERE
Contact: Pro-Canada - Canada, 1-416-445-8700

JESUS OF MONTREAL Max Films International, 1989, Canadian-French

FRANCIS LAI
b. 1932 - Nice, France
Agent: Bart-Milander - North Hollywood, 818/761-4040

CIRCLE OF LOVE *LA RONDE* Continental, 1964, French
A MAN AND A WOMAN ★★ Allied Artists, 1966, French
THE BOBO Warner Bros., 1967, British
LIVE FOR LIFE United Artists, 1967, French
THE ACTION MAN *LE SOLEIL DES VOYOUS* H .K. Film Distribution, 1967, French
I'LL NEVER FORGET WHAT'S 'IS NAME Regional, 1968, British
LIFE LOVE DEATH Lopert, 1969, French
THREE INTO TWO WON'T GO Universal, 1969, British
HOUSE OF THE CARDS Universal, 1969
MAYERLING MGM, 1969, British-French
HANNIBAL BROOKS United Artists, 1969, British
THE GAMES 20th Century-Fox, 1970, British
HELLO - GOODBYE 20th Century-Fox, 1970
LE PETIT MATIN 1970, French
LOVE IS A FUNNY THING *UN HOMME QUI ME PLAIT* United Artists, 1970, French-Italian
RIDER IN THE RAIN Avco Embassy, 1970, French-Italian
LOVE STORY ★★ Paramount, 1970
BERLIN AFFAIR (TF) Universal TV, 1970
DU SOLEIL PLEIN LES YEUX 1970, French
SMIC, SMAC, SMOC GSF, 1971, French
THE CROOK United Artists, 1971, French
...AND HOPE TO DIE *LA COURSE DU LIEVRE A TRAVAERS LESCHAMPS* 20th Century-Fox, 1972, French
MONEY MONEY MONEY *L'AVENTURE C'EST L'AVENTURE* GSF, 1972, French
LE PETIT POUCET *TOM THUMB* 1972, French
LA LOUVE SOLITAIRE French
LA LECON PARTICULIERE French
L'ODEUR DES FAUVES French
DANS LA POUSSIERE DU SOLEIL French
LES PEIROLEUSES French
UN HOMME LIBRE *A FREE MAN* 1973, French
HAPPY NEW YEAR *LA BONNE ANNEE* Avco Embassy, 1973, French-Italian
LES HOMMES Cocinor, 1973, French-Italian
PAR LE SANG DES AUTRES 1973, French
UN AMOUR DE PLUIE 1973, French
VISIT TO A CHIEF'S SON United Artists, 1974
LA BABY-SITTER Titanus, 1975, Italian-French-Monacan
CAT AND MOUSE Quartet, 1975, French
CHILD UNDER A LEAF Cinema National, 1975, Canadian
MARIAGE 1975, French
AND NOW MY LOVE *TOUTE UNE VIE* Avco Embassy, 1975, French-Italian
EMMANUELLE II 1975, French
SECOND CHANCE *SI C'ETAIT A REFAIRE* United Artists Classics, 1976, French
LE CORPS DE MON ENNEMI AMLF, 1976, French
THE GOOD AND THE BAD Paramount, 1976, French
BILITIS Topar, 1976, French
ANOTHER MAN, ANOTHER CHANCE United Artists, 1977, U.S.-French
ANIMA PERSA Dean Film/Les Productions Fox Europe, 1977, Italian-French
WIDOWS' NEST Navarro Prods., 1977, U.S.-Spanish
ROBERT ET ROBERT Quartet, 1978, French
INTERNATIONAL VELVET MGM/United Artists, 1978, British
OLIVER'S STORY co-composer with Lee Holdridge, Paramount, 1979
LES RINGARDS 1978, French
PASSION FLOWER HOTEL 1978, West German
A NOUS DEUX AMLF, 1979, French-Canadian
LES BORSALINI French-Italian
INDIAN SUMMER French
SEA KILLER Italian
BEYOND THE REEF Universal, 1981

BOLERO *LES UNS ET LES AUTRES/WITHIN MEMORY* co-composer with Michel Legrand, Double 13/Sharp Features, 1982, French
EDITH AND MARCEL Miramax, 1983, French
SALUT LA PUCE Naja Film, 1983, French
CANICULE *DOG DAY* UGC, 1984, French
LES RIPOUX AMLF, 1984, French
MADAME CLAUDE 2 1985, French
HERE COMES SANTA CLAUS *J'AI RECONTRE LE PERE NOEL* New World, 1985, French
MARIE MGM/UA, 1985
SINS (MS) New World TV/The Greif-Dore Company/ Collins-Holm Productions, 1986
A MAN AND A WOMAN: 20 YEARS LATER Warner Bros., 1986, French
BANDITS *ATTENTION BANDITS* Grange Communications/Jerry Winters, 1987, French
DARK EYES Island Pictures, 1987, Italian-French
BERNADETTE Cannon, 1988, French
LES PYRAMIDES BLEUES Sofracima/FR3 Films/ Mexico Inc., French
ITINERAIRE D'UN ENFANT GATE Films 13/Cerito Films/TFI Films, French
KEYS TO FREEDOM RPB Pictures/Queen's Cross Productions, 1989, U.S.-Malaysian
MY NEW PARTNER 2 AMLF, 1990, French

FRANK LaLOGGIA

Business: LaLaoggia Productions - Los Angeles, 213/462-3055

FEAR NO EVIL co-composer with David Spear, Avco Embassy, 1981
THE LADY IN WHITE New Century Vista, 1988

JERRY LAMBERT

Contact: BMI - Los Angeles, 213/659-9109

THE TEXAS CHAINSAW MASSACRE PART 2 co-composer with Tobe Hooper, Cannon, 1986

PHILLIP LAMBRO

Contact: ASCAP - Los Angeles, 213/466-7681

AND NOW MIGUEL Paramount, 1966
LIVE A LITTLE, STEAL A LOT American International, 1975

JOHN LANCHBERY

b. 1923 - London, England
Contact: PRS - London, England, 011-44-1-580-5544

THE TURNING POINT 20th Century-Fox, 1977
NIJINSKY Paramount, 1980
EVIL UNDER THE SUN adaptation, Universal/AFD, 1982, British

MICHAEL LANG

Contact: ASCAP - Los Angeles, 213/466-7681

HOLLYWOOD HARRY Shapiro Entertainment, 1985

BRUCE LANGHORNE

Contact: BMI - Los Angeles, 213/659-9109

IDAHO TRANSFER Cinemation, 1975
FIGHTING MAD 20th Century-Fox, 1976
STAY HUNGRY co-composer with Byron Berline, United Artists, 1976

OUTLAW BLUES co-composer with Charles Fox, Warner Bros., 1977
JIMMY B. & ANDRE (TF) Georgian Bay Productions, 1980
MELVIN AND HOWARD Universal, 1980
WORD OF HONOR (TF) Georgian Bay Productions, 1981
NIGHT WARNING Comworld, 1983
HOLLYWOOD DREAMING co-composer, American Twist/ Boulevard Productions, 1986

HENRI LANOE

b. France
Contact: SACEM - France, 011-33-14-747-5650

LA RIVIERE DU HIBOU 1961, French
AU COEUR DE LA VIE 1962, French
LA BELLE VIE 1963, French
THE THIEF OF PARIS *LE VOLEUR* Lopert, 1967, French-Italian
NO JOUEZ PAS AVEC LES MARTIENS 1967, French

TITO LARRIVA

Contact: BMI - Los Angeles, 213/659-9109

REPO MAN co-composer with Steven Hufsteter, Universal, 1984

GLEN A. LARSON

Contact: BMI - Los Angeles, 213/659-9109

THE MURDER THAT WOULDN'T DIE (TF) co-composer with Joe Harnell, Glen A. Larson Productions/ Universal TV, 1980

RICHARD LaSALLE

Contact: BMI - Los Angeles, 213/659-9109

SPEED CRAZY Allied Artists, 1959
THE BIG NIGHT Paramount, 1960
THE BOY WHO CAUGHT A CROOK United Artists, 1961
THE FLIGHT THAT DISAPPEARED United Artists, 1961
SECRET OF DEEP HARBOR United Artists, 1961
SNIPER'S RIDGE 20th Century-Fox, 1961
WHEN THE CLOCK STRIKES United Artists, 1961
YOU HAVE TO RUN FAST United Artists, 1961
DEADLY DUO United Artists, 1962
BROKEN LAND 20th Century-Fox, 1962
THE FIREBRAND 20th Century-Fox, 1962
GUN STREET United Artists, 1962
HANDS OF A STRANGER Allied Artists, 1962
INCIDENT IN AN ALLEY United Artists, 1962
SAINTLY SINNERS United Artists, 1962
THE DAY MARS INVADED EARTH 20th Century-Fox, 1962
POLICE NURSE 20th Century-Fox, 1963
DIARY OF A MADMAN United Artists, 1963
TWICE-TOLD TALES United Artists, 1963
APACHE RIFLES 20th Century-Fox, 1964
BLOOD ON THE ARROW Allied Artists, 1964
THE TIME TRAVELERS American International, 1964
THE QUICK GUN Columbia, 1964
A YANK IN VIET-NAM *YEAR OF THE TIGER* Allied Artists, 1964
FORT COURAGEOUS 20th Century-Fox, 1965
ARIZONA RAIDERS Columbia, 1965
WAR PARTY 20th Century-Fox, 1965
CONVICT STAGE 20th Century-Fox, 1965
AMBUSH BAY United Artists, 1966
BOY, DID I GET THE WRONG NUMBER! United Artists, 1966

CITY BENEATH THE SEA (TF) 20th Century-Fox TV/ Motion Pictures International/Kent Productions, 1971
DAUGHTERS OF SATAN United Artists, 1972
SUPERBEAST United Artists, 1972
DOCTOR DEATH, SEEKER OF SOULS 20th Century-Fox, 1973
ALICE DOESN'T LIVE HERE ANYMORE Warner Bros., 1974
SWISS FAMILY ROBINSON (TF) Irwin Allen Productions/20th Century-Fox TV, 1975
ADVENTURES OF THE QUEEN (TF) Irwin Allen Productions/20th Century-Fox TV, 1975
FLOOD (TF) Irwin Allen Productions/Warner Bros. TV, 1976
FIRE! (TF) Irwin Allen Productions/Warner Bros. TV, 1977
HANGING BY A THREAD (TF) Irwin Allen Productions/ Warner Bros. TV, 1979
KEN MURRAY SHOOTING STARS Royal Oak, 1979
THE MEMORY OF EVA RYKER (TF) Irwin Allen Productions, 1980
CODE RED (TF) Irwin Allen Productions/Columbia Pictures TV, 1981
CAVE-IN! (TF) Irwin Allen Productions/Warner Bros. Television, 1983
THE NIGHT THE BRIDGE FELL DOWN (TF) Irwin Allen Productions/Warner Bros. Television, 1983

KEN LAUBER

SCRATCH HARRY 1969
BRAND X 1970
CRY PANIC (TF) Spelling-Goldberg Productions, 1974
THINGS IN THEIR SEASON (TF) Tomorrow Entertainment, 1974
THE HATFIELDS AND THE MCCOYS (TF) Charles Fries Productions, 1975
JOURNEY FROM DARKNESS (TF) Bob Banner Associates, 1975
RETURNING HOME (TF) Samuel Goldwyn Productions/ Lorimar Productions, 1975
HEARTS OF THE WEST United Artists, 1975
THE CHICKEN CHRONICLES Avco Embassy, 1977
STUDS LONIGAN (MS) Lorimar Productions, 1979
WANDA NEVADA United Artists, 1979
HEAD OVER HEELS *CHILLY SCENES OF WINTER* United Artists, 1979
THE LITTLE DRAGONS Aurora, 1980
KENT STATE (TF) Inter Planetary Productions/ Osmond TV Productions, 1981

BOBBY LAUREL

Contact: ASCAP - Los Angeles, 213/466-7681

THE ROSARY MURDERS co-composer with Don Sebesky, Samuel Goldwyn Company, 1987

TOM LAVIN

Contact: Pro-Canada - Canada, 1-416-445-8700

OUT OF THE BLUE Discovery Films, 1980, Canadian

ELLIOT LAWRENCE

Contact: ASCAP - Los Angeles, 213/466-7681

YOUR MONEY OR YOUR WIFE (TF) Brentwood Productions, 1972
NETWORK United Artists, 1976
THE CRADLE WILL FALL (TF) Cates Films Inc./ Procter & Gamble Productions, 1983

STEPHEN LAWRENCE

Contact: BMI - Los Angeles, 213/659-9109

JENNIFER ON MY MIND United Artists, 1971
BANG THE DRUM SLOWLY Paramount, 1973
HURRY UP OR I'LL BE THIRTY Avco Embassy, 1973
DRAGONFLY American International, 1976
ALICE, SWEET ALICE *COMMUNION/HOLY TERROR* Allied Artists, 1977
IT HAPPENED ONE CHRISTMAS (TF) Daisy Productions/ Universal TV, 1977
SOONER OR LATER (TF) Laughing Willow Company, 1979
TRACKDOWN: FINDING THE GOODBAR KILLER (TF) Grosso-Jacobson Productions/Centerpoint Productions, 1983
MEET THE MUNCEYS (TF) Walt Disney TV, 1988

MAURY LAWS

THE DAYDREAMER Embassy, 1966
MAD MONSTER PARTY (AF) Embassy, 1967
THE LAST DINOUSAUR (TF) Rankin-Bass Productions, 1977, U.S.-Japanese
THE HOBBIT (ATF) Rankin-Bass Productions, 1977
THE BERMUDA DEPTHS (TF) Rankin-Bass Productions, 1978
THE RETURN OF THE KING (ATF) Rankin-Bass Productions, 1979
THE IVORY APE (TF) co-composer with Bernard Hoffer, Rankin-Bass Productions, 1980
THE BUSHIDO BLADE Aquarius, 1982, U.S.-Japanese

JULIAN LAXTON

Contact: SAMRO - South Africa, 011-27-11-725-1425

PURGATORY New Star Entertainment, 1989
RISING STORM Gibraltar Releasing, 1989

BILL LEE

Contact: BMI - Los Angeles, 213/659-9109

JOE'S BED-STUY BARBERSHOP: WE CUT HEADS First Run Features, 1983
SHE'S GOTTA HAVE IT Island Pictures, 1986
SCHOOL DAZE Columbia, 1988
DO THE RIGHT THING Universal, 1989
MO' BETTER BLUES Universal, 1990

DAVID LEE

THE MASQUE OF THE RED DEATH American International, 1964, British-U.S.

GERALD LEE

Contact: BMI - Los Angeles, 213/659-9109

SATAN'S CHEERLEADERS World Amusement, 1977

CAROL LEES

Contact: BMI - Los Angeles, 213/659-9109

THE LAST WORD Samuel Goldwyn Company, 1979

MICHEL LEGRAND

b. 1932 - Paris, France
Agent: Gorfaine-Schwartz - Burbank, 818/954-9500

BEAU FIXE 1953, French
LES AMANTS DU TAGE 1954, French

L'AMERICAIN SE DETEND (TF) 1958, French
L'AMERIQUE INSOLITE (FD) 1960, French
TERRAIN VAGUE co-composer with Francis Lemarque, 1960, French
LE COEUR BATTANT 1960, French
LOLA Films Around the World, 1961, French
UN COEUR GROS COMME CA (FD) co-composer with Georges Delerue, 1961, French
A WOMAN IS A WOMAN Pathe Contemporary, 1961, French
CLEO FROM 5 TO 7 Zenith, 1962, French
SEVEN CAPITAL SINS co-composer, Embassy, 1962, French-Italian
RETOUR A NEW YORK (FD) 1962, French
EVA Times, 1962, French-Italian
MY LIFE TO LIVE Pathe Contemporary, 1962, French
L'AMERIQUE LUNAIRE (FD) 1962, French
HISTOIRE D'UN PETIT GARCON DEVENU GRAND 1962, French
ILLUMINATIONS (FD) 1963, French
LE GRAND ESCROC 1963, French
L'EMPIRE DE LA NUIT 1963, French
BAY OF THE ANGELS Pathe Contemporary, 1964, French
THE UMBRELLAS OF CHERBOURG ★ Landau, 1964, French-West German
UNE RAVISSANTE IDIOTE 1964, French
BAND OF OUTSIDERS Royal Films International, 1964, French
LES AMOUREUX DU "FRANCE" (FD) 1964, French
LA DOUCEUR DU VILLAGE (FD) 1964, French
LA VIE DE CHATEAU 1965, French
QUAND PASSENT LES FAISANS 1965, French
MONNAIRE DE SINGE 1965, French
L'AN 2000 1966, French
TENDRE VOYOU 1966, French
QUI ETES-VOUS POLLY MAGGOO? 1966, French
L'OR ET LE PLUMB *GOLD AND LEAD* 1966, French
SWEET NOVEMBER Warner Bros., 1967
THE YOUNG GIRLS OF ROCHEFERT ★ Warner Bros., 1968, French
A MATTER OF INNOCENCE *PRETTY POLLY* Universal, 1968, British
THE THOMAS CROWN AFFAIR ★ United Artists, 1968
LA PISCINE 1968, French
PLAY DIRTY United Artists, 1968, British
ICE STATION ZEBRA MGM, 1968
HOW TO SAVE A MARRIAGE AND RUIN YOUR LIFE Columbia, 1968
CASTLE KEEP Columbia, 1969
THE HAPPY ENDING United Artists, 1969
THE PICASSO SUMMER Warner Bros., 1969
THE LADY IN THE CAR WITH GLASSES AND A GUN Columbia, 1970, French-U.S.
LE MANS National General, 1970
PIECES OF DREAMS United Artists, 1970
THE MAGIC GARDEN OF STANLEY SWEETHEART MGM, 1970
DONKY SKIN *PEAU D'ANE* Janus, 1971, French
THE GO-BETWEEN Columbia, 1971, British
WUTHERING HEIGHTS American International, 1971, British
SUMMER OF '42 ★★ Warner Bros., 1971
BRIAN'S SONG (TF) ☆ Screen Gems/Columbia TV, 1971
LADY SINGS THE BLUES Paramount, 1972
ONE IS A LONELY NUMBER MGM, 1972
PORTNOY'S COMPLAINT Warner Bros., 1972
THE ADVENTURES OF DON QUIXOTE (TF) Universal TV/BBC, 1973, U.S.-British
COPS AND ROBBERS United Artists, 1973
THE IMPOSSIBLE OBJECT Valoria, 1973, French-Italian
40 CARATS Columbia, 1973
BREEZY Universal, 1973
THE OUTSIDE MAN *UN HOMME EST MORT* United Artists, 1973, French-Italian
LE GANG DES OTAGES Gaumont, 1973, French
L'EVENEMENT LE PLUS IMPORTANT DEPUIS QUE L'HOMME A MARCHE SUR LA LUNE Lira Films/Roas Productions, 1973, French-Italian
THE THREE MUSKETEERS *THE QUEEN'S DIAMONDS* 20th Century-Fox, 1974, British
IT'S GOOD TO BE ALIVE (TF) Metromedia Producers Corporation/Larry Harmon Pictures Corporation, 1974
F FOR FAKE Specialty Films, 1974, French-Iranian-West German
OUR TIME Warner Bros., 1974
CAGE WITHOUT A KEY (TF) Columbia TV, 1975
SHEILA LEVINE IS DEAD AND LIVING IN NEW YORK Paramount, 1975
LE SAUVAGE 1975, French
ODE TO BILLY JOE Warner Bros., 1976
GABLE AND LOMBARD Universal, 1976
LE VOYAGE DE NOCES 1976, French
LA FLUTE A SIX SCHTROUMPFS 1976, French
THE OTHER SIDE OF MIDNIGHT 20th Century-Fox, 1977
GULLIVER'S TRAVELS EMI, 1977, British-Belgian
LES ROUTES DU SUD Parafrance, 1978, French
LES FABULEUSES AVENTURES DU LEGENDAIRE BARON MICHAUSEN (AF) 1979, French
THE HUNTER Paramount, 1980
FALLING IN LOVE AGAIN International Picture Show Company, 1980
THE MOUNTAIN MEN Columbia, 1980
HINOTORI co-composer with Jun Fukamachi, Toho, 1980, Japanese
YOUR TICKET IS NO LONGER VALID RSL Productions/ Ambassador, 1981, Canadian
ATLANTIC CITY Paramount, 1981, Canadian-French
A WOMAN CALLED GOLDA (TF) ☆ Harve Bennett Productions/Paramount TV, 1982
BEST FRIENDS Warner Bros., 1982
THE GIFT Samuel Goldwyn Company, 1982, French-Italian
NEVER SAY NEVER AGAIN Warner Bros., 1983
YENTL ★★ MGM/UA, 1983
A LOVE IN GERMANY Triumph/Columbia, 1983, West German-French
LE REVANCHE DES HUMANOIDES (AF) Planfilm, 1983, French
THE SMURFS AND THE MAGIC FLUTE (AF) Atlantic Releasing, 1984, Belgian-French
SECRET PLACES TLC Films/20th Century-Fox, 1984, British
THE JESSE OWENS STORY (TF) Harve Bennett Productions/Paramount TV, 1984
PAROLES ET MUSIQUES A.A.A., 1984, French
PROMISES TO KEEP (TF) Sandra Harmon Productions/ Green-Epstein Productions/Telepictures, 1985
PARTIR REVENIR UGC, 1985, French
PARKING A.M. Films, 1985, French
SINS (MS) additional music, New World TV/The Greif-Dore Company/Collins-Holm Productions, 1986
CROSSINGS (MS) Aaron Spelling Productions, 1986
AS SUMMERS DIE (CTF) HBO Premiere Films/Chris-Rose Productions/Baldwin/Aldrich Productions/Lorimar-Telepictures Productions, 1986
CASANOVA (TF) Konigsberg-Sanitsky Productions/ Reteitalia, 1987
SWITCHING CHANNELS Columbia, 1988
NOT A PENNY MORE, NOT A PENNY LESS (CTF) BBC/ Paramount TV Ltd./Revcom, 1990, U.S.-British

MITCH LEIGH
Contact: ASCAP - Los Angeles, 213/466-7681

ONCE IN PARIS... Atlantic Releasing Corporation, 1978

JEAN-FRANCOIS LEON
b. France
Contact: SACEM - France, 011-33-14-747-5650

LES LONGS MANTEAUX Fechner-Gaumont, 1986, French

MICHAEL LEONARD
BILLION DOLLAR HOBO International Picture Show Company, 1978
THEY WENT THAT-A-WAY AND THAT-A-WAY International Picture Show Company, 1978

PATRICK LEONARD
Agent: CAA - Los Angeles, 213/288-4545

AT CLOSE RANGE Orion, 1986
NOTHING IN COMMON Tri-Star, 1986
HEART CONDITION New Line Cinema, 1990

RAYMOND LEPPARD
b. 1927
Contact: PRS - London, England, 011-44-1-580-5544

LORD OF THE FLIES Continental, 1963, British
PENALTY PHASE (TF) Tamara Asseyev Productions/New World TV, 1986

CORY LERIOS
Agent: Gorfaine-Schwartz - Burbank, 818/954-9500

ONE CRAZY SUMMER Warner Bros., 1986
NIGHT ANGEL Fries Entertainment, 1990

MICHAEL LEVANIOS III
UNCLE SCAM New World, 1981

SYLVESTER LEVAY
Agent: Gorfaine-Schwartz - Burbank, 818/954-9500

INVITATION TO HELL (TF) Moonlight Productions II, 1984
TIME BOMB (TF) Barry Weitz Films/Universal TV, 1984
WET GOLD (TF) Telepictures Productions, 1984
WHERE THE BOYS ARE '84 Tri-Star, 1984
AIRWOLF (TF) Belisarius Productions/Universal TV, 1984
A TOUCH OF SCANDAL (TF) Doris M. Keating Productions/Columbia TV, 1984
SINS OF THE FATHER (TF) Freies Entertainment, 1985
CREATOR Universal, 1985
COBRA Warner Bros., 1986
INTIMATE ENCOUNTERS (TF) Larry A. Thompson Productions/Donna Mills Productions/Columbia TV, 1986
CHOKE CANYON United Film Distribution, 1986
THE ANNIHILATOR (TF) Universal TV, 1986
INVADERS FROM MARS co-composer with Christopher Young, Cannon, 1986
HOWARD THE DUCK co-composer with John Barry, Universal, 1986
WHERE ARE THE CHILDREN? Columbia, 1986
TOUCH & GO Tri-Star, 1986
THE ABDUCTION OF KARI SWENSON (TF) NBC Productions, 1987
MANNEQUIN 20th Century Fox, 1987
WEREWOLF (TF) Lycanthrope Productions/Tri-Star TV, 1987
BURGLAR Warner Bros., 1987
THREE O'CLOCK HIGH additional music, Universal, 1987
PROBE (TF) MCA TV Ltd., 1988
THE TRACKER (CTF) HBO Pictures/Lance Hool Productions, 1988
SOMETHING IS OUT THERE (TF) Columbia TV, 1988
THE COVER GIRL AND THE COP (TF) Barry-Enright Productions/Alexander Productions, 1988
POLICE STORY: GLADIATOR SCHOOL (TF) Columbia Pictures TV, 1988
MANHUNT: SEARCH FOR THE NIGHT STALKER (TF) Leonard Hill Films, 1989
COURAGE MOUNTAIN Triumph Releasing Corporation, 1989, U.S.-French
THE LAKER GIRLS (TF) Viacom Productions/Finnegan-Pinchuk Co./Valente-Hamilton Productions, 1990
SNOW KILL (CTF) Wilshire Court Productions, 1990
NAVY SEALS Orion, 1990

GEOFF LEVIN
Contact: ASCAP - Los Angeles, 213/466-7681

HEART co-composer with Chris Many, New World, 1987
PERSONAL CHOICE co-composer with Chris Smart, Moviestore Entertainment, 1989

KEITH LEVINE
HOLLYWOOD VICE co-composer with Michael Convertino, Concorde/Cinema Group, 1986

WALT LEVINSKY
Contact: ASCAP - Los Angeles, 213/466-7681

BREAKING UP (TF) Time-Life Productions/Talent Associates Ltd., 1978

JAY LEVY
Contact: BMI - Los Angeles, 213/659-9109

HARDBODIES 2 co-composer with Ed Arkin, CineTel Films, 1986
MODERN GIRLS co-composer with Ed Arkin, Atlantic Releasing Corporation, 1986
THUNDER RUN Cannon, 1986
PRETTY SMART New World, 1987
LADY AVENGER Marco Colombo, 1989

LOU LEVY
OUTSIDE CHANCE (TF) co-composer with Murphy Dunne, New World Pictures/Miller-Begun TV, 1978

SHUKI LEVY
Contact: BMI - Los Angeles, 213/659-9109

DAWN OF THE MUMMY Harmony Gold Ltd., 1981
LE SECRET DES SELENITES (AF) co-composer, 1983, French
HERE COME THE LITTLES (AF) Atlantic Releasing, 1985
RAINBOW BRITE AND THE STAR STEALER (AF) co-composer with Haim Saban, Warner Bros., 1985
BAY COVEN (TF) Guber-Peters Entertainment/Phoenix Entertainment Group, 1987

HERSCHELL GORDON LEWIS
Contact: BMI - Los Angeles, 213/659-9109

BLOOD FEAST Box Office Spectaculars, 1963
2000 MANIACS co-composer with Larry Wellington, Box Office Spectaculars, 1964
SHE-DEVILS ON WHEELS 1968
THE GORE-GORE GIRLS *BLOOD ORGY* Lewis Motion Picture Enterprises, 1972

MICHAEL J. LEWIS
Contact: Triad Artists - Los Angeles, 213/556-2727

THE MAN WHO HAUNTED HIMSELF Levitt-Pickman, 1970, British
UNMAN, WITTERING & ZIGO Paramount, 1971, British
THEATRE OF BLOOD United Artists, 1973, British
Il HARROWHOUSE 20th Century-Fox, 1974, British
92 IN THE SHADE United Artists, 1975
RUSSIAN ROULETTE Avco Embassy, 1975
THE MEDUSA TOUCH Warner Bros., 1978, British
THE STICK UP *MUD* Trident-Barber, 1978, British
THE PASSAGE United Artists, 1979
THE LEGACY Universal, 1979
ffolkes *NORTH SEAS HIJACK* Universal, 1980, British
THE UNSEEN World Northal, 1981
SPHINX Orion/Warner Bros., 1981
YES, GIORGIO MGM/UA, 1982
THE NAKED FACE Cannon, 1985
THE ROSE AND THE JACKAL (CTF) Steve White Productions/PWD Productions/Spectator Films/TNT, 1990

W. MICHAEL LEWIS
Agent: Richard Emler - Los Angeles, 213/651-0222

ENTER THE NINJA co-composer with Laurin Rinder, Cannon, 1981
FIRECRACKER co-composer with Laurin Rinder, New World, 1981, U.S.-Filipino
SHOGUN ASSASSIN co-composer with Laurin Rinder, New World, 1981, Japanese-U.S.
HOT BUBBLEGUM *LEMON POPSICLE III* co-composer with Laurin Rinder, Noah Films, 1981, Israeli
NEW YEAR'S EVIL co-composer with Laurin Rinder, Cannon, 1981
THE KILLING OF AMERICA (FD) co-composer with Mark Lindsay, Filmlink Corp., 1982, U.S.-Japanese
THE KULIES co-composer with Laurin Rinder, Global
THE BALLAD OF GREGORIO CORTEZ co-composer with Laurin Rinder, Embassy, 1983
REVENGE OF THE NINJA additional music, MGM/UA/Cannon, 1983
NINJA III—THE DOMINATION co-composer with Laurin Rinder, Cannon, 1984
BAD MANNERS *GROWING PAINS* co-composer with Laurin Rinder, New World, 1984
HOT CHILD IN THE CITY co-composer with Laurin Rinder, Mediacom Filmworks, 1987

WEBSTER LEWIS
Contact: BMI - Los Angeles, 213/659-9109

THE HEARSE Crown International, 1980
BODY AND SOUL Cannon, 1981
MY TUTOR Crown International, 1983
GO TELL IT ON THE MOUNTAIN (TF) Learning in Focus, 1984

MARK LINDSAY
Contact: BMI - Los Angeles, 213/659-9109

THE KILLING OF AMERICA co-composer with W. Michael Lewis, Filmlink Corp., 1982, U.S.-Japanese

MORT LINDSEY
Contact: ASCAP - Los Angeles, 213/466-7681

40 POUNDS OF TROUBLE Universal, 1962
I COULD GO ON SINGING United Artists, 1963, British
STOLEN HOURS United Artists, 1963
THE BEST MAN United Artists, 1964
REAL LIFE Paramount, 1979

STEVE LINDSEY
Contact: ASCAP - Los Angeles, 213/466-7681

BEHIND ENEMY LINES (TF) co-composer with Jack Chipman, MTM Enterprises/TVS, 1985

DAVID LINDUP
Contact: PRS - London, England, 011-44-1-580-5544

THE SPIRAL STAIRCASE Warner Bros., 1975, British

PETER LINK
NIGHTMARE (TF) Mark Carliner Productions/CBS Entertainment, 1974

MICHAEL J. LINN
Contact: Robert Light - Los Angeles, 213/651-1777

BREAKIN' 2: ELECTRIC BOOGALOO Tri-Star/Cannon, 1984
AMERICAN NINJA Cannon, 1985
DUET FOR ONE Cannon, 1986
SURVIVAL GAME Trans World Entertainment, 1987
ALLAN QUARTERMAIN AND THE LOST CITY OF GOLD Cannon, 1987

ALAN LISK
Contact: PRS - London, England, 011-44-1-580-5544

CODENAME: KYRIL (TF) Incito Productions/HTV, 1989, British

ZDENEK LISKA
b. Czechoslovakia
Contact: OSA - Tr. Cs. Armady 20, 160-56 Prague 6-Bubene, Czechoslovakia

POKLAD NA PTACIM OSTROVE *THE TREASURE OF BIRD ISLAND* (AF) 1952, Czech
PAN PROKOUK PRITEL ZVIRATEK (AF) 1953, Czech
FLICEK THE BALL *THE NAUGHTY BALL* (AF) 1956, Czech
THE FABULOUS WORLD OF JULES VERNE 1958, Czech
DEN ODPLATY *THE DAY OF RECKONING* (AF) 1960, Czech
WHERE THE DEVIL CANNOT GO 1960, Czech
THE FABULOUS BARON MUNCHAUSEN 1961, Czech
THE SHOP ON MAIN STREET *THE SHOP ON HIGH STREET* 1965, Czech
VRAZDA PO CESKY *MURDER, CZECH STYLE* 1966, Czech
BYT *THE FLAT* 1968, Czech
THE VALLEY OF THE BEES 1968, Czech

MARKETA LAZAROVA 1969, Czech
OVOCE STROMJ RAJSHYCH JIME 1970, Czech
PRIPAD PRO ZACINAJICHO KATA *A CASE FOR A YOUNG HANGMAN* 1970, Czech
WE'LL EAT THE FRUIT OF PARADISE 1970, Czech
ADRIFT 1971, Czech
JUMPING OVER PUDDLES AGAIN 1971, Czech
THE TRICKY GAME OF LOVE 1971, Czech
QUITE GOOD CHAPS 1972
DAYS OF BETRAYAL 1974
PAVLINKA 1974
WHO LEAVES IN THE RAIN 1976
THE LITTLE MERMAID 1977
SMOKE IN THE POTATO FIELDS 1977
SHADOWS OF A HOT SUMMER 1978

RUSS LITTLE

Contact: Pro-Canada - Canada, 1-416-445-8700

TOO OUTRAGEOUS! Spectrafilm, 1987

CHARLES LLOYD

Contact: BMI - Los Angeles, 213/659-9109

ALMOST SUMMER co-composer with Ron Altbach, Universal, 1978

MICHAEL LLOYD

Contact: ASCAP - Los Angeles, 213/466-7681

THE POM POM GIRLS Crown International, 1976
LOVE'S DARK RIDE (TF) co-composer with John D'Andrea, Mark VII Ltd./Worldvision Enterprises, 1978
STRANGER IN OUR HOUSE (TF) co-composer with John D'Andrea, Inter Planetary Pictures/Finnegan Associates, 1978
GRAMBLING'S WHITE TIGER (TF) co-composer with John D'Andrea, Inter Planetary Productions/Jenner/Wallach Productions, 1981
THE BEACH GIRLS Crown International, 1982
TOUGH ENOUGH co-composer with Steve Wax, 20th Century-Fox, 1983
SAVAGE STREETS co-composer with John D'Andrea, MPM, 1984
BODY SLAM co-composer with John D'Andrea, DEG, 1987
THE GARBAGE PAIL KIDS MOVIE Atlantic Entertainment Group, 1987
SWIMSUIT (TF) co-composer with John D'Andrea, Musifilm Productions/American First Run Studios, 1989

MALCOM LOCKYER

Contact: PRS - London, England, 011-44-1-580-5544

THE LITTLE ONES Columbia, 1965, British
TEN LITTLE INDIANS 1965, British
BANG BANG, YOU'RE DEAD! *OUR MAN IN MARRAKESH* American International, 1966, British
DEADLIER THAN THE MALE Universal, 1966, British
ISLAND OF TERROR Universal, 1966, British
THE VENGEANCE OF FU-MANCHU Warner Bros., 1968, British

JOE LO DUCA

Contact: ASCAP - Los Angeles, 213/466-7681

THE EVIL DEAD New Line Cinema, 1983
EVIL DEAD 2 Rosebud Releasing Corporation, 1987

GARY LOGAN

Contact: ASCAP - Los Angeles, 213/466-7681

THE HUMAN FACTOR co-composer with Richard Logan, MGM/UA, 1979

RICHARD LOGAN

THE HUMAN FACTOR co-composer with Gary Logan, MGM/UA, 1979

PAUL LOOMIS

THE PASSAGE Manson International, 1988
RIVERBEND Intercontinental Releasing, 1989

WILLIAM LOOSE

Contact: BMI - Los Angeles, 213/659-9109

LOVE AND KISSES co-composer with Jimmie Haskell, Universal, 1965
NAVAJO RUN co-composer with Emil Cadkin, American International, 1966, Italian-Spanish
TARZAN AND THE GREAT RIVER Paramount, 1967
TARZAN AND THE JUNGLE BOY Paramount, 1968
THE BIG BIRD CAGE co-composer with William Castleman, 1972
THE EROTIC ADVENTURES OF ZORRO co-composer with Betty Allen, 1972, French-West German
THE WONDER OF IT ALL 1973
DEVIL TIMES FIVE *PEOPLE TOYS/THE HORRIBLE HOUSE ON THE HILL* 1974
SWEET SUZY! *BLACKSNAKE* co-composer with Al Teeter, Signal 166, 1975
RUSS MEYER'S UP! RM Films, 1976
MYSTERIOUS ISLAND OF BEAUTIFUL WOMEN (TF) co-composer with Jack Tillar, Alan Landsburg Productions, 1979
THE MAN WHO SAW TOMORROW co-composer with Jack Tillar, Warner Bros., 1981

JEFF LORBER

Contact: BMI - Los Angeles, 213/659-9109

SIDE OUT Tri-Star, 1990

DIANE LOUIE

Contact: Pro-Canada - Canada, 1-416-445-8700

LATINO Cinecom, 1985

MUNDELL LOWE

Contact: ASCAP - Los Angeles, 213/466-7681

EVERYTHING YOU WANTED TO KNOW ABOUT SEX (BUT WERE AFRAID TO ASK) United Artists, 1972
ATTACK ON TERROR: THE FBI VERSUS THE KU KLUX KLAN (TF) QM Productions/Warner Bros. TV, 1975
SIDEWINDER 1 Avco Embassy, 1977
THE GIRL IN THE EMPTY GRAVE (TF) Manteo Enterprises/MGM TV, 1977
TARANTULAS: THE DEADLY CARGO (TF) Alan Landsburg Productions, 1977
DEADLY GAME (TF) Manteo Enterprises/MGM TV, 1977

JEREMY LUBBOCK

THE COLOR PURPLE ★ co-composer, Warner Bros., 1985
ANY MAN'S DEATH INI Entertainment, 1990

KEN LUBER
WORLD GONE WILD Lorimar, 1988

DONAL LUNNY
b. Ireland
Contact: PRS - London, England, 011-44-1-580-5544

EAT THE PEACH Skouras Pictures, 1986, Irish
THE RETURN (TF) Spectre Productions, 1988, Irish

JOHN LURIE
Contact: BMI - Los Angeles, 213/659-9109

SUBWAY RIDERS co-composer, Hep Pictures, 1981
PERMANENT VACATION co-composer, Gray City Inc., 1982
STRANGER THAN PARADISE Samuel Goldwyn Company, 1984
VARIETY Horizon Films, 1985
DOWN BY LAW Island Pictures, 1986
POLICE STORY: MONSTER MANOR (TF) Columbia Pictures TV, 1988
MYSTERY TRAIN Orion Classics, 1989

M

TONY MACAULEY
Contact: PRS - London, England, 011-44-1-580-5544

THE BEAST IN THE CELLAR 1971, British
IT'S NOT THE SIZE THAT COUNTS *PERCY'S PROGRESS* Joseph Brenner Associates, 1974, British
MIDDLE AGE CRAZY 20th Century-Fox, 1980, Canadian

EGISTO MACCHI
Contact: SIAE - Rome, Italy, 011-39-6-59-90-1

MUSSOLINI: THE DECLINE AND FALL OF IL DUCE (CTF) HBO Premiere Films/RAI/Antenne-2/ Beta Film/TVE/RTSI, 1985, U.S.-Italian-French-West German
THE ROSE GARDEN 21st Century, 1989, West German-U.S.

GEOFF MacCORMACK
WILD ORCHID Triumph Releasing Corporation, 1990

TEO MACERO
Contact: BMI - Los Angeles, 213/659-9109

TOP SECRET (TF) co-composer with Stu Gardner, Jemmin Productions/Sheldon Leonard Productions, 1978
SERGEANT MATLOVICH VS. THE U.S. AIR FORCE (TF) Tomorrow Entertainment, 1978
FRIDAY THE 13TH...THE ORPHAN World Northal, 1979, Japanese
VIRUS Haruki Kadokawa, 1980, Japanese
THE TED KENNEDY JR. STORY (TF) Entertainment Partners, 1986
A SPECIAL FRIENDSHIP (TF) Entertainment Partners, 1987

JOHN MADARA
Contact: BMI - Los Angeles, 213/659-9109

HEY, GOOD LOOKIN' co-composer with Ric Sandler, Warner Bros., 1982

MAURO MALAVASI
b. Italy
Contact: SIAE - Rome, Italy, 011-39-6-59-90-1

MARIO PUZO'S THE FORTUNATE PILGRIM (MS) co-composer with Mauro Malavasi, Carlo & Alex Ponti Productions/Reteitalia S.P.A., 1988, Italian

BOB MAMET
NECROMANCER co-composer with Gary Stockdale and Kevin Klinger, Bonnaire Films, 1989

NORMAN MAMEY
Contact: Michael Dalling Co.

MALEDICTION Henry Plott Productions, 1989

HENRY MANCINI
b. April 16, 1924 - Cleveland, Ohio
Agent: ICM - Los Angeles, 213/550-4000

LOST IN ALASKA co-composer, Universal, 1952
BACK FROM THE FRONT co-composer with Herman Stein, Universal, 1952
HAS ANYBODY SEEN MY GAL? co-composer, Universal, 1952
HORIZONS WEST co-composer, Universal, 1952
MEET ME AT THE FAIR co-composer, Universal, 1952
THE RAIDERS co-composer, Universal, 1952
ALL I DESIRE co-composer, Universal, 1953
CITY BENEATH THE SEA co-composer, Universal, 1953
COLUMN SOUTH co-composer, Universal, 1953
IT CAME FROM OUTER SPACE co-composer, Universal, 1953
EAST OF SUMATRA co-composer, Universal, 1953
GIRLS IN THE NIGHT co-composer, Universal, 1953
THE GOLDEN BLADE co-composer, Universal, 1953
THE GREAT SIOUX UPRISING co-composer, Universal, 1953
GUNSMOKE co-composer, Universal, 1953
WALKING MY BABY BACK HOME Universal, 1953
IT HAPPENS EVERY THURSDAY Universal, 1953
LAW AND ORDER co-composer, Universal, 1953
THE LONE HAND co-composer, Universal, 1953
TAKE ME TO TOWN co-composer, Universal, 1953
TUMBLEWEED co-composer, Universal, 1953
THE VEILS OF BAGDAD co-composer, Universal, 1953
THE WORLD'S MOST BEAUTIFUL GIRLS Universal, 1953
THE CREATURE FROM THE BLACK LAGOON co-composer, 1954
FIREMAN SAVE MY CHILD co-composer, Universal, 1954
FOUR GUNS TO THE BORDER co-composer, Universal, 1954
THIS ISLAND EARTH co-composer, Universal, 1954
THE GLENN MILLER STORY ★ co-composer, Universal, 1954
JOHNNY DARK co-composer, Universal, 1954
MA AND PA KETTLE AT HOME co-composer, Universal, 1954
SO THIS IS PARIS co-composer with Herman Stein, Universal, 1954
TANGANYIKA co-composer, Universal, 1954
YELLOW MOUNTAIN co-composer, Universal, 1954

ABBOTT & COSTELLO MEET THE KEYSTONE COPS co-composer, Universal, 1955
THE FAR COUNTRY co-composer, Universal, 1955
THE PRIVATE WAR OF MAJOR BENSON co-composer, Universal, 1955
THE SPOILERS co-composer, Universal, 1955
THE SECOND GREATEST SEX Universal, 1955
THE BENNY GOODMAN STORY Universal, 1955
AIN'T MISBEHAVIN' Universal, 1955
THE CREATURE WALKS AMONG US co-composer, Universal, 1956
A DAY OF FURY co-composer, Universal, 1956
EVERYTHING BUT THE TRUTH co-composer, Universal, 1956
FRANCIS IN THE HAUNTED HOUSE Universal, 1956
THE GREAT MAN co-composer, Universal, 1956
ROCK PRETTY BABY Universal, 1956
THE TOY TIGER co-composer, Universal, 1956
THE UNGUARDED MOMENT co-composer, Universal, 1956
JOE DAKOTA co-composer, Universal, 1957
THE KETTLES ON OLD MACDONALD'S FARM co-composer, Universal, 1957
THE LAND UNKNOWN co-composer, Universal, 1957
MISTER CORY co-composer, Universal, 1957
THE MONOLITH MONSTERS co-composer, Universal, 1957
THE NIGHT RUNNER co-composer, Universal, 1957
MAN AFRAID Universal, 1957
DAMN CITIZEN co-composer, Universal, 1958
SUMMER LOVE Universal, 1958
FLOOD TIME Universal, 1958
DAMN CITIZEN Universal, 1958
THE THING THAT COULDN'T DIE co-composer, Universal, 1958
VOICE IN THE MIRROR Universal, 1958
TOUCH OF EVIL Universal, 1958
NEVER STEAL ANYTHING SMALL Universal, 1959
HIGH TIME 20th Century-Fox, 1960
THE GREAT IMPOSTOR 1960
BREAKFAST AT TIFFANY'S ★★ Paramount, 1961
BACHELOR IN PARADISE MGM, 1961
HATARI! Paramount, 1962
EXPERIMENT IN TERROR Warner Bros., 1962
DAYS OF WINE AND ROSES Warner Bros., 1962
MR. HOBBS TAKES A VACATION 20th Century-Fox, 1962
SOLDIER IN THE RAIN Allied Artists, 1963
THE PINK PANTHER ★ United Artists, 1964
CHARADE Universal, 1964
MAN'S FAVORITE SPORT? Universal, 1964
A SHOT IN THE DARK United Artists, 1964
DEAR HEART Warner Bros., 1964
THE GREAT RACE Warner Bros., 1965
ARABESQUE Universal, 1966, British-U.S.
MOMENT TO MOMENT Universal, 1966
WHAT DID YOU DO IN THE WAR, DADDY? United Artists, 1966
TWO FOR THE ROAD 20th Century-Fox, 1967, British-U.S.
WAIT UNTIL DARK Warner Bros., 1967
GUNN Warner Bros., 1967
THE PARTY United Artists, 1968
GAILY, GAILY United Artists, 1969
ME, NATALIE Cinema Center, 1969
SUNFLOWER ★ Avco Embassy, 1969, Italian-French
DARLING LILI Paramount, 1970
THE HAWAIIANS United Artists, 1970
THE MOLLY MAGUIRES Paramount, 1970
SOMETIMES A GREAT NOTION *NEVER GIVE AN INCH* Universal, 1971
THE NIGHT VISITOR UMC, 1971
THE THIEF WHO CAME TO DINNER Warner Bros., 1972
VISIONS OF EIGHT Cinema 5, 1973
OKLAHOMA CRUDE Columbia, 1973
THE GIRL FROM PETROVKA Universal, 1974
THAT'S ENTERTAINMENT! (FD) MGM/United Artists, 1974
99 & 44/100% DEAD 20th Century-Fox, 1974
THE WHITE DAWN Paramount, 1974
RETURN OF THE PINK PANTHER United Artists, 1975, British
THE BLUE NIGHT (TF) Lorimar Productions, 1975
THE GREAT WALDO PEPPER Universal, 1975
JACQUELINE SUSANN'S ONCE IS NOT ENOUGH *ONCE IS NOT ENOUGH* Paramount, 1975
SILVER STREAK 20th Century-Fox, 1976
THE PINK PANTHER STRIKES AGAIN United Artists, 1976, British
W.C. FIELDS AND ME Universal, 1976
ALEX & THE GYPSY 20th Century-Fox, 1976
ANGELA Embassy Home Entertainment, 1976, Canadian
ARTHUR HAILEY'S 'THE MONEYCHANGERS' (MS) Ross Hunter Productions/Paramount Pictures TV, 1976
REVENGE OF THE PINK PANTHER United Artists, 1978, British
SUDDENLY, LOVE (TF) Ross Hunter Productions, 1978
A FAMILY UPSIDE DOWN (TF) Ross Hunter-Jacques Mapes Film/Paramount TV, 1978
HOUSE CALLS Universal, 1978
WHO IS KILLING THE GREAT CHEFS OF EUROPE? Warner Bros., 1978
THE PRISONER OF ZENDA Universal, 1979
THE BEST PLACE TO BE (TF) Ross Hunter Productions, 1979
NIGHTWING Columbia, 1979
10 ★ Orion/Warner Bros., 1979
LITTLE MISS MARKER Universal, 1980
THE SHADOW BOX (TF) The Shadow Box Film Company, 1980
A CHANGE OF SEASONS 20th Century-Fox, 1980
BACK ROADS Warner Bros., 1981
S.O.B. Paramount, 1981
CONDORMAN Buena Vista, 1981
MOMMIE DEAREST Paramount, 1981
VICTOR/VICTORIA ★★ MGM/United Artists, 1982
TRAIL OF THE PINK PANTHER MGM/UA, 1982
SECOND THOUGHTS Universal, 1983
BETTER LATE THAN NEVER Warner Bros., 1983, British
CURSE OF THE PINK PANTHER MGM/UA, 1983
THE THORN BIRDS (MS) ☆ David L. Wolper-Stan Margulies Productions/Edward Lewis Productions/Warner Bros. TV, 1983
THE MAN WHO LOVED WOMEN Columbia, 1983
HARRY & SON Orion, 1984
THAT'S DANCING! (FD) MGM/UA, 1985
LIFEFORCE Tri-Star, 1985, British
SANTA CLAUS: THE MOVIE Tri-Star, 1985, U.S.-British
THE GREAT MOUSE DETECTIVE Buena Vista, 1986
A FINE MESS Columbia, 1986
THAT'S LIFE! Columbia, 1986
BLIND DATE Tri-Star, 1987
THE GLASS MENAGERIE Cineplex Odeon, 1987
SUNSET Tri-Star, 1988
WITHOUT A CLUE Orion, 1988
JUSTIN CASE (TF) The Blake Edwards Company/Walt Disney TV, 1988
PHYSICAL EVIDENCE Columbia, 1989
PETER GUNN (TF) The Blake Edwards Co./New World TV, 1989
SKIN DEEP 20th Century Fox, 1989
WELCOME HOME Columbia, 1989
FEAR (CTF) Vestron, 1990
GHOST DAD Universal, 1990

JOHNNY MANDEL

b. November 23, 1935 - New York, New York
Agent: Carol Faith - Beverly Hills, 213/274-0776

I WANT TO LIVE! United Artists, 1958
THE THIRD VOICE 20th Century Fox, 1959
DRUMS OF AFRICA MGM, 1963
THE AMERICANIZATION OF EMILY MGM, 1964
THE SANDPIPER MGM, 1965
THE RUSSIANS ARE COMING THE RUSSIANS ARE COMING United Artists, 1966
HARPER Warner Bros., 1966
AN AMERICAN DREAM Warner Bros., 1966
POINT BLANK MGM, 1967
PRETTY POISON 20th Century-Fox, 1968
HEAVEN WITH A GUN MGM, 1969
THAT COLD DAY IN THE PARK Commonwealth United, 1969, Canadian-U.S.
SOME KIND OF A NUT United Artists, 1969
M HA HS HH 20th Century-Fox, 1970
THE MAN WHO HAD POWER OVER WOMEN Avco Embassy, 1971, British
A NEW LEAF Paramount, 1971
CACTUS MOLLY AND LAWLESS JOHN Malibu Productions, 1971
THE TRACKERS (TF) Aaron Spelling Productions, 1971
JOURNEY THROUGH ROSEBUD GSF, 1972
SUMMER WISHES, WINTER DREAMS Columbia, 1973
THE LAST DETAIL Columbia, 1973
"W" Cinerama Releasing Corporation, 1974, British
THE TURNING POINT OF JIM MALLOY (TF) David Gerber Productions/Columbia Pictures TV, 1975
ESCAPE TO WITCH MOUNTAIN Buena Vista, 1975
THE SAILOR WHO FELL FROM GRACE WITH THE SEA Avco Embassy, 1976, British
FREAKY FRIDAY Buena Vista, 1976
AGATHA Warner Bros., 1979, British
BEING THERE United Artists, 1979
THE BALTIMORE BULLET Avco Embassy, 1980
CADDYSHACK Orion/Warner Bros., 1980
EVITA PERON (TF) Hartwest Productions/Zephyr Productions, 1981
DEATHTRAP Warner Bros., 1982
SOUP FOR ONE additional music, Warner Bros., 1982
LOOKIN' TO GET OUT Paramount, 1982
THE VERDICT 20th Century-Fox, 1982
STAYING ALIVE Paramount, 1983
A LETTER TO THREE WIVES (TF) ☆ 20th Century Fox TV, 1985
CHRISTMAS EVE (TF) NBC Productions, 1986
BRENDA STARR New World, 1987
LBJ: THE EARLY YEARS (TF) Louis Rudolph Films/ Fries Entertainment, 1987
ASSAULT AND MATRIMONY (TF) Michael Filerman Productions/NBC Productions, 1987
FOXFIRE (TF) ☆ Marian Rees Associates, 1987
THE GREAT ESCAPE II: THE UNTOLD STORY (TF) Spectator Films/Michael Jaffe Films, 1988
SINGLE MEN, MARRIED WOMEN (TF) Michele Lee Productions/CBS Entertainment, 1989

TOMMY MANDEL

DEADLY HERO co-composer with Brad Fiedel, Avco Embassy, 1976

HARRY MANFREDINI

Contact: BMI - Los Angeles, 213/659-9109

HERE COME THE TIGERS American International, 1978
THE KIRLIAN WITNESS 1978
NIGHT FLOWERS Willow Production Co., 1979
THE CHILDREN 1980
FRIDAY THE 13TH Paramount, 1980
FRIDAY THE 13TH PART 2 Paramount, 1981
FRIDAY THE 13TH PART 3 Paramount, 1982
SWAMP THING Avco Embassy, 1982
SPRING BREAK Columbia, 1983
THE RETURNING Willow Films, 1983
THE LAST PICNIC 1983
FRIDAY THE 13TH - THE FINAL CHAPTER Paramount, 1984
FRIDAY THE 13TH PART V - A NEW BEGINNING Paramount, 1985
THE HILLS HAVE EYES PART II Castle Prods., 1985, British-U.S.
HOUSE New World, 1986
FRIDAY THE 13TH PART VI: JASON LIVES Paramount, 1986
HOUSE II: THE SECOND STORY New World, 1987
FRIDAY THE 13TH PART VII - THE NEW BLOOD co-composer with Fred Mollin, Paramount, 1988
DOUBLE REVENGE Smart Egg Releasing, 1988
THE HORROR SHOW MGM/UA, 1989
DEEP STAR SIX Tri-Star, 1989
CAMERON'S CLOSET SVS Films, 1989
DOUBLE REVENGE Smart Egg Pictures, 1990

CHUCK MANGIONE

b. November 29, 1940 - Rochester, New York
Contact: BMI - Los Angeles, 213/659-9109

THE CHILDREN OF SANCHEZ Lone Star, 1978, U.S.-Mexican

BARRY MANN

Contact: BMI - Los Angeles, 213/659-9109

I NEVER SANG FOR MY FATHER co-composer with Al Gorgoni, Columbia, 1970

HUMMIE MANN

Contact: ASCAP - Los Angeles, 213/466-7681

STOOGEMANIA Atlantic Releasing Corporation, 1985

FRANCO MANNINO

b. 1924 - Palermo, Italy
Contact: SIAE - Rome, Italy, 011-39-6-59-90-1

DOMANI E UN ALTRO GIORNO 1951, Italian
BELLISSIMA Italian Films Export, 1951, Italian
CINEMA D'ALTRI TEMPI 1953, Italian
LA PROVINCIALE 1953, Italian
IL SOLE NEGLI OCCHI 1953, Italian
AI MARGINI DELLA METROPOLI 1953, Italian
BEAT THE DEVIL co-composer with Lambert Williamson, United Artists, 1954, British
VESTIRE GLI INUDI 1954, Italian
I VAMPIRI 1956, Italian
MORGAN THE PIRATE MGM, 1961, Italian
SEVEN SEAS TO CALAIS *IL DOMINATORE DEI SETTE MARI* MGM, 1962, Italian
GOLD FOR THE CAESARS Colorama, 1962, Italian-French

MADEMOISELLE DE MAUPIN Jolly Film/Consortium Pathe/Tecisa, 1965, Italian-French-Spanish
LOVE IN FOUR DIMENSIONS 1965, Italian
DEATH IN VENICE adaptation, Warner Bros., 1971, Italian-French
LUDWIG adaptation, MGM, 1972, Italian-French-West German
IDENTIKIT 1974, Italian
CONVERSATION PIECE *GRUPPO DI FAMIGLIAIN UNO INTERNO* New Line Cinema, 1975, Italian-French
UN CUORE SEMPLICE 1976, Italian
THE INNOCENT 1976, Italian
A SIMPLE HEART 1978, Italian

DAVID MANSFIELD

Agent: CAA - Los Angeles, 213/288-4545

HEAVEN'S GATE United Artists, 1980
YEAR OF THE DRAGON MGM/UA, 1985
CLUB PARADISE co-composer with Van Dyke Parks, Warner Bros., 1986
THE SICILIAN 20th Century Fox, 1987
INTO THE HOMELAND (CTF) Kevin McCormick/Anna Hamilton Phelan Productions, 1987
FRESH HORSES Columbia/WEG, 1988
MISS FIRECRACKER Firecracker Co. Productions/ Corsair Pictures, 1989
THE DESPERATE HOURS 1990

KEITH MANSFIELD

Contact: PRS - London, England, 011-44-1-580-5544

FIST OF FEAR TOUCH OF DEATH Aquarius, 1980

EDDIE LAWRENCE MANSON

b. May 9, 1925 - New York, New York
Contact: ASCAP - Los Angeles, 213/466-7681

THE LITTLE FUGITIVE 1953
LOVERS AND LOLLIPOPS 1956
DAY OF THE PAINTER 1960
THREE BITES OF THE APPLE 1967
A LOVE AFFAIR: THE ELEANOR AND LOU GEHRIG STORY (TF) Charles Fries Productions/Stonehenge Productions, 1978
CRASH (TF) Charles Fries Productions, 1978
TIGER TOWN (CTF) Thompson Street Pictures, 1983
EYE ON THE SPARROW (TF) Sarabande Productions/Republic Pictures, 1987

CHRIS MANY

HEART co-composer with Geoff Levin, New World, 1987

JIM MANZIE

Agent: Robert Light - Los Angeles, 213/651-1777

PUBERTY BLUES Universal Classics, 1982, Australian
RUNNING FROM THE GUNS 1987, Australian
THE OFFSPRING *FROM A WHISPER TO A SCREAM* TMS Pictures, 1987
STEPFATHER II co-composer with Pat Regan, Millimeter Films, 1989
LEATHERFACE: THE TEXAS CHAINSAW MASSACRE III co-composer with Pat Regan, New Line Cinema, 1990
TALES FROM THE DARKSIDE: THE MOVIE co-composer, Paramount, 1990

MARC MARDER

Agent: Bart-Milander - North Hollywood, 818/761-4040

SIDEWALK STORIES Island Pictures, 1989

SUSAN MARDER

Contact: BMI - Los Angeles, 213/659-9109

THE TAKE (CTF) co-composer with David Bell, Cine-Nevada Inc./MCA-TV, 1990

MITCH MARGO

Contact: ASCAP - Los Angeles, 213/466-7681

THE GODDESS OF LOVE (TF) co-composer with Dennis Dreith and A.S. Diamond, Phil Margo Enterprises/New World TV/Phoenix Entertainment Group, 1988

STUART MARGOLIN

b. January 31 - Davenport, Iowa
Home: Box 478, Ganges, Salt Spring Island, British Columbia VOS 1E0, Canada, 604/537-4224
Agent: Lou Pitt, ICM - Los Angeles, 213/550-4000

THE LONG SUMMER OF GEORGE ADAMS (TF) co-composer, Cherokee Productions/Warner Bros. TV, 1982
THE GLITTER DOME (CTF) HBO Premiere Films/ Telepictures Corporation/Trincomali Film Productions, 1984

ANTHONY MARINELLI

Agent: William Morris Agency - Beverly Hills, 213/274-7451

EPILOGUE OF DOOM co-composer with Brian Banks, Odette Productions, 1984
RIGGED co-composer with Brian Banks, CineStar, 1985
NICE GIRLS DON'T EXPLODE co-composer with Brian Banks, New World, 1987
PINOCCHIO AND THE EMPEROR OF THE NIGHT (AF) co-composer with Brian Banks, New World, 1987
YOUNG GUNS co-composer with Brian Banks, 20th Century Fox, 1988
SPOONER (TF) co-composer with Brian Banks, Walt Disney Productions, 1989
INTERNAL AFFAIRS co-composer with Mike Figgis and Brian Banks, Paramount, 1990
STEPHEN KING'S GRAVEYARD SHIFT co-composer with Brian Banks, Paramount, 1990

RICHARD MARKOWITZ

b. 1926
Agent: Robert Light - Los Angeles, 213/651-1777

STAKE-OUT ON DOPE STREET Warner Bros., 1958
THE HOT ANGEL Paramount, 1958
THE YOUNG CAPTIVES Paramount, 1959
OPERATION DAMES American International, 1959
ROAD RACERS American International, 1960
THE HOODLUM PRIEST United Artists, 1961
THE MAGIC SWORD United Artists, 1962
CRY OF BATTLE Allied Artists, 1963
A FACE IN THE RAIN Embassy, 1963
ONE MAN'S WAY Columbia, 1964
BUS RILEY'S BACK IN TOWN Universal, 1965
THE WILD SEED Universal, 1965
SCALPLOCK (TF) Columbia Pictures TV, 1966
THE SHOOTING American International, 1966
RIDE BEYOND VENGEANCE Columbia, 1966
A BLACK VEIL FOR LISA Commonwealth United, 1969, Italian-West German

WEEKEND OF TERROR (TF) Paramount TV, 1970
CRY FOR ME, BILLY *COUNT YOUR BULLETS/FACE TO THE WIND/APACHE MASSACRE/THE LONG TOMORROW* Brut Productions, 1972
THE VOYAGE OF THE YES (TF) Bing Crosby Productions, 1973
THE STRANGER (TF) Bing Crosby Productions, 1973
THE HANGED MAN (TF) Fenady Associates/Bing Crosby Productions, 1974
PANIC ON THE 5:22 (TF) QM Productions, 1974
THE GIRL ON THE LATE, LATE SHOW (TF) Screen Gems/Columbia TV, 1974
WINNER TAKE ALL (TF) The Jozak Company, 1975
THE RETURN OF JOE FORRESTER (TF) David Gerber Productions/Columbia Pictures TV, 1975
BRINK'S: THE GREAT ROBBERY (TF) QM Productions/Warner Bros. TV, 1976
KISS ME...KILL ME (TF) The Writers Company/ Columbia Pictures TV, 1976
MAYDAY AT 40,000 FEET (TF) Andrew J. Fenady Associates/Warner Bros. TV, 1976
WASHINGTON, BEHIND CLOSED DOORS (MS) composer of Parts 4 and 6 only, Paramount TV, 1977
DOCTORS' PRIVATE LIVES (TF) David Gerber Company/Columbia TV, 1978
STANDING TALL (TF) QM Productions, 1978
HUNTERS OF THE REEF (TF) Writers Company Productions/Paramount TV, 1978
THE BOSS' SON The Boss' Son Prods., 1978
DEATH CAR ON THE FREEWAY (TF) Shpetner Productions, 1979
THE NEIGHBORHOOD (TF) David Gerber Company/ Columbia TV, 1982
CIRCLE OF POWER *MYSTIQUE/BRAINWASH/THE NAKED WEEKEND* QUI Productions, 1983
A MASTERPIECE OF MURDER (TF) 20th Century Fox TV, 1986
THE LAW & HARRY MCGRAW (TF) Universal TV, 1987

WYNTON MARSALIS

Agent: CAA - Los Angeles, 213/288-4545

SHANNON'S DEAL (TF) Stan Rogaw Productions/ NBC Productions, 1989

JACK MARSHALL

Contact: BMI - Los Angeles, 213/659-9109

THE MISSOURI TRAVELER Buena Vista, 1958
THE RABBIT TRAP United Artists, 1959
TAKE A GIANT STEP United Artists, 1959
MY DOG BUDDY Columbia, 1960
MUNSTER, GO HOME Universal, 1966
TAMMY AND THE MILLIONAIRE Universal, 1967
KONA COAST Warner Bros., 1968
STAY AWAY, JOE MGM, 1968
SOMETHING FOR A LONELY MAN (TF) Universal TV, 1968

JULIAN MARSHALL

Contact: PRS - London, England, 011-44-1-580-5544

OLD ENOUGH Orion Classics, 1984

PHIL MARSHALL

Agent: Gorfaine-Schwartz - Burbank, 818/954-9500

PRIME RISK Almi Pictures, 1985
THE LAST OF PHILIP BANTER Tesauro, 1986, Spanish-Swiss

FULL MOON IN BLUE WATER Trans World Entertainment, 1988
ILLEGALLY YOURS MGM/UA, 1988
FLYING BLIND (TF) NBC Productions, 1990

GEORGE MARTIN

b. 1926
Contact: BMI - Los Angeles, 213/659-9109

A HARD DAY'S NIGHT ★ adaptation, United Artists, 1964, British
YELLOW SUBMARINE United Artists, 1968, British
PULP United Artists, 1972, British
LIVE AND LET DIE United Artists, 1973, British
THE OPTIMISTS *THE OPTIMISTS OF NINE ELMS* Paramount, 1973, British
HONKY TONK FREEWAY co-composer with Elmer Bernstein, Universal/AFD, 1981

GEORGE PORTER MARTIN

THE WHITE GIRL Tony Brown Productions, 1990

PETER MARTIN

Contact: PRS - London, England, 011-44-1-580-5544

HOPE AND GLORY Columbia, 1987, British

SIMON MICHAEL MARTIN

Contact: Pro-Canada - Canada, 1-416-445-8700

HEARTACHES Rising Star, 1981, Canadian

CLIFF MARTINEZ

b. February 2, 1954 - New York, New York
Agent: ICM - Los Angeles, 213/550-4000

sex, lies and videotape Outlaw Productions, 1989
PUMP UP THE VOLUME New Line, 1990

BILL MARX

Contact: ASCAP - Los Angeles, 213/466-7681

WALK THE ANGRY BEACH 1961
COUNT YORGA, VAMPIRE American International, 1970
THE RETURN OF COUNT YORGA American International, 1971
THE DEATHMASTER American International, 1972
THE FOLKS AT RED WOLF INN *TERROR HOUSE* Scope III, 1972
SCREAM, BLACULA, SCREAM American International, 1973
JOHNNY VIK 1973
ACT OF VENGEANCE American International, 1974

NICK MASON

Contact: PRS - London, England, 011-44-1-580-5544

WHITE OF THE EYE co-composer with Rick Fenn, Palisades Entertainment, 1988

JOHN MASSARI

Contact: Stu Yahm Management

KILLER KLOWNS FROM OUTER SPACE Trans World Entertainment, 1988

GEORGE MASSENBURG
Contact: Pro-Canada - Canada, 1-416-445-8700

CERTAIN FURY co-composer with Bill Payne and Russ Kunkel, New World, 1985, Canadian
SMOOTH TALK co-composer with Bill Payne and Russ Kunkel, Spectrafilm, 1985

MICHAEL MASSER
Contact: ASCAP - Los Angeles, 213/466-7681

MAHOGANY co-composer with Gil Askey and Lee Holdridge, Paramount, 1975
THE GREATEST co-composer with Lee Holdridge, Columbia, 1977

ALEJANDRO MASSO
Contact: Luis Mas, SGAE - New York, 212/752-7230

THE WITCHING HOUR Serva Films, 1985, Spanish

GREG MATHIESON
Contact: BMI - Los Angeles, 213/659-9109

AMERICAN FLYERS co-composer with Lee Ritenour, Warner Bros., 1985

SASHA MATSON
Agent: Robert Light - Los Angeles, 213/651-1777

DADDY'S BOYS Concorde, 1988
LOBSTER MAN FROM MARS Electric Pictures, 1989
RED SURF Arrowhead Entertainment, 1990

DAVID MATTHEWS
THE FIGHTERS 1974
STONY ISLAND World-Northal, 1978

PETER MATZ
b. November 6, 1928 - Pittsburgh, Pennsylvania
Agent: Carol Faith - Beverly Hills, 213/274-0776

BYE BYE BRAVERMAN Warner Bros., 1968
MARLOWE MGM, 1969
RIVALS *SINGLE PARENT* Avco Embassy, 1972
EMERGENCY! (TF) Mark VII Ltd./Universal TV, 1972
I HEARD THE OWL CALL MY NAME (TF) Tomorrow Entertainment, 1973
LARRY (TF) Tomorrow Entertainment, 1974
FUNNY LADY ★ adaptation, Columbia, 1975
IN THIS HOUSE OF BREDE (TF) Tomorrow Entertainment, 1975
THE DARK SIDE OF INNOCENCE (TF) Warner Bros. TV, 1976
JUST AN OLD SWEET SONG (TF) MTM Enterprises, 1976
THE CALL OF THE WILD (TF) Charles Fries Productions, 1976
THE GREAT HOUDINIS (TF) ABC Circle Films, 1976
TERRACES (TF) Charles Fries Productions/ Worldvision, 1977
THE LAST HURRAH (TF) O'Connor-Becker Productions/Columbia TV, 1977
SPECIAL OLYMPICS (TF) Roger Gimbel Productions/ EMI TV, 1978
ONE IN A MILLION: THE RON LeFLORE STORY (TF) Roger Gimbel Productions/EMI TV, 1978
HAPPILY EVER AFTER (TF) Tri-Media II, Inc./Hamel-Somers Entertainment, 1978
THE GRASS IS ALWAYS GREENER OVER THE SEPTIC TANK (TF) Joe Hamilton Productions, 1978
FIRST YOU CRY (TF) ☆ MTM Enterprises, 1978
LOVE FOR RENT (TF) Warren V. Bush Productions, 1979
CAN YOU HEAR THE LAUGHTER? THE STORY OF FREDDIE PRINZE (TF) Roger Gimbel Productions/ EMI TV, 1979
I KNOW WHY THE CAGED BIRD SINGS (TF) Tomorrow Entertainment, 1979
THE TENTH MONTH (TF) Joe Hamilton Productions, 1979
THE PRIZE FIGHTER New World, 1979
THE MAN IN THE SANTA CLAUS SUIT (TF) Dick Clark Productions, 1979
VALENTINE MAGIC ON LOVE ISLAND (TF) Dick Clark Productions/PKO Television/Osmond TV Productions, 1980
THE PRIVATE EYES New World, 1980
WHITE MAMA (TF) Tomorrow Entertainment, 1980
FUN AND GAMES (TF) Kanin-Gallo Productions/Warner Bros. TV, 1980
DAMIEN: THE LEPER PRIEST (TF) ☆ Tomorrow Entertainment, 1980
CRAZY TIMES (TF) Kayden-Gleason Productions/George Reeves Productions/Warner Bros. TV, 1981
THE KILLING OF RANDY WEBSTER (TF) Roger Gimbel Productions/EMI TV, 1981
TAKE YOUR BEST SHOT (TF) Levinson-Link Productions/ Robert Papazian Productions, 1982
DROP-OUT FATHER (TF) ☆ CBS Entertainment, 1982
LUST IN THE DUST New World, 1985
MRS. DELAFIELD WANTS TO MARRY (TF) Schaefer-Karpf Productions/Gaylord Production Company, 1986
STONE FOX (TF) co-composer with Allyn Ferguson, Hanna-Barbera Productions/Allarcom Ltd./Taft Entertainment TV, 1987, U.S.-Canadian
MERCY OR MURDER? (TF) John J. McMahon Productions/MGM-UA TV, 1987
LAURA LANSING SLEPT HERE (TF) Schaefer-Karpf-Eckstein Productions/Gaylord Production Company, 1988
TORCH SONG TRILOGY adaptation, New Line Cinema, 1988
WHEN WE WERE YOUNG (TF) Richard & Esther Shapiro Entertainment, 1989
THE GUMSHOE KID Skouras Pictures, 1989

BILLY MAY
b. November 10, 1916 - Pittsburgh, Pennsylvania
Contact: BMI - Los Angeles, 213/659-9109

THE FUZZY PINK NIGHTGOWN United Artists, 1957
SERGEANTS 3 United Artists, 1962
JOHNNY COOL United Artists, 1963
THE PLEASURE SEEKERS 20th Century-Fox, 1964
TONY ROME 20th Century-Fox, 1967
THE SECRET LIFE OF AN AMERICAN WIFE 20th Century-Fox, 1968
THE BALLAD OF ANDY CROCKER (TF) Thomas-Spelling Productions, 1969
THE PIGEON (TF) Thomas-Spelling Productions, 1969
THE FRONT PAGE Universal, 1974
THE SPECIALISTS (TF) Mark VII Ltd./Universal TV, 1975
TAIL GUNNER JOE (TF) Universal TV, 1977
LITTLE MO (TF) co-composer with Carl Brandt, Mark VII Ltd./Worldvision Enterprises, 1978
RETURN OF THE BEVERLY HILLBILLIES (TF) The Energy Venture, 1981

BRIAN MAY

b. Australia
Agent: Robert Light - Los Angeles, 213/651-1777

THE TRUE STORY OF ESKIMO NELL *DICK DOWN UNDER* Quest Films/Filmways Australasian Distributors, 1975, Australian
NO ROOM TO RUN (TF) Australian Broadcasting Commission/Trans-Atlantic Enterprises, 1977, Australian
BARNABY AND ME Trans-Atlantic Enterprises, 1978
PATRICK Cinema Shares International, 1979, Australian
THE DAY AFTER HALLOWEEN *SNAPSHOT* Group 1, 1979, Australian
THIRST 1979, Australian
MAD MAX American International, 1979, Australian
HARLEQUIN New Image, 1980, Australian
THE LAST OUTLAW (MS) Network Seven/Pegasus Productions, 1980, Australian
NIGHTMARES Australian
THE SURVIVOR Hemdale, 1981, Australian
DEADLINE Australian
GALLIPOLI Paramount, 1981, Australian
ROAD GAMES Avco Embassy, 1981
DANGEROUS SUMMER Filmco Ltd., 1982, Australian
TREASURE OF THE YANKEE ZEPHYR *RACE TO THE YANKEE ZEPHYR* Artists Releasing Corporation/Film Ventures International, 1984, New Zealand-British
THE KILLING OF ANGEL STREET Forest Home Films, 1981, Australian
BREAKFAST IN PARIS 1982, Australian
THE ROAD WARRIOR *MAD MAX II* Warner Bros., 1982, Australian
TURKEY SHOOT Second FGH Film Consortium, 1982, Australian
KITTY & THE BAGMAN Quartet/Films Incorporated, 1982, Australian
RETURN TO EDEN (MS) McElroy & McElroy/Hanna-Barbera Australia Productions, 1983, Australian
A SLICE OF LIFE Australian
VOYEUR Australian
CLOAK & DAGGER Universal, 1984
MISSING IN ACTION II: THE BEGINNING Cannon, 1984
FROG DREAMING Middle Reef Productions, 1985
THE LAST FRONTIER (TF) McElroy & McElroy Productions, 1986, Australian
SKY PIRATES John Lamond Motion Pictures, 1986, Australian
DEATH BEFORE DISHONOR New World, 1987
STEEL DAWN Vestron, 1987
A DANGEROUS LIFE (CTF) HBO/McElroy & McElroy/FilmAccord Corporation/Australian Broadcasting Corporation/Zenith Productions, 1988, U.S.-Australian

DANIEL MAY

Contact: BMI - Los Angeles, 213/659-9109

ZOMBIE HIGH Cinema Group, 1987
SEVERANCE Fox/Lorber Films, 1989

LYLE MAYERS

THE SEARCH FOR SOLUTIONS (FD) co-composer with Pat Metheny, Playback Associates, 1979

CURTIS MAYFIELD

b. June 3, 1942 - Chicago, Illinois
Contact: BMI - Los Angeles, 213/659-9109

SUPERFLY Warner Bros., 1972
CLAUDINE 20th Century-Fox, 1974
LET'S DO IT AGAIN Warner Bros., 1975
SPARKLE Warner Bros., 1976
A PIECE OF THE ACTION Warner Bros., 1977
SHORT EYES *SLAMMER* The Film League, 1977

DOUG MAYNARD

PATTI ROCKS FilmDallas, 1987

LINCOLN MAYORGA

Contact: ASCAP - Los Angeles, 213/466-7681

NICKEL MOUNTAIN Ziv International, 1985

LYLE MAYS

Contact: BMI - Los Angeles, 213/659-9109

THE FALCON AND THE SNOWMAN co-composer with Pat Metheny, Orion, 1985

JOHN McCABE

Contact: PRS - London, England, 011-44-1-580-5544

FEAR IN THE NIGHT International Co-Productions, 1972, British

PAUL McCALLUM

Contact: BMI - Los Angeles, 213/659-9109

DEATH WISH 4: THE CRACKDOWN co-composer with Valentine McCallum and John Bisharat, Cannon, 1988

VALENTINE McCALLUM

Contact: BMI - Los Angeles, 213/659-9109

MURPHY'S LAW co-composer with Marc Donahue, Cannon, 1986
ASSASSINATION co-composer with Robert O. Ragland, Cannon, 1987
DEATH WISH 4: THE CRACKDOWN co-composer with Paul McCallum and John Bisharat, Cannon, 1988

DENNIS McCARTHY

Agent: Gorfaine-Schwartz - Burbank, 818/954-9500

PRAY TV (TF) ABC Circle Films, 1982
THE KID WITH THE 200 I.Q. (TF) Guillaume-Margo Productions/Zephyr Productions, 1983
OFF THE WALL Jensen Farley Pictures, 1983
V: THE FINAL BATTLE (MS) composer of parts 2 and 3, Blatt-Singer Productions/Warner Bros. TV, 1984
PLAYING WITH FIRE (TF) Zephyr Productions/New World Pictures, 1985
HOUSTON: THE LEGEND OF TEXAS (TF) Taft Entertainment TV/J.D. Feigelson Productions, 1986
HOUSTON KNIGHTS (TF) Jay Bernstein Productions/Columbia Pictures TV, 1987
SWORN TO SILENCE (TF) Daniel H. Blatt-Robert Singer Productions, 1987
STAR TREK: THE NEXT GENERATION (TF) Paramount TV, 1987
THE LOVE BOAT: A VALENTINE VOYAGE (TF) Aaron Spelling Productions/Douglas S. Cramer Co., 1990

PAUL McCARTNEY
b. June 18, 1942 - Liverpool, England
Contact: PRS - London, England, 011-44-1-580-5544

THE FAMILY WAY Warner Bros., 1967, British

MICHAEL McCARTY
Contact: ASCAP - Los Angeles, 213/466-7681

DANGEROUSLY CLOSE Cannon, 1986

MATTHEW McCAULEY
Agent: Bart-Milander - North Hollywood, 818/761-4040

BETWEEN FRIENDS Eudon Productions, 1973, Canadian
SUDDEN FURY Filmscan, 1975, Canadian
CITY ON FIRE! Avco Embassy, 1979, Canadian
RIEL CBC/Green River Productions, 1979, Canadian
MIDDLE AGE CRAZY 20th Century-Fox, 1980, Canadian-U.S.
IN THE CUSTODY OF STRANGERS (TF) Moonlight Productions/Filmways, 1982
THE LAST UNICORN (AF) Jensen Farley Pictures, 1982
A MATTER OF SEX (CTD) Willmar 8 Productions/ Orion TV, 1984
OBSESSIVE LOVE (TF) Onza Inc./Moonlight Productions, 1984
THE UNDERGRADS (CTF) Sharmhill Productions/ The Disney Channel, 1985, U.S.-Canadian
MANY HAPPY RETURNS (TF) Alan M. Levin & Steven H. Stern Films, 1986, U.S.-Canadian
THUNDER RUN Cannon, 1986
STATE PARK ITC, 1987, Canadian

TIM McCAULEY
Contact: Pro-Canada - Canada, 1-416-445-8700

LOVE Velvet Films, 1982, Canadian
SCREWBALLS New World, 1983

STEPHEN McCURDY
Contact: APRA - Australia, 011-61-2-922-6422

SHAKER RUN Challenge Film Corporation, 1985, New Zealand

JOHN McEUEN
MAN OUTSIDE Virgin Vision, 1988

DAVID McHUGH
Agent: ICM - Los Angeles, 213/550-4000

NOBODY'S PERFEKT Columbia, 1981
GO FOR THE GOLD Go for the Gold Productions, 1984
MOSCOW ON THE HUDSON Columbia, 1984
PUMPING IRON II: THE WOMEN (FD) Cinecom, 1985
ONE MORE SATURDAY NIGHT Columbia, 1986
SOMETHING SPECIAL *WILLY MILLY/I WAS A TEENAGE BOY* Cinema Group, 1986
WELCOME HOME, BOBBY (TF) Titus Productions, 1986
A YEAR IN THE LIFE (MS) Universal TV, 1986
JOCKS Crown International, 1987
MR. NORTH Heritage Entertainment, 1988
MYSTIC PIZZA Samuel Goldwyn Company, 1988
THREE FUGITIVES Buena Vista, 1989
THE DREAM TEAM Universal, 1989
MONTANA (CTF) HBO Productions/Zoetrope Studios/ Roger Gimbel Productions, 1990
DADDY'S DYIN'...WHO'S GOT THE WILL? MGM/UA, 1990

TOM McINTOSH
Contact: BMI - Los Angeles, 213/659-9109

SLITHER MGM, 1973
A HERO AIN'T NOTHIN' BUT A SANDWICH New World, 1977

FRANK McKELVEY
BOGGY CREEK II Howco International, 1985

ROD McKUEN
b. April 29, 1933 - Oakland, California
Contact: ASCAP - Los Angeles, 213/466-7681

JOANNA 20th Century-Fox, 1968, British
A BOY NAMED CHARLIE BROWN (AF) National General, 1968
THE PRIME OF MISS JEAN BRODIE 20th Century-Fox, 1969, British
COME TO YOUR SENSES 1971
SCANDALOUS JOHN Buena Vista, 1971
THE BORROWERS (TF) co-composer with Billy Byers, Walt DeFaria Productions/20th Century-Fox TV, 1973
LISA, BRIGHT AND DARK (TF) Bob Banner Associates, 1973
EMILY 1976, British

DON McLEAN
Contact: BMI - Los Angeles, 213/659-9109

FRATERNITY ROW Paramount, 1977

GERARD McMAHON
Contact: BMI - Los Angeles, 213/659-9109

DEFIANCE co-composer with Basil Poledouris, American International, 1980

JOEL McNEELY
Agent: Gorfaine-Schwartz - Burbank, 818/954-9500

YOU TALKIN' TO ME MGM/UA, 1987
SPLASH, TOO (TF) Mark H. Ovitz Productions/Walt Disney TV, 1988
DAVY CROCKETT: RAINBOW IN THE THUNDER (TF) Echo Cove Productions/Walt Disney TV, 1988
APPEARNCES (TF) Echo Cove Productions/ Touchstone TV, 1990

ABIGAIL MEAD
Contact: PRS - London, England, 011-44-1-580-5544

FULL METAL JACKET Warner Bros., 1987

PADDY MEEGAN
Contact: PRS - London, England, 011-44-1-580-5544

DANNY BOY *ANGEL* Triumph/Columbia, 1983, Irish

GIL MELLE

b. December 31, 1935 - Jersey City, New Jersey
Agent: Robert Light - Los Angeles, 213/651-1777

MY SWEET CHARLIE (TF) Bob Banner Associates/ Universal TV, 1970
THE ANDROMEDA STRAIN Universal, 1971
THE ORGANIZATION United Artists, 1971
IF TOMORROW COMES (TF) Aaron Spelling Productions/American Broadcasting Company, 1971
THE ASTRONAUT (TF) Universal TV, 1972
YOU'LL LIKE MY MOTHER Universal, 1972
BONE Jack H. Harris Enterprises, 1972
THE VICTIM (TF) Universal TV, 1972
LIEUTENANT SCHUSTER'S WIFE (TF) Universal TV, 1972
THE JUDGE AND JAKE WYLER (TF) Universal TV, 1972
A COLD NIGHT'S DEATH (TF) ABC Circle Films, 1973
TENAFLY (TF) Universal TV, 1973
SAVAGE (TF) Universal TV, 1973
PARTNERS IN CRIME (TF) Fairmont/Foxcroft Productions/Universal TV, 1973
THE SIX-MILLION DOLLAR MAN (TF) Universal TV, 1973
TRAPPED (TF) Universal TV, 1973
THE PRESIDENT'S PLANE IS MISSING (TF) ABC Circle Films, 1973
FRANKENSTEIN: THE TRUE STORY (TF) Universal TV, 1973
THE QUESTOR TAPES (TF) Universal TV, 1974
HITCHHIKE! (TF) Universal TV, 1974
THE LAST ANGRY MAN (TF) The Jozak Company/ Screen Gems/Columbia Pictures TV, 1974
KILLDOZER (TF) Universal TV, 1974
THE SAVAGE IS LOOSE Campbell Devon, 1974
THE MISSING ARE DEADLY (TF) Lawrence Gordon Productions, 1975
A CRY FOR HELP (TF) Fairmont-Foxcroft Productions/ Universal TV, 1975
THE IMPOSTER (TF) Warner Bros. TV, 1975
CRIME CLUB (TF) Universal TV, 1975
DEATH SCREAM (TF) RSO Films, 1975
JAMES MICHENER'S DYNASTY (TF) David Paradine TV, 1976
THE ULTIMATE WARRIOR Warner Bros., 1976
PERILOUS VOYAGE (TF) Universal TV, 1976
EMBRYO Cine Artists, 1976
THE SENTINEL Universal, 1977
STARSHIP INVASIONS Warner Bros., 1977, Canadian
GOLD OF THE AMAZON WOMEN (TF) MI-KA Productions Inc., 1979
ATTICA (TF) ABC Circle Films, 1980
BORDERLINE ITC, 1980
THE CURSE OF KING TUT'S TOMB (TF) Stromberg-Kerby Productions/Columbia TV/ HTV West, 1980
RAPE AND MARRIAGE—THE RIDEOUT CASE (TF) Dick Berg/Stonehenge Productions/Lorimar Productions, 1980
BLOOD BEACH Jerry Gross Organization, 1981
THE INTRUDER WITHIN (TF) Furia-Oringer Productions, 1981
THE LAST CHASE Crown International, 1981, Canadian
WORLD WAR III (TF) Finnegan Associates/David Greene Productions, 1982
THROUGH NAKED EYES (TF) Charles Fries Productions, 1983
JEALOUSY (TF) co-composer with Jimmie Haskell, Charles Fries Productions/Alan Sacks Productions, 1984
FLIGHT 90: DISASTER ON THE POTOMAC (TF) Sheldon Pinchuk Productions/Finnegan Associates, 1984
BEST KEPT SECRETS (TF) ABC Circle Films, 1984
SWEET REVENGE (TF) David Greene Productions/Robert Papazian Productions, 1984
FATAL VISION (TF) NBC Entertainment, 1984
STARCROSSED (TF) Fries Entertainment, 1985
WHEN DREAMS COME TRUE (TF) I&C Productions, 1985
HOT TARGET Crown International, 1985, New Zealand
KILLER IN THE MIRROR (TF) Litke-Grossbart Productions/ Warner Bros. TV, 1986
THE DELIBERATE STRANGER (TF) Stuart Phoenix Productions/Lorimar-Telepictures, 1986
RESTLESS Endeavour Productions, 1986, Australian
CIRCLE OF VIOLENCE: A FAMILY DRAMA (TF) Sheldon Pinchuk Productions/Rafshoon Communications Inc./ Finnegan Associates/Telepictures Productions, 1986
STILLWATCH (TF) Zev Braun Pictures/Potomac Productions/Interscope Communications, 1987
THE TAKING OF FLIGHT 847: THE ULI DERICKSON STORY (TF) Columbia TV, 1988
FROM THE DEAD OF NIGHT (TF) Shadowplay Films/ Phoenix Entertainment Group, 1989
THE CASE OF THE HILLSIDE STRANGLER (TF) Kenwood Productions/Fries Entertainment, 1989
SO PROUDLY WE HAIL (TF) Lionel Chetwynd Productions/ CBS Entertainment, 1990

PETER MELNICK

GET SMART, AGAIN! (TF) IndieProd Productions/Phoenix Entertainment Group, 1989

MICHAEL MELVOIN

Agent: Robert Light - Los Angeles, 213/651-1777

MONGO'S BACK IN TOWN (TF) Bob Banner Associates, 1971
THE LAST SURVIVORS (TF) Bob Banner Associates, 1975
ASPEN (MS) co-composer with Tom Scott, Universal TV, 1977
ASHANTI Columbia, 1979, Swiss-U.S.
THE MAIN EVENT Warner Bros., 1979
BLIND FEAR Allegro Films, 1980
PICKING UP THE PIECES Saratoga Films, 1981
KING OF THE MOUNTAIN Universal, 1981
RETURN OF THE REBELS (TF) Moonlight Productions/ Filmways, 1981
ARMED AND DANGEROUS Columbia, 1986
THE BIG TOWN Columbia, 1987
SHARING RICHARD (TF) Houston Motion Picture Entertainment/CBS Entertainment, 1988

JAIME MENDOZA-NAVA

BOOTLEGGERS Howco International, 1974
PSYCHO FROM TEXAS New American Films, 1974
TEARS OF HAPPINESS 1974
THE TOWN THAT DREADED SUNDOWN American International, 1977
GRAYEAGLE American International, 1977
THE BOYS IN COMPANY C Columbia, 1978
THE NORSEMAN American International, 1978
THE EVICTORS American International, 1979
MAUSOLEUM MPM, 1983

ALAN MENKEN
Agent: The Shukat Company - New York, 212/582-7614

THE LITTLE MERMAID (AF) ★★ Buena Vista, 1989

JOEY MENNONNA
BAD BLOOD Platinum Pictures, 1989

DALE MENTEN
Contact: BMI - Los Angeles, 213/659-9109

LIFEGUARD Paramount, 1976

PAT METHENY
Agent: Gorfaine-Schwartz - Burbank, 818/954-9500

THE SEARCH FOR SOLUTIONS (FD) co-composer with Lyle Mayers, Playback Associates, 1979
TWICE IN A LIFETIME The Yorkin Company, 1985
THE FALCON AND THE SNOWMAN co-composer with Lyle Mays, Orion, 1985
LEMON SKY American Playhouse, 1987

BILL MEYERS
Contact: BMI - Los Angeles, 213/659-9109

ARMED AND DANGEROUS Columbia, 1986

LANNY MEYERS
Contact: ASCAP - Los Angeles, 213/466-7681

THE FIRST TIME New Line Cinema, 1983
BEIRUT: THE LAST HOME MOVIE (FD) Zohe Film, 1987

FRANCO MICALIZZI
b. Italy
Contact: SIAE - Rome, Italy, 011-39-6-59-90-1

LO CHIAMAVANO TRINITA 1970, Italian
BEYOND THE DOOR 1974, U.S.-Italian
IL FOGLIO DELLA SEPOLTA VIVA 1974, Italian
L'ULTIMA NEVE DI PRIMAVERA 1974, Italian
IL PIATTO PIANGE 1974, Italian
ALLA MIA CARA MAMMA NEL GIORNO DEL SUO COMPLEANNO 1974, Italian
L'ALBERO DALLE FOGLIE ROSA 1974, Italian
BIANCHI CAVALLI D'AGOSTO 1975, Italian
GIOVANNINO 1975, Italian
IL GIUSTIZIERE SFIDA LA CITTA 1975, Italian
TRE SUPERMEN CONTRO LE AMAZZONI 1975, Italian
LAURE 1975, Italian
LEZIONI PRIVATE 1975, Italian
SYNDICATE SADISTS Summit Associates Ltd., 1975, Italian
IL CINICO, L'INFAME, IL VIOLENTO 1976, Italian
GENOVA A MANO ARMATA 1976, Italian
ITALIA A MANO ARMATA 1976, Italian
NAPOLI VIOLENTA 1976, Italian
THE LAST HUNTER *HUNTER OF THE APOCALYPSE* World Northal, 1980, Italian
FOREVER EMMANUELLE Movies for Cable, 1982, Italian-French
THE CURSE Trans World Entertainment, 1987

GEORGE MICHALSKI
Contact: ASCAP - Los Angeles, 213/466-7681

KANDYLAND New World, 1988

HARRY MIDDLEBROOKS
Contact: BMI - Los Angeles, 213/659-9109

GUS BROWN AND MIDNIGHT BREWSTER (TF) Kaledonia Productions/SCOMI, 1985

FRANKIE MILLER
ACT OF VENGEANCE (CTF) Telepic Canada Corporation Productions/Frank Koenigsberg Productions/ Lorimar-Telepictures Productions, 1986

MARCUS MILLER
HOUSE PARTY co-composer with Lenny White, New Line Cinema, 1990

RANDY MILLER
Contact: BMI - Los Angeles, 213/659-9109

DR. HACKENSTEIN Vista Street Productions, 1988
WITCHCRAFT Film Mirage, 1988, Italian

MARIO MILLO
Contact: APRA - Australia, 011-61-2-922-6422

THE LIGHTHORSEMAN Cinecom International, 1988

JOHN MILLS-COCKELL
Contact: Pro-Canada - Canada, 1-416-445-8700

TERROR TRAIN 20th Century-Fox, 1980, Canadian
HUMONGOUS Avco Embassy, 1982, Canadian

DAN MILNER
Contact: BMI - Los Angeles, 213/659-9109

HAPPY HOUR TMS Pictures, 1987

MICHAEL MINARD
Contact: ASCAP - Los Angeles, 213/466-7681

SPECIAL EFFECTS New Line Cinema, 1985

DAVID MINDEL
Contact: PRS - London, England, 011-44-1-580-5544

REAL LIFE Bedford, 1984, British

RICHARD MITCHELL
Contact: ASCAP - Los Angeles, 213/466-7681

BORN AMERICAN Concorde, 1986, Finnish-U.S.

VIC MIZZY
b. 1922 - Brooklyn, New York
Contact: ASCAP - Los Angeles, 213/466-7681

THE NIGHT WALKER Universal, 1965
A VERY SPECIAL FAVOR Universal, 1965
THE GHOST AND MR. CHICKEN Universal, 1966
THE BUSY BODY Paramount, 1967
THE CAPER OF THE GOLDEN BULLS Embassy, 1967
THE RELUCTANT ASTRONAUT Universal, 1967

DON'T MAKE WAVES MGM, 1967
THE SPIRIT IS WILLING Paramount, 1967
THE PERILS OF PAULINE Universal, 1967
DID YOU HEAR THE ONE ABOUT THE TRAVELING SALESLADY? Universal, 1968
THE SHAKIEST GUN IN THE WEST Universal, 1968
HOW TO FRAME A FIGG Universal, 1971
THE DEADLY HUNT (TF) Four Star International, 1971
A VERY MISSING PERSON (TF) Universal TV, 1972
GETTING AWAY FROM IT ALL (TF) Palomar Productions, 1972
HURRICANE (TF) Montagne Productions/Metromedia Producers Corporation, 1974
TERROR ON THE 40TH FLOOR (TF) Montagne Productions/Metromedia Producers Corporation, 1974
THE MILLION DOLLAR RIP-OFF (TF) Charles Fries Productions/Montagne Productions, 1976
THE MUNSTERS' REVENGE (TF) Universal TV, 1981

MARK MOFFIATT
Contact: APRA - Australia, 011-61-2-922-6422

HIGH TIDE co-composer with Ricky Fataar, Hemdale, 1987, Australian

FRED MOLLIN
Agent: Robert Light - Los Angeles, 213/651-1777

SPRING FEVER Comworld, 1983, Canadian
FRIDAY THE 13TH, PART VII - THE NEW BLOOD co-composer with Harry Manfredini, Paramount, 1988
FRIDAY THE 13th, PART VIII - JASON TAKES MANHATTAN Paramount, 1989

FRANCIS MONKMAN
Contact: PRS - London, England, 011-44-1-580-5544

THE LONG GOOD FRIDAY Embassy, 1982, British

DOUG MOODY
DU BEAT-E-O H-Z-H Presentation, 1984

HAL MOONEY
Contact: ASCAP - Los Angeles, 213/466-7681

THE LONGEST NIGHT (TF) Universal TV, 1972
TOM SAWYER (TF) Hal Roach Productions/ Universal TV, 1973
RUNAWAY! (TF) Universal TV, 1973
MY DARLING DAUGHTERS' ANNIVERSARY (TF) Groverton Productions/Universal TV, 1973
THE CHADWICK FAMILY (TF) Universal TV, 1974
THE TRIBE (TF) Universal TV, 1974
THE STORYTELLER (TF) co-composer with David Shire, Fairmount/Foxcroft Productions/ Universal TV, 1977

DUDLEY MOORE
b. April 19, 1935 - London, England
Contact: PRS - London, England, 011-44-1-580-5544

BEDAZZLED 20th Century-Fox, 1967, British
30 IS A DANGEROUS AGE, CYNTHIA Columbia, 1968, British
INADMISSABLE EVIDENCE Paramount, 1968, British
STAIRCASE 20th Century-Fox, 1969, British
THE HOUND OF THE BASKERVILLES Atlantic Releasing Corporation, 1979, British
DEREK AND CLIVE GET THE HORN Peter Cook Productions, 1981, British
SIX WEEKS Universal, 1982

JACQUES MORALI
Contact: SACEM - France, 011-33-14-747-5650

CRAZY HORSE PARIS—FRANCE SNC, 1977, French
I'VE GOT YOU, YOU'VE GOT ME BY THE HAIRS OF MY CHINNY CHIN CHIN 1979, French
CAN'T STOP THE MUSIC AFD, 1980

MIKE MORAN
Contact: PRS - London, England, 011-44-1-580-5544

TIME BANDITS Avco Embassy, 1981, British
THE MISSIONARY Columbia, 1982, British
WATER Atlantic Releasing Corporation, 1984, British

PATRICK MORAZ
Contact: SUISA - Zurich, Switzerland, 011-41-1-482-6666

THE STEPFATHER New Century/Vista, 1987

HOWARD MORGAN
Contact: BMI - Los Angeles, 213/659-9109

MERCENARY FIGHTERS Cannon, 1988

JOHN W. MORGAN
b. October 21, 1946 - Los Angeles, California
Contact: Tarzana, 818/344-0930

THE AFTERMATH Prism Entertainment, 1982
FLICKS United Film Distribution Co., 1987
BACK FROM THE PAST additional music, 1990
EVIL NIGHT Nautilus Film Co., 1990

KUROUDO MORI
b. Japan
Contact: JASRAC - Tokyo, Japan, 011-81-3-502-6551

MUDDY RIVER Japan Film Center, 1981, Japanese

KEN-ICHIRO MORIOKA
b. Japan
Contact: JASRAC - Tokyo, Japan, 011-81-3-502-6551

MESSAGE FROM SPACE (AF) United Artists, 1978, Japanese

ANGELA MORLEY
(Wally Stott)
Agent: Carol Faith - Beverly Hills, 213/274-0776

THE LOOKING GLASS WAR Columbia, 1970, British
CAPTAIN NEMO AND THE UNDERWATER CITY MGM, 1970, British
WHEN EIGHT BELLS TOLL Cinerama Releasing Corporation, 1971, British
THE LITTLE PRINCE ★ Paramount, 1974, British
THE SLIPPER AND THE ROSE: THE STORY OF CINDERELLA ★ adaptation, Universal, 1976, Brtiish
WATERSHIP DOWN (AF) Avco Embassy, 1978, British
LA COLINA DEI COMALI 1979, Italian
FRIENDSHIPS, SECRETS AND LIES (TF) Wittman-Riche Productions/Warner Bros. TV, 1979

MADAME X (TF) Levenback-Riche Productions/ Universal TV, 1981
SUMMER GIRL (TF) Bruce Lansbury Productions/ Roberta Haynes Productions/Finnegan Associates, 1983
TWO MARRIAGES (TF) Lorimar Productions/Raven's Claw Productions, 1983
THREESOME (TF) CBS Entertainment, 1984

GIORGIO MORODER

b. April 26, 1940 - Ortisei, Italy
Agent: Bart-Milander - North Hollywood, 818/761-4040

MIDNIGHT EXPRESS ★★ Columbia, 1978, British
FOXES Paramount, 1980
AMERICAN GIGOLO Paramount, 1980
CAT PEOPLE Universal, 1982
D.C. CAB Universal, 1983
FLASHDANCE Paramount, 1983
METROPOLIS new score for 1926 silent, 1983
SCARFACE Universal, 1983
THE NEVERENDING STORY co-composer with Klaus Doldinger, Warner Bros., 1984, West German
ELECTRIC DREAMS MGM/UA, 1984
OVER THE TOP Cannon, 1987
FAIR GAME 1988
LET IT RIDE Paramount, 1989

ENNIO MORRICONE

b. October 11, 1928 - Rome, Italy
Agent: Gorfaine-Schwartz - Burbank, 818/954-9500

THE FASCIST 1961, Italian
CRAZY DESIRE *LA VOGLIE MATTA* 1962, Italian
DICIOTTENNI AL SOLE 1962, Italian
I MOTORIZATTI 1962, Italian
LA CUCCAGNA *A GIRL...AND A MILLION* 1963, Italian
THE HOURS OF LOVE *LE ORE DELL'AMORE* 1963, Italian
IL SUCCESSO 1963, Italian
I BASILISCHI 1963, Italian
LE MONASCHINE *THE LITTLE NUNS* 1963, French
GRINGO *DUELLO NEL TEXAS/GUNFIGHT AT RED SANDS* 1963, Italian
I MANIACI 1964, Italian
I MALAMONDO 1964, Italian
IN GINOCCHIO DA TE 1964, Italian
BEFORE THE REVOLUTION New Yorker, 1964, Italian
I MARZIANI HANNO 12 MANI 1964, Italian
I DUE EVASI DI SING SING 1964, Italian
LE PISTOLE NON DISCUTUNO 1964, Italian
A FISTFUL OF DOLLARS United Artists, 1964, Italian-Spanish-West German
NON SON DEGNO DI TE 1965, Italian
UNA PISTOLA PER RINGO 1965, Italian
ALTISSIMA PRESSIONE co-composer with Luis Bacalov, 1965, Italian
I PUGNI IN TASCA 1965, Italian
SLALOM 1965, Italian
NIGHTMARE CASTLE *AMANTI D'OLTRE TOMBA* 1965, Italian
FOR A FEW DOLLARS MORE United Artists, 1965, Italian-Spanish-West German
IL RITORNO DI RINGO 1965, Italian
MENAGE ALL'ITALIANA 1965, Italian
SETTE PISTOLE PER I MACGREGOR 1965, Italian
EL GRECO 1966, Italian
SE NON AVESSI PIU TE 1966, Italian
IDOLI CONTROLUCE 1966, Italian
MI VEDRAI TORNARE 1966, Italian
TOO SOON TO DIE *SVEGLIATI E UCCIDI* 1966, Italian
ADULTERIO ALL'ITALIANA 1966, Italian
THE HAWKS AND THE SPARROWS *UCCELLACI E UCCELLINI* 1966, Italian
NAVAJO JOE *UN DOLLARO A TESTA* 1966, Italian
UN UOMO A META 1966, Italian
THE HILLS RUN RED *I FIUME DI DOLLARI* 1966, Italian
THE HELLBENDERS *I CRUDELLI* 1966, Italian
RIFIFI IM BEIRUT 1966, Italian
THE BIG GUNDOWN *LA RESA DEI CONTI* 1966, Italian
THE GOOD, THE BAD AND THE UGLY United Artists, 1966, Italian
THE BATTLE OF ALGIERS Rizzoli, 1967, Italian-Algerian
COME IMPARI AD AMARE LE DONNE 1967, Italian
UP THE MACGREGORS *SETTE DONNE PER I MACGREGOR* 1967, Italian
THE WITCHES co-composer with Pierro Piccioni, Lopert, 1967, Italian-French
OPERATION KID BROTHER co-composer with Bruno Nicolai, 1967, Italian
THE GIRL AND THE GENERAL *LA RAGAZZA E IL GENERALE* 1967, Italian
GRAND SLAM *AD OGNI COSTO* 1967, Italian
DEATH RIDES A HORSE *DA UOMO A UOMO* 1967, Italian
CHINA IS NEAR *LA CINE E VICINA* 1967, Italian
MATCHLESS 1967, Italian
DANGER: DIABOLIK *DIABOLIK* 1967, Italian
THE ROVER *L'AVVENTURIERO* 1967, Italian
HAREM 1967, Italian
ARABELLA Cram Film, 1967, Italian
ESCALATION 1967, Italian
FACCIA A FACCIA 1967, Italian
THE DIRTY HEROES *DALLE ARDENNE ALL'INFERNO* co-composer with Bruno Nicolai, 1968, Italian
GUNS FOR SAN SEBASTIAN 1968, Italian
COME PLAY WITH ME *GRAZIE ZIA* 1968, Italian
A FINE PAIR *RUBA AL PROSSIMO TUO* 1968, Italian
FRAULEIN DOKTOR 1968, West German
GALILEO 1968
THEOREM *TEOREMA* 1968, Italian
COMANDEMENTI PER UN GANGSTER 1968, Italian
LISTEN, LET'S MAKE LOVE 1968, Italian
THAT SPLENDID NOVEMBER 1968, Italian
E PER TETTO UN CIELO DI STELLE 1968, Italian
IL GRANDE SILENZIO 1968, Italian
PARTNER 1968
ROME LIKE CHICAGO co-composer with Bruno Nicolai, 1968, Italian
MACHINE GUN McCAIN *GLI INTOCCABILI* 1968, Italian
A QUIET PLACE IN THE COUNTRY 1968, Italian
VERGOGNA SCHIFOSI 1968, Italian
MOTHER'S HEART *CUORE DI MAMMA* 1968, Italian
TEPEPA 1968, Italian
EAT IT *MANGIALA* 1968, Italian
H-2-S 1968, Italian
ECCE HOMO 1968, Italian
SENZA SAPERE NIENTE DI LEI 1968, Italian
THE MERCENARY co-composer with Bruno Nicolai, 1969, Italian
THE AWFUL STORY OF THE NUN OF MONZA 1969, Italian
ONCE UPON A TIME IN THE WEST Paramount, 1969, Italian-U.S.
METTI UNA SERA A CENA *LOVE CIRCLE* 1969, Italian
LA STAGIONE DEI SENSI 1969, Italian
SAI COSA FACEVA STALIN ALLE DONNE? 1969, Italian
UNA BREVE STAGIONE 1969, Italian
THE YEAR OF THE CANNIBALS *I CANNIBALI* American International, 1969, Italian

UCCIDETE IL VITELLO GRASSO E ARROSTITELO 1969, Italian
L'ASSOLUTO NATURALE *SHE AND HE* 1969, Italian
LA NOTTE DEI SERPENTI 1969, Italian
GOTT MIT UNS *THE LAST FIVE DAYS OF PEACE* 1969, Italian
THE SICILLIAN CLAN 20th Century-Fox, 1970, Italian
THE FIVE MAN ARMY MGM, 1970, Italian
TWO MULES FOR SISTER SARAH Universal, 1970, U.S.-Mexican
BURN! QUEIMADA! United Artists, 1970, Italian-French
INVESTIGATION OF A CITIZEN ABOVE SUSPICION Columbia, 1970, Italian
METELLO 1970, Italian
THE BIRD WITH THE CRYSTAL PLUMAGE UMC, 1970, Italian-West German
LUI PER LEI 1970, Italian
LA MOGLIE PIU BELLA 1970, Italian
VERUSCHKA, POESIA DI UNA DONNA 1970, Italian
HORNET'S NEST United Artists, 1970
QUANDO LE DONNE AVEVANO LA CODA *WHEN WOMEN HAD TAILS* 1970, Italian
CITTA VIOLENTA *THE FAMILY* 1970, Italian
VAMOS A MATAR, COMPANEROS 1970, Italian
GIOCHI PARTICOLARI 1970, Italian
FORZA G *WINGED DEVILS* 1970, Italian
LE FOTO PROIBITE DI UNA SIGNORA PER BENE 1970, Italian
TRE NEL MILLE 1970, French
LA CALIFFA 1970, Italian
THE RED TENT Paramount, 1971, Italian-Russian
CAT O'NINE TAILS National General, 1971, Italian-West German-French
MADDALENA 1971, Italian
SACCO AND VANZETTI 1971, Italian
IL DECAMERONE 1971, Italian
OCEANO 1971, Italian
GLI OCCHI FEDDI DELLA PAURA 1971, Italian
GIU LA TESTA 1971, Italian
GIORNATA NERA PER L'ARIETE 1971, Italian
ADDIO, FRATELLO CRUDELE *'TIS A PITY SHE'S A WHORE* 1971, Italian
LA CLASE OPERAIA VA IN PARADISO *LULU THE TOOL* 1971, Italian
SANS MOBILE APPARENT 1971, Italian
INCONTRO 1971, Italian
LE CASSE *THE BURGLARS* 1971, Italian
LA CORTA NOTTE DELLE BAMBOLE DI VETRO 1971, Italian
LA TARANTOLA DAL VENTRO NERO *THE BLACK BELLY OF THE TARANTULA* 1971, Italian
L'ISTRUTTORIA E' CHIUSA: DIMENTICHI co-composer with Walter Branchi, 1971, Italian
IMPUTAZIONE DI OMICIDIO PER UNO STUDENTE 1971, Italian
QUATTRO MOSCHE DI VELLUTO GRIGIO *FOUR FLIES ON GREY VELVET* 1971, Italian
IL DIAVOLO NEL CERVELLO 1971, Italian
LA VIOLENZA: QUNITO POTERE 1971, Italian
QUANDO LE DONNE PERSERO LA CODA *WHEN WOMEN LOST THEIR TAILS* co-composer with Bruno Nicolai, 1971, Italian
...CORREVA L'ANNO DI GRAZIE 1870 1972, Italian
I BAMBINI CI CHIEDONO PERCHE 1972, Italian
QUESTA SPECIE D'AMORE 1972, Italian
COSA AVETE FATTO A SOLANGE? 1972, Italian
MIO CARO ASSASSINO 1972, Italian
ANCHE SE VOLESSI LAVORARE, CHE COSA FACCIO? 1972, Italian
CHI L'HA VISTA MORIRE? 1972, Italian
THE CANTERBURY TALES United Artists, 1972, Italian
IL MAESTRO E MARGHERITA 1972, Italian
LES DEUX SAISONS DE LA VIE 1972, Italian
BARBABLU BLUEBEARD 1972, Hungarian
L'ATTENTAT *THE FRENCH CONSPIRACY* 1972, French
LA VITA, A VOLTE, E MOLTO DURO NEL WEST, VERO PROVVIDENZA? 1972, Italian
SBATTI IL MONSTRO IN PRIMA PAGINA 1972, Italian
LA COSA BUFFA 1972, Italian
LA BANDA J & S: CRONACA CRIMINALE DEL FAR WEST *SONNY AND JED* 1972, Italian
UN UOMO DA RISPETTARE *THE MASTER TOUCH/ HEARTS AND MINDS/A MAN TO RESPECT* 1972, Italian
CHE C'ENTRIAMO NOI CON LA RIVOLUZIONE? 1972, Italian
DUCK! YOU SUCKER *FISTFUL OF DYNAMITE* United Artists, 1972, Italian-U.S.
QUANDO L'AMORE E SENSUALITA Gemini, 1972, Italian
D'AMORE SI MUORE 1973, Italian
THE SERPENT *NIGHT FLIGHT TO MOSCOW* Avco Embassy, 1973, French-Italian-West German
FORSE UN FIORE theme only, 1973, Italian
REVOLVER BLOOD IN THE STREETS 1973
CRESCETTE E MOLTIPLICATEVI 1973, Italian
VIA RASELLA MASSACRE IN ROME 1973, Italian
LA PROPRIETA NON PIU UN FURTO 1973, Italian
SPOGLIATI, PROTESTA, UCCIDI 1973, Italian
L'ULTIMO UOMO DI SARA 1973, Italian
SEPOLTA VIVA 1973, Italian
GIORDANO BRUNO 1973, Italian
CI RISIAMO, VERO PROVVIDENZA? co-composer with Bruno Nicolai, 1973, Italian
SESSO IN CONFESSIONALE 1973, Italian
VAARWEL *THE ROMANTIC AGONY* 1974, Dutch
MY NAME IS NOBODY 1974, Italian-French-West German
THE TEMPTER Euro International, 1974, British-Italian
THE LAST DAYS OF MUSSOLINI *MUSSOLINI: ULTIMO ATTO* Paramount, 1974, Italian
SPASMO 1974, Italian
THE DEATH DEALER *MILANO ODIA: LA POLIZIA NON PUO SPARARE* 1974, Italian
LE TRIO INFERNAL 1974, French
LA CUGINA 1974
LE SECRET 1974, French
L'ANTICRISTO 1974
MACCIE SOLARI 1974, Italian
LA FAILLE 1974, French
LAST STOP ON THE NIGHT TRAIN *L'ULTIMO TRENO DELLA NOTTE* 1974, Italian
THE MASTER TOUCH Warner Bros., 1974, Italian
LA GRANDE BOURGEOISE 1974, French-Italian
ALLONSANFAN Cinematographic Cooperative, 1975, Italian
DRAMA OF THE RICH *FATTI DI GENTE PERBENE* PAC, 1975, Italian-French
LIBERA, AMORE MIO *LIBERA, MY LOVE* Italnoleggio, 1975, Italian
THE DEVIL IS A WOMAN 1975, British-Italian
THE NIGHT CALLER *PEUR SUR LA VILLE* 1975, French
STORIE DI VITA E MALAVITA 1975, Italian
LEONOR 1975
DOWN THE ANCIENT STAIRS *PER LE ANTICHE SCALE* 1975, Italian
END OF THE GAME *DER RICHTER UND SEIN HENKER* 20th Century-Fox, 1975, German-Italian
THE HUMAN FACTOR Bryanston, 1975
ATTENTI AL BUFFONE 1975, Italian
DIVINA CREATURA 1975

LABBRA DI LURIDO BLU 1975, Italian
SALO OR THE 120 DAYS OF SODOM United Artists, 1975, Italian
LA DONNA DELLA DOMENICA 1975, Italian
MOSES (MS) ITC/RAI, 1975, British-Italian
UN GENIO, DUE COMPARI, UN POLLO Titanus, 1976, Italian
NOVECENTO 1976, Italian
SAN BABILA ORE 20: UN DELITTO INUTILE 1976, Italian
L'EREDITA FERRAMONTI 1976, Italian
L'AGNESE VA A MORIRE 1976, Italian
BLOOD IN THE STREETS Independent-International, 1976, Italian-French-West German
SUNDAY WOMAN 20th Century-Fox, 1976, Italian-French
EREDITA FERRAMONTI 1976, Italian
L'UOMO E LA MAGIA (TF) 1976, Italian
THE THRUSTER 1976, Belgian
PARTNER 1977
THE DESERT OF THE TARTARS *IL DESIERTO DEI TARTARI* Gaumont, 1977, French-Italian-Iranian
1900 Paramount, 1977, Italian
EXORCIST II: THE HERETIC Warner Bros., 1977
ORCA Paramount, 1977
RENE LA CANNE *RENE THE CANE* AMLF, 1977, French
PEDRO PERAMO 1977, Mexican
HOLOCAUST 2000 1977, British-Italian
DAYS OF HEAVEN ★ Paramount, 1978
THE TEMPTER Avco Embassy, 1978, Italian
TRAVELS WITH ANITA 1979
SIDNEY SHELDON'S BLOODLINE Paramount, 1979
LUNA 20th Century-Fox, 1979, Italian-U.S.
WINDOWS United Artists, 1980
MILANO ODIA: LA POLIZIA NON PUO' SPARARE Joseph Brenner, 1980, Italian
THE ISLAND Universal, 1980
TODO MODO Nu-Image, 1980, Italian
LA CAGE AUX FOLLES II United Artists, 1981, French-Italian
LOVERS AND LIARS Levitt-Pickman, 1981
BUTTERFLY Analysis, 1981
SO FINE Warner Bros., 1981
WHITE DOG Paramount, 1982
MARCO POLO (MS) RAI/Franco Cristaldi Productions/ Vincenzo Labella Productions, 1982, Italian
THE THING Universal, 1982
TREASURE OF THE FOUR CROWNS Cannon, 1983, U.S.-Spanish
THE SCARLET AND THE BLACK (TF) Bill McCutchen Productions/ITC Productions/RAI, 1983
LE MARGINAL *THE OUTSIDER* Gaumont, 1983, Italian
NANA Cannon, 1983, Italian
A TIME TO DIE *SEVEN GRAVES FOR ROGAN* additional music, Almi Films, 1983
SAHARA MGM/UA, 1983
LA CHIAVE *THE KEY* San Francisco Films, 1983, Italian
LE RUFFIAN AMLF, 1983, French
ORDER OF DEATH 1983, Italian
ONCE UPON A TIME IN AMERICA The Ladd Company/Warner Bros., 1984, U.S.-Italian-Canadian
RED SONJA MGM/UA, 1985
LA CAGE AUX FOLLES 3 Warner Bros./Columbia, 1985, French
C.A.T. SQUAD (TF) NBC Productions/Filmline International, 1986
THE MISSION ★ Warner Bros., 1986, British
MOSCA ADDIO Istituto Luce/Italnoleggio, 1987, Italian
THE UNTOUCHABLES ★ Paramount, 1987
RAMPAGE DEG, 1987
MAMBA Eidoscope/Reteitalia, 1988, Italian
C.A.T. SQUAD: PYTHON WOLF (TF) NBC Productions, 1988
A TIME OF DESTINY Columbia, 1988
FRANTIC Warner Bros., 1988
CASUALTIES OF WAR Columbia, 1989
FAT MAN AND LITTLE BOY Paramount, 1989
TEMPO DI UCCIDERE *THE SHORT CUT* Titanus, 1989, Italian-French
CINEMA PARADISO Miramax, 1989, Italian
ENDLESS GAME (CTF) Showtime/Telso International/ Roteitalia, 1990
TO FORGET PALERMO Penta, 1990, Italian
THE ACHILLE LAURO AFFAIR (TF) Mike Robe Productions, 1990
EVERYBODY'S FINE Miramax, 1990, Italian-French
TIE ME UP! TIE ME DOWN! Miramax, 1990, Spanish
STATE OF GRACE 1990

JOHN MORRIS

b. October 18, 1926 - Elizabeth, New Jersey
Agent: Gorfaine-Schwartz - Burbank, 818/954-9500

THE PRODUCERS Avco Embassy, 1968
THE TWELVE CHAIRS UMC, 1970
THE GAMBLERS 20th Century-Fox, 1969
BLAZING SADDLES Warner Bros., 1973
THE BANK SHOT United Artists, 1974
YOUNG FRANKENSTEIN 20th Century-Fox, 1974
THE ADVENTURE OF SHERLOCK HOLMES' SMARTER BROTHER 20th Century-Fox, 1975
SILENT MOVIE 20th Century-Fox, 1976
THE LAST REMAKE OF BEAU GESTE Universal, 1977
THE WORLD'S GREATEST LOVER 20th Century-Fox, 1977
HIGH ANXIETY 20th Century-Fox, 1977
THE IN-LAWS Columbia, 1979
IN GOD WE TRUST Universal, 1980
THE MATING SEASON (TF) Highgate Pictures, 1980
THE ELEPHANT MAN ★ Paramount, 1980, British-U.S.
THE HISTORY OF THE WORLD, PART 1 20th Century-Fox, 1981
SPLENDOR IN THE GRASS (TF) Katz-Gallin Productions/ Half-Pint Productions/Warner Bros. TV, 1981
THE ELECTRIC GRANDMOTHER (TF) Highgate Pictures, 1982
YELLOWBEARD Orion, 1983, British
TABLE FOR FIVE co-composer with Miles Goodman, Warner Bros., 1983
TO BE OR NOT TO BE 20th Century-Fox, 1983
GHOST DANCING (TF) Herbert Brodkin Productions/ The Eugene O'Neill Memorial Theatre Center/Titus Productions, 1983
JOHNNY DANGEROUSLY 20th Century Fox, 1984
THE WOMAN IN RED Orion, 1984
THE DOCTOR AND THE DEVILS 20th Century Fox, 1985, British
CLUE Paramount, 1985
HAUNTED HONEYMOON Orion, 1986
FRESNO (MS) MTM Productions, 1986
DIRTY DANCING Vestron, 1987
SPACEBALLS MGM/UA, 1987
IRONWEED Tri-Star, 1987
THE LITTLE MATCH GIRL (TF) NBC Productions, 1987
THE WASH Skouras Pictures, 1988
FAVORITE SON (MS) NBC Productions, 1988
SECOND SIGHT Warner Bros., 1989
STELLA Buena Vista, 1990

VAN MORRISON
b. 1945
Contact: BMI - Los Angeles, 213/659-9109

SLIPSTREAM co-composer, 1974, Canadian
LAMB Limehouse/Flickers/Channel Four, 1985, British

JONATHAN MORSE
(Fuzzbee Morse)
Agent: Richard Emler - Los Angeles, 213/651-0222

DOLLS Empire Pictures, 1987
EVOLUTION (FD) Elan Vital Production
GHOULIES II Empire Pictures, 1988

ARTHUR MORTON
Contact: BMI - Los Angeles, 213/659-9109

NIGHT LIFE OF THE GODS Universal, 1935
PRINCESS O'HARA Universal, 1935
PICK A STAR co-composer with T. Marvin Hatley, MGM, 1937
RIDING ON AIR RKO Radio, 1937
FIT FOR A KING RKO Radio, 1937
THE DAY THE BOOKIES WEPT RKO Radio, 1939
TURNABOUT United Artists, 1940
MILLIE'S DAUGHTER Columbia, 1947
IT HAD TO BE YOU co-composer with Heinz Roemheld, Columbia, 1947
THE THIRTEENTH HOUR Columbia, 1947
THE WALKING HILLS Columbia, 1949
THE NEVADAN Columbia, 1950
FATHER IS A BACHELOR Columbia, 1950
ROGUES OF SHERWOOD FOREST co-composer with Heinz Roemheld, Columbia, 1950
NEVER TRUST A GAMBLER Columbia, 1951
THE HARLEM GLOBETROTTERS Columbia, 1951
MEDICAL STORY (TF) David Gerber Productions/ Columbia Pictures TV, 1975

TONY MOTTOLA
Contact: ASCAP - Los Angeles, 213/466-7681

RUNNING ON EMPTY Warner Bros., 1988

WILLIAM MOTZIG
Contact: APRA - Australia, 011-61-2-922-6422

THE RETURN OF CAPTAIN INVINCIBLE *LEGEND IN LEOTARDS* New World, 1983, Australian
THE COCA COLA KID Cinecom/Film Gallery, 1985, Australian
THE FIRST KANGAROOS (TF) Roadshow/Channel 4, 1987, Australian
ECHOES OF PARADISE SHADOWS OF THE PEACOCK Castle Hill Productions/Quartet Films, 1987, Australian
YOUNG EINSTEIN co-composer, Warner Bros., 1989, Australian

ROB MOUNSEY
TAKEN AWAY (TF) Hart, Thomas & Berlin Productions, 1989
DANGEROUS PASSION (TF) Stormy Weathers Production/Davis Entertainment, 1990

JAMES MTUME
Contact: BMI - Los Angeles, 213/659-9109

NATIVE SON Cinecom, 1986

MARK MUELLER
Agent: Bart-Milander - North Hollywood, 818/761-4040

BERLIN BLUES Cannon, 1988

DOMINIC MULDOWNEY
Contact: PRS - London, England, 011-44-1-580-5544

BETRAYAL 20th Century-Fox International Classics, 1983, British
THE PLOUGHMAN'S LUNCH Samuel Goldwyn Company, 1983, British
LOOSE CONNECTIONS co-composer with Andy Roberts, Orion Classics, 1983, British
LAUGHTER HOUSE (TF) Film Four International, 1984, British
1984 co-composer with Eurythmics, Atlantic Releasing Corporation, 1984, British

DAVID MUNROW
Contact: PRS - London, England, 011-44-1-580-5544

THE DEVILS additional music only, Warner Bros., 1971, British
ZARDOZ 20th Century Fox, 1974, British

MURRAY MUNRO
Contact: PRS - London, England, 011-44-1-580-5544

PRIVATE INVESTIGATIONS MGM/UA, 1987

JUDY MUNSEN
STREET MUSIC co-composer with Ed Bogas, Specialty Films, 1983

MICHAEL MARTIN MURPHEY
Contact: BMI - Los Angeles, 213/659-9109

HARD COUNTRY co-composer with Jimmie Haskell, Universal/AFD, 1981

WALTER MURPHY
Agent: Jim Preminger - Los Angeles

THE SAVAGE BEES (TF) Landsburg-Kirshner Productions/ NBC, 1976
THE NIGHT THEY TOOK MISS BEAUTIFUL (TF) Don Kirshner Productions/LaRose Productions, 1977
RAW FORCE American Panorama, 1982
TRICKS OF THE TRADE (TF) Leonard Hill Films, 1988
THE LADY FORGETS (TF) Leonard Hill Films, 1989

SEAN MURRAY
Contact: BMI - Los Angeles, 213/659-9109

SCORPION Crown International, 1986

JOHN MUSSER
SOME KIND OF WONDERFUL co-composer with Stephen Hague, Paramount, 1987

JEAN MUSY

Contact: SACEM - France, 011-33-14-747-5650

CLAIRE DE FEMME Atlantic Releasing Corporation, 1979, French-Italian-West German
CHANEL SOLITAIRE United Film Distribution, 1981, French-British
TANYA'S ISLAND International Film Exchange/Fred Baker Films, 1981, Canadian
LA PALOMBIERE THE BIRD WATCH Gaumont, 1983, French
PRENDS TON PASSE-MONTAGNE ON VA A LA PLAGE! UGC, 1983, French
ITINERAIRE BIS *SIDEROADS* 1983, French

BILL MYERS

Contact: BMI - Los Angeles, 213/659-9109

ALL'S FAIR Moviestore Entertainment, 1989

PETER MYERS

Agent: Bart-Milander - North Hollywood, 818/761-4040

STUNT SEVEN (TF) additional music, Martin Poll Productions, 1979
STARK (TF) CBS Entertainment, 1985
DEATH OF AN ANGEL 20th Century Fox, 1985
STARK: MIRROR IMAGE (TF) CBS Entertainment, 1986

STANLEY MYERS

b. 1939
Agent: Bart-Milander - North Hollywood, 818/761-4040

KALEIDOSCOPE Warner Bros., 1966, British
ULYSSES Continental, 1967
NO WAY TO TREAT A LADY Paramount, 1968
OTLEY Columbia, 1969, British
TWO GENTLEMEN *SHARING* American International, 1969, British
AGE OF CONSENT Columbia, 1970, Australian
TROPIC OF CANCER Paramount, 1970
THE WALKING STICK MGM, 1970, British
A SEVERED HEAD Columbia, 1971, British
LONG AGO TOMORROW *THE RAGING MOON* Cinema 5, 1971, British
SUMMER LIGHTNING 1972, West German
SITTING TARGET MGM, 1972, British
KING, QUEEN, KNAVE Avco Embassy, 1972, West German-British
X, Y, ZEE *ZEE & CO.* Columbia, 1972, British
DIVORCE HIS/DIVORCE HERS (TF) World Films Services, 1973
LITTLE MALCOLM AND HIS STRUGGLE AGAINST THE EUNUCHS Multicetera Investments, 1974, British
FRIGHTMARE Miracle, 1974, British
THE APPRENTICESHIP OF DUDLEY KRAVITZ Paramount, 1974, Canadian
HOUSE OF WHIPCORD Miracle, 1974, British
THE WILBY CONSPIRACY United Artists, 1975, British
CARAVAN TO VACCARES Bryanston, 1976, British-French
COUP DE GRACE Cinema 5, 1976, West German
THE COMEBACK *THE DAY THE SCREAMING STOPPED* Enterprise, 1978, British
THE GREEK TYCOON Universal, 1978
THE CLASS OF MISS MacMICHAELS Brut Prods., 1978, British
THE DEER HUNTER Universal, 1978
SUMMER OF MY GERMAN SOLDIER (TF) Highgate Productions, 1978
A PORTRAIT OF THE ARTIST AS A YOUNG MAN Howard Mahler Films, 1979
THE CLASS OF MISS MacMICHAEL Brut Productions, 1979, British
ABSOLUTION Trans World Entertainment, 1979, British
YESTERDAY'S HERO EMI, 1979, British
THE WATCHER IN THE WOODS Buena Vista, 1980, British
THE MARTIAN CHRONICLES (TF) Charles Fries Productions/Stonehenge Productions, 1980
THE GENTLEMAN BANDIT (TF) Highgate Pictures, 1981
LADY CHATTERLEY'S LOVER Cannon, 1982, French-British
THE INCUBUS Artists Releasing Corporation/Film Ventures International, 1982, Canadian
MOONLIGHTING co-composer with Hans Zimmer, Universal Classics, 1982, British
BEYOND THE LIMIT *THE HONORARY CONSUL* Paramount, 1983, British
BLIND DATE New Line Cinema, 1984, British-Greek
SUCCESS IS THE BEST REVENGE co-composer with Hans Zimmer, Triumph/Columbia, 1984, British
EUREKA MGM/UA Classics, 1984, British
THE ZANY ADVENTURES OF ROBIN HOOD (TF) Bobka Productions/Charles Fries Entertainment, 1984
BLACK ARROW (TF) Harry Towers Productions/ Pan-Atlantic Pictures Productions, 1985
THE CHAIN Rank, 1985, British
THE LIGHTSHIP Castle Hill Productions, 1985, U.S.-West German
FLORENCE NIGHTENGALE (TF) Cypress Point Productions, 1985
INSIGNIFICANCE co-composer with Hans Zimmer, Island Alive, 1985, British
THE RUSSIAN SOLDIER (TF) BBC, 1985, British
CONDUCT UNBECOMING Allied Artists, 1985, British
DREAMCHILD Universal, 1985, British
MY BEAUTIFUL LAUNDRETTE (TF) Orion Classics, 1985, British
WILD HORSES (TF) co-composer with Hans Zimmer, Wild Horses Productions/Telepictures Productions, 1985
SEPARATE VACATIONS RSL Entertainment, 1986, Canadian
CASTAWAY Cannon, 1986, British
STRONG MEDICINE (TF) Telepictures Productions/ TVS Ltd. Productions, 1986, U.S.-British
MONTE CARLO (TF) New World TV/Phoenix Entertainment Group/Collins-Holm Productions/ Highgate Pictures, 1986
RAINY DAY WOMEN (TF) BBC, 1986, British
PACK OF LIES (TF) Robert Halmi Inc., 1987
THE SECOND VICTORY Filmworld Distributors, 1987, Australian-British
PRICK UP YOUR EARS Samuel Goldwyn Company, 1987, British
SAMMIE & ROSIE GET LAID Cinecom, 1987, British
WISH YOU WERE HERE Atlantic Releasing Corporation, 1987, British
SCOOP (TF) London Weekend TV, 1987, British
TAFFIN co-composer with Hans Zimmer, MGM/UA, 1988, U.S.-Irish
STARS AND BARS Columbia, 1988

THE NATURE OF THE BEAST co-composer with Stanley Myers, Rosso Productions, 1988, British
TRADING HEARTS Cineworld, 1988
BAJA OKLAHOMA (CTF) HBO Pictures/Rastar Productions, 1988
TIDY ENDINGS (CTF) HBO Showcase/Sandollar Productions, 1988
THE MOST DANGEROUS MAN IN THE WORLD (TF) BBC/Iberoamericana/Celtic Films, 1988, British
STONES FOR IBARRA (TF) Titus Productions, 1988
TRACK 29 Island Pictures, 1988
THE BOOST Hemdale, 1988
DANNY: CHAMPION OF THE WORLD (CTF) Portobello Productions/British Screen/Thames TV/ The Disney Channel/WonderWorks/Children's Film & Television Foundation, 1989, British-U.S.
SCENES FROM THE CLASS STRUGGLE IN BEVERLY HILLS Cinecom, 1989
LADDER OF SWORDS Film Four International, 1989
A MONTH OF SUNDAYS (CTF) HBO Showcase, 1989
THE WITCHES Warner Bros., 1989, British
AGE-OLD FRIENDS (CTF) Granger Productions/ HBO Showcase, 1989
TORRENTS OF SPRING Millimeter, 1990, Italian

FRED MYROW

Contact: Richard Emler - Los Angeles, 213/651-0222

LEO THE LAST United Artists, 1970, British
IN SEARCH OF AMERICA (TF) Four Star International, 1971
THE STEAGLE Avco Embassy, 1971
SOYLENT GREEN co-composer with Gerald Fried, MGM, 1972
SCARECROW Warner Bros., 1973
A REFLECTION OF FEAR Columbia, 1973, British
LOLLY-MADONNA XXX MGM, 1973
MESSAGE TO MY DAUGHTER (TF) Charles Fries Productions/Metromedia Producers Corporation, 1973
PRAY FOR THE WILDCATS (TF) ABC Circle Films, 1974
JIM, THE WORLD'S GREATEST Universal, 1976
BLUE ANGELS 1976
KENNY & COMPANY 20th Century-Fox, 1976
THE SECRET LIFE OF JOHN CHAPMAN (TF) The Jozak Company, 1976
PHANTASM co-composer with Malcolm Seagrave, Avco Embassy, 1979
ON THE NICKEL Rose's Park, 1980
HOUR OF THE ASSASSIN Concorde, 1987, U.S.-Peruvian
PHANTASM II Universal, 1988
JOURNEY TO SPIRIT ISLAND Pal Prods.-Seven Wonders Entertainment, 1988

YURIKO NAKAMURA

b. Japan
Contact: JASRAC - Tokyo, Japan, 011-81-3-502-6551

SUMMER VACATION: 1999 New Yorker, 1989, Japanese

ANDY NARRELL

SIGNAL 7 Myron-Taylor Productions, 1986

MARIO NASCIMBENE

b. November 28, 1913 - Milan, Italy

L'AMORE CANTA 1941, Italian
SE LO FOSSI ONESTO 1942, Italian
I FANTASMI DEL MARE 1948, Italian
CAPITAN DEMONIO 1949, Italian
IL SOGNO DI ZORRO 1951, Italian
E L'AMOR CHE MI ROVINA 1951, Italian
O.K. NERO! 1951, Italian
AMOR NON HO, PERO PERO 1951, Italian
LE AVVENTURE DI MANDRIN 1952, Italian
ROME 11 O'CLOCK 1953, Italian
IT HAPPENED IN THE PARK *VILLA BORGHESE* 1953, Italian
LOVE IN THE CITY Italian Films Export, 1953
TOO YOUNG FOR LOVE *L'ETA DELL'AMORE* 1954, Italian
THE BAREFOOT CONTESSA United Artists, 1954, U.S.-Italian
ANGELA 20th Century-Fox, 1955
DON JUAN'S NIGHT OF LOVE 1955
UOMINI E LUPI 1956, Italian
ALEXANDER THE GREAT United Artists, 1956
L'ULTIMA VIOLENZA 1957, Italian
A FAREWELL TO ARMS 20th Century-Fox, 1957
THAT NIGHT Universal, 1957
THE QUIET AMERICAN United Artists, 1958
THE VIKINGS United Artists, 1958
SUBWAY IN THE SKY 1959, West German
MORTE DI UN AMICO 1959, Italian
ESTATE VIOLENTA 1959, Italian
CARTHAGE IN FLAMES 1959, Italian
ROOM AT THE TOP Continental, 1959
SOLOMON AND SHEBA United Artists, 1959
LA GARCONNIERE 1960, Italian
LAS BACCANTI *THE BACCHANTES* 1960, Italian
SCENT OF MYSTERY Todd, 1960, British
SONS AND LOVERS 20th Century-Fox, 1960, British
FRANCIS OF ASSISI 20th Century-Fox, 1961
ROMANOFF AND JULIET Universal, 1961
THE SWORDSMAN OF SIENA 1961, Italian
JOSEPH AND HIS BRETHREN *GIUSEPPE VENDUTO DAI FRATELLI* Colorama, 1962, Italian
BARABBAS Columbia, 1962, Italian
CONSTANTINE AND THE CROSS 1962, Italian
THE HAPPY THIEVES United Artists, 1962
JESSICA United Artists, 1962, U.S.-Italian-French
LIGHT IN THE PIAZZA MGM, 1962
IL DISORDINE 1962, Italian
QUATTRO NOTTI CON ALBA 1962, Italian

LA BANDA CASAROLI 1962, Italian
THE GOLDEN ARROW MGM, 1962, Italian-U.S.
L'ARCIERE DELLE MILLE E UNA NOTTE 1963, Italian
IL PROCESSO DI VERONA 1963, Italian
TEARS ARE FOR TOMORROW 1964
THE CAMP FOLLOWERS *LE SOLDATESSE* 1964, French-Italian
WHERE THE SPIES ARE MGM, 1965, British
DICK SMART 2/007 1966
ONE MILLION YEARS B.C. 20th Century-Fox, 1967, British
KISS THE GIRLS AND MAKE THEM DIE *SE TUTTE LE DONNE DEL MONDO/OPERAZIONE PARADISO* Columbia, 1967, Italian-U.S.
DOCTOR FAUSTUS 1968, British
SUMMIT 1968, French-Italian
THE VENGEANCE OF SHE 20th Century-Fox, 1968, British
SOCRATES New Yorker, 1969, Italian, originally made for television
WHEN DINOSAURS RULED THE EARTH Warner Bros., 1969, British
GRADINA 1970, Italian
LA LOTTA DELL'VORRO PER LE SOPRA VIVENZ (TF) 1970, Italian T.V.
CREATURES THE WORLD FORGOT Columbia, 1971, British
AGOSTINO DI IPPONA 1972, Italian
BLAISE PASCAL (TF) Orizzonte 2000, 1972, Italian
LA PRIMA NOTTE DI QUIETE 1972, Italian
ANNO UNO *YEAR ONE* Italnoleggio, 1974, Italian
THE MESSIAH 1978, Italian

LOUIS NATALE

Contact: CAPAC - Ontario, Canada, 1-416-924-4427

COWBOYS DON'T CRY Cineplex Odeon, 1988, Canadian
LAST TRAIN HOME (CTF) Atlantis Films/Great North Productions/CBC, 1990, Canadian-U.S.

CHRIS NEAL

b. Australia
Contact: APRA - Australia, 011-61-2-922-6422

BUDDIES 1983, Australian
REBEL Vestron, 1985, Australian
SHORT CHANGED Greater Union, 1986, Australian
BULLSEYE Cinema Group, 1987, Australian
GROUND ZERO Avenue Pictures, 1987, Australian
THE SHIRALEE (MS) SAFC Productions, 1988, Australian
GRIEVOUS BODILY HARM International Film Management, 1988, Australian
EMERALD CITY Greater Union, 1989, Australian
CELIA Hoyts, 1989, Australian
TROUBLE IN PARADISE (TF) Qintex Entertainment, 1989, U.S.-Australian

BILL NELSON

Contact: PRS - London, England, 011-44-1-580-5544

DREAM DEMON Spectrafilm, 1988, British

STEVE NELSON

Contact: BMI - Los Angeles, 213/659-9109

LAST RESORT co-composer with Thom Sharp, Concorde, 1986

WILLIE NELSON

b. April 30, 1933 - Abbott, Texas
Contact: BMI - Los Angeles, 213/659-9109

HONEYSUCKLE ROSE co-composer with Richard Baskin, Warner Bros., 1980
STAGECOACH (TF) co-composer with David Allan Coe, Raymond Katz Productions/Heritage Entertainment, 1986

JOHN NESCHLING

Contact: SICAM - Brazil, 011-55-11-223-8555

LUCIO FLAVIO Unifilm/Embrafilme, 1978, Brazilian
KISS OF THE SPIDER WOMAN Island Alive/Film Dallas, 1985, Brazillian-U.S.

MICHAEL NESMITH

Contact: BMI - Los Angeles, 213/659-9109

TIMERIDER Jensen Farley Pictures, 1983

ETHAN NEUBURG

BUM RAP co-composer with Robert Kessler, Millennium, 1988

OSCAR CASTRO NEVES

BLAME IT ON RIO co-composer with Ken Wannberg, 20th Century-Fox, 1984

IRA NEWBORN

Agent: ICM - Los Angeles, 213/550-4000

THE BLUES BROTHERS Universal, 1980
ALL NIGHT LONG co-composer with Richard Hazard, Universal, 1981
SIXTEEN CANDLES Universal, 1984
INTO THE NIGHT Universal, 1985
WEIRD SCIENCE Universal, 1985
FERRIS BUELLER'S DAY OFF Paramount, 1986
WISE GUYS MGM/UA, 1986
DRAGNET Universal, 1987
AMAZON WOMEN ON THE MOON Universal, 1987
PLANES, TRAINS AND AUTOMOBILES Paramount, 1987
CADDYSHACK II Warner Bros., 1988
THE NAKED GUN: FROM THE FILES OF POLICE SQUAD! Paramount, 1988
UNCLE BUCK Universal, 1989
CAST THE FIRST STONE (TF) Mench Productions/ Columbia Pictures TV, 1989
SHORT TIME 20th Century-Fox, 1990
MY BLUE HEAVEN Warner Bros., 1990

DAVID NEWMAN

b. 1954
Agent: Lawrence B. Marks - Northridge, 818/831-1830

CRITTERS New Line Cinema, 1985
VENDETTA Concorde, 1986
THE KINDRED FM Entertainment, 1987
THE BRAVE LITTLE TOASTER (TF) Hyperion-Kushner-Locke Productions, 1987
MALONE Orion, 1987
MY DEMON LOVER New Line Cinema, 1987
THROW MOMMA FROM THE TRAIN Orion, 1987
HEATHERS New World, 1989
BILL & TED'S EXCELLENT ADVENTURE Orion, 1989
DISORGANIZED CRIME Buena Vista, 1989
LITTLE MONSTERS Vestron, 1989

THE WAR OF THE ROSES 20th Century Fox, 1989
MADHOUSE Orion, 1990
FIRE BIRDS Buena Visa, 1990
THE FRESHMAN Tri-Star, 1990
DUCK TALES (AF) Buena Vista, 1990
MARRYING MAN Buena Vista, 1990

RANDY NEWMAN

b. November 28, 1943 - Los Angeles, California
Agent: Gorfaine-Schwartz - Burbank, 818/954-9500

COLD TURKEY United Artists, 1971
RAGTIME ★ Paramount, 1981
THE NATURAL ★ Tri-Star, 1984
PARENTHOOD Universal, 1989
AVALON Columbia, 1990
AWAKENINGS Columbia, 1990

THOMAS NEWMAN

Agent: Gorfaine-Schwartz - Burbank, 818/954-9500

GRANDVIEW, U.S.A. Warner Bros., 1984
THE SEDUCTION OF GINA (TF) Bertinelli-Jaffee Productions, 1984
RECKLESS MGM/UA, 1984
REVENGE OF THE NERDS 20th Century Fox, 1984
GIRLS JUST WANT TO HAVE FUN New World, 1985
DESPERATELY SEEKING SUSAN Orion, 1985
THE MAN WITH ONE RED SHOE 20th Century Fox, 1985
REAL GENIUS Tri-Star, 1985
GUNG HO Paramount, 1986
JUMPIN' JACK FLASH 20th Century Fox, 1986
LIGHT OF DAY Tri-Star, 1987
THE LOST BOYS Warner Bros., 1987
LESS THAN ZERO 20th Century Fox, 1987
THE GREAT OUTDOORS Universal, 1988
THE PRINCE OF PENNSYLVANIA New Line Cinema, 1988
COOKIE Warner Bros., 1989
MEN DON'T LEAVE The Geffen Company/Warner Bros., 1990
WELCOME BACK, ROXY CARMICHAEL ITC, 1990
NAKED TANGO 1990

DAVID NICHTERN

Contact: ASCAP - Los Angeles, 213/466-7681

THE BIG PICTURE Columbia, 1989

BRUNO NICOLAI

b. 1926 - Italy
Contact: SIAE - Rome, Italy, 011-39-6-59-90-1

MONDO CANE #2 co-composer with Nino Olivieri, 1963, Italian
IL PELO NEL MONDO co-composer with Nino Olivieri, 1963, Italian
VITA DI MICHELANGELO (TF) 1964, Italian
10,000 DOLLARI PER RINGO 1965, Italian
MISSIONE SPEZIALE LADY CHAPLIN 1966, Italian
EL CISCO 1966, Italian
DA BERLINO L'APOCALISSE 1966, Italian-West German
99 WOMEN 1966, Italian
THE CHRISTMAS THAT ALMOST WASN'T 1966, Italian-U.S.
ROMEO AND JULIET adaptation, 1966, Italian
DJANGO SPARA PER PRIMO 1966, Italian
AGENTE SPEZIALE - OPERAZIONE RE MIDA 1966, Italian
KISS KISS BANG BANG 1966, Spanish
LUCKY EL INTREPIDO 1967, Italian
OPERATION KID BROTHER *O.K. CONNERY* co-composer with Ennio Morricone, 1967, Italian
I GIORNI DELLA VIOLENZA 1967, Italian
THE DITY HEROES *DALLE ARDENNE ALL'INFERNO* co-composer with Ennio Morricone, 1968, Italian
RUN MAN RUN! 1968, Italian
FLASHBACK 1968
JUSTINE OVVERO LE DISAVVENTURE DELLA VIRTU 1968, Italian
GIUGNO '44, SBARCHEREMO IN NORMANDIA 1968, Italian
LA BATTAGLIA DEL DESERTO 1968, Italian
ROME LIKE CHICAGO co-composer with Ennio Morricone, 1968, Italian
RINGO, DOVE VAI? 1968, Italian
GENTLEMAN JO...UCCIDI 1968, Italian
THE MERCENARY co-composer with Ennio Morricone, 1969, Italian
THE INSATIABLES *FEMMINE INSAZIABILI* 1969, Italian
LA SFIDA DI MACKENNA 1969, Italian
LOVE BIRDS 1969, Italian
THE LAST MERCENARY 1969, Italian
LAND RAIDERS 1969, Italian
ZENABEL 1969, Italian
EUGENIE...THE STORY OF HER JOURNEY INTO PERVERSION *MARQUIS DE SADE* 1969, Italian
REBUS (TF) 1969, Italian
LES CAUCHEMARS NAISSENT LA NUIT 1970, Italian
GEMINUS (TF) 1970, Italian
COUNT DRACULA *NIGHTS OF DRACULA* 1970, Spanish
SEX CHARADE 1970, Italian
X312 FLUG ZUR HOLLE co-composer with Wolf Hartmayer, 1970, West German
PAOLO E FRANCESCA 1970, Italian
DIO IN CIELO, ARIZONA IN TERRA 1970, Italian
ADIOS, SABATA 1970, Italian
AMERICA...COSI NUDA, COSI VIOLENTA 1970, Italian
I DUE MAGHI DELL PALLONE 1970, Italian
ROBIN HOOD, L'INVINCIBILE ARCIERE 1970, Italian
ARIZONA SI SCATENO...E LI FECE FUORI TUTTI 1970, Italian
BUON FUNERALE, AMIGOS...PAGE SARTANA 1970, Italian
DUE BIANCHI NELL 'AFRICA NERA 1970, Italian
UNA NUVOLA DI POLVERE 1970, Italian
UN UOMO CHIAMATO APOCALISSE JOE 1970, Italian
ANDA MUCHACHO, SPARA! 1971, Italian
LA CODA DELLO SCORPIONE 1971, Italian
GLI FUMAVANO LE COLT 1971, Italian
IL SOLE SOTTO TERRA 1971, Italian
LO CHIAMAVANO SPIRITO SANTO 1971, Italian
LOS BUITRES CARAVAN TU FOSA 1971, Spanish
CHRISTINA PRINCESSE DE L'EROTISME co-composer with Jesus Franco, 1971, Italian-French
DRACULA CONTRA EL DR. FRANKENSTEIN co-composer with Daniel J. White, 1971, Italian-West German
EL CRISTO DEL OCEANO *CHRIST OF THE OCEAN* 1971, Italian
ROBINSON UND SEINE WILDEN SKLAVINNEN co-composer with Daniel J. White, 1971, West German
LA PREDA E L'AVVOLTOIO 1972, Italian
QUANDO LE DONNE PERSERO LA CODA co-composer with Ennio Morricone, 1972, Italian
UNE JOURNEE BIEN REMPLIE 1972, French-Italian

COSI SIA 1972, Italian
DOMANI PASSERO A SALUTARE LA TUA VEDOVA...PAROLIA DI EPIDEMIA! 1972, Italian
IL TUO VIZIO E UNA STANZA CHIUSA E SOLO IO NE HO LA CHIAVE *EXCITE ME* 1972, Italian
L'ALPIN L'E SEMPRE QUEL 1972, French-Italian
LOS AMANTES DE LA ISLA DEL DIABLO 1972, Spanish
UN CAPITAN DE QUINCE ANOS co-composer with Daniel J. White, 1972, Spanish
QUEL GRAN PEZZO DELL'UBALDA, TUTTA NUDA E TUTTA CALDA 1972, Italian
LA DAMA ROSSA UCCIDE SETTE VOLTE 1972, Italian
NIGHT OF THE BLOOD MONSTER *THRONE OF FIRE* 1972, Italian
PERCHE QUELLE STRANE GOCCI DE SANGUE SIL CORPE DE JENNIFER? *WHAT ARE THOSE STRANGE DROPS OF BLOOD ON THE BODY OF JENNIFER?* 1972, Italian
TUTTI I COLORI DEL BUIO *ALL THE COLORS OF DARKNESS/THEY'RE COMING TO GET YOU* 1972, Italian
DEFENSE DE SAVOIR 1973, French-Italian
IL MIO NOME E SHANGHAI JOE 1973, Italian
LE CHEMIN SOLITAIRE 1973, French-Italian
CI RISIAMO, VERO PROVVIDENZA? co-composer with Ennio Morricone, 1973, Italian
LO CHIAMAVANO "TRESETTE" 1973, Italian
L'ONORATO FAMIGLIA UCCIDERE E COSA NOSTRA 1973, Italian
ELEANORA (TF) 1973, Italian
THE NIGHT EVELYN CAME OUT OF THE GRAVE 1973, Italian
L'ANTICRISTO *ANTICHRIST/THE TEMPTER* co-composer with Ennio Morricone, 1974, Italian
DON GIOVANNI IN SICILIA (TF) 1974, Italian
I FIGLI CHIEDONE PERCHE 1974, Italian
ALLORA IL TRENO 1974, Italian
TEN LITTLE INDIANS Talia Films, 1975, Italian-French-Spanish-German
GATTI ROSSI IN UN LABIRINTO DI VETRO 1975, Italian
L'UOMO DELLA STRADA FA GIUSTIZIA 1975, Italian
LA FURIE DU DESIR 1975, French
I MIEI AMICI (TF) 1976, Italian
IL MAESTRO DI VIOLINO 1976, Italian
DUE MAGNUM 38 PER UNA CITTA DI CAROGNE 1976, Italian
LEZIONI DI VIOLONCELLO 1976, Italian
LUCA, BAMBINO MIO 1977, Italian
OLTRE LA NOTTE 1977, Italian
EYEBALL 1978, Italian
IL CAPPOTTO DI ASTRAKAN 1980, Italian
GOODBYE MARY (TF) 1980, Italian
CAMMINA CAMMINA Gaumont, 1983, Italian

LENNIE NIEHAUS

Agent: Robert Light - Los Angeles, 213/651-1777

TIGHTROPE Warner Bros., 1984
CITY HEAT Warner Bros., 1984
SESAME STREET PRESENTS: FOLLOW THAT BIRD co-composer with Van Dyke Parks, Warner Bros., 1985
PALE RIDER Warner Bros., 1985
NEVER TOO YOUNG TO DIE Paul Releasing 1986
RATBOY Warner Bros., 1986
HEARTBREAK RIDGE Warner Bros., 1986
EMANON Paul Releasing 1987
THE CHILD SAVER (TF) Michael Filerman Productions/ NBC Productions, 1988
BIRD Warner Bros., 1988
HOT MEN 1989
WHITE HUNTER, BLACK HEART Warner Bros., 1990

STEFAN NILSSON

Contact: STIM - Sweden, 011-46-8-783-8800

PELLE THE CONQUEROR Miramax Films, 1988, Danish-Swedish

JACK NITZSCHE

b. 1937 - Chicago, Illinois
Agent: Gorfaine-Schwartz - Burbank, 818/954-9500

THE T.A.M.I. SHOW 1964
VILLAGE OF THE GIANTS Embassy, 1965
PERFORMANCE Warner Bros., 1970, British
GREASER'S PALACE Greaser's Palace, 1972
THE EXORCIST co-composer, Warner Bros., 1973
ONE FLEW OVER THE CUCKOO'S NEST ★ United Artists, 1976
HEROES co-composer with Richard Hazard, Universal, 1977
BLUE COLLAR Universal, 1978
HARDCORE Columbia, 1979
WHEN YOU COMIN' BACK, RED RYDER? Columbia, 1979
HEART BEAT Orion/Warner Bros., 1980
CRUISING United Artists, 1980
CUTTER'S WAY *CUTTER AND BONE* United Artists Classics, 1981
CANNERY ROW MGM/UA, 1982
PERSONAL BEST co-composer with Jill Fraser, The Geffen Company/Warner Bros., 1982
AN OFFICER AND A GENTLEMAN ★ Paramount, 1982
BREATHLESS Orion, 1983
WITHOUT A TRACE 20th Century-Fox, 1983
THE RAZOR'S EDGE Columbia, 1984
STARMAN Columbia, 1984
WINDY CITY Warner Bros., 1984
STRIPPER co-composer with Buffy Sainte-Marie, 20th Century Fox, 1985
JEWEL OF THE NILE 20th Century-Fox, 1985
9-1/2 WEEKS MGM/UA, 1986
STAND BY ME Columbia, 1986
THE WHOOPEE BOYS Paramount, 1986
STREETS OF GOLD 20th Century Fox, 1986
THE SEVENTH SIGN Tri-Star, 1988
REVENGE Columbia, 1989
NEXT OF KIN Warner Bros., 1989
REVENGE Columbia, 1990
THE LAST OF THE FINEST Orion, 1990
MERMAIDS 1990

NAZ NOMAD

GIVE DADDY THE KNIFE 1984

ERIC NORDGREN

b. 1913 - Sweden
Contact: STIM - Sweden, 011-46-8-783-8800

KVINNA UTAN ANSIKTE 1947, Swedish
EVA 1948, Swedish
THREE STRANGE LOVES *THIRST* Janus, 1949, Swedish
DIVORCE 1951, Swedish

THIS CAN'T HAPPEN HERE Svensk Filmindustri, 1951, Swedish
ILLICIT INTERLUDE *SOMMARLEK* Janus, 1951, Swedish
SECRETS OF WOMEN Janus, 1952, Swedish
MONIKA Janus, 1953, Swedish
SMILES OF A SUMMER NIGHT Janus, 1955, Swedish
LAST PAIR OUT 1956, Swedish
THE SEVENTH SEAL Janus, 1957, Swedish
WILD STRAWBERRIES Janus, 1957, Swedish
THE MAGICIAN Janus, 1958, Swedish
FACE OF FIRE Allied Artists, 1959
THE VIRGIN SPRING Janus, 1960, Swedish
PLEASURE GARDEN 1961, Swedish
ALL THESE WOMEN Janus, 1964, Swedish
THE ISLAND 1966, Swedish

MONTY NORMAN

Contact: PRS - London, England, 011-44-1-580-5544

HOUSE OF FRIGHT *THE TWO FACES OF DR. JEKYLL* co-composer with David Heneker, American International, 1960, British
DR. NO co-composer with John Barry, United Artists, 1962, British

ALEX NORTH

b. December 4, 1910 - Chester, Pennsylvania
Agent: Gorfaine-Schwartz - Burbank, 818/954-9500

[In 1986, Mr. North was the first composer to receive an honorary Academy Award for his lifetime achievement.]

A STREETCAR NAMED DESIRE ★ Warner Bros., 1951
THE 13TH LETTER 20th Century-Fox, 1951
DEATH OF A SALESMAN ★ Columbia, 1951
VIVA ZAPATA! ★ 20th Century-Fox, 1952
LES MISERABLES 20th Century-Fox, 1952
PONY SOLDIER 20th Century-Fox, 1952
THE MEMBER OF THE WEDDING Columbia, 1953
GO, MAN, GO United Artists, 1954
DESIREE 20th Century Fox, 1954
DADDY LONG LEGS ballet music only, 20th Century-Fox, 1955
THE RACERS 20th Century-Fox, 1955
UNCHAINED Warner Bros., 1955
MAN WITH THE GUN United Artists, 1955
I'LL CRY TOMORROW MGM, 1956
THE ROSE TATTOO ★ Paramount, 1955
THE BAD SEED Warner Bros., 1956
THE RAINMAKER ★ Paramount, 1956
FOUR GIRLS IN TOWN Universal, 1956
THE KING AND FOUR QUEENS United Artists, 1956
THE BACHELOR PARTY United Artists, 1957
THE LONG, HOT SUMMER MGM, 1958
STAGE STRUCK RKO Radio, 1958
HOT SPELL Paramount, 1958
SOUTH SEAS ADVENTURE Cinerama Releasing Corporation, 1958
THE SOUND AND THE FURY 20th Century Fox, 1959
THE WONDERFUL COUNTRY United Artists, 1959
SPARTACUS ★ Universal, 1960
THE CHILDREN'S HOUR United Artists, 1961
SANCTUARY 20th Century Fox, 1961
THE MISFITS United Artists, 1961
ALL FALL DOWN MGM, 1962
CLEOPATRA ★ 20th Century Fox, 1963
THE OUTRAGE MGM, 1964
CHEYENNE AUTUMN Warner Bros., 1964
THE AGONY AND THE ECSTASY ★ 20th Century Fox, 1965
WHO'S AFRAID OF VIRGINIA WOOLF? ★ Warner Bros., 1966
AFRICA (FD) ABC, 1967
THE DEVIL'S BRIGADE United Artists, 1968
THE SHOES OF THE FISHERMAN ★ MGM, 1968
HARD CONTRACT 20th Century Fox, 1969
A DREAM OF KINGS National General, 1969
WILLARD Cinerama Releasing Corporation, 1971
REBEL JESUS 1972
POCKET MONEY National General, 1972
ONCE UPON A SCOUNDREL Image International, 1974, U.S.-Mexican
SHANKS ★ Paramount, 1974
LOST IN THE STARS American Film Theatre, 1974
JOURNEY INTO FEAR Stirling Gold, 1975, Canadian
BITE THE BULLET ★ Columbia, 1975
RICH MAN, POOR MAN (MS) ☆☆ Universal TV, 1976
THE PASSOVER PLOT Atlas, 1976, U.S.-Israeli
THE WORD (MS) ☆ Charles Fries Productions/ Stonehenge Productions, 1978
SOMEBODY KILLED HER HUSBAND Columbia, 1978
WISE BLOOD New Line Cinema, 1979
CARNY United Artists, 1980
DRAGONSLAYER ★ Paramount, 1981, U.S.-British
SISTER, SISTER (TF) 20th Century-Fox TV, 1982
UNDER THE VOLCANO ★ Universal, 1984
PRIZZI'S HONOR 20th Century Fox, 1985
DEATH OF A SALESMAN (TF) ☆ Roxbury and Punch Productions, 1985
THE DEAD Vestron, 1987
GOOD MORNING VIETNAM Buena Vista, 1987
THE PENITENT New Century Vista, 1988

PAUL NOVOTNY

Contact: CAPAC - Ontario, Canada, 1-416-924-4427

BLUE MONKEY co-composer with Patrick Coleman, Spectrafilm, 1987, Canadian

MICHAEL NYMAN

Agent: Bart-Milander - North Hollywood, 818/761-4040

THE DRAUGHTSMAN'S CONTRACT United Artists Classics, 1982, British
NELLY'S VERSION Mithras Films, 1983, British
THE COLD ROOM (TD) Jethro Films/Mark Forstater Productions, 1984, British
A ZED AND TWO NOUGHTS Skouras Pictures, 1985, British-Dutch
DROWNING BY NUMBERS Galaxy International, 1988, British
THE COOK, THE THIEF, HIS WIFE & HER LOVER Recorded Releasing, 1989, British

LAURA NYRO

Contact: BMI - Los Angeles, 213/659-9109

BROKEN RAINBOW (FD) Earthworks, 1985

ARLON OBER
Contact: BMI - Los Angeles, 213/659-9109

ILLUSIONS OF A LADY 1974
THROUGH THE LOOKING GLASS Mature Pictures, 1976
THE INCREDIBLE MELTING MAN American International, 1977
X-RAY *HOSPITAL MASSACRE* Cannon, 1981
HAPPY BIRTHDAY *BLOODY BIRTHDAY/ CREEPS* 1980
EATING RAOUL 20th Century Fox International Classics, 1982
NIGHTBEAST co-composer, 1982
HOSPITAL MASSACRE Cannon, 1983
CRIMEWAVE *BROKEN HEARTS AND NOSES* Columbia, 1985
IN THE SHADOW OF KILIMANJARO Scotti Brothers, 1986

OSCAR CARDOZO OCAMPO
b. Argentina
Contact: SADAIC - Buenos Aires, Argentina, 011-54-1-35-7132

THERE WILL BE NO MORE SORROWS NOR OBLIVION Aries, 1983, Argentine
LOS FIERECILLOS SE DIVIERTEN Aries, 1983, Argentine
DEATHSTALKER New World, 1984

SHINNOSUKA OKAWA
b. Japan
Contact: JASRAC - Tokyo, Japan, 011-81-3-502-6551

THE MAKIOKA SISTERS RS/58, 1983, Japanese

JOHN O'KENNEDY
Contact: ASCAP - Los Angeles, 213/466-7681

STRIPPED TO KILL Concorde, 1987

ALAN OLDFIELD
Contact: ASCAP - Los Angeles, 213/466-7681

THE FOREST *TERROR IN THE FOREST* co-composer with Richard Hieronymous, Fury Film Distribution Ltd., 1983
INVISIBLE STRANGLER co-composer with Richard Hieronymous, Seymour Borde & Associates, 1984

MIKE OLDFIELD
b. 1953
Contact: PRS - London, England, 011-44-1-580-5544

CHARLOTTE 1975
THE SPACE MOVIE (FD) International Harmony, 1980, British
THE KILLING FIELDS Warner Bros., 1984, British

STEPHEN OLIVER
Contact: BMI - Los Angeles, 213/659-9109

LADY JANE Paramount, 1986, British

ALBERT LLOYD OLSON
THE TRIP American International, 1967

KEITH OLSEN
Contact: ASCAP - Los Angeles, 213/466-7681

THAT WAS THEN...THIS IS NOW co-composer with Bill Cuomo, Paramount, 1985

WILLIAM OLVIS
Agent: Gorfaine-Schwartz - Burbank, 818/954-9500

NIGHTINGALES (TF) Aaron Spelling Productions, 1988
EVIL IN CLEAR RIVER (TF) The Steve Tisch Company/ Lionel Chetwynd Productions/Phoenix Entertainment Group, 1988
BABYCAKES (TF) The Konigsburg-Sanitsky Co., 1989
FINISH LINE (CTF) Guber-Peters Entertainment Productions/Phoenix Entertainment Group, 1989
DREAM STREET (TF) Bedford Falls Co./Finnegan Pinchuk/MGM/UA, 1989
KILL ME AGAIN MGM/UA, 1990
PAIR OF ACES (TF) Pedernales Films/Once Upon a Time Films Ltd., 1990
EL DIABLO (CTF) Wizan-Black Film Productions, 1990
FRAMED (CTF) HBO Pictures, 1990

RUSSELL O'MALLEY
UP FROM THE DEPTHS New World, 1979

WILLIAM ORBIT
Contact: PRS - London, England, 011-44-1-580-5544

YOUNGBLOOD MGM/UA, 1986
HOTSHOT International Film Marketing, 1987

CYRIL ORNADEL
Contact: PRS - London, England, 011-44-1-580-5544

BRIEF ENCOUNTER (TF) Carlo Ponti Productions/Cecil Clarke Productions, 1974, British

FRANK ORTEGA
Contact: ASCAP - Los Angeles, 213/466-7681

ROSIE: THE ROSEMARY CLOONEY STORY (TF) Charles Fries Productions/Alan Sacks Productions, 1982

LUIS PERICO ORTIZ
Contact: BMI - Los Angeles, 213/659-9109

MONDO NEW YORK co-composer with Johnny Pacheco, Fourth and Broadway Films/Island Pictures, 1988

RIZ ORTOLANI
b. 1926 - Pesaro, Italy
Contact: SIAE - Rome, Italy, 011-39-6-59-90-1

MONDO CANE co-composer with Nino Oliviero, 1962, Italian
THE EASY LIFE *IL SORPASSO* Embassy, 1962, Italian
LA DONNA NEL MONDO 1963, Italian

LE VERGINE DI NUREMBERG Atlantica Cinematografica, 1964, Italian
THE SEVENTH DAWN United Artists, 1964, U.S.-British
LE ORE NUDE 1964, Italian
AFRICA ADDIO 1965, Italian
THE YELLOW ROLLS-ROYCE MGM, 1965, British
THE GLORY GUYS United Artists, 1965
MAYA MGM, 1966
TIFFANY MEMORANDUM 1966, British
WOMAN TIMES SEVEN Avco Embassy, 1967, French-Italian-U.S.
REQUIESCANT Castoro Film, 1967, Italian
THE VIOLENT FOUR *BANDITI A MILANO* Paramount, 1968, Italian
SEQUESTRO DI PERSONA 1968, Italian
ANZIO Columbia, 1968, Italian
LES AMOURS DE LADY HAMILTON 1968, French-Italian
AL DI LA DELLA LEGGE 1968, Italian
THE BLISS OF MRS. BLOSSOM Paramount, 1969, British
PERVERSION STORY 1969, Italian
O CANGACEIRO 1969, Italian
BORA BORA 1969, Italian
LA CATTURA 1969, Italian
THE ADVENTURES OF GIRARD United Artists, 1969, British-Swiss
LA PRIMA NOTTA DEL DOTTOR DANIELI, INDUSTRIALE, COL COMPLESSO DEL... GIOCATTOLO 1970, Italian
L'INVASION 1970, French-Italian
THE HUNTING PARTY United Artists, 1970
CONFESSIONS OF A POLICE CAPTAIN *CONFESSIONE DI UN COMMISSARIO* 1970, Italian
THE STATUE Cinerama Releasing Corporation, 1971, British
ADDIO ZIO TOM 1971, Italian
IL MERLO MASCHIO 1971, Italian
FRATELLO SOLE, SORELLA LUNA co-composer with Donovan, 1972, Italian
GLI EROI *THE HEROES* 1972, Italian-French-Spanish
UNA RAGIONE PER VIVERE E UNA PER MORIRE 1972, Italian-French-Spanish-West German
GIROLIMONI - IL MOSTRO DI ROMA Dino De Laurentiis Cinematografica, 1972, Italian
THE VALACHI PAPERS *JOE VILACHI: I SEGRETI DI COSA NOSTRA* Columbia, 1972, Italian-French
E GUERRIERE DAL SENO NUDA *THE AMAZONS* EMI, 1973, Italian-French
TERESA LA LADRA 1973, Italian
BISTURI, MAFIA BIANCA 1973, Italian
LE MATAF 1973, French-Italian
GLI EROI 1973, Italian
DIO, SEI UN PADRETERNO! 1973, Italian
MONDO CANDIDO 1975, Italian
LA FACCIA VIOLENTA DI NEW YORK 1975, Italian
PASSI DI MORTE PERDUTI NEL BUIO 1976, Italian
SUBMISSION *SCANDALO* Joseph Brenner Associates, 1977, Italian
BRUTES AND SAVAGES 1978, Italian
DOUBLE MURDER 1978, Italian
FIRST LOVE 1978
THE GIRL IN YELLOW PAJAMAS 1978, Italian
THE RETURN OF CASANOVA 1978, Italian
TIGERS IN LIPSTICK *WILD BEDS/HIJINKS* Castle Hill, 1978, Italian
UN DRAMMA BORGHESE MIMI 1979, Italian
THE 5TH MUSKETEER Columbia, 1979
FROM HELL TO VICTORY 1979, French-Italian-Spanish
CANNIBAL HOLOCAUST Trans Continental Film, 1979, Italian
HOUSE ON THE EDGE OF THE PARK Bedford Entertainment, 1979, Italian
UNA GITA SCOLASTICA *A SCHOOL OUTING* 1983, Italian
1919 1983, Spanish
LA RAGAZZA DI TRIESTE 1983, Italian
CHRISTOPHER COLUMBUS (MS) RAI/Clesi Cinematografica Productions/Antenne 2/Bavaria Atelier/Lorimar Productions, 1985, Italian-West German-U.S.-French

DANIEL OSBORN

SMILE United Artists, 1975

JASON OSBORN

Contact: PRS - London, England, 011-44-1-580-5544

HIGH SEASON Hemdale, 1987, British

VYECHESLAV OVCHINNIKOV

b. 1937 - U.S.S.R.
Contact: VAAP - U.S.S.R., Telex: 871-411327

THE ROLLER AND THE VIOLIN Mosfilm, 1961, Soviet
MY NAME IS IVAN Shore International, 1962, Soviet
THE FIRST TEACHER Mosfilm/Kirghizfilm, 1965, Soviet
ASYA'S HAPPINESS Mosfilm, 1967, Soviet
WAR AND PEACE Continental, 1968, Soviet
ANDREI RUBLEV Columbia, 1968, Soviet
A NEST OF GENTRY Corinth, 1969, Soviet
ARSENAL new score for 1929 silent film, 1971, Soviet
OPERATION LIBERTY 1973, Soviet
THEY FOUGHT FOR THEIR MOTHERLAND Mosfilm, 1974, Soviet
THE STEPPE IFEX Film/Sovexport film, 1977, Soviet

JOHNNY PACHECO

Contact: BMI - Los Angeles, 213/659-9109

MONDO NEW YORK co-composer with Luis Perico Ortiz, Fourth and Broadway Films/Island Pictures, 1988

CHRIS PAGE

Contact: Midiland Studios - Glendale, 818/507-7982

JUST A LITTLE MORE LOVE (TF) NBC, 1981
STEEP AND DEEP 1982
GUS BROWN AND MIDNITE BREWSTER (TF) NBC, 1985
HEAT OF THE NIGHT (TF) main title song only, 1985
BEEKMAN'S PLACE (TF) NBC, 1988

GENE PAGE

Contact: BMI - Los Angeles, 213/659-9109

BREWSTER McCLOUD MGM, 1970
BLACULA American International, 1972

JIMMY PAGE

Contact: ASCAP - Los Angeles, 213/466-7681

DEATH WISH II Filmways, 1982
DEATH WISH 3 Cannon, 1985

MARTY PAICH

b. January 23, 1925 - Oakland, California
Contact: Francis & Freedman Corp., 328 S. Beverly Drive, Beverly Hills, 90212, 213/277-7351

HEY THERE, IT'S YOGI BEAR (AF) Hanna-Barbera, 1964
THE SWINGER Paramount, 1966
CHANGES Cinerama Releasing Corporation, 1969
DUNE additional music, Universal, 1984

CHRISTOPHER PALMER

b. England
Contact: PRS - London, England, 011-44-1-580-5544

VALMONT Orion, 1989

DAVID PALMER

THE ROYAL ROMANCE OF CHARLES AND DIANA (TF) Chrysalis-Yellen Productions, 1982

GERULF PANNACH

Contact: SACEM - France, 011-33-14-747-5650

SINGING THE BLUES IN RED *FATHERLAND* co-composer with Christian Kunert, Angelika Films, 1986, British-West German-French

DANIELE PARIS

b. 1921
Contact: SIAE - Rome, Italy, 011-39-6-59-90-1

EVERY DAY EXCEPT CHRISTMAS 1957, British
LA STORIA DEL TERZO REICH (TD) 1971, Italian
STORIA DELLA BOMBA ATOMICA (TD) 1971, Italian
MILAREPA Lotar Film, 1974, Italian
THE NIGHT PORTER Avco Embassy, 1974, Italian
BEYOND GOOD AND EVIL United Artists, 1977, Italian-French-West German

SIMON PARK

Contact: PRS - London, England, 011-44-1-580-5544

NUTCRACKER Jezshaw Film, 1982, British

ALAN PARKER

Contact: BMI - Los Angeles, 213/659-9109

JAWS 3-D Universal, 1983
AMERICAN GOTHIC Vestron, 1988
OUT OF TIME Motion Picture International, 1989
VOICE OF THE HEART (TF) Portman Productions/ HTV, 1990

CLIFTON PARKER

Contact: PRS - London, England, 011-44-1-580-5544

TARZAN AND THE LOST SAFARI MGM, 1957, British-U.S.
CURSE OF THE DEMON *NIGHT OF THE DEMON* Columbia, 1957, British
SCREAM OF FEAR *TASTE OF FEAR* Columbia, 1961, British

JIM PARKER

Contact: PRS - London, England, 011-44-1-580-5544

TIME AFTER TIME BBC-TV, 1985, British
DEADLINE (TF) BBC Enterprises, 1988, British

JOHN PARKER

Agent: Gorfaine-Schwartz - Burbank, 818/954-9500

LAUREL AND HARDY'S LAUGHING '20s MGM, 1965
THE FURTHER PERILS OF LAUREL AND HARDY MGM, 1968
DARKER THAN AMBER National General, 1970
CUTTER'S TRAIL (TF) CBS Studio Center, 1970
HUNGRY WIVES Jack H. Harris Enterprises, 1973
THE MAN WHO DIED TWICE (TF) Cinema Center, 1973
STRANGE HOMECOMING (TF) Alpine Productions/ Worldvision, 1974
THE SECRET NIGHT CALLER (TF) Charles Fries Productions/ Penthouse Productions, 1975
LAW OF THE LAND (TF) QM Productions, 1976
IN THE GLITTER PALACE (TF) The Writer's Company/ Columbia TV, 1977
SECRETS OF THREE HUNGRY WIVES (TF) Penthouse Productions, 1978
THE GIRLS IN THE OFFICE (TF) ABC Circle Films, 1979
THE GREAT CASH GIVEAWAY GETAWAY (TF) Penthouse Productions/Cine Guarantors, 1980

VAN DYKE PARKS

Agent: CAA - Los Angeles, 213/288-4545

GOIN' SOUTH co-composer with Perry Botkin, Paramount, 1978
POPEYE Paramount, 1980
SESAME STREET PRESENTS: FOLLOW THAT BIRD co-composer, Warner Bros., 1985
CLUB PARADISE co-composer with David Mansfield, Warner Bros., 1986
RENTED LIPS New Century Vista, 1988
CASUAL SEX? Universal, 1988
THE TWO JAKES also appears as prosecutor, Paramount, 1990

STEVE PARSONS

Contact: PRS - London, England, 011-44-1-580-5544

HOWLING II...YOUR SISTER IS A WEREWOLF Thorn-EMI, 1985, British
RECRUITS Concorde, 1986

ARVO PART

Contact: GEMA - West Germany, 011-49-89-621400

RACHEL RIVER Taurus Entertainment, 1987

JOHNNY PATE

Contact: BMI - Los Angeles, 213/659-9109

SHAFT IN AFRICA MGM, 1973
BROTHER ON THE RUN 1974
SATAN'S TRIANGLE (TF) Danny Thomas Productions, 1975
BUCKTOWN American International, 1975
DR. BLACK, MR. HYDE Dimension, 1976
THE WATTS MONSTER Dimension, 1979

RICK PATTERSON
Contact: Pro-Canada - Canada, 1-416-445-8700

YOUNG GIANTS Entertainment Enterprises, 1983

CHARLES PAVLOSKY
Contact: BMI - Los Angeles, 213/659-9109

NINJA TURF co-composer with Gary Falcone and Chris Stone, Ascot Entertainment Group, 1986

GLENN PAXTON
Contact: ASCAP - Los Angeles, 213/466-7681

THE CLONE MASTER (TF) Mel Ferber Productions/ Paramount Pictures TV, 1978
THE TWO WORLDS OF JENNIE LOGAN (TF) Joe Wizan TV Productions/Charles Fries Productions, 1979
DARK NIGHT OF THE SCARECROW (TF) Wizan Productions, 1981
ISABEL'S CHOICE (TF) Stuart Miller Productions/ Pantheon Television, 1981
VITAL SIGNS (TF) CBS Entertainment, 1986
DREAM BREAKERS (TF) CBS Entertainment, 1989

BILL PAYNE
CERTAIN FURY co-composer with Russ Kunkel and George Massenburg, New World, 1985, Canadian
SMOOTH TALK co-composer with Russ Kunkel and George Massenburg, Spectrafilm, 1985

DON PEAKE
Contact: Robert Light - Los Angeles, 213/651-1777

HAROLD LLOYD: SAFETY LAST new score for 1923 silent, Time-Life Films, 1974
HAROLD LLOYD: WHY WORRY? new score for 1923 silent, Time-Life Films
HAROLD LLOYD: THE FRESHMAN new score for 1925 silent, Time-Life Films
HAROLD LLOYD: HOT WATER new score for 1924 silent, Time-Life Films
THE LEGEND OF BIGFOOT Palladium Productions, 1975
BAD GEORGIA ROAD Dimension, 1976
MOVING VIOLATION 20th Century-Fox, 1976
BLACK OAK CONSPIRACY New World, 1977
THE HILLS HAVE EYES Vanguard, 1977
BATTERED (TF) Henry Jaffe Enterprises, 1978
WALK PROUD Universal, 1979
FLATBED ANNIE AND SWEETIE PIE: LADY TRUCKERS (TF) Moonlight Productions/ Filmways, 1979
FAST FRIENDS (TF) Columbia TV, 1979
DELUSION New Line Cinema, 1981
I, DESIRE (TF) Green-Epstein Productions/ Columbia TV, 1982
THE HOUSE WHERE DEATH LIVES New American, 1984
CODE OF VENGEANCE (TF) Universal TV, 1985
DALTON: CODE OF VENGEANCE II (TF) Universal TV, 1986
MODERN LOVE Skouras Pictures, 1990

KEVIN PEAK
Contact: APRA - Australia, 011-61-2-922-6422

BATTLETRUCK *WARLORDS OF THE 21ST CENTURY* New World, 1982, U.S.-New Zealand
WINDRIDER Hoyts, 1986, Australian

BOB PEGG
Contact: PRS - London, England, 011-44-1-580-5544

BLACK JACK Kestrel Films, 1979, British

LEON PENDARVIS
Contact: BMI - Los Angeles, 213/659-9109

AMERICA ASA Communications, 1986

THE PENGUIN CAFE ORCHESTRA
Contact: APRA - Australia, 011-61-2-922-6422

MALCOLM Vestron, 1986, Australian

COLERIDGE-TAYLOR PERKINSON
Contact: ASCAP - Los Angeles, 213/466-7681

IF HE HOLLERS, LET HIM GO Cinerama Releasing Corporation, 1968
THE McMASTERS Chevron, 1970
TOGETHER FOR DAYS Olas, 1973
A WARM DECEMBER National General, 1973
AMAZING GRACE United Artists, 1974
THOMASINE AND BUSHROD Columbia, 1974
THE EDUCATION OF SONNY CARSON Paramount, 1974
LOVE IS NOT ENOUGH (TF) Universal TV, 1978
A WOMAN CALLED MOSES (TF) Henry Jaffe Enterprises/ IKE Productions, 1978
FREEDOM ROAD (TF) co-composer with Terrence James, Zev Braun TV/Freedom Road Films, 1979

FREDDIE PERREN
Contact: ASCAP - Los Angeles, 213/466-7681

HELL UP IN HARLEM co-composer with Fonce Mizell, American International, 1973
COOLEY HIGH American International, 1975

MARC PERRONE
LA TRACE co-composer with Nicole Piovani, Fox-Hachette, 1984, French-Swiss

ALEXANDER PESKANOV
HE KNOWS YOU'RE ALONE co-composer with Mark Peskanov, MGM/United Artists, 1980

MARK PESKANOV
HE KNOWS YOU'RE ALONE co-composer with Alexander Peskanov, MGM/United Artists, 1980

OSCAR PETERSON
b. August 15, 1925 - Montreal, Canada
Contact: BMI - Los Angeles, 213/659-9109

THE SILENT PARTNER EMC Film/Aurora, 1979, Canadian

RANDY PETERSEN
Agent: Robert Light - Los Angeles, 213/651-1777

THE ZOO GANG New World, 1985

JEAN-CLAUDE PETIT

b. France
Agent: Bart-Milander - North Hollywood, 818/761-4040

VIVE LA SOCIALE! Fox-Hachette, 1983, French
JEAN DE FLORETTE Orion Classics, 1987, French
MANON OF THE SPRING Orion Classics, 1987, French
THE RETURN OF THE MUSKETEERS Universal, 1989, British

ANDREY PETROVIC

b. U.S.S.R.
Contact: VAAP - U.S.S.R., Telex: 871-411327

THE BLUE BIRD 20th Century-Fox, 1976, U.S.-Soviet

HERB PHILHOFER

ON THE EDGE Skouras Pictures, 1985

ART PHILIPPS

Contact: BMI - Los Angeles, 213/659-9109

THE LUCKY STAR Pickman Films, 1980, Canadian

JOHN PHILLIPS

Contact: PRS - London, England, 011-44-1-580-5544

MYRA BRECKENRIDGE 20th Century-Fox, 1971
THE MAN WHO FELL TO EARTH Cinema 5, 1976, British

MARY PHILLIPS

Contact: PRS - London, England, 011-44-1-580-5544

CARAVAGGIO co-composer with Simon Fisher Turner, British Film Institute, 1986, British

STU PHILLIPS

Agent: Richard Emler - Los Angeles, 213/651-0222

MAD DOG COLL Columbia, 1961
THE MAN FROM THE DINER'S CLUB Columbia, 1963
RIDE THE WILD SURF Columbia, 1964
DEAD HEAT ON A MERRY-GO-ROUND Columbia, 1966
HELL'S ANGELS ON WHEELS American International, 1967
THE NAME OF THE GAME IS TO KILL *THE FEMALE TRAP* Fanfare, 1968
ANGELS FROM HELL American International, 1968
RUN, ANGEL, RUN! Fanfare, 1969
THE APPOINTMENT MGM, 1969
2000 YEARS LATER Warner Bros., 1969
THE GAY DECEIVERS Fanfare, 1969
FOLLOW ME! Cinerama, 1969
THE LOSERS Fanfare, 1970
BEYOND THE VALLEY OF THE DOLLS 20th Century-Fox, 1970
SIMON, KING OF THE WITCHES Fanfare, 1971
THE SEVEN MINUTES 20th Century-Fox, 1971
JUD Duque Films, 1971
HOW TO SEDUCE A WOMAN Cinerama, 1974
MACON COUNTY LINE American International, 1974
SWITCH (TF) Glen Larson Productions/ Universal TV, 1975
THE MEAL *DEADLY ENCOUNTER* Ambassador Releasing, 1975
BENNY AND BARNEY: LAS VEGAS UNDERCOVER (TF) Glen A. Larson Productions/Universal TV, 1977
EVENING IN BYZANTIUM (TF) Universal TV, 1978
FAST CHARLIE, THE MOONBEAM RIDER *FAST CHARLIE AND THE MOONBEAM* Universal, 1979
BUCK ROGERS Universal, 1979
WAIKIKI (TF) Aaron Spelling Productions, 1980
MIDNIGHT LACE (TF) Four R. Productions/ Universal TV, 1981
ROOSTER (TF) Glen A. Larson Productions/Tugboat Productions/20th Century-Fox TV, 1982
TERROR AT ALCATRAZ (TF) Glen A. Larson Productions/ Universal TV, 1982
IN LIKE FLYNN (TF) Glen A. Larson Productions/20th Century-Fox TV, 1985
THE HIGHWAYMAN (TF) Glen A. Larson Productions/20th Century Fox TV, 1987
THE ROAD RAIDERS (TF) New East Entertainment/ Universal TV, 1989

ASTOR PIAZ

Contact: SIAE - Rome, Italy, 011-39-6-59-90-1

HENRY IV Orion Classics, 1984, Italian

PIERO PICCIONI

b. 1921 - Turin, Italy
Contact: SIAE - Rome, Italy, 011-39-6-59-90-1

SAMPAN BOY 1950, Italian
IL MONDO LE CONDANNA 1952, Italian
LA SPIAGGIA 1954, Italian
LA DONNA CHE VENNE DEL MARE 1956, Italian
POOR BUT BEAUTIFUL Trans-Lux, 1956, Italian-French
GUENDALINA Carlo Ponti/Les Films Marceau, 1957, Italian-French
BELLE, MA POVERE Titanus, 1957, Italian
LA FINESTRA SUL LUNA PARK Noria Film, 1957, Italian
IL SEGRETO DELLA SIERRA DORADA 1957, Italian
TEMPEST Paramount, 1958, Italian-French-Yugoslavian
LA BALLERINA ED IL BUON DIO 1958, Italian
I RAGAZZI DEL PARIOLI 1958, Italian
AVVENTURA A CAPRI 1958, Italian
I TARTASSATI 1958, Italian
LA NOTTE BRAVA *ON ANY STREET/BAD GIRLS DON'T CRY* Ajace Film/Franco London Film, 1959, Italian-French
RUN WITH THE DEVIL *VIA MARGUTTA* 1959, Italian
RACCONTI D'ESTATE 1959, Italian
I DOLCI INGANNI 1959, Italian
L'IMPIEGATO 1959, Italian
I MAGLIARI Vides/Titanus, 1959, Italian
NATA DI MARZO 1959, Italian
ADUA E LE COMPAGNE 1960, Italian
IL BELL'ANTONIO Cino Del Duca/Arco Film/Lyre Cinematographique, 1960, Italian-French
FROM A ROMAN BALCONY *LA GIORNATA BALORDA/ LOVE IS A DAY'S WORK/PICKUP IN ROME* Continental, 1960, Italian-French
LA VIACCIA adaptation, Embassy, 1960, Italian
IL GOBBO Dino De Laurentiis Cinematografica, 1960, Italian
L'ASSASSINO *THE LADY KILLER OF ROME* Manson, 1961, Italian-French
SENILITA Zebra Film/Aera Film, 1961, Italian-French
SALVATORE GIULIANO CCM Films, 1962, Italian-French
ANNI RUGGENTI 1962, Italian
CONGO VIVO 1962, Italian
THE SLAVE *IL FIGLIO DI SPARTACUS* 1962, Italian
LA MANI SULLA CITTA Galatea Film, 1963, Italian

FILM COMPOSERS

L'ATTICO 1963, Italian
CHI LAVORA E'PERDUTO *IN CAPO AL MONDO* Zebra Film/Franco London Film, 1963, Italian-French
LA PARMIGIANA 1963, Italian
IL TERRORISTA 22 Dicembre/Galatea, 1964, Italian
LA FUGA 1964, Italian
THE TENTH VICTIM Embassy, 1965, Italian
THE MOMENT OF TRUTH Rizzoli, 1965, Italian-Spanish
CACCIA ALLA VOLPE 1966, Italian
MATCHLESS United Artists, 1966, Italian
THE STRANGER Paramount, 1967, Italian-French-Algerian
THE WITCHES Lopert, 1967, Italian-French
IL MEDICO DELLA MUTUA 1968, Italian
CAPRICCIO ALL'ITALIANA De Laurentiis, 1968, Italian
SARTANA 1968
PAS DE ROSES POUR OSS 117 1968, Italian
TO'E MORTA LA NONNA Vides, 1969, Italian
UOMINI CONTRO Prima Cinematografica/Jadran Film, 1970, Italian-Yugoslavian
LA CONTESTAZIONE GENERALE 1970, Italian
BELLO, ONESTO, EMIGRATO AUSTRALIA SPOSEREBBE COMPAESANA ILLIBATA 1970, Italian
ER PIU, STORIA D'AMORE E DI COLTELLO 1970, Italian
THE LIGHT AT THE EDGE OF THE WORLD National General, 1971, U.S.-Spanish
THE SEDUCTION OF MIMI *MIMI METALLURGICO FERITO NELL'ONORE* New Line Cinema, 1972, Italian
LE MOINE *THE MONK* Rank, 1972, French-Italian-West German
LO SCOPIONE SCIENTIFICO De Laurentiis, 1972, Italian
LE MONACHE DI SANT' ARCANGELO Miracle, 1973, Italian-French
THE MATTEI AFFAIR Paramount, 1973, Italian
POLVERE DI STELLE Capitolina Produzioni Cinematografiche, 1973, Italian
LUCKY LUCIANO Avco Embassy, 1974, Italian
ALL SCREWED UP *TUTTO A POSTO, NIENTE IN ORDINE* New Line Cinema, 1974, Italian
APPASSIONATA 1974, Italian
IL DIO SOTTO LA PELLE 1974, Italian
SWEPT AWAY BY AN UNUSUAL DESTINY IN THE BLUE SEA OF AUGUST Cinema 5, 1974, Italian
CHI DICE DONNA DICE...DONNA 1975, Italian
CUORE DI CANE Italnoleggio, 1975, Italian
FRATELLO MARE 1975, Italian
CADAVERI ECCELENTI United Artists, 1976, Italian-French
IL COMUNE SENSO DEL PUDORE Rizzoli Film, 1976, Italian
I VIZI MORBOSI DI UNA GOVERNANTE 1976, Italian
QUELLE STRANE OCCASIONI Cineriz, 1977, Italian
STRANGE EVENTS 1977, Italian
THE WITNESS 1978, Italian
DOVE VAI IN VACANZA? co-composer, Rizzoli, 1978, Italian
THE HYPOCHONDRIAC 1979, Italian
EBOLI *CHRIST STOPPED AT EBOLI* Franklin Media, 1980, Italian-French
IL MALATO IMMAGINARIO 1980, Italian
FIGHTING BACK Paramount, 1982

MICHAEL PICCIRILLO
Contact: BMI - Los Angeles, 213/659-9109

CRACK HOUSE Cannon, 1989

TOM PIERSON
Contact: BMI - Los Angeles, 213/659-9109

QUINTET 20th Century-Fox, 1979

NICHOLAS PIKE
Agent: Bart-Milander - North Hollywood, 818/761-4040

GRAVEYARD SHIFT Shapiro/Virgin, 1986, Canadian
CRITTERS 2: THE MAIN COURSE New Line Cinema, 1988
TALES FROM THE CRYPT (CTF) co-composer, Tales from the Crypt Holdings, 1989
CHUD II: BUD THE CHUD Vestron, 1989

CHUCK PINNELL
LAST NIGHT AT THE ALAMO co-composer with Wayne Bell, Alamo Films, 1983

NICOLA PIOVANI
b. 1946 - Italy
Contact: SIAE - Rome, Italy, 011-39-6-59-90-1

NEL NOME DEL PADRE 1970, Italian
LA REGAZZA DI LATTA 1970, Italian
DANIELE E MARIA 1972, Italian
N.P. IL SEGRETO 1972, Italian
SBATTI IL MOSTRO IN PRIMA PAGINA 1972, Italian
LA VITA IN GIOCO 1973, Italian
THE REBEL NUN *FLAVIA LA MONACA MUSULMANA* 1974, Italian
L'INVENZIONE DI MOREL 1974, Italian
IL PROFUMO DELLA SIGNORA IN NERO 1974, Italian
LE ORME 1975, Italian
VERMISAT 1975, Italian
VICTORY MARCH Summit Features, 1976, Italian-French
MORIRE A ROMA 1976, Italian
IL GABBIANO (TF) RAI, 1976, Italian
HYENA'S SUN *ACH CHAMS WADHDHIBA* 1977, Algerian-British
GLI ULTIMI TRE GIORNI 1977, Italian
NEL PIU ALTO DEI CIELI 1977, Italian
LE SOLEIL DES HYENES 1977, Dutch-Algerian
SALTO NEL VUOTO 1980, Italian
VACANZE IN VAL TREBBIA 1980, Italian
IL MINESTRONE 1981, Italian
HET MEISJE MET HET RODE HAAR 1981, Dutch
IL MARCHESE DEL GRILLO 1981, Italian
THE NIGHT OF THE SHOOTING STARS *LA NOTTE DI SAN LORENZO* United Artists Classics, 1981, Italian
LA VELA INCANTATA 1982, Italian
GIL OCCHI, LA BOCCA *THE EYES, THE MOUTH* Gaumont, 1982, Italian-French
DE SCHORPIOEN 1983, Dutch
LA TRACE co-composer with Marc Perrone, Fox-Hachette, 1984, French-Swiss
GINGER AND FRED MGM/UA, 1986, Italian-French-West German
DEVIL IN THE FLESH Istituto Luce/Italnoleggio, 1986, Italian-French
GOOD MORNING, BABYLON Vestron, 1987, Italian-French-U.S.
MANIFESTO Cannon, 1989
THE VOICE OF THE MOON Penta Distribuzione, 1990, Italian

GIANFRANCO PLENIZIO
b. Italy
Contact: SIAE - Rome, Italy, 011-39-6-59-90-1

BELLA DI GIORNO, MOGLIE DI NOTTE 1971, Italian
I LEONI DI SAN PETERSBURG 1972, Italian
NO...SONO VERGINE 1973, Italian
AH SI? E IO LO DICO A ZZZORO! 1975, Italian
LIBERI, ARMATI, PERICOLOSI 1976, Italian
MASOCH Difilm, 1980, Italian
AND THE SHIP SAILS ON Triumph/Columbia, 1983, Italian-French

TERRY PLUMERI
Contact: BMI - Los Angeles, 213/659-9109

ANGEL TOWN Taurus Entertainment Company, 1990
BODY CHEMISTRY Concorde, 1990

BASIL POLEDOURIS
b. 1945
Agent: ICM - Los Angeles, 213/550-4000

CONGRATULATIONS, IT'S A BOY! (TF) co-composer with Richard Baskin, Aaron Spelling Productions, 1971
EXTREME CLOSE-UP National General, 1973
TINTORERA - THE SILENT DEATH 1977, British-Mexican
BIG WEDNESDAY Warner Bros., 1978
DOLPHIN (FD) Michael Wiese Film Productions, 1979
90028 1979
DEFIANCE co-composer with Gerard McMahon, American International, 1980
THE BLUE LAGOON Columbia, 1980
THE HOUSE OF GOD *(H.O.G.)* United Artists, 1981
A WHALE FOR THE KILLING (TF) Play Productions/ Beowulf Productions, 1981
FIRE ON THE MOUNTAIN (TF) Bonnard Productions, 1982
CONAN THE BARBARIAN Universal, 1982
SUMMER LOVERS Filmways, 1982
AMAZONS (TF) ABC Circle Films, 1984
CONAN THE DESTROYER Universal, 1984
SINGLE BARS, SINGLE WOMEN (TF) Carsey Werner Productions/Sunn Classic Pictures, 1984
MAKING THE GRADE MGM/UA/Cannon, 1984
RED DAWN MGM/UA, 1984
PROTOCOL Warner Bros., 1984
ALFRED HITCHCOCK PRESENTS (TF) co-composer, Universal TV, 1985
FLESH *I BLOOD* Orion, 1985, U.S.-Dutch
IRON EAGLE Tri-Star, 1986
CHERRY 2000 Orion, 1986
AMERIKA (MS) ABC Circle Films, 1987
ISLAND SONS (TF) Universal TV, 1987
ROBOCOP Orion, 1987
NO MAN'S LAND Orion, 1987
SPELLBINDER *WITCHING HOUR* MGM/UA, 1988
INTRIGUE (TF) Crew Neck Productions/Linnea Productions/Columbia Pictures TV, 1988
SPLIT DECISIONS New Century/Vista, 1988
FAREWELL TO THE KING Orion, 1989
LONESOME DOVE (MS) ☆☆ Motown Productions/ Pangaea/Qintex Entertainment, Inc., 1989
WIRED The Wired Joint Venture, 1989
WHY ME? Trans World Entertainment, 1989
L.A. TAKEDOWN (TF) additional music, AJAR/ Mories Film Productions, 1989
THE HUNT FOR RED OCTOBER Paramount, 1990
QUIGLEY DOWN UNDER Warner Bros., 1990, Australian
THE FLIGHT OF THE INTRUDER Paramount, 1990

TIBAR POLGAR
Contact: Pro-Canada - Canada, 1-416-445-8700

IN PRAISE OF OLDER WOMEN Avco Embassy, 1978, Canadian

POPOL VUH
Contact: GEMA - West Germany, 011-49-89621400

AGUIRRE, THE WRATH OF GOD New Yorker, 1973, West German-Mexican-Peruvian
HEART OF GLASS New Yorker, 1976, West German
NOSFERATU THE VAMPYRE 20th Century-Fox, 1979, West German-French-U.S.
FITZCARRALDO New World, 1982, West German
COBRA VERDE DEG, 1988, West German

GREG POREE
Contact: BMI - Los Angeles, 213/659-9109

AND THE CHILDREN SHALL LEAD (TF) Rainbow TV Workshop, 1985

MICHEL PORTAL
b. 1935 - Bayonne, France
Contact: SACEM - France, 011-33-14-747-5650

CINEMATOGRAPHIE co-composer, 1966, French
LE VIOL *A QUESTION OF RAPE* 1967, French
GROMAIRE (FD) 1967, French
SOLEIL DE PIERRE 1967, French
HAXAN WITCHCRAFT THROUGH THE AGES 1968, French
HOA-BINH 1969, French
FEU *FIRE* 1970, French
ALECHINSKY D'APRES NATURE 1970, French
FRANCE SOCIETE ANONYME 1973, French
LA CECILIA 1974, French
LES CONQUISTADORS 1975, French
SERAIL 1975, French
FOR CLEMENCE 1977, French
THE ADOPTION 1978, French
LES CAVALIERS DE L'ORAGE 1983, French-Yugoslavian
BALLES PERDUES *STRAY BULLETS* Films Galatee, 1983, French
SORCERESS *LA MOINE ET LA SORCIERE* European Classics, 1987, French-U.S.

RACHEL PORTMAN
Contact: PRS - London, England, 011-44-1-580-5544

SHARMA AND BEYOND Cinecom International, 1986, British
YOUNG CHARLIE CHAPLIN (TF) Thames TV Productions/ WonderWorks, 1989, British-U.S.

MIKE POST
Agent: Gorfaine-Schwartz - Burbank, 818/954-9500

GIDGET GETS MARRIED (TF) co-composer with Pete Carpenter, Screen Gems/Columbia Pictures TV, 1972
THE MORNING AFTER (TF) co-composer with Pete Carpenter, Wolper Productions, 1974
LOCUSTS (TF) co-composer with Pete Carpenter, Carson Productions/Paramount Pictures TV, 1974

THE INVASION OF JOHNSON COUNTY (TF) co-composer with Pete Carpenter, Roy Huggins Productions/Universal TV, 1976
SCOTT FREE (TF) co-composer with Pete Carpenter, Cherokee Productions/Universal TV, 1976
RICHIE BROCKELMAN: MISSING 24 HOURS (TF) co-composer with Pete Carpenter, Universal TV, 1976
DR. SCORPION (TF) co-composer with Pete Carpenter, Universal TV, 1978
RABBIT TEST co-composer with Pete Carpenter, Avco Embassy, 1978
CAPTAIN AMERICA (TF) co-composer with Pete Carpenter, Universal TV, 1979
THE NIGHT RIDER (TF) co-composer with Pete Carpenter, Stephen J. Cannell Productions/ Universal TV, 1979
CAPTAIN AMERICA II (TF) co-composer with Pete Carpenter, Universal TV, 1979
SCOUT'S HONOR (TF) Zephyr Productions, 1980
COACH OF THE YEAR (TF) co-composer with Pete Carpenter, Shane Company Productions/NBC Entertainment, 1980
DEEP IN THE HEART *HANDGUN* Warner Bros., 1981
WILL, G. GORDON LIDDY (TF) co-composer with Pete Carpenter, Shayne Company Productions, 1982
ADAM (TF) Alan Landsburg Productions, 1983
RUNNING BRAVE Buena Vista, 1983, Canadian
HARD KNOX (TF) co-composer with Pete Carpenter, Shane Company Productions, 1984
NO MAN'S LAND (TF) co-composer with Pete Carpenter, JADDA Productions/Warner Bros. TV, 1984
HADLEY'S REBELLION American Film Distributors, 1984
RHINESTONE adaptation, 20th Century Fox, 1984
THE RIVER RAT Paramount, 1984
HEART OF A CHAMPION: THE RAY MANCINI STORY (TF) Rare Titles Productions/Robert Papazian Productions, 1985
STINGRAY (TF) co-composer with Pete Carpenter, Stephen J. Cannell Productions, 1985
THE LAST PRECINCT (TF) co-composer with Pete Carpenter, Stephen J. Cannell Productions, 1986
ADAM: HIS SONG CONTINUES (TF) Alan Landsburg Productions, 1986
L.A. LAW (TF) 20th Century Fox TV, 1986
DESTINATION: AMERICA (TF) Stephen J. Cannell Productions, 1987
WISEGUY (TF) Stephen J. Cannell Productions, 1987
J.J. STARBUCK (TF) Stephen J. Cannell Productions, 1987
THE RYAN WHITE STORY (TF) The Landsburg Co., 1989
B.L. STRYKER: THE DANCER'S TOUCH (TF) Blue Period Productions/TWS Productions/ Universal TV, 1989
QUANTUM LEAP (TF) Belisarius Productions/ Universal TV, 1989
UNSPEAKABLE ACTS (TF) Alan Landsburg Productions, 1990
WITHOUT HER CONSENT (TF) Raymond Katz Enterprises/Half Pint Productions/Carla Singer Productions, 1990

ANDREW POWELL

Contact: PRS - London, England, 011-44-1-580-5544

LADYHAWKE Warner Bros., 1985
ROCKET GIBRALTAR Columbia, 1988

DON PRESTON

Contact: Richard Emler - Los Angeles, 213/651-0222

ANDROID Island Alive/New Realm, 1982
THE BEING Embassy, 1983
NIGHT PATROL New World, 1984
SILENT WITNESS (TF) Robert Greenwald Productions, 1985
EYE OF THE TIGER Scotti Brothers, 1986
BLOOD DINER Vestron, 1987
THE UNDERACHIEVERS Vestron, 1987
TIPS Paragon Arts, 1987

JAN PRESTON

Contact: APRA - Australia, 011-61-2-922-6422

ILLUSTRIOUS ENERGY Mirage Entertainment, 1988, New Zealand

ANDRE PREVIN

b. April 6, 1929 - Berlin, Germany
Contact: ASCAP - Los Angeles, 213/466-7681

THE SUN COMES UP MGM, 1949
SCENE OF THE CRIME MGM, 1949
BORDER INCIDENT MGM, 1949
CHALLENGE TO LASSIE MGM, 1949
TENSION MGM, 1949
SHADOW ON THE WALL MGM, 1950
THE OUTRIDERS MGM, 1950
THREE LITTLE WORDS ★ adaptation, MGM, 1950
DIAL 1119 MGM, 1950
KIM MGM, 1950
CAUSE FOR ALARM MGM, 1951
SMALL TOWN GIRL MGM, 1953
THE GIRL WHO HAD EVERYTHING MGM, 1953
KISS ME KATE ★ adaptation, MGM, 1953
GIVE A GIRL A BREAK MGM, 1953
BAD DAY AT BLACK ROCK MGM, 1955
IT'S ALWAYS FAIR WEATHER MGM, 1955
KISMET adaptation, MGM, 1955
THE CATERED AFFAIR MGM, 1956
THE FASTEST GUN ALIVE MGM, 1956
HOT SUMMER NIGHT MGM, 1957
DESIGNING WOMAN MGM, 1957
SILK STOCKINGS adaptation, MGM, 1957
HOUSE OF NUMBERS Columbia, 1957
GIGI ★★ adaptation, MGM, 1958
PORGY AND BESS ★★ adaptation, Columbia, 1959
WHO WAS THAT LADY? Columbia, 1960
THE SUBTERRANEANS MGM, 1960
BELLS ARE RINGING ★ adaptation, MGM, 1960
ELMER GANTRY ★ United Artists, 1960
ALL IN A NIGHT'S WORK Paramount, 1961
ONE, TWO, THREE United Artists, 1961
THE FOUR HORSEMEN OF THE APOCALYPSE MGM, 1962
LONG DAY'S JOURNEY INTO NIGHT Embassy, 1962
TWO FOR THE SEESAW United Artists, 1962
IRMA LA DOUCE ★★ United Artists, 1963
DEAD RINGER Warner Bros., 1964
MY FAIR LADY ★★ adaptation, Warner Bros., 1964
GOODBYE CHARLIE 20th Century-Fox, 1964
KISS ME, STUPID Lopert, 1964
INSIDE DAISY CLOVER Warner Bros., 1965
THE FORTUNE COOKIE United Artists, 1966
ROLLERBALL supervision, United Artists, 1975

ALAN PRICE

b. 1942
Contact: PRS - London, England, 011-44-1-580-5544

OH, LUCKY MAN! Warner Bros., 1973, British
ALFIE DARLING *OH! ALFIE* EMI Films, 1975, British
BRITTANIA HOSPITAL United Artists Classics, 1982, British
THE WHALES OF AUGUST Alive Films, 1987

GEORGE S. PRICE

Contact: BMI - Los Angeles, 213/659-9109

GUYANA, CULT OF THE DAMNED co-composer with Nelson Riddle and Robert Summers, Universal, 1980

FRANK PRIMATA

MAUSOLEUM MPM, 1983

ROBERT PRINCE

Contact: ASCAP - Los Angeles, 213/466-7681

A LITTLE GAME (TF) Universal TV, 1971
WHAT'S A NICE GIRL LIKE YOU...? (TF) Universal TV, 1971
GARGOYLES (TF) Tomorrow Entertainment, 1972
COOL MILLION (TF) Universal TV, 1972
SCREAM, PRETTY PEGGY (TF) Universal TV, 1973
A CRY IN THE WILDERNESS (TF) Universal TV, 1974
WHERE HAVE ALL THE PEOPLE GONE? (TF) Metromedia Producers Corporation/The Jozak Company, 1974
THE STRANGE AND DEADLY OCCURRENCE (TF) Metromedia Productions, 1974
BIG ROSE (TF) 20th Century-Fox TV, 1974
NEWMAN'S LAW Universal, 1974
THE STRANGE AND DEADLU OCCURRENCE (TF) Metromedia Producers Corporation/Alpine Productions, 1974
WHERE HAVE ALL THE PEOPLE GONE? (TF) Metromedia Productions, 1974
THE DEAD DON'T DIE (TF) Douglas S. Cramer Productions, 1975
J.D.'S REVENGE American International, 1976
SQUIRM American International, 1976
SNOWBEAST (TF) Douglas Cramer Productions, 1977
HAPPINESS IS A WARM CLUE *THE RETURN OF CHARLIE CHAN* (TF) Charlie Chan Company/ Universal TV, 1979
THE GATHERING, PART II (TF) Hanna-Barbera Productions, 1979
THE SEDUCTION OF MISS LEONA (TF) Edgar J. Scherick Associates, 1980
THE VIOLATION OF SARAH McDAVID (TF) CBS Entertainment, 1981

JEAN PRODROMIDES

b. July 3, 1927 - Neuilly-sur-Seine, France
Contact: SACEM - France, 011-33-14-747-5650

L'HOMME DANS LA MUIERE 1952, French
GENEVIEVE A GAGNE SON PARI 1953, French
DANS L'OMBRE DES COMBATS 1954, French
UN JARDIN PUBLIC 1955, French
COURTE TETE 1955, French
LES BIENS DE CE MONDE 1957, French
ARCHIMEDE LE CLOCHARD 1958, French
LE VOYAGE EN BALLON 1958, French
MAIGRET ET L'AFFAIRE SAINT-FIACRE 1959, French
LE BARON DE L'ECLUSE 1959, French
BLOOD AND ROSES *ET MOURIR DE PLAISIR* Paramount, 1960, Italian
LES PERSES 1961, French
SPIRITS OF THE DEAD composer of "Metzengerstein" segment, American International, 1967, Italian-French
SOUS LE SIGNE DU TAUREAU 1968, French
24 HEURES DE LA VIE D'UNE FEMME 1968, French
THE EDUCATION IN LOVE OF VALENTIN 1975, French
DANTON Triumph/Columbia, 1983, French-Polish

Q

QUEEN

Contact: PRS - London, England, 011-44-1-580-5544

FLASH GORDON co-composers with Howard Blake, Universal, 1980, British
HIGHLANDER additional music, 20th Century Fox, 1986, British-U.S.

PEER RABEN

Contact: GEMA - West Germany, 011-49-89621400

GODS OF PESTILENCE 1970, West German
THE AMERICAN SOLDIER New Yorker, 1970, West German
RECRUITS IN INGOLSTADT 1971, West German
WHITY 1971, West German
CHETAN, INDIAN BOY 1973, West German
THE TENDERNESS OF WOLVES 1973, West German
ICE-AGE 1975, West German
MIGHT MAKES RIGHT 1975, West German
CHINESE ROULETTE New Yorker, 1976, West German
FEAR OF FEAR 1976, West German
GAME PASS 1976, West German
SATAN'S BREW New Yorker, 1976, West German
VIOLANTA 1976, West German
DESPAIR New Line Cinema, 1978, West German
FIFTY-FIFTY 1978, West German
THE THIRD GENERATION 1979, West German
LILI MARLEEN Luggi Waldleitner, 1981, West German
VERONIKA VOSS Laura Film, 1982, West German
QUERELLE Triumph/Columbia, 1982, West German-French
THE WIZARD OF BABYLON (FD) Planet, 1982, West German
THE SWING 1983, West German
GLUT *EMBERS* 1983, Swiss-West German
LES TRICHEURS Films du Galatee, 1983, French-West German

GRENZENLOS *OPEN ENDS* 1983, West German
A WOMAN FLAMBEE 1983, West German
NOTHING LEFT TO LOVE 1983, West German
SINS OF THE FATHERS (CTF) Bavaria Atelier GmbH/ Taurus-Film/RAI/RETE, 1988, West German

HARRY RABINOWITZ

Contact: PRS - London, England, 011-44-1-580-5544

REILLY - ACE OF SPIES (MS) Euston Films Ltd., 1984, British

ROBERT O. RAGLAND

b. July 3, 1931 - Chicago, Illinois
Contact: ASCAP - Los Angeles, 213/466-7681

THE THING WITH TWO HEADS American International, 1972
THE TOUCH OF SATAN Embassy, 1973
ABBY American International, 1974
RETURN TO MACON COUNTY American International, 1975
SEVEN ALONE Doty-Dayton, 1975
SHARK'S TREASURE United Artists, 1975
GRIZZLY Film Ventures International, 1976
MANSION OF THE DOOMED 1977
JAGUAR LIVES! American International, 1979
DEADLY GAMES Monterey Films, 1979
ONLY ONCE IN A LIFETIME 1979
MOUNTAIN FAMILY ROBINSON Pacific International, 1979
HIGH ICE (TF) ESJ Productions, 1980
THE GLOVE *BLOOD MAD* Pro International, 1981
Q United Film Distribution, 1982
10 TO MIDNIGHT Cannon, 1983
BRAIN WAVES Motion Picture Marketing, 1983
A TIME TO DIE *SEVEN GRAVES FOR ROGAN* Almi Films, 1983
LOVELY BUT DEADLY Juniper Releasing Co., 1983
HYSTERICAL co-composer with Robert Alcivar, Embassy, 1983
THE GUARDIAN (CTF) HBO Premiere Films/Robert Cooper Productions/Stanely Chase Productions, 1984, U.S.-Canadian
THE SUPERNATURALS Republic Entertainment/ Sandy Howard Productions, 1985
PRETTYKILL Spectrafilm, 1987
ASSASSINATION co-composer with Valentine McCallum, Cannon, 1987
NIGHTSTICK Production Distribution Co., 1987
MESSENGER OF DEATH Cannon, 1988

TONY RAINS

AN INVASION OF PRIVACY (TF) Dick Berg-Stonehenge Productions/Embassy TV, 1983

DAVID RAKSIN

b. August 4, 1912 - Philadelphia, Pennsylvania
Agent: Robert Light - Los Angeles, 213/651-1777

MARRY THE GIRL Warner Bros., 1937
MIDNIGHT COURT co-composer, Warner Bros., 1937
MARKED WOMAN co-composer, Warner Bros., 1937
52ND STREET co-composer, 1937
DON'T PULL YOUR PUNCHES co-composer, 1937
THE MIGHTY TREVE Universal, 1937
LET THEM LIVE 1937
AS GOOD AS MARRIED 1937
SHE'S DANGEROUS Universal, 1937
SAN QUENTIN Warner Bros., 1937
WINGS OVER HONOLULU Universal, 1937
THE KID COMES BACK co-composer, Warner Bros., 1938
FRONTIER MARSHALL co-composer, 20th Century-Fox, 1939
THE ADVENTURES OF SHERLOCK HOLMES co-composer, 20th Century-Fox, 1939
HOLLYWOOD CAVALCADE co-composer, 20th Century-Fox, 1939
MR. MOTO'S LAST WARNING co-composer, 20th Century-Fox, 1939
STANLEY AND LIVINGSTONE co-composer, 20th Century-Fox, 1939
SUEZ co-composer, 20th Century-Fox, 1939
STORM WARNING 1940
DEAD MEN TELL 20th Century-Fox, 1940
THE MEN IN HER LIFE Columbia, 1941
RIDE ON, VAQUERO co-composer, 20th Century-Fox, 1941
DR. RENAULT'S SECRET co-composer, 20th Century-Fox, 1942
JUST OFF BROADWAY co-composer, 20th Century-Fox, 1942
THE MAN WHO WOULDN'T DIE 20th Century-Fox, 1942
THE MAGNICIENT DOPE 20th Century-Fox, 1942
MANILA CALLING co-composer, 20th Century-Fox, 1942
THE UNDYING MONSTER 20th Century-Fox, 1942
WHISPERING GHOSTS co-composer, 20th Century-Fox, 1942
WHO IS HOPE SCHUYLER? co-composer, 20th Century-Fox, 1942
CITY WITHOUT MEN Columbia, 1943
SOMETHING TO SHOUT ABOUT adaptation, Columbia, 1943
LAURA 20th Century-Fox, 1944
TAMPICO 20th Century-Fox, 1944
ATTACK IN THE PACIFIC (FD) U.S. Navy, 1945
DON JUAN QUILLIGAN 20th Century-Fox, 1945
FALLEN ANGEL 20th Century-Fox, 1945
WHERE DO WE GO FROM HERE? 20th Century-Fox, 1945
SMOKY 20th Century-Fox, 1946
THE SHOCKING MISS PILGRIM adaptation, 20th Century-Fox, 1947
FOREVER AMBER ★ 20th Century-Fox, 1947
DAISY KENYON 20th Century-Fox, 1947
THE HOMESTRETCH 20th Century-Fox, 1947
THE SECRET LIFE OF WALTER MITTY RKO Radio, 1947
APARTMENT FOR PEGGY 20th Century-Fox, 1948
FURY AT FURNACE CREEK 20th Century-Fox, 1948
FORCE OF EVIL MGM, 1948
WHIRLPOOL 20th Century-Fox, 1950
GROUNDS FOR MARRIAGE co-composer with Bronislau Kaper, MGM, 1950
A LADY WITHOUT PASSPORT MGM, 1950
THE MAGNIFICENT YANKEE MGM, 1950
THE NEXT VOICE YOU HEAR MGM, 1950
THE REFORMER AND THE REDHEAD MGM, 1950
RIGHT CROSS MGM, 1950
ACROSS THE WIDE MISSOURI MGM, 1951
KIND LADY MGM, 1951
THE MAN WITH A CLOAK MGM, 1951
IT'S A BIG COUNTRY co-composer, MGM, 1952
THE BAD AND THE BEAUTIFUL MGM, 1952
CARRIE Paramount, 1952
BLOODHOUNDS OF BROADWAY 20th Century-Fox, 1952
THE GIRL IN WHITE MGM, 1952
PAT AND MIKE MGM, 1952
A BLUEPRINT FOR MURDER 20th Century-Fox, 1953

APACHE United Artists, 1954
SUDDENLY United Artists, 1954
THE BIG COMBO Allied Artists, 1955
BIGGER THAN LIFE 20th Century-Fox, 1956
HILDA CRANE 20th Century-Fox, 1956
JUBAL Columbia, 1956
SEVEN WONDERS OF THE WORLD co-composer, Stanley Warner Cinema Corporation, 1956
GUNSIGHT RIDGE United Artists, 1957
MAN ON FIRE MGM, 1957
UNTIL THEY SAIL MGM, 1957
THE VINTAGE MGM, 1957
TWILIGHT FOR THE GODS Universal, 1958
SEPARATE TABLES ★ United Artists, 1958
AL CAPONE Allied Artists, 1959
PAY OR DIE Allied Artists, 1960
TOO LATE BLUES Paramount, 1962
TWO WEEKS IN ANOTHER TOWN MGM, 1962
NIGHT TIDE Universal, 1963
INVITATION TO A GUNFIGHTER United Artists, 1964
THE PATSY Paramount, 1964
LOVE HAS MANY FACES Columbia, 1965
SYLVIA Paramount, 1965
THE REDEEMER Empire, 1966
A BIG HAND FOR THE LITTLE LADY Warner Bros., 1966
WILL PENNY Paramount, 1968
THE OVER-THE-HILL GANG RIDES AGAIN (TF) Thomas-Spelling Productions, 1970
WHAT'S THE MATTER WITH HELEN? United Artists, 1971
GLASS HOUSES Columbia, 1972
THE GHOST OF FLIGHT 401 (TF) Paramount TV, 1978
THE SUICIDE'S WIFE (TF) Factor-Newland Production Corporation, 1979
THE DAY AFTER (TF) ABC Circle Films, 1983
LADY IN A CORNER (TF) Fries Entertainment, 1989

RON RAMIN

STRANGER ON MY LAND (TF) Edgar J. Scherick Associates/Taft Entertainment TV, 1988
FROG (TF) Platypus Productions, 1988
THE DIAMOND TRAP (TF) Jay Bernstein Productions/ Columbia TV, 1988
MICKEY SPILLANE'S MIKE HAMMER: MURDER TAKES ALL (TF) Jay Bernstein Productions/ Columbia Pictures TV, 1989

KENNARD RAMSEY

THE HEAVENLY KID Orion, 1985
UNCLE TOM'S CABIN (CTF) Edgar J. Scherick Productions/Taft Entertainment TV, 1987

WILLIS ALAN RAMSEY

Contact: BMI - Los Angeles, 213/659-9109

SECOND-HAND HEARTS Lorimar, 1980

ROBERT RANDLES

Contact: BMI - Los Angeles, 213/659-9109

NOBODY'S PERFECT Moviestore Entertainment, 1989

SATYAJIT RAY

b. May 2, 1921 - Calcutta, India
Address: Flat 8, 1/1 Bishop Lefroy Road, Calcutta 20, India
Contact: Films Division, Ministry of Information & Broadcasting, 24 Dr G Beshmukh Marg, Bombay 40026, India, 36-1461

KANCHENJUNGHA Harrison, 1962, Indian
NAYAK 1966, Indian
SHAKESPEARE WALLAH Continental, 1966, Indian
DAYS AND NIGHTS IN THE FOREST Pathe Contemporary, 1970, Indian
THE ADVERSARY Audio Brandon, 1971, Indian
SIMABADDHA 1972, Indian
DISTANT THUNDER Cinema 5, 1973, Indian
THE GOLDEN FORTRESS 1975, Indian
THE CHESS PLAYERS Creative, 1977, Indian
THE ELEPHANT GOD R.D. Bansal & Company, 1979, Indian
PHATIK AND THE JUGGLER 1983, Indian
THE HOME AND THE WORLD European Classics, 1984, Indian

EDDIE RAYNOR

Contact: APRA - Australia, 011-61-2-922-6422

RIKKY AND PETE co-composer with Phil Judd, MGM/UA, 1988, Australian

CHRIS REA

Contact: ASCAP - Los Angeles, 213/466-7681

CROSS COUNTRY New World, 1983

COBY RECHT

Contact: SACEM - France, 011-33-14-747-5650

THE APPLE co-composer with Iris Recht, Cannon, 1980, U.S.-West German

IRIS RECHT

Contact: SACEM - France, 011-33-14-747-5650

THE APPLE co-composer with Coby Recht, Cannon, 1980, U.S.-West German

LEON REDBONE

EVERYBODY WINS additional music, Orion, 1990

RED CLAY RAMBLERS

FAR NORTH Alive Films, 1988

J.A.C. REDFORD

Agent: Gorfaine-Schwartz - Burbank, 818/954-9500

STINGRAY Avco Embassy, 1978
THE LONG SUMMER OF GEORGE ADAMS (TF) co-composer, Warner Bros. TV, 1982
HONEYBOY (TF) Fan Fares Inc. Productions/Estrada Productions, 1982
HAPPY ENDINGS (TF) Blinn-Thorpe Productions, 1983
HELEN KELLER - THE MIRACLE CONTINUES (TF) Castle Combe Productions/20th Century-Fox TV, 1984, U.S.-British
THE TRIP TO BOUNTIFUL Island Pictures/Film Dallas, 1985

GOING FOR THE GOLD: THE BILL JOHNSON STORY (TF) ITC Productions/Sullivan-Carter Interests/Goodman-Rosen Productions, 1985
THE KEY TO REBECCA (TF) Taft Entertainment TV/ Castle Combe Productions, 1985, U.S.-British
EXTREMITIES Atlantic Releasing Corporation, 1986
CRY FROM THE MOUNTAIN World Wide, 1986
ALEX: THE LIFE OF A CHILD (TF) Mandy Productions, 1986
EASY PREY (TF) New World TV/Rene Malo Productions, 1986, U.S.-Canadian
INDEPENDENCE (TF) Sunn Classic Pictures, 1987
THE LONG JOURNEY HOME (TF) Andrea Baynes Productions/Grail Productions/ Lorimar-Telepictures, 1987
OLIVER & CO. (AF) Buena Vista, 1988
SAVE THE DOG (CTF) The Disney Channel, 1988
BREAKING POINT (CTF) Avnet/Kerner Co., 1989
A SON'S PROMISE (TF) Marian Rees Associates, 1990

JERRY REED

b. March 20, 1937
Contact: BMI - Los Angeles, 213/659-9109

SMOKEY AND THE BANDIT Universal, 1977

LES REED

Contact: PRS - London, England, 011-44-1-580-5544

THE GIRL ON A MOTORCYCLE *NAKED UNDER LEATHER* Claridge, 1968, British-French
LES BICYCLETTES DE BELSIZE 1969, British-French
THE BUSHBABY MGM, 1970
ONE MORE TIME United Artists, 1970
CREEPSHOW 2 New World, 1987

PAT REGAN

Contact: ASCAP - Los Angeles, 213/466-7681

STEPFATHER II co-composer with Jim Manzie, Millimeter Films, 1989
LEATHERFACE: THE TEXAS CHAINSAW MASSACRE III co-composer with Jim Manzie, New Line Cinema, 1990
TALES FROM THE DARKSIDE: THE MOVIE co-composer, Paramount, 1990

GARY REMAL

Contact: BMI - Los Angeles, 213/659-9109

DARK CIRCLE (FD) co-composer with Bernard Krause, Independent Documentary Group, 1982
BREAKIN' co-composer with Michael Boyd, MGM/UA, 1984
MARIA'S LOVERS MGM/UA/Cannon, 1984

ROBERT RENFROW

FUTURE-KILL International Film Marketing, 1985

RUTH RENNIE

Contact: PRS - London, England, 011-44-1-580-5544

WHEN THE WHALES CAME additional music, 20th Century Fox, 1989, British

JOE RENZETTI

Contact: BMI - Los Angeles, 213/659-9109

THE BUDDY HOLLY STORY ★★ Columbia, 1978
COTTON CANDY (TF) Major H Productions, 1978
ELVIS (TF) Dick Clark Productions, 1979
DIARY OF A HITCHHIKER (TF) The Shpetner Company, 1979
MARATHON (TF) Alan Landsburg Productions, 1980
FATSO 20th Century-Fox, 1980
THE EXTERMINATOR Avco Embassy, 1980
DEAD AND BURIED Avco Embassy, 1981
UNDER THE RAINBOW Orion/Warner Bros., 1981
THROUGH THE MAGIC PYRAMID (TF) Major H Productions, 1981
MYSTERIOUS TWO (TF) Alan Landsburg Productions, 1982
WANTED: DEAD OR ALIVE New World, 1987
CHILD'S PLAY MGM/UA, 1988
POLTERGEIST 3 MGM/UA, 1988
LISA United Artists, 1989
BASKET CASE 2 Shapiro-Glickenhaus Entertainment, 1990
FRANKENHOOKER Shapiro-Glickenhaus Entertainment, 1990

GRAEME REVELL

Agent: ICM - Los Angeles, 213/550-4000

DEAD CALM Warner Bros., 1989, Australian
SPONTANEOUS COMBUSTION Taurus Entertainment, 1990
UNTIL THE END OF THE WORLD 1990
CHILD'S PLAY 2 Universal, 1990

GIAN REVERBERI

Contact: SIAE - Rome, Italy, 011-39-6-59-90-1

NOT QUITE PARADISE *NOT QUITE JERUSALEM* New World, 1985, British

KEN RICHMOND

IT HAPPENED AT LAKEWOOD MANOR (TF) Alan Landsburg Productions, 1977

DAVID RICKETS

ECHO PARK Atlantic Releasing Corporation, 1985, U.S.-Austrian

LAURIN RINDER

Agent: Richard Emler - Los Angeles, 213/651-0222

ENTER THE NINJA co-composer with W. Michael Lewis, Cannon, 1981
FIRECRACKER co-composer with W. Michael Lewis, New World, 1981, U.S.-Filipino
SHOGUN ASSASSIN co-composer with W. Michael Lewis, New World, 1981, Japanese-U.S.
HOT BUBBLEGUM *LEMON POPSICLE III* co-composer with W. Michael Lewis, Noah Films, 1981, Israeli
NEW YEAR'S EVIL co-composer with W. Michael Lewis, Cannon, 1981
THE KILLING OF AMERICA co-composer with W. Michael Lewis, Toho, 1982, Japanese
THE KULIES co-composer with W. Michael Lewis, Global
THE BALLAD OF GREGORIO CORTEZ co-composer with W. Michael Lewis, Embassy, 1983

REVENGE OF THE NINJA additional music, MGM/UA/ Cannon, 1983
NINJA III—THE DOMINATION co-composer with W. Michael Lewis, Cannon, 1984
BAD MANNERS *GROWING PAINS* co-composer with W. Michael Lewis, New World, 1984
HOT CHILD IN THE CITY co-composer with W. Michael Lewis, Mediacom Filmworks, 1987

PAUL RISER
Contact: ASCAP - Los Angeles, 213/466-7681

WHICH WAY IS UP? co-composer with Mark Davis, Universal, 1977

LEE RITENOUR
Agent: Bart-Milander - North Hollywood, 818/761-4040

AMERICAN FLYERS co-composer with Greg Mathieson, Warner Bros., 1985
ROCK'N'ROLL MOM (TF) Walt Disney TV, 1988

WALTER RIZZATI
Contact: SIAE - Rome, Italy, 011-39-6-59-90-1

THE HOUSE BY THE CEMETARY Almi Pictures, 1981, Italian
1990: THE BRONX United Film Distribution, 1983, Italian

RICHARD ROBBINS
Contact: CAA - Los Angeles, 213/288-4545

THE EUROPEANS Levitt-Pickman, 1979, British
JANE AUSTEN IN MANHATTAN Contemporary, 1980
QUARTET New World, 1981, British-French
HEAT AND DUST Universal Classics, 1983, British
THE BOSTONIANS Almi Pictures, 1984
A ROOM WITH A VIEW Cinecom, 1986, British
MY LITTLE GIRL Hemdale, 1986
SWEET LORRAINE Angelika Films, 1987
MAURICE Cinecom, 1987, British
THE PERFECT MURDER Merchant Ivory Productions, 1988, British-Indian
SLAVES OF NEW YORK Tri-Star, 1989
BAIL JUMPER Angelika Films, 1990

JIM ROBERGE
JOEY Satori Entertainment, 1985

GUY ROBERT
b. France
Contact: SACEM - France, 011-33-14-747-5650

PERCEVAL LE GALLOIS Gaumont, 1978, French

MAX ROBERT
Contact: BMI - Los Angeles, 213/659-9109

RUMPELSTILTSKIN Cannon, 1987

ANDY ROBERTS
Contact: PRS - London, England, 011-44-1-580-5544

LOOSE CONNECTIONS co-composer with Dominic Muldowney, Orion Classics, 1983, British

BRUCE ROBERTS
Contact: ASCAP - Los Angeles, 213/466-7681

JINXED co-composer with Miles Goodman, MGM/UA, 1982

B.A. ROBERTSON
Contact: PRS - London, England, 011-44-1-580-5544

GOSPEL ACCORDING TO VIC *JUST ANOTHER MIRACLE* Skouras Pictures, 1986, British

ERIC N. ROBERTSON
Contact: Pro-Canada - Canada, 1-416-445-8700

SPASMS Producers Distribution Company, 1983, Canadian
SPECIAL PEOPLE (TF) Joe Cates Productions, 1986
HOME IS WHERE THE HART IS Atlantic Entertainment Group, 1987
MILLENNIUM 20th Century Fox, 1989

HARRY ROBERTSON
b. Scotland
Contact: PRS - London, England, 011-44-1-580-5544

THE OBLONG BOX American International, 1969, British
THE VAMPIRE LOVERS American International, 1970, British
LUST FOR A VAMPIRE American Continental, 1971, British
THE JOHNSTOWN MONSTER Sebastian Films, Ltd., 1971, British
FRIGHT 1971, British
TWINS OF EVIL Universal, 1972, British
COUNTESS DRACULA 20th Century-Fox, 1972, British
DEMONS OF THE MIND MGM-EMI, 1972, British
THE HOUSE IN NIGHTMARE PARK MGM-EMI, 1973, British
THE GHOUL Rank, 1974, British
LEGEND OF THE WEREWOLF Tyburn, 1975, British
HAWK THE SLAYER ITC, 1980, British
PRISONER OF THE LOST UNIVERSE (CTF) Marcel-Robertson Productions/United Media Finance, 1983

ROBBIE ROBERTSON
Contact: ASCAP - Los Angeles, 213/466-7681

THE KING OF COMEDY 20th Century-Fox, 1983
THE COLOR OF MONEY Buena Vista, 1986

EARL ROBINSON
Contact: ASCAP - Los Angeles, 213/466-7681

MAYBE HE'LL COME HOME IN THE SPRING (TF) Metromedia Producers Corporation, 1971
THE GREAT MAN'S WHISKERS (TF) Universal TV, 1973
HUCKLEBERRY FINN (TF) ABC Circle Films, 1975

HARRY ROBINSON
Contact: BMI - Los Angeles, 213/659-9109

THERE GOES THE BRIDE Vanguard Releasing, 1980

J. PETER ROBINSON
Agent: Bart-Milander - North Hollywood, 818/761-4040

DEADLY ENCOUNTER (TF) Roger Gimbel Productions/EMI TV, 1982
KATE'S SECRET (TF) Andrea Baynes Productions/ Columbia TV, 1986
THE WRAITH New Century/Vista, 1986
J. EDGAR HOOVER (CTF) RLC Productions/ Finnegan Co., 1987
THE BELIVERS Orion, 1987
THE GATE co-composer with Michael Hoenig, New Century/Vista, 1987, Canadian
BATES MOTEL (TF) Universal TV, 1987
RETURN OF THE LIVING DEAD PART II Lorimar, 1988
COCKTAIL Buena Vista, 1988
DESERT RATS (TF) Universal TV, 1988
THE KISS Tri-Star, 1988, U.S.-Canadian
BLIND FURY Tri-Star, 1989
THE GIFTED ONE (TF) Richard Rothstein Productions/NBC Productions, 1989
THE WIZARD Universal, 1989
CADILLAC MAN Orion, 1990

PETE ROBINSON
Contact: BMI - Los Angeles, 213/659-9109

RADIOACTIVE DREAMS DEG, 1986
PIN New World, 1989, Canadian

PETER MANNING ROBINSON
THE PENTHOUSE (TF) Greene-White Productions/ Spectacor Films, 1989
SMALL SACRIFICES (TF) Louis Rudolph Silms/ Motown/Allarcom Ltd./Fries Entertainment, 1989
IN THE BEST INTEREST OF THE CHILD (TF) Papazian-Hirsch Entertainment, 1990

NILE RODGERS
Contact: BMI - Los Angeles, 213/659-9109

SOUP FOR ONE co-composer with Bernard Edwards, Warner Bros., 1982
ALPHABET CITY Atlantic Releasing, 1984
WHITE HOT *CRACK IN THE MIRROR* Triax Entertainment Group, 1988
COMING TO AMERICA Universal, 1988
EARTH GIRLS ARE EASY Vestron, 1989

SCOTT ROEWE
Contact: BMI - Los Angeles, 213/659-9109

VIPER Fries Distribution, 1988
TRUE BLOOD Fries Entertainment, 1989
MINISTRY OF VENGEANCE Concorde, 1989

SHORTY ROGERS
Agent: Carol Faith - Beverly Hills, 213/274-0776

GIDGET GROWS UP (TF) Screen Gems/Columbia Pictures TV, 1969
BREAKOUT (TF) Universal TV, 1970
THE RETURN OF THE MOD SQUAD (TF) co-composer with Mark Snow, Thomas-Spelling Productions, 1979

SIMON ROGERS
DADDY (TF) Robert Greenwald Productions, 1987

GEORGE ROMANIS
Contact: BMI - Los Angeles, 213/659-9109

CRIME CLUB (TF) CBS Entertainment, 1973
MANEATER (TF) Universal TV, 1973
LIVE AGAIN, DIE AGAIN (TF) Universal TV, 1974
THE FAMILY NOBODY WANTED (TF) Groverton Productions/Universal TV, 1975
SHARK KILL (TF) D'Antoni-Weitz Productions, 1976
NEVER CON A KILLER (TF) Larry White Productions/ Columbia Pictures TV, 1977
SHE'S DRESSED TO KILL (TF) Grant-Case-McGrath Enterprises/Barry Weitz Films, 1979
REUNION (TF) Barry Weitz Films, 1980
THE MONKEY MISSION (TF) Mickey Productions/ Filmways, 1981
THE BIG BLACK PILL (TF) Filmways/Micky Productions/ NBC Entertainment, 1981
OF MICE AND MEN (TF) Of Mice and Men Productions, 1981
KENTUCKY WOMAN (TF) Walter Doniger Productions/ 20th Century-Fox TV, 1983
MURDER 1, DANCER 0 (TF) Mickey Productions/ Filmways, 1983

ALAIN ROMANS
b. France
Contact: SACEM - France, 011-33-14-747-5650

MR. HULOT'S HOLIDAY G-B-D International, 1953, French
MY UNCLE, MR. HULOT *MON ONCLE* Continental, 1956, French
FADILA 1961

RICHARD ROMANUS
SITTING DUCKS Speciality Films, 1980

EARL ROSE
Agent: Carol Faith - Beverly Hills, 213/274-0776

THIN ICE (TF) CBS Entertainment, 1981

MILTON ROSEN
b. 1906

ENTER ARSENE LUPIN Universal, 1944
SUDAN Universal, 1945
SWING OUT, SISTER Universal, 1945
ON STAGE EVERYBODY co-composer, Universal, 1945
SHADY LADY Universal, 1945
MEN IN HER DIARY Universal, 1945
TANGIER Universal, 1945
THE SPIDER WOMAN STRIKES BACK co-composer, Universal, 1946
DRESSED TO KILL co-composer, Universal, 1946
CUBAN PETE co-composer, Universal, 1946
SLIGHTLY SCANDALOUS co-composer, Universal, 1946
RUSTLER'S ROUND-UP co-composer, Universal, 1946
THE TIME OF THEIR LIVES Universal, 1946
LAWLESS BREED co-composer, Universal, 1946
WHITE TIE AND TAILS Universal, 1946
SLAVE GIRL Universal, 1947
PIRATES OF MONTEREY Universal, 1947
ABRAHAM AND ISAAC Churchcraft, 1948
DANIEL IN THE LION'S DEN Churchcraft, 1948
OF SUCH IS THE KINGDOM Churchcraft, 1948
THE RAISING OF LAZARUS Churchcraft, 1948
BOB AND SALLY Social Guidance, 1948

THE CHALLENGE 20th Century-Fox, 1948
13 LEAD SOLDIERS 20th Century-Fox, 1948
THE CREEPER 20th Century-Fox, 1948
THE MILKMAN Universal, 1950
SON OF ALI BABA co-composer with Herman Stein, Universal, 1951
CITY BENEATH THE SEA co-composer with Herman Stein and Henry Mancini, Universal, 1952
FRANCIS GOES TO WEST POINT co-composer with Herman Stein and Frank Skinner, Universal, 1952
EVERYTHING BUT THE TRUTH Universal, 1956
OUTSIDE THE LAW Universal, 1956
DEATH RACE (TF) Silverton Productions/ Universal TV, 1973

JOEL ROSENBAUM

Agent: Robert Light - Los Angeles, 213/651-1777

PSYCHO GIRLS Cannon, 1985, Canadian
THE COLOR PURPLE ★ co-composer, Warner Bros., 1985
BILLY GALVIN Vestron, 1986
THE OUTING *THE LAMP* TMS Pictures, 1987
WACO AND RINEHART (TF) Touchstone Films TV, 1987
FATHER DOWLING: THE MISSING BODY MYSTERY (TF) The Fred Silverman Company/ Dean Hargrove Productions/Viacom, 1989

LEONARD ROSENMAN

b. Sept. 7, 1924 - Brooklyn, New York
Agent: Gorfaine-Schwartz - Burbank, 818/954-9500

EAST OF EDEN Warner Bros., 1955
THE COBWEB MGM, 1955
REBEL WITHOUT A CAUSE Warner Bros., 1955
BOMBERS B-52 Warner Bros., 1957
EDGE OF THE CITY MGM, 1957
THE YOUNG STRANGER Universal, 1957
LAFAYETTE ESCADRILLE Warner Bros., 1958
THE HIDDEN WORLD (FD) Small World, 1958
PORK CHOP HILL United Artists, 1959
THE SAVAGE EYE Trans-Lux, 1959
THE RISE AND FALL OF LEGS DIAMOND Warner Bros., 1960
THE BRAMBLE BUSH Warner Bros., 1960
THE CROWDED SKY Warner Bros., 1960
THE PLUNDERERS Allied Artists, 1960
THE OUTSIDER Universal, 1961
HELL IS FOR HEROES Paramount, 1962
CONVICTS FOUR Allied Artists, 1962
THE CHAPMAN REPORT Warner Bros., 1962
FANTASTIC VOYAGE 20th Century-Fox, 1966
A COVENANT WITH DEATH Warner Bros., 1966
STRANGER ON THE RUN (TF) Universal TV, 1967
SHADOW OVER ELVERON (TF) Universal TV, 1968
COUNTDOWN Warner Bros., 1968
HELLFIGHTERS Universal, 1969
ANY SECOND NOW (TF) Public Arts Productions/ Universal TV, 1969
MARCUS WELBY, M.D. (TF) Universal TV, 1969
A MAN CALLED HORSE National General, 1970
BENEATH THE PLANET OF THE APES 20th Century-Fox, 1970
BANYON (TF) Warner Bros. TV, 1971
VANISHED (TF) Universsal TV, 1971
SKIPPER National General, 1971
IN BROAD DAYLIGHT (TF) Aaron Spelling Productions, 1971
THE BRAVOS (TF) Groverton Productions/ Universal TV, 1972
CONQUEST OF THE PLANET OF THE APES 20th Century-Fox, 1972
BATTLE FOR THE PLANET OF THE APES 20th Century-Fox, 1973
THE CAT CREATURE (TF) Screen Gems/ Columbia TV, 1973
THE PHANTOM OF HOLLYWOOD (TF) MGM TV, 1974
NAKIA (TF) David Gerber Productions/Screen Gems/ Columbia Pictures TV, 1974
JUDGE DEE AND THE MONASTERY MURDERS (TF) ABC Circle Films, 1974
BARRY LYNDON ★★ adaptation, Warner Bros., 1975, British
SKY HEIST (TF) A J Fenady Associates/Warner Bros. TV, 1975
RACE WITH THE DEVIL 20th Century-Fox, 1975
BIRCH INTERVAL Gamma III, 1976
BOUND FOR GLORY ★★ adaptation, United Artists, 1976
LANIGAN'S RABBI (TF) Hayday Productions/ Universal TV, 1976
KINGSTON: THE POWER PLAY (TF) Groverton Productions/Universal TV, 1976
SYBIL (TF) ☆☆ Lorimar Productions, 1976
THE CAR Universal, 1977
THE POSSESSED (TF) Warner Bros. TV, 1977
9/30/55 *SEPTEMBER 30, 1955* Universal, 1977
MARY WHITE (TF) Radnitz-Mattel Productions, 1977
AN ENEMY OF THE PEOPLE Warner Bros., 1978
THE LORD OF THE RINGS (AF) United Artists, 1978
FRIENDLY FIRE (TF) ☆☆ Marble Arch Productions, 1979
PROPHECY Paramount, 1979
PROMISES IN THE DARK Orion, 1979
NERO WOLFE (TF) Emmet Lavery Jr. Productions/ Paramount Pictures TV, 1979
CITY IN FEAR (TF) Trans World International, 1980
HIDE IN PLAIN SIGHT United Artists, 1980
THE JAZZ SINGER AFD, 1980
MURDER IN TEXAS (TF) Dick Clark Productions/Billy Hale Films, 1981
MAKING LOVE 20th Century-Fox, 1981
THE WALL (TF) Cinetex International/Time-Life Productions, 1982
CROSS CREEK ★ Universal/AFD, 1983
MISS LONELYHEARTS H. Jay Holman Productions/ American Film Institute, 1983
CELEBRITY (MS) NBC Productions, 1984
THE RETURN OF MARCUS WELBY, M.D. (TF) Marstar Productions/Universal TV, 1984
HEARTSOUNDS (TF) Embassy TV, 1984
HEART OF THE STAG New World, 1984, New Zealand
FIRST STEPS (TF) CBS Entertainment, 1985
SYLVIA MGM/UA Classics, 1985, New Zealand
STAR TREK IV: THE VOYAGE HOME ★ Paramount, 1986
PROMISED A MIRACLE (TF) Dick Clark Productions/ Republic Pictures Roni Weisberg Productions, 1988
WHERE PIGEONS GO TO DIE (TF) Michael Landon Productions/World International Network, 1990
ROBOCOP 2 Orion, 1990

LAURENCE ROSENTHAL

b. November 4, 1926 - Detroit, Michigan
Agent: Gorfaine-Schwartz - Burbank, 818/954-9500

YELLOWNECK Republic, 1955
NAKED IN THE SUN Allied Artists, 1957
A RAISIN IN THE SUN Columbia, 1961
DARK ODYSSEY Era, 1961
THE MIRACLE WORKER United Artists, 1962

REQUIEM FOR A HEAVYWEIGHT Columbia, 1962
BECKET ★ Paramount, 1964
HOTEL PARADISO MGM, 1966, British
THE COMEDIANS MGM, 1967
THREE United Artists, 1969
HOW AWFUL ABOUT ALLAN (TF) Aaron Spelling Productions, 1970
THE HOUSE THAT WOULD NOT DIE (TF) Aaron Spelling Productions, 1970
NIGHT CHASE (TF) Cinema Center 100, 1970
THE LAST CHILD (TF) Aaron Spelling Productions, 1971
A GUNFIGHT Paramount, 1971
THE AFRICAN ELEPHANT *KING ELEPHANT* (FD) 1972
MAN OF LA MANCHA ★ adaptation, United Artists, 1972
HEC RAMSEY (TF) Universal TV/Mark VII Ltd., 1972
CALL TO DANGER (TF) Paramount Pictures TV, 1973
THE DEVIL'S DAUGHTER (TF) Paramount Pictures Television, 1973
SATAN'S SCHOOL FOR GIRLS (TF) Spelling-Goldberg Productions, 1973
DEATH SENTENCE (TF) Spelling-Goldberg Productions, 1974
THE LOG OF THE BLACK PEARL (TF) Mark VII Ltd./Universal TV, 1975
THE WILD PARTY American International, 1975
ROOSTER COGBURN Universal, 1975
YOUNG PIONEERS (TF) ABC Circle Films, 1976
THE RETURN OF A MAN CALLED HORSE United Artists, 1976
21 HOURS AT MUNICH (TF) Moonlight Productions/Filmways Pictures, 1976
YOUNG PIONEERS' CHRISTMAS (TF) ABC Circle Films, 1976
THE AMAZING HOWARD HUGHES (TF) Roger Gimbel Productions/EMI TV, 1977
MURDER IN PEYTON PLACE (TF) 20th Century-Fox TV, 1977
THE ISLAND OF DR. MOREAU American International, 1977
FANTASY ISLAND (TF) Spelling-Goldberg Productions, 1977
LOGAN'S RUN (TF) Goff-Roberts-Steiner Productions/MGM TV, 1977
WHO'LL STOP THE RAIN United Artists, 1978
BRASS TARGET MGM/United Artists, 1978
AND I ALONE SURVIVED (TF) Jerry Leider/OJL Productions, 1978
MEETINGS WITH REMARKABLE MEN Libra, 1979, British
METEOR American International, 1979
ORPHAN TRAIN (TF) EMI TV, 1979
THE DAY CHRIST DIED (TF) Martin Manulis Productions/20th Century-Fox TV, 1980
F.D.R.—THE LAST YEAR (TF) Titus Productions, 1980
RAGE (TF) Diane Silver Productions/Charles Fries Productions, 1980
REVENGE OF THE STEPFORD WIVES (TF) Edgar J. Scherick Productions, 1980
CLASH OF THE TITANS MGM/United Artists, 1981, British
THE LETTER (TF) ☆ partial adaptation, Hajeno Productions/Warner Bros. TV, 1982
WHO WILL LOVE MY CHILDREN? (TF) ☆ ABC Circle Films, 1983
HEART LIKE A WHEEL 20th Century-Fox, 1983
EASY MONEY Orion, 1983
LICENSE TO KILL (TF) Marian Rees Associates/D. Petrie Productions, 1984
THE LOST HONOR OF KATHERINE BECK (TF) Open Road Productions, 1984
GEORGE WASHINGTON (MS) David Gerber Productions/MGM Television, 1984
CONSENTING ADULT (TF) Starger Company/Lawrence-Aghayan Productions, 1985
EVERGREEN (MS) Edgar J. Scherick Associates/Metromedia Producers Corporation, 1985
BLACKOUT (CTF) HBO Premiere Films/Roger Gimbel Productions/Peregrine Entertainment Ltd./Lee Buck Industries/Alexander Smith & Parks, 1985, U.S.-Canadian
MUSSOLINI: THE UNTOLD STORY (MS) Trian Productions, 1985
PETER THE GREAT (MS) ☆☆ PTG Productions/NBC Productions, 1986
STRANGER IN MY BED (TF) Taft Entertainment TV/Edgar J. Sherick Productions, 1986
ON WINGS OF EAGLES (MS) Edgar J. Scherick Productions/Taft Entertainment TV, 1986
ANASTASIA: THE MYSTERY OF ANNA (TF) ☆☆ Telecom Entertainment/Consolidated Productions/Reteitalia, 1986, U.S.-Italian
FIGHT FOR LIFE (TF) Fries Entertainment, 1987
DOWNPAYMENT ON MURDER (TF) Adam Productions/20th Century Fox TV, 1987
PROUD MEN (TF) Cowboy Productions/Agamemnon Films Productions/von Zerneck-Samuels Productions, 1987
FREEDOM FIGHTER (TF) HTV/Columbia TV/Embassy TV, 1988, U.S.-British
TO HEAL A NATION (TF) Lionel Chetwynd Productions/Orion TV/von Zerneck-Samuels Productions, 1988
MY FATHER, MY SON (TF) Fred Weintraub Productions/John J. McMahon Productions, 1988
STREET OF DREAMS (TF) Bill Stratton-Myrtos Productions/Phoenix Entertainment Group, 1988
THE BOURNE IDENTITY (TF) ☆☆ Alan Shayne Productions/Warner Bros. TV, 1988
BLACKOUT Ambient Light Entertainment, 1988
IN THE LINE OF DUTY: THE FBI MURDERS (TF) Telecom Entertainment/World International Network, 1988
TWIST OF FATE (TF) Henry Plitt-Larry White Productions/HTV/Columbia TV, 1989, British-U.S.
BROTHERHOOD OF THE ROSE (TF) NBC Productions, 1989
MY NAME IS BILL W. (TF) Garner/Duchow Productions, 1989
GORE VIDAL'S BILLY THE KID (CTF) von Zerneck-Sertner Productions, 1989
BLIND FAITH (TF) NBC Productions, 1990
THE INCIDENT (TF) Qintex Entertainment, 1990
THE KISSING PLACE (CTF) Cynthia A. Cherbak Production/Wilshire Court Productions, 1990

BRUCE ROWLAND

b. Australia
Agent: Bart-Milander - North Hollywood, 818/761-4040

FREE ENTERPRISE Burrowes Film Group, Australian
THE MAN FROM SNOWY RIVER 20th Century-Fox, 1982, Australian
COOL CHANGE Hoyts, 1986, Australian
NOW AND FOREVER Klevand Productions, 1983, Australian
PHAR LAP 20th Century-Fox, 1983, Australian
ALL THE RIVERS RUN (CMS) Crawford Productions/Nine Network, 1984, Australian
REBEL Vestron, 1985, Australian

COOL CHANGE Hoyts, 1986, Australian
LES PATTERSON SAVES THE WORLD Hoyts Distribution, 1987, Australian
BIGFOOT (TF) Walt Disney TV, 1987
RUNNING FROM THE GUNS 1987, Australian
ANZACS: THE WAR DOWN UNDER (MS) Orbis Communications/Hal Roach Studios, 1987, Australian
THE CHRISTMAS VISITOR *BUSHFIRE MOON* (CTF) Entertainment Media/The Disney Channel/ WonderWorks, 1987, Australian-U.S.
BACKSTAGE Hoyts, Australian, 1988
RETURN TO SNOWY RIVER Buena Vista, 1988, Australian
DANGER DOWN UNDER (TF) Weintraub Entertainment Group/Hoyts Productions Ltd., 1988, U.S.-Australian
CHEETAH Buena Vista, 1989
ALL THE RIVERS RUN II (CTF) Crawford Productions/ HBO, 1989
GUNSMOKE: THE LAST APACHE (TF) CBS Entertainment Productions/Galatea Productions, 1990

MIKLOS ROZSA

b. April 18, 1907 - Budapest, Hungary
Agent: Bart-Milander - North Hollywood, 818/761-4040

KNIGHT WITHOUT ARMOUR United Artists, 1937, British
THUNDER IN THE CITY Columbia, 1937, British
THE SQUEAKER *MURDER ON DIAMOND ROAD* United Artists, 1937, British
THE GREEK COCKATOO *FOUR DARK HOURS* New World, 1937, British
THE DIVORCE OF LADY X United Artists, 1938, British
THE FOUR FEATHERS United Artists, 1939, British
THE SPY IN BLACK *U BOAT 29* Columbia, 1939, British
TEN DAYS IN PARIS Columbia, 1939, British
THE THIEF OF BAGHDAD ★ United Artists, 1940, British
THAT HAMILTON WOMAN *LADY HAMILTON* United Artists, 1941, British
LYDIA ★ United Artists, 1941
SUNDOWN ★ United Artists, 1941
NEW WINE adaptation, United Artists, 1941
JUNGLE BOOK ★ United Artists, 1942, British
JACARE United Artists, 1942
FIVE GRAVES TO CAIRO Paramount, 1943
SO PROUDLY WE HAIL! Paramount, 1943
SAHARA Columbia, 1943
WOMAN OF THE TOWN ★ United Artists, 1943
THE HOUR BEFORE THE DAWN Paramount, 1944
DOUBLE INDEMNITY ★ Paramount, 1944
DARK WATERS United Artists, 1944
THE MAN IN HALF MOON STREET Paramount, 1944
A SONG TO REMEMBER ★ adaptation, Columbia, 1945
BLOOD ON THE SUN United Artists, 1945
THE LOST WEEKEND ★ Paramount, 1945
LADY ON A TRAIN Universal, 1945
SPELLBOUND ★★ United Artists, 1945
BECAUSE OF HIM Universal, 1946
THE STRANGE LOVE OF MARTHA IVERS Paramount, 1946
THE KILLERS ★ Universal, 1946
THE RED HOUSE United Artists, 1947
SONG OF SCHEHERAZADE adaptation, Universal, 1947
THE MACOMBER AFFAIR United Artists, 1947
TIME OUT OF MIND Universal, 1947
DESERT FURY Paramount, 1947
BRUTE FORCE Universal, 1947
THE OTHER LOVE United Artists, 1947
A WOMAN'S VENGEANCE Universal, 1947
A DOUBLE LIFE ★★ Universal, 1947
SECRET BEYOND THE DOOR Universal, 1948
THE NAKED CITY Universal, 1948
KISS THE BLOOD OFF MY HANDS Universal, 1948
COMMAND DECISION MGM, 1948
CRISS CROSS Universal, 1949
THE BRIBE MGM, 1949
MADAME BOVARY MGM, 1949
THE RED DANUBE MGM, 1949
EAST SIDE, WEST SIDE MGM, 1949
ADAM'S RIB MGM, 1949
THE MINIVER STORY adaptation, MGM, 1950
THE ASPHALT JUNGLE MGM, 1950
CRISIS MGM, 1950
THE LIGHT TOUCH MGM, 1951
QUO VADIS ★ MGM, 1951
IVANHOE ★ MGM, 1952
PLYMOUTH ADVENTURE MGM, 1952
JULIUS CAESAR ★ MGM, 1953
THE STORY OF THREE LOVES MGM, 1953
YOUNG BESS MGM, 1953
ALL THE BROTHERS WERE VALIANT MGM, 1953
KNIGHTS OF THE ROUND TABLE MGM, 1953
MEN OF THE FIGHTING LADY MGM, 1954
VALLEY OF THE KINGS MGM, 1954
CREST OF THE WAVE *GREEN FIRE* MGM, 1954, British
MOONFLEET MGM, 1955
THE KING'S THIEF MGM, 1955
DIANE MGM, 1956
TRIBUTE TO A BAD MAN MGM, 1956
BHOWANI JUNCTION MGM, 1956, U.S.-British
LUST FOR LIFE MGM, 1956
SOMETHING OF VALU MGM, 1957
THE SEVENTH SIN MGM, 1957
TIP ON A DEAD JOCKEY MGM, 1957
A TIME TO LOVE AND A TIME TO DIE Universal, 1958
THE WORLD, THE FLESH AND THE DEVIL MGM, 1959
BEN HUR ★★ MGM, 1959
KING OF KINGS MGM, 1961
EL CID ★ Allied Artists, 1961
SODOM AND GOMORRAH 20th Century-Fox, 1962, Italian-French-U.S.
THE V.I.P.'S MGM, 1963, British
THE POWER MGM, 1968
THE GREEN BERETS Warner Bros., 1968
THE PRIVATE LIFE OF SHERLOCK HOLMES also cameo as ballet conductor, United Artists, 1970, U.S.-British
THE GOLDEN VOYAGE OF SINBAD Columbia, 1974, British
PROVIDENCE Cinema 5, 1977, French-Swiss
THE SECRET FILES OF J. EDGAR HOOVER American International, 1978
FEDORA United Artists, 1979, West German-French
LAST EMBRACE United Artists, 1979
TIME AFTER TIME Warner Bros., 1979
EYE OF THE NEEDLE United Artists, 1981, U.S.-British
DEAD MEN DON'T WEAR PLAID Universal, 1982

LANCE RUBIN

Agent: Carol Faith - Beverly Hills, 213/274-0776

LEO AND LOREE United Artists, 1980
MOTEL HELL United Artists, 1980
HAPPY BIRTHDAY TO ME co-composer with Bo Harwood, Columbia, 1981, Canadian
MODERN ROMANCE Columbia, 1981
HEAR NO EVIL (TF) Paul Pompian Productions/ MGM TV, 1982
THE INCREDIBLE HULK RETURNS (TF) B&B Productions/New World TV, 1988
THE TRIAL OF THE INCREDIBLE HULK (TF) Bixby-Brandon Productions/New World TV, 1989
THE DEATH OF THE INCREDIBLE HULK (TF) Bixby-Brandon Productions/New World TV, 1990

MICHEL RUBINI

Contact: Carol Faith - Beverly Hills, 213/274-0776

RACQUET Cal-Am Artists, 1979
THE HUNGER co-composer with Danny Jaeger, MGM/UA, 1983, British
WHAT WAITS BELOW Blossom Pictures, 1984
THE NEW KIDS Columbia, 1985
BAND OF THE HAND Tri-Star, 1986
ABDUCTED InterPictures, 1986, Canadian
MANHUNTER DEG, 1986
HANDS OF A STRANGER (TF) Taft Entertainment TV, 1987
MOVING TARGET (TF) Lewis B. Chesler Productions/ Bateman Company Productions/Finnegan-Pinchuk Company/MGM-UA TV, 1988
UNHOLY MATRIMONY (TF) Edgar J. Scherick Associates/Taft Entertainment TV, 1988
TOO GOOD TO BE TRUE (TF) Newland-Raynor Productions, 1988
CROSSING THE MOB (TF) Bateman Company Productions/Interscope Communications, 1988
THE EDGE (CTF) Lewis B. Chesler Productions/The Christopher Morgan Co./MGM/UA, 1989

ARTHUR B. RUBINSTEIN

Agent: Gorfaine-Schwartz - Burbank, 818/954-9500

THE PRINCE OF CENTRAL PARK (TF) Lorimar Productions, 1977
THE GREAT BANK HOAX *SHENANIGANS* Warner Bros., 1978
PORTRAIT OF A STRIPPER (TF) Moonlight Productions/Filmways, 1979
AUNT MARY (TF) Henry Jaffe Enterprises, 1979
THE GREAT AMERICAN TRAFFIC JAM *GRIDLOCK* (TF) Ten-Four Productions, 1980
PORTRAIT OF A REBEL: MARGARET SANGER (TF) Marvin Minoff Productions/David Paradine TV, 1980
ON THE RIGHT TRACK 20th Century-Fox, 1981
THE PHOENIX (TF) Mark Carliner Productions, 1981
RIVKIN, BOUNTY HUNTER (TF) Chiarascurio Productions/Ten-Four Productions, 1981
WHOSE LIFE IS IT ANYWAY? MGM/United Artists, 1981
NOT JUST ANOTHER AFFAIR (TF) Ten-Four Productions, 1982
FAKE OUT Analysis, 1982
SKEEZER (TF) Margie-Lee Enterprises/The Blue Marble Company/Marble Arch Productions, 1982
DEAL OF THE CENTURY Warner Bros., 1983
BLUE THUNDER Columbia, 1983
WARGAMES MGM/UA, 1983
IT CAME UPON THE MIDNIGHT CLEAR (TF) Schenck-Cardea Productions/Columbia TV/LBS Communications, 1984
SINS OF THE PAST (TF) Sinpast Entertainment Company Productions, 1984
THE PARADE (TF) Hill-Mandelker Productions, 1984
THE CARTIER AFFAIR (TF) Hill-Mandelker Productions, 1984
LOST IN AMERICA The Geffen Company/Warner Bros., 1985
MURDER IN SPACE (CTF) Robert Cooper/Zenith Productions, 1985
DOUBLETAKE (TF) Titus Productions, 1985
DOING LIFE (TF) Castillian Productions/Phoenix Entertainment Group, 1986
HYPER SAPIEN Taliafilm II, 1986
THE BEST OF TIMES Universal, 1986
LOVE AMONG THIEVES (TF) Robert A. Papazian Productions, 1987
STAKEOUT Buena Vista, 1987
ROSES ARE FOR THE RICH (TF) Phoenix Entertainment Group, 1987
THE BETTY FORD STORY (TF) David L. Wolper Productions/Warner Bros. TV, 1987
ONCE UPON A TEXAS TRAIN (TF) CBS Entertainment, 1988
DEFENSE PLAY Trans World Entertainment, 1988
INHERIT THE WIND (TF) Vincent Pictures Productions/ David Greene-Robert Papazian Productions, 1988
INTERNAL AFFAIRS (TF) Titus Productions, 1988
WHERE THE HELL'S THAT GOLD?!! (TF) Willie Nelson Productions/Brigade Productions/Konigsberg-Sanitsky Company, 1988
NIGHTMARE AT BITTER CREEK (TF) Swanton Films/ Guber-Peters Entertainment/Phoenix Entertainment Group, 1988
INDISCREET (TF) Karen Mack Productions/HTV/Republic Pictures, 1988, U.S.-British
AGATHA CHRISTIE'S THE MAN IN THE BROWN SUIT (TF) Alan Shayne Productions/Warner Bros. TV, 1989
UNCONQUERED (TF) Alexandra Film Productions, 1989
GIDEON OLIVER: SLEEP WELL, PROFESSOR OLIVER (TF) Wolf Films/Crescendo Productions/ Universal TV, 1989
BAYWATCH: PANIC AT MALIBU PIER (TF) GTG Entertainment/NBC, 1989
GUTS AND GLORY: THE RISE AND FALL OF OLIVER NORTH (TF) Mike Rob Productions/Papazian-Hirsch Entertainment, 1989

DONALD RUBINSTEIN

Contact: ASCAP - Los Angeles, 213/466-7681

MARTIN Libra, 1978
KNIGHTRIDERS United Film Distribution, 1981
TALES FROM THE DARKSIDE: THE MOVIE co-composer, Paramount, 1990

JOHN RUBINSTEIN

b. December 8, 1946
Contact: ASCAP - Los Angeles, 213/466-7681

KID BLUE co-composer with Tim McIntire, 20th Century-Fox, 1973
ALL TOGETHER NOW (TF) RSO Films, 1975
STALK THE WILD CHILD (TF) Charles Fries Productions, 1976
THE KILLER INSIDE ME co-composer with Tim McIntire, Warner Bros., 1976

STICKING TOGETHER (TF) Blinn-Thorpe Productions/ Viacom Productions, 1978
THE NEW MAVERICK (TF) Cherokee Productions/ Warner Bros. TV, 1978
CHAMPIONS: A LOVE STORY (TF) Warner Bros. TV, 1979
TO RACE THE WIND (TF) Walter Grauman Productions, 1980
AMBER WAVES (TF) Time-Life Productions, 1980
JOHNNY BELINDA (TF) Dick Berg/Stonehenge Productions/Lorimar Productions, 1982
SECRETS OF A MOTHER AND DAUGHTER (TF) The Shpetner Company/Sunrise Productions, 1983
CHOICES OF THE HEART (TF) Katz-Gallin Associates/Half-Pint Productions/Metromedia Producers Corporation/NBC Entertainment, 1983
THE DOLLMAKER (TF) Finnegan Associates/IPC Films/Dollmaker Productions, 1984
CITY KILLER (TF) Stan Shpetner Productions, 1984
CONSPIRACY OF LOVE (TF) New World TV, 1987
CHINA BEACH (TF) Sacret Inc./Warner Bros. TV, 1988

KEITH RUBINSTEIN

Contact: ASCAP - Los Angeles, 213/466-7681

VICE SQUAD Avco Embassy, 1982

STEVE RUCKER

Agent: Robert Light - Los Angeles, 213/651-1777

CREATURE *TITAN FIND* co-composer with Tom Chase, Cardinal Releasing, 1985
FEEL THE HEAT co-composer with Tom Chase, Trans World Entertainment, 1987
ALIEN PREDATOR co-composer with Tom Chase, Trans World Entertainment, 1987
AND GOD CREATED WOMAN co-composer with Tom Chase, Vestron, 1988
976-EVIL co-composer with Tom Chase, New Line Cinema, 1988
BULLETPROOF co-composer with Tom Chase, Cinetel, 1988
LITTLE NEMO (AF) co-composer with Tom Chase, 1990
SYNGENOR co-composer with Tom Chase, Syngenor Production Co., 1990

PETE RUGOLO

b. December 25, 1915 - Sicily, Italy
Contact: BMI - Los Angeles, 213/659-9109

JACK THE RIPPER composer of U.S. version, 1960
THE OUTSIDER (TF) Public Arts Productions/ Universal TV, 1967
THE SWEET RIDE 20th Century-Fox, 1968
THE SOUND OF ANGER (TF) Public Arts Productions/ Universal TV, 1968
THE WHOLE WORLD IS WATCHING (TF) Public Arts Productions/Universal TV, 1969
THE LONELY PROFESSION (TF) Universal TV/ Public Arts Productions, 1969
THE YOUNG COUNTRY (TF) Public Arts Productions/ Universal TV, 1970
THE CHALLENGERS (TF) ☆☆ Universal TV, 1970
DO YOU TAKE THIS STRANGER? (TF) ☆ Universal TV/Public Arts Productions, 1971
SAM HILL: WHO KILLED THE MYSTERIOUS MR. FOSTER? (TF) Public Arts Productions/Universal TV, 1971
THE DEATH OF ME YET (TF) Aaron Spelling Productions, 1971
HOW TO STEAL AN AIRPLANE (TF) Universal TV, 1972
SET THIS TOWN ON FIRE (TF) Public Arts Productions/ Universal TV, 1973
TOMA (TF) Universal TV, 1973
THE LETTERS Spelling-Goldberg Productions/ABC Circle Films, 1973
DRIVE HARD, DRIVE FAST (TF) Public Arts Productions/ Universal TV, 1973
LETTERS FROM THREE LOVERS Spelling-Goldberg Productions, 1973
THE STORY OF PRETTY BOY FLOYD (TF) Public Arts Productions/Universal TV, 1974
DEATH CRUISE (TF) Spelling-Goldberg Productions, 1974
LAST HOURS BEFORE MORNING (TF) Charles Fries Productions/MGM Television, 1975
DEATH STALK (TF) Herman Rush Associates/David L. Wolper Productions, 1975
FOXTROT THE OTHER SIDE OF PARADISE New World, 1976, Mexican-Swiss
THE SAN PEDRO BUMS (TF) Aaron Spelling Productions, 1977
THE JORDAN CHANCE (TF) Universal TV, 1978
THE LAST CONVERTIBLE (MS) ☆ Roy Huggins Productions/Universal TV, 1979
CHU CHU AND THE PHILLY FLASH 20th Century-Fox, 1981
FOR LOVERS ONLY (TF) Henerson-Hirsch Productions/ Caesar Palace Productions, 1982

TODD RUNDGREN

b. 1948
Agent: ICM - Los Angeles, 213/550-4000

COLD FEET Cinecom International, 1983
UNDER COVER Cannon, 1987

PATRICE RUSHEN

Contact: ASCAP - Los Angeles, 213/466-7681

HOLLYWOOD SHUFFLE co-composer with Udi Harpaz, Samuel Goldwyn Co., 1987

RAY RUSSELL

Contact: PRS - London, England, 011-44-1-580-5544

THAT SUMMER! Columbia, 1979, British

WILLY RUSSELL

Contact: PRS - London, England, 011-44-1-580-5544

MR. LOVE (TF) Enigma/Goldcrest Films & TV, 1986, British
SHIRLEY VALENTINE co-composer with George Hatzinassios, Paramount, 1989

DAVID RUSSO

Contact: BMI - Los Angeles, 213/659-9109

SPACED INVADERS Buena Vista, 1990

GUS RUSSO

BASKET CASE Analysis, 1982

WILLIAM RUSSO

Contact: ASCAP - Los Angeles, 213/466-7681

THE COSMIC EYE (AF) 1985

CARLO RUSTICHELLI

b. December 24, 1916 - Emilia, Italy

GLI ULTIMI FILIBUSTIERI co-composer, 1941, Italian
IL FIGLIO DEL CORSARO NERO co-composer, 1941, Italian
GRAN PREMIO 1943, Italian
GIOVENTU PERDUTA *LOST YOUTH* 1947, Italian
IN NOME DELLA LEGGE 1948, Italian
THE WHITE LINE *CUORI SENZA FRONTIERE* 1949, Italian
TOTO CERCA CASA ATA, 1949, Italian
BARRIERA A SETTENTRIONE 1949, Italian
CINTURA DI CASTITA 1949, Italian
PERSIANE CHIUSE 1950, Italian
ATTO DI ACCUSA 1950, Italian
IL CAMINO DELLA SPERANZA 1950, Italian
CAVALCATA DI MEZZO SECOLO 1950, Italian
IL LEONE DI AMALFI 1950, Italian
DOMANI E UN ALTRO GIORNO co-composer, 1950, Italian
I FALSARI 1950, Italian
LA CITTA SI DIFENDE *FOUR WAYS OUT* 1951, Italian
LORENZACCIO 1951, Italian
IL BILVIO 1951, Italian
REVENGE OF THE PIRATES *LA VENDETTA DEL CORSARO* 1951, Italian
IL BRIGANTE DI TACCA DEL LUPO 1951, Italian
PERSIANE CHIUSE Rovere Film, 1951, Italian
LA CIECA DI SORRENTO 1952, Italian
TI HO SEMPRE AMATO 1952, Italian
PRIGIONIERA DELLA TORRE DI FUOCO 1952, Italian
LA PRESIDENTESSA 1952, Italian
TOTO E LE DONNE 1952, Italian
HIS TWO LOVES *PUCCINI* adaptation, 1952, Italian
PERDONAMI! 1952, Italian
BLACK 13 1953, British
CAPTAIN FANTASMA, IL TESORO DELLE INDIE 1953, Italian
LA NEMICA 1953, Italian
LA FIGLIA DEL DIAVOLO 1953, Italian
CANZONI, CANZONI, CANZONI 1953, Italian
GELOSIA 1953, Italian
GRAN VARIETA 1953, Italian
L'OMBRA 1954, Italian
PIETA PER CHI CADE 1955, Italian
DISPERATO ADDIO 1955, Italian
WILD LOVE *GLI INNAMORATI* Jacovoni, 1955, Italian
LA VENA D'ORO Athena Cinematografica, 1955, Italian
THE RAILROAD MAN *IL FERROVIERE* Continental, 1956, Italian
GUARDIA, GUARDIA SCELTA, BRIGADIERE E MARESCIALLO Imperial Film, 1956, Italian
SINFONIA D'AMORE adaptation, 1956, Italian
IL TESORO DI ROMMEL 1956, Italian
LAZZARELLA 1957, Italian
THE TAILOR'S MAID *PADRI E FIGLI* Trans-Lux, 1957, Italian
LA MINA 1957, Italian
MARISA LA CIVETTA Ponti/Balcazar, 1957, Italian-Spanish
DINANZI A NOI IL CIELO 1957, Italian
L'UOMO DI PAGLIA 1957, Italian
SAMIR E IL MARE 1958, Italian
TOTO E MARCELLINO 1958, Italian
THE DAY THE SKY EXPLODED *LA MORTE VIENE DALLO SPAZIO* 1958, Italian
ANNIBALE 1958, Italian
LE SECRET DU CHEVALIER D'EON 1959, French-Italian
ARRANGIATEVI Cineriz, 1959, Italian
NON SIAMO DUE EVASI 1959, Italian-French
THE FACTS OF MURDER *UN MALEDETTO IMBROGLIO* Seven Arts, 1959, Italian
LOVE THE ITALIAN WAY *FEMMINE DI LUSSO* 1959, Italian
ESTERINA 1959, Italian
UN UOMO FACILE co-composer, 1959, Italian
LA NOTTE DEL GRANDE ASSALTO 1959, Italian
I GIGANTI DELLA TESSAGLIA 1959, Italian
KAPO 1959, Italian
L'UOMO DAI CALZONI CORTI 1960, Italian
OLIMPIADI DEI MARITI 1960, Italian
LETTO A TRE PIAZZE 1960, Italian
A NOI PIACE FREDDO 1960, Italian
ROBIN HOOD AND THE PIRATES 1960, Italian
CATERINA SFORZA 1960, Italian
THE MINOTAUR *TESEO CONTRO IL MINOTAURO* 1960, Italian
UN AMORE A ROMA CEI Incom/Fair Film/Laetitia Film/Les Films Cocinor/Alpha Film, 1960, Italian-French-West German
LA VENERE DEI PIRATI 1960, Italian
LA LUNGA NOTTE DEL '43 1960, Italian
IL LADRO DI BAGDAD 1960, Italian
JOURNEY BENEATH THE DESERT *ANTINEA - L'AMANTE DELLA CITTA SEPOLTA* Embassy, 1961, Italian-French
ACCATONE! adaptation, Brandon, 1961, Italian
UN GIORNO DA LEONI 1961, Italian
IL COLPO SEGRETO DI D'ARTAGNAN 1961, Italian
GIORNO PER GIORNO DISPERATAMENTE 1961, Italian
QUEEN OF THE NILE *NEFERTITE, REGINA DEL NILO* 1961, Italian
DIVORCE ITALIAN STYLE Embassy, 1961, Italian
TIRO AL PICCIONE 1961, Italian
THE BLACK PIRATE 1961, Italian
PSYCOSISSIMO 1961, Italian
ROMULUS AND THE SABINES *IL RATTO DELLE SABINE* 1961, Italian
SWORD OF THE CONQUEROR *ROSMUNDA E ALBOINO* 1961, Italian
IL COMMISSARIO 1962, Italian
MAMMA ROMA adaptation, 1962, Italian
I MISCHETTIERI DEL MARE 1962, Italian
PASTACIATTA NEL DESERTO 1962, Italian
PELLA VIVA 1962, Italian
VENERE CREOLA co-composer, 1962, Italian
LA TIGRE DEI SETTE MARI 1962, Italian
I TROMBONI DI FRAI DIAVOLO 1962, Italian
AGOSTINO Baltea Film, 1962, Italian
LA BELLEZZA D'IPPOLITA 1962, Italian
MY SON THE HERO *ARRIVANO I TITANI* 1962, Italian
ROGOPAG co-composer, 1962, Italian
THE EYE OF THE NEEDLE *LA SMANIA ADOSSO* 1962, Italian
ARTURO'S ISLAND MGM, 1962, Italian
LE QUATTRE GIORNATE DI NAPOLI 1962, Italian

TRIUMPH OF THE SON OF HERCULES *IL TRIONFO DI MACISTE* 1963, Italian
FINCHE DURA LA TEMPESTA 1963, Italian
THE ORGANIZER *I COMPAGNI* Continental, 1963, Italian-French-Yugoslavian
ATLAS AGAINST THE TSAR *MACISTE ALLA CORTE DELLO ZAR* 1963, Italian
IL BOIA DI VENEZIA 1963, Italian
MARE MATTO 1963, Italian
CONQUEST OF MYCENE *ERCOLE CONTRO MOLOCH* 1963, Italian
CORIOLANO, EROE SENZA PATRIA 1963, Italian
LA FASDIZIOSA 1963, Italian
I GIGANTI DI ROMA 1963, Italian
SEDUCED AND ABANDONED Continental, 1964, Italian-French
GLI IMBROGLIANI Produzione D.S./Tecisa Film, 1963, Italian-Spanish
TERROR OF THE STEPPE *I PREDONI DELLA STEPPA* 1963, Italian
BEBO'S GIRL Continental, 1963, Italian-French
IL TERRORE DEI MANTELLI ROSSI 1963, Italian
LOS DINAMITEROS 1963, Italian
ADULTERO LUI *...ADULTERO LEI* 1963, Italian
TOTO E CLEOPATRA 1963, Italian
LA MANE SUL FUCILE 1963, Italian
IL CRIMINALE 1963, Italian
GLI ULTIMI 1963, Italian
TOTO CONTRO IL PIRATA NERO 1963, Italian
WHAT! LA FRUSTRA E IL CORPO 1963, Italian
LA CARICA DEL 7 CAVALLEGGERI 1964, Italian
THE WARM LIFE *LA CALDA VITA* 1964, Italian
THE CAVERN *SETTE CONTRO LA MORTE* 1964, Italian
I PROMESSI SPOSI 1964, Italian
SEDOTTI E BIDONATI 1964, Italian
IL LEONE DI SAN MARCO 1964, Italian
L'ANTIMIRACOLO 1964, Italian
LOS MANGANTES 1964, Spanish-Italian
AMORI PERICOLOSI co-composer, 1964, Italian
LA DONNA E UNA COSA MERAVIGLIOSA 1964, Italian
BAFFALO BILL, L'EROE DEL FAR WEST 1964, Italian
SANDOKAN FIGHTS BACK 1964, Italian
BLOOD AND BLACK LACE *SEI DONNE PER L'ASSASSINO* 1964, Italian
GLI EROI DI FORT WORTH 1964, Italian
SANDOKAN CONTRO IL LEOPARDO DI SARAWAK 1964, Italian
DESERT RAIDERS *IL DOMINATORE DEL DESERTO* 1964, Italian
TRE NOTTI D'AMORE co-composer, 1964, Italian
I LUNGHI CAPELLI DELLA MORTE 1964, Italian
HERCULES OF THE DESERT *LA VALLE DELL'ECO TONANTE* 1964, Italian
GENOVEVA DE BRABANTE 1965, Italian
LETTI SBAGLIATI 1965, Italian
L'AVVENTURIERO DELLA TORTUGA 1965, Italian
IL FIGLIO DI CLEOPATRA 1965, Italian
LIBIDO 1965, Italian
MADE IN ITALY co-composer, 1965, Italian
ON A VOLE LA JOCONDE 1965, Italian
THE MYSTERY OF THUG ISLAND 1965, Italian
I CAVALIERI DELLA VENDETTA 1965, Italian
LE NOTTE DEL DESPERADO 1965, Italian
LE STAGIONI DEL NOSTRO AMORE 1965, Italian
FORT ALESIA 1965, Italian
THE BIRDS, THE BEES AND THE ITALIANS *SIGNORE E SIGNORI* Claridge, 1966, Italian
FOR LOVE AND GOLD *L'ARMATA BRANCALEONE* Fair Film, 1966, Italian
MONDO SOMMERSO 1966, Italian
IO, IO, IO E GLI ALTRI 1966, Italian
KILL, BABY, KILL *OPERAZIONE PAURA* 1966, Italian
LA GRANDE NOTTE DI RINGO 1966, Itlaian
KILL OR BE KILLED *UCCIDI E MUORI* 1966, Italian
DELITTO QUASI PERFETTO 1966, Italian
THE CLIMAX *L'IMMORALE* Lopert, 1967, Italian-French
I DUE VIGILI 1967, Italian
ASSICURASI VERGINE 1967, Italian
I DIAMANTI CHE NESSUNO VOLEVA ROBARE 1967, Italian
A MINUTE TO PRAY, A SECOND TO DIE 1967, Italian
IL PADRE DI FAMIGLIA 1967, Italian
L'UOMO, L'ORGIGLIO, LA VENDETTA 1967, Italian
COLPO DOPPIO DEL CAMALEONTE D'ORO 1967, Italian
DIO PERDONA, IO NO 1967, Italian
UN TRENO PER DURANGO 1967, Italian
THE SECRET WAR OF HARRY FRIGG Universal, 1968
HEROES A LA FUERZA 1968, Italian
BATTAGLIE SUI MARI 1968, Italian
DUE PISTOLE E UN VIGLIACCIO 1968, Italian
THE RUTHLESS FOUR *EVERY MAN FOR HIMSELF/SAM COOPER'S GOLD* 1968, Italian-West German
SERAFINO Royal Films International, 1968, Italian-French
L'ISOLA 1968, Italian
VADO, VERO E SPARO 1968, Italian
MEGLIO VEDOVA 1968, Italian
LA BATTAGLIA DI EL ALAMEIN 1968, Italian
DAI NEMICI MI GUARDO IO 1968, Italian
I 7 FRATELLI CERVI 1968, Italian
ACE HIGH *I QUATTRO DELL'AVE MARIA* 1969, Italian
GLI INTERMIERI DELLA MUTUA 1969, Italian
LA PORTA DEL CANNONE 1969, Italian
STUNTMAN 1969, Italian
CRIMINAL SYMPHONY 1969, Italian
SCACCO INTERNAZIONALE 1969, Italian
IL TERRIBILE ISPETTORE 1969, Italian
CERTO, CERTISSIMI, ANZI...PROBABILE 1969, Italian
IL RAGAZZO CHE SORRIDE 1969, Italian
PROBABILITA ZERO 1969, Italian
PER UN PUGNO DI DIAMANTI 1969, Italian
UN ESTATE IN QUATTRO 1969, Italian
A DOPPIA FACCIA 1969, Italian
IL PISTOLERO SEGNATO DA DIO 1969, Italian
SATYRICON 1969, Italian
LA COLLINA DEGLI STIVALI 1970, Italian
BASTARDO! VAMOS A MATAR 1970, Italian
SATYRICOSISSIMO 1970, Italian
E VENNE IL GIORNO DEI LIMONI NERI 1970, Italian
UNA SPADA PER BRANDO 1970, Italian
NINI TIRABUSCIO, LA DONNA CHE INVENTO LA MOSSA 1970, Italian
TILL DIVORCE DO YOU PART *LE CASTAGNE SONO BUONO* 1970, Italian
ROSOLINO PATERNO, SOLDATO 1970, Italian
ER PIU, STORIA D'AMORE E DI COLTELLO 1970, Italian
MA CHI T'HA DATE LA PATENTE? 1970, Italian
BUBU' BRC, 1970, Italian
BRANCALEONE ALLE CROCIATE Fair Film, 1970, Italian
IL SERGENTE KLEMS 1971, Italian
DETENUTO IN ATTESA DI GIUDIZIO 1971, Italian
LA BETIA, OVVERO IN AMORE PER OGNI GAUDENZA 1971, Italian

ARMIAMOCI E PARTITE! 1971, Italian
BELLA, RICCA, LIEVE DIFETTO FISICO, CERCA, ANIMA GEMELLA 1972, Italian
DON CAMILLO E I GIOVANI D'OGGI 1972, Italian
IN NOME DEL POPOLO ITALIANO Apollo International Film, 1972, Italian
BOCCACCIO 1972, Italian
CAUSA DI DIVORZIO 1972, Italian
CALL OF THE WILD Constantin, 1972, West German-Spanish
AVANTI! United Artists, 1972, U.S.-Italian
ALFREDO ALFREDO Paramount, 1973, Italian
TRE RAMAZZE IN FUORI GIOCO 1973, Italian
UNA MATTA MATTA CORSA IN RUSSIA 1973, Italian
LE FUHRER EN FOLIE 1973, French
IL FIGLIOCCIO DEL PADRINO 1973, Italian
MILANO ROVENTE 1973, Italian
LA MANO NERA 1973, Italian
VOGLIAMO I COLONELLI Dean Film, 1973, Italian
MORDI E FUGGE C.C. Champion/Les Films Concordia, 1973, Italian-French
L'EMIGRANTE 1973, Italian
MING, RAGAZZI! 1973, Italian
TUTTI PER UNO, BOTTE PER TUTTI 1973, Italian
UN UOMO, UNA CITTA 1974, Italian
ZANNA BIANCA 1974, Italian
IL RITORNO DI ZANNA BIANCA 1974, Italian
DELITTO D'AMORE Documento Film, 1974, Italian
PERMETTO SIGNORA CHE AMI VOSTRA FIGLIA? 1974, Italian
IL GATTO MAMMONE 1975, Italian
ZANNA BIANCA ALLA RISCOSSA 1975, Italian
GIUBBE ROSSE 1975, Italian
M TUTTI W NOI 1975, Italian
FIGHT TO THE DEATH *METRALLETA STEIN* co-composer, 1975, Italian
MY FRIENDS Allied Artists, 1975, Italian
LES RANGERS DEFIENT LES KARATEKAS 1975, French
SALVO D'ACQUISTO 1975, French
UNE FEMME A SA FENETRE 1976, French
LE GANG Warner-Columbia, 1977, French
L'HOMME PRESSE AMLF, 1977, French
LE BEAUJOLAIS NOUVEAU EST ARRIVE 1978, French
ASSASSINIO SUL TEVERE 1980, Italian
AMICI MIEII II Sacis, 1982, Italian
CLARETTA AND BEN Aquarius Films, 1983, Italian-French
HEADS OR TAILS co-composer with Paolo Rustichelli, CIDIF, 1983, Italian

MICHAEL RUTHERFORD

Contact: PRS - London, England, 011-44-1-580-5544

THE SHOUT co-composer with Rupert Hine and Anthony Banks, Films Inc., 1979, British

HAIM SABAN

Contact: BMI - Los Angeles, 213/659-9109

RAINBOW BRITE AND THE STAR STEALER (AF) co-composer with Shuki Levy, Warner Bros., 1985

CRAIG SAFAN

Agent: ICM - Los Angeles, 213/550-4000

THE CALIFORNIA REICH (FD) City Life Films, 1975
THE GREAT TEXAS DYNAMITE CHASE New World, 1976
THE GREAT SMOKEY ROADBLOCK *THE LAST OF THE COWBOYS* Dimension, 1976
THE BAD NEWS BEARS IN BREAKING TRAINING Paramount, 1977
ACAPULCO GOLD R.C. Riddell, 1978
GETTING MARRIED (TF) Paramount TV, 1978
CORVETTE SUMMER MGM/United Artists, 1978
GOOD GUYS WEAR BLACK American Cinema, 1979
THE SURVIVAL OF DANA (TF) Roger Gimbel Productions/ Marc Trabulus Enterprises/EMI TV, 1979
ROLLER BOOGIE United Artists, 1979
DIE LAUGHING co-composer with Robby Benson and Jerry Segal, Orion, 1980
FADE TO BLACK American Cinema, 1980
T.A.G.: THE ASSASSINATION GAME New World, 1982
NIGHTMARES Universal, 1983
ANGEL New World, 1984
THE LAST STARFIGHTER Universal, 1984
THE IMPOSTER (TF) Gloria Monty Productions/Comworld Productions, 1984
WARNING SIGN 20th Century Fox, 1985
ALFRED HITCHCOCK PRESENTS (TF) co-composer, Universal TV, 1985
THE LEGEND OF BILLIE JEAN Tri-Star, 1985
MIRRORS (TF) Leonard Hill Films, 1985
REMO WILLIAMS: THE ADVENTURE BEGINS... Orion, 1985
MIRRORS (TF) Leonard Hill Films, 1985
HELP WANTED: KIDS (TF) Stan Rogow Productions, 1986
I-MAN (TF) Mark H. Ovitz Productions/Walt Disney TV, 1986
SAMARITAN (TF) Levine-Robins Productions/Fries Entertainment, 1986
COURAGE (TF) Highgate Pictures/New World TV, 1986
TIMESTALKERS (TF) Fries Entertainment/Newland-Raynor Productions, 1987
LADY BEWARE Scotti Brothers, 1987
THE STRANGER Columbia, 1987, U.S.-Argentine
NIGHTMARE ON ELM STREET PART 4: THE DREAM MASTER New Line Cinema, 1988
ALMOST GROWN (TF) Universal TV/Atlantis Films, 1988
SUPERCARRIER (TF) Fries Entertainment/Richard Hayward-Real Tinsel Productions, 1988
SHOOTDOWN (TF) Leonard Hill Films, 1988
STAND AND DELIVER Warner Bros., 1988
THE COMEBACK (TF) CBS Entertainment, 1989
THE REVENGE OF AL CAPONE (TF) Unity Productions/ River City, 1989
ENID IS SLEEPING Vestron, 1990

MICHAEL SAHL
BLOODSUCKING FREAKS Troma, 1982

BUFFY SAINTE-MARIE
Contact: ASCAP - Los Angeles, 213/466-7681

STRIPPER (FD) co-composer with Jack Nitzsche, 20th Century Fox

RYUICHI SAKAMOTO
b. Japan
Contact: CAA - Los Angeles, 213/288-4545

MERRY CHRISTMAS, MR. LAWRENCE Universal, 1983, British-Japanese
THE LAST EMPEROR ★★ co-composer with David Byrne and Cong Su, Columbia, 1987, British-Chinese
THE HANDMAID'S TALE Cinecom, 1990

GARY SALES
MADMAN co-composer with Stephen Horelick, Jensen Farley Pictures, 1982

BARRY SALMON
SILENT MADNESS Almi Pictures, 1984

HANS J. SALTER
b. Jan. 14, 1896 - Vienna, Austria

(Between the late 1930s and 1950s Mr. Salter contributed music to over 150 films for Universal, almost all of them in collaboration.)

YOUNG FUGITIVE Universal, 1938
BIG GUY Universal, 1939
CALL A MESSENGER Universal, 1939
THE GREAT COMMANDMENT Universal, 1939
ALIAS THE DEACON Universal, 1940
BLACK DIAMONDS Universal, 1940
BLACK FRIDAY Universal, 1940
THE DEVIL'S PIPELINE Universal, 1940
ENEMY AGENT Universal, 1940
FIRST LOVE Universal, 1940
FRAMED Universal, 1940
GIVE US WINGS Universal, 1940
I CAN'T GIVE YOU ANYTHING BUT LOVE, BABY Universal, 1940
I'M NOBODY'S SWEETHEART NOW Universal, 1940
THE INVISIBLE MAN RETURNS Universal, 1940
SEVEN SINNERS Universal, 1940
LAW AND ORDER Universal, 1940
THE LEATHER PUSHERS Universal, 1940
LOVE, HONOR AND OH, BABY! Universal, 1940
MARGIE Universal, 1940
MEET THE WILDCAT Universal, 1940
MIRACLE ON MAIN STREET Universal, 1940
THE MUMMY'S HAND Universal, 1940
PRIVATE AFFAIRS Universal, 1940
SANDY GETS HER MAN Universal, 1940
SEVEN SINNERS Universal, 1940
SKI PATROL Universal, 1940
SLIGHTLY TEMPTED Universal, 1940
SOUTH TO KARANGA Universal, 1940
SPRING PARADE Universal, 1940
TRAIL OF THE VIGILANTES Universal, 1940
YOU'RE NOT SO TOUGH Universal, 1940
ZANZIBAR Universal, 1940
ARIZONA CYCLONE Universal, 1941
BACHELOR DADDY Universal, 1941
BADLANDS OF DAKOTA Universal, 1941
THE BLACK CAT Universal, 1941
BURMA CONVOY Universal, 1941
A DANGEROUS GAME Universal, 1941
DARK STREETS OF CAIRO Universal, 1941
DOUBLE DATE Universal, 1941
THE WOLF MAN Universal, 1941
FLYING CADETS Universal, 1941
HELLO SUCKER Universal, 1941
HIT THE ROAD Universal, 1941
HOLD THAT GHOST Universal, 1941
HORROR ISLAND Universal, 1941
IT STARTED WITH EVE Universal, 1941
LUCKY DEVILS Universal, 1941
MAN-MADE MONSTER Universal, 1941
THE MAN WHO LOST HIMSELF Universal, 1941
MEET THE CHUMP Universal, 1941
MEN OF THE TIMBERLAND Universal, 1941
MR. DYNAMITE Universal, 1941
MOB TOWN Universal, 1941
MODEL WIFE Universal, 1941
MUTINY IN THE ARCTIC Universal, 1941
RAIDERS OF THE DESERT Universal, 1941
ROAD AGENT Universal, 1941
SAN FRANCISCO DOCKS Universal, 1941
SEALED LIPS Universal, 1941
TIGHT SHOES Universal, 1941
WHERE DID YOU GET THAT GIRL? Universal, 1941
DESTINATION UNKNOWN Universal, 1942
FRISCO LIL Universal, 1942
HALF WAY TO SHANGHAI Universal, 1942
THE INVISIBLE AGENT Universal, 1942
THE MAD DOCTOR OF MARKET STREET Universal, 1942
MADAME SPY Universal, 1942
THE OLD CHISHOLM TRAIL Universal, 1942
PITTSBURGH Universal, 1942
SHERLOCK HOLMES AND THE SECRET WEAPON Universal, 1942
WHO DONE IT? Universal, 1942
BOMBAY CLIPPER Universal, 1942
DANGER IN THE PACIFIC Universal, 1942
DEEP IN THE HEART OF TEXAS Universal, 1942
DRUMS OF THE CONGO Universal, 1942
FIGHTING BILL FARGO Universal, 1942
THE GHOST OF FRANKENSTEIN Universal, 1942
LITTLE JOE, THE WRANGLER Universal, 1942
THE MUMMY'S TOMB Universal, 1942
THE MYSTERY OF MARIE ROGET Universal, 1942
NIGHT MONSTER Universal, 1942
NORTH TO THE KLONDIKE Universal, 1942
PITTSBURGH Universal, 1942
THE SILVER BULLET Universal, 1942
SIN TOWN Universal, 1942
THE SPOILERS Universal, 1942
STAGECOACH BUCKAROO Universal, 1942
THE STRANGE CASE OF DR. RX Universal, 1942
THERE'S ONE BORN EVERY MINUTE Universal, 1942
TIMBER Universal, 1942
TOP SERGEANT Universal, 1942
TOUGH AS THEY COME Universal, 1942
TREAT 'EM ROUGH Universal, 1942
YOU'RE TELLING ME Universal, 1942
THE AMAZING MRS. HOLIDAY ★ co-composer with Frank Skinner, Universal, 1943
ARIZONA TRAIL Universal, 1943
CALLING DR. DEATH Universal, 1943
EYES OF THE UNDERWORLD Universal, 1943

FRONTIER BADMEN Universal, 1943
BOSS OF HANGTOWN MESA Universal, 1943
CAPTIVE WILD WOMAN Universal, 1943
CHEYENNE ROUNDUP Universal, 1943
COWBOY IN MANHATTAN Universal, 1943
FRANKENSTEIN MEETS THE WOLFMAN Universal, 1943
GET GOING Universal, 1943
HIS BUTLER'S SISTER Universal, 1943
HI YA, CHUM Universal, 1943
HI'YA, SAILOR Universal, 1943
KEEP 'EM SLUGGING Universal, 1943
LONE STAR TRAIL Universal, 1943
THE MAD GHOUL Universal, 1943
MUG TOWN Universal, 1943
NEVER A DULL MOMENT Universal, 1943
RAIDERS OF SAN JOAQUIN Universal, 1943
SHERLOCK HOLMES FACES DEATH Universal, 1943
SON OF DRACULA Universal, 1943
THE STRANGE DEATH OF ADOLPH HITLER Universal, 1943
TENTING TONIGHT ON THE OLD CAMP GROUND Universal, 1943
ALLERGIC TO LOVE Universal, 1944
BOSS OF BOOMTOWN Universal, 1944
CAN'T HELP SINGING Universal, 1944
CHRISTMAS HOLIDAY ★ Universal, 1944
HAT CHECK HONEY Universal, 1944
THE HOUSE OF FEAR Universal, 1944
HI, GOOD LOOKIN' Universal, 1944
HOUSE OF FRANKENSTEIN Universal, 1944
THE INVISIBLE MAN'S REVENGE Universal, 1944
JUNGLE CAPTIVE Universal, 1944
SHERLOCK HOLMES AND THE SPIDER WOMAN Universal, 1944
JUNGLE WOMAN Universal, 1944
THE MERRY MONAHANS ★ Universal, 1944
MARSHAL OF GUNSMOKE Universal, 1944
THE MUMMY'S GHOST Universal, 1944
PARDON MY RHYTHM Universal, 1944
THE PEARL OF DEATH Universal, 1944
SAN DIEGO, I LOVE YOU Universal, 1944
THE SCARLET CLAW Universal, 1944
TWILIGHT ON THE PRAIRIE Universal, 1944
WEIRD WOMAN Universal, 1944
HOUSE OF DRACULA Universal, 1945
EASY TO LOOK AT Universal, 1945
THE FROZEN GHOST Universal, 1945
PURSUIT TO ALGIERS Universal, 1945
THE STRANGE AFFAIR OF UNCLE HARRY Universal, 1945
THE WOMAN IN GREEN Universal, 1945
I'LL TELL THE WORLD Universal, 1945
PATRICK THE GREAT Universal, 1945
THE RIVER GANG Universal, 1945
SCARLET STREET Universal, 1945
SEE MY LAWYER Universal, 1945
THAT NIGHT WITH YOU Universal, 1945
THAT'S THE SPIRIT Universal, 1945
THIS LOVE OF OURS ★ Universal, 1945
THE BRUTE MAN Universal, 1946
DRESSED TO KILL Universal, 1946
GUNG HO! Universal, 1946
THE MAGNIFICENT DOLL Universal, 1946
THE DARK HOUSE Universal, 1946
HER ADVENTUROUS NIGHT Universal, 1946
TERROR BY NIGHT Universal, 1946
HOUSE OF HORRORS Universal, 1946
LITTLE MISS BIG Universal, 1946
LOVER COME BACK Universal, 1946
SO GOES MY LOVE Universal, 1946
THE MICHIGAN KID Universal, 1947
THAT'S MY MAN Universal, 1947
THE WEB Universal, 1947
LOVE FROM A STRANGER Universal, 1947
THE SIGN OF THE RAM Universal, 1948
MAN-EATER OF KUMAON Universal, 1948
DON'T TRUST YOUR HUSBAND Universal, 1948
AN INNOCENT AFFAIR Universal, 1948
COVER-UP Universal, 1949
THE RECKLESS MOMENT Universal, 1949
BORDERLINE Universal, 1950
PLEASE BELIEVE ME Universal, 1950
THE KILLER THAT STALKED NEW YORK Universal, 1950
FRENCHIE Universal, 1950
WOMAN FROM HEADQUARTERS Universal, 1950
FINDERS KEEPERS Universal, 1951
ABBOTT AND COSTELLO MEET THE INVISIBLE MAN Universal, 1951
THE PRINCE WHO WAS A THIEF Universal, 1951
THUNDER ON THE HILL Universal, 1951
TOMAHAWK Universal, 1951
APACHE DRUMS Universal, 1951
YOU CAN NEVER TELL Universal, 1951
THE GOLDEN HORDE Universal, 1951
AGAINST ALL FLAGS Universal, 1952
THE BLACK CASTLE Universal, 1952
THE BATTLE OF APACHE PASS Universal, 1952
BEND OF THE RIVER Universal, 1952
THE DUEL AT SILVER CREEK Universal, 1952
FLESH AND FURY Universal, 1952
UNTAMED FRONTIER Universal, 1952
ABBOTT AND COSTELLO MEET DR. JEYKLL AND MR. HYDE Universal, 1953
THE 5,000 FINGERS OF DR. T co-composer with Frederick Hollander and Heinz Roemheld, Columbia, 1953
BENGAL BRIDE Universal, 1954
BLACK HORSE CANYON Universal, 1954
THE BLACK SHIELD OF FALWORTH Universal, 1954
THE CREATURE FROM THE BLACK LAGOON co-composer, Universal, 1954
THE FAR COUNTRY Universal, 1954
FOUR GUNS TO THE BORDER Universal, 1954
JOHNNY DARK Universal, 1954
NAKED ALIBI Universal, 1954
SASKATCHEWAN Universal, 1954
SIGN OF THE PAGAN Universal, 1954
TANGANYIKA Universal, 1954
YANKEE PASHA Universal, 1954
THE HUMAN JUNGLE Universal, 1954
ABBOTT AND COSTELLO MEET THE MUMMY Universal, 1955
CAPTAIN LIGHTFOOT Universal, 1955
MAN WITHOUT A STAR Universal, 1955
THIS ISLAND EARTH Universal, 1955
THE FAR HORIZONS Universal, 1955
WICHITA Universal, 1955
LADY GODIVA Universal, 1956
AUTUMN LEAVES Universal, 1956
HOLD BACK THE NIGHT Universal, 1956
THE MOLE PEOPLE Universal, 1956
NAVY WIFE Universal, 1956
THE RAW EDGE Universal, 1956
THE RAWHIDE YEARS Universal, 1956
WALK THE PROUD LAND Universal, 1956
RED SUNDOWN Universal, 1956
THE OKLAHOMAN Universal, 1957
THE INCREDIBLE SHRINKING MAN Universal, 1957
JOE DAKOTA Universal, 1957
THE LAND UNKNOWN Universal, 1957

THE MAN IN THE SHADOW Universal, 1957
THE MIDNIGHT STORY Universal, 1957
THE TALL STRANGER Universal, 1957
THREE BRAVE MEN Universal, 1957
DAY OF THE BAD MAN Universal, 1958
THE FEMALE ANIMAL Universal, 1958
APPOINTMENT WITH A SHADOW Universal, 1958
SUMMER LOVE Universal, 1958
RAW WIND IN EDEN Universal, 1958
THE GUNFIGHT AT DODGE CITY Universal, 1959
MAN IN THE NET Universal, 1959
THE WILD AND THE INNOCENT Universal, 1959
COME SEPTEMBER Universal, 1961
FOLLOW THAT DREAM Universal, 1962
HITLER Universal, 1962
IF A MAN ANSWERS Universal, 1962
SHOWDOWN Universal, 1963
BEDTIME STORY Universal, 1964
THE WAR LORD Universal, 1965
BEAU GESTE Universal, 1966
GUNPOINT Universal, 1966
I KNEW HER WELL Universal, 1966
INCIDENT AT PHANTOM HILL Universal, 1966
RETURN OF THE GUNFIGHTER (TF) King Brothers/ MGM TV, 1967

BENNETT SALVAY
Contact: BMI - Los Angeles, 213/659-9109

ALOHA SUMMER co-composer with Jesse Frederick, Spectrafilm, 1988
BURNING BRIDGES (TF) co-composer with W.G. Snuffy Walden, Andrea Baynes Productions/ Lorimar TV, 1990

LEONARDO SALZEDO
b. 1921 - London
Contact: PRS - London, England, 011-44-1-580-5544

SHADOW OF FEAR *BEFORE I WAKE* 1956, British
THE REVENGE OF FRANKENSTEIN Columbia, 1958, British
THE STEEL BAYONET United Artists, 1958, British

DAVID SANBORN
b. 1945
Contact: BMI - Los Angeles, 213/659-9109

FINNEGAN BEGIN AGAIN (CTF) co-composer with Michael Colina, HBO Premiere Films/Zenith Productions/Jennie & Co. Film Productions, 1985, U.S.-British
LETHAL WEAPON II co-composer with Michael Kamen and Eric Clapton, Warner Bros., 1989

RIC SANDLER
Contact: BMI - Los Angeles, 213/659-9109

HEY, GOOD LOOKIN' co-composer with John Madara, Warner Bros., 1982

PETER SANDLOFF
Contact: GEMA - West Germany, 011-49-89621400

MAEDCHEN IN UNIFORM 1965, West German
MICHAEL KOHLHAAS Horst Film, 1979, West German

CARLOS SANTOS
Contact: SICAM - Brazil, 011-55-11-223-8555

JETLAG Wieland Schulz-Keil/Figaro Films, 1981, U.S.-Spanish

ANDREA SAPAROFF
Agent: Robert Light - Los Angeles, 213/651-1777

NO MAN IS AN ISLAND Dana Productions
THE JOY OF ACHIEVEMENT Dana Productions
THE JOYS OF COMMUNICATION Dana Productions
AMERICA'S PEOPLE Dana Productions
HOME ALONE Hi-Tops Productions
A SIMPLE MATTER OF JUSTICE PS Films
APPOINTMENT WITH FEAR Galaxy International, 1985
DEADLY PRESENCE Trancas International

FRANK SARAFINE
Contact: ASCAP - Los Angeles, 213/466-7681

NIGHTFALL Concorde, 1988

PHILIPPE SARDE
b. June 21, 1945 - Neuilly-sur-Seine, France
Agent: CAA - Los Angeles, 213/288-4545

LES CHOSES DE LA VIE *THE THINGS OF LIFE* Columbia, 1970, French
SORTIE DE SECOURS 1970, French
LA LIBERTE EN CROUPE 1970, French
MAX ET LES FERRAILLEURS CFDC, 1971, French
LE CHAT 1971, French
LA VEUVE COUDERC 1972, French
LIZA Horizon, 1972, French-Italian
LE FILS 1972, French
HELLE Cocinor, 1972, French
LE DROIT D'AIMER 1972, French
CESAR AND ROSALIE Cinema 5, 1972, French-Italian-West German
LA GRANDE BOUFFE ABKCO, 1973, French-Italian
LE TRAIN 1973, French
TOUCHE PAS A LA FEMME BLANCHE! *HANDS OFF WHITE WOMEN* CFDC, 1974, French
LES CORPS CELESTES Les Productions Carle-Lamy, 1973, Canadian
LA VALISE 1973, French
LE MARIAGE A LA MODE 1973, French
CHARLIE ET SES DEUX NENETTES 1973, French
THE CLOCKMAKER OF ST. PAUL Joseph Green Pictures, 1974, French
DOROTHEA 1974, French
LA RACE DES SEIGNEURS 1974, French
DEUX HOMMES DANS LA VILLE 1974, French
LES SEINS DE GLACE 1974, French
VINCENT, FRANCOIS, PAUL AND THE OTHERS Joseph Green Pictures, 1974, French-Italian
SOUVENIRS D'EN FRANCE adaptation, 1974, French
LANCELOT OF THE LAKE New Yorker, 1975, French-Italian
UN DIVORCE HEUREUX CFDC, 1975, French-Danish
LA CAGE 1975, French
PAS DE PROBLEME *NO PROBLEM* 1975, French
FOLLE A TUER 1975, French
UN SAC DE BILLES 1975, French
LES GALETTES DE PONT-AVEN adaptation, 1975, French
THE FRENCH DETECTIVE 1975, French
THE JUDGE AND THE ASSASSIN Libra, 1976, French

THE LAST WOMAN Columbia, 1976, Italian-French
ADIEU, POULET 1976, French
ON AURA TOUT VU 1976, French
SEPT MORTS SUR ORDONNANCE 1976, French
THE TENANT Paramount, 1976, French-U.S.
MARIE POUPEE 1976, French
BAROCCO 1976, French
MADO Joseph Green Pictures, 1976, French
LE JUGE FAYARD DIT LE SHERIFF CCFC, 1977, French
VIOLETTE ET FRANCOIS 1977, French
LE DIABLE PROBABLEMENT Gaumont, 1977, French
UN TAXI MAUVE *THE PURPLE TAXI* Parafrance Films, 1977, French-Italian-Irish
COMME LA LUNE... 1977, Italian
DES ENFANTS GATES *SPOILED CHILDREN* Gaumont, 1977, French
LE CRABE-TAMBOUR 1977, French
MADAME ROSA *LA VIE DEVANT SOI* Atlantic Releasing Corporation, 1978, French
BYE BYE MONKEY Gaumont, 1978, Italian-French
ILS SONT FOUS CES SORCIERS! 1978, French
PASSE MONTAGNE 1978, French
LE SUCRE 1978, French
LA CLE SUR LA PORTE *THE KEY IS IN THE DOOR* 1978, French
L'ADOLESCENTE 1978, French
A SIMPLE STORY Quartet, 1979, French
THE BRONTE SISTERS Gaumont, 1979, French
LE TOUBIB 1979, French
FLIC OU VOYOU 1979, French
TESS ★ Columbia, 1979, French-British
CHIEDO ASILO *MY ASYLUM* 1979
LA FEMME-FLIC 1980, French
BUFFET FROID *COLD CUTS* adaptation, 1980, French
I SENT A LETTER TO MY LOVE *CHERE INCONNUE* Atlantic Releasing Corporation, 1980, French
LE GUIGNOLO 1980, French
BEAU PERE New Line Cinema, 1981, French
GHOST STORY Universal, 1981
CHOICE OF ARMS 1981, French
COUP DE TORCHON *CLEAN SLATE* Biograph/ Quartet/Films Inc./The Frank Moreno Company, 1982
L'ETOILE DU NORD *THE NORTH STAR* Parafrance, 1982, French
A STRANGE AFFAIR Parafrance, 1982, French
QUEST FOR FIRE 20th Century-Fox, 1982, Canadian-French
LOVESICK The Ladd Company/Warner Bros., 1983
J'AI ESPOUSE UN OMBRE AMLF, 1983, French
ATTENTION, UME FEMME PEUT EN CACHER UNE AUTRE Gaumont, 1983, French
GARCON Sara Film/Renn Productions, 1983, French
FIRST DESIRES AMLF, 1983, French
A FRIEND OF VINCENT AMLF, 1983, French
STELLA Fox-Hachette, 1983, French
FORT SAGANNE A.A.A., 1984, French
SUNDAY IN THE COUNTRY MGM/UA Classics, 1984, French
JOSHUA, THEN AND NOW 20th Century Fox, 1985, Canadian
RENDEZVOUS UGC, 1985, French
HAREM Sara Films, 1985, French
DEVIL IN THE FLESH World Film Alliance, 1986, Australian
MON BEAU-FRERE A TUE MA SOEUR World Marketing, 1986, French
THE SCENE OF THE CRIME AMLF, 1986, French
THE MANHATTAN PROJECT 20th Century Fox, 1986
PIRATES Cannon, 1986, French-Tunisian
EVERY TIME WE SAY GOODBYE Tri-Star, 1987, Israeli
LES MOIS D'AVRIL SONT MEURTRIERS Sara/CDF, 1987, French
A FEW DAYS WITH ME Galaxy International, 1988, French
LOST ANGELS Orion, 1989
REUNION Les Films Ariane-FR3 Films, 1989, French
THE BEAR Tri-Star, 1989, French
THE MUSIC BOX Tri-Star, 1989
LA BAULE-LES PINS UGC, 1990, French
LORD OF THE FLIES Columbia, 1990

MASARU SATO

b. 1928 - Hokkaido, Japan
Contact: JASRAC - Tokyo, Japan, 011-81-3-502-6551

RECORD OF A LIVING BEING co-composer with Fumio Hayasaka, 1956, Japanese
THE LOWER DEPTHS Brandon, 1957, Japanese
THRONE OF BLOOD *THE CASTLE OF THE SPIDER'S WEB* Brandon, 1957, Japanese
HALF HUMAN DCA, 1957, Japanese
THE HIDDEN FORTRESS *THREE BAD MEN IN A HIDDEN FORTRESS* Toho, 1958, Japanese
GIGANTIS THE FIRE MONSTER 1959, Japanese
THE H-MAN Columbia, 1959, Japanese
THE BAD SLEEP WELL Toho, 1960, Japanese
YOJIMBO Seneca International, 1961, Japanese
SANJURO Toho, 1962, Japanese
HIGH AND LOW East West Classics, 1963, Japanese
THE LOST WORLD OF SINBAD 1964
RED BEARD Toho, 1965, Japanese
THE EMPEROR AND THE GENERAL *THE LONGEST DAY IN JAPAN* Toho, 1967, Japanese
THREE SISTERS 1967, Japanese
SATSUJINYO JUDAI *THE AGE OF ASSASSINS* 1967, Japanese
THE SWORD OF DOOM Toho, 1967, Japanese
GODZILLA VS. THE SEA MONSTER *EBIRAH, HORROR OF THE DEEP* 1968, Japanese
KILL! 1968, Japanese
PORTRAIT OF CHICKO 1968, Japanese
SON OF GODZILLA 1969, Japanese
SAMURAI BANNERS 1969, Japanese
RED LION 1969, Japanese
OUTLAWS 1970, Japanese
KAZOKU 1971, Japanese
THE BATTLE OF OKINAWA 1971, Japanese
SAPPORO WINTER OLYMPICS 1972, Japanese
THE WOLVES 1972, Japanese
SUBMERSION OF JAPAN *TIDAL WAVE* 1973, Japanese
MAN AND WAR, PART III 1974, Japanese
GODZILLA VS. MECHA-GODZILLA *GODZILLA VS. BIONIC MONSTER/GODZILLA VS. COSMIC MONSTER* 1976, Japanese
A PORTRAIT OF SHUNKIN 1977, Japanese
THE YELLOW HANDKERCHIEF OF HAPPINESS 1978, Japanese
U.F.O. BLUE CHRISTMAS *BLOOD TYPE BLUE* 1979
THE GLACIER FOX (FD) Sanrio Film, 1979
OH! THE NOMUGI PASS 1979, Japanese
TOWARD THE TERRA 1980, Japanese
SENSEI THE TEACHER Daiei, 1983, Japanese
IREZUMI: SPIRIT OF TATTOO Daiei, 1983, Japanese
SHOGUN'S SHADOW Toei, 1989, Japanese

EDDIE SAUTER
Contact: ASCAP - Los Angeles, 213/466-7681

MICKEY ONE Columbia, 1965
BEGGERMAN, THIEF (TF) Universal TV, 1979

TOM SAVIANO
Agent: Andi Howard - Los Angeles, 213/278-6483

DEFIANCE American International, 1980

CARLO SAVINA
b. 1919 - Turin, Italy
Contact: SIAE - Rome, Italy, 011-39-6-59-90-1

ERODE IL GRANDE 1958, Italian
EUROPA DI NOTTE 1959, Italian
IL MORALISTA 1959, Italian
IL PRINCIPE FUSTO 1960, Italian
LA RAGAZZA SOTTO IL LENZUOLO 1961, Italian
L'IRA DI ACHILLE 1962, Italian
LIOLA 1964, Italian
SFIDA AL RE DI CASTIGLIA 1964, Italian
LE SPIE UCCIDONO A BEIRUT 1965, Italian
GLI AMANTI LATINI 1965, Italian
FURIA A MARRAKESCH 1966, Italian
L'UOME CHE RIDE 1966, Italian
JOHNNY ORO 1966, Italian
A 077 SFIDA AL KILLERS Aenit/Flora/Regina, 1967, Italian
PROCESSO A STALIN...? 1967, Italian
JOE L'IMPLACABILE Seven/Hispamer, 1967, Italian-Spanish
JOKO INVOCA DIO E MUORI 1968, Italian
SIMON BOLIVAR 1969, Italian
HYPNOS 1969, Italian
EHI AMIGO SEI MORTO 1970, Italian
E LO CHIAMARONO SPIRITO SANTO 1971, Italian
LE CALDE NOTTE DI DON GIOVANNI 1971, Italian
FINALMENTE...LE MILLE E UNA NOTTE Pink Medusa, 1972, Italian
UN ANIMAL CHIAMATO UOMO 1972, Italian
TRINITA E SARTANA: FIGLI DI... 1972, Italian
JESSE E LESTER DUE FRATELLI IN UN POSTO CHIAMOTO TRINITA 1972, Italian
INGRID SULLA STRADA 1973, Italian
MING, RAGAZZI! 1973, Italian
MR. HERCULES AGAINST KARATE *MR. HERCULES AGAINST KUNG FU* United Artists, 1973, Italian
MANONE IL LADRONE Laser Film, 1974, Italian
CARNALITA 1974, Italian
LA PROFANAZIONE 1974, Italian
L'ASSASSINO HA RISERVATO 9 POLTRONE 1974, Italian
LA DOVE NON BATTE IL SOLE 1975, Italian
LA BOLOGNESE 1975, Italian
LA NUORA GIOVANE 1975, Italian
LA NIPOTE 1975, Italian
LA NIPOTE DEL PRETE 1975, Italian
ORDINE FIRMATO IN BIANCO 1975, Italian
IL VIZIO HA LE CALZE NERE 1975, Italian
UNA VERGINE IN FAMIGLIA 1975, Italian
L'INGENUA 1975, Italian
ULTIME GRIDA DALLA SAVANA (FD) 1975, Italian
CALORE IN PROVINCIA 1975, Italian
CARI MOSTRI DEL MARE 1976, Italian
COMIN' AT YA! Filmways, 1981, Italian-U.S.
THE HUNTERS OF THE GOLDEN COBRA *THE RAIDERS OF THE GOLDEN COBRA* World Northal, 1982, Italian

WALTER SCHARF
b. August 1, 1910 - New York, New York
Contact: ASCAP - Los Angeles, 213/466-7681

MERCY ISLAND ★ co-composer with Cy Feuer, Republic, 1941
JOHNNY DOUGHBOY ★ adaptation, Republic, 1942
CHATTERBOX Republic, 1943
HIT PARADE OF 1943 ★ Republic, 1943
NOBODY'S DARLING Republic, 1943
SECRETS OF THE UNDERGROUND Republic, 1943
HANDS ACROSS THE BORDER Republic, 1943
SHANTYTOWN Republic, 1943
SLEEPY LAGOON Republic, 1943
SOMEONE TO REMEMBER Republic, 1943
IN OLD OKLAHOMA ★ Republic, 1943
THUMBS UP Republic, 1943
ATLANTIC CITY Republic, 1944
THE FIGHTING SEABEES ★ Republic, 1944
THE COWBOY AND THE SENORITA Republic, 1944
CASANOVA IN BURLESQUE Republic, 1944
BRAZIL ★ Republic, 1944
LAKE PLACID SERENADE Republic, 1944
THE LADY AND THE MONSTER Republic, 1944
STORM OVER LISBON Republic, 1944
THE CHEATERS Republic, 1945
DAKOTA Republic, 1945
EARL CARROLL'S VANITIES Repubic, 1945
I'VE ALWAYS LOVED YOU Republic, 1946
THE SAXON CHARM United Artists, 1948
THE COUNTESS OF MONTE CRISTO United Artists, 1948
ARE YOU WITH IT? Universal, 1948
RED CANYON United Artists, 1949
CITY ACROSS THE RIVER Universal, 1949
TAKE ONE FALSE STEP Universal, 1949
YES SIR, THAT'S MY BABY Universal, 1949
ABANDONED Universal, 1949
SOUTH SEA SINNER Universal, 1950
BUCCANNEER'S GIRL Universal, 1950
CURTAIN CALL AT CACTUS CREEK Universal, 1950
SIERRA Universal, 1950
SPY HUNT Universal, 1950
DEPORTED Universal, 1950
TWO TICKETS TO BROADWAY RKO Radio, 1951
HANS CHRISTIAN ANDERSON adaptation, RKO Radio, 1952
THE FRENCH LINE RKO Radio, 1953
LIVING IT UP Paramount, 1954
THREE RING CIRCUS Paramount, 1954
ARTISTS AND MODELS Paramount, 1955
YOU'RE NEVER TOO YOUNG Paramount, 1955
THE BIRDS AND THE BEES Paramount, 1956
HOLLYWOOD OR BUST Paramount, 1956
THREE FOR JAMIE DAWN Allied Artists, 1956
TIMETABLE United Artists, 1956
THREE VIOLENT PEOPLE Paramount, 1957
THE JOKER IS WILD ALL THE WAY Paramount, 1957
LOVING YOU Paramount, 1957
THE SAD SACK Paramount, 1957
ROCK-A-BYE BABY Paramount, 1958
KING CREOLE Paramount, 1958
THE GEISHA BOY Paramount, 1958
DON'T GIVE UP THE SHIP Paramount, 1959
THE BELLBOY Paramount, 1960
CINDERFELLA Paramount, 1960
THE LADIES' MAN Paramount, 1961
POCKETFUL OF MIRACLES United Artists, 1961
THE ERRAND BOY Paramount, 1962

HAROLD LLOYD'S WORLD OF COMEDY Continental, 1962
IT'S ONLY MONEY Paramount, 1962
MY SIX LOVES Paramount, 1963
THE NUTTY PROFESSOR Paramount, 1963
HONEYMOON HOTEL MGM, 1964
WHERE LOVE HAS GONE Paramount, 1964
TICKLE ME Allied Artists, 1965
FUNNY GIRL ★ adaptation, Columbia, 1968
PENDULUM Columbia, 1969
THE CHEYENNE SOCIAL CLUB National General, 1970
BEN Cinerama Releasing Corporation, 1972
WALKING TALL Cinerama Releasing Corporation, 1973
PART 2, WALKING TALL American International, 1975
FINAL CHAPTER—WALKING TALL American International, 1977
GASP! Avala Films, 1977, Yugoslavian
NUNZIO Universal, 1978
WHEN EVERY DAY WAS THE FOURTH OF JULY (TF) Dan Curtis Productions, 1978
A REAL AMERICAN HERO (TF) Bing Crosby Productions, 1978
THE TRIANGLE FACTORY FIRE SCANDAL (TF) Alan Landsburg Productions/Don Kirshner Productions, 1979
SALVAGE (TF) Bennett-Katleman Productions/ Columbia Pictures TV, 1979
FROM HERE TO ETERNITY (MS) Bennett-Katleman Productions/Columbia Pictures TV, 1979
BLIND AMBITION (MS) Time-Life Productions Inc., 1979
MOVIOLA: THE SCARLETT O'HARA WAR (TF) David Wolper-Stan Margulies Productions/Warner Bros. TV, 1980
THE LONG DAYS OF SUMMER (TF) Dan Curtis Productions, 1980
THIS IS ELVIS (FD) Warner Bros., 1981
MIDNIGHT OFFERINGS (TF) Stephen J. Cannell Productions, 1981
TWILIGHT TIME MGM/UA, 1983, U.S.-Yugoslavian

TON SCHERPENZEEL

b. Denmark
Contact: KODA - Denmark, 011-45-31-68-38-00

SPETTERS Samuel Goldwyn Company, 1980, Dutch

PETER SCHICKELE

b. 1935 - Ames, Iowa
Contact: ASCAP - Los Angeles, 213/466-7681

FUNNYMAN New Yorker, 1967
SILENT RUNNING Universal, 1972
OH CALCUTTA! co-composer, Tigon, 1972

LALO SCHIFRIN

b. 1932 - Buenos Aires, Argentina
Agent: CAA - Los Angeles, 213/288-4545

EL JEFE 1957, Argentine
JOY HOUSE *LES FELINS* MGM, 1964, French
RHINO! MGM, 1964
SEE HOW THEY RUN (TF) Universal TV, 1964
ONCE A THIEF MGM, 1965
THE CINCINATTI KID MGM, 1965
GONE WITH THE WAVE (FD) 1965
DARK INTRUDER Universal, 1965
THE LIQUIDATOR MGM, 1966, British
I DEAL IN DANGER 20th Century-Fox, 1966
THE DOOMSDAY FLIGHT (TF) Universal TV, 1966
BLINDFOLD Universal, 1966
WAY...WAY OUT! 20th Century-Fox, 1966
HOW I SPENT MY SUMMER VACATION (TF) Universal TV, 1967
MURDERERS' ROW Columbia, 1967
SULLIVAN'S EMPIRE Universal, 1967
THE PRESIDENT'S ANALYST Paramount, 1967
WHO'S MINDING THE MINT? Columbia, 1967
COOL HAND LUKE ★ Warner Bros., 1967
THE VENETIAN AFFAIR MGM, 1967
THE FOX ★ Claridge, 1968
WHERE ANGELS GO...TROUBLE FOLLOWS! Columbia, 1968
SOL MADRID MGM, 1968
THE BROTHERHOOD Paramount, 1968
BULLITT Warner Bros., 1968
COOGAN'S BLUFF Universal, 1968
HELL IN THE PACIFIC Cinerama Releasing Corporation, 1968
U.M.C. (TF) MGM TV, 1969
CHE! 20th Century-Fox, 1969
EYE OF THE CAT Universal, 1969
THE YOUNG LAWYERS (TF) Paramount Pictures TV, 1969
PUSSYCAT, PUSSYCAT, I LOVE YOU United Artists, 1970, British
IMAGO Emerson, 1970
THE MASK OF SHEBA (TF) MGM TV, 1970
KELLY'S HEROES MGM, 1970, U.S.-Yugoslavian
THE AQUARIANS (TF) Universal TV, 1970
WUSA Paramount, 1970
I LOVE MY WIFE Universal, 1970
MRS. POLIFAX - SPY United Artists, 1971
THE BEGUILED Universal, 1971
ESCAPE (TF) Paramount TV, 1971
PRETTY MAIDS ALL IN A ROW MGM, 1971
THX-1138 Warner Bros., 1971
THE CHRISTIAN LICORICE STORE National General, 1971
THE HELLSTROM CHRONICLE (FD) Cinema 5, 1971
EARTH II (TF) MGM TV, 1971
DIRTY HARRY Warner Bros., 1972
WELCOME HOME, JOHNNY BRISTOL (TF) Cinema Center, 1972
THE WRATH OF GOD MGM, 1972
RAGE Warner Bros., 1972
JOE KID Universal, 1972
PRIME CUT National General, 1972
HUNTER (TF) CBS Entertainment, 1973
CHARLIE VARRICK Universal, 1973
ENTER THE DRAGON Warner Bros., 1973, U.S.-Hong Kong
HARRY IN YOUR POCKET United Artists, 1973
HIT! Paramount, 1973
MAGNUM FORCE Warner Bros., 1973
THE NEPTUNE FACTOR 20th Century-Fox, 1973
NIGHT GAMES (TF) Paramount TV, 1974
MAN ON A SWING Paramount, 1974
GOLDEN NEEDLES American International, 1974
THE FOUR MUSKETEERS *MILADY'S REVENGE* 20th Century-Fox, 1975, British
STARSKY AND HUTCH (TF) Spelling-Goldberg Productions, 1975
DELANCEY STREET: THE CRISIS WITHIN (TF) Paramount TV, 1975
THE MASTER GUNFIGHTER Taylor-Laughlin, 1975
GUILTY OR INNOCENT: THE SAM SHEPPARD MURDER CASE (TF) Universal TV, 1975

FOSTER AND LAURIE (TF) Charles Fries Productions, 1975
SKY RIDERS 20th Century-Fox, 1976
ST. IVES Warner Bros., 1976
SPECIAL DELIVERY American International, 1976
BRENDA STARR (TF) Wolper Productions, 1976
VOYAGE OF THE DAMNED ★ Avco Embassy, 1976, British
THE EAGLE HAS LANDED Columbia, 1977, British
DAY OF THE ANIMALS Film Ventures, 1977
ROLLERCOASTER Universal, 1977
GOOD AGAINST EVIL (TF) Frankel-Bolen Productions/ 20th Century-Fox TV, 1977
TELEFON MGM/United Artists, 1977
THE MANITOU Avco Embassy, 1978
THE PRESIDENT'S MISTRESS (TF) Stephen Friedman/ Kings Road Productions, 1978
NUNZIO Universal, 1978
RETURN FROM WITCH MOUNTAIN Buena Vista, 1978
THE CAT FROM OUTER SPACE Buena Vista, 1978
THE NATIVITY (TF) D'Angelo-Bullock-Allen Productions/ 20th Century-Fox TV, 1978
LOVE AND BULLETS AFD, 1979
INSTITUTE FOR REVENGE (TF) Gold-Driskill Productions/Columbia TV, 1979
ESCAPE TO ATHENA AFD, 1979, British
BOULEVARD NIGHTS Warner Bros., 1979
THE CONCORDE - AIRPORT '79 Universal, 1979
THE AMITYVILLE HORROR ★ American International, 1979
SERIAL Paramount, 1980
WHEN TIME RAN OUT Warner Bros., 1980
THE NUDE BOMB Universal, 1980
BRUBAKER 20th Century-Fox, 1980
THE BIG BRAWL Warner Bros., 1980
THE COMPETITION ★ Columbia, 1980
LOOPHOLE MGM/United Artists, 1981, British
THE CHICAGO STORY (TF) Eric Bercovici Productions/MGM TV, 1981
CAVEMAN United Artists, 1981
LA PELLE 1981, Italian
BUDDY BUDDY MGM/United Artists, 1981
THE SEDUCTION Avco Embassy, 1981
VICTIMS (TF) Hajeno Productions/Warner Bros. TV, 1982
THE CLASS OF 1984 United Film Distribution, 1982, Canadian
LAS VIERNES DE LA ETERNIDAD 1982, Argentine
FAST-WALKING Pickman Films, 1982
A STRANGER IS WATCHING MGM/United Artists, 1982
AMITYVILLE II: THE POSSESSION Orion, 1982
FALCON'S GOLD (CTF) Paul Heller Productions/ Schulz Productions/Sonesta Productions/Intrepid Productions, 1982
STARFLIGHT: THE PLANE THAT COULDN'T LAND (TF) Orgolini-Nelson Productions, 1983
DOCTOR DETROIT Universal, 1983
THE STING II ★ adaptation, Universal, 1983
SUDDEN IMPACT Warner Bros., 1983
THE OSTERMAN WEEKEND 20th Century-Fox, 1983
RITA HAYWORTH: THE LOVE GODDESS (TF) The Susskind Company, 1983
PRINCESS DAISY (TF) Steve Krantz Productions/NBC Entertainment, 1983
TANK Universal, 1984
SPRAGGUE (TF) MG Productions/Lorimar Productions, 1984
THE NEW KIDS Columbia, 1985
A.D. (TF) Procter & Gamble Productions/International Film Productions, 1985
HOLLYWOOD WIVES (MS) Aaron Spelling Productions, 1985
PRIVATE SESSIONS (TF) Raven's Claw Productions/ Seltzer-Gimbel Productions/Comworld Productions, 1985
THE MEAN SEASON Orion, 1985
BAD MEDICINE 20th Century Fox, 1985
COMMAND 5 (TF) Paramount Pictures TV, 1985
BRIDGE ACROSS TIME (TF) Fries Entertainment, 1985
KUNG FU: THE MOVIE (TF) Lou-Step Productions/Warner Bros. TV, 1986
TRIPLECROSS (TF) Tisch-Avnet Productions/ABC Circle Films, 1986
THE LADIES CLUB New Line Cinema, 1986
BEVERLY HILLS MADAM (TF) BLS Productions/Orion TV Productions, 1986
BLACK MOON RISING New World, 1986
OUT ON A LIMB (TF) Stan Margulies Co./ABC Circle Films, 1987
THE FOURTH PROTOCOL Lorimar, 1987, British
EARTH*STAR VOYAGER (TF) Walt Disney TV/Marstar Productions, 1988
SHAKEDOWN ON THE SUNSET STRIP (TF) CBS Entertainment, 1988
THE SILENCE AT BETHANY Keener Productions/ American Playhouse Theatrical Films, 1988
THE DEAD POOL Warner Bros., 1988
LITTLE SWEETHEART Columbia, 1988, U.S.-British
FRIDAYS OF ETERNITY Aires, 1989
ORIGINAL SIN (TF) The Larry Thompson Organization/ New World TV, 1989
THE NEON EMPIRE (CTF) Fries Entertainment, 1989
LITTLE WHITE LIES (TF) Larry A. Thompson Organization/ New World TV, 1989

BARRY SCHRADER

GALAXY OF TERROR *MINDWARP: AN INFINITY OF TERROR/PLANET OF HORRORS* New World, 1981

GREG SCHULTZ

Contact: APRA - Australia, 011-61-2-922-6422

FRAN Harron Films, 1985, Australian

KLAUS SCHULZE

BARRACUDA *THE LUCIFER PROJECT* 1978

GERARD SCHURMANN

b. January 19, 1928 - Dutch East Indies
Contact: Carolyn Nott, Los Angeles - 213/850-0744

BUT NOT IN VAIN 1948, British-Dutch
THE THIRD KEY *THE LONG ARM* Ealing, 1956, British
DECISION AGAINST TIME *THE MAN IN THE SKY* MGM, 1956, British
THE RUTHLESS ONE 1957, British
THE CAMP ON BLOOD ISLAND Columbia, 1958, British
THE NUMBER SEVEN British Lion, 1959, British
THE HEADLESS GHOST American International, 1959
THE TWO-HEADED SPY Columbia, 1959
HORRORS OF THE BLACK MUSEUM American International, 1959, British
THE DESPERATE MAN 1959, British
CONE OF SILENCE Bryanston, 1960, British
THE LIVING EARTH (FD) Buena Vista, 1961
PAYROLL 1961, British
KONGA American International, 1961, British
DR. SYN, ALIAS THE SCARECROW Buena Vista, 1962, originally made for television
DAY IN DAY OUT 1965, British

THE BEDFORD INCIDENT Columbia, 1965
ATTACK ON THE IRON COAST United Artists, 1968, U.S.-British
THE LOST CONTINENT Warner Bros., 1968
CLARETTA Trans World, 1984, Italian

NAN SCHWARTZ

Agent: Gorfaine-Schwartz - Burbank, 818/954-9500

HOME (TF) Leonard Goldberg Productions, 1986
UNDER THE INFLUENCE (TF) ☆ CBS Entertainment, 1986
SHE WAS MARKED FOR MURDER (TF) Jack Grossbart Productions, 1988
TURN BACK THE CLOCK (TF) Michael Filerman Productions/Republic/NBC Productions, 1989

STEPHEN SCHWARTZ

Contact: ASCAP - Los Angeles, 213/466-7681

ECHOES Continental, 1983

GARRY SCHYMAN

Agent: Carol Faith - Beverly Hills, 213/274-0776

TALES OF THE GOLD MONKEY (TF) Universal TV/ Belisarius Productions, 1982
ASSASSIN (TF) co-composer, Sankan\ Productions, 1986
NEVER TOO YOUNG TO DIE Paul Releasing, 1986
PENITENTIARY III Cannon, 1987
HIT LIST New Line Cinema, 1989
JUDGMENT Juvie Productions, 1989

ILONA SCKACZ

BACK HOME (CTF) TVS Films/Verronmead Productions/Citadel, 1990, British-U.S.

GARY SCOTT

b. Los Angeles, California
Agent: Richard Emler - Los Angeles, 213/651-0222

FINAL EXAM MPM, 1981
DEADLY FORCE Embassy, 1983
ROADHOUSE 66 Atlantic Releasing, 1984
THE FULFILLMENT OF MARY GRAY (TF) Mary Gray Inc./Lee Caplin Productions/Indian Neck Entertainment, 1989
DECEPTIONS (CTF) Republic Pictures, 1990

JOHN SCOTT

b. November 1, 1930 - Bristol, England
Agent: Gorfaine-Schwartz - Burbank, 818/954-9500

A STUDY IN TERROR Columbia, 1965, British
CARNABY, M.D. *DOCTOR IN CLOVER* Continental, 1966, British
THE LONG DUEL Paramount, 1967, British
THE 1,000 EYES OF SU-MURU 1967, Japanese
COP-OUT *STRANGER IN THE HOUSE* Rank, 1967, British
THOSE FANTASTIC FLYING FOOLS *BLAST OFF/ JULES VERNE'S ROCKET TO THE MOON* American International, 1967, British
BERSERK! Columbia, 1968, British
AMSTERDAM AFFAIR Lippert, 1968, British
SOPHIE'S PLACE *CROOKS AND CORONETS* Warner Bros., 1969, British
THE VIOLENT ENEMY 1969, British
TROG Warner Bros., 1970, British
LOLA *TWINKY* American International, 1970, British-Italian
CONQUISTA 1971
GIRL STROKE BOY London Screen Distributors, 1971, British
OUTBACK *WAKE IN FRIGHT* United Artists, 1971, Australian
BILLY TWO HATS United Artists, 1972, British
DOOMWATCH Avco Embassy, 1972, British
WILD DOG IN AMERICA (TD) ☆☆ 1972
THE JERUSALEM FILE MGM, 1972, U.S.-Israeli
ANTONY AND CLEOPATRA Rank, 1973, British-Spanish-Swiss
ENGLAND MADE ME Cine Globe, 1973, British
CRAZE Warner Bros., 1974, British
S HP HY HS European version only, 20th Century-Fox, 1974, British-U.S.
SYMPTOMS *THE BLOOD VIRGIN* 1974
HENNESSY American International, 1975, British
THAT LUCKY TOUCH Allied Artists, 1975, British
SATAN'S SLAVE 1976
THE PEOPLE THAT TIME FORGOT American International, 1977, British
THE QUINNS (TF) Daniel Wilson Productions, 1977
NORTH DALLAS FORTY Paramount, 1979
THE HOSTAGE TOWER (TF) Jerry Leider Productions, 1980
THE FINAL COUNTDOWN United Artists, 1980
HORROR PLANET *INSEMINOID* Almi Films, 1982, British
YOR, THE HUNTER FROM THE FUTURE co-composer, Columbia, 1983, Italian-Turkish-U.S.
GREYSTOKE: THE LEGEND OF TARZAN, LORD OF THE APES Warner Bros., 1984, British-U.S.
THE SHOOTING PARTY European Classics, 1984, British
WET GOLD (TF) Telepictures Corporation, 1984
BLOOD ROYAL (TF) Goldcrest Films, British
MOUNTBATTEN: THE LAST VICEROY (MS) George Walker TV Productions, 1986, British
HAREM (TS) Highgate Pictures, 1986
KING KONG LIVES DEG, 1986
THE WHISTLE BLOWER Hemdale, 1987
MAN ON FIRE Tri-Star, 1987, Italian-French
THE DECEIVERS Cinecom, 1988
SHOOT TO KILL Buena Vista, 1988
WINTER PEOPLE Columbia, 1989
RED KING, WHITE KNIGHT (CTF) John Kemeny Citdale Entertainment/Zenith, 1989
DOG TAGS Cinecrest Entertainment Group, 1990

TOM SCOTT

b. 1948
Agent: Gorfaine-Schwartz - Burbank, 818/954-9500

THE CULPEPPER CATTLE CO. 20th Century-Fox, 1972
CONQUEST OF THE PLANET OF THE APES 20th Century-Fox, 1972
TROUBLE COMES TO TOWN (TF) ABC Circle Films, 1973
THE GIRLS OF HUNTINGTON HOUSE (TF) Lorimar Productions, 1973
FIREHOUSE (TF) Metromedia Producers Corporation/ Stonehenge Productions, 1973
CLASS OF '63 (TF) Metromedia Productions/Stonehenge Productions, 1973
THE NINE LIVES OF FRITZ THE CAT (AF) American International, 1974
SIDECAR RACERS Universal, 1975, Australian

TWIN DETECTIVES (TF) Charles Fries Productions, 1976
ASPEN (MS) co-composer with Michael Melvoin, Universal TV, 1977
THE COMPANY COMEDY (TF) Malloy-Adler Productions/MGM TV, 1978
AMERICATHON United Artists, 1979
STIR CRAZY Columbia, 1980
OUR FAMILY BUSINESS (TF) Lorimar Productions, 1981
HANKY PANKY Columbia, 1982
CLASS additional music, Orion, 1983
GOING BERSERK Universal, 1983, Canadian
HARD TO HOLD Universal, 1984
FAST FORWARD co-composer with Jack Hayes, Columbia, 1985
THE SURE THING Embassy, 1985
JUST ONE OF THE GUYS Columbia, 1985
FAMILY TIES VACATION (TF) UBU Productions/ Paramount Pictures TV, 1985
BADGE OF THE ASSASSIN (TF) Daniel H. Blatt/Robert Singer Productions, 1985
SOUL MAN New World, 1986
THE LEFTOVERS (TF) Walt Disney TV, 1986
NOT QUITE HUMAN (CTF) Sharmhill Productions/Walt Disney TV, 1987
A FATHER'S HOMECOMING (TF) NBC Productions, 1988
RUN TILL YOU FALL (TF) CBS Entertainment, 1988

BILLY SCREAM

MARK TWAIN (AF) Atlantic Releasing Corporation, 1985

EARL SCRUGGS

Contact: BMI - Los Angeles, 213/659-9109

WHERE THE LILLIES BLOOM United Artists, 1974

PETER SCULTHORPE

Contact: APRA - Australia, 011-61-2-922-6422

BURKE & WILLIS Hemdale, 1985, Australian

JAY SEAGRAVE

THE CENSUS TAKER Argentum Prods., 1984

MALCOLM SEAGRAVE

PHANTASM co-composer with Fred Myrow, Avco Embassy, 1979

WALTER SEAR

DR. BUTCHER, M.D. Aquarius, 1982, Italian
THE ORACLE co-composer, Reeltime Distributing, 1987
LURKERS Concorde, 1988

JOHN SEBASTIAN

Agent: BMI - Los Angeles, 213/659-9109

YOU'RE A BIG BOY NOW 7 Arts, 1966
THE JERK, TOO (TF) co-composer with Phil Galston, Share Productions/Universal TV, 1984
THE CARE BEARS MOVIE (AF) Samuel Goldwyn Company, 1985

DON SEBESKY

Contact: ASCAP - Los Angeles, 213/466-7681

F. SCOTT FITZGERALD AND "THE LAST OF THE BELLES" (TF) Titus Productions, 1974
HOW TO PICK UP GIRLS! (TF) King-Hitzig Productions, 1978
HOLLOW IMAGE (TF) Titus Productions, 1979
THE ROSARY MURDERS co-composer with Bobby Laurel, Samuel Goldwyn Company, 1987

JERRY SEGAL

Contact: BMI - Los Angeles, 213/659-9109

DIE LAUGHING co-composer with Robby Benson and Craig Safan, Orion, 1980

MISHA SEGAL

Contact: BMI - Los Angeles, 213/659-9109

TWO HEARTBEATS 1972, Israeli
THE FACTS OF LIFE GOES TO PARIS (TF) Embassy TV, 1982
BERRY GORDY'S THE LAST DRAGON *THE LAST DRAGON* Tri-Star, 1985
LETHAL *KGB—THE SECRET WAR* Cinema Group, 1985
KNIGHTS OF THE CITY New World, 1986
UNSETTLED LAND *ONCE WE WERE DREAMERS* Hemdale, 1987, U.S.-Israeli
LENA: MY 100 CHILDREN (TF) Robert Greenwald Productions, 1987
THE NEW ADVENTURES OF PIPPI LONGSTALKING Columbia, 1988
THE PHANTOM OF THE OPERA 21st Century, 1989

BERNARDO SEGALL

THE GREAT ST. LOUIS BANK ROBBERY United Artists, 1959
THE LUCK OF GINGER COFFEY Continental, 1964, Canadian
HALLUCINATION GENERATION 1966
CUSTER OF THE WEST Cinerama Releasing Corporation, 1968, U.S.-Spanish
LOVING Columbia, 1970
NIGHT SLAVES (TF) Bing Crosby Productions, 1970
THE JESUS TRIP EMCO, 1971
MOON OF THE WOLF (TF) Filmways, 1972
THE GIRL MOST LIKELY TO... (TF) ABC Circle Films, 1973
HOMEBODIES Avco Embassy, 1974
TURNOVER SMITH (TF) Wellington Productions, 1980

MATYAS SEIBER

Contact: PRS - London, England, 011-44-1-580-5544

THE MAGIC CANVAS (AF) 1949, British
THE FAKE adaptation, 1953
THE DIAMOND WIZARD 1954
ANIMAL FARM (AF) 1954, British
THE OWL AND THE PUSSYCAT (FD) 1954
A TOWN LIKE ALICE *RAPE OF MALAYA* 1956, British
THE SHIRALEE 1956, British
CHASE A CROOKED SHADOW Warner Bros., 1958, British
THE MARK OF THE HAWK 1958, British
ROBBERY UNDER ARMS 1958, British
MALAGA *MOMENT OF DANGER* Warner Bros., 1959

LEON SEITH
OH HEAVENLY DOG 20th Century-Fox, 1980

ILONA SEKACZ
Contact: PRS - London, England, 011-44-1-580-5544

INTIMATE CONTACT (CTF) Zenith Productions/ Central TV, 1987, British

WLADIMIR SELINSKY
GOODBYE RAGGEDY ANN (TF) Metromedia Producers Corporation, 1971
SOMETHING EVIL (TF) Belford Productions/CBS International, 1972
MILES TO GO BEFORE I SLEEP (TF) Roger Gimbel Productions/Tomorrow Entertainment, 1975
FAMILY REUNION (TF) Creative Projects/Columbia Pictures TV, 1981

DOV SELTZER
Contact: ACUM - Tel Aviv, Israel, Telex: 922-342471

TRUNK TO CAIRO American International, 1967, Israeli-West German
EAGLES ATTACK AT DAWN 1970, Israeli
HIGHWAY QUEEN 1971, Israeli
ESCAPE TO THE SUN Cinevision, 1972, Israeli-West German-French
I LOVE YOU, ROSA 1972, Israeli
KAZABLAN MGM, 1973, Israeli
MOSES (MS) additional music, ITC/RAI, 1975, British-Italian
THE RABBI AND THE SHIKSE 1976, Israeli
OPERATION THUNDERBOLT 1977, Israeli
MILLIONAIRE IN TROUBLE 1978, Israeli
KUNI LEMI IN TEL AVIV 1978, Israeli
THE AMBASSADOR MGM/UA/Cannon, 1984
HAME'AHEV *THE LOVER* Cannon, 1986
HANNA'S WAR Cannon, 1988

CAIPHUS SEMENYA
THE COLOR PURPLE ★ co-composer, Warner Bros., 1985

FRANK SERAFINE
Agent: Robert Light - Los Angeles, 213/651-1777

NIGHTFALL Concorde, 1988

RENATO SERIO
Contact: SIAE - Rome, Italy, 011-39-6-59-90-1

ALONE IN THE DARK New Line Cinema, 1982
SILHOUETTES Primi Piani Enterprises, 1982

ERIC SERRA
Contact: SACEM - France, 011-33-14-747-5650

LE DERNIER COMBAT Gaumont/Les Films du Loup/ Constantin Alexandrof Productions, 1983, French
SUBWAY Island Pictures, 1985, French
THE BIG BLUE composer of European version, Columbia/WEG, 1988, French

FRANCIS SEYRIG
Contact: SACEM - France, 011-33-14-747-5650

LAST YEAR AT MARIENBAD Astor, 1961, French-Italian
THE TRIAL OF JOAN OF ARC Pathe Contemporary, 1962, French
MARIE SOLEIL 1964, French

MARC SHAIMAN
Agent: ICM - Los Angeles, 213/550-4000

WHEN HARRY MET SALLY... adaptation, Columbia, 1989

RAVI SHANKAR
b. 1920 - Varanasi, Uttar Pradesh, India
Agent: Robert Light - Los Angeles, 213/651-1777

PANTHER PANCHALI 1956, Indian
APARAJITO 1958, Indian
THE WORLD OF APU 1959, Indian
CHAPPAQUA Hunter, 1966, Indian
CHARLY Cinerama Releasing Corporation, 1968
RAGA 1971, Indian
GANDHI ★ co-composer with George Fenton, Columbia, 1982, British-Indian
GENESIS Scarabee Films, 1986, Indian-French-Belgian-Swiss

RAY SHANKLIN
Contact: BMI - Los Angeles, 213/659-9109

BLACK GIRL Cinerama Releasing Corporation, 1972
FRITZ THE CAT (AF) co-composer with Ed Bogas, American International, 1972
HEAVY TRAFFIC (AF) co-composer with Ed Bogas, American International, 1973

TED SHAPIRO
BLOODEATERS Parker National, 1980

THOM SHARP
LAST RESORT co-composer with Steve Nelson, Concorde, 1986

AVERY SHARPE
AN UNREMARKABLE LIFE Continental Film Group, 1989

JONATHAN SHEFFER
Agent: ICM - Los Angeles, 213/550-4000

ON VALENTINE'S DAY Angelika Films, 1986
VIETNAM WAR STORY (CTF) Nexus Productions, 1987
IN A SHALLOW GRAVE Skouras Pictures, 1988
LIKEWISE Cinema Group, 1988
BLOODHOUNDS OF BROADWAY Columbia, 1989
DINNER AT EIGHT (CTF) Think Entertainment/Turner Network TV, 1989

BERT A. SHEFTER
b. 1904 - Russia

ONE TOO MANY co-composer with Nelly Coletti, 1950
HOLIDAY RHYTHM Lippert, 1950
DANGER ZONE Lippert, 1951
LEAVE IT TO THE MARINES Lippert, 1951
PIER 23 Lippert, 1951
ROARING CITY Lippert, 1951
SKY HIGH Lippert, 1951

M Columbia, 1951
NO ESCAPE United Artists, 1953
SCANDAL, INC. co-composer with Paul Sawtell, Republic, 1956
THE DESPERADOES ARE IN TOWN co-composer with Paul Sawtell, 20th Century-Fox, 1956
THE DEERSLAYER co-composer with Paul Sawtell, 20th Century-Fox, 1957
GHOST DIVER co-composer with Paul Sawtell, 20th Century-Fox, 1957
GUN DUEL IN DURANGO co-composer with Paul Sawtell, United Artists, 1957
HELL SHIP MUTINY co-composer with Paul Sawtell, Republic, 1957
THE BLACK SCORPION co-composer with Paul Sawtell and Jack Cookerly, Warner Bros., 1957
SHE DEVIL co-composer with Paul Sawtell, 20th Century-Fox, 1957
KRONOS co-composer with Paul Sawtell, 20th Century-Fox, 1957
MONKEY ON MY BACK co-composer with Paul Sawtell, United Artists, 1957
AMBUSH AT CIMARRON PASS co-composer with Paul Sawtell, 20th Century-Fox, 1958
THE FLY co-composer with Paul Sawtell, 20th Century-Fox, 1958
CATTLE EMPIRE co-composer with Paul Sawtell, 20th Century-Fox, 1958
HONG KONG CONFIDENTIAL co-composer with Paul Sawtell, United Artists, 1958
IT! THE TERROR FROM BEYOND SPACE co-composer with Paul Sawtell, United Artists, 1958
MACHETE co-composer with Paul Sawtell, United Artists, 1958
SIERRA BARON co-composer with Paul Sawtell, 20th Century-Fox, 1958
VILLA! co-composer with Paul Sawtell, 20th Century-Fox, 1958
THE COSMIC MAN co-composer with Paul Sawtell, Allied Artists, 1959
COUNTERPLOT co-composer with Paul Sawtell, United Artists, 1959
THE MIRACLE OF THE HILLS co-composer with Paul Sawtell, 20th Century-Fox, 1959
THE SAD HORSE co-composer with Paul Sawtell, 20th Century-Fox, 1959
VICE RAID co-composer with Paul Sawtell, United Artists, 1959
RETURN OF THE FLY co-composer with Paul Sawtell, 20th Century-Fox, 1959
A DOG OF FLANDERS co-composer with Paul Sawtell, 20th Century-Fox, 1959
THE BIG CIRCUS co-composer with Paul Sawtell, Allied Artists, 1959
A DOG'S BEST FRIEND co-composer with Paul Sawtell, United Artists, 1960
THE LOST WORLD co-composer, 20th Century-Fox, 1960
TESS OF THE STORM COUNTRY co-composer with Paul Sawtell, 20th Century-Fox, 1960
THREE CAME TO KILL United Artists, 1960
FIVE GUNS TO TOMBSTONE co-composer with Paul Sawtell, United Artists, 1960
FRONTIER UPRISING co-composer with Paul Sawtell, United Artists, 1961
VOYAGE TO THE BOTTOM OF THE SEA co-composer with Paul Sawtell, 20th Century-Fox, 1961
THE LONG ROPE co-composer with Paul Sawtell, 20th Century-Fox, 1961
PIRATES OF TORTUGA co-composer with Paul Sawtell, 20th Century-Fox, 1961
JACK THE GIANT KILLER co-composer with Paul Sawtell, United Artists, 1962
THUNDER ISLAND co-composer with Paul Sawtell, 20th Century-Fox, 1963
THE LAST MAN ON EARTH co-composer with Paul Sawtell, 1964, U.S.-Italian
THE CURSE OF THE FLY 20th Century-Fox, 1965
MOTOR PSYCHO co-composer with Paul Sawtell, Eve, 1965
THE BUBBLE *FANTASTIC INVASION OF THE PLANET EARTH* co-composer with Paul Sawtell, Oboler Films, 1967
THE LAST SHOT YOU HEAR 20th Century-Fox, 1969, British
THE CHRISTINE JORGENSEN STORY co-composer with Paul Sawtell, United Artists, 1970

MARK SHEKTER

Contact: Pro-Canada - Canada, 1-416-445-8700

B.S. I LOVE YOU 20th Century-Fox, 1971

ERNIE SHELDON

Contact: ASCAP - Los Angeles, 213/466-7681

HARD TRAVELING New World, 1986

KIRBY SHELSTAD

Contact: BMI - Los Angeles, 213/659-9109

ERNEST GOES TO JAIL co-composer with Bruce Arnstson, Buena Vista, 1990

THOMAS Z. SHEPARD

Contact: BMI - Los Angeles, 213/659-9109

SUCH GOOD FRIENDS Paramount, 1971

BOBBY SHERMAN

Contact: BMI - Los Angeles, 213/659-9109

THE DAY THE EARTH MOVED (TF) ABC Circle Films, 1974

GARRY SHERMAN

Contact: ASCAP - Los Angeles, 213/466-7681

ALICE'S RESTAURANT United Artists, 1969
BEEN DOWN SO LONG IT LOOKS LIKE UP TO ME Paramount, 1971
THE HEARTBREAK KID 20th Century-Fox, 1972
PARADES Cinerama Releasing Corporation, 1972
JOHNNY, WE HARDLY KNEW YE (TF) Talent Associates/Jamel Productions, 1977
THE KID FROM NOWHERE (TF) Cates-Bridges Company, 1982
CHILD'S CRY (TF) Shoot the Moon Enterprises/Phoenix Entertainment Group, 1986
WHATEVER IT TAKES Aquarius Films, 1986

JOE SHERMAN

Contact: ASCAP - Los Angeles, 213/466-7681

BRASS (TF) Carnan Productions/Jaygee Productions/Orion TV, 1985

DAVID SHIRE

b. July 3, 1937 - Buffalo, New York
Agent: Gorfaine-Schwartz - Burbank, 818/954-9500

HARPY (TF) Cinema Center 100, 1970
McCLOUD: WHO KILLED MISS U.S.A.? (TF) Universal TV, 1970
MARRIAGE: YEAR ONE (TF) Universal TV, 1971
THE IMPATIENT HEART (TF) Universal TV, 1971
ONE MORE TRAIN TO ROB Universal, 1971
THE PRIEST KILLER (TF) Universal TV, 1971
SUMMERTREE Columbia, 1971
SKIN GAME Warner Bros., 1971
DRIVE, HE SAID Columbia, 1971
SEE THE MAN RUN (TF) Universal TV, 1971
TO FIND A MAN *THE BOY NEXT DOOR/SEX AND THE TEENAGER* Columbia, 1972
ISN'T IT SHOCKING? (TF) ABC Circle Films, 1973
STEELYARD BLUES adaptation, Warner Bros., 1973
TWO PEOPLE Universal, 1973
SHOWDOWN Universal, 1973
CLASS OF '44 Warner Bros., 1973
KILLER BEES (TF) RSO Films, 1974
SIDEKICKS (TF) Warner Bros. TV, 1974
THE TRIBE (TF) Universal TV, 1974
TELL ME WHERE IT HURTS (TF) Tomorrow Entertainment, 1974
THE CONVERSATION Paramount, 1974
LUCAS TANNER (TF) Universal TV, 1974
THE HEALERS (TF) Warner Bros. TV, 1974
THE TAKING OF PELHAM 1-2-3 United Artists, 1974
THE GODCHILD (TF) MGM TV, 1974
WINNER TAKE ALL (TF) The Jozak Company, 1975
THE FORTUNE adaptation, Columbia, 1975
FAREWELL, MY LOVELY Avco Embassy, 1975
THE HINDENBERG Universal, 1975
OREGON TRAIL (TF) Universal TV, 1976
ALL THE PRESIDENT'S MEN Warner Bros., 1976
McNAUGHTON'S DAUGHTER (TF) Universal TV, 1976
AMELIA EARHART (TF) Universal TV, 1976
THE BIG BUS Paramount, 1976
HARRY AND WALTER GO TO NEW YORK Columbia, 1976
SOMETHING FOR JOEY (TF) MTM Productions, 1977
THE GREATEST THING THAT ALMOST HAPPENED (TF) Charles Fries Productions, 1977
SATURDAY NIGHT FEVER Paramount, 1977
RAID ON ENTEBBE (TF) ☆ Edgar J. Scherick Associates/20th Century-Fox TV, 1977
THE STORYTELLER (TF) co-composer with Hal Mooney, Universal TV, 1977
STRAIGHT TIME Warner Bros., 1978
DADDY, I DON'T LIKE IT LIKE THIS (TF) CBS Entertainment, 1978
THE DEFECTION OF SIMAS KUDIRKA (TF) ☆ The Jozak Company/Paramount TV, 1978
THE PROMISE Universal, 1979
OLD BOYFRIENDS Avco Embassy, 1979
FAST BREAK Columbia, 1979
NORMA RAE 20th Century-Fox, 1979
NEIL SIMON'S ONLY WHEN I LAUGH Columbia, 1981
THE NIGHT THE LIGHTS WENT OUT IN GEORGIA Avco Embassy, 1981
PATERNITY Paramount, 1981
THE WORLD ACCORDING TO GARP Warner Bros., 1982
MAX DUGAN RETURNS 20th Century-Fox, 1983
OH, GOD! YOU DEVIL Warner Bros., 1984
2010 MGM/UA, 1984
DO YOU REMEMBER LOVE (TF) ☆ Dave Bell Productions, 1985
RETURN TO OZ Buena Vista, 1985
TIME FLYER (TF) Three Blind Mice Productions, 1986
SHORT CIRCUIT Tri-Star, 1986
PROMISE (TF) Garner-Duchow Productions/Warner Bros. TV, 1986
'NIGHT, MOTHER Universal, 1986
BACKFIRE New Century/Vista, 1987
CONVICTED: A MOTHER'S STORY (TF) NBC Productions, 1987
MAYFLOWER MADAM (TF) Robert Halmi Inc., 1987
JOSEPH WAMBAUGH'S ECHOES IN THE DARKNESS *ECHOES IN THE DARKNESS (MS)* Litke-Grossbart Productions/New World TV, 1987
VICE VERSA Columbia, 1988
MONKEY SHINES Orion, 1988
JESSE (TF) Turman-Foster Company/Jordan Productions/ Republic Pictures, 1988
GOD BLESS THE CHILD (TF) Indieprod Company/Phoenix Entertainment Group, 1988
THE WOMEN OF BREWSTER PLACE (MS) Phoenix Entertainment Group, 1989
I KNOW MY FIRST NAME IS STEVEN (TF) Lorimar/NBC Productions, 1989
THE KENNEDYS OF MASSACHUSETTS (MS) ☆ Edgar J. Scherick Associates/Orion TV, 1990

SHELDON SHKOLNIK

TELL ME A RIDDLE Filmways, 1980

HOWARD SHORE

b. Canada
Agent: Triad Artists - Los Angeles, 213/556-2727

I MISS YOU, HUGS AND KISSES 1978, Canadian
THE BROOD New World, 1979, Canadian
SCANNERS Avco Embassy, 1981, Canadian
VIDEODROME Universal, 1983, Canadian
PLACES IN THE HEART Tri-Star, 1984
AFTER HOURS The Geffen Company/Warner Bros., 1985
BELIZAIRE THE CAJUN Skouras Pictures, 1986
FIRE WITH FIRE Paramount, 1986
THE FLY 20th Century Fox, 1986, U.S.-Canadian
HEAVEN (FD) Island Pictures, 1987
NADINE Tri-Star, 1987
MOVING Warner Bros., 1988
BIG 20th Century Fox, 1988
DEAD RINGERS 20th Century Fox, 1988, Canadian
AN INNOCENT MAN Buena Vista, 1989
SHE DEVIL Orion, 1989
QUICK CHANGE additional music, Warner Bros., 1990
THE SILENCE OF THE LAMBS Orion, 1990

RICHARD SHORES

Contact: ASCAP - Los Angeles, 213/466-7681

LOOK IN ANY WINDOW Allied Artists, 1961
TOMBOY AND THE CHAMP Universal, 1961
THE LAST CHALLENGE MGM, 1967
A MATTER OF WIFE...AND DEATH (TF) Robert M. Weitman Productions/Columbia Pictures TV, 1976
THE QUEST (TF) David Gerber Productions/Columbia Pictures TV, 1976
A KILLING AFFAIR (TF) David Gerber Productions/ Columbia Pictures TV, 1977
COVER GIRLS (TF) David Gerber Productions/Columbia Pictures TV, 1977
THE COURAGE AND THE PASSION (TF) David Gerber Productions/Columbia Pictures TV, 1978
THE BILLION DOLLAR THREAT (TF) David Gerber Productions/Columbia Pictures TV, 1979

PHYLLIS SHOTWELL
CALIFORNIA SPLIT Columbia, 1974

MARK SHREEVE
Agent: Bart-Milander - North Hollywood, 818/761-4040

TURNAROUND Major/Rose Productions, 1987
BUY AND CELL Trans World Entertainment, 1989
HONOR BOUND MGM/UA, 1989, U.S.-French

MICHAEL SHRIEVE
Contact: BMI - Los Angeles, 213/659-9109

THE CHILDREN OF TIMES SQUARE (TF) Gross-Weston Productions/Fries Entertainment, 1986
THE BEDROOM WINDOW co-composer with Patrick Gleeson, DEG, 1987
THE TAKE (CTF) co-composer with David Beal, Cine-Nevada Inc./MCA-TV, 1990

WATAZUMIDO SHUOO
THE SACRIFICE Orion Classics, 1986, Swedish-French

ELIE SIEGMEISTER
b. 1909 - New York

THEY CAME TO CORDURA Columbia, 1959

JEFFREY SILVERMAN
Contact: ASCAP - Los Angeles, 213/466-7681

AND ONCE UPON A TIME *FANTASIES* Joseph Brenner Associates, 1973

STANLEY SILVERMAN
Contact: BMI - Los Angeles, 213/659-9109

SIMON Orion, 1980
EYEWITNESS 20th Century-Fox, 1981
I'M DANCING AS FAST AS I CAN Paramount, 1982

ALAN SILVESTRI
Agent: Lawrence B. Marks - Northridge, 818/831-1830

LAS VEGAS LADY Crown International, 1976
THE AMAZING DOBERMANS Golden, 1976
PAR OU TES RENTRE...*ON TA PAS VU SORTIR* Carthago Films, 1984, French
ROMANCING THE STONE 20th Century Fox, 1984
FANDANGO Warner Bros., 1985
STEPHEN KING'S CAT'S EYE *CAT'S EYE* MGM/UA, 1985
BACK TO THE FUTURE Universal, 1985
SUMMER RENTAL Paramount, 1985
DELTA FORCE Cannon, 1986
AMERICAN ANTHEM Columbia, 1986
CLAN OF THE CAVE BEAR Warner Bros., 1986
FLIGHT OF THE NAVIGATOR Buena Vista, 1986
NO MERCY Tri-Star, 1987
CRITICAL CONDITION Paramount, 1987
OUTRAGEOUS FORTUNE Buena Vista, 1987
PREDATOR 20th Century Fox, 1987
OVERBOARD MGM/UA, 1987
MAC AND ME Orion, 1988
WHO FRAMED ROGER RABBIT? Buena Vista, 1988
MY STEPMOTHER IS AN ALIEN Columbia/WEG, 1988
SHE'S OUT OF CONTROL Columbia/WEG, 1989
THE ABYSS 20th Century Fox, 1989
TALES FROM THE CRYPT (CTF) co-composer, Tales from the Crypt Holdings, 1989
BACK TO THE FUTURE 2 Universal, 1989
DOWNTOWN 20th Century-Fox, 1990
BACK TO THE FUTURE 3 Universal, 1990
YOUNG GUNS II 20th Century-Fox, 1990

CARLY SIMON
b. June 25, 1945
Contact: ASCAP - Los Angeles, 213/466-7681

HEARTBURN Paramount, 1986
POSTCARDS FROM THE EDGE Columbia, 1990

MARTY SIMON
Agent: Derek Power

EDDIE AND THE CRUISERS II: EDDIE LIVES co-composer with Leon Aronson, Scotti Bros. Pictures/ Aurora Film Partners, 1989
GEORGE'S ISLAND Salter Street Films/Telefilm Canada/ National Film Board of Canada, 1989, Canadian

PAUL SIMON
b. November 8, 1942 - Newark, New Jersey
Contact: BMI - Los Angeles, 213/659-9109

ONE TRICK PONY Warner Bros., 1980

MICHAEL SIMPSON
Contact: Pro-Canada - Canada, 1-416-445-8700

HOT ROD (TF) ABC Circle Films, 1979

IVOR SLANEY
Contact: PRS - London, England, 011-44-1-580-5544

TERROR Crown International, 1979, British

DAN SLIDER
Agent: Robert Light - Los Angeles, 213/651-1777

KID NINJAS Reel Movies
FORCE OF THE NINJA Reel Movies
UNINVITED Amazing Movies, 1988
DEMONWARP Vidmark, 1988
SKINHEADS Amazing Movies, 1989

TOM SLOCUM
Contact: BMI - Los Angeles, 213/659-9109

CATTLE ANNIE AND LITTLE BRITCHES co-composer with Sanh Berti, Universal, 1981

GEORGE SMALL
LAST RITES *DRACULA'S LAST RITES* co-composer with Paul Jost, Cannon, 1980

MICHAEL SMALL
b. 1939
Agent: Gorfaine-Schwartz - Burbank, 818/954-9500

OUT OF IT United Artists, 1969
PUZZLE OF A DOWNFALL CHILD Universal, 1970
JENNY Cinerama Releasing Corporation, 1970
THE REVOLUTIONARY United Artists, 1970
THE SPORTING CLUB Avco Embassy, 1971

KLUTE Warner Bros., 1971
CHILD'S PLAY Paramount, 1972
DEALING: OR THE BERKELEY-TO-BOSTON FORTY-BRICK LOST-BAG BLUES Warner Bros., 1972
LOVE AND PAIN AND THE WHOLE DAMNED THING Columbia, 1973, British-U.S.
THE PARALLAX VIEW Paramount, 1974
THE DROWNING POOL co-composer with Charles Fox, Warner Bros., 1975
THE STEPFORD WIVES Columbia, 1975
NIGHT MOVES Warner Bros., 1975
MARATHON MAN Paramount, 1976
PUMPING IRON (FD) Cinema 5. 1977
AUDREY ROSE United Artists, 1977
GIRLFRIENDS Warner Bros., 1978
THE DRIVER 20th Century-Fox, 1978
COMES A HORSEMAN United Artists, 1978
GOING IN STYLE Warner Bros., 1979
THE BOY WHO DRANK TOO MUCH (TF) MTM Enterprises Inc., 1980
THOSE LIPS, THOSE EYES United Artists, 1980
THE POSTMAN ALWAYS RINGS TWICE Paramount, 1981
CONTINENTAL DIVIDE Universal, 1981
ROLLOVER Orion/Warner Bros., 1981
THE STAR CHAMBER 20th Century-Fox, 1983
CHIEFS (MS) Highgate Pictures, 1983
KIDCO 20th Century-Fox, 1984
FIRSTBORN Paramount, 1984
TARGET Warner Bros., 1985
DREAM LOVER MGM/UA, 1986
NOBODY'S CHILD (TF) Joseph Feury Productions/ Gaylord Production Company, 1986
BRIGHTON BEACH MEMOIRS Universal, 1986
BLACK WIDOW 20th Century Fox, 1987
ORPHANS Lorimar, 1987
JAWS THE REVENGE Universal 1987
1969 Atlantic Releasing Corporation, 1988
SEE YOU IN THE MORNING Warner Bros., 1989
MOUNTAINS OF THE MOON Tri-Star, 1990

JACK SMALLEY
Contact: BMI - Los Angeles, 213/659-9109

TOURIST (TF) Castle Combe Productions/20th Century-Fox TV, 1980

SCOTT SMALLEY
Contact: 818/784-9182

THE UNSINKABLE SHECKY The Landmark Organization, 1989
MARTIAL MARSHALL The Landmark Organization, 1989
DISTURBED I.V.E., 1990

CHRIS SMART
PERSONAL CHOICE co-composer with Geoff Levin, Moviestore Entertainment, 1989

BRUCE SMEATON
b. Australia
Agent: ICM - Los Angeles, 213/550-4000

THE CARS THAT EAT PEOPLE *THE CARS THAT ATE PARIS* New Line Cinema, 1974, Australian
PICNIC AT HANGING ROCK Atlantic Releasing Corporation, 1975, Australian
THE GREAT MacARTHY 1975, Australian
THE DEVIL'S PLAYGROUND Entertainment Marketing, 1976, Australian
ELIZA FRASER Hexagon Productions, 1976, Australian
THE TRESPASSERS Vega Film Productions, 1976, Australian
SUMMERFIELD 1977, Australian
THE CHANT OF JIMMIE BLACKSMITH New Yorker, 1978, Australian
THE LAST OF THE KNUCKLEMEN Hexagon, 1978, Australian
CIRCLE OF IRON *THE SILENT FLUTE* Avco Embassy, 1979
GRENDEL, GRENDEL, GRENDEL (AF) Victorian Film Corp., 1980, Australian
DOUBLE DEAL Samuel Goldwyn Company, 1981, Australian
BARBAROSA Universal/AFD, 1982, West German
THE WINDS OF JARRAH 1983, Australian
UNDERCOVER Filmco, 1983, Australian
THE NAKED COUNTRY Naked Country Productions, 1984, Australian
ICEMAN Universal, 1984
PLENTY 20th Century-Fox, 1985, British
ELENI Warner Bros., 1985
ROXANNE Columbia, 1987
A CRY IN THE DARK Warner Bros., 1988, Australian

ARTHUR SMITH
Contact: BMI - Los Angeles, 213/659-9109

LADY GREY co-composer with Clay Smith, Maverick Pictures, 1980

CLAY SMITH
Contact: BMI - Los Angeles, 213/659-9109

SEABO co-composer, 1977
LADY GREY co-composer with Arthur Smith, Maverick Pictures, 1980

CLIVE SMITH
LIQUID SKY co-composer with Slava Tsukerman amd Brenda Hutchinson, Cinevista, 1982

MAURICIO SMITH
CROSSOVER DREAMS Crossover Films, 1985

MARK SNOW
Agent: Bart-Milander - North Hollywood, 818/761-4040

THE BOY IN THE PLASTIC BUBBLE (TF) Spelling-Goldberg Productions, 1976
BIG BOB JOHNSON AND HIS FANTASTIC SPEED CIRCUS (TF) Playboy Productions/Paramount TV, 1978
OVERBOARD (TF) Factor-Newland Production Corporation, 1978
THE RETURN OF THE MOD SQUAD (TF) co-composer with Shorty Rogers, Thomas-Spelling Productions, 1979
SOMETHING SHORT OF PARADISE American International, 1979
ANGEL CITY (TF) Factor-Newland Productions, 1980
CASINO (TF) Aaron Spelling Productions/Metromedia Producers Corporation, 1980
CAGNEY AND LACEY (TF) Mace Neufeld Productions/ Filmways, 1981
HIGH RISK American Cinema, 1981

GAMES MOTHER NEVER TAUGHT YOU (TF) CBS Entertainment, 1982
PAPER DOLLS (TF) Leonard Goldberg Productions, 1982
TWO KINDS OF LOVE (TF) CBS Entertainment, 1983
PACKIN' IT IN (TF) Roger Gimbel Productions/Thorn EMI TV/Jones-Reiker Ink Corporation, 1983
THE WINTER OF OUR DISCONTENT (TF) Lorimar Productions, 1983
MALIBU (TF) Hamner Productions/Columbia TV, 1983
SECRETS OF A MARRIED MAN (TF) ITC Productions, 1984
A GOOD SPORT (TF) Ralph Waite Productions/ Warner Bros. TV, 1984
SOMETHING ABOUT AMELIA (TF) ☆ Leonard Goldberg Productions, 1984
CHALLENGE OF A LIFETIME (TF) 20th Century-Fox TV, 1985
INTERNATIONAL AIRPORT (TF) Aaron Spelling Productions, 1985
CALIFORNIA GIRLS (TF) ABC Circle Films, 1985
THE LADY FROM YESTERDAY (TF) Barry Weitz Films/Comworld Productions, 1985
I DREAM OF JEANNIE...15 YEARS LATER (TF) Can't Sing Can't Dance Production/Columbia Pictures TV, 1985
BEVERLY HILLS COWGIRL BLUES (TF) Leonard Goldberg Company, 1985
NOT MY KID (TF) Beth Polson Productions/Finnegan Associates, 1985
ACCEPTABLE RISKS (TF) ABC Circle Films, 1986
JAKE SPEED New World, 1986
MURDER BY THE BOOK (TF) TVS Ltd./Benton Evans Productions, 1986, British
ONE POLICE PLAZA (TF) CBS Entertainment, 1986
ONE TERRIFIC GUY (TF) CBS Entertainment, 1986
THE GIRL WHO SPELLED FREEDOM (TF) Knopf-Simons Productions/ITC Productions/Walt Disney Productions, 1986
NEWS AT ELEVEN (TF) Turman-Foster Productions/ Finnegan Associates, 1986
BLOOD AND ORCHIDS (MS) Lorimar Productions, 1986
DOWN THE LONG HILLS (TF) The Finnegan Company/Walt Disney TV, 1986
WARM HEARTS, COLD FEET (TF) Lorimar-Telepictures, 1987
PALS (TF) Robert Halmi, Inc., 1987
STILL CRAZY LIKE A FOX (TF) Schenck-Cardea Productions/Columbia TV, 1987
CRACKED UP (TF) Aaron Spelling Productions, 1987
ROMAN HOLIDAY (TF) Jerry Ludwig Enterprises/ Paramount TV, 1987
VIETNAM WAR STORIES (CTF) Nexus Productions, 1987
MURDER ORDAINED (MS) Zev Braun Productions/ Interscope Communications, 1987
KIDS LIKE THESE (TF) Taft Entertainment TV/Nexus Productions, 1987
THE FATHER CLEMENTS STORY (TF) Zev Braun Productions/Interscope Communications, 1987
A HOBO'S CHRISTMAS (TF) Joe Byrnne-Falrose Productions/Phoenix Entertainment, 1987
AARON'S WAY: THE HARVEST (TF) Blinn-Thorpe Productions/Lorimar Telepictures, 1988
BLUEGRASS (TF) co-composer with Don Davis, The Landsburg Company, 1988
THE IN-CROWD Orion, 1988
ALONE IN THE NEON JUNGLE (TF) Robert Halmi Inc., 1988
SCANDAL IN A SMALL TOWN (TF) Carliner-Rappoport Productions, 1988
ERNEST SAVES CHRISTMAS Buena Vista, 1988
THOSE SHE LEFT BEHIND (TF) NBC Productions, 1989
EVERYBODY'S BABY: THE RESCUE OF JESSIE McCLURE (TF) Interscope, 1989
STUCK WITH EACH OTHER (TF) Nexus Productions, 1989
SETTLE THE SCORE (TF) Steve Sohmer Productions/ ITC, 1989
MIRACLE LANDING (TF) CBS Entertainment, 1990
CHILD IN THE NIGHT (TF) Mike Robe Productions, 1990
ARCHIE: TO RIVERDALE AND BACK AGAIN (TF) Patchett Kaufman Entertainment/DIC, 1990
THE GIRL WHO CAME BETWEEN (TF) Saban/Scherick Productions/Saban International, 1990
DEAD RECKONING (CTF) Houston Lady Productions, 1990

CURT SOBEL

Agent: BMI - Los Angeles, 213/659-9109

ALIEN NATION 20th Century Fox, 1988

STEPHEN SONDHEIM

b. March 22, 1930 - New York, New York
Contact: ASCAP - Los Angeles, 213/466-7681

STAVISKY Cinemation, 1974, French
REDS theme only, Paramount, 1981

DAVID SPEAR

Agent: Richard Emler - Los Angeles, 213/651-0222

FEAR NO EVIL co-composer with Frank LaLoggia, Avco Embassy, 1981
SPACESHIP *THE CREATURE WASN'T NICE* Almi Cinema 5, 1982
EXTERMINATOR 2 Cannon, 1984
THE RATINGS GAME (TF) Imagination-New Street Productions, 1984
NO RETREAT, NO SURRENDER New World, 1986, Hong Kong
MORTUARY ACADEMY Landmark Releasing, 1987
ARAB AND JEW Rob Gardner Productions
NO RETREAT, NO SURRENDER II Shapiro Glickenhaus Entertainment, 1989

CHRIS SPEDDING

Contact: PRS - London, England, 011-44-1-580-5544

HOLLYWOOD VICE SQUAD Concorde/Cinema Group, 1986

JOHN SPENCE

Contact: PRS - London, England, 011-44-1-580-5544

PANIC IN ECHO PARK (TF) Edgar J. Scherick Associates, 1977
THE AMAZING SPIDERMAN (TF) Charles Fries Productions/Dan Goodman Productions, 1977

ATILIO STAMPONE

Contact: SADAIC - Buenos Aires, Argentina, 011-54-1-35-7132

TANGO BAR Beco Films/Zaga Films, 1988, Puerto-Rican, Argentine

STANISLAS
Contact: PRS - London, England, 011-44-1-580-5544

THE HOLCROFT COVENANT Universal, 1985, British
BIGGLES Compact Yellowbill/Tambarle, 1986, British

VIVIAN STANSHALL
Contact: PRS - London, England, 011-44-1-580-5544

SIR HENRY AT RAWLINSON END Charisma Films, 1980, British

DAVID STEELE
TIN MEN co-composer with Andy Cox, Buena Vista, 1987

ANDREW STEIN
Contact: BMI - Los Angeles, 213/659-9109

HOLLYWOOD BOULEVARD New World, 1976
THUNDER AND LIGHTNING American International, 1977
DEATHSPORT New World, 1978
NATIONAL LAMPOON'S MOVIE MADNESS United Artists, 1981

CHRIS STEIN
Contact: ASCAP - Los Angeles, 213/466-7681

UNION CITY Kinesis, 1980
POLYESTER co-composer with Michael Kamen, New Line Cinema, 1981
WILD STYLE co-composer with Fred Brathwaite, Wild Style, 1983

HERMAN STEIN
b. 1915 - Philadelphia, Pennsylvania

BACK AT THE FRONT co-composer with Henry Mancini, Universal, 1952
THE DUEL AT SILVER CREEK co-composer, Universal, 1952
FRANCIS GOES TO WEST POINT co-composer, Universal, 1952
HAS ANYBODY SEEN MY GAL? co-composer, Universal, 1952
HERE COME THE NELSONS co-composer, Universal, 1952
HORIZONS WEST co-composer, Universal, 1952
JUST ACROSS THE STREET co-composer, Universal, 1952
THE LAWLESS BREED co-composer, Universal, 1952
MEET ME AT THE FAIR co-composer, Universal, 1952
THE RAIDERS co-composer, Universal, 1952
THE REDHEAD FROM WYOMING co-composer, Universal, 1952
SON OF ALI BABA co-composer, Universal, 1952
ABBOTT & COSTELLO GO TO MARS co-composer, Universal, 1953
ABBOTT & COSTELLO MEET DR. JEKYLL & MR. HYDE co-composer, Universal, 1953
ALL I DESIRE co-composer, Universal, 1953
CITY BENEATH THE SEA co-composer, Universal, 1953
COLUMN SOUTH co-composer, Universal, 1953
EAST OF SUMATRA co-composer, Universal, 1953
FRANCIS COVERS THE BIG TOWN co-composer, Universal, 1953
GIRLS IN THE NIGHT co-composer, Universal, 1953
THE GLASS WEB co-composer, Universal, 1953
THE GOLDEN BLADE co-composer, Universal, 1953
THE GREAT SIOUX UPRISING co-composer, Universal, 1953
GUNSMOKE co-composer, Universal, 1953
IT CAME FROM OUTER SPACE co-composer with Irving Gertz and Henry Mancini, Universal, 1953
THE LONE HAND co-composer, Universal, 1953
TAKE ME TO TOWN co-composer, Universal, 1953
TUMBLEWEED co-composer, Universal, 1953
THE VEILS OF BAGDAD co-composer, Universal, 1953
WAR ARROW co-composer, Universal, 1953
BENGAL BRIGADE co-composer, Universal, 1954
BLACK HORSE CANYON co-composer, Universal, 1954
THE BLACK SHIELD OF FALWORTH co-composer, Universal, 1954
BORDER RIVER co-composer, Universal, 1954
THE CREATURE FROM THE BLACK LAGOON co-composer, Universal, 1954
DESTRY co-composer, Universal, 1954
DRUMS ACROSS THE RIVER co-composer, Universal, 1954
FIREMAN SAVE MY CHILD co-composer, Universal, 1954
FOUR GUNS TO THE BORDER co-composer, Universal, 1954
THE GLENN MILLER STORY co-composer, Universal, 1954
JOHNNY DARK co-composer, Universal, 1954
MA AND PA KETTLE AT HOME co-composer, Universal, 1954
NAKED ALIBI co-composer, Universal, 1954
PLAYGIRL co-composer, Universal, 1954
RAILS INTO LARAMIE co-composer, Universal, 1954
RIDE CLEAR OF DIABLO co-composer, Universal, 1954
SASKATCHEWAN co-composer, Universal, 1954
SIGN OF THE PAGAN co-composer, Universal, 1954
SO THIS IS PARIS co-composer with Henry Mancini, Universal, 1954
TANGANYIKA co-composer, Universal, 1954
YELLOW MOUNTAIN co-composer, Universal, 1954
ABBOTT & COSTELLO MEET THE KEYSTONE COPS co-composer, Universal, 1955
CAPTAIN LIGHTFOOT co-composer, Universal, 1955
THE FAR COUNTRY co-composer, Universal, 1955
FEMALE ON THE BEACH co-composer, Universal, 1955
KISS OF FIRE co-composer, Universal, 1955
MA AND PA KETTLE AT WAIKIKI co-composer, Universal, 1955
MAN WITHOUT A STAR co-composer, Universal, 1955
THE PRIVATE WAR OF MAJOR BENSON co-composer, Universal, 1955
THE PURPLE MASK co-co mposer, Universal, 1955
REVENGE OF THE CREATURE main title only, Universal, 1955
SIX BRIDGES TO CROSS co-composer, Universal, 1955
THE SPOILERS co-composer, Universal, 1955
TARANTULA co-composer, Universal, 1955
THIS ISLAND EARTH co-composer with Henry Mancini and Hans J. Salter, Universal, 1955
BACKLASH Universal, 1956
THE CREATURE WALKS AMONG US co-composer, Universal, 1956
A DAY OF FURY co-composer, Universal, 1956
EVERYTHING BUT THE TRUTH co-composer, Universal, 1956
FOUR GIRLS IN TOWN co-composer, Universal, 1956
FRANCIS IN THE HAUNTED HOUSE Universal, 1956
THE GREAT MAN co-composer, Universal, 1956
I'VE LIVED BEFORE co-composer with Don Roseland and Ray Cormier, Universal, 1956

THE KETTLES IN THE OZARKS co-composer, Universal, 1956
THE MOLE PEOPLE co-composer, Universal, 1956
THERE'S ALWAYS TOMORROW co-composer, Universal, 1956
THE TOY TIGER co-composer, Universal, 1956
THE UNGUARDED MOMENT co-composer, Universal, 1956
WALK THE PROUD LAND co-composer, Universal, 1956
THE INCREDIBLE SHRINKING MAN co-composer, Universal, 1957
ISTANBUL co-composer, Universal, 1957
JOE DAKOTA co-composer, Universal, 1957
THE LAND UNKNOWN co-composer, Universal, 1957
LOVE SLAVES OF THE AMAZON co-composer, Universal, 1957
MAN IN THE SHADOW co-composer, Universal, 1957
MISTER CORY co-composer, Universal, 1957
THE MONOLITH MOSTERS co-composer, Universal, 1957
THE NIGHT RUNNER co-composer, Universal, 1957
QUANTEZ Universal, 1957
SLIM CARTER Universal, 1957
THE LADY TAKES A FLYER co-composer, Universal, 1958
LAST OF THE FAST GUNS *THE WESTERN STORY* co-composer with Hans J. Salter, Universal, 1958
MONEY, WOMEN & GUNS co-composer, Universal, 1958
THE SAGA OF HEMP BROWN Universal, 1958
THIS IS RUSSIA (FD) co-composer, Universal, 1958
NO NAME ON THE BULLET co-composer with Irving Gertz, Universal, 1959
THE INTRUDER *I HATE YOUR GUTS!/SHAME* Pathe American, 1961

FRED STEINER

b. February 24, 1923 - New York, New York
Contact: ASCAP - Los Angeles, 213/466-7681

RUN FOR THE SUN United Artists, 1956, British
MAN FROM DEL RIO United Artists, 1956
TIME LIMIT United Artists, 1957
THE COLOSSUS OF NEW YORK uncredited co-composer with Nathan Van Cleave, Paramount, 1958
ROBINSON CRUSOE ON MARS uncredited co-composer with Nathan Van Cleave, Paramount, 1964
FIRST TO FIGHT Warner Bros., 1967
THE ST. VALENTINE'S DAY MASSACRE 20th Century-Fox, 1967
WAKE ME WHEN THE WAR IS OVER (TF) Thomas-Spelling Productions, 1969
CARTER'S ARMY (TF) Thomas-Spelling Productions, 1970
RIVER OF GOLD (TF) Aaron Spelling Productions, 1971
FAMILY FLIGHT (TF) Silverton Productions/Universal TV, 1972
HEC RAMSEY (TF) Mark VII Ltd./Universal TV, 1972
HEATWAVE! (TF) Universal TV, 1974
NIGHT TERROR (TF) Charles Fries Productions, 1977
THE SEA GYPSIES Warner Bros., 1978
BLOOD FEUD (TF) 20th Century-Fox TV/ Glickman-Selznick Productions, 1983
THE COLOR PURPLE ★ co-composer, Warner Bros., 1985

JIM STEINMAN

Contact: BMI - Los Angeles, 213/659-9109

A SMALL CIRCLE OF FRIENDS United Artists, 1980

JAMES WESLEY STEMPLE

b. July 3, 1955 - Arlington, Virginia
Agent: Robert Light - Los Angeles, 213/651-1777

THE LAST RIDE (CTF) Fitzgerald/Hartley Films, 1988
DAMNED RIVER MGM/UA, 1989

JAKE STERN

FEEDBACK Feedback Company, 1979

DARYL STEVENETT

KILLPOINT co-composer with Herman Jeffreys, Crown International, 1984

MORTON STEVENS

b. 1929 - New Jersey
Agent: Bart-Milander - North Hollywood, 818/761-4040

WILD AND WONDERFUL Universal, 1964
HAWAII FIVE-O (TF) ☆ Leonard Freeman Productions/CBS Entertainment, 1968
A DEATH OF INNOCENCE (TF) Mark Carliner Productions, 1971
THE FACE OF FEAR (TF) QM Productions, 1971
SHE WAITS (TF) Metromedia Productions, 1972
DEADLY HARVEST (TF) CBS Entertainment, 1972
THE STRANGERS IN 7A (TF) Palomar Pictures International, 1972
VISIONS... (TF) CBS Entertainment, 1972
HORROR AT 37,000 FEET (TF) CBS Entertainment, 1973
GUESS WHO'S SLEEPING IN MY BED? (TF) ABC Circle Films, 1973
POOR DEVIL (TF) Paramount TV, 1973
COFFEE, TEA OR ME? (TF) CBS, Inc., 1973
JURY OF ONE 1974, French-Italian
THE DISAPPEARANCE OF FLIGHT 412 (TF) Cine Films/ Cinemobile Productions, 1974
BANJO HACKETT: ROAMIN' FREE (TF) Bruce Lansbury Productions/Columbia TV, 1976
THE TIME TRAVELERS (TF) Irwin Allen Productions/20th Century-Fox TV, 1976
THE STRANGE POSSESSION OF MRS. OLIVER (TF) The Shpetner Company, 1977
PETER LUNDY AND THE MEDICINE HAT STALLION (TF) Ed Friendly Productions, 1977
CODE NAME: DIAMOND HEAD (TF) QM Productions, 1977
ARTHUR HAILEY'S WHEELS (MS) ☆ Universal TV, 1978
WOMEN IN WHITE (MS) NBC, 1979
MANDRAKE (TF) Universal TV, 1979
THE FLAME IS LOVE (TF) Ed Friendly Productions/ Friendly-O'Herlihy Ltd., 1979
BACKSTAIRS AT THE WHITE HOUSE (MS) Ed Friendly Productions, 1979
UNDERCOVER WITH THE KKK *FREEDOM RIDERS* (TF) Columbia TV, 1979
DETOUR TO TERROR (TF) Orenthal Productions/Playboy Productions/Columbia TV, 1980
M STATION: HAWAII (TF) Lord and Lady Enterprises, 1980
FUGITIVE FAMILY (TF) Aubrey-Hamner Productions, 1980
HARDLY WORKING 20th Century-Fox, 1981
THE MILLION DOLLAR FACE (TF) Nephi-Hamner Productions, 1981

THE MANIONS OF AMERICA (MS) Roger Gimbel Productions/EMI TV/Argonaut Films Ltd., 1981
MASADA (MS) ☆ composer of Parts 3 and 4, Arnon Milchan Productions/Universal TV, 1981
GREAT WHITE co-composer with Guido & Maurizio De Angelis, Film Ventures International, 1982
MEMORIES NEVER DIE (TF) Groverton Productions/ Scholastic Productions/Universal TV, 1982
I MARRIED WYATT EARP (TF) Osmond TV Productions/Comworld Productions, 1983
COCAINE AND BLUE EYES (TF) Orenthal Productions/ Columbia TV, 1983
SMORGASBORD Warner Bros., 1983
SLAPSTICK OF ANOTHER KIND *SLAPSTICK* Entertainment Releasing Corporation/International Film Marketing, 1983
THE LADIES (TF) NBC, 1987, filmed in 1983
ALICE IN WONDERLAND (TF) Irwin Allen Productions/ Procter & Gamble Productions/Columbia TV, 1985
OUTRAGE! (TF) Irwin Allen Productions/ Columbia TV, 1986
THEY STILL CALL ME BRUCE Shapiro Entertainment, 1987
ACT OF PIRACY The Movie Group, 1988

DAVID A. STEWART

ROOFTOPS co-composer with Michael Kamen, New Century/Vista, 1989

STING
(Gordon Matthew Summer)

Contact: BMI - Los Angeles, 213/659-9109

BRIMSTONE AND TREACLE United Artists Classics, 1982, British

JON ST. JAMES

Contact: BMI - Los Angeles, 213/659-9109

CAVE GIRL Crown International, 1985

GARY STOCKDALE

Contact: BMI - Los Angeles, 213/659-9109

DANCE OF THE DAMNED Concorde, 1989
STRIPPED TO KILL 2 Concorde, 1989
NECROMANCER co-composer with Kevin Klinger and Bob Mamet, Bonnaire Films, 1989
SAVAGE BEACH (TF) Malibu Bay Films, 1989

CHRISTOPHER L. STONE

Agent: Robert Light - Los Angeles, 213/651-1777

NEVER PUT IT IN WRITING Allied Artists, 1964, British
THE SECRET OF MY SUCCESS MGM, 1965, British
THE TREASURE OF JAMAICA REEF MGM, 1974
MONEY TO BURN Victoria Films
GONE WITH THE WEST International Cinefilm, 1975
CHOICES Choices Company, 1981, Canadian
COVERGIRL New World, 1984, Canadian
NADIA (TF) Dave Bell Productions/Tribune Entertainment Company/Jadran Film, 1984, U.S.-Yugoslavian
SWORD OF HEAVEN Trans World Entertainment, 1985
NINJA TURF co-composer with Charles Pavlosky and Gary Falcone, Ascot Entertainment Group, 1986
TERRORVISION Empire Pictures, 1986
THE NAKED CAGE Cannon, 1986
PRISON Empire Pictures, 1988
PHANTASM II co-composer with Fred Myrow Universal, 1988
FELIX THE CAT (AF) New World, 1989

HOWARD STONE

SIGNS OF LIFE Avenue Pictures, 1989

RICHARD STONE

Agent: ICM - Los Angeles - 213/550-4000

NORTH SHORE Universal, 1987
SUMMER HEAT Atlantic Releasing Corporation, 1987
LONGARM (TF) Universal TV, 1988
NEVER ON TUESDAY Cinema Group, 1988
ELVIS AND ME (TF) Navarone Productions/New World TV, 1988
PUMPKINHEAD MGM/UA, 1988
HIROSHIMA MAIDEN (TF) Arnold Shapiro Productions, 1988
SUNDOWN Vestron, 1989
VIETNAM TEXAS Trans World Entertainment, 1990

MICHAEL STOREY

Contact: PRS - London, England, 011-44-1-580-5544

ANOTHER COUNTRY Orion Classics, 1984, British
COMING UP ROSES *RHOSYN A RHITH* Red Rooster, 1986, British
A PERFECT SPY (MS) BBC, 1987, British

DAVID STORRS

P.O.W. THE ESCAPE Cannon, 1986

WALLY STOTT
(See Angela Morley)

TED STOVALL

Contact: BMI - Los Angeles, 213/659-9109

THE BOY WHO CRIED WEREWOLF Universal, 1973

FRANK STRANGIO

Contact: APRA - Australia, 011-61-2-922-6422

THE BLUE LIGHTNING (TF) Alan Sloan Productions/The Seven Network/Coote-Carroll Australia/Roadshow, 1986, U.S.-Australian

JOHN STRAUSS

Contact: ASCAP - Los Angeles, 213/466-7681

MIKEY AND NICKY Paramount, 1976

BARBRA STREISAND

b. April 24, 1942 - New York, New York
Agent: CAA - Los Angeles, 213/277-4545

NUTS Universal, 1987

WILLIAM T. STROMBERG

b. May 23, 1964 - Oceanside, California
Contact: 818/769-9272

ORDER OF THE EAGLE AIP, 1989
BACK FROM THE PAST AIP, 1990
ODDBALL HALL, 1990

CHARLES STROUSE

b. 1929
Contact: ASCAP - Los Angeles, 213/466-7681

BONNIE AND CLYDE Warner Bros., 1967
THE NIGHT THEY RAIDED MINSKY'S United Artists, 1968
THERE WAS A CROOKED MAN Warner Bros., 1970
JUST TELL ME WHAT YOU WANT Columbia, 1980

JOE STRUMMER

Contact: PRS - London, England, 011-44-1-580-5544

RUDE BOY co-composer with Mick Jones, Atlantic Releasing Corporation, 1980
WALKER Universal, 1987
PERMANENT RECORD Paramount, 1988

JEFF STURGES

Agent: Carol Faith - Beverly Hills, 213/274-0776

HELLHOLE Arkoff International Pictures, 1985

JERRY STYNE

SKI FEVER co-composer with Guy Hemric, Allied Artists, 1969
CYCLE SAVAGES Trans American, 1970
THE MAGIC GARDEN OF STANLEY SWEETHEART MGM, 1970
CORKY MGM, 1972
THE GENESIS CHILDREN 1972
BLACK JACK *WILD IN THE SKY* 1972
JENNIFER American International, 1978

JULE STYNE
(Jules Stein)

b. December 31, 1905 - London, England
Contact: ASCAP - Los Angeles, 213/466-7681

THIEVES Paramount, 1977

ANDY SUMMERS

Agent: ICM - Los Angeles, 213/550-4000

DOWN AND OUT IN BEVERLY HILLS Buena Vista, 1986
OUT OF TIME (TF) Columbia TV, 1988
END OF THE LINE Orion Classics, 1988
WEEKEND AT BERNIE'S 20th Century Fox, 1989

BOB SUMMERS

Agent: Robert Light - Los Angeles, 213/651-1777

MURDER BY NUMBERS Burnhill, 1990

ROBERT SUMMERS

GUARDIAN OF THE WILDERNESS Sunn Classic, 1977
THE LINCOLN CONSPIRACY Sunn Classic, 1977
SIXTH AND MAIN National Cinema, 1977
THE INCREDIBLE ROCKY MOUNTAIN RACE (TF) Schick Sunn Classics Productions, 1977
THE LAST OF THE MOHICANS (TF) Schick Sunn Classics Productions, 1977
BEYOND AND BACK Sunn Classic, 1978
DONNER PASS: THE ROAD TO SURVIVAL (TF) Schick Sunn Classics Productions, 1978
THE DEERSLAYER (TF) co-composer with Andrew Belling, Schick Sunn Classics Productions, 1978
BEYOND DEATH'S DOOR Sunn Classic, 1979
THE LEGEND OF SLEEPY HOLLOW Sunn Classic, 1979
IN SEARCH OF HISTORIC JESUS Sunn Classic, 1980
GUYANA, CULT OF THE DAMNED co-composer with Nelson Riddle and George S. Price, Universal, 1980
THE LEGEND OF SLEEPY HOLLOW (TF) Schick Sunn Classics Productions/Taft International Pictures, 1980
THE ADVENTURES OF NELLIE BLY (TF) Schick Sunn Classics Productions/Taft International Pictures, 1981
THE ADVENTURES OF HUCKLEBERRY FINN (TF) Schick Sunn Classics Productions/Taft International Pictures, 1981
THE BOOGENS Jensen Farley Pictures, 1981
THE CAPTURE OF GRIZZLY ADAMS (TF) Schick Sunn Classics Productions/Taft International Pictures, 1982
THE FALL OF THE HOUSE OF USHER (TF) Schick Sunn Classics Productions/Taft International Pictures, 1982
ONE DARK NIGHT Comworld, 1983
UNCOMMON VALOR (TF) Brademan-Self Productions/ Sunn Classic, 1983
THE ANNIHILATORS New World, 1986
THE BIKINI SHOP *THE MALIBU BIKINI SHOP* International Film Marketing, 1986

WILL SUMNER

Contact: BMI - Los Angeles, 213/659-9100

THE PERSONALS New World, 1982

PAUL SUNDFOR

ATTACK OF THE KILLER TOMATOES co-composer with Gordon Goodwin, 1979

KEN SUTHERLAND

Contact: ASCAP - Los Angeles, 213/466-7681

SAVANNAH SMILES Embassy, 1982
DARK BEFORE DAWN PSM Entertainment, 1989

ELIZABETH SWADOS

Contact: BMI - Los Angeles, 213/659-9109

TOO FAR TO GO (TF) Sea Cliff Productions/Polytel Films, 1979
OHMS (TF) Grant-Case-McGrath Enterprises, 1980
FOUR FRIENDS Filmways, 1982
SEIZE THE DAY (TF) Learning in Focus, 1986
A YEAR IN THE LIFE (MS) Falsey/Austin Street Productions/Universal TV, 1986
FAMILY SINS (TF) London Films, 1987

STANISLAS SYREWICZ

Agent: Bart-Milander - North Hollywood, 818/761-4040

BEWITCHED EYES 1980, French
LE PART DU CHOSE 1983, French
L'AMOUR BRAQUE 1985, French
THE HOLCROFT COVENANT Universal, 1985
BIGGLES Compact Yellowbill/Tambarle, 1986, British
THE FANTASIST ITC, 1986, Irish
THE LAIR OF THE WHITE WORM Vestron, 1988, British

T

TAJ MAHAL

SOUNDER 20th Century-Fox, 1972
PART 2, SOUNDER Gamma III, 1976
BROTHERS Warner Bros., 1977

TORU TAKEMITSU

b. October 8, 1930 - Manchuria
Contact: JASRAC - Tokyo, Japan, 011-81-3-502-6551

JUVENILE PASSIONS 1958, Japanese
BAD BOYS 1960, Japanese
THE INHERITANCE Shochiku, 1962, Japanese
PALE FLOWER Shochiku, 1963, Japanese
HARIKARI *SEPPUKU* Shochiku, 1963, Japanese
WOMAN OF THE DUNES 1964, Japanese
KWAIDAN Continental, 1964, Japanese
BWANA TOSHI 1965, Japanese
MINATOMO YOSHITSUNE 1966, Japanese
CLOUDS AT SUNSET Hyogensha/Shochiku, 1967, Japanese
REBELLION *SAMURAI REBELLION* Toho, 1967, Japanese
DOUBLE SUICIDE Toho, 1969, Japanese
DODES'KA'DEN Janus, 1970, Japanese
CLICKETY-CLACK 1970, Japanese
SILENCE Toho, 1971, Japanese
HE DIED AFTER THE WAR 1971, Japanese
INN OF EVIL Toho, 1971, Japanese
DEAR SUMMER SISTER 1972, Japanese
A SILENCE 1972, Japanese
THE PETRIFIED FOREST Hyogensha/Toho, 1973, Japanese
SUMMER SOLDIERS 1972, Japanese
TIME WITHIN MEMORY 1973, Japanese
HIMIKO Hyogensha/ATG, 1974, Japanese
KASEKI Haiyuza Films, 1975, Japanese
SHIAWASE 1975, Japanese
PHANTOM LOVE 1978, Japanese
BANISHED Toho, 1978, Japanese
THE LOUVRE MUSEUM 1979, Japanese
EMPIRE OF PASSION *CORRIDA OF LOVE* Barbary Coast, 1980, Japanese
RAN Orion Classics, 1985, Japanese-French
ARASHI GA OKA *ONIMARU* Toho, 1988, Japanese-Swiss
BLACK RAIN Toei, 1989, Japanese

FREDERIC TALGORN

b. July 2, 1961 - Toulouse, France
Agent: Jacques Fiorentino, LH-81 Entertainment - Beverly Hills, 213/658-1094

EDGE OF SANITY August Entertainment, 1989, British
BURIED ALIVE The Movie Group, 1989, British
STRANGLEHOLD: DELTA FORCE II Cannon, 1989
ROBOTJOX Trans World Entertainment, 1990
LE BRASIER 1990, French

TANGERINE DREAM

Agent: ICM - Los Angeles, 213/550-4000

SORCERER Universal/Paramount, 1977
KNEUSS 1978, West German-Swiss
THIEF United Artists, 1981
IDENTIFICATION OF A WOMAN Iter Film/Gaumont, 1982, Italian-French
THE SOLDIER Embassy, 1982
RISKY BUSINESS The Geffen Company/Warner Bros., 1983
THE KEEP Paramount, 1983
WAVELENGTH New World, 1983
HEARTBREAKERS Orion, 1984
FLASHPOINT Tri-Star, 1984
TRIBES Queensland Pictures
FIRESTARTER Universal, 1984
FORBIDDEN (CTF) HBO Premiere Films/Mark Forstater Productions/Clasart/Anthea Productions, 1985, U.S.-British-West German
VISION QUEST Warner Bros., 1985
STREET HAWK (TF) Limekiln and Templar Productions/ Universal TV, 1985
THE PARK IS MINE (CTF) Astral Film Enterprises/HBO Premiere Films, 1985
LEGEND U.S. version only, Universal, 1986
TONIGHT'S THE NIGHT (TF) Phoenix Entertainment Group, 1987
DEADLY CARE (TF) Universal TV, 1987
NEAR DARK DEG, 1987
KAMIKAZE Gaumont, 1987, French
SHY PEOPLE Cannon, 1987
DEAD SOLID PERFECT (CTF) HBO Pictures/David Merrick Productions, 1988
MIRACLE MILE Hemdale, 1988
CATCH ME IF YOU CAN MCEG, 1989
RAINBOW ITC, 1990

JOHN ANDREW TARTAGLIA

Contact: ASCAP - Los Angeles, 213/466-7681

POWDERKEG (TF) Filmways/Rodphi Productions, 1971
THE ADVENTURES OF NICK CARTER (TF) Universal TV, 1972
THE BARBARY COAST (TF) Paramount Pictures TV, 1975
THE ISLANDER (TF) Glen A. Larson Productions/ Universal TV, 1978
GRACE KELLY (TF) Takota Productions/Embassy TV, 1983

DUANE TATRO

Contact: BMI - Los Angeles, 213/659-9109

THE HOUSE ON GREENAPPLE ROAD (TF) QM Productions, 1970
KEEFER (TF) David Gerber Productions/Columbia Pictures TV, 1978

BOB TELSON

Contact: BMI - Los Angeles, 213/659-9109

BAGDAD CAFE OUT OF ROSENHEIM Island Pictures, 1987, West German-U.S.
ROSALIE GOES SHOPPING Futura Filmverlag/Pelemele Film, 1989, West German-U.S.

ROD TEMPERTON
THE COLOR PURPLE ★ co-composer, Warner Bros., 1985
RUNNING SCARED MGM/UA, 1986

DENNIS TENNEY
Contact: BMI - Los Angeles, 213/659-9109

WITCHBOARD Cinema Group, 1986
NIGHT OF THE DEMONS International Film Marketing, 1988

SONNY TERRY
Contact: BMI - Los Angeles, 213/659-9109

STROSZEK co-composer with Chet Atkins, New Yorker, 1977, West German

JOHN TESH
Agent: Carol Faith - Beverly Hills, 213/274-0776

LIMIT UP MCEG, 1990

MIKIS THEODORAKIS
b. 1925 - Khios, Greece
Contact: SACEM - France, 011-33-14-747-5650

EVA 1953, Greek
NIGHT AMBUSH *ILL MET BY MOONLIGHT* Rank, 1957, British
HONEYMOON RKO Radio, 1958, Spanish
THE SHADOW OF THE CAT 1961, British
THE LOVERS OF TERUEL co-composer, 1962, French
ELECTRA Lopert, 1962, Greek
PHAEDRA Lopert, 1962, Greek-U.S.-French
FIVE MILES TO MIDNIGHT United Artists, 1963, U.S.-French-Italian
ZORBA THE GREEK International Classics, 1964, Greek
THE ISLAND OF APHRODITE 1966, Greek
THE DAY THE FISH CAME OUT 20th Century-Fox, 1967, British-Greek
Z Cinema 5, 1969, French-Algerian
THE TROJAN WOMEN Cinerama Releasing Corporation, 1971, U.S.-Greek
BIRIBI 1971, French
STATE OF SIEGE Cinema 6, 1973, French
SERPICO Paramount, 1973
SUTJESKA 1973, Yugoslavian
THE STORY OF JACOB AND JOSEPH (TF) Milberg Theatrical Productions/Columbia Pictures TV, 1974
HELL RIVER 1974
PARTISANS 1974, Yugoslavian
LETTERS FROM MARUSIA Azteca Films, 1975, Mexican
IPHIGENIA Cinema 5, 1977, Greek
EASY ROAD co-composer with George Thoedorakis, 1979, Greek

THE THIRD EAR BAND
MACBETH Columbia, 1971, British

PETER THOMAS
Contact: GEMA - West Germany, 011-81-3-502-6551

THE INDIAN SCARF 1963, West German
STOP TRAIN 349 1964, West German-French
THE LAST OF THE MOHICANS 1965, West German
THE SHOT FROM A VIOLIN CASE 1965, West German
UNCLE TOM'S CABIN 1965, West German
THE BLOOD DEMON 1967, West German
JACK OF DIAMONDS MGM, 1967, U.S.-West German
WINNETOU AND HIS FRIEND, OLD FIREHAND 1967, West German
THE SNAKE PIT AND THE PENDULUM 1967
THE TRYGON FACTOR 1967, British
INTIMATE DESIRES OF WOMEN Gemini, 1968, West German
DEADLY SHOTS ON BROADWAY 1969, West German
TO HELL WITH SCHOOL 1969, West German
DIE WEIBCHEN *THE FEMALES* 1970, West German
GENTLEMEN IN WHITE VESTS 1970, West German
MEMORIES OF THE FUTURE 1970, West German
THE DEAD ONE IN THE THAMES RIVER 1971, West German
OUR WILLI IS THE BEST 1972, West German
SOHO GORILLA 1972, West German
HAND OF POWER 1972, West German
THE STUFF THAT DREAMS ARE MADE OF 1972, West German
CHARIOTS OF THE GODS (FD) 1973, West German
TEMPTATIONS IN THE SUMMER WIND 1973, West German
BOTTSCHEFT DER GOETTER *MYSTERIES OF THE GODS* 1976, West German
ONCE UPON A TIME *MARIA D'ORO UND BELLO BLUE* (AF) G.G. Communications, 1976, Italian-West German
BREAKTHROUGH *SERGEANT STEINER* Maverick Pictures International, 1978, West German

ANDY THOMPSON
INTO THE FIRE Moviestore Entertainment, 1988, Canadian

KEN THORNE
Agent: Bart-Milander - North Hollywood, 818/761-4040

HELP United Artists, 1965, British
A FUNNY THING HAPPENED ON THE WAY TO THE FORUM ★★ United Artists, 1966, British
HOW I WON THE WAR United Artists, 1967, British
INSPECTOR CLOUSEAU United Artists, 1968, British
HEAD Columbia, 1968
THE TOUCHABLES 20th Century-Fox, 1968, British
THE BED SITTING ROOM United Artists, 1969, British
SINFUL DAVEY United Artists, 1969, British
A TALENT FOR LOVING The Mirisch Company, 1969
THE MAGIC CHRISTIAN Commonwealth United, 1970, British
HANNIE CAULDER Paramount, 1971, British
MURPHY'S WAR Paramount, 1971, British
JUGGERNAUT United Artists, 1974, British
ROYAL FLASH 20th Century-Fox, 1976, British
ASSAULT ON AGATHON Nine Network, 1976
THE RITZ Warner Bros., 1976
POWER PLAY Magnum International Pictures/Cowry Film Productions, 1978, Canadian-British
ARABIAN ADVENTURE AFD, 1979, British
THE OUTSIDER Paramount, 1980, U.S.-Irish
SUPERMAN II adaptation, Warner Bros., 1981, U.S.-British
WOLF LAKE *THE HONOR GUARD* Filmcorp Distribution, 1981, Canadian
THE HOUSE WHERE EVIL DWELLS MGM/UA, 1982, U.S.-Japanese
THE HUNCHBACK OF NOTRE DAME (TF) Norman Rosemont Productions/Columbia TV, 1982, U.S.-British

SUPERMAN III adaptation, Warner Bros., 1983, U.S.-British
WHITE WATER REBELS (TF) CBS Entertainment, 1983
THE EVIL THAT MEN DO Tri-Star, 1984
LASSITER Warner Bros., 1984
FINDERS KEEPERS Warner Bros., 1984
THE PROTECTOR Warner Bros., 1985, U.S.-Hong Kong
MY WICKED, WICKED WAYS: THE LEGEND OF ERROL FLYNN (TF) CBS Entertainment, 1985
LOST IN LONDON (TF) Emmanuel Lewis Entertainment Enterprises/D'Angelo Productions/ Group W. Productions, 1985
THE TROUBLE WITH SPIES DEG, 1987
THE RETURN OF SHERLOCK HOLMES (TF) CBS Entertainment, 1987, British
IF IT'S TUESDAY, IT STILL MUST BE BELGIUM (TF) Eisenstock & Mintz Productions, 1987
GREAT EXPECTATIONS (CTF) The Disney Channel/ Harlech TV/Primetime TV, 1989, U.S.-British

JUHA TIKKA

b. Finland
Contact: TEOSTO - Finland, 358-0-692-2511

TALVISOTA National-Filmi Oy, 1989, Finnish

JACK TILLAR

Contact: BMI - Los Angeles, 213/659-9109

THE MAN WHO SAW TOMORROW co-composer with William Loose, Warner Bros., 1981

COLIN TIMMS

Contact: APRA - Australia, 011-61-2-922-6422

AUSTRALIAN DREAM Ronin Films, 1987, Australian

KEITH TIPPET

Contact: PRS - London, England, 011-44-1-580-5544

THE SUPERGRASS Hemdale, 1985, British

SIR MICHAEL TIPPETT

b. 1905 - London, England
Contact: PRS - London, England, 011-44-1-580-5544

AKENFIELD (FD) Angle Films, 1975, British

GEORGE ALICESON TIPTON

NO PLACE TO RUN (TF) Spelling-Goldberg Productions/ABC Circle Films, 1972
HOME FOR THE HOLIDAYS (TF) Spelling-Goldberg Productions/ABC Circle Films, 1972
THE AFFAIR (TF) Spelling-Goldberg Productions, 1973
THE STRANGER WHO LOOKS LIKE ME (TF) Lillian Gallo Productions/Filmways, 1974
THE GUN AND THE PULPIT (TF) Cine Television/ Danny Thomas Productions, 1974
REMEMBER WHEN (TF) Danny Thomas Productions/The Raisin Company, 1974
BADLANDS Warner Bros., 1974
PHANTOM OF THE PARADISE ★ co-composer with Paul Williams, 20th Century-Fox, 1974
HIT LADY (TF) Spelling-Goldberg Productions, 1974
GRIFFIN AND PHOENIX (TF) ABC Circle Films, 1976
I WANT TO KEEP MY BABY! (TF) CBS Entertainment, 1976
SECRETS (TF) The Jozak Company, 1977
RED ALERT (TF) The Jozak Company/Paramount Pictures TV, 1977
MULLIGAN'S STEW (TF) Christiana Productions/ Paramount Pictures TV, 1977
THREE ON A DATE (TF) ABC Circle Films, 1978
WITH THIS RING (TF) co-composer with Richard Hazard, The Jozak Company/Paramount Pictures TV, 1978
CHRISTMAS LILLIES OF THE FIELD (TF) Rainbow Productions/Osmond Television Productions, 1979
SEIZURE: THE STORY OF KATHY MORRIS (TF) The Jozak Company, 1980
TROUBLE IN HIGH TIMBER COUNTRY (TF) Witt-Thomas Productions/Warner Bros. TV, 1980
SIDE BY SIDE: THE TRUE STORY OF THE OSMOND FAMILY (TF) Osmond TV Productions/Comworld Productions, 1982
THE DEMON MURDER CASE (TF) Dick Clark Productions/ Len Steckler Productions, 1983

GERRY TOLAND

Contact: APRA - Australia, 011-61-2-922-6422

THE PLUMBER Barbary Coast, 1978, Australian, originally made for television

ISAO TOMITA

b. Japan
Contact: JASRAC - Tokyo, Japan, 011-81-3-502-6551

THE HEAVENS AND THE EARTH 1969, Japanese
THE STORY OF THE TAIRA FAMILY 1972, Japanese
KATSU TAIHEIKI 1974, Japanese
CATASTROPHE 1999 New World, 1977
DEMON POND Shochiku, 1980, Japanese

TIM TORRANCE

Contact: BMI - Los Angeles, 213/659-9109

MUTANT ON THE BOUNTY Skouras Pictures, 1989

TOTO

DUNE co-composer with Brian Eno, Universal, 1984

OLIVER TOUISSAINT

b. France
Contact: SACEM - France, 011-33-14-747-5650

MAID FOR PLEASURE co-composer with Bernard Gerard, 1974, French
CELESTINE, MAID AT YOUR SERVICE co-composer with Paul de Senneville, 1974, French
IRRECONCILABLE DIFFERENCES co-composer with Paul De Senneville, Warner Bros., 1984

COLIN TOWNS

Agent: Bart-Milander - North Hollywood, 818/761-4040

THE HAUNTING OF JULIA *FULL CIRCLE* Discovery Films, 1977, British-Canadian
SLAYGROUND Universal/AFD, 1983, British
SHADEY Skouras Pictures, 1986, British
KNIGHTS AND EMERALDS Warner Bros., 1986, British
BORN OF FIRE Film Four International
BELLMAN AND TRUE Island Pictures, 1987, British
RAWHEAD REX Empire Pictures, 1987, British
THE FEAR (MS) Euston Films, 1988, British
CHASE Zenith Films

VAMPIRE'S KISS Hemdale, 1988
THE WOLVES OF WILLOUGHBY CHASE Atlantic Releasing Corporation, 1989, British
GETTING IT RIGHT MCEG, 1989, U.S.-British
DAUGHTER OF DARKNESS (TF) King Phoenix Entertainment, 1990
FELLOW TRAVELLER (CTF) 1990
HANDS OF A MURDERER (TF) Storke/Fuisz Productions/Yorkshire TV, 1990, U.S.-British

DOMENIC TROIANO

Agent: BMI - Los Angeles, 213/659-9109

THE GUNFIGHTERS (TF) Grosso-Jacobson Productions/Alliance Entertainment/Tribune Entertainment, 1987, U.S.-Canadian
TRUE BLUE (CTF) Grosso-Jacobson Productions/ NBC Productions, 1989

ERNEST TROOST

Contact: BMI - Los Angeles, 213/659-9109

MUNCHIES Concorde, 1987
SWEET REVENGE Concorde, 1987
DEAD HEAT New World, 1988
TIGER WARSAW Sony Pictures, 1988
TREMORS Universal, 1990

ARMANDO TROVAJOLI

b. 1917 - Rome, Italy
Contact: SIAE - Rome, Italy, 011-39-6-59-90-1

LA TRATTA DELLE BIANCHE *GIRLS MARKED FOR DANGER* 1952, Italian
LE INFIDELI 1952, Italian
DUE NOTTI CON CLEOPATRA *TWO NIGHTS WITH CLEOPATRA* 1953, Italian
UN GIORNO IN PRETURA *A DAY IN COURT* 1954, Italian
QUESTA E LA VITA *OF LIFE AND LOVE* co-composer with Carlo Innocenzi, 1954, Italian
LA DONNA DEL FIUME *THE WOMAN OF THE RIVER* co-composer with Angelo Francesco Lavagnino, 1954, Italian
LE DICIOTENNI 1956, Italian
IL COCCO DI MAMMA 1957, Italian
CAMPINE 1957, Italian
POVERI MILIONARI 1958, Italian
IL VEDOVO 1959, Italian
A QUALCUNO PIACE CALVO 1959, Italian
VACANZE D'INVERNO 1959, Italian
NOSTALGIE ROMANE 1959, Italian
LA NOTTE DEI TEDDY-BOYS 1959, Italian
TEMPI DURI PER I VAMPIRI 1959, Italian
IL CARRO ARMATO DELL' 8 SETTEMBRE 1959, Italian
UN MILITARE E MEZZO 1960, Italian
TU CHE NE DICI? 1960, Italian
LA CENTO CHILOMETRI 1960, Italian
QUESTO AMORE AL CONFINI DEL MONDO 1960, Italian
I PIACERE DEL SABATO NOTTE *CALL-GIRLS OF ROME* 1960, Italian
I PIACERE DELLO SCAPOLO 1960, Italian
IL CORAZZIERE 1960, Italian
LE PILLOLE DI ERCOLE *THE HERCULES PILLS* 1960, Italian
LA CIOCIARA *TWO WOMEN* 1960, Italian
ANONIMA COCOTTES *THE CALL-GIRL BUSINESS* 1960, Italian
CHIAMATA 22-22 TENENTE SHERIDAN 1960, Italian
THE GRAND OLYMPICS co-composer with Angelo Francesco Lavagnino, 1960
A PORTE CHIUSE Fair Film/Cinematografica Rire/Societe Generale de Cinematographie/Ultra Film/Lyre Film/Roxy Film, 1960, Italian-French-West German
BLOOD OF THE WARRIORS *LA SCHIAVA DI ROMA* 1960, Italian
ATOM AGE VAMPIRE *SEDDOK, L'EREDE DI SATANA* 1961, Italian
TOTO, PEPPINO E LA DOLCE VITA 1961, Italian
THE PLANETS AGAINST US *I PIANETI CONTRO DI NOI* 1961, Italian
HERCULES IN THE HAUNTED WORLD *ERCOLE AL CENTRO DELLA TERRA* 1961, Italian
GLI ATTENDENTI 1961, Italian
TOGNAZZI E LA MINORENNE 1961, Italian
LA RAGAZZA DI MILLE MESI 1961, Italian
MOLEMEN VS. THE SON OF HERCULES 1961, Italian
THE MAGIC WORLD OF TOPO GIGIO (AF) 1961, Italian
IL MANTENUTO *HIS WOMEN* 1961, Italian
PUGNI, PUPE E MARINAI 1961, Italian
WEREWOLF IN A GIRLS' DORMITORY *LUCANTROPUS* 1961, Italian
HERCULES AND THE CAPTIVE WOMEN co-composer with Gino Marinuzzi, 1961, Italian
WARRIORS FIVE *LA GUERRA CONTINUA* 1962, Italian
RUGANTINO co-composer with Gianfranco Plenizio, 1962, Italian
UNA DOMENICA D'ESTATE 1962, Italian
BOCCACCIO '70 composer of "The Raffle" segment, Embassy, 1962, Italian
TOTO DI NOTTE 1962, Italian
IL MIO AMICO BENITO 1962, Italian
OGGI A BERLINO 1962, Italian
DIECI ITALIANI PER UN TEDESCO 1962, Italian
I QUATTRO MONACI 1962, Italian
ALONE AGAINST ROME *SOLO CONTRO ROMA* 1962, Italian
TOTO E PEPPINO DIVISI A BERLINO 1962, Italian
THE GIANT OF METROPOLIS 1962, Italian
IL GIOVEDI 1962, Italian
LA VISITA 1963, Italian
IL MONACA DI MONZA 1963, Italian
IN ITALIA SI CHIAMA AMORE 1963, Italian
TOTO SEXY 1963, Italian
IL FORNARETTO DI VENEZIA 1963, Italian
GLI ONOREVOLI 1963, Italian
OPIATE '67 *I MOSTRI* 1963, Italian
YESTERDAY, TODAY AND TOMORROW Embassy, 1963, Italian-French
IL VUOTO 1963, Italian
ASSASSINO MADE IN ITALY 1963, Italian
ITALIANI BRAVA GENTE 1963, Italian
I TABU (FD) co-composer with Francesco Lavagnino, 1963, Italian
I TERRIBILI SETTE 1964, Italian
I CAGASOTTO 1964, Italian
HIGH INFIDELITY Magna, 1964, Italian-French
IL GAUCHO Fair Film/Clemente Lococo, 1964, Italian-Argentinian
LA MIA SIGNORA 1964, Italian
THE MAGNIFICENT CUCKOLD co-composer with Roman Vlad, 1964, Italian
MARRIAGE ITALIAN STYLE Embassy, 1964, Italian-French
LA BELLE FAMIGLIE 1964, Italian
THE DOLLS *LE BAMBOLE* 1964, Italian
ENGAGEMENT ITALIANO *LA RAGAZZA IN PRESTITO* 1964, Italian

LA CONGIUNTURA 1965, Italian
OGGI, DOMANI, DOPODOMANI co-composer, 1965, Italian
CASANOVA '70 co-composer with Franco Bassi, Embassy, 1965, Italian-French
SEVEN GOLDEN MEN *SETTE UOMINI D'ORO* 1965, Italian
I COMPLESSI Documento Film/SPCE, 1965, Italian-French
GUGLIELMO IL DENTONE 1965, Italian
I LUNGHI GIORNI DELLA VENDETTA co-composer with Ennio Morricone, 1965, Italian
THE DEVIL IN LOVE *L'ARCODIAVOLO* 1966, Italian
UNA STORIA DI NOTTE 1966, Italian
LE SPIE AMANO I FIORI co-composer with Francesco Lavagnino, 1966, Italian
IL PANE AMARO co-composer with Francesco Lavagnino, 1966, Italian
AMERICA - PAESE DI DIO (FD) co-composer with Francesco Lavagnino, 1966, Italian
THE QUEENS *LE FATE* Royal Films International, 1966, Italian-French
MAIGRET A PIGALLE 1966, Italian
ADULTERIO ALL'ITALIANA 1966, Italian
SIGNOR DYANMITE 1966, Italian
TREASURE OF SAN GENNARO *OPERAZIONE SAN GENNARO* Paramount, 1966, Italian-French-West German
THE 7 GOLDEN MEN STRIKE AGAIN 1966, Italian
I NOSTRI MARITI Documento Film, 1966, Italian
IL PROFETA *MR. KINKY* 1967, Italian
ACID *DELIRIO DEI SENSI* co-composer with Francesco Lavagnino, 1967, Italian
DON GIOVANNI IN SICILIA 1967, Italian
DROP DEAD, MY LOVE 1967, Italian
ANYONE CAN PLAY *LE DOLCE SIGNORE* 1967, Italian
WITH BATED BREATH *COL CUORE IN GOLA* 1967, Italian
RAPPORTE FULLER BASE STOCCOLMA 1967, Italian
7 VOLTE 7 1967, Italian
OMICIDIO PER APPUNTAMENTO 1967, Italian
TORTURE ME, BUT KILL ME WITH KISSES 1968, Italian
FAUSTINA 1968, Italian
NELL'ANNO DEL SIGNORE 1968, Italian
THE LIBERTINE *LA MATRIARCA* 1968, Italian
L'URLO DEI GIGANTI 1968, Italian
RIUSCIRANNO I NOSTRI EROI A TROVARE L'AMICO MISTERIOSAMENTE SCOMPARSO IN AFRICA? Documento Film, 1968, Italian
LOVEMAKER - L'UOMO PER FARE L'AMORE 1969, Italian
WHERE ARE YOU GOING ALL NAKED? 1969, Italian
IL COMMISSARIO PEPE Dean Film, 1969, Italian
VEDO NUDO Dean Film/Jupiter Generale Cinematografica, 1969, Italian
LA FAMIGLIA BENVENUTI (TF) 1969, Italian
IL GIOVANE NORMALE Dean Film/Italnoleggio, 1969, Italian
MAY MORNING 1969, Italian
QUELLA CHIARA NOTTE D'OTTOBRE 1970, Italian
THE PRIEST'S WIFE Warner Bros., 1970, Italian-French
THE MOTIVE WAS JEALOUSY 1970, Italian
THE SWINGING CONFESSORS *IL PRETE SPOSATO* 1970, Italian
NOI DONNE SIAMO FATTI COSI Apollo International Film, 1971, Italian
LA CONTROFIGURA 1971, Italian
EXCUSE ME, MY NAME IS ROCCO PAPALEO Rumson, 1971, Italian
HOMO EROTICUS 1971, Italian
IL VICHINGO VENUTO DAL SUD 1971, Italian
STANZA 17-17: PALAZZO DEL TASSE-UFFICIO DELLA IMPOSTE 1971, Italian
THE ITALIAN CONNECTION *LA MALA ORDINA* 1972, Italian
L'UCCELLO MIGRATORE 1972, Italian
SONO STATO IO 1973, Italian
AMORE E GIMNISTICA 1973, Italian
THE SENSUOUS SICILIAN *PAOLO IL CALDO* 1973, Italian
LA VIA DEI BABBUINI 1974, Italian
THERE IS NO. 13 1974, Italian
UN AMOUR COMME LE NOTRE 1974, Italian
HOW, WHEN AND WITH WHOM Warner Bros., 1974, Italian
SESSO MATTO 1974, Italian
DI MAMMA NON CE N'E UNA SOLA 1974, Italian
WE ALL LOVED EACH OTHER SO MUCH Cinema 5, 1975, Italian
LA MOGLIE VERGINE 1975, Italian
DUCK IN ORANGE SAUCE 1975, Italian
TELEFONI BIANCHI Dean Film, 1975, Italian
SCENT OF A WOMAN 20th Century-Fox, 1976, Italian
STRANGE SHADOWS IN AN EMPTY ROOM 1976, Italian
BASTE CHE NON SI SAPPIA IN GIRO 1976, Italian
PRIMA NOTTE DI NOZZE 1976, Italian
LUNA DI MIELE IN TRE 1976, Italian
BRUTTI SPORCHI E CATTIVI 1976, Italian
DIMMI CHE FAI TUTTO PER ME 1976, Italian
LA BANCA DI MONATE 1976, Italian
CATTIVI PENSIERI 1976, Italian
IL MARITO IN COLLEGIO 1976, Italian
E UNA BANCA RAPINAMMO PER FATAL CAMBINAZION co-composer with Renato Serio, 1976, Italian
THE BISHOP'S ROOM 1976, Italian
A SPECIAL DAY Cinema 5, 1977, Italian
RENATA 1977, Italian
LA PIU BELLA SERATA DELLA MIA VITA 1977, Italian
IN NOME DEL PAPA RE 1977, Italian
WIFEMISTRESS *MOGLIAMENTE* 1977, Italian
I NUOVI MOSTRI 1977, Italian
VIVA ITALIA! *I NUOVI MOSTRI* Cinema 6, 1978, Italian
DOTTORE JEKYLL E GENTILE SIGNORA co-composer with Renato Serio, 1978, Italian
DAS FUENFTE GEBOT 1979, West German
AMORE MIEI 1979, Italian
LA TERRAZZA United Artists, 1980, Italian-French
LA VITA E BELLA 1980, Italian
ARRIVANO I BERSAGLIERI 1980, Italian
PASSIONE D'AMORE 1980, Italian
PORQUE NO HACEMOS EL AMOR 1981, Italian-Spanish
A PIEDI NUDI NEL PARCO 1981, Italian
IL PARAMEDICO 1982, Italian
VIULENTEMENTE MIA 1982, Italian
IL MONDO NUOVO 1982, Italian
GRAND HOTEL EXCELSIOR 1982, Italian
LA BALLADE DE MAMLOUK 1982, Tunisian-Czech
PLUS BEAU QUE MOI TU MEURS 1983, French-Italian
IL CONTE TACCHIA Gaumont, 1983, Italian
MYSTERE Titanus, 1983, Italian
MACARONI Paramount, 1985, Italian

TIM TRUMAN

Agent: Bart-Milander - North Hollywood, 818/761-4040

L.A. TAKEDOWN (TF) AJAR/Mories Film Productions, 1989

SULKHAN TSINTSADZE

DRAGON LORD Golden Harvest, 1982, Hong Kong

SLAVA TSUKERMAN

LIQUID SKY co-composer with Brenda Hutchinson and Clive Smith, Cinevista, 1982

GIORGIO TUCCI

b. Italy
Contact: SIAE - Rome, Italy, 011-39-6-59-90-1

ZOMBI 2 *ZOMBIE FLESH EATERS* co-composer with Fabbio Frizzi, Variety Film, 1979, Italian

COLIN TULLY

Contact: PRS - London, England, 011-44-1-580-5544

THAT SINKING FEELING Samuel Goldwyn Company, 1979, Scottish
GREGORY'S GIRL Samuel Goldwyn Company, 1982, British

JONATHAN TUNICK

Agent: Bart-Milander - North Hollywood, 818/761-4040

A LITTLE NIGHT MUSIC ★★ adaptation, New World, 1978, Austrian-U.S.
FLYING HIGH (TF) Mark Carliner Productions, 1978
RENDEZVOUS HOTEL (TF) Mark Carliner Productions, 1979
SWAN SONG (TF) Renee Valente Productions/ Topanga Services Ltd./20th Century-Fox, 1980
THE JILTING OF GRANNY WEATHERALL (TF) Learning in Focus/American Short Story, 1980
BLINDED BY THE LIGHT (TF) Time-Life Films, 1980
ENDLESS LOVE Universal, 1981
FORT APACHE THE BRONX 20th Century-Fox, 1981
I AM THE CHEESE Libra Cinema 5, 1983
CONCEALED ENEMIES (TF) ☆ WGBH-Boston/ Goldcrest Films and Television/Comworld Productions, 1984, U.S.-British
BROTHERLY LOVE (TF) CBS Entertainment, 1985
THE B.R.A.T. PATROL (TF) Mark H. Ovitz Productions/ Walt Disney Productions, 1986
YOU RUINED MY LIFE (TF) Lantana-Kosberg Productions/Mark H. Ovitz Productions/Walt Disney TV, 1987

SIMON FISHER TURNER

Contact: PRS - London, England, 011-44-1-580-5544

CARAVAGGIO co-composer with Mary Phillips, British Film Institute, 1986, British

JONATHAN TURRIN

A NEW LIFE Paramount, 1988

STEVE TYRELL

Contact: BMI - Los Angeles, 213/659-9109

MIDNIGHT CROSSING Vestron, 1988
POUND PUPPIES AND THE LEGEND OF BIG PAW (AF) Tri-Star, 1988

IAN UNDERWOOD

Contact: BMI - Los Angeles, 213/659-9109

THE ARCHER—FUGITIVE FROM THE EMPIRE *FUGITIVE FROM THE EMPIRE* (TF) Mad-Dog Productions/ Universal TV, 1981

MARKUS URCHS

Contact: GEMA - West Germany, 011-49-89621400

THE LAST YEAR OF CHILDHOOD 1979, West German

TEO USUELLI

b. 1920 - Milan, Italy
Contact: SIAE - Rome, Italy, 011-39-6-59-90-1

DONNE E SOLDATI 1952, Italian
ITALIA K2 1955, Italian
MICHELE STROGOFF 1956, Italian
UN GIORNO IN EUROPA (FD) 1958, Italian
MADRI PERICOLOSE 1960, Italian
THE CONJUGAL BED *UNA STORIA MODERNA - L'APE REGINA* Embassy, 1963, Italian-French
I PATRIARCHI DELLA BIBBIA *THE PATRIARCHS OF THE BIBLE* co-composer with Gino Marinuzzi, Italian, 1963
THE APE WOMAN Embassy, 1964, Italian
SAUL E DAVID 1965, Italian
PARANOIA 1966, Italian
THE MAN WITH THE BALLOONS Sigma III, 1968, French-Italian
DILLINGER E MORTO Pegaso Film, 1969, Italian
THE SEED OF MAN SRL, 1970, Italian
L'UDIENZA Vides, 1971, Italian
TROIS MILLIARDS SANS ASCENSEUR 1972, Italian
R.S.I.: LA REPUBBLICA DI MUSSOLINI (FD) 1976, Italian
IL VOLCO DI PESCA 1976, Italian

RYUDO UZAKI

b. Japan
Contact: JASRAC - Tokyo, Japan, 011-81-3-502-6551

DOUBLE SUICIDE OF SONEZAKI 1978, Japanese
GOODBYE, FLICKMANIA Nippon Herald, 1979, Japanese

WARREN VACHE
THE LUCKIEST MAN IN THE WORLD co-composer with Jack Gale, Co-Star Entertainment, 1989

JEAN-LOUIS VALERO
Contact: SACEM - France, 011-33-14-747-5650

PAULINE AT THE BEACH Orion Classics, 1983, French
SUMMER *LE RAYON VERT* Orion Classics, 1986, French

CELSO VALLI
b. Italy
Contact: SIAE - Rome, Italy, 011-39-6-59-90-1

BLOOD TIES (CTF) RAI Channel One/Racing Pictures/Viacom International, 1986, Italian-U.S.

BERINGTON VAN CAMPEN
IN DANGEROUS COMPANY Manson International, 1988

KENNY VANCE
Agent: ICM - Los Angeles, 213/550-4000

HAIRSPRAY New Line Cinema, 1988
EDDIE AND THE CRUISERS II Embassy, 1989
HEART OF DIXIE Orion, 1989

VANGELIS
(Vangelis Papathinassou)
b. Greece
Contact: SACEM - France, 011-33-14-747-5650

APOCALYPSE DES ANIMA... 1970
CHARIOTS OF FIRE ★★ The Ladd Company/Warner Bros., 1981, British
BLADE RUNNER The Ladd Company/Warner Bros., 1982
MISSING Universal, 1982
ANTARTICA TLC Films, 1984, Japanese
THE BOUNTY Orion, 1984, British
FRANCESCO Istituto Luce/Italnoleggio, 1989, West German-Italian

ROSS VANNELLI
Contact: BMI - Los Angeles, 213/659-9109

BORN TO RACE MGM/UA, 1988

MELVIN VAN PEEBLES
b. 1932 - Chicago, Illinois
Home: 353 West 56th Street - Apt. 10F, New York, NY 10019, 212/489-6570

WATERMELON MAN Columbia, 1970

LAURENS VAN ROOYEN
b. Denmark
Contact: KODA - Denmark, 011-45-31-68-38-00

REMBRANDT: FECIT 1668 1978, Dutch
MYSTERIES 1979, Dutch
DEAR BOYS Sigma Films, 1980, Dutch
A WOMAN LIKE EVE Sigma Films, 1980, Dutch
FLIGHT OF THE RAINBIRD Dutch

DAVID VAN TIEGHEM
Contact: ASCAP - Los Angeles, 213/466-7681

WORKING GIRLS Miramax Films, 1987

PAOLO VASILE
b. Italy
Contact: SIAE - Rome, Italy, 011-39-6-59-90-1

THE SQUEEZE *THE RIP-OFF* Maverick International, 1976, Italian-U.S.

DIDIER VASSEUR
Contact: SACEM - France, 011-33-14-747-5650

SWEET REVENGE (CTF) Turner Pictures/Chrysalide Films/Canal/The Movie Group, 1990

CLEM VICARI
THE REDEEMER...SON OF SATAN! co-composer with Phil Gallo, 1978
MOTHER'S DAY co-composer with Phil Gallo, United Film Distribution, 1980

MICHAEL VICKERS
Contact: PRS - London, England, 011-44-1-580-5544

DRACULA TODAY *DRACULA A.D. 1972* Warner Bros., 1972, British
THE SEX THIEF 1974, British
AT THE EARTH'S CORE American International, 1976, British
WARRIORS OF ATLANTIS EMI, 1978, British

TOMMY VIG
Contact: ASCAP - Los Angeles, 213/466-7681

SWEET SIXTEEN CI Films, 1981
THE KID WITH THE BROKEN HALO (TF) Satellite Productions, 1982
THEY CALL ME BRUCE? *A FISTFUL OF CHOPSTICKS* Artists Releasing Corporation/Film Ventures International, 1982

STAN VINCENT
Contact: BMI - Los Angeles, 213/659-9109

FOREPLAY Cinema National Corporation, 1975

JOSEPH VITARELLI
Agent: CAA - Los Angeles, 213/288-4545

BIG MAN ON CAMPUS Vestron, 1989
HOW I GOT INTO COLLEGE 20th Century Fox, 1989

GYORGY VUKAN
Contact: ARTISJUS - Budapest, Hungary, Telex: 861-226527

HANUSSEN Studio Objektiv/CCC Filmkunst/Hungarofilm/MOKEP, 1988, Hungarian-West German

BOB WAHLER

A DIFFERENT STORY Avco Embassy, 1978

TOM WAITS

b. 1949
Contact: ASCAP - Los Angeles, 213/466-7681

ONE FROM THE HEART ★ Columbia, 1982
STREETWISE (FD) Angelika Films, 1985

RICK WAKEMAN

b. 1949
Contact: PRS - London, England, 011-44-1-580-5544

LISZTOMANIA Warner Bros., 1975, British
WHITE ROCK (FD) Shueisha Publishing Co., 1977
THE BURNING Orion, 1982
G'OLE (FD) IVECO, 1983, British
SHE American National Enterprises, 1983, Italian
CRIMES OF PASSION New World, 1984
CREEPSHOW II additional music, New World, 1987

NATHAN WAKS

Contact: APRA - Australia, 011-61-2-922-6422

MY BRILLIANT CAREER Analysis, 1980, Australian

DANA WALDEN

Agent: Robert Light - Los Angeles, 213/651-1777

DEAD RINGER co-composer with Barry Fasman, Stock Grange Productions, 1988
MY MOM'S A WEREWOLF co-composer with Barry Fasman, Crown International, 1988
THE IMMORTALIZER co-composer with Barry Fasman, Filmwest Productions, 1989
WHISPERS co-composer with Barry Fasman, Distant Horizon, 1989
HELLGATE co-composer with Barry Fasman, New World, 1989
RICH GIRL co-composer with Barry Fasman, Filmwest Productions, 1989
STREET HUNTER co-composer with Barry Fasman, 21st Century, 1989
NIGHT CLUB co-composer with Barry Fasman, Crown International, 1990

W.G. SNUFFY WALDEN

Agent: Gorfaine-Schwartz - Burbank, 818/954-9500

WINNIE (TF) All Girls Productions/NBC Productions, 1988
ROE VS. WADE (TF) The Manheim Co./NBC Productions, 1989
BURNING BRIDGES (TF) co-composer with Bennett Salvay, Andrea Baynes Productions/Lorimar TV, 1990

JACK WALDMAN

Contact: BMI - Los Angeles, 213/659-9109

A MARRIAGE Cinecom, 1983

SHIRLEY WALKER

Agent: Bart-Milander - North Hollywood, 818/761-4040

BLUE MOON Winfield Films
TOUCHED Lorimar Productions/Wildwoods Partners, 1983
THE VIOLATED The Violated Co., 1984
GHOULIES co-composer with Richard H. Band, Empire Pictures, 1985
THE DUNGEONMASTER co-composer with Richard H. Band, Empire Pictures, 1985
THE END OF AUGUST Quartett Films
STRIKE IT RICH co-composer with Cliff Eidelman, Millimeter Films, 1990
CHICAGO JOE AND THE SHOWGIRL co-composer with Hans Zimmer, 1990, British

SIMON WALKER

Contact: APRA - Australia, 011-61-2-922-6422

THE WILD DUCK RKR Releasing, 1983, Australian

BENNIE WALLACE

Agent: Bart-Milander - North Hollywood, 818/761-4040

BLAZE Buena Vista, 1989

ROB WALLACE

Contact: BMI - Los Angeles, 213/659-9109

KILL AND GO HIDE *THE CHILD* Boxoffice International, 1977

ROBERT J. WALSH

Agent: Bart-Milander - North Hollywood, 818/761-4040

THE GALACTIC CONNECTION Barrich Corporation, 1979
THE LOONEY, LOONEY, LOONEY BUGS BUNNY MOVIE (AF) Warner Bros., 1981
BLOOD SONG Allstate Films, 1981
REVENGE OF THE SHOGUN WOMEN 21st Century, 1982, Taiwanese
BUGS BUNNY'S 3RD MOVIE: 1001 RABBIT TALES (AF) Warner Bros., 1982
NOMAD RIDERS Windjammer Productions, 1982
THE DAFFY DUCK MOVIE: FANTASTIC ISLAND (AF) Warner Bros., 1982
HEARTBREAKER Monarex/Emerson Film Enterprises, 1983
LOVE YA FLORENCE NIGHTINGALE TPL Productions, 1983
THE WITCHING Associated Entertainment, 1983
YOUNG WARRIORS Cannon, 1983
REVENGE OF THE NINJA MGM/UA/Cannon, 1983
MY LITTLE PONY - THE MOVIE (AF) DEG, 1986
BLOOD MONEY Shapiro Entertainment, 1987
OVERKILL Manson International, 1987
DIGGIN' UP BUSINESS Curb Esquire Films, 1990

NATHAN WANG
b. August 8, 1956
Contact: North Light Sound, 213/467-8513

SPELLCASTER Empire Pictures, 1987
SCREWBALL HOTEL Maurice Smith Productions/ Avatar Film, 1988, Canadian

WANG CHUNG
Agent: ICM - Los Angeles, 213/550-4000

TO LIVE AND DIE IN L.A. MGM/UA, 1985

KEN WANNBERG
Agent: Bart-Milander - North Hollywood, 818/761-4040

THE TENDER WARRIOR Safari, 1971
THE PEACE KILLERS co-composer with Ruthann Friedman, 1971
WELCOME HOME, SOLDIER BOYS 20th Century-Fox, 1972
THE GREAT AMERICAN BEAUTY CONTEST (TF) ABC Circle Films, 1973
THE FOUR DEUCES Avco Embassy, 1974
LEPKE Warner Bros., 1975
BITTERSWEET LOVE Avco Embassy, 1976
THE LATE SHOW Warner Bros., 1977
THE CHANGELING AFD, 1980, Canadian
TRIBUTE 20th Century-Fox, 1980, U.S.-Canadian
THE AMATEUR 20th Century-Fox, 1982, Canadian
MOTHER LODE Agamemnon Films, 1982, Canadian
LOSIN' IT Embassy, 1983, Canadian-U.S.
OF UNKNOWN ORIGIN Warner Bros., 1983, Canadian
BLAME IT ON RIO co-composer with Oscar Castro Neves, 20th Century Fox, 1984
THE PHILADELPHIA EXPERIMENT New World, 1984
DRAW! (CTF) HBO Premiere Films/Astral Film Productions/Bryna Company, 1984, U.S.-Canadian
VANISHING ACT (TF) Robert Cooper Productions/ Levinson-Link Productions, 1986
MILES TO GO... (TF) Keating-Shostak Productions, 1986, U.S.-Canadian
RED RIVER (TF) Catalina Production Group/ MGM-UA TV, 1988

WAR
THE RIVER BIGER Cine Artists Pictures, 1976
YOUNGBLOOD American International, 1978

DALE O. WARREN
Contact: BMI - Los Angeles, 213/659-9109

THE KLANSMAN co-composer with Stu Gardner, Paramount, 1974

RICHARD LEWIS WARREN
Agent: Carol Faith - Beverly Hills, 213/274-0776

CARLY'S WEB (TF) MTM Enterprises, 1987

CHUMEI WATANABE
b. Japan
Contact: JASRAC - Tokyo, Japan, 011-81-3-502-6551

SUPER-GIANT 2 *SPACEMEN AGAINST THE VAMPIRES FROM SPACE* 1956, Japanese
THE NIGHT OF THE SEAGULL 1970, Japanese
EIJANAIKA Shochiku, 1981, Japanese

WAVEMAKER
THE TEMPEST Boyd's Co., 1979, British

STEVE WAX
TOUGH ENOUGH co-composer with Michael Lloyd, 20th Century-Fox, 1983

SAM WAYMON
Contact: BMI - Los Angeles, 213/659-9109

GANJA AND HESS Kelly-Jordan, 1973
JUST CRAZY ABOUT HORSES (FD) Fred Baker Films, 1979

JEFF WAYNE
Contact: PRS - London, England, 011-44-1-580-5544

McVICAR Crown International, 1981, British

MICHAEL WETHERWAX
CAGE New Century/Vista, 1989
MIDNIGHT SVS, 1989

JIMMY WEBB
THE NAKED APE Universal, 1973
VOICES United Artists, 1979
THE LAST UNICORN (AF) Jensen Farley Pictures, 1982
THE HANOI HILTON Cannon, 1987

ROGER WEBB
Contact: Pro-Canada: Canada, 1-416-445-8700

THE GODSEND Cannon, 1980
DEATH OF A CENTERFOLD: THE DOROTHY STRATTEN STORY (TF) Wilcox Productions/MGM TV, 1981
THE BOY IN BLUE 20th Century Fox, 1986, Canadian

ANDREW LLOYD WEBBER
b. England
Contact: BMI - Los Angeles, 213/659-9109

GUMSHOE Columbia, 1971, British
THE ODESSA FILE Columbia, 1974, British-West German

JULIUS WECHTER
Contact: ASCAP - Los Angeles, 213/466-7681

MIDNIGHT MADNESS Buena Vista, 1980

JOHN WEISMAN
LOOKING FOR MIRACLES (CTF) Sullivan Films, 1989

JOSEPH WEISS
Contact: ASCAP - Los Angeles, 213/466-7681

GIDEON'S TRUMPET (TF) Gideon Productions/Worldvision Enterprises, 1980

ED WELCH
Contact: PRS - London, England, 011-44-1-580-5544

STAND UP, VIRGIN SOLDIERS Warner Bros., 1977, British
THE 39 STEPS International Picture Show Company, 1978, British
THE SHILLINGBURY BLOWERS *...AND THE BAND PLAYED ON* Inner Circle, 1980, British

DANGEROUS DAVIES - THE LAST DETECTIVE ITC/ Inner Circle/Maidenhead Films, 1980, British
THE BOYS IN BLUE MAM Ltd./Apollo Leisure Group, 1983, British

KEN WELCH

MOVERS & SHAKERS co-composer with Mitzie Welch, MGM/UA, 1985

MITZIE WELCH

MOVERS & SHAKERS co-composer with Ken Welch, MGM/UA, 1985

LARRY WELLINGTON

Contact: BMI - Los Angeles, 213/659-9109

2000 MANIACS co-composer with Herschell Gordon Lewis, Box Office Spectaculars, 1964
HOW TO MAKE A DOLL 1967
A TASTE OF BLOOD *THE SECRET OF DR. ALUCARD* Creative Film Enterprises, 1967
THE WIZARD OF GORE Mayflower Pictures, 1970

RICK WENTWORTH

Contact: PRS - London, England, 011-44-1-580-5544

HOW TO GET AHEAD IN ADVERTISING co-composer with David Dundas, Warner Bros., 1989, British

FRED WERNER

Contact: ASCAP - Los Angeles, 213/466-7681

HUCKLEBERRY FINN United Artists, 1974
MOONSHINE COUNTY EXPRESS New World, 1977
THE DEATH OF OCEAN VIEW PARK (TF) Furia-Oringer Productions/Playboy Productions, 1979
A SMALL KILLING (TF) Orgolini-Nelson Productions/ Motown Productions, 1981

JIM WETZEL

HOMEWORK co-composer with Tony Jones, Jensen Farley Pictures, 1982

DAVID WHEATLEY

Agent: Richard Emler - Los Angeles, 213/651-0222

TOUGH ENOUGH co-composer with Michael Lloyd, 20th Century-Fox, 1983
AVENGING ANGEL co-composer with Paul Antonelli, Weitraub Productions, 1985
PRINCESS ACADEMY co-composer with Paul Antonelli, Weintraub Productions, 1987, U.S.-French-Yugoslav
MANY CLASSIC MOMENTS Da Capo Films
THE WOMEN'S CLUB co-composer with Paul Antonelli, Weintraub-Cloverleaf/Scorsese Productions, 1987
CHINA O'BRIEN co-composer with Paul Antonelli, Golden Harvest, 1989, U.S.-Hong Kong
OUT OF THE DARK co-composer with Paul Antonelli, New Line Cinema, 1989
SPEED ZONE Orion, 1989

JACK W. WHEATON

PENITENTIARY II MGM/UA, 1982

HAROLD WHEELER

Contact: ASCAP - Los Angeles, 213/466-7681

BENNY'S PLACE (TF) Titus Productions, 1982

DAVID WHITAKER

Contact: PRS - London, England, 011-44-1-580-5544

HAMMERHEAD Columbia, 1968, British
DON'T RAISE THE BRIDGE - LOWER THE RIVER Columbia, 1968, British
RUN WILD, RUN FREE Columbia, 1969, British
SCREAM AND SCREAM AGAIN American International, 1970, British
THE DEATH WHEELERS *PSYCHOMANIA* Scotia International, 1971, British
DR. JEKYLL AND SISTER HYDE American International, 1972, British
VAMPIRE CIRCUS Rank, 1972, British
OLD DRACULA *VAMPIRA* American International, 1975, British
DOMINIQUE Sword and Sworcery Productions, 1979, British
THE SWORD AND THE SORCERER Group 1, 1982

LENNY WHITE

HOUSE PARTY co-composer with Marcus Miller, New Line Cinema, 1990

MAURICE WHITE

THAT'S THE WAY OF THE WORLD United Artists, 1975

NORMAN WHITFIELD

CAR WASH Universal, 1976

STACY WIDELITZ

Agent: Triad Artists - Los Angeles, 213/556-2727

RETURN TO HORROR HIGH New World, 1987
STRANDED New Line Cinema, 1987
DARK TOWER Spectrafilm, 1987, Canadian
PHANTOM OF THE MALL Fries Distribution, 1989

ROLF WILHELM

b. Germany
Contact: GEMA - Munich, 011-49-89621400

THE REVOLT OF GUNNER ASCH 1955, West German
SIEGFRIED *WHOM THE GODS WISH TO DESTROY/DIE NIBELUNGEN* 1967, West German
HURRAH! THE SCHOOL IS BURNING 1970, West German
LUDWIG ON THE LOOKOUT FOR A WIFE 1970, West German
WE CHOP THE TEACHERS INTO MINCE MEAT 1970, West German
THE SERPENT'S EGG Paramount, 1978, West German-U.S.
FROM THE LIFE OF THE MARIONETTES Universal/AFD, 1980, West German

SCOTT WILK

Contact: ASCAP - Los Angeles, 213/466-7681

PLAIN CLOTHES Paramount, 1988

GEORGE WILKINS

Contact: ASCAP - Los Angeles, 213/466-7681

BLACK MARKET BABY (TF) co-composer with Richard Bellis, Brut Productions, 1977

RICK WILKINS

Contact: Pro-Canada - Canada, 1-416-445-8700

THE CHANGELING AFD, 1980, Canadian

MARC WILKINSON

Contact: PRS - London, England, 011-44-1-580-5544

IF... Paramount, 1969, British
THE ROYAL HUNT OF THE SUN National General, 1969, British
BLOOD ON SATAN'S CLAW *SATAN'S SKIN* Cannon, 1971, British
EAGLE IN A CAGE National General, 1971, British-Yugoslavian
THE DARWIN ADVENTURE 20th Century-Fox, 1972, British
THE MAN AND THE SNAKE 1972
THE RETURN 1973
THE HIRELING Columbia, 1973, British
THE MANGO TREE 1977, Australian
THE QUARTERMASS CONCLUSION co-composer with Nic Rowley, Euston Films Ltd., 1979, British
EAGLE'S WING International Picture Show, 1979, British
THE FIENDISH PLOT OF DR. FU MANCHU Orion/ Warner Bros., 1980, British
ENIGMA Embassy, 1983
KIM (TF) London Films, 1984

DAVID C. WILLIAMS

Agent: Robert Light - Los Angeles, 213/651-1777

DELIRIUM Maris Entertainment, 1980
HARMONY Anvil Productions, 1981
FREE RIDE Galaxy International, 1986
TERROR SQUAD The Matterhorn Group, 1987
BEFORE GOD Quest Productions, 1987
SIDE ROADS Side Roads Productions, 1988
DEADLY INNOCENCE Universal, 1988
AFTER SCHOOL Moviestore Entertainment, 1988

JACK ERIC WILLIAMS

NIGHTMARE 21st Century, 1981

JOHN WILLIAMS

b. 1932 - Long Island, New York
Agent: Gorfaine-Schwartz - Burbank, 818/954-9500

I PASSED FOR WHITE Allied Artists, 1960
BECAUSE THEY'RE YOUNG Columbia, 1960
THE SECRET WAYS Universal, 1961
BACHELOR FLAT 20th Century-Fox, 1962
DIAMOND HEAD Columbia, 1963
GIDGET GOES TO ROME Columbia, 1963
NONE BUT THE BRAVE Warner Bros., 1964, U.S.-Japanese
THE KILLERS Universal, 1964
JOHN GOLDFARB, PLEASE COME HOME 20th Century-Fox, 1965
HOW TO STEAL A MILLION Columbia, 1966
NOT WITH MY WIFE, YOU DON'T! Warner Bros., 1966
THE PLAINSMAN Universal, 1966
PENELOPE MGM, 1966
THE RARE BREED Universal, 1966
A GUIDE FOR THE MARRIED MAN 20th Century-Fox, 1967
FITZWILLY United Artists, 1967
VALLEY OF THE DOLLS ★ adaptation, 20th Century-Fox, 1967
SERGEANT RYKER *THE CASE AGAINST PAUL RYKER* Universal, 1968, originally filmed for television in 1963
HEIDI (TF) ☆☆ Omnibus-Biography Productions, 1968
DADDY'S GONE A-HUNTING National General, 1969
THE REIVERS ★ National General, 1969
GOODBYE, MR. CHIPS ★ adaptation, MGM, 1969, British
THE STORY OF A WOMAN 1970, Italian
JANE EYRE (TF) ☆☆ Omnibus Productions/Sagittarius Productions, 1971, British-U.S.
FIDDLER ON THE ROOF ★★ adaptation, United Artists, 1971
THE SCREAMING WOMAN (TF) Universal TV, 1972
THE COWBOYS Warner Bros., 1972
THE POSEIDON ADVENTURE ★ 20th Century-Fox, 1972
PETE N'TILLIE Universal, 1972
IMAGES ★ Columbia, 1972, Irish
THE MAN WHO LOVED CAT DANCING MGM, 1973
TOM SAWYER ★ adaptation, United Artists, 1973
THE PAPER CHASE 20th Century-Fox, 1973
THE LONG GOODBYE United Artists, 1973
CINDERELLA LIBERTY ★ 20th Century-Fox, 1974
THE TOWERING INFERNO ★ 20th Century-Fox, 1974
EARTHQUAKE Universal, 1974
THE SUGERLAND EXPRESS Universal, 1974
CONRACK 20th Century-Fox, 1974
CALIFORNIA SPLIT Columbia, 1974
THE EIGER SANCTION Universal, 1975
JAWS ★★ Universal, 1975
THE MISSOURI BREAKS United Artists, 1976
FAMILY PLOT Universal, 1976
MIDWAY Universal, 1976
BLACK SUNDAY Universal, 1976
STAR WARS ★★ 20th Century-Fox, 1977
CLOSE ENCOUNTERS OF THE THIRD KIND ★ Columbia, 1977
SUPERMAN ★ Warner Bros., 1978, U.S.-British
JAWS 2 Universal, 1978
THE FURY 20th Century-Fox, 1978
DRACULA Universal, 1979
1941 Universal/Columbia, 1979
THE EMPIRE STRIKES BACK ★ 20th Century-Fox, 1980
RAIDERS OF THE LOST ARK ★ Paramount, 1981
HEARTBEEPS Universal, 1981
E.T. THE EXTRA-TERRESTRIAL ★★ Universal, 1982
MONSIGNOR 20th Century-Fox, 1982
THE RETURN OF THE JEDI ★ 20th Century-Fox, 1983
INDIANA JONES AND THE TEMPLE OF DOOM ★ Paramount, 1984
THE RIVER ★ Universal, 1984
SPACECAMP 20th Century Fox, 1986
THE WITCHES OF EASTWICK ★ Warner Bros., 1987
EMPIRE OF THE SUN ★ Warner Bros., 1987
THE ACCIDENTAL TOURIST ★ Warner Bros., 1988
INDIANA JONES AND THE LAST CRUSADE ★ Paramount, 1989
ALWAYS Universal, 1989
BORN ON THE FOURTH OF JULY ★ Universal, 1989
STANLEY AND IRIS MGM/UA, 1990
PRESUMED INNOCENT Warner Bros., 1990

PATRICK WILLIAMS

b. April 23, 1939 - Bonne Terre, Missouri
Agent: Gorfaine-Schwartz - Burbank, 818/954-9500

HOW SWEET IT IS! Buena Vista, 1968
DON'T DRINK THE WATER Avco Embassy, 1969
A NICE GIRL LIKE ME Avco Embassy, 1969, British

PIGEONS *THE SIDELONG GLANCES OF A PIGEON KICKER* MGM, 1970
SAN FRANCISCO INTERNATIONAL (TF) Universal TV, 1970
MACHO CALLAHAN Avco Embassy, 1970
INCIDENT IN SAN FRANCISCO (TF) QM Productions/ American Broadcasting Company, 1971
TRAVIS LOGAN, D.A. (TF) QM Productions, 1971
THE FAILING OF RAYMOND (TF) Universal TV, 1971
LOCK, STOCK AND BARREL (TF) Universal TV, 1971
TERROR IN THE SKY (TF) Paramount Pictures TV, 1971
HARDCASE (TF) Hanna-Barbera Productions, 1972
EVEL KNIEVEL Fanfare, 1972
THE STREETS OF SAN FRANCISCO (TF) QM Productions/Warner Bros. TV, 1972
SHORT WALK TO DAYLIGHT (TF) Universal TV, 1972
THE MAGICIAN (TF) B&B Productions/Paramount Pictures TV, 1973
HITCHED (TF) Universal TV, 1973
SSSSSSS Universal, 1973
ORDEAL *INFERNO* (TF) 20th Century-Fox TV, 1973
MRS. SUNDANCE (TF) 20th Century-Fox TV, 1974
MURDER OR MERCY (TF) QM Productions, 1974
MOONCHILD co-composer with Billy Byers, Filmmakers Ltd./American Films Ltd., 1974
HARRAD SUMMER Cinerama Releasing Corporation, 1974
FRAMED Paramount, 1974
STOWAWAY TO THE MOON (TF) 20th Century-Fox TV, 1975
CROSSFIRE (TF) QM Productions, 1975
HEX 1975
THE LIVES OF JENNY DOLAN (TF) Ross Hunter Productions/Paramount Pictures TV, 1975
MOST WANTED (TF) QM Productions, 1976
STONESTREET: WHO KILLED THE CENTERFOLD MODEL? (TF) Universal TV, 1977
THE MAN WITH THE POWER (TF) Universal TV, 1977
THE ONE AND ONLY Paramount, 1978
THE CHEAP DETECTIVE Columbia, 1978
CASEY'S SHADOW Columbia, 1978
BREAKING AWAY ★ adaptation, 20th Century-Fox, 1979
BUTCH AND SUNDANCE: THE EARLY DAYS 20th Century-Fox, 1979
HOT STUFF Columbia, 1979
CUBA United Artists, 1979
CHARLIE CHAN AND THE CURSE OF THE DRAGON QUEEN American Cinema, 1980
WHOLLY MOSES Columbia, 1980
HERO AT LARGE MGM/United Artists, 1980
USED CARS Columbia, 1980
IT'S MY TURN Columbia, 1980
HOW TO BEAT THE HIGH COST OF LIVING American International, 1980
THE MIRACLE OF KATHY MILLER (TF) Rothman-Wohl Productions/Universal TV, 1981
THE PRINCESS AND THE CABBIE (TF) ☆☆ Freyda Rothstein Productions/Time-Life Productions, 1981
TOMORROW'S CHILD (TF) 20th Century-Fox TV, 1982
SOME KIND OF HERO Paramount, 1982
THE BEST LITTLE WHOREHOUSE IN TEXAS adaptation, Universal, 1982
MOONLIGHT (TF) Universal TV, 1982
THE TOY Columbia, 1982
SWING SHIFT Warner Bros., 1983
THE FIGHTER (TF) Martin Manulis Productions/The Catalina Production Group, 1983
MARVIN AND TIGE *LIKE FATHER AND SON* 20th Century-Fox International Classics, 1983
THE BUDDY SYSTEM 20th Century Fox, 1984
BEST DEFENSE Paramount, 1984
ALL OF ME Universal, 1984
THE SLUGGER'S WIFE Columbia, 1985
SEDUCED (TF) ☆ Catalina Production Group/Comworld Productions, 1985
JUST BETWEEN FRIENDS Orion, 1986
VIOLETS ARE BLUE Columbia, 1986
OCEANS OF FIRE (TF) Catalina Production Group, 1986
KOJAK: THE PRICE OF JUSTICE (TF) Universal TV, 1987
LAGUNA HEAT (CTF) HBO Pictures/Jay Weston Productions, 1987
FRESH HORSES co-composer with David Foster, Columbia/WEG, 1988
DOUBLE STANDARD (TF) Louis Randolph Productions/ Fenton Entertainment Group/Fries Entertainment, 1988
MAYBE BABY (TF) Perry Lafferty Productions/von Zerneck-Samuels Productions, 1988
WORTH WINNING 20th Century Fox, 1989
COLUMBO: MURDER - SELF-PORTRAIT (TF) Universal TV, 1989
LOVE AND LIES (TF) Fredya Rothstein Productions, 1990
CRY BABY Universal, 1990
IN THE SPIRIT Castle Hill, 1990

PAUL WILLIAMS

b. September 19, 1940 - Omaha, Nebraska
Contact: ASCAP - Los Angeles, 213/466-7681

PHANTOM OF THE PARADISE ★ co-composer with George Aliceson Tipton, 20th Century-Fox, 1974
BUGSY MALONE ★ Paramount, 1976, British
A STAR IS BORN co-composer, Warner Bros., 1976
FLIGHT TO HOLOCAUST (TF) Aycee Productions/First Artists Production Company, 1977
THE END United Artists, 1978
THE MUPPET MOVIE ★ co-composer with Kenny Ascher, AFD, 1979

MALCOLM WILLIAMSON

b. 1931 - Mosmon Bay, Australia
Contact: PRS - London, England, 011-44-1-580-5544

THE BRIDES OF DRACULA Universal, 1960, British
THE HORROR OF FRANKENSTEIN Levitt-Pickman, 1970, British
CRESCENDO Warner Bros., 1972, British
NOTHING BUT THE NIGHT Cinema Systems, 1975, British
WATERSHIP DOWN (AF) co-composer, Avco Embassy, 1978, British

ANDREW WILSON

Contact: APRA - Australia, 011-61-2-922-6422

CHAIN REACTION 1980, Australian

SAM WINANS

Contact: BMI - Los Angeles, 213/659-9109

PARTY LINE SVS Films, 1988

ALAIN WISNIAK

Contact: SACEM - France, 011-33-14-747-5650

FEMME PUBLIQUE 1984, French

DAVID WOLINSKI
Contact: ASCAP - Los Angeles, 213/466-7681

SEASON OF FEAR MGM/UA, 1989

HAWK WOLINSKI
Contact: ASCAP - Los Angeles, 213/466-7681

WILDCATS co-composer with James Newton Howard, Warner Bros., 1986

STEVIE WONDER
(Steveland Morris)
Contact: ASCAP - Los Angeles, 213/466-7681

THE SECRET LIFE OF PLANTS (FD) Paramount, 1978

GUY WOOLFENDEN
Contact: PRS - London, England, 011-44-1-580-5544

SECRETS Samuel Goldwyn Company, 1983, British

TOM WORRALL
Contact: ASCAP - Los Angeles, 213/466-7681

THE WILD WOMEN OF CHASTITY GULCH (TF) co-composer with Frank De Vol, Aaron Spelling Productions, 1982

JODY TAYLOR WORTH
UP THE ACADEMY Warner Bros., 1980

CLIVE WRIGHT
Contact: BMI - Los Angeles, 213/659-9109

SOUTH TO RENO co-composer with Nigel Holton, Open Road Productions/Pendulum Productions, 1987

GARY WRIGHT
Contact: ASCAP - Los Angeles, 213/466-7681

BENJAMIN 1973, West German
ENDANGERED SPECIES MGM/UA, 1982

BILL WYMAN
Contact: PRS - London, England, 011-44-1-580-5544

GREEN ICE ITC Films, 1981, British

DAN WYMAN
WITHOUT WARNING Filmways, 1980
THE RETURN *THE ALIEN'S RETURN* 1981
HELL NIGHT Compass International, 1981

STAVROS XARCHAKOS
b. Greece
Contact: AEPI - Athens, Greece, 011-30-1-821-9512

RED LANTERNS 1964, Greek
THE STONE 1965, Greek
THE HOT MONTH OF AUGUST 1966, Greek
SIGNS OF LIFE 1968, Greek
GIRLS IN THE SUN 1968, Greek
LYCISTRATA 1972, Greek
REBETICO 1983, Greek
SWEET COUNTRY Cinema Group, 1987

SHOJI YAMASHIRO
Contact: JASRAC - Tokyo, Japan, 011-81-3-502-6551

AKIRA (AF) Streamline Pictures, 1990, Japanese

STOMU YAMASHITA
Contact: JASRAC - Tokyo, Japan, 011-81-3-502-6551

ONE BY ONE *EAST WIND* 1974
ART OF KILLING 1978, Japanese
THE MAN WHO FELL TO EARTH Cinema 5, 1976, British
THE TEMPEST Columbia, 1982

YANNI
Agent: Gorfaine-Schwartz - Burbank, 818/954-9500

HEART OF MIDNIGHT Samuel Goldwyn Company, 1988
STEAL OF THE SKY (CTF) Yorma Ben-Ami/ Paramount, 1988
FRANK NITTI: THE ENFORCER (TF) Leonard Hill Films, 1988

GABRIEL YARED
b. France
Agent: Bart-Milander - North Hollywood, 818/761-4040

MISS O'GYNIE AND THE FLOWER MAN 1974, Belgian
EVERY MAN FOR HIMSELF *SAUVE QUI PEUT LA VIE* New Yorker/Zoetrope, 1980, Swiss-French
MELEVIL UGC, 1981, French-West German
INVITATION AU VOYAGE Mel Difussion/Filmalpha, 1982, French-Italian
THE MOON AND THE GUTTER Triumph/Columbia, 1983, French-Italian
LUCIE SUR SEINE Nicole Jouve Interama, 1983, French
HANNA K. Universal Classics, 1983, French

LA JAVA DES OMBRES *SHADOW DANCE* 1983, French
SARAH UGC, 1983, French
AL HOUROB AL SAGHIRA *LITTLE WARS* 1983, Lebanese
LA SCARLATINE UGC, 1984, French
DANGEROUS MOVES Arthur Cohn Productions, 1984, Swiss
DREAM ONE *NEMO* NEF, 1984, British
ADIEU, BONAPARTE AMLF, 1985, French-Egyptian
ZONE ROUGE *RED ZONE* AAA/Revcom Films, 1986, French
FLAGRANT DESIR *A CERTAIN DESIRE* UGC, 1986, French
BETTY BLUE *37.2 DEGREES LE MATIN* Alive Films, 1986, French
DESORDRE Forum Distribution, 1986, French
BEYOND THERAPY New World, 1987
CLEAN AND SOBER Warner Bros., 1988
CAMILLE CLAUDEL Orion Classics, 1988, French
ROMERO Four Seasons Entertainment, 1989
THE KING'S WHORE J&M Entertainment, 1990, French-Italian-U.S.

YELLO

Agent: Bart-Milander - North Hollywood, 818/761-4040

THE ADVENTURES OF FORD FAIRLANE 20th Century-Fox, 1990

CHRISTOPHER YOUNG

Agent: Lawrence B. Marks Agency - Northridge, 818/831-1830

THE DORM THAT DRIPPED BLOOD *DEATH DORM/ PRANKS* New Image, 1983
THE POWER Artists Releasing Corporation/Film Ventures International, 1984
A SAVAGE HUNGER *THE OASIS* Shapiro Entertainment, 1984
HIGHPOINT New World, 1984
WHEELS OF FIRE New Horizons, 1984
WIZARDS OF THE LOST KINGDOM Concorde/ Cinema Group, 1985, U.S.-Argentine
BARBARIAN QUEEN Concorde/Cinema Group, 1985, U.S.-Argentine
AVENGING ANGEL New World, 1985
DEF-CON 4 New World, 1985, Canadian
DESERT WARRIOR Concorde, 1985, U.S.-Filipino
NIGHTMARE ON ELM STREET, PART 2: FREDDY'S REVENGE New Line Cinema, 1985
TORMENT New World, 1986
GETTING EVEN American Distribution Group, 1986
INVADERS FROM MARS co-composer with Sylvester LeVay, Cannon, 1986
TRICK OR TREAT DEG, 1986
AMERICAN HARVEST (TF) Ruth-Stratton Productions/ The Finnegan Company, 1987
HELLRAISER New World, 1987, British
FLOWERS IN THE ATTIC New World, 1987
THE TELEPHONE New World, 1988
BAT-21 Tri-Star, 1988
HAUNTED SUMMER Cannon, 1988
HELLBOUND: HELLRAISER II New World, 1988, British-U.S.
THE FLY II 20th Century Fox, 1989, U.S.-Canadian
HIDER IN THE HOUSE Vestron, 1989
LAST FLIGHT OUT (TF) ☆ The Mannheim Co./Co-Star Entertainment/NBC Productions, 1990

NEIL YOUNG

b. November 12, 1945 - Toronto, Canada
Contact: ASCAP - Los Angeles, 213/466-7681

JOURNEY THROUGH THE PAST 1973
WHERE THE BUFFALO ROAM Universal, 1980
HUMAN HIGHWAY co-composer with Devo, Shakey Pictures, 1982

PATRICK YOUNG

Contact: PRS - London, England, 011-44-1-580-5544

STEVIE First Artists, 1978, British

NORIO YUASA

b. Japan
Contact: JASRAC - Tokyo, Japan, 011-81-3-502-6551

ISLAND OF THE EVIL SPIRITS Kadokawa/Toei, 1981, Japanese

Z

FRANK ZAPPA

b. December 21, 1940 - Baltimore, Maryland
Agent: ICM - Los Angeles, 213/550-4000

200 MOTELS United Artists, 1971, British
BABY SNAKES Intercontinental Absurdities, 1979

ALLAN ZAVOD

b. Australia
Agent: Robert Light - Los Angeles, 213/651-1777

DEATH OF A SOLDIER Scotti Brothers, 1986, Australian
THE BIG HURT Valhalla Films, 1986, Australian
THE RIGHT HAND MAN FilmDallas, 1987, Australian
THE HOWLING III *THE MARSUPIALS: THE HOWLING III* Square Pictures, 1987, Australian
THE TIME GUARDIAN Hemdale, 1987, Australian
SEBASTIAN AND THE SPARROW Kino Films, 1988
COMMUNION co-composer with Eric Clapton, New Line Cinema, 1989
MARTIANS GO HOME Taurus Entertainment Co., 1989

PAUL ZAZA

Contact: CAPAC - Ontario, Canada, 1-416-924-4427

TITLE SHOT 1979, Canadian
MURDER BY DECREE co-composer with Carl Zittrer, Avco Embassy, 1979, Canadian-British
PROM NIGHT co-composer with Carl Zittrer, Avco Embassy, 1980, Canadian
THE KIDNAPPING OF THE PRESIDENT Crown International, 1980, Canadian
GAS Paramount, 1981
MY BLOODY VALENTINE Paramount, 1981, Canadian
PORKY'S co-composer with Carl Zittrer, 20th Century-Fox, 1981, U.S.-Canadian
MELANIE Embassy, 1982, Canadian
CURTAINS Jensen Farley Pictures, 1983, Canadian

A CHRISTMAS STORY co-composer with Paul Zittrer, MGM/UA, 1983, Canadian
TURK 182 20th Century Fox, 1985
BREAKING ALL THE RULES New World, 1985, Canadian
ISAAC LITTLEFEATHERS Lauron Productions, 1985, Canadian
THE VINDICATOR *FRANKENSTEIN '88* 20th Century Fox, 1985, Canadian
BULLIES Universal, 1986, Canadian
THE PINK CHIQUITAS Shapiro Entertainment, 1986, Canadian
FROM THE HIP DEG, 1987
MEATBALLS III Movie Store, 1987
FORD: THE MAN AND THE MACHINE (TF) Lantana Productions/Robert Halmi, Inc., 1987
LOOSE CANNONS Tri-Star, 1990

DENNY ZEITLIN
Contact: BMI - Los Angeles, 213/659-9109

INVASION OF THE BODY SNATCHERS United Artists, 1978

AL ZIMA
SOUTH BRONX HEROES Continental, 1985

HANS ZIMMER
Agent: Gorfaine-Schwartz - Burbank, 818/954-9500

MOONLIGHTING co-composer with Stanley Myers, Universal Classics, 1982, British
SUCCESS IS THE BEST REVENGE co-composer with Stanely Myers, Triumph/Columbia, 1984, British
INSIGNIFICANCE co-composer with Stanley Myers, Island Alive, 1985, British
WILD HORSES (TF) co-composer with Stanley Myers, Wild Horses Productions/Telepictures Productions, 1985
DOUBLE EXPOSURE United Film Distribution Co., 1987
THE NATURE OF THE BEAST co-composer with Stanley Myers, Rosso Productions, 1988, British
A WORLD APART Atlantic Releasing Corporation, 1988, British
BURNING SECRET Vestron, 1988, U.S.-British-West German
ELPHIDA Working Title Films, 1988, British
WONDERLAND *THE FRUIT MACHINE* Vestron, 1988, British
PAPERHOUSE Vestron, 1988, British
THE PRISONER OF RIO Multi Media AG/Samba Corporation, 1988, Swiss
VARDO Working Title Films, 1988, British
RAIN MAN ★ MGM/UA, 1988
TWISTER Vestron, 1989, British
S.P.O.O.K.S. Vestron, 1989
DIAMOND SKULLS Film Four International/British Screen/Working Title, 1989, British
BLACK RAIN Paramount, 1989
DRIVING MISS DAISY Warner Bros., 1989
FOOLS OF FORTUNE New Line Cinema, 1990, British
BIRD ON A WIRE Universal, 1990
CHICAGO JOE AND THE SHOWGIRL co-composer with Shirley Walker, 1990, British
DAYS OF THUNDER Paramount, 1990
GREEN CARD Buena Vista, 1990
PACIFIC HEIGHTS 20th Century-Fox, 1990
BACKDRAFT 1991

DON ZIMMERS
Contact: BMI - Los Angeles, 213/659-9109

SCREAMS OF A WINTER NIGHT Dimension Pictures, 1979

CARL ZITTRER
Contact: CAPAC - Ontario, Canada, 1-416-924-4427

CHILDREN SHOULDN'T PLAY WITH DEAD THINGS Gemini Film, 1972, Canadian
BLOOD ORGY OF THE SHE DEVILS Gemini Films, 1973
DERANGED American International, 1974
DEATH DREAM *DEAD OF NIGHT/THE NIGHT ANDY CAME HOME* Europix International, 1974, Canadian
BLACK CHRISTMAS *SILENT NIGHT, EVIL NIGHT/ STRANGER IN THE HOUSE* Warner Bros., 1975, Canadian
MURDER BY DECREE co-composer with Paul Zaza, Avco Embassy, 1979, Canadian-British
PROM NIGHT co-composer wih Paul Zaza, Avco Embassy, 1980, Canadian
PORKY'S co-composer with Paul Zaza, 20th Century-Fox, 1981, U.S.-Canadian
PORKY'S II: THE NEXT DAY 20th Century-Fox, 1983, U.S.-Canadian
A CHRISTMAS STORY co-composer with Paul Zaza, MGM/UA, 1983, Canadian

★★★★

NOTABLE COMPOSERS OF THE PAST

LISTINGS

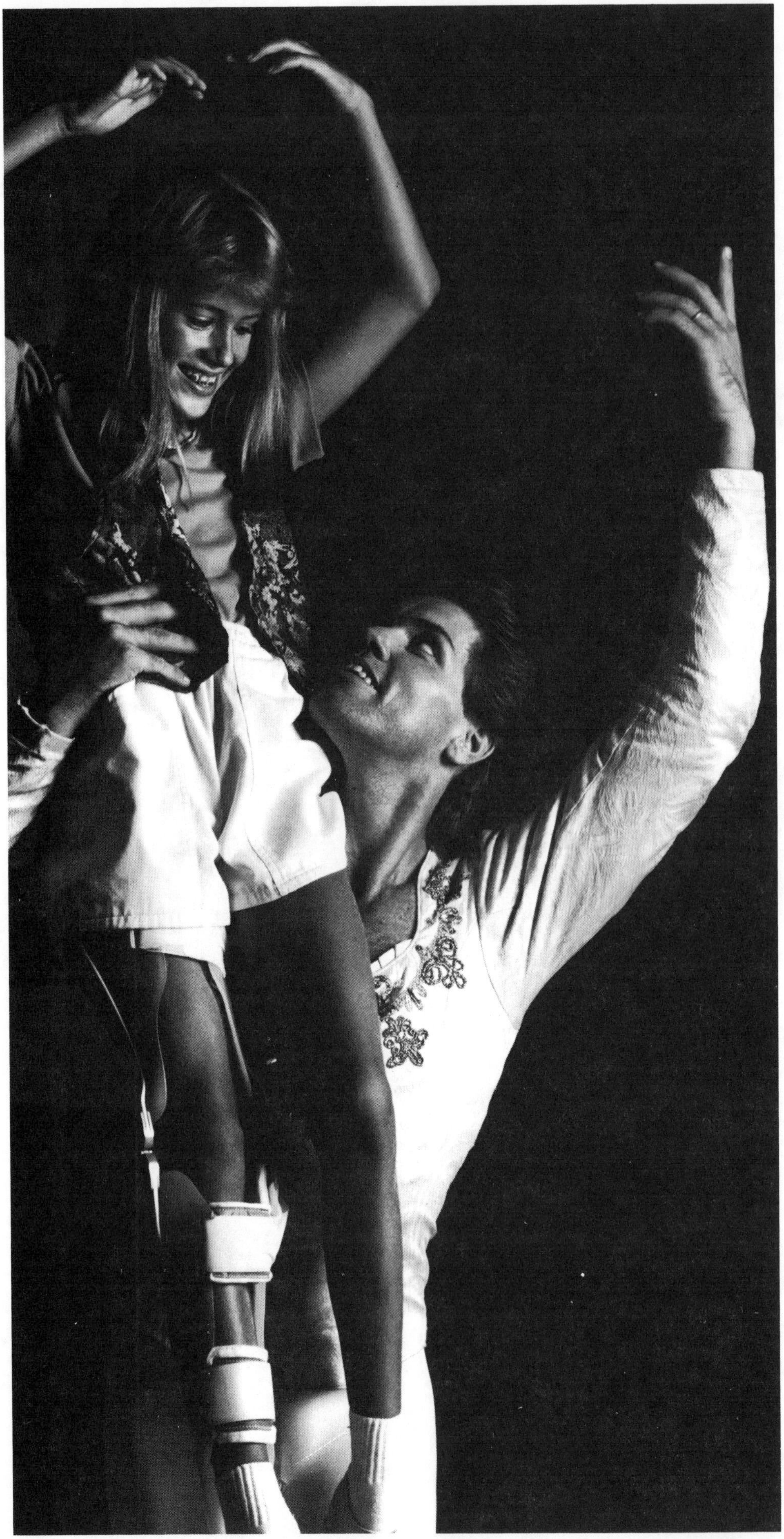

"For a second, I felt just like a ballet dancer, too."

This little girl had a wish come true, thanks to the help of people who care at the Make-A-Wish Foundation. She met a real dancer, saw a real ballet, and was given a pair of toe shoes all her own.

A simple wish means more than most of us could ever imagine for a child with a life-threatening illness. A wish is a special moment and an unforgettable memory for a grateful family.

If you would like to help make a child's wish come true, please, call or write the Make-A-Wish Foundation and find out how you can help. Somewhere a little dreamer is counting on you.

Make-A-Wish
Foundation® of America

RICHARD ADDINSELL

b. January 13, 1904 - London, England
d. November 15, 1977 - Chelsea, England

AMATEUR GENTLEMAN co-composer with Walter Goehr, United Artists, 1936, British
DARK JOURNEY 1937, British
FAREWELL AGAIN 1937, British
FIRE OVER ENGLAND 1937, British
THE BEACHCOMBER *VESSEL OF WRATH* 1937, British
SOUTH RIDING 1938, British
GOODBYE MR. CHIPS MGM, 1939
THE LION HAS WINGS United Artists, 1939, British
GASLIGHT ANGEL STREET 1939, British
BRITAIN AT BAY 1940, British
CONTRABAND *BLACKOUT* Anglo-American, 1940, British
THIS ENGLAND 1940, British
CAMOUFLAGE 1940, British
SPECIAL DISPATCH 1940, British
MEN OF THE LIGHTSHIP 1940, British
THE GREEN BELT 1941, British
LOVE ON THE DOLE 1941, British
SUICIDE SQUADRON *DANGEROUS MOONLIGHT* RKO Radio, 1941, British
THE BIG BLOCKADE 1942, British
THE SIEGE OF TOBRUK 1942, British
THE DAY WILL DAWN 1942, British
THE AVENGERS 1942, British
WE SAIL AT MIDNIGHT 1943, British
A.T.S. 1943, British
THE NEW LOT 1943, British
BLITHE SPIRIT United Artists, 1945, British
A DIARY FOR TIMOTHY 1945, British
ONE WOMAN'S STORY *THE PASSIONATE FRIENDS* Universal, 1949, British
UNDER CAPRICORN Warner Bros., 1949, British-U.S.
THE BLACK ROSE 20th Century-Fox, 1950, British-U.S.
RING AROUND THE MOON 1950, British
TOM BROWN'S SCHOOLDAYS United Artists, 1951, British
A CHRISTMAS CAROL *SCROOGE* United Artists, 1951, British
HIGHLY DANGEROUS Lippert, 1951, British
ENCORE 1952, British
SEA DEVILS RKO Radio, 1953
BEAU BRUMMEL MGM, 1954
OUT OF THE CLOUDS Rank, 1954, British
THE PRINCE AND THE SHOWGIRL Warner Bros., 1957, U.S.-British
A TALE OF TWO CITIES Rank, 1958, British
LOSS OF INNOCENCE *THE GREENGAGE SUMMER* Columbia, 1961, British
MACBETH British Lion, 1961, British
THE ROMAN SPRING OF MRS. STONE Warner Bros., 1961
WALTZ OF THE TOREADORS Continental, 1962, British
THE WAR LOVER Columbia, 1962, British
LIFE AT THE TOP Columbia, 1965, British

JEFF ALEXANDER

b. 1910 - Seattle, Washington
d. December 23, 1989 - Seattle, Washington

WESTWARD THE WOMEN MGM, 1952
AFFAIRS OF DOBIE GILLIS MGM, 1953
ESCAPE FROM FORT BRAVO MGM, 1953
REMAINS TO BE SEEN MGM, 1953
PRISONER OF WAR MGM, 1954
ROGUE COP MGM, 1954
THE TENDER TRAP MGM, 1955
THE GREAT AMERICAN PASTIME MGM, 1956
RANSOM MGM, 1956
SLANDER MGM, 1956
THESE WILDER YEARS MGM, 1956
GUN GLORY MGM, 1957
JAILHOUSE ROCK MGM, 1957
THE WINGS OF EAGLES MGM, 1957
THE HIGH COST OF LOVING MGM, 1958
PARTY GIRL MGM, 1958
SADDLE THE WIND MGM, 1958
THE SHEEPMAN MGM, 1958
THE MATING GAME MGM, 1959
ASK ANY GIRL MGM, 1959
IT STARTED WITH A KISS MGM, 1959
THE GAZEBO MGM, 1959
ALL THE FINE YOUNG CANNIBALS MGM, 1960
THE GEORGE RAFT STORY Allied Artists, 1961
KID GALAHAD United Artists, 1962
THE ROUNDERS MGM, 1965
DOUBLE TROUBLE MGM, 1967
DAY OF THE EVIL GUN MGM, 1968
SPEEDWAY MGM, 1968
SUPPORT YOUR LOCAL SHERIFF! MGM, 1969
DIRTY DINGUS MAGEE MGM, 1970
THE DAUGHTERS OF JOSHUA CABE (TF) Spelling-Goldberg Productions, 1972
THE SEX SYMBOL (TF) The Douglas Cramer Company/ Columbia Pictures TV, 1974
THE DAUGHTERS OF JOSHUA CABE RETURN (TF) Spelling-Goldberg Productions, 1975
THE NEW DAUGHTERS OF JOSHUA CABE (TF) Spelling-Goldberg Productions, 1976
KATE BLISS AND THE TICKER TAPE KID (TF) Aaron Spelling Productions, 1978
THE WILD WILD WEST REVISITED (TF) CBS Entertainment, 1979
MORE WILD WILD WEST (TF) CBS Entertainment, 1980

VICTOR ALLIX

THE PASSION OF JOAN OF ARC M.J. Gourland, 1928, French

WILLIAM ALWYN

b. November 7, 1905 - Northampton, England
d. September 12, 1985 - Southwold, England

THE REMARKABLE MR. KIPP *KIPP* 20th Century-Fox, 1941, British
THE YOUNG MR. PITT 20th Century-Fox, 1942, British
DESERT VICTORY 1943, British
THE WAY AHEAD *THE IMMORTAL BATTALION* 20th Century-Fox, 1944, British
NOTORIOUS GENTLEMAN *THE RAKE'S PROGRESS* 1945, British
THE TRUE GLORY (FD) Columbia, 1945, British
GREEN FOR DANGER 1946, British
ODD MAN OUT General Film Distributors, 1947, British
CAPTAIN BOYCOTT 1947, British

THE WINSLOW BOY British Lion Film Corporation, 1947, British
THE OCTOBER MAN Eagle Lion, 1947, British
TAKE MY LIFE Eagle Lion, 1947, British
I SEE A DARK STRANGER 1947, British
THE FALLEN IDOL Selznick Releasing, 1948, British
SO EVIL MY LOVE co-composer with Victor Young, Paramount, 1948
OPERATION DISASTER *MORNING DEPARTURE* Universal, 1950, British
MADELINE Universal, 1950, British
THE ROCKING HORSE WINNER 1950, British
THE MUDLARK 20th Century-Fox, 1950
STATE SECRET 1950, British
THE GOLDEN SALAMANDER Eagle Lion, 1951, British
I'LL NEVER FORGET YOU *THE HOUSE IN THE SQUARE* 20th Century-Fox, 1951, British
THE MAGNET 1951, British
THE MAGIC BOX Rank, 1951, British
THE CRIMSON PIRATE Warner Bros., 1952, U.S.-British
NO RESTING PLACE 1952
THE PROMOTER *THE CARD* Universal, 1952, British
CRASH OF SILENCE *MANDY* Universal, 1952, British
THE MASTER OF BALLANTRAE Warner Bros., 1953, British
THE MALTA STORY Universal, 1953, British
MAN WITH A MILLION *THE MILLION POUND NOTE* United Artists, 1954, British
A PERSONAL AFFAIR United Artists, 1954, British
THE CONSTANT HUSBAND 1954, British
BEDEVILLED MGM, 1955
LAND OF FURY 1955, British
SVENGALI MGM, 1955, British
THE SHIP THAT DIED OF SHAME *P.T. RAIDERS* Continental, 1955, British
SAFARI Columbia, 1956
ZARAK Columbia, 1956, British
THE BLACK TENT Rank, 1956, British
SEA WIFE 20th Century-Fox, 1957, British
THE SMALLEST SHOW ON EARTH Times Film Corporation, 1957, British
SMILEY 1957, Australian
STOWAWAY GIRL *MANUELA* Paramount, 1957, British
CARVE HER NAME WITH PRIDE Lopert, 1958, British
I ACCUSE! MGM, 1958, British
A NIGHT TO REMEMBER Rank, 1958, British
SHE PLAYED WITH FIRE Columbia, 1958, British
THE SILENT ENEMY Universal, 1958, British
SHAKE HANDS WITH THE DEVIL United Artists, 1959, British
THIRD MAN ON THE MOUNTAIN Buena Vista, 1959, U.S.-British
SWISS FAMILY ROBINSON Buena Vista, 1960
THE NAKED EDGE United Artists, 1961
BURN WITCH BURN *NIGHT OF THE EAGLE* American International, 1962, British
IN SEARCH OF THE CASTAWAYS Buena Vista, 1962, British-U.S.
WALK IN THE SHADOW *LIFE FOR RUTH* Continental, 1962, British
THE RUNNING MAN Columbia, 1963, British

DANIELE AMFITHEATROF

b. 1901 - St. Petersburg, Russia
d. June 7, 1983 - Rome, Italy

LA SIGNORA DI TUTTI 1934, Italian
FAST AND FURIOUS MGM, 1939
THE MAN FROM DAKOTA co-composer with David Snell, MGM, 1940
AND ONE WAS BEAUTIFUL MGM, 1940
KEEPING COMPANY MGM, 1940
THE GET-AWAY MGM, 1941
JOE SMITH, AMERICAN MGM, 1942
CALLING DR. GILLESPIE MGM, 1942
DR. GILLESPIE'S NEW ASSISTANT MGM, 1942
ANDY HARDY'S DOUBLE LIFE MGM, 1942
NORTHWEST RANGERS co-composer with David Snell, MGM, 1943
A STRANGER IN TOWN co-composer with Nathaniel Shilkret, MGM, 1943
AERIAL GUNNER Paramount, 1943
HIGH EXPLOSIVE Paramount, 1943
HARRIGAN'S KID MGM, 1943
DR. GILLESPIE'S CRIMINAL CASE MGM, 1943
LASSIE COME HOME MGM, 1943
LOST ANGEL MGM, 1943
CRY HAVOC MGM, 1943
DAYS OF GLORY RKO Radio, 1944
I'LL BE SEEING YOU RKO Radio, 1944
GUEST WIFE ★ United Artists, 1945
MISS SUSIE SLAGLE'S Paramount, 1946
THE VIRGINIAN Paramount, 1946
SUSPENSE Monogram, 1946
O.S.S. Paramount, 1946
SONG OF THE SOUTH ★ co-composer with Paul Smith, RKO Radio, 1946
TEMPTATION Universal, 1946
THE BEGINNING OR THE END MGM, 1947
SMASH-UP, THE STORY OF A WOMAN Universal, 1947
IVY Universal, 1947
SINGAPORE Universal, 1947
THE LOST MOMENT Universal, 1947
THE SENATOR WAS INDISCREET Universal, 1947
LETTER FROM AN UNKNOWN WOMAN Universal, 1948
ANOTHER PART OF THE FOREST Universal, 1948
ROGUE'S REGIMENT Universal, 1948
YOU GOTTA STAY HAPPY Universal, 1948
AN ACT OF MURDER Universal, 1948
THE FAN 20th Century-Fox, 1948
SAND 20th Century-Fox, 1949
HOUSE OF STRANGERS 20th Century-Fox, 1949
BACKFIRE Warner Bros., 1950
UNDER MY SKIN 20th Century-Fox, 1950
THE CAPTURE RKO Radio, 1950
THE DAMNED DON'T CRY Warner Bros., 1950
DEVIL'S DOORWAY MGM, 1950
COPPER CANYON Paramount, 1950
STORM WARNING Warner Bros., 1951
BIRD OF PARADISE 20th Century-Fox, 1951
THE PAINTED HILLS MGM, 1951
GOODBYE MY FANCY Warner Bros., 1951
ANGELS IN THE OUTFIELD MGM, 1951
TOMORROW IS ANOTHER DAY Warner Bros., 1951
THE DESERT FOX 20th Century-Fox, 1951
DEVIL'S CANYON RKO Radio, 1953
SALOME co-composer with George Duning, Columbia, 1953
THE BIG HEAT Columbia, 1953
SCANDAL AT SCOURIE MGM, 1953
DAY OF TRIUMPH 1954
HUMAN DESIRE Columbia, 1954
THE NAKED JUNGLE Paramount, 1954
TRIAL MGM, 1955
THE LAST HUNT MGM, 1956
THE MOUNTAIN Paramount, 1956
THE UNHOLY WIFE Universal, 1957
FRAULEIN 20th Century-Fox, 1958
FROM HELL TO TEXAS 20th Century-Fox, 1958
SPANISH AFFAIR Paramount, 1958, Spanish
EDGE OF ETERNITY Columbia, 1959

HELLER IN PINK TIGHTS Paramount, 1960
MAJOR DUNDEE Columbia, 1965

GEORGE ANTHEIL

b. June 8, 1900 - Trenton, New Jersey
d. 1959 - New York

BALLET MECHANIQUE 1924, French
ONCE IN A BLUE MOON Paramount, 1935
THE SCOUNDREL Paramount, 1935
THE PLAINSMAN Paramount, 1937
MAKE WAY FOR TOMORROW Paramount, 1937
THE BUCCANEER Paramount, 1938
ANGELS OVER BROADWAY Columbia, 1940
SPECTER OF THE ROSE Republic, 1946
PLAINSMAN AND THE LADY Republic, 1946
THAT BRENNAN GIRL Republic, 1946
REPEAT PERFORMANCE Eagle Lion, 1947
KNOCK ON ANY DOOR Columbia, 1949
WE WERE STRANGERS Columbia, 1949
THE FIGHTING KENTUCKIAN Republic, 1949
TOKYO JOE Columbia, 1949
HOUSE BY THE RIVER Republic, 1950
IN A LONELY PLACE Columbia, 1950
SIROCCO Columbia, 1951
THE SNIPER Columbia, 1952
ACTORS AND SIN United Artists, 1952
THE JUGGLER Columbia, 1953
DEMENTIA Parker, 1953
HUNTERS OF THE DEEP (FD) DCA, 1954
NOT AS A STRANGER United Artists, 1955
THE YOUNG DON'T CRY Columbia, 1957
THE PRIDE AND THE PASSION United Artists, 1957

GEORGES AURIC

b. February 15, 1899 - Lodeve, France
d. 1983

THE BLOOD OF A POET Brandon, 1930, French
A NOUS LA LIBERTE 1931, French
LAC AUX DAMES 1934, French
LES MYSTERES DE PARIS 1935, French
L'AFFAIRE LAFARGE 1936, French
SOUS LES YEUX D'OCCIDENT 1936, French
GRIBOUILLE *HEART OF PARIS* 1937, French
ORAGE 1937, French
ENTREE DES ARTISTS *THE CURTAIN RISES* 1938, French
L'ALIBI 1938, French
L'ENFER DU JEU 1939, French
L'ETERNEL RETOUR *THE ETERNAL RETURN* 1943, French
LE BOSSU 1944, French
LA BELLE AVENTURE *TWILIGHT* 1945, French
DEAD OF NIGHT Universal, 1945, British
CAESAR AND CLEOPATRA United Artists, 1945, British
LA PART DE L'OMBRE 1945, French
BEAUTY AND THE BEAST Lopert, 1946, French
RUY BLAS 1947, French
LES JEUX SONT FAITS *THE CHIPS ARE DOWN* 1947, French
HUE AND CRY Fine Arts, 1947, British
IT ALWAYS RAINS ON SUNDAY General Film Distributors, 1947, British
CORRIDOR OF MIRRORS Universal, 1948, British
L'AIGLE A DEUX TETES *EAGLE WITH TWO HEADS* 1948, French
ANOTHER SHORE 1948
BLIND DESIRE 1948
LES PARENTS TERRIBLES 1948, French
THE QUEEN OF SPADES 1948, British
LA SYMPHONIE PASTORALE 1948, French
AUX YEUX DU SOUVENIR 1949, French
PASSPORT TO PIMLICO 1949, British
THE SPIDER AND THE FLY General Film Distributors, 1949, British
TIGHT LITTLE ISLAND *WHISKEY GALORE!* Rank, 1949, British
ORPHEE *ORPHEUS* Discina International, 1950, French
MAYA 1950
LES AMANTS DE BRAS-MORT 1950, French
NEZ DE CUIR 1951, French
CAROLINE CHERIE 1951, French
THE LAVENDER HILL MOB Universal, 1951, British
THE GALLOPING MAJOR 1951, British
LA PUTAIN RESPECTUEUSE *THE RESPECTFUL PROSTITUTE* 1952, French
DAUGHTER OF THE SANDS 1952
MOULIN ROUGE United Artists, 1952, British
L'ESCLAVE 1953, French
ROMAN HOLIDAY Paramount, 1953
THE TITFIELD THUNDERBOLT Universal, 1953, British
LA FETE A HENRIETTE *HOLIDAY FOR HENRIETTE* 1953, French
THE WAGES OF FEAR DCA, 1953, French
RIFIFI Pathe, 1954, French
THE DIVIDED HEART Republic, 1954, British
THE GOOD DIE YOUNG United Artists, 1954, British
FATHER BROWN *THE DETECTIVE* Columbia, 1954, British
THE BESPOKE OVERCOAT 1955
FLESH AND DESIRE 1955, French
LOLA MONTES *THE SINS OF LOLA MONTES* Brandon, 1955, French-West German
ABDULLAH'S HAREM 20th Century-Fox, 1956, Egyptian
GERVAISE Continental, 1956, French
THE MYSTERY OF PICASSO (FD) Samuel Goldwyn Company, 1956, French
LES HUSSARDS 1956, French
THE HUNCHBACK OF NOTRE DAME *NOTRE DAME DE PARIS* RKO Radio, 1956, French
THE CRUCIBLE 1957, French-East German
HEAVEN KNOWS, MR. ALLISON 20th Century-Fox, 1957
THE STORY OF ESTHER COSTELLO Columbia, 1957
WALK INTO HELL 1957, Australian
DANGEROUS EXILE Rank, 1957, British
LES ESPIONS 1957, French
THE NIGHT HEAVEN FELL *LES BIJOUTIERS DU CLAIR DE LUNES* Kingsley International, 1957, French-Italian
LES AVENTURES DE TILL L'ESPIEGLE 1957, French
BONJOUR TRISTESSE Columbia, 1958
CELUI QUI DOIT MOURIR *HE WHO MUST DIE* 1958, French
NEXT TO NO TIME! 1958, British
THE JOURNEY MGM, 1959
S.O.S. PACIFIC Universal, 1960, British
LE TESTAMENT D'ORPHEE 1960, French
BRIDGE TO THE SUN MGM, 1961, U.S.-French
GOODBYE AGAIN *AIMEZ-VOUS BRAHMS?* United Artists, 1961, French-U.S.
THE INNOCENTS 20th Century-Fox, 1961, British
LA RENDEZ-VOUS DE MINUIT 1962, French
LA CHAMBRE ARDENTE *THE BURNING COURT* 1962, French
THE MIND BENDERS American International, 1963, British
DON'T LOOK NOW...WE'RE BEING SHOT AT *LA GRANDE VADROVILLE* Cinepix, 1966, French-British
THE POPPY IS ALSO A FLOWER Comet, 1966, European

THERESE AND ISABELLE Audubon, 1968, West German-U.S.
THE CHRISTMAS TREE Continental, 1969, French-Italian

WILLIAM AXT

b. 1882
d. February 13, 1959 - Ukiah, California

THE BIG PARADE co-composer with David Mendoza, MGM, 1925
BEN-HUR co-composer with David Mendoza, MGM, 1926
DON JUAN co-composer with David Mendoza, MGM, 1926
THE FIRE BRIGADE MGM, 1926
MARE NOSTRUM MGM, 1926
THE SCARLET LETTER MGM, 1926
ANNIE LAURIE MGM, 1927
CAMILLE MGM, 1927
SLIDE, KELLY SLIDE MGM, 1927
WHITE SHADOWS OF THE SOUTH SEAS co-composer with David Mendoza, MGM, 1928
OUR DANCING DAUGHTERS co-composer with David Mendoza, MGM, 1928
THE TRAIL OF '98 co-composer with David Mendoza, MGM, 1929
THUNDER MGM, 1929
THE SINGLE STANDARD MGM, 1929
OUR MODERN MAIDENS MGM, 1929
SPEEDWAY MGM, 1929
THE KISS MGM, 1929
POLLY OF THE CIRCUS MGM, 1932
SEA SPIDERS MGM, 1932
THE WET PARADE MGM, 1932
WASHINGTON MASQUERADE MGM, 1932
SMILIN' THROUGH MGM, 1932
THE SECRET OF MADAME BLANCHE MGM, 1933
GABRIEL OVER THE WHITE HOUSE MGM, 1933
REUNION IN VIENNA MGM, 1933
MIDNIGHT MARY MGM, 1933
STORM AT DAYBREAK MGM, 1933
PENTHOUSE MGM, 1933
BROADWAY TO HOLLYWOOD MGM, 1933
DINNER AT EIGHT MGM, 1933
ESKIMO MGM, 1933
YOU CAN'T BUY EVERYTHING MGM, 1934
THIS SIDE OF HEAVEN MGM, 1934
LAZY RIVER MGM, 1934
MEN IN WHITE MGM, 1934
MANHATTAN MELODRAMA MGM, 1934
SADIE McKEE MGM, 1934
THE THIN MAN MGM, 1934
OPERATOR 13 MGM, 1934
THE GIRL FROM MISSOURI MGM, 1934
STRAIGHT IS THE WAY MGM, 1934
HIDE-OUT MGM, 1934
A WICKED WOMAN MGM, 1934
FORSAKING ALL OTHERS MGM, 1934
THE MURDER MAN MGM, 1935
WOMAN WANTED MGM, 1935
PURSUIT MGM, 1935
O'SHAUGHNESSY'S BOY MGM, 1935
IT'S IN THE AIR MGM, 1935
RENDEZVOUS MGM, 1935
THE PERFECT GENTLEMAN MGM, 1935
DAVID COPPERFIELD co-composer with Herbert Stothart, MGM, 1935
THE LAST OF THE PAGANS MGM, 1935
WHIPSAW MGM, 1935
THREE LIVE GHOSTS MGM, 1936
TOUGH GUY MGM, 1936
THE PERFECT SET-UP MGM, 1936
THE GARDEN MURDER CASE MGM, 1936
THE THREE GODFATHERS MGM, 1936
PETTICOAT FEVER MGM, 1936
THE UNGUARDED HOUR MGM, 1936
THREE WISE GUYS MGM, 1936
WE WENT TO COLLEGE MGM, 1936
SUZY MGM, 1936
PICCADILLY JIM MGM, 1936
OLD HUTCH MGM, 1936
LIBELED LADY MGM, 1936
ALL-AMERICAN CHUMP MGM, 1936
MAD HOLIDAY MGM, 1936
UNDER COVER OF NIGHT MGM, 1937
THE LAST OF MRS. CHEYNEY MGM, 1937
ESPIONAGE MGM, 1937
SONG OF THE CITY MGM, 1937
PARNELL MGM, 1937
BETWEEN TWO WOMEN MGM, 1937
LONDON BY NIGHT MGM, 1937
BIG CITY MGM, 1937
THOROUGHBREDS DON'T CRY MGM, 1937
BEG, BORROW OR STEAL MGM, 1937
BAD MAN OF BRIMSTONE MGM, 1937
FRIEND INDEED MGM, 1938
EVERYBODY SING MGM, 1938
THE FIRST HUNDRED YEARS MGM, 1938
YELLOW JACK MGM, 1938
WOMAN AGAINST WOMAN MGM, 1938
FAST COMPANY MGM, 1938
RICH MAN, POOR GIRL MGM, 1938
THREE LOVES HAS NANCY MGM, 1938
LISTEN, DARLING MGM, 1938
SPRING MADNESS MGM, 1938
PYGMALION additional music for U.S. version, MGM, 1938, British
THE GIRL DOWNSTAIRS MGM, 1939
STAND UP AND FIGHT MGM, 1939
WITHIN THE LAW MGM, 1939
SERGEANT MADDEN MGM, 1939
THE KID FROM TEXAS MGM, 1939
TELL NO TALES MGM, 1939

B

MISCHA BAKALEINIKOFF

b. Russia
d. 1960

(The following is an incomplete list of Mr. Bakaleinikoff's credits.)

CRY OF THE WEREWOLF Columbia, 1944
MY NAME IS JULIA ROSS Columbia, 1945
BLONDIE KNOWS BEST Columbia, 1946
BARBARY PIRATE Columbia, 1949
LAST OF THE BUCCANEERS Columbia, 1950
THE MAGIC CARPET Columbia, 1951
SMUGGLER'S GOLD Columbia, 1951
WHIRLWIND Columbia, 1951
OKINAWA Columbia, 1952
HANGMAN'S KNOT Columbia, 1952
THE PATHFINDER Columbia, 1952

VOODOO TIGER Columbia, 1952
THE BIG HEAT Columbia, 1953
THE 49TH MAN Columbia, 1953
KILLER APE Columbia, 1953
GUN FURY Columbia, 1953
THE STRANGER WORE A GUN Columbia, 1953
MISSION OVER KOREA Columbia, 1953
PRINCE OF PIRATES Columbia, 1953
BAD FOR EACH OTHER Columbia, 1954
THE BAMBOO PRISON Columbia, 1954
BATTLE OF ROGUE RIVER Columbia, 1954
THE IRON GLOVE Columbia, 1954
CELL 2455, DEATH ROW Columbia, 1955
CREATURE WITH THE ATOM BRAIN Columbia, 1955
THE CROOKED WEB Columbia, 1955
DEVIL GODDESS Columbia, 1955
DUEL ON THE MISSISSIPPI Columbia, 1955
INSIDE DETROIT Columbia, 1955
IT CAME FROM BENEATH THE SEA Columbia, 1955
EARTH VS. THE FLYING SAUCERS Columbia, 1956
THE FLYING FONTAINES Columbia, 1956
THE WEREWOLF Columbia, 1956
SEVENTH CAVALRY Columbia, 1956
THE 27TH DAY Columbia, 1956
HELLCATS OF THE NAVY Columbia, 1957
NO TIME TO BE YOUNG Columbia, 1957
THE PHANTOM STAGECOACH Columbia, 1957
THE TIJUANA STORY Columbia, 1957
20 MILLION MILES TO EARTH Columbia, 1957
ZOMBIES OF MORA-TAU Columbia, 1957
THE CASE AGAINST BROOKLYN Columbia, 1958
CRASH LANDING Columbia, 1958
HAVE ROCKET, WILL TRAVEL Columbia, 1959
COMANCHE STATION Columbia, 1960
THE ENEMY GENERAL Columbia, 1960

LOUIS BARRON

FORBIDDEN PLANET co-composer with Bebe Barron, MGM, 1956
THE VERY EDGE OF NIGHT co-composer with Bebe Barron, 1959
SPACEBOY co-composer with Bebe Barron, 1972

R.H. BASSETT

WHAT PRICE GLORY? Fox, 1926
SEVENTH HEAVEN Fox, 1927
TRANSATLANTIC Fox, 1931
SHERLOCK HOLMES Fox, 1932
DANTE'S INFERNO MGM, 1935
THE PRISONER OF SHARK ISLAND 20th Century-Fox, 1936
SINS OF MAN 20th Century-Fox, 1936

HUBERT BATH

b. England
d. April 24, 1945 - Middlesex, England

KITTY British International, 1929, British
BLACKMAIL British International Pictures, 1929, British
THE THIRTY-NINE STEPS Gaumont-British, 1935, British
RHODES OF AFRICA 1936, British
NINE DAYS A QUEEN *TUDOR ROSE* Gaumont, 1936, British
SILENT BARRIERS 1937, British
A YANK AT OXFORD MGM, 1938
MILLIONS LIKE US 1943, British
LOVE STORY 1944, British

SIR ARNOLD BAX

b. November 8, 1883 - Streatham, England
d. October 3, 1953 - Cork, Ireland

MALTA, G.C. (D) 1942, British
OLIVER TWIST United Artists, 1948, British
JOURNEY INTO HISTORY (D) British Transport Films, 1951, British

GIUSEPPE BECCE

b. 1881 - Padua, Italy

DER MUDE TOD *DESTINY* 1921, German
TARTUFFE 1926, German
DER GUNSTLING VON SCHONBRUNN 1929, German
DER SOHN DER WEISSEN BERGE 1930, German
DAS BLAUE LICHT 1932, German
DER REBELL 1932, German
EXTASE 1932, German
PEER GYNT 1933, German
HAN WESTMAR 1933, German
DER VERLORENE SOHN 1934, German
HUNDERT TAGE 1935, German
DER EWIGE TRAUM 1935, German
DER LAUFER VON MARATHON 1935, German
DER KAISER VON KALIFORNIEN 1936, German
CONDOTTIERI 1937, German
DER BERG RUFT 1937, German
MADAME BOVARY 1937, German
DU BIST MEIN GLUCK 1937, German
LIEBESBRIEFE AUS DEM ENGADIN 1938, German
FRAU IM STROM 1939, German
DER FEUERTEUFEL 1940, German
LA CENA DELLA BEFFE 1941, Italian
VIEL LARM UM NICHTS 1942, German
EIN ABENTEUER AM THUNERSEE 1942, German
TIEFLAND 1945, German
DAS SCHWEIGEN IM WALDE 1955, German
DER JAGER VON FALL 1957, German
DER SCHAFER VON TRUTKBERG 1958, German

ARTHUR BENJAMIN

b. 1893 - Sydney, Australia
d. 1960 - London, England

THE MAN WHO KNEW TOO MUCH Gaumont-British, 1934, British
THE SCARLET PIMPERNEL 1934, British
THE TURN OF THE TIDE 1935, British
THE CLAIRVOYANT 1936, British
UNDER THE RED ROBE 20th Century-Fox, 1937, British
WINGS OF THE MORNING 1937, British
THE RETURN OF THE SCARLET PIMPERNEL 1938, British
THE CUMBERLAND STORY 1947, British
AN IDEAL HUSBAND 20th Century-Fox, 1947, British
STEPS OF THE BALLET 1948, British
THE CONQUEST OF EVEREST 1953, British
UNTERNEHMEN XARIFA 1954
ABOVE US THE WAVES Republic, 1955, British
THE MAN WHO KNEW TOO MUCH new main title and "Storm Clouds" cantata from 1934 version, Paramount, 1956
FIRE DOWN BELOW Columbia, 1957
THE NAKED EARTH 20th Century-Fox, 1959

ROBERT RUSSELL BENNETT

b. 1894 - Kansas City
d. August 18, 1981 - New York

FUGITIVES FOR A NIGHT RKO Radio, 1938
ANNABEL TAKES A TOUR RKO Radio, 1938
PACIFIC LINER ★ RKO Radio, 1938
CAREER RKO Radio, 1939
FIFTH AVENUE GIRL RKO Radio, 1939

LORD BERNERS

(Gerald Hugh Tyrwhitt-Wilson)

b. 1883 - Shropshire, England
d. 1950 - Berks, England

HALFWAY HOUSE Ealing, 1944, British
NICHOLAS NICKLEBY 1946, British

LEONARD BERNSTEIN

b. August 25, 1918 - Lawrence, Massachusetts
d. 1990

ON THE WATERFRONT ★ Columbia, 1954

SIR ARTHUR BLISS

b. 1891 - London, England
d. 1975 - London, England

THINGS TO COME United Artists, 1936, British
CONQUEST OF THE AIR 1938, British
MEN OF TWO WORLDS 1946, British
CHRISTOPHER COLUMBUS 1949, British
WELCOME TO THE QUEEN (FD) 1954, British

MARC BLITZSTEIN

b. 1905 - Philadelphia, Pennsylvania
d. 1964 - Martinique, France

SURF AND SEAWEED Ralph Steiner, 1931
CHESAPEAKE BAY RETRIEVER Pedigreed Pictures, 1936
THE SPANISH EARTH Contemporary Historians, 1937
VALLEY TOWN Willard Van Dyke, 1940
NATIVE LAND Frontier Films, 1942
NIGHT SHIFT O.W.I., 1942

JOSEPH CARL BRIEL

b. 1870 - Pittsburgh, Pennsylvania
d. January 24, 1926 - Los Angeles, California

QUEEN ELIZABETH Paramount, 1912
CABIRIA 1913
THE PRISONER OF ZENDA 1913
THE BIRTH OF A NATION Mutual, 1915
DOUBLE TROUBLE 1915
THE LILY AND THE ROSE 1915
THE MARTYRS OF THE ALAMO 1915
LOS PENITENTES 1915
INTOLERANCE Triangle, 1916
THE WOOD NYMPH 1916
THE DRAMATIC LIFE OF ABRAHAM LINCOLN 1923
THE WHITE ROSE United Artists, 1923
AMERICA United Artists, 1924

BENJAMIN BRITTEN

b. November 22, 1913 - Lowestoft, England
d. December 4, 1976 - Aldeburgh, England

COAL FACE 1935, British
THE CALENDAR OF THE YEAR 1936, British
NIGHT MAIL 1936, British
THE SAVING OF BILL BLEWETT 1936, British
LINE TO THE TSCHIERVA HUT 1937, British
LOVE FROM A STRANGER United Artists, 1937, British
THE TOCHER (FD) 1938, British
VILLAGE HARVEST (FD) 1938, British
INSTRUMENTS OF THE ORCHESTRA 1946, British

NICHOLAS BRODZSKY

b. 1905 - Odessa, Russia
d. December 25, 1958 - Hollywood, California

FRENCH WITHOUT TEARS Paramount, 1940, British
A VOICE IN THE NIGHT *FREEDOM RADIO* Columbia, 1941, British
THE DEMI-PARADISE *ADVENTURE FOR TWO* General Film Distributors, 1943, British
THE WAY TO THE STARS *JOHNNY IN THE CLOUDS* United Artists, 1945, British
CARNIVAL 1946, British
BEWARE OF PITY 1946, British
WHILE THE SUN SHINES Pathe, 1947, British
A MAN ABOUT THE HOUSE 1947, British
HER MAN GILBEY 1948, British
THE TOAST OF NEW ORLEANS MGM, 1950
RICH, YOUNG AND PRETTY MGM, 1951
THE STUDENT PRINCE MGM, 1954
THE OPPOSITE SEX MGM, 1956
LET'S BE HAPPY Allied Artists, 1957, British

DAVID BROEKMAN

b. 1902 - Holland
d. April 1, 1958 - New York

MISSISSIPPI GAMBLER Universal, 1929
TONIGHT AT TWELVE Universal, 1929
THE PHANTOM OF THE OPERA additional music for 1930 release, Universal, 1925
OUTSIDE THE LAW Universal, 1930
ALL QUIET ON THE WESTERN FRONT Universal, 1930
THE OLD DARK HOUSE main title only, Universal, 1932
GIMME MY QUARTERBACK Educational, 1934

DAVID BUTTOLPH

b. August 3, 1902 - New York, New York

THIS IS THE LIFE co-composer, 20th Century-Fox, 1935
NAVY WIFE co-composer, 20th Century-Fox, 1935
SHOW THEM NO MERCY co-composer, 20th Century-Fox, 1935
EVERYBODY'S OLD MAN co-composer, 20th Century-Fox, 1936
LOVE IS NEWS co-composer, 20th Century-Fox, 1937
NANCY STEELS IS MISSING co-composer, 20th Century-Fox, 1937
FIFTY ROADS TO TOWN co-composer, 20th Century-Fox, 1937
YOU CAN'T HAVE EVERYTHING co-composer, 20th Century-Fox, 1937
DANGER! LOVE AT WORK co-composer, 20th Century-Fox, 1937
SECOND HONEYMOON 20th Century-Fox, 1937
JOSETTE co-composer, 20th Century-Fox, 1938

THE THREE MUSKETEERS co-composer, 20th Century-Fox, 1939
HUSBAND, WIFE AND FRIEND co-composer, 20th Century-Fox, 1939
THE GORILLA co-composer, 20th Century-Fox, 1939
HOTEL FOR WOMEN co-composer, 20th Century-Fox, 1939
BARRICADE co-composer, 20th Century-Fox, 1939
STANLEY AND LIVINGSTONE co-composer, 20th Century-Fox, 1939
HOLLYWOOD CAVALCADE 20th Century-Fox, 1939
THE ADVENTURES OF SHERLOCK HOLMES co-composer, 20th Century-Fox, 1939
BARRICADE co-composer, 20th Century-Fox, 1939
HE MARRIED HIS WIFE co-composer, 20th Century-Fox, 1940
STAR DUST co-composer, 20th Century-Fox, 1940
I WAS AN ADVENTURESS co-composer, 20th Century-Fox, 1940
FOUR SONS co-composer, 20th Century-Fox, 1940
THE MAN I MARRIED co-composer, 20th Century-Fox, 1940
THE RETURN OF FRANK JAMES co-composer, 20th Century-Fox, 1940
CHAD HANNA 20th Century-Fox, 1940
WESTERN UNION co-composer, 20th Century-Fox, 1941
TOBACCO ROAD co-composer, 20th Century-Fox, 1941
CONFIRM OR DENY co-composer, 20th Century-Fox, 1941
SWAMP WATER 20th Century-Fox, 1941
BAHAMA PASSAGE Paramount, 1941
LADY FOR A NIGHT Republic, 1942
MY FAVORITE BLONDE Paramount, 1942
THIS GUN FOR HIRE Paramount, 1942
MOONTIDE co-composer with Cyril J. Mockridge, 20th Century-Fox, 1942
IN OLD CALIFORNIA Republic, 1942
WAKE ISLAND Paramount, 1942
MANILA CALLING co-composer with Cyril J. Mockridge and David Raksin, 20th Century-Fox, 1942
THUNDER BIRDS 20th Century-Fox, 1942
STREET OF CHANCE Paramount, 1942
THE IMMORTAL SERGEANT 20th Century-Fox, 1943
CRASH DIVE 20th Century-Fox, 1943
BOMBER'S MOON 20th Century-Fox, 1943
CORVETTE K-225 Universal, 1943
GUADALCANAL DIARY 20th Century-Fox, 1943
BUFFALO BILL 20th Century-Fox, 1944
THE HITLER GANG Paramount, 1944
TILL WE MEET AGAIN Paramount, 1944
IN THE MEANTIME, DARLING 20th Century-Fox, 1944
THE FIGHTING LADY (FD) 20th Century-Fox, 1944
CIRCUMSTANTIAL EVIDENCE 20th Century-Fox, 1945
THE BULLFIGHTERS 20th Century-Fox, 1945
NOB HILL 20th Century-Fox, 1945
WITHIN THESE WALLS 20th Century-Fox, 1945
JUNIOR MISS 20th Century-Fox, 1945
THE CARIBBEAN MYSTERY 20th Century-Fox, 1945
THE HOUSE ON 92ND STREET 20th Century-Fox, 1945
THE SPIDER 20th Century-Fox, 1945
SHOCK 20th Century-Fox, 1946
JOHNNY COMES FLYING HOME 20th Century-Fox, 1946
SOMEWHERE IN THE NIGHT 20th Century-Fox, 1946
STRANGE TRIANGLE 20th Century-Fox, 1946
IT SHOULDN'T HAPPEN TO A DOG 20th Century-Fox, 1946
HOME SWEET HOMICIDE 20th Century-Fox, 1946
13 RUE MADELINE 20th Century-Fox, 1947
BOOMERANG 20th Century-Fox, 1947
THE BRASHER DOUBLOON 20th Century-Fox, 1947
MOSS ROSE 20th Century-Fox, 1947
KISS OF DEATH 20th Century-Fox, 1947
THE FOXES OF HARROW 20th Century-Fox, 1947
BILL AND COO Republic, 1947
TO THE VICTOR Warner Bros., 1948
SMART GIRLS DON'T TALK Warner Bros., 1948
JUNE BRIDE Warner Bros., 1948
ONE SUNDAY AFTERNOON Warner Bros., 1948
ROPE Warner Bros., 1948
JOHN LOVES MARY Warner Bros., 1949
COLORADO TERRITORY Warner Bros., 1949
THE GIRL FROM JONES BEACH Warner Bros., 1949
ONE LAST FLING Warner Bros., 1949
ROSEANNA McCOY RKO Radio, 1949
THE STORY OF SEABISCUIT Warner Bros., 1949
MONTANA Warner Bros., 1950
CHAIN LIGHTNING Warner Bros., 1950
RETURN OF THE FRONTIERSMAN Warner Bros., 1950
PRETTY BABY Warner Bros., 1950
THREE SECRETS Warner Bros., 1950
THE DAUGHTER OF ROSIE O'GRADY Warner Bros., 1950
THE ENFORCER Warner Bros., 1951
THE REDHEAD AND THE COWBOY Paramount, 1951
FIGHTING COAST GUARD Republic, 1951
ALONG THE GREAT DIVIDE Warner Bros., 1951
FORT WORTH Warner Bros., 1951
SUBMARINE COMMAND Paramount, 1951
TEN TALL MEN Columbia, 1951
THE SELLOUT MGM, 1951
LONE STAR MGM, 1952
THIS WOMAN IS DANGEROUS Warner Bros., 1952
TALK ABOUT A STRANGER MGM, 1952
CARSON CITY Warner Bros., 1952
THE WINNING TEAM Warner Bros., 1952
MY MAN AND I MGM, 1952
THE MAN BEHIND THE GUN Warner Bros., 1953
HOUSE OF WAX Warner Bros., 1953
SOUTH SEA WOMAN Warner Bros., 1953
THUNDER OVER THE PLAINS Warner Bros., 1953
THE SYSTEM Warner Bros., 1953
THE BEAST FROM 20,000 FATHOMS Warner Bros., 1953
RIDING SHOTGUN Warner Bros., 1954
THE CITY IS DARK Warner Bros., 1954
THE BOUNTY HUNTER Warner Bros., 1954
PHANTOM OF THE RUE MORGUE Warner Bros., 1954
SECRET OF THE INCAS Warner Bros., 1954
I DIE A THOUSAND TIMES Warner Bros., 1955
JUMP INTO HELL Warner Bros., 1955
TARGET ZERO Warner Bros., 1955
THE LONE RANGER Warner Bros., 1956
A CRY IN THE NIGHT Warner Bros., 1956
THE BURNING HILLS Warner Bros., 1956
SANTIAGO Warner Bros., 1956
THE STEEL JUNGLE Warner Bros., 1956
THE BIG LAND Warner Bros., 1957
THE D.I. Warner Bros., 1957
THE DEEP SIX Warner Bros., 1958
ONIONHEAD Warner Bros., 1958
THE HORSE SOLDIERS United Artists, 1959
WESTBOUND Warner Bros., 1959
GUNS OF THE TIMBERLAND Warner Bros., 1960
PT-109 co-composer with William Lava, Warner Bros., 1963
THE MAN FROM GALVESTON Warner Bros., 1964

C

PETE CARPENTER
d. October 18, 1987

TWO ON A BENCH (TF) co-composer with Mike Post, Universal TV, 1971
GIDGET GETS MARRIED (TF) co-composer with Mike Post, Screen Gems/Columbia Pictures TV, 1972
THE ROCKFORD FILES (TF) Cherokee Productions/Roy Huggins Productions/Universal TV, 1974
THE MORNING AFTER (TF) co-composer with Mike Post, David L. Wolper Productions, 1974
LOCUSTS (TF) co-composer with Mike Post, Carson Productions/Paramount Pictures TV, 1974
THE INVASION OF JOHNSON COUNTY (TF) co-composer with Mike Post, Roy Huggins Productions/Universal TV, 1976
SCOTT FREE (TF) co-composer with Mike Post, Cherokee Productions/Universal TV, 1976
RICHIE BROCKELMAN: MISSING 24 HOURS (TF) co-composer with Mike Post, Universal TV, 1976
CHARLIE COBB: NICE NIGHT FOR A HANGING (TF) co-composer with Mike Post, Fairmount/Foxcroft Productions/Universal TV, 1977
DR. SCORPION (TF) co-composer with Mike Post, Stephen J. Cannell Productions/Universal TV, 1978
RABBIT TEST co-composer with Mike Post, Avco Embassy, 1978
CAPTAIN AMERICA (TF) co-composer with Mike Post, Universal TV, 1979
THE NIGHT RIDER (TF) co-composer with Mike Post, Stephen J. Cannell Productions/Universal TV, 1979
STONE (TF) co-composer with Mike Post, Stephen J. Cannell/Universal TV, 1979
CAPTAIN AMERICA II (TF) co-composer with Mike Post, Universal TV, 1979
COACH OF THE YEAR (TF) co-composer with Mike Post, Shane Company Productions/NBC Entertainment, 1980
WILL, G. GORDON LIDDY (TF) co-composer with Mike Post, Shayne Company Productions, 1982
THE ROUSTERS (TF) Stephen J. Cannell Productions, 1983
NO MAN'S LAND (TF) co-composer with Mike Post, JADDA Productions/Warner Bros. TV, 1984
HARD KNOX (TF) co-composer with Mike Post, Shane Company Productions, 1984
BROTHERS-IN-LAW (TF) co-composer with Mike Post, Stephen J. Cannell Productions, 1985
STINGRAY (TF) co-composer with Mike Post, Stephen J. Cannell Productions, 1985
THE LAST PRECINCT (TF) co-composer with Mike Post, Stephen J. Cannell Productions, 1986

MARIO CASTELNUOVO-TEDESCO
b. 1895 - Florence
d. 1968 - Los Angeles, California

THE RETURN OF THE VAMPIRE Columbia, 1943
TWO-MAN SUBMARINE Columbia, 1944
THE BLACK PARACHUTE Columbia, 1944
SHE'S A SOLDIER, TOO Columbia, 1944
I LOVE A MYSTERY Columbia, 1945
THE CRIME DOCTOR'S COURAGE Columbia, 1945
AND THEN THERE WAS NONE 20th Century-Fox, 1945
PRISON SHIP Columbia, 1945
THE PICTURE OF DORIAN GRAY uncredited co-composer with Herbert Stothart, MGM, 1945
NIGHT EDITOR Columbia, 1946
DANGEROUS BUSINESS Columbia, 1946
TIME OUT OF MIND co-composer with Miklos Rozsa, Universal, 1947
THE LOVES OF CARMEN Columbia, 1948
EVERYBODY DOES IT 20th Century-Fox, 1949
MASK OF THE AVENGER Columbia, 1951
THE BRIGAND Columbia, 1952
THE LONG WAIT United Artists, 1954

FRANCES CHAGRIN
(Alexander Paucker)
b. 1905 - Bucharest, Hungary
d. 1972 - London, England

LAST HOLIDAY 1950, British
AN INSPECTOR CALLS Associated Artists, 1954, British
THE MONSTER OF HIGHGATE PONDS 1966, British

CHARLES CHAPLIN
b. April 16, 1889 - Walworth, England
d. 1977 - Switzerland

SHOULDER ARMS United Artists, 1918
THE KID United Artists, 1921
THE PILGRIM United Artists, 1923
THE GOLD RUSH arranged by Carli D. Elinor, United Artists, 1925
THE CIRCUS United Artists, 1928
CITY LIGHTS arranged by Arthur Johnston, United Artists, 1931
MODERN TIMES arranged by David Raksin, United Artists, 1936
THE GREAT DICTATOR ★ arranged by Meredith Willson, United Artists, 1940
MONSIEUR VERDOUX arranged by Rudolph Schrager, United Artists, 1947
LIMELIGHT ★★ arranged by Ray Rasch, United Artists, 1952
A KING IN NEW YORK Archway, 1957, British
THE COUNTESS FROM HONG KONG Universal, 1967, British

FRANK CHURCHILL
d. 1941

SNOW WHITE AND THE SEVEN DWARFS (AF) ★ co-composer with Leigh Harline and Paul Smith, RKO Radio, 1938
THE RELUCTANT DRAGON (AF) RKO Radio, 1941
DUMBO ★★ co-composer with Oliver Wallace, RKO Radio, 1941
BAMBI ★ co-composer with Edward Plumb, RKO Radio, 1942

ALESSANDRO CICOGNINI
b. January 25,1906 - Pescara, Italy

NAPOLI D'ALTRI TEMPI 1937, Italian
ETTORE FIERAMOSCA 1938, Italian
NAPOLI CHE NON MUORE 1938, Italian
UN'AVVENTURA DI SALVATORE ROSA 1939, Italian

UNA ROMANTICA AVVENTURA 1940, Italian
PRIMO AMORE 1941, Italian
LA CORONDA DI FERRO 1941, Italian
QUATTRO PASSI NELLE NUVOLE 1942, Italian
DUE LETTERE ANONIME 1945, Italian
I MISERABILI *LES MISERABLES* 1948, Italian
THE BICYCLE THIEF *LADRI DI BICICLETTE* Mayer-Burstyn, 1949, Italian
PRIMA COMMUNIONE 1949, Italian
DOMANI E TROPPO TARDI 1950, Italian
THE THIEF OF VENICE 1950, Italian
MIRACLE IN MILAN *MIRACOLO A MILANO* Joseph Burstyn, 1951, Italian
ALTRI TEMPI 1951, Italian
GUARDIE E LADRI 1951, Italian
THE LITTLE WORLD OF DON CAMILLO Italian Films Export, 1951, French
UMBERTO D. Harrison Pictures, 1952, Italian
BUONGIORNO, ELEFANTE 1952, Italian
INDISCRETION OF AN AMERICAN WIFE *STAZIONE TERMINI* Columbia, 1953, U.S.-Italian
THE RETURN OF DON CAMILLO 1953, French-Italian
MOGLIE PER UNA NOTTE 1953, Italian
BREAD, LOVE AND DREAMS *PANE, AMORE E FANTASIA* Italian Film Export, 1953, Italian
ULISSE *ULYSSES* 1954, Italian
FRISKY *PANE, AMORE E GELOSIA* DCA, 1954, Italian
GOLD OF NAPLES *L'ORO DI NAPOLI* DCA, 1955, Italian
SUMMERTIME *SUMMER MADNESS* United Artists, 1955, British
SCANDAL IN SORRENTO *PANE, AMORE E...* DCA, 1955, Italian
THE ROOF *IL TETTO* Trans-Lux, 1956, Italian
ANNA DE BROOKLYN 1958, Italian
VACANZE A ISCHIA 1958, Italian
THE BLACK ORCHID Paramount, 1959
IL GIUDIZIO UNIVERSALE 1960, Italian
A BREATH OF SCANDAL Paramount, 1960
IT STARTED IN NAPLES Paramount, 1960
DON CAMILLO MONSIGNORE MA NON TROPPO 1961
THE PIGEON THAT TOOK ROME Paramount, 1962
IL COMPAGNO DON CAMILLO Rizzoli Film/Francoriz/ Omnia Film, 1965, Italian-West German

ANTHONY COLLINS

b. 1903 - Hastings, England
d. 1963 - Los Angeles, California

VICTORIA THE GREAT RKO Radio, 1937
THE RAT RKO Radio, 1938
SIXTY GLORIOUS YEARS RKO Radio, 1938
A ROYAL DIVORCE Paramount, 1938
NURSE EDITH CAVELL ★ RKO Radio, 1939
ALLEGHENY UPRISING RKO Radio, 1939
SWISS FAMILY ROBINSON RKO Radio, 1940
IRENE ★ adaptation, RKO Radio, 1940
TOM BROWN'S SCHOOLDAYS RKO Radio, 1940
NO, NO, NANETTE adaptation, RKO Radio, 1940
SUNNY ★ RKO Radio, 1941
UNEXPECTED UNCLE RKO Radio, 1941
FOREVER AND A DAY RKO Radio, 1943
THE DESTROYER Columbia, 1943
A YANK IN LONDON 20th Century-Fox, 1946
PICCADILLY INCIDENT Pathe, 1946, British
THE FABULOUS TEXAN Republic, 1947
THE COURTNEY AFFAIR *THE COURTNEYS OF CURZON STREET* British Lion, 1947, British
ODETTE British Lion, 1950, British
THE LADY WITH THE LAMP British Lion, 1951, British
MACAO RKO Radio, 1952
TRENT'S LAST CASE British Lion, 1952, British
THE ADVENTURES OF ROBINSON CRUSOE United Artists, 1952, Mexican
LAUGHING ANNE Republic, 1953, British

RAY COOK

b. 1937 - Australia
d. March 20, 1989 - London, England

CAREFUL HE MIGHT HEAR YOU TLC Films/20th Century Fox, 1983, Australian

FRANK CORDELL

d. July 6, 1980 - Sussex, England

THE CAPTAIN'S TABLE 20th Century-Fox, 1960
FLIGHT FROM ASHIYA United Artists, 1964
NEVER PUT IT IN WRITING Allied Artists, 1964, British
KHARTOUM United Artists, 1966, British
RING OF BRIGHT WATER Cinerama Releasing Corporation, 1969, British
MOSQUITO SQUADRON United Artists, 1970, British
CROMWELL ★ Columbia, 1970, British
DIRTY KNIGHT'S WORK *TRIAL BY COMBAT/A CHOICE OF WEAPONS* Gamma III, 1976, British
DEMON *GOD TOLD ME TO* New World, 1977

SIR NOEL COWARD

b. December 16, 1899 - Teddington, England
d. 1973 - Blue Harbor, Jamaica

IN WHICH WE SERVE Universal, 1942, British
THE ASTONISHED HEART GFD, 1950, British

SIDNEY CUTNER

d. September 20, 1971 - Hollywood, California

HOLIDAY Columbia, 1938
CITY STREETS Columbia, 1938
THE LADY OBJECTS Columbia, 1938
FLIGHT TO FAME Columbia, 1938
HOMICIDE BUREAU Columbia, 1939
MUSIC IN MY HEART Columbia, 1940
THE LONE WOLF STRIKES Columbia, 1940
THE LONE WOLF MEETS A LADY Columbia, 1940
HIS GIRL FRIDAY Columbia, 1940
THE LONE WOLF KEEPS A DATE Columbia, 1940
THE FACE BEHIND THE MASK Columbia, 1941
THE LONE WOLF TAKES A CHANCE Columbia, 1941
TEXAS Columbia, 1941
HOLD BACK TOMORROW Universal, 1955
GUNSMOKE IN TUCSON Allied Artists, 1958

D

PAUL DESSAU

b. 1894 - Germany
d. June 28, 1979 - East Berlin, East Germany

HOUSE OF FRANKENSTEIN co-composer, Universal, 1944
HOUSE OF DRACULA co-composer, Universal, 1945

ADOLPH DEUTSCH

b. October 20, 1897 - London, England
d. January 1, 1980

MR. DODD TAKES THE AIR Warner Bros., 1937
THEY WON'T FORGET Warner Bros., 1937
THE GREAT GARRICK Warner Bros., 1937
SUBMARINE D-1 Warner Bros., 1937
SWING YOUR LADY Warner Bros., 1938
RACKET BUSTERS Warner Bros., 1938
VALLEY OF THE GIANTS co-compose with Hugo Friedhofer, Warner Bros., 1938
BROADWAY MUSKETEERS Warner Bros., 1938
FOUR'S A CROWD Warner Bros., 1938
HEART OF THE NORTH Warner Bros., 1938
OFF THE RECORD Warner Bros., 1939
THE KID FROM KOKOMO Warner Bros., 1939
INDIANAPOLIS SPEEDWAY Warner Bros., 1939
ANGELS WASH THEIR FACES Warner Bros., 1939
ESPIONAGE AGENT Warner Bros., 1939
THE FIGHTING 69TH Warner Bros., 1940
CASTLE ON THE HUDSON Warner Bros., 1940
THREE CHEERS FOR THE IRISH Warner Bros., 1940
SATURDAY'S CHILDREN Warner Bros., 1940
TORRID ZONE Warner Bros., 1940
THEY DRIVE BY NIGHT Warner Bros., 1940
FLOWING GOLD Warner Bros., 1940
TUGBOAT ANNIE SAILS AGAIN Warner Bros., 1940
EAST OF THE RIVER Warner Bros., 1940
HIGH SIERRA Warner Bros., 1941
THE GREAT MR. NOBODY Warner Bros., 1941
SINGAPORE WOMAN Warner Bros., 1941
UNDERGROUND Warner Bros., 1941
KISSES FOR BREAKFAST Warner Bros., 1941
MANPOWER Warner Bros., 1941
THE MALTESE FALCON Warner Bros., 1941
ALL THROUGH THE NIGHT Warner Bros., 1941
LARCENY, INC. Warner Bros., 1942
JUKE GIRL Warner Bros., 1942
THE BIG SHOT Warner Bros., 1942
ACROSS THE PACIFIC Warner Bros., 1942
YOU CAN'T ESCAPE FOREVER Warner Bros., 1942
GEORGE WASHINGTON SLEPT HERE Warner Bros., 1942
LUCKY JORDAN Paramount, 1942
ACTION IN THE NORTH ATLANTIC Warner Bros., 1943
NORTHERN PURSUIT Warner Bros., 1943
UNCERTAIN GLORY Warner Bros., 1944
THE MASK OF DIMITRIOS Warner Bros., 1944
THE DOUGHGIRLS Warner Bros., 1944
ESCAPE IN THE DESERT Warner Bros., 1945
DANGER SIGNAL Warner Bros., 1945
THREE STRANGERS Warner Bros., 1946
SHADOW OF A WOMAN Warner Bros., 1946
NOBODY LIVES FOREVER Warner Bros., 1945
RAMROD United Artists, 1947
BLAZE OF NOON Paramount, 1947
JULIA MISBEHAVES MGM, 1948
WHISPERING SMITH Paramount, 1949
LITTLE WOMEN MGM, 1949
THE STRATTON STORY MGM, 1949
INTRUDER IN THE DUST MGM, 1949
STARS IN MY CROWN MGM, 1950
THE BIG HANGOVER MGM, 1950
TAKE ME OUT TO THE BALL GAME MGM, 1949
ANNIE GET YOUR GUN ★★ adaptation, MGM, 1950
FATHER OF THE BRIDE MGM, 1950
MRS. O'MALLEY AND MR. MALONE MGM, 1950
THE YELLOW CAB MAN MGM, 1950
SOLDIERS THREE MGM, 1951
SHOW BOAT ★ adaptation, MGM, 1951
THE BAND WAGON ★ adaptation, MGM, 1953
TORCH SONG MGM, 1953
SEVEN BRIDES FOR SEVEN BROTHERS ★★ adaptation, MGM, 1954
THE LONG, LONG TRAILER MGM, 1954
INTERRUPTED MELODY MGM, 1955
OKLAHOMA! ★★ adaptation, 20th Century-Fox, 1955
THE RACK MGM, 1956
TEA AND SYMPATHY MGM, 1956
FUNNY FACE adaptation, Paramount, 1957
LES GIRLS MGM, 1957
THE MATCHMAKER Paramount, 1958
SOME LIKE IT HOT United Artists, 1959
THE APARTMENT United Artists, 1960
GO NAKED INTO THE WORLD MGM, 1961

ROBERT EMMETT DOLAN

b. 1906 - Hartford, Connecticut
d. September 25, 1972 - Westwood, California

BIRTH OF THE BLUES ★ adaptation, Paramount, 1941
ARE HUSBANDS NECESSARY? Paramount, 1942
THE MAJOR AND THE MINOR Paramount, 1942
ONCE UPON A HONEYMOON Paramount, 1942
HOLIDAY INN ★ adaptation, Paramount, 1942
STAR SPANGLED RHYTHM ★ Paramount, 1943
HAPPY GO LUCKY Paramount, 1943
DIXIE Paramount, 1943
GOING MY WAY Paramount, 1944
HERE COME THE WAVES Paramount, 1944
STANDING ROOM ONLY Paramount, 1944
LADY IN THE DARK ★ adaptation, Paramount, 1944
I LOVE A SOLDIER Paramount, 1944
SALTY O'ROURKE Paramount, 1945
BRING ON THE GIRLS Paramount, 1945
MURDER, HE SAYS Paramount, 1945
INCENDIARY BLONDE ★ Paramount, 1945
THE BELLS OF ST. MARY'S ★ RKO Radio, 1945
DUFFY'S TAVERN Paramount, 1945
THE STORK CLUB Paramount, 1945
BLUE SKIES ★ adaptation, Paramount, 1946
MONSIEUR BEAUCAIRE Paramount, 1946
CROSS MY HEART Paramount, 1947
MY FAVORITE BRUNETTE Paramount, 1947
THE ROAD TO RIO ★ superivision, Paramount, 1947
WELCOME STRANGER Paramount, 1947
THE TROUBLE WITH WOMEN Paramount, 1947
THE PERILS OF PAULINE Paramount, 1947
DEATH RUTH Paramount, 1947
SAIGON Paramount, 1948
MR. PEABODY AND THE MERMAID Universal, 1948
GOOD SAM RKO Radio, 1948

MY OWN TRUE LOVE Paramount, 1948
SORROWFUL JONES Paramount, 1949
THE GREAT GATSBY Paramount, 1949
TOP O' THE MORNING supervision, Paramount, 1949
LET'S DANCE supervision, Paramount, 1950
AARON SLICK FROM PUMPKIN CRICK Paramount, 1952
MY SON JOHN Paramount, 1952
THE THREE FACES OF EVE 20th Century-Fox, 1957
THE MAN WHO UNDERSTOOD WOMEN 20th Century-Fox, 1959

CARMEN DRAGON

d. March 28, 1984

COVER GIRL ★★ adaptation, Columbia, 1943
MR. WINKLE GOES TO WAR Columbia, 1944
YOUNG WIDOW United Artists, 1946
THE STRANGE WOMAN United Artists, 1946
DISHONORED LADY United Artists, 1947
OUT OF THE BLUE Eagle Lion, 1947
THE TIME OF YOUR LIFE United Artists, 1948
KISS TOMORROW GOODBYE Warner Bros., 1950
NIGHT INTO MORNING MGM, 1951
THE LAW AND THE LADY MGM, 1951
THE PEOPLE AGAINST O'HARA MGM, 1951
WHEN IN ROME MGM, 1952
AT GUNPOINT Allied Artists, 1955
INVASION OF THE BODY SNATCHERS Allied Artists, 1956

HANNS EISLER

b. July 6, 1898 - Leipzig, Germany
d. 1962 - Berlin, West Germany

OPUS 3 1928, German
NO MAN'S LAND 1930
WAR IS HELL 1930
KUHLE WAMPE 1931
A SONG ABOUT HEROES 1932, French
ABDUL THE DAMNED 1934, French
LE GRAND JEU 1934, French
NEW EARTH 1934
THE 400 MILLION 1939
PETE ROLEUM AND HIS COUSINS co-composer with Oscar Levant, 1939
SOIL (FD) Department of Agriculture, 1939
WHITE FLOOD Frontier Films, 1940
RAIN Joris Ivens, 1940
THE FORGOTTEN VILLAGE (FD) 1941
HANGMEN ALSO DIE ★ United Artists, 1943
NONE BUT THE LONELY HEART ★ RKO Radio, 1944
JEALOUSY Republic, 1945
THE SPANISH MAIN RKO Radio, 1945
DEADLINE AT DAWN RKO Radio, 1946
A SCANDAL IN PARIS United Artists, 1946
THE WOMAN ON THE BEACH RKO Radio, 1947
SO WELL REMEMBERED RKO Radio, 1948
RAT DER GOTTER 1951, German
BEL AMI 1955, French
NIGHT AND FOG 1955
SCHICKSAL AM LENKRAD 1956
MAITRE PUNTILA ET SON VALET MATTI 1956, French
THE CRUCIBLE 1957, French-East German
LES ARRIVISTES 1960, French

CARLI D. ELINOR

THE BIRTH OF A NATION Mutual, 1915 [Note: Two scores were written for this film; the other is by Joseph Carl Briel.]

DUKE ELLINGTON
(Edward Kennedy)

b. April 29, 1899 - Washington, D.C.
d. May 24, 1974 - New York

JONAS 1957, German
ANATOMY OF A MURDER Columbia, 1959
PARIS BLUES ★ United Artists, 1961
ASSAULT ON A QUEEN Paramount, 1966
RACING WORLD 1968
CHANGE OF MIND Cinerama Releasing Corporation, 1969

DON ELLIS

b. 1934
d. December 17, 1978

MOON ZERO TWO Warner Bros., 1970, British
THE FRENCH CONNECTION 20th Century-Fox, 1971
KANSAS CITY BOMBER MGM, 1972
THE SEVEN UPS 20th Century-Fox, 1973
IN TANDEM (TF) D'Antoni-Weitz TV Productions, 1974
THE FRENCH CONNECTION II 20th Century-Fox, 1975
THE DEADLY TOWER (TF) MGM TV, 1975
RUBY Dimension, 1977
NATURAL ENEMIES Cinema 5, 1979

LEHMAN ENGEL

b. 1910 - Jackson, Mississippi
d. August 29, 1982 - New York, New York

THE FLEET THAT CAME TO STAY Paramount, 1946
ROOGIE'S RUMP 1954

LEO ERDODY

d. April 5, 1949 - Los Angeles, California

BABY FACE MORGAN Producers Releasing Corp., 1942
TOMORROW WE LIVE Producers Releasing Corp., 1942
CITY OF SILENT MEN Producers Releasing Corp., 1942
PRISONER OF JAPAN Producers Releasing Corp., 1942
DEAD MEN WALK Producers Releasing Corp., 1943
QUEEN OF BROADWAY Producers Releasing Corp., 1942
CORREGIDOR Producers Releasing Corp., 1943
MY SON, THE HERO Producers Releasing Corp., 1943
WILD HORSE RUSTLERS Producers Releasing Corp., 1943
GIRLS IN CHAINS Producers Releasing Corp., 1943
ISLE OF FORGOTTEN SINS *MONSOON* Producers Releasing Corp., 1943
FUGITIVE OF THE PLAINS Producers Releasing Corp., 1943
BLUEBEARD Producers Releasing Corp., 1944
MINSTREL MAN ★ co-composer with Ferde Grofe, Producers Releasing Corp., 1944
STRANGE ILLUSION *OUT OF THE NIGHT* Producers Releasing Corp., 1945

APOLOGY FOR MURDER Producers Releasing Corp., 1945
WHITE PONGO Producers Releasing Corp., 1945
DETOUR Producers Releasing Corp., 1945
THE FLYING SERPENT Producers Releasing Corp., 1946
I RING DOORBELLS Producers Releasing Corp., 1946
MURDER IS MY BUSINESS Producers Releasing Corp., 1946
LARCENY IN HER HEART Producers Releasing Corp., 1946
BLONDE FOR A DAY Producers Releasing Corp., 1946
GAS HOUSE KIDS Producers Releasing Corp., 1946
THE RETURN OF RIN TIN TIN Eagle Lion, 1947
BLONDE SAVAGE Eagle Lion, 1947
MONEY MADNESS Film Classics, 1948
LADY AT MIDNIGHT Eagle Lion, 1948
MIRACULOUS JOURNEY Film Classics, 1948

HANS ERDMANN

b. Germany

NOSFERATU THE VAMPIRE *NOSFERATU - EINE SYMPHONIE DES GRAUENS* Film Arts Guild, 1922, German
THE TESTAMENT DES DR. MABUSE Janus, 1933, German

JERRY FIELDING

b. June 17, 1922 - Pittsburgh, Pennsylvania
d. February 17, 1980

ADVISE AND CONSENT Columbia, 1962
THE NUN AND THE SERGEANT United Artists, 1962
FOR THOSE WHO THINK YOUNG United Artists, 1964
McHALE'S NAVY Universal, 1964
McHALE'S NAVY JOINS THE AIR FORCE Universal, 1965
THE CRAZY WORLD OF LAUREL & HARDY MGM, 1967
THE WILD BUNCH ★ Warner Bros., 1969
HUNTERS ARE FOR KILLING (TF) Cinema Center 100, 1970
SUPPOSE THEY GAVE A WAR AND NOBODY CAME? Cinerama Releasing Corporation, 1970
LAWMAN United Artists, 1971
JOHNNY GOT HIS GUN Cinemation, 1971
ELLERY QUEEN: DON'T LOOK BEHIND YOU (TF) Universal TV, 1971
ONCE UPON A DEAD MAN (TF) Universal TV, 1971
STRAW DOGS ★ Cinerama Releasing Corporation, 1971, British
CHATO'S LAND United Artists, 1972
THE NIGHTCOMERS Avco Embassy, 1972, British
THE MECHANIC United Artists, 1972
A WAR OF CHILDREN (TF) Tomorrow Entertainment, 1972
JUNIOR BONNER Cinerama Releasing Corporation, 1973
SCORPIO United Artists, 1973
THE DEADLY TRACKERS Warner Bros., 1973
SHIRTS/SKINS (TF) MGM TV, 1973
UNWED FATHER (TF) David L. Wolper Productions, 1974
THE OUTFIT MGM, 1974
HONKY-TONK (TF) Douglas Heyes Productions/MGM TV, 1974
THE SUPER COPS MGM, 1974
THE GAMBLER Paramount, 1974
BRING ME THE HEAD OF ALFREDO GARCIA United Artists, 1974
HUSTLING (TF) Filmways/Lillian Gallo Productions, 1975
THE BLACK BIRD Columbia, 1975
MATT HELM (TF) Meadway Productions/Columbia Pictures TV, 1975
ONE OF OUR OWN (TF) Universal TV, 1975
THE KILLER ELITE United Artists, 1975
THE BAD NEWS BEARS adaptation, Paramount, 1976
THE OUTLAW JOSEY WALES ★ Warner Bros., 1976
THE ENFORCER Warner Bros., 1976
LITTLE LADIES OF THE NIGHT (TF) Spelling-Goldberg Productions, 1977
THE GAUNTLET Warner Bros., 1977
DEMON SEED MGM/United Artists, 1977
SEMI-TOUGH United Artists, 1978
GRAY LADY DOWN Universal, 1978
THE BIG SLEEP United Artists, 1978, British
LOVEY: A CIRCLE OF CHILDREN, PART II (TF) Time-Life Productions, 1978
MR. HORN (TF) Lorimar Productions, 1979
ESCAPE FROM ALCATRAZ Paramount, 1979
BEYOND THE POSEIDON ADVENTURE Warner Bros., 1979
HIGH MIDNIGHT (TF) ☆☆ The Mirisch Corporation/Universal TV, 1979
BELOW THE BELT Atlantic Releasing, 1980
FUNERAL HOME 1981, scored in 1979

BENJAMIN FRANKEL

b. 1906 - London, England
d. 1973 - London, England

THE SEVENTH VEIL Universal, 1945, British
DEAR MURDERER 1947, British
MINE OWN EXECUTIONER 1947, British
DULCIMER STREET *LONDON BELONGS TO ME* 1948, British
PORTRAIT FROM LIFE *THE GIRL IN THE PAINTING* Universal, 1948, British
SLEEPING CAR TO TRIESTE 1948, British
THE AMAZING MR. BEECHAM 1948, British
THE GAY LADY *TROTTIE TRUE* Eagle Lion, 1949, British
SALT TO THE DEVIL 1949, British
SO LONG AT THE FAIR GFD, 1950, British
THE CLOUDED YELLOW General Film Distributors, 1950, British
HOTEL SAHARA United Artists, 1951, British
THE LONG DARK HALL 1951, British
ISLAND RESCUE *APPOINTMENT WITH VENUS* Universal, 1951, British
THE IMPORTANCE OF BEING ERNEST Universal, 1952, British
THE MAN IN THE WHITE SUIT Rank, 1952, British
THE FINAL TEST 1953, British
PROJECT M-7 *THE NET* Universal, 1953, British
MAD ABOUT MEN General Film Distributors, 1954, British
ALWAYS A BRIDE 1954, British
FIRE OVER AFRICA Columbia, 1954
CHANCE MEETING 1955, British
THE END OF THE AFFAIR Columbia, 1955
FOOTSTEPS IN THE FOG Columbia, 1955

THE MAN WHO LOVED REDHEADS United Artists, 1955, British
THE PRISONER Columbia, 1955, British
A KID FOR TWO FARTHINGS Lopert, 1956, British
THE IRON PETTICOAT MGM, 1956, British
SIMON AND LAURA 1956, British
STORM OVER THE NILE Columbia, 1956, British
TEARS FOR SIMON *LOST* Republic, 1956, British
ORDERS TO KILL United Motion Picture Organization, 1958, British
HAPPY IS THE BRIDE Kassler, 1959, British
LIBEL MGM, 1959, British
SURPRISE PACKAGE Columbia, 1960
THE CURSE OF THE WEREWOLF Universal, 1961, British
SEASON OF PASSION United Artists, 1961, British
GUNS OF DARKNESS Warner Bros., 1962, British
THE OLD DARK HOUSE Columbia, 1963, British-U.S.
NIGHT OF THE IGUANA MGM, 1964
BATTLE OF THE BULGE Warner Bros., 1965

HUGO FRIEDHOFER

b. May 3, 1902 - San Francisco, California
d. May 17, 1981 - Los Angeles, California

JUST IMAGINE Fox, 1930
SHERLOCK HOLMES co-composer with R.H. Bassett, Fox, 1932
MY LIPS BETRAY Fox, 1933
THE ADVENTURES OF MARCO POLO United Artists, 1938
VALLEY OF THE GIANTS co-composer with Adolph Deutsch, Warner Bros., 1938
TOPPER TAKES A TRIP co-composer with Edward Powell, MGM, 1939
CHINA GIRL 20th Century-Fox, 1943
CHETNIKS! 20th Century-Fox, 1943
THEY CAME TO BLOW UP AMERICA 20th Century-Fox, 1943
PARIS AFTER DARK 20th Century-Fox, 1943
THE LODGER 20th Century-Fox, 1944
LIFEBOAT 20th Century-Fox, 1944
ROGER TOUHY, GANGSTER 20th Century-Fox, 1944
HOME IN INDIANA 20th Century-Fox, 1944
WING AND A PRAYER 20th Century-Fox, 1944
BREWSTER'S MILLIONS United Artists, 1945
GETTING GERTIE'S GARTER United Artists, 1945
THE WOMAN IN THE WINDOW ★ RKO Radio, 1945
THE BANDIT OF SHERWOOD FOREST Columbia, 1946
GILDA Columbia, 1946
SO DARK THE NIGHT Columbia, 1946
THE BEST YEARS OF OUR LIVES ★★ RKO Radio, 1946
BODY AND SOUL United Artists, 1947
WILD HARVEST Paramount, 1947
THE BISHOP'S WIFE ★ RKO Radio, 1947
THE SWORDSMAN Columbia, 1947
A SONG IS BORN RKO Radio, 1948
THE ADVENTURES OF CASANOVA Eagle Lion, 1948
BLACK BART Universal, 1948
SEALED VERDICT Paramount, 1948
JOAN OF ARC ★ RKO Radio, 1948
ENCHANTMENT RKO Radio, 1948
BRIDE OF VENGEANCE Paramount, 1949
ROSEANNA McCOY RKO Radio, 1949
GUILTY OF TREASON Eagle Lion, 1950
THREE CAME HOME 20th Century-Fox, 1950
CAPTAIN CAREY, U.S.A. Paramount, 1950
NO MAN OF HER OWN Paramount, 1950
BROKEN ARROW 20th Century-Fox, 1950
EDGE OF DOOM RKO Radio, 1950
TWO FLAGS WEST 20th Century-Fox, 1950
THE SOUND OF FURY United Artists, 1951
QUEEN FOR A DAY United Artists, 1951
ACE IN THE HOLE Paramount, 1951
RANCHO NOTORIOUS RKO Radio, 1952
THE MARRYING KIND Columbia, 1952
THE OUTCASTS OF POKER FLAT 20th Century-Fox, 1952
LYDIA BAILEY 20th Century-Fox, 1952
JUST FOR YOU Paramount, 1952
ABOVE AND BEYOND ★ MGM, 1952
FACE TO FACE RKO Radio, 1952
THUNDER IN THE EAST Paramount, 1953
ISLAND IN THE SKY Warner Bros., 1953
HONDO Warner Bros., 1953
VERA CRUZ United Artists, 1954
WHITE FEATHER 20th Century-Fox, 1955
VIOLENT SATURDAY 20th Century-Fox, 1955
SOLDIER OF FORTUNE 20th Century-Fox, 1955
SEVEN CITIES OF GOLD 20th Century-Fox, 1955
THE RAINS OF RANCHIPUR 20th Century-Fox, 1955
THE HARDER THEY FALL Columbia, 1956
THE REVOLT OF MAMIE STOVER 20th Century-Fox, 1956
BETWEEN HEAVEN AND HELL ★ 20th Century-Fox, 1956
OH, MEN! OH, WOMEN! 20th Century-Fox, 1957
BOY ON A DOLPHIN ★ 20th Century-Fox, 1957
AN AFFAIR TO REMEMBER ★ 20th Century-Fox, 1957
THE SUN ALSO RISES 20th Century-Fox, 1957
THE YOUNG LIONS ★ 20th Century-Fox, 1958
THE BRAVADOS 20th Century-Fox, 1958
THE BARBARIAN AND THE GEISHA 20th Century-Fox, 1958
IN LOVE AND WAR 20th Century-Fox, 1958
WOMAN OBSESSED 20th Century-Fox, 1959
THIS EARTH IS MINE Universal, 1959
THE BLUE ANGEL 20th Century-Fox, 1959
NEVER SO FEW MGM, 1959
ONE-EYED JACKS Paramount, 1960
HOMICIDAL Columbia, 1961
GERONIMO United Artists, 1962
BEAUTY AND THE BEAST United Artists, 1962
THE SECRET INVASION United Artists, 1964
THE OVER-THE-HILL GANG (TF) Thomas-Spelling Productions, 1969
VON RICHTOFEN AND BROWN United Artists, 1971
PRIVATE PARTS MGM, 1972

PAUL GIOVANNI

d. June 17, 1990

THE WICKER MAN Warner Bros., 1975, British

JACKIE GLEASON

b. February 26, 1916 - New York, New York
d. June 24, 1987 - Los Angeles, California

IZZY AND MOE (TF) Robert Halmi Productions, 1985

MORT GLICKMAN

d. 1953

(In addition to the titles below, Mr. Glickman scored dozens of low-budget films, mostly westerns, for Republic.)

PREHISTORIC WOMEN uncredited co-composer with Rene Kraushaar, United Artists, 1950
BRIDE OF THE GORILLA uncredited co-composer with Rene Kraushaar, Realart, 1951
UNTAMED WOMEN uncredited co-composer with Rene Kraushaar, United Artists, 1952
INVADERS FROM MARS uncredited co-composer with Rene Kraushaar, 20th Century-Fox, 1953

LUD GLUSKIN

d. 1989

THE HOUSEKEEPER'S DAUGHTER United Artists, 1939
THE MAN IN THE IRON MASK ★ co-composer with Lucien Moraweck, United Artists, 1939
ABROAD WITH TWO YANKS United Artists, 1944
HIGH CONQUEST Monogram, 1947
MICHAEL O'HALLORAN Monogram, 1948
MIRACLE IN HARLEM Screen Guild, 1948
MASSACRE RIVER Allied Artists, 1949
BOY FROM INDIANA Eagle Lion, 1950

WALTER GOEHR

d. December 4, 1960 - Sheffield, England

AMATEUR GENTLEMAN co-composer with Richard Addinsell, United Artists, 1936, British
GREAT EXPECTATIONS Universal, 1947, British
STOP PRESS GIRL 1949, British
LUCKY NICK CAIN 20th Century-Fox, 1951
BETRAYED MGM, 1954

PERCY GRAINGER

b. 1882 - Brighton, Victoria
d. 1961 - White Plains, New York

FLYING FEET 1929

ALLAN GRAY

b. 1904

EMIL AND THE DETECTIVES 1931, German
BERLIN ALEXANDER PLATZ 1931, German
DIE GRAFFIN VON MONTE-CRISTO 1931, German
F.P.I. ANTWORTET NICHT 1932, German
SANS LENDEMAIN 1939, French
THE LIFE AND DEATH OF COLONEL BLIMP *COLONEL BLIMP* GFO, 1943, British
A CANTERBURY TALE Eagle-Lion, 1944, British
I KNOW WHERE I'M GOING Universal, 1945, British
STAIRWAY TO HEAVEN *A MATTER OF LIFE AND DEATH* Universal, 1946, British
THIS MAN IS MINE 1946, British
MR. PERRIN AND MR. TRAILL 1948, British
MADNESS OF THE HEART 1949, British
THE RELUCTANT WIDOW 1951, British
NO PLACE FOR JENNIFER 1951, British
THE OBSESSED 1951
HER PANELLED DOOR 1951, British
THE AFRICAN QUEEN United Artists, 1951
OUTPOST IN MALAYA *THE PLANTER'S WIFE* United Artists, 1952, British

TWILIGHT WOMEN Lippert, 1953
THE GENIE 1953
SOLANG 'ES HUBSCHE MADCHEN GIBT 1955, West German

JOHN GREEN

b. October 10, 1908 - New York, New York
d. 1989 - Los Angeles, California

(Mr. Green was arranger, music director or supervisor for dozens of films in the 1940s and 1950s. This list is limited to scores composed or adapted by Mr. Green.)

SECRETS OF A SECRETARY Paramount, 1931
MY SIN Paramount, 1931
WAYWARD Paramount, 1931
THE WISER SEX Paramount, 1931
BROADWAY RHYTHM MGM, 1944
BATHING BEAUTY MGM, 1944
WEEKEND AT THE WALDORF MGM, 1945
THE SAILOR TAKES A WIFE MGM, 1945
EASY TO WED MGM, 1946
FIESTA ★ adaptation, MGM, 1947
IT HAPPENED IN BROOKLYN MGM, 1947
SOMETHING IN THE WIND Universal, 1947
EASTER PARADE ★★ adaptation, MGM, 1948
UP IN CENTRAL PARK Universal, 1948
THE INSPECTOR GENERAL Warner Bros., 1949
SUMMER STOCK MGM, 1950
ROYAL WEDDING MGM, 1951
THE GREAT CARUSO ★ MGM, 1951
AN AMERICAN IN PARIS ★★ adaptation, MGM, 1951
TOO YOUNG TO KISS MGM, 1951
BECAUSE YOU'RE MINE MGM, 1952
BRIGADOON adaptation, MGM, 1954
RHAPSODY MGM, 1954
HIGH SOCIETY ★ adaptation, MGM, 1956
MEET ME IN LAS VEGAS ★ adaptation, MGM, 1956
RAINTREE COUNTY ★ MGM, 1957
PEPE ★ Columbia, 1960
WEST SIDE STORY ★ adaptation, United Artists, 1961
BYE BYE BIRDIE ★ adaptation, Columbia, 1963
TWILIGHT OF HONOR MGM, 1963
ALVAREZ KELLY Columbia, 1966
JOHNNY TIGER Universal, 1966
OLIVER! ★★ adaptation, Columbia, 1968, British
THEY SHOOT HORSES, DON'T THEY? Cinerama Releasing Corporation, 1969

JOHN GREENWOOD

b. 1889

THE CONSTANT NYMPH co-composer with Eugene Goossens, 1933, British
MAN OF ARAN (FD) Gaumont-British, 1934, British
ELEPHANT BOY United Artists, 1937, British
THE DRUM United Artists, 1938, British
PIMPERNEL SMITH *MISTER V* Anglo-American, 1941, British
NINE MEN 1943, British
HUNGRY HILL Universal, 1947, British
FRIEDA Universal, 1947, British
THE LAST DAYS OF DOLWYN *WOMAN OF DOLWYN* 1948, British
TRIO Paramount, 1950, British
EUREKA STOCKADE 1950, British
FAMILY PORTRAIT 1950, British
ANOTHER MAN'S POISON United Artists, 1952, British
THE GENTLE GUNMAN Universal, 1952, British
WICKED WIFE Allied Artists, 1955, British

FERDE GROFE
(Ferdinand Rudolf von Grofe)
b. 1892 - New York
d. 1972 - Santa Monica, California

KING OF JAZZ Universal, 1930
DIAMOND JIM co-composer with Franz Waxman, Universal, 1935
KNUTE ROCKNE, ALL AMERICAN Warner Bros., 1940
MINSTREL MAN ★ co-composer with Leo Erdody, Producers Releasing Corp., 1944
ROCKETSHIP X-M Lippert, 1950

LOUIS GRUENBERG
b. 1884 - Brest-Litovsk, Russia
d. June 6, 1964 - Los Angeles, California

THE FIGHT FOR LIFE ★ Columbia, 1940
SO ENDS OUR NIGHT ★ United Artists, 1941
COMMANDOS STRIKE AT DAWN ★ Columbia, 1943
AN AMERICAN ROMANCE MGM, 1944
COUNTER-ATTACK Columbia, 1945
THE GANGSTER Allied Artists, 1947
ARCH OF TRIUMPH United Artists, 1948
SMART WOMAN Allied Artists, 1948
ALL THE KING'S MEN Columbia, 1949
QUICKSAND United Artists, 1950

RICHARD HAGEMAN
d. March 6, 1966

IF I WERE KING ★ Paramount, 1938
HOTEL IMPERIAL Paramount, 1939
STAGECOACH ★★ co-composer, United Artists, 1939
RULERS OF THE SEA Paramount, 1939
THE HOWARDS OF VIRGINIA ★ Columbia, 1940
THE LONG VOYAGE HOME ★ United Artists, 1940
THIS WOMAN IS MINE ★ Universal, 1941
PARIS CALLING Universal, 1942
THE SHANGHAI GESTURE ★ United Artists, 1942
ANGEL AND THE BADMAN Republic, 1947
THE FUGITIVE RKO Radio, 1947
FORT APACHE RKO Radio, 1948
MOURNING BECOMES ELECTRA RKO Radio, 1947
THREE GODFATHERS MGM, 1948
SHE WORE A YELLOW RIBBON RKO Radio, 1949
WAGON MASTER RKO Radio, 1950

KARL HAJOS
b. 1889 - Budapest, Hungary
d. 1950 - Los Angeles, California

LOVES OF AN ACTRESS Paramount, 1928
BEGGARS OF LIFE Paramount, 1928
MOROCCO Paramount, 1930
SUPERNATURAL co-composer, Paramount, 1933
FOUR FRIGHTENED PEOPLE Paramount, 1934
MANHATTAN MOON Universal, 1935
WEREWOLF OF LONDON Universal, 1935
TWO WISE MAIDS Republic, 1937
HITLER'S HANGMAN MGM, 1943
THE SULTAN'S DAUGHTER Monogram, 1943
CHARLIE CHAN IN THE SECRET SERVICE Monogram, 1944
SUMMER STORM ★ United Artists, 1944
THE MAN WHO WALKED ALONE ★ Producers Releasing Corp., 1945
THE PHANTOM OF 42ND STREET Producers Releasing Corp., 1945
THE MISSING CORPSE Producers Releasing Corp., 1945
DANGEROUS INTRUDER Producers Releasing Corp., 1945
SHADOW OF TERROR Producers Releasing Corp., 1945
FOG ISLAND Universal, 1945
THE MASK OF DIIJON Producers Releasing Corp., 1946
QUEEN OF BURLESQUE Producers Releasing Corp., 1946
SECRETS OF A SORORITY GIRL Producers Releasing Corp., 1946
DOWN MISSOURI WAY Producers Releasing Corp., 1946
DRIFTIN' RIVER Producers Releasing Corp., 1946
STARS OVER TEXAS Producers Releasing Corp., 1946
WILD WEST Producers Releasing Corp., 1946
TUMBLEWEED TRAIL Producers Releasing Corp., 1948
APPOINTMENT WITH MURDER Producers Releasing Corp., 1948
SEARCH FOR DANGER Film Classics, 1949
THE LOVABLE CHEAT Film Classics, 1949
KILL OR BE KILLED Eagle Lion, 1950
IT'S A SMALL WORLD Eagle Lion, 1950

LEIGH HARLINE
b. March 26, 1907 - Salt Lake City, Utah
d. 1969

SNOW WHITE AND THE SEVEN DWARFS (AF) ★ co-composer with Frank Churchill and Paul Smith, RKO Radio, 1938
BEWARE, SPOOKS! main and end title, 1939
PINOCCHIO (AF) ★★ co-composer with Paul Smith, RKO Radio, 1940
BLONDIE ON A BUDGET Columbia, 1940
BLONDIE HAS SERVANT TROUBLE Columbia, 1940
SO YOU WON'T TALK Columbia, 1940
BLONDIE PLAYS CUPID Columbia, 1940
MR. BUG GOES TO TOWN *HOPPITY GOES TO TOWN* (AF) Paramount, 1941
THE LADY HAS PLANS co-composer with Leo Shuken, Paramount, 1942
WHISPERING GHOSTS co-composer, 20th Century-Fox, 1942
THE PRIDE OF THE YANKEES ★ RKO Radio, 1942
CAREFUL, SOFT SHOULDER 20th Century-Fox, 1942
YOU WERE NEVER LOVELIER ★ Columbia, 1942
THEY GOT ME COVERED RKO Radio, 1943
MARGIN FOR ERROR 20th Century-Fox, 1943
THE MORE THE MERRIER Columbia, 1943
THE SKY'S THE LIMIT ★ RKO Radio, 1943
JOHNNY COME LATELY ★ United Artists, 1943
GOVERNMENT GIRL RKO Radio, 1943
TENDER COMRADE RKO Radio, 1944
FOLLOW THE BOYS Universal, 1944
A NIGHT OF ADVENTURE RKO Radio, 1944
HEAVENLY DAYS RKO Radio, 1944
MUSIC IN MANHATTAN RKO Radio, 1944
WHAT A BLONDE RKO Radio, 1945
HAVING WONDERFUL CRIME RKO Radio, 1945
CHINA SKY RKO Radio, 1945

THE BRIGHTON STRANGLER co-composer, RKO Radio, 1945
GEORGE WHITE'S SCANDALS RKO Radio, 1945
JOHNNY ANGEL RKO Radio, 1945
MAMA LOVES PAPA RKO Radio, 1945
FIRST YANK INTO TOKYO RKO Radio, 1945
ISLE OF THE DEAD RKO Radio, 1945
MAN ALIVE RKO Radio, 1945
ROAD TO UTOPIA Paramount, 1946
FROM THIS DAY FORWARD RKO Radio, 1946
THE TRUTH ABOUT MURDER RKO Radio, 1946
TILL THE END OF TIME RKO Radio, 1946
CRACK-UP RKO Radio, 1946
CHILD OF DIVORCE RKO Radio, 1946
LADY LUCK RKO Radio, 1946
NOCTURNE RKO Radio, 1946
THE FARMER'S DAUGHTER RKO Radio, 1947
A LIKELY STORY RKO Radio, 1947
HONEYMOON RKO Radio, 1947
THE BACHELOR AND THE BOBBY-SOXER RKO Radio, 1947
TYCOON RKO Radio, 1947
THE MIRACLE OF THE BELLS RKO Radio, 1948
MR. BLANDINGS BUILDS HIS DREAM HOUSE RKO Radio, 1948
THE VELVET TOUCH RKO Radio, 1948
EVERY GIRL SHOULD BE MARRIED RKO Radio, 1948
THE BOY WITH GREEN HAIR RKO Radio, 1948
IT HAPPENS EVERY SPRING 20th Century-Fox, 1949
THE JUDGE STEPS OUT RKO Radio, 1949
THE BIG STEAL RKO Radio, 1949
THEY LIVE BY NIGHT RKO Radio, 1949
THE WOMAN ON PIER 13 RKO Radio, 1950
PERFECT STRANGERS Warner Bros., 1950
MY FRIEND IRMA GOES WEST Paramount, 1950
THE HAPPY YEARS MGM, 1950
UNION STATION Paramount, 1950
THE COMPANY SHE KEEPS RKO Radio, 1950
CALL ME MISTER 20th Century-Fox, 1951
THE GUY WHO CAME BACK 20th Century-Fox, 1951
THAT'S MY BOY Paramount, 1951
HIS KIND OF WOMAN RKO Radio, 1951
ON THE LOOSE RKO Radio, 1951
BEHAVE YOURSELF RKO Radio, 1951
DOUBLE DYNAMITE RKO Radio, 1951
I WANT YOU RKO Radio, 1951
PICK-UP ON SOUTH STREET 20th Century-Fox, 1951
THE LAS VEGAS STORY RKO Radio, 1952
MONKEY BUSINESS 20th Century-Fox, 1952
MY WIFE'S BEST FRIEND 20th Century-Fox, 1952
MY PAL GUS 20th Century-Fox, 1952
TAXI 20th Century-Fox, 1953
THE DESERT RATS 20th Century-Fox, 1953
VICKI 20th Century-Fox, 1953
BLACK WIDOW 20th Century-Fox, 1954
BROKEN LANCE 20th Century-Fox, 1954
MONEY FROM HOME Paramount, 1954
SUSAN SLEPT HERE RKO Radio, 1954
THE GIRL IN THE RED VELVET SWING 20th Century-Fox, 1955
GOOD MORNING, MISS DOVE 20th Century-Fox, 1955
THE LAST FRONTIER Columbia, 1956
THE BOTTOM OF THE BOTTLE 20th Century-Fox, 1956
GREAT DAY IN THE MORNING RKO Radio, 1956
TEEN-AGE REBEL 20th Century-Fox, 1956
23 PACES TO BAKER STREET 20th Century-Fox, 1956, British-U.S.
THE ENEMY BELOW 20th Century-Fox, 1957
NO DOWN PAYMENT 20th Century-Fox, 1957
THE TRUE STORY OF JESSE JAMES 20th Century-Fox, 1957
THE WAYWARD BUS 20th Century-Fox, 1957
MAN OF THE WEST United Artists, 1958
TEN NORTH FREDERICK 20th Century-Fox, 1958
THE REMARKABLE MR. PENNYPACKER 20th Century-Fox, 1958
HOLIDAY FOR LOVERS 20th Century-Fox, 1959
THESE THOUSAND HILLS 20th Century-Fox, 1959
WARLOCK 20th Century-Fox, 1959
THE FACTS OF LIFE United Artists, 1960
VISIT TO A SMALL PLANET Paramount, 1960
THE HONEYMOON MACHINE MGM, 1961
THE WONDERFUL WORLD OF THE BROTHERS GRIMM ★ MGM/Cinerama, 1962
THE SEVEN FACES OF DR. LAO MGM, 1964
STRANGE BEDFELLOWS Universal, 1965

W. FRANKE HARLING

b. 1887
d. November 22, 1958 - Sierra Madre, California

HONEY Paramount, 1930
MONTE CARLO Paramount, 1930
THE RIGHT TO LOVE Paramount, 1930
RANGO Paramount, 1931
SHANGHAI EXPRESS Paramount, 1932
BROKEN LULLABY Paramount, 1932
FIREMAN, SAVE MY CHILD Warner Bros., 1932
THE EXPERT Warner Bros., 1932
PLAY GIRL Warner Bros., 1932
ONE HOUR WITH YOU co-composer, Paramount, 1932
THE MIRACLE MAN Paramount, 1932
THIS IS THE NIGHT Paramount, 1932
THE RICH ARE ALWAYS WITH US Warner Bros., 1932
TWO SECONDS Warner Bros., 1932
STREET OF WOMEN Warner Bros., 1932
WEEK-END MARRIAGE Warner Bros., 1932
WINNER TAKE ALL Warner Bros., 1932
TROUBLE IN PARADISE Paramount, 1932
ONE WAY PASSAGE theme only, Warner Bros., 1932
MEN ARE SUCH FOOLS RKO Radio, 1932
MADAME BUTTERFLY Paramount, 1932
THE BITTER TEA OF GENERAL YEN Columbia, 1933
DESTINATION UNKNOWN Universal, 1933
A KISS BEFORE THE MIRROR Universal, 1933
CRADLE SONG Paramount, 1933
A MAN'S CASTLE Columbia, 1933
BY CANDLELIGHT Universal, 1933
ONE MORE RIVER Universal, 1933
THE SCARLETT EMPRESS co-composer with John Leipold, Paramount, 1934
THE CHURCH MOUSE Warner Bros., 1934
SO RED THE ROSE Paramount, 1935
I MARRIED A DOCTOR Warner Bros., 1936
THE GOLDEN ARROW Warner Bros., 1936
CHINA CLIPPER Warner Bros., 1936
MOUNTAIN JUSTICE Warner Bros., 1937
SOULS AT SEA ★ co-composer with Milan Roder, 1937
MEN WITH WINGS co-composer with Gerard Carbonara, Paramount, 1938
STAGECOACH ★★ co-composer, United Artists, 1939
ADAM HAD FOUR SONS Columbia, 1941
PENNY SERENADE Columbia, 1941
ADVENTURE IN WASHINGTON Columbia, 1941
THE LADY IS WILLING Columbia, 1942
I ESCAPED FROM THE GESTAPO Monogram, 1943
SOLDIERS OF THE SOIL Du Pont, 1943
THREE RUSSIAN GIRLS ★ United Artists, 1944
JOHNNY DOESN'T LIVE HERE ANYMORE King Bros./Mon., 1944
WHEN THE LIGHTS GO ON AGAIN Producers Releasing Corp., 1944

RED WAGON   American Film Center, 1945
THE BACHELOR'S DAUGHTERS   United Artists, 1946

ROY HARRIS

b. 1898 - Lincoln County, Nebraska
d. October 1, 1979 - Santa Monica, California

ONE-TENTH OF A NATION (FD)   Rockefeller, 1940

T. MARVIN HATLEY

d. August 26, 1986

KELLY THE SECOND   MGM, 1936
MISTER CINDERELLA   MGM, 1936
GENERAL SPANKY   MGM, 1936
WAY OUT WEST ★   MGM, 1937
NOBODY'S BABY   MGM, 1937
PICK A STAR   MGM, 1937
TOPPER   MGM, 1937
MERRILY WE LIVE   MGM, 1938
SWISS MISS   MGM, 1933
BLOCKHEADS ★   MGM, 1938
THERE GOES MY HEART ★   United Artists, 1938
ZENOBIA   United Artists, 1939
CAPTAIN FURY   United Artists, 1939
A CHUMP AT OXFORD   United Artists, 1940
SAPS AT SEA   United Artists, 1940

FUMIO HAYASAKA

b. August 19, 1914 - Sendai, Japan
d. 1955 - Japan

DRUNKEN ANGEL   Toho, 1948, Japanese
RASHOMON   RKO Radio, 1950, Japanese
THE PICTURE OF MADAME YUKI   1950, Japanese
WOMAN OF MUSAHINO   1951, Japanese
IKIRU   Brandon, 1952, Japanese
UGETSU   Harrison Pictures, 1953, Japanese
SANSHO THE BAILIFF   1954, Japanese
SEVEN SAMURAI   Landmark Releasing, 1954, Japanese
TALES OF THE TAIRA CLAN   1955, Japanese
I LIVE IN FEAR   Brandon, 1955, Japanese
YANG KWEI FEI   1955, Japanese

CHARLES HENDERSON

b. 1907 - Boston, Massachusetts
d. March 7, 1970 - Laguna Beach, California

BLACK FRIDAY   co-composer, Universal, 1940
HORROR ISLAND   co-composer, Universal, 1941
THE BLACK CAT   co-composer, Universal, 1941
THE MAD GHOUL   co-composer, Universal, 1943
HOUSE OF DRACULA   co-composer, Universal, 1945
STATE FAIR ★   adaptation, 20th Century-Fox, 1945

VICTOR HERBERT

b. 1859 - Dublin, Ireland
d. 1924 - New York

THE FALL OF A NATION   National Films, 1916

BERNARD HERRMANN

b. June 30, 1911 - New York, New York
d. December 24, 1975 - Los Angeles, California

CITIZEN KANE ★   RKO Radio, 1941
ALL THAT MONEY CAN BUY   *THE DEVIL AND DANIEL WEBSTER* ★★   RKO Radio, 1941
THE MAGNIFICENT AMBERSONS   RKO Radio, 1942
JANE EYRE   20th Century-Fox, 1943
HANGOVER SQUARE   20th Century-Fox, 1945
ANNA AND THE KING OF SIAM ★   20th Century-Fox, 1946
THE GHOST AND MRS. MUIR   20th Century-Fox, 1947
PORTRAIT OF JENNIE   composer of Jennie's theme, Selznick, 1948
THE DAY THE EARTH STOOD STILL   20th Century-Fox, 1951
ON DANGEROUS GROUND   RKO Radio, 1952
THE SNOWS OF KILIMANJARO   20th Century-Fox, 1952
FIVE FINGERS   20th Century-Fox, 1952
WHITE WITCH DOCTOR   20th Century-Fox, 1953
BENEATH THE TWELVE-MILE REEF   20th Century-Fox, 1953
KING OF THE KHYBER RIFLES   20th Century-Fox, 1954
GARDEN OF EVIL   20th Century-Fox, 1954
THE EGYPTIAN   co-composer with Alfred Newman, 20th Century-Fox, 1954
PRINCE OF PLAYERS   20th Century-Fox, 1954
THE TROUBLE WITH HARRY   Paramount, 1955
THE KENTUCKIAN   Paramount, 1955
THE MAN WHO KNEW TOO MUCH   also appears as conductor in Albert Hall sequence, Paramount, 1956
THE MAN IN THE GRAY FLANNEL SUIT   20th Century-Fox, 1956
THE WRONG MAN   Warner Bros., 1956
WILLIAMSBURG: THE STORY OF A PATRIOT   Paramount, 1956
A HATFUL OF RAIN   20th Century-Fox, 1957
VERTIGO   Paramount, 1958
THE NAKED AND THE DEAD   Warner Bros., 1958
THE SEVENTH VOYAGE OF SINBAD   Columbia, 1958
NORTH BY NORTHWEST   MGM, 1959
BLUE DENIM   20th Century-Fox, 1959
JOURNEY TO THE CENTER OF THE EARTH   20th Century-Fox, 1959
PSYCHO   Paramount, 1960
THE THREE WORLDS OF GULLIVER   Columbia, 1960
MYSTERIOUS ISLAND   Columbia, 1961
TENDER IS THE NIGHT   20th Century-Fox, 1962
CAPE FEAR   Universal, 1962
JASON AND THE ARGONAUTS   Columbia, 1963
THE BIRDS   sound-consultant only, Universal, 1963
MARNIE   Universal, 1964
JOY IN THE MORNING   MGM, 1965
TORN CURTAIN   score not used, Universal, 1965
FAHRENHEIT 451   Universal, 1966, British
THE BRIDE WORE BLACK   Lopert, 1968, French-Italian
TWISTED NERVE   National General, 1969, British
THE NIGHT DIGGER   MGM, 1971, British
THE BATTLE OF NERETVA   American International, 1971, Yugoslavian-U.S.-Italian-German
ENDLESS NIGHT   Rank, 1971, British
SISTERS   American International, 1973
IT'S ALIVE   Warner Bros., 1974
OBSESSION ★   Columbia, 1976
TAXI DRIVER ★   Columbia, 1976

(Several films use "tracked" [pre-existing] music by Herrmann, including "Obsessions" [1969] and "The Hound of the Baskervilles" [1972]. Scores for "It Lives Again" (1978) and "It's Alive III: Island of the Alive" (1987) are based on Herrmann's score for "It's Alive.")

WERNER R. HEYMANN

b. Germany

THE SPY   1927
MELODIE DES HERZENS   1929, German
LIEBESWALZER   1929, German

DER SIEGER 1931, German
DER BALL 1931, German
EIN BLONDER TRAUM 1932, German
ICH BEI TAG, DU BEI NACHT 1932, German
LA PETITE SAUVAGE 1933, German
ADORABLE Fox, 1933
CARAVAN Fox, 1934
THE KING AND THE CHORUS GIRL Warner Bros., 1937
BLUEBEARD'S EIGHTH WIFE co-composer with Frederick Hollander, Paramount, 1938
NINOTCHKA MGM, 1939
THE EARL OF CHICAGO MGM, 1940
THE SHOP AROUND THE CORNER MGM, 1940
PRIMROSE PATH RKO Radio, 1940
ONE MILLION B.C. ★ United Artists, 1940
HE STAYED FOR BREAKFAST Columbia, 1940
THIS THING CALLED LOVE Columbia, 1941
TOPPER RETURNS United Artists, 1941
THAT UNCERTAIN FEELING ★ United Artists, 1941
MY LIFE WITH CAROLINE RKO Radio, 1941
BEDTIME STORY Columbia, 1941
TO BE OR NOT TO BE ★ United Artists, 1942
THE WIFE TAKES A FLYER Columbia, 1942
THEY ALL KISSED THE BRIDE Columbia, 1942
FLIGHT LIEUTENANT Columbia, 1942
A NIGHT TO REMEMBER Columbia, 1942
APPOINTMENT IN BERLIN Columbia, 1943
KNICKERBOCKER HOLIDAY ★ adaptation, United Artists, 1944
HAIL THE CONQUERING HERO Paramount, 1944
MADEMOISELLE FIFI RKO Radio, 1944
OUR HEARTS WERE YOUNG AND GAY Paramount, 1944
MY PAL, WOLF RKO Radio, 1944
THREE IS A FAMILY United Artists, 1944
TOGETHER AGAIN Columbia, 1944
IT'S IN THE BAG United Artists, 1945
KISS AND TELL Columbia, 1945
LOST HONEYMOON Eagle Lion, 1947
THE SIN OF HAROLD DIDDLEBOCK *MAD WEDNESDAY* RKO Radio, 1947
ALWAYS TOGETHER Warner Bros., 1948
THE MATING OF MILLIE Columbia, 1948
LET'S LIVE A LITTLE Eagle Lion, 1948
A KISS FOR CORLISS United Artists, 1949
TELL IT TO THE JUDGE Columbia, 1949
A WOMAN OF DISTINCTION Columbia, 1949
EMERGENCY WEDDING Columbia, 1950
HEIDELBERGER ROMANZE 1951, West German
ALRAUNE 1952, West German
EIN HAUS VOLL LIEBE 1952, West German
DER KONGRESS TANZT 1955, West German

PAUL HINDEMITH

b. 1895 - Hanau, Germany
d. 1963 - Frankfurt, West Germany

VORMITTAGSPUK 1928, German

GUSTAV HINRICHS

b. 1850 - Germany

THE PHANTOM OF THE OPERA Universal, 1925

FREDERICK HOLLANDER

(Friedrich Hollander)

b. October 18, 1896 - London, England
d. 1976

THE BLUE ANGEL UFA, 1930, German
I AM SUZANNE Fox, 1934
SHANGHAI Paramount, 1935
DESIRE Paramount, 1936
TILL WE MEET AGAIN Paramount, 1936
VALIANT IS THE WORD FOR CARRIE Paramount, 1936
JOHN MEADE'S WOMAN Paramount, 1937
TRUE CONFESSION Paramount, 1937
BLUEBEARD'S EIGHTH WIFE co-composer with Werner R. Heymann, Paramount, 1938
MIDNIGHT Paramount, 1939
INVITATION TO HAPPINESS Paramount, 1939
DISPUTED PASSAGE Paramount, 1939
REMEMBER THE NIGHT Paramount, 1940
TOO MANY HUSBANDS Columbia, 1940
THE DOCTOR TAKES A WIFE Columbia, 1940
TYPHOON Paramount, 1940
THE BISCUIT EATER Paramount, 1940
SAFARI Paramount, 1940
THE GREAT McGINTY Paramount, 1940
RANGERS OF FORTUNE Paramount, 1940
SOUTH OF SUEZ Warner Bros., 1940
VICTORY Paramount, 1941
LIFE WITH HENRY Paramount, 1941
THERE'S MAGIC IN MUSIC Paramount, 1941
FOOTSTEPS IN THE DARK Warner Bros., 1941
MILLION DOLLAR BABY Warner Bros., 1941
HERE COMES MR. JORDAN Columbia, 1941
YOU BELONG TO ME Columbia, 1942
THE MAN WHO CAME TO DINNER Warner Bros., 1942
WINGS FOR THE EAGLE Warner Bros., 1942
TALK OF THE TOWN ★ Columbia, 1942
BACKGROUND TO DANGER Warner Bros., 1943
PRINCESS O'ROURKE Warner Bros., 1943
ONCE UPON A TIME Columbia, 1944
THE AFFAIRS OF SUSAN Paramount, 1945
PILLOW TO POST Warner Bros., 1945
CONFLICT Warner Bros., 1945
CHRISTMAS IN CONNECTICUT Warner Bros., 1945
CINDERELLA JONES Warner Bros., 1946
THE BRIDE WORE BOOTS Paramount, 1946
JANIE GETS MARRIED Warner Bros., 1946
TWO GUYS FROM MILWAUKEE Warner Bros., 1946
NEVER SAY GOODBYE Warner Bros., 1946
THE VERDICT Warner Bros., 1946
THE TIME, THE PLACE AND THE GIRL Warner Bros., 1946
THE PERFECT MARRIAGE Paramount, 1947
THAT WAY WITH WOMEN Warner Bros., 1947
STALLION ROAD Warner Bros., 1947
THE RED STALLION Eagle Lion, 1947
BERLIN EXPRESS RKO Radio, 1948
WALLFLOWER Warner Bros., 1948
A FOREIGN AFFAIR Paramount, 1948
A WOMAN'S SECRET RKO Radio, 1949
CAUGHT MGM, 1949
ADVENTURE IN BALTIMORE RKO Radio, 1949
STRANGE BARGAIN RKO Radio, 1949
BRIDE FOR SALE RKO Radio, 1949
A DANGEROUS PROFESSION RKO Radio, 1949
BORN TO BE BAD RKO Radio, 1950
WALK SOFTLY, STRANGER RKO Radio, 1950
NEVER A DULL MOMENT RKO Radio, 1950
BORN YESTERDAY Columbia, 1950

MY FORBIDDEN PAST RKO Radio, 1951
DARLING, HOW COULD YOU? Paramount, 1951
THE FIRST TIME Columbia, 1952
ANDROCLES AND THE LION RKO Radio, 1952
THE 5,000 FINGERS OF DR. T ★ co-composer with Heinz Roemheld and Hans J. Salter, Columbia, 1953
IT SHOULD HAPPEN TO YOU Columbia, 1954
PHFFFT Columbia, 1954
SABRINA Paramount, 1954
WE'RE NO ANGELS Paramount, 1955
DAS SPUKSCHLOSS IN SPESSART *THE SPOOK CASTLE IN SPESSART* 1960, West German

ARTHUR HONEGGER

b. March 10, 1892 - Le Havre, France
d. 1955 - Paris, France

LA ROUE 1922, French
FAIT DIVERS 1924, French
NAPOLEON 1926, French
L'IDEE 1926, French
PACIFIC 231 1931
LES MISERABLES 1934
CRIME AND PUNISHMENT 1935
L'EQUIPAGE *FLIGHT INTO DARKNESS* 1935, French
MADEMOISELLE DOCTEUR 1935, French
NITCHEVO 1936, French
MAYERLING 1936, French
REGAIN 1937, French
LA CITADELLE DU SILENCE co-composer with Darius Milhaud, 1937, French
THE WOMAN I LOVE RKO Radio, 1937
PYGMALION MGM, 1938, British
JE T'ATTENDRAI 1939, French
CAVALCADE d'AMOUR co-composer with Darius Milhaud, 1939, French
LE CAPITAINE FRACASSE 1942, French
SECRETS 1942, French
UN SEUL AMOUR 1943, French
UN AMI VIENDRA CE SOIR 1945, French
UN REVENANT 1946, French
STORM OVER TIBET Columbia, 1951
JOAN OF ARC AT THE STAKE 1954, French

GOTTFRIED HUPPERTZ

b. Germany

DIE NIBELUNGEN UFA, 1924, German
METROPOLIS UFA, 1926, German

I

JACQUES IBERT

b. August 15, 1890 - Paris, France
d. 1962 - Paris, France

UN CHAPEAU DE PAILLE D'ITALIE *THE ITALIAN STRAW HAT* 1927, French
LES CINQ GENTLEMAN MAUDITS 1930, French
S.O.S. FOCH 1931, French
LES DEUX ORPHELINES 1932, French
DON QUIXOTE 1933, British
JUSTIN DE MARSEILLES co-composer, 1935, French
GOLGOTHA 1935, French
MATERNITE 1935, French
KOENIGSMARK 1935, French
LE COUPABLE 1936, French
PARIS 1936, French
ANNE-MARIE 1936, French
COURRIER SUD co-composer with Maurice Thiriet, 1936, French
L'HOMME DE NULLE PART 1936, French
LA MAISON DU MALTAIS 1937, French
LE PERE LEBONNARD 1937, French
ANGELICA 1938, French
LE HEROS DE LA MARNE 1938, French
LE PATRIOTE 1938, French
THERESE MARTIN 1938, French
LE COMEDIE DU BONHEUR 1939, French
LA CHARRETTE FANTOME 1939, French
FELICIE NANTEUIL 1942, French
LES PETITES DU QUAI AUX FLEURS 1943, French
LE PERE SERGE 1945, French
PANIC Tricolore, 1946, French
MACBETH Republic, 1948
EQUILIBRE 1952, French
MARIANNE OF MY YOUTH United Motion Picture Organization, 1955, French

JOHN IRELAND

b. 1879 - Bowden, England
d. 1962 - Sussex, England

THE OVERLANDERS 1946, Australian-British

J

GORDON JENKINS

b. May 12, 1910 - Webster Groves, Missouri
d. May 1, 1984 - Los Angeles, California

STRANGE HOLIDAY Producers Releasing Corporation, 1946
BWANA DEVIL United Artists, 1952
THE FIRST DEADLY SIN Filmways Pictures, 1980

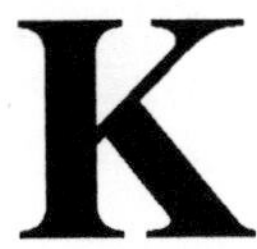

DMITRI KABALEVSKY

b. 1904 - St. Petersburg, Russia
d. 1987 - Moscow, U.S.S.R.

AEROGRAD FRONTIER 1936, Soviet
SHORS 1939, Soviet
ACADEMICIAN IVAN PAVLOV 1949, Soviet
IVAN PAVLOV 1950, Soviet
FLAMES ON THE VOLGA 1950, Soviet
THE GADFLY 1955, Soviet
THE SISTERS 1957, Soviet
1918 1958, Soviet
BLEAK MORNING 1959, Soviet

BRONISLAU KAPER

b. February 5, 1902 - Warsaw, Poland
d. 1983

DIE LUSTIGEN MUSIKANTEN 1930, German
ALRAUNE *DAUGHTER OF EVIL* 1930, German
DIE GROSSE ATTRAKTION 1931, German
MELODIE DER LIEBE 1932, German
EIN LIED FUR DICH 1933, German
MADAME WUNSCHT KEINE KINDER 1933, German
I TAKE THIS WOMAN MGM, 1940
THE MORTAL STORM MGM, 1940
THE CAPTAIN IS A LADY MGM, 1940
WE WHO ARE YOUNG MGM, 1940
DULCY MGM, 1940
COMRADE X MGM, 1940
BLONDE INSPIRATION MGM, 1941
RAGE IN HEAVEN MGM, 1941
A WOMAN'S FACE MGM, 1941
I'LL WAIT FOR YOU MGM, 1941
BARNACLE BILL MGM, 1941
WHISTLING IN THE DARK MGM, 1941
DR. KILDARE'S WEDDING DAY MGM, 1941
WHEN LADIES MEET MGM, 1941
THE CHOCOLATE SOLDIER ★ adaptation, MGM, 1941
H.M. PULHAM, ESQUIRE MGM, 1941
JOHNNY EAGER MGM, 1941
TWO-FACED WOMAN MGM, 1942
WE WERE DANCING MGM, 1942
FINGERS AT THE WINDOW MGM, 1942
CROSSROADS MGM, 1942
THE AFFAIRS OF MARTHA MGM, 1942
SOMEWHERE I'LL FIND YOU MGM, 1942
A YANK AT EATON MGM, 1942
WHITE CARGO MGM, 1942
KEEPER OF THE FLAME MGM, 1942
SLIGHTLY DANGEROUS MGM, 1943
ABOVE SUSPICION MGM, 1943
BATAAN MGM, 1943
THE CROSS OF LORRAINE MGM, 1943
THE HEAVENLY BODY MGM, 1944
GASLIGHT MGM, 1944
MARRIAGE IS A PRIVATE AFFAIR MGM, 1944
MRS. PARKINGTON MGM, 1945
WITHOUT LOVE MGM, 1945
BEWITCHED MGM, 1945
OUR VINES HAVE TENDER GRAPES MGM, 1945
THREE WISE FOOLS MGM, 1946
THE STRANGER RKO Radio, 1946
COURAGE OF LASSIE MGM, 1946
THE SECRET HEART MGM, 1946
CYNTHIA MGM, 1947
SONG OF LOVE MGM, 1947
GREEN DOLPHIN STREET MGM, 1947
HIGH WALL MGM, 1948
B.F.'S DAUGHTER MGM, 1948
HOMECOMING MGM, 1948
THE SECRET LAND (FD) MGM, 1948
ACT OF VIOLENCE MGM, 1948
THE SECRET GARDEN MGM, 1949
THE GREAT SINNER MGM, 1949
THAT FORSYTE WOMAN MGM, 1949
MALAYA MGM, 1949
KEY TO THE CITY MGM, 1950
THE SKIPPER SURPRISED HIS WIFE MGM, 1950
A LIFE OF HER OWN MGM, 1950
TO PLEASE A LADY MGM, 1950
GROUNDS FOR MARRIAGE MGM, 1950
THREE GUYS NAMED MIKE MGM, 1951
MR. IMPERIUM MGM, 1951
THE RED BADGE OF COURAGE MGM, 1951
TOO YOUNG TO KISS MGM, 1951
IT'S A BIG COUNTRY MGM, 1951
SHADOW IN THE SKY MGM, 1951
INVITATION MGM, 1952
THE WILD NORTH MGM, 1952
THE NAKED SPUR MGM, 1953
LILI ★★ MGM, 1953
RIDE, VAQUERO! MGM, 1953
THE ACTRESS MGM, 1953
SAADIA MGM, 1953
THEM! Warner Bros., 1954
HER TWELVE MEN MGM, 1954
THE GLASS SLIPPER MGM, 1955
THE PRODIGAL MGM, 1955
QUENTIN DURWARD MGM, 1955
FOREVER, DARLING MGM, 1955
THE SWAN MGM, 1956
THE POWER AND THE PRIZE MGM, 1956
SOMEBODY UP THERE LIKES ME MGM, 1956
THE BARRETTS OF WIMPOLE STREET MGM, 1957
JET PILOT RKO Radio, 1957
DON'T GO NEAR THE WATER MGM, 1957
THE BROTHERS KARAMAZOV MGM, 1957
AUNTIE MAME Warner Bros., 1958
THE SCAPEGOAT MGM, 1958
GREEN MANSIONS MGM, 1959
HOME FROM THE HILL MGM, 1959
THE ANGEL WORE RED MGM, 1960
BUTTERFIELD 8 MGM, 1960
TWO LOVES MGM, 1961
ADA MGM, 1961
MUTINY ON THE BOUNTY ★ MGM, 1962
KISSES FOR MY PRESIDENT Warner Bros., 1964
LORD JIM Columbia, 1965
TOBRUK Universal, 1967
THE WAY WEST United Artists, 1967
COUNTERPOINT Universal, 1968
A FLEA IN HER EAR 20th Century-Fox, 1968

ANTON KARAS

d. January 10, 1985

THE THIRD MAN Selznick Releasing, 1949, British

BERNHARD KAUN

b. 1899 - Germany
d. January 3, 1980

HEAVEN ON EARTH Universal, 1931
FRANKENSTEIN Universal, 1931
DR. X Warner Bros., 1932
ONE WAY PASSAGE Warner Bros., 1932
THE MYSTERY OF THE WAX MUSEUM Warner Bros., 1933
20,000 YEARS IN SING SING Warner Bros., 1933
DEATH TAKES A HOLIDAY additional music, Paramount, 1934
RETURN OF THE TERROR Warner Bros., 1934
THE STORY OF LOUIS PASTEUR Warner Bros., 1936
THE WALKING DEAD Warner Bros., 1936
THE INVISIBLE MENACE Warner Bros., 1937
THE RETURN OF DR. X Warner Bros., 1939
THE BODY DISAPPEARS additional music, 1941
THE SMILING GHOST co-composer with William Lava, 1941
SPECIAL DELIVERY VON HIMM *EL GEFALLEN* Columbia, 1955, West German-U.S.

ARAM KHACHATURIAN

b. 1903 - Tbilisi, Russia
d. May 2, 1978 - Moscow, U.S.S.R.

PEPO 1935, Soviet
SALAVAT YULAYEV 1941, Soviet
GIRL NO. 217 1944, Soviet
THE RUSSIAN QUESTION 1948, Soviet
THE BATTLE OF STALINGRAD 1949, Soviet
ADMIRAL USHAKOV 1953, Soviet
ATTACK FROM THE SEA 1953, Soviet
SALTANAT 1955, Soviet
OTHELLO 1955, Soviet

CHRISTOPHER KOMEDA

(Krzysztof T. Komeda)

b. April 27, 1937 - Poland
d. April 23, 1969 - Los Angeles, California

THE GLASS MOUNTAIN 1960
INNOCENT SORCERERS 1960
SEE YOU TOMORROW 1960
THE FAT AND THE LEAN 1961
KNIFE IN THE WATER Kanawha, 1962, Polish
AMBULANCE 1962
MAMMALS 1962
OPENING TOMORROW 1962
EPILOGUE 1963
NEW CLOTHES 1963
THE BEAUTIFUL SWINDLERS *LES PLUS BELLES ESCROQUERIES DU MONDE* composer of Polanski segment, Jack Ellis Films, 1964, French-Italian-Japanese-Dutch
CATS *KATTORNA* 1964
THE PENGUIN 1965
BARRIER Film Polski, 1966, Polish
LE DEPART Pathe Contemporary, 1966, Belgian
HUNGER 1966
CUL-DE-SAC Sigma III, 1966, British
PEOPLE MEET AND SWEET MUSIC FILLS THE AIR 1967
THE FEARLESS VAMPIRE KILLERS, OR PARDON ME BUT YOUR TEETH ARE IN MY NECK *DANCE OF THE VAMPIRES* MGM, 1967, British
ROSEMARY'S BABY Paramount, 1968
RIOT Paramount, 1969

ERICH WOLFGANG KORNGOLD

b. May 29, 1897 - Brno, Czechoslovakia
d. 1957 - Los Angeles, California

A MIDSUMMER NIGHT'S DREAM adaptation, Warner Bros., 1935
CAPTAIN BLOOD Warner Bros., 1935
GIVE US THIS NIGHT Paramount, 1936
THE GREEN PASTURES Warner Bros., 1936
ANTHONY ADVERSE ★★ Warner Bros., 1936
THE PRINCE AND THE PAUPER Warner Bros., 1937
ANOTHER DAWN Warner Bros., 1937
THE ADVENTURES OF ROBIN HOOD ★★ Warner Bros., 1938
JUAREZ Warner Bros., 1939
THE PRIVATE LIVES OF ELIZABETH AND ESSEX ★ Warner Bros., 1939
THE SEA HAWK ★ Warner Bros., 1940
THE SEA WOLF Warner Bros., 1941
KINGS ROW Warner Bros., 1942
THE CONSTANT NYMPH Warner Bros., 1943
BETWEEN TWO WORLDS Warner Bros., 1944
DEVOTION Warner Bros., 1946
OF HUMAN BONDAGE Warner Bros., 1946
DECEPTION Warner Bros., 1946
ESCAPE ME NEVER Warner Bros., 1947
MAGIC FIRE adaptation, Republic, 1956

JOSEPH KOSMA

b. 1905 - Budapest, Hungary
d. 1969 - Paris, France

JENNY co-composer with Lionel Cazaux, 1936, French
A DAY IN THE COUNTRY *UN PARTIE DE CAMPAGNE* 1936, French
GRAND ILLUSION World Pictures, 1937, French
LA BETE HUMAINE *THE HUMAN BEAST* 1938, French
LA MARSEILLAISE 1938, French
THE RULES OF THE GAME Janus, 1939, French
THE DEVIL'S ENVOYS *LES VISITEURS DU SOIR* 1942, French
ADIEU LEONARD 1943, French
CHILDREN OF PARADISE Tricolore, 1944, French
LES PORTES DE LA NUIT 1945, French
AUBERVILLIERS 1945, French
L'HOMME 1945, French
LES CHOUANS 1946, French
VOYAGE SURPRISE 1946, French
PETRUS 1946, French
L'ARCHE DE NOE 1946, French
L'AMOUR AUTOUR DE LA MAISON 1946, French
MONSIEUR LUDOVIC 1946, French
BETHSABEE 1947, French
LE PETIT SOLDAT 1947, French
LA DAME D'ONZE HEURES 1947, French
LE PARADIS DES PILOTES PERDUS 1947, French
L'ECOLE BUISSONNIERE 1947, French
BAGARRES 1948, French
D'HOMMES A HOMMES 1948, French
LES AMANTS DE VERONE 1948, French
HANS LE MARIN 1948, French
LE SANG DES BETES 1948, French
AU GRAND BALCON 1949, French
VENDETTA EN CAMARGUE 1949, French
LA MARIE DU PORT 1949, French
LA GRAND RENDEZ-VOUS 1949, French
LA BELLE QUE VOILA 1949, French
LA CIGALE ET LA FOURMI 1949, French
LE LOUP ET L'AGNEAU 1949, French

SOUVENIRS PERDUS 1950, French
TROIS TELEGRAMMES 1950, French
SANS LAISSER D'ADRESSE 1950, French
OMBRE ET LUMIERE 1950, French
CAPTAIN BLACK JACK United Artists, 1950, French-British-Spanish
DESORDRES 1950, French
JULIETTE OU LA CLE DES SONGES 1951, French
UN GRAN PATRON 1951, French
THE GREEN GLOVE *LE GANTELET VERT* United Artists, 1952
LA BERGERE ET LE RAMONEUR 1952, French
LE RIDEAU ROUGE 1952, French
AGENCE MATRIMONIALE 1952, French
LES FRUITS SAUVAGES 1953, French
FRANCOIS LE RHINOCEROS 1953, French
HUIS CLOS 1954, French
LES EVADES 1954, French
LES CHIFFONNIERS d'EMMAUS 1954, French
LE PORT DU DESIR 1954, French
LE VILLAGE MAGIQUE 1954, French
LOUIS LUMIERE 1954, French
INNOCENTS IN PARIS 1955, British
MONSIEUR LA CAILLE 1955, French
DES GENS SANS IMPORTANCE 1955, French
L'AMANT DE LADY CHATTERLEY 1955, French
MA JEANNETTE ET MES COPAINS 1955, French
MERMOZ 1955, French
CELA S'APPELLE L'AURORE 1956, French-Italian
PARIS DOES STRANGE THINGS *ELENA ET LES HOMMES* Warner Bros., 1956, French
CALLE MAYOR 1956, French
JE REVIENDRAI A KANDARA 1956, French
LE LONG DES TROTTOIRS 1956, French
L'INSPECTEUR AIME LA BAGARRE 1956, French
LES LOUVES 1956, French
THE CASE OF DR. LAURENT 1957, French
TAMANGO Valiant, 1957, French
DEMONIAQUE 1958, French
THE DOCTOR'S DILEMMA 1958, French
THE LOVEMAKER 1958, French
THE WILD FRUIT 1958, French
PICNIC ON THE GRASS Kingsley-Union, 1959, French
LE HUITIEME JOUR 1959, French
LOVE AND THE FRENCHWOMAN Kingsley International, 1960, French
LE PAVE DE PARIS 1961, French
LE TESTAMENT DU DR. CORDELIER (TF) 1961, French
LA PUPEE 1962, French
THE ELUSIVE CORPORAL *LE CAPORAL EPINGLE* Pathe Contemporary, 1962, French
IN THE FRENCH STYLE Columbia, 1963, French-U.S.
THE MAGNIFICENT SUMMER 1963, French
THANK HEAVEN FOR SMALL FAVORS 1965, French
BITTER FRUIT 1967, French
THE LITTLE THEATRE OF JEAN RENOIR (TF) Phoenix Films, 1969, French-Italian-West German

SIGMUND KRUMGOLD

DEATH TAKES A HOLIDAY co-composer, Paramount, 1934
WE'RE NOT DRESSING co-composer, Paramount, 1934
SHE LOVES ME NOT co-composer, Paramount, 1934
COLLEGE RHYTHM co-composer, Paramount, 1934
MISSISSIPPI co-composer, Paramount, 1935
STOLEN HARMONY co-composer, Paramount, 1935
PARIS IN SPRING Paramount, 1935
THE BIG BROADCAST OF 1936 co-composer, Paramount, 1935
UNION PACIFIC co-composer, Paramount, 1939

GAIL KUBIK

b. 1914 - S. Coffeyville, Oklahoma
d. July 20, 1984 - Covina, California

MEN AND SHIPS (FD) U.S. Maritime Commission, 1940
THE WORLD AT WAR (FD) O.W.I., 1942
PARATROOPS (FD) O.W.I., 1942
MANPOWER (FD) O.W.I., 1942
DOVER (FD) O.W.I., 1942
COLLEGES AT WAR (FD) O.W.I., 1942
EARTHQUAKERS (FD) A.A.F., 1943
THE MEMPHIS BELLE (FD) A.A.F., 1943
AIR PATTERN—PACIFIC (FD) A.A.F., 1944
THUNDERBOLT (FD) A.A.F., 1945
C-MAN Film Classics, 1949
THE MINER'S DAUGHTER (AS) Columbia, 1950
GERALD McBOING BOING (AS) Columbia, 1950
TWO GALS AND A GUY United Artists, 1951
THE DESPERATE HOURS Paramount, 1955
I THANK A FOOL MGM, 1962, British

L

WILLIAM LAVA

b. March 18, 1911 - Minnesota
d. February 20, 1971

HAWK OF THE WILDERNESS serial, Republic, 1938
SANTA FE STAMPEDE Republic, 1938
RED RIVER RANGE Republic, 1938
DAREDEVILS OF THE RED CIRCLE serial, Republic, 1939
THE NIGHT RAIDERS Republic, 1939
DICK TRACY'S G-MEN serial, Republic, 1939
THREE TEXAS STEERS Republic, 1939
WYOMING OUTLAW Republic, 1939
NEW FRONTIER Republic, 1939
THE LONE RANGER RIDES AGAIN serial, Republic, 1939
THE KANSAS TERRORS Republic, 1939
COWBOYS FROM TEXAS Republic, 1939
ZORRO'S FIGHTING LEGION serial, Republic, 1939
THE COURAGEOUS DR. CHRISTIAN RKO Radio, 1940
THE SMILING GHOST co-composer with Bernhard Kraun, 1941
THE MYSTERIOUS DOCTOR co-composer with Howard Jackson, 1943
THE INVISIBLE MAN'S REVENGE co-composer with Hans J. Salter, Eric Zeisl, Universal, 1944
JUNGLE CAPTIVE co-composer, Universal, 1944
HOUSE OF DRACULA co-composer, Universal, 1945
SHE-WOLF OF LONDON Universal, 1946
MOONRISE Republic, 1948
THE BIG PUNCH Warner Bros., 1948
EMBRACEABLE YOU Warner Bros., 1948
FLAXI MARTIN Warner Bros., 1949
HOMICIDE Warner Bros., 1949
THE YOUNGER BROTHERS Warner Bros., 1949
THE HOUSE ACROSS THE STREET Warner Bros., 1949
BARRICADE Warner Bros., 1950
COLT .45 Warner Bros., 1950
THIS SIDE OF THE LAW Warner Bros., 1950

THE GREAT JEWEL ROBBER Warner Bros., 1950
BREAKTHROUGH Warner Bros., 1950
HIGHWAY 301 Warner Bros., 1951
INSIDE THE WALLS OF FOLSOM PRISON Warner Bros., 1951
THE TANKS ARE COMING Warner Bros., 1951
RETREAT, HELL! Warner Bros., 1952
CATTLE TOWN Warner Bros., 1952
PHANTOM FROM SPACE 1952
TOBOR THE GREAT co-composer with Howard Jackson, Republic, 1954
REVENGE OF THE CREATURE co-composer, Universal, 1955
THE LITTLEST OUTLAW Buena Vista, 1955
THE DEADLY MANTIS Universal, 1957
HELL BENT FOR LEATHER Universal, 1960
SEVEN WAYS FROM SUNDOWN co-composer, Universal, 1960
THE SIGN OF ZORRO Buena Vista, 1960
PT-109 co-composer with David Buttolph, Warner Bros., 1963
WALL OF NOISE Warner Bros., 1963
THE TATTOOED POLICE HORSE Buena Vista, 1964
CHAMBER OF HORRORS Warner Bros., 1966
ASSIGNMENT TO KILL Warner Bros., 1968
CHUBASCO Warner Bros., 1968
IN ENEMY COUNTRY Universal, 1968
THE GOOD GUYS AND THE BAD GUYS Warner Bros., 1969
O'HARA, UNITED STATES TREASURY: OPERATION COBRA (TF) co-composer with Ray Heindorf, Mark VII Ltd./Universal TV, 1971
DRACULA VS. FRANKENSTEIN *BLOOD OF FRANKENSTEIN* Independent-International, 1971

ANGELO FRANCESCO LAVAGNINO

b. 1909 - Italy
d. September, 1987

STRANO APPUNTAMENTO *STRANGE APPOINTMENT* 1950, Italian
OTHELLO co-composer with Alberto Barberis, United Artists, 1952, U.S.-Italian
JUNGLE SPELL *MAGIA VERDE* (FD) 1953, Italian
MAMBO co-composer with Nino Rota, Paramount, 1954, U.S.-Italian
SINS OF CASANOVA 1954, Italian
LA DONNA DEL FIUME *THE WOMAN OF THE RIVER* co-composer with Armando Trovajoli, 1954, Italian
RICE GIRL *LA RISAIA* 1955, Italian
THE MILLER'S BEAUTIFUL WIFE *LA BELLA MUGNAIA* 1955, Italian
THE LAST PARADISE (FD) 1956, Italian
NERO'S WEEKEND *MIO FIGLIO NERONE* 1956, Italian
LEGEND OF THE LOST United Artists, 1957
IL CIELO BRUCIA co-composer with Francesco De Masi, 1957, Italian
CALYPSO (FD) 1958, Italian
BEHIND THE GREAT WALL *LA MURAGLIA CINESE* (FD) 1958, Italian
THE NAKED MAJA United Artists, 1959
MESSALINA 1959, Italian
POLICARPO 1959, Italian
CHE GIOIA VIVERE 1960, Italian
CONSPIRACY OF HEARTS Paramount, 1960, British
ESTHER AND THE KING co-composer with Roberto Nicolosi, 1960, Italian
FIVE BRANDED WOMEN 1960, Italian
THE GRAND OLYMPICS (FD) co-composer with Armando Trovajoli, 1960
THE LAST DAYS OF POMPEII United Artists, 1960, Italian
THE SAVAGE INNOCENTS Paramount, 1960, Italian
HERCULES AGAINST ROME 1960, Italian
THE NIGHT THEY KILLED RASPUTIN *L'ULTIMO ZAR* 1960, Italian
NUDE ODYSSEY 1961, Italian
THE WARRIOR EMPRESS 1961, Italian
THE COLOSSUS OF RHODES 1961, Italian
GORGO MGM, 1961, British
THE REVOLT OF THE SLAVES 1961, Italian
ULYSSES AGAINST THE SONS OF HERCULES 1961, Italian
THE WONDERS OF ALADDIN MGM, 1961, Italian-U.S.
THE CORSICAN BROTHERS 1961, Italian
GOLIATH AND THE VAMPIRES Italian version only, 1961, Italian
DAMON AND PYTHIAS 1962, Italian
MARCO POLO 1962, Italian
THE SIEGE OF SYRACUSE Paramount, 1962, Italian
MADAME 1962, French-Italian
COMMANDO *MARCIA O CREPA* 1963, Italian
SAMSON & THE SLAVE QUEEN composer of Italian version only, 1963, Italian
SAMSON CONTRO I PARATI *SAMSON VS. THE PIRATES* 1963, Italian
AGENT 8 3/4 *HOT ENOUGH FOR JUNE* Continental, 1963, British
DARK PURPOSE *L'INTRIGO* 1964, Italian
THE CASTLE OF THE LIVING DEAD 1964, Italian-French
HERCULES AND THE TYRANTS OF BABYLON 1964, Italian
GLI INVINCIBILI TRE *THE INVINCIBLE THREE* 1964, Italian
TOTO DE ARABIA 1964, Italian
THE HERO OF ROME 1964, Italian
L'INVINCIBILE CAVALIERE MASCHERATO 1964, French-Italian
McGUIRE GO HOME *THE HIGH BRIGHT SUN* 1964, British-Italian
GUNMEN OF THE RIO GRANDE 1965, Italian
I TABU #2 (FD) 1965, Italian
I PREDONI DEL SAHARA 1965, Italian
IL MISTERO DELL'ISOLA MALEDETTA 1965, Italian
IL CASTELLO DEI MORTI VIVI 1965, Italian
JOHNNY WEST IL MANCINO 1965, Italian
HERCULES, SAMSON & ULYSSES 1965, Italian
SEVEN HOURS OF GUNFIRE 1965, Italian
SNOW DEVILS 1965, Italian
SALADINO 1966, Italian
CHIMES AT MIDNIGHT *FALSTAFF* Peppercorn-Wormser, 1966, Spanish-Swiss
WILD WILD PLANET *I CRIMINALI DELLA GELASSIA* MGM, 1966, Italian
WAR BETWEEN THE PLANETS *MISSIONE PIANETA ERRANTE* Fanfare, 1966, Italian
GUNGALA, LA VIRGINE DELLS GIUNGLA *GUNGALA, THE VIRGIN OF THE JUNGLE* 1967, Italian
ACID co-composer with Armando Trovajoli, 1967, Italian
OGGI A ME, DOMANI A TE 1968, Italian
SCUSI, LEI CONOSCE IL SESSO? co-composer with Piero Umiliani, 1968, Italian
REQUIEM PER UN GRINGO 1968, Italian
STORY OF A GIRL ALONE 1969, Spanish
GLI SPECIALISTI 1969, French-Italian
QUALCOSA STRISCIA NEL BUIO *SOMETHING IS CREEPING IN THE DARK* 1970, Italian
ZORRO, MARCHESE DI NAVARRE 1971, Italian

QUEENS OF EVIL *IL DELITTO DEL DIAVOLO* 1971, Italian
AFRICA NUDA, AFRICA VIOLENTA (FD) 1973, Italian
NAKED MAGIC *SHOCKING CANNIBALS* Fury Films, 1974, Italian
L'ITALIA IN PIGIAMA 1976, Italian

JOHN LEIPOLD

STAGECOACH ★★ co-composer, United Artists, 1939
DISPUTED PASSAGE co-composer, Paramount, 1939
THE FLYING DEUCES co-composer, RKO Radio, 1939
UNION PACIFIC co-composer, Paramount, 1939
THE PARSON OF PANAMINT Paramount, 1941
SHUT MY BIG MOUTH Columbia, 1942
TWO YANKS IN TRINIDAD Columbia, 1942
THE DARING YOUNG MAN Columbia, 1943
THE DESPERADOES Columbia, 1943
GOOD LUCK, MR. YATES Columbia, 1943
NINE GIRLS Columbia, 1944

OSCAR LEVANT

b. December 27, 1906 - Pittsburgh, Pennsylvania
d. 1972 - Beverly Hills, California

CRIME WITHOUT PASSION co-composer with Frank Tours, Paramount, 1934
CHARLIE CHAN AT THE OPERA opera sequence, 20th Century-Fox, 1937
NOTHING SACRED United Artists, 1937
MADE FOR EACH OTHER United Artists, 1939
PETE ROLEUM AND HIS COUSINS co-composer with Hans Eisler, 1939

LOUIS LEVY

b. 1893
d. August 18, 1957

EVENSONG 1934, British
ALIAS BULLDOG DRUMMOND 1935, British
MR. HOBO 1935, British
TRANSATLANTIC TUNNEL 1935, British
EAST MEETS WEST 1936, British
IT'S LOVE AGAIN co-composer, 1936, British
NINE DAYS A QUEEN 1936, British
THE PASSING OF THE THIRD FLOOR BACK 1936, British
THE SECRET AGENT Gaumont-British, 1936, British
SEVEN SINNERS 1936, British
SABOTAGE *A WOMAN ALONE* Gaumont-British, 1936, British
HEAD OVER HEELS IN LOVE 1937, British
YOUNG AND INNOCENT *THE GIRL WAS YOUNG* Gaumont-British, 1937, British
MAN OF AFFAIRS 1937, British
THE CITADEL MGM, 1938
NIGHT TRAIN *NIGHT TRAIN TO MUNICH* MGM, 1940, British
HAUNTED HONEYMOON MGM, 1941, British
THE HASTY HEART Warner Bros., 1949
WOMAN IN A DRESSING GOWN Warner Bros., 1957, British

LEIGHTON LUCAS

b. 1903 - London, England
d. 1982 - London, England

TARGET FOR TONIGHT 1941, British
STAGE FRIGHT Warner Bros., 1950
THE WEAK AND THE WICKED Allied Artists, 1954, British
THE DAM BUSTERS Warner Bros., 1955, British
BATTLE HELL *YANGTSE INCIDENT* DCA, 1957, British
DESERT ATTACK *ICE COLD IN ALEX* 20th Century-Fox, 1958, British
THE SON OF ROBIN HOOD 20th Century-Fox, 1959, British

ELISABETH LUYTENS

b. 1906 - London, England
d. 1983 - London, England

A STRING OF BEADS 1947, British
THE BOY KUMASENU 1951, British
EL DORADO 1951, British
WORLD WITHOUT END 1953, British
THE MALPAS MYSTERY Anglo-Amalgamated, 1960, British
PARANOIAC Universal, 1964, British
THE EARTH DIES SCREAMING 20th Century-Fox, 1964, British
WHY BOTHER TO KNOCK? 1964, British
DR. TERROR'S HOUSE OF HORRORS Paramount, 1965, British
THE SKULL Paramount, 1965, British
SPACEFLIGHT IC-1 1965, British
THE PSYCHOPATH Paramount, 1966, British
THEATRE OF DEATH *BLOOD FIEND* 1967, British
THE TERRORNAUTS 1967, British
MIJN HACHTEN MET SUSAN OLGA ALBERT JULIE PIET & SANDRA 1975, Dutch

MICHEL MAGNE

b. 1930 - Lisieux, France
d. France

LE PAIN VIVANT 1954, French
LES PIQUE-ASSIETTES 1959, French
LES LIVREURS 1960, French
UN SINGE EN HIVER 1961, French
LES BRICOLEURS 1961, French
LOVE ON A PILLOW *LE REPOS DU GEURRIER* Royal Films International, 1962, French-Italian
GIGOT ★ 20th Century-Fox, 1962
LE VICE ET LA VERTU 1962, French
ANY NUMBER CAN WIN *MELODIE EN SOUS-SOL* MGM, 1963, French
GERMINAL 1963, French
LES GRANDS CHEMINS 1963, French
LES TONTONS FLINGLEURS 1963, French
LE MONOCLE RIT JAUNE 1963, French
LA MARQUISE DES ANGES 1963, French
CIRCLE OF LOVE *LA RONDE* Continental, 1964, French
FANTOMAS 1964, French
MARVEILLEUSE ANGELIQUE 1964, French
PAR UN BEAU MATIN D'ETE 1964, French
SYMPHONY FOR A MASSACRE 7 Arts, 1965, French-Italian
LE JOURNAL D'UNE FEMME EN BLANC 1965, French
GALIA 1965, French
THE SLEEPING CAR MURDERS 7 Arts, 1966, French

LES BONS VIVANTS 1966, French
ANGELIQUE ET LE ROI 1966, French
LE NOUVEAU JOURNAL D'UNE FEMME EN BLANC 1966, French
AVEC LA PEAU AUTRES 1967, French
TWO WEEKS IN SEPTEMBER *A COEUR JOIE* Paramount, 1967, French
BELLE DE JOUR Allied Artists, 1967, French-Italian
FLEUR D'OSEILLE 1968, French
ANGELIQUE ET LE SULTAN 1969, French
LA ROUTE DE SALINA 1970, French
MANON 70 1970, French
UN FEMME EN BLANC SE REVOLTE 1970, French
COLD SWEAT *DE LA PART DES COPAINS* Emerson, 1970, French
CRAN D'ARRET 1971, French
TOUT LE MONDE IL EST BEAU... 1973, French
MS. DON JUAN *DON JUAN ETAIT UNE FEMME* Scotia American, 1973, French
MOI Y'EN A VOULOIR DES SOUS 1973, French
UN ANGE AU PARADIS 1973, French
LES CHINOIS A PARIS 1974, French
LE COMPLOT CIC, 1975, French
NEA *NEA - A YOUNG EMMANUELLE* Libra, 1976, French
SURPRISE PARTY co-composer, Uranium Films, 1982, French
L'INDIC *THE INFORMER* GEF/CCFC, 1983, French
S.A.S. A SAN SALVADOR *S.A.S. - TERMINATE WITH EXTREME PREJUDICE* UGC, 1983, West German-French
EMMANUELLE 4 AAA/Sedpa, 1984, French

EDMUND MEISEL

d. 1930

THE BATTLESHIP POTEMKIN *POTEMKIN* Amkino, 1925, Soviet
BERLIN—SYMPHONY OF A GREAT CITY 1927
OCTOBER *TEN DAYS THAT SHOOK THE WORLD* Amkino, 1928,

MICHEL MICHELET

b. June 27, 1899 - Kiev, Russia

THE END OF THE WORLD 1930, French
LE MONT SAINT-MICHEL 1934, French
LES YEUX NOIRS 1935, French
NOSTALGIE 1935, French
LES BATELIERS DE LA VOLGA 1935, French
SOUS LA TERREUR 1935, French
FORFAITURE 1936, French
LE MENSONGE DE NINA PETROVNA 1937, French
ALERTE EN MEDITERRANEE 1938, French
LE DERNIER TOURNANT 1939, French
VOICE IN THE WIND United Artists, 1944
THE HAIRY APE ★ United Artists, 1944
UP IN MABEL'S ROOM United Artists, 1944
MUSIC FOR MILLIONS MGM, 1944
THe DIARY OF A CHAMBERMAID United Artists, 1946
THE CHASE United Artists, 1946
LURED *PERSONAL COLUMN* Universal, 1947
SIREN OF ATLANTIS United Artists, 1948
IMPACT United Artists, 1949
OUTPOST IN MOROCCO United Artists, 1949
THE MAN ON THE EIFFEL TOWER RKO Radio, 1949
ONCE A THIEF United Artists, 1950
DOUBLE DEAL RKO Radio, 1950
M Columbia, 1951
TARZAN'S PERIL RKO Radio, 1951
FORT ALGIERS United Artists, 1953
UN MISSIONNAIRE 1955, French
LE SECRET DE SOEUR ANGELE 1955, French
LA VENERE DI CHERONEA 1957, French
DER TIGER VON ESCHNAPUR *JOURNEY TO THE LOST CITY* American International, 1959, West German-French-Italian
GODDESS OF LOVE 1960, Italian
CAPTAIN SINDBAD MGM, 1963
THE CHALLENGE OF GREATNESS 1976

DARIUS MILHAUD

b. September 4, 1892 - Aix-en-Provence, France
d. 1974 - Geneva, Switzerland

L'INHUMAINE 1925, French
ACTUALITIES 1928, French
LA PETITE LILI 1929, French
HALLO EVERYBODY 1933, French
L'HIPPOCAMPE 1934, French
TARTARIN DE TARASCON French, 1934
MADAME BOVARY C.I.D., 1934, French
THE SEA HORSE 1934, French
THE BELOVED VAGABOND 1934, British
GRANDS FEUX 1937, French
LA CITADELLE DU SILENCE co-composer with Arthur Honegger, 1937, French
A LA CONQUETE DU CIEL 1937, French
MOLLENARD *HATRED* 1938, French
LA TRAGEDIE IMPERIALE 1938, French
LES OTAGES 1938, French
GULF STREAM 1939, French
CAVALCADE d'AMOUR co-composer with Arthur Honegger, 1939, French
L'ESPOIR 1939, French
THE ISLANDERS 1939, British
THE PRIVATE AFFAIRS OF BEL AMI United Artists, 1947
DREAMS THAT MONEY CAN BUY co-composer, Films International of America, 1948
LIFE BEGINS TOMORROW *LA VIE COMMENCE DEMAIN* 1950, French
ILS ETAIENT TOUS DES VOLONTAIRES (FD) 1954, French
CELLE QUI N'ETAIT PLUS co-composer with Pierre Henry, 1957, French

PAUL MISRAKI

b. 1908 - Constantinople

CLAUDINE A L'ECOLE 1936, French
TOUT VA TRES BIEN MADAME LA MARQUISE 1936, French
PRINCE BOUBOULE 1938, French
CHERI-BIBI 1938, French
LE CHANTEUR DE MINUIT 1938, French
J'ETAIS UNE AVENTURIERE 1938, French
FEUX DE JOIE 1938, French
RETOUR A LAUBE 1939, French
TOURBILLONS DE PARIS 1939, French
BATTEMENTS DE COEUR 1939, French
STELLA 1943
SIETE MUJERES 1943
LA PETITE FEMME DU MOULIN ROUGE 1943, French
PASSEPORT POUR RIO 1944, French
ECLIPSE DE SOL 1944, French
HEARTBEAT RKO Radio, 1946, French
LA FOIRE AUX CHIMERES 1946, French
SI JEUNESSE SAVAIT 1947, French
MADEMOISELLE S'AMUSE 1948, French
MANON 1949, French

NOUS IRONS A PARIS 1949, French
TOUS LE CHEMINS MENENT A ROME 1949, French
MANEGES 1949, French
LE ROSIER DE MADAME HUSSON 1950, French
KNOCK 1950, French
NOUS IRONS A MONTE-CARLO 1950, French
PIGALLE SAINT-GERMAIN-DES-PRES 1950, French
UTOPIA *ATOLL K* 1950, French
UNE HISTOIRE D'AMOUR 1951, French
LES MAINS SALES 1951, French
LE GARCON SAUVAGE 1951, French
COIFFEUR POUR DAMES 1952, French
LA JEUNE FOLLE 1952, French
ELLE ET MOI 1952, French
LE TROU NORMAND 1952, French
THE MOMENT OF TRUTH Arlan Pictures, 1952, French
LES ORGUEILLEUX 1953, French
LA ROUTE NAPOLEON 1953, French
ALI-BABA ET LES 40 VOLEURS 1954, French
MR. ARKADIN *CONFIDENTIAL REPORT* Warner Bros., 1955, Spanish-Swiss
OBSESSION Gibe Films, 1954, French-Italian
LES FEMMES S'EN BALANCENT 1954, French
FORTUNE CARREE 1954, French
OASIS 1954, French
LA REINE MARGOT 1954, French
LE FIL A LA PATTE co-composer with Rene Cloerec, 1954, French
ESCALE A ORLY 1955, French
CHIENS PERDUS SANS COLLIER 1955, French
LA MEILLEURE PART 1955, French
LE COUTURIER DE CES DAMES 1956, French
AND GOD CREATED WOMAN Kingsley International, 1956, French
EN EFFEUILLANT LA MARGUERITE 1956, French
DEATH IN THE GARDEN Bauer International, 1956, French-Mexican
LA CHATELAINE DU LIBAN 1956, French
SOUS LE CIEL DE PROVENCE 1956, French
MEFIEZ-VOUS FILLETTES 1957, French
A PIED A CHEVAL ET EN VOITURE 1957, French
QUAND LA FEMME S'EN MELE 1957, French
LES FANATIQUES 1957, French
INSPECTOR MAIGRET *MAIGRET TEND UN PIEGE* Lopert, 1958, French-Italian
SANS FAMILE 1958, French
A DOG, A MOUSE AND A SPUTNIK 1958, French
UN DROLE DE DIMANCHE 1958, French
MONTPARNASSE 19 1958, French
THE COUSINS Films Around the World, 1959, French
FAIBLES FEMMES 1959, French
LE CHEMINS DES ECOLIERS 1959, French
LEDA *WEB OF PASSION/A DOUBLE TOUR* Times, 1959, French
COMMENT QU'ELLE EST 1960, French
LE CAID 1960, French
LOVE AND THE FRENCHWOMAN Kingsley International, 1960, French
LES BONNES FEMMES Robert Hakim, 1960, French-Italian
LES 3 MOUSQUETAIRES 1961, French
LE RENDEZ-VOUS 1961, French
LENNY POUR LES DAMES 1962, French
LE DOULOUS 1962, French
LE CHEVALIER DE PARDAILLAN 1962, French
HARDI PARDAILLAN 1963, French
L'ASSASSIN CONNAIT LA MUSIQE 1963, French
A TOI DE FAIRE MIGNONNE 1963, French
LA MARJOLAINE 1965, French
ALPHAVILLE Pathe Contemporary, 1965, French
DIS-MOI QUI TU ES 1965, French
CARTES SUR TABLE 1966, French
SEVEN HOMMES ET UNE GARCE 1966, French
A MURDER IS A MURDER 1972, French
LES VOLETS CLOS 1972, French
JULIETTE ET JULIETTE 1973, French
LA MAIN A COUPER 1974, French
LE CHASSEUR DE CHEZ MAXIM 1975, French
LE MAESTRO 1975, French
LA PART DU FEU 1977, French
SUCH A LOVELY TOWN... 1979, French

CYRIL J. MOCKRIDGE

b. August 6, 1896 - London, England
d. January 18, 1979

THE ADVENTURES OF SHERLOCK HOLMES co-composer, 20th Century-Fox, 1939
WHISPERING GHOSTS co-composer, 20th Century-Fox, 1942
THE UNDYING MONSTER co-composer, 20th Century-Fox, 1942
MOONTIDE co-composer with David Buttolph, 20th Century-Fox, 1942
MANILA CALLING co-composer with David Buttolph and David Raksin, 20th Century-Fox, 1942
THE MAN IN THE TRUNK 20th Century-Fox, 1942
THE MEANEST MAN IN THE WORLD 20th Century-Fox, 1943
OVER MY DEAD BODY 20th Century-Fox, 1943
TONIGHT WE RAID CALAIS 20th Century-Fox, 1943
THE OX-BOW INCIDENT 20th Century-Fox, 1943
HOLY MATRIMONY 20th Century-Fox, 1943
HAPPY LAND 20th Century-Fox, 1943
THE SULLIVANS 20th Century-Fox, 1944
THE EVE OF ST. MARK 20th Century-Fox, 1944
LADIES OF WASHINGTON 20th Century-Fox, 1944
THE BIG NOISE 20th Century-Fox, 1944
THUNDERHEAD—SON OF FLICKA 20th Century-Fox, 1945
MOLLY AND ME 20th Century-Fox, 1945
CAPTAIN EDDIE 20th Century-Fox, 1945
COLONEL EFFINGHAM'S RAID 20th Century-Fox, 1946
SENTIMENTAL JOURNEY 20th Century-Fox, 1946
THE DARK CORNER 20th Century-Fox, 1946
CLUNY BROWN 20th Century-Fox, 1946
CLAUDIA AND DAVID 20th Century-Fox, 1946
MY DARLING CLEMENTINE 20th Century-Fox, 1946
WAKE UP AND DREAM 20th Century-Fox, 1946
THE LATE GEORGE APLEY 20th Century-Fox, 1947
MIRACLE ON 34TH STREET 20th Century-Fox, 1947
NIGHTMARE ALLEY 20th Century-Fox, 1947
THUNDER IN THE VALLEY 20th Century-Fox, 1947
SCUDDA HOO! SCUDDA HAY! 20th Century-Fox, 1948
GREEN GRASS OF WYOMING 20th Century-Fox, 1948
DEEP WATERS 20th Century-Fox, 1948
THE WALLS OF JERICHO 20th Century-Fox, 1948
LUCK OF THE IRISH 20th Century-Fox, 1948
ROAD HOUSE 20th Century-Fox, 1948
THAT WONDERFUL URGE 20th Century-Fox, 1949
THE BEAUTIFUL BLONDE FROM BASHFUL BEND 20th Century-Fox, 1949
SLATTERY'S HURRICANE 20th Century-Fox, 1949
COME TO THE STABLE 20th Century-Fox, 1949
I WAS A MALE WAR BRIDE 20th Century-Fox, 1949
FATHER WAS A FULLBACK 20th Century-Fox, 1949
MOTHER DIDN'T TELL ME 20th Century-Fox, 1950
CHEAPER BY THE DOZEN 20th Century-Fox, 1950
A TICKET TO TOMAHAWK 20th Century-Fox, 1950
LOVE THAT BRUTE 20th Century-Fox, 1950

WHERE THE SIDEWALK ENDS 20th Century-Fox, 1950
STELLA 20th Century-Fox, 1950
AMERICAN GUERRILLA IN THE PHILIPPINES 20th Century-Fox, 1950
YOU'RE IN THE NAVY NOW 20th Century-Fox, 1951
FOLLOW THE SUN 20th Century-Fox, 1951
HALF ANGEL 20th Century-Fox, 1951
AS YOUNG AS YOU FEEL 20th Century-Fox, 1951
THE FROGMEN 20th Century-Fox, 1951
MR. BELVEDERE RINGS THE BELL 20th Century-Fox, 1951
LOVE NEST 20th Century-Fox, 1951
LET'S MAKE IT LEGAL 20th Century-Fox, 1951
ELOPEMENT 20th Century-Fox, 1951
THE MODEL AND THE MARRIAGE BROKER 20th Century-Fox, 1952
DEADLINE U.S.A. 20th Century-Fox, 1952
BELLES ON THEIR TOES 20th Century-Fox, 1952
WE'RE NOT MARRIED 20th Century-Fox, 1952
DREAMBOAT 20th Century-Fox, 1952
NIGHT WITHOUT SLEEP 20th Century-Fox, 1952
MISTER SCOUTMASTER 20th Century-Fox, 1953
HOW TO MARRY A MILLIONAIRE 20th Century-Fox, 1953
NIGHT PEOPLE 20th Century-Fox, 1954
WOMAN'S WORLD 20th Century-Fox, 1954
RIVER OF NO RETURN 20th Century-Fox, 1954
THE LIEUTENANT WORE SKIRTS 20th Century-Fox, 1956
DESK SET 20th Century-Fox, 1957
OH, MEN! OH, WOMEN! 20th Century-Fox, 1957
WILL SUCCESS SPOIL ROCK HUNTER? 20th Century-Fox, 1957
THE GIFT OF LOVE 20th Century-Fox, 1958
I MARRIED A WOMAN Universal, 1958
RALLY 'ROUND THE FLAG, BOYS! 20th Century-Fox, 1958
HOUND-DOG MAN 20th Century-Fox, 1959
A PRIVATE'S AFFAIR 20th Century-Fox, 1959
THUNDER IN THE SUN Paramount, 1959
TALL STORY Warner Bros., 1960
WAKE ME WHEN IT'S OVER 20th Century-Fox, 1960
ALL HANDS ON DECK 20th Century-Fox, 1961
THE MAN WHO SHOT LIBERTY VALANCE Paramount, 1962
DONOVAN'S REEF Paramount, 1963

THELONIOUS MONK

d. February 17, 1982 - Englewood, New Jersey

LES LIASONS DANGEREUSES co-composer with Jack Murray, Astor, 1959, French-Italian

LUCIEN MORAWECK

d. October 20, 1973

THE MAN IN THE IRON MASK ★ co-composer with Lud Gluskin, United Artists, 1939
THE LADY IN QUESTION Columbia, 1940
DREAMING OUT LOUD RKO Radio, 1940
INTERNATIONAL LADY United Artists, 1941
FRIENDLY ENEMIES United Artists, 1942
AVALANCHE Producers Releasing Corp., 1946
STRANGE VOYAGE Monogram, 1946
THE RETURN OF MONTE CRISTO Small/Col., 1946
HIGH CONQUEST co-composer with Rene Garriguenc and Lyn Murray, Monogram, 1947
16 FATHOMS DEEP co-composer with Rene Garriguenc, Lake/Mon., 1948
MASSACRE RIVER co-composer with John Leipold, Allied Artists, 1949
NEW MEXICO co-composer with Rene Garriguenc, United Artists, 1951

JEROME MOROSS

b. August 1, 1913 - Brooklyn, New York
d. July 25, 1983 - Miami, Florida

CLOSE-UP Eagle Lion, 1948
WHEN I GROW UP United Artists, 1951
CAPTIVE CITY United Artists, 1952
HANS CHRISTIAN ANDERSEN ballet music only, RKO Radio, 1952
SEVEN WONDERS OF THE WORLD co-composer with David Raksin and Sol Kaplan, Cinerama, 1956
THE SHARKFIGHTERS United Artists, 1956
THE PROUD REBEL Buena Vista, 1958
THE BIG COUNTRY ★ United Artists, 1958
THE JAYHAWKERS Paramount, 1959
THE MOUNTAIN ROAD Columbia, 1960
THE ADVENTURES OF HUCKLEBERRY FINN MGM, 1960
FIVE FINGER EXERCISE Columbia, 1962
THE CARDINAL Columbia, 1963
THE WAR LORD Universal, 1965
RACHEL RACHEL Warner Bros., 1968
VALLEY OF THE GWANGI Warner Bros., 1969
HAIL, HERO! National General, 1969

LYN MURRAY
(Lionel Breeze)

b. December 6, 1909 - London, England
d. May 20, 1989 - Los Angeles, California

HIGH CONQUEST co-composer with Rene Garriguenc and Lucien Moraweck, Monogram, 1947
THE PROWLER United Artists, 1951
THE BIG NIGHT United Artists, 1951
THE RETURN OF GILBERT & SULLIVAN United Artists, 1951
SON OF PALEFACE Paramount, 1952
THE GIRLS OF PLEASURE ISLAND Paramount, 1952
HERE COME THE GIRLS Paramount, 1953
CASANOVA'S BIG NIGHT Paramount, 1954
THE BRIDGES AT TOKO-RI Paramount, 1955
TO CATCH A THIEF Paramount, 1955
D-DAY, THE SIXTH OF JUNE 20th Century-Fox, 1956
ON THE THRESHHOLD OF SPACE 20th Century-Fox, 1956
SNOW WHITE AND THE THREE STOOGES Columbia, 1961
ESCAPE FROM ZAHRAIN Paramount, 1962
PERIOD OF ADJUSTMENT MGM, 1962
COME FLY WITH ME MGM, 1963
WIVES AND LOVERS Paramount, 1963
SIGNPOST TO MURDER MGM, 1965
PROMISE HER ANYTHING Paramount, 1966
ROSIE! Universal, 1967
ESCAPE TO MINDANAO (TF) Universal TV, 1968
NOW YOU SEE IT, NOW YOU DON'T (TF) Universal TV, 1968
THE SMUGGLERS (TF) Universal TV, 1968
DRAGNET (TF) Mark VII Ltd./Universal TV, 1969
STRATEGY OF TERROR *IN DARKNESS WAITING* Universal, 1969, originally made for television

COCKEYED COWBOYS OF CALICO COUNTY Universal, 1970
LOVE, HATE, LOVE (TF) Aaron Spelling Productions, 1971
MAGIC CARPET (TF) Westwood Productions/ Universal TV, 1972
DON'T PUSH, I'LL CHARGE WHEN I'M READY (TF) Universal TV, 1977, filmed in 1969

OLIVER NELSON

b. June 4, 1932 - Saint Louis, Missouri
d. October 28, 1975 - Los Angeles, California

DEATH OF A GUNFIGHTER Universal, 1967
ISTANBUL EXPRESS (TF) Universal TV, 1968
DIAL HOT LINE (TF) Universal TV, 1970
SKULLDUGGERY Universal, 1970
ZIGZAG Universal, 1970
CUTTER (TF) Universal TV, 1972
CHASE (TF) CBS Entertainment, 1973
LAST TANGO IN PARIS United Artists, 1973, Italian-French
INSIDE JOB 1973
MONEY TO BURN (TF) Silverton Productions/ Universal TV, 1973

ALFRED NEWMAN

b. March 17, 1901 - New Haven, Connecticut
d. February, 1970

THE DEVIL TO PAY United Artists, 1931
REACHING FOR THE MOON United Artists, 1931
KIKI United Artists, 1931
INDISCREET United Artists, 1931
STREET SCENE United Artists, 1931
THE UNHOLY GARDEN United Artists, 1931
THE AGE FOR LOVE United Artists, 1931
CORSAIR United Artists, 1931
AROUND THE WORLD IN EIGHTY MINUTES United Artists, 1931
TONIGHT OR NEVER United Artists, 1931
ARROWSMITH United Artists, 1931
COCK OF THE AIR United Artists, 1932
THE GREEKS HAD A WORD FOR THEM United Artists, 1932
SKY DEVILS United Artists, 1932
MR. ROBINSON CRUSOE United Artists, 1932
RAIN United Artists, 1932
CYNARA United Artists, 1932
SECRETS United Artists, 1933
I COVER THE WATERFRONT United Artists, 1933
THE MASQUERADER United Artists, 1933
THE BOWERY United Artists, 1933
BLOOD MONEY United Artists, 1933
ADVICE TO THE LOVELORN United Artists, 1933
GALLANT LADY United Artists, 1934
LOOKING FOR TROUBLE United Artists, 1934
NANA United Artists, 1934
THE HOUSE OF ROTHSCHILD United Artists, 1934
BORN TO BE BAD United Artists, 1934
THE AFFAIRS OF CELLINI United Artists, 1934
THE LAST GENTLEMAN United Artists, 1934
BULLDOG DRUMMOND STRIKES BACK United Artists, 1934
THE CAT'S PAW 20th Century-Fox, 1934
OUR DAILY BREAD United Artists, 1934
WE LIVE AGAIN United Artists, 1934
THE COUNT OF MONTE CRISTO United Artists, 1934
THE MIGHTY BARNUM United Artists, 1935
CLIVE OF INDIA United Artists, 1935
THE WEDDING NIGHT United Artists, 1935
LES MISERABLES United Artists, 1935
CARDINAL RICHELIEU United Artists, 1935
THE CALL OF THE WILD United Artists, 1935
THE DARK ANGEL United Artists, 1935
BARBARY COAST United Artists, 1935
THE MELODY LINGERS ON United Artists, 1935
SPLENDOR United Artists, 1935
THESE THREE United Artists, 1936
RAMONA 20th Century-Fox, 1936
DODSWORTH United Artists, 1936
COME AND GET IT United Artists, 1936
BELOVED ENEMY United Artists, 1937
YOU ONLY LIVE ONCE United Artists, 1937
HISTORY IS MADE AT NIGHT United Artists, 1937
WOMAN CHASES MAN United Artists, 1937
SLAVE SHIP 20th Century-Fox, 1937
WEE WILLIE WINKIE 20th Century-Fox, 1937
STELLA DALLAS United Artists, 1937
DEAD END United Artists, 1937
THE PRISONER OF ZENDA ★ United Artists, 1937
THE HURRICANE ★ United Artists, 1938
ALEXANDER'S RAGTIME BAND ★★ adaptation, 20th Century-Fox, 1938
THE COWBOY AND THE LADY ★ United Artists, 1938
TRADE WINDS United Artists, 1938
GUNGA DIN RKO Radio, 1939
WUTHERING HEIGHTS ★ United Artists, 1939
YOUNG MR. LINCOLN 20th Century-Fox, 1939
BEAU GESTE Paramount, 1939
THE RAINS CAME ★ 20th Century-Fox, 1939
THE REAL GLORY United Artists, 1939
THEY SHALL HAVE MUSIC ★ United Artists, 1939
DRUMS ALONG THE MOHAWK 20th Century-Fox, 1939
THE HUNCHBACK OF NOTRE DAME ★ RKO Radio, 1939
THE BLUE BIRD 20th Century-Fox, 1940
THE GRAPES OF WRATH 20th Century-Fox, 1940
VIGIL IN THE NIGHT RKO Radio, 1940
LITTLE OLD NEW YORK 20th Century-Fox, 1940
EARTHBOUND 20th Century-Fox, 1940
FOREIGN CORRESPONDENT United Artists, 1940
BRIGHAM YOUNG 20th Century-Fox, 1940
THEY KNEW WHAT THEY WANTED RKO Radio, 1940
THE MARK OF ZORRO ★ 20th Century-Fox, 1940
HUDSON'S BAY 20th Century-Fox, 1940
THAT NIGHT IN RIO 20th Century-Fox, 1941
BLOOD AND SAND 20th Century-Fox, 1941
A YANK IN THE R.A.F. 20th Century-Fox, 1941
BALL OF FIRE ★ United Artists, 1941
HOW GREEN WAS MY VALLEY ★ 20th Century-Fox, 1941
SON OF FURY 20th Century-Fox, 1942
ROXIE HART 20th Century-Fox, 1942
TO THE SHORES OF TRIPOLI 20th Century-Fox, 1942
THIS ABOVE ALL 20th Century-Fox, 1942
THE PIED PIPER 20th Century-Fox, 1942
GIRL TROUBLE 20th Century-Fox, 1942
THE BLACK SWAN ★ 20th Century-Fox, 1942
LIFE BEGINS AT EIGHT-THIRTY 20th Century-Fox, 1942

THE MOON IS DOWN 20th Century-Fox, 1943
MY FRIEND FLICKA 20th Century-Fox, 1943
HEAVEN CAN WAIT 20th Century-Fox, 1943
CLAUDIA 20th Century-Fox, 1943
THE SONG OF BERNADETTE ★★ 20th Century-Fox, 1943
THE PURPLE HEART 20th Century-Fox, 1944
WILSON ★ 20th Century-Fox, 1944
SUNDAY DINNER FOR A SOLDIER 20th Century-Fox, 1944
THE KEYS OF THE KINGDOM ★ 20th Century-Fox, 1944
A TREE GROWS IN BROOKLYN 20th Century-Fox, 1945
STATE FAIR ★ adaptation, 20th Century-Fox, 1945
A ROYAL SCANDAL 20th Century-Fox, 1945
A BELL FOR ADANO 20th Century-Fox, 1945
LEAVE HER TO HEAVEN 20th Century-Fox, 1945
DRAGONWYCK 20th Century-Fox, 1946
CENTENNIAL SUMMER ★ 20th Century-Fox, 1946
MARGIE 20th Century-Fox, 1946
THE RAZOR'S EDGE 20th Century-Fox, 1946
GENTLEMAN'S AGREEMENT 20th Century-Fox, 1947
CAPTAIN FROM CASTILE ★ 20th Century-Fox, 1947
MOTHER WORE TIGHTS ★★ adaptation, 20th Century-Fox, 1947
CALL NORTHSIDE 777 20th Century-Fox, 1948
SITTING PRETTY 20th Century-Fox, 1948
THE WALLS OF JERICHO 20th Century-Fox, 1948
CRY OF THE CITY 20th Century-Fox, 1948
THE SNAKE PIT ★ 20th Century-Fox, 1948
YELLOW SKY 20th Century-Fox, 1948
WHEN MY BABY SMILES AT ME ★ adaptation, 20th Century-Fox, 1948
CHICKEN EVERY SUNDAY 20th Century-Fox, 1948
A LETTER TO THREE WIVES 20th Century-Fox, 1949
DOWN TO THE SEA IN SHIPS 20th Century-Fox, 1949
MOTHER IS A FRESHMAN 20th Century-Fox, 1949
MR. BELVEDERE GOES TO COLLEGE 20th Century-Fox, 1949
YOU'RE IN EVERYTHING 20th Century-Fox, 1949
PINKY 20th Century-Fox, 1949
PRINCE OF FOXES 20th Century-Fox, 1949
TWELVE O'CLOCK HIGH 20th Century-Fox, 1949
WHEN WILLIE COMES MARCHING HOME 20th Century-Fox, 1950
THE BIG LIFT 20th Century-Fox, 1950
THE GUNFIGHTER 20th Century-Fox, 1950
PANIC IN THE STREETS 20th Century-Fox, 1950
NO WAY OUT 20th Century-Fox, 1950
ALL ABOUT EVE ★ 20th Century-Fox, 1950
FOR HEAVEN'S SAKE 20th Century-Fox, 1950
FOURTEEN HOURS 20th Century-Fox, 1951
TAKE CARE OF MY LITTLE GIRL 20th Century-Fox, 1951
DAVID AND BATHSHEBA ★ 20th Century-Fox, 1951
ON THE RIVIERA ★ 20th Century-Fox, 1951
WITH A SONG IN MY HEART ★★ 20th Century-Fox, 1952
WAIT 'TILL THE SUN SHINES, NELLIE 20th Century-Fox, 1952
WHAT PRICE GLORY? 20th Century-Fox, 1952
O. HENRY'S FULL HOUSE 20th Century-Fox, 1952
STARS AND STRIPES FOREVER 20th Century-Fox, 1952
TONIGHT WE SING 20th Century-Fox, 1953
CALL ME MADAM ★★ adaptation, 20th Century-Fox, 1953
THE PRESIDENT'S LADY 20th Century-Fox, 1953
THE ROBE 20th Century-Fox, 1953
HELL AND HIGH WATER 20th Century-Fox, 1954
THE EGYPTIAN co-composer with Bernard Herrmann, 20th Century-Fox, 1954
THERE'S NO BUSINESS LIKE SHOW BUSINESS ★ 20th Century-Fox, 1954
A MAN CALLED PETER 20th Century-Fox, 1955
THE SEVEN YEAR ITCH 20th Century-Fox, 1955
LOVE IS A MANY SPLENDORED THING ★★ 20th Century-Fox, 1955
ANASTASIA ★ 20th Century-Fox, 1956
A CERTAIN SMILE 20th Century-Fox, 1958
THE DIARY OF ANNE FRANK ★ 20th Century-Fox, 1959
THE BEST OF EVERYTHING 20th Century-Fox, 1959
THE PLEASURE OF HIS COMPANY Paramount, 1961
THE COUNTERFEIT TRAITOR Paramount, 1962
HOW THE WEST WAS WON ★ MGM, 1962
THE GREATEST STORY EVER TOLD ★ United Artists, 1965
NEVADA SMITH Paramount, 1966
FIRECREEK Warner Bros., 1968
AIRPORT ★ Universal, 1970

EMIL NEWMAN

d. August 30, 1984 - Woodland Hills, California

REUNION MGM, 1936
RISE AND SHINE 20th Century-Fox, 1941
TALL, DARK AND HANDSOME 20th Century-Fox, 1941
BERLIN CORRESPONDENT 20th Century-Fox, 1941
SUN VALLEY SERENADE ★ adaptation, 20th Century-Fox, 1941
THE LOVES OF EDGAR ALLAN POE 20th Century-Fox, 1942
THE MAGNIFICENT DOPE co-composer, 20th Century-Fox, 1942
THE MAN WHO WOULDN'T DIE 20th Century-Fox, 1942
TIME TO KILL 20th Century-Fox, 1942
DIXIE DUGAN 20th Century-Fox, 1943
TONIGHT WE RAID CALAIS 20th Century-Fox, 1943
PIN-UP GIRL 20th Century-Fox, 1944
BEDSIDE MANNER 20th Century-Fox, 1945
NOB HILL 20th Century-Fox, 1945
BEHIND GREEN LIGHTS 20th Century-Fox, 1946
RENDEZVOUS 24 20th Century-Fox, 1946
TEXAS, BROOKLYN AND HEAVEN United Artists, 1948
GUILTY OF TREASON Eagle Lion, 1949
CRY DANGER co-composer with Paul Dunlap, RKO Radio, 1951
THE LADY SAYS NO United Artists, 1951
BIG JIM McLAIN Warner Bros., 1952
THE CAPTIVE CITY United Artists, 1952
JAPANESE WAR BRIDE 20th Century-Fox, 1952
JUST FOR YOU Paramount, 1952
THE SAN FRANCISCO STORY Warner Bros., 1952
RANCHO NOTORIOUS RKO Radio, 1952
ISLAND IN THE SKY Warner Bros., 1953
THE STEEL LADY United Artists, 1953
WAR PAINT United Artists, 1953
99 RIVER STREET United Artists, 1953
BEACHHEAD co-composer with Arthur Lange, United Artists, 1954
THE MAD MAGICIAN co-composer with Arthur Lange, Columbia, 1954
RING OF FEAR co-composer with Arthur Lange, Warner Bros., 1954
SOUTHWEST PASSAGE co-composer with Arthur Lange, United Artists, 1954
THE NAKED STREET United Artists, 1955
CHICAGO CONFIDENTIAL United Artists, 1957
THE IRON SHERIFF United Artists, 1957

DEATH IN SMALL DOSES Allied Artists, 1957
UNWED MOTHER Allied Artists, 1958
RIOT IN JUVENILE PRISON United Artists, 1959
THE GREAT SIOUX MASSACRE Columbia, 1965

LIONEL NEWMAN

b. January 4, 1916
d. February 3, 1989 - Los Angeles, California

THE STREET WITH NO NAME 20th Century-Fox, 1948
I'LL GET BY ★ adaptation, 20th Century-Fox, 1950
CHEAPER BY THE DOZEN 20th Century-Fox, 1950
THE JACKPOT 20th Century-Fox, 1950
MISTER 880 20th Century-Fox, 1950
MOTHER DIDN'T TELL ME 20th Century-Fox, 1950
WHERE THE SIDEWALK ENDS 20th Century-Fox, 1950
THE FROGMEN 20th Century-Fox, 1951
DEADLINE - U.S.A. MGM, 1952
DIPLOMATIC COURIER 20th Century-Fox, 1952
DON'T BOTHER TO KNOCK 20th Century-Fox, 1952
LYDIA BAILEY 20th Century-Fox, 1952
MONKEY BUSINESS 20th Century-Fox, 1952
THE OUTCASTS OF POKER FLAT 20th Century-Fox, 1952
RED SKIES OF MONTANA 20th Century-Fox, 1952
RETURN OF THE TEXAN 20th Century-Fox, 1952
WE'RE NOT MARRIED 20th Century-Fox, 1952
DANGEROUS CROSSING 20th Century-Fox, 1953
THE FARMER TAKES A WIFE 20th Century-Fox, 1953
THE KID FROM LEFT FIELD 20th Century-Fox, 1953
GORILLA AT LARGE 20th Century-Fox, 1954
THE ROCKET MAN 20th Century-Fox, 1954
THERE'S NO BUSINESS LIKE SHOW BUSINESS ★ 20th Century-Fox, 1954
HOUSE OF BAMBOO 20th Century-Fox, 1955
HOW TO BE VERY, VERY POPULAR 20th\ Century-Fox, 1955
VIOLENT SATURDAY 20th Century-Fox, 1955
THE KILLER IS LOOSE United Artists, 1956
THE BEST THINGS IN LIFE ARE FREE ★ adaptation, 20th Century-Fox, 1956
THE LAST WAGON 20th Century-Fox, 1956
LOVE ME TENDER 20th Century-Fox, 1956
THE PROUD ONES 20th Century-Fox, 1956
BERNADINE 20th Century-Fox, 1957
KISS THEM FOR ME 20th Century-Fox, 1957
MARDI GRAS 20th Century-Fox, 1958
THE BRAVADOS 20th Century-Fox, 1958
COMPULSION 20th Century-Fox, 1959
SAY ONE FOR ME ★ 20th Century-Fox, 1959
LET'S MAKE LOVE ★ 20th Century-Fox, 1960
NORTH TO ALASKA 20th Century-Fox, 1960
MOVE OVER, DARLING 20th Century-Fox, 1963
THE PLEASURE SEEKERS ★ 20th Century-Fox, 1964
HELLO, DOLLY! ★★ adaptation, 20th Century-Fox, 1969
THE GREAT WHITE HOPE 20th Century-Fox, 1970
FIREBALL FORWARD (TF) 20th Century-Fox, 1972
WHEN MICHAEL CALLS (TF) Palomar Productions/20th Century-Fox TV, 1972
THE SALZBURG CONNECTION 20th Century-Fox, 1972

P

LOTHAR PERL

b. Germany
d. April 28, 1975 - New York

THIS LAND IS MINE RKO Radio, 1943

EDWARD PLUMB

b. 1907 - Streator, Illinois
d. April, 1958

BAMBI (AF) ★ co-composer with Frank Churchill, RKO Radio, 1942
SALUDOS AMIGOS ★ co-composer with Paul J. Smith, RKO Radio, 1943
VICTORY THROUGH AIR POWER co-composer with Paul J. Smith and Oliver Wallace, United Artists, 1943
THE THREE CABALLEROS (AF) ★ co-composer, RKO Radio, 1944
THE PHANTOM SPEAKS Republic, 1945
THE WOMAN WHO CAME BACK Republic, 1945
QUEBEC co-composer with Van Cleave, Paramount, 1951

CHARLES PREVIN

b. 1888 - Brooklyn, New York
d. September 22, 1973 - Hollywood, California

THE MAGNIFICENT BRUTE Universal, 1936
TWO IN A CROWD Universal, 1936
THREE SMART GIRLS Universal, 1937
WHEN LOVE IS YOUNG Universal, 1937
WINGS OVER HONOLULU Universal, 1937
MAD ABOUT MUSIC ★ co-composer with Frank Skinner, Universal, 1938
MIDNIGHT INTRUDER Universal, 1938
RIO Universal, 1939
TOWER OF LONDON Universal, 1939
THE BANK DICK Universal, 1940
IT'S A DATE Universal, 1940
SEVEN SINNERS Universal, 1940
THE INVISIBLE WOMAN Universal, 1940
BLACK FRIDAY co-composer, Universal, 1940
MODEL WIFE Universal, 1941
THE WOLF MAN co-composer, Universal, 1941
HORROR ISLAND co-composer, Universal, 1941
NICE GIRL? Universal, 1941
THE BLACK CAT co-composer, Universal, 1941
HOLD THAT GHOST co-composer, Universal, 1941
DRUMS OF THE CONGO co-composer, Universal, 1941
BUCK PRIVATES ★ adaptation, Universal, 1941
MAN-MADE MONSTER co-composer, Universal, 1941
INVISIBLE AGENT co-composer, Universal, 1942
THE MUMMY'S TOMB co-composer, Universal, 1942
FRANKENSTEIN MEETS THE WOLF MAN co-composer, Universal, 1943
SON OF DRACULA co-composer, Universal, 1943
THE MAD GHOUL co-composer, Universal, 1943
HOUSE OF FRANKENSTEIN co-composer, Universal, 1944
JUNGLE CAPTIVE co-composer, Universal, 1944
THE MUMMY'S GHOST co-composer, Universal, 1944
SONG OF THE OPEN ROAD ★ Universal, 1944
HOUSE OF DRACULA co-composer, Universal, 1945

SERGEI PROKOFIEV
b. April 23, 1891 - Sontsovka, Russia
d. March 5, 1953 - Moscow, U.S.S.R.

LIEUTENANT KIJE 1934, Soviet
ALEXANDER NEVSKY Amkino, 1938, Soviet
KOTOVSKY 1943, Soviet
LERMONTOV 1944, Soviet
IVAN THE TERRIBLE, PART I Artkino, 1945, Soviet
IVAN THE TERRIBLE, PART II Artkino, 1946, Soviet

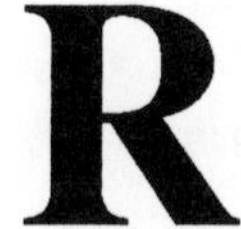

JOE RAPOSO
b. February 8, 1937 - Far River, Massachusetts
d. February 4, 1989 - Bronxville, New York

THE POSSESSION OF JOEL DELANEY Paramount, 1972
SAVAGES Angelika, 1972
RAGGEDY ANN AND ANDY (AF) 20th Century-Fox, 1977
THE GREAT MUPPET CAPER Universal/AFD, 1981, British

KAROL RATHAUS
b. 1895 - Tarnopol, Poland
d. 1954 - New York

THE BROTHERS KARAMAZOV 1931, German
THE DICTATOR *THE LOVE AFFAIR OF A DICTATOR/ LOVES OF A DICTATOR* 1935, British
LET US LIVE Columbia, 1939
JAGUAS (D) Viking Fund, 1942
HISTADRUTH (D) Palestine Labor Union, 1945

ALAN RAWSTHORNE
b. 1905 - Haslingden, England
d. 1971 - Cambridge, England

BURMA VICTORY (FD) Army Film Init, 1945, British
THE CAPTIVE HEART Universal, 1946, British
SARABAND *SARABAND FOR DEAD LOVERS* Eagle Lion, 1948, British
THE DANCING FLEECE 1950, British
WATERS OF TIME 1951, British
PANDORA AND THE FLYING DUTCHMAN MGM, 1951, British
IVORY HUNTER *WHERE NO VULTURES FLY* 1951, British
THE CRUEL SEA 1953, British
WEST OF ZANZIBAR 1954, British
THE DRAWINGS OF LEONARDO DA VINCI 1954, British
LEASE OF LIFE 1954, British
THE MAN WHO NEVER WAS 20th Century-Fox, 1956, British
FLOODS OF FEAR Universal, 1958, British

FRANZ REIZENSTEIN
b. 1911 - Nuremberg, Germany
d. 1968 - London, England

THE MUMMY Universal, 1959, British
CIRCUS OF HORRORS American International, 1960, British

NELSON RIDDLE
b. 1921 - Hackensack, New Jersey
d. 1985

JOHNNY CONCHO United Artists, 1956
LISBON Republic, 1956
A HOLE IN THE HEAD United Artists, 1959
LI'L ABNER ★ adaptation, Paramount, 1959
CAN-CAN ★ adaptation, 20th Century-Fox, 1960
LOLITA co-composer with Bob Harris, MGM, 1962, British
COME BLOW YOUR HORN Paramount, 1963
FOUR FOR TEXAS Warner Bros., 1963
PARIS WHEN IT SIZZLES Paramount, 1964
ROBIN AND THE SEVEN HOODS ★ Warner Bros., 1964
WHAT A WAY TO GO! 20th Century-Fox, 1964
HARLOW co-composer with Al Ham, Magna, 1965
MARRIAGE ON THE ROCKS Warner Bros., 1965
A RAGE TO LIVE United Artists, 1965
RED LINE 7000 Paramount, 1965
BATMAN 20th Century-Fox, 1966
ONE SPY TOO MANY MGM, 1966
EL DORADO Paramount, 1967
HOW TO SUCCEED IN BUSINESS WITHOUT REALLY TRYING adaptation, United Artists, 1967
PAINT YOUR WAGON ★ adaptation, Paramount, 1969
THE GREAT BANK ROBBERY Warner Bros., 1969
THE MALTESE BIPPY MGM, 1969
HELL'S BLOODY DEVILS *THE FAKERS/SMASHING THE CRIME SYNDICATE* Independent-International, 1970
EMERGENCY! (TF) Mark VII Ltd./Universal TV, 1972
THE BLUE KNIGHT (TF) Lorimar Productions, 1973
THE GREAT GATSBY ★★ Paramount, 1974
THE RUNAWAY BARGE (TF) Lorimar Productions, 1975
PROMISE HIM ANYTHING... (TF) ABC Circle Films, 1975
MOBILE TWO (TF) Mark VII Ltd./Universal TV, 1975
AMERICA AT THE MOVIES (FD) American Film Institute, 1976
THAT'S ENTERTAINMENT, PART 2 MGM/United Artists, 1976
HOW TO BREAK UP A HAPPY DIVORCE (TF) Charles Fries Productions, 1976
SEVENTH AVENUE (MS) Universal TV, 1977
A CIRCLE OF CHILDREN (TF) Edgar J. Scherick Associates/20th Century-Fox TV, 1977
HARPER VALLEY PTA April Fools, 1978
GOIN' COCOANUTS Osmond Distribution, 1978
GUYANA, CULT OF THE DAMNED co-composer with Robert Summers and George S. Price, Universal, 1980
ROUGH CUT adaptation, Paramount, 1980
MICKEY SPILLANE'S MARGIN FOR MURDER (TF) Hamner Productions, 1981
HELP WANTED: MALE (TF) Brademan-Self Productions/ QM Productions, 1982

RICHARD RODGERS
b. June 28, 1902 - New York, New York
d. December 30, 1979 - New York

LOVE ME TONIGHT Paramount, 1932

MILAN RODER

b. 1878
d. 1956

SILVER DOLLAR Warner Bros., 1932
SUPERNATURAL co-composer with Karl Hajos and Howard Jackson, Paramount, 1933
DEATH TAKES A HOLIDAY co-composer with John Leipold and Bernhard Kaun, Paramount, 1934
THE LAST OF THE PAGANS MGM, 1935
THE LIVES OF A BENGAL LANCER Paramount, 1935
ALL THE KING'S HORSES Paramount, 1935
THE LAST OUTPOST Paramount, 1935
TOO MANY PARENTS Paramount, 1936
EASY LIVING Paramount, 1937
EXCLUSIVE Paramount, 1937
SOULS AT SEA ★ co-composer with W. Franke Harling, Paramount, 1937
BULLDOG DRUMMOND IN AFRICA Paramount, 1938
NEVER SAY DIE Paramount, 1939

HEINZ ROEMHELD

b. 1901 - Milwaukee
d. February 11, 1985

THE HUNCHBACK OF NOTRE DAME co-composer of score for 1931 reissue with Sam Perry, Universal, 1923
GOLDEN HARVEST Paramount, 1933
THE INVISIBLE MAN Universal, 1933
THE BLACK CAT Universal, 1934
IMITATION OF LIFE Universal, 1934
THE MAN WHO RECLAIMED HIS HEAD Universal, 1934
KLIOU *THE TIGER* RKO Radio, 1935
MARY BURNS, FUGITIVE Paramount, 1935
DRACULA'S DAUGHTER Universal, 1936
THREE SMART GIRLS Universal, 1936
STAND-IN United Artists, 1937
I MET MY LOVE AGAIN United Artists, 1938
FOUR'S A CROWD Warner Bros., 1938
COMET OVER BROADWAY Warner Bros., 1938
NANCY DREW, REPORTER Warner Bros., 1939
YOU CAN'T GET AWAY WITH MURDER Warner Bros., 1939
INVISIBLE STRIPES Warner Bros., 1939
A CHILD IS BORN Warner Bros., 1940
BROTHER RAT AND BABY Warner Bros., 1940
BRITISH INTELLIGENCE Warner Bros., 1940
BROTHER ORCHID Warner Bros., 1940
THE MAN WHO TALKED TOO MUCH Warner Bros., 1940
MY LOVE CAME BACK Warner Bros., 1940
NO TIME FOR COMEDY Warner Bros., 1940
LADY WITH RED HAIR Warner Bros., 1940
FOUR MOTHERS Warner Bros., 1941
HONEYMOON FOR THREE Warner Bros., 1941
FLIGHT FROM DESTINY Warner Bros., 1941
THE STRAWBERRY BLONDE ★ Warner Bros., 1941
THE WAGONS ROLL AT NIGHT Warner Bros., 1941
AFFECTIONATELY YOURS Warner Bros., 1941
BLUES IN THE NIGHT Warner Bros., 1941
ALWAYS IN MY HEART Warner Bros., 1942
THE MALE ANIMAL Warner Bros., 1942
GENTLEMAN JIM Warner Bros., 1942
YANKEE DOODLE DANDY ★★ adaptation, Warner Bros., 1942
THE MUMMY'S TOMB co-composer, Universal, 1942
THE HARD WAY Warner Bros., 1943
THE DESERT SONG adaptation, Warner Bros., 1944
SHINE ON, HARVEST MOON Warner Bros., 1944
MAKE YOUR OWN BED Warner Bros., 1944
JANIE Warner Bros., 1944
TOO YOUNG TO KNOW Warner Bros., 1945
O.S.S. co-composer with Daniele Amfitheatrof, Paramount, 1946
MR. ACE United Artists, 1947
CURLEY United Artists, 1947
THE FABULOUS JOE United Artists, 1947
HEAVEN ONLY KNOWS United Artists, 1947
DOWN TO EARTH co-composer with George Duning, Columbia, 1947
CHRISTMAS EVE United Artists, 1947
THE FLAME Republic, 1947
IT HAD TO BE YOU co-composer with Arthur Morton, Columbia, 1947
HERE COMES TROUBLE United Artists, 1948
WHO KILLED DOC ROBBIN? United Artists, 1948
THE LADY FROM SHANGHAI Columbia, 1948
I, JANE DOE Republic, 1948
ON OUR MERRY WAY United Artists, 1948
THE FULLER BRUSH MAN Columbia, 1948
THE GIRL FROM MANHATTAN United Artists, 1948
STATION WEST RKO Radio, 1948
MY DEAR SECRETARY United Artists, 1948
THE LUCKY STIFF United Artists, 1949
MR. SOFT TOUCH Columbia, 1949
MISS GRANT TAKES RICHMOND Columbia, 1949
KILL THE UMPIRE Columbia, 1950
THE GOOD HUMOR MAN Columbia, 1950
ROGUES OF SHERWOOD FOREST Columbia, 1950
THE FULLER BRUSH GIRL Columbia, 1950
VALENTINO Columbia, 1951
CHICAGO CALLING United Artists, 1952
THE BIG TREES Warner Bros., 1952
JACK AND THE BEANSTALK Warner Bros., 1952
THREE FOR BEDROOM C Warner Bros., 1952
RUBY GENTRY 20th Century-Fox, 1953
THE 5,000 FINGERS OF DR. T co-composer with Hans Salter and Frederick Hollander, Columbia, 1953
THE MOONLIGHTER Warner Bros., 1953
HELL'S HORIZON Columbia, 1955
THE SQUARE JUNGLE Universal, 1956
THERE'S ALWAYS TOMORROW Universal, 1956
THE CREATURE WALKS AMONG US co-composer, Universal, 1956
THE MOLE PEOPLE co-composer with Hans Salter and Herman Stein, Universal, 1956
THE LAND UNKNOWN co-composer, Universal, 1957
THE MONSTER THAT CHALLENGED THE WORLD United Artists, 1957
THE TALL T Columbia, 1957
DECISION AT SUNDOWN Columbia, 1958
RIDE LONESOME Columbia, 1959
LAD: A DOG Warner Bros., 1961

ERIC ROGERS

b. England
d. April 8, 1981 - Buckinghamshire, England

THE SWINGIN' MAIDEN *THE IRON MAIDEN* Columbia, 1962, British
CARRY ON SPYING Governor, 1964, British
CARRY ON CLEO Governor, 1964, British
CARRY ON COWBOY Anglo-Amalgamated/Warner-Pathe, 1966, British
CARRY ON SCREAMING Anglo-Amalgamated/Warner-Pathe, 1966, British
DON'T LOSE YOUR HEAD 1967, British
FOLLOW THAT CAMEL Schoenfeld Film Distributing, 1967, British
CARRY ON DOCTOR Rank, 1968, British

CARRY ON...UP THE KHYBER Rank, 1969, British
CARRY ON CAMPING Rank, 1969, British
CARRY ON UP THE JUNGLE Rank, 1970, British
CARRY ON AGAIN, DOCTOR Rank, 1970, British
DOCTOR IN TROUBLE Rank, 1970, British
IN THE DEVIL'S GARDEN *ASSAULT* Hemisphere, 1971, British
QUEST FOR LOVE Rank, 1971, British
CARRY ON DICK Rank, 1974, British
CARRY ON EMMANUELLE Rank, 1978, British

SIGMUND ROMBERG

b. 1887 - Szeged, Hungary
d. 1951 - New York

FOOLISH WIVES Universal, 1922

DAVID ROSE

b. June 24, 1910 - London, England
d. August 23, 1990 - Los Angeles, California

THE PRINCESS AND THE PIRATE ★ RKO Radio, 1944
WINGED VICTORY 20th Century-Fox, 1944
THE WHIPPED United Artists, 1950
THE UNDERWORLD STORY United Artists, 1950
RICH, YOUNG AND PRETTY MGM, 1951
TEXAS CARNIVAL MGM, 1951
JUST THIS ONCE MGM, 1952
YOUNG MAN WITH IDEAS MGM, 1952
EVERYTHING I HAVE IS YOURS MGM, 1952
THE CLOWN MGM, 1953
CONFIDENTIALLY YOURS MGM, 1953
BRIGHT ROAD MGM, 1953
JUPITER'S DARLING MGM, 1955
PUBLIC PIGEON NO. ONE Universal, 1957
OPERATION PETTICOAT Universal, 1959
PLEASE DON'T EAT THE DAISIES MGM, 1960
THIS REBEL BREED Warner Bros., 1960
QUICK, BEFORE IT MELTS MGM, 1965
NEVER TOO LATE Warner Bros., 1965
HOMBRE 20th Century-Fox, 1967
ALONG CAME A SPIDER (TF) 20th Century-Fox TV, 1970
THE DEVIL AND MISS SARAH (TF) Universal TV, 1971
THE BIRDMEN (TF) Universal TV, 1971
A DREAM FOR CHRISTMAS (TF) Lorimar Productions, 1973
LITTLE HOUSE ON THE PRAIRIE (TF) NBC Entertainment, 1974
THE LONELIEST RUNNER (TF) NBC TV, 1976
RANSOM FOR ALICE! (TF) Universal TV, 1977
KILLING STONE (TF) Universal TV, 1978
SUDDENLY, LOVE (TF) Ross Hunter Productions, 1978
LITTLE HOUSE: LOOK BACK TO YESTERDAY (TF) NBC Productions/Ed Friendly Productions, 1983
SAM'S ROSE Invictus Entertainment, 1984
LITTLE HOUSE: THE LAST FAREWELL (TF) Ed Friendly Productions/NBC Entertainment, 1984
LITTLE HOUSE: BLESS ALL THE DEAR CHILDREN (TF) NBC Productions/Ed Friendly Productions, 1984

NINO ROTA

b. December 31, 1911 - Milan, Italy
d. April 10, 1979 - Rome, Italy

TRENO POPOLARE 1933, Italian
GIORNO DI NOZZE 1942, Italian
IL BIRICHINO DI PAPA 1942, Italian
ZAZA 1943, Italian
THE ARROW *LA FRECCIA NEL FIANCO* 1943, Italian
LA DONNA DELLA MONTAGNA 1943, Italian
HIS YOUNG WIFE *LE MISERIE DEL SIGNOR TRAVET* 1945, Italian
SOTTO IL SOLE DI ROMA 1946, Italian
ROMA, CITTA LIBERA 1946, Italian
ALBERGO LUNA, CAMERA 34 1946, Italian
MIO FIGLIO PROFESSORE 1946, Italian
UN AMERICANO IN VAZANZA co-composer with Giovanni d'Anzi, 1946, Italian
VIVERE IN PACE 1947, Italian
AMANTI SENZA AMORE 1947, Italian
DANIELE CORTIS 1947, Italian
FLESH WILL SURRENDER *IL DELITTO DI GIOVANNI EPISCOPO* 1947, Italian
SPRINGTIME IN ITALY *E PRIMAVERA* 1947, Italian
COME PERSI LA GUERRA 1947, Italian
ARRIVEDERCI PAPA 1948, Italian
SENZA PIETA 1948, Italian
FUGA IN FRANCIA 1948, Italian
CAMPANE A MARTELLO 1948, Italian
SOTTO IL SOLE DI ROMA 1948, Italian
L'EROE DELLA STRADA 1948, Italian
PROIBITO RUBARE Lux Film, 1948, Italian
THE PIRATES OF CAPRI *CAPTAIN SIROCCO* Film Classics, 1949, Italian
THE GLASS MOUNTAIN 1949, British
THE HIDDEN ROOM *OBSESSION* British Lion, 1949, British
COME SCOPERSI L'AMERICA 1949, Italian
DUE MOGLI SONO TROPPE 1950, Italian
NAPOLI MILIONARIA 1950, Italian
A DOG'S LIFE *VITA DA CANI* ATA, 1950, Italian
E PIU FACILE CHE UN CAMELLO... 1950, Italian
VALLEY OF THE EAGLES 1951
FILUMENA MARTURANO 1951, Italian
ANNA Italian Films Export, 1951, Italian
DONNE E BRIGANTI 1951, Italian
ERA LUI...SI! SI! 1951, Italian
PEPPINO E VIOLETTA 1951, Italian
TOTO E IL RE DI ROMA 1951, Italian
IL MONELLO DELLA STRADA *STREET URCHIN* 1951, Italian
THE WHITE SHIEK Pathe Contemporary, 1952, Italian
SOMETHING MONEY CAN'T BUY 1952, Italian
JOLANDA, LA FIGLIA DEL CORSARO NERO 1952, Italian
LA REGINA DI SABA 1952, Italian
DUE SOLDI DI SPERANZA 1952, Italian
LA MANO DEL STRANIERO 1952, Italian
MARITO E MOGLIE 1952, Italian
LE MERAVIGLIOSE AVVENTURE DI GUERRIN MESCHINO 1952, Italian
HELL RAIDERS OF THE DEEP 1952, Italian
THE ASSASSIN *VENETIAN BIRD* 1952, Italian
SCAMPOLO 53' 1953, Italian
I VITELLONI API Productions, 1953, Italian
ANNI DIFICILI 1953, Italian
RISCATTO 1953, Italian
NOI DUE SOLI 1953, Italian
LUXURY GIRLS *FANCIULLE DI LUSSO* 1953, Italian
STAR OF INDIA 1953
MUSODURO 1954, Italian
MAMBO co-composer with Francesco Lavagnino, Paramount, 1954, U.S.-Italian
LA STRADA Trans-Lux, 1954, Italian
LA VERGINE MODERNA 1954, Italian
LE DUE ORFANELLE 1954, Italian
PROIBITO Documento Film/UGC/Cormoran Film, 1954, Italian

ENNEMI PUBLIC #1 co-composer with Raymond Legrand, 1954, Italian
CENTO ANNI D'AMORE co-composer, 1954, Italian
LOVES OF THREE QUEENS *HELEN OF TROY—THE FACE THAT LAUNCHED A THOUSAND SHIPS* 1954, Italian
LA DOMENICA DELLA BUONA GENTE 1954, Italian
LA GRANDE SPERANZA 1954, Italian
VIA PADOVA, 46 1954, Italian
FRIENDS FOR LIFE *AMICI PER LA PELLE* 1955, Italian
THE SWINDLE *IL BIDONE* Astor, 1955, Italian
LA BELLA DI ROMA Lux Film, 1955, Italian
UN EROE DEI BOSTRI TEMPI 1955, Italian
THE MOST WONDERFUL MOMENT 1956, Italian
CITTA DI NOTTE 1956, Italian
WAR AND PEACE Paramount, 1956, Italian
NIGHTS OF CABIRIA Lopert, 1957, Italian
THE HOUSE OF INTRIGUE 1957, Italian
ITALIA PICCOLA 1957, Italian
WHITE NIGHTS *LE NOTTI BIANCHE* United Motion Picture Organization, 1957, Italian-French
IL MEDICO E LO STREGONE 1957, Italian
FORTUNELLA 1957, Italian
THIS ANGRY AGE Columbia, 1958, Italian-French
GLI ITALIANI SONO MATTI 1958, Italian
THE LAW IS THE LAW *LA LOI C'EST LA LOI* 1958, French
THE GREAT WAR United Artists, 1959, Italian
UN ETTARO DI CIELO 1959, Italian
LA DOLCE VITA Astor, 1960, Italian
UNDER TEN FLAGS *SOTTO DIECI BANDIERE* 1960, U.S.-Italian
PURPLE NOON Times, 1960, French-Italian
PHANTOM LOVERS *FANTASMI A ROMA* 1960, Italian
ROCCO AND HIS BROTHERS Astor, 1960, Italian-French
ITALIAN BRIGANDS *IL BRIGANTE* 1961, Italian
THE RELUCTANT SAINT Davis-Royal, 1962, Italian-U.S.
THE BEST OF ENEMIES *IL DUE NEMICI* Columbia, 1962, Italian-British
MAFIOSO 1962, Italian
BOCCACCIO '70 composer of Fellini and Visconti segments, Embassy, 1962, Italian
ARTURO'S ISLAND MGM, 1962, Italian
8-1/2 Embassy, 1963, Italian
THE LEOPARD 20th Century-Fox, 1963, Italian-French
IL MAESTRO DI VIGEVANO 1963, Italian
JULIET OF THE SPIRITS Rizzoli, 1965, Italian-French-West German
SHOOT LOUD...LOUDER, I DON'T UNDERSTAND 1966, Italian
THE TAMING OF THE SHREW Columbia, 1967, Italian-British
KISS THE OTHER SHEIK *OGGI, DOMANI E DOPODAMANI* 1968, Italian-French
ROMEO AND JULIET Paramount, 1968, Italian-British
SPIRITS OF THE DEAD *HISTOIRES EXTRAORDINAIRES* composer of "Toby Dammit" segment, American International, 1969, French-Italian
FELLINI SATYRICON United Artists, 1970, Italian-French
THE CLOWNS Levitt-Pickman, 1971, Italian-French-West German, originally made for television
WATERLOO Paramount, 1971, Italian-Soviet
FELLINI'S ROMA United Artists, 1972, Italian-French
THE GODFATHER Paramount, 1972
LOVE AND ANARCHY *FILM D'AMORE E D'ANARCHIA* co-composer with Carlo Savina, Peppercorn-Wormser, 1973, Italian
SUNSET, SUNRISE 1973, Italian
AMARCORD New World, 1974, Italian
THE ABDICATION Warner Bros., 1974, British
THE GODFATHER, PART II ★★ co-composer with Carmine Coppola, Paramount, 1974
BOY FROM THE SUBURBS *RAGAZZO DI BORGATA* co-composer with Carlo Savina, Italneggio, 1976, Italian
CARO MICHELE Cineriz, 1976, Italian
CASANOVA *IL CASANOVA DI FEDERICO FELLINI* Universal, 1976, Italian
DEATH ON THE NILE Paramount, 1978, British
HURRICANE Paramount, 1979
ORCHESTRA REHEARSAL New Yorker, 1979, Italian-West German, originally made for television

CAMILLE SAINT-SAENS

b. 1835 - Paris, France
d. 1921 - Algiers

THE ASSASSINATION OF THE DUC DE GUISE Le Film d'Art, 1908, French

PHILIP SAINTON

b. England
d. 1967

MOBY DICK United Artists, 1956, British

CONRAD SALINGER

d. June 18, 1962 - Hollywood, California

THE UNKNOWN MAN MGM, 1951
CARBINE WILLIAMS MGM, 1952
WASHINGTON STORY MGM, 1952
THE PRISONER OF ZENDA adaptation of 1937 score by Alfred Newman, MGM, 1952
DREAM WIFE MGM, 1953
THE LAST TIME I SAW PARIS MGM, 1954
TENNESSEE CHAMP MGM, 1954
THE SCARLET COAT MGM, 1955
GABY MGM, 1956
LONELYHEARTS United Artists, 1958

PAUL SAWTELL

b. 1906 - Poland
d. 1970

(The following is an incomplete list of Mr. Sawtell's credits.)

LEGION OF THE LAWLESS RKO Radio, 1940
MEXICAN SPITFIRE RKO Radio, 1940
NO HANDS ON THE CLOCK Paramount, 1941
RED RIVER RIDING HOOD RKO Radio, 1942
THE GREAT GILDERSLEEVE RKO Radio, 1943
CALLING DR. DEATH RKO Radio, 1943
THE SCARLET CLAW Universal, 1944

GILDERSLEEVE'S GHOST RKO Radio, 1944
MR. WINKLE GOES TO WAR co-composer with Carmen Dragon, Columbia, 1944
THE PEARL OF DEATH co-composer with Hans J. Salter, Universal, 1944
DEAD MAN'S EYES Universal, 1944
JUNGLE CAPTIVE co-composer, Universal, 1944
JUNGLE WOMAN co-composer with Hans J. Salter, Universal, 1944
THE MUMMY'S CURSE co-composer, Universal, 1945
THE HOUSE OF FEAR Universal, 1945
THE POWER OF THE WHISTLER Columbia, 1945
CRIME DOCTOR'S WARNING Columbia, 1945
GENIUS AT WORK co-composer with Roy Webb, RKO Radio, 1946
TARZAN AND THE LEOPARD WOMAN RKO Radio, 1946
THE CAT CREEPS Universal, 1946
DICK TRACY MEETS GRUESOME RKO Radio, 1947
THE BLACK ARROW Columbia, 1948
THE DOOLINS OF OKLAHOMA co-composer with George Duning, Columbia, 1949
DAVY CROCKETT, INDIAN SCOUT United Artists, 1950
THE WHIP HAND RKO, 1951
THE SON OF DR. JEKYLL Columbia, 1951
TARZAN'S SAVAGE FURY RKO Radio, 1952
TARZAN AND THE SHE-DEVIL RKO Radio, 1953
ABBOTT & COSTELLO MEET DR. JEKYLL AND MR. HYDE co-composer, Universal, 1953
CAPTAIN KIDD AND THE SLAVE GIRL United Artists, 1954
RETURN TO TREASURE ISLAND United Artists, 1954
THE LIVING SWAMP 20th Century-Fox, 1955
SCANDAL, INC. co-composer with Bert A. Shefter, Republic, 1956
THE DEERSLAYER co-composer with Bert A. Shefter, 20th Century-Fox, 1957
THE BLACK SCORPION co-composer with Bert A. Shefter and Jack Cookerly, Warner Bros., 1957
SHE DEVIL co-composer with Bert A. Shefter, 20th Century-Fox, 1957
KRONOS co-composer with Bert A. Shefter, 20th Century-Fox, 1957
THE FLY co-composer with Bert A. Shefter, 20th Century-Fox, 1958
IT! THE TERROR FROM BEYOND SPACE co-composer with Bert A. Shefter, United Artists, 1958
THE COSMIC MAN co-composer with Bert A. Shefter, Allied Artists, 1959
RETURN OF THE FLY co-composer with Bert A. Shefter, 20th Century-Fox, 1959
A DOG OF FLANDERS co-composer with Bert A. Shefter, 20th Century-Fox, 1959
GIGANTIS THE FIRE MONSTER co-composer of U.S. version only, 1959, Japanese
THE BIG CIRCUS co-composer with Bert A. Shefter, Allied Artists, 1959
THE LOST WORLD co-composer, 20th Century-Fox, 1960
VOYAGE TO THE BOTTOM OF THE SEA co-composer with Bert A. Shefter, 20th Century-Fox, 1961
MISTY 20th Century-Fox, 1961
JACK THE GIANT KILLER co-composer with Bert A. Shefter, United Artists, 1962
FIVE WEEKS IN A BALLOON 20th Century-Fox, 1962
THUNDER ISLAND co-composer with Bert A. Shefter, 20th Century-Fox, 1963
ISLAND OF THE BLUE DOLPHINS Universal, 1964
THE LAST MAN ON EARTH co-composer with Bert A. Shefter, 1964, U.S.-Italian
MOTOR PSYCHO co-composer with Bert A. Shefter, Eve, 1965
FASTER, PUSSYCAT, KILL! KILL! Eve, 1965
THE BUBBLE *FANTASTIC INVASION OF THE PLANET EARTH* co-composer with Bert A. Shefter, Oboler Films, 1967
THE CHRISTINE JORGENSEN STORY co-composer with Bert A. Shefter, United Artists, 1970

VICTOR SCHERTZINGER

b. April 8, 1880 - Mahanoy City, Pennsylvania
d. 1941

BETWEEN MEN co-composer, Triangle, 1915
D'ARTAGNAN co-composer, Triangle, 1915
THE GOLDEN CLAW co-composer, Triangle, 1915
THE WINGED IDOL co-composer, Triangle, 1915
THE EDGE OF THE ABYSS Triangle, 1916
THE BECKONING FLAME Triangle, 1916
THE CONQUEROR Triangle, 1916
PEGGY Triangle, 1916
CIVILIZATION Ince, 1916
THE PRINCESS OF THE DARK Ince, 1917
ROBIN HOOD United Artists, 1922
BELOVED co-composer with Howard Jackson, Universal, 1934
ONE NIGHT OF LOVE ★ co-composer with Gus Kahn, Columbia, 1937
SOMETHING TO SING ABOUT ★ Grand National, 1937

WALTER SCHUMANN

d. August 21, 1958 - Minneapolis

THE NIGHT OF THE HUNTER United Artists, 1955

HUMPHREY SEARLE

b. 1915 - Oxford, England
d. May 12, 1982 - London, England

BEYOND MOMBASA Columbia, 1956, British-U.S.
THE ABOMINABLE SNOWMAN OF THE HIMALAYAS *ABOMINABLE SNOWMAN* uncredited, 20th Century-Fox, 1957, British
ACTION OF THE TIGER MGM, 1957, British
LAW AND DISORDER Continental, 1958, British
LEFT, RIGHT AND CENTER 1961, British
THE HAUNTING MGM, 1963, British-U.S.

ANDREA SETARO

b. November 11, 1886 - Philadelphia, Pennsylvania

BOLERO co-composer, Paramount, 1934
THE OLD-FASHIONED WAY co-composer, Paramount, 1934
BELLE OF THE NINETIES co-composer, Paramount, 1934
GOIN' TO TOWN co-composer, Paramount, 1935
COLLEGE SCANDAL co-composer, Paramount, 1935

NATHANIEL SHILKRET

b. 1895

BATTLE OF THE SEXES United Artists, 1928
LILAC TIME First National, 1928
THE BIG GAME RKO Radio, 1936
MARY OF SCOTLAND RKO Radio, 1936
THE SMARTEST GIRL IN TOWN RKO Radio, 1936
THE LAST OF THE MOHICANS United Artists, 1936
THAT GIRL FROM PARIS RKO Radio, 1936

WALKING ON AIR RKO Radio, 1936
WINTERSET ★ RKO Radio, 1936
THE SOLDIER AND THE LADY RKO Radio, 1937
BORDER CAFE RKO Radio, 1937
THE TOAST OF NEW YORK RKO Radio, 1937
...ONE THIRD OF A NATION... Paramount, 1939
FRANK BUCK'S JUNGLE CAVALCADE RKO Radio, 1941
STOLEN PARADISE RKO Radio, 1941
A STRANGER IN TOWN co-composer with Daniele Amfitheatrof, MGM, 1943
AIR RAD WARDENS MGM, 1943
BLONDE FEVER MGM, 1944
NOTHING BUT TROUBLE MGM, 1944
THREE MEN IN WHITE MGM, 1944
SHE WENT TO THE RACES MGM, 1945
THIS MAN'S NAVY MGM, 1945
BOY'S RANCH MGM, 1946
FAITHFUL IN MY FASHION MGM, 1946
THE HOODLUM SAINT MGM, 1946

DMITRI SHOSTAKOVITCH

b. September 25, 1906 - St. Petersburg, Russia
d. 1975 - U.S.S.R.

THE NEW BABYLON 1929, Soviet
ALONE 1930, Soviet
GOLDEN MOUNTAINS 1931, Soviet
HAMLET 1931, Soviet
COUNTERPLAN 1932, Soviet
THE YOUTH OF MAXIM 1934, Soviet
GIRL FRIENDS 1936, Soviet
THE RETURN OF MAXIM GORKY 1936, Soviet
A GREAT CITIZEN 1938, Soviet
THE MAN WITH A GUN 1938, Soviet
VOLOCHAYEVSK DAYS 1938, Soviet
THE VYBORG SIDE 1939, Soviet
THE BATTLE FOR SIBERIA 1940, Soviet
ZOYA 1944, Soviet
THE FALL OF BERLIN 1945, Soviet
PLAIN PEOPLE 1945, Soviet
MICHURIN 1947, Soviet
PIROGOV 1947, Soviet
YOUNG GUARD 1947, Soviet
MEETING ON THE ELBA 1949, Soviet
THE UNFORGETTABLE YEAR—1919 1952, Soviet
THE GADFLY 1955, Soviet
THE FIRST ECHELON 1956, Soviet
FIVE DAYS AND FIVE NIGHTS 1960, Soviet
KHOVANSHCHINA H Artkino, 1961, Soviet
THE CONDEMNED OF ALTONA 1963, Soviet
HAMLET United Artists, 1964, Soviet
KING LEAR Artkino, 1971, Soviet

LEO SHUKEN

b. December 8, 1906 - Los Angeles, California
d. July 24, 1976 - Santa Monica, California

WAIKIKI WEDDING Paramount, 1937
EVERY DAY'S A HOLIDAY Paramount, 1938
ARTISTS AND MODELS ABROAD Paramount, 1938
PARIS HONEYMOON Paramount, 1939
CAFE SOCIETY Paramount, 1939
STAGECOACH ★★ co-composer, United Artists, 1939
THE LADY FROM KENTUCKY United Artists, 1939
THE FLYING DEUCES co-composer, RKO Radio, 1939
ADVENTURE IN DIAMONDS Paramount, 1940
THE LADY EVE Paramount, 1941
WEST POINT WIDOW Paramount, 1941
OUR WIFE Columbia, 1941
NEW YORK TOWN Paramount, 1941
SULLIVAN'S TRAVELS co-composer with Charles Bradshaw, Paramount, 1941
THE LADY HAS PLANS co-composer with Leigh Harline, Paramount, 1942
MEET THE STEWARTS Columbia, 1942
HENRY ALDRICH, EDITOR Paramount, 1942
THE GOOD FELLOWS Paramount, 1943
THE MIRACLE OF MORGAN'S CREEK co-composer with Charles Bradshaw, Paramount, 1944
THE FABULOUS DORSEYS United Artists, 1947
THOSE REDHEADS FROM SEATTLE Paramount, 1953

LOUIS SILVERS

d. March 26, 1954 - Hollywood, California

WAY DOWN EAST United Artists, 1920
DREAM STREET Griffith, 1921
ISN'T LIFE WONDERFUL? co-composer, United Artists, 1924
THE JAZZ SINGER Warner Bros., 1927
NOAH'S ARK Warner Bros., 1929
DANCING LADY MGM, 1933
ONE NIGHT OF LOVE Columbia, 1934
LOVE ME FOREVER Columbia, 1935
CAPTAIN JANUARY 20th Century-Fox, 1936
DIMPLES 20th Century-Fox, 1936
LADIES IN LOVE 20th Century-Fox, 1936
A MESSAGE TO GARCIA 20th Century-Fox, 1936
POOR LITTLE RICH GIRL 20th Century-Fox, 1936
PRIVATE NUMBER 20th Century-Fox, 1936
PROFESSIONAL SOLDIER 20th Century-Fox, 1936
ROAD TO GLORY 20th Century-Fox, 1936
TO MARY, WITH LOVE 20th Century-Fox, 1936
UNDER TWO FLAGS 20th Century-Fox, 1936
CAFE METROPOLE 20th Century-Fox, 1937
LLOYDS OF LONDON 20th Century-Fox, 1937
SEVENTH HEAVEN 20th Century-Fox, 1937
STOWAWAY 20th Century-Fox, 1937
FOUR MEN AND A PRAYER 20th Century-Fox, 1937
IN OLD CHICAGO ★ 20th Century-Fox, 1938
KENTUCKY 20th Century-Fox, 1938
KENTUCKY MOONSHINE 20th Century-Fox, 1938
SUEZ ★ 20th Century-Fox, 1938
HOLLYWOOD CAVALCADE co-composer, 20th Century-Fox, 1939
SECOND FIDDLE 20th Century-Fox, 1939
SUSANNAH OF THE MOUNTIES 20th Century-Fox, 1939
SWANEE RIVER ★ adaptation, 20th Century-Fox, 1939

FRANK SKINNER

b. 1897 - Meredosia, Illinois
d. 1968 - Los Angeles, California

MAD ABOUT MUSIC ★ co-composer with Charles Previn, Universal, 1938
SON OF FRANKENSTEIN co-composer with Hans J. Salter and Charles Previn, Universal, 1939
THE SUN NEVER SETS Universal, 1939
CHARLIE McCARTHY, DETECTIVE Universal, 1939
DESTRY RIDES AGAIN Universal, 1939
TOWER OF LONDON Universal, 1939
THE INVISIBLE MAN RETURNS co-composer with Hans J. Salter, Universal, 1940
MY LITTLE CHICKADEE Universal, 1940
THE HOUSE OF THE SEVEN GABLES ★ Universal, 1940
HIRED WIFE Universal, 1940
WHEN THE DALTONS RODE Universal, 1940
BLACK FRIDAY co-composer, Universal, 1940

THE MUMMY'S HAND co-composer with Hans J. Salter, Universal, 1940
BACK STREET ★ Universal, 1941
THE LADY FROM CHEYENNE Universal, 1941
THE FLAME OF NEW ORLEANS Universal, 1941
NEVER GIVE A SUCKER AN EVEN BREAK Universal, 1941
APPOINTMENT FOR LOVE Universal, 1941
KEEP 'EM FLYING Universal, 1941
HELZAPOPPIN Universal, 1941
THE WOLF MAN co-composer with Hans J. Salter, Universal, 1941
HORROR ISLAND co-composer, Universal, 1941
THE BLACK CAT co-composer, Universal, 1941
HOLD THAT GHOST co-composer, Universal, 1941
MAN-MADE MONSTER co-composer with Hans J. Salter and Charles Henderson, Universal, 1941
JAIL HOUSE BLUES Universal, 1942
RIDE 'EM COWBOY Universal, 1942
SABOTEUR Universal, 1942
BROADWAY Universal, 1942
LADY IN A JAM Universal, 1942
EAGLE SQUADRON Universal, 1942
SHERLOCK HOLMES AND THE VOICE OF TERROR Universal, 1942
WHO DONE IT? Universal, 1942
PITTSBURGH co-composer with Hans J. Salter, Universal, 1942
ARABIAN NIGHTS ★ Universal, 1942
SHERLOCK HOLMES AND THE SECRET WEAPON Universal, 1943
THE AMAZING MRS. HOLLIDAY H co-composer with Hans J. Salter, Universal, 1943
WHITE SAVAGE Universal, 1943
SHERLOCK HOLMES IN WASHINGTON Universal, 1943
TWO TICKETS IN LONDON Universal, 1943
HERS TO HOLD Universal, 1943
WE'VE NEVER BEEN LICKED Universal, 1943
FIRED WIFE Universal, 1943
GUNG HO! Universal, 1943
FRANKENSTEIN MEETS THE WOLF MAN co-composer with Hans J. Salter and Charles Previn, Universal, 1943
SON OF DRACULA co-composer with Hans J. Salter and Charles Previn, Universal, 1943
THE MAD GHOUL co-composer, Universal, 1943
CALLING DR. DEATH co-composer with Hans J. Salter and Paul Sawtell, Universal, 1943
HI, BEAUTIFUL Universal, 1944
HOUSE OF FRANKENSTEIN co-composer, Universal, 1944
DESTINY co-composer with Alexander Tansman, Universal, 1944
THE MUMMY'S GHOST co-composer with Hans J. Salter and Charles Previn, Universal, 1944
THE SUSPECT Universal, 1945
UNDER WESTERN SKIES co-composer, Universal, 1945
BLONDE RANSOM co-composer, Universal, 1945
STRANGE CONFESSION co-composer, Universal, 1945
THE DALTONS RIDE AGAIN co-composer, Universal, 1945
PILLOW OF DEATH co-composer, Universal, 1945
FRONTIER GAL Universal, 1945
IDEA GIRL co-composer, Universal, 1946
NIGHT IN PARADISE Universal, 1946
THE RUNAROUND Universal, 1946
WHITE SAVAGE co-composer, Universal, 1946
CANYON PASSAGE Universal, 1946
BLACK ANGEL Universal, 1946
SWELL GUY Universal, 1947
I'LL BE YOURS Universal, 1947
THE EGG AND I Universal, 1947
RIDE THE PINK HORSE Universal, 1947
THE EXILE Universal, 1947
THE NAKED CITY co-composer with Miklos Rozsa, Universal, 1948
HAZARD Universal, 1948
ABBOTT AND COSTELLO MEET FRANKENSTEIN Universal, 1948
TAP ROOTS Universal, 1948
FOR THE LOVE OF MARY Universal, 1948
THE FIGHTING O'FLYNN Universal, 1949
FAMILY HONEYMOON Universal, 1949
THE LIFE OF RILEY Universal, 1949
TULSA Eagle Lion, Universal, 1949
THE LADY GAMBLES Universal, 1949
THE GAL WHO TOOK THE WEST Universal, 1949
SWORD IN THE DESERT Universal, 1949
FREE FOR ALL Universal, 1949
WOMAN IN HIDING Universal, 1950
FRANCIS Universal, 1950
ONE-WAY STREET Universal, 1950
COMANCHE TERRITORY Universal, 1950
THE DESERT HAWK Universal, 1950
LOUISA Universal, 1950
THE SLEEPING CITY Universal, 1950
HARVEY Universal, 1950
BEDTIME FOR BONZO Universal, 1951
DOUBLE CROSSBONES Universal, 1951
KATIE DID IT Universal, 1951
FRANCIS GOES TO THE RACES Universal, 1951
MARK OF THE RENEGADE Universal, 1951
BRIGHT VICTORY Universal, 1951
THE LADY PAYS OFF Universal, 1951
THE RAGING TIDE Universal, 1951
WEEKEND WITH FATHER Universal, 1951
NO ROOM FOR THE GROOM Universal, 1952
SALLY AND SAINT ANNE Universal, 1952
THE WORLD IN HIS ARMS Universal, 1952
BONZO GOES TO COLLEGE Universal, 1952
BECAUSE OF YOU Universal, 1952
IT GROWS ON TREES Universal, 1952
MISSISSIPPI GAMBLER Universal, 1953
THE MAN FROM THE ALAMO Universal, 1953
THUNDER BAY Universal, 1953
WINGS OF THE HAWK Universal, 1953
TAZA, SON OF COCHISE Universal, 1954
MAGNIFICENT OBSESSION Universal, 1954
SIGN OF THE PAGAN Universal, 1954
CHIEF CRAZY HORSE Universal, 1955
FOXFIRE Universal, 1955
ALL THAT HEAVEN ALLOWS Universal, 1956
FRANCIS IN THE HAUNTED HOUSE Universal, 1956
AWAY ALL BOATS Universal, 1956
NEVER SAY GOODBYE Universal, 1956
THE RAWHIDE YEARS Universal, 1956
STAR IN THE DUST Universal, 1956
WRITTEN ON THE WIND Universal, 1957
BATTLE HYMN Universal, 1957
INTERLUDE Universal, 1957
MAN OF A THOUSAND FACES Universal, 1957
MY MAN GODFREY Universal, 1957
THE TARNISHED ANGELS Universal, 1958
THIS HAPPY FEELING Universal, 1958
THE SNOW QUEEN (AF) composer of U.S. version only, Universal, 1959
THE PERFECT FURLOUGH Universal, 1959
IMITATION OF LIFE Universal, 1959

PAUL J. SMITH

b. October 30, 1906 - Calumet, Michigan
d. January 25, 1985

SNOW WHITE AND THE SEVEN DWARFS (AF) ★ co-composer with Frank Churchill and Leigh Harline, RKO Radio, 1938
PINOCCHIO (AF) ★★ co-composer with Leigh Harline, RKO Radio, 1940
SALUDOS AMIGOS ★ co-composer with Edward Plumb, RKO Radio, 1943
VICTORY THROUGH AIR POWER ★ co-composer with Edward Plumb and Oliver Wallace, United Artists, 1943
THE THREE CABALLEROS (AF) ★ co-composer, RKO Radio, 1944
SONG OF THE SOUTH ★ co-composer with Daniele Amfitheatrof, RKO Radio, 1946
FUN AND FANCY FREE co-composer with Eliot Daniel and Oliver Wallace, RKO Radio, 1947
THE STRANGE MRS. CRANE Eagle Lion, 1948
SO DEAR TO MY HEART RKO Radio, 1948
CINDERELLA (AF) ★ co-composer with Oliver Wallace, RKO Radio, 1950
BEAVER VALLEY RKO Radio, 1950
NATURE'S HALF ACRE RKO Radio, 1951
THE OLYMPIC ELK RKO Radio, 1952
WATER BIRDS RKO Radio, 1952
20,000 LEAGUES UNDER THE SEA Buena Vista, 1954
PERRI ★ Buena Vista, 1957
THE SHAGGY DOG Buena Vista, 1959
MOON PILOT Buena Vista, 1962
THE THREE LIVES OF THOMASINA Buena Vista, 1963

MISCHA SPOLIANSKY

d. June 29, 1985

THE GHOST GOES WEST 1936, British
THE MAN WHO COULD WORK MIRACLES 1937, British

RONALD STEIN

b. April 12, 1930 - St. Louis, Missouri
d. August 15, 1988

THE APACHE WOMAN American International, 1955
THE DAY THE WORLD ENDED American International, 1956
THE PHANTOM FROM 10,000 LEAGUES 1956
THE OKLAHOMA WOMAN American International, 1956
THE GUNSLINGER ARC, 1956
GIRLS IN PRISON American International, 1956
IT CONQUERED THE WORLD American International, 1956
THE SHE CREATURE American International, 1956
FLESH AND THE SPUR American International, 1957
SHE GODS OF SHARK REEF American International, 1957
NOT OF THIS EARTH Allied Artists, 1957
THE UNDEAD American International, 1957
THUNDER OVER HAWAII *NAKED PARADISE* American International, 1957
RUNAWAY DAUGHTERS American International, 1957
ATTACK OF THE CRAB MONSTERS Allied Artists, 1957
DRAGSTRIP GIRL American International, 1957
INVASION OF THE SAUCER-MEN American International, 1957
REFORM SCHOOL GIRL American International, 1957
ROCK ALL NIGHT American International, 1957
SORORITY GIRL American International, 1957
JET ATTACK American International, 1958
SUICIDE BATTALION American International, 1958
THE ATTACK OF THE 50 FOOT WOMAN American International, 1958
THE BONNIE PARKER STORY American International, 1958
HOT ROD GANG American International, 1958
HIGH SCHOOL HELLCATS American International, 1958
THE LITTLEST HOBO Allied Artists, 1958
THE DEVIL'S PARTNER Filmgroup, 1959
PARATROOP COMMAND American International, 1959
TANK COMMANDOS American International, 1959
THE VIOLENT EVIL 1959
THE DEVIL'S PARTNER Filmgroup, 1959
DIAL 111 - JUVENILE SQUAD 1959
THE LEGEND OF TOM DOOLEY Columbia, 1959
DIARY OF A HIGH SCHOOL BRIDE American International, 1959
GHOST OF DRAGSTRIP HOLLOW American International, 1959
TOO SOON TO LOVE Universal, 1960
RAYMIE Allied Artists, 1960
THE THREAT Warner Bros., 1960
THE LAST WOMAN ON EARTH Filmgroup, 1960
DINOSAURUS! Universal, 1960
STAKEOUT 1960
ATLAS Filmgroup, 1961
JUST BETWEEN US 1961
THE PREMATURE BURIAL American International, 1962
THE BASHFUL ELEPHANT Allied Artists, 1962
THE UNDERWATER CITY Columbia, 1962
OF LOVE AND DESIRE 20th Century-Fox, 1963
DEMENTIA 13 American International, 1963
THE TERROR American International, 1963
DIME WITH A HALO MGM, 1963
THE HAUNTED PALACE American International, 1963
THE YOUNG AND THE BRAVE MGM, 1963
WAR HERO *WAR IS HELL* Allied Artists, 1963
THE BASHFUL BIKINI 1964
MY SOUL RUNS NAKED *RAT FINK/WILD AND WILLING* Genesis, 1964
SPIDER BABY *THE LIVER EATERS/CANNIBAL ORGY* 1965
THE BOUNTY KILLER Embassy, 1965
REQUIEM FOR A GUNFIGHTER Embassy, 1965
PORTRAIT IN TERROR American International, 1966
PSYCH-OUT American International, 1968
TARGETS co-composer, Paramount, 1968
THE RAIN PEOPLE Warner Bros., 1969
GETTING STRAIGHT Columbia, 1970
THE PRISONER 1973
FRANKENSTEIN'S GREAT AUNT TILLIE 1984
RASCAL DAZZLE 1985

MAX STEINER

b. May 10, 1888 - Vienna, Austria
d. 1971

RIO RITA RKO Radio, 1929
DIXIANA RKO Radio, 1930
HALF SHOT AT SUNRISE RKO Radio, 1930
CHECK AND DOUBLE CHECK RKO Radio, 1930
BEAU IDEAL RKO Radio, 1930
CIMARRON RKO Radio, 1931
KEPT HUSBANDS RKO Radio, 1931
CRACKED NUTS RKO Radio, 1931
YOUNG DONOVAN'S KID RKO Radio, 1931
TRANSGRESSION RKO Radio, 1931
THE PUBLIC DEFENDER RKO Radio, 1931

TRAVELING HUSBANDS RKO Radio, 1931
THE RUNAROUND RKO Radio, 1931
THE GAY DIPLOMAT RKO Radio, 1931
FANNY FOLEY HERSELF RKO Radio, 1931
CONSOLATION MARRIAGE RKO Radio, 1931
WAY BACK HOME RKO Radio, 1931
ARE THESE OUR CHILDREN? RKO Radio, 1931
SECRET SERVICE RKO Radio, 1931
MEN OF CHANCE RKO Radio, 1932
GIRL OF THE RIO RKO Radio, 1932
LADIES OF THE JURY RKO Radio, 1932
THE LOST SQUADRON RKO Radio, 1932
YOUNG BRIDE RKO Radio, 1932
SYMPHONY OF SIX MILLION RKO Radio, 1932
STATE'S ATTORNEY RKO Radio, 1932
WESTWARD PASSAGE RKO Radio, 1932
IS MY FACE RED? RKO Radio, 1932
WHAT PRICE HOLLYWOOD RKO Radio, 1932
ROAR OF THE DRAGON RKO Radio, 1932
BIRD OF PARADISE RKO Radio, 1932
THE MOST DANGEROUS GAME RKO Radio, 1932
A BILL OF DIVORCEMENT RKO Radio, 1932
THIRTEEN WOMEN RKO Radio, 1932
THE PHANTOM OF CRESTWOOD RKO Radio, 1932
LITTLE ORPHAN ANNIE RKO Radio, 1932
RENEGADES OF THE WEST RKO Radio, 1932
SECRETS OF THE FRENCH POLICE RKO Radio, 1932
THE CONQUERORS RKO Radio, 1932
THE SPORT PARADE RKO Radio, 1932
ROCKABYE RKO Radio, 1932
THE HALF NAKED TRUTH also cameo as conductor, RKO Radio, 1932
PENGUIN POOL MURDER RKO Radio, 1932
THE ANIMAL KINGDOM RKO Radio, 1932
THE MONKEY'S PAW RKO Radio, 1932
NO OTHER WOMAN RKO Radio, 1933
THE CHEYENNE KID RKO Radio, 1933
LUCKY DEVILS RKO Radio, 1933
THE GREAT JASPER RKO Radio, 1933
TOPAZE RKO Radio, 1933
OUR BETTERS RKO Radio, 1933
KING KONG RKO Radio, 1933
CHRISTOPHER STRONG RKO Radio, 1933
SWEEPINGS RKO Radio, 1933
DIPLOMANIACS RKO Radio, 1933
THE SILVER CORD RKO Radio, 1933
SON OF THE BORDER RKO Radio, 1933
EMERGENCY CALL RKO Radio, 1933
PROFESSIONAL SWEETHEART RKO Radio, 1933
FLYING DEVILS RKO Radio, 1933
MELODY CRUISE RKO Radio, 1933
BED OF ROSES RKO Radio, 1933
DOUBLE HARNESS RKO Radio, 1933
HEADLINE SHOOTER RKO Radio, 1933
BEFORE DAWN RKO Radio, 1933
NO MARRIAGE TIES RKO Radio, 1933
MORNING GLORY RKO Radio, 1933
BLIND ADVENTURE RKO Radio, 1933
ONE MAN'S JOURNEY RKO Radio, 1933
RAFTER ROMANCE RKO Radio, 1933
MIDSHIPMAN JACK RKO Radio, 1933
ANN VICKERS RKO Radio, 1933
ACE OF ACES RKO Radio, 1933
CHANCE AT HEAVEN RKO Radio, 1933
AFTER TONIGHT RKO Radio, 1933
LITTLE WOMEN RKO Radio, 1933
THE RIGHT TO ROMANCE RKO Radio, 1933
AGGIE APPLEBY RKO Radio, 1933
IF I WERE FREE RKO Radio, 1933
THE SON OF KONG RKO Radio, 1933
FLYING DOWN TO RIO RKO Radio, 1933
MAN OF TWO WORLDS RKO Radio, 1934
THE MEANEST GAL IN TOWN RKO Radio, 1934
LONG LOST FATHER RKO Radio, 1934
TWO ALONE RKO Radio, 1934
THE LOST PATROL ★ RKO Radio, 1934
KEEP 'EM ROLLING RKO Radio, 1934
SPITFIRE RKO Radio, 1934
SUCCESS AT ANY PRICE RKO Radio, 1934
THIS MAN IS MINE RKO Radio, 1934
SING AND LIKE IT RKO Radio, 1934
THE CRIME DOCTOR RKO Radio, 1934
FINISHING SCHOOL RKO Radio, 1934
STRICTLY DYNAMITE RKO Radio, 1934
WHERE SINNERS MEET RKO Radio, 1934
STINGAREE RKO Radio, 1934
MURDER ON THE BLACKBOARD RKO Radio, 1934
THE LIFE OF VERGIE MINTERS RKO Radio, 1934
LET'S TRY AGAIN RKO Radio, 1934
OF HUMAN BONDAGE RKO Radio, 1934
WE'RE RICH AGAIN RKO Radio, 1934
HIS GREATEST GAMBLE RKO Radio, 1934
HAT, COAT AND GLOVE RKO Radio, 1934
BACHELOR BAIT RKO Radio, 1934
THEIR BIG MOMENT RKO Radio, 1934
DOWN TO THEIR LAST YACHT RKO Radio, 1934
THE FOUNTAIN RKO Radio, 1934
THE AGE OF INNOCENCE RKO Radio, 1934
THE RICHEST GIRL IN THE WORLD RKO Radio, 1934
THE GAY DIVORCEE RKO Radio, 1934
DANGEROUS CORNER RKO Radio, 1934
GRIDIRON FLASH RKO Radio, 1934
WEDNESDAY'S CHILD RKO Radio, 1934
KENTUCKY KERNELS RKO Radio, 1934
BY YOUR LEAVE RKO Radio, 1934
ANNE OF GREEN GABLES RKO Radio, 1934
THE LITTLE MINISTER RKO Radio, 1934
ROMANCE IN MANHATTAN RKO Radio, 1935
ENCHANTED APRIL RKO Radio, 1935
ROBERTA RKO Radio, 1935
LADDIE RKO Radio, 1935
STAR OF MIDNIGHT RKO Radio, 1935
THE INFORMER ★★ RKO Radio, 1935
BREAK OF HEARTS RKO Radio, 1935
SHE RKO Radio, 1935
ALICE ADAMS RKO Radio, 1935
TOP HAT RKO Radio, 1935
THE THREE MUSKETEERS RKO Radio, 1935
I DREAM TOO MUCH RKO Radio, 1935
FOLLOW THE FLEET RKO Radio, 1936
TWO IN REVOLT RKO Radio, 1936
M'LISS RKO Radio, 1936
LITTLE LORD FAUNTLEROY United Artists, 1936
THE CHARGE OF THE LIGHT BRIGADE ★ Warner Bros., 1936
THE GARDEN OF ALLAH ★ United Artists, 1936
GOD'S COUNTRY AND THE WOMAN Warner Bros., 1936
GREEN LIGHT Warner Bros., 1937
SLIM Warner Bros., 1937
KID GALAHAD Warner Bros., 1937
A STAR IS BORN United Artists, 1937
THE LIFE OF EMILE ZOLA ★ Warner Bros., 1937
THAT CERTAIN WOMAN Warner Bros., 1937
FIRST LADY Warner Bros., 1937
SUBMARINE D-I Warner Bros., 1937
TOVARICH Warner Bros., 1937
GOLD IS WHERE YOU FIND IT Warner Bros., 1938
JEZEBEL ★ Warner Bros., 1938
THE ADVENTURES OF TOM SAWYER Warner Bros., 1938

CRIME SCHOOL Warner Bros., 1938
WHITE BANNERS Warner Bros., 1938
THE AMAZING DR. CLITTERHOUSE Warner Bros., 1938
FOUR DAUGHTERS Warner Bros., 1938
THE SISTERS Warner Bros., 1938
ANGELS WITH DIRTY FACES Warner Bros., 1938
THE DAWN PATROL Warner Bros., 1938
THEY MADE ME A CRIMINAL Warner Bros., 1939
THE OKLAHOMA KID Warner Bros., 1939
DODGE CITY Warner Bros., 1939
CONFESSIONS OF A NAZI SPY Warner Bros., 1939
DAUGHTERS COURAGEOUS Warner Bros., 1939
EACH DAWN I DIE Warner Bros., 1939
THE OLD MAID Warner Bros., 1939
DARK VICTORY ★ Warner Bros., 1939
DUST BE MY DESTINY Warner Bros., 1939
INTERMEZZO United Artists, 1939
WE ARE NOT ALONE Warner Bros., 1939
GONE WITH THE WIND ★ MGM, 1939
FOUR WIVES Warner Bros., 1940
DR. ERLICH'S MAGIC BULLET Warner Bros., 1940
VIRGINIA CITY Warner Bros., 1940
ALL THIS AND HEAVEN TOO Warner Bros., 1940
CITY FOR CONQUEST Warner Bros., 1940
A DISPATCH FROM REUTER'S Warner Bros., 1940
THE LETTER ★ Warner Bros., 1940
SANTA FE TRAIL Warner Bros., 1940
THE GREAT LIE Warner Bros., 1941
SHINING VICTORY Warner Bros., 1941
THE BRIDE CAME C.O.D. Warner Bros., 1941
DIVE BOMBER Warner Bros., 1941
SERGEANT YORK ★ Warner Bros., 1941
ONE FOOT IN HEAVEN Warner Bros., 1941
THEY DIED WITH THEIR BOOTS ON Warner Bros., 1942
CAPTAINS OF THE CLOUDS Warner Bros., 1942
IN THIS OUR LIFE Warner Bros., 1942
THE GAY SISTERS Warner Bros., 1942
DESPERATE JOURNEY Warner Bros., 1942
NOW, VOYAGER ★★ Warner Bros., 1942
CASABLANCA ★ Warner Bros., 1943
MISSION TO MOSCOW Warner Bros., 1943
WATCH ON THE RHINE Warner Bros., 1943
THIS IS THE ARMY Warner Bros., 1943
PASSAGE TO MARSEILLE Warner Bros., 1944
THE ADVENTURES OF MARK TWAIN ★ Warner Bros., 1944
SINCE YOU WENT AWAY ★★ United Artists, 1944
ARSENIC AND OLD LACE Warner Bros., 1944
THE CONSPIRATORS Warner Bros., 1944
ROUGHLY SPEAKING Warner Bros., 1945
THE CORN IS GREEN Warner Bros., 1945
RHAPSODY IN BLUE ★ adaptation, Warner Bros., 1945
MILDRED PIERCE Warner Bros., 1945
TOMORROW IS FOREVER RKO Radio, 1946
SAN ANTONIO Warner Bros., 1946
MY REPUTATION Warner Bros., 1946
SARATOGA TRUNK Warner Bros., 1946
ONE MORE TOMORROW Warner Bros., 1946
A STOLEN LIFE Warner Bros., 1946
THE BIG SLEEP Warner Bros., 1946
NIGHT AND DAY ★ adaptation, Warner Bros., 1946
CLOAK AND DAGGER Warner Bros., 1946
THE MAN I LOVE Warner Bros., 1947
THE BEAST WITH FIVE FINGERS Warner Bros., 1947
PURSUED Warner Bros., 1947
LOVE AND LEARN Warner Bros., 1947
MY WILD IRISH ROSE ★ adaptation, Warner Bros., 1947
CHEYENNE Warner Bros., 1947
THE UNFAITHFUL Warner Bros., 1947
DEEP VALLEY Warner Bros., 1947
LIFE WITH FATHER ★ Warner Bros., 1947
THE VOICE OF THE TURTLE Warner Bros., 1947
THE TREASURE OF THE SIERRA MADRE Warner Bros., 1948
MY GIRL TISA Warner Bros., 1948
WINTER MEETING Warner Bros., 1948
THE WOMAN IN WHITE Warner Bros., 1948
SILVER RIVER Warner Bros., 1948
KEY LARGO Warner Bros., 1948
JOHNNY BELINDA ★ Warner Bros., 1948
FIGHTER SQUADRON Warner Bros., 1948
THE DECISION OF CHRISTOPHER BLAKE Warner Bros., 1948
A KISS IN THE DARK Warner Bros., 1949
ADVENTURES OF DON JUAN Warner Bros., 1949
SOUTH OF ST. LOUIS Warner Bros., 1949
FLAMINGO ROAD Warner Bros., 1949
THE FOUNTAINHEAD Warner Bros., 1949
WITHOUT HONOR United Artists, 1949
BEYOND THE FOREST H Warner Bros., 1949
WHITE HEAT Warner Bros., 1949
MRS. MIKE United Artists, 1949
THE LADY TAKES A SAILOR Warner Bros., 1949
CAGED Warner Bros., 1950
THE FLAME AND THE ARROW ★ Warner Bros., 1950
THE GLASS MENAGERIE Warner Bros., 1950
ROCKY MOUNTAIN Warner Bros., 1950
SUGARFOOT Warner Bros., 1950
DALLAS Warner Bros., 1950
OPERATION PACIFIC Warner Bros., 1951
LIGHTNING STRIKES TWICE Warner Bros., 1951
RATON PASS Warner Bros., 1951
I WAS A COMMUNIST FOR THE F.B.I. Warner Bros., 1951
ON MOONLIGHT BAY Warner Bros., 1951
JIM THORPE—ALL AMERICAN Warner Bros., 1951
FORCE OF ARMS Warner Bros., 1951
CLOSE TO MY HEART Warner Bros., 1951
DISTANT DRUMS Warner Bros., 1951
ROOM FOR ONE MORE Warner Bros., 1952
THE LION AND THE HORSE Warner Bros., 1952
MARA MARU Warner Bros., 1952
THE MIRACLE OF OUR LADY OF FATIMA ★ Warner Bros., 1952
SPRINGFIELD RIFLE Warner Bros., 1952
THE IRON MISTRESS Warner Bros., 1952
THIS IS CINERAMA uncredited, Cinerama, 1952
THE JAZZ SINGER ★ Warner Bros., 1953
TROUBLE ALONG THE WAY Warner Bros., 1953
BY THE LIGHT OF THE SILVERY MOON Warner Bros., 1953
THE DESERT SONG Warner Bros., 1953
THE CHARGE AT FEATHER RIVER Warner Bros., 1953
SO THIS IS LOVE Warner Bros., 1953
SO BIG Warner Bros., 1953
THE BOY FROM OKLAHOMA Warner Bros., 1954
THE CAINE MUTINY ★ Columbia, 1954
KING RICHARD AND THE CRUSADERS Warner Bros., 1954
THE VIOLENT MEN Columbia, 1954
BATTLE CRY ★ Warner Bros., 1955
THE LAST COMMAND Republic, 1955
THE McCONNELL STORY Warner Bros., 1955
ILLEGAL Warner Bros., 1955
COME NEXT SPRING Republic, 1956
HELL ON FRISCO BAY Warner Bros., 1956
HELEN OF TROY Warner Bros., 1956
THE SEARCHERS Warner Bros., 1956

BANDIDO Warner Bros., 1956
DEATH OF A SCOUNDREL RKO Radio, 1956
CHINA GATE co-composer with Victor Young, 20th Century-Fox, 1957
BAND OF ANGELS Warner Bros., 1957
ESCAPADE IN JAPAN Universal, 1957
ALL MINE TO GIVE *THE DAY THEY GAVE BABIES AWAY* Universal, 1958
FORT DOBBS Warner Bros., 1958
DARBY'S RANGERS Warner Bros., 1958
MARJORIE MORNINGSTAR Warner Bros., 1958
THE HANGING TREE Warner Bros., 1959
JOHN PAUL JONES Warner Bros., 1959
THE FBI STORY Warner Bros., 1959
A SUMMER PLACE Warner Bros., 1959
CASH McCALL Warner Bros., 1960
ICE PALACE Warner Bros., 1960
THE DARK AT THE TOP OF THE STAIRS Warner Bros., 1960
THE SINS OF RACHEL CADE Warner Bros., 1961
PORTRAIT OF A MOBSTER Warner Bros., 1961
PARRISH Warner Bros., 1961
SUSAN SLADE Warner Bros., 1961
A MAJORITY OF ONE Warner Bros., 1961
ROME ADVENTURE Warner Bros., 1962
SPENCER'S MOUNTAIN Warner Bros., 1963
A DISTANT TRUMPET Warner Bros., 1964
FBI CODE 98 Warner Bros., 1964
YOUNGBLOOD HAWKE Warner Bros., 1964
THOSE CALLOWAYS Buena Vista, 1965
TWO ON A GUILLOTINE Warner Bros., 1965

LEITH STEVENS

b. 1909 - Mount Moriah, Missouri
d. 1970

SYNCOPATION RKO Radio, 1942
NIGHT SONG RKO Radio, 1947
BLACK BART Universal, 1948
ALL MY SONS Universal, 1948
FEUDIN', FUSSIN' AND A'FIGHTIN' Universal, 1948
LARCENY Universal, 1948
NOT WANTED Film Classics, 1949
NEVER FEAR Eagle Lion, 1950
THE GREAT RUPERT Eagle Lion, 1950
DESTINATION MOON Eagle Lion, 1950
THE SUN SETS AT DAWN Eagle Lion, 1951
NO QUESTIONS ASKED MGM, 1951
WHEN WORLDS COLLIDE Paramount, 1951
STORM OVER TIBET additional music, Columbia, 1951
NAVAJO (FD) Lippert, 1952
THE ATOMIC CITY Paramount, 1952
BEWARE, MY LOVELY RKO Radio, 1952
EIGHT IRON MEN Columbia, 1952
THE GLASS WALL Columbia, 1953
THE HITCHHIKER RKO Radio, 1953
SCARED STIFF Paramount, 1953
WAR OF THE WORLDS Paramount, 1953
THE BIGAMIST Filmmakers, 1953
THE BOB MATHIAS STORY Allied Artists, 1954
PRIVATE HELL 36 RKO Radio, 1954
THE WILD ONE Columbia, 1954
THE TREASURE OF PANCHO VILLA RKO Radio, 1955
CRASHOUT Filmakers, 1955
MAD AT THE WORLD Filmmakers, 1955
JULIE MGM, 1956
GREAT DAY IN THE MORNING RKO Radio, 1956
WORLD WITHOUT END Allied Artists, 1956
THE SCARLET HOUR Paramount, 1956
THE CARELESS YEARS United Artists, 1957
THE GARMENT JUNGLE Columbia, 1957
EIGHTEEN AND ANXIOUS Republic, 1957
THE GREEN-EYED BLONDE Warner Bros., 1957
LIZZIE MGM, 1957
RIDE OUT FOR REVENGE United Artists, 1957
THE JAMES DEAN STORY Warner Bros., 1957
BULLWHIP Allied Artists, 1958
THE GUN RUNNERS United Artists, 1958
COP HATER United Artists, 1958
SEVEN GUNS TO MESA Allied Artists, 1958
VIOLENT ROAD Warner Bros., 1958
THE GENE KRUPA STORY Columbia, 1959
BUT NOT FOR ME Paramount, 1959
THE FIVE PENNIES ★ Paramount, 1959
HELL TO ETERNITY Allied Artists, 1960
MAN TRAP Paramount, 1961
ON THE DOUBLE Paramount, 1961
THE INTERNS Columbia, 1962
IT HAPPENED AT THE WORLD'S FAIR MGM, 1963
A NEW KIND OF LOVE ★ Paramount, 1963
THE NIGHT OF THE GRIZZLY Paramount, 1966
SMOKY 20th Century-Fox, 1966
CHUKA Paramount, 1967
THE SILENT GUN (TF) Paramount Pictures TV, 1969
ASSAULT ON THE WAYNE (TF) Paramount Pictures TV, 1971

WILLIAM GRANT STILL

b. 1895 - Woodville, Miss.
d. December 3, 1978 - Los Angeles, California

LADY OF SECRETS Columbia, 1936
THEODORA GOES WILD Columbia, 1936
PENNIES FROM HEAVEN Columbia, 1936

HERBERT STOTHART

b. September 11, 1885 - Milwaukee, Wisconsin
d. February 1, 1949

DEVIL MAY CARE MGM, 1930
MONTANA MOON MGM, 1930
THE ROGUE SONG MGM, 1930
IN GAY MADRID MGM, 1930
THE FLORADORA GIRL MGM, 1930
CALL OF THE FLESH MGM, 1930
MADAM SATAN MGM, 1930
A LADY'S MORALS MGM, 1930
NEW MOON MGM, 1931
THE PRODIGAL MGM, 1931
THE SQUAW MAN MGM, 1931
THE CUBAN LOVE SONG MGM, 1931
THE SON-DAUGHTER MGM, 1932
RASPUTIN AND THE EMPRESS MGM, 1932
THE WHITE SISTER MGM, 1933
THE BARBARIAN MGM, 1933
PEG O' MY HEART MGM, 1933
TURN BACK THE CLOCK MGM, 1933
NIGHT FLIGHT MGM, 1933
GOING HOLLYWOOD MGM, 1933
QUEEN CHRISTINA MGM, 1934
THE CAT AND THE FIDDLE MGM, 1934
RIPTIDE MGM, 1934
LAUGHING BOY MGM, 1934
VIVA VILLA! MGM, 1934
TREASURE ISLAND MGM, 1934
CHAINED MGM, 1934
THE BARRETTS OF WIMPOLE STREET MGM, 1934
WHAT EVERY WOMAN KNOWS MGM, 1934
THE MERRY WIDOW adaptation, MGM, 1934
THE PAINTED VEIL MGM, 1934

BIOGRAPHY OF A BACHELOR GIRL MGM, 1935
THE NIGHT IS YOUNG MGM, 1935
DAVID COPPERFIELD MGM, 1935
SEQUOIA MGM, 1935
VANESSA, HER LOVE STORY MGM, 1935
NAUGHTY MARIETTA adaptation, MGM, 1935
CHINA SEAS MGM, 1935
ANNA KARENINA MGM, 1935
MUTINY ON THE BOUNTY ★ MGM, 1935
A NIGHT AT THE OPERA MGM, 1935
AH, WILDERNESS! MGM, 1935
A TALE OF TWO CITIES MGM, 1935
ROSE MARIE adaptation, MGM, 1936
WIFE VS. SECRETARY co-composer with Edward Ward, MGM, 1936
MOONLIGHT MURDER co-composer with Edward Ward, MGM, 1936
SMALL TOWN GIRL co-composer with Edward Ward, MGM, 1936
THE ROBIN HOOD OF EL DORADO MGM, 1936
SAN FRANCISCO MGM, 1936
THE GORGEOUS HUSSY MGM, 1936
THE DEVIL IS A SISSY MGM, 1936
AFTER THE THIN MAN co-composer with Edward Ward, MGM, 1936
ROMEO AND JULIET MGM, 1936
CAMILLE MGM, 1937
MAYTIME ★ adaptation, MGM, 1937
THE GOOD EARTH MGM, 1937
CONQUEST MGM, 1937
THE FIREFLY MGM, 1937
ROSALIE MGM, 1937
OF HUMAN HEARTS MGM, 1938
THE GIRL OF THE GOLDEN WEST MGM, 1938
MARIE ANTOINETTE ★ MGM, 1938
SWEETHEARTS ★ MGM, 1938
IDIOT'S DELIGHT MGM, 1939
BROADWAY SERENADE MGM, 1939
THE WIZARD OF OZ ★★ adaptation, MGM, 1939
BALALAIKA MGM, 1939
NORTHWEST PASSAGE MGM, 1940
EDISON, THE MAN MGM, 1940
WATERLOO BRIDGE ★ MGM, 1940
SUSAN AND GOD MGM, 1940
NEW MOON adaptation, MGM, 1940
PRIDE AND PREJUDICE MGM, 1940
BITTER SWEET adaptation, MGM, 1940
COME LIVE WITH ME MGM, 1941
ANDY HARDY'S PRIVATE SECRETARY MGM, 1941
MEN OF BOYS TOWN MGM, 1941
ZIEGFELD GIRL MGM, 1941
THEY MET IN BOMBAY MGM, 1941
BLOSSOMS IN THE DUST MGM, 1941
SMILIN' THROUGH MGM, 1941
THE CHOCOLATE SOLDIER ★ adaptation, MGM, 1941
RIO RITA adaptation, MGM, 1942
I MARRIED AN ANGEL MGM, 1942
MRS. MINIVER MGM, 1942
CAIRO MGM, 1942
RANDOM HARVEST ★ MGM, 1942
TENNESSEE JOHNSON MGM, 1943
THREE HEARTS FOR JULIA MGM, 1943
THE HUMAN COMEDY MGM, 1943
THOUSANDS CHEER ★ MGM, 1944
MADAME CURIE ★ MGM, 1944
SONG OF RUSSIA MGM, 1944
A GUY NAMED JOE MGM, 1944
THE WHITE CLIFFS OF DOVER MGM, 1944
DRAGON SEED MGM, 1944
KISMET ★ MGM, 1944
THIRTY SECONDS OVER TOKYO MGM, 1945
NATIONAL VELVET MGM, 1945
THE PICTURE OF DORIAN GRAY co-composer with Mario Castelnuovo-Tedesco, MGM, 1945
THE VALLEY OF DECISION ★ MGM, 1945
SON OF LASSIE MGM, 1945
THEY WERE EXPENDABLE MGM, 1945
ADVENTURE MGM, 1946
THE GREEN YEARS MGM, 1946
UNDERCURRENT MGM, 1946
THE SEA OF GRASS MGM, 1947
THE YEARLING based on music by Delius, MGM, 1947
HIGH BARBAREE MGM, 1947
THE UNFINISHED DANCE MGM, 1947
DESIRE ME MGM, 1947
IF WINTER COMES MGM, 1948
THREE DARING DAUGHTERS MGM, 1948
THE THREE MUSKETEERS based on music by Tchaikovsky, MGM, 1948
HILLS OF HOME MGM, 1948
BIG JACK MGM, 1949

HARRY SUKMAN

b. 1912
d. December 4, 1984 - Palm Springs, California

GOG United Artists, 1954
RIDERS TO THE STARS United Artists, 1954
BATTLE TAXI United Artists, 1955
A BULLET FOR JOEY United Artists, 1955
THE PHENIX CITY STORY Allied Artists, 1955
SCREAMING EAGLES Allied Artists, 1956
FORTY GUNS 20th Century-Fox, 1957
FURY AT SUNDOWN United Artists, 1957
SABU AND THE MAGIC RING Allied Artists, 1957
OUTCASTS OF THE CITY Republic, 1958
UNDERWATER WARRIOR MGM, 1958
VERBOTEN! Columbia, 1958
THE HANGMAN Paramount, 1959
THE CRIMSON KIMONO Columbia, 1959
SONG WITHOUT END adaptation, Columbia, 1960
UNDERWORLD, U.S.A. Columbia, 1961
A THUNDER OF DRUMS MGM, 1961
FANNY Warner Bros., 1961
BELLE SOMERS Columbia, 1962
MADISON AVENUE 20th Century-Fox, 1962
AROUND THE WORLD UNDER THE SEA MGM, 1966
THE SINGING NUN MGM, 1966
THE NAKED RUNNER Warner Bros., 1967
WELCOME TO HARD TIMES MGM, 1967
IF HE HOLLERS, LET HIM GO Cinerama Releasing Corporation, 1968
THE PRIVATE NAVY OF SGT. O'FARRELL United Artists, 1968
MISTER KINGSTREET'S WAR H.R.S. Films, 1971
GENESIS II (TF) Warner Bros. TV, 1973
THE FAMILY KOVAK (TF) Playboy Productions, 1974
PLANET EARTH (TF) Warner Bros. TV, 1974
BEYOND THE BERMUDA TRIANGLE (TF) Playboy Productions, 1975
SOMEONE IS WATCHING ME (TF) Warner Bros. TV, 1978
SALEM'S LOT (TF) ☆ Warner Bros. TV, 1979

T

ALEXANDRE TANSMAN

b. 1897 - Lodz, Poland
d. November 15, 1986

POIL DE CAROTTE 1932, French
FLESH AND FANTASY Universal, 1943
DESTINY co-composer with Frank Skinner, Universal, 1944
PARIS—UNDERGROUND ★ United Artists, 1945
SISTER KENNY RKO Radio, 1946

DEEMS TAYLOR

b. 1885 - New York
d. 1966 - New York

JANICE MEREDITH MGM, 1924

VIRGIL THOMSON

b. November 25, 1896 - Kansas City, Missouri
d. 1989

THE PLOW THAT BROKE THE PLAINS (D) U.S. Government, 1936
THE SPANISH EARTH (D) Contemporary Historians, 1937
THE RIVER (D) U.S. Government, 1937
TUESDAY IN NOVEMBER (D) U.S. Government, 1945
LOUISIANA STORY (D) Lopert, 1948
THE GODDESS Columbia, 1958
POWER AMONG MEN (D) United Nations, 1959
VOYAGE TO AMERICA (D) N.Y. World's Fair, 1964

DOUG TIMM

d. July 29, 1989

MISSION HILL Atlantic Releasing Corporation, 1983
TERROR IN THE AISLES additional music, Universal, 1984
STREETWALKIN' co-composer with Matthew Ender, Concorde, 1985
FORTUNE DANE (TF) Stormy Weathers Productions/ The Movie Company Enterprises/The Rosenzweig Company, 1986
U.S. MARSHALS: WACO & RHINEHART (TF) co-composer, Touchstone Films, 1987
WINNERS TAKE ALL Apollo Pictures, 1987
THE MAN WHO FELL TO EARTH (TF) David Gerber Productions/MGM TV, 1987
NIGHTFLYERS New Century/Vista, 1987
DIRTY DOZEN: DANKO'S DOZEN (TF) MGM-UA TV/ Jadran Films/TV Espanola, 1988, U.S.-Yugoslavian

DIMITRI TIOMKIN

b. May 10, 1894 - near St. Petersburg, Russia
d. November 11, 1979 - London, England

DEVIL MAY CARE ballet music only, MGM, 1930
LORD BYRON OF BROADWAY ballet music only, MGM, 1930
THE ROGUE SONG ballet music only, MGM, 1930
OUR BLUSHING BRIDES ballet music only, MGM, 1930
RESURRECTION Universal, 1931
BROADWAY TO HOLLYWOOD ballet only, Universal, 1933
ALICE IN WONDERLAND Paramount, 1933
NAUGHTY MARIETTA ballet only, MGM, 1935
CASINO MURDER CASE MGM, 1935
MAD LOVE MGM, 1935
I LIVE MY LIFE MGM, 1935
MR. DEEDS GOES TO TOWN Columbia, 1936
LOST HORIZON ★ Columbia, 1937
THE ROAD BACK Universal, 1937
SPAWN OF THE NORTH Paramount, 1938
YOU CAN'T TAKE IT WITH YOU Columbia, 1938
THE GREAT WALTZ MGM, 1938
ONLY ANGELS HAVE WINGS Columbia, 1939
MR. SMITH GOES TO WASHINGTON ★ Columbia, 1939
LUCKY PARTNERS RKO Radio, 1940
THE WESTERNER United Artists, 1940
MEET JOHN DOE Warner Bros., 1941
FORCED LANDING Paramount, 1941
SCATTERGOOD MEETS BROADWAY RKO Radio, 1941
FLYING BLIND Paramount, 1941
THE CORSICAN BROTHERS ★ United Artists, 1942
GENTLEMAN AFTER DARK United Artists, 1942
TWIN BEDS United Artists, 1942
THE MOON AND SIXPENCE ★ United Artists, 1942
SHADOW OF A DOUBT Universal, 1943
THE UNKNOWN GUEST Monogram, 1943
THE IMPOSTER Universal, 1944
THE BRIDGE OF SAN LUIS REY ★ United Artists, 1944
LADIES COURAGEOUS Universal, 1944
WHEN STRANGERS MARRY Monogram, 1944
FOREVER YOURS Monogram, 1944
DILLINGER Monogram, 1945
CHINA'S LITTLE DEVILS Monogram, 1945
PARDON MY PAST Columbia, 1945
WHISTLE STOP United Artists, 1946
BLACK BEAUTY 20th Century-Fox, 1946
ANGEL ON MY SHOULDER United Artists, 1946
THE DARK MIRROR Universal, 1946
DUEL IN THE SUN Selznick Releasing, 1946
IT'S A WONDERFUL LIFE RKO Radio, 1946
THE LONG NIGHT RKO Radio, 1947
TARZAN AND THE MERMAIDS RKO Radio, 1948
THE DUDE GOES WEST Allied Artists, 1948
SO THIS IS NEW YORK United Artists, 1948
RED RIVER United Artists, 1948
PORTRAIT OF JENNIE adaptation of Debussy, Selznick, 1948
CANADIAN PACIFIC 20th Century-Fox, 1949
CHAMPION ★ United Artists, 1949
HOME OF THE BRAVE United Artists, 1949
RED LIGHT United Artists, 1949
D.O.A. United Artists, 1949
DAKOTA LIL 20th Century-Fox, 1950
GUILTY BYSTANDER Film Classics, 1950
CHAMPAGNE FOR CAESAR United Artists, 1950
THE MEN United Artists, 1950
CYRANO DE BERGERAC United Artists, 1950
MR. UNIVERSE United Artists, 1951
THE THING RKO Radio, 1951
STRANGERS ON A TRAIN Warner Bros., 1951
PEKING EXPRESS Paramount, 1951
THE WELL United Artists, 1951
DRUMS IN THE DEEP SOUTH RKO Radio, 1951
BUGLES IN THE AFTERNOON Warner Bros., 1952
MUTINY United Artists, 1952
MY SIX CONVICTS Columbia, 1952
LADY IN THE IRON MASK 20th Century-Fox, 1952

THE HAPPY TIME Columbia, 1952
THE BIG SKY RKO Radio, 1952
HIGH NOON ★★ United Artists, 1952
THE FOUR POSTER Columbia, 1952
THE STEEL TRAP 20th Century-Fox, 1952
ANGEL FACE RKO Radio, 1953
JEOPARDY MGM, 1953
I CONFESS Warner Bros., 1953
RETURN TO PARADISE United Artists, 1953
BLOWING WILD Warner Bros., 1953
TAKE THE HIGH GROUND MGM, 1953
CEASE FIRE! Paramount, 1953
HIS MAJESTY O'KEEFE Warner Bros., 1953
THE COMMAND Warner Bros., 1954
DIAL M FOR MURDER Warner Bros., 1954
THE HIGH AND THE MIGHTY ★★ Warner Bros., 1954
A BULLET IS WAITING Columbia, 1954
THE ADVENTURES OF HAJJI BABA 20th Century-Fox, 1954
STRANGE LADY IN TOWN Warner Bros., 1955
LAND OF THE PHARAOHS Warner Bros., 1955
THE COURT-MARTIAL OF BILLY MITCHELL Warner Bros., 1955
FRIENDLY PERSUASION Allied Artists, 1956
TENSION AT TABLE ROCK RKO Radio, 1956
GIANT ★ Warner Bros., 1956
GUNFIGHT AT THE O.K. CORRAL Paramount, 1957
NIGHT PASSAGE Universal, 1957
SEARCH FOR PARADISE Cinerama Releasing Corporation, 1957
WILD IS THE WIND Paramount, 1957
THE OLD MAN AND THE SEA ★★ Warner Bros., 1958
THE YOUNG LAND Columbia, 1959
RIO BRAVO Warner Bros., 1959
LAST TRAIN FROM GUN HILL Paramount, 1959
THE UNFORGIVEN United Artists, 1960
THE ALAMO ★ United Artists, 1960
THE SUNDOWNERS Warner Bros., 1960
THE GUNS OF NAVARONE ★ Columbia, 1961
TOWN WITHOUT PITY United Artists, 1961
WITHOUT EACH OTHER Allen Klein, 1962
55 DAYS AT PEKING ★ Allied Artists, 1963
THE FALL OF THE ROMAN EMPIRE ★ Paramount, 1964
CIRCUS WORLD Paramount, 1964
36 HOURS MGM, 1964
THE WAR WAGON Universal, 1967
GREAT CATHERINE Warner Bros., 1968, British
TCHAIKOVSKY ★ adaptation, Mosfilm, 1971, Soviet

ERNST TOCH

b. 1887 - Vienna, Austria
d. 1964 - Santa Monica, California

CATHERINE THE GREAT United Artists, 1934
THE PRIVATE LIFE OF DON JUAN United Artists, 1934
LITTLE FRIEND Gaumont-British, 1934
PETER IBBETSON ★ Paramount, 1935
OUTCAST Paramount, 1937
ON SUCH A NIGHT Paramount, 1937
THE CAT AND THE CANARY Paramount, 1939
DR. CYCLOPS co-composer, Paramount, 1940
GHOST BREAKERS Paramount, 1940
LADIES IN RETIREMENT ★ Columbia, 1941
FIRST COMES COURAGE Columbia, 1943
NONE SHALL ESCAPE Columbia, 1944
ADDRESS UNKNOWN Columbia, 1944
THE UNSEEN Paramount, 1945

V

NATHAN VAN CLEAVE

b. 1910
d. July 2, 1970 - Hollywood, California

THE SAINTED SISTERS Paramount, 1948
DEAR WIFE co-composer, Paramount, 1949
FANCY PANTS Paramount, 1950
MOLLY Paramount, 1951
QUEBEC co-composer, Paramount, 1951
DEAR BRAT Paramount, 1951
RHUBARB Paramount, 1951
OFF LIMITS Paramount, 1953
CONQUEST OF SPACE Paramount, 1955
LUCY GALLANT Paramount, 1955
THE DEVIL'S HAIRPIN Paramount, 1957
THE LONELY MAN Paramount, 1957
THE COLOSSUS OF NEW YORK co-composer with Fred Steiner, Paramount, 1958
THE SPACE CHILDREN Paramount, 1958
THAT KIND OF WOMAN Paramount, 1959
BLUEPRINT FOR ROBBERY Paramount, 1961
ROBINSON CRUSOE ON MARS co-composer with Fred Steiner, Paramount, 1964
PROJECT X Paramount, 1968

ROGIER VAN OTTERLOO

b. Netherlands

TURKISH DELIGHT Cinemation, 1973, Dutch
KEETJE TIPPEL 1975, Dutch
SOLDIER OF ORANGE Rank, 1979, Dutch
GRIJPSTRA & DE GLER Verenigade Nederland Filmcompagnie, 1983, Dutch

GEORGES VAN PARYS

b. 1902 - Paris, France
d. 1971 - Paris, France

LA FEMME ET LE PANTIN 1929, French
UN SOIR DE RAFLE co-composer, 1931, French
LE MILLION 1931, French
MADEMOISELLE JOSETTE MA FEMME 1933, French
CETTE VIELLE CANAILLE 1933, French
JEUNESSE 1934, French
L'OR DANS LA RUE co-composer, 1934, French
QUELLE DROLE DE GOSSE co-composer with Jean Lenoir, 1934, French
LES BEUX JOURS 1935, French
LA ROUTE HEUREUSE 1935, French
PRENDS LA ROUTE 1936, French
UN MAUVAIS GARCON 1936, French
ABUS DE CONFIANCE 1937, French
L'ENTRAINEUSE 1938, French
CIRCONSTANCES ATTENUANTES 1939, French
PREMIER BAL 1941, French
LA MAISON DES SEPT JEUNES FILLES 1941, French
LE BIENFAITEUR 1942, French
CAPRICES 1942, French
MARIE-MARTINE 1943, French
L'HOMME DE LONDRES 1943, French

LE COUPLE IDEAL 1945, French
SILENCE EST D'OR 1947, French
LA VIE EN ROSE 1947, French
L'ARMOIRE VOLANTE 1948, French
PARIS AU PRINTEMPS 1948, French
JEAN DE LA LUNE 1948, French
UNE FEMME PAR JOUR 1948, French
HISTORIES EXTRAORDINAIRES 1949, French
MONSEIGNEUR 1949, French
LADY PANAME 1949, French
UN CERTAIN MONSIEUR 1949, French
LE 84 PREND DES VACANCES 1949, French
LES ANCIENS DE SAINT-LOUP 1950, French
LA VIE DRAMATIQUE DE MAURICE UTRILLO 1950, French
LE PASSE-MURAILLE 1950, French
REMAKE 1950, French
DEUX SOUS DE VIOLETTES 1951, French
L'AFFAIRE MANET 1951, French
LA MAISON BONNADIEU 1951, French
CASQUE D'OR 1951, French
TROIS FEMMES co-composer with Louis Beydts, 1951, French
FANFAN LA TULIPE co-composer with Maurice Thiriet, 1951, French
ADORABLES CREATURES 1952, French
LE GRAND MELIES THE GREAT MELIES 1952, French
DORTOIR DES GRANDES 1952, French
RECONTRES SUR LE RHIN 1952, French
AVANT LE DELUGE 1953, French
ON TRIAL *L'AFFAIRE MAURIZIUS* co-composer, New Realm, 1953, French-Italian
VIRGILE 1953, French
FLESH AND THE WOMAN *LE GRAND JEU* Dominant Pictures, 1954, French-Italian
ESCALIERDESERVICE 1954, French
SECRETS D'ALCOVE 1954, French
THE SHEEP HAS FIVE LEGS United Motion Picture Organization, 1954, French
A NOUS DEUX PARIS 1954, French
MADAME DU BARRY 1954, French
PAPA, MAMA, THE MAID AND I 1954, French
NANA 1954, French
FRENCH CAN-CAN *ONLY THE FRENCH CAN* United Motion Picture Organization, 1954, French
LES GRANDES MANOEUVRES 1955, French
PARIS LA NUIT 1955, French
L'ARCHITECTE MAUDIT 1955, French
DIABOLIQUE United Motion Picture Organization, 1955, French
LES TRUANDS 1956, French
C'EST ARRIVE A ADEN 1956, French
THE MAN IN THE RAINCOAT Kingsley International, 1956, French-Italian
COMME EN CHEVEU SUR LA SOUPE 1957, French
FILOUS ET COMPAGNIE 1957, French
LE GORILLE VOUS SALUE BIEN 1958, French
NINA 1958, French
GUINGUETTE 1958, French
RUE DES PRAIRIES 1959, French
THE MILLIONAIRESS 20th Century-Fox, 1960, British
ALL THE GOLD IN THE WORLD 1961, French
I LIKE MONEY 1962, British

CLIFFORD VAUGHAN

b. 1893 - New Jersey
d. November 23, 1987 - Arcadia, California

THE RAVEN Universal, 1935
WHITE BONDAGE 1937

RALPH VAUGHAN WILLIAMS

b. 1872 - Gloustershire, England
d. 1958 - London, England

THE FORTY-NINTH PARALLEL *THE INVADERS* Columbia, 1941, British
COASTAL COMMAND 1942, British
THE PEOPLE'S LAND 1942, British
THE FLEMISH FARM 1943, British
STRICKEN PENINSULA 1944, British
THE LOVES OF JOANNA GODDEN 1946, British
SCOTT OF THE ANTARCTIC 1948, British
DIM LITTLE ISLAND 1949, British

HEITOR VILLA-LOBOS

b. 1887 - Rio de Janeiro, Brazil
d. 1959 - Rio de Janeiro, Brazil

GREEN MANSIONS MGM, 1959

OLIVER WALLACE

b. 1887 - London, England
d. 1963

MURDER BY TELEVISION 1935
DUMBO (AF) HH co-composer with Frank Churchill, RKO Radio, 1941
VICTORY THROUGH AIR POWER ★ co-composer, 1943, United Artists
FUN AND FANCY FREE co-composer, RKO Radio, 1947
THE ADVENTURES OF ICHABOD AND MR. TOAD (AF) RKO Radio, 1949
CINDERELLA (AF) ★ co-composer with Paul J. Smith, RKO Radio, 1950
SEAL ISLAND RKO Radio, 1950
ALICE IN WONDERLAND (AF) ★ RKO Radio, 1951
PETER PAN (AF) RKO Radio, 1953
LADY AND THE TRAMP (AF) Buena Vista, 1955
SAMOA Buena Vista, 1956
OLD YELLER Buena Vista, 1957
TONKA Buena Vista, 1958
WHITE WILDERNESS ★ Buena Vista, 1958
DARBY O'GILL AND THE LITTLE PEOPLE Buena Vista, 1959
JUNGLE CAT Buena Vista, 1960
TEN WHO DARED Buena Vista, 1960
NIKKI, WILD DOG OF THE NORTH Buena Vista, 1961
BIG RED Buena Vista, 1962
THE LEGEND OF LOBO Buena Vista, 1962
THE INCREDIBLE JOURNEY Buena Vista, 1963
SAVAGE SAM Buena Vista, 1963

SIR WILLIAM WALTON

b. March 29, 1902 - Oldham, England
d. March 8, 1983 - Ischia

ESCAPE ME NEVER United Artists, 1935, British
AS YOU LIKE IT 20th Century-Fox, 1936, British
STOLEN LIFE Paramount, 1939, British
MAJOR BARBARA United Artists, 1941, British

THE FOREMAN WENT TO FRANCE 1941, British
SPITFIRE *THE FIRST OF THE FEW* RKO Radio, 1942, British
NEXT OF KIN 1942, British
HENRY V ★ Rank, 1945, British
HAMLET ★ Universal, 1946, British
RICHARD III Lopert, 1956, British
BATTLE OF BRITAIN score unused except for "Battle in Air" sequence, United Artists, 1969, British
THREE SISTERS American Film Theatre, 1970, British

EDWARD WARD

d. September 26, 1971 - Hollywood, California

PARIS Warner Bros., 1929
SHOW OF SHOWS Warner Bros., 1929
WEDDING RINGS Warner Bros., 1930
SONG OF THE FLAME Warner Bros., 1930
BRIDE OF THE REGIMENT Warner Bros., 1930
KISMET Warner Bros., 1931
HYPNOTIZED World Wide, 1932
I LIKE IT THAT WAY Universal, 1934
EMBARRASSING MOMENTS Universal, 1934
ROMANCE IN THE RAIN Universal, 1934
GIFT OF GAB Universal, 1934
GREAT EXPECTATIONS Universal, 1934
CHEATING CHEATERS Universal, 1934
GIRL O' MY DREAMS Monogram, 1934
THE MYSTERY OF EDWIN DROOD Universal, 1935
TIMES SQUARE LADY MGM, 1935
RECKLESS MGM, 1935
AGE OF INDISCRETION MGM, 1935
PUBLIC HERO NO. 1 MGM, 1935
NO MORE LADIES MGM, 1935
HERE COMES THE BAND MGM, 1935
THE BISHOP MISBEHAVES MGM, 1935
KIND LADY MGM, 1935
RIFF RAFF MGM, 1936
EXCLUSIVE STORY MGM, 1936
WIFE VS. SECRETARY co-composer with Herbert Stothart, MGM, 1936
MOONLIGHT MURDER co-composer with Herbert Stothart, MGM, 1936
SMALL TOWN GIRL co-composer with Herbert Stothart, MGM, 1936
SPEED MGM, 1936
WOMEN ARE TROUBLE MGM, 1936
SWORN ENEMY MGM, 1936
THE LONGEST NIGHT MGM, 1936
SINNER TAKE ALL MGM, 1936
AFTER THE THIN MAN co-composer with Herbert Stothart, MGM, 1936
MAN OF THE PEOPLE MGM, 1937
MAMA STEPS OUT MGM, 1937
THE GOOD OLD SOAK MGM, 1937
NIGHT MUST FALL MGM, 1937
SARATOGA MGM, 1937
BAD GUY MGM, 1937
THE WOMEN MEN MARRY MGM, 1937
DOUBLE WEDDING MGM, 1937
LIVE, LOVE AND LEARN MGM, 1937
THE LAST GANGSTER MGM, 1937
NAVY BLUE AND GOLD MGM, 1937
LOVE IS A HEADACHE MGM, 1938
MANNEQUIN MGM, 1938
PARADISE FOR THREE MGM, 1938
A YANK AT OXFORD co-composer with Hubert Bath, MGM, 1938
HOLD THAT KISS MGM, 1938
THE TOY WIFE MGM, 1938
LORD JEFF MGM, 1938
THE SHOPWORN ANGEL MGM, 1938
THE CROWN ROARS MGM, 1938
BOYS TOWN MGM, 1938
MEET THE MAYOR Times Exchange, 1938
VACATION FROM LOVE MGM, 1938
STABLEMATES MGM, 1938
SOCIETY LAWYER MGM, 1939
IT'S A WONDERFUL WORLD MGM, 1939
6,000 ENEMIES MGM, 1939
MAISIE MGM, 1939
STRONGER THAN DESIRE co-composer with David Snell, MGM, 1939
THEY ALL COME OUT co-composer with David Snell, MGM, 1939
ANDY HARDY GETS SPRING FEVER co-composer with David Snell, MGM, 1939
THESE GLAMOUR GIRLS co-composer with David Snell, MGM, 1939
THE WOMEN co-composer with David Snell, MGM, 1939
BLACKMAIL co-composer with David Snell, MGM, 1939
THUNDER AFLOAT co-composer with David Snell, MGM, 1939
DANCING CO-ED co-composer with David Snell, MGM, 1939
BAD LITTLE ANGEL MGM, 1939
REMEMBER? MGM, 1939
ANOTHER THIN MAN MGM, 1939
JOE AND ETHEL TURP CALL ON THE PRESIDENT co-composer with David Snell, MGM, 1939
NICK CARTER, MASTER DETECTIVE MGM, 1939
CONGO MAISIE MGM, 1940
YOUNG TOM EDISON MGM, 1940
MY SON, MY SON United Artists, 1940
SOUTH OF PAGO PAGO United Artists, 1940
DANCE, GIRL, DANCE RKO Radio, 1940
KIT CARSON United Artists, 1940
THE SON OF MONTE CRISTO United Artists, 1941
MR. AND MRS. SMITH RKO Radio, 1941
CHEERS FOR MISS BISHOP ★ United Artists, 1941
TANKS A MILLION ★ United Artists, 1941
NIAGRA FALLS United Artists, 1941
ALL-AMERICAN CO-ED ★ United Artists, 1941
MISS POLLY United Artists, 1941
HAY FOOT United Artists, 1942
BROOKLYN ORCHID United Artists, 1942
DUDES ARE PRETTY PEOPLE United Artists, 1942
ABOUT FACE United Artists, 1942
FLYING WITH MUSIC ★ United Artists, 1942
MEN OF TEXAS Universal, 1942
THE DEVIL WITH HITLER United Artists, 1942
THE McGUERINS FROM BROOKLYN United Artists, 1942
CALABOOSE United Artists, 1943
FALL IN United Artists, 1943
TAXI, MISTER United Artists, 1943
PRAIRIE CHICKENS United Artists, 1943
YANKS AHOY United Artists, 1943
THAT NATZY NUISANCE United Artists, 1943
PHANTOM OF THE OPERA ★ Universal, 1943
MOONLIGHT IN VERMONT Universal, 1943
ALI BABA AND THE FORTY THIEVES Universal, 1944
HER PRIMITIVE MAN Universal, 1944
COBRA WOMAN Universal, 1944
GHOST CATCHERS Universal, 1944
GYPSY WILDCAT Universal, 1944
THE CLIMAX Universal, 1944
BOWERY TO BROADWAY Universal, 1944
FRISCO SAL Universal, 1945
SONG OF THE SARONG Universal, 1945
SALOME, WHERE SHE DANCED Universal, 1945
IT HAPPENED ON FIFTH AVENUE Allied Artists, 1947
COPACABANA United Artists, 1947
THE BABE RUTH STORY Allied Artists, 1948

FRANZ WAXMAN

b. December 24, 1906 - Konigshutte, Germany
d. February 24, 1967 - Los Angeles, California

LILLIOM Fox-Europa, 1934, French
THE BRIDE OF FRANKENSTEIN Universal, 1935
DIAMOND JIM co-composer with Ferde Grofe, Universal, 1935
THE AFFAIR OF SUSAN Universal, 1935
HIS NIGHT OUT Universal, 1935
THREE KIDS AND A QUEEN Universal, 1935
REMEMBER LAST NIGHT? Universal, 1935
EAST OF JAVA Universal, 1935
THE GREAT IMPERSONATION Universal, 1935
MAGNIFICENT OBSESSION Universal, 1935
THE INVISIBLE RAY Universal, 1936
NEXT TIME WE LOVE Universal, 1936
DON'T GET PERSONAL Universal, 1936
LOVE BEFORE BREAKFAST Universal, 1936
SUTTER'S GOLD Universal, 1936
ABSOLUTE QUIET MGM, 1936
TROUBLE FOR TWO MGM, 1936
FURY MGM, 1936
THE DEVIL-DOLL MGM, 1936
HIS BROTHER'S WIFE MGM, 1936
LOVE ON THE RUN MGM, 1936
PERSONAL PROPERTY MGM, 1937
CAPTAINS COURAGEOUS MGM, 1937
THE EMPEROR'S CANDLESTICKS MGM, 1937
THE BRIDE WORE RED MGM, 1937
MAN-PROOF MGM, 1938
ARSENE LUPIN RETURNS MGM, 1938
TEST PILOT MGM, 1938
PORT OF SEVEN SEAS MGM, 1938
THREE COMRADES MGM, 1938
TOO HOT TO HANDLE MGM, 1938
THE SHINING HOUR MGM, 1938
THE YOUNG IN HEART ★ Selznick International, 1938
DRAMATIC SCHOOL MGM, 1938
A CHRISTMAS CAROL MGM, 1938
HONOLULU MGM, 1939
HUCKLEBERRY FINN MGM, 1939
ON BORROWED TIME MGM, 1939
LADY OF THE TROPICS MGM, 1939
STRANGE CARGO MGM, 1940
FLORIAN MGM, 1940
REBECCA ★ United Artists, 1940
SPORTING BLOOD MGM, 1940
BOOM TOWN MGM, 1940
I LOVE YOU AGAIN MGM, 1940
ESCAPE MGM, 1940
THE PHILADELPHIA STORY MGM, 1940
FLIGHT COMMAND MGM, 1940
THE BAD MAN MGM, 1941
DR. JEKYLL AND MR. HYDE ★ MGM, 1941
UNFINISHED BUSINESS MGM, 1941
THE FEMININE TOUCH MGM, 1941
HONKY TONK MGM, 1941
KATHLEEN MGM, 1941
SUSPICION ★ RKO Radio, 1941
DESIGN FOR SCANDAL MGM, 1941
WOMAN OF THE YEAR MGM, 1942
TORTILLA FLAT MGM, 1942
HER CARDBOARD LOVER MGM, 1942
SEVEN SWEETHEARTS MGM, 1942
JOURNEY FOR MARGARET MGM, 1942
REUNION IN FRANCE MGM, 1942
AIR FORCE Warner Bros., 1943
EDGE OF DARKNESS Warner Bros., 1943
OLD ACQUAINTANCE Warner Bros., 1943
DESTINATION TOKYO Warner Bros., 1943
IN OUR TIME Warner Bros., 1944
MR. SKEFFINGTON Warner Bros., 1944
THE VERY THOUGHT OF YOU Warner Bros., 1944
TO HAVE AND HAVE NOT Warner Bros., 1944
OBJECTIVE, BURMA! ★ Warner Bros., 1945
HOTEL BERLIN Warner Bros., 1945
GOD IS MY CO-PILOT Warner Bros., 1945
THE HORN BLOWS AT MIDNIGHT Warner Bros., 1945
PRIDE OF THE MARINES Warner Bros., 1945
CONFIDENTIAL AGENT Warner Bros., 1945
HER KIND OF MAN Warner Bros., 1946
HUMORESQUE ★ Warner Bros., 1946
NORA PRENTISS Warner Bros., 1947
THE TWO MRS. CARROLLS Warner Bros., 1947
POSSESSED Warner Bros., 1947
CRY WOLF Warner Bros., 1947
DARK PASSAGE Warner Bros., 1947
THE UNSUSPECTED Warner Bros., 1947
THAT HAGEN GIRL Warner Bros., 1947
THE PARADINE CASE Selznick Releasing, 1947
SORRY, WRONG NUMBER Paramount, 1948
NO MINOR VICES MGM, 1948
WHIPLASH Warner Bros., 1948
ALIAS NICK BEAL Paramount, 1949
ROPE OF SAND Paramount, 1949
NIGHT UNTO NIGHT Warner Bros., 1949
TASK FORCE Warner Bros., 1949
JOHNNY HOLIDAY United Artists, 1949
NIGHT AND THE CITY 20th Century-Fox, 1950
THE FURIES Paramount, 1950
SUNSET BOULEVARD ★★ Paramount, 1950
DARK CITY Paramount, 1950
ONLY THE VALIANT Warner Bros., 1951
HE RAN ALL THE WAY United Artists, 1951
A PLACE IN THE SUN ★★ Paramount, 1951
ANNE OF THE INDIES 20th Century-Fox, 1951
THE BLUE VEIL RKO Radio, 1951
RED MOUNTAIN Paramount, 1951
DECISION BEFORE DAWN 20th Century-Fox, 1951
PHONE CALL FROM A STRANGER 20th Century-Fox, 1952
LURE OF THE WILDERNESS 20th Century-Fox, 1952
MY COUSIN RACHEL 20th Century-Fox, 1952
COME BACK, LITTLE SHEBA Paramount, 1952
MAN ON A TIGHTROPE 20th Century-Fox, 1953
STALAG 17 Paramount, 1953
I, THE JURY United Artists, 1953
A LION IS IN THE STREETS Warner Bros., 1953
BOTANY BAY Paramount, 1953
PRINCE VALIANT 20th Century-Fox, 1954
ELEPHANT WALK Paramount, 1954
DEMETRIUS AND THE GLADIATORS 20th Century-Fox, 1954
REAR WINDOW Paramount, 1954
THIS IS MY LOVE RKO Radio, 1954
THE SILVER CHALICE ★ Warner Bros., 1954
UNTAMED 20th Century-Fox, 1955
MISTER ROBERTS Warner Bros., 1955
THE VIRGIN QUEEN 20th Century-Fox, 1955
THE INDIAN FIGHTER United Artists, 1955
MIRACLE IN THE RAIN Warner Bros., 1956
CRIME IN THE STREETS Allied Artists, 1956
BACK FROM ETERNITY RKO Radio, 1956
THE SPIRIT OF ST. LOUIS Warner Bros., 1957
LOVE IN THE AFTERNOON Allied Artists, 1957
PEYTON PLACE 20th Century-Fox, 1957
SAYONARA Warner Bros., 1957
RUN SILENT, RUN DEEP United Artists, 1958
HOME BEFORE DARK Warner Bros., 1958

COUNT YOUR BLESSINGS MGM, 1959
THE NUN'S STORY ★ Warner Bros., 1959
CAREER Paramount, 1959
BELOVED INFIDEL 20th Century-Fox, 1959
THE STORY OF RUTH 20th Century-Fox, 1960
SUNRISE AT CAMPOBELLO Warner Bros., 1960
CIMARRON MGM, 1960
RETURN TO PEYTON PLACE 20th Century-Fox, 1961
KING OF THE ROARING '20's—THE STORY OF ARNOLD ROTHSTEIN Allied Artists, 1961
MY GEISHA Paramount, 1962
HEMINGWAY'S ADVENTURES OF A YOUNG MAN 20th Century-Fox, 1962
TARAS BULBA ★ United Artists, 1962
LOST COMMAND Columbia, 1966
THE LONGEST HUNDRED MILES (TF) Universal TV, 1967

ROY WEBB

b. 1888 - New York, New York
d. 1982

PROFESSIONAL SWEETHEART RKO Radio, 1933
COCKEYED CAVALIERS RKO Radio, 1934
KENTUCKY KERNELS RKO Radio, 1934
LIGHTNING STRIKES TWICE RKO Radio, 1934
ENCHANTED APRIL RKO Radio, 1935
CAPTAIN HURRICANE RKO Radio, 1935
LADDIE RKO Radio, 1935
STRANGERS ALL RKO Radio, 1935
THE NITWITS RKO Radio, 1935
THE ARIZONIAN RKO Radio, 1935
BECKY SHARP RKO Radio, 1935
OLD MAN RHYTHM RKO Radio, 1935
THE LAST DAYS OF POMPEII RKO Radio, 1935
THE RAINMAKERS RKO Radio, 1935
ANOTHER FACE RKO Radio, 1935
WE'RE ONLY HUMAN RKO Radio, 1935
SYLVIA SCARLETT RKO Radio, 1936
THE LADY CONSENTS RKO Radio, 1936
MUSS 'EM UP RKO Radio, 1936
SILLY BILLIES RKO Radio, 1936
MURDER ON A BRIDLE PATH RKO Radio, 1936
THE WITNESS CHAIR RKO Radio, 1936
SPECIAL INVESTIGATOR RKO Radio, 1936
THE EX-MRS. BRADFORD RKO Radio, 1936
BUNKER BEAN RKO Radio, 1936
THE BRIDE WALKS OUT RKO Radio, 1936
SECOND WIFE RKO Radio, 1936
THE LAST OF THE MOHICANS United Artists, 1936
MUMMY'S BOYS RKO Radio, 1936
THE PLOUGH AND THE STARS RKO Radio, 1937
RACING LADY RKO Radio, 1937
SEA DEVILS RKO Radio, 1937
QUALITY STREET ★ RKO Radio, 1937
THE OUTCASTS OF POKER FLAT RKO Radio, 1937
MEET THE MISSUS RKO Radio, 1937
NEW FACES OF 1937 RKO Radio, 1937
ON AGAIN—OFF AGAIN RKO Radio, 1937
THE LIFE OF THE PARTY RKO Radio, 1937
FORTY NAUGHTY GIRLS RKO Radio, 1937
STAGE DOOR RKO Radio, 1937
HIGH FLYERS RKO Radio, 1937
BRINGING UP BABY RKO Radio, 1938
NIGHT SPOT RKO Radio, 1938
CONDEMNED WOMEN RKO Radio, 1938
GO CHASE YOURSELF RKO Radio, 1938
VIVACIOUS LADY RKO Radio, 1938
GUN LAW RKO Radio, 1938
BLOND CHEAT RKO Radio, 1938
BORDER G-MAN RKO Radio, 1938
HAVING WONDERFUL TIME RKO Radio, 1938
CRIME RING RKO Radio, 1938
SKY GIANT RKO Radio, 1938
I'M FROM THE CITY RKO Radio, 1938
PAINTED DESERT RKO Radio, 1938
THE AFFAIRS OF ANNABEL RKO Radio, 1938
THE RENEGADE RANGER RKO Radio, 1938
ROOM SERVICE RKO Radio, 1938
MR. DOODLE KICKS OFF RKO Radio, 1938
A MAN TO REMEMBER RKO Radio, 1938
THE MAD MISS MANTON RKO Radio, 1938
LAWLESS VALLEY RKO Radio, 1938
THE LAW WEST OF TOMBSTONE RKO Radio, 1938
NEXT TIME I MARRY RKO Radio, 1938
THE GREAT MAN VOTES RKO Radio, 1939
ARIZONA LEGION RKO Radio, 1939
TWELVE CROWDED HOURS RKO Radio, 1939
THE SAINT STRIKES BACK RKO Radio, 1939
THE FLYING IRISHMAN RKO Radio, 1939
TROUBLE IN SUNDOWN RKO Radio, 1939
LOVE AFFAIR RKO Radio, 1939
THEY MADE HER A SPY RKO Radio, 1939
FIXER DUGAN RKO Radio, 1939
THE ROOKIE COP RKO Radio, 1939
SORORITY HOUSE RKO Radio, 1939
PANAMA LADY RKO Radio, 1939
RACKETEERS OF THE RANGE RKO Radio, 1939
THE GIRL FROM MEXICO RKO Radio, 1939
THE GIRL AND THE GAMBLER RKO Radio, 1939
FIVE CAME BACK RKO Radio, 1939
TIMBER STAMPEDE RKO Radio, 1939
BACHELOR MOTHER RKO Radio, 1939
BAD LANDS RKO Radio, 1939
IN NAME ONLY RKO Radio, 1939
THE FIGHTING GRINGO RKO Radio, 1939
FULL CONFESSION RKO Radio, 1939
THREE SONS RKO Radio, 1939
SUED FOR LIBEL RKO Radio, 1939
RENO RKO Radio, 1939
TWO THOROUGHBREDS RKO Radio, 1939
MARRIED AND IN LOVE RKO Radio, 1940
THE SAINT'S DOUBLE TROUBLE RKO Radio, 1940
THE MARINES FLY HIGH RKO Radio, 1940
ABE LINCOLN IN ILLINOIS RKO Radio, 1940
CURTAIN CALL RKO Radio, 1940
MY FAVORITE WIFE ★ RKO Radio, 1940
YOU CAN'T FOOL YOUR WIFE RKO Radio, 1940
A BILL OF DIVORCEMENT RKO Radio, 1940
THE SAINT TAKES OVER RKO Radio, 1940
ANNE OF WINDY POPLARS RKO Radio, 1940
CROSS COUNTRY ROMANCE RKO Radio, 1940
MILLIONAIRES IN PRISON RKO Radio, 1940
ONE CROWDED NIGHT RKO Radio, 1940
THE STRANGER ON THE THIRD FLOOR RKO Radio, 1940
I'M STILL ALIVE RKO Radio, 1940
LADDIE RKO Radio, 1940
MEXICAN SPITFIRE OUT WEST RKO Radio, 1940
YOU'LL FIND OUT RKO Radio, 1940
KITTY FOYLE RKO Radio, 1941
LITTLE MEN RKO Radio, 1941
LET'S MAKE MUSIC RKO Radio, 1941
THE SAINT IN PALM SPRINGS RKO Radio, 1941
A GIRL, A GUY AND A GOB RKO Radio, 1941
THE DEVIL AND MISS JONES RKO Radio, 1941
HURRY, CHARLIE, HURRY RKO Radio, 1941
TOM, DICK AND HARRY RKO Radio, 1941
PARACHUTE BATTALION RKO Radio, 1941
FATHER TAKES A WIFE RKO Radio, 1941

LOOK WHO'S LAUGHING RKO Radio, 1941
WEEKEND FOR THREE RKO Radio, 1941
PLAYMATES RKO Radio, 1941
OBLIGING YOUNG LADY RKO Radio, 1942
JOAN OF PARIS ★ RKO Radio, 1942
THE TUTTLES OF TAHITI RKO Radio, 1942
MY FAVORITE SPY RKO Radio, 1942
THE MAGNIFICENT AMBERSONS additional music, RKO Radio, 1942
POWDER TOWN RKO Radio, 1942
MEXICAN SPITFIRE SEES A GHOST RKO Radio, 1942
THE BIG STREET RKO Radio, 1942
MEXICAN SPITFIRE'S ELEPHANT RKO Radio, 1942
HERE WE GO AGAIN RKO Radio, 1942
HIGHWAYS BY NIGHT RKO Radio, 1942
THE NAVY COMES THROUGH RKO Radio, 1942
I MARRIED A WITCH ★ United Artists, 1942
THE FALCON'S BROTHER RKO Radio, 1942
SEVEN DAYS' LEAVE RKO Radio, 1942
ARMY SURGEON RKO Radio, 1942
CAT PEOPLE RKO Radio, 1942
SEVEN MILES FROM ALCATRAZ RKO Radio, 1943
JOURNEY INTO FEAR RKO Radio, 1943
HITLER'S CHILDREN RKO Radio, 1943
FLIGHT FOR FREEDOM RKO Radio, 1943
LADIES' DAY RKO Radio, 1943
I WALKED WITH A ZOMBIE RKO Radio, 1943
THE FALCON STRIKES BACK RKO Radio, 1943
BOMBARDIER RKO Radio, 1943
MR. LUCKY RKO Radio, 1943
THE LEOPARD MAN RKO Radio, 1943
PETTICOAT LARCENY RKO Radio, 1943
THE FALCON IN DANGER RKO Radio, 1943
BEHIND THE RISING SUN RKO Radio, 1943
A LADY TAKES A CHANCE RKO Radio, 1943
THE FALLEN SPARROW ★ RKO Radio, 1943
THE SEVENTH VICTIM RKO Radio, 1943
GANGWAY FOR TOMORROW RKO Radio, 1943
THE IRON MAJOR RKO Radio, 1943
THE GHOST SHIP RKO Radio, 1943
PASSPORT TO DESTINY RKO Radio, 1944
CURSE OF THE CAT PEOPLE RKO Radio, 1944
ACTION IN ARABIA RKO Radio, 1944
THE FALCON OUT WEST RKO Radio, 1944
MARINE RAIDERS RKO Radio, 1944
BRIDE BY MISTAKE RKO Radio, 1944
THE SEVENTH CROSS MGM, 1944
RAINBOW ISLAND Paramount, 1944
TALL IN THE SADDLE RKO Radio, 1944
THE MASTER RACE RKO Radio, 1944
MURDER, MY SWEET RKO Radio, 1944
EXPERIMENT PERILOUS RKO Radio, 1945
THE ENCHANTED COTTAGE ★ RKO Radio, 1945
BETRAYAL FROM THE EAST RKO Radio, 1945
THOSE ENDEARING YOUNG CHARMS RKO Radio, 1945
ZOMBIES ON BROADWAY RKO Radio, 1945
THE BODY SNATCHER RKO Radio, 1945
BACK TO BATAAN RKO Radio, 1945
TWO O'CLOCK COURAGE RKO Radio, 1945
LOVE, HONOR AND GOODBYE Republic, 1945
CORNERED RKO Radio, 1945
DICK TRACY RKO Radio, 1945
THE SPIRAL STAIRCASE RKO Radio, 1945
BADMAN'S TERRITORY RKO Radio, 1946
BEDLAM RKO Radio, 1946
THE WELL GROOMED BRIDE Paramount, 1946
WITHOUT RESERVATIONS RKO Radio, 1946
NOTORIOUS RKO Radio, 1946
EASY COME, EASY GO Paramount, 1947
THE LOCKET RKO Radio, 1947
SINBAD THE SAILOR RKO Radio, 1947
THEY WON'T BELIEVE ME RKO Radio, 1947
CROSSFIRE RKO Radio, 1947
RIFFRAFF RKO Radio, 1947
MAGIC TOWN RKO Radio, 1947
OUT OF THE PAST RKO Radio, 1947
CASS TIMBERLANE MGM, 1948
I REMEMBER MAMA RKO Radio, 1948
FIGHTING FATHER DUNNE RKO Radio, 1948
RACE STREET RKO Radio, 1948
RACHEL AND THE STRANGER RKO Radio, 1948
BLOOD ON THE MOON RKO Radio, 1948
BAD MEN OF TOMBSTONE Allied Artists, 1949
THE WINDOW RKO Radio, 1949
ROUGHSHOD RKO Radio, 1949
MIGHTY JOE YOUNG RKO Radio, 1949
EASY LIVING RKO Radio, 1949
MY FRIEND IRMA Paramount, 1949
HOLIDAY AFFAIR RKO Radio, 1949
THE SECRET FURY RKO Radio, 1950
THE WHITE TOWER RKO Radio, 1950
WHERE DANGER LIVES RKO Radio, 1950
VENDETTA RKO Radio, 1950
BRANDED Paramount, 1951
GAMBLING HOUSE RKO Radio, 1951
SEALED CARGO RKO Radio, 1951
HARD, FAST AND BEAUTIFUL RKO Radio, 1951
FLYING LEATHERNECKS RKO Radio, 1951
FIXED BAYONETS! 20th Century-Fox, 1951
A GIRL IN EVERY PORT RKO Radio, 1952
AT SWORD'S POINT RKO Radio, 1952
CLASH BY NIGHT RKO Radio, 1952
THE LUSTY MEN RKO Radio, 1952
OPERATION SECRET Warner Bros., 1952
SECOND CHANCE RKO Radio, 1953
SHE COULDN'T SAY NO RKO Radio, 1953
HOUDINI Paramount, 1953
DANGEROUS MISSION RKO Radio, 1954
TRACK OF THE CAT Warner Bros., 1954
BENGAZI RKO Radio, 1955
THE AMERICANO Columbia, 1955
BLOOD ALLEY Warner Bros., 1955
MARTY United Artists, 1955
THE SEA CHASE Warner Bros., 1955
UNDERWATER! RKO Radio, 1955
THE GIRL HE LEFT BEHIND Warner Bros., 1956
THE FIRST TEXAN Allied Artists, 1956
OUR MISS BROOKS Warner Bros., 1956
THE RIVER CHANGES Warner Bros., 1956
SHOOT-OUT AT MEDICINE BEND Warner Bros., 1957
TOP SECRET AFFAIR Warner Bros., 1957
TEACHER'S PET Paramount, 1958

KURT WEILL

b. March 2, 1900 - Dessau, Germany
d. April 3, 1950 - New York

YOU AND ME Paramount, 1938

JEAN WIENER

b. March 19, 1896 - Paris, France
d. June 8, 1982 - Paris France

KNOCK 1932, French
L'HOMME A L'HISPANO *THE MAN FROM SPAIN* 1932, French
THE GREAT GLASS BLOWER 1933, French
L'AVENTURIER 1934, French
LA PAQUEBOT "TENACITY" 1934, French

MARIA CHAPDELAINE 1934, French
LES AFFAIRES PUBLIQUES Arc Films, 1934, French
LA CATHEDRALE DES MORTES 1935, French
LA BANDERA 1935, French
LE CLOWN BUX co-composer with Roger Desormieres, 1935, French
THE CRIME OF MONSIEUR LANGE co-composer with Joseph Kosma, Brandon, 1936, French
L'HOMME DU JOUR 1936, French
LES BAS-FONDS *THE LOWER DEPTHS* 1936, French
ROSE 1936, French
LA LETTRE 1938, French
NUITS DE FEU 1939, French
DERRIERE LA FACADE 1939, French
LES PASSAGERS DE LA GRANDE OUISE 1939, French
UNTEL, PERE ET FILS *HEART OF A NATION* 1940, French
LA VOYAGEUR DE LA TOUSSAINT 1942, French
SUITE FRANCAISE 1943, French
LE PERE GORIOT 1944, French
LE VOLEUR DE PARATONNERRES 1944, French
LA FILLE AUX YEUX GRIS 1945, French
LE CAPITAN 1945, French
PATRIE 1946, French
CONTRE-ENQUETE 1946, French
POUR UNE NUIT D'AMOUR 1946, French
MACADAM 1946, French
LES FRERES BOUQUINQUANT 1947, French
LE DIABLE SOUFFLE 1947, French
LA CARCASSE ET LE TORD-COU 1947, French
L'ESCADRON BLANC 1948, French
LE POINT DU JOUR 1948, French
ZANZABELLE A PARIS 1948, French
RENDEZ-VOUS DE JUILLET 1949, French
LE PARFUM DE LA DAME EN NOIR 1949, French
MAITRE APRES DIEU 1950, French
UN SOURIRE DANS LA TEMPETE 1950, French
SOUS LE CIEL DE PARIS *UNDER THE PARIS SKY* Discina International, 1951, French
LE CHEMIN DE l'ETOILE 1953, French
LE COMTE DE MONTE-CRISTO 1953, French
LA RAFLE EST POUR CE SOIR 1953, French
TOUCHEZ PAS AU GRISBI 1953, French
LES POUSSIERES 1954, French
FUTURES VEDETTES 1954, French
DEADLIER THAN THE MALE *VOICI LE TEMPS DES ASSASSINS* Continental, 1955, French
LA VIE EST BELLE 1956, French
LA GARCONNE 1956, French
MOTRE-DAME, CATHEDRALE DE PARIS 1957, French
POT-BOUILLE *THE HOUSE OF LOVERS* Continental, 1957, French
A WOMAN LIKE SATAN *THE FEMALE/LA FEMME ET LA PANTIN* Lopert, 1958, French-Italian
PANTALASKAS 1959, French
ILS ONT TUE JAURES 1962, French
LADY L MGM, 1965, U.S.-Italian-French
AU HASARD, BALTHAZAR Cinema Ventures, 1966, French
LES FILOUS 1966, French
MOUCHETTE 1967, French
LA REVOLUTION D'OCTOBRE 1968, French
DIEU A CHOISI PARIS 1968, French
LA FAUTE DE L'ABBE MOURET 1970, French

MEREDITH WILLSON

b. 1902 - Mason City, Iowa
d. June 15, 1984 - Santa Monica, California

THE LITTLE FOXES ★ RKO Radio, 1941

MORTIMER WILSON

d. January 27, 1932 - New York

THE THIEF OF BAGDAD United Artists, 1924

VICTOR YOUNG

b. August 8, 1900 - Chicago, Illinois
d. 1956 - Los Angeles, California

CHAMPAGNE WALTZ Paramount, 1937
MAID OF SALEM Paramount, 1937
SWING HIGH, SWING LOW Paramount, 1937
VOGUES *VOGUES OF 1938* United Artists, 1937
EBB TIDE Paramount, 1937
WELLS FARGO Paramount, 1937
ARMY GIRL ★ Republic, 1938
BREAKING THE ICE ★ RKO Radio, 1938
PECK'S BAD BOY WITH THE CIRCUS RKO Radio, 1938
FLIRTING WITH FATE MGM, 1938
FISHERMAN'S WHARF RKO Radio, 1939
MAN OF CONQUEST ★ Republic, 1939
HERITAGE OF THE DESERT Paramount, 1939
WAY DOWN SOUTH ★ RKO Radio, 1939
GOLDEN BOY ★ Columbia, 1939
RANGE WAR Paramount, 1939
OUR NEIGHBORS—THE CARTERS Paramount, 1939
THE NIGHT OF NIGHTS Paramount, 1939
THE LLANO KID Paramount, 1939
GULLIVER'S TRAVELS (AF) ★ Paramount, 1939
THE LIGHT THAT FAILED Paramount, 1939
RAFFLES United Artists, 1940
DARK COMMAND Republic, 1940
BUCK BENNY RIDES AGAIN Paramount, 1940
THE WAY OF ALL FLESH Paramount, 1940
THREE FACES WEST Republic, 1940
UNTAMED Paramount, 1940
I WANT A DIVORCE Paramount, 1940
MOON OVER BURMA Paramount, 1940
ARISE, MY LOVE ★ Paramount, 1940
THREE MEN FROM TEXAS Paramount, 1940
NORTHWEST MOUNTED POLICE ★ Paramount, 1940
ARIZONA ★ Columbia, 1940
THE MAD DOCTOR Paramount, 1940
VIRGINIA Paramount, 1941
REACHING FOR THE SUN Paramount, 1941
CAUGHT IN THE DRAFT Paramount, 1941
I WANTED WINGS Paramount, 1941
ALOMA OF THE SOUTH SEAS Paramount, 1941
HOLD BACK THE DAWN ★ Paramount, 1941
SKYLARK Paramount, 1941
THE REMARKABLE ANDREW Paramount, 1942
REAP THE WILD WIND Paramount, 1942

THE GREAT MAN'S LADY Paramount, 1942
BEYOND THE BLUE HORIZON Paramount, 1942
TAKE A LETTER, DARLING ★ Paramount, 1942
THE FOREST RANGERS Paramount, 1942
MRS. WIGGS OF THE CABBAGE PATCH Paramount, 1942
FLYING TIGERS ★ Republic, 1942
THE GLASS KEY Paramount, 1942
THE PALM BEACH STORY Paramount, 1942
SILVER QUEEN ★ United Artists, 1942
THE OUTLAW United Artists, 1943
BUCKSKIN FRONTIER United Artists, 1943
THE CRYSTAL BALL United Artists, 1943
YOUNG AND WILLING United Artists, 1943
CHINA Paramount, 1943
FOR WHOM THE BELL TOLLS ★ Paramount, 1943
HOSTAGES Paramount, 1943
TRUE TO LIFE Paramount, 1943
NO TIME FOR LOVE Paramount, 1943
THE UNINVITED Paramount, 1944
THE STORY OF DR. WASSELL Paramount, 1944
THE GREAT MOMENT Paramount, 1944
FRENCHMAN'S CREEK Paramount, 1944
MINISTRY OF FEAR Paramount, 1944
PRACTICALLY YOURS Paramount, 1944
AND NOW TOMORROW Paramount, 1944
A MEDAL FOR BENNY Paramount, 1945
THE GREAT JOHN L. United Artists, 1945
YOU CAME ALONG Paramount, 1945
KITTY Paramount, 1945
LOVE LETTERS ★ Paramount, 1945
MASQUERADE IN MEXICO Paramount, 1945
HOLD THAT BLONDE Paramount, 1945
THE BLUE DAHLIA Paramount, 1946
THE SEARCHING WIND Paramount, 1946
OUR HEARTS WERE GROWING UP Paramount, 1946
TO EACH HIS OWN Paramount, 1946
TWO YEARS BEFORE THE MAST Paramount, 1946
SUDDENLY, IT'S SPRING Paramount, 1947
CALIFORNIA Paramount, 1947
THE IMPERFECT LADY Paramount, 1947
CALCUTTA Paramount, 1947
THE TROUBLE WITH WOMEN Paramount, 1947
I WALK ALONE Paramount, 1947
UNCONQUERED Paramount, 1947
GOLDEN EARRINGS Paramount, 1947
STATE OF THE UNION MGM, 1948
THE BIG CLOCK Paramount, 1948
THE EMPEROR WALTZ ★ Paramount, 1948
DREAM GIRL Paramount, 1948
SO EVIL MY LOVE co-composer with William Alwyn, Paramount, 1948
BEYOND GLORY Paramount, 1948
THE NIGHT HAS A THOUSAND EYES Paramount, 1948
MISS TATLOCK'S MILLIONS Paramount, 1948
THE PALEFACE Paramount, 1948
THE ACCUSED Paramount, 1948
A CONNECTICUT YANKEE IN KING ARTHUR'S COURT Paramount, 1949
STREETS OF LAREDO Paramount, 1949
THE FILE ON THELMA JORDAN *THELMA JORDAN* Paramount, 1949
SONG OF SURRENDER Paramount, 1949
CHICAGO DEADLINE Paramount, 1949
SANDS OF IWO JIMA Republic, 1949
GUN CRAZY *DEADLY IS THE FEMALE* United Artists, 1949
MY FOOLISH HEART RKO Radio, 1949
SAMSON AND DELILAH ★ Paramount, 1949
OUR VERY OWN RKO Radio, 1950
PAID IN FULL Paramount, 1950
BRIGHT LEAF Warner Bros., 1950
THE FIREBALL 20th Century-Fox, 1950
RIO GRANDE Republic, 1950
SEPTEMBER AFFAIR Paramount, 1950
BELLE LE GRAND Republic, 1951
PAYMENT ON DEMAND RKO Radio, 1951
THE BULLFIGHTER AND THE LADY Republic, 1951
THE LEMON DROP KID Paramount, 1951
APPOINTMENT WITH DANGER Paramount, 1951
HONEYCHILE Republic, 1951
A MILLIONAIRE FOR CHRISTY 20th Century-Fox, 1951
THE WILD BLUE YONDER Republic, 1951
MY FAVORITE SPY Paramount, 1951
THE QUIET MAN Republic, 1952
ANYTHING CAN HAPPEN Paramount, 1952
SOMETHING TO LIVE FOR Paramount, 1952
THE GREATEST SHOW ON EARTH Paramount, 1952
SCARAMOUCHE MGM, 1952
THE STORY OF WILL ROGERS Warner Bros., 1952
ONE MINUTE TO ZERO RKO Radio, 1952
THUNDERBIRDS Republic, 1952
BLACKBEARD, THE PIRATE RKO Radio, 1952
THE STAR 20th Century-Fox, 1952
FAIR WIND TO JAVA Republic, 1953
A PERILOUS JOURNEY Republic, 1953
THE SUN SHINES BRIGHT Republic, 1953
SHANE Paramount, 1953
LITTLE BOY LOST Paramount, 1953
FOREVER FEMALE Paramount, 1953
TROUBLE IN THE GLEN Republic, 1953, British
FLIGHT NURSE Republic, 1954
JUBILEE TRAIL Republic, 1954
JOHNNY GUITAR Republic, 1954
THREE COINS IN THE FOUNTAIN 20th Century-Fox, 1954
ABOUT MRS. LESLIE Paramount, 1954
DRUM BEAT Warner Bros., 1954
THE COUNTRY GIRL Paramount, 1954
TIMBERJACK Republic, 1955
STRATEGIC AIR COMMAND Paramount, 1955
SON OF SINBAD RKO Radio, 1955
A MAN ALONE Republic, 1955
THE LEFT HAND OF GOD 20th Century-Fox, 1955
THE TALL MEN 20th Century-Fox, 1955
THE CONQUEROR RKO Radio, 1956
THE MAVERICK QUEEN Republic, 1956
THE VAGABOND KING Paramount, 1956
THE PROUD AND PROFANE Paramount, 1956
AROUND THE WORLD IN 80 DAYS ★★ United Artists, 1956
THE BRAVE ONE RKO Radio, 1956
THE BUSTER KEATON STORY Paramount 1957
OMAR KHAYYAM Paramount, 1957
RUN OF THE ARROW RKO Radio, 1957
CHINA GATE co-composer with Max Steiner, 20th Century-Fox, 1957

Z

JOHN S. ZAMECNIK
d. June 13, 1953 - Los Angeles, California

OLD IRONSIDES Paramount, 1926
WINGS Paramount, 1927
ABIE'S IRISH ROSE Paramount, 1928
THE WEDDING MARCH Paramount, 1928
BETRAYAL Paramount, 1929
REDSKIN Paramount, 1929

WOLFGANG ZELLER
b. Germany
d. 1967 - West Germany

ADVENTURES OF PRINCE ACHMED 1926, German
WELTMELODIE 1929, German
VAMPYR *VAMPYR OU L'ETRANGE AVENTURE DE DAVID GRAY* 1932, French-German
L'ATLANTIDE *LOST ATLANTIS* 1932, French-German
WAJAN *SON OF A WITCH* 1934, German
DIE UNJEIMLICHEN WUNSCHE *THE UNHOLY WITCH* 1939, German
MARRIAGE IN THE SHADOWS 1947
CHINA GATE co-composer with Max Steiner, 20th Century -Fox, 1957
SERENGETI SHALL NOT DIE 1960

★★★★

INDICES

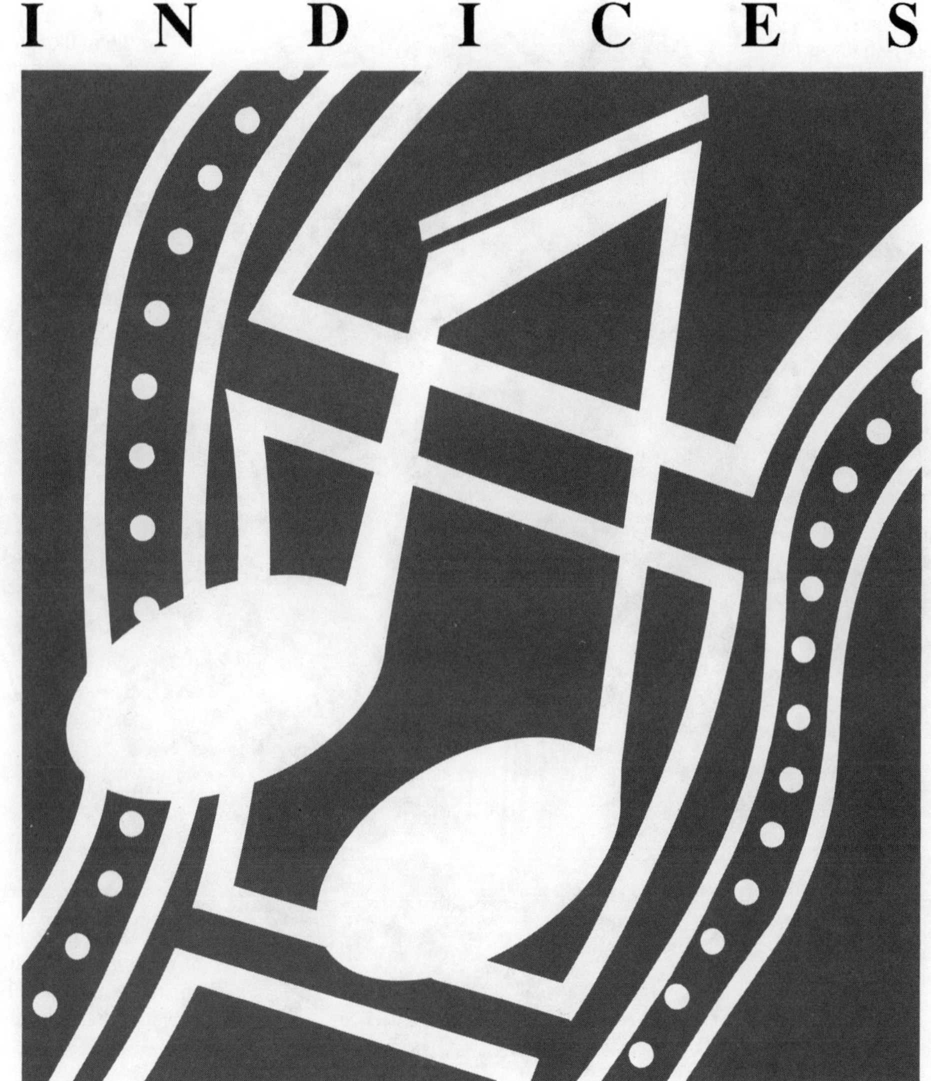

FILM TITLES • AGENTS & MANAGERS

TAKE A FEW MINUTES TO GO THROUGH YOUR GARBAGE.

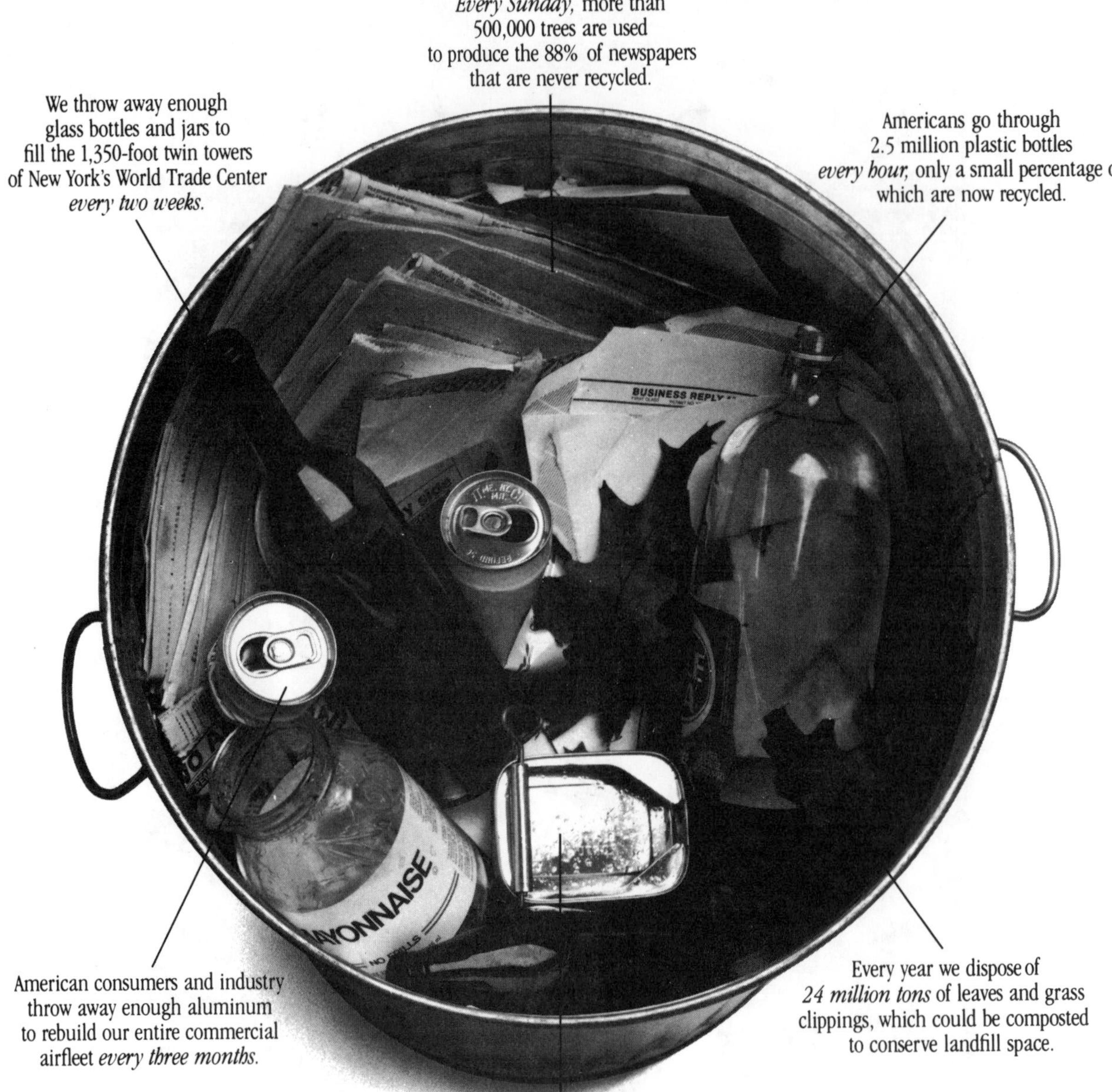

Every Sunday, more than 500,000 trees are used to produce the 88% of newspapers that are never recycled.
We throw away enough glass bottles and jars to fill the 1,350-foot twin towers of New York's World Trade Center *every two weeks.*
Americans go through 2.5 million plastic bottles *every hour,* only a small percentage of which are now recycled.
BUSINESS REPLY
American consumers and industry throw away enough aluminum to rebuild our entire commercial airfleet *every three months.*
Every year we dispose of *24 million tons* of leaves and grass clippings, which could be composted to conserve landfill space.
We throw away enough iron and steel to *continuously* supply all the nation's automakers.

The ordinary bag of trash you throw away is slowly becoming a serious problem for everybody.

Because the fact is, not only are we running out of resources to make the products we need, we're running out of places to put what's left over.

Write the Environmental Defense Fund at: 257 Park Avenue South, New York, NY 10010, for a free brochure that will tell you virtually everything you'll need to know about recycling.

One thing's for certain, the few minutes you take to learn how to recycle will spare us all a lot of garbage later.

IF YOU'RE NOT RECYCLING℠ YOU'RE THROWING IT ALL AWAY.

EDF™ Ad Council

INDEX OF FILM TITLES - FILM COMPOSERS

NOTE: This is not an index of every film ever made, only those listed in this directory.

† = deceased

A

ADVENTURE ..... Herbert Stothart†
ADVENTURE FOR TWO ..... Nicholas Brodzsky†
ADVENTURE IN BALTIMORE ..... Frederick Hollander†
ADVENTURE IN DIAMONDS ..... Leo Shuken†
ADVENTURE IN WASHINGTON ..... W. Franke Harling†
ADVENTURE OF SHERLOCK HOLMES' SMARTER BROTHER, THE ..... John Morris
ADVENTURES IN BABYSITTING ..... Michael Kamen
ADVENTURES OF BARON MUNCHAUSEN, THE ..... Michael Kamen
ADVENTURES OF BUCKAROO BANZAI: ACROSS THE 8TH DIMENSION, THE ..... Michael Boddicker
ADVENTURES OF BULLWHIP GRIFFIN, THE ..... George Bruns
ADVENTURES OF CASANOVA, THE ..... Hugo Friedhofer†
ADVENTURES OF DON JUAN ..... Max Steiner†
ADVENTURES OF DON QUIXOTE, THE (TF) ..... Michel Legrand
ADVENTURES OF FORD FAIRLANE, THE ..... Yello
ADVENTURES OF GALLANT BESS, THE ..... Irving Gertz
ADVENTURES OF GIRARD, THE ..... Riz Ortolani
ADVENTURES OF HAJJI BABA, THE ..... Dimitri Tiomkin†
ADVENTURES OF HUCKLEBERRY FINN, THE ..... Jerome Moross†
ADVENTURES OF HUCKLEBERRY FINN, THE (TF) ..... Robert Summers
ADVENTURES OF ICHABOD AND MR. TOAD, THE (AF) ..... Oliver Wallace†
ADVENTURES OF MARCO POLO, THE ..... Hugo Friedhofer†
ADVENTURES OF MARK TWAIN, THE ..... ★ Max Steiner†
ADVENTURES OF MILO & OTIS, THE ..... Michael Boddicker
ADVENTURES OF NELLIE BLY, THE (TF) ..... Robert Summers
ADVENTURES OF NICK CARTER, THE (TF) ..... John Andrew Tartaglia
ADVENTURES OF PRINCE ACHMED ..... Wolfgang Zeller†
ADVENTURES OF ROBIN HOOD, THE ..... ★★ Erich Wolfgang Korngold†
ADVENTURES OF ROBINSON CRUSOE, THE ..... Anthony Collins†
ADVENTURES OF SHERLOCK HOLMES, THE ..... David Raksin
ADVENTURES OF SHERLOCK HOLMES, THE ..... David Buttolph†
ADVENTURES OF SHERLOCK HOLMES, THE ..... Cyril J. Mockridge†
ADVENTURES OF TAKLA MAKAN ..... Akira Ifukube
ADVENTURES OF THE QUEEN (TF) ..... Richard LaSalle
ADVENTURES OF THE WILDERNESS FAMILY, THE ..... Gene Kauer
ADVENTURES OF THE WILDERNESS FAMILY, THE ..... Douglas Lackey
ADVENTURES OF TOM SAWYER, THE ..... Max Steiner†
ADVERSARY, THE ..... Satyajit Ray
ADVICE TO THE LOVELORN ..... Alfred Newman†
ADVICE TO THE LOVELORN (TF) ..... James Di Pasquale
ADVISE AND CONSENT ..... Jerry Fielding†
AEODROME, THE (TF) ..... Carl Davis
AERIAL GUNNER ..... Daniele Amfitheatrof†
AEROGRAD ..... Dmitri Kabalevsky†
AFFAIR IN HAVANA ..... Ernest Gold
AFFAIR OF SUSAN, THE ..... Franz Waxman†
AFFAIR TO REMEMBER, AN ..... ★ Hugo Friedhofer†
AFFAIR, THE (TF) ..... George Aliceson Tipton
AFFAIRS OF ANNABEL, THE ..... Roy Webb†
AFFAIRS OF CELLINI, THE ..... Alfred Newman†
AFFAIRS OF DOBIE GILLIS ..... Jeff Alexander†
AFFAIRS OF MARTHA, THE ..... Bronislau Kaper†
AFFAIRS OF SUSAN, THE ..... Frederick Hollander†
AFFECTIONATELY YOURS ..... Heinz Roemheld†
AFRICA (FD) ..... Alex North
AFRICA - TEXAS STYLE! ..... Malcolm Arnold
AFRICA ADDIO ..... Riz Ortolani
AFRICA NUDA, AFRICA VIOLENTA (FD) ..... Angelo Francesco Lavagnino†
AFRICAN ELEPHANT, THE (FD) ..... Laurence Rosenthal
AFRICAN QUEEN, THE ..... Allan Gray†
AFTER DARK, MY SWEET ..... Maurice Jarre
AFTER HOURS ..... Howard Shore
AFTER SCHOOL ..... David C. Williams
AFTER THE AXE (FD) ..... Patricia Cullen
AFTER THE FOX ..... Burt Bacharach
AFTER THE PROMISE (TF) ..... Ralph Burns
AFTER THE THIN MAN ..... Herbert Stothart†
AFTER THE THIN MAN ..... Edward Ward†
AFTER TONIGHT ..... Max Steiner†
AFTERMATH, THE ..... John W. Morgan
AFTERNOON OF A PEASANT, THE ..... Alfi Kabiljo
AFTERSHOCK ..... Kevin Klinger
AGAINST ALL FLAGS ..... Hans J. Salter
AGAINST ALL ODDS ..... Larry Carlton
AGAINST ALL ODDS ..... Michel Colombier
AGATHA ..... Johnny Mandel
AGATHA CHRISTIE'S THE MAN IN THE BROWN SUIT (TF) ..... Arthur B. Rubinstein
AGATHA CHRISTIE'S 'A CARIBBEAN MYSTERY' (TF) ..... Lee Holdridge
AGATHA CHRISTIE'S 'DEAD MAN'S FOLLY' (TF) ..... John Addison
AGATHA CHRISTIE'S 'MURDER IN THREE ACTS' (TF) ..... Alf Clausen
AGATHA CHRISTIE'S 'MURDER WITH MIRRORS' ..... ☆ Richard Rodney Bennett
AGATHA CHRISTIE'S 'SPARKLING CYANIDE' (TF) ..... James Di Pasquale
AGATHA CHRISTIE'S 'THIRTEEN AT DINNER' (TF) ..... John Addison
AGE FOR LOVE, THE ..... Alfred Newman†
AGE OF ASSASSINS, THE ..... Masaru Sato
AGE OF CONSENT ..... Stanley Myers
AGE OF INDISCRETION ..... Edward Ward†
AGE OF INNOCENCE, THE ..... Max Steiner†
AGE-OLD FRIENDS (CTF) ..... Stanley Myers
AGENCE MATRIMONIALE ..... Joseph Kosma†
AGENCY ..... Lewis Furey
AGENT 8 3/4 ..... Angelo Francesco Lavagnino†
AGENTE SPEZIALE - OPERAZIONE RE MIDA ..... Bruno Nicolai
AGGIE APPLEBY ..... Max Steiner†
AGNES OF GOD ..... ★ Georges Delerue
AGONY AND THE ECSTASY, THE ..... Jerry Goldsmith
AGONY AND THE ECSTASY, THE ..... ★ Alex North
AGOSTINO ..... Carlo Rustichelli
AGOSTINO DI IPPONA ..... Mario Nascimbene
AGUIRRE, THE WRATH OF GOD ..... Popol Vuh
AH SI? E IO LO DICO A ZZZOROI ..... Gianfranco Plenizio
AH, WILDERNESS! ..... Herbert Stothart†
AI MARGINI DELLA METROPOLI ..... Franco Mannino
AIMEZ-VOUS BRAHMS? ..... Georges Auric†
AIN'T MISBEHAVIN' ..... Henry Mancini
AIR AMERICA ..... Charles Gross
AIR FORCE ..... Franz Waxman†
AIR PATROL ..... Albert Glasser
AIR PATTERN—PACIFIC (FD) ..... Gail Kubik†
AIR RAD WARDENS ..... Nathaniel Shilkret†
AIRPLANE II ..... Richard Hazard
AIRPLANE II: THE SEQUEL ..... Elmer Bernstein
AIRPLANE! ..... Elmer Bernstein
AIRPORT ..... ★ Alfred Newman†
AIRPORT 1975 ..... John Cacavas
AIRPORT '77 ..... John Cacavas
AIRWOLF (TF) ..... Sylvester Levay
AKAZA, GOD OF VENGEANCE ..... Andrew Belling
AKENFIELD (FD) ..... Sir Michael Tippett
AKIRA (AF) ..... Shoji Yamashiro
AKIRA KUROSAWA'S DREAMS ..... Shinchiro Ikebe
AL CAPONE ..... David Raksin
AL DI LA DELLA LEGGE ..... Riz Ortolani
AL HOUROB AL SAGHIRA ..... Gabriel Yared
ALADDIN ..... Fabio Frizzi
ALAKAZAM THE GREAT ..... Les Baxter
ALAMO BAY ..... Ry Cooder
ALAMO, THE ..... ★ Dimitri Tiomkin†
ALAMO: 13 DAYS TO GLORY, THE (TF) ..... Peter Bernstein
ALASKA: AN AMERICAN CHILD (FD) ..... Lee Holdridge
ALBERGO LUNA, CAMERA 34 ..... Nino Rota†
ALBERT R.N. ..... Malcolm Arnold
ALCATRAZ: THE WHOLE SHOCKING STORY (TF) ..... Jerrold Immel
ALCHEMIST, THE ..... Richard H. Band
ALECHINSKY D'APRES NATURE ..... Michel Portal
ALERTE EN MEDITERRANEE ..... Michel Michelet†
ALEX & THE GYPSY ..... Henry Mancini
ALEX: THE LIFE OF A CHILD (TF) ..... J.A.C. Redford
ALEXANDER ..... Vladimir Cosma
ALEXANDER NEVSKY ..... Sergei Prokofiev†
ALEXANDER THE GREAT ..... Mario Nascimbene
ALEXANDER'S RAGTIME BAND ..... ★★ Alfred Newman†
ALEXANDER: THE OTHER SIDE OF DAWN (TF) ..... Fred Karlin
ALFIE DARLING ..... Alan Price
ALFRED HITCHCOCK PRESENTS (TF) ..... Peter Bernstein
ALFRED HITCHCOCK PRESENTS (TF) ..... John Goux
ALFRED HITCHCOCK PRESENTS (TF) ..... Basil Poledouris
ALFRED HITCHCOCK PRESENTS (TF) ..... Craig Safan
ALFREDO ALFREDO ..... Carlo Rustichelli
ALI BABA AND THE FORTY THIEVES ..... Edward Ward†
ALI-BABA ET LES 40 VOLEURS ..... Paul Misraki†
ALIAS BULLDOG DRUMMOND ..... Louis Levy†
ALIAS NICK BEAL ..... Franz Waxman†
ALIAS THE DEACON ..... Hans J. Salter
ALICE ADAMS ..... Max Steiner†
ALICE DOESN'T LIVE HERE ANYMORE ..... Richard LaSalle
ALICE IN WONDERLAND ..... Sol Kaplan
ALICE IN WONDERLAND ..... Dimitri Tiomkin†
ALICE IN WONDERLAND (AF) ..... ★ Oliver Wallace†
ALICE IN WONDERLAND (TF) ..... Morton Stevens
ALICE OR THE LAST ESCAPADE ..... Pierre Jansen
ALICE OU LA DERNIERE FUGUE ..... Pierre Jansen
ALICE'S ADVENTURES IN WONDERLAND ..... John Barry
ALICE'S RESTAURANT ..... Garry Sherman
ALICE, SWEET ALICE ..... Stephen Lawrence
ALIEN ..... Jerry Goldsmith
ALIEN CONTAMINATION ..... Goblin
ALIEN NATION ..... Curt Sobel
ALIEN PREDATOR ..... Tom Chase
ALIEN PREDATOR ..... Steve Rucker
ALIEN THUNDER ..... Georges Delerue
ALIEN'S RETURN, THE ..... Dan Wyman
ALIENS ..... ★ James Horner
ALIENS ARE COMING, THE (TF) ..... William Goldstein
ALIKI ..... Manos Hadjidakis
ALL ABOUT EVE ..... ★ Alfred Newman†
ALL ASHORE ..... George Duning
ALL CREATURES GREAT AND SMALL (TF) ..... Wilfred Josephs
ALL DOGS GO TO HEAVEN (AF) ..... Ralph Burns
ALL FALL DOWN ..... Alex North
ALL GOD'S CHILDREN (TF) ..... Billy Goldenberg
ALL HANDS ON DECK ..... Cyril J. Mockridge†
ALL I DESIRE ..... Herman Stein
ALL I DESIRE ..... Henry Mancini
ALL IN A NIGHT'S WORK ..... Andre Previn
ALL MINE TO GIVE ..... Max Steiner†
ALL MY SONS ..... Leith Stevens†
ALL NIGHT LONG ..... Richard Hazard
ALL NIGHT LONG ..... Ira Newborn
ALL OF ME ..... Patrick Williams
ALL QUIET ON THE WESTERN FRONT ..... David Broekman†
ALL QUIET ON THE WESTERN FRONT (TF) ..... Allyn Ferguson
ALL SCREWED UP ..... Piero Piccioni
ALL THAT HEAVEN ALLOWS ..... Frank Skinner†
ALL THAT JAZZ ..... ★★ Ralph Burns
ALL THAT MONEY CAN BUY ..... ★★ Bernard Herrmann†
ALL THE BROTHERS WERE VALIANT ..... Miklos Rozsa
ALL THE COLORS OF DARKNESS ..... Bruno Nicolai
ALL THE FINE YOUNG CANNIBALS ..... Jeff Alexander†
ALL THE GOLD IN THE WORLD ..... Georges Van Parys†
ALL THE KING'S HORSES ..... Milan Roder†
ALL THE KING'S MEN ..... Louis Gruenberg†
ALL THE LOVING COUPLES ..... Les Baxter
...ALL THE MARBLES ..... Frank De Vol
ALL THE PRESIDENT'S MEN ..... David Shire
ALL THE RIGHT MOVES ..... David Campbell
ALL THE RIVERS RUN (CMS) ..... Bruce Rowland
ALL THE RIVERS RUN II (CTF) ..... Bruce Rowland
ALL THE WAY ..... Walter Scharf
ALL THE WAY HOME ..... Bernard Green
ALL THESE WOMEN ..... Eric Nordgren
ALL THIS AND HEAVEN TOO ..... Max Steiner†
ALL THROUGH THE NIGHT ..... Adolph Deutsch†
ALL TOGETHER NOW (TF) ..... John Rubinstein
ALL'S FAIR ..... Bill Myers
ALL-AMERICAN CHUMP ..... William Axt†
ALL-AMERICAN CO-ED ..... ★ Edward Ward†
ALL-AMERICAN WOMAN, THE ..... Bruce Kimmel
ALLA MIA CARA MAMMA NEL GIORNO DEL SUO COMPLEANNO ..... Franco Micalizzi
ALLAN QUARTERMAIN AND THE LOST CITY OF GOLD ..... Michael J. Linn

ALLEGHENY UPRISING .... Anthony Collins†
ALLERGIC TO LOVE .... Hans J. Salter
ALLES IN EIMER .... Jurgen Knieper
ALLIGATOR .... Craig Hundley
ALLIGATOR PEOPLE, THE .... Irving Gertz
ALLNIGHTER, THE .... Charles Bernstein
ALLONSANFAN .... Ennio Morricone
ALLORA IL TRENO .... Bruno Nicolai
ALMOST GROWN (TF) .... Craig Safan
ALMOST PARTNERS (TF) .... Paul Chihara
ALMOST PERFECT AFFAIR, AN .... Georges Delerue
ALMOST SUMMER .... Ron Altbach
ALMOST SUMMER .... Charles Lloyd
ALMOST YOU .... Jonathan Elias
ALOHA MEANS GOODBYE (TF) .... Charles Fox
ALOHA SUMMER .... Jesse Frederick
ALOHA SUMMER .... Bennett Salvay
ALOMA OF THE SOUTH SEAS .... Victor Young†
ALONE .... Dmitri Shostakovitch†
ALONE AGAINST ROME .... Armando Trovajoli
ALONE IN THE DARK .... Renato Serio
ALONE IN THE NEON JUNGLE (TF) .... Mark Snow
ALONG CAME A SPIDER (TF) .... David Rose†
ALONG THE GREAT DIVIDE .... David Buttolph†
ALPHABET CITY .... Nile Rodgers
ALPHABET MURDERS, THE .... Ron Goodwin
ALPHAVILLE .... Paul Misraki†
ALRAUNE .... Werner R. Heymann†
ALRAUNE .... Bronislau Kaper†
ALTERED STATES .... John Corigliano
ALTISSIMA PRESSIONE .... Luis Bacalov
ALTISSIMA PRESSIONE .... Ennio Morricone
ALTRI TEMPI .... Alessandro Cicognini†
ALVAREZ KELLY .... John Green†
ALWAYS .... John Williams
ALWAYS A BRIDE .... Benjamin Frankel†
ALWAYS IN MY HEART .... Heinz Roemheld†
ALWAYS TOGETHER .... Werner R. Heymann†
AMANTI .... Manuel De Sica
AMANTI D'OLTRE TOMBA .... Ennio Morricone
AMANTI SENZA AMORE .... Nino Rota†
AMARCORD .... Nino Rota†
AMATEUR GENTLEMAN .... Walter Goehr†
AMATEUR, THE .... Ken Wannberg
AMAZING COLOSSAL MAN, THE .... Albert Glasser
AMAZING DR. CLITTERHOUSE, THE .... Max Steiner†
AMAZING GRACE .... Coleridge-Taylor Perkinson
AMAZING GRACE AND CHUCK .... Elmer Bernstein
AMAZING HOWARD HUGHES, THE (TF) .... Laurence Rosenthal
AMAZING MR. BEECHAM, THE .... Benjamin Frankel†
AMAZING MR. BLUNDEN, THE .... Elmer Bernstein
AMAZING MRS. HOLIDAY, THE .... ★ Hans J. Salter
AMAZING MRS. HOLLIDAY, THE .... ★ Frank Skinner†
AMAZING SPIDERMAN, THE (TF) .... John Spence
AMAZON WOMEN ON THE MOON .... Ira Newborn
AMAZONS (TF) .... Basil Poledouris
AMAZONS, THE .... Riz Ortolani
AMBASSADOR, THE .... Alfi Kabiljo
AMBASSADOR, THE .... Dov Seltzer
AMBER WAVES (TF) .... John Rubinstein
AMBULANCE .... Christopher Komeda†
AMBUSH AT CIMARRON PASS .... Bert A. Shefter
AMBUSH BAY .... Richard LaSalle
AMELIA EARHART (TF .... David Shire
AMERICA .... Leon Pendarvis
AMERICA .... Joseph Carl Breil†
AMERICA - PAESE DI DIO (FD) .... Armando Trovajoli
AMERICA 3000 .... Tony Berg
AMERICA AT THE MOVIES (FD) .... Nelson Riddle†
AMERICA'S DISINHERITED .... Paul Bowles
AMERICA'S PEOPLE .... Andrea Saparoff
AMERICA, AMERICA .... Manos Hadjidakis
AMERICA...COSI NUDA, COSI VIOLENTA .... Bruno Nicolai
AMERICAN ANTHEM .... Alan Silvestri
AMERICAN BUILT .... Jay Ferguson
AMERICAN CHRISTMAS CAROL, AN (TF) .... Hagood Hardy
AMERICAN DREAM (TF) .... Artie Butler
AMERICAN DREAM, AN .... Johnny Mandel
AMERICAN DREAMER .... Lewis Furey
AMERICAN FLYERS .... Lee Ritenour
AMERICAN FLYERS .... Greg Mathieson
AMERICAN FRIEND, THE .... Jurgen Knieper
AMERICAN GEISHA (TF) .... Miles Goodman
AMERICAN GIGOLO .... Giorgio Moroder
AMERICAN GOTHIC .... Alan Parker
AMERICAN GUERRILLA IN THE PHILIPPINES .... Cyril J. Mockridge†
AMERICAN HARVEST (TF) .... Christopher Young
AMERICAN IN PARIS, AN .... ★★ John Green†
AMERICAN JUSTICE .... Paul Chihara
AMERICAN NINJA .... George S. Clinton
AMERICAN NINJA .... Michael J. Linn
AMERICAN NINJA 3: BLOOD HUNT .... George S. Clinton
AMERICAN POP (AF) .... Lee Holdridge
AMERICAN ROMANCE, AN .... Louis Gruenberg†
AMERICAN ROULETTE .... Michael Gibbs
AMERICAN SCREAM, THE .... Robert Cox
AMERICAN SOLDIER, THE .... Peer Raben
AMERICAN SUCCESS COMPANY, THE .... Maurice Jarre
AMERICAN TAIL, AN (AF) .... James Horner
AMERICAN WEREWOLF IN LONDON, AN .... Elmer Bernstein
AMERICANA .... David Carradine
AMERICANA .... Craig Hundley
AMERICANIZATION OF EMILY, THE .... Johnny Mandel
AMERICANO, THE .... Roy Webb†
AMERICATHON .... Earl Brown, Jr.
AMERICATHON .... Tom Scott
AMERIKA (MS) .... Basil Poledouris
AMICI MIEI II .... Carlo Rustichelli
AMICI PER LA PELLE .... Nino Rota†
AMITYVILLE 3-D .... Howard Blake
AMITYVILLE HORROR, THE .... ★ Lalo Schifrin
AMITYVILLE II: THE POSSESSION .... Howard Blake
AMITYVILLE II: THE POSSESSION .... Lalo Schifrin
AMITYVILLE: THE EVIL ESCAPES (TF) .... Rick Conrad
AMMAZZALI TUTTI E TORNA SOLO .... Francesco De Masi
AMOR NON HO, PERO PERO .... Mario Nascimbene
AMORE E GIMNISTICA .... Armando Trovajoli
AMORE LIBERO .... Fabio Frizzi
AMORE MIEI .... Armando Trovajoli
AMORI PERICOLOSI .... Carlo Rustichelli
AMOROUS ADVENTURES OF MOLL FLANDERS, THE .... John Addison
AMOROUS MR. PRAWN, THE .... John Barry
AMOS (TF) .... Georges Delerue
AMSTERDAM AFFAIR .... John Scott
AMY .... Robert F. Brunner
ANA-TA-HAN .... Akira Ifukube
ANASTASIA .... ★ Alfred Newman†
ANASTASIA: THE MYSTERY OF ANNA (TF) .... ☆ Laurence Rosenthal
ANATOMY OF A MURDER .... Duke Ellington†
ANATOMY OF A SEDUCTION (TF) .... Hagood Hardy
ANATOMY OF AN ILLNESS (TF) .... Brad Fiedel
ANCHE SE VOLESSI LAVORARE, CHE COSA FACCIO? .... Ennio Morricone
AND BABY MAKES SIX (TF) .... Fred Karlin
AND BABY MAKES THREE .... George Duning
AND GOD CREATED WOMAN .... Tom Chase
AND GOD CREATED WOMAN .... Steve Rucker
AND GOD CREATED WOMAN .... Paul Misraki†
...AND HOPE TO DIE .... Francis Lai
AND I ALONE SURVIVED (TF) .... Laurence Rosenthal
...AND JUSTICE FOR ALL .... Dave Grusin
AND NO ONE COULD SAVE HER (TF) .... Ron Grainer
AND NOW MIGUEL .... Phillip Lambro
AND NOW MY LOVE .... Francis Lai
AND NOW THE SCREAMING STARTS .... Douglas Gamley
AND NOW TOMORROW .... Victor Young†
AND ONCE UPON A TIME .... Jeffrey Silverman
AND ONE WAS BEAUTIFUL .... Daniele Amfitheatrof†
AND PIGS MUST FLY (TF) .... Trevor Jones
...AND THE BAND PLAYED ON .... Ed Welch
AND THE CHILDREN SHALL LEAD (TF) .... Greg Poree
AND THEN THERE WAS NONE .... Mario Castelnuovo-Tedesco†
...AND YOUR NAME IS JONAH (TF) .... Fred Karlin
ANDERSON TAPES, THE .... Quincy Jones
ANDREI RUBLEV .... Vyecheslav Ovchinnikov
ANDROCLES AND THE LION .... Frederick Hollander†
ANDROID .... Don Preston
ANDROMEDA STRAIN, THE .... Gil Melle
ANDY HARDY COMES HOME .... Van Alexander
ANDY HARDY GETS SPRING FEVER .... Edward Ward†
ANDY HARDY'S DOUBLE LIFE .... Daniele Amfitheatrof†
ANDY HARDY'S PRIVATE SECRETARY .... Herbert Stothart†
ANDY WARHOL'S DRACULA .... Claudio Gizzi
ANDY WARHOL'S FRANKENSTEIN .... Claudio Gizzi
ANGEL .... Craig Safan
ANGEL .... Paddy Meegan
ANGEL AND THE BADMAN .... Richard Hageman†
ANGEL CITY (TF) .... Mark Snow
ANGEL DUSTED (TF) .... James Horner
ANGEL FACE .... Dimitri Tiomkin†
ANGEL HEART .... Trevor Jones
ANGEL III: THE FINAL CHAPTER .... Eric Allaman
ANGEL III: THE FINAL CHAPTER .... Berlin Game
ANGEL III: THE FINAL CHAPTER .... Alan Ett
ANGEL III: THE FINAL CHAPTER .... Don Great
ANGEL IN GREEN (TF) .... Allyn Ferguson
ANGEL ON MY SHOULDER .... Dimitri Tiomkin†
ANGEL ON MY SHOULDER (TF) .... Artie Butler
ANGEL STREET .... Richard Addinsell†
ANGEL TOWN .... Terry Plumeri
ANGEL WHO PAWNED HER HARP, THE .... Antony Hopkins
ANGEL WORE RED, THE .... Bronislau Kaper†
ANGELA .... Georges Delerue
ANGELA .... Henry Mancini
ANGELA .... Mario Nascimbene
ANGELICA .... Jacques Ibert†
ANGELIQUE ET LE ROI .... Michel Magne†
ANGELIQUE ET LE SULTAN .... Michel Magne†
ANGELO, MY LOVE .... Michael Kamen
ANGELS FROM HELL .... Stu Phillips
ANGELS IN THE OUTFIELD .... Daniele Amfitheatrof†
ANGELS OVER BROADWAY .... George Antheil†
ANGELS WASH THEIR FACES .... Adolph Deutsch†
ANGELS WITH DIRTY FACES .... Max Steiner†
ANGKOR-CAMBODIA EXPRESS .... Stelvio Cipriani
ANGRY HILLS, THE .... Richard Rodney Bennett
ANGRY MAN, THE .... Claude Bolling
ANGRY RED PLANET, THE .... Paul Dunlap
ANGRY SILENCE, THE .... Malcolm Arnold
ANIMA PERSA .... Francis Lai
ANIMAL BEHAVIOR .... Cliff Eidelman
ANIMAL FARM (AF) .... Matyas Seiber
ANIMAL KINGDOM, THE .... Max Steiner†
ANIMAL, THE .... Vladimir Cosma
ANIMALS, THE .... Rupert Holmes
ANN VICKERS .... Max Steiner†
ANNA .... Greg Hawkes
ANNA .... Nino Rota†
ANNA AND THE KING OF SIAM .... ★ Bernard Herrmann†
ANNA AND THE WOLVES .... Luis De Pablo
ANNA DE BROOKLYN .... Alessandro Cicognini†
ANNA KARENINA .... Herbert Stothart†
ANNA KARENINA (TF) .... Patrick Gowers
ANNA LUCASTA .... Elmer Bernstein
ANNA LUCASTA .... David Diamond
ANNABEL TAKES A TOUR .... Robert Russell Bennett†
ANNE (TF) .... Vladimir Cosma
ANNE DEVLIN .... Robert Boyle
ANNE OF A THOUSAND DAYS .... ★ Georges Delerue
ANNE OF AVONLEA: THE CONTINUING STORY OF ANNE OF GREEN GABLES (MS) .... Hagood Hardy
ANNE OF GREEN GABLES .... Max Steiner†
ANNE OF GREEN GABLES (MS) .... Hagood Hardy
ANNE OF THE INDIES .... Franz Waxman†
ANNE OF WINDY POPLARS .... Roy Webb†
ANNE-MARIE .... Jacques Ibert†
ANNI DIFICILI .... Nino Rota†
ANNI RUGGENTI .... Piero Piccioni
ANNIBALE .... Carlo Rustichelli
ANNIE .... ★ Ralph Burns
ANNIE GET YOUR GUN .... ★★ Adolph Deutsch†
ANNIE LAURIE .... William Axt†
ANNIHILATOR, THE (TF) .... Udi Harpaz
ANNIHILATOR, THE (TF) .... Sylvester Levay
ANNIHILATORS, THE .... Robert Summers
ANNO DOMINI 1573 .... Alfi Kabiljo
ANNO UNO .... Mario Nascimbene
ANONIMA COCOTTES .... Armando Trovajoli
ANONYMOUS VENETIAN, THE .... Stelvio Cipriani
ANOTHER 48 HOURS .... James Horner
ANOTHER COUNTRY .... Michael Storey
ANOTHER DAWN .... Erich Wolfgang Korngold†
ANOTHER FACE .... Roy Webb†
ANOTHER LIFE .... Vladimir Horunzhy
ANOTHER MAN'S POISON .... John Greenwood†
ANOTHER MAN, ANOTHER CHANCE .... Francis Lai
ANOTHER PART OF THE FOREST .... Daniele Amfitheatrof†
ANOTHER SHORE .... Georges Auric†
ANOTHER THIN MAN .... Edward Ward†
ANOTHER TIME, ANOTHER PLACE .... Douglas Gamley
ANTARTICA .... Vangelis
ANTHONY ADVERSE .... ★★ Erich Wolfgang Korngold†
ANTICHRIST .... Bruno Nicolai

ANTINEA - L'AMANTE DELLA CITTA SEPOLTA ..... Carlo Rustichelli
ANTONY AND CLEOPATRA ..... John Scott
ANY MAN'S DEATH ..... Jeremy Lubbock
ANY NUMBER CAN WIN ..... Michel Magne†
ANY SECOND NOW (TF) ..... Leonard Rosenman
ANY WEDNESDAY ..... George Duning
ANY WHICH WAY YOU CAN ..... Snuff Garrett
ANYONE CAN PLAY ..... Armando Trovajoli
ANYTHING CAN HAPPEN ..... Victor Young†
ANYTHING TO SURVIVE (TF) ..... Michael Conway Baker
ANZACS: THE WAR DOWN UNDER (MS) ..... Bruce Rowland
ANZIO ..... Riz Ortolani
APACHE ..... David Raksin
APACHE CHIEF ..... Albert Glasser
APACHE DRUMS ..... Hans J. Salter
APACHE MASSACRE ..... Richard Markowitz
APACHE RIFLES ..... Richard LaSalle
APACHE TRAIL ..... Sol Kaplan
APACHE UPRISING ..... Jimmie Haskell
APACHE WARRIOR ..... Paul Dunlap
APACHE WOMAN, THE ..... Ronald Stein†
APARAJITO ..... Ravi Shankar
APARTMENT FOR PEGGY ..... David Raksin
APARTMENT ZERO ..... Elia Cmiral
APARTMENT, THE ..... Adolph Deutsch†
APE WOMAN, THE ..... Teo Usuelli
APOCALYPSE DES ANIMA ..... Vangelis
APOCALYPSE NOW ..... Carmine Coppola
APOLOGY (CTF) ..... Maurice Jarre
APOLOGY FOR MURDER ..... Leo Erdody†
APPASSIONATA ..... Piero Piccioni
APPEARANCES (TF) ..... Joel McNeely
APPLE DUMPLING GANG RIDES AGAIN, THE ..... Buddy Baker
APPLE DUMPLING GANG, THE ..... Buddy Baker
APPLE PIE ..... Brad Fiedel
APPLE, THE ..... Coby Recht
APPLE, THE ..... Iris Recht
APPOINTMENT FOR LOVE ..... Frank Skinner†
APPOINTMENT IN BERLIN ..... Werner R. Heymann†
APPOINTMENT WITH A SHADOW ..... Hans J. Salter
APPOINTMENT WITH DANGER ..... Victor Young†
APPOINTMENT WITH DEATH ..... Pino Donaggio
APPOINTMENT WITH FEAR ..... Andrea Saparoff
APPOINTMENT WITH MURDER ..... Karl Hajos†
APPOINTMENT WITH VENUS ..... Benjamin Frankel†
APPOINTMENT, THE ..... John Barry
APPOINTMENT, THE ..... Stu Phillips
APPRENTICE TO MURDER ..... Charles Gross
APPRENTICESHIP OF DUDLEY KRAVITZ, THE ..... Stanley Myers
APRIL FOOL'S DAY ..... Charles Bernstein
APRIL FOOLS, THE ..... Marvin Hamlisch
APRIL MORNING (TF) ..... ☆ Allyn Ferguson
AQUARIANS, THE (TF) ..... Lalo Schifrin
ARAB AND JEW ..... David Spear
ARABELLA ..... Ennio Morricone
ARABESQUE ..... Henry Mancini
ARABIAN ADVENTURE ..... Ken Thorne
ARABIAN NIGHTS ..... ★ Frank Skinner†
ARABISCHE NACHTE ..... Jurgen Knieper
ARACHNOPHOBIA ..... Trevor Jones
ARASHI GA OKA ONIMARU ..... Toru Takemitsu
ARCH OF TRIUMPH ..... Louis Gruenberg†
ARCH OF TRIUMPH (TF) ..... Georges Delerue
ARCHER—FUGITIVE FROM THE EMPIRE, THE (TF) ..... Ian Underwood
ARCHIE: TO RIVERDALE AND BACK AGAIN (TF) ..... Mark Snow
ARCHIMEDE LE CLOCHARD ..... Jean Prodromides
ARE HUSBANDS NECESSARY? ..... Robert Emmett Dolan†
ARE THESE OUR CHILDREN? ..... Max Steiner†
ARE WE WINNING, MOMMY? AMERICA & THE COLD WAR (FD) ..... Wendy Blackstone
ARE YOU IN THE HOUSE ALONE? (TF) ..... Charles Bernstein
ARE YOU WITH IT? ..... Walter Scharf
ARENA, THE ..... Francesco De Masi
ARISE, MY LOVE ..... ★ Victor Young†
ARISTOCATS, THE (AF) ..... George Bruns
ARIZONA ..... ★ Victor Young†
ARIZONA BUSHWACKERS ..... Jimmie Haskell
ARIZONA COLT ..... Francesco De Masi
ARIZONA CYCLONE ..... Hans J. Salter
ARIZONA HEAT ..... Kevin Klinger
ARIZONA LEGION ..... Roy Webb†
ARIZONA RAIDERS ..... Richard LaSalle
ARIZONA SI SCATENO...E LI FECE FUORI TUTTI ..... Bruno Nicolai
ARIZONA TRAIL ..... Hans J. Salter
ARIZONIAN, THE ..... Roy Webb†
ARMED AND DANGEROUS ..... Bill Meyers
ARMED AND DANGEROUS ..... Michael Melvoin
ARMIAMOCI E PARTITE! ..... Carlo Rustichelli
ARMORED ATTACK ..... ★ Aaron Copland
ARMY GIRL ..... ★ Victor Young†
ARMY SURGEON ..... Roy Webb†
ARNELO AFFAIR, THE ..... George Bassman
ARNOLD ..... George Duning
AROUND THE WORLD IN 80 DAYS ..... ★★ Victor Young†
AROUND THE WORLD IN 80 DAYS (MS) ..... Billy Goldenberg
AROUND THE WORLD IN EIGHTY MINUTES ..... Alfred Newman†
AROUND THE WORLD UNDER THE SEA ..... Harry Sukman†
ARRANGEMENT, THE ..... David Amram
ARRANGIATEVI ..... Carlo Rustichelli
ARRETEZ LES TAMBOURS ..... Georges Delerue
ARRIVANO I BERSAGLIERI ..... Armando Trovajoli
ARRIVANO I TITANI ..... Carlo Rustichelli
ARRIVEDERCI PAPA ..... Nino Rota†
ARRIVEDERCI, BABY! ..... Dennis Farnon
ARROW, THE ..... Nino Rota†
ARROWSMITH ..... Alfred Newman†
ARSENAL ..... Vyecheslav Ovchinnikov
ARSENE LUPIN RETURNS ..... Franz Waxman†
ARSENIC AND OLD LACE ..... Max Steiner†
ART OF KILLING ..... Stomu Yamashita
ART OF LOVE, THE ..... Cy Coleman
ARTHUR ..... Burt Bacharach
ARTHUR 2 - ON THE ROCKS ..... Burt Bacharach
ARTHUR HAILEY'S WHEELS (MS) ..... ☆ Morton Stevens
ARTHUR HAILEY'S 'THE MONEYCHANGERS' (MS) ..... Henry Mancini
ARTHUR THE KING (TF) ..... Charles Gross
ARTISTS AND MODELS ..... Walter Scharf
ARTISTS AND MODELS ABROAD ..... Leo Shuken†
ARTURO'S ISLAND ..... Carlo Rustichelli
ARTURO'S ISLAND ..... Nino Rota†
AS GOOD AS MARRIED ..... David Raksin
AS SUMMERS DIE (CTF) ..... Michel Legrand
AS YOU LIKE IT ..... Sir William Walton†
AS YOUNG AS YOU FEEL ..... Cyril J. Mockridge†
ASCENSEUR POUR L'ECHAFAUD ..... Miles Davis
ASH WEDNESDAY ..... Maurice Jarre
ASHANTI ..... Michael Melvoin
ASK ANY GIRL ..... Jeff Alexander†
ASK ME AGAIN (TF) ..... Dick Hyman
ASPEN (MS) ..... Tom Scott
ASPEN (MS) ..... Michael Melvoin
ASPHALT JUNGLE, THE ..... Miklos Rozsa
ASSAM GARDEN, THE ..... Richard Harvey
ASSASSIN (TF) ..... Anthony Guefen
ASSASSIN (TF) ..... Gary Schyman
ASSASSIN, THE ..... Nino Rota†
ASSASSINATION ..... Robert O. Ragland
ASSASSINATION ..... Valentine McCallum
ASSASSINATION BUREAU, THE ..... Ron Grainer
ASSASSINATION OF THE DUC DE GUISE, THE ..... Camille Saint-Saens†
ASSASSINIO SUL TEVERE ..... Carlo Rustichelli
ASSASSINO MADE IN ITALY ..... Armando Trovajoli
ASSAULT ..... Eric Rogers†
ASSAULT AND MATRIMONY (TF) ..... Johnny Mandel
ASSAULT ON A QUEEN ..... Duke Ellington†
ASSAULT ON AGATHON ..... Ken Thorne
ASSAULT ON PRECINCT 13 ..... John Carpenter
ASSAULT ON THE WAYNE (TF) ..... Leith Stevens†
ASSICURASI VERGINE ..... Carlo Rustichelli
ASSIGNED TO DANGER ..... Albert Glasser
ASSIGNMENT K ..... Basil Kirchin
ASSIGNMENT TO KILL ..... William Lava†
ASSIGNMENT—PARIS ..... George Duning
ASSISI UNDERGROUND, THE ..... Pino Donaggio
ASTERIX VS. CAESAR (AF) ..... Vladimir Cosma
ASTONISHED HEART, THE ..... Sir Noel Coward†
ASTRONAUT, THE (TF) ..... Gil Melle
ASYA'S HAPPINESS ..... Vyecheslav Ovchinnikov
ASYLUM ..... Douglas Gamley
AT CLOSE RANGE ..... Patrick Leonard
AT GUNPOINT ..... Carmen Dragon†
AT HOME AMONG STRANGERS ..... Eduard Artemyev
AT LONG LAST LOVE ..... Artie Butler
AT MOTHER'S REQUEST (TF) ..... Charles Gross
AT SWORD'S POINT ..... Roy Webb†
AT THE EARTH'S CORE ..... Michael Vickers
ATLANTA CHILD MURDERS, THE (TF) ..... Billy Goldenberg
ATLANTIC CITY ..... Michel Legrand
ATLANTIC CITY ..... Walter Scharf
ATLANTIS, THE LOST CONTINENT, THE ..... Russell Garcia
ATLAS ..... Ronald Stein†
ATLAS AGAINST THE TSAR ..... Carlo Rustichelli
ATOLL K ..... Paul Misraki†
ATOM AGE VAMPIRE ..... Armando Trovajoli
ATOMIC CITY, THE ..... Leith Stevens†
ATOMIC KID, THE ..... Van Alexander
ATOR ..... Maria Cordio
ATTACK FROM THE SEA ..... Aram Khachaturian†
ATTACK IN THE PACIFIC (FD) ..... David Raksin
ATTACK OF THE 50 FOOT WOMAN, THE ..... Ronald Stein†
ATTACK OF THE CRAB MONSTERS ..... Ronald Stein†
ATTACK OF THE KILLER TOMATOES ..... Gordon Goodwin
ATTACK OF THE KILLER TOMATOES ..... Paul Sundfor
ATTACK OF THE PUPPET PEOPLE ..... Albert Glasser
ATTACK ON FEAR (TF) ..... Tony Berg
ATTACK ON TERROR: THE FBI VERSUS THE KU KLUX KLAN (TF) ..... Mundell Lowe
ATTACK ON THE IRON COAST ..... Gerard Schurmann
ATTACK! ..... Frank De Vol
ATTENTI AL BUFFONE ..... Ennio Morricone
ATTENTION BANDITS ..... Francis Lai
ATTENTION, UME FEMME PEUT EN CACHER UNE AUTRE ..... Philippe Sarde
ATTIC: THE HIDING OF ANNE FRANK, THE (TF) ..... Richard Rodney Bennett
ATTICA (TF) ..... Gil Melle
ATTO DI ACCUSA ..... Carlo Rustichelli
ATTRAGON ..... Akira Ifukube
AU COEUR DE LA VIE ..... Henri Lanoe
AU GRAND BALCON ..... Joseph Kosma†
AU HASARD, BALTHAZAR ..... Jean Wiener†
AU PLAISIR DE DIEU (TF) ..... Antoine Duhamel
AU-DELA DE LA PEUR ..... Alain Gorraguer
AUBERVILLIERS ..... Joseph Kosma†
AUDREY ROSE ..... Michael Small
AUF BIEGEN UND BRECH ..... Jurgen Knieper
AUNT MARY (TF) ..... Arthur B. Rubinstein
AUNTIE MAME ..... Bronislau Kaper†
AURORA (TF) ..... Georges Delerue
AUSTRALIAN DREAM ..... Colin Timms
AUTHOR! AUTHOR! ..... Dave Grusin
AUTOBIOGRAPHY OF MISS JANE PITTMAN, THE (TF) ..... ☆☆ Fred Karlin
AUTOUR D'UNE TROMPETTE (FD) ..... Claude Bolling
AUTUMN LEAVES ..... Hans J. Salter
AUX YEUX DU SOUVENIR ..... Georges Auric†
AVALANCHE ..... William Kraft
AVALANCHE ..... Lucien Moraweck†
AVALANCHE EXPRESS ..... Allyn Ferguson
AVALANCHE PATROL (FD) ..... Malcolm Arnold
AVALON ..... Randy Newman
AVANT LE DELUGE ..... Georges Van Parys†
AVANTI! ..... Carlo Rustichelli
AVEC LA PEAU AUTRES ..... Michel Magne†
AVENGERS, THE ..... Richard Addinsell†
AVENGING ANGEL ..... David Wheatley
AVENGING ANGEL ..... Christopher Young
AVENGING FORCE ..... George S. Clinton
AVIATOR, THE ..... Dominic Frontiere
AVONLEA (CTF) ..... Hagood Hardy
AVVENTURA A CAPRI ..... Piero Piccioni
AVVOLTOI SULLA CITTA ..... Stelvio Cipriani
AWAKENING LAND, THE (MS) ..... ☆ Fred Karlin
AWAKENING OF CANADA, THE (TF) ..... Billy Goldenberg
AWAKENING, THE ..... Claude Bolling
AWAKENINGS ..... Randy Newman
AWAY ALL BOATS ..... Frank Skinner†
AWFUL STORY OF THE NUN OF MONZA, THE ..... Ennio Morricone

B

BEASTS ARE ON THE STREETS, THE (TF) ... Gerald Fried
BEAT ... Carter Burwell
BEAT GENERATION, THE ... Albert Glasser
BEAT GIRL ... John Barry
BEAT THE DEVIL ... Franco Mannino
BEATI E RICCHI ... Luis Bacalov
BEATRICE ... Lili Boulanger
BEATRICE ... Ron Carter
BEAU BRUMMEL ... Richard Addinsell†
BEAU FIXE ... Michel Legrand
BEAU GESTE ... Hans J. Salter
BEAU GESTE ... Alfred Newman†
BEAU IDEAL ... Max Steiner†
BEAU PERE ... Philippe Sarde
BEAUTIFUL BLONDE FROM BASHFUL BEND, THE ... Cyril J. Mockridge†
BEAUTIFUL STRANGER, THE ... Malcolm Arnold
BEAUTIFUL SWINDLERS, THE .. Christopher Komeda†
BEAUTY AND THE BEAST ... Georges Auric†
BEAUTY AND THE BEAST ... Hugo Friedhofer†
BEAUTY AND THE BEAST (TF) ... Don Davis
BEAUTY AND THE BEAST (TF) ... Ron Goodwin
BEAVER VALLEY ... Paul J. Smith†
BEBO'S GIRL ... Carlo Rustichelli
BECAUSE OF HIM ... Miklos Rozsa
BECAUSE OF YOU ... Frank Skinner†
BECAUSE THEY'RE YOUNG ... John Williams
BECAUSE YOU'RE MINE ... John Green†
BECKET ... ★ Laurence Rosenthal
BECKONING FLAME, THE ... Victor Schertzinger†
BECKY SHARP ... Roy Webb†
BED AND BOARD ... Antoine Duhamel
BED OF GRASS ... Manos Hadjidakis
BED OF ROSES ... Max Steiner†
BED SITTING ROOM, THE ... Ken Thorne
BEDAZZLED ... Dudley Moore
BEDEVILLED ... William Alwyn†
BEDFORD INCIDENT, THE ... Gerard Schurmann
BEDKNOBS AND BROOMSTICKS ... ★ Irwin Kostal
BEDLAM ... Roy Webb†
BEDROOM WINDOW, THE ... Patrick Gleeson
BEDROOM WINDOW, THE ... Michael Shrieve
BEDSIDE MANNER ... Emil Newman†
BEDTIME FOR BONZO ... Frank Skinner†
BEDTIME STORY ... Hans J. Salter
BEDTIME STORY ... Werner R. Heymann†
BEEKMANS PLACE (TF) ... Chris Page
BEEN DOWN SO LONG IT LOOKS LIKE UP TO ME ... Garry Sherman
BEER ... Bill Conti
BEETLEJUICE ... Danny Elfman
BEFORE & AFTER ... Steve Bernstein
BEFORE AND AFTER (TF) ... Jimmie Haskell
BEFORE DAWN ... Max Steiner†
BEFORE GOD ... David C. Williams
BEFORE I WAKE ... Leonardo Salzedo
BEFORE THE REVOLUTION ... Gato Barbieri
BEFORE THE REVOLUTION ... Ennio Morricone
BEFORE WINTER COMES ... Ron Grainer
BEG, BORROW OR STEAL ... William Axt†
BEGGARS OF LIFE ... Karl Hajos†
BEGGERMAN, THIEF (TF) ... Eddie Sauter
BEGINNING OF THE END ... Albert Glasser
BEGINNING OR THE END, THE ... Daniele Amfitheatrof†
BEGUILED, THE ... Lalo Schifrin
BEHAVE YOURSELF ... Leigh Harline†
BEHIND ENEMY LINES (TF) ... Jack Chipman
BEHIND ENEMY LINES (TF) ... Steve Lindsey
BEHIND GREEN LIGHTS ... Emil Newman†
BEHIND LOCKED DOORS ... Albert Glasser
BEHIND THE GREAT WALL (FD) ... Angelo Francesco Lavagnino†
BEHIND THE RISING SUN ... Roy Webb†
BEHOLD A PALE HORSE ... Maurice Jarre
BEING THERE ... Johnny Mandel
BEING, THE ... Don Preston
BEIRUT: THE LAST HOME MOVIE (FD) ... Lanny Meyers
BEL AMI ... Hanns Eisler†
BELIEVE IN ME ... Fred Karlin
BELIVERS, THE ... J. Peter Robinson
BELIZAIRE THE CAJUN ... Michael Doucet
BELIZAIRE THE CAJUN ... Howard Shore
BELL FOR ADANO, A ... Alfred Newman†
BELL JAR, THE ... Gerald Fried
BELL, BOOK AND CANDLE ... George Duning
BELLA DI GIORNO, MOGLIE DI NOTTE ... Gianfranco Plenizio
BELLA, RICCA, LIEVE DIFETTO FISICO, CERCA, ANIMA GEMELLA ... Carlo Rustichelli
BELLBOY, THE ... Walter Scharf
BELLE ... Frederic Devreese
BELLE DE JOUR ... Michel Magne†
BELLE LE GRAND ... Victor Young†
BELLE OF THE NINETIES ... Andrea Setaro†
BELLE SOMERS ... Harry Sukman†
BELLE STARR (TF) ... Dana Kaproff
BELLE, MA POVERE ... Piero Piccioni
BELLES OF ST. TRINIAN'S ... Malcolm Arnold
BELLES ON THEIR TOES ... Cyril J. Mockridge†
BELLISSIMA ... Franco Mannino
BELLMAN AND TRUE ... Colin Towns
BELLO, ONESTO, EMIGRATO AUSTRALIA SPOSEREBBE COMPAESANA ILLIBATA ... Piero Piccioni
BELLS ... John Barry
BELLS ARE RINGING ... ★ Andre Previn
BELLS OF ST. MARY'S, THE ... ★ Robert Emmett Dolan†
BELOVED ... Victor Schertzinger†
BELOVED ENEMY ... Alfred Newman†
BELOVED INFIDEL ... Franz Waxman†
BELOVED VAGABOND, THE ... Darius Milhaud†
BELOW THE BELT ... Jerry Fielding†
BELPHEGOR (TF) ... Antoine Duhamel
BELSTONE FOX, THE ... Laurie Johnson
BEN ... Walter Scharf
BEN HUR ... Carl Davis
BEN HUR ... ★★ Miklos Rozsa
BEN-HUR ... William Axt†
BEND OF THE RIVER ... Hans J. Salter
BENEATH THE PLANET OF THE APES ... Leonard Rosenman
BENEATH THE TWELVE-MILE REEF ... Bernard Herrmann†
BENEFICIARY, THE ... Trevor Jones
BENGAL BRIDE ... Hans J. Salter
BENGAL BRIGADE ... Herman Stein
BENGAZI ... Roy Webb†
BENJAMIN ... Gary Wright
BENJI ... Euel Box
BENJI, THE HUNTED ... Euel Box
BENNY AND BARNEY: LAS VEGAS UNDERCOVER (TF) ... Stu Phillips
BENNY GOODMAN STORY, THE ... Henry Mancini
BENNY'S PLACE (TF) ... Harold Wheeler
BENVENUTA ... Frederic Devreese
BERLIN AFFAIR (TF) ... Francis Lai
BERLIN AFFAIR, THE ... Pino Donaggio
BERLIN ALEXANDER PLATZ ... Allan Gray†
BERLIN BLUES ... Mark Mueller
BERLIN CORRESPONDENT ... Emil Newman†
BERLIN EXPRESS ... Frederick Hollander†
BERLIN TUNNEL 21 (TF) ... Dana Kaproff
BERLIN—SYMPHONY OF A GREAT CITY ... Edmund Meisel†
BERMUDA DEPTHS, THE (TF) ... Maury Laws
BERMUDA TRIANGLE, THE ... John Cameron
BERNADETTE ... Francis Lai
BERNADINE ... Lionel Newman†
BERRY GORDY'S THE LAST DRAGON ... Misha Segal
BERSAGLIO ALTEZZA UOMO ... Stelvio Cipriani
BERSERK! ... John Scott
BERT RIGBY, YOU'RE A FOOL ... Ralph Burns
BERYL MARKHAM: A SHADOW ON THE SUN (TF) ... John Addison
BESPOKE OVERCOAT, THE ... Georges Auric†
BEST DEFENSE ... Patrick Williams
BEST FOOT FORWARD ... George Bassman
BEST FRIENDS ... Michel Legrand
BEST KEPT SECRETS (TF) ... Gil Melle
BEST LITTLE GIRL IN THE WORLD, THE (TF) ... Billy Goldenberg
BEST LITTLE WHOREHOUSE IN TEXAS, THE ... Patrick Williams
BEST MAN, THE ... Mort Lindsey
BEST OF ENEMIES, THE ... Nino Rota†
BEST OF EVERYTHING, THE ... Alfred Newman†
BEST OF THE BEST ... Paul Gilman
BEST OF TIMES, THE ... Arthur B. Rubinstein
BEST PLACE TO BE, THE (TF) ... Henry Mancini
BEST REVENGE ... Keith Emerson
BEST SELLER ... Jay Ferguson
BEST THINGS IN LIFE ARE FREE, THE ... ★ Lionel Newman†
BEST YEARS OF OUR LIVES, THE ... ★★ Hugo Friedhofer†
BETHSABEE ... Joseph Kosma†
BETRAYAL ... Dominic Muldowney
BETRAYAL ... John S. Zamecnik†
BETRAYAL (TF) ... Paul Chihara
BETRAYAL (TF) ... Ernest Gold
BETRAYAL FROM THE EAST ... Roy Webb†
BETRAYED ... Bill Conti
BETRAYED ... Walter Goehr†
BETRAYED BY INNOCENCE (TF) ... Charles Fox
BETSY'S WEDDING ... Bruce Broughton
BETSY, THE ... John Barry
BETTER LATE THAN NEVER ... Henry Mancini
BETTER LATE THAN NEVER (TF) ... Charles Fox
BETTER OFF DEAD ... Rupert Hine
BETTY BLUE ... Gabriel Yared
BETTY FORD STORY, THE (TF) ... Arthur B. Rubinstein
BETWEEN FRIENDS ... Matthew McCauley
BETWEEN FRIENDS (CTF) ... James Horner
BETWEEN HEAVEN AND HELL ... ★ Hugo Friedhofer†
BETWEEN MEN ... Victor Schertzinger†
BETWEEN MIDNIGHT AND DAWN ... George Duning
BETWEEN THE DARKNESS AND THE DAWN (TF) ... Dana Kaproff
BETWEEN THE LINES ... Michael Kamen
BETWEEN TWO BROTHERS (TF) ... Richard Hazard
BETWEEN TWO WOMEN ... William Axt†
BETWEEN TWO WOMEN (TF) ... Charles Gross
BETWEEN TWO WORLDS ... Erich Wolfgang Korngold†
BEULAH LAND (TF) ... Allyn Ferguson
BEVERLY HILLS BRATS ... Barry Goldberg
BEVERLY HILLS COP ... Harold Faltermeyer
BEVERLY HILLS COP II ... Harold Faltermeyer
BEVERLY HILLS COWGIRL BLUES (TF) ... Mark Snow
BEVERLY HILLS MADAM (TF) ... Lalo Schifrin
BEWARE OF PITY ... Nicholas Brodzsky†
BEWARE! THE BLOB ... Mort Garson
BEWARE, MY LOVELY ... Leith Stevens†
BEWARE, SPOOKS! ... Leigh Harline†
BEWITCHED ... Bronislau Kaper†
BEWITCHED EYES ... Stanislas Syrewicz
BEYOND A REASONABLE DOUBT ... Herschel Burke Gilbert
BEYOND AND BACK ... Robert Summers
BEYOND DEATH'S DOOR ... Robert Summers
BEYOND EVIL ... Pino Donaggio
BEYOND GLORY ... Victor Young†
BEYOND GOOD AND EVIL ... Daniele Paris
BEYOND MOMBASA ... Humphrey Searle†
BEYOND THE BERMUDA TRIANGLE (TF) ... Harry Sukman†
BEYOND THE BLUE HORIZON ... Victor Young†
BEYOND THE DOOR ... Franco Micalizzi
BEYOND THE FOG ... Kenneth V. Jones
BEYOND THE FOREST ... ★ Max Steiner†
BEYOND THE LIMIT ... Richard Harvey
BEYOND THE LIMIT ... Stanley Myers
BEYOND THE POSEIDON ADVENTURE ... Jerry Fielding†
BEYOND THE REEF ... Francis Lai
BEYOND THE VALLEY OF THE DOLLS ... Stu Phillips
BEYOND THERAPY ... Gabriel Yared
BEYOND THIS PLACE ... Douglas Gamley
BHOWANI JUNCTION ... Miklos Rozsa
BIANCHI CAVALLI D'AGOSTO ... Franco Micalizzi
BICYCLE THIEF, THE ... Alessandro Cicognini†
BIG ... Howard Shore
BIG BAD MAMA II ... Chuck Cirino
BIG BANG, THE (AF) ... Roy Budd
BIG BIRD CAGE, THE ... William Loose
BIG BLACK PILL, THE (TF) ... George Romanis
BIG BLOCKADE, THE ... Richard Addinsell†
BIG BLUE, THE ... Bill Conti
BIG BLUE, THE ... Eric Serra
BIG BOB JOHNSON AND HIS FANTASTIC SPEED CIRCUS (TF) ... Mark Snow
BIG BOUNCE, THE ... Mike Curb
BIG BRAWL, THE ... Lalo Schifrin
BIG BROADCAST OF 1936, THE ... Sigmund Krumgold†
BIG BUS, THE ... David Shire
BIG BUSINESS ... Lee Holdridge
BIG CAPER, THE ... Albert Glasser
BIG CIRCUS, THE ... Bert A. Shefter
BIG CIRCUS, THE ... Paul Sawtell†
BIG CITY ... William Axt†
BIG CLOCK, THE ... Victor Young†
BIG COMBO, THE ... David Raksin
BIG COUNTRY, THE ... ★ Jerome Moross†
BIG DOLL HOUSE, THE ... Les Baxter
BIG EASY, THE ... Brad Fiedel
BIG FIX, THE ... Bill Conti
BIG GAMBLE, THE ... Maurice Jarre

BIG GAME, THE ... Nathaniel Shilkret†
BIG GUNDOWN, THE ... Ennio Morricone
BIG GUY ... Hans J. Salter
BIG HAND FOR THE LITTLE LADY, A ... David Raksin
BIG HANGOVER, THE ... Adolph Deutsch†
BIG HEAT, THE ... Daniele Amfitheatrof†
BIG HEAT, THE ... Mischa Bakaleinikoff †
BIG HOUSE, U.S.A. ... Paul Dunlap
BIG HURT, THE ... Allan Zavod
BIG JACK ... Herbert Stothart†
BIG JAKE ... Elmer Bernstein
BIG JIM McLAIN ... Paul Dunlap
BIG JIM McLAIN ... Emil Newman†
BIG KNIFE, THE ... Frank De Vol
BIG LAND, THE ... David Buttolph†
BIG LIFT, THE ... Alfred Newman†
BIG MAD MAMA ... David Grisman
BIG MAN ON CAMPUS ... Joseph Vitarelli
BIG MOUTH, THE ... Harry Betts
BIG NIGHT, THE ... Richard LaSalle
BIG NIGHT, THE ... Lyn Murray†
BIG NOISE, THE ... Cyril J. Mockridge†
BIG OPERATOR, THE ... Van Alexander
BIG PARADE, THE ... Carl Davis
BIG PARADE, THE ... William Axt†
BIG PICTURE, THE ... David Nichtern
BIG PUNCH, THE ... William Lava†
BIG RED ... Oliver Wallace†
BIG RED ONE, THE ... Dana Kaproff
BIG RIPOFF, THE (TF) ... Richard DeBenedictis
BIG RISK, THE ... Georges Delerue
BIG ROSE (TF) ... Robert Prince
BIG SCORE, THE ... Jay Chattaway
BIG SENTIMENTS MAKE FOR GOOD SPORTS ... Vladimir Cosma
BIG SHOT, THE ... Adolph Deutsch†
BIG SHOTS ... Bruce Broughton
BIG SKY, THE ... Dimitri Tiomkin†
BIG SLEEP, THE ... Jerry Fielding†
BIG SLEEP, THE ... Max Steiner†
BIG STEAL, THE ... Leigh Harline†
BIG STORE, THE ... George Bassman
BIG STREET, THE ... Roy Webb†
BIG TOP PEE WEE ... Danny Elfman
BIG TOWN, THE ... Michael Melvoin
BIG TREES, THE ... Heinz Roemheld†
BIG TROUBLE ... Bill Conti
BIG TROUBLE IN LITTLE CHINA ... John Carpenter
BIG WEDNESDAY ... Basil Poledouris
BIGAMIST, THE ... Leith Stevens†
BIGFOOT (TF) ... Bruce Rowland
BIGGER SPLASH, A ... Patrick Gowers
BIGGER THAN LIFE ... David Raksin
BIGGLES ... Stanislas
BIGGLES ... Stanislas Syrewicz
BIKINI SHOP, THE ... Robert Summers
BILITIS ... Francis Lai
BILL & TED'S EXCELLENT ADVENTURE ... David Newman
BILL (TF) ... William Kraft
BILL AND COO ... David Buttolph†
BILL OF DIVORCEMENT, A ... Max Steiner†
BILL OF DIVORCEMENT, A ... Roy Webb†
BILL: ON HIS OWN (TF) ... Lee Curreri
BILLIE ... Dominic Frontiere
BILLION DOLLAR BRAIN ... Richard Rodney Bennett
BILLION DOLLAR HOBO ... Michael Leonard
BILLION DOLLAR THREAT, THE (TF) ... Richard Shores
BILLY BUDD ... Antony Hopkins
BILLY GALVIN ... Joel Rosenbaum
BILLY JACK GOES TO WASHINGTON ... Elmer Bernstein
BILLY LIAR ... Richard Rodney Bennett
BILLY TWO HATS ... John Scott
BILLY: PORTRAIT OF A STREET KID (TF) ... Fred Karlin
BILOXI BLUES ... Georges Delerue
BINGO LONG TRAVELING ALL STARS AND MOTOR KINGS, THE ... William Goldstein
BIOGRAPHY OF A BACHELOR GIRL ... Herbert Stothart†
BIRCH INTERVAL ... Leonard Rosenman
BIRD ... Lennie Niehaus
BIRD OF PARADISE ... Daniele Amfitheatrof†
BIRD OF PARADISE ... Max Steiner†
BIRD ON A WIRE ... Hans Zimmer
BIRD WATCH, THE ... Jean Musy
BIRD WITH THE CRYSTAL PLUMAGE, THE ... Ennio Morricone
BIRDMAN OF ALCATRAZ ... Elmer Bernstein
BIRDMEN, THE (TF) ... David Rose†
BIRDS AND THE BEES, THE ... Walter Scharf
BIRDS DO IT, BEES DO IT ... ★ Gerald Fried
BIRDS OF PREY (TF) ... Jack Elliott
BIRDS OF PREY (TF) ... Allyn Ferguson
BIRDS, THE ... Bernard Herrmann†
BIRDS, THE BEES AND THE ITALIANS, THE ... Carlo Rustichelli
BIRDY ... Peter Gabriel
BIRIBI ... Mikis Theodorakis
BIRTH OF A NATION, THE ... Joseph Carl Briel†
BIRTH OF A NATION, THE ... Carli D. Elinor†
BIRTH OF THE BEATLES (TF) ... Carl Davis
BIRTH OF THE BLUES ... ★ Robert Emmett Dolan†
BISCUIT EATER, THE ... Robert F. Brunner
BISCUIT EATER, THE ... Frederick Hollander†
BISHOP MISBEHAVES, THE ... Edward Ward†
BISHOP'S ROOM, THE ... Armando Trovajoli
BISHOP'S WIFE, THE ... ★ Hugo Friedhofer†
BISTURI, MAFIA BIANCA ... Riz Ortolani
BIT BETWEEN THE TEETH ... Antoine Duhamel
BITE THE BULLET ... ★ Alex North
BITTER FRUIT ... Joseph Kosma†
BITTER HARVEST (TF) ... Fred Karlin
BITTER SWEET ... Herbert Stothart†
BITTER TEA OF GENERAL YEN, THE ... W. Franke Harling†
BITTERSWEET LOVE ... Ken Wannberg
BJ & THE BEAR ... John Cacavas
BLACK 13 ... Carlo Rustichelli
BLACK AND WHITE IN COLOR ... Pierre Bachelet
BLACK ANGEL ... Frank Skinner†
BLACK ARROW (TF) ... Stanley Myers
BLACK ARROW, THE ... Paul Sawtell†
BLACK BART ... Hugo Friedhofer†
BLACK BART ... Leith Stevens†
BLACK BEAUTY ... Lionel Bart
BLACK BEAUTY ... Dimitri Tiomkin†
BLACK BEAUTY (MS) ... John Addison
BLACK BELLY OF THE TARANTULA, THE ... Ennio Morricone
BLACK BIRD, THE ... Jerry Fielding†
BLACK CASTLE, THE ... Hans J. Salter
BLACK CAT, THE ... Pino Donaggio
BLACK CAT, THE ... Hans J. Salter
BLACK CAT, THE ... Charles Henderson†
BLACK CAT, THE ... Charles Previn†
BLACK CAT, THE ... Heinz Roemheld†
BLACK CAT, THE ... Frank Skinner†
BLACK CAULDRON, THE (AF) ... Elmer Bernstein
BLACK CHRISTMAS ... Carl Zittrer
BLACK DIAMONDS ... Hans J. Salter
BLACK EYE ... Mort Garson
BLACK FRIDAY ... Hans J. Salter
BLACK FRIDAY ... Charles Henderson†
BLACK FRIDAY ... Charles Previn†
BLACK FRIDAY ... Frank Skinner†
BLACK GIRL ... Ed Bogas
BLACK GIRL ... Ray Shanklin
BLACK HOLE, THE ... John Barry
BLACK HORSE CANYON ... Hans J. Salter
BLACK HORSE CANYON ... Herman Stein
BLACK JACK ... Bob Pegg
BLACK JACK ... Jerry Styne
BLACK KNIGHT , THE ... John Addison
BLACK MAMA, WHITE MAMA ... Harry Betts
BLACK MARBLE, THE ... Maurice Jarre
BLACK MARKET BABY (TF) ... Richard Bellis
BLACK MARKET BABY (TF) ... George Wilkins
BLACK MOON RISING ... Lalo Schifrin
BLACK NARCISSUS ... Brian Easdale
BLACK NOON (TF) ... George Duning
BLACK OAK CONSPIRACY ... Don Peake
BLACK ORCHID, THE ... Alessandro Cicognini†
BLACK PARACHUTE, THE ... Mario Castelnuovo-Tedesco†
BLACK PATCH ... Jerry Goldsmith
BLACK PIRATE, THE ... Carlo Rustichelli
BLACK RAIN ... Toru Takemitsu
BLACK RAIN ... Hans Zimmer
BLACK ROSE, THE ... Richard Addinsell†
BLACK SABBATH ... Les Baxter
BLACK SCORPION, THE ... Bert A. Shefter
BLACK SCORPION, THE ... Paul Sawtell†
BLACK SHEEP, THE ... Luis Bacalov
BLACK SHIELD OF FALWORTH, THE ... Hans J. Salter
BLACK SHIELD OF FALWORTH, THE ... Herman Stein
BLACK SLEEP, THE ... Les Baxter
BLACK SPURS ... Jimmie Haskell
BLACK STALLION RETURNS, THE ... Georges Delerue
BLACK STALLION, THE ... Carmine Coppola
BLACK SUNDAY ... Les Baxter
BLACK SUNDAY ... John Williams
BLACK SWAN, THE ... ★ Alfred Newman†
BLACK TENT, THE ... William Alwyn†
BLACK TUESDAY ... Paul Dunlap
BLACK VEIL FOR LISA, A ... Richard Markowitz
BLACK WATER GOLD (TF) ... Mike Curb
BLACK WIDOW ... Michael Small
BLACK WIDOW ... Leigh Harline†
BLACK WINDMILL, THE ... Roy Budd
BLACK ZOO ... Paul Dunlap
BLACKBEARD'S GHOST ... Robert F. Brunner
BLACKBEARD, THE PIRATE ... Victor Young†
BLACKMAIL ... Hubert Bath†
BLACKMAIL ... Edward Ward†
BLACKOUT ... Don Davis
BLACKOUT ... Laurence Rosenthal
BLACKOUT ... Richard Addinsell†
BLACKOUT (CTF) ... Laurence Rosenthal
BLACKSNAKE ... William Loose
BLACULA ... Gene Page
BLADE ... John Cacavas
BLADE IN HONG KONG (TF) ... David Kurtz
BLADE RUNNER ... Vangelis
BLAGUE DANS LE COIN ... Alain Gorraguer
BLAISE PASCAL (TF) ... Mario Nascimbene
BLAME IT ON RIO ... Ken Wannberg
BLAME IT ON RIO ... Oscar Castro Neves
BLAST OFF ... John Scott
BLAZE ... Bennie Wallace
BLAZE OF NOON ... Adolph Deutsch†
BLAZING SADDLES ... John Morris
BLEAK HOUSE (MS) ... Geoffrey Burgon
BLEAK MORNING ... Dmitri Kabalevsky†
BLESS THE BEASTS AND CHILDREN ... Perry Botkin
BLIND ADVENTURE ... Max Steiner†
BLIND AMBITION (MS) ... Fred Karlin
BLIND AMBITION (MS) ... Walter Scharf
BLIND DATE ... Richard Rodney Bennett
BLIND DATE ... Henry Mancini
BLIND DATE ... Stanley Myers
BLIND DESIRE ... Georges Auric†
BLIND FAITH (TF) ... Laurence Rosenthal
BLIND FEAR ... Michael Melvoin
BLIND FURY ... J. Peter Robinson
BLIND GODDESS ... Bernard Green
BLIND JUSTICE (TF) ... Miles Goodman
BLIND WITNESS (TF) ... Robert Alcivar
BLINDED BY THE LIGHT (TF) ... Jonathan Tunick
BLINDFOLD ... Lalo Schifrin
BLISS OF MRS. BLOSSOM, THE ... Riz Ortolani
BLITHE SPIRIT ... Richard Addinsell†
BLOB, THE ... Michael Hoenig
BLOCKADE ... ★ Werner Janssen
BLOCKHEADS ... ★ T. Marvin Hatley†
BLOND CHEAT ... Roy Webb†
BLONDE FEVER ... Nathaniel Shilkret†
BLONDE FOR A DAY ... Leo Erdody†
BLONDE ICE ... Irving Gertz
BLONDE INSPIRATION ... Bronislau Kaper†
BLONDE RANSOM ... Frank Skinner†
BLONDE SAVAGE ... Leo Erdody†
BLONDIE HAS SERVANT TROUBLE ... Leigh Harline†
BLONDIE KNOWS BEST ... Mischa Bakaleinikoff †
BLONDIE ON A BUDGET ... Leigh Harline†
BLONDIE PLAYS CUPID ... Leigh Harline†
BLONDY ... Stelvio Cipriani
BLOOD ALLEY ... Roy Webb†
BLOOD AND BLACK LACE ... Carlo Rustichelli
BLOOD AND HONOR: YOUTH UNDER HITLER (MS) ... Ernst Bradner
BLOOD AND ORCHIDS (MS) ... Mark Snow
BLOOD AND ROSES ... Jean Prodromides
BLOOD AND SAND ... Alfred Newman†
BLOOD BEACH ... Gil Melle
BLOOD DEMON, THE ... Peter Thomas
BLOOD DINER ... Don Preston
BLOOD FEAST ... Herschell Gordon Lewis
BLOOD FEUD (TF) ... Fred Steiner
BLOOD FIEND ... Elisabeth Luytens†
BLOOD FOR DRACULA ... Claudio Gizzi
BLOOD FROM THE MUMMY'S TOMB ... Tristram Cary
BLOOD IN THE STREETS ... Ennio Morricone
BLOOD MAD ... Robert O. Ragland
BLOOD MONEY ... Gerald Fried
BLOOD MONEY ... Robert J. Walsh
BLOOD MONEY ... Alfred Newman†
BLOOD OF A POET, THE ... Georges Auric†
BLOOD OF DRACULA ... Paul Dunlap
BLOOD OF FRANKENSTEIN ... William Lava†
BLOOD OF HEROES, THE ... Todd Boekelheide

BLOOD OF OTHERS, THE (CTF) ... Francois Dompierre
BLOOD OF THE WARRIORS ... Armando Trovajoli
BLOOD ON SATAN'S CLAW ... Marc Wilkinson
BLOOD ON THE ARROW ... Richard LaSalle
BLOOD ON THE MOON ... Roy Webb†
BLOOD ON THE SUN ... Miklos Rozsa
BLOOD ORGY ... HerschellGordon Lewis
BLOOD ORGY OF THE SHE DEVILS ... Carl Zittrer
BLOOD ROYAL (TF) ... John Scott
BLOOD SABBATH ... Les Baxter
BLOOD SIMPLE ... Carter Burwell
BLOOD SONG ... Robert J. Walsh
BLOOD SPORT (TF) ... John Davis
BLOOD SPORT (TF) ... Randy Edelman
BLOOD TIES (CTF) ... Celso Valli
BLOOD TYPE BLUE ... Masaru Sato
BLOOD VIRGIN, THE ... John Scott
BLOOD VOWS: THE STORY OF A MAFIA WIFE (TF) ... William Goldstein
BLOODBROTHERS ... Elmer Bernstein
BLOODEATERS ... Ted Shapiro
BLOODHOUNDS OF BROADWAY ... David Raksin
BLOODHOUNDS OF BROADWAY ... Jonathan Sheffer
BLOODSPORT ... Paul Hertzog
BLOODSUCKING FREAKS ... Michael Sahl
BLOODY BIRTHDAY ... Arlon Ober
BLOSSOMS IN THE DUST ... Herbert Stothart†
BLOW OUT ... Pino Donaggio
BLOWBACK ... Wendy Blackstone
BLOWING WILD ... Dimitri Tiomkin†
BLOWUP ... Herbie Hancock
BLUE ... Manos Hadjidakis
BLUE AND THE GRAY, THE (MS) ... ☆ Bruce Broughton
BLUE ANGEL, THE ... Hugo Friedhofer†
BLUE ANGEL, THE ... Frederick Hollander†
BLUE ANGELS ... Fred Myrow
BLUE BIRD, THE ... Irwin Kostal
BLUE BIRD, THE ... Andrey Petrovic
BLUE BIRD, THE ... Alfred Newman†
BLUE CITY ... Ry Cooder
BLUE COLLAR ... Jack Nitzsche
BLUE COUNTRY, THE ... Gerard Anfosso
BLUE DAHLIA, THE ... Victor Young†
BLUE De VILLE (TF) ... Don Felder
BLUE DENIM ... Bernard Herrmann†
BLUE FIN ... Michael Carlos
BLUE IGUANA, THE ... Ethan James
BLUE KNIGHT, THE (TF) ... Nelson Riddle†
BLUE LAGOON, THE ... Basil Poledouris
BLUE LIGHTNING, THE (TF) ... Frank Strangio
BLUE MAX, THE ... Jerry Goldsmith
BLUE MONEY (TF) ... Richard Hartley
BLUE MONKEY ... Patrick Coleman
BLUE MONKEY ... Paul Novotny
BLUE MOON ... Shirley Walker
BLUE MURDER AT ST. TRINIAN'S ... Malcolm Arnold
BLUE NIGHT, THE (TF) ... Henry Mancini
BLUE SKIES ... ★ Robert Emmett Dolan†
BLUE SKIES AGAIN ... John Kander
BLUE STEEL ... Brad Fiedel
BLUE THUNDE ... Arthur B. Rubinstein
BLUE VEIL, THE ... Franz Waxman†
BLUE VELVET ... Angelo Badalamenti
BLUEBEARD ... Ennio Morricone
BLUEBEARD ... Leo Erdody†
BLUEBEARD'S EIGHTH WIFE ... Frederick Hollander†
BLUEBEARD'S EIGHTH WIFE ... Werner R. Heymann†
BLUEGRASS (TF) ... Don Davis
BLUEGRASS (TF) ... Mark Snow
BLUEPRINT FOR MURDER, A ... David Raksin
BLUEPRINT FOR ROBBERY ... Nathan Van Cleave†
BLUES BROTHERS, THE ... Ira Newborn
BLUES IN THE NIGHT ... Heinz Roemheld†
BLUFFING IT (TF) ... Brad Fiedel
BLUME IN LOVE ... Bill Conti
BOARDWALK ... Joel Dorn
BOAT, THE ... Klaus Doldinger
BOATNIKS, THE ... Robert F. Brunner
BOB & CAROL & TED & ALICE ... Quincy Jones
BOB AND SALLY ... Milton Rosen
BOB MATHIAS STORY, THE ... Leith Stevens†
BOBBIE JO AND THE OUTLAW ... Barry De Vorzon
BOBBY DEERFIELD ... Dave Grusin
BOBO, THE ... Francis Lai
BOCCACCIO ... Carlo Rustichelli
BOCCACCIO '70 ... Armando Trovajoli
BOCCACCIO '70 ... Nino Rota†
BODY AND SOUL ... Webster Lewis
BODY AND SOUL ... Hugo Friedhofer†
BODY CHEMISTRY ... Terry Plumeri
BODY DISAPPEARS, THE ... Bernhard Kaun†
BODY DOUBLE ... Pino Donaggio
BODY HEAT ... John Barry
BODY OF EVIDENCE (TF) ... John Cacavas
BODY SLAM ... John D'Andrea
BODY SLAM ... Michael Lloyd
BODY SNATCHER, THE ... Roy Webb†
BOEING BOEING ... Neal Hefti
BOFORS GUN, THE ... Carl Davis
BOGGY CREEK II ... Frank McKelvey
BOGIE: THE LAST HERO (TF) ... Charles Bernstein
BOKYO ... Akira Ifukube
BOLD AND THE BRAVE, THE ... Herschel Burke Gilbert
BOLERO ... Peter Bernstein
BOLERO ... Francis Lai
BOLERO ... Andrea Setaro†
BOMBARDIER ... Roy Webb†
BOMBAY CLIPPER ... Hans J. Salter
BOMBER'S MOON ... David Buttolph†
BOMBERS B-52 ... Leonard Rosenman
BON VOYAGE, CHARLIE BROWN (AND DON'T COME BACK) ... Ed Bogas
BONA COME IL PANO ... Stelvio Cipriani
BONANZA: THE NEXT GENERATION (TF) ... Bob Cobert
BONE ... Gil Melle
BONFIRE OF THE VANITIES ... Dave Grusin
BONGO MAN ... Jimmy Cliff
BONJOUR CINEMA ... Claude Bolling
BONJOUR TRISTESSE ... Georges Auric†
BONNIE AND CLYDE ... Charles Strouse
BONNIE PARKER STORY, THE ... Ronald Stein†
BONZO GOES TO COLLEGE ... Frank Skinner†
BOOGENS, THE ... Robert Summers
BOOGEY MAN, THE ... Tim Krog
BOOGEYMAN II ... Craig Hundley
BOOGEYMAN II ... Tim Krog
BOOM TOWN ... Franz Waxman†
BOOM! ... John Barry
BOOMERANG ... David Buttolph†
BOOST, THE ... Stanley Myers
BOOTLEGGERS ... Jaime Mendoza-Nava
BOOTS MALONE ... Elmer Bernstein
BOP GIRL ... Les Baxter
BOP GIRL GOES CALYPSO ... Les Baxter
BORA BORA ... Les Baxter
BORA BORA ... Riz Ortolani
BORDER CAFE ... Nathaniel Shilkret†
BORDER FEUD ... Albert Glasser
BORDER G-MAN ... Roy Webb†
BORDER INCIDENT ... Andre Previn
BORDER RADIO ... Dave Alvin
BORDER RANGERS ... Albert Glasser
BORDER RIVER ... Herman Stein
BORDER, THE ... Ry Cooder
BORDERLINE ... Hans J. Salter
BORDERLINE ... Gil Melle
BORGIA STICK, THE (TF) ... Kenyon Hopkins
BORIS AND NATASHA ... David Kitay
BORN AGAIN ... Les Baxter
BORN AMERICAN ... Richard Mitchell
BORN BEAUTIFUL (TF) ... Brad Fiedel
BORN FREE ... ★★ John Barry
BORN IN EAST L.A. ... Lee Holdridge
BORN INNOCENT (TF) ... Fred Karlin
BORN LOSERS ... Mike Curb
BORN OF FIRE ... Colin Towns
BORN ON THE FOURTH OF JULY ... ★ John Williams
BORN TO BE BAD ... Frederick Hollander†
BORN TO BE BAD ... Alfred Newman†
BORN TO BE SOLD (TF) ... Johnny Harris
BORN TO KILL ... Michael Franks
BORN TO RACE Ross ... Vannelli
BORN TO RUN ... Ron Goodwin
BORN YESTERDAY ... Frederick Hollander†
BORROWERS, THE (TF) ... Billy Byers
BORROWERS, THE (TF) ... Rod McKuen
BORSALINO ... Claude Bolling
BORSALINO AND CO. ... Claude Bolling
BOSS OF BOOMTOWN ... Hans J. Salter
BOSS OF HANGTOWN MESA ... Hans J. Salter
BOSS' SON, THE ... Richard Markowitz
BOSS'S WIFE, THE ... Bill Conti
BOSS, THE ... Albert Glasser
BOSTONIANS, THE ... Richard Robbins
BOTANY BAY ... Franz Waxman†
BOTTOM OF THE BOTTLE, THE ... Leigh Harline†
BOTTSCHEFT DER GOETTER ... Peter Thomas
BOULEVARD NIGHTS ... Lalo Schifrin
BOUND FOR GLORY ... ★★ Leonard Rosenman
BOUNTY HUNTER, THE ... David Buttolph†
BOUNTY KILLER, THE ... Ronald Stein†
BOUNTY, THE ... Vangelis
BOURNE IDENTITY, THE (TF) ... ☆ Laurence Rosenthal
BOWERY TO BROADWAY ... Edward Ward†
BOWERY, THE ... Alfred Newman†
BOY AND THE BRIDGE ... Malcolm Arnold
BOY AND THE PIRATES, THE ... Albert Glasser
BOY FROM INDIANA ... Lud Gluskin†
BOY FROM OKLAHOMA, THE ... Max Steiner†
BOY FROM THE SUBURBS ... Nino Rota†
BOY IN BLUE, THE ... Roger Webb
BOY IN THE PLASTIC BUBBLE, THE (TF) ... Mark Snow
BOY IN THE TREE ... Quincy Jones
BOY KUMASENU, THE ... Elisabeth Luytens†
BOY NAMED CHARLIE BROWN, A (AF) ... Rod McKuen
BOY NEXT DOOR, THE ... David Shire
BOY ON A DOLPHIN ... ★ Hugo Friedhofer†
BOY TEN FEET TALL, A ... Les Baxter
BOY TEN FEET TALL, A ... Tristram Cary
BOY WHO CAUGHT A CROOK, THE ... Richard LaSalle
BOY WHO COULD FLY, THE ... Bruce Broughton
BOY WHO CRIED WEREWOLF, THE ... Ted Stovall
BOY WHO DRANK TOO MUCH, THE (TF) ... Michael Small
BOY WHO STOLE A MILLION, THE ... Tristram Cary
BOY WITH GREEN HAIR, THE ... Leigh Harline†
BOY'S NIGHT OUT ... Frank De Vol
BOY'S RANCH ... Nathaniel Shilkret†
BOY, DID I GET THE WRONG NUMBER! ... Richard LaSalle
BOYFRIEND SCHOOL ... Michael Gore
BOYS FROM BRAZIL, THE ... ★ Jerry Goldsmith
BOYS IN BLUE, THE ... Ed Welch
BOYS IN COMPANY C, THE ... Jaime Mendoza-Nava
BOYS NEXT DOOR, THE ... George S. Clinton
BOYS TOWN ... Edward Ward†
BOYS WILL BE BOYS (TF) ... Rik Howard
BRADDOCK: MISSING IN ACTION III ... Jay Chattaway
BRADY'S ESCAPE ... Charles Gross
BRADYS, THE (TF) ... Laurence Juber
BRAIN WAVES ... Robert O. Ragland
BRAIN, THE ... Georges Delerue
BRAIN, THE ... Kenneth V. Jones
BRAINSTORM ... James Horner
BRAINWASH ... Richard Markowitz
BRAKER (TF) ... Brad Fiedel
BRAMBLE BUS, THE ... Leonard Rosenman
BRANCALEONE ALLE CROCIATE ... Carlo Rustichelli
BRAND NEW LIFE, A (TF ... ☆ Billy Goldenberg
BRAND X ... Ken Lauber
BRANDED ... Roy Webb†
BRANNIGAN ... Dominic Frontiere
BRASHER DOUBLOON, THE ... David Buttolph†
BRASS (TF) ... Joe Sherman
BRASS BOTTLE, THE ... Bernard Green
BRASS LEGEND, THE ... Paul Dunlap
BRASS TARGET ... Laurence Rosenthal
BRAVADOS, THE ... Hugo Friedhofer†
BRAVADOS, THE ... Lionel Newman†
BRAVE LITTLE TOASTER, THE (TF) ... David Newman
BRAVE NEW WORLD (TF) ... Paul Chihara
BRAVE ONE, THE ... Victor Young†
BRAVO ALFA ... Maurice Jarre
BRAVOS, THE (TF) ... Leonard Rosenman
BRAZIL ... Michael Kamen
BRAZIL ... ★ Walter Scharf
BREACH OF CONTRACT ... John Davis
BREAD, LOVE AND DREAMS ... Alessandro Cicognini†
BREAK OF DAWN ... Mark Adler
BREAK OF HEARTS ... Max Steiner†
BREAK TO FREEDOM ... Malcolm Arnold
BREAKDOWN ... Paul Dunlap
BREAKER MORANT ... Eric Cook
BREAKFAST AT TIFFANY'S ... ★★ Henry Mancini
BREAKFAST CLUB, THE ... Gary Chang
BREAKFAST IN PARIS ... Brian May
BREAKHEART PASS ... Jerry Goldsmith
BREAKIN' ... Michael Boyd
BREAKIN' ... Gary Remal
BREAKIN' 2: ELECTRIC BOOGALOO ... Michael J. Linn
BREAKING ALL THE RULES ... Paul Zaza
BREAKING AWAY ... ★ Patrick Williams
BREAKING IN ... Michael Gibbs
BREAKING POINT (CTF) ... J.A.C. Redford
BREAKING THE ICE ... ★ Victor Young†
BREAKING THE SOUND BARRIER ... Malcolm Arnold

C

CAHILL, U.S. MARSHALL .... Elmer Bernstein
CAINE MUTINY, THE .... ★ Max Steiner†
CAIRO .... Herbert Stothart†
CAL .... Mark Knopfler
CALABOOSE .... Edward Ward†
CALAMITY JANE (TF) .... Fred Karlin
CALCUTTA .... Victor Young†
CALENDAR GIRL MURDERS (TF) .... Brad Fiedel
CALENDAR OF THE YEAR, THE ...... Benjamin Britten†
CALIFORNIA .... Victor Young†
CALIFORNIA DREAMING .... Fred Karlin
CALIFORNIA GIRLS (TF) .... Mark Snow
CALIFORNIA KID, THE (TF) .... Luchi DeJesus
CALIFORNIA REICH, THE (FD) .... Craig Safan
CALIFORNIA SPLIT .... Phyllis Shotwell
CALIFORNIA SPLIT .... John Williams
CALIFORNIA SUITE .... Claude Bolling
CALIGULA .... Paul Clemente
CALL A MESSENGER .... Hans J. Salter
CALL ME .... David Frank
CALL ME MADAM .... ★ Alfred Newman†
CALL ME MISTER .... Leigh Harline†
CALL NORTHSIDE 777 .... Alfred Newman†
CALL OF THE FLESH .... Herbert Stothart†
CALL OF THE JUNGLE .... Albert Glasser
CALL OF THE WILD .... Carlo Rustichelli
CALL OF THE WILD, THE .... Alfred Newman†
CALL OF THE WILD, THE (TF) .... Peter Matz
CALL TO DANGER (TF) .... Laurence Rosenthal
CALL-GIRL BUSINESS, THE .... Armando Trovajoli
CALL-GIRLS OF ROME .... Armando Trovajoli
CALLAN .... Wilfred Josephs
CALLE MAYOR .... Joseph Kosma†
CALLER, THE .... Richard H. Band
CALLIE & SON (TF) .... Billy Goldenberg
CALLING DR. DEATH .... Hans J. Salter
CALLING DR. DEATH .... Paul Sawtell†
CALLING DR. DEATH .... Frank Skinner†
CALLING DR. GILLESPIE .... Daniele Amfitheatrof†
CALMOS .... Georges Delerue
CALORE IN PROVINCIA .... Carlo Savina
CALYPSO (FD) .... Angelo Francesco Lavagnino†
CAMARENA STORY, THE (TF) .... Charles Bernstein
CAMERON'S CLOSET .... Harry Manfredini
CAMILLE .... William Axt†
CAMILLE .... Herbert Stothart†
CAMILLE (TF) .... ☆☆ Allyn Ferguson
CAMILLE CLAUDEL .... Gabriel Yared
CAMMINA CAMMINA .... Bruno Nicolai
CAMORRA .... Manuel De Sica
CAMOUFLAGE .... Wojciech Kilar
CAMOUFLAGE .... Richard Addinsell†
CAMP FOLLOWERS, THE .... Mario Nascimbene
CAMP ON BLOOD ISLAND, THE .... Gerard Schurmann
CAMPANE A MARTELLO .... Nino Rota†
CAMPINE .... Armando Trovajoli
CAMPUS MAN .... James Newton Howard
CAN BE DONE, AMIGO .... Luis Bacalov
CAN SHE BAKE A CHERRY PIE? .... Karen Black
CAN YOU FEEL ME DANCING? (TF) ...... Johnny Harris
CAN YOU HEAR THE LAUGHTER? THE
  STORY OF FREDDIE PRINZE (TF) .... Peter Matz
CAN'T BUY ME LOVE .... Robert Folk
CAN'T HELP SINGING .... Hans J. Salter
CAN'T STOP THE MUSIC .... Jacques Morali
CAN-CAN .... ★ Nelson Riddle†
CANADIAN PACIFIC .... Dimitri Tiomkin†
CANADIANS, THE .... Ken Darby
CANADIANS, THE (MS) .... Hagood Hardy
CANDIDATE PER UN ASSASSINO .... Bill Conti
CANDLESHOE .... Ron Goodwin
CANDY .... Dave Grusin
CANICULE .... Francis Lai
CANNABIS .... Serge Gainsbourg
CANNERY ROW .... Jack Nitzsche
CANNIBAL HOLOCAUST .... Riz Ortolani
CANNIBAL ORGY .... Ronald Stein†
CANNIBAL WOMEN IN THE
  AVOCADO JUNGLE OF DEATH .... Carl Dante
CANNON (TF) .... Robert Drasnin
CANNON FOR CORDOBA .... Elmer Bernstein
CANNONBALL .... David A. Axelrod
CANNONBALL RUN II .... Al Capps
CANNONBALL RUN II .... Steve Dorff
CANNONBALL RUN,THE .... Snuff Garrett
CANTERBURY TALE, A .... Allan Gray†
CANTERBURY TALES, THE .... Ennio Morricone
CANTERVILLE GHOST, THE .... George Bassman
CANTERVILLE GHOST, THE (TF) .... Howard Blake
CANYON CROSSROADS .... George Bassman
CANYON PASSAGE .... Frank Skinner†
CANZONI, CANZONI, CANZONI .... Carlo Rustichelli
CAPE FEAR .... Bernard Herrmann†
CAPER OF THE GOLDEN BULLS, THE .... Vic Mizzy
CAPITAL NEWS (TF) .... Jan Hammer
CAPITAN DEMONIO .... Mario Nascimbene
CAPONE .... David Grisman
CAPRICCIO ALL'ITALIANA .... Piero Piccioni
CAPRICE .... Frank De Vol
CAPRICES .... Georges Van Parys†
CAPRICORN ONE .... Jerry Goldsmith
CAPTAIN AMERICA (TF) .... Mike Post
CAPTAIN AMERICA (TF) .... Pete Carpenter†
CAPTAIN AMERICA II (TF) .... Mike Post
CAPTAIN AMERICA II (TF) .... Pete Carpenter†
CAPTAIN BLACK JACK .... Joseph Kosma†
CAPTAIN BLOOD .... Erich Wolfgang Korngold†
CAPTAIN BOYCOTT .... William Alwyn†
CAPTAIN CAREY, U.S.A. .... Hugo Friedhofer†
CAPTAIN CLEGG .... Don Banks
CAPTAIN EDDIE .... Cyril J. Mockridge†
CAPTAIN FANTASMA, IL
  TESORO DELLE INDIE .... Carlo Rustichelli
CAPTAIN FROM CASTILE .... ★ Alfred Newman†
CAPTAIN FURY .... T. Marvin Hatley†
CAPTAIN HORATIO HORNBLOWER ..... Robert Farnon
CAPTAIN HURRICANE .... Roy Webb†
CAPTAIN IS A LADY, THE .... Bronislau Kaper†
CAPTAIN JANUARY .... Louis Silvers†
CAPTAIN JOHN SMITH AND
  POCAHONTAS .... Albert Glasser
CAPTAIN KIDD .... ★ Werner Janssen
CAPTAIN KIDD AND THE
  SLAVE GIRL .... Paul Sawtell†
CAPTAIN KRONOS:
  VAMPIRE HUNTER .... Laurie Johnson
CAPTAIN LIGHTFOOT .... Hans J. Salter
CAPTAIN LIGHTFOOT .... Herman Stein
CAPTAIN NEMO AND THE
  UNDERWATER CITY .... Angela Morley
CAPTAIN PIRATE .... George Duning
CAPTAIN SINDBAD .... Michel Michelet†
CAPTAIN SIROCCO .... Nino Rota†
CAPTAIN'S PARADISE, THE .... Malcolm Arnold
CAPTAIN'S TABLE, THE .... Frank Cordell†
CAPTAINS AND THE KINGS (MS) ... ☆ Elmer Bernstein
CAPTAINS COURAGEOUS .... Franz Waxman†
CAPTAINS COURAGEOUS (TF) .... Allyn Ferguson
CAPTAINS OF THE CLOUDS .... Max Steiner†
CAPTIVE CITY .... Jerome Moross†
CAPTIVE CITY, THE .... Emil Newman†
CAPTIVE HEART, THE .... Alan Rawsthorne†
CAPTIVE HEARTS .... David Benoit
CAPTIVE HEARTS .... Osamu Kitajima
CAPTIVE WILD WOMAN .... Hans J. Salter
CAPTURE OF GRIZZLY
  ADAMS, THE (TF) .... Robert Summers
CAPTURE, THE .... Daniele Amfitheatrof†
CAR WASH .... Norman Whitfield
CAR, THE .... Leonard Rosenman
CARAVAGGIO .... Mary Phillips
CARAVAGGIO .... Simon Fisher Turner
CARAVAN .... Werner R. Heymann†
CARAVAN TO VACCARES .... Stanley Myers
CARAVANS .... Mike Batt
CARBINE WILLIAMS .... Conrad Salinger†
CARBON COPY .... Bill Conti
CARD, THE .... William Alwyn†
CARDINAL RICHELIEU .... Alfred Newman†
CARDINAL, THE .... Jerome Moross†
CARE BEARS MOVIE II: A NEW
  GENERATION (AF) .... Patricia Cullen
CARE BEARS MOVIE, THE (AF) .... Patricia Cullen
CARE BEARS MOVIE, THE (AF) .... John Sebastian
CAREER .... Robert Russell Bennett†
CAREER .... Franz Waxman†
CAREFUL HE MIGHT HEAR YOU .... Ray Cook†
CAREFUL, SOFT SHOULDER .... Leigh Harline†
CARELESS YEARS, THE .... Leith Stevens†
CARETAKER, THE .... Ron Grainer
CARETAKERS, THE .... Elmer Bernstein
CAREY TREATMENT, THE .... Roy Budd
CARGO TO CAPETOWN .... George Duning
CARI MOSTRI DEL MARE .... Carlo Savina
CARIBBEAN MYSTERY, THE .... David Buttolph†
CARLTON BROWN OF THE F.O. .... John Addison
CARLY'S WEB (TF) .... Richard Lewis Warren
CARMEN .... Paco De Lucia
CARMEN JONES .... ★ Herschel Burke Gilbert
CARNABY, M.D. .... John Scott
CARNALITA .... Carlo Savina
CARNIVAL .... Nicholas Brodzsky†
CARNY .... Alex North
CARO MICHELE .... Nino Rota†
CARO PAPA .... Manuel De Sica
CAROLINE CHERIE .... Georges Garvarentz
CAROLINE CHERIE .... Georges Auric†
CAROLINE? (TF) .... ☆ Charles Bernstein
CARPETBAGGERS, THE .... Elmer Bernstein
CARPOOL (TF) .... Jimmie Haskell
CARRIE .... Pino Donaggio
CARRIE .... David Raksin
CARROT QUEEN, THE .... Luis De Pablo
CARRY ON AGAIN, DOCTOR .... Eric Rogers†
CARRY ON CAMPING .... Eric Rogers†
CARRY ON CLEO .... Eric Rogers†
CARRY ON COWBOY .... Eric Rogers†
CARRY ON DICK .... Eric Rogers†
CARRY ON DOCTOR .... Eric Rogers†
CARRY ON EMMANUELLE .... Eric Rogers†
CARRY ON SCREAMING .... Eric Rogers†
CARRY ON SPYING .... Eric Rogers†
CARRY ON UP THE JUNGLE .... Eric Rogers†
CARRY ON...UP THE KHYBER .... Eric Rogers†
CARS THAT ATE PARIS, THE .... Bruce Smeaton
CARS THAT EAT PEOPLE, THE .... Bruce Smeaton
CARSON CITY .... David Buttolph†
CARTER'S ARMY (TF) .... Fred Steiner
CARTES SUR TABLE .... Paul Misraki†
CARTHAGE IN FLAMES .... Mario Nascimbene
CARTIER AFFAIR, THE (TF) .... Arthur B. Rubinstein
CARTOUCHE .... Georges Delerue
CARVE HER NAME WITH PRIDE .... William Alwyn†
CASABLANCA .... ★ Max Steiner†
CASANOVA .... Georges Delerue
CASANOVA .... Nino Rota†
CASANOVA '70 .... Armando Trovajoli
CASANOVA (TF) .... Michel Legrand
CASANOVA IN BURLESQUE .... Walter Scharf
CASANOVA'S BIG NIGHT .... Lyn Murray†
CASE AGAINST
  BROOKLYN, THE .... Mischa Bakaleinikoff †
CASE AGAINST FERRO, THE .... Georges Delerue
CASE AGAINST PAUL RYKER, THE .... John Williams
CASE FOR A YOUNG HANGMAN, A .... Zdenek Liska
CASE OF DEADLY FORCE, A (TF) .... Paul Chihara
CASE OF DR. LAURENT, THE .... Joseph Kosma†
CASE OF THE HILLSIDE
  STRANGLER, THE (TF) .... Gil Melle
CASE OF THE MUKKINESE
  BATTLEHORN, THE .... Edwin Astley
CASEY'S SHADOW .... Patrick Williams
CASH McCALL .... Max Steiner†
CASH ON DEMAND .... Wilfred Josephs
CASINO (TF) .... Mark Snow
CASINO MURDER CASE .... Dimitri Tiomkin†
CASINO ROYALE .... Burt Bacharach
CASQUE D'OR .... Georges Van Parys†
CASS TIMBERLANE .... Roy Webb†
CASSANDRA CROSSING, THE .... Jerry Goldsmith
CAST A GIANT SHADOW .... Elmer Bernstein
CAST A LONG SHADOW .... Gerald Fried
CAST THE FIRST STONE (TF) .... Ira Newborn
CASTAWAY .... Stanley Myers
CASTAWAY COWBOY, THE .... Robert F. Brunner
CASTAWAYS OF GILLIGAN'S
  ISLAND, THE (TF) .... Gerald Fried
CASTLE KEEP .... Michel Legrand
CASTLE OF EVIL .... Paul Dunlap
CASTLE OF THE LIVING
  DEAD, THE .... Angelo Francesco Lavagnino†
CASTLE OF THE SPIDER'S WEB, THE .... Masaru Sato
CASTLE ON THE HUDSON .... Adolph Deutsch†
CASUAL SEX? .... Van Dyke Parks
CASUALTIES OF WAR .... Ennio Morricone
CAT AND MOUSE .... Francis Lai
CAT AND MOUSE (TF) .... Ron Grainer
CAT AND THE CANARY, THE .... Steven Cagan
CAT AND THE CANARY, THE .... Ernst Toch†
CAT AND THE FIDDLE, THE .... Herbert Stothart†
CAT BALLOU .... Frank De Vol
CAT CHASER .... Ted Cochran
CAT CREATURE, THE (TF) .... Leonard Rosenman
CAT CREEPS, THE .... Paul Sawtell†
CAT FROM OUTER SPACE, THE .... Lalo Schifrin
CAT O'NINE TAILS .... Ennio Morricone
CAT PEOPLE .... Giorgio Moroder
CAT PEOPLE .... Roy Webb†
CAT WOMEN OF THE MOON .... Elmer Bernstein
CAT'S EYE .... Alan Silvestri
CAT'S PAW, THE .... Alfred Newman†
CATACOMBS .... Pino Donaggio

CHOKE CANYON ... Sylvester Levay
CHOPPING MALL ... Chuck Cirino
CHORUS LINE, A ... Ralph Burns
CHORUS OF DISAPPROVAL, A ... John Du Prez
CHOSEN SURVIVORS ... Fred Karlin
CHOSEN, THE ... Elmer Bernstein
CHOUANS ... Georges Delerue
CHRIST OF THE OCEAN ... Bruno Nicolai
CHRIST STOPPED AT EBOLI ... Piero Piccioni
CHRISTIAN LICORICE STORE, THE ... Lalo Schifrin
CHRISTIANE F. ... Jurgen Knieper
CHRISTINA PRINCESSE DE L'EROTISME ... Bruno Nicolai
CHRISTINE ... John Carpenter
CHRISTINE ... Alan Howarth
CHRISTINE CROMWELL (TF) ... Lee Holdridge
CHRISTINE JORGENSEN STORY, THE ... Bert A. Shefter
CHRISTINE JORGENSEN STORY, THE ... Paul Sawtell†
CHRISTMAS CAROL, A ... Franz Waxman†
CHRISTMAS CAROL, A ... Richard Addinsell†
CHRISTMAS CAROL, A (TF) ... Nick Bicat
CHRISTMAS COMES TO WILLOW CREEK (TF) ... Charles Fox
CHRISTMAS EVE ... Heinz Roemheld†
CHRISTMAS EVE (TF) ... Johnny Mandel
CHRISTMAS GIFT, THE (TF) ... Allyn Ferguson
CHRISTMAS HOLIDAY ... ★ Hans J. Salter
CHRISTMAS IN CONNECTICUT ... Frederick Hollander†
CHRISTMAS LILLIES OF THE FIELD (TF) ... George Aliceson Tipton
CHRISTMAS STAR, THE (TF) ... Ralph Burns
CHRISTMAS STORY, A ... Carl Zittrer
CHRISTMAS STORY, A ... Paul Zaza
CHRISTMAS THAT ALMOST WASN'T, THE ... Bruno Nicolai
CHRISTMAS TO REMEMBER, A (TF) ... Jimmie Haskell
CHRISTMAS TREE, THE ... Georges Auric†
CHRISTMAS VISITOR, THE (TF) ... Bruce Rowland
CHRISTMAS WITHOUT SNOW, A (TF) ... Ed Bogas
CHRISTOPHER COLUMBUS ... Sir Arthur Bliss†
CHRISTOPHER COLUMBUS (MS) ... Riz Ortolani
CHRISTOPHER STRONG ... Max Steiner†
CHRONICLE OF A CRIME ... Alfi Kabiljo
CHRONIQUE PROVINCIALE ... Maurice Jarre
CHU CHU AND THE PHILLY FLASH ... Pete Rugolo
CHUBASCO ... William Lava†
CHUD II: BUD THE CHUD ... Nicholas Pike
CHUKA ... Leith Stevens†
CHUMP AT OXFORD, A ... T. Marvin Hatley†
CHURCH MOUSE, THE ... W. Franke Harling†
CHUSHINGURA ... Akira Ifukube
CI RISIAMO, VERO PROVVIDENZA? ... Ennio Morricone
CI RISIAMO, VERO PROVVIDENZA? ... Bruno Nicolai
CIMARRON ... Max Steiner†
CIMARRON ... Franz Waxman†
CINCINATTI KID, THE ... Lalo Schifrin
CINDERELLA ... Andrew Belling
CINDERELLA (AF) ... ★ Paul J. Smith†
CINDERELLA (AF) ... ★ Oliver Wallace†
CINDERELLA JONES ... Frederick Hollander†
CINDERELLA LIBERTY ... ★ John Williams
CINDERFELLA ... Walter Scharf
CINEMA D'ALTRI TEMPI ... Franco Mannino
CINEMA PARADISO ... Ennio Morricone
CINEMATOGRAPHIE ... Michel Portal
CINTURA DI CASTITA ... Carlo Rustichelli
CIRCLE OF CHILDREN, A (TF) ... Nelson Riddle†
CIRCLE OF DECEIT ... Maurice Jarre
CIRCLE OF IRON ... Bruce Smeaton
CIRCLE OF LOVE ... Francis Lai
CIRCLE OF LOVE ... Michel Magne†
CIRCLE OF POWER ... Richard Markowitz
CIRCLE OF TWO ... Paul Hoffert
CIRCLE OF VIOLENCE: A FAMILY DRAMA (TF) ... Gil Melle
CIRCONSTANCES ATTENUANTES ... Georges Van Parys†
CIRCUMSTANTIAL EVIDENCE ... David Buttolph†
CIRCUS OF HORRORS ... Franz Reizenstein†
CIRCUS WORLD ... Dimitri Tiomkin†
CIRCUS, THE ... Charles Chaplin†
CISCO KID IN OLD NEW MEXICO, THE ... Albert Glasser
CISCO KID RETURNS, THE ... Albert Glasser
CITADEL, THE ... Louis Levy†
CITIZEN KANE ... ★ Bernard Herrmann†
CITIZENS BAND ... Bill Conti
CITTA DI NOTTE ... Nino Rota†
CITTA VIOLENTA ... Ennio Morricone
CITY ACROSS THE RIVER ... Walter Scharf
CITY BENEATH THE SEA ... Milton Rosen
CITY BENEATH THE SEA ... Herman Stein
CITY BENEATH THE SEA ... Henry Mancini
CITY BENEATH THE SEA (TF) ... Richard LaSalle
CITY FOR CONQUEST ... Max Steiner†
CITY HEAT ... Lennie Niehaus
CITY IN FEAR (TF) ... Leonard Rosenman
CITY IS DARK, THE ... David Buttolph†
CITY KILLER (TF) ... John Rubinstein
CITY LIGHTS ... Charles Chaplin†
CITY OF FEAR ... Jerry Goldsmith
CITY OF SILENT MEN ... Leo Erdody†
CITY OF THE DEAD ... Douglas Gamley
CITY OF THE DEAD, THE ... Kenneth V. Jones
CITY OF THE WALKING DEAD ... Stelvio Cipriani
CITY OF WOMEN ... Luis Bacalov
CITY ON FIRE! ... Matthew McCauley
CITY STREETS ... Sidney Cutner†
CITY UNDER THE SEA, THE ... Stanley Black
CITY WITHOUT MEN ... David Raksin
CITY, THE (D) ... Aaron Copland
CITY, THE (TF) ... ohn Elizalde
CIVILIZATION ... Victor Schertzinger†
CLAIRE DE FEMME ... Jean Musy
CLAIRVOYANT, THE ... Arthur Benjamin†
CLAN OF THE CAVE BEAR ... Alan Silvestri
CLARA'S HEART ... Dave Grusin
CLARETTA ... Gerard Schurmann
CLARETTA AND BEN ... Carlo Rustichelli
CLASH BY NIGHT ... Roy Webb†
CLASH OF LOYALTIES ... Ron Goodwin
CLASH OF THE TITANS ... Laurence Rosenthal
CLASS ... Elmer Bernstein
CLASS ... Tom Scott
CLASS ACTION ... James Horner
CLASS CRUISE (TF) ... Mark Davis
CLASS OF 1984, THE ... Lalo Schifrin
CLASS OF 1999 ... Michael Hoenig
CLASS OF MISS MacMICHAELS, THE ... Stanley Myers
CLASS OF '44 ... David Shire
CLASS OF '63 (TF) ... Tom Scott
CLASSIFIED LOVE (TF) ... Artie Butler
CLAUDIA ... Alfred Newman†
CLAUDIA AND DAVID ... Cyril J. Mockridge†
CLAUDINE ... Curtis Mayfield
CLAUDINE A L'ECOLE ... Paul Misraki†
CLEAN AND SOBER ... Gabriel Yared
CLEAN MACHINE , THE (TF) ... Cameron Allan
CLEAN SLATE ... Philippe Sarde
CLEO FROM 5 TO 7 ... Michel Legrand
CLEOPATRA ... ★ Alex North
CLEOPATRA JONES ... Dominic Frontiere
CLEOPATRA JONES ... J.J. Johnson
CLEOPATRA JONES AND THE CASINO OF GOLD ... Dominic Frontiere
CLEREMBARD ... Vladimir Cosma
CLICKETY-CLACK ... Toru Takemitsu
CLIMAX, THE ... Carlo Rustichelli
CLIMAX, THE ... Edward Ward†
CLIMB AN ANGRY MOUNTAIN (TF) ... George Duning
CLINTON AND NADINE (CTF) ... Jan Hammer
CLIVE OF INDIA ... Alfred Newman†
CLOAK & DAGGER ... Brian May
CLOAK AND DAGGER ... Max Steiner†
CLOCK, THE ... George Bassman
CLOCKMAKER OF ST.PAUL, THE ... Philippe Sarde
CLOCKWISE ... George Fenton
CLOCKWORK ORANGE, A ... Wendy Carlos
CLONE MASTER, THE (TF) ... Glenn Paxton
CLOSE ENCOUNTERS OF THE THIRD KIND ... ★ John Williams
CLOSE TO MY HEART ... Max Steiner†
CLOSE-UP ... Jerome Moross†
CLOUD DANCER ... Fred Karlin
CLOUDED YELLOW, THE ... Benjamin Frankel†
CLOUDS AT SUNSET ... Toru Takemitsu
CLOWN, THE ... David Rose†
CLOWNS, THE ... Nino Rota†
CLUB MED (TF) ... Peter Bernstein
CLUB PARADISE ... Van Dyke Parks
CLUB PARADISE ... David Mansfield
CLUE ... John Morris
CLUE OF THE NEW PIN, THE ... Ron Goodwin
CLUNY BROWN ... Cyril J. Mockridge†
COACH ... Anthony Harris
COACH OF THE YEAR (TF) ... Mike Post
COACH OF THE YEAR (TF) ... Pete Carpenter†
COAL FACE ... Benjamin Britten†
COAL MINER'S DAUGHTER ... Owen Bradley
COAST TO COAST ... Charles Bernstein
COASTAL COMMAND ... Ralph Vaughan Williams†
COBRA ... Sylvester Levay
COBRA STRIKES, THE ... Albert Glasser
COBRA VERDE ... Popol Vuh
COBRA WOMAN ... Edward Ward†
COBWEB, THE ... Leonard Rosenman
COCA COLA KID, THE ... William Motzig
COCAINE AND BLUE EYES (TF) ... Morton Stevens
COCAINE: ONE MAN'S SEDUCTION (TF) ... Brad Fiedel
COCK OF THE AIR ... Alfred Newman†
COCKEYED CAVALIERS ... Roy Webb†
COCKEYED COWBOYS OF CALICO COUNTY ... Lyn Murray†
COCKLESHELL HEROES, THE ... John Addison
COCKTAIL ... J. Peter Robinson
COCOON ... James Horner
COCOON: THE RETURN ... James Horner
CODE NAME: DIAMOND HEAD (TF) ... Morton Stevens
CODE NAME: EMERALD ... John Addison
CODE OF SILENCE ... David Frank
CODE OF VENGEANCE (TF) ... Don Peake
CODE RED (TF) ... Richard LaSalle
CODENAME: KYRIL (TF) ... Alan Lisk
COFFEE, TEA OR ME? (TF) ... Morton Stevens
COFFY ... Roy Ayers
COHEN & TATE ... Bill Conti
COIFFEUR POUR DAMES ... Paul Misraki†
COL CUORE IN GOLA ... Armando Trovajoli
COLD CUTS ... Philippe Sarde
COLD FEET ... Tom Bahler
COLD FEET ... Todd Rundgren
COLD HOMELAND ... Jurgen Knieper
COLD NIGHT'S DEATH, A (TF) ... Gil Melle
COLD ROOM, THE (TD) ... Michael Nyman
COLD SASSY TREE (CTF) ... Brad Fiedel
COLD STEEL ... David A. Jackson
COLD SWEAT ... Michel Magne†
COLD TURKEY ... Randy Newman
COLD WIND IN AUGUST,A ... Gerald Fried
COLLECTOR, THE ... Maurice Jarre
COLLEGE RHYTHM ... Sigmund Krumgold†
COLLEGE SCANDAL ... Andrea Setaro†
COLLEGES AT WAR (FD) ... Gail Kubik†
COLOMBO GOES TO THE GUILLOTINE (TF) ... John Cacavas
COLONEL BLIMP ... Allan Gray†
COLONEL EFFINGHAM'S RAID ... Cyril J. Mockridge†
COLOR OF MONEY, THE ... Robbie Robertson
COLOR PURPLE, THE ... ★ Chris Boardman
COLOR PURPLE, THE ... ★ Jorge Calandrelli
COLOR PURPLE, THE ... ★ Andrae Crouch
COLOR PURPLE, THE ... ★ Jack Hayes
COLOR PURPLE, THE ... ★ Jerry Hey
COLOR PURPLE, THE ... ★ Quincy Jones
COLOR PURPLE, THE ... ★ Randy Kerber
COLOR PURPLE, THE ... ★ Jeremy Lubbock
COLOR PURPLE, THE ... ★ Joel Rosenbaum
COLOR PURPLE, THE ... ★ Caiphus Semenya
COLOR PURPLE, THE ... ★ Fred Steiner
COLOR PURPLE, THE ... ★ Rod Temperton
COLORADO TERRITORY ... David Buttolph†
COLORS ... Herbie Hancock
COLOSSUS OF NEW YORK, THE ... Fred Steiner
COLOSSUS OF NEW YORK, THE ... Nathan Van Cleave†
COLOSSUS OF RHODES, THE ... Angelo Francesco Lavagnino†
COLOSSUS: THE FORBIN PROJECT ... Michel Colombier
COLPITA DA IMPROVVISO BENESSERE ... Luis Bacalov
COLPO DOPPIO DEL CAMALEONTE D'ORO ... Carlo Rustichelli
COLPO IN CANNA ... Luis Bacalov
COLT .45 ... William Lava†
COLUMBO: MURDER - SELF-PORTRAIT (TF) ... Patrick Williams
COLUMN SOUTH ... Herman Stein
COLUMN SOUTH ... Henry Mancini
COMA ... Jerry Goldsmith
COMANCHE ... Herschel Burke Gilbert
COMANCHE STATION ... Mischa Bakaleinikoff†
COMANCHE TERRITORY ... Frank Skinner†
COMANCHEROS, THE ... Elmer Bernstein
COMANDEMENTI PER UN GANGSTER ... Ennio Morricone
COMBAT HIGH (TF) ... Robert Folk

COMBAT SQUAD ... Paul Dunlap
COME AND GET IT ... Alfred Newman†
COME BACK, LITTLE SHEBA ... Franz Waxman†
COME BLOW YOUR HORN ... Nelson Riddle†
COME FLY WITH ME ... Lyn Murray†
COME HOME AND MEET MY WIFE ... Enzo Jannacci
COME IMPARI AD AMARE LE DONNE ... Ennio Morricone
COME LIVE WITH ME ... Herbert Stothart†
COME NEXT SPRING ... Max Steiner†
COME PERSI LA GUERRA ... Nino Rota†
COME PLAY WITH ME ... Ennio Morricone
COME SCOPERSI L'AMERICA ... Nino Rota†
COME SEE THE PARADISE ... Randy Edelman
COME SEPTEMBER ... Hans J. Salter
COME TO THE STABLE ... Cyril J. Mockridge†
COME TO YOUR SENSES ... Rod McKuen
COME-ON, THE ... Paul Dunlap
COMEBACK ... Eric Burdon
COMEBACK (TF) ... Klaus Doldinger
COMEBACK KID, THE (TF) ... Barry De Vorzon
COMEBACK TRAIL, THE ... Igo Kantor
COMEBACK, THE ... Stanley Myers
COMEBACK, THE (TF) ... Craig Safan
COMEDIANS, THE ... Laurence Rosenthal
COMEDY OF TERRORS, THE ... Les Baxter
COMES A HORSEMAN ... Michael Small
COMET OVER BROADWAY ... Heinz Roemheld†
COMFORT AND JOY ... Mark Knopfler
COMFORT OF STRANGERS, THE ... Angelo Badalamenti
COMIC, THE ... Jack Elliott
COMIN' AT YA! ... Carlo Savina
COMING, THE ... Arthur Kempel
COMING ATTRACTIONS ... Murphy Dunne
COMING OUT OF THE ICE (TF) ... Maurice Jarre
COMING TO AMERICA ... Nile Rodgers
COMING UP ROSES ... Michael Storey
COMMAND 5 (TF) ... Lalo Schifrin
COMMAND DECISION ... Miklos Rozsa
COMMAND, THE ... Dimitri Tiomkin†
COMMANDO ... James Horner
COMMANDO ... Angelo Francesco Lavagnino†
COMMANDOS STRIKE AT DAWN ... ★ Louis Gruenberg†
COMME EN CHEVEU SUR LA SOUPE ... Georges Van Parys†
COMME LA LUNE ... Philippe Sarde
COMME UN BOOMERANG ... Georges Delerue
COMMENT QU'ELLE EST ... Paul Misraki†
COMMENT REUSSIR EN AMOUR ... Georges Garvarentz
COMMENT TROUVEZ-VOUS MA SOEUR? ... Serge Gainsbourg
COMMUNION ... Eric Clapton
COMMUNION ... Stephen Lawrence
COMMUNION ... Allan Zavod
HOUSE OF FRANKENSTEIN ... Paul Dessau†
COMPANY COMEDY, THE (TF) ... Tom Scott
COMPANY OF WOLVES, THE ... George Fenton
COMPANY SHE KEEPS, THE ... Leigh Harline†
COMPETITION, THE ... ★ Lalo Schifrin
COMPROMISING POSITIONS ... Brad Fiedel
COMPTES A REBOURS ... Georges Delerue
COMPULSION ... Lionel Newman†
COMPUTER WORE TENNIS SHOES, THE ... Robert F. Brunner
COMPUTERSIDE (TF) ... Jack Elliott
COMPUTERSIDE (TF) ... Allyn Ferguson
COMRADE X ... Bronislau Kaper†
COMRADES ... David Graham
COMRADES ... Hans Werner Henze
CONAN THE BARBARIAN ... Basil Poledouris
CONAN THE DESTROYER ... Basil Poledouris
CONCEALED ENEMIES (TF) ... ☆ Jonathan Tunick
CONCERTO PER PISTOLA SOLISTA ... Francesco De Masi
CONCORDE - AIRPORT '79, THE ... Lalo Schifrin
CONCORDE AFFAIR '79 ... Stelvio Cipriani
CONCRETE BEAT (TF) ... Artie Kane
CONCRETE JUNGLE, THE ... Joseph Conlan
CONCRETE JUNGLE, THE ... John Dankworth
CONDEMNED OF ALTONA, THE ... Dmitri Shostakovitch†
CONDEMNED WOMEN ... Roy Webb†
CONDOMINIUM (TF) ... Gerald Fried
CONDORMAN ... Henry Mancini
CONDOTTIERI ... Giuseppe Becce†
CONDUCT UNBECOMING ... Stanley Myers
CONE OF SILENCE ... Gerard Schurmann
CONFESSIONE DI UN COMMISSARIO ... Riz Ortolani
CONFESSIONS OF A NAZI SPY ... Max Steiner†
CONFESSIONS OF A POLICE CAPTAIN ... Riz Ortolani
CONFESSIONS OF AN OPIUM EATER ... Albert Glasser
CONFESSOR, THE ... Chico Hamilton
CONFIDENCES POUR CONFIDENCES ... Vladimir Cosma
CONFIDENTIAL AGENT ... Franz Waxman†
CONFIDENTIAL REPORT ... Paul Misraki†
CONFIDENTIALLY YOURS ... Georges Delerue
CONFIDENTIALLY YOURS ... David Rose†
CONFIRM OR DENY ... David Buttolph†
CONFLICT ... Frederick Hollander†
CONFORMIST, THE ... Georges Delerue
CONGO MAISIE ... Edward Ward†
CONGO VIVO ... Piero Piccioni
CONGO, THE (D) ... Paul Bowles
CONGRATULATIONS, IT'S A BOY! (TF) ... Richard Baskin
CONGRATULATIONS, IT'S A BOY! (TF) ... Basil Poledouris
CONJUGAL BED, THE ... Teo Usuelli
CONNECTICUT YANKEE IN KING ARTHUR'S COURT,A ... Victor Young†
CONQUEROR WORM, THE ... Paul Ferris
CONQUEROR, THE ... Victor Schertzinger†
CONQUEROR, THE ... Victor Young†
CONQUERORS, THE ... Max Steiner†
CONQUEST ... Herbert Stothart†
CONQUEST OF EVEREST, THE ... Arthur Benjamin†
CONQUEST OF MYCENE ... Carlo Rustichelli
CONQUEST OF SPACE ... Nathan Van Cleave†
CONQUEST OF THE AIR ... Sir Arthur Bliss†
CONQUEST OF THE PLANET OF THE APES ... Leonard Rosenman
CONQUEST OF THE PLANET OF THE APES ... Tom Scott
CONQUISTA ... John Scott
CONRACK ... John Williams
CONSEIL DE FAMILLE ... Georges Delerue
CONSENTING ADULT (TF) ... Laurence Rosenthal
CONSOLATION MARRIAGE ... Max Steiner†
CONSPIRACY OF HEARTS ... Angelo Francesco Lavagnino†
CONSPIRACY OF LOVE (TF) ... John Rubinstein
CONSPIRACY OF TERROR (TF) ... Neal Hefti
CONSPIRATORS, THE ... Max Steiner†
CONSTANT HUSBAND, THE ... Malcolm Arnold
CONSTANT HUSBAND, THE ... William Alwyn†
CONSTANT NYMPH, THE ... John Greenwood†
CONSTANT NYMPH, THE ... Erich Wolfgang Korngold†
CONSTANTINE AND THE CROSS ... Mario Nascimbene
CONSUMING PASSIONS ... Richard Hartley
CONTEMPT ... Georges Delerue
CONTENDER, THE ... Albert Glasser
CONTENDER, THE (TF) ... James Di Pasquale
CONTINENTAL DIVIDE ... Michael Small
CONTINUAVAMO A METTERE LO DIAVOLO NE LO INFERNO ... Stelvio Cipriani
CONTRABAND ... Richard Addinsell†
CONTRACT ON CHERRY STREET (TF) ... Jerry Goldsmith
CONTRARY WARRIORS (FD) ... Todd Boekelheide
CONTRE-ENQUETE ... Jean Wiener†
CONVERSATION PIECE ... Franco Mannino
CONVERSATION, THE ... David Shire
CONVICT STAGE ... Richard LaSalle
CONVICTED ... George Duning
CONVICTED (TF) ... Steve Dorff
CONVICTED: A MOTHER'S STORY (TF) ... David Shire
CONVICTS FOUR ... Leonard Rosenman
CONVOY BUSTERS ... Stelvio Cipriani
COOGAN'S BLUFF ... Lalo Schifrin
COOK & PEARY: THE RACE TO THE POLE (TF) ... Charles Gross
COOK, THE THIEF, HIS WIFE & HER LOVER, THE ... Michael Nyman
COOKIE ... Thomas Newman
Bruce Rowland
COOL HAND LUKE ... ★ Lalo Schifrin
COOL MILLION (TF) ... Robert Prince
COOLANGATTA GOLD, THE ... Bill Conti
COOLEY HIGH ... Freddie Perren
COONSKIN ... Chico Hamilton
COP ... Michel Colombier
COP HATER ... Leith Stevens†
COP-OUT ... John Scott
COPACABANA ... Edward Ward†
COPACABANA (TF) ... Artie Butler
COPPER CANYON ... Daniele Amfitheatrof†
COPS AND ROBBERS ... Michel Legrand
CORIOLANO, EROE SENZA PATRIA ... Carlo Rustichelli
CORKY ... Jerry Styne
CORN IS GREEN, THE ... Max Steiner†
CORN IS GREEN, THE (TF) ... John Barry
CORNBREAD, EARL AND ME ... Donald Byrd
CORNERED ... Roy Webb†
CORPSE CAME C.O.D., THE ... George Duning
CORREGIDOR ... Leo Erdody†
...CORREVA L'ANNO DI GRAZIE 1870 ... Ennio Morricone
CORRIDA OF LOVE ... Toru Takemitsu
CORRIDOR OF MIRRORS ... Georges Auric†
CORRUPTION IN THE HALLS OF JUSTICE ... Pino Donaggio
CORSAIR ... Alfred Newman†
CORSICAN BROTHERS, THE ... Angelo Francesco Lavagnino†
CORSICAN BROTHERS, THE ... ★ Dimitri Tiomkin†
CORSICAN BROTHERS, THE (TF) ... George S. Clinton
CORSICAN BROTHERS, THE (TF) ... Allyn Ferguson
CORVETTE K-225 ... David Buttolph†
CORVETTE SUMMER ... Craig Safan
COSA AVETE FATTO A SOLANGE? ... Ennio Morricone
COSE DI COSA NOSTRA ... Manuel De Sica
COSI SIA ... Bruno Nicolai
COSMIC EYE, THE (AF) ... William Russo
COSMIC MAN, THE ... Bert A. Shefter
COSMIC MAN, THE ... Paul Sawtell†
COTTON CANDY (TF) ... Joe Renzetti
COTTON CLUB, THE ... John Barry
COUCH TRIP, THE ... Michel Colombier
COUNT DRACULA ... Bruno Nicolai
COUNT DRACULA AND HIS VAMPIRE BRIDE ... John Cacavas
COUNT OF MONTE CRISTO, THE ... Alfred Newman†
COUNT OF MONTE CRISTO, THE (TF) ... Allyn Ferguson
COUNT YORGA, VAMPIRE ... Bill Marx
COUNT YOUR BLESSINGS ... Franz Waxman†
COUNT YOUR BULLETS ... Richard Markowitz
COUNTDOWN ... Georges Delerue
COUNTDOWN ... Leonard Rosenman
COUNTER-ATTACK ... Louis Gruenberg†
COUNTERFEIT COMMANDOS ... Francesco De Masi
COUNTERFEIT KILLER, THE ... Quincy Jones
COUNTERFEIT TRAITOR, THE ... Alfred Newman†
COUNTERFEITERS, THE ... Irving Gertz
COUNTERPLAN ... Dmitri Shostakovitch†
COUNTERPLOT ... Bert A. Shefter
COUNTERPOINT ... Bronislau Kaper†
COUNTESS DRACULA ... Harry Robertson
COUNTESS FROM HONG KONG, THE ... Charles Chaplin†
COUNTESS OF MONTE CRISTO, THE ... Walter Scharf
COUNTRY ... Charles Gross
COUNTRY DANCE ... John Addison
COUNTRY GIRL, THE ... Victor Young†
COUNTRY GOLD (TF) ... Billy Goldenberg
COUNTRY MAN ... Wally Badarou
COUP D'ETAT ... Pierre Bachelet
COUP DE FOUDRE ... Luis Bacalov
COUP DE GRACE ... Stanley Myers
COUP DE TORCHON ... Philippe Sarde
COUPE DE VILLE ... James Newton Howard
COUPLE TAKES A WIFE, THE ... Richard DeBenedictis
COURAGE (TF) ... Craig Safan
COURAGE - LET'S RUN! ... Vladimir Cosma
COURAGE AND THE PASSION, THE (TF) ... Richard Shores
COURAGE FUYONS ... Vladimir Cosma
COURAGE MOUNTAIN ... Sylvester Levay
COURAGE OF LASSIE ... Bronislau Kaper†
COURAGEOUS DR. CHRISTIAN, THE ... William Lava†
COURRIER SUD ... Jacques Ibert†
COURT-MARTIAL OF BILLY MITCHELL, THE ... Dimitri Tiomkin†
COURTE TETE ... Jean Prodromides
COURTNEY AFFAIR, THE ... Anthony Collins†
COURTNEYS OF CURZON STREET, THE ... Anthony Collins†
COUSIN, COUSINE ... Gerard Anfosso
COUSINS ... Angelo Badalamenti
COUSINS, THE ... Paul Misraki†
COVENANT (TF) ... Charles Bernstein
COVENANT WITH DEATH, A ... Leonard Rosenman
COVER GIRL ... ★★ Carmen Dragon†

INDEX OF FILM TITLES

COVER GIRL AND THE COP, THE (TF) ... Sylvester Levay
COVER GIRLS (TF) ... Richard Shores
COVER UP (TF) ... Paul Chihara
COVER-UP ... Hans J. Salter
COVERGIRL ... Christopher L. Stone
COVERUP: BEHIND THE IRAN CONTRA AFFAIR (FD) ... Richard Elliott
COWARD OF THE COUNTY (TF) ... Larry Cansler
COWBOY ... George Duning
COWBOY (TF) ... Bruce Broughton
COWBOY AND THE BALLERINA, THE (TF) ... Bruce Broughton
COWBOY AND THE LADY, THE ... ★ Alfred Newman†
COWBOY AND THE SENORITA, THE ... Walter Scharf
COWBOY IN MANHATTAN ... Hans J. Salter
COWBOYS DON'T CRY ... Louis Natale
COWBOYS FROM TEXAS ... William Lava†
COWBOYS, THE ... John Williams
CRACK HOUSE ... Michael Piccirillo
CRACK IN THE MIRROR ... Maurice Jarre
CRACK IN THE MIRROR ... Nile Rodgers
CRACK IN THE WORLD ... Johnny Douglas
CRACK-UP ... Leigh Harline†
CRACKED NUTS ... Max Steiner†
CRACKED UP (TF) ... Mark Snow
CRACKER FACTORY, THE (TF) ... Billy Goldenberg
CRACKERS ... Paul Chihara
CRACKSMAN, THE ... Ron Goodwin
CRADLE SONG ... W. Franke Harling†
CRADLE WILL FALL, THE (TF) ... Elliot Lawrence
CRAN D'ARRET ... Michel Magne†
CRASH (TF) ... Eddie Lawrence Manson
CRASH COURSE (TF) ... Mark Davis
CRASH DIVE ... David Buttolph†
CRASH LANDING ... Mischa Bakaleinikoff †
CRASH OF SILENCE ... William Alwyn†
CRASH! ... Andrew Belling
CRASHOUT ... Leith Stevens†
CRAWLING EYE, THE ... Stanley Black
CRAWLSPACE ... Pino Donaggio
CRAWLSPACE (TF) ... Jerry Goldsmith
CRAZE ... John Scott
CRAZY DESIRE ... Ennio Morricone
CRAZY HORSE PARIS—FRANCE ... Jacques Morali
CRAZY PEOPLE ... Cliff Eidelman
CRAZY TIMES (TF) ... Peter Matz
CRAZY WORLD OF JULUIS VROODER, THE ... Robert Alcivar
CRAZY WORLD OF LAUREL & HARDY, THE ... Jerry Fielding†
CREATOR ... Sylvester Levay
CREATURE ... Tom Chase
CREATURE ... Steve Rucker
CREATURE FROM THE BLACK LAGOON, THE ... Hans J. Salter
CREATURE FROM THE BLACK LAGOON, THE ... Herman Stein
CREATURE FROM THE BLACK LAGOON, THE ... Henry Mancini
CREATURE WALKS AMONG US, THE ... Irving Gertz
CREATURE WALKS AMONG US, THE ... Herman Stein
CREATURE WALKS AMONG US, THE ... Henry Mancini
CREATURE WALKS AMONG US, THE ... Heinz Roemheld†
CREATURE WASN'T NICE, THE ... David Spear
CREATURE WITH THE ATOM BRAIN ... Mischa Bakaleinikoff †
CREATURES THE WORLD FORGOT ... Mario Nascimbene
CREATURES, THE ... Douglas Gamley
CREEPER, THE ... Milton Rosen
CREEPERS ... Goblin
CREEPING FLESH, THE ... Paul Ferris
CREEPING UNKNOWN, THE ... James Bernard
CREEPS ... Arlon Ober
CREEPSHOW ... John Harrison
CREEPSHOW 2 ... Les Reed
CREEPSHOW II ... Rick Wakeman
CREMATORS, THE ... Albert Glasser
CRESCENDO ... Malcolm Williamson
CRESCETTE E MOLTIPLICATEVI ... Ennio Morricone
CREST OF THE WAVE ... Miklos Rozsa
CRIME AGAINST JOE ... Paul Dunlap
CRIME AND PUNISHMENT ... Arthur Honegger†
CRIME AND PUNISHMENT, USA ... Herschel Burke Gilbert
CRIME CLUB (TF) ... George Romanis
CRIME CLUB (TF) ... Gil Melle
CRIME DOCTOR'S COURAGE, THE ... Mario Castelnuovo-Tedesco†
CRIME DOCTOR'S WARNING ... Paul Sawtell†
CRIME DOCTOR, THE ... Max Steiner†
CRIME DOES NOT PAY ... Georges Delerue
CRIME IN THE STREETS ... Franz Waxman†
CRIME OF INNOCENCE (TF) ... Paul Chihara
CRIME OF MONSIEUR LANGE, THE ... Jean Wiener†
CRIME OF PASSION ... Paul Dunlap
CRIME RING ... Roy Webb†
CRIME SCHOOL ... Max Steiner†
CRIME WITHOUT PASSION ... Oscar Levant†
CRIME ZONE ... Rick Conrad
CRIMEBUSTER, THE ... Jerry Goldsmith
CRIMES OF PASSION ... Rick Wakeman
CRIMES OF THE HEART ... Georges Delerue
CRIMEWAVE ... Arlon Ober
CRIMINAL LAW ... Jerry Goldsmith
CRIMINAL SYMPHONY ... Carlo Rustichelli
CRIMINAL, THE ... John Dankworth
CRIMSON KIMONO, THE ... Harry Sukman†
CRIMSON PIRATE, THE ... William Alwyn†
CRISIS ... Miklos Rozsa
CRISIS AT CENTRAL HIGH (TF) ... Billy Goldenberg
CRISIS IN MID-AIR (TF) ... Robert Drasnin
CRISIS IN SUN VALLEY (TF) ... Richard DeBenedictis
CRISS CROSS ... Miklos Rozsa
CRITICAL CONDITION ... Alan Silvestri
CRITICAL LIST, THE (TF) ... James Di Pasquale
CRITTERS ... David Newman
CRITTERS 2: THE MAIN COURSE ... Nicholas Pike
CROCODILE DUNDEE ... Peter Best
CROCODILE DUNDEE II ... Peter Best
CROMWELL ... ★ Frank Cordell†
CROOK, THE ... Francis Lai
CROOKED WEB, THE ... Mischa Bakaleinikoff †
CROOKS AND CORONETS ... John Scott
CROSS COUNTRY ... Chris Rea
CROSS COUNTRY ROMANCE ... Roy Webb†
CROSS CREEK ... ★ Leonard Rosenman
CROSS MY HEART ... Bruce Broughton
CROSS MY HEART ... Robert Emmett Dolan†
CROSS OF FIRE (TF) ... William Goldstein
CROSS OF IRON ... Ernest Gold
CROSS OF LORRAINE, THE ... Bronislau Kaper†
CROSSED SWORDS ... Maurice Jarre
CROSSFIRE ... Roy Webb†
CROSSFIRE (TF) ... Patrick Williams
CROSSING DELANCEY ... Paul Chihara
CROSSING THE MOB (TF) ... Michel Rubini
CROSSING TO FREEDOM (TF) ... Carl Davis
CROSSINGS (MS) ... Michel Legrand
CROSSOVER DREAMS ... Mauricio Smith
CROSSROADS ... Ry Cooder
CROSSROADS ... Bronislau Kaper†
CROWD, THE ... Carl Davis
CROWDED SKY, THE ... Leonard Rosenman
CROWHAVEN FARM (TF) ... Robert Drasnin
CROWN ROARS, THE ... Edward Ward†
CRUCIBLE, THE ... Georges Auric†
CRUCIBLE, THE ... Hanns Eisler†
CRUEL SEA, THE ... Alan Rawsthorne†
CRUEL TOWER, THE ... Paul Dunlap
CRUISE INTO TERROR (TF) ... Gerald Fried
CRUISING ... Jack Nitzsche
CRUSOE ... Michael Kamen
CRY BABY ... Patrick Williams
CRY BABY KILLER ... Gerald Fried
CRY BLOOD, APACHE ... Elliot Kaplan
CRY DANGER ... Paul Dunlap
CRY DANGER ... Emil Newman†
CRY FOR HELP, A (TF) ... Gil Melle
CRY FOR LOVE, A (TF) ... Jimmie Haskell
CRY FOR ME, BILLY ... Richard Markowitz
CRY FOR THE STRANGERS (TF) ... John Cacavas
CRY FREEDOM ... ★ George Fenton
CRY FREEDOM ... ★ Jonas Gwangwa
CRY FROM THE MOUNTAIN ... J.A.C. Redford
CRY FROM THE STREETS, A ... Larry Adler
CRY HAVOC ... Daniele Amfitheatrof†
CRY IN THE DARK, A ... Bruce Smeaton
CRY IN THE NIGHT, A ... David Buttolph†
CRY IN THE WILD, A ... Arthur Kempel
CRY IN THE WILDERNESS, A (TF) ... Robert Prince
CRY OF BATTLE ... Richard Markowitz
CRY OF THE BANSHEE ... Les Baxter
CRY OF THE CITY ... Alfred Newman†
CRY OF THE INNOCENT (TF) ... Allyn Ferguson
CRY OF THE PENGUINS ... John Addison
CRY OF THE WEREWOLF ... Mischa Bakaleinikoff†
CRY PANIC (TF) ... Ken Lauber
CRY WOLF ... Franz Waxman†
CRYSTAL BALL, THE ... Victor Young†
CRYSTAL EYES ... Greg Forrest
CRYSTAL HEART ... Joel Goldsmith
CUBA ... Patrick Williams
CUBAN LOVE SONG, THE ... Herbert Stothart†
CUBAN PETE ... Milton Rosen
CUJO ... Charles Bernstein
CUL-DE-SAC ... Christopher Komeda†
CULPEPPER CATTLE CO., THE ... Jerry Goldsmith
CULPEPPER CATTLE CO., THE ... Tom Scott
CUMBERLAND STORY, THE ... Arthur Benjamin†
CUMMINGTON STORY, THE (D) ... Aaron Copland
CUORE DI CANE ... Piero Piccioni
CUORE DI MAMMA ... Ennio Morricone
CUORE FREDDO, A ... Stelvio Cipriani
CUORI SENZA FRONTIERE ... Carlo Rustichelli
CUORI SOLITARI ... Luis Bacalov
CURIOSITY KILLS (CTF) ... Jan Hammer
CURLEY ... Heinz Roemheld†
CURSE OF DRACULA, THE ... Gerald Fried
CURSE OF FRANKENSTEIN, THE ... James Bernard
CURSE OF KING TUT'S TOMB, THE (TF) ... Gil Melle
CURSE OF THE BLACK WIDOW (TF) ... Bob Cobert
CURSE OF THE CAT PEOPLE ... Roy Webb†
CURSE OF THE DEMON ... Clifton Parker
CURSE OF THE FACELESS MAN ... Gerald Fried
CURSE OF THE FLY, THE ... Bert A. Shefter
CURSE OF THE PINK PANTHER ... Henry Mancini
CURSE OF THE UNDEAD ... Irving Gertz
CURSE OF THE WEREWOLF, THE ... Benjamin Frankel†
CURSE, THE ... Franco Micalizzi
CURTAIN CALL ... Roy Webb†
CURTAIN CALL AT CACTUS CREEK ... Walter Scharf
CURTAIN RISES, THE ... Georges Auric†
CURTAIN UP ... Malcolm Arnold
CURTAINS ... Paul Zaza
CUSTER OF THE WEST ... Bernardo Segall
CUTTER (TF) ... Oliver Nelson†
CUTTER AND BONE ... Jack Nitzsche
CUTTER'S TRAIL (TF) ... John Parker
CUTTER'S WAY ... Jack Nitzsche
CUTTING CLASS ... Jill Fraser
CYBELE OU LES DIMANCHES DE VILLE d'AVRAY ... ★ Maurice Jarre
CYBORG ... Kevin Bassinson
CYBORG 2087 ... Paul Dunlap
CYCLE SAVAGES ... Jerry Styne
CYCLONE ... David A. Jackson
CYCLOPS ... Albert Glasser
CYNARA ... Alfred Newman†
CYNTHIA ... Bronislau Kaper†
CYRANO DE BERGERAC ... Dimitri Tiomkin†

D

D'AMORE SI MUORE ... Ennio Morricone
D'ARTAGNAN ... Victor Schertzinger†
D'HOMMES A HOMMES ... Joseph Kosma†
D-DAY, THE SIXTH OF JUNE ... Lyn Murray†
D.A.: CONSPIRACY TO KILL, THE (TF) ... Frank Comstock
D.A.: MURDER ONE, THE (TF) ... Frank Comstock
D.A.R.Y.L. ... Marvin Hamlisch
D.C. CAB ... Giorgio Moroder
D.I., THE ... David Buttolph†
D.O.A. ... Chaz Jankel
D.O.A. ... Dimitri Tiomkin†
DA ... Elmer Bernstein
DA BERLINO L'APOCALISSE ... Bruno Nicolai
DA UOMO A UOMO ... Ennio Morricone
DABBEL TRABBEL ... Jurgen Knieper
DAD ... James Horner
DADAH IS DEATH (TF) ... Fred Karlin
DADDY (TF) ... Simon Rogers
DADDY LONG LEGS ... Alex North
DADDY NOSTALGIE ... Antoine Duhamel
DADDY'S BOYS ... Sasha Matson
DADDY'S DEADLY DARLING ... Charles Bernstein
DADDY'S DYIN'...WHO'S GOT THE WILL? ... David McHugh
DADDY'S GONE A-HUNTING ... John Williams
DADDY, I DON'T LIKE IT LIKE THIS (TF) ... David Shire
DAFFY DUCK MOVIE: FANTASTIC ISLAND, THE (AF) ... Robert J. Walsh
DAGMAR'S HOT PANTS, INC. ... Jimmie Haskell
DAGORA, THE SPACE MONSTER ... Akira Ifukube

DAI NEMICI MI GUARDO IO ... Carlo Rustichelli
DAIN CURSE, THE (MS) ... Charles Gross
DAISY KENYON ... David Raksin
DAKOTA ... Chris Christian
DAKOTA ... Walter Scharf
DAKOTA LIL ... Dimitri Tiomkin†
DALLAS ... Max Steiner†
DALLAS COWBOY CHEERLEADERS (TF) ... Jimmie Haskell
DALLAS COWBOY CHEERLEADERS II (TF) ... Jimmie Haskell
DALLAS: THE EARLY YEARS (TF) ... Jerrold Immel
DALLE ARDENNE ALL'INFERNO ... Ennio Morricone
DALLE ARDENNE ALL'INFERNO ... Bruno Nicolai
DALTON GIRLS, THE ... Les Baxter
DALTON: CODE OF VENGEANCE II (TF) ... Don Peake
DALTONS RIDE AGAIN, THE ... Frank Skinner†
DAM BUSTERS, THE ... Leighton Lucas†
DAMIEN: OMEN II ... Jerry Goldsmith
DAMIEN: THE LEPER PRIEST (TF) ... ☆ Peter Matz
DAMN CITIZEN ... Henry Mancini
DAMNATION ALLEY ... Jerry Goldsmith
DAMNED DON'T CRY, THE ... Daniele Amfitheatrof†
DAMNED IN VENICE ... Pino Donaggio
DAMNED RIVER ... James Wesley Stemple
DAMNED, THE ... James Bernard
DAMNED, THE ... Maurice Jarre
DAMNSEL IN DISTRESS, A ... George Bassman
DAMON AND PYTHIAS ... Angelo Francesco Lavagnino†
DAN CANDY'S LAW ... Georges Delerue
DANCE OF HOPE (FD) ... Wendy Blackstone
DANCE OF THE DAMNED ... Gary Stockdale
DANCE OF THE DWARFS ... Perry Botkin
DANCE OF THE VAMPIRES ... Christopher Komeda†
DANCE WITH A STRANGER ... Richard Hartley
DANCE WITH ME, HENRY ... Paul Dunlap
DANCE, GIRL, DANCE ... Edward Ward†
DANCERS ... Pino Donaggio
DANCES WITH WOLVES ... John Barry
DANCING CO-ED ... Edward Ward†
DANCING FLEECE, THE ... Alan Rawsthorne†
DANCING LADY ... Louis Silvers†
DANDY IN ASPIC, A ... Quincy Jones
DANDY, THE ALL AMERICAN GIRL ... Paul Chihara
DANGER DOWN UNDER (TF) ... Bruce Rowland
DANGER IN PARADISE (TF) ... Jack Elliott
DANGER IN PARADISE (TF) ... Allyn Ferguson
DANGER IN THE PACIFIC ... Hans J. Salter
DANGER SIGNAL ... Adolph Deutsch†
DANGER USA ... Jeffrey Ainis
DANGER ZONE ... Bert A. Shefter
DANGER! LOVE AT WORK ... David Buttolph†
DANGER: DIABOLIK ... Ennio Morricone
DANGEROUS BUSINESS ... Mario Castelnuovo-Tedesco†
DANGEROUS COMPANY (TF) ... Creed Bratton
DANGEROUS CORNER ... Max Steiner†
DANGEROUS CROSSING ... Lionel Newman†
DANGEROUS DAVIES - THE LAST DETECTIVE ... Ed Welch
DANGEROUS EXILE ... Georges Auric†
DANGEROUS GAME, A ... Hans J. Salter
DANGEROUS INTRUDER ... Karl Hajos†
DANGEROUS LIASONS ... ★ George Fenton
DANGEROUS LIFE, A (CTF) ... Brian May
DANGEROUS LOVE ... Paul Hertzog
DANGEROUS MISSION ... Roy Webb†
DANGEROUS MOONLIGHT ... Richard Addinsell†
DANGEROUS MOVES ... Gabriel Yared
DANGEROUS OBSESSION ... Simon Boswell
DANGEROUS PASSION (TF) ... Rob Mounsey
DANGEROUS PROFESSION, A ... Frederick Hollander†
DANGEROUS SUMMER ... Brian May
DANGEROUS TYPE, THE ... Carl Dante
DANGEROUSLY CLOSE ... Michael McCarty
DANIEL IN THE LION'S DEN ... Milton Rosen
DANIELE CORTIS ... Nino Rota†
DANIELE E MARIA ... Nicola Piovani
DANNY BOY ... Paddy Meegan
DANNY: CHAMPION OF THE WORLD (CTF) ... Stanley Myers
DANS L'OMBRE DES COMBATS ... Jean Prodromides
DANS LA POUSSIERE DU SOLEIL ... Francis Lai
DANTE'S INFERNO ... R.H. Bassett†
DANTON ... Jean Prodromides
DARBY O'GILL AND THE LITTLE PEOPLE ... Oliver Wallace†
DARBY'S RANGERS ... Max Steiner†
DAREDEVIL IN THE CASTLE ... Akira Ifukube
DAREDEVILS OF THE RED CIRCLE ... William Lava†
DARING CABALLERO, THE ... Albert Glasser
DARING GAME ... George Bruns
DARING YOUNG MAN, THE ... John Leipold†
DARK ANGEL, THE ... Alfred Newman†
DARK AT THE TOP OF THE STAIRS, THE ... Max Steiner†
DARK BEFORE DAWN ... Ken Sutherland
DARK CIRCLE (FD) ... Bernard Krause
DARK CIRCLE (FD) ... Gary Remal
DARK CITY ... Franz Waxman†
DARK COMMAND ... Victor Young†
DARK CORNER, THE ... Cyril J. Mockridge†
DARK CRYSTAL, THE ... Trevor Jones
DARK EYES ... Francis Lai
DARK HOLIDAY (TF) ... Paul Chihara
DARK HOUSE, THE ... Hans J. Salter
DARK INTRUDER ... Lalo Schifrin
DARK JOURNEY ... Richard Addinsell†
DARK MANSIONS (TF) ... Ken Harrison
DARK MIRROR (TF) ... Dominic Frontiere
DARK MIRROR, THE ... Dimitri Tiomkin†
DARK NIGHT OF THE SCARECROW (TF) ... Glenn Paxton
DARK ODYSSEY ... Laurence Rosenthal
DARK PASSAGE ... Franz Waxman†
DARK PAST, THE ... George Duning
DARK PLACES ... Wilfred Josephs
DARK PURPOSE ... Angelo Francesco Lavagnino†
DARK SIDE OF INNOCENCE, THE (TF) ... Peter Matz
DARK STAR ... John Carpenter
DARK STREETS OF CAIRO ... Hans J. Salter
DARK TOWER ... Stacy Widelitz
DARK VICTORY ... ★ Max Steiner†
DARK VICTORY (TF) ... ☆ Billy Goldenberg
DARK WATERS ... Miklos Rozsa
DARK, THE ... Roger Kellaway
DARKER SIDE OF TERROR, THE (TF) ... Paul Chihara
DARKER THAN AMBER ... John Parker
DARKMAN ... Danny Elfman
DARLING ... John Dankworth
DARLING LILI ... Henry Mancini
DARLING, HOW COULD YOU? ... Frederick Hollander†
DARWIN ADVENTURE, THE ... Marc Wilkinson
DAS BLAUE LICHT ... Giuseppe Becce†
DAS BOOT ... Klaus Doldinger
DAS FUENFTE GEBOT ... Armando Trovajoli
DAS INDISCHE GRABMAL ... Michel Michelet†
DAS SCHWEIGEN IM WALDE ... Giuseppe Becce†
DAS SPUKSCHLOSS IN SPESSART ... Frederick Hollander†
DATE WITH AN ANGEL ... Randy Kerber
DAUGHTER OF DARKNESS (TF) ... Colin Towns
DAUGHTER OF EVIL ... Bronislau Kaper†
DAUGHTER OF ROSIE O'GRADY, THE ... David Buttolph†
DAUGHTER OF THE MIND (TF) ... Robert Drasnin
DAUGHTER OF THE SANDS ... Georges Auric†
DAUGHTER OF THE STREETS (TF) ... Lee Holdridge
DAUGHTER OF THE SUN GOD ... Les Baxter
DAUGHTERS COURAGEOUS ... Max Steiner†
DAUGHTERS OF JOSHUA CABE , THE (TF), ... Jeff Alexander†
DAUGHTERS OF JOSHUA CABE RETURN, THE (TF) ... Jeff Alexander†
DAUGHTERS OF SATAN ... Richard LaSalle
DAVID ... Wojciech Kilar
DAVID (TF) ... Marvin Hamlisch
DAVID AND BATHSHEBA ... ★ Alfred Newman†
DAVID COPPERFIELD ... William Axt†
DAVID COPPERFIELD ... Herbert Stothart†
DAVID COPPERFIELD (TF) ... Malcolm Arnold
DAVY CROCKETT AND THE RIVER PIRATES ... George Bruns
DAVY CROCKETT, INDIAN SCOUT ... Paul Sawtell†
DAVY CROCKETT, KING OF THE WILD FRONTIER ... George Bruns
DAVY CROCKETT: RAINBOW IN THE THUNDER (TF) ... Joel McNeely
DAWN OF THE DEAD ... Goblin
DAWN OF THE MUMMY ... Shuki Levy
DAWN PATROL, THE ... Max Steiner†
DAWN: PORTRAIT OF A TEENAGE RUNAWAY (TF) ... Fred Karlin
DAY AFTER HALLOWEEN, THE ... Brian May
DAY AFTER, THE (TF) ... David Raksin
DAY AND THE HOUR, THE ... Claude Bolling
DAY AT THE RACES, A ... George Bassman
DAY CHRIST DIED, THE (TF) ... Laurence Rosenthal
DAY FOR NIGHT ... Georges Delerue
DAY FOR THANKS ON WALTONS MOUNTAIN, A (TF) ... Alexander Courage
DAY IN COURT, A ... Armando Trovajoli
DAY IN DAY OUT ... Gerard Schurmann
DAY IN THE COUNTRY, A ... Joseph Kosma†
DAY MARS INVADED EARTH, THE ... Richard LaSalle
DAY OF FURY, A ... Herman Stein
DAY OF FURY, A ... Henry Mancini
DAY OF RECKONING, THE (AF) ... Zdenek Liska
DAY OF THE ANIMALS ... Lalo Schifrin
DAY OF THE BAD MAN ... Hans J. Salter
DAY OF THE DEAD ... John Harrison
DAY OF THE DOLPHIN, THE ... ★ Georges Delerue
DAY OF THE EVIL GUN ... Jeff Alexander†
DAY OF THE JACKAL, THE ... Georges Delerue
DAY OF THE LOCUST, THE ... John Barry
DAY OF THE OUTLAW ... Alexander Courage
DAY OF THE PAINTER ... Eddie Lawrence Manson
DAY OF THE TRIFFIDS, THE ... Ron Goodwin
DAY OF TRIUMPH ... Daniele Amfitheatrof†
DAY ONE (TF) ... Mason Daring
DAY THE BOOKIES WEPT, THE ... Arthur Morton
DAY THE BUBBLE BURST, THE (TF) ... Jack Elliott
DAY THE EARTH MOVED, THE (TF) ... Bobby Sherman
DAY THE EARTH STOOD STILL, THE ... Bernard Herrmann†
DAY THE FISH CAME OUT, THE ... Mikis Theodorakis
DAY THE LOVING STOPPED, THE (TF) ... Lee Holdridge
DAY THE SCREAMING STOPPED, THE ... Stanley Myers
DAY THE SKY EXPLODED, THE ... Carlo Rustichelli
DAY THE WOMEN GOT EVEN, THE (TF) ... Brad Fiedel
DAY THE WORLD ENDED, THE ... Ronald Stein†
DAY THEY GAVE BABIES AWAY, THE ... Max Steiner†
DAY THEY ROBBED THE BANK OF ENGLAND, THE ... Edwin Astley
DAY TIME ENDED, THE ... Richard H. Band
DAY WILL DAWN, THE ... Richard Addinsell†
DAYDREAMER, THE ... Vladimir Cosma
DAYDREAMER, THE ... Maury Laws
DAYS AND NIGHTS IN THE FOREST ... Satyajit Ray
DAYS OF BETRAYAL ... Zdenek Liska
DAYS OF GLORY ... Daniele Amfitheatrof†
DAYS OF HEAVEN ... Leo Kottke
DAYS OF HEAVEN ... ★ Ennio Morricone
DAYS OF THUNDER ... Hans Zimmer
DAYS OF WINE AND ROSES ... Henry Mancini
DE CRIADA A SIGNORA ... Stelvio Cipriani
DE LA PART DES COPAINS ... Michel Magne†
DE SCHORPIOEN ... Nicola Piovani
DEAD AND BURIED ... Joe Renzetti
DEAD CALM ... Graeme Revell
DEAD CERT ... John Addison
DEAD DON'T DIE, THE (TF) ... Robert Prince
DEAD END ... Alfred Newman†
DEAD END KIDS (FD) ... David Byrne
DEAD END KIDS (FD) ... Philip Glass
DEAD HEAT ... Ernest Troost
DEAD HEAT ON A MERRY-GO-ROUND ... Stu Phillips
DEAD MAN ON THE RUN (TF) ... Harry Geller
DEAD MAN OUT (CTF) ... Cliff Eidelman
DEAD MAN'S EYES ... Paul Sawtell†
DEAD MEN DON'T WEAR PLAID ... Miklos Rozsa
DEAD MEN TELL ... David Raksin
DEAD MEN WALK ... Leo Erdody†
DEAD OF NIGHT ... Carl Zittrer
DEAD OF NIGHT ... Georges Auric†
DEAD OF WINTER ... Richard Einhorn
DEAD ON COURSE ... Malcolm Arnold
DEAD ONE IN THE THAMES RIVER, THE ... Peter Thomas
DEAD POETS SOCIETY ... Maurice Jarre
DEAD POOL, THE ... Lalo Schifrin
DEAD RECKONING (CTF) ... Mark Snow
DEAD RINGER ... Barry Fasman
DEAD RINGER ... Dana Walden
DEAD RINGER ... Andre Previn
DEAD RINGERS ... Howard Shore
DEAD SOLID PERFECT (CTF) ... Tangerine Dream
DEAD ZONE, THE ... Michael Kamen
DEAD, THE ... Alex North
DEAD-BANG ... Gary Chang
DEAD-BANG ... Michael Kamen
DEADFALL ... John Barry
DEADHEAD MILES ... Tom T. Hall
DEADLIER THAN THE MALE ... Malcom Lockyer
DEADLIER THAN THE MALE ... Jean Wiener†
DEADLIEST SEASON, THE (TF) ... Dick Hyman
DEADLINE ... Brian May
DEADLINE (TF) ... Larry Carlton

DEADLINE (TF) ... Jim Parker
DEADLINE - U.S.A. ... Lionel Newman†
DEADLINE AT DAWN ... Hanns Eisler†
DEADLINE U.S.A. ... Cyril J. Mockridge†
DEADLY AFFAIR, THE ... Quincy Jones
DEADLY BEES, THE ... Wilfred Josephs
DEADLY BLESSING ... James Horner
DEADLY BUSINESS, A (TF) ... Paul Chihara
DEADLY CARE (TF) ... Tangerine Dream
DEADLY DREAM, THE (TF) ... Dave Grusin
DEADLY DUO ... Richard LaSalle
DEADLY ENCOUNTER ... Stu Phillips
DEADLY ENCOUNTER (TF) ... Michael Hoenig
DEADLY ENCOUNTER (TF) ... Fred Karlin
DEADLY ENCOUNTER (TF) ... J. Peter Robinson
DEADLY EYES ... Anthony Guefen
DEADLY FORCE ... Gary Scott
DEADLY FRIEND ... Charles Bernstein
DEADLY GAME (TF) ... Mundell Lowe
DEADLY GAMES ... Robert O. Ragland
DEADLY HARVEST (TF) ... Morton Stevens
DEADLY HERO ... Brad Fiedel
DEADLY HERO ... Tommy Mandel
DEADLY HONEYMOON ... Elmer Bernstein
DEADLY HUNT, THE (TF) ... Vic Mizzy
DEADLY ILLUSION ... Patrick Gleeson
DEADLY INNOCENCE ... David C. Williams
DEADLY INTENT ... Ethan James
DEADLY INTENTIONS (TF) ... Georges Delerue
DEADLY IS THE FEMALE ... Victor Young†
DEADLY LESSONS (TF) ... Ian Freebairn-Smith
DEADLY MANTIS, THE ... William Lava†
DEADLY MESSAGES (TF) ... Brad Fiedel
DEADLY PRESENCE ... Andrea Saparoff
DEADLY SHOTS ON BROADWAY ... Peter Thomas
DEADLY SILENCE, A (TF) ... Richard Gibbs
DEADLY STRANGERS ... Ron Goodwin
DEADLY TOWER, THE (TF) ... Don Ellis†
DEADLY TRACKERS, THE ... Jerry Fielding†
DEADLY TRIANGLE (TF) ... Richard DeBenedictis
DEADMAN'S CURVE (TF) ... Fred Karlin
DEAL OF THE CENTUR ... Arthur B. Rubinstein
DEALERS ... Richard Hartley
DEALING: OR THE BERKELEY-TO-
BOSTON FORTY-BRICK LOST-
BAG BLUES ... Michael Small
DEAR AMERICA: LETTERS HOME
FROM VIETNAM (FD) ... Todd Boekelheide
DEAR BOYS ... Laurens Van Rooyen
DEAR BRAT ... Nathan Van Cleave†
DEAR DETECTIVE ... Georges Delerue
DEAR HEART ... Henry Mancini
DEAR MURDERER ... Benjamin Frankel†
DEAR SUMMER SISTER ... Toru Takemitsu
DEAR WIFE ... Nathan Van Cleave†
DEATH AMONG FRIENDS (TF) ... Jim Helms
DEATH BE NOT PROUD (TF) ... Fred Karlin
DEATH BEFORE DISHONOR ... Brian May
DEATH CAR ON THE
FREEWAY (TF) ... Richard Markowitz
DEATH CORPS ... Richard Einhorn
DEATH CRUISE (TF) ... Pete Rugolo
DEATH DEALER, THE ... Ennio Morricone
DEATH DORM ... Christopher Young
DEATH DREAM ... Carl Zittrer
DEATH GAME ... Jimmie Haskell
DEATH HUNT ... Jerrold Immel
DEATH IN CALIFORNIA, A (TF) ... John Cacavas
DEATH IN SMALL DOSES ... Emil Newman†
DEATH IN THE GARDEN ... Paul Misraki†
DEATH IN VENICE ... Franco Mannino
DEATH MOON (TF) ... Paul Chihara
DEATH OF A CENTERFOLD: THE DOROTHY
STRATTEN STORY (TF) ... Roger Webb
DEATH OF A GUNFIGHTER ... Oliver Nelson†
DEATH OF A SALESMAN ... ★ Alex North
DEATH OF A SALESMAN (TF) ... ☆ Alex North
DEATH OF A SCOUNDREL ... Max Steiner†
DEATH OF A SOLDIER ... Allan Zavod
DEATH OF AN ANGEL ... Jay Ferguson
DEATH OF AN ANGEL ... Peter Myers
DEATH OF AN EXPERT
WITNESS (MS) ... Richard Harvey
DEATH OF INNOCENCE, A (TF) ... Morton Stevens
DEATH OF ME YET, THE (TF) ... Pete Rugolo
DEATH OF OCEAN VIEW
PARK, THE (TF) ... Fred Werner
DEATH OF RICHIE, THE (TF) ... Fred Karlin
DEATH OF THE INCREDIBLE
HULK, THE (TF) ... Lance Rubin
DEATH ON THE NILE ... Nino Rota†

DEATH PLAY ... Rupert Holmes
DEATH RACE (TF) ... Milton Rosen
DEATH RACE 2000 ... Paul Chihara
DEATH RAY 2000 (TF) ... John Elizalde
DEATH RIDE TO OSAKA (TF) ... Brad Fiedel
DEATH RIDES A HORSE ... Ennio Morricone
DEATH RUTH ... Robert Emmett Dolan†
DEATH SCREAM (TF) ... Gil Melle
DEATH SENTENCE (TF) ... Laurence Rosenthal
DEATH STALK (TF) ... Pete Rugolo
DEATH TAKES A HOLIDAY ... Bernhard Kaun†
DEATH TAKES A HOLIDAY ... Sigmund Krumgold†
DEATH TAKES A HOLIDAY ... Milan Roder†
DEATH TRAP ... Wayne Bell
DEATH VALLEY ... Dana Kaproff
DEATH WHEELERS, THE ... David Whitaker
DEATH WISH ... Herbie Hancock
DEATH WISH 3 ... Jimmy Page
DEATH WISH 4: THE CRACKDOWN ... Paul Callum
DEATH WISH 4: THE CRACKDOWN ... Paul McCallum
DEATH WISH 4: THE
CRACKDOWN ... Valentine McCallum
DEATH WISH II ... Jimmy Page
DEATHHOUSE ... Gershon Kingsley
DEATHMASTER, THE ... Bill Marx
DEATHSPORT ... Andrew Stein
DEATHSTALKER ... Chuck Cirino
DEATHSTALKER ... Oscar Cardozo Ocampo
DEATHTRAP ... Johnny Mandel
DECAMERON NIGHTS ... Antony Hopkins
DECEIVERS, THE ... John Scott
DECEPTION ... Erich Wolfgang Korngold†
DECEPTIONS (CTF) ... Gary Scott
DECEPTIONS (TF) ... Nigel Hess
DECISION AGAINST TIME ... Gerard Schurmann
DECISION AT SUNDOWN ... Heinz Roemheld†
DECISION BEFORE DAWN ... Franz Waxman†
DECISION OF CHRISTOPHER
BLAKE, THE ... Max Steiner†
DECLINE AND FALL OF A
BIRD WATCHER ... Ron Goodwin
DEEP IN THE HEART ... Mike Post
DEEP IN THE HEART OF TEXAS ... Hans J. Salter
DEEP SIX, THE ... David Buttolph†
DEEP STAR SIX ... Harry Manfredini
DEEP VALLEY ... Max Steiner†
DEEP WATERS ... Cyril J. Mockridge†
DEEP, BLUE SEA, THE ... Malcolm Arnold
DEEP, THE ... John Barry
DEER HUNTER, THE ... Stanley Myers
DEERSLAYER, THE ... Bert A. Shefter
DEERSLAYER, THE ... Paul Sawtell†
DEERSLAYER, THE (TF) ... Andrew Belling
DEERSLAYER, THE (TF) ... Robert Summers
DEF-CON 4 ... Christopher Young
DEFECTION OF SIMAS
KUDIRKA, THE (TF) ... ☆ David Shire
DEFENSE DE SAVOIR ... Bruno Nicolai
DEFENSE OF THE REALM ... Richard Harvey
DEFENSE PLAY ... Arthur B. Rubinstein
DEFENSELESS ... Trevor Jones
DEFIANCE ... Dominic Frontiere
DEFIANCE ... Basil Poledouris
DEFIANCE ... Tom Saviano
DEFIANCE ... Gerard McMahon
DEFIANT ONES, THE ... Ernest Gold
DEFIANT ONES, THE (TF) ... Steve Dorff
DEJA VU ... Pino Donaggio
DELANCEY STREET: THE CRISIS
WITHIN (TF) ... Lalo Schifrin
DELIBERATE STRANGER, THE (TF) ... Gil Melle
DELIGHTFULLY DANGEROUS ... Morton Gould
DELIRIO DEI SENSI ... Armando Trovajoli
DELIRIUM ... David C. Williams
DELITTO D'AMORE ... Carlo Rustichelli
DELITTO QUASI PERFETTO ... Carlo Rustichelli
DELIVER US FROM EVIL (TF) ... Andrew Belling
DELTA COUNTY U.S.A. (TF) ... Jack Elliott
DELTA COUNTY U.S.A. (TF) ... Allyn Ferguson
DELTA FORCE ... Alan Silvestri
DELUSION ... Don Peake
DEMENTIA ... George Antheil†
DEMENTIA 13 ... Ronald Stein†
DEMETRIUS AND THE
GLADIATORS ... Franz Waxman†
DEMI-PARADISE, THE ... Nicholas Brodzsky†
DEMON ... Frank Cordell†
DEMON MURDER
CASE, THE (TF) ... George Aliceson Tipton
DEMON OF THE ISLE, THE ... Christian Gaubert
DEMON POND ... Isao Tomita

DEMON SEED ... Jerry Fielding†
DEMONIAQUE ... Joseph Kosma†
DEMONOID ... Richard Gillis
DEMONS OF THE MIND ... Harry Robertson
DEMONWARP ... Dan Slider
DEMPSEY (TF) ... Billy Goldenberg
DEN ODPLATY (AF) ... Zdenek Liska
DENNIS THE MENACE (TF) ... Randy Edelman
DEPORTED ... Walter Scharf
DEPS ... Alfi Kabiljo
DER AUFENTHALT ... Guenther Fischer
DER BALL ... Werner R. Heymann†
DER BERG RUFT ... Giuseppe Becce†
DER EWIGE TRAUM ... Giuseppe Becce†
DER FEUERTEUFEL ... Giuseppe Becce†
DER GUNSTLING VON
SCHONBRUNN ... Giuseppe Becce†
DER HIMMEL UBER BERLIN ... Jurgen Knieper
DER JAGER VON FALL ... Giuseppe Becce†
DER KAISER VON KALIFORNIEN ... Giuseppe Becce†
DER KLEINE BRUDER ... Jurgen Knieper
DER KONGRESS TANZT ... Werner R. Heymann†
DER LAUFER VON MARATHON ... Giuseppe Becce†
DER MUDE TOD ... Giuseppe Becce†
DER REBELL ... Giuseppe Becce†
DER RICHTER UND SEIN HENKER ... Ennio Morricone
DER SCHAFER VON
TRUTKBERG ... Giuseppe Becce†
DER SEXBOMBER ... Stelvio Cipriani
DER SIEGER ... Werner R. Heymann†
DER SOHN DER
WEISSEN BERGE ... Giuseppe Becce†
DER STEINERNE FLUSS ... Guenther Fischer
DER TIGER VON ESCHNAPUR ... Michel Michelet†
DER VERLORENE SOHN ... Giuseppe Becce†
DERANGED ... Carl Zittrer
DERBY FIEBER USA ... Jurgen Knieper
DEREK AND CLIVE GET THE HORN ... Dudley Moore
DERRIERE LA FACADE ... Jean Wiener†
DERRIERE LA FENETRE ... Georges Delerue
DES ENFANTS GATES ... Philippe Sarde
DES GENS SANS IMPORTANCE ... Joseph Kosma†
DES HOMMES...UNE DOCTRINE ... Georges Delerue
DES PISSENLITS PAR LA RACINE ... Georges Delerue
DES TEUFELS PARADIES ... Jurgen Knieper
DESERT ATTACK ... Leighton Lucas†
DESERT BLOOM ... Brad Fiedel
DESERT FOX, THE ... Daniele Amfitheatrof†
DESERT FURY ... Miklos Rozsa
DESERT HAWK, THE ... Frank Skinner†
DESERT OF THE TARTARS, THE ... Ennio Morricone
DESERT RAIDERS ... Carlo Rustichelli
DESERT RATS (TF) ... J. Peter Robinson
DESERT RATS, THE ... Leigh Harline†
DESERT SANDS ... Paul Dunlap
DESERT SONG, THE ... Heinz Roemheld†
DESERT SONG, THE ... Max Steiner†
DESERT VICTORY ... William Alwyn†
DESERT WARRIOR ... Christopher Young
DESERTERS ... Michael Conway Baker
DESIGN FOR SCANDAL ... Franz Waxman†
DESIGNING WOMAN ... Andre Previn
DESIRE ... Frederick Hollander†
DESIRE ME ... Herbert Stothart†
DESIRE UNDER THE ELMS ... Elmer Bernstein
DESIREE ... Alex North
DESK SET ... Cyril J. Mockridge†
DESORDRE ... Gabriel Yared
DESORDRES ... Joseph Kosma†
DESPAIR ... Peer Raben
DESPERADO (TF) ... Michel Colombier
DESPERADO: AVALANCHE AT
DEVIL'S RIDGE (TF) ... Michel Colombier
DESPERADOES ARE IN TOWN, THE ... Bert A. Shefter
DESPERADOES, THE ... John Leipold†
DESPERATE (TF) ... Lee Holdridge
DESPERATE FOR LOVE (TF) ... Charles Bernstein
DESPERATE HOURS, THE ... David Mansfield
DESPERATE HOURS, THE ... Gail Kubik†
DESPERATE JOURNEY ... Max Steiner†
DESPERATE LIVES (TF) ... Bruce Broughton
DESPERATE MAN, THE ... Gerard Schurmann
DESPERATE MISSION (TF) ... Robert Drasnin
DESPERATE VOYAGE (TF) ... Bruce Broughton
DESPERATE WOMEN (TF) ... Richard DeBenedictis
DESPERATELY SEEKING SUSAN ... Thomas Newman
DESTINATION 60,000 ... Albert Glasser
DESTINATION INNER SPACE ... Paul Dunlap
DESTINATION MOON ... Leith Stevens†
DESTINATION MURDER ... Irving Gertz
DESTINATION TOKYO ... Franz Waxman†

DESTINATION UNKNOWN ..... Hans J. Salter
DESTINATION UNKNOWN ..... W. Franke Harling†
DESTINATION: AMERICA (TF) ..... Mike Post
DESTINY ..... Giuseppe Beccet
DESTINY ..... Frank Skinner†
DESTINY ..... Alexandre Tansman†
DESTINY OF A SPY (TF) ..... Ron Grainer
DESTROY ALL MONSTERS ..... Akira Ifukube
DESTROYER, THE ..... Anthony Collins†
DESTRUCTORS, THE ..... Roy Budd
DESTRUCTORS, THE ..... Paul Dunlap
DESTRY ..... Herman Stein
DESTRY RIDES AGAIN ..... Frank Skinner†
DETECTIVE, THE ..... Jerry Goldsmith
DETECTIVE, THE ..... Georges Auric†
DETENUTO IN ATTESA
DI GIUDIZIO ..... Carlo Rustichelli
DETOUR ..... Leo Erdody†
DETOUR TO TERROR (TF) ..... Morton Stevens
DEUTSCHLAND, BLEICHE ..... Jurgen Knieper
DEUX GRANDES FILLES
DANS UN PYJAMA ..... Claude Bolling
DEUX HOMMES DANS LA VILLE ..... Philippe Sarde
DEUX SOUS DE VIOLETTES ..... Georges Van Paryst
DEVIL AND DANIEL WEBSTER, THE ..... ★★ Bernard Herrmann†
DEVIL AND LEROY BASSETT, THE ..... Les Baxter
DEVIL AND MAX DEVLIN, THE ..... Buddy Baker
DEVIL AND MAX DEVLIN, THE ..... Marvin Hamlisch
DEVIL AND MISS JONES, THE ..... Roy Webb†
DEVIL AND MISS SARAH, THE (TF) ..... David Rose†
DEVIL AT 4 O'CLOCK, THE ..... George Duning
DEVIL BY THE TAIL, THE ..... Georges Delerue
DEVIL DOG: THE HOUND OF HELL (TF) ..... Artie Kane
DEVIL GODDESS ..... Mischa Bakaleinikoff †
DEVIL IN LOVE, THE ..... Armando Trovajoli
DEVIL IN THE FLESH ..... Carlo Crivelli
DEVIL IN THE FLESH ..... Nicola Piovani
DEVIL IN THE FLESH ..... Philippe Sarde
DEVIL IS A SISSY, THE ..... Herbert Stothart†
DEVIL IS A WOMAN, THE ..... Ennio Morricone
DEVIL MAY CARE ..... Herbert Stothart†
DEVIL MAY CARE ..... Dimitri Tiomkin†
DEVIL ON HORSEBACK ..... Malcolm Arnold
DEVIL RIDES OUT, THE ..... James Bernard
DEVIL TIMES FIVE ..... William Loose
DEVIL TO PAY, THE ..... Alfred Newman†
DEVIL WITH HITLER, THE ..... Edward Ward†
DEVIL WITHIN HER, THE ..... Ron Grainer
DEVIL'S ANGELS ..... Mike Curb
DEVIL'S BRIDE, THE ..... James Bernard
DEVIL'S BRIGADE, THE ..... Alex North
DEVIL'S CANYON ..... Daniele Amfitheatrof†
DEVIL'S DAUGHTER, THE (TF) ..... Laurence Rosenthal
DEVIL'S DISCIPLE, THE ..... Richard Rodney Bennett
DEVIL'S DOORWAY ..... Daniele Amfitheatrof†
DEVIL'S ENVOYS, THE ..... Joseph Kosma†
DEVIL'S HAIRPIN, THE ..... Nathan Van Cleave†
DEVIL'S MASK, THE ..... George Duning
DEVIL'S MASK, THE ..... Irving Gertz
DEVIL'S MEN, THE ..... Brian Eno
DEVIL'S ODDS ..... John Debney
DEVIL'S OWN, THE ..... Richard Rodney Bennett
DEVIL'S PARTNER, THE ..... Ronald Stein†
DEVIL'S PIPELINE, THE ..... Hans J. Salter
DEVIL'S PLAYGROUND, THE ..... Bruce Smeaton
DEVIL'S RAIN, THE ..... Al DeLory
DEVIL-DOLL, THE ..... Franz Waxman†
DEVILS, THE ..... Peter Maxwell Davies
DEVILS, THE ..... David Munrow
DEVONSHIRE TERROR, THE ..... Ray Colcord
DEVOTION ..... Erich Wolfgang Korngold†
DI MAMMA NON CE
N'E UNA SOLA ..... Armando Trovajoli
DIABOLIK ..... Ennio Morricone
DIABOLIQUE ..... Georges Van Paryst
DIAL 111 - JUVENILE SQUAD ..... Ronald Stein†
DIAL 1119 ..... Andre Previn
DIAL HOT LINE (TF) ..... Oliver Nelson†
DIAL M FOR MURDER ..... Dimitri Tiomkin†
DIAL M FOR MURDER (TF) ..... Billy Goldenberg
DIAMANTI SPORCHI DI SANGUE ..... Luis Bacalov
DIAMOND HEAD ..... John Williams
DIAMOND JIM ..... Ferde Grofe†
DIAMOND JIM ..... Franz Waxman†
DIAMOND ON WHEELS ..... Ron Goodwin
DIAMOND SKULLS ..... Hans Zimmer
DIAMOND TRAP, THE (TF) ..... Ron Ramin
DIAMOND WIZARD, THE ..... Matyas Seiber
DIAMONDS ..... Roy Budd
DIAMONDS ARE FOREVER ..... John Barry
DIANE ..... Miklos Rozsa
DIARY FOR TIMOTHY, A ..... Richard Addinsell†
DIARY OF A CHAMBERMAID, THE ..... Michel Michelet†
DIARY OF A HIGH SCHOOL BRIDE ..... Ronald Stein†
DIARY OF A HITCHHIKER (TF) ..... Joe Renzetti
DIARY OF A MADMAN ..... Richard LaSalle
DIARY OF A PERFECT
MURDER (TF) ..... Richard DeBenedictis
DIARY OF ANNE FRANK, THE ..... ★ Alfred Newman†
DIARY OF ANNE FRANK, THE (TF) ..... Billy Goldenberg
DICIOTTENNI AL SOLE ..... Ennio Morricone
DICK DOWN UNDER ..... Brian May
DICK SMART 2/007 ..... Mario Nascimbene
DICK TRACY ..... Danny Elfman
DICK TRACY ..... Roy Webb†
DICK TRACY MEETS GRUESOME ..... Paul Sawtell†
DICK TRACY'S G-MEN ..... William Lava†
DICTATOR, THE ..... Karol Rathaus†
DID YOU HEAR THE ONE ABOUT THE
TRAVELING SALESLADY? ..... Vic Mizzy
DIE ANGST DES TORMAN ..... Jurgen Knieper
DIE FALSCHUNG ..... Maurice Jarre
DIE GRAFFIN VON MONTE-CRISTO ..... Allan Gray†
DIE GROSSE ATTRAKTION ..... Bronislau Kaper†
DIE HARD ..... Michael Kamen
DIE HARD II ..... Michael Kamen
DIE LAUGHING ..... Robby Benson
DIE LAUGHING ..... Craig Safan
DIE LAUGHING ..... Jerry Segal
DIE LUSTIGEN MUSIKANTEN ..... Bronislau Kaper†
DIE NIBELUNGEN ..... Rolf Wilhelm
DIE NIBELUNGEN ..... Gottfried Huppertz†
DIE UNJEIMLICHEN WUNSCHE ..... Wolfgang Zeller†
DIE WEIBCHEN ..... Peter Thomas
DIE WILDEN FUENZIGER ..... Klaus Doldinger
DIEI DIEI MY DARLING ..... Wilfred Josephs
DIE, MONSTER, DIEI ..... Don Banks
DIECI ITALIANI PER UN TEDESCO ..... Armando Trovajoli
DIEU A CHOISI PARIS ..... Jean Wiener†
DIFFERENT AFFAIR, A (TF) ..... Jim Gross
DIFFERENT STORY, A ..... Bob Wahler
DIFFERENT STORY, A ..... David Frank
DIGBY, THE BIGGEST DOG
IN THE WORLD ..... Edwin Astley
DIGGIN' UP BUSINESS ..... Robert J. Walsh
DIGITAL DREAMS ..... Mike Batt
DILLINGER ..... Barry De Vorzon
DILLINGER ..... Dimitri Tiomkin†
DILLINGER E MORTO ..... Teo Usuelli
DIM LITTLE ISLAND ..... Ralph Vaughan Williams†
DIM SUM: A LITTLE
BIT OF HEART ..... Todd Boekelheide
DIME WITH A HALO ..... Ronald Stein†
DIMMI CHE FAI TUTTO PER ME ..... Armando Trovajoli
DIMPLES ..... Louis Silvers†
DINANZI A NOI IL CIELO ..... Carlo Rustichelli
DINNER AT EIGHT ..... William Axt†
DINNER AT EIGHT (CTF) ..... Jonathan Sheffer
DINO ..... Gerald Fried
DINOSAURUSI ..... Ronald Stein†
DIO IN CIELO, ARIZONA IN TERRA ..... Bruno Nicolai
DIO PERDONA, IO NO ..... Carlo Rustichelli
DIO, SEI UN PADRETERNOI ..... Riz Ortolani
DION BROTHERS, THE ..... Fred Karlin
DIPLOMANIACS ..... Max Steiner†
DIPLOMATIC COURIER ..... Sol Kaplan
DIPLOMATIC COURIER ..... Lionel Newman†
DIRT ..... Dick Halligan
DIRTY DANCING ..... John Morris
DIRTY DINGUS MAGEE ..... Jeff Alexander†
DIRTY DOZEN, THE ..... Frank De Vol
DIRTY DOZEN: DANKO'S DOZEN (TF) ..... Doug Timm†
DIRTY DOZEN: THE DEADLY
MISSION, THE (TF) ..... John Cacavas
DIRTY DOZEN: THE FATAL
MISSION, THE (TF) ..... John Cacavas
DIRTY DOZEN: THE NEXT
MISSION (TF) ..... Richard Harvey
DIRTY HANDS ..... Pierre Jansen
DIRTY HARRY ..... Lalo Schifrin
DIRTY HEROES, THE ..... Ennio Morricone
DIRTY KNIGHT'S WORK ..... Frank Cordell†
DIRTY MARY CRAZY LARRY ..... Jimmie Haskell
DIRTY MONEY ..... Michel Colombier
DIRTY ROTTEN SCOUNDRELS ..... Miles Goodman
DIRTY TRICKS ..... Hagood Hardy
DIS-MOI QUE TU M'AIMES ..... Claude Bolling
DIS-MOI QUI TU ES ..... Paul Misraki†
DISAPPEARANCE ..... Craig Hundley
DISAPPEARANCE OF
FLIGHT 412, THE (TF) ..... Morton Stevens
DISASTER ON THE COASTLINER (TF) ..... Gerald Fried
DISCO GODFATHER ..... Ernie Fields
DISCRETAMENTE UNA
SERA D'ESTATE ..... Stelvio Cipriani
DISHONORED LADY ..... Carmen Dragon†
DISORDERLIES ..... Anne Dudley
DISORGANIZED CRIME ..... David Newman
DISPATCH FROM REUTER'S,A ..... Max Steiner†
DISPERATO ADDIO ..... Carlo Rustichelli
DISPUTED PASSAGE ..... Frederick Hollander†
DISPUTED PASSAGE ..... John Leipold†
DISTANT DRUMS ..... Max Steiner†
DISTANT THUNDER ..... Maurice Jarre
DISTANT THUNDER ..... Satyajit Ray
DISTANT TRUMPET, A ..... Max Steiner†
DISTURBED ..... Scott Smalley
DITES-LE AVEC DES FLEURS ..... Claude Bolling
DITES-LUI QUE JE L'AIME ..... Alain Jomy
DITY HEROES, THE ..... Bruno Nicolai
DIVA ..... Vladimir Cosma
DIVE ..... David Michael Frank
DIVE BOMBER ..... Max Steiner†
DIVIDED HEART, THE ..... Georges Auric†
DIVINA CREATURA ..... Ennio Morricone
DIVINE NYMPH, THE ..... Cesare Bixio
DIVORCE ..... Eric Nordgren
DIVORCE AMERICAN STYLE ..... Dave Grusin
DIVORCE HIS/DIVORCE HERS (TF) ..... Stanley Myers
DIVORCE ITALIAN STYLE ..... Carlo Rustichelli
DIVORCE OF LADY X, THE ..... Miklos Rozsa
DIVORCE WARS: A LOVE STORY (TF) ..... Paul Chihara
DIXIANA ..... Max Steiner†
DIXIE ..... Robert Emmett Dolan†
DIXIE DUGAN ..... Emil Newman†
DIXIE: CHANGING HABITS (TF) ..... Jimmie Haskell
DJANGO ..... Luis Bacalov
DJANGO SPARA PER PRIMO ..... Bruno Nicolai
DO NOT FOLD, SPINDLE OR
MUTILATE (TF) ..... Jerry Goldsmith
DO THE RIGHT THING ..... Bill Lee
DO YOU KNOW THE
MUFFIN MAN? (TF) ..... ☆ Lee Holdridge
DO YOU REMEMBER LOVE (TF) ..... ☆ David Shire
DO YOU TAKE THIS
STRANGER? (TF) ..... ☆ Pete Rugolo
DOC SAVAGE, THE MAN OF BRONZE ..... Frank De Vol
DOCTEUR POPAUL ..... Pierre Jansen
DOCTOR AND THE DEVILS, THE ..... John Morris
DOCTOR DEATH, SEEKER
OF SOULS ..... Richard LaSalle
DOCTOR DETROIT ..... Lalo Schifrin
DOCTOR FAUSTUS ..... Mario Nascimbene
DOCTOR FISCHER OF GENEVA (TF) ..... Trevor Jones
DOCTOR IN CLOVER ..... John Scott
DOCTOR IN TROUBLE ..... Eric Rogers†
DOCTOR JUDYM ..... Andrzej Korzynski
DOCTOR TAKES A WIFE, THE ..... Frederick Hollander†
DOCTOR ZHIVAGO ..... ★★ Maurice Jarre
DOCTOR'S DILEMMA, THE ..... Joseph Kosma†
DOCTOR'S STORY, A (TF) ..... Randy Edelman
DOCTOR, YOU'VE GOT TO
BE KIDDING ..... Kenyon Hopkins
DOCTORS WILDE (TF) ..... Dana Kaproff
DOCTORS' PRIVATE LIVES (TF) ..... Richard Markowitz
DOCTORS' WIVES ..... Elmer Bernstein
DOCUMENTEUR: AN EMOTION
PICTURE (FD) ..... Georges Delerue
DODES'KA'DEN ..... Toru Takemitsu
DODGE CITY ..... Max Steiner†
DODSWORTH ..... Alfred Newman†
DOG, A MOUSE AND A SPUTNIK, A ..... Paul Misraki†
DOG AND CAT (TF) ..... Barry De Vorzon
DOG DAY ..... Francis Lai
DOG IT WAS THAT DIED, THE (TF) ..... Nigel Hess
DOG OF FLANDERS, A ..... Bert A. Shefter
DOG OF FLANDERS, A ..... Paul Sawtell†
DOG TAGS ..... John Scott
DOG'S BEST FRIEND, A ..... Bert A. Shefter
DOG'S LIFE, A ..... Nino Rota†
DOG, A MOUSE AND A SPUTNIK, A ..... Paul Misraki†
DOGS OF WAR, THE ..... Geoffrey Burgon
DOIN' TIME ..... Charles Fox
DOIN' TIME ON PLANET EARTH ..... Dana Kaproff
DOING LIFE (TF ..... Arthur B. Rubinstein
DOLL SQUAD, THE ..... Nicholas Carras
DOLL'S HOUSE, A ..... John Barry
DOLLARS ..... Quincy Jones
DOLLMAKER, THE (TF) ..... John Rubinstein
DOLLS ..... Richard H. Band
DOLLS ..... Jonathan Morse
DOLLS, THE ..... Armando Trovajoli

DOLPHIN (FD) ... Basil Poledouris
DOMANI E TROPPO TARDI ... Alessandro Cicognini†
DOMANI E UN ALTRO GIORNO ... Carlo Rustichelli
DOMANI E UN ALTRO GIORNO ... Franco Mannino
DOMANI PASSERO A SALUTARE LA TUA VEDOVA...PAROLIA DI EPIDEMIA! ... Bruno Nicolai
DOMICILE CONJUGAL ... Antoine Duhamel
DOMINICK AND EUGENE ... Trevor Jones
DOMINIQUE ... David Whitaker
DOMINO PRINCIPLE, THE ... Billy Goldenberg
DON CAMILLO ... Pino Donaggio
DON CAMILLO E I GIOVANI D'OGGI ... Carlo Rustichelli
DON CAMILLO MONSIGNORE MA NON TROPPO ... Alessandro Cicognini†
DON GIOVANNI IN SICILIA ... Armando Trovajoli
DON GIOVANNI IN SICILIA (TF) ... Bruno Nicolai
DON IS DEAD, THE ... Jerry Goldsmith
DON JUAN ... William Axt†
DON JUAN ETAIT UNE FEMME ... Michel Magne†
DON JUAN QUILLIGAN ... David Raksin
DON JUAN'S NIGHT OF LOVE ... Mario Nascimbene
DON QUIXOTE ... Jacques Ibert†
DON RAMIRO ... Luis De Pablo
DON'T ANSWER THE PHONE! ... Byron Allred
DON'T BOTHER TO KNOCK ... Lionel Newman†
DON'T CRY WITH YOUR MOUTH FULL ... Vladimir Cosma
DON'T CRY, IT'S ONLY THUNDER ... Maurice Jarre
DON'T DRINK THE WATER ... Patrick Williams
DON'T GET PERSONAL ... Franz Waxman†
DON'T GIVE UP THE SHIP ... Walter Scharf
DON'T GO IN THE HOUSE ... Richard Einhorn
DON'T GO NEAR THE WATER ... Bronislau Kaper†
DON'T GO TO SLEEP (TF) ... Dominic Frontiere
DON'T LOOK BACK (TF) ... Jack Elliott
DON'T LOOK IN THE BASEMENT ... Robert Farrar
DON'T LOOK NOW ... Pino Donaggio
DON'T LOOK NOW...WE'RE BEING SHOT AT ... Georges Auric†
DON'T LOSE YOUR HEAD ... Eric Rogers†
DON'T MAKE WAVES ... Vic Mizzy
DON'T PULL YOUR PUNCHES ... David Raksin
DON'T PUSH, I'LL CHARGE WHEN I'M READY (TF) ... Lyn Murray†
DON'T RAISE THE BRIDGE - LOWER THE RIVER ... David Whitaker
DON'T TRUST YOUR HUSBAND ... Hans J. Salter
DONA FLOR AND HER TWO HUSBANDS ... Chico Buarque
DONA FLOR AND HER TWO HUSBANDS ... Frances Hime
DONDE TU ESTES ... Luis Bacalov
DONKY SKIN ... Michel Legrand
DONNE E BRIGANTI ... Nino Rota†
DONNE E SOLDATI ... Teo Usuelli
DONNER PASS: THE ROAD TO SURVIVAL (TF) ... Robert Summers
DONOVAN'S REEF ... Cyril J. Mockridge†
DOOLINS OF OKLAHOMA, THE ... George Duning
DOOLINS OF OKLAHOMA, THE ... Paul Sawtell†
DOOMSDAY 2000 ... William Goldstein
DOOMSDAY FLIGHT, THE (TF) ... Lalo Schifrin
DOOMWATCH ... John Scott
DOOR IN THE WALL, THE ... James Bernard
DOPPLEGANGER ... Barry Gray
DORM THAT DRIPPED BLOOD, THE ... Christopher Young
DOROTHEA ... Philippe Sarde
DORTOIR DES GRANDES ... Georges Van Parys†
DOTTIE (TF) ... Paul Chihara
DOTTORE JEKYLL E GENTILE SIGNORA ... Armando Trovajoli
DOUBLE AGENT (TF) ... Alf Clausen
DOUBLE CROSSBONES ... Frank Skinner†
DOUBLE DATE ... Hans J. Salter
DOUBLE DEAL ... Bruce Smeaton
DOUBLE DEAL ... Michel Michelet†
DOUBLE DYNAMITE ... Leigh Harline†
DOUBLE EXPOSURE ... Hans Zimmer
DOUBLE HARNESS ... Max Steiner†
DOUBLE INDEMNITY ... ★ Miklos Rozsa
DOUBLE LIFE, A ... ★★ Miklos Rozsa
DOUBLE McGUFFIN, THE ... Euel Box
DOUBLE MURDER ... Riz Ortolani
DOUBLE NEGATIVE ... Paul Hoffert
DOUBLE REVENGE ... Harry Manfredini
DOUBLE STANDARD (TF) ... Patrick Williams
DOUBLE SUICIDE ... Toru Takemitsu
DOUBLE SUICIDE OF SONEZAKI ... Ryudo Uzaki
DOUBLE SWITCH (TF) ... Michel Colombier
DOUBLE TOUR, A ... Paul Misraki†
DOUBLE TROUBLE ... Jeff Alexander†
DOUBLE TROUBLE ... Joseph Carl Briel†
DOUBLE WEDDING ... Edward Ward†
DOUBLETAKE (TF) ... Arthur B. Rubinstein
DOUCEMENT LES BASSES! ... Claude Bolling
DOUGHGIRLS, THE ... Adolph Deutsch†
DOVE VAI IN VACANZA? ... Piero Piccioni
DOVE, THE ... John Barry
DOVER (FD) ... Gail Kubik†
DOVER (FD) ... Gail Kubik†
DOWN AND OUT IN BEVERLY HILLS ... Andy Summers
DOWN BY LAW ... John Lurie
DOWN MEMORY LANE ... Sol Kaplan
DOWN MISSOURI WAY ... Karl Hajos†
DOWN THE ANCIENT STAIRS ... Ennio Morricone
DOWN THE LONG HILLS (TF) ... Mark Snow
DOWN TO EARTH ... George Duning
DOWN TO EARTH ... Heinz Roemheld†
DOWN TO THE SEA IN SHIPS ... Alfred Newman†
DOWN TO THEIR LAST YACHT ... Max Steiner†
DOWN TWISTED ... Eric Allaman
DOWN TWISTED ... Berlin Game
DOWNHILL RACER ... Kenyon Hopkins
DOWNPAYMENT ON MURDER (TF) ... Laurence Rosenthal
DOWNTOWN ... Akira Ifukube
DOWNTOWN ... Alan Silvestri
DR. BLACK, MR. HYDE ... Johnny Pate
DR. BUTCHER, M.D. ... Walter Sear
DR. COOK'S GARDEN (TF) ... Robert Drasnin
DR. CRIPPEN ... Kenneth V. Jones
DR. CYCLOPS ... Ernst Toch†
DR. DOOLITTLE ... ★ Leslie Bricusse
DR. ERLICH'S MAGIC BULLET ... Max Steiner†
DR. FRANKENSTEIN ON CAMPUS ... Paul Hoffert
DR. GILLESPIE'S CRIMINAL CASE ... Daniele Amfitheatrof†
DR. GILLESPIE'S NEW ASSISTANT ... Daniele Amfitheatrof†
DR. GOLDFOOT AND THE BIKINI MACHINE ... Les Baxter
DR. GOLDFOOT AND THE GIRL BOMBS ... Les Baxter
DR. HACKENSTEIN ... Randy Miller
DR. HECKLE AND MR. HYPE ... Richard H. Band
DR. JEKYLL AND MR. HYDE ... ★ Franz Waxman†
DR. JEKYLL AND SISTER HYDE ... David Whitaker
DR. KILDARE'S WEDDING DAY ... Bronislau Kaper†
DR. NO ... John Barry
DR. NO ... Monty Norman
DR. PHIBES RISES AGAIN ... John Gale
DR. RENAULT'S SECRET ... David Raksin
DR. SCORPION (TF) ... Mike Post
DR. SCORPION (TF) ... Pete Carpenter†
DR. STRANGE (TF) ... Paul Chihara
DR. STRANGELOVE OR: HOW I LEARNED TO STOP WORRYING AND LOVE THE BOMB ... Laurie Johnson
DR. SYN, ALIAS THE SCARECROW ... Gerard Schurmann
DR. TERROR'S HOUSE OF HORRORS ... Elisabeth Luytens†
DR. X ... Bernhard Kaun†
DRACULA ... James Bernard
DRACULA ... John Williams
DRACULA (TF) ... Bob Cobert
DRACULA - PRINCE OF DARKNESS ... James Bernard
DRACULA A.D. 1972 ... Michael Vickers
DRACULA AND SON ... Vladimir Cosma
DRACULA CONTRA EL DR. FRANKENSTEIN ... Bruno Nicolai
DRACULA HAS RISEN FROM THE GRAVE ... James Bernard
DRACULA IN THE PROVINCES ... Fabio Frizzi
DRACULA TODAY ... Michael Vickers
DRACULA VS. FRANKENSTEIN ... William Lava†
DRACULA'S DAUGHTER ... Heinz Roemheld†
DRACULA'S DOG ... Andrew Belling
DRACULA'S LAST RITES ... Paul Jost
DRACULA'S LAST RITES ... George Small
DRACULA'S WIDOW ... James Campbell
DRAGNET ... Irving Gertz
DRAGNET ... Ira Newborn
DRAGNET (TF) ... Lyn Murray†
DRAGON LORD ... Sulkham Tsintsadze
DRAGON SEED ... Herbert Stothart†
DRAGON WELLS MASSACRE ... Paul Dunlap
DRAGON'S GOLD ... Albert Glasser
DRAGONFLY ... Stephen Lawrence
DRAGONFLY SQUADRON ... Paul Dunlap
DRAGONSLAYER ... ★ Alex North
DRAGONWYCK ... Alfred Newman†
DRAGSTRIP GIRL ... Ronald Stein†
DRAMA OF THE RICH ... Ennio Morricone
DRAMATIC LIFE OF ABRAHAM LINCOLN, THE ... Joseph Carl Briel†
DRAMATIC SCHOOL ... Franz Waxman†
DRANGO ... Elmer Bernstein
DRAUGHTSMAN'S CONTRACT, THE ... Michael Nyman
DRAW! (CTF) ... Ken Wannberg
DRAWINGS OF LEONARDO DA VINCI, THE ... Alan Rawsthorne†
DREAM A LITTLE DREAM ... John William Dexter
DREAM BREAKERS (TF) ... Glenn Paxton
DREAM DATE (TF) ... Peter Bernstein
DREAM DEMON ... Bill Nelson
DREAM FOR CHRISTMAS, A (TF) ... David Rose†
DREAM GIRL ... Victor Young†
DREAM HOUSE (TF) ... Brad Fiedel
DREAM LOVER ... Michael Small
DREAM MERCHANTS, THE (TF) ... George Duning
DREAM OF KINGS, A ... Alex North
DREAM ONE ... Gabriel Yared
DREAM ROSE, THE ... Alfi Kabiljo
DREAM STREET ... Louis Silvers†
DREAM STREET (TF) ... William Olvis
DREAM TEAM, THE ... David McHugh
DREAM WEST (MS) ... Fred Karlin
DREAM WIFE ... Conrad Salinger†
DREAMBOAT ... Cyril J. Mockridge†
DREAMCHILD ... Max Harris
DREAMCHILD ... Stanley Myers
DREAMER ... Bill Conti
DREAMING OUT LOUD ... Lucien Moraweck†
DREAMS DON'T DIE (TF) ... Brad Fiedel
DREAMS OF GOLD: THE MEL FISHER STORY (TF) ... Ernest Gold
DREAMS THAT MONEY CAN BUY ... Paul Bowles
DREAMS THAT MONEY CAN BUY ... John Cage
DREAMS THAT MONEY CAN BUY ... David Diamond
DREAMS THAT MONEY CAN BUY ... Darius Milhaud†
DREAMSCAPE ... Maurice Jarre
DRESS GRAY (TS) ... Billy Goldenberg
DRESSED TO KILL ... Pino Donaggio
DRESSED TO KILL ... Milton Rosen
DRESSED TO KILL ... Hans J. Salter
DRESSER, THE ... James Horner
DRESSMAKER, THE ... George Fenton
DRIFTER, THE ... Rick Conrad
DRIFTIN' RIVER ... Karl Hajos†
DRILLER KILLER ... Joseph Delia
DRIVE HARD, DRIVE FAST (TF) ... Pete Rugolo
DRIVE, HE SAID ... David Shire
DRIVER, THE ... Michael Small
DRIVING MISS DAISY ... Hans Zimmer
DROP DEAD, DARLING ... Dennis Farnon
DROP DEAD, MY LOVE ... Armando Trovajoli
DROP-OUT FATHER (TF) ... ☆ Peter Matz
DROP-OUT MOTHER (TF) ... Gerald Fried
DROWNING BY NUMBERS ... Michael Nyman
DROWNING POOL, THE ... Charles Fox
DROWNING POOL, THE ... Michael Small
DRUGSTORE COWBOY ... Elliot Goldenthal
DRUG WARS (TF) ... Charles Bernstein
DRUM BEAT ... Victor Young†
DRUM, THE ... John Greenwood†
DRUMS ACROSS THE RIVER ... Herman Stein
DRUMS ALONG THE MOHAWK ... Alfred Newman†
DRUMS IN THE DEEP SOUTH ... Dimitri Tiomkin†
DRUMS OF AFRICA ... Johnny Mandel
DRUMS OF THE CONGO ... Hans J. Salter
DRUMS OF THE CONGO ... Charles Previn†
DRUNKEN ANGEL ... Fumio Hayasaka †
DRY WHITE SEASON, A ... Dave Grusin
DU BEAT-E-O ... Doug Moody
DU BIST MEIN GLUCK ... Giuseppe Becce†
DU BOUT DES LEVRES ... Frederic Devreese
DU GRABUGE CHEZ LES VEUVES ... Georges Delerue
DU SOLEIL PLEIN LES YEUX ... Francis Lai
DUCHESS AND THE DIRTWATER FOX, THE ... Charles Fox
DUCK IN ORANGE SAUCE ... Armando Trovajoli
DUCK TALES (AF) ... David Newman
DUCK! YOU SUCKER ... Ennio Morricone
DUDE GOES WEST, THE ... Dimitri Tiomkin†
DUDES ... Charles Bernstein
DUDES ARE PRETTY PEOPLE ... Edward Ward†
DUE BIANCHI NELL 'AFRICA NERA ... Bruno Nicolai
DUE CUORI, UNA CAPPELLA ... Stelvio Cipriani

E

ENEMY BELOW, THE ... Leigh Harline†
ENEMY FROM SPACE ... James Bernard
ENEMY GENERAL, THE ... Mischa Bakaleinikoff †
ENEMY MINE ... Maurice Jarre
ENEMY OF THE PEOPLE, AN ... Leonard Rosenman
ENFORCER, THE ... David Buttolph†
ENFORCER, THE ... Jerry Fielding†
ENGAGEMENT ITALIANO ... Armando Trovajoli
ENGLAND MADE ME ... John Scott
ENGLISHMAN ABROAD, AN (TF) ... George Fenton
ENID IS SLEEPING ... Craig Safan
ENIGMA ... Marc Wilkinson
ENNEMI PUBLIC #1 ... Nino Rota†
ENOLA GAY (TF) ... Maurice Jarre
ENTER ARSENE LUPIN ... Milton Rosen
ENTER LAUGHING ... Quincy Jones
ENTER THE DRAGON ... Lalo Schifrin
ENTER THE NINJA ... W. Michael Lewis
ENTER THE NINJA ... Laurin Rinder
ENTERTAINER, THE ... John Addison
ENTERTAINER, THE (TF) ... Marvin Hamlisch
ENTITY, THE ... Charles Bernstein
ENTRE NOUS ... Luis Bacalov
ENTREE DES ARTISTS ... Georges Auric†
EPILOGUE ... Christopher Komeda†
EPILOGUE OF DOOM ... Brian Banks
EPILOGUE OF DOOM ... Anthony Marinelli
EQUAL JUSTICE (TF) ... David Bell
EQUATOR ... Serge Gainsbourg
EQUILIBRE ... Jacques Ibert†
EQUINOZIO ... Fiorenzo Carpi
EQUUS ... Richard Rodney Bennett
ER PIU, STORIA D'AMORE
E DI COLTELLO ... Piero Piccioni
ER PIU, STORIA D'AMORE
E DI COLTELLO ... Carlo Rustichelli
ERA LUI...SII SII ... Nino Rota†
ERASERHEAD ... Peter Ivers
ERCOLE AL CENTRO
DELLA TERRA ... Armando Trovajoli
ERCOLE CONTRO MOLOCH ... Carlo Rustichelli
EREDITA FERRAMONTI ... Ennio Morricone
ERIC (TF) ... Dave Grusin
ERIC THE CONQUEROR ... Les Baxter
ERIC THE VIKING ... Neil Innes
ERNEST GOES TO CAMP ... Shane Keister
ERNEST GOES TO JAIL ... Bruce Arnstson
ERNEST GOES TO JAIL ... Kirby Shelstad
ERNEST HEMINGWAY'S THE OLD
MAN AND THE SEA (TF) ... ☆ Bruce Broughton
ERNEST SAVES CHRISTMAS ... Mark Snow
ERNIE KOVACS - BETWEEN
THE LAUGHTER (TF) ... Ralph Burns
ERODE IL GRANDE ... Carlo Savina
EROTIC ADVENTURES
OF ZORRO, THE ... William Loose
ERRAND BOY, THE ... Walter Scharf
ESCALATION ... Ennio Morricone
ESCALE A ORLY ... Paul Misraki†
ESCALIER DE SERVICE ... Georges Van Parys†
ESCAPADE IN JAPAN ... Max Steiner†
ESCAPE ... Franz Waxman†
ESCAPE (TF) ... James Di Pasquale
ESCAPE (TF) ... Lalo Schifrin
ESCAPE ARTIST, THE ... Georges Delerue
ESCAPE FROM ALCATRAZ ... Jerry Fielding†
ESCAPE FROM BOGEN
COUNTY (TF) ... Charles Bernstein
ESCAPE FROM FORT BRAVO ... Jeff Alexander†
ESCAPE FROM IRAN: THE
CANADIAN CAPER (TF) ... Peter Jermyn
ESCAPE FROM NEW YORK ... John Carpenter
ESCAPE FROM NEW YORK ... Alan Howarth
ESCAPE FROM RED ROCK ... Les Baxter
ESCAPE FROM SOBIBOR (TF) ... Georges Delerue
ESCAPE FROM THE BRONX ... Francesco De Masi
ESCAPE FROM THE DARK ... Ron Goodwin
ESCAPE FROM THE PLANET
OF THE APES ... Jerry Goldsmith
ESCAPE FROM ZAHRAIN ... Lyn Murray†
ESCAPE IN THE DESERT ... Adolph Deutsch†
ESCAPE ME NEVER ... Erich Wolfgang Korngold†
ESCAPE ME NEVER ... Sir William Walton†
ESCAPE TO ATHENA ... Lalo Schifrin
ESCAPE TO MINDANAO (TF) ... Lyn Murray†
ESCAPE TO THE SUN ... Dov Seltzer
ESCAPE TO WITCH MOUNTAIN ... Johnny Mandel
ESKIMO ... William Axt†
ESPIONAGE ... William Axt†
ESPIONAGE AGENT ... Adolph Deutsch†
ESTATE VIOLENTA ... Mario Nascimbene
ESTERINA ... Carlo Rustichelli
ESTHER AND
THE KING ... Angelo Francesco Lavagnino†
ESTRATTO DAGLI ARCHIVI SEGRETI
DELLA POLIZIA DI UNA
CAPITALE EUROPA ... Stelvio Cipriani
ET MOURIR DE PLAISIR ... Jean Prodromides
ETERNAL RETURN, THE ... Georges Auric†
ETERNAL SEA, THE ... Elmer Bernstein
ETERNALLY YOURS ... ★ Werner Janssen
ETTORE FIERAMOSCA ... Alessandro Cicognini†
EUGENIE...THE STORY OF HER
JOURNEY INTO PERVERSION ... Bruno Nicolai
EUREKA ... Stanley Myers
EUREKA STOCKADE ... John Greenwood†
EUROPA DI NOTTE ... Carlo Savina
EUROPEANS, THE ... Richard Robbins
EVA ... Michel Legrand
EVA ... Mikis Theodorakis
EVA ... Eric Nordgren
EVARISTE GALOIS ... Antoine Duhamel
EVE OF ST. MARK, THE ... Cyril J. Mockridge†
EVEL KNIEVEL ... Patrick Williams
EVENING IN BYZANTIUM (TF) ... Stu Phillips
EVENSONG ... Louis Levy†
EVERGREEN (MS) ... Laurence Rosenthal
EVERY DAY EXCEPT CHRISTMAS ... Daniele Paris
EVERY DAY'S A HOLIDAY ... Leo Shuken†
EVERY GIRL SHOULD BE MARRIED ... Leigh Harline†
EVERY HOME SHOULD HAVE ONE ... John Cameron
EVERY LITTLE CROOK AND NANNY ... Fred Karlin
EVERY MAN FOR HIMSELF ... Carlo Rustichelli
EVERY MAN FOR HIMSELF ... Gabriel Yared
EVERY MAN NEEDS ONE (TF) ... Jack Elliott
EVERY MAN NEEDS ONE (TF) ... Allyn Ferguson
EVERY TIME WE SAY GOODBYE ... Philippe Sarde
EVERY WHICH WAY BUT LOOSE ... Steve Dorff
EVERYBODY DOES IT ... Mario Castelnuovo-Tedesco†
EVERYBODY SING ... George Bassman
EVERYBODY SING ... William Axt†
EVERYBODY WINS ... Mark Isham
EVERYBODY WINS ... Leon Redbone
EVERYBODY'S ALL
AMERICAN ... James Newton Howard
EVERYBODY'S BABY: THE RESCUE
OF JESSIE McCLURE (TF) ... Mark Snow
EVERYBODY'S DANCIN' ... Albert Glasser
EVERYBODY'S FINE ... Ennio Morricone
EVERYBODY'S OLD MAN ... David Buttolph†
EVERYTHING BUT THE TRUTH ... Milton Rosen
EVERYTHING BUT THE TRUTH ... Herman Stein
EVERYTHING BUT THE TRUTH ... Henry Mancini
EVERYTHING I HAVE IS YOURS ... David Rose†
EVERYTHING YOU WANTED TO
KNOW ABOUT SEX (BUT WERE
AFRAID TO ASK) ... Mundell Lowe
EVERYTHING'S DUCKY ... Bernard Green
EVICTORS, THE ... Jaime Mendoza-Nava
EVIL DEAD 2 ... Joe Lo Duca
EVIL DEAD, THE ... Joe Lo Duca
EVIL EYE ... Les Baxter
EVIL IN CLEAR RIVER (TF) ... William Olvis
EVIL NIGHT ... John W. Morgan
EVIL OF FRANKENSTEIN, THE ... Don Banks
EVIL THAT MEN DO, THE ... Ken Thorne
EVIL UNDER THE SUN ... John Lanchberry
EVIL, THE ... Johnny Harris
EVILS OF CHINATOWN ... Albert Glasser
EVITA PERON (TF) ... Johnny Mandel
EVOLUTION (FD) ... Jonathan Morse
EVW'S (FD) ... Malcolm Arnold
EWOK ADVENTURE, THE (TF) ... Peter Bernstein
EWOKS: THE BATTLE
FOR ENDOR (TF) ... Peter Bernstein
EX-MRS. BRADFORD, THE ... Roy Webb†
EXCALIBUR ... Trevor Jones
EXCITE ME ... Bruno Nicolai
EXCLUSIVE ... Milan Roder†
EXCLUSIVE STORY ... Edward Ward†
EXCUSE ME, MY NAME IS
ROCCO PAPALEO ... Armando Trovajoli
EXECUTION, THE (TF) ... Georges Delerue
EXECUTIONER'S SONG, THE (TF) ... John Cacavas
EXECUTIONER, THE ... Ron Goodwin
EXECUTIVE ACTION ... Randy Edelman
EXILE, THE ... Frank Skinner†
EXO-MAN (TF) ... Dana Kaproff
EXODUS ... ★★ Ernest Gold
EXORCIST II: THE HERETIC ... Ennio Morricone
EXORCIST III ... Barry De Vorzon
EXORCIST, THE ... Jack Nitzsche
EXPERIMENT ALCATRAZ ... Irving Gertz
EXPERIMENT IN TERROR ... Henry Mancini
EXPERIMENT PERILOUS ... Roy Webb†
EXPERT, THE ... W. Franke Harling†
EXPERTS, THE ... Marvin Hamlisch
EXPLORERS ... Jerry Goldsmith
EXPLOSION ... Sol Kaplan
EXPOSED ... Georges Delerue
EXPOSED ... Ernest Gold
EXPRESSO BONGO ... Robert Farnon
EXTASE ... Giuseppe Becce†
EXTERMINATOR 2 ... David Spear
EXTERMINATOR, THE ... Joe Renzetti
EXTRA CONJUGALE ... Luis Bacalov
EXTRAORDINARY SEAMAN, THE ... Maurice Jarre
EXTREME CLOSE-UP ... Basil Poledouris
EXTREME PREJUDICE ... Jerry Goldsmith
EXTREMES (FD) ... Roy Budd
EXTREMITIES ... J.A.C. Redford
EYE FOR AN EYE, AN ... William Goldstein
EYE OF THE CAT ... Lalo Schifrin
EYE OF THE NEEDLE ... Miklos Rozsa
EYE OF THE NEEDLE, THE ... Carlo Rustichelli
EYE OF THE TIGER ... Don Preston
EYE ON THE
SPARROW (TF) ... Eddie Lawrence Manson
EYE WITNESS ... Malcolm Arnold
EYEBALL ... Bruno Nicolai
EYES OF A STRANGER ... Richard Einhorn
EYES OF FIRE ... Brad Fiedel
EYES OF LAURA MARS ... Artie Kane
EYES OF THE UNDERWORLD ... Hans J. Salter
EYES, THE MOUTH, THE ... Nicola Piovani
EYEWITNESS ... Stanley Silverman

F

F FOR FAKE ... Michel Legrand
F. SCOTT FITZGERALD AND THE
LAST OF THE BELLES (TF) ... Don Sebesky
F. SCOTT FIZTGERALD IN
HOLLYWOOD (TF) ... Morton Gould
F.B.I. OPERAZIONE PAKISTAN ... Francesco De Masi
F.B.I. OPERAZIONE
VIPERA GIALLA ... Francesco De Masi
F.D.R.—THE LAST YEAR (TF) ... Laurence Rosenthal
F.I.S.T. ... Bill Conti
F.P.I. ANTWORTET NICHT ... Allan Gray†
F/X ... Bill Conti
FABULOUS BAKER BOYS, THE ... ★ Dave Grusin
FABULOUS BARON
MUNCHAUSEN, THE ... Zdenek Liska
FABULOUS DORSEYS, THE ... Leo Shuken†
FABULOUS JOE, THE ... Heinz Roemheld†
FABULOUS TEXAN, THE ... Anthony Collins†
FABULOUS WORLD OF
JULES VERNE, THE ... Zdenek Liska
FACCIA A FACCIA ... Ennio Morricone
FACE BEHIND THE MASK, THE ... Sidney Cutner†
FACE IN THE RAIN, A ... Richard Markowitz
FACE OF A FUGITIVE ... Jerry Goldsmith
FACE OF FEAR, THE (TF) ... Morton Stevens
FACE OF FIRE ... Eric Nordgren
FACE OF RAGE, THE (TF) ... Miles Goodman
FACE TO FACE ... Hugo Friedhofer†
FACE TO THE WIND ... Richard Markowitz
FACES ... Jack Ackerman
FACES OF FEAR ... Joel Goldsmith
FACTS OF LIFE GOES
TO PARIS, THE (TF) ... Misha Segal
FACTS OF LIFE, THE ... Leigh Harline†
FACTS OF MURDER, THE ... Carlo Rustichelli
FADE TO BLACK ... Craig Safan
FADILA ... Alain Romans
FAHRENHEIT 451 ... Bernard Herrmann†
FAIBLES FEMMES ... Paul Misraki†
FAILING OF RAYMOND, THE (TF) ... Patrick Williams
FAIR GAME ... Giorgio Moroder
FAIR WIND TO JAVA ... Victor Young†
FAIRY TALES ... Andrew Belling
FAIT DIVERS ... Arthur Honegger†
FAITHFUL IN MY FASHION ... Nathaniel Shilkret†
FAKE OUT ... Arthur B. Rubinstein
FAKE, THE ... Matyas Seiber
FAKERS, THE ... Nelson Riddle†
FALCON AND THE SNOWMAN, THE ... Lyle Mays
FALCON AND THE SNOWMAN, THE ... Pat Metheny
FALCON IN DANGER, THE ... Roy Webb†
FALCON OUT WEST, THE ... Roy Webb†

FIRE OVER AFRICA ... Benjamin Frankel†
FIRE OVER ENGLAND ... Richard Addinsell†
FIRE SALE ... Dave Grusin
FIRE WITH FIRE ... Howard Shore
FIRE! (TF) ... Richard LaSalle
FIREBALL 500 ... Les Baxter
FIREBALL FORWARD (TF) ... Lionel Newman†
FIREBALL, THE ... Victor Young†
FIREBRAND, THE ... Richard LaSalle
FIRECRACKER ... W. Michael Lewis
FIRECRACKER ... Laurin Rinder
FIRECREEK ... Alfred Newman†
FIRED WIFE ... Frank Skinner†
FIREFIGHTER (TF) ... Dana Kaproff
FIREFLY, THE ... Herbert Stothart†
FIREFOX ... Maurice Jarre
FIREHOUSE (TF) ... Tom Scott
FIREMAN SAVE MY CHILD ... Herman Stein
FIREMAN SAVE MY CHILD ... Henry Mancini
FIREMAN, SAVE MY CHILD ... W. Franke Harling†
FIREPOWER ... Gato Barbieri
FIRESTARTER ... Tangerine Dream
FIREWALKER ... Gary Chang
FIRST AFFAIR (TF) ... Lee Holdridge
FIRST AMONG EQUALS (MS) ... Richard Harvey
FIRST BLOOD ... Jerry Goldsmith
FIRST COMES COURAGE ... Ernst Toch†
FIRST DEADLY SIN, THE ... Gordon Jenkins†
FIRST DESIRES ... Philippe Sarde
FIRST ECHELON, THE ... Dmitri Shostakovitch†
FIRST FAMILY ... Ralph Burns
FIRST HUNDRED YEARS, THE ... William Axt†
FIRST KANGAROOS, THE (TF) ... William Motzig
FIRST LADY ... Max Steiner†
FIRST LOVE ... John Barry
FIRST LOVE ... Hans J. Salter
FIRST LOVE ... Riz Ortolani
FIRST MEN IN THE MOON ... Laurie Johnson
FIRST MONDAY IN OCTOBER ... Ian Fraser
FIRST NUDIE MUSICAL, THE ... Bruce Kimmel
FIRST OF THE FEW, THE ... Sir William Walton†
FIRST OLYMPICS - ATHENS 1896, THE (MS) ... ☆☆ Bruce Broughton
FIRST POWER, THE ... Stewart Copeland
FIRST STEPS (TF) ... Leonard Rosenman
FIRST TEACHER, THE ... Vyecheslav Ovchinnikov
FIRST TEXAN, THE ... Roy Webb†
FIRST TIME, THE ... Kenyon Hopkins
FIRST TIME, THE ... Lanny Meyers
FIRST TIME, THE ... Frederick Hollander†
FIRST TO FIGHT ... Fred Steiner
FIRST YANK INTO TOKYO ... Leigh Harline†
FIRST YOU CRY (TF) ... ☆ Peter Matz
FIRSTBORN ... Michael Small
FISH CALLED WANDA, A ... John Du Prez
FISH THAT SAVED PITTSBURGH, THE ... Thom Bell
FISHERMAN'S WHARF ... Victor Young†
FIST OF FEAR TOUCH OF DEATH ... Keith Mansfield
FISTFIGHTER ... Emilio Kauderer
FISTFUL OF CHOPSTICKS, A ... Tommy Vig
FISTFUL OF DOLLARS, A ... Ennio Morricone
FISTFUL OF DYNAMITE ... Ennio Morricone
FIT FOR A KING ... Arthur Morton
FITZCARRALDO ... Popol Vuh
FITZWILLY ... John Williams
FIVE A.M. ... Wendy Blackstone
FIVE BRANDED WOMEN ... Angelo Francesco Lavagnino†
FIVE CAME BACK ... Roy Webb†
FIVE CORNERS ... James Newton Howard
FIVE DAY LOVER, THE ... Georges Delerue
FIVE DAYS AND FIVE NIGHTS ... Dmitri Shostakovitch†
FIVE DAYS FROM HOME ... Bill Conti
FIVE DAYS ONE SUMMER ... Elmer Bernstein
FIVE DESPERATE WOMEN (TF) ... Paul Glass
FIVE FINGER EXERCISE ... Jerome Moross†
FIVE FINGERS ... Bernard Herrmann†
FIVE GRAVES TO CAIRO ... Miklos Rozsa
FIVE GUNS TO TOMBSTONE ... Bert A. Shefter
FIVE MAN ARMY, THE ... Ennio Morricone
FIVE MILES TO MIDNIGHT ... Mikis Theodorakis
FIVE MILLION YEARS TO EARTH ... Tristram Cary
FIVE OF ME, THE (TF) ... Fred Karlin
FIVE PENNIES, THE ... ★ Leith Stevens†
FIVE WEEKS IN A BALLOON ... Paul Sawtell†
FIXED BAYONETS! ... Roy Webb†
FIXER DUGAN ... Roy Webb†
FIXER, THE ... Maurice Jarre
FLAGRANT DESIR ... Gabriel Yared
FLAME AND THE ARROW, THE ... ★ Max Steiner†

FLAME BARRIER, THE ... Gerald Fried
FLAME IS LOVE, THE (TF) ... Morton Stevens
FLAME OF NEW ORLEANS, THE ... Frank Skinner†
FLAME, THE ... Heinz Roemheld†
FLAMES ON THE VOLGA ... Dmitri Kabalevsky†
FLAMINGO ROAD ... Max Steiner†
FLAMINGO ROAD (TF) ... Gerald Fried
FLAP ... Marvin Hamlisch
FLAREUP ... Les Baxter
FLASH GORDON ... Howard Blake
FLASH GORDON ... Queen
FLASH OF GREEN, A ... Charles Engstrom
FLASHBACK ... Barry Goldberg
FLASHBACK ... Bruno Nicolai
FLASHDANCE ... Giorgio Moroder
FLASHPOINT ... Tangerine Dream
FLAT, THE ... Zdenek Liska
FLATBED ANNIE AND SWEETIE PIE: LADY TRUCKERS (TF) ... Don Peake
FLATLINERS ... James Newton Howard
FLAXI MARTIN ... William Lava†
FLEA IN HER EAR, A ... Bronislau Kaper†
FLEET THAT CAME TO STAY, THE ... Lehman Engel†
FLEMISH FARM, THE ... Ralph Vaughan Williams†
FLESH + BLOOD ... Basil Poledouris
FLESH AND BLOOD (TF) ... Billy Goldenberg
FLESH AND DESIRE ... Georges Auric†
FLESH AND FANTASY ... Alexandre Tansman†
FLESH AND FLAME ... Albert Glasser
FLESH AND FURY ... Hans J. Salter
FLESH AND THE DEVIL ... Carl Davis
FLESH AND THE SPUR ... Ronald Stein†
FLESH AND THE WOMAN ... Georges Van Parys†
FLESH FOR FRANKENSTEIN ... Claudio Gizzi
FLESH WILL SURRENDER ... Nino Rota†
FLESHBURN ... Don Felder
FLESHBURN ... Arthur Kempel
FLETCH ... Harold Faltermeyer
FLETCH LIVES ... Harold Faltermeyer
FLEUR D'OSEILLE ... Michel Magne†
FLIC OU VOYOU ... Philippe Sarde
FLIC STORY ... Claude Bolling
FLICEK THE BALL (AF) ... Zdenek Liska
FLICK ... Paul Hoffert
FLICKS ... John W. Morgan
FLIGHT 90: DISASTER ON THE POTOMAC (TF) ... Gil Melle
FLIGHT COMMAND ... Franz Waxman†
FLIGHT FOR FREEDOM ... Roy Webb†
FLIGHT FROM ASHIYA ... Frank Cordell†
FLIGHT FROM DESTINY ... Heinz Roemheld†
FLIGHT INTO DARKNESS ... Arthur Honegger†
FLIGHT LIEUTENANT ... Werner R. Heymann†
FLIGHT NURSE ... Victor Young†
FLIGHT OF THE DOVES ... Roy Budd
FLIGHT OF THE INTRUDER, THE ... Basil Poledouris
FLIGHT OF THE NAVIGATOR ... Alan Silvestri
FLIGHT OF THE PHOENIX, THE ... Frank De Vol
FLIGHT OF THE RAINBIRD ... Laurens Van Rooyen
FLIGHT THAT DISAPPEARED, THE ... Richard LaSalle
FLIGHT TO FAME ... Sidney Cutner†
FLIGHT TO HOLOCAUST (TF) ... Paul Williams
FLIGHT, THE ... Guenther Fischer
FLIM FLAM MAN, THE ... Jerry Goldsmith
FLIRTING WITH FATE ... Victor Young†
FLOOD (TF) ... Richard LaSalle
FLOOD TIME ... Henry Mancini
FLOODS OF FEAR ... Alan Rawsthorne†
FLORADORA GIRL, THE ... Herbert Stothart†
FLORENCE NIGHTENGALE (TF) ... Stanley Myers
FLORIAN ... Franz Waxman†
FLORIDA STRAITS (CTF) ... Michel Colombier
FLOWERS IN THE ATTIC ... Christopher Young
FLOWING GOLD ... Adolph Deutsch†
FLUGEL UND FESSELN ... Jurgen Knieper
FLY AWAY HOME (TF) ... Lee Holdridge
FLY II, THE ... Christopher Young
FLY, THE ... Bert A. Shefter
FLY, THE ... Howard Shore
FLY, THE ... Paul Sawtell†
FLYERS OF THE OPEN SKIES ... Alfi Kabiljo
FLYING BLIND ... Dimitri Tiomkin†
FLYING BLIND (TF) ... Phil Marshall
FLYING CADETS ... Hans J. Salter
FLYING DEUCES, THE ... John Leipold†
FLYING DEUCES, THE ... Leo Shuken†
FLYING DEVILS ... Max Steiner†
FLYING DOWN TO RIO ... Max Steiner†
FLYING FEET ... Percy Grainger†
FLYING FONTAINES, THE ... Mischa Bakaleinikoff †
FLYING HIGH (TF) ... Jonathan Tunick

FLYING IRISHMAN, THE ... Roy Webb†
FLYING LEATHERNECKS ... Roy Webb†
FLYING MISSILE, THE ... George Duning
FLYING SERPENT, THE ... Leo Erdody†
FLYING TIGERS ... ★ Victor Young†
FLYING WITH MUSIC ... ★ Edward Ward†
FOG ISLAND ... Karl Hajos†
FOG, THE ... John Carpenter
FOLIES BOURGEOISES ... Manuel De Sica
FOLKS AT RED WOLF INN, THE ... Bill Marx
FOLLE A TUER ... Philippe Sarde
FOLLOW ME! ... Stu Phillips
FOLLOW ME, BOYS! ... George Bruns
FOLLOW THAT CAMEL ... Eric Rogers†
FOLLOW THAT DREAM ... Hans J. Salter
FOLLOW THE BOYS ... Ron Goodwin
FOLLOW THE BOYS ... Leigh Harline†
FOLLOW THE FLEET ... Max Steiner†
FOLLOW THE SUN ... Cyril J. Mockridge†
FOND MEMORIES ... Jean Cousineau
FOOD OF THE GODS, THE ... Elliot Kaplan
FOOL FOR LOVE ... George Burt
FOOLIN' AROUND ... Charles Bernstein
FOOLISH WIVES ... Sigmund Romberg†
FOOLS OF FORTUNE ... Hans Zimmer
FOOTLOOSE ... Miles Goodman
FOOTSTEPS (TF) ... Ernest Gold
FOOTSTEPS IN THE DARK ... Frederick Hollander†
FOOTSTEPS IN THE FOG ... Benjamin Frankel†
FOR A FEW DOLLARS MORE ... Ennio Morricone
FOR ALL MANKIND (FD) ... Brian Eno
FOR CLEMENCE ... Michel Portal
FOR HEAVEN'S SAKE ... Alfred Newman†
FOR KEEPS ... Bill Conti
FOR LADIES ONLY (TF) ... Lee Holdridge
FOR LOVE AND GOLD ... Carlo Rustichelli
FOR LOVE OF IVY ... Quincy Jones
FOR LOVE OR MONEY ... Frank De Vol
FOR LOVE OR MONEY (TF) ... Billy Goldenberg
FOR LOVERS ONLY (TF) ... Pete Rugolo
FOR ME AND MY GAL ... George Bassman
FOR PETE'S SAKE ... Artie Butler
FOR QUEEN AND COUNTRY ... Michael Kamen
FOR THE LOVE OF BENJI ... Euel Box
FOR THE LOVE OF IT (TF) ... Jimmie Haskell
FOR THE LOVE OF MARY ... Frank Skinner†
FOR THOSE I LOVED ... Maurice Jarre
FOR THOSE WHO THINK YOUNG ... Jerry Fielding†
FOR US, THE LIVING (TF) ... Gerald Fried
FOR WHOM THE BELL TOLLS ... ★ Victor Young†
FOR YOUR EYES ONLY ... Bill Conti
FORBBIDEN GAMES ... Greg De Belles
FORBIDDEN (CTF) ... Tangerine Dream
FORBIDDEN DANCE, THE ... Vladimir Horunzhy
FORBIDDEN LOVE (TF) ... Hagood Hardy
FORBIDDEN NIGHTS (TF) ... Lucia Hwong
FORBIDDEN PLANET ... Bebe Barron
FORBIDDEN PLANET ... Louis Barron†
FORBIDDEN STREET, THE ... Malcolm Arnold
FORBIDDEN WORLD ... Susan Justin
FORBIDDEN ZONE ... Danny Elfman
FORCE 10 FROM NAVARONE ... Ron Goodwin
FORCE FIVE (TF) ... James Di Pasquale
FORCE OF ARMS ... Max Steiner†
FORCE OF EVIL ... David Raksin
FORCE OF ONE, A ... Dick Halligan
FORCE OF THE NINJA ... Dan Slider
FORCE: FIVE ... William Goldstein
FORCED LANDING ... Dimitri Tiomkin†
FORCED VENGEANCE ... William Goldstein
FORD: THE MAN AND THE MACHINE (TF) ... Paul Zaza
FORE PLAY ... Gary William Friedman
FOREIGN AFFAIR, A ... Frederick Hollander†
FOREIGN BODY ... Ken Howard
FOREIGN CORRESPONDENT ... Alfred Newman†
FOREMAN WENT TO FRANCE, THE ... Sir William Walton†
FOREPLAY ... Stan Vincent
FOREST RANGERS, THE ... Victor Young†
FOREST, THE ... Richard Hieronymous
FOREST, THE ... Alan Oldfield
FOREVER (TF) ... Fred Karlin
FOREVER AMBER ... ★ David Raksin
FOREVER AND A DAY ... Anthony Collins†
FOREVER EMMANUELLE ... Franco Micalizzi
FOREVER FEMALE ... Victor Young†
FOREVER YOUNG, FOREVER FREE ... Lee Holdridge
FOREVER YOURS ... Dimitri Tiomkin†
FOREVER, DARLING ... Bronislau Kaper†
FORFAITURE ... Michel Michelet†

FORGOTTEN MAN, THE (TF) ... Dave Grusin
FORGOTTEN VILLAGE, THE (FD) ... Hanns Eisler†
FORMULA FOR MURDER ... Francesco De Masi
FORMULA, THE ... Bill Conti
FORSAKING ALL OTHERS ... William Axt†
FORSE UN FIORE ... Ennio Morricone
FORT ALESIA ... Carlo Rustichelli
FORT ALGIERS ... Michel Michelet†
FORT APACHE ... Richard Hageman†
FORT APACHE THE BRONX ... Jonathan Tunick
FORT BOWIE ... Les Baxter
FORT COURAGEOUS ... Richard LaSalle
FORT DOBBS ... Max Steiner†
FORT SAGANNE ... Philippe Sarde
FORT UTAH ... Jimmie Haskell
FORT VENGEANCE ... Paul Dunlap
FORT WORTH ... David Buttolph†
FORT YUMA ... Paul Dunlap
FORTRESS (CTF) ... Danny Beckerman
FORTUNE CARREE ... Paul Misraki†
FORTUNE COOKIE, THE ... Andre Previn
FORTUNE DANE (TF) ... Doug Timm†
FORTUNE, THE ... David Shire
FORTUNELLA ... Nino Rota†
FORTY DEUCE ... Manu Dibango
FORTY GUNS ... Harry Sukman†
FORTY NAUGHTY GIRLS ... Roy Webb†
FORTY-NINTH PARALLEL, THE ... Ralph Vaughan Williams†
FORZA G ... Ennio Morricone
FOSTER AND LAURIE (TF) ... Lalo Schifrin
FOUL PLAY ... Charles Fox
FOUND MONEY (TF) ... Jack Elliott
FOUNTAIN, THE ... Max Steiner†
FOUNTAINHEAD, THE ... Max Steiner†
FOUR BOYS AND A GUN ... Albert Glasser
FOUR DARK HOURS ... Miklos Rozsa
FOUR DAUGHTERS ... Max Steiner†
FOUR DAYS IN NOVEMBER (FD) ... Elmer Bernstein
FOUR DEUCES, THE ... Ken Wannberg
FOUR FEATHERS, THE ... Miklos Rozsa
FOUR FEATHERS, THE (TF) ... Allyn Ferguson
FOUR FLIES ON GREY VELVET ... Ennio Morricone
FOUR FOR TEXAS ... Nelson Riddle†
FOUR FRIENDS ... Elizabeth Swados
FOUR FRIGHTENED PEOPLE ... Karl Hajos†
FOUR GIRLS IN TOWN ... Herman Stein
FOUR GIRLS IN TOWN ... Alex North
FOUR GUNS TO THE BORDER ... Hans J. Salter
FOUR GUNS TO THE BORDER ... Herman Stein
FOUR GUNS TO THE BORDER ... Henry Mancini
FOUR HORSEMEN OF THE APOCALYPSE, THE ... Andre Previn
FOUR IN THE MORNING ... John Barry
FOUR MEN AND A PRAYER ... Louis Silvers†
FOUR MINUTE MILE, THE (TF) ... Richard Hartley
FOUR MOTHERS ... Heinz Roemheld†
FOUR MUSKETEERS, THE ... Lalo Schifrin
FOUR POSTER, THE ... Dimitri Tiomkin†
FOUR SKULLS OF JONATHAN DRAKE, THE ... Paul Dunlap
FOUR SONS ... David Buttolph†
FOUR WAYS OUT ... Carlo Rustichelli
FOUR WIVES ... Max Steiner†
FOUR'S A CROWD ... Adolph Deutsch†
FOUR'S A CROWD ... Heinz Roemheld†
FOUR-SIDED TRIANGLE ... Malcolm Arnold
FOURTEEN HOURS ... Alfred Newman†
FOURTH PROTOCOL, THE ... Lalo Schifrin
FOURTH WAR, THE ... Bill Conti
FOX AND THE HOUND, THE (AF) ... Buddy Baker
FOX, THE ... ★ Lalo Schifrin
FOXBAT ... Roy Budd
FOXES ... Giorgio Moroder
FOXES OF HARROW, THE ... David Buttolph†
FOXFIRE ... Frank Skinner†
FOXFIRE (TF) ... ☆ Johnny Mandel
FOXTROT ... Pete Rugolo
FRAMED ... Hans J. Salter
FRAMED ... Patrick Williams
FRAMED (CTF) ... William Olvis
FRAN ... Greg Schultz
FRANCE SOCIETE ANONYME ... Michel Portal
FRANCES ... John Barry
FRANCESCO ... Vangelis
FRANCIS ... Frank Skinner†
FRANCIS COVERS THE BIG TOWN ... Herman Stein
FRANCIS GARY POWERS: THE TRUE STORY OF THE U-2 SPY INCIDENT (TF) ... Gerald Fried
FRANCIS GOES TO THE RACES ... Frank Skinner†
FRANCIS GOES TO WEST POINT ... Milton Rosen
FRANCIS GOES TO WEST POINT ... Herman Stein
FRANCIS IN THE HAUNTED HOUSE ... Herman Stein
FRANCIS IN THE HAUNTED HOUSE ... Henry Mancini
FRANCIS IN THE HAUNTED HOUSE ... Frank Skinner†
FRANCIS OF ASSISI ... Mario Nascimbene
FRANCOIS LE RHINOCEROS ... Joseph Kosma†
FRANK BUCK'S JUNGLE CAVALCADE ... Nathaniel Shilkret†
FRANK NITTI: THE ENFORCER (TF) ... Yanni
FRANKENHOOKER ... Joe Renzetti
FRANKENSTEIN ... Bernhard Kaun†
FRANKENSTEIN '88 ... Paul Zaza
FRANKENSTEIN (TF) ... Bob Cobert
FRANKENSTEIN - 1970 ... Paul Dunlap
FRANKENSTEIN AND THE MONSTER FROM HELL ... James Bernard
FRANKENSTEIN CONQUERS THE WORLD ... Akira Ifukube
FRANKENSTEIN CREATED WOMAN ... James Bernard
FRANKENSTEIN MEETS THE WOLF MAN ... Charles Previn†
FRANKENSTEIN MEETS THE WOLF MAN ... Frank Skinner†
FRANKENSTEIN MEETS THE WOLFMAN ... Hans J. Salter
FRANKENSTEIN MUST BE DESTROYED! ... James Bernard
FRANKENSTEIN UNBOUND ... Carl Davis
FRANKENSTEIN'S GREAT AUNT TILLIE ... Ronald Stein†
FRANKENSTEIN—ITALIAN STYLE ... Stelvio Cipriani
FRANKENSTEIN: THE TRUE STORY (TF) ... Gil Melle
FRANTIC ... Miles Davis
FRANTIC ... Ennio Morricone
FRATELLO MARE ... Piero Piccioni
FRATELLO SOLE, SORELLA LUNA ... Riz Ortolani
FRATERNITY ROW ... Don McLean
FRATERNITY VACATION ... Brad Fiedel
FRAU IM STROM ... Giuseppe Becce†
FRAULEIN ... Daniele Amfitheatrof†
FRAULEIN DOKTOR ... Ennio Morricone
FREAKY FRIDAY ... Johnny Mandel
FREDDOM ROAD (TF) ... Terrence James
FREE ENTERPRISE ... Bruce Rowland
FREE FOR ALL ... Frank Skinner†
FREE MAN, A ... Francis Lai
FREE RETURN, THE ... Carl Dante
FREE RIDE ... David C. Williams
FREE SPIRIT ... Laurie Johnson
FREEBIE AND THE BEAN ... Dominic Frontiere
FREEDOM (TF) ... Lee Holdridge
FREEDOM FIGHTER (TF) ... Laurence Rosenthal
FREEDOM RADIO ... Nicholas Brodzsky†
FREEDOM RIDERS (TF) ... Morton Stevens
FREEDOM ROAD (TF) ... Coleridge-Taylor Perkinson
FREEWAY ... Joseph Delia
FRENCH CAN-CAN ... Georges Van Parys†
FRENCH CONNECTION II, THE ... Don Ellis†
FRENCH CONNECTION, THE ... Don Ellis†
FRENCH CONSPIRACY, THE ... Ennio Morricone
FRENCH DETECTIVE, THE ... Philippe Sarde
FRENCH DRESSING ... Georges Delerue
FRENCH LIEUTENANT'S WOMAN, THE ... Carl Davis
FRENCH LINE, THE ... Walter Scharf
FRENCH POSTCARDS ... Lee Holdridge
FRENCH REVOLUTION, THE ... Georges Delerue
FRENCH WITHOUT TEARS ... Nicholas Brodzsky†
FRENCH WOMAN, THE ... Serge Gainsbourg
FRENCHIE ... Hans J. Salter
FRENCHMAN'S CREEK ... Victor Young†
FRENZY ... Ron Goodwin
FRESH FROM PARIS ... Frank De Vol
FRESH HORSES ... David Foster
FRESH HORSES ... Patrick Williams
FRESH HORSES ... David Mansfield
FRESHMAN, THE ... David Newman
FRESNO (MS) ... John Morris
FREUD ... ★ Jerry Goldsmith
FRIDAY THE 13TH ... Harry Manfredini
FRIDAY THE 13TH - THE FINAL CHAPTER ... Harry Manfredini
FRIDAY THE 13TH PART 2 ... Harry Manfredini
FRIDAY THE 13TH PART 3 ... Harry Manfredini
FRIDAY THE 13TH PART V - A NEW BEGINNING ... Harry Manfredini
FRIDAY THE 13TH PART VI: JASON LIVES ... Harry Manfredini
FRIDAY THE 13TH PART VII - THE NEW BLOOD ... Harry Manfredini
FRIDAY THE 13TH, PART VII - THE NEW BLOOD ... Fred Mollin
FRIDAY THE 13th, PART VIII - JASON TAKES MANHATTAN ... Fred Mollin
FRIDAY THE 13TH...THE ORPHAN ... Teo Macero
FRIDAYS OF ETERNITY ... Lalo Schifrin
FRIEDA ... John Greenwood†
FRIEND INDEED ... William Axt†
FRIEND OF VINCENT, A ... Philippe Sarde
FRIENDLY ENEMIES ... Lucien Moraweck†
FRIENDLY FIRE (TF) ... ☆☆ Leonard Rosenman
FRIENDLY PERSUASION ... Dimitri Tiomkin†
FRIENDLY PERSUASION (TF) ... John Cacavas
FRIENDS FOR LIFE ... Nino Rota†
FRIENDS OF EDDIE COYLE, THE ... Dave Grusin
FRIENDSHIP IN VIENNA, A (CTF) ... Lee Holdridge
FRIENDSHIPS, SECRETS AND LIES (TF) ... Angela Morley
FRIGHT ... Harry Robertson
FRIGHT NIGHT ... Brad Fiedel
FRIGHT NIGHT PART 2 ... Brad Fiedel
FRIGHTMARE ... Stanley Myers
FRISCO KID, THE ... Frank De Vol
FRISCO LIL ... Hans J. Salter
FRISCO SAL ... Edward Ward†
FRISKY ... Alessandro Cicognini†
FRITZ THE CAT (AF) ... Ed Bogas
FRITZ THE CAT (AF) ... Ray Shanklin
FROG (TF) ... Ron Ramin
FROG DREAMING ... Brian May
FROGMEN, THE ... Cyril J. Mockridge†
FROGMEN, THE ... Lionel Newman†
FROGS ... Les Baxter
FROM A FAR COUNTRY (TF) ... Wojciech Kilar
FROM A ROMAN BALCONY ... Piero Piccioni
FROM A WHISPER TO A SCREAM ... Jim Manzie
FROM BEYOND ... Richard H. Band
FROM BEYOND THE GRAVE ... Douglas Gamley
FROM HELL TO TEXAS ... Daniele Amfitheatrof†
FROM HELL TO VICTORY ... Riz Ortolani
FROM HERE TO ETERNITY ... ★ George Duning
FROM HERE TO ETERNITY (MS) ... Walter Scharf
FROM HOLLYWOOD TO DEADWOOD ... Alex Gibson
FROM NOON TILL THREE ... Elmer Bernstein
FROM RUSSIA WITH LOVE ... John Barry
FROM THE DEAD OF NIGHT (TF) ... Gil Melle
FROM THE HIP ... Paul Zaza
FROM THE LIFE OF THE MARIONETTES ... Rolf Wilhelm
FROM THE POLICE, WITH THANKS ... Stelvio Cipriani
FROM THE TERRACE ... Elmer Bernstein
FROM THIS DAY FORWARD ... Leigh Harline†
FRONT PAGE, THE ... Billy May
FRONT, THE ... Dave Grusin
FRONTIER ... Dmitri Kabalevsky†
FRONTIER BADMEN ... Hans J. Salter
FRONTIER GAL ... Frank Skinner†
FRONTIER GUN ... Paul Dunlap
FRONTIER MARSHALL ... David Raksin
FRONTIER UPRISING ... Bert A. Shefter
FROZEN DEAD, THE ... Don Banks
FROZEN GHOST, THE ... Hans J. Salter
FRUIT MACHINE, THE ... Hans Zimmer
FUGA IN FRANCIA ... Nino Rota†
FUGITIVE FAMILY (TF) ... Morton Stevens
FUGITIVE FROM THE EMPIRE (TF) ... Ian Underwood
FUGITIVE KIND, THE ... Kenyon Hopkins
FUGITIVE OF THE PLAINS ... Leo Erdody†
FUGITIVE, THE ... Richard Hageman†
FUGITIVES FOR A NIGHT ... Robert Russell Bennett†
FUGUE ... Antoine Duhamel
FULFILLMENT OF MARY GRAY, THE (TF) ... Gary Scott
FULL CIRCLE ... Colin Towns
FULL CONFESSION ... Roy Webb†
FULL EXPOSURE: THE SEX TAPES SCANDAL (TF) ... Dana Kaproff
FULL METAL JACKET ... Abigail Mead
FULL MOON HIGH ... Gary William Friedman
FULL MOON IN BLUE WATER ... Phil Marshall
FULLER BRUSH GIRL, THE ... Heinz Roemheld†
FULLER BRUSH MAN, THE ... Heinz Roemheld†
FUN AND FANCY FREE ... Paul J. Smith†
FUN AND FANCY FREE ... Oliver Wallace†
FUN AND GAMES (TF) ... Peter Matz
FUN WITH DICK AND JANE ... Ernest Gold
FUNERAL HOME ... Jerry Fielding†
FUNHOUSE, THE ... John Beal
FUNNY COMPANY (AF) ... Vladimir Horunzhy
FUNNY FACE ... Adolph Deutsch†
FUNNY FARM ... Elmer Bernstein

FUNNY GIRL ... ★ Walter Scharf
FUNNY LADY ... ★ Peter Matz
FUNNY THING HAPPENED ON THE WAY TO THE FORUM, A ... ★★ Ken Thorne
FUNNYMAN ... Peter Schickele
FURIA A MARRAKESCH ... Carlo Savina
FURIES, THE ... Franz Waxman†
FURTHER ADVENTURES OF TENNESSEE BUCK, THE ... John Debney
FURTHER ADVENTURES OF THE WILDERNESS FAMILY ... Gene Kauer
FURTHER ADVENTURES OF THE WILDERNESS FAMILY ... Douglas Lackey
FURTHER PERILS OF LAUREL AND HARDY, THE ... John Parker
FURY ... Franz Waxman†
FURY AT FURNACE CREEK ... David Raksin
FURY AT SUNDOWN ... Harry Sukman†
FURY, THE ... John Williams
FUTURE-KILL ... Robert Renfrow
FUTURES VEDETTES ... Jean Wiener†
FUTUREWORLD ... Fred Karlin
FUZZ ... Dave Grusin
FUZZY PINK NIGHTGOWN, THE ... Billy May

G

G'OLE (FD) ... Rick Wakeman
G.I. EXECUTIONER, THE ... Elliot Chiprut
G.I. EXECUTIONER,THE ... Jason Garfield
G.I. WAR BRIDES ... Ernest Gold
GABLE AND LOMBARD ... Michel Legrand
GABRIEL OVER THE WHITE HOUSE ... William Axt†
GABY ... Conrad Salinger†
GABY - A TRUE STORY ... Maurice Jarre
GADFLY, THE ... Dmitri Kabalevsky†
GADFLY, THE ... Dmitri Shostakovitch†
GAILY, GAILY ... Henry Mancini
GAL WHO TOOK THE WEST, THE ... Frank Skinner†
GALA ... Antoine Duhamel
GALACTIC CONNECTION, THE ... Robert J. Walsh
GALAXY OF TERROR ... Barry Schrader
GALIA ... Michel Magne†
GALILEO ... Richard Hartley
GALILEO ... Ennio Morricone
GALLANT BLADE, THE ... George Duning
GALLANT LADY ... Alfred Newman†
GALLIPOLI ... Brian May
GALLOPING MAJOR, THE ... Georges Auric†
GAMBIT ... Maurice Jarre
GAMBLER, THE ... Jerry Fielding†
GAMBLERS, THE ... John Morris
GAMBLING HOUSE ... Roy Webb†
GAME IS OVER, THE ... Jean Bouchety
GAME OF DEATH ... John Barry
GAME PASS ... Peer Raben
GAME, SET AND MATCH (MS) ... Richard Harvey
GAMES MOTHER NEVER TAUGHT YOU (TF) ... Mark Snow
GAMES, THE ... Francis Lai
GANDHI ... ★ George Fenton
GANDHI ... ★ Ravi Shankar
GANG WAR ... Paul Dunlap
GANGSTER CHRONICLES, THE (TF) ... John Cacavas
GANGSTER, THE ... Louis Gruenberg†
GANGWAY FOR TOMORROW ... Roy Webb†
GANJA AND HESS ... Sam Waymon
GARBAGE PAIL KIDS MOVIE, THE ... Michael Lloyd
GARBO TALKS ... Cy Coleman
GARCON ... Philippe Sarde
GARDE A VUE ... Georges Delerue
GARDEN MURDER CASE, THE ... William Axt†
GARDEN OF ALLAH, THE ... ★ Max Steiner†
GARDEN OF EVIL ... Bernard Herrmann†
GARDEN OF THE FINZI-CONTINIS, THE ... Manuel De Sica
GARDENER'S SON, THE (TF) ... Charles Gross
GARDENER, THE ... Marc Fredericks
GARDENS OF STONE ... Carmine Coppola
GARGOYLES (TF) ... Robert Prince
GARMENT JUNGLE, THE ... Leith Stevens†
GAS ... Paul Zaza
GAS HOUSE KIDS ... Leo Erdody†
GAS HOUSE KIDS GO WEST ... Albert Glasser
GAS HOUSE KIDS IN HOLLYWOOD ... Albert Glasser
GASLIGHT ... Richard Addinsell†
GASLIGHT ... Bronislau Kaper†
GASPI ... Walter Scharf
GATE, THE ... Michael Hoenig
GATE, THE ... J. Peter Robinson
GATES OF HELL, THE ... Fabio Frizzi
GATHERING OF EAGLES, A ... Jerry Goldsmith
GATHERING OF OLD MEN, A (TF) ... Ron Carter
GATHERING, PART II, THE (TF) ... Robert Prince
GATHERING, THE (TF) ... John Barry
GATOR ... Charles Bernstein
GATTI ROSSI IN UN LABIRINTO DI VETRO ... Bruno Nicolai
GAUNTLET, THE ... Jerry Fielding†
GAWAIN AND THE GREEN KNIGHT ... Ron Goodwin
GAY AMIGO, THE ... Albert Glasser
GAY DECEIVERS, THE ... Stu Phillips
GAY DIPLOMAT, THE ... Max Steiner†
GAY DIVORCEE, THE ... Max Steiner†
GAY LADY, THE ... Benjamin Frankel†
GAY SISTERS, THE ... Max Steiner†
GAZEBO, THE ... Jeff Alexander†
GEISHA BOY, THE ... Walter Scharf
GEISHA GIRL ... Albert Glasser
GELOSIA ... Carlo Rustichelli
GEMINI, THE TWIN STARS ... Nigel Holton
GEMINUS (TF) ... Bruno Nicolai
GENE KRUPA STORY, THE ... Leith Stevens†
GENERAL DIED AT DAWN, THE ... Werner Janssen
GENERAL SPANKY ... T. Marvin Hatley†
GENERAL, THE ... Carl Davis
GENERATION ... Dave Grusin
GENERATION (TF) ... Charles Bernstein
GENESIS ... Ravi Shankar
GENESIS CHILDREN, THE ... Jerry Styne
GENESIS II (TF) ... Harry Sukman†
GENEVIEVE ... ★ Larry Adler
GENEVIEVE A GAGNE SON PARI ... Jean Prodromides
GENIE, THE ... Allan Gray†
GENIUS AT WORK ... Paul Sawtell†
GENOCIDE (FD) ... Elmer Bernstein
GENOVA A MANO ARMATA ... Franco Micalizzi
GENOVEVA DE BRABANTE ... Carlo Rustichelli
GENTLE GUNMAN, THE ... John Greenwood†
GENTLEMAN AFTER DARK ... Dimitri Tiomkin†
GENTLEMAN BANDIT, THE (TF) ... Stanley Myers
GENTLEMAN JIM ... Heinz Roemheld†
GENTLEMAN JO...UCCIDI ... Bruno Nicolai
GENTLEMAN'S AGREEMENT ... Alfred Newman†
GENTLEMEN IN WHITE VESTS ... Peter Thomas
GENTLEMEN MARRY BRUNETTES ... Robert Farnon
GEORGE McKENNA STORY, THE (TF) ... Herbie Hancock
GEORGE RAFT STORY, THE ... Jeff Alexander†
GEORGE STEVENS: A FILMMAKER'S JOURNEY (FD) ... Carl Davis
GEORGE WASHINGTON (MS) ... Laurence Rosenthal
GEORGE WASHINGTON SLEPT HERE ... Adolph Deutsch†
GEORGE WASHINGTON: THE FORGING OF A NATION (TF) ... Bruce Broughton
GEORGE WHITE'S SCANDALS ... Leigh Harline†
GEORGE'S ISLAND ... Marty Simon
GEORGIA PEACHES, THE (TF) ... R. Donovan Fox
GERALD McBOING BOING (AS) ... Gail Kubik†
GERMINAL ... Michel Magne†
GERONIMO ... Hugo Friedhofer†
GERVAISE ... Georges Auric†
GET CARTER ... Roy Budd
GET CHARLIE TULLY ... Christopher Gunning
GET CHRISTIE LOVE! (TF) ... Jack Elliott
GET CHRISTIE LOVE! (TF) ... Allyn Ferguson
GET CRAZY ... Michael Boddicker
GET GOING ... Hans J. Salter
GET IT MAN ... Alfi Kabiljo
GET OUT YOUR HANDKERCHIEFS ... Georges Delerue
GET SMART, AGAIN! (TF) ... Peter Melnick
GET TO KNOW YOUR RABBIT ... Jack Elliott
GET-AWAY, THE ... Daniele Amfitheatrof†
GETAWAY, THE ... Vladimir Cosma
GETAWAY, THE ... Quincy Jones
GETEILTE LIEBE ... Jurgen Knieper
GETTING AWAY FROM IT ALL (TF) ... Vic Mizzy
GETTING EVEN ... Richard Greene
GETTING EVEN ... Christopher Young
GETTING GERTIE'S GARTER ... Hugo Friedhofer†
GETTING IT ON ... Rickey Keller
GETTING IT RIGHT ... Colin Towns
GETTING MARRIED (TF) ... Craig Safan
GETTING PHYSICAL (TF) ... William Goldstein
GETTING STRAIGHT ... Ronald Stein†
GHIDRAH, THE THREE-HEADED MONSTER ... Akira Ifukube
GHOST ... Maurice Jarre
GHOST AND MR. CHICKEN, THE ... Vic Mizzy
GHOST AND MRS. MUIR, THE ... Bernard Herrmann†
GHOST BREAKERS ... Ernst Toch†
GHOST CATCHERS ... Edward Ward†
GHOST DAD ... Henry Mancini
GHOST DANCING (TF) ... John Morris
GHOST DIVER ... Bert A. Shefter
GHOST FEVER ... James Hart
GHOST GOES WEST, THE ... Mischa Spoliansky†
GHOST IN MONTE CARLO, A (CTF) ... Laurie Johnson
GHOST IN THE INVISIBLE BIKINI ... Les Baxter
GHOST OF A CHANCE (TF) ... Charles Bernstein
GHOST OF DRAGSTRIP HOLLOW ... Ronald Stein†
GHOST OF FLIGHT 401, THE (TF) ... David Raksin
GHOST OF FRANKENSTEIN, THE ... Hans J. Salter
GHOST SHIP, THE ... Roy Webb†
GHOST STORY ... Philippe Sarde
GHOST TOWN ... Harvey R. Cohen
GHOST TOWN ... Paul Dunlap
GHOST WARRIOR ... Richard H. Band
GHOSTBUSTERS ... Elmer Bernstein
GHOSTBUSTERS II ... Randy Edelman
GHOSTS CAN'T DO IT ... Junior Homrich
GHOSTS ITALIAN STYLE ... Luis Bacalov
GHOSTS OF BUXLEY HALL, THE (TF) ... Frank De Vol
GHOUL, THE ... Harry Robertson
GHOULIES ... Richard H. Band
GHOULIES ... Shirley Walker
GHOULIES II ... Jonathan Morse
GIANT ... ★ Dimitri Tiomkin†
GIANT BEHEMOTH, THE ... Edwin Astley
GIANT FROM THE UNKNOWN ... Albert Glasser
GIANT OF DEVIL'S CRAG, THE ... Albert Glasser
GIANT OF METROPOLIS, THE ... Armando Trovajoli
GIDEON OF SCOTLAND YARD ... Douglas Gamley
GIDEON OLIVER: SLEEP WELL, PROFESSOR OLIVER (TF) ... Arthur B. Rubinstein
GIDEON'S DAY ... Douglas Gamley
GIDEON'S TRUMPET (TF) ... Joseph Weiss
GIDGET GETS MARRIED (TF) ... Mike Post
GIDGET GETS MARRIED (TF) ... Pete Carpenter†
GIDGET GOES TO ROME ... John Williams
GIDGET GROWS UP (TF) ... Shorty Rogers
GIFT OF GAB ... Edward Ward†
GIFT OF LIFE, THE (TF) ... Billy Goldenberg
GIFT OF LOVE, THE ... Cyril J. Mockridge†
GIFT OF LOVE: A CHRISTMAS STORY, THE (TF) ... Fred Karlin
GIFT, THE ... Michel Legrand
GIFTED ONE, THE (TF) ... J. Peter Robinson
GIGANTIS THE FIRE MONSTER ... Masaru Sato
GIGANTIS THE FIRE MONSTER ... Paul Sawtell†
GIGI ... ★★ Andre Previn
GIGOT ... ★ Michel Magne†
GIL OCCHI, LA BOCCA ... Nicola Piovani
GILDA ... Hugo Friedhofer†
GILDERSLEEVE'S GHOST ... Paul Sawtell†
GIMME AN F ... Jan Hammer
GIMME MY QUARTERBACK ... David Broekman†
GINGER ALE AFTERNOON ... Willie Dixon
GINGER AND FRED ... Nicola Piovani
GIOCHI PARTICOLARI ... Ennio Morricone
GIORDANO BRUNO ... Ennio Morricone
GIORNATA NERA PER L'ARIETE ... Ennio Morricone
GIORNO DI NOZZE ... Nino Rota†
GIORNO PER GIORNO DISPERATAMENTE ... Carlo Rustichelli
GIOVANNINO ... Franco Micalizzi
GIOVENTU PERDUTA ... Carlo Rustichelli
GIRL AND THE GAMBLER, THE ... Roy Webb†
GIRL AND THE GENERAL, THE ... Ennio Morricone
GIRL DOWNSTAIRS, THE ... William Axt†
GIRL FRIENDS ... Dmitri Shostakovitch†
GIRL FROM JONES BEACH, THE ... David Buttolph†
GIRL FROM MANHATTAN, THE ... Heinz Roemheld†
GIRL FROM MEXICO, THE ... Roy Webb†
GIRL FROM MISSOURI, THE ... William Axt†
GIRL FROM PETROVKA, THE ... Henry Mancini
GIRL FROM SAN LORENZO, THE ... Albert Glasser
GIRL HE LEFT BEHIND, THE ... Roy Webb†
GIRL IN BLACK STOCKINGS, THE ... Les Baxter
GIRL IN EVERY PORT, A ... Roy Webb†
GIRL IN THE EMPTY GRAVE, THE (TF) ... Mundell Lowe
GIRL IN THE PAINTING, THE ... Benjamin Frankel†
GIRL IN THE PICTURE, THE ... Alfi Kabiljo
GIRL IN THE RED VELVET SWIN, THE ... Leigh Harline†
GIRL IN THE SWING, THE ... Carl Davis
GIRL IN THE WOODS ... Albert Glasser
GIRL IN WHITE, THE ... David Raksin

GIRL IN YELLOW PAJAMAS, THE .... Riz Ortolani
GIRL MOST LIKELY TO..., THE (TF) .... Bernardo Segall
GIRL NAMED SOONER, A (TF) .... Jerry Goldsmith
GIRL NAMED TAMIKO, A .... Elmer Bernstein
GIRL NO. 217 .... Aram Khachaturian†
GIRL O' MY DREAMS .... Edward Ward†
GIRL OF THE GOLDEN WEST, THE .... Herbert Stothart†
GIRL OF THE LIMBERLOST, THE .... Ernest Gold
GIRL OF THE NIGHT .... Sol Kaplan
GIRL OF THE RIO .... Max Steiner†
GIRL ON A MOTORCYCLE, THE .... Les Reed
GIRL ON THE LATE, LATE SHOW, THE (TF) .... Richard Markowitz
GIRL STROKE BOY .... John Scott
GIRL TROUBLE .... Alfred Newman†
GIRL WAS YOUNG, THE .... Louis Levy†
GIRL WHO CAME BETWEEN, THE (TF) .... Mark Snow
GIRL WHO CAME GIFT-WRAPPED, THE (TF) .... Jack Elliott
GIRL WHO CAME GIFT-WRAPPED, THE (TF) .... Allyn Ferguson
GIRL WHO HAD EVERYTHING, THE .... Andre Previn
GIRL WHO SPELLED FREEDOM, THE (TF) .... Mark Snow
GIRL WITH GREEN EYES, THE .... John Addison
GIRL, A GUY AND A GOB, A .... Roy Webb†
GIRL, THE GOLD WATCH AND DYNAMITE, THE (TF) .... Bruce Broughton
GIRL...AND A MILLION, A .... Ennio Morricone
GIRLFRIENDS .... Michael Small
GIRLS IN CHAINS .... Leo Erdody†
GIRLS IN PRISON .... Ronald Stein†
GIRLS IN THE NIGHT .... Herman Stein
GIRLS IN THE NIGHT .... Henry Mancini
GIRLS IN THE OFFICE, THE (TF) .... John Parker
GIRLS IN THE SUN .... Stavros Xarchakos
GIRLS JUST WANT TO HAVE FUN .... Thomas Newman
GIRLS MARKED FOR DANGER .... Armando Trovajoli
GIRLS OF HUNTINGTON HOUSE, THE (TF) .... Tom Scott
GIRLS OF PLEASURE ISLAND, THE .... Lyn Murray†
GIRLS OF THE WHITE ORCHID (TF) .... Brad Fiedel
GIRLS TOWN .... Van Alexander
GIRLY .... Bernard Ebbinghouse
GIRO CITY .... Alun Francis
GIROLIMONI - IL MOSTRO DI ROMA .... Riz Ortolani
GIU LA TESTA .... Ennio Morricone
GIUBBE ROSSE .... Carlo Rustichelli
GIUGNO '44, SBARCHEREMO IN NORMANDIA .... Bruno Nicolai
GIUSEPPE VENDUTO DAI FRATELLI .... Mario Nascimbene
GIVE A GIRL A BREAK .... Andre Previn
GIVE DADDY THE KNIFE .... Naz Nomad
GIVE GOD A CHANCE ON SUNDAYS .... Patrick Gowers
GIVE HER THE MOON .... Georges Delerue
GIVE US THIS NIGHT .... Erich Wolfgang Korngold†
GIVE US WINGS .... Hans J. Salter
GLACIER FOX, THE (FD) .... Masaru Sato
GLADIATOR (TF) .... David Frank
GLASS BOTTOM BOAT, THE .... Frank De Vol
GLASS HOUSE, THE (TF) .... Billy Goldenberg
GLASS HOUSES .... David Raksin
GLASS KEY, THE .... Victor Young†
GLASS MENAGERIE, THE .... Henry Mancini
GLASS MENAGERIE, THE .... Max Steiner†
GLASS MENAGERIE, THE (TF) .... John Barry
GLASS MOUNTAIN, THE .... Christopher Komeda†
GLASS MOUNTAIN, THE .... Nino Rota†
GLASS SLIPPER, THE .... Bronislau Kaper†
GLASS SPHINX, THE .... Les Baxter
GLASS WALL, THE .... Leith Stevens†
GLASS WEB, THE .... Herman Stein
GLEAMING THE CUBE .... Jay Ferguson
GLENN MILLER STORY, THE .... Herman Stein
GLENN MILLER STORY, THE .... ★ Henry Mancini
GLI AMANTI LATINI .... Carlo Savina
GLI AMICI DI NICK HEZARD .... Luis Bacalov
GLI ANGELI DALLE MANI BENDATE .... Stelvio Cipriani
GLI ATTENDENTI .... Armando Trovajoli
GLI EROI .... Riz Ortolani
GLI EROI DI FORT WORTH .... Carlo Rustichelli
GLI ESECUTORI .... Luis Bacalov
GLI FUMAVANO LE COLT .... Bruno Nicolai
GLI IMBROGLIANI .... Carlo Rustichelli
GLI INNAMORATI .... Carlo Rustichelli
GLI INTERMIERI DELLA MUTUA .... Carlo Rustichelli
GLI INTOCCABILI .... Ennio Morricone
GLI INVASORI/FURY OF THE VIKINGS .... Les Baxter
GLI INVINCIBILI TRE .... Angelo Francesco Lavagnino†
GLI ITALIANI SONO MATTI .... Nino Rota †
GLI OCCHI FEDDI DELLA PAURA .... Ennio Morricone
GLI ONOREVOLI .... Armando Trovajoli
GLI SCHIAVI PIU FORTI DEL MONDO .... Francesco De Masi
GLI SPECIALISTI .... Angelo Francesco Lavagnino†
GLI ULTIMI .... Carlo Rustichelli
GLI ULTIMI FILIBUSTIERI .... Carlo Rustichelli
GLI ULTIMI TRE GIORNI .... Nicola Piovani
GLITTER DOME, THE (CTF) .... Stuart Margolin
GLITZ (TF) .... Dana Kaproff
GLORIA .... Bill Conti
GLORY .... James Horner
GLORY DAYS (TF) .... Robert Folk
GLORY GUYS, THE .... Riz Ortolani
GLORY STOMPERS, THE .... Mike Curb
GLORY! GLORY! (CTF) .... Christopher Dedrick
GLOVE, THE .... Robert O. Ragland
GLUT .... Peer Raben
GLYKIA SYMMORIA .... George Hatzinassios
GNOME-MOBILE, THE .... Buddy Baker
GO CHASE YOURSELF .... Roy Webb†
GO FOR IT .... Dennis Dragon
GO FOR THE GOLD .... David McHugh
GO KART GO! .... Ron Goodwin
GO NAKED INTO THE WORLD .... Adolph Deutsch†
GO TELL IT ON THE MOUNTAIN (TF) .... Webster Lewis
GO TELL THE SPARTANS .... Dick Halligan
GO TOWARD THE LIGHT (TF) .... James Newton Howard
GO WEST .... George Bassman
GO WEST, YOUNG GIRL! (TF) .... Jerrold Immel
GO, MAN, GO .... Alex North
GO-BETWEEN, THE .... Michel Legrand
GOBOTS: BATTLE OF THE ROCK LORDS (AF) .... Hoyt Curtin
GOD BLESS THE CHILD (TF) .... David Shire
GOD IS MY CO-PILOT .... Franz Waxman†
GOD IS MY PARTNER .... Paul Dunlap
GOD TOLD ME TO .... Frank Cordell†
GOD'S COUNTRY AND THE WOMAN .... Max Steiner†
GOD'S LITTLE ACRE .... Elmer Bernstein
GOD'S WILL .... Christopher Cameron
GODCHILD, THE (TF) .... David Shire
GODDESS OF LOVE .... Michel Michelet†
GODDESS OF LOVE, THE (TF) .... A.S. Diamond
GODDESS OF LOVE, THE (TF) .... Dennis Dreith
GODDESS OF LOVE, THE (TF) .... Mitch Margo
GODDESS, THE .... Virgil Thomson†
GODFATHER, THE .... Nino Rota†
GODFATHER PART III, THE .... Carmine Coppola
GODFATHER, PART II, THE .... ★★ Carmine Coppola
GODFATHER, PART II, THE .... ★★ Nino Rota†
GODS MUST BE CRAZY II, THE .... Charles Fox
GODS MUST BE CRAZY, THE .... Johnny Bishop
GODS MUST BE CRAZY, THE .... John Boshoff
GODS OF PESTILENCE .... Peer Raben
GODSEND, THE .... Roger Webb
GODZILLA 1985 .... Reijiro Koroku
GODZILLA VS. BIONIC MONSTER .... Masaru Sato
GODZILLA VS. COSMIC MONSTER .... Masaru Sato
GODZILLA VS. MECHA-GODZILLA .... Masaru Sato
GODZILLA VS. MOTHRA .... Akira Ifukube
GODZILLA VS. THE SEA MONSTER .... Masaru Sato
GODZILLA VS. THE THING .... Akira Ifukube
GODZILLA, KING OF THE MONSTERS .... Akira Ifukube
GOG .... Harry Sukman†
GOIN' COCOANUTS .... Nelson Riddle†
GOIN' HOME .... Lee Holdridge
GOIN' SOUTH .... Perry Botkin
GOIN' SOUTH .... Van Dyke Parks
GOIN' TO TOWN .... Andrea Setaro†
GOING APE! .... Elmer Bernstein
GOING BERSERK .... Tom Scott
GOING FOR THE GOLD: THE BILL JOHNSON STORY (TF) .... J.A.C. Redford
GOING HOLLYWOOD .... Herbert Stothart†
GOING IN STYLE .... Michael Small
GOING MY WAY .... Robert Emmett Dolan†
GOING SANE .... Cameron Allan
GOING TO THE CHAPEL (TF) .... Charles Fox
GOJIRA .... Akira Ifukube
GOLD .... Elmer Bernstein
GOLD AND LEAD .... Michel Legrand
GOLD FOR THE CAESARS .... Franco Mannino
GOLD IS WHERE YOU FIND IT .... Max Steiner†
GOLD OF NAPLES .... Alessandro Cicognini†
GOLD OF THE AMAZON WOMEN (TF) .... Gil Melle
GOLD RUSH, THE .... Charles Chaplin†
GOLDEN ARROW, THE .... W. Franke Harling†
GOLDEN ARROW, THE .... Mario Nascimbene
GOLDEN BLADE, THE .... Herman Stein
GOLDEN BLADE, THE .... Henry Mancini
GOLDEN BOY .... ★ Victor Young†
GOLDEN CHILD, THE .... Michel Colombier
GOLDEN CLAW, THE .... Victor Schertzinger†
GOLDEN EARRINGS .... Victor Young†
GOLDEN FORTRESS, THE .... Satyajit Ray
GOLDEN GATE (TF) .... Ralph Burns
GOLDEN GATE MURDERS, THE (TF) .... Sol Kaplan
GOLDEN HARVEST .... Heinz Roemheld†
GOLDEN HORDE, THE .... Hans J. Salter
GOLDEN LADY,THE .... Georges Garvarentz
GOLDEN MISTRESS, THE .... Raoul Kraushaar
GOLDEN MOMENT: AN OLYMPIC LOVE STORY, THE (TF) .... Perry Botkin
GOLDEN MOUNTAINS .... Dmitri Shostakovitch†
GOLDEN NEEDLES .... Lalo Schifrin
GOLDEN NIGHTS .... Pierre Jansen
GOLDEN SALAMANDER .... William Alwyn†
GOLDEN SEAL, THE .... John Barry
GOLDEN SEAL, THE .... Dana Kaproff
GOLDEN VOYAGE OF SINBAD, THE .... Miklos Rozsa
GOLDENGIRL .... Bill Conti
GOLDFINGER .... John Barry
GOLDIE AND THE BOXER (TF) .... Jimmie Haskell
GOLDIE AND THE BOXER GO HOLLYWOOD (TF) .... Jimmie Haskell
GOLGOTHA .... Jacques Ibert†
GOLIATH AND THE BARBARIANS .... Les Baxter
GOLIATH AND THE DRAGON .... Les Baxter
GOLIATH AND THE VAMPIRES .... Les Baxter
GOLIATH AND THE VAMPIRES .... Angelo Francesco Lavagnino†
GOLIATH AWAITS (TF) .... George Duning
GONE IN 60 SECONDS .... Ronald Halicki
GONE TO EARTH .... Brian Easdale
GONE WITH THE WAVE (FD) .... Lalo Schifrin
GONE WITH THE WEST .... Christopher L. Stone
GONE WITH THE WIND .... ★ Max Steiner†
GONG SHOW MOVIE, THE .... Milton DeLugg
GOOD AGAINST EVIL (TF) .... Lalo Schifrin
GOOD AND THE BAD, THE .... Francis Lai
GOOD DIE YOUNG, THE .... Georges Auric†
GOOD EARTH, THE .... Herbert Stothart†
GOOD FATHER, THE .... Richard Hartley
GOOD FELLOWS, THE .... Leo Shuken†
GOOD FIGHT, THE (FD) .... Wendy Blackstone
GOOD FOR NOTHING .... Hans Werner Henze
GOOD GUYS AND THE BAD GUYS, THE .... William Lava†
GOOD GUYS WEAR BLACK .... Craig Safan
GOOD HUMOR MAN, THE .... Heinz Roemheld†
GOOD LUCK, MISS WYCKOFF .... Ernest Gold
GOOD LUCK, MR. YATES .... John Leipold†
GOOD MORNING VIETNAM .... Alex North
GOOD MORNING, BABYLON .... Nicola Piovani
GOOD MORNING, MISS DOVE .... Leigh Harline†
GOOD MORNING...AND GOODBYE .... Igo Kantor
GOOD MOTHER, THE .... Elmer Bernstein
GOOD NEIGHBOR SAM .... Frank De Vol
GOOD OLD SOAK, THE .... Edward Ward†
GOOD SAM .... Robert Emmett Dolan†
GOOD SPORT, A (TF) .... Mark Snow
GOOD TO GO .... Wally Badarou
GOOD WIFE, THE .... Cameron Allan
GOOD, THE BAD AND THE UGLY, THE .... Ennio Morricone
GOOD-BYE, CRUEL WORLD .... Tom Jenkins
GOODBYE AGAIN .... Georges Auric†
GOODBYE CHARLIE .... Andre Previn
GOODBYE COLUMBUS .... Charles Fox
GOODBYE EMMANUELLE .... Serge Gainsbourg
GOODBYE GEMINI .... Christopher Gunning
GOODBYE GIRL, THE .... Dave Grusin
GOODBYE MARY (TF) .... Bruno Nicolai
GOODBYE MR. CHIPS .... Richard Addinsell†
GOODBYE MY FANCY .... Daniele Amfitheatrof†
GOODBYE NEW YORK .... Michael Abene
GOODBYE RAGGEDY ANN (TF) .... Wladimir Selinsky
GOODBYE, FLICKMANIA .... Ryudo Uzaki
GOODBYE, MR. CHIPS .... ★ Leslie Bricusse
GOODBYE, MR. CHIPS .... ★ John Williams
GOODBYE, NORMA JEAN .... Joe Beck
GOODNIGHT MY LOVE (TF) .... Harry Betts
GOONIES .... Dave Grusin
GORDON'S WAR .... Angelo Badalamenti

GORE VIDAL'S BILLY THE KID (CTF) ... Laurence Rosenthal
GORE VIDAL'S LINCOLN (MS) ... Ernest Gold
GORE-GORE GIRLS, THE ... Herschell Gordon Lewis
GORGEOUS HUSSY, THE ... Herbert Stothart†
GORGO ... Angelo Francesco Lavagnino†
GORGON, THE ... James Bernard
GORILLA AT LARGE ... Lionel Newman†
GORILLA, THE ... David Buttolph†
GORILLAS IN THE MIST ... ★ Maurice Jarre
GORKY PARK ... James Horner
GOSPEL ACCORDING TO ST. MATTHEW, THE ... ★ Luis Bacalov
GOSPEL ACCORDING TO VIC ... B.A. Robertson
GOSSIP COLUMNIST, THE (TF) ... Allyn Ferguson
GOTCHA! ... Bill Conti
GOTHAM (CTF) ... George S. Clinton
GOTHIC ... Thomas Dolby
GOTT MIT UNS ... Ennio Morricone
GOTTERDAMERUNG ... Maurice Jarre
GOVERNMENT GIRL ... Leigh Harline†
GOYA ... Luis De Pablo
GRACE KELLY (TF) ... John Andrew Tartaglia
GRACE QUIGLEY ... John Addison
GRADINA ... Mario Nascimbene
GRADUATE, THE ... Dave Grusin
GRADUATION DAY ... Arthur Kempel
GRAMBLING'S WHITE TIGER (TF) ... John D'Andrea
GRAMBLING'S WHITE TIGER (TF) ... Michael Lloyd
GRAN PREMIO ... Carlo Rustichelli
GRAN VARIETA ... Carlo Rustichelli
GRAND CANYON ... Albert Glasser
GRAND DUEL, THE ... Luis Bacalov
GRAND HOTEL EXCELSIOR ... Armando Trovajoli
GRAND ILLUSION ... Joseph Kosma†
GRAND OLYMPICS, THE ... Armando Trovajoli
GRAND OLYMPICS, THE (FD) ... Angelo Francesco Lavagnino†
GRAND PRIX ... Maurice Jarre
GRAND SLAM ... Ennio Morricone
GRAND THEFT AUTO ... Peter Ivers
GRANDEUR NATURE ... Maurice Jarre
GRANDMOTHER'S HOUSE ... Nigel Holton
GRANDS FEUX ... Darius Milhaud†
GRANDVIEW, U.S.A. ... Thomas Newman
GRAPES OF WRATH, THE ... Alfred Newman†
GRASS IS ALWAYS GREENER OVER THE SEPTIC TANK, THE (TF) ... Peter Matz
GRASSHOPPER, THE ... Billy Goldenberg
GRAVEYARD SHIFT ... Nicholas Pike
GRAVY TRAIN, THE ... Fred Karlin
GRAY LADY DOWN ... Jerry Fielding†
GRAY OF ABSENCE ... Emilio Kauderer
GRAYEAGLE ... Jaime Mendoza-Nava
GRAZIE TANTE E ARRIVEDERCI ... Luis Bacalov
GRAZIE ZIA ... Ennio Morricone
GREASE 2 ... Artie Butler
GREASED LIGHTNING ... Fred Karlin
GREASER'S PALACE ... Jack Nitzsche
GREAT ALLIGATOR, THE ... Stelvio Cipriani
GREAT AMERICAN BEAUTY CONTEST, THE (TF) ... Ken Wannberg
GREAT AMERICAN PASTIME, THE ... Jeff Alexander†
GREAT AMERICAN TRAFFIC JAM, THE (TF) ... Arthur B. Rubinstein
GREAT AMERICAN TRAGEDY, A (TF) ... George Duning
GREAT BANK HOAX, THE ... Arthur B. Rubinstein
GREAT BANK ROBBERY, THE ... Nelson Riddle†
GREAT BRAIN, THE ... Don Costa
GREAT CARUSO, THE ... ★ John Green†
GREAT CASH GIVEAWAY GETAWAY, THE (TF) ... John Parker
GREAT CATHERINE ... Dimitri Tiomkin†
GREAT CHASE, THE ... Larry Adler
GREAT CITIZEN, A ... Dmitri Shostakovitch†
GREAT COMMANDMENT, THE ... Hans J. Salter
GREAT DAY IN THE MORNING ... Leigh Harline†
GREAT DAY IN THE MORNING ... Leith Stevens†
GREAT DICTATOR, THE ... ★ Charles Chaplin†
GREAT ESCAPE II: THE UNTOLD STORY, THE (TF) ... Johnny Mandel
GREAT ESCAPE, THE ... Elmer Bernstein
GREAT EXPECTATIONS ... Maurice Jarre
GREAT EXPECTATIONS ... Walter Goehr†
GREAT EXPECTATIONS ... Edward Ward†
GREAT EXPECTATIONS (CTF) ... Ken Thorne
GREAT GARRICK, THE ... Adolph Deutsch†
GREAT GATSBY, THE ... Robert Emmett Dolan†
GREAT GATSBY, THE ... ★★ Nelson Riddle†
GREAT GILDERSLEEVE, THE ... Paul Sawtell†
GREAT GLASS BLOWER, THE ... Jean Wiener†
GREAT HOUDINIS, THE (TF) ... Peter Matz
GREAT ICE RIP-OFF, THE (TF) ... Bob Cobert
GREAT IMPERSONATION, THE ... Franz Waxman†
GREAT IMPOSTOR, THE ... Henry Mancini
GREAT JASPER, THE ... Max Steiner†
GREAT JEWEL ROBBER, THE ... William Lava†
GREAT JOHN L., THE ... Victor Young†
GREAT LIE, THE ... Max Steiner†
GREAT MacARTHY, THE ... Bruce Smeaton
GREAT MAN VOTES, THE ... Roy Webb†
GREAT MAN'S LADY, THE ... Victor Young†
GREAT MAN'S WHISKERS, THE (TF) ... Earl Robinson
GREAT MAN, THE ... Herman Stein
GREAT MAN, THE ... Henry Mancini
GREAT McGINTY, THE ... Frederick Hollander†
GREAT MELIES, THE ... Georges Van Parys†
GREAT MOMENT, THE ... Victor Young†
GREAT MOUSE DETECTIVE, THE ... Henry Mancini
GREAT MR. NOBODY, THE ... Adolph Deutsch†
GREAT MUPPET CAPER, THE ... Joe Raposo†
GREAT NORTHFIELD, MINNESOTA RAID, THE ... Dave Grusin
GREAT OUTDOORS, THE ... Nicky Holland
GREAT OUTDOORS, THE ... Thomas Newman
GREAT RACE, THE ... Henry Mancini
GREAT RUPERT, THE ... Leith Stevens†
GREAT SANTINI, THE ... Elmer Bernstein
GREAT SCOUT AND CATHOUSE THURSDAY, THE ... John Cameron
GREAT SINNER, THE ... Bronislau Kaper†
GREAT SIOUX MASSACRE, THE ... Emil Newman†
GREAT SIOUX UPRISING, THE ... Herman Stein
GREAT SIOUX UPRISING, THE ... Henry Mancini
GREAT SMOKEY ROADBLOCK, THE ... Craig Safan
GREAT ST. LOUIS BANK ROBBERY, THE ... Bernardo Segall
GREAT ST. TRINIAN'S TRAIN ROBBERY, THE ... Malcolm Arnold
GREAT TEXAS DYNAMITE CHASE, THE ... Craig Safan
GREAT TRAIN ROBBERY, THE ... Jerry Goldsmith
GREAT WALDO PEPPER, THE ... Henry Mancini
GREAT WALTZ, THE ... Dimitri Tiomkin†
GREAT WAR, THE ... Nino Rota†
GREAT WHITE ... Guido De Angelis
GREAT WHITE ... Maurizio De Angelis
GREAT WHITE ... Morton Stevens
GREAT WHITE HOPE, THE ... Lionel Newman†
GREATEST GIFT, THE (TF) ... Richard DeBenedictis
GREATEST KIDNAPPING IN THE WEST, THE ... Luis Bacalov
GREATEST SHOW ON EARTH, THE ... Victor Young†
GREATEST STORY EVER TOLD, THE ... ★ Alfred Newman†
GREATEST THING THAT ALMOST HAPPENED, THE (TF) ... David Shire
GREATEST, THE ... Lee Holdridge
GREATEST, THE ... Michael Masser
GREECE, LAND OF DREAMS ... Manos Hadjidakis
GREED ... Carl Davis
GREED IN THE SUN ... Georges Delerue
GREEK COCKATOO, THE ... Miklos Rozsa
GREEK TYCOON, THE ... Stanley Myers
GREEKS HAD A WORD FOR THEM, THE ... Alfred Newman†
GREEN BELT, THE ... Richard Addinsell†
GREEN BERETS, THE ... Miklos Rozsa
GREEN CARD ... Hans Zimmer
GREEN DOLPHIN STREET ... Bronislau Kaper†
GREEN EYES (TF) ... Fred Karlin
GREEN FIRE ... Miklos Rozsa
GREEN FOR DANGER ... William Alwyn†
GREEN GLOVE, THE ... Joseph Kosma†
GREEN GRASS OF WYOMING ... Cyril J. Mockridge†
GREEN HELMET, THE ... Kenneth V. Jones
GREEN ICE ... Bill Wyman
GREEN JACKET, THE ... Luis Bacalov
GREEN LIGHT ... Max Steiner†
GREEN MANSIONS ... Bronislau Kaper†
GREEN MANSIONS ... Heitor Villa-Lobos†
GREEN PASTURES, THE ... Erich Wolfgang Korngold†
GREEN SCARF, THE ... Brian Easdale
GREEN YEARS, THE ... Herbert Stothart†
GREEN-EYED BLONDE, THE ... Leith Stevens†
GREENGAGE SUMMER, THE ... Richard Addinsell†
GREGORY'S GIRL ... Colin Tully
GREMLINS ... Jerry Goldsmith
GREMLINS II ... Jerry Goldsmith
GRENDEL, GRENDEL, GRENDEL (AF) ... Bruce Smeaton
GRENZENLOS ... Peer Raben
GREY FOX, THE ... Michael Conway Baker
GREYSTOKE: THE LEGEND OF TARZAN, LORD OF THE APES ... John Scott
GRIBOUILLE ... Georges Auric†
GRIDIRON FLASH ... Max Steiner†
GRIDLOCK (TF) ... Arthur B. Rubinstein
GRIEVOUS BODILY HARM ... Chris Neal
GRIFFIN AND PHOENIX (TF) ... George Aliceson Tipton
GRIFTERS, THE ... Elmer Bernstein
GRIJPSTRA & DE GLER ... Rogier Van Otterloo†
GRINGO ... Ennio Morricone
GRISSOM GANG, THE ... Gerald Fried
GRIZZLY ... Robert O. Ragland
GROMAIRE (FD) ... Michel Portal
GROUND ZERO ... Chris Neal
GROUNDS FOR MARRIAGE ... David Raksin
GROUNDS FOR MARRIAGE ... Bronislau Kaper†
GROUNDSTAR CONSPIRACY, THE ... Paul Hoffert
GROUP, THE ... Charles Gross
GROWING PAINS ... W. Michael Lewis
GROWING PAINS ... Laurin Rinder
GRUNT! THE WRESTLING MOVIE ... Susan Justin
GRUPPO DI FAMIGLIAIN UNO INTERNO ... Franco Mannino
GUADALCANAL DIARY ... David Buttolph†
GUARDIA, GUARDIA SCELTA, BRIGADIERE E MARESCIALLO ... Carlo Rustichelli
GUARDIAN OF THE WILDERNESS ... Robert Summers
GUARDIAN, THE ... Jack Hues
GUARDIAN, THE (CTF) ... Robert O. Ragland
GUARDIE E LADRI ... Alessandro Cicognini†
GUENDALINA ... Piero Piccioni
GUESS WHO'S COMING TO DINNER ... ★ Frank De Vol
GUESS WHO'S SLEEPING IN MY BED? (TF) ... Morton Stevens
GUEST IN THE HOUSE ... ★ Werner Janssen
GUEST WIFE ... ★ Daniele Amfitheatrof†
GUEST, THE ... Ron Grainer
GUEULETONS ... Vladimir Cosma
GUGLIELMO IL DENTONE ... Armando Trovajoli
GUIDE FOR THE MARRIED MAN, A ... John Williams
GUIDE FOR THE MARRIED WOMAN, A (TF) ... Jack Elliott
GUIDE FOR THE MARRIED WOMAN,A (TF) ... Allyn Ferguson
GUILT OF JANET AMES, THE ... George Duning
GUILTY BYSTANDER ... Dimitri Tiomkin†
GUILTY OF TREASON ... Hugo Friedhofer†
GUILTY OF TREASON ... Emil Newman†
GUILTY OR INNOCENT: THE SAM SHEPPARD MURDER CASE (TF) ... Lalo Schifrin
GUINEA PIG COUPLE, THE ... Michel Colombier
GUINEA PIG, THE ... John Addison
GUINGUETTE ... Georges Van Parys†
GULAG (CTF) ... Elmer Bernstein
GULF STREAM ... Darius Milhaud†
GULLIVER'S TRAVELS ... Michel Legrand
GULLIVER'S TRAVELS (AF) ... ★ Victor Young†
GULLIVER'S TRAVELS BEYOND THE MOON (AF) ... Milton DeLugg
GUMBALL RALLY ... Dominic Frontiere
GUMSHOE ... Andrew Lloyd Webber
GUMSHOE KID, THE ... Peter Matz
GUN AND THE PULPIT, THE (TF) ... George Aliceson Tipton
GUN CRAZY ... Victor Young†
GUN DUEL IN DURANGO ... Bert A. Shefter
GUN FEVER ... Paul Dunlap
GUN FURY ... Mischa Bakaleinikoff †
GUN GLORY ... Jeff Alexander†
GUN HAWK, THE ... Jimmie Haskell
GUN IN THE HOUSE, A (TF) ... Jimmie Haskell
GUN LAW ... Roy Webb†
GUN RUNNERS, THE ... Leith Stevens†
GUN STREET ... Richard LaSalle
GUN, A ... Michel Legrand
GUNFIGHT AT DODGE CITY, THE ... Hans J. Salter
GUNFIGHT AT RED SANDS ... Ennio Morricone
GUNFIGHT AT THE O.K. CORRAL ... Dimitri Tiomkin†
GUNFIGHT, A ... Laurence Rosenthal
GUNFIGHTER, THE ... Alfred Newman†
GUNFIGHTERS OF ABILENE ... Paul Dunlap
GUNFIGHTERS, THE (TF) ... Domenic Troiano
GUNFIRE ... Albert Glasser
GUNG HO ... Thomas Newman
GUNG HO! ... Hans J. Salter
GUNG HO! ... Frank Skinner†
GUNGA DIN ... Alfred Newman†

GUNGALA, LA VIRGINE DELLS GIUNGLA ... Angelo Francesco Lavagnino†
GUNGALA, THE VIRGIN OF THE JUNGLE ... Angelo Francesco Lavagnino†
GUNMEN OF THE RIO GRANDE ... Angelo Francesco Lavagnino†
GUNN ... Henry Mancini
GUNPOINT ... Hans J. Salter
GUNS AT BATASI ... John Addison
GUNS FOR SAN SEBASTIAN ... Ennio Morricone
GUNS OF AUGUST, THE (FD) ... Sol Kaplan
GUNS OF DARKNESS ... Benjamin Frankel†
GUNS OF NAVARONE, THE ... ★ Dimitri Tiomkin†
GUNS OF THE BLACK WITCH ... Les Baxter
GUNS OF THE MAGNIFICENT SEVEN ... Elmer Bernstein
GUNS OF THE TIMBERLAND ... David Buttolph†
GUNSIGHT RIDGE ... David Raksin
GUNSLINGER, THE ... Ronald Stein†
GUNSMOKE ... Herman Stein
GUNSMOKE ... Henry Mancini
GUNSMOKE IN TUCSON ... Sidney Cutner†
GUNSMOKE: RETURN TO DODGE (TF) ... Jerrold Immel
GUNSMOKE: THE LAST APACHE (TF) ... Bruce Rowland
GUS ... Robert F. Brunner
GUS BROWN AND MIDNIGHT BREWSTER (TF) ... Harry Middlebrooks
GUTS AND GLORY: THE RISE AND FALL OF OLIVER NORTH (TF) ... Arthur B. Rubinstein
GUY NAMED JOE, A ... Herbert Stothart†
GUY WHO CAME BACK, THE ... Leigh Harline†
GUYANA TRAGEDY: THE STORY OF JIM JONES (TF) ... Elmer Bernstein
GUYANA, CULT OF THE DAMNED ... George S. Price
GUYANA, CULT OF THE DAMNED ... Robert Summers
GUYANA, CULT OF THE DAMNED ... Nelson Riddle†
GWENDOLINE ... Pierre Bachelet
GYMKATA ... Alfi Kabiljo
GYPSY GIRL ... Malcolm Arnold
GYPSY MOTHS, THE ... Elmer Bernstein
GYPSY WILDCAT ... Edward Ward†

H

H-2-S ... Ennio Morricone
H-MAN, THE ... Masaru Sato
H.M. PULHAM, ESQUIRE ... Bronislau Kaper†
H.O.T.S. ... David Davis
H.P. LOVECRAFT'S REANIMATOR ... Richard H. Band
HADLEY'S REBELLION ... Mike Post
HAIL THE CONQUERING HERO ... Werner R. Heymann†
HAIL, HERO! ... Jerome Moross†
HAIRSPRAY ... Kenny Vance
HAIRY APE, THE ... ★ Michel Michelet†
HALF ANGEL ... Cyril J. Mockridge†
HALF HUMAN ... Masaru Sato
HALF MOON STREET ... Richard Harvey
HALF NAKED TRUTH, THE ... Max Steiner†
HALF SHOT AT SUNRISE ... Max Steiner†
HALF WAY TO SHANGHAI ... Hans J. Salter
HALFWAY HOUSE ... Lord Berners†
HALLELUJAH TRAIL, THE ... Elmer Bernstein
HALLO EVERYBODY ... Darius Milhaud†
HALLOWEEN ... John Carpenter
HALLOWEEN 4: THE RETURN OF MICHAEL MYERS ... Alan Howarth
HALLOWEEN 5: THE REVENGE OF MICHAEL MYERS ... Alan Howarth
HALLOWEEN II ... John Carpenter
HALLOWEEN II ... Alan Howarth
HALLOWEEN III: SEASON OF THE WITCH ... John Carpenter
HALLOWEEN III: SEASON OF THE WITCH ... Alan Howarth
HALLS OF ANGER ... Dave Grusin
HALLS OF MONTEZUMA ... Sol Kaplan
HALLUCINATION GENERATION ... Bernardo Segall
HAMBURGER HILL ... Philip Glass
HAMBURGER...THE MOTION PICTURE ... Peter Bernstein
HAME'AHEV ... Dov Seltzer
HAMLET ... Dmitri Shostakovitch†
HAMLET ... ★ Sir William Walton†
HAMMERHEAD ... David Whitaker
HAMMERSMITH IS OUT ... Dominic Frontiere
HAMMETT ... John Barry
HAN WESTMAR ... Giuseppe Becce†
HAND OF POWER ... Peter Thomas
HAND, THE ... James Horner
HANDFUL OF DUST,A ... George Fenton
HANDGUN ... Mike Post
HANDLE WITH CARE ... Alexander Courage
HANDLE WITH CARE ... Bill Conti
HANDMAID'S TALE, THE ... Ryuichi Sakamoto
HANDS ACROSS THE BORDER ... Walter Scharf
HANDS OF A MURDERER (TF) ... Colin Towns
HANDS OF A STRANGER ... Richard LaSalle
HANDS OF A STRANGER (TF) ... Michel Rubini
HANDS OF ORLAC, THE ... Claude Bolling
HANDS OF THE RIPPER ... Christopher Gunning
HANDS OFF WHITE WOMEN ... Philippe Sarde
HANG 'EM HIGH ... Dominic Frontiere
HANGAR 18 ... John Cacavas
HANGED MAN, THE (TF) ... Benny Carter
HANGED MAN, THE (TF) ... Richard Markowitz
HANGING BY A THREAD (TF) ... Richard LaSalle
HANGING TREE, THE ... Max Steiner†
HANGMAN'S KNOT ... Mischa Bakaleinikoff †
HANGMAN, THE ... Harry Sukman†
HANGMEN ALSO DIE ... ★ Hanns Eisler†
HANGOVER SQUARE ... Bernard Herrmann†
HANKY PANKY ... Tom Scott
HANNA K. ... Gabriel Yared
HANNA'S WAR ... Dov Seltzer
HANNIBAL BROOKS ... Francis Lai
HANNIE CAULDER ... Ken Thorne
HANOI HILTON, THE ... Jimmy Webb
HANOVER STREET ... John Barry
HANS CHRISTIAN ANDERSEN ... Jerome Moross†
HANS CHRISTIAN ANDERSON ... Walter Scharf
HANS LE MARIN ... Joseph Kosma†
HANUSSEN ... Gyorgy Vukan
HAPPENING, THE ... Frank De Vol
HAPPILY EVER AFTER (TF) ... Peter Matz
HAPPINESS IS A WARM CLUE (TF) ... Robert Prince
HAPPY (TF) ... Billy Goldenberg
HAPPY ANNIVERSARY ... Sol Kaplan
HAPPY BIRTHDAY ... Arlon Ober
HAPPY BIRTHDAY TO ME ... Bo Harwood
HAPPY BIRTHDAY TO ME ... Lance Rubin
HAPPY ENDING, THE ... Michel Legrand
HAPPY ENDINGS (TF) ... William Goldstein
HAPPY ENDINGS (TF) ... J.A.C. Redford
HAPPY GO LUCKY ... Robert Emmett Dolan†
HAPPY HOOKER, THE ... Don Elliott
HAPPY HOUR ... Dan Milner
HAPPY IS THE BRIDE ... Benjamin Frankel†
HAPPY LAND ... Cyril J. Mockridge†
HAPPY NEW YEAR ... Bill Conti
HAPPY NEW YEAR ... Francis Lai
HAPPY PRINCE, THE (AF) ... Ron Goodwin
HAPPY THIEVES, THE ... Mario Nascimbene
HAPPY TIME, THE ... Dimitri Tiomkin†
HAPPY TOGETHER ... Robert Folk
HAPPY YEARS, THE ... Leigh Harline†
HARD CHOICES ... Jay Chattaway
HARD CONTRACT ... Alex North
HARD COUNTRY ... Jimmie Haskell
HARD COUNTRY ... Michael Martin Murphey
HARD DAY'S NIGHT, A ... ★ George Martin
HARD KNOX (TF) ... Mike Post
HARD KNOX (TF) ... Pete Carpenter†
HARD TICKET TO HAWAII ... Kevin Klinger
HARD TIMES ... Barry De Vorzon
HARD TO HOLD ... Tom Scott
HARD TO KILL ... David Michael Frank
HARD TRAVELING ... Ernie Sheldon
HARD WAY, THE ... Heinz Roemheld†
HARD, FAST AND BEAUTIFUL ... Roy Webb†
HARDBODIES 2 ... Eddie Arkin
HARDBODIES 2 ... Jay Levy
HARDCASE (TF) ... Patrick Williams
HARDCORE ... Jack Nitzsche
HARDER THEY COME, THE ... Jimmy Cliff
HARDER THEY FALL, THE ... Hugo Friedhofer†
HARDHAT AND LEGS (TF) ... Brad Fiedel
HARDI PARDAILLAN ... Paul Misraki†
HARDLY WORKING ... Morton Stevens
HARDWARE ... Simon Boswell
HAREM ... Philippe Sarde
HAREM ... Ennio Morricone
HAREM (TS) ... John Scott
HARIKARI ... Toru Takemitsu
HARLEM GLOBETROTTERS ON GILLIGAN'S ISLAND, THE (TF) ... Gerald Fried
HARLEM GLOBETROTTERS, THE ... Arthur Morton
HARLEM NIGHTS ... Herbie Hancock
HARLEQUIN ... Brian May
HARLOW ... Neal Hefti
HARLOW ... Nelson Riddle†
HARMONY ... David C. Williams
HARNESS, THE (TF) ... Billy Goldenberg
HAROLD LLOYD'S WORLD OF COMEDY ... Walter Scharf
HAROLD LLOYD: WHY WORRY? ... Don Peake
HAROLD LLOYD: HOT WATER ... Don Peake
HAROLD LLOYD: SAFETY LAST ... Don Peake
HAROLD LLOYD: THE FRESHMAN ... Don Peake
HAROLD ROBBINS' THE PIRATE (TF) ... Bill Conti
HARP IN THE SOUTH, THE (MS) ... Peter Best
HARP OF BURMA ... Akira Ifukube
HARPER ... Johnny Mandel
HARPER VALLEY PTA ... Nelson Riddle†
HARPY (TF) ... David Shire
HARRAD EXPERIMENT, THE ... Artie Butler
HARRAD SUMMER ... Patrick Williams
HARRIET CRAIG ... George Duning
HARRIGAN'S KID ... Daniele Amfitheatrof†
HARRY & SON ... Henry Mancini
HARRY AND THE HENDERSONS ... Bruce Broughton
HARRY AND TONTO ... Bill Conti
HARRY AND WALTER GO TO NEW YORK ... David Shire
HARRY IN YOUR POCKET ... Lalo Schifrin
HARRY'S HONG KONG (TF) ... Dominic Frontiere
HARRY'S WAR ... Merrill B. Jensen
HARVEY ... Frank Skinner†
HARVEY MIDDLEMAN, FIREMAN ... Bernard Green
HAS ANYBODY SEEN MY GAL? ... Herman Stein
HAS ANYBODY SEEN MY GAL? ... Henry Mancini
HASTY HEART, THE ... Louis Levy†
HAT CHECK HONEY ... Hans J. Salter
HAT, COAT AND GLOVE ... Max Steiner†
HATARI! ... Henry Mancini
HATFIELDS AND THE MCCOYS, THE (TF) ... Ken Lauber
HATFUL OF RAIN, A ... Bernard Herrmann†
HATRED ... Darius Milhaud†
HAUNTED BY HER PAST (TF) ... Paul Chihara
HAUNTED HONEYMOON ... John Morris
HAUNTED HONEYMOON ... Louis Levy†
HAUNTED PALACE, THE ... Ronald Stein†
HAUNTED SUMMER ... Christopher Young
HAUNTING OF JULIA, THE ... Colin Towns
HAUNTING PASSION, THE (TF) ... Paul Chihara
HAUNTING, THE ... Humphrey Searle†
HAUNTS ... Pino Donaggio
HAUNTS OF THE VERY RICH (TF) ... Dominic Frontiere
HAUSER'S MEMORY (TF) ... Billy Byers
HAVANA ... Dave Grusin
HAVE ROCKET, WILL TRAVEL ... Mischa Bakaleinikoff†
HAVING BABIES (TF) ... Earle Hagen
HAVING BABIES II (TF) ... Fred Karlin
HAVING BABIES III (TF) ... Lee Holdridge
HAVING IT ALL (TF) ... Miles Goodman
HAVING WONDERFUL CRIME ... Leigh Harline†
HAVING WONDERFUL TIME ... Roy Webb†
HAWAII ... ★ Elmer Bernstein
HAWAII FIVE-O (TF) ... ☆ Morton Stevens
HAWAIIANS, THE ... Henry Mancini
HAWK OF THE WILDERNESS ... William Lava†
HAWK THE SLAYER ... Harry Robertson
HAWKINS ON MURDER (TF) ... Jerry Goldsmith
HAWKS ... Barry Gibb
HAWKS AND THE SPARROWS, THE ... Ennio Morricone
HAWMPS ... Euel Box
HAXAN WITCHCRAFT THROUGH THE AGES ... Michel Portal
HAY FOOT ... Edward Ward†
HAYWIRE (TF) ... Billy Goldenberg
HAZARD ... Frank Skinner†
HAZARD OF HEARTS, A (TF) ... Laurie Johnson
HE DIED AFTER THE WAR ... Toru Takemitsu
HE KNOWS YOU'RE ALONE ... Alexander Peskanov
HE KNOWS YOU'RE ALONE ... Mark Peskanov
HE MARRIED HIS WIFE ... David Buttolph†
HE RAN ALL THE WAY ... Franz Waxman†
HE STAYED FOR BREAKFAST ... Werner R. Heymann†
HE WHO MUST DIE ... Georges Auric†
HE'S FIRED, SHE'S HIRED (TF) ... Lee Holdridge
HEAD ... Ken Thorne
HEAD OFFICE ... James Newton Howard
HEAD OVER HEELS ... Ken Lauber

HEAD OVER HEELS IN LOVE ... Louis Levy†
HEADIN' FOR BROADWAY ... Joseph Brooks
HEADLESS GHOST, THE ... Gerard Schurmann
HEADLINE SHOOTER ... Max Steiner†
HEADS OR TAILS ... Carlo Rustichelli
HEALERS, THE (TF) ... David Shire
HEALTH ... Joseph Byrd
HEAR NO EVIL (TF) ... Lance Rubin
HEARSE, THE ... Webster Lewis
HEART ... Geoff Levin
HEART ... Chris Many
HEART BEAT ... Jack Nitzsche
HEART CONDITION ... Patrick Leonard
HEART IS A LONELY HUNTER, THE ... Dave Grusin
HEART LIKE A WHEEL ... Laurence Rosenthal
HEART OF A CHAMPION: THE RAY MANCINI STORY (TF) ... Mike Post
HEART OF A NATION ... Jean Wiener†
HEART OF DIXIE ... Kenny Vance
HEART OF GLASS ... Popol Vuh
HEART OF MIDNIGHT ... Yanni
HEART OF PARIS ... Georges Auric†
HEART OF STEEL (TF) ... Brad Fiedel
HEART OF THE NORTH ... Adolph Deutsch†
HEART OF THE STAG ... Leonard Rosenman
HEARTACHES ... Simon Michael Martin
HEARTBEAT ... Paul Misraki†
HEARTBEAT (TF) ... Peter Bernstein
HEARTBEAT (TF) ... Ken Harrison
HEARTBEEPS ... John Williams
HEARTBREAK HOTEL ... Georges Delerue
HEARTBREAK KID, THE ... Garry Sherman
HEARTBREAK RIDGE ... Lennie Niehaus
HEARTBREAKER ... Robert J. Walsh
HEARTBREAKERS ... Tangerine Dream
HEARTBURN ... Carly Simon
HEARTLAND ... Charles Gross
HEARTS AND MINDS ... Ennio Morricone
HEARTS OF FIRE ... John Barry
HEARTS OF THE WEST ... Ken Lauber
HEARTSOUNDS (TF) ... Leonard Rosenman
HEAT ... Michael Gibbs
HEAT AND DUST ... Richard Robbins
HEAT OF THE NIGHT (TF) ... Chris Page
HEATHERS ... David Newman
HEATWAVE! (TF) ... Fred Steiner
HEAVEN (FD) ... Howard Shore
HEAVEN CAN WAIT ... ★ Dave Grusin
HEAVEN CAN WAIT ... Alfred Newman†
HEAVEN HELP US ... James Horner
HEAVEN KNOWS, MR. ALLISON ... Georges Auric†
HEAVEN ON EARTH ... Bernhard Kaun†
HEAVEN ONLY KNOWS ... Heinz Roemheld†
HEAVEN WITH A GUN ... Johnny Mandel
HEAVEN'S GATE ... David Mansfield
HEAVENLY BODY, THE ... Bronislau Kaper†
HEAVENLY DAYS ... Leigh Harline†
HEAVENLY KID, THE ... Kennard Ramsey
HEAVENS ABOVE ... Richard Rodney Bennett
HEAVENS AND THE EARTH, THE ... Isao Tomita
HEAVY METAL (AF) ... Elmer Bernstein
HEAVY TRAFFIC (AF) ... Ed Bogas
HEAVY TRAFFIC (AF) ... Ray Shanklin
HEC RAMSEY (TF) ... Laurence Rosenthal
HEC RAMSEY (TF) ... Fred Steiner
HEDDA ... Laurie Johnson
HEIDELBERGER ROMANZE ... Werner R. Heymann†
HEIDI (TF) ... ☆☆ John Williams
HEIDI'S SONG (AF) ... Hoyt Curtin
HEIRESS, THE ... ★★ Aaron Copland
HEIST, THE (TF) ... Robert Drasnin
HELEN KELLER - THE MIRACLE CONTINUES (TF) ... J.A.C. Redford
HELEN OF TROY ... Max Steiner†
HELEN OF TROY—THE FACE THAT LAUNCHED A THOUSAND SHIPS ... Nino Rota†
HELL AND HIGH WATER ... Alfred Newman†
HELL BENT FOR LEATHER ... William Lava†
HELL BOUND ... Les Baxter
HELL CAMP ... Marc Donahue
HELL HIGH ... Christopher Hyans-Hart
HELL IN KOREA ... Malcolm Arnold
HELL IN THE PACIFIC ... Lalo Schifrin
HELL IS FOR HEROES ... Leonard Rosenman
HELL NIGHT ... Dan Wyman
HELL ON FRISCO BAY ... Max Steiner†
HELL RAIDERS OF THE DEEP ... Nino Rota†
HELL RIVER ... Mikis Theodorakis
HELL SHIP MUTINY ... Bert A. Shefter
HELL SQUAD ... Charles P. Barnett
HELL TO ETERNITY ... Leith Stevens†
HELL UP IN HARLEM ... Freddie Perren
HELL WITH HEROES, THE ... Quincy Jones
HELL'S ANGELS ON WHEELS ... Stu Phillips
HELL'S BELLES ... Les Baxter
HELL'S BLOODY DEVILS ... Nelson Riddle†
HELL'S HORIZON ... Heinz Roemheld†
HELLBENDERS, THE ... Ennio Morricone
HELLBOUND: HELLRAISER II ... Christopher Young
HELLCATS OF THE NAVY ... Mischa Bakaleinikoff †
HELLE ... Philippe Sarde
HELLER IN PINK TIGHTS ... Daniele Amfitheatrof†
HELLFIGHTERS ... Leonard Rosenman
HELLGATE ... Barry Fasman
HELLGATE ... Paul Dunlap
HELLGATE ... Dana Walden
HELLHOLE ... Jeff Sturges
HELLINGER'S LAW (TF) ... John Cacavas
HELLIONS, THE ... Larry Adler
HELLO - GOODBYE ... Francis Lai
HELLO AGAIN ... William Goldstein
HELLO SUCKER ... Hans J. Salter
HELLO, DOLLY! ... ★★ Lionel Newman†
HELLRAISER ... Christopher Young
HELLSTROM CHRONICLE, THE (FD) ... Lalo Schifrin
HELP ... Ken Thorne
HELP WANTED: KIDS (TF) ... Craig Safan
HELP WANTED: MALE (TF) ... Nelson Riddle†
HELTER SKELTER (TF) ... ☆ Billy Goldenberg
HELZAPOPPIN ... Frank Skinner†
HEMINGWAY'S ADVENTURES OF A YOUNG MAN ... Franz Waxman†
HENDERSON MONSTER, THE (TF) ... Dick Hyman
HENNESSY ... John Scott
HENRY ALDRICH, EDITOR ... Leo Shuken†
HENRY IV ... Astor Piaz
HENRY SOLUTION, THE ... Tom Canning
HENRY V ... Patrick Doyle
HENRY V ... ★ Sir William Walton†
HER ADVENTUROUS NIGHT ... Hans J. Salter
HER ALIBI ... Georges Delerue
HER CARDBOARD LOVER ... Franz Waxman†
HER HUSBAND'S AFFAIRS ... George Duning
HER KIND OF MAN ... Franz Waxman†
HER MAN GILBEY ... Nicholas Brodszky†
HER PANELLED DOOR ... Allan Gray†
HER PRIMITIVE MAN ... Edward Ward†
HER SECRET LIFE (TF) ... Georges Delerue
HER TWELVE MEN ... Bronislau Kaper†
HERBIE GOES TO MONTE CARLO ... Frank De Vol
HERBIE RIDES AGAIN ... George Bruns
HERCULES ... Pino Donaggio
HERCULES AGAINST ROME ... Angelo Francesco Lavagnino†
HERCULES AND THE CAPTIVE WOMEN ... Armando Trovajoli
HERCULES AND THE TYRANTS OF BABYLON ... Angelo Francesco Lavagnino†
HERCULES II ... Pino Donaggio
HERCULES IN THE HAUNTED WORLD ... Armando Trovajoli
HERCULES OF THE DESERT ... Carlo Rustichelli
HERCULES PILLS, THE ... Armando Trovajoli
HERCULES, SAMSON & ULYSSES ... Angelo Francesco Lavagnino†
HERE ARE LADIES (FD) ... David Fanshawe
HERE COME THE GIRLS ... Lyn Murray†
HERE COME THE JETS ... Paul Dunlap
HERE COME THE LITTLES (AF) ... Shuki Levy
HERE COME THE NELSONS ... Herman Stein
HERE COME THE TIGERS ... Harry Manfredini
HERE COME THE WAVES ... Robert Emmett Dolan†
HERE COMES MR. JORDAN ... Frederick Hollander†
HERE COMES SANTA CLAUS ... Francis Lai
HERE COMES THE BAND ... Edward Ward†
HERE COMES TROUBLE ... Heinz Roemheld†
HERE WE GO AGAIN ... Roy Webb†
HERITAGE OF THE DESERT ... Victor Young†
HERO AIN'T NOTHIN' BUT A SANDWICH, A ... Tom McIntosh
HERO AND THE TERROR ... David Frank
HERO AT LARGE ... Patrick Williams
HERO IN THE FAMILY (TF) ... William Goldstein
HERO OF ROME, THE ... Angelo Francesco Lavagnino†
HERO'S ISLAND ... Dominic Frontiere
HEROES ... Richard Hazard
HEROES ... Jack Nitzsche
HEROES A LA FUERZA ... Carlo Rustichelli
HEROES OF TELEMARK , THE ... Malcolm Arnold
HEROES, THE ... Riz Ortolani
HEROINES OF EVIL, THE ... Oliver Dassault
HERS TO HOLD ... Frank Skinner†
HESTER STREET ... William Bolcom
HET MEISJE MET HET RODE HAAR ... Nicola Piovani
HEUREUX QUI COMME ULYSSE ... Georges Delerue
HEX ... Charles Bernstein
HEX ... Patrick Williams
HEY THERE, IT'S YOGI BEAR (AF) ... Marty Paich
HEY, GOOD LOOKIN' ... Ric Sandler
HEY, GOOD LOOKIN' ... John Madara
HEY, I'M ALIVE! (TF) ... Frank De Vol
HI YA, CHUM ... Hans J. Salter
HI'YA, SAILOR ... Hans J. Salter
HI, BEAUTIFUL ... Frank Skinner†
HI, GOOD LOOKIN' ... Hans J. Salter
HI-JACKED ... Paul Dunlap
HIBERNATUS ... Georges Delerue
HIDDEN AGENDA ... Stewart Copeland
HIDDEN FORTRESS, THE ... Masaru Sato
HIDDEN ROOM, THE ... Nino Rota†
HIDDEN WORLD, THE (FD) ... Leonard Rosenman
HIDDEN, THE ... Michael Convertino
HIDE IN PLAIN SIGHT ... Leonard Rosenman
HIDE-OUT ... William Axt†
HIDER IN THE HOUSE ... Christopher Young
HIDING OUT ... Anne Dudley
HIGH AND LOW ... Masaru Sato
HIGH AND THE MIGHTY, THE ... ★★ Dimitri Tiomkin†
HIGH ANXIETY ... John Morris
HIGH BARBAREE ... Herbert Stothart†
HIGH BRIGHT SUN, THE ... Angelo Francesco Lavagnino†
HIGH COMMISSIONER, THE ... Georges Delerue
HIGH CONQUEST ... Lud Gluskin†
HIGH CONQUEST ... Lucien Moraweck†
HIGH CONQUEST ... Lyn Murray†
HIGH COST OF LOVING, THE ... Jeff Alexander†
HIGH EXPLOSIVE ... Daniele Amfitheatrof†
HIGH FLYERS ... Roy Webb†
HIGH HEELS ... Pierre Jansen
HIGH HOPES ... Andrew Dixon
HIGH ICE (TF) ... Robert O. Ragland
HIGH INFIDELITY ... Armando Trovajoli
HIGH MIDNIGHT (TF) ... ☆☆ Jerry Fielding†
HIGH MOUNTAIN RANGERS (TF) ... Robert Folk
HIGH NOON ... ★★ Dimitri Tiomkin†
HIGH PLAINS DRIFTER ... Dee Barton
HIGH POINT ... John Addison
HIGH POWERED-RIFLE, THE ... Albert Glasser
HIGH PRICE OF PASSION, THE (TF) ... Joseph Conlan
HIGH RISK ... Mark Snow
HIGH ROAD TO CHINA ... John Barry
HIGH SCHOOL CONFIDENTIAL ... Albert Glasser
HIGH SCHOOL HELLCATS ... Ronald Stein†
HIGH SCHOOL U.S.A. (TF) ... Tony Berg
HIGH SCHOOL U.S.A. (TF) ... Miles Goodman
HIGH SEASON ... Jason Osborn
HIGH SIERRA ... Adolph Deutsch†
HIGH SOCIETY ... ★ John Green†
HIGH SPIRITS ... George Fenton
HIGH TIDE ... Peter Best
HIGH TIDE ... Ricky Fataar
HIGH TIDE ... Mark Moffiatt
HIGH TIME ... Henry Mancini
HIGH TREASON ... John Addison
HIGH VELOCITY ... Jerry Goldsmith
HIGH WALL ... Bronislau Kaper†
HIGH WIND IN JAMAICA, A ... Larry Adler
HIGH-BALLIN' ... Paul Hoffert
HIGHER GROUND (TF) ... Lee Holdridge
HIGHLANDER ... Michael Kamen
HIGHLANDER ... Queen
HIGHLY DANGEROUS ... Richard Addinsell†
HIGHPOINT ... Christopher Young
HIGHWAY 301 ... William Lava†
HIGHWAY PICKUP ... Georges Delerue
HIGHWAY QUEEN ... Dov Seltzer
HIGHWAYMAN, THE ... Herschel Burke Gilbert
HIGHWAYMAN, THE (TF) ... Stu Phillips
HIGHWAYS BY NIGHT ... Roy Webb†
HIJACK! (TF) ... Jack Elliott
HIJACK! (TF) ... Allyn Ferguson
HIJACKING OF THE ACHILLE LAURO, THE (TF) ... ☆ Chris Boardman
HIJINKS ... Riz Ortolani
HILDA CRANE ... David Raksin
HILL IN KOREA, A ... Malcolm Arnold
HILLS HAVE EYES PART II, THE ... Harry Manfredini
HILLS HAVE EYES, THE ... Don Peake
HILLS OF HOME ... Herbert Stothart†
HILLS RUN RED, THE ... Ennio Morricone
HIMIKO ... Toru Takemitsu

HOUSE IN NIGHTMARE PARK, THE ... Harry Robertson
HOUSE IN THE SQUARE, THE ... William Alwyn†
HOUSE OF BAMBOO ... Lionel Newman†
HOUSE OF DARK SHADOWS ... Bob Cobert
HOUSE OF DRACULA ... Hans J. Salter
HOUSE OF DRACULA ... Paul Dessau†
HOUSE OF DRACULA ... Charles Henderson†
HOUSE OF DRACULA ... William Lava†
HOUSE OF DRACULA ... Charles Previn†
HOUSE OF FEAR, THE ... Hans J. Salter
HOUSE OF FEAR, THE ... Paul Sawtell†
HOUSE OF FRANKENSTEIN ... Hans J. Salter
HOUSE OF FRANKENSTEIN ... Charles Previn†
HOUSE OF FRANKENSTEIN ... Frank Skinner†
HOUSE OF FRIGHT ... Monty Norman
HOUSE OF GAMES ... Alaric Jans
HOUSE OF GOD, THE ... Basil Poledouris
HOUSE OF HORRORS ... Hans J. Salter
HOUSE OF INTRIGUE, THE ... Nino Rota†
HOUSE OF LOVERS, THE ... Jean Wiener†
HOUSE OF MYSTERY ... Stanley Black
HOUSE OF NUMBERS ... Andre Previn
HOUSE OF ROTHSCHILD, THE ... Alfred Newman†
HOUSE OF SAND, A ... Les Baxter
HOUSE OF STRANGERS ... Daniele Amfitheatrof†
HOUSE OF THE CARDS ... Francis Lai
HOUSE OF THE LONG SHADOWS ... Richard Harvey
HOUSE OF THE SEVEN GABLES, THE ... ★ Frank Skinner†
HOUSE OF USHER ... Les Baxter
HOUSE OF WAX ... David Buttolph†
HOUSE OF WHIPCORD ... Stanley Myers
HOUSE ON 92ND STREET, THE ... David Buttolph†
HOUSE ON CARROLL STREET, THE ... Georges Delerue
HOUSE ON GARIBALDI STREET, THE (TF) ... Charles Bernstein
HOUSE ON GREENAPPLE ROAD, THE (TF) ... Duane Tatro
HOUSE ON HAUNTED HILL ... Von Dexter
HOUSE ON SKULL MOUNTAIN, THE ... Jerrold Immel
HOUSE ON SORORITY ROW, THE ... Richard H. Band
HOUSE ON TELEGRAPH HILL ... Sol Kaplan
HOUSE ON THE EDGE OF THE PARK ... Riz Ortolani
HOUSE PARTY ... Lenny White
HOUSE PARTY ... Marcus Miller
HOUSE THAT CRIED MURDER, THE ... Peter Bernstein
HOUSE THAT DRIPPED BLOOD, THE ... Michael Dress
HOUSE THAT WOULD NOT DIE, THE (TF) ... Laurence Rosenthal
HOUSE WHERE DEATH LIVES, THE ... Don Peake
HOUSE WHERE EVIL DWELLS, THE ... Ken Thorne
HOUSEBOAT ... George Duning
HOUSEKEEPER'S DAUGHTER, THE ... Lud Gluskin†
HOUSEKEEPING ... Michael Gibbs
HOUSTON KNIGHTS (TF) ... Dennis McCarthy
HOUSTON, WE'VE GOT A PROBLEM (TF) ... Richard Clements
HOUSTON: THE LEGEND OF TEXAS (TF) ... Dennis McCarthy
HOW AWFUL ABOUT ALLAN (TF) ... Laurence Rosenthal
HOW GREEN WAS MY VALLEY ... ★ Alfred Newman†
HOW I GOT INTO COLLEGE ... Joseph Vitarelli
HOW I SPENT MY SUMMER VACATION (TF) ... Lalo Schifrin
HOW I WON THE WAR ... Ken Thorne
HOW SWEET IT IS! ... Patrick Williams
HOW THE WEST WAS WON ... ★ Alfred Newman†
HOW THE WEST WAS WON (MS) ... Richard DeBenedictis
HOW TO BE VERY, VERY POPULAR ... Lionel Newman†
HOW TO BEAT THE HIGH COST OF LIVING ... Patrick Williams
HOW TO BECOME A CITIZEN OF THE UNITED STATES ... Paul Bowles
HOW TO BREAK UP A HAPPY DIVORCE (TF) ... Nelson Riddle†
HOW TO FRAME A FIGG ... Vic Mizzy
HOW TO GET AHEAD IN ADVERTISING ... David Dundas
HOW TO GET AHEAD IN ADVERTISING ... Rick Wentworth
HOW TO MAKE A DOLL ... Larry Wellington
HOW TO MAKE A MONSTER ... Paul Dunlap
HOW TO MAKE IT ... Les Baxter
HOW TO MARRY A MILLIONAIRE ... Cyril J. Mockridge†
HOW TO MURDER A MILLIONAIRE (TF) ... Richard Gibbs
HOW TO MURDER A RICH UNCLE ... Kenneth V. Jones
HOW TO MURDER YOUR WIFE ... Neal Hefti
HOW TO PICK UP GIRLS! (TF) ... Don Sebesky
HOW TO SAVE A MARRIAGE AND RUIN YOUR LIFE ... Michel Legrand
HOW TO SEDUCE A WOMAN ... Stu Phillips
HOW TO STEAL A MILLION ... John Williams
HOW TO STEAL AN AIRPLANE (TF) ... Pete Rugolo
HOW TO STUFF A WILD BIKINI ... Les Baxter
HOW TO SUCCEED IN BUSINESS WITHOUT REALLY TRYING ... Nelson Riddle†
HOW WONDERFUL TO DIE ASSASSINATED ... Roberto De Simone
HOW, WHEN AND WITH WHOM ... Armando Trovajoli
HOWARD BEACH: MAKING THE CASE FOR MURDER (TF) ... Jonathan Elias
HOWARD THE DUCK ... John Barry
HOWARD THE DUCK ... Sylvester Levay
HOWARDS OF VIRGINIA, THE ... ★ Richard Hageman†
HOWLING II...YOUR SISTER IS A WEREWOLF ... Steve Parsons
HOWLING III, THE ... Allan Zavod
HOWLING IN THE WOODS, A (TF) ... Dave Grusin
HOWLING, THE ... Pino Donaggio
HUCKLEBERRY FINN ... Fred Werner
HUCKLEBERRY FINN ... Franz Waxman†
HUCKLEBERRY FINN (TF) ... Earl Robinson
HUD ... Elmer Bernstein
HUDSON'S BAY ... Alfred Newman†
HUE AND CRY ... Georges Auric†
HUEY LONG (FD) ... John Colby
HUGHES LE LOUP (TF) ... Vladimir Cosma
HUIS CLOS ... Joseph Kosma†
HUK ... Albert Glasser
HULLABALOO OVER GEORGIE AND BONNIE'S PICTURES ... Vic Flick
HUMAN BEAST, THE ... Joseph Kosma†
HUMAN COMEDY, THE ... Herbert Stothart†
HUMAN DESIRE ... Daniele Amfitheatrof†
HUMAN FACTOR, THE ... Gary Logan
HUMAN FACTOR, THE ... Richard Logan
HUMAN FACTOR, THE ... Ennio Morricone
HUMAN FEELINGS (TF) ... John Cacavas
HUMAN HIGHWAY ... Devo
HUMAN HIGHWAY ... Neil Young
HUMAN JUNGLE, THE ... Hans J. Salter
HUMAN REVOLUTION, THE ... Akira Ifukube
HUMANOIDS FROM THE DEEP ... James Horner
HUMONGOUS ... John Mills-Cockell
HUMORESQUE ... ★ Franz Waxman†
HUNCHBACK OF NOTRE DAME, THE ... Georges Auric†
HUNCHBACK OF NOTRE DAME, THE ... Heinz Roemheld†
HUNCHBACK OF NOTRE DAME, THE ... ★ Alfred Newman†
HUNCHBACK OF NOTRE DAME, THE (TF) ... Ken Thorne
HUNDERT TAGE ... Giuseppe Becce†
HUNGER ... Christopher Komeda†
HUNGER, THE ... Denny Jaeger
HUNGER, THE ... Michel Rubini
HUNGRY HILL ... John Greenwood†
HUNGRY WIVES ... John Parker
HUNK ... David Kurtz
HUNT FOR RED OCTOBER, THE ... Basil Poledouris
HUNTER (TF) ... Lalo Schifrin
HUNTER OF THE APOCALYPSE ... Franco Micalizzi
HUNTER, THE ... Charles Bernstein
HUNTER, THE ... Michel Legrand
HUNTERS ARE FOR KILLING (TF) ... Jerry Fielding†
HUNTERS OF THE DEEP (FD) ... George Antheil†
HUNTERS OF THE GOLDEN COBRA, THE ... Carlo Savina
HUNTERS OF THE REEF (TF) ... Richard Markowitz
HUNTING PARTY, THE ... Riz Ortolani
HURRAH! THE SCHOOL IS BURNING ... Rolf Wilhelm
HURRICANE ... Nino Rota†
HURRICANE (TF) ... Vic Mizzy
HURRICANE, THE ... ★ Alfred Newman†
HURRY UP OR I'LL BE THIRTY ... Stephen Lawrence
HURRY, CHARLIE, HURRY ... Roy Webb†
HUSBAND, WIFE AND FRIEND ... David Buttolph†
HUSH...HUSH SWEET CHARLOTTE ... ★ Frank De Vol
HUSSY ... George Fenton
HUSSY, THE ... Alain Jomy
HUSTLE ... Frank De Vol
HUSTLER OF MUSCLE BEACH, THE (TF) ... Earle Hagen
HUSTLING (TF) ... Jerry Fielding†
HYENA'S SUN ... Nicola Piovani
HYPER SAPIEN ... Arthur B. Rubinstein
HYPERSPACE ... Don Davis
HYPNOS ... Carlo Savina
HYPNOTIZED ... Edward Ward†
HYPOCHONDRIAC, THE ... Piero Piccioni
HYSTERIA ... Don Banks
HYSTERICAL ... Robert Alcivar
HYSTERICAL ... Robert O. Ragland

I

I 7 FRATELLI CERVI ... Carlo Rustichelli
I ACCUSE! ... William Alwyn†
I AIM AT THE STARS ... Laurie Johnson
I AM A CAMERA ... Malcolm Arnold
I AM SUZANNE ... Frederick Hollander†
I AM THE CHEESE ... Jonathan Tunick
I BAMBINI CI CHIEDONO PERCHE ... Ennio Morricone
I BAMBINI E NOI (TF) ... Fiorenzo Carpi
I BASILISCHI ... Ennio Morricone
I BURY THE LIVING ... Gerald Fried
I CAGASOTTO ... Armando Trovajoli
I CAN GET IT FOR YOU WHOLESALE ... Sol Kaplan
I CAN'T GIVE YOU ANYTHING BUT LOVE, BABY ... Hans J. Salter
I CANNIBALI ... Ennio Morricone
I CAVALIERI DELLA VENDETTA ... Carlo Rustichelli
I COMPAGNI ... Carlo Rustichelli
I COMPLESSI ... Armando Trovajoli
I CONFESS ... Dimitri Tiomkin†
I COULD GO ON SINGING ... Mort Lindsey
I COVER THE WATERFRONT ... Alfred Newman†
I CRIMINALI DELLA GELASSIA ... Angelo Francesco Lavagnino†
I CRUDELLI ... Ennio Morricone
I DEAL IN DANGER ... Lalo Schifrin
I DIAMANTI CHE NESSUNO VOLEVA ROBARE ... Carlo Rustichelli
I DIE A THOUSAND TIMES ... David Buttolph†
I DISMEMBER MAMA ... Herschel Burke Gilbert
I DOLCI INGANNI ... Piero Piccioni
I DON'T WANT TO BE BORN ... Ron Grainer
I DREAM OF JEANNIE...15 YEARS LATER (TF) ... Mark Snow
I DREAM TOO MUCH ... Max Steiner†
I DUE DELLA LEGIONE ... Luis Bacalov
I DUE EVASI DI SING SING ... Ennio Morricone
I DUE MAGHI DELL PALLONE ... Bruno Nicolai
I DUE VIGILI ... Carlo Rustichelli
I ESCAPED FROM DEVIL'S ISLAND ... Les Baxter
I ESCAPED FROM THE GESTAPO ... W. Franke Harling†
I FALSARI ... Carlo Rustichelli
I FANTASMI DEL MARE ... Mario Nascimbene
I FIGLI CHIEDONE PERCHE ... Bruno Nicolai
I FIUME DI DOLLARI ... Ennio Morricone
I FIX AMERICA AND RETURN ... Luis Bacalov
I GIGANTI DELLA TESSAGLIA ... Carlo Rustichelli
I GIGANTI DI ROMA ... Carlo Rustichelli
I GIORNI DELLA VIOLENZA ... Bruno Nicolai
I HATE YOUR GUTS! ... Herman Stein
I HEARD THE OWL CALL MY NAME (TF) ... Peter Matz
I KILLED RASPUTIN ... Don Banks
I KNEW HER WELL ... Hans J. Salter
I KNOW MY FIRST NAME IS STEVEN (TF) ... David Shire
I KNOW WHERE I'M GOING ... Allan Gray†
I KNOW WHY THE CAGED BIRD SINGS (TF) ... Peter Matz
I LEONI DI SAN PETERSBURG ... Gianfranco Plenizio
I LIKE IT THAT WAY ... Edward Ward†
I LIKE MONEY ... Georges Van Parys†
I LIVE IN FEAR ... Fumio Hayasaka †
I LIVE MY LIFE ... Dimitri Tiomkin†
I LOVE A MYSTERY ... Mario Castelnuovo-Tedesco†
I LOVE A SOLDIER ... Robert Emmett Dolan†
I LOVE MY WIFE ... Lalo Schifrin
I LOVE N.Y. ... Bill Conti
I LOVE TROUBLE ... George Duning
I LOVE YOU AGAIN ... Franz Waxman†
I LOVE YOU TO DEATH ... James Horner
I LOVE YOU, ALICE B. TOKLAS ... Elmer Bernstein

K

K-9 .... Miles Goodman
KAGEMUSHA: THE SHADOW WARRIOR .... Shinchiro Ikebe
KAIDEN YUKUJORO .... Akira Ifukube
KALEIDOSCOPE .... Stanley Myers
KALTE HEIMAT .... Jurgen Knieper
KAMIKAZE .... Tangerine Dream
KAMIKAZE 1989 .... Edgar Froese
KANCHENJUNGHA .... Satyajit Ray
KANDYLAND .... George Michalski
KANE & ABEL (MS) .... Billy Goldenberg
KANGAROO .... Sol Kaplan
KANSAS .... Pino Donaggio
KANSAS CITY BOMBER .... Don Ellis†
KANSAS CITY MASSACRE, THE (TF) .... Bob Cobert
KANSAS TERRORS, THE .... William Lava†
KAPO .... Carlo Rustichelli
KARAMOJA (FD) .... Ernest Gold
KARATE KID II, THE .... Bill Conti
KARATE KID III .... Bill Conti
KARATE KID, THE .... Bill Conti
KAREN CARPENTER STORY, THE (TF) .... David Kole
KASEKI .... Toru Takemitsu
KATE BLISS AND THE TICKER TAPE KID (TF) .... Jeff Alexander†
KATE McSHANE (TF) .... John Cacavas
KATE'S SECRET (TF) .... J. Peter Robinson
KATHLEEN .... Franz Waxman†
KATIE DID IT .... Frank Skinner†
KATIE: PORTRAIT OF A CENTERFOLD (TF) .... Charles Bernstein
KATSU TAIHEIKI .... Isao Tomita
KATTORNA .... Christopher Komeda†
KAUBERGERG .... Jurgen Knieper
KAZABLAN .... Dov Seltzer
KAZOKU .... Masaru Sato
KEEFER (TF) .... Duane Tatro
KEEGANS, THE (TF) .... Paul Chihara
KEEP 'EM FLYING .... Frank Skinner†
KEEP 'EM ROLLING .... Max Steiner†
KEEP 'EM SLUGGING .... Hans J. Salter
KEEP, THE .... Tangerine Dream
KEEPER OF THE FLAME .... Bronislau Kaper†
KEEPING COMPANY .... Daniele Amfitheatrof†
KEETJE TIPPEL .... Rogier Van Otterloo†
KELLY THE SECO .... T. Marvin Hatley†
KELLY'S HEROES .... Lalo Schifrin
KEN MURRAY SHOOTING STARS .... Richard LaSalle
KENNEDY (MS) .... Richard Hartley
KENNEDYS OF MASSACHUSETTS, THE (MS) .... ☆ David Shire
KENNY & COMPANY .... Fred Myrow
KENNY ROGERS AS THE GAMBLER (TF) .... Larry Cansler
KENNY ROGERS AS THE GAMBLER - THE ADVENTURE CONTINUES (TF) .... Larry Cansler
KENNY ROGERS AS THE GAMBLER III: THE LEGEND CONTINUES (TF) .... Larry Cansler
KENT STATE (TF) .... Ken Lauber
KENTUCKIAN, THE .... Bernard Herrmann†
KENTUCKY .... Louis Silvers†
KENTUCKY KERNELS .... Max Steiner†
KENTUCKY KERNELS .... Roy Webb†
KENTUCKY MOONSHINE .... Louis Silvers†
KENTUCKY WOMAN (TF) .... George Romanis
KEPT HUSBANDS .... Max Steiner†
KES .... John Cameron
KETTLES IN THE OZARKS, THE .... Herman Stein
KETTLES ON OLD MACDONALD'S FARM, THE .... Henry Mancini
KEY EXCHANGE .... Mason Daring
KEY EXCHANGE .... Jonathan Elias
KEY IS IN THE DOOR, THE .... Philippe Sarde
KEY LARGO .... Max Steiner†
KEY MAN, THE .... Les Baxter
KEY TO REBECCA, THE (TF) .... J.A.C. Redford
KEY TO THE CITY .... Bronislau Kaper†
KEY WEST (TF) .... Frank De Vol
KEY, THE .... Malcolm Arnold
KEY, THE .... Ennio Morricone
KEYS OF THE KINGDOM, THE .... ★ Alfred Newman†
KEYS TO FREEDOM .... Francis Lai
KGB—THE SECRET WAR .... Misha Segal
KHARTOUM .... Frank Cordell†
KHOVANSHCHINA .... ★ Dmitri Shostakovitch†
KICKBOXER .... Paul Hartzop
KICKBOXER .... Paul Hertzog
KICKS .... Peter Bernstein
KID BLUE .... John Rubinstein
KID COMES BACK, THE .... David Raksin
KID FOR TWO FARTHINGS, A .... Benjamin Frankel†
KID FROM KOKOMO, THE .... Adolph Deutsch†
KID FROM LEFT FIELD, THE .... Lionel Newman†
KID FROM LEFT FIELD, THE (TF) .... David Frank
KID FROM NOT-SO-BIG, THE .... Ron Grant
KID FROM NOWHERE, THE (TF) .... Garry Sherman
KID FROM TEXAS, THE .... William Axt†
KID GALAHAD .... Jeff Alexander†
KID GALAHAD .... Max Steiner†
KID MONK BARONI .... Herschel Burke Gilbert
KID NINJAS .... Dan Slider
KID SISTER, THE .... Albert Glasser
KID WITH THE 200 I.Q., THE (TF) .... Dennis McCarthy
KID WITH THE BROKEN HALO, THE (TF) .... Tommy Vig
KID, THE .... Charles Chaplin†
KIDCO .... Michael Small
KIDNAPPED .... Roy Budd
KIDNAPPED .... Ron Jones
KIDNAPPING OF THE PRESIDENT, THE .... Paul Zaza
KIDS DON'T TELL (TF) .... Fred Karlin
KIDS LIKE THESE (TF) .... Mark Snow
KIEZ .... Carl Dante
KIGANJO NO BOKEN .... Akira Ifukube
KIKI .... Alfred Newman†
KILL AND GO HIDE .... Rob Wallace
KILL HER GENTLY .... Edwin Astley
KILL ME AGAIN .... William Olvis
KILL ME IF YOU CAN (TF) .... Bill Conti
KILL OR BE KILLED .... Carlo Rustichelli
KILL OR BE KILLED .... Karl Hajos†
KILL OR CURE .... Ron Goodwin
KILL SQUAD .... Joseph Conlan
KILL THE UMPIRE .... Heinz Roemheld†
KILLI .... Masaru Sato
KILL, BABY, KILL .... Carlo Rustichelli
KILLDOZER (TF) .... Gil Melle
KILLER APE .... Mischa Bakaleinikoff †
KILLER AT LARGE .... Albert Glasser
KILLER BEES (TF) .... David Shire
KILLER BY NIGHT (TF) .... Quincy Jones
KILLER ELITE, THE .... Jerry Fielding†
KILLER FISH .... Guido De Angelis
KILLER FISH .... Maurizio De Angelis
KILLER FORCE .... Georges Garvarentz
KILLER IN THE FAMILY (TF) .... Gerald Fried
KILLER IN THE MIRROR (TF) .... Gil Melle
KILLER INSIDE ME, THE .... John Rubinstein
KILLER INSTINCT (TF) .... Paul Chihara
KILLER IS LOOSE, THE .... Lionel Newman†
KILLER KLOWNS FROM OUTER SPACE .... John Massari
KILLER ON BOARD (TF) .... Earle Hagen
KILLER PARTY .... John Beal
KILLER SPY .... Georges Delerue
KILLER THAT STALKED NEW YORK, THE .... Hans J. Salter
KILLER WHO WOULDN'T DIE,THE (TF) .... Georges Garvarentz
KILLER'S KISS .... Gerald Fried
KILLERS, THE .... ★ Miklos Rozsa
KILLERS, THE .... John Williams
KILLING AFFAIR, A .... John Barry
KILLING AFFAIR, A (TF) .... Richard Shores
KILLING AT HELL'S GATE (TF) .... David Bell
KILLING DAD (TF) .... Chaz Jankel
KILLING FIELDS, THE .... Mike Oldfield
KILLING IN A SMALL TOWN (TF) .... Richard Gibbs
KILLING KIND, THE .... Andrew Belling
KILLING OF A CHINESE BOOKIE, THE .... Anthony Harris
KILLING OF A CHINESE BOOKIE, THE .... Bo Harwood
KILLING OF AMERICA, THE .... Mark Lindsay
KILLING OF AMERICA, THE .... Laurin Rinder
KILLING OF AMERICA, THE (FD) .... W. Michael Lewis
KILLING OF ANGEL STREET, THE .... Brian May
KILLING OF RANDY WEBSTER, THE (TF) .... Peter Matz
KILLING OF SISTER GEORGE, THE .... Gerald Fried
KILLING STONE (TF) .... David Rose†
KILLING TIME, THE .... Paul Chihara
KILLING, THE .... Gerald Fried
KILLJOY (TF) .... ☆ Bruce Broughton
KILLPOINT .... Herman Jeffreys
KILLPOINT .... Daryl Stevenett
KIM .... Andre Previn
KIM (TF) .... Marc Wilkinson
KIND LADY .... David Raksin
KIND LADY .... Edward Ward†
KIND OF LOVING, A .... Ron Grainer
KINDRED, THE .... David Newman
KING (MS) .... ☆☆ Billy Goldenberg
KING AND COUNTRY .... Larry Adler
KING AND FOUR QUEENS, THE .... Alex North
KING AND THE CHORUS GIRL, THE .... Werner R. Heymann†
KING AND THE MOCKINGBIRD, THE .... Wojciech Kilar
KING CRAB (TF) .... Dick Hyman
KING CREOLE .... Walter Scharf
KING DAVID .... Carl Davis
KING ELEPHANT (FD) .... Laurence Rosenthal
KING IN NEW YORK, A .... Charles Chaplin†
KING JAMES VERSION .... Wendy Blackstone
KING KONG .... John Barry
KING KONG .... Max Steiner†
KING KONG ESCAPES .... Akira Ifukube
KING KONG LIVES .... John Scott
KING KONG VS. GODZILLA .... Akira Ifukube
KING LEAR .... Dmitri Shostakovitch†
KING OF COMEDY, THE .... Robbie Robertson
KING OF HEARTS, THE .... Georges Delerue
KING OF JAZZ .... Ferde Grofe†
KING OF KINGS .... Miklos Rozsa
KING OF LOVE, THE (TF) .... Paul Chihara
KING OF NEW YORK .... Joseph Delia
KING OF THE GYPSIES .... David Grisman
KING OF THE KHYBER RIFLES .... Bernard Herrmann†
KING OF THE MOUNTAIN .... Michael Melvoin
KING OF THE OLYPMICS (TF) .... Paul Chihara
KING OF THE ROARING '20's—THE STORY OF ARNOLD ROTHSTEIN .... Franz Waxman†
KING RALPH .... James Newton Howard
KING RAT .... John Barry
KING RICHARD AND THE CRUSADERS .... Max Steiner†
KING SOLOMON'S MINES .... Jerry Goldsmith
KING'S THIEF, THE .... Miklos Rozsa
KING'S WHORE, THE .... Gabriel Yared
KING, QUEEN, KNAVE .... Stanley Myers
KINGS GO FORTH .... Elmer Bernstein
KINGS OF THE SUN .... Elmer Bernstein
KINGS ROW .... Erich Wolfgang Korngold†
KINGSTON: THE POWER PLAY (TF) .... Leonard Rosenman
KINJITE .... Greg De Belles
KIPPERBANG .... David Earl
KIPPS .... William Alwyn†
KIRLIAN WITNESS, THE .... Harry Manfredini
KISMET .... Andre Previn
KISMET .... ★ Herbert Stothart†
KISMET .... Edward Ward†
KISS AND TELL .... Werner R. Heymann†
KISS BEFORE THE MIRROR, A .... W. Franke Harling†
KISS FOR CORLISS, A .... Werner R. Heymann†
KISS IN THE DARK, A .... Max Steiner†
KISS KISS BANG BANG .... Bruno Nicolai
KISS ME DEADLY .... Frank De Vol
KISS ME GOODBYE .... Ralph Burns
KISS ME KATE .... ★ Andre Previn
KISS ME, STUPID .... Andre Previn
KISS ME...KILL ME (TF) .... Richard Markowitz
KISS MEETS THE PHANTOM OF THE PARK (TF) .... Hoyt Curtin
KISS MEETS THE PHANTOM OF THE PARK (TF) .... Fred Karlin
KISS OF DEATH .... David Buttolph†
KISS OF FIRE .... Herman Stein
KISS OF THE SPIDER WOMAN .... John Neschling
KISS OF THE VAMPIRE, THE .... James Bernard
KISS SHOT (TF) .... Steve Dorff
KISS THE BLOOD OFF MY HANDS .... Miklos Rozsa
KISS THE GIRLS AND MAKE THEM DIE .... Mario Nascimbene
KISS THE OTHER SHEIK .... Nino Rota†
KISS THEM FOR ME .... Lionel Newman†
KISS TOMORROW GOODBYE .... Carmen Dragon†
KISS, THE .... Tom Canning
KISS, THE .... J. Peter Robinson
KISS, THE .... William Axt†
KISSES FOR BREAKFAST .... Adolph Deutsch†
KISSES FOR MY PRESIDENT .... Bronislau Kaper†
KISSING PLACE, THE (CTF) .... Laurence Rosenthal
KIT CARSON .... Edward Ward†
KITCHEN TOTO, THE .... John Keane
KITTY .... Hubert Bath†
KITTY .... Victor Young†
KITTY & THE BAGMAN .... Brian May
KITTY FOYLE .... Roy Webb†

KLANSMAN, THE ... Stu Gardner
KLANSMAN, THE ... Dale O. Warren
KLIOU ... Heinz Roemheld†
KLONDIKE FEVER ... Hagood Hardy
KLUTE ... Michael Small
KNACK...AND HOW TO GET IT, THE ... John Barry
KNEUSS ... Tangerine Dream
KNICKERBOCKER
HOLIDAY ... ★ Werner R. Heymann†
KNIFE IN THE WATER ... Christopher Komeda†
KNIGHT WITHOUT ARMOUR ... Miklos Rozsa
KNIGHTRIDERS ... Donald Rubinstein
KNIGHTS AND EMERALDS ... Colin Towns
KNIGHTS OF THE CITY ... Misha Segal
KNIGHTS OF THE ROUND TABLE ... Miklos Rozsa
KNOCK ... Jean Wiener†
KNOCK ... Paul Misraki†
KNOCK ON ANY DOOR ... George Antheil†
KNUTE ROCKNE, ALL AMERICAN ... Ferde Grofe†
KOENIGSMARK ... Jacques Ibert†
KOJAK (TF) ... Cameron Allan
KOJAK: THE BELARUS FILE (TF) ... Joseph Conlan
KOJAK: THE BELARUS FILE (TF) ... Barry De Vorzon
KOJAK: THE PRICE OF
JUSTICE (TF) ... Patrick Williams
KOMMISSAR X, DREI
GRUNE HUNDE ... Francesco De Masi
KONA COAST ... Jack Marshall
KONGA ... Gerard Schurmann
KORCZAK ... Wojciech Kilar
KOTCH ... Marvin Hamlisch
KOTOVSKY ... Sergei Prokofiev†
KOYAANISQATSI ... Philip Glass
KRAKATOA, EAST OF JAVA ... Frank De Vol
KRAMER VS. KRAMER ... John Kander
KRAYS, THE ... Michael Kamen
KREMLIN LETTER, THE ... Robert Drasnin
KRONOS ... Bert A. Shefter
KRONOS ... Paul Sawtell†
KRULL ... James Horner
KUHLE WAMPE ... Hanns Eisler†
KULIES, THE ... W. Michael Lewis
KULIES, THE ... Laurin Rinder
KUNG FU (TF) ... Jim Helms
KUNG FU: THE MOVIE (TF) ... Lalo Schifrin
KUNI LEMI IN TEL AVIV ... Dov Seltzer
KVINNA UTAN ANSIKTE ... Eric Nordgren
KWAIDAN ... Toru Takemitsu

L

L BOSS ... Luis Bacalov
L'ABOMINABLE GOMME
DES DOUANES ... Georges Delerue
L'ACROBATE ... Antoine Duhamel
L'ADOLESCENTE ... Philippe Sarde
L'AFFAIRE CRAZY CAPO ... Vladimir Cosma
L'AFFAIRE DOMINICI ... Alain Gorraguer
L'AFFAIRE LAFARGE ... Georges Auric†
L'AFFAIRE MANET ... Georges Van Parys†
L'AFFAIRE MAURIZIUS ... Georges Van Parys†
L'AFFAIRE NINA B ... Georges Delerue
L'AFRICAIN ... Georges Delerue
L'AGE INGRAT ... Georges Delerue
L'AGNESE VA A MORIRE ... Ennio Morricone
L'AIGLE A DEUX TETES ... Georges Auric†
L'AILE OU LA CUISSE ... Vladimir Cosma
L'AINE DES FERCHAUX ... Georges Delerue
L'ALBERO DALLE FOGLIE ROSA ... Franco Micalizzi
L'ALIBI ... Georges Auric†
L'ALPAGUEUR ... Michel Colombier
L'ALPIN L'E SEMPRE QUEL ... Bruno Nicolai
L'AMANT DE LADY CHATTERLEY ... Joseph Kosma†
L'AMERICAIN SE DETEND (TF) ... Michel Legrand
L'AMERIQUE INSOLITE (FD) ... Michel Legrand
L'AMERIQUE LUNAIRE (FD) ... Michel Legrand
L'AMICA ... Luis Bacalov
L'AMORE CANTA ... Mario Nascimbene
L'AMOUR A LA CHAINE ... Georges Delerue
L'AMOUR A MORT ... Hans Werner Henze
L'AMOUR AUTOUR DE LA MAISON ... Joseph Kosma†
L'AMOUR BRAQUE ... Stanislas Syrewicz
L'AN 2000 ... Michel Legrand
L'ANIMAL ... Vladimir Cosma
L'ANNEE PROCHAINE,
SI TOUT VA BIEN ... Vladimir Cosma
L'ANNEE SAINTE ... Claude Bolling
L'ANTICRISTO ... Ennio Morricone
L'ANTICRISTO ... Bruno Nicolai
L'ANTIMIRACOLO ... Carlo Rustichelli
L'ARCHE DE NOE ... Joseph Kosma†
L'ARCHITECTE MAUDIT ... Georges Van Parys†
L'ARCIERE DELLE MILLE
E UNA NOTTE ... Mario Nascimbene
L'ARCODIAVOLO ... Armando Trovajoli
L'ARMATA BRANCALEONE ... Carlo Rustichelli
L'ARME A GAUCHE ... Michel Colombier
L'ARMOIRE VOLANTE ... Georges Van Parys†
L'ART D'AIMER ... Luis Bacalov
L'AS DES AS ... Vladimir Cosma
L'ASSASSIN CONNAIT LA MUSIQE ... Paul Misraki†
L'ASSASSINO ... Piero Piccioni
L'ASSASSINO E AL TELEFONO ... Stelvio Cipriani
L'ASSASSINO HA RISERVATO 9
POLTRONE ... Carlo Savina
L'ASSOLUTO NATURALE ... Ennio Morricone
L'ATLANTIDE ... Wolfgang Zeller†
L'ATTENTAT ... Ennio Morricone
L'ATTICO ... Piero Piccioni
L'AUTRE FEMME ... Georges Delerue
L'AVENTURE C'EST L'AVENTURE ... Francis Lai
L'AVENTURIER ... Jean Wiener†
L'AVVENTURIERO ... Ennio Morricone
L'AVVENTURIERO
DELLA TORTUGA ... Carlo Rustichelli
L'EAU A LA BOUCHE ... Serge Gainsbourg
L'ECOLE BUISSONNIERE ... Joseph Kosma†
L'EFFRONTEE ... Alain Jomy
L'EMIGRANTE ... Carlo Rustichelli
L'EMPIRE DE LA NUIT ... Michel Legrand
L'ENFER DES AUTRES ... Vladimir Cosma
L'ENFER DU JEU ... Georges Auric†
L'ENTRAINEUSE ... Georges Van Parys†
L'EQUIPAGE ... Arthur Honegger†
L'EREDITA FERRAMONTI ... Ennio Morricone
L'EROE DELLA STRADA ... Nino Rota†
L'ESCADRON BLANC ... Jean Wiener†
L'ESCLAVE ... Georges Auric†
L'ESPOIR ... Darius Milhaud†
L'ETA DELL'AMORE ... Mario Nascimbene
L'ETA DI COSIMO (TF) ... Manuel De Sica
L'ETAT SAUVAGE ... Pierre Jansen
L'ETE MEURTRIER ... Georges Delerue
L'ETERNEL RETOUR ... Georges Auric†
L'ETINCELLE ... Vladimir Cosma
L'ETOILE DU NORD ... Philippe Sarde
L'EVENEMENT LE PLUS IMPORTANT
DEPUIS QUE L'HOMME A MARCHE
SUR LA LUNE ... Michel Legrand
L'HERITIER ... Michel Colombier
L'HIPPOCAMPE ... Darius Milhaud†
L'HOMME ... Joseph Kosma†
L'HOMME A FEMMES ... Claude Bolling
L'HOMME A L'HISPANO ... Jean Wiener†
L'HOMME AU CRANE RASE ... Frederic Devreese
L'HOMME DANS LA MUIERE ... Jean Prodromides
L'HOMME DE LONDRES ... Georges Van Parys†
L'HOMME DE MARRAKECH ... Alain Gorraguer
L'HOMME DE NULLE PART ... Jacques Ibert†
L'HOMME DU JOUR ... Jean Wiener†
L'HOMME PRESSE ... Carlo Rustichelli
L'HOMME QUI VALAIT
DES MILLIARDS ... Georges Garvarentz
L'HONORABLE STANISLAS,
AGENT SECRET ... Georges Delerue
L'HORIZON ... Serge Gainsbourg
L'HOROSCOPE ... Claude Bolling
L'IDEE ... Arthur Honegger†
L'IGUANA DALLA LINGUA
DI FUOCO ... Stelvio Cipriani
L'IMMORALE ... Carlo Rustichelli
L'IMMORTELLE ... Georges Delerue
L'IMPIEGATO ... Piero Piccioni
L'IMPORTANT C'EST D'AIMER ... Georges Delerue
L'IMPRECATEUR ... Richard Rodney Bennett
L'INCONNU DE SHANDIGOR ... Serge Gainsbourg
L'INDIC ... Michel Magne†
L'INGENU ... Georges Delerue
L'INGENUA ... Carlo Savina
L'INHUMAINE ... Darius Milhaud†
L'INSOUMIS ... Georges Delerue
L'INSPECTEUR AIME LA BAGARRE ... Joseph Kosma†
L'INTRIGO ... Angelo Francesco Lavagnino†
L'INTRUS ... Georges Garvarentz
L'INVASION ... Riz Ortolani
L'INVENZIONE DI MOREL ... Nicola Piovani
L'INVINCIBILE CAVALIERE
MASCHERATO ... Angelo Francesco Lavagnino†
L'INVITEE ... Georges Garvarentz
L'IRA DI ACHILLE ... Carlo Savina
L'ISOLA ... Carlo Rustichelli
L'ISTRUTTORIA E' CHIUSA:
DIMENTICHI ... Ennio Morricone
L'ITALIA IN PIGIAMA ... Angelo Francesco Lavagnino†
L'ODEUR DES FAUVES ... Francis Lai
L'OISEAU DE PARADIS ... Maurice Jarre
L'OMBRA ... Carlo Rustichelli
L'ONORATO FAMIGLIA UCCIDERE
E COSA NOSTRA ... Bruno Nicolai
L'OR DANS LA RUE ... Georges Van Parys†
L'OR ET LE PLUMB ... Michel Legrand
L'ORDINATEUR DES
POMPES FUNEBRES ... Claude Bolling
L'ORO DEI BRAVADOS ... Luis Bacalov
L'ORO DI NAPOLI ... Alessandro Cicognini†
L'UCCELLO MIGRATORE ... Armando Trovajoli
L'UDIENZA ... Teo Usuelli
L'ULTIMA CHANCE ... Luis Bacalov
L'ULTIMA NEVE DI PRIMAVERA ... Franco Micalizzi
L'ULTIMA VIOLENZA ... Mario Nascimbene
L'ULTIMA VOLTA INSIEME ... Stelvio Cipriani
L'ULTIMO HAREM ... Stelvio Cipriani
L'ULTIMO TRENO DELLA NOTTE ... Ennio Morricone
L'ULTIMO UOMO DI SARA ... Ennio Morricone
L'ULTIMO ZAR ... Angelo Francesco Lavagnino†
L'UOME CHE RIDE ... Carlo Savina
L'UOMO CHE SFIDO
L'ORGANIZZAZIONE ... Luis Bacalov
L'UOMO DAI CALZONI CORTI ... Carlo Rustichelli
L'UOMO DELLA STRADA
FA GIUSTIZIA ... Bruno Nicolai
L'UOMO DI PAGLIA ... Carlo Rustichelli
L'UOMO E LA MAGIA (TF) ... Ennio Morricone
L'UOMO, L'ORGIGLIO,
LA VENDETTA ... Carlo Rustichelli
L'URLO DEI GIGANTI ... Armando Trovajoli
L-SHAPED ROOM, THE ... John Barry
L.A. LAW (TF) ... Mike Post
L.A. TAKEDOWN (TF) ... Basil Poledouris
L.A. TAKEDOWN (TF) ... Tim Truman
LA 317 SECTION ... Pierre Jansen
LA BABY-SITTER ... Francis Lai
LA BALANCE ... Roland Bocquet
LA BALLADE DE MAMLOUK ... Armando Trovajoli
LA BALLERINA ED IL BUON DIO ... Piero Piccioni
LA BAMBA ... Miles Goodman
LA BAMBOLONA ... Luis Bacalov
LA BANCA DI MONATE ... Armando Trovajoli
LA BANDA CASAROLI ... Mario Nascimbene
LA BANDA DEL BUCO ... Luis Bacalov
LA BANDA J & S: CRONACA
CRIMINALE DEL FAR WEST ... Ennio Morricone
LA BANDERA ... Jean Wiener†
LA BARRICADE DU
POINT DU JOUR ... Antoine Duhamel
LA BATTAGLIA DEL DESERTO ... Bruno Nicolai
LA BATTAGLIA DI EL ALAMEIN ... Carlo Rustichelli
LA BAULE-LES PINS ... Philippe Sarde
LA BELLA DI ROMA ... Nino Rota†
LA BELLA MUGNAIA ... Angelo Francesco Lavagnino†
LA BELLE AVENTURE ... Georges Auric†
LA BELLE FAMIGLIE ... Armando Trovajoli
LA BELLE QUE VOILA ... Joseph Kosma†
LA BELLE VIE ... Henri Lanoe
LA BELLE VIE (TF) ... Vladimir Cosma
LA BELLEZZA D'IPPOLITA ... Carlo Rustichelli
LA BELVA ... Stelvio Cipriani
LA BERGERE ET LE RAMONEUR ... Joseph Kosma†
LA BETE A L'AFFUT ... Maurice Jarre
LA BETE HUMAINE ... Joseph Kosma†
LA BETIA, OVVERO IN AMORE
PER OGNI GAUDENZA ... Carlo Rustichelli
LA BOLOGNESE ... Carlo Savina
LA BONNE ANNEE ... Francis Lai
LA BOUM ... Vladimir Cosma
LA BOUM II ... Vladimir Cosma
LA BRIDE SUR LE COU ... Maurice Jarre
LA CADUTA DEGLI DEI ... Maurice Jarre
LA CAGE ... Philippe Sarde
LA CAGE AUX FOLLES 3 ... Ennio Morricone
LA CAGE AUX FOLLES II ... Ennio Morricone
LA CALDA VITA ... Carlo Rustichelli
LA CALIFFA ... Ennio Morricone
LA CARCASSE ET LE TORD-COU ... Jean Wiener†
LA CARICA DEL 7 CAVALLEGGERI ... Carlo Rustichelli
LA CASA DEL TAPPETO GIALLO ... Stelvio Cipriani
LA CATHEDRALE DES MORTES ... Jean Wiener†
LA CATTURA ... Riz Ortolani
LA CECILIA ... Michel Portal
LA CENA DELLA BEFFE ... Giuseppe Becce†
LA CENTO CHILOMETRI ... Armando Trovajoli

LA CHAIR DE L'ORCHIDEE .... Fiorenzo Carpi
LA CHAMBRE ARDENTE .... Georges Auric†
LA CHANSON DE ROLAND .... Antoine Duhamel
LA CHARRETTE FANTOME .... Jacques Ibert†
LA CHATELAINE DU LIBAN .... Paul Misraki†
LA CHEVRE .... Vladimir Cosma
LA CHIAVE .... Ennio Morricone
LA CIECA DI SORRENTO .... Carlo Rustichelli
LA CIGALE ET LA FOURMI .... Joseph Kosma†
LA CINE E VICINA .... Ennio Morricone
LA CIOCIARA .... Armando Trovajoli
LA CITADELLE DU SILENCE .... Arthur Honegger†
LA CITADELLE DU SILENCE .... Darius Milhaud†
LA CITTA SCONVOLTA: CACCIA
SPIETATA AI RAPITORI .... Luis Bacalov
LA CITTA SI DIFENDE .... Carlo Rustichelli
LA CIUDAD SAGRADA .... Les Baxter
LA CLASE OPERAIA VA
IN PARADISO .... Ennio Morricone
LA CLASSE .... Stelvio Cipriani
LA CLE SUR LA PORTE .... Philippe Sarde
LA CODA DELLO SCORPIONE .... Bruno Nicolai
LA COLINA DEI COMALI .... Angela Morley
LA COLLINA DEGLI STIVALI .... Carlo Rustichelli
LA CONGIUNTURA .... Luis Bacalov
LA CONGIUNTURA .... Armando Trovajoli
LA CONTESTAZIONE GENERALE .... Piero Piccioni
LA CONTROFIGURA .... Armando Trovajoli
LA CORDE RAIDE .... Maurice Jarre
LA CORONDA DI FERRO .... Alessandro Cicognini†
LA CORTA NOTTE DELLE BAMBOLE
DI VETRO .... Ennio Morricone
LA COSA BUFFA .... Ennio Morricone
LA COUPE A DIX FRANCS .... Antoine Duhamel
LA COURSE A L'ECHALOTE .... Vladimir Cosma
LA COURSE DU LIEVRE A TRAVAERS
LESCHAMPS .... Francis Lai
LA CROISIERE DU NAVIGATOR .... Claude Bolling
LA CUCCAGNA .... Ennio Morricone
LA CUGINA .... Ennio Morricone
LA CUREE .... Jean Bouchety
LA DAMA ROSSA UCCIDE
SETTE VOLTE .... Bruno Nicolai
LA DAME D'ONZE HEURES .... Joseph Kosma†
LA DECADE PRODIGIEUSE .... Pierre Jansen
LA DENTELLIERE .... Pierre Jansen
LA DERNIERE BOURREE A PARIS ..... Vladimir Cosma
LA DEROBADE .... Vladimir Cosma
LA DESCENTE AUX ENFERS .... Georges Delerue
LA DISCOTECA DEL AMOR .... Emilio Kauderer
LA DOLCE VITA .... Nino Rota†
LA DOMENICA DELLA BUONA GENTE ...... Nino Rota†
LA DONNA CHE VENNE DEL MARE .... Piero Piccioni
LA DONNA DEL FIUME .... Armando Trovajoli
LA DONNA
DEL FIUME .... Angelo Francesco Lavagnino†
LA DONNA DELLA DOMENICA .... Ennio Morricone
LA DONNA DELLA MONTAGNA .... Nino Rota†
LA DONNA E UNA COSA
MERAVIGLIOSA .... Carlo Rustichelli
LA DONNA NEL MONDO .... Riz Ortolani
LA DOUBLE VIE DE THEOPHRASTE
LONGUET (TF) .... Vladimir Cosma
LA DOUCEUR DU VILLAGE (FD) .... Michel Legrand
LA DOVE NON BATTE IL SOLE .... Carlo Savina
LA FACCIA VIOLENTA DI NEW YORK ...... Riz Ortolani
LA FAILLE .... Ennio Morricone
LA FAMIGLIA BENVENUTI (TF) .... Armando Trovajoli
LA FASDIZIOSA .... Carlo Rustichelli
LA FAUTE DE L'ABBE MOURET .... Jean Wiener†
LA FEMME DE JEAN .... Georges Delerue
LA FEMME ET LA PANTIN .... Jean Wiener†
LA FEMME ET LE PANTIN .... Georges Van Parys†
LA FEMME INFIDELE .... Pierre Jansen
LA FEMME-ENFANT .... Vladimir Cosma
LA FEMME-FLIC .... Philippe Sarde
LA FETE A HENRIETTE .... Georges Auric†
LA FIGLIA DEL DIAVOLO .... Carlo Rustichelli
LA FILLE AUX YEUX GRIS .... Jean Wiener†
LA FINESTRA SUL LUNA PARK .... Piero Piccioni
LA FLUTE A SIX SCHTROUMPFS .... Michel Legrand
LA FOIRE AUX CHIMERES .... Paul Misraki†
LA FOLLE DE CHAILLOT (TF) .... Georges Delerue
LA FRANCAISE ET L'AMOUR .... Georges Delerue
LA FRECCIA NEL FIANCO .... Nino Rota†
LA FRUSTRA E IL CORPO .... Carlo Rustichelli
LA FUGA .... Piero Piccioni
LA FURIE DU DESIR .... Bruno Nicolai
LA GARCONNE .... Jean Wiener†
LA GARCONNIERE .... Mario Nascimbene
LA GENERATION DU DESERT .... Maurice Jarre
LA GIFLE .... Georges Delerue
LA GIORNATA BALORDA .... Piero Piccioni
LA GRAND RENDEZ-VOUS .... Joseph Kosma†
LA GRANDE BOUFFE .... Philippe Sarde
LA GRANDE BOURGEOISE .... Ennio Morricone
LA GRANDE NOTTE DI RINGO .... Carlo Rustichelli
LA GRANDE SCROFA NERA .... Luis Bacalov
LA GRANDE SPERANZA .... Nino Rota†
LA GRANDE VADROVILLE .... Georges Auric†
LA GUERRA CONTINUA .... Armando Trovajoli
LA GUEULE DE L'EMPLOI .... Vladimir Cosma
LA HORSE .... Serge Gainsbourg
LA JAVA DES OMBRES .... Gabriel Yared
LA JEUNE FOLLE .... Paul Misraki†
LA LAMA NEL CORPO .... Francesco De Masi
LA LECON PARTICULIERE .... Francis Lai
LA LETTRE .... Jean Wiener†
LA LIBERTE EN CROUPE .... Philippe Sarde
LA LIGNE DE DEMARCATION .... Pierre Jansen
LA LOI C'EST LA LOI .... Nino Rota†
LA LONGUE MARCHE .... Antoine Duhamel
LA LOTTA DELL'VORRO PER LE SOPRA
VIVENZ (TF) .... Mario Nascimbene
LA LOUVE SOLITAIRE .... Francis Lai
LA LUMIERE DES JUSTES .... Georges Garvarentz
LA LUNGA NOTTE DEL '43 .... Carlo Rustichelli
LA MADAMA .... Manuel De Sica
LA MAESTRA DI SCI .... Stelvio Cipriani
LA MAIN A COUPER .... Paul Misraki†
LA MAISON BONNADIEU .... Georges Van Parys†
LA MAISON DES SEPT
JEUNES FILLES .... Georges Van Parys†
LA MAISON DU MALTAIS .... Jacques Ibert†
LA MALA ORDINA .... Armando Trovajoli
LA MANDARINE .... Claude Bolling
LA MANE SUL FUCILE .... Carlo Rustichelli
LA MANI SULLA CITTA .... Piero Piccioni
LA MANO DEL STRANIERO .... Nino Rota†
LA MANO NERA .... Carlo Rustichelli
LA MANO SPIETATA DELLA LEGGE .... Stelvio Cipriani
LA MARIE DU PORT .... Joseph Kosma†
LA MARJOLAINE .... Paul Misraki†
LA MARQUISE DES ANGES .... Michel Magne†
LA MARSEILLAISE .... Joseph Kosma†
LA MATRIARCA .... Armando Trovajoli
LA MEILLEURE FACON DE MARCHER ...... Alain Jomy
LA MEILLEURE PART .... Paul Misraki†
LA MIA SIGNORA .... Armando Trovajoli
LA MINA .... Carlo Rustichelli
LA MOGLIE PIU BELLA .... Ennio Morricone
LA MOGLIE VERGINE .... Armando Trovajoli
LA MOINE ET LA SORCIERE .... Michel Portal
LA MORT DE BELLE .... Georges Delerue
LA MORTE CAMMINA
CON I TACCHI ALTI .... Stelvio Cipriani
LA MORTE SAISON DES AMOUR ..... Georges Delerue
LA MORTE SULL' ALTA COLLINA .... Luis Bacalov
LA MORTE VIENE DA MANILA .... Francesco De Masi
LA MORTE VIENE DALLO SPAZIO ..... Carlo Rustichelli
LA MOUTARDE ME
MONTE AU NEZ .... Vladimir Cosma
LA MURAGLIA
CINESE (FD) .... Angelo Francesco Lavagnino†
LA NEMICA .... Carlo Rustichelli
LA NIPOTE .... Carlo Savina
LA NIPOTE DEL PRETE .... Carlo Savina
LA NOIA .... Luis Bacalov
LA NOTTE BRAVA .... Piero Piccioni
LA NOTTE DEI SERPENTI .... Ennio Morricone
LA NOTTE DEI TEDDY-BOYS .... Armando Trovajoli
LA NOTTE DEL
GRANDE ASSALTO .... Carlo Rustichelli
LA NOTTE DELL'ULTIMO GIORNO .... Stelvio Cipriani
LA NOTTE DI SAN LORENZO .... Nicola Piovani
LA NUIT AMERICAINE .... Georges Delerue
LA NUORA GIOVANE .... Carlo Savina
LA ORGIA DE LOS MUERTOS .... Francesco De Masi
LA PACHA .... Serge Gainsbourg
LA PALOMBIERE .... Jean Musy
LA PAQUEBOT TENACITY .... Jean Wiener†
LA PARMIGIANA .... Piero Piccioni
LA PART DE L'OMBRE .... Georges Auric†
LA PART DU FEU .... Paul Misraki†
LA PASSANTE .... Georges Delerue
LA PASSION BEATRICE .... Lili Boulanger
LA PASSION BEATRICE .... Ron Carter
LA PECORA NERA .... Luis Bacalov
LA PELLE .... Lalo Schifrin
LA PETITE FEMME DU
MOULIN ROUGE .... Paul Misraki†
LA PETITE FILLE EN
VELOURS BLEU .... Georges Delerue
LA PETITE LILI .... Darius Milhaud†
LA PETITE SAUVAGE .... Werner R. Heymann†
LA PETITE VERTU .... Georges Delerue
LA PISCINE .... Michel Legrand
LA PIU BELLA SERATA
DELLA MIA VITA .... Armando Trovajoli
LA PLANETE SAUVAGE .... Alain Gorraguer
LA POLIZIA E AL SERVIZIO
DEL CITTADINO? .... Luis Bacalov
LA POLIZIA RINGRAZIA .... Stelvio Cipriani
LA PORTA DEL CANNONE .... Carlo Rustichelli
LA PREDA E L'AVVOLTOIO .... Bruno Nicolai
LA PRESIDENTESSA .... Carlo Rustichelli
LA PRIMA NOTTA DEL DOTTOR DANIELI,
INDUSTRIALE, COL COMPLESSO DEL...
GIOCATTOLO .... Riz Ortolani
LA PRIMA NOTTE DI QUIETE .... Mario Nascimbene
LA PROFANAZIONE .... Carlo Savina
LA PROPRIETA NON
PIU UN FURTO .... Ennio Morricone
LA PROVINCIALE .... Franco Mannino
LA PUPEE .... Joseph Kosma†
LA PUTAIN RESPECTUEUSE .... Georges Auric†
LA QUESTION .... Antoine Duhamel
LA RACE DES SEIGNEURS .... Philippe Sarde
LA RAFLE EST POUR CE SOIR .... Jean Wiener†
LA RAGAZZA DI MILLE MESI .... Armando Trovajoli
LA RAGAZZA DI TRIESTE .... Riz Ortolani
LA RAGAZZA DI VIA MILLE LIRE .... Luis Bacalov
LA RAGAZZA E IL GENERALE .... Ennio Morricone
LA RAGAZZA IN PRESTITO .... Armando Trovajoli
LA RAGAZZA SOTTO IL
LENZUOLO .... Carlo Savina
LA RAISON D'ETAT .... Vladimir Cosma
LA RAISON DU PLUS FOU .... Vladimir Cosma
LA REGAZZA DI LATTA .... Nicola Piovani
LA REGINA DI SABA .... Nino Rota†
LA REINE MARGOT .... Paul Misraki†
LA RENDEZ-VOUS DE MINUIT .... Georges Auric†
LA RESA DEI CONTI .... Ennio Morricone
LA REVOLUTION D'OCTOBRE .... Jean Wiener†
LA RISAIA .... Angelo Francesco Lavagnino†
LA RIVALE .... Vladimir Cosma
LA RIVIERE DU HIBOU .... Henri Lanoe
LA RONDE .... Francis Lai
LA RONDE .... Michel Magne†
LA ROSA ROSSA .... Luis Bacalov
LA ROUE .... Arthur Honegger†
LA ROUTE DE CORINTHE .... Pierre Jansen
LA ROUTE DE SALINA .... Michel Magne†
LA ROUTE HEUREUSE .... Georges Van Parys†
LA ROUTE NAPOLEON .... Paul Misraki†
LA RUMBA .... Claude Bolling
LA RUPTURE .... Pierre Jansen
LA SCARLATINE .... Gabriel Yared
LA SCHIAVA DI ROMA .... Armando Trovajoli
LA SEDUZIONE .... Luis Bacalov
LA SERVANTE (TF) .... Vladimir Cosma
LA SFIDA DI MACKENNA .... Bruno Nicolai
LA SIGNORA DI TUTTI .... Daniele Amfitheatrof†
LA SMANIA ADOSSO .... Carlo Rustichelli
LA SPIAGGIA .... Piero Piccioni
LA STAGIONE DEI SENSI .... Ennio Morricone
LA STORIA DEL TERZO REICH (TD) .... Daniele Paris
LA STRADA .... Nino Rota†
LA STREGA IN AMORE .... Luis Bacalov
LA SUPERTESTIMONE .... Luis Bacalov
LA SUPPLENTE VA IN CITTA .... Stelvio Cipriani
LA SURPRISE DU CHEF .... Vladimir Cosma
LA SYMPHONIE PASTORALE .... Georges Auric†
LA TARANTOLA DAL
VENTRO NERO .... Ennio Morricone
LA TECNICA E IL RITO .... Francesco De Masi
LA TERRAZZA .... Armando Trovajoli
LA TETE CONTRE LES MURS .... Maurice Jarre
LA TIGRE DEI SETTE MARI .... Carlo Rustichelli
LA TRACE .... Marc Perrone
LA TRACE .... Nicola Piovani
LA TRAGEDIE IMPERIALE .... Darius Milhaud†
LA TRATTA DELLE BIANCHE .... Armando Trovajoli
LA TRUITE .... Richard Hartley
LA VACANZA .... Fiorenzo Carpi
LA VALISE .... Philippe Sarde
LA VALLE DELL'ECO TONANTE .... Carlo Rustichelli
LA VEDOVA DEL TRULLO .... Stelvio Cipriani
LA VELA INCANTATA .... Nicola Piovani
LA VENA D'ORO .... Carlo Rustichelli
LA VENDETTA DEL CORSARO .... Carlo Rustichelli
LA VENERE DEI PIRATI .... Carlo Rustichelli

LA VENERE DI CHERONEA ... Michel Michelet†
LA VERGINE MODERNA ... Nino Rota†
LA VEUVE COUDERC ... Philippe Sarde
LA VIA DEI BABBUINI ... Armando Trovajoli
LA VIACCIA ... Piero Piccioni
LA VICTOIRE EN CHANTANT ... Pierre Bachelet
LA VIE COMMENCE DEMAIN ... Darius Milhaud†
LA VIE CONTINUE ... Georges Delerue
LA VIE DE CHATEAU ... Michel Legrand
LA VIE DEVANT SOI ... Philippe Sarde
LA VIE DRAMATIQUE DE MAURICE UTRILLO ... Georges Van Parys†
LA VIE EN ROSE ... Georges Van Parys†
LA VIE EST BELLE ... Jean Wiener†
LA VIE ET RIEN D'AUTRE ... Oswald D'Andrea
LA VIEREE SUPERBE ... Vladimir Cosma
LA VIOLENZA: QUNITO POTERE ... Ennio Morricone
LA VISITA ... Armando Trovajoli
LA VITA E BELLA ... Armando Trovajoli
LA VITA IN GIOCO ... Nicola Piovani
LA VITA INTERIORE ... Pino Donaggio
LA VITA, A VOLTE, E MOLTO DURO NEL WEST, VERO PROVVIDENZA? ... Ennio Morricone
LA VITTIMA DESIGNATA ... Luis Bacalov
LA VOCE ... Stelvio Cipriani
LA VOGLIE MATTA ... Ennio Morricone
LA VOYAGEUR DE LA TOUSSAINT ... Jean Wiener†
LA ZIZANIE ... Vladimir Cosma
LAAT DE DOCKTER MAAR SCHUIVENI ... Vladimir Cosma
LABBRA DI LURIDO BLU ... Ennio Morricone
LABYRINTH ... Trevor Jones
LAC AUX DAMES ... Georges Auric†
LACE (MS) ... Nick Bicat
LACE II (TF) ... Nick Bicat
LACEMAKER, THE ... Pierre Jansen
LACY AND THE MISSISSIPPI QUEEN (TF) ... Barry De Vorzon
LAD: A DOG ... Heinz Roemheld†
LADDER OF SWORDS ... Stanley Myers
LADDIE ... Max Steiner†
LADDIE ... Roy Webb†
LADIES CLUB, THE ... Lalo Schifrin
LADIES COURAGEOUS ... Dimitri Tiomkin†
LADIES IN LOVE ... Louis Silvers†
LADIES IN RETIREMENT ... ★ Ernst Toch†
LADIES OF THE JURY ... Max Steiner†
LADIES OF WASHINGTON ... Cyril J. Mockridge†
LADIES WHO DO ... Ron Goodwin
LADIES' DAY ... Roy Webb†
LADIES' MAN, THE ... Walter Scharf
LADIES, THE (TF) ... Morton Stevens
LADRI DI BICICLETTE ... Alessandro Cicognini†
LADY AND THE BANDIT, THE ... George Duning
LADY AND THE HIGHWAYMAN, THE (TF) ... Laurie Johnson
LADY AND THE MONSTER, THE ... Walter Scharf
LADY AND THE TRAMP (AF) ... Oliver Wallace†
LADY AT MIDNIGHT ... Leo Erdody†
LADY AVENGER ... Jay Levy
LADY BE GOOD ... George Bassman
LADY BEWARE ... Craig Safan
LADY BLUE (TF) ... John Cacavas
LADY CAROLINE LAMB ... Richard Rodney Bennett
LADY CHATTERLEY'S LOVER ... Stanley Myers
LADY CONSENTS, THE ... Roy Webb†
LADY EVE, THE ... Leo Shuken†
LADY FOR A NIGHT ... David Buttolph†
LADY FORGETS, THE (TF) ... Walter Murphy
LADY FROM CHEYENNE, THE ... Frank Skinner†
LADY FROM KENTUCKY, THE ... Leo Shuken†
LADY FROM SHANGHAI, THE ... Heinz Roemheld†
LADY FROM YESTERDAY, THE (TF) ... Mark Snow
LADY GAMBLES, THE ... Frank Skinner†
LADY GODIVA ... Hans J. Salter
LADY GREY ... Arthur Smith
LADY GREY ... Clay Smith
LADY HAMILTON ... Miklos Rozsa
LADY HAS PLANS, THE ... Leigh Harline†
LADY HAS PLANS, THE ... Leo Shuken†
LADY ICE ... Perry Botkin
LADY IN A CAGE ... Paul Glass
LADY IN A CORNER (TF) ... David Raksin
LADY IN A JAM ... Frank Skinner†
LADY IN QUESTION, THE ... Lucien Moraweck†
LADY IN RED, THE ... James Horner
LADY IN THE DARK ... ★ Robert Emmett Dolan†
LADY IN THE IRON MASK ... Dimitri Tiomkin†
LADY IN WHITE, THE ... Frank LaLoggia
LADY IS WILLING, THE ... W. Franke Harling†
LADY JANE ... Stephen Oliver
LADY KILLER OF ROME, THE ... Piero Piccioni
LADY L ... Jean Wiener†
LADY LUCK ... Leigh Harline†
LADY MOBSTER (TF) ... Fred Karlin
LADY OBJECTS, THE ... Sidney Cutner†
LADY OF SECRETS ... William Grant Still†
LADY OF THE HOUSE (TF) ... Fred Karlin
LADY OF THE TROPICS ... Franz Waxman†
LADY ON A TRAIN ... Miklos Rozsa
LADY PANAME ... Georges Van Parys†
LADY PAYS OFF, THE ... Frank Skinner†
LADY SAYS NO, THE ... Emil Newman†
LADY SINGS THE BLUES ... Michel Legrand
LADY TAKES A CHANCE, A ... Roy Webb†
LADY TAKES A FLYER, THE ... Herman Stein
LADY TAKES A SAILOR, THE ... Max Steiner†
LADY VANISHES, THE ... Richard Hartley
LADY WITH RED HAIR ... Heinz Roemheld†
LADY WITH THE LAMP, THE ... Anthony Collins†
LADY WITHOUT PASSPORT, A ... David Raksin
LADY'S MORALS, A ... Herbert Stothart†
LADYBUG, LADYBUG ... Bob Cobert
LADYHAWKE ... Andrew Powell
LADYKILLERS, THE ... Tristram Cary
LAFAYETTE ESCADRILL ... Leonard Rosenman
LAGUNA HEAT (CTF) ... Patrick Williams
LAIR OF THE WHITE WORM, THE ... Stanislas Syrewicz
LAKE PLACID SERENADE ... Walter Scharf
LAKER GIRLS, THE ... Sylvester Levay
LAMB ... Van Morrison
LAMBADA ... Greg De Belles
LAMP, THE ... Joel Rosenbaum
LANCELOT AND GUINEVERE ... Ron Goodwin
LANCELOT OF THE LAKE ... Philippe Sarde
LAND BEFORE TIME, THE (AF) ... James Horner
LAND OF FURY ... William Alwyn†
LAND OF NO RETURN, THE ... Ralph Geddes
LAND OF PROMISE ... Wojciech Kilar
LAND OF THE MINOTAUR ... Brian Eno
LAND OF THE PHARAOHS ... Dimitri Tiomkin†
LAND RAIDERS ... Bruno Nicolai
LAND THAT TIME FORGOT, THE ... Douglas Gamley
LAND UNKNOWN, THE ... Hans J. Salter
LAND UNKNOWN, THE ... Herman Stein
LAND UNKNOWN, THE ... Henry Mancini
LAND UNKNOWN, THE ... Heinz Roemheld†
LANDRU ... Pierre Jansen
LANIGAN'S RABBI (TF) ... Leonard Rosenman
LARCENY ... Leith Stevens†
LARCENY IN HER HEART ... Leo Erdody†
LARCENY, INC ... Adolph Deutsch†
LARRY (TF) ... Peter Matz
LAS BACCANTI ... Mario Nascimbene
LAS VEGAS LADY ... Alan Silvestri
LAS VEGAS STORY, THE ... Leigh Harline†
LAS VIERNES DE LA ETERNIDAD ... Lalo Schifrin
LASERBLAST ... Richard H. Band
LASERBLAST ... Joel Goldsmith
LASERMAN, THE ... Mason Daring
LASSIE COME HOME ... Daniele Amfitheatrof†
LASSITER ... Ken Thorne
LAST AMERICAN HERO, THE ... Charles Fox
LAST ANGRY MAN, THE (TF) ... Gil Melle
LAST CHALLENGE, THE ... Richard Shores
LAST CHASE, THE ... Gil Melle
LAST CHILD, THE (TF) ... Laurence Rosenthal
LAST COMMAND, THE ... Max Steiner†
LAST CONVERTIBLE, THE (MS) ... ☆ Pete Rugolo
LAST CRY FOR HELP, A (TF) ... Miles Goodman
LAST DAY, THE (TF) ... Carmine Coppola
LAST DAYS OF DOLWYN, THE ... John Greenwood†
LAST DAYS OF FRANK AND JESSE JAMES, THE (TF) ... Paul Chihara
LAST DAYS OF MUSSOLINI, THE ... Ennio Morricone
LAST DAYS OF PATTON, THE (TF) ... ☆ Allyn Ferguson
LAST DAYS OF POMPEII, THE ... Angelo Francesco Lavagnino†
LAST DAYS OF POMPEII, THE ... Roy Webb†
LAST DAYS OF POMPEII, THE (MS) ... Trevor Jones
LAST DETAIL, THE ... Johnny Mandel
LAST DINOUSAUR, THE (TF) ... Maury Laws
LAST DRAGON, THE ... Misha Segal
LAST ELECTRIC KNIGHT, THE (TF) ... David Kurtz
LAST ELEPHANT, THE ... Charles Bernstein
LAST EMBRACE ... Miklos Rozsa
LAST EMPEROR, THE ... ★★ David Byrne
LAST EMPEROR, THE ... ★★ Cong Su
LAST EMPEROR, THE ... ★★ Ryuichi Sakamoto
LAST EXIT TO BROOKLYN ... Mark Knopfler
LAST FIGHT, THE ... Jay Chattaway
LAST FIVE DAYS OF PEACE, THE ... Ennio Morricone
LAST FLIGHT OF NOAH'S ARK, THE ... Maurice Jarre
LAST FLIGHT OUT (TF) ... ☆ Christopher Young
LAST FLING, THE (TF) ... Charles Bernstein
LAST FRONTIER, THE ... Leigh Harline†
LAST FRONTIER, THE (TF) ... Brian May
LAST GANGSTER, THE ... Edward Ward†
LAST GENTLEMAN, THE ... Alfred Newman†
LAST GRENADE, THE ... John Dankworth
LAST HARD MEN, THE ... Jerry Goldsmith
LAST HOLIDAY ... Francis Chagrin†
LAST HORROR FILM, THE ... Udi Harpaz
LAST HORROR SHOW, THE ... Arthur Kempel
LAST HOURS BEFORE MORNING (TF) ... Pete Rugolo
LAST HOUSE ON THE LEFT ... David Alex Hess
LAST HUNT, THE ... Daniele Amfitheatrof†
LAST HUNTER, THE ... Franco Micalizzi
LAST HURRAH, THE (TF) ... Peter Matz
LAST IMAGES OF THE SHIPWRECK ... Pedro Aznar
LAST INNOCENT MAN, THE (CTF) ... Brad Fiedel
LAST MAN ON EARTH, THE ... Bert A. Shefter
LAST MARRIED COUPLE IN AMERICA, THE ... Charles Fox
LAST MERCENARY, THE ... Bruno Nicolai
LAST METRO, THE ... Georges Delerue
LAST NIGHT AT THE ALAMO ... Wayne Bell
LAST NIGHT AT THE ALAMO ... Chuck Pinnell
LAST NINJA, THE (TF) ... Bob Cobert
LAST OF MRS. CHEYNEY, THE ... William Axt†
LAST OF PHILIP BANTER, THE ... Phil Marshall
LAST OF SHEILA, THE ... Billy Goldenberg
LAST OF THE BUCCANEERS ... Mischa Bakaleinikoff†
LAST OF THE COMMANCES ... George Duning
LAST OF THE COWBOYS, THE ... Craig Safan
LAST OF THE FAST GUNS ... Herman Stein
LAST OF THE FINEST, THE ... Jack Nitzsche
LAST OF THE GOOD GUYS, THE (TF) ... Dana Kaproff
LAST OF THE GREAT SURVIVORS (TF) ... Artie Butler
LAST OF THE KNUCKLEMEN, THE ... Bruce Smeaton
LAST OF THE MOBILE HOT-SHOTS ... Quincy Jones
LAST OF THE MOHICANS, THE ... Peter Thomas
LAST OF THE MOHICANS, THE ... Nathaniel Shilkret†
LAST OF THE MOHICANS, THE ... Roy Webb†
LAST OF THE MOHICANS, THE (TF) ... Robert Summers
LAST OF THE PAGANS, THE ... William Axt†
LAST OF THE PAGANS, THE ... Milan Roder†
LAST OF THE RED HOT LOVERS ... Neal Hefti
LAST OF THE WILD HORSES ... Albert Glasser
LAST OUTLAW, THE (MS) ... Brian May
LAST OUTPOST, THE ... Milan Roder†
LAST PAIR OUT ... Eric Nordgren
LAST PARADISE, THE (FD) ... Angelo Francesco Lavagnino†
LAST PICNIC, THE ... Harry Manfredini
LAST PLACE ON EARTH, THE (MS) ... Trevor Jones
LAST PRECINCT, THE(TF) ... Pete Carpenter†
LAST PRECINCT, THE (TF) ... Mike Post
LAST REMAKE OF BEAU GESTE, THE ... John Morris
LAST RESORT ... Thom Sharp
LAST RESORT ... Steve Nelson
LAST RIDE OF THE DALTON GANG, THE (TF) ... Bob Cobert
LAST RIDE, THE (CTF) ... James Wesley Stemple
LAST RITES ... Bruce Broughton
LAST RITES ... Paul Jost
LAST RITES ... George Small
LAST ROUND, THE ... Luis Bacalov
LAST RUN, THE ... Jerry Goldsmith
LAST SAFARI, THE ... John Dankworth
LAST SHOT YOU HEAR, THE ... Bert A. Shefter
LAST SONG, THE (TF) ... Johnny Harris
LAST STARFIGHTER, THE ... Craig Safan
LAST STOP ON THE NIGHT TRAIN ... Ennio Morricone
LAST SUNSET, THE ... Ernest Gold
LAST SURVIVORS, THE (TF) ... Michael Melvoin
LAST TANGO IN PARIS ... Gato Barbieri
LAST TANGO IN PARIS ... Oliver Nelson†
LAST TEMPTATION OF CHRIST, THE ... Peter Gabriel
LAST TENANT, THE (TF) ... Dick Hyman
LAST TIME I SAW ARCHIE, THE ... Frank Comstock
LAST TIME I SAW PARIS,THE ... Conrad Salinger†
LAST TRAIN FROM GUN HILL ... Dimitri Tiomkin†
LAST TRAIN HOME (CTF) ... Louis Natale
LAST TYCOON, THE ... Maurice Jarre
LAST UNICORN, THE (AF) ... Jimmy Webb
LAST UNICORN, THE (AF) ... Matthew McCauley
LAST VALLEY, THE ... John Barry
LAST WAGON, THE ... Lionel Newman†
LAST WARRIOR, THE ... Marvin Hamlisch

LAST WOMAN ON EARTH, THE ... Ronald Stein†
LAST WOMAN, THE ... Philippe Sarde
LAST WORD, THE ... Carol Lees
LAST YEAR AT MARIENBAD ... Francis Seyrig
LAST YEAR OF CHILDHOOD, THE ... Markus Urchs
LATE GEORGE APLEY, THE ... Cyril J. Mockridge†
LATE GREAT PLANET EARTH, THE (FD) ... Dana Kaproff
LATE SHOW, THE ... Ken Wannberg
LATINO ... Diane Louie
LATITUDE ZERO ... Akira Ifukube
LAUGHING ANNE ... Anthony Collins†
LAUGHING BOY ... Herbert Stothart†
LAUGHING POLICEMAN, THE ... Charles Fox
LAUGHTER HOUSE (TF) ... Dominic Muldowney
LAURA ... David Raksin
LAURA LANSING SLEPT HERE (TF) ... Peter Matz
LAURE ... Franco Micalizzi
LAUREL AND HARDY'S LAUGHING '20s ... John Parker
LAVENDER HILL MOB, THE ... Georges Auric†
LAW & HARRY MCGRAW, THE (TF) ... Richard Markowitz
LAW AND DISORDER ... Angelo Badalamenti
LAW AND DISORDER ... Humphrey Searle†
LAW AND ORDER ... Hans J. Salter
LAW AND ORDER ... Henry Mancini
LAW AND ORDER (TF) ... Richard Hazard
LAW AND THE LADY, THE ... Carmen Dragon†
LAW IS THE LAW, THE ... Nino Rota†
LAW OF THE LAND (TF) ... John Parker
LAW OF THE LASH ... Albert Glasser
LAW WEST OF TOMBSTONE, THE ... Roy Webb†
LAWLESS BREED ... Milton Rosen
LAWLESS BREED, THE ... Herman Stein
LAWLESS VALLEY ... Roy Webb†
LAWMAN ... Jerry Fielding†
LAWRENCE OF ARABIA ... ★★ Maurice Jarre
LAZY RIVER ... William Axt†
LAZZARELLA ... Carlo Rustichelli
LBJ: THE EARLY YEARS (TF) ... ☆ Johnny Mandel
LE 84 PREND DES VACANCES ... Georges Van Parys†
LE AVVENTURE DI MANDRIN ... Mario Nascimbene
LE AVVENTURE DI PINNOCHIO ... Fiorenzo Carpi
LE BAISER AU LEPREUX (TF) ... Vladimir Cosma
LE BAL ... Vladimir Cosma
LE BAMBOLE ... Armando Trovajoli
LE BAR DU TELEPHONE ... Vladimir Cosma
LE BARON DE L'ECLUSE ... Jean Prodromides
LE BEAUJOLAIS NOUVEAU EST ARRIVE ... Carlo Rustichelli
LE BEL AGE ... Georges Delerue
LE BEL AGE ... Alain Gorraguer
LE BESTIAIRE D'AMOUR (FD) ... Georges Delerue
LE BIENFAITEUR ... Georges Van Parys†
LE BON PLAISIR ... Georges Delerue
LE BONHEUR EST POUR DEMAIN ... Georges Delerue
LE BOSSU ... Georges Auric†
LE BOUCHER ... Pierre Jansen
LE BRACONNIER DE DIEU ... Claude Bolling
LE BRASIER ... Frederic Talgorn
LE CADRAN SOLAIRE (TF) ... Georges Delerue
LE CAID ... Paul Misraki†
LE CALDE NOTTE DI DON GIOVANNI ... Carlo Savina
LE CAPITAINE FRACASSE ... Arthur Honegger†
LE CAPITAN ... Jean Wiener†
LE CAPORAL EPINGLE ... Joseph Kosma†
LE CASSE ... Ennio Morricone
LE CASTAGNE SONO BUONO ... Carlo Rustichelli
LE CAVALEUR ... Georges Delerue
LE CHANTEUR DE MINUIT ... Paul Misraki†
LE CHAPEAU DE PAILLE D'ITALIE ... Georges Delerue
LE CHASSEUR DE CHEZ MAXIM ... Paul Misraki†
LE CHAT ... Philippe Sarde
LE CHAUD LAPIN ... Vladimir Cosma
LE CHEMIN DE l'ETOILE ... Jean Wiener†
LE CHEMIN SOLITAIRE ... Bruno Nicolai
LE CHEMINS DES ECOLIERS ... Paul Misraki†
LE CHEVAL D'ORGEUIL ... Pierre Jansen
LE CHEVALIER DE PARDAILLAN ... Paul Misraki†
LE CLOWN BUX ... Jean Wiener†
LE COEUR BATTANT ... Michel Legrand
LE COMEDIE DU BONHEUR ... Jacques Ibert†
LE COMPLOT ... Michel Magne†
LE COMTE DE MONTE-CRISTO ... Jean Wiener†
LE CONNETABLE DE BOURBON (TF) ... Vladimir Cosma
LE COPPIE ... Manuel De Sica
LE CORBUSIER ... Alain Gorraguer
LE CORPS DE MON ENNEMI ... Francis Lai
LE COUP DU PARAPLUIE ... Vladimir Cosma
LE COUPABLE ... Jacques Ibert†
LE COUPLE IDEAL ... Georges Van Parys†
LE COUTURIER DE CES DAMES ... Paul Misraki†
LE CRABE-TAMBOUR ... Philippe Sarde
LE DENONCIATION ... Georges Delerue
LE DEPART ... Christopher Komeda†
LE DERNIER COMBAT ... Eric Serra
LE DERNIER TOURNANT ... Michel Michelet†
LE DIABLE PROBABLEMENT ... Philippe Sarde
LE DIABLE SOUFFLE ... Jean Wiener†
LE DICIOTENNI ... Armando Trovajoli
LE DIMANCHE DE LA VIE ... Georges Delerue
LE DINGUE ... Vladimir Cosma
LE DISTRAIT ... Vladimir Cosma
LE DOLCE SIGNORE ... Armando Trovajoli
LE DOULOUS ... Paul Misraki†
LE DROIT D'AIMER ... Philippe Sarde
LE DUE ORFANELLE ... Nino Rota†
LE FATE ... Armando Trovajoli
LE FIL A LA PATTE ... Paul Misraki†
LE FILS ... Philippe Sarde
LE FOTO PROIBITE DI UNA SIGNORA PER BENE ... Ennio Morricone
LE FRANCISCAIN DE BOURGES ... Antoine Duhamel
LE FUHRER EN FOLIE ... Carlo Rustichelli
LE GANG ... Carlo Rustichelli
LE GANG DES OTAGES ... Michel Legrand
LE GANTELET VERT ... Joseph Kosma†
LE GARCON SAUVAGE ... Paul Misraki†
LE GITAN ... Claude Bolling
LE GORILLE VOUS SALUE BIEN ... Georges Van Parys†
LE GRAIN DE SABLE ... Antoine Duhamel
LE GRAND CARNIVAL ... Serge Franklin
LE GRAND DADAIS ... Antoine Duhamel
LE GRAND DADAIS ... Georges Garvarentz
LE GRAND ESCOGRIFFE ... Georges Delerue
LE GRAND ESCROC ... Michel Legrand
LE GRAND JEU ... Hanns Eisler†
LE GRAND JEU ... Georges Van Parys†
LE GRAND MELIES ... Georges Van Parys†
LE GRAND OUEVRE ... Maurice Jarre
LE GRAND SILENCE ... Maurice Jarre
LE GROS COUP ... Georges Delerue
LE GUIGNOLO ... Philippe Sarde
LE HASARD ET LA VIOLENCE ... Michel Colombier
LE HEROS DE LA MARNE ... Jacques Ibert†
LE HUITIEME JOUR ... Joseph Kosma†
LE INFIDELI ... Armando Trovajoli
LE JARDINIER D'ARGENTEUIL ... Serge Gainsbourg
LE JEU DE LA PUCE ... Georges Delerue
LE JEU DU SOLITAIRE ... Georges Delerue
LE JEUNE MARIE ... Luis Bacalov
LE JOUET ... Vladimir Cosma
LE JOURNAL D'UN FOU ... Georges Delerue
LE JOURNAL D'UNE FEMME EN BLANC ... Michel Magne†
LE JOURNAL INTIME D'UNE NYMPHOMANE ... Vladimir Cosma
LE JUGE ... Luis Bacalov
LE JUGE FAYARD DIT LE SHERIFF ... Philippe Sarde
LE JUMEAU ... Vladimir Cosma
LE LEOPARD ... Claude Bolling
LE LONG DES TROTTOIRS ... Joseph Kosma†
LE LOUP ET L'AGNEAU ... Joseph Kosma†
LE MAESTRO ... Paul Misraki†
LE MAESTRO (TF) ... Luis Bacalov
LE MAGNIFIQUE ... Claude Bolling
LE MAIN CHAUDE ... Maurice Jarre
LE MANS ... Michel Legrand
LE MARGINAL ... Ennio Morricone
LE MARIAGE A LA MODE ... Philippe Sarde
LE MATAF ... Riz Ortolani
LE MECREANT (TF) ... Georges Delerue
LE MENSONGE DE NINA PETROVNA ... Michel Michelet†
LE MEPRIS ... Georges Delerue
LE MERAVIGLIOSE AVVENTURE DI GUERRIN MESCHINO ... Nino Rota†
LE MILLE-PATTES FAIT DES CLAQUETTES ... Claude Bolling
LE MILLION ... Georges Van Parys†
LE MISERIE DEL SIGNOR TRAVET ... Nino Rota†
LE MISTRAL ... Antoine Duhamel
LE MOINE ... Piero Piccioni
LE MONACHE DI SANT' ARCANGELO ... Piero Piccioni
LE MONASCHINE ... Ennio Morricone
LE MONOCLE RIT JAUNE ... Michel Magne†
LE MONT SAINT-MICHEL ... Michel Michelet†
LE MONTE-CHARGE ... Georges Delerue
LE MUR DE L'ATLANTIQUE ... Claude Bolling
LE NAUFRAGE DE MONTE CRISTO (TF) ... Georges Delerue
LE NOTTE DEL DESPERADO ... Carlo Rustichelli
LE NOTTI BIANCHE ... Nino Rota†
LE NOUVEAU JOURNAL D'UNE FEMME EN BLANC ... Michel Magne†
LE ORE DELL'AMORE ... Ennio Morricone
LE ORE NUDE ... Riz Ortolani
LE ORME ... Nicola Piovani
LE PAIN VIVANT ... Michel Magne†
LE PAIN VIVANT ... Michel Magne†
LE PARADIS DES PILOTES PERDUS ... Joseph Kosma†
LE PARFUM DE LA DAME EN NOIR ... Jean Wiener†
LE PART DU CHOSE ... Stanislas Syrewicz
LE PASSE-MURAILLE ... Georges Van Parys†
LE PATRIOTE ... Jacques Ibert†
LE PAVE DE PARIS ... Joseph Kosma†
LE PAYS BLEU ... Gerard Anfosso
LE PERE GORIOT ... Jean Wiener†
LE PERE LEBONNARD ... Jacques Ibert†
LE PERE SERGE ... Jacques Ibert†
LE PETIT GARCON DE L'ASCENSEUR ... Georges Delerue
LE PETIT MATIN ... Francis Lai
LE PETIT POUCET ... Francis Lai
LE PETIT SOLDAT ... Joseph Kosma†
LE PIEGE ... Alain Gorraguer
LE PILLOLE DI ERCOLE ... Armando Trovajoli
LE PISTOLE NON DISCUTUNO ... Ennio Morricone
LE POINT DE MIRE ... Georges Delerue
LE POINT DU JOUR ... Jean Wiener†
LE PORT DU DESIR ... Joseph Kosma†
LE POUVOIR DU MAL ... Wojciech Kilar
LE PRESIDENT ... Maurice Jarre
LE PRIX DU DANGER ... Vladimir Cosma
LE PUITS AUX TROIS VERITES ... Maurice Jarre
LE PUITS ET LE PENDULE ... Antoine Duhamel
LE QUATTRE GIORNATE DI NAPOLI ... Carlo Rustichelli
LE RAT D'AMERIQUE ... Georges Garvarentz
LE RAYON VERT ... Jean-Louis Valero
LE RECREATION ... Georges Delerue
LE RENDEZ-VOUS ... Paul Misraki†
LE REPOS DU GEURRIER ... Michel Magne†
LE REVANCHE DES HUMANOIDES (AF) ... Michel Legrand
LE RIDEAU ROUGE ... Joseph Kosma†
LE ROSE DI DANZICA ... Luis Bacalov
LE ROSIER DE MADAME HUSSON ... Paul Misraki†
LE RUFFIAN ... Ennio Morricone
LE SANG DES BETES ... Joseph Kosma†
LE SAUVAGE ... Michel Legrand
LE SAUVEUR ... Pierre Jansen
LE SCANDALE ... Pierre Jansen
LE SECRET ... Ennio Morricone
LE SECRET DE SOEUR ANGELE ... Michel Michelet†
LE SECRET DE WILHELM STORITZ (TF) ... Georges Delerue
LE SECRET DES SELENITES (AF) ... Shuki Levy
LE SECRET DU CHEVALIER D'EON ... Carlo Rustichelli
LE SEX SHOP ... Serge Gainsbourg
LE SOLDATESSE ... Mario Nascimbene
LE SOLEIL DES HYENES ... Nicola Piovani
LE SOLEIL DES VOYOUS ... Francis Lai
LE SOLITAIRE ... Claude Bolling
LE SPIE AMANO I FIORI ... Armando Trovajoli
LE SPIE UCCIDONO A BEIRUT ... Carlo Savina
LE SPIE VENGONO DAL SEMIFREDDO ... Les Baxter
LE STAGIONI DEL NOSTRO AMORE ... Carlo Rustichelli
LE SUCRE ... Philippe Sarde
LE TAPIS VOLANT ... Maurice Jarre
LE TATOUE ... Georges Garvarentz
LE TELEPHONE ROSE ... Vladimir Cosma
LE TEMPS DES LOUPS ... Georges Garvarentz
LE TEMPS DU GHETTO ... Maurice Jarre
LE TEMPS REDONNE ... Georges Delerue
LE TESTAMENT D'ORPHEE ... Georges Auric†
LE TESTAMENT DU DR. CORDELIER (TF) ... Joseph Kosma†
LE TIGRE AIME LA CHAIR FRAICHE ... Pierre Jansen
LE TOUBIB ... Philippe Sarde
LE TRAIN ... Philippe Sarde
LE TRANSFUGE ... Luis Bacalov
LE TRIO INFERNAL ... Ennio Morricone
LE TROU NORMAND ... Paul Misraki†
LE VERGINE DI NUREMBERG ... Riz Ortolani
LE VICE ET LA VERTU ... Michel Magne†

LE VIEL HOMME ET L'ENFANT .... Georges Delerue
LE VILLAGE AU MILIEU DES BRUMES .... Georges Delerue
LE VILLAGE MAGIQUE .... Joseph Kosma†
LE VIOL .... Michel Portal
LE VOLEUR .... Henri Lanoe
LE VOLEUR DE PARATONNERRES .... Jean Wiener†
LE VOLEUR DE TIBIDABO .... Antoine Duhamel
LE VOYAGE DE NOCES .... Michel Legrand
LE VOYAGE EN BALLON .... Jean Prodromides
LEADBELLY .... Fred Karlin
LEADER OF THE BAND .... Dick Hyman
LEAN ON ME .... Bill Conti
LEAP OF FAITH (TF) .... Charles Gross
LEASE OF LIFE .... Alan Rawsthorne†
LEATHER PUSHERS, THE .... Hans J. Salter
LEATHERFACE: THE TEXAS CHAINSAW MASSACRE III .... Pat Regan
LEATHERFACE: THE TEXAS CHAINSAW MASSACRE III .... Jim Manzie
LEAVE 'EM LAUGHING (TF) .... Jimmie Haskell
LEAVE HER TO HEAVEN .... Alfred Newman†
LEAVE IT TO THE MARINES .... Bert A. Shefter
LEAVE YESTERDAY BEHIND (TF) .... Fred Karlin
LECTURE ON MAN, A .... Tristram Cary
LEDA .... Paul Misraki†
LEECH WOMAN, THE .... Irving Gertz
LEFT HAND OF GOD, THE .... Victor Young†
LEFT, RIGHT AND CENTER .... Humphrey Searle†
LEFT-HANDED GUN, THE .... Alexander Courage
LEFTOVERS, THE (TF) .... Tom Scott
LEGACY .... Roger Kellaway
LEGACY, THE .... Michael J. Lewis
LEGAL EAGLES .... Elmer Bernstein
LEGEND .... Jerry Goldsmith
LEGEND .... Tangerine Dream
LEGEND IN LEOTARDS .... William Motzig
LEGEND OF BIGFOOT, THE .... Don Peake
LEGEND OF BILLIE JEAN, THE .... Craig Safan
LEGEND OF HELL HOUSE, THE .... Delia Derbyshire
LEGEND OF HELL HOUSE, THE .... Brian Hodgson
LEGEND OF HILLBILLY JOHN, THE .... Roger Kellaway
LEGEND OF LIZZIE BORDEN, THE (TF) .... Billy Goldenberg
LEGEND OF LOBO, THE .... Oliver Wallace†
LEGEND OF LYLAH CLARE, THE .... Frank De Vol
LEGEND OF SLEEPY HOLLOW, THE .... Robert Summers
LEGEND OF SLEEPY HOLLOW, THE (TF) .... Robert Summers
LEGEND OF THE GOLDEN GUN, THE (TF) .... Jerrold Immel
LEGEND OF THE LONE RANGER, THE .... John Barry
LEGEND OF THE LOST .... Angelo Francesco Lavagnino†
LEGEND OF THE SEVEN GOLDEN VAMPIRES, THE .... James Bernard
LEGEND OF THE WEREWOLF .... Harry Robertson
LEGEND OF TOM DOOLEY, THE .... Ronald Stein†
LEGEND OF WALKS FAR WOMAN, THE (TF) .... Paul Chihara
LEGION OF THE LAWLESS .... Paul Sawtell†
LEGS (TF) .... Lee Holdridge
LEMON DROP KID, THE .... Victor Young†
LEMON POPSICLE III .... W. Michael Lewis
LEMON POPSICLE III .... Laurin Rinder
LEMON SKY .... Pat Metheny
LENA: MY 100 CHILDREN (TF) .... Misha Segal
LENNY .... Ralph Burns
LENNY POUR LES DAMES .... Paul Misraki†
LEO AND LOREE .... Lance Rubin
LEO THE LAST .... Fred Myrow
LEONARD PART 6 .... Elmer Bernstein
LEONI AL SOLE .... Fiorenzo Carpi
LEONOR .... Ennio Morricone
LEOPARD MAN, THE .... Roy Webb†
LEOPARD, THE .... Nino Rota†
LEPER .... Wojciech Kilar
LEPKE .... Ken Wannberg
LERMONTOV .... Sergei Prokofiev†
LES 11,000 VERGES .... Michel Colombier
LES 3 MOUSQUETAIRES .... Paul Misraki†
LES AFFAIRES PUBLIQUES .... Jean Wiener†
LES AMANTS DE BRAS-MORT .... Georges Auric†
LES AMANTS DE VERONE .... Joseph Kosma†
LES AMANTS DU TAGE .... Michel Legrand
LES AMOUREUX DU FRANCE (FD) .... Michel Legrand
LES AMOURS CELEBRES .... Maurice Jarre
LES AMOURS DE LADY HAMILTON .... Riz Ortolani
LES ANCIENS DE SAINT-LOUP .... Georges Van Parys†
LES ANIMAUX (FD) .... Maurice Jarre
LES ARRIVISTES .... Hanns Eisler†
LES ASSASSINS DE L'ORDE .... Michel Colombier
LES AVENTURES DE TILL L'ESPIEGLE .... Georges Auric†
LES AVEUX LES PLUS DOUX .... Georges Delerue
LES BAS-FONDS .... Jean Wiener†
LES BATELIERS DE LA VOLGA .... Michel Michelet†
LES BEAUX SOUVENIRS .... Jean Cousineau
LES BEUX JOURS .... Georges Van Parys†
LES BICHES .... Pierre Jansen
LES BICYCLETTES DE BELSIZE .... Les Reed
LES BIENS DE CE MONDE .... Jean Prodromides
LES BIJOUTIERS DU CLAIR DE LUNES .... Georges Auric†
LES BONNES CAUSES .... Georges Garvarentz
LES BONNES FEMMES .... Pierre Jansen
LES BONNES FEMMES .... Paul Misraki†
LES BONS VIVANTS .... Michel Magne†
LES BORSALINI .... Francis Lai
LES BRICOLEURS .... Michel Magne†
LES CAPRICES DE MARIE .... Georges Delerue
LES CAUCHEMARS NAISSENT LA NUIT .... Bruno Nicolai
LES CAVALIERS DE L'ORAGE .... Michel Portal
LES CHEMINS DE KATMANDOU .... Serge Gainsbourg
LES CHIFFONNIERS d'EMMAUS .... Joseph Kosma†
LES CHINOIS A PARIS .... Michel Magne†
LES CHOSES DE LA VIE .... Philippe Sarde
LES CHOUANS .... Joseph Kosma†
LES CINQ GENTLEMAN MAUDITS .... Jacques Ibert†
LES COMPRES .... Vladimir Cosma
LES CONQUISTADORS .... Michel Portal
LES CORPS CELESTES .... Philippe Sarde
LES CRACKS .... Georges Delerue
LES DEUX ANGLAISES ET LE CONTINENT .... Georges Delerue
LES DEUX ORPHELINES .... Jacques Ibert†
LES DEUX SAISONS DE LA VIE .... Ennio Morricone
LES DEUX TIMIDES .... Georges Delerue
LES DRAGUEURS .... Maurice Jarre
LES ESPIONS .... Georges Auric†
LES ETOILES DU MIDI .... Maurice Jarre
LES EVADES .... Joseph Kosma†
LES EXPERIENCES EROTIQUES DE FRANKENSTEIN .... Vladimir Cosma
LES FABULEUSES AVENTURES DU LEGENDAIRE BARON MICHAUSEN (AF) .... Michel Legrand
LES FANATIQUES .... Paul Misraki†
LES FANTOMES DU CHAPELIER .... Mathieu Chabrol
LES FELINES .... Vladimir Cosma
LES FELINS .... Lalo Schifrin
LES FEMMES S'EN BALANCENT .... Paul Misraki†
LES FILOUS .... Jean Wiener†
LES FRERES BOUQUINQUANT .... Jean Wiener†
LES FRUITS SAUVAGES .... Joseph Kosma†
LES FUGITIFS .... Vladimir Cosma
LES GALETS D'ETRETAT .... Georges Garvarentz
LES GALETTES DE PONT-AVEN .... Philippe Sarde
LES GIRLS .... Adolph Deutsch†
LES GODELUREAUX .... Pierre Jansen
LES GOMMES .... Georges Delerue
LES GRANDES MANOEUVRES .... Georges Van Parys†
LES GRANDS CHEMINS .... Michel Magne†
LES GRANDS SENTIMENTS FONT LES BONS .... Vladimir Cosma
LES HOMMES .... Francis Lai
LES HUSSARDS .... Georges Auric†
LES INNOCENTS AUX MAIN SALES .... Pierre Jansen
LES JEUDIS D'ADRIENNE (TF) .... Georges Delerue
LES JEUX DE L'AMOUR .... Georges Delerue
LES JEUX SONT FAITS .... Georges Auric†
LES LIASONS DANGEREUSES .... Thelonious Monk†
LES LIENS DE SANG .... Pierre Jansen
LES LIVREURS .... Michel Magne†
LES LONGS MANTEAUX .... Jean-Francois Leon
LES LOUVES .... Joseph Kosma†
LES MAINS SALES .... Paul Misraki†
LES MAITRES SONNEURS (TF) .... Vladimir Cosma
LES MALHEURS d'ALFRED .... Vladimir Cosma
LES MIETTES .... Antoine Duhamel
LES MISERABLES .... Alex North
LES MISERABLES .... Alessandro Cicognini†
LES MISERABLES .... Arthur Honegger†
LES MISERABLES .... Alfred Newman†
LES MISERABLES (TF) .... Allyn Ferguson
LES MOIS D'AVRIL SONT MEURTRIERS .... Philippe Sarde
LES MORFALOUS .... Georges Delerue
LES MYSTERES DE PARIS .... Georges Auric†
LES NOCES ROUGES .... Pierre Jansen
LES OEUFS BROUILLES .... Vladimir Cosma
LES OLIVIERS DE LA JUSTICE .... Maurice Jarre
LES ORGUEILLEUX .... Paul Misraki†
LES OTAGES .... Darius Milhaud†
LES PARENTS TERRIBLES .... Georges Auric†
LES PASSAGERS .... Claude Bolling
LES PASSAGERS DE LA GRANDE OUISE .... Jean Wiener†
LES PATTERSON SAVES THE WORLD .... Bruce Rowland
LES PEIROLEUSES .... Francis Lai
LES PERSES .... Jean Prodromides
LES PETITES DU QUAI AUX FLEURS .... Jacques Ibert†
LES PIQUE-ASSIETTES .... Michel Magne†
LES PLUS BELLES ESCROQUERIES DU MONDE .... Pierre Jansen
LES PLUS BELLES ESCROQUERIES DU MONDE .... Christopher Komeda†
LES PORTES DE LA NUIT .... Joseph Kosma†
LES POUSSIERES .... Jean Wiener†
LES PRISONNIERS DE LA LIBERTE .... Vladimir Cosma
LES PYRAMIDES BLEUES .... Francis Lai
LES RANGERS DEFIENT LES KARATEKAS .... Carlo Rustichelli
LES RINGARDS .... Francis Lai
LES RIPOUX .... Francis Lai
LES ROUTES DU SUD .... Michel Legrand
LES SEINS DE GLACE .... Philippe Sarde
LES TONTONS FLINGLEURS .... Michel Magne†
LES TRAVESTIS DU DIABLE .... Maurice Jarre
LES TRIBULATIONS D'UN CHINOIS EN CHINE .... Georges Delerue
LES TRICHEURS .... Peer Raben
LES TRUANDS .... Georges Van Parys†
LES UNS ET LES AUTRES .... Francis Lai
LES VISITEURS DU SOIR .... Joseph Kosma†
LES VOLETS CLOS .... Paul Misraki†
LES YEUX NOIRS .... Michel Michelet†
LES YEUX SANS VISAGE .... Maurice Jarre
LES ZOZOS .... Vladimir Cosma
LESS THAN ZERO .... Thomas Newman
LET IT RIDE .... Giorgio Moroder
LET JOY REIGN SUPREME .... Antoine Duhamel
LET THEM LIVE .... David Raksin
LET US LIVE .... Karol Rathaus†
LET'S BE HAPPY .... Nicholas Brodzsky†
LET'S DANCE .... Robert Emmett Dolan†
LET'S DO IT AGAIN .... Curtis Mayfield
LET'S GET HARRY .... Brad Fiedel
LET'S LIVE A LITTLE .... Werner R. Heymann†
LET'S MAKE IT LEGAL .... Cyril J. Mockridge†
LET'S MAKE LOVE .... ★ Lionel Newman†
LET'S MAKE MUSIC .... Roy Webb†
LET'S MAKE UP .... Robert Farnon
LET'S SWITCH (TF) .... Harry Geller
LET'S TALK ABOUT MEN .... Luis Bacalov
LET'S TRY AGAIN .... Max Steiner†
LETHAL .... Misha Segal
LETHAL WEAPON .... Eric Clapton
LETHAL WEAPON .... Michael Kamen
LETHAL WEAPON 2 .... Michael Kamen
LETHAL WEAPON II .... Eric Clapton
LETHAL WEAPON II .... David Sanborn
LETTER FOR EVIE, A .... George Bassman
LETTER FROM AN UNKNOWN WOMAN .... Daniele Amfitheatrof†
LETTER TO THREE WIVES, A .... Alfred Newman†
LETTER TO THREE WIVES, A (TF) .... ☆ Johnny Mandel
LETTER, THE .... ★ Max Steiner†
LETTER, THE (TF) .... ☆ Laurence Rosenthal
LETTERS FROM FRANK (TF) .... Ernest Gold
LETTERS FROM MARUSIA .... Mikis Theodorakis
LETTERS FROM THREE LOVERS .... Pete Rugolo
LETTERS, THE .... Pete Rugolo
LETTI SBAGLIATI .... Carlo Rustichelli
LETTING GO (TF) .... Lee Holdridge
LETTO A TRE PIAZZE .... Carlo Rustichelli
LEVA LO DIAVOLO TUO DAL CONVENTO .... Stelvio Cipriani
LEVIATHAN .... Jerry Goldsmith
LEZIONI DI VIOLONCELLO .... Bruno Nicolai
LEZIONI PRIVATE .... Franco Micalizzi
LI'L ABNER .... ★ Nelson Riddle†
LIANNA .... Mason Daring
LIBEL .... Benjamin Frankel†
LIBELED LADY .... William Axt†

LUCKY JORDAN ... Adolph Deutsch†
LUCKY LADY ... Ralph Burns
LUCKY LUCIANO ... Piero Piccioni
LUCKY LUKE ... Claude Bolling
LUCKY NICK CAIN ... Walter Goehr†
LUCKY PARTNERS ... Dimitri Tiomkin†
LUCKY PIERRE ... Vladimir Cosma
LUCKY STAR, THE ... Art Philipps
LUCKY STIFF, THE ... Heinz Roemheld†
LUCY GALLANT ... Nathan Van Cleave†
LUDWIG ... Franco Mannino
LUDWIG ON THE LOOKOUT FOR A WIFE ... Rolf Wilhelm
LUI E PEGGIO DI ME ... Manuel De Sica
LUI PER LEI ... Ennio Morricone
LULU THE TOOL ... Ennio Morricone
LUNA ... Ennio Morricone
LUNA DI MIELE IN TRE ... Armando Trovajoli
LUNDI (TF) ... Georges Delerue
LURE OF THE SWAMP ... Paul Dunlap
LURE OF THE WILDERNESS ... Franz Waxman†
LURED ... Michel Michelet†
LURKERS ... Walter Sear
LUST FOR A VAMPIRE ... Harry Robertson
LUST FOR GOLD ... George Duning
LUST FOR LIFE ... Miklos Rozsa
LUST IN THE DUST ... Peter Matz
LUSTY MEN, THE ... Roy Webb†
LUTHER ... John Addison
LUXURY GIRLS ... Nino Rota†
LYCISTRATA ... Stavros Xarchakos
LYDIA ... ★ Miklos Rozsa
LYDIA BAILEY ... Hugo Friedhofer†
LYDIA BAILEY ... Lionel Newman†

M

M ... Bert A. Shefter
M ... Michel Michelet†
M STATION: HAWAII (TF) ... Morton Stevens
M TUTTI W NOI ... Carlo Rustichelli
M'LISS ... Max Steiner†
M*A*S*H ... Johnny Mandel
M. COMME MATHIEU ... Antoine Duhamel
M.A.D.D.: MOTHERS AGAINST DRUNK DRIVERS (TF) ... Bruce Broughton
MA AND PA KETTLE AT HOME ... Herman Stein
MA AND PA KETTLE AT HOME ... Henry Mancini
MA AND PA KETTLE AT WAIKIKI ... Herman Stein
MA CHI T'HA DATE LA PATENTE? ... Carlo Rustichelli
MA JEANNETTE ET MES COPAINS ... Joseph Kosma†
MAC AND ME ... Alan Silvestri
MACABRE ... Les Baxter
MACADAM ... Jean Wiener†
MACAHANS, THE (TF) ... Jerrold Immel
MACAO ... Anthony Collins†
MACARONI ... Armando Trovajoli
MacARTHUR ... Jerry Goldsmith
MacARTHUR'S CHILDREN (FD) ... Shinchiro Ikebe
MACBETH ... The Third Ear Band
MACBETH ... Richard Addinsell†
MACBETH ... Jacques Ibert†
MACCIE SOLARI ... Ennio Morricone
MACGRUDER AND LOUD (TF) ... Paul Chihara
MACHETE ... Bert A. Shefter
MACHINE GUN KELLY ... Gerald Fried
MACHINE GUN McCAIN ... Ennio Morricone
MACHO CALLAHAN ... Patrick Williams
MACISTE ALLA CORTE DELLO ZAR ... Carlo Rustichelli
MACISTE IL GLADIATORE PIU FORTE DEL MONDO ... Francesco De Masi
MACISTE L'EROE PIU GRANDE DEL MONDO ... Francesco De Masi
MACKENNA'S GOLD ... Quincy Jones
MACKINTOSH & T.J. ... Waylon Jennings
MACKINTOSH MAN, THE ... Maurice Jarre
MACOMBER AFFAIR, THE ... Miklos Rozsa
MACON COUNTY LINE ... Stu Phillips
MAD ABOUT MEN ... Benjamin Frankel†
MAD ABOUT MUSIC ... ★ Charles Previn†
MAD ABOUT MUSIC ... ★ Frank Skinner†
MAD ADVENTURES OF 'RABBI' JACOB, THE ... Vladimir Cosma
MAD AT THE WORLD ... Leith Stevens†
MAD BULL (TF) ... Al DeLory
MAD DOCTOR OF MARKET STREET, THE ... Hans J. Salter
MAD DOCTOR, THE ... Victor Young†
MAD DOG COLL ... Stu Phillips
MAD GHOUL, THE ... Hans J. Salter
MAD GHOUL, THE ... Charles Henderson†
MAD GHOUL, THE ... Charles Previn†
MAD GHOUL, THE ... Frank Skinner†
MAD HOLIDAY ... William Axt†
MAD LOVE ... Dimitri Tiomkin†
MAD MAGICIAN, THE ... Emil Newman†
MAD MAX ... Brian May
MAD MAX BEYOND THUNDERDOME ... Maurice Jarre
MAD MAX II ... Brian May
MAD MISS MANTON, THE ... Roy Webb†
MAD MONSTER PARTY (AF) ... Maury Laws
MAD ROOM, THE ... Dave Grusin
MAD WEDNESDAY ... Werner R. Heymann†
MADAM SATAN ... Herbert Stothart†
MADAME ... Angelo Francesco Lavagnino†
MADAME BOVARY ... Miklos Rozsa
MADAME BOVARY ... Giuseppe Becce†
MADAME BOVARY ... Darius Milhaud†
MADAME BUTTERFLY ... W. Franke Harling†
MADAME CLAUDE ... Serge Gainsbourg
MADAME CLAUDE 2 ... Francis Lai
MADAME CURIE ... ★ Herbert Stothart†
MADAME DU BARRY ... Georges Van Parys†
MADAME ROSA ... Philippe Sarde
MADAME SIN (TF) ... Michael Gibbs
MADAME SOUSATZKA ... Gerald Gouriet
MADAME SPY ... Hans J. Salter
MADAME WUNSCHT KEINE KINDER ... Bronislau Kaper†
MADAME X (TF) ... Angela Morley
MADDALENA ... Ennio Morricone
MADE ... John Cameron
MADE FOR EACH OTHER ... Oscar Levant†
MADE IN HEAVEN ... Mark Isham
MADE IN ITALY ... Carlo Rustichelli
MADELINE ... William Alwyn†
MADEMOISELLE DE MAUPIN ... Franco Mannino
MADEMOISELLE DE SADE E I SUOVI VIZI ... Bill Conti
MADEMOISELLE DOCTEUR ... Arthur Honegger†
MADEMOISELLE FIFI ... Werner R. Heymann†
MADEMOISELLE JOSETTE MA FEMME ... Georges Van Parys†
MADEMOISELLE S'AMUSE ... Paul Misraki†
MADHOUSE ... Douglas Gamley
MADHOUSE ... David Newman
MADIGAN ... Don Costa
MADISON AVENUE ... Harry Sukman†
MADMAN ... Stephen Horelick
MADMAN ... Gary Sales
MADNESS OF THE HEART ... Allan Gray†
MADO ... Philippe Sarde
MADRI PERICOLOSE ... Teo Usuelli
MAE WEST (TF) ... Brad Fiedel
MAEDCHEN IN UNIFORM ... Peter Sandloff
MAERKISCHE FORSCHUNGEN ... Guenther Fischer
MAFIA PRINCESS (TF) ... Lee Holdridge
MAFIA, UNA LEGGE CHE NON PERDONA ... Stelvio Cipriani
MAFIOSO ... Nino Rota†
MAFU CAGE, THE ... Roger Kellaway
MAGIA VERDE (FD) ... Angelo Francesco Lavagnino†
MAGIC ... Jerry Goldsmith
MAGIC BOX, THE ... William Alwyn†
MAGIC CANVAS, THE (AF) ... Matyas Seiber
MAGIC CARPET (TF) ... Lyn Murray†
MAGIC CARPET, THE ... Mischa Bakaleinikoff †
MAGIC CHRISTIAN, THE ... Ken Thorne
MAGIC FACE, THE ... Herschel Burke Gilbert
MAGIC FIRE ... Erich Wolfgang Korngold†
MAGIC GARDEN OF STANLEY SWEETHEART, THE ... Michel Legrand
MAGIC GARDEN OF STANLEY SWEETHEART, THE ... Jerry Styne
MAGIC MOMENTS (CTF) ... Alan Hawkshaw
MAGIC SWORD, THE ... Richard Markowitz
MAGIC TOWN ... Roy Webb†
MAGIC WORLD OF TOPO GIGIO, THE (AF) ... Armando Trovajoli
MAGICIAN OF LUBLIN, THE ... Maurice Jarre
MAGICIAN, THE ... Eric Nordgren
MAGICIAN, THE (TF) ... Patrick Williams
MAGNET, THE ... William Alwyn†
MAGNICIENT DOPE, THE ... David Raksin
MAGNIFICENT AMBERSONS, THE ... Bernard Herrmann†
MAGNIFICENT AMBERSONS, THE ... Roy Webb†
MAGNIFICENT BRUTE, THE ... Charles Previn†
MAGNIFICENT CUCKOLD, THE ... Armando Trovajoli
MAGNIFICENT DOLL, THE ... Hans J. Salter
MAGNIFICENT DOPE, THE ... Emil Newman†
MAGNIFICENT MAGICAL MAGNET OF SANTA MESA, THE (TF) ... Allyn Ferguson
MAGNIFICENT MAGICAL MAGNET OFSANTA MESA, THE (TF) ... Jack Elliott
MAGNIFICENT OBSESSION ... Frank Skinner†
MAGNIFICENT OBSESSION ... Franz Waxman†
MAGNIFICENT ONE, THE ... Claude Bolling
MAGNIFICENT ROUGHNECKS ... Paul Dunlap
MAGNIFICENT SEVEN DEADLY SINS, THE ... Roy Budd
MAGNIFICENT SEVEN RIDEI, THE ... Elmer Bernstein
MAGNIFICENT SEVEN, THE ... Elmer Bernstein
MAGNIFICENT SUMMER, THE ... Joseph Kosma†
MAGNIFICENT TWO, THE ... Ron Goodwin
MAGNIFICENT YANKEE, THE ... David Raksin
MAGNUM FORCE ... Lalo Schifrin
MAGUS, THE ... John Dankworth
MAHOGANY ... Lee Holdridge
MAHOGANY ... Michael Masser
MAID FOR PLEASURE ... Oliver Touissaint
MAID IN AMERICA (TF) ... David Frank
MAID OF SALEM ... Victor Young†
MAID TO ORDER ... Georges Delerue
MAIDS, THE ... Laurie Johnson
MAIGRET A PIGALLE ... Armando Trovajoli
MAIGRET ET L'AFFAIRE SAINT-FIACRE ... Jean Prodromides
MAIGRET TEND UN PIEGE ... Paul Misraki†
MAIL ORDER BRIDE ... George Bassman
MAIN EVENT, THE ... Michael Melvoin
MAIN STREET AFTER DARK ... George Bassman
MAIS OU ET DONC ORNICAR ... Antoine Duhamel
MAISIE ... Edward Ward†
MAITRE APRES DIEU ... Jean Wiener†
MAITRE PUNTILA ET SON VALET MATTI ... Hanns Eisler†
MAJIN STRIKES AGAIN ... Akira Ifukube
MAJIN, THE HIDEOUS IDOL ... Akira Ifukube
MAJOR AND THE MINOR, THE ... Robert Emmett Dolan†
MAJOR BARBARA ... Sir William Walton†
MAJOR DUNDEE ... Daniele Amfitheatrof†
MAJOR LEAGUE ... James Newton Howard
MAJORITY OF ONE, A ... Max Steiner†
MAKE HASTE TO LIVE ... Elmer Bernstein
MAKE ME AN OFFER (TF) ... Ralph Burns
MAKE WAY FOR TOMORROW ... George Antheil†
MAKE YOUR OWN BED ... Heinz Roemheld†
MAKING LOVE ... Leonard Rosenman
MAKING MR. RIGHT ... Chaz Jankel
MAKING OF A MALE MODEL, THE (TF) ... Artie Butler
MAKING OF THE PRESIDENT, THE (TD) ... ☆☆ Elmer Bernstein
MAKING THE GRADE ... Basil Poledouris
MAKIOKA SISTERS, THE ... Shinnosuka Okawa
MALAGA ... Matyas Seiber
MALAYA ... Bronislau Kaper†
MALCOLM ... Penguin Cafe Orchestra
MALDONNE ... Vladimir Cosma
MALE ANIMAL, THE ... Heinz Roemheld†
MALE COMPANION ... Georges Delerue
MALEDICTION ... Norman Mamey
MALIBU (TF) ... Mark Snow
MALIBU BIKINI SHOP, THE ... Robert Summers
MALICE IN WONDERLAND (TF) ... Charles Bernstein
MALLORY: CIRCUMSTANTIAL EVIDENCE (TF) ... James Di Pasquale
MALONE ... David Newman
MALPAS MYSTERY, THE ... Elisabeth Luytens†
MALPERTUIS: HISTOIRE D'UNE MAISON MAUDITE ... Georges Delerue
MALRIF, AIGLE ROYAL ... Maurice Jarre
MALTA STORY, THE ... William Alwyn†
MALTA, G.C. (D) ... Sir Arnold Bax†
MALTESE BIPPY, THE ... Nelson Riddle†
MALTESE FALCON, THE ... Adolph Deutsch†
MAMA LOVES PAPA ... Leigh Harline†
MAMA STEPS OUT ... Edward Ward†
MAMA'S DIRTY GIRLS ... Don Bagley
MAMBA ... Ennio Morricone
MAMBO ... Angelo Francesco Lavagnino†
MAMBO ... Nino Rota†
MAMMA DRACULA ... Roy Budd
MAMMA ROMA ... Carlo Rustichelli
MAMMALS ... Christopher Komeda†
MAN ABOUT THE HOUSE ... Christopher Gunning
MAN ABOUT THE HOUSE, A ... Nicholas Brodzsky†
MAN AFRAID ... Henry Mancini
MAN AGAINST THE MOB: THE CHINATOWN MURDERS (TF) ... Artie Kane
MAN ALIVE ... Leigh Harline†

MAN ALONE, A ..... Victor Young†
MAN AND A WOMAN, A ..... ★★ Francis Lai
MAN AND A WOMAN: 20 YEARS LATER, A ..... Francis Lai
MAN AND BOY ..... J.J. Johnson
MAN AND BOY ..... Quincy Jones
MAN AND THE SNAKE, THE ..... Marc Wilkinson
MAN AND WAR, PART III ..... Masaru Sato
MAN AT THE CARLTON TOWER, THE ..... Ron Goodwin
MAN BEHIND THE GUN, THE ..... David Buttolph†
MAN BETWEEN , THE ..... John Addison
MAN CALLED ADAM, A ..... Benny Carter
MAN CALLED HORSE, A ..... Leonard Rosenman
MAN CALLED INTREPID, A (MS) ..... Robert Farnon
MAN CALLED NOON , THE ..... Luis Bacalov
MAN CALLED PETER, A ..... Alfred Newman†
MAN CRAZY ..... Ernest Gold
MAN FACING SOUTHEAST ..... Pedro Aznar
MAN FOR ALL SEASONS, A ..... Georges Delerue
MAN FOR ALL SEASONS, A (CTF) ..... Julia Downes
MAN FRIDAY ..... Carl Davis
MAN FROM ATLANTIS, THE (TF) ..... Fred Karlin
MAN FROM BUTTON WILLOW, THE (AF) ..... George Bruns
MAN FROM COLORADO, THE ..... George Duning
MAN FROM DAKOTA, THE ..... Daniele Amfitheatrof†
MAN FROM DEL RIO ..... Fred Steiner
MAN FROM GALVESTON, THE ..... David Buttolph†
MAN FROM SNOWY RIVER, THE ..... Bruce Rowland
MAN FROM SPAIN, THE ..... Jean Wiener†
MAN FROM THE ALAMO, THE ..... Frank Skinner†
MAN FROM THE DINER'S CLUB, THE ..... Stu Phillips
MAN I LOVE, THE ..... Max Steiner†
MAN I MARRIED, THE ..... David Buttolph†
MAN IN A COCKED HAT ..... John Addison
MAN IN HALF MOON STREET, THE ..... Miklos Rozsa
MAN IN LOVE, A ..... Georges Delerue
MAN IN THE GRAY FLANNEL SUIT, THE ..... Bernard Herrmann†
MAN IN THE IRON MASK, THE ..... ★ Lud Gluskin†
MAN IN THE IRON MASK, THE ..... ★ Lucien Moraweck†
MAN IN THE IRON MASK, THE (TF) ..... Allyn Ferguson
MAN IN THE MIDDLE ..... John Barry
MAN IN THE NET ..... Hans J. Salter
MAN IN THE RAINCOAT, THE ..... Georges Van Parys†
MAN IN THE SADDLE ..... George Duning
MAN IN THE SANTA CLAUS SUIT, THE (TF) ..... Peter Matz
MAN IN THE SHADOW ..... Herman Stein
MAN IN THE SHADOW, THE ..... Hans J. Salter
MAN IN THE SKY, THE ..... Gerard Schurmann
MAN IN THE TRUNK, THE ..... Cyril J. Mockridge†
MAN IN THE WHITE SUIT, THE ..... Benjamin Frankel†
MAN IN THE WILDERNESS ..... Johnny Harris
MAN INSIDE, THE ..... Richard Rodney Bennett
MAN OF A THOUSAND FACES ..... Frank Skinner†
MAN OF AFFAIRS ..... Louis Levy†
MAN OF AFRICA ..... Malcolm Arnold
MAN OF ARAN (FD) ..... John Greenwood†
MAN OF CONFLICT ..... Albert Glasser
MAN OF CONQUEST ..... ★ Victor Young†
MAN OF IRON ..... Andrzej Korzynski
MAN OF LA MANCHA ..... ★★ Laurence Rosenthal
MAN OF MARBLE ..... Andrzej Korzynski
MAN OF PASSION, A ..... Vladimir Horunzhy
MAN OF THE PEOPLE ..... Edward Ward†
MAN OF THE WEST ..... Leigh Harline†
MAN OF TWO WORLDS ..... Max Steiner†
MAN ON A SWING ..... Lalo Schifrin
MAN ON A TIGHTROPE ..... Franz Waxman†
MAN ON EARTH, THE ..... Paul Sawtell†
MAN ON FIRE ..... David Raksin
MAN ON FIRE ..... John Scott
MAN ON THE EIFFEL TOWER, THE ..... Michel Michelet†
MAN ON THE MOVE (TF) ..... Robert Drasnin
MAN ON THE OUTSIDE (TF) ..... Elliot Kaplan
MAN ON THE PROWL ..... Ernest Gold
MAN OUTSIDE ..... John McEuen
MAN TO REMEMBER, A ..... Roy Webb†
MAN TO RESPECT, A ..... Ennio Morricone
MAN TRAP ..... Leith Stevens†
MAN WHO BROKE 1,000 CHAINS, THE (CTF) ..... Charles Bernstein
MAN WHO CAME TO DINNER, THE ..... Frederick Hollander†
MAN WHO COULD CHEAT DEATH, THE ..... Richard Rodney Bennett
MAN WHO COULD TALK TO KIDS, THE (TF) ..... Fred Karlin
MAN WHO COULD WORK MIRACLES, THE ..... Mischa Spoliansky†
MAN WHO DIED TWICE, THE (TF) ..... John Parker
MAN WHO FELL TO EARTH, THE ..... John Phillips
MAN WHO FELL TO EARTH, THE ..... Stomu Yamashita
MAN WHO FELL TO EARTH, THE (TF) ..... Doug Timm†
MAN WHO HAD POWER OVER WOMEN, THE ..... Johnny Mandel
MAN WHO HAUNTED HIMSELF, THE ..... Michael J. Lewis
MAN WHO KNEW TOO MUCH, THE ..... Arthur Benjamin†
MAN WHO KNEW TOO MUCH, THE ..... Bernard Herrmann†
MAN WHO LOST HIMSELF, THE ..... Hans J. Salter
MAN WHO LOVED CAT DANCING, THE ..... John Williams
MAN WHO LOVED REDHEADS, THE ..... Benjamin Frankel†
MAN WHO LOVED WOMEN, THE ..... Henry Mancini
MAN WHO NEVER WAS, THE ..... Alan Rawsthorne†
MAN WHO RECLAIMED HIS HEAD, THE ..... Heinz Roemheld†
MAN WHO SAW TOMORROW, THE ..... William Loose
MAN WHO SAW TOMORROW, THE ..... Jack Tillar
MAN WHO SHOT LIBERTY VALANCE, THE ..... Cyril J. Mockridge†
MAN WHO TALKED TOO MUCH, THE ..... Heinz Roemheld†
MAN WHO UNDERSTOOD WOMEN, THE ..... Robert Emmett Dolan†
MAN WHO WALKED ALONE, THE ..... ★ Karl Hajos†
MAN WHO WASN'T THERE, THE ..... Miles Goodman
MAN WHO WOULD BE KING, THE ..... Maurice Jarre
MAN WHO WOULDN'T DIE, THE ..... David Raksin
MAN WHO WOULDN'T DIE, THE ..... Emil Newman†
MAN WITH A CLOAK, THE ..... David Raksin
MAN WITH A GUN, THE ..... Dmitri Shostakovitch†
MAN WITH A MILLION ..... William Alwyn†
MAN WITH BOGART'S FACE, THE ..... George Duning
MAN WITH ONE RED SHOE, THE ..... Thomas Newman
MAN WITH THE BALLOONS, THE ..... Teo Usuelli
MAN WITH THE GOLDEN ARM, THE ..... ★ Elmer Bernstein
MAN WITH THE GOLDEN GUN, THE ..... John Barry
MAN WITH THE GREEN CARNATION, THE ..... Ron Goodwin
MAN WITH THE GUN ..... Alex North
MAN WITH THE POWER, THE (TF) ..... Patrick Williams
MAN WITH TWO BRAINS, THE ..... Joel Goldsmith
MAN WITHOUT A COUNTRY, THE (TF) ..... Jack Elliott
MAN WITHOUT A COUNTRY, THE (TF) ..... Allyn Ferguson
MAN WITHOUT A STAR ..... Hans J. Salter
MAN WITHOUT A STAR ..... Herman Stein
MAN'S CASTLE, A ..... W. Franke Harling†
MAN'S FAVORITE SPORT? ..... Henry Mancini
MAN, A WOMAN, AND A BANK, A ..... Bill Conti
MAN, THE ..... Jerry Goldsmith
MAN, WOMAN AND CHILD ..... Georges Delerue
MAN-EATER OF KUMAON ..... Hans J. Salter
MAN-MADE MONSTER ..... Hans J. Salter
MAN-MADE MONSTER ..... Charles Previn†
MAN-MADE MONSTER ..... Frank Skinner†
MAN-PROOF ..... Franz Waxman†
MANBEAST (TF) ..... William Goldstein
MANCHU EAGLE MURDER CAPER MYSTERY, THE ..... Richard DeBenedictis
MANCHURIAN CANDIDATE, THE ..... David Amram
MANDELA (CTF) ..... Richard Hartley
MANDINGO ..... Maurice Jarre
MANDRAKE (TF) ..... Morton Stevens
MANDY ..... William Alwyn†
MANEATER (TF) ..... George Romanis
MANEATERS ARE LOOSE! (TF) ..... Gerald Fried
MANEGES ..... Paul Misraki†
MANEUVERS ..... Jurgen Knieper
MANGIALA ..... Ennio Morricone
MANGO TREE, THE ..... Marc Wilkinson
MANHATTAN BABY ..... Fabio Frizzi
MANHATTAN MELODRAMA ..... William Axt†
MANHATTAN MOON ..... Karl Hajos†
MANHATTAN PROJECT, THE ..... Philippe Sarde
MANHUNT FOR CLAUDE DALLAS (TF) ..... Steve Dorff
MANHUNT, THE ..... Francesco De Masi
MANHUNT: SEARCH FOR THE NIGHT STALKER (TF) ..... Sylvester Levay
MANHUNTER ..... Michel Rubini
MANHUNTER (TF) ..... Benny Carter
MANIA ..... Stanley Black
MANIAC ..... Stanley Black
MANIAC ..... Jay Chattaway
MANIAC COP ..... Jay Chattaway
MANIAC COP 2 ..... Jay Chattaway
MANIFESTO ..... Nicola Piovani
MANILA CALLING ..... David Raksin
MANILA CALLING ..... David Buttolph†
MANILA CALLING ..... Cyril J. Mockridge†
MANIMAL (TF) ..... Paul Chihara
MANIONS OF AMERICA, THE (MS) ..... Morton Stevens
MANITOU, THE ..... Lalo Schifrin
MANNEQUIN ..... Sylvester Levay
MANNEQUIN ..... Edward Ward†
MANON ..... Paul Misraki†
MANON 70 ..... Serge Gainsbourg
MANON 70 ..... Michel Magne†
MANON OF THE SPRING ..... Jean-Claude Petit
MANONE IL LADRONE ..... Carlo Savina
MANPOWER ..... Adolph Deutsch†
MANPOWER (FD) ..... Gail Kubik†
MANSION OF THE DOOMED ..... Robert O. Ragland
MANUELA ..... William Alwyn†
MANY CLASSIC MOMENTS ..... David Wheatley
MANY HAPPY RETURNS (TF) ..... Matthew McCauley
MARA MARU ..... Max Steiner†
MARATHON (TF) ..... Joe Renzetti
MARATHON MAN ..... Michael Small
MARCH OR DIE ..... Maurice Jarre
MARCHE FRANCAISE ..... Georges Delerue
MARCHE OU CREVE ..... Georges Delerue
MARCIA O CREPA ..... Angelo Francesco Lavagnino†
MARCIANO (TF) ..... Ernest Gold
MARCO POLO ..... Les Baxter
MARCO POLO ..... Angelo Francesco Lavagnino†
MARCO POLO (MS) ..... Ennio Morricone
MARCUS WELBY, M.D. (TF) ..... Leonard Rosenman
MARDI GRAS ..... Lionel Newman†
MARE MATTO ..... Carlo Rustichelli
MARE NOSTRUM ..... William Axt†
MARGARET-BOURKE WHITE (CTF) ..... John Cacavas
MARGIE ..... Hans J. Salter
MARGIE ..... Alfred Newman†
MARGIN FOR ERROR ..... Leigh Harline†
MARIA CHAPDELAINE ..... Jean Wiener†
MARIA D'ORO UND BELLO BLUE (AF) ..... Peter Thomas
MARIA'S LOVERS ..... Gary Remal
MARIAGE ..... Francis Lai
MARIANNE OF MY YOUTH ..... Jacques Ibert†
MARIE ..... Francis Lai
MARIE ANTOINETTE ..... ★ Herbert Stothart†
MARIE POUPEE ..... Philippe Sarde
MARIE SOLEIL ..... Francis Seyrig
MARIE-CHANTAL CONTRE LE DOCTEUR KHA ..... Pierre Jansen
MARIE-MARTINE ..... Georges Van Parys†
MARILYN: THE UNTOLD STORY (TF) ..... William Goldstein
MARINE RAIDERS ..... Roy Webb†
MARINES FLY HIGH, THE ..... Roy Webb†
MARIO PUZO'S THE FORTUNATE PILGRIM (MS) ..... Mauro Malavasi
MARIO PUZO'S THE FORTUNE PILGRIM (MS) ..... Lucio Dalla
MARION ROSE WHITE (TF) ..... Billy Goldenberg
MARISA LA CIVETTA ..... Carlo Rustichelli
MARITO E MOGLIE ..... Nino Rota†
MARJORIE MORNINGSTAR ..... Max Steiner†
MARK COLPISCE ANCORA ..... Stelvio Cipriani
MARK DI SUVERO, SCULPTOR (FD) ..... Philip Glass
MARK IL POLIZIOTTO ..... Stelvio Cipriani
MARK OF THE HAWK, THE ..... Matyas Seiber
MARK OF THE RENEGADE ..... Frank Skinner†
MARK OF THE VAMPIRE ..... Gerald Fried
MARK OF ZORRO, THE ..... ★ Alfred Newman†
MARK OF ZORRO, THE (TF) ..... Dominic Frontiere
MARK TWAIN (AF) ..... Billy Scream
MARK, I LOVE YOU (TF) ..... Jimmie Haskell
MARK, THE ..... Richard Rodney Bennett
MARKED WOMAN ..... David Raksin
MARKETA LAZAROVA ..... Zdenek Liska
MARLET'S TALE, THE ..... Manos Hadjidakis
MARLOWE ..... Peter Matz
MARNIE ..... Bernard Herrmann†
MAROC 7 ..... Kenneth V. Jones
MARQUIS DE SADE ..... Bruno Nicolai
MARRIAGE IN THE SHADOWS ..... Wolfgang Zeller†
MARRIAGE IS A PRIVATE AFFAIR ..... Bronislau Kaper†
MARRIAGE IS ALIVE AND WELL (TF) ..... Fred Karlin
MARRIAGE ITALIAN STYLE ..... Armando Trovajoli
MARRIAGE OF A YOUNG STOCKBROKER ..... Fred Karlin

MARRIAGE ON THE ROCKS ... Nelson Riddle†
MARRIAGE, A ... Jack Waldman
MARRIAGE: YEAR ONE (TF) ... David Shire
MARRIED AND IN LOVE ... Roy Webb†
MARRIED MAN, A (TF) ... Elliot Kaplan
MARRY THE GIRL ... David Raksin
MARRYING KIND, THE ... Hugo Friedhofer†
MARRYING MAN ... David Newman
MARSEILLES CONTRACT, THE ... Roy Budd
MARSHAL OF GUNSMOKE ... Hans J. Salter
MARSUPIALS: THE HOWLING III, THE ... Allan Zavod
MARTIAL MARSHALL ... Scott Smalley
MARTIAN CHRONICLES, THE (TF) ... Richard Harvey
MARTIAN CHRONICLES, THE (TF) ... Stanley Myers
MARTIANS GO HOME ... Allan Zavod
MARTIN ... Donald Rubinstein
MARTIN'S DAY ... Wilfred Josephs
MARTY ... Roy Webb†
MARTYRS OF THE ALAMO, THE ... Joseph Carl Briel†
MARVEILLEUSE ANGELIQUE ... Michel Magne†
MARVIN AND TIGE ... Patrick Williams
MARY AND JOSEPH: A STORY OF FAITH (TF) ... Robert Farnon
MARY BURNS, FUGITIVE ... Heinz Roemheld†
MARY JANE HARPER CRIED LAST NIGHT (TF) ... Billy Goldenberg
MARY OF SCOTLAND ... Nathaniel Shilkret†
MARY POPPINS ... ★ Irwin Kostal
MARY WHITE (TF) ... Leonard Rosenman
MARY, MARY, BLOODY MARY ... Tom Bahler
MARY, QUEEN OF SCOTS ... ★ John Barry
MASADA (MS) ... ☆☆ Jerry Goldsmith
MASADA (MS) ... ☆ Morton Stevens
MASK OF DIIJON, THE ... Karl Hajos†
MASK OF DIMITRIOS, THE ... Adolph Deutsch†
MASK OF SHEBA, THE (TF) ... Lalo Schifrin
MASK OF THE AVENGER ... Mario Castelnuovo-Tedesco†
MASOCH ... Gianfranco Plenizio
MASQUE OF THE RED DEATH ... Mark Governor
MASQUE OF THE RED DEATH, THE ... David Lee
MASQUERADE ... John Barry
MASQUERADE IN MEXICO ... Victor Young†
MASQUERADER, THE ... Alfred Newman†
MASS APPEAL ... Bill Conti
MASSACRE IN ROME ... Ennio Morricone
MASSACRE RIVER ... Lud Gluskin†
MASSACRE RIVER ... Lucien Moraweck†
MASSARATI AND THE BRAIN (TF) ... Billy Goldenberg
MASTER GUNFIGHTER, THE ... Lalo Schifrin
MASTER OF BALLANTRAE, THE ... William Alwyn†
MASTER OF BALLANTRAE, THE (TF) ... Bruce Broughton
MASTER OF THE GAME (TF) ... ☆ Allyn Ferguson
MASTER OF THE WORLD ... Les Baxter
MASTER RACE, THE ... Roy Webb†
MASTER TOUCH, THE ... Ennio Morricone
MASTERPIECE OF MURDER, A (TF) ... Richard Markowitz
MASTERS OF THE UNIVERSE ... Bill Conti
MATA HARI ... Wilfred Josephs
MATA-HARI AGENT H21 ... Georges Delerue
MATCHLESS ... Piero Piccioni
MATCHLESS ... Ennio Morricone
MATCHMAKER, THE ... Adolph Deutsch†
MATERNALE ... Stelvio Cipriani
MATERNITE ... Jacques Ibert†
MATEWAN ... Mason Daring
MATILDA ... Jerrold Immel
MATING GAME, THE ... Jeff Alexander†
MATING OF MILLIE, THE ... Werner R. Heymann†
MATING SEASON, THE (TF) ... John Morris
MATT HELM (TF) ... Jerry Fielding†
MATTEI AFFAIR, THE ... Piero Piccioni
MATTER OF HONOR, A ... Luis Bacalov
MATTER OF INNOCENCE, A ... Michel Legrand
MATTER OF LIFE AND DEATH, A ... Allan Gray†
MATTER OF SEX, A (CTF) ... Matthew McCauley
MATTER OF WHO, A ... Edwin Astley
MATTER OF WIFE...AND DEATH, A (TF) ... Richard Shores
MAURICE ... Richard Robbins
MAUSOLEUM ... Frank Primata
MAUSOLEUM ... Jaime Mendoza-Nava
MAVERICK QUEEN, THE ... Victor Young†
MAX DUGAN RETURNS ... David Shire
MAX ET LES FERRAILLEURS ... Philippe Sarde
MAXIE ... Georges Delerue
MAXIMUM OVERDRIVE ... AC/DC
MAY FOOLS ... Stephane Grappelli
MAY MORNING ... Armando Trovajoli
MAYA ... Riz Ortolani
MAYA ... Georges Auric†
MAYBE BABY (TF) ... Patrick Williams
MAYBE HE'LL COME HOME IN THE SPRING (TF) ... Earl Robinson
MAYDAY AT 40,000 FEET (TF) ... Richard Markowitz
MAYERLING ... Francis Lai
MAYERLING ... Arthur Honegger†
MAYFLOWER MADAM (TF) ... David Shire
MAYFLOWER: THE PILGRIM'S ADVENTURE (TF) ... Brad Fiedel
MAYTIME ... ★ Herbert Stothart†
McCLOUD: WHO KILLED MISS U.S.A.? (TF) ... David Shire
McCONNELL STORY, THE ... Max Steiner†
McGUERINS FROM BROOKLYN, THE ... Edward Ward†
McGUFFIN, THE (TF) ... Richard Hartley
McGUIRE GO HOME ... Angelo Francesco Lavagnino†
McHALE'S NAVY ... Jerry Fielding†
McHALE'S NAVY JOINS THE AIR FORCE ... Jerry Fielding†
McLINTOCK! ... Frank De Vol
McMASTERS, THE ... Coleridge-Taylor Perkinson
McNAUGHTON'S DAUGHTER (TF) ... David Shire
McQ ... Elmer Bernstein
McVICAR ... Jeff Wayne
ME AND HIM ... Klaus Doldinger
ME, NATALIE ... Henry Mancini
MEAL, THE ... Stu Phillips
MEAN DOG BLUES ... Fred Karlin
MEAN SEASON, THE ... Lalo Schifrin
MEANEST GAL IN TOWN, THE ... Max Steiner†
MEANEST MAN IN THE WORLD, THE ... Cyril J. Mockridge†
MEANTIME ... Andrew Dixon
MEATBALLS ... Elmer Bernstein
MEATBALLS III ... Paul Zaza
MEATBALLS PART II ... Ken Harrison
MECHANIC, THE ... Jerry Fielding†
MEDAL FOR BENNY, A ... Victor Young†
MEDECINS DE NUIT: AMALGINE (TF) ... Vladimir Cosma
MEDECINS DE NUIT: HENRI GILLOT, RETRAITE (TF) ... Vladimir Cosma
MEDECINS DE NUIT: L'ENTREPOT (TF) ... Vladimir Cosma
MEDECINS DE NUIT: L'USINE CA STEL (TF) ... Vladimir Cosma
MEDECINS DE NUIT: LA DECAPOTABLE (TF) ... Vladimir Cosma
MEDECINS DE NUIT: LA PENSION MICHEL (TF) ... Vladimir Cosma
MEDECINS DE NUIT: LEGITIME DEFENSE (TF) ... Vladimir Cosma
MEDECINS DE NUIT: UN PLAT CUISINE (TF) ... Vladimir Cosma
MEDICAL STORY (TF) ... Arthur Morton
MEDITERRANEE ... Antoine Duhamel
MEDUSA TOUCH, THE ... Michael J. Lewis
MEET JOHN DOE ... Dimitri Tiomkin†
MEET ME AT THE FAIR ... Herman Stein
MEET ME AT THE FAIR ... Henry Mancini
MEET ME IN LAS VEGAS ... ★ John Green†
MEET THE CHUMP ... Hans J. Salter
MEET THE HOLLOWHEADS ... Glenn Jordan
MEET THE MAYOR ... Edward Ward†
MEET THE MISSUS ... Roy Webb†
MEET THE MUNCEYS (TF) ... Stephen Lawrence
MEET THE STEWARTS ... Leo Shuken†
MEET THE WILDCAT ... Hans J. Salter
MEETING ON THE ELBA ... Dmitri Shostakovitch†
MEETINGS WITH REMARKABLE MEN ... Laurence Rosenthal
MEFIEZ-VOUS FILLETTES ... Paul Misraki†
MEGAFORCE ... Jerrold Immel
MEGLIO VEDOVA ... Carlo Rustichelli
MELANIE ... Paul Zaza
MELEVIL ... Gabriel Yared
MELODIE DER LIEBE ... Bronislau Kaper†
MELODIE DES HERZENS ... Werner R. Heymann†
MELODIE EN SOUS-SOL ... Michel Magne†
MELODY CRUISE ... Max Steiner†
MELODY LINGERS ON, THE ... Alfred Newman†
MELVIN AND HOWARD ... Bruce Langhorne
MELVIN PURVIS: G-MAN (TF) ... Bob Cobert
MEMBER OF THE WEDDING, THE ... Alex North
MEMORIAL DAY (TF) ... Billy Goldenberg
MEMORIES NEVER DIE (TF) ... Morton Stevens
MEMORIES OF ME ... Georges Delerue
MEMORIES OF MURDER (CTF) ... Joseph Conlan
MEMORIES OF THE FUTURE ... Peter Thomas
MEMORIES WITHIN MISS AGGIE ... Rupert Holmes
MEMORY OF EVA RYKER, THE (TF) ... Richard LaSalle
MEMPHIS BELLE ... George Fenton
MEMPHIS BELLE, THE (FD) ... Gail Kubik†
MEN AND SHIPS (FD) ... Gail Kubik†
MEN AND WOMEN ... Claude Bolling
MEN ARE SUCH FOOLS ... W. Franke Harling†
MEN DON'T LEAVE ... Thomas Newman
MEN IN DANGER ... Brian Easdale
MEN IN HER DIARY ... Milton Rosen
MEN IN HER LIFE, THE ... David Raksin
MEN IN WAR ... Elmer Bernstein
MEN IN WHITE ... William Axt†
MEN OF BOYS TOWN ... Herbert Stothart†
MEN OF CHANCE ... Max Steiner†
MEN OF TEXAS ... Edward Ward†
MEN OF THE DRAGON (TF) ... Elmer Bernstein
MEN OF THE FIGHTING LADY ... Miklos Rozsa
MEN OF THE LIGHTSHIP ... Richard Addinsell†
MEN OF THE TIMBERLAND ... Hans J. Salter
MEN OF TWO WORLDS ... Sir Arthur Bliss†
MEN WITH WINGS ... W. Franke Harling†
MEN'S CLUB, THE ... Lee Holdridge
MEN, THE ... Dimitri Tiomkin†
MENACE IN THE NIGHT ... Richard Rodney Bennett
MENAGE ... Serge Gainsbourg
MENAGE ALL'ITALIANA ... Ennio Morricone
MENSCHEN AUS GLASS ... Jurgen Knieper
MEPHISTO WALTZ, THE ... Jerry Goldsmith
MERCENARY FIGHTERS ... Howard Morgan
MERCENARY, THE ... Ennio Morricone
MERCENARY, THE ... Bruno Nicolai
MERCI NATERCIA ... Georges Delerue
MERCY ISLAND ... ★ Walter Scharf
MERCY OR MURDER? (TF) ... Peter Matz
MERIDIAN ... Pino Donaggio
MERMAIDS ... Jack Nitzsche
MERMOZ ... Joseph Kosma†
MERRILY WE LIVE ... T. Marvin Hatley†
MERRY CHRISTMAS, MR. LAWRENCE ... Ryuichi Sakamoto
MERRY MONAHANS, THE ... ★ Hans J. Salter
MERRY WIDOW, THE ... Herbert Stothart†
MESA OF LOST WOMEN, THE ... Hoyt Curtin
MESSAGE FROM SPACE (AF) ... Ken-Ichiro Morioka
MESSAGE TO GARCIA, A ... Louis Silvers†
MESSAGE TO MY DAUGHTER (TF) ... Fred Myrow
MESSAGE, THE ... Maurice Jarre
MESSALINA ... Angelo Francesco Lavagnino†
MESSENGER OF DEATH ... Robert O. Ragland
MESSIAH, THE ... Mario Nascimbene
MESSIEURS DE VOUOUS: LE CONCIERGE REVIENT DE SUITE (TF) ... Georges Delerue
METALSTORM: THE DESTRUCTION OF JARED SYN ... Richard H. Band
METELLO ... Ennio Morricone
METEOR ... Laurence Rosenthal
METRALLETA STEIN ... Carlo Rustichelli
METROPOLIS ... Giorgio Moroder
METROPOLIS ... Gottfried Huppertz†
METTI LO DIAVOLO TUO NE LO MIO INFERNO ... Stelvio Cipriani
METTI UNA SERA A CENA ... Ennio Morricone
MEXICAN SPITFIRE ... Paul Sawtell†
MEXICAN SPITFIRE OUT WEST ... Roy Webb†
MEXICAN SPITFIRE SEES A GHOST ... Roy Webb†
MEXICAN SPITFIRE'S ELEPHANT ... Roy Webb†
MGM'S BIG PARADE OF COMEDY ... Bernard Green
MI VEDRAI TORNARE ... Luis Bacalov
MI VEDRAI TORNARE ... Ennio Morricone
MIAMI BLUES ... Gary Chang
MICHAEL KOHLHAAS ... Peter Sandloff
MICHAEL O'HALLORAN ... Lud Gluskin†
MICHELE STROGOFF ... Teo Usuelli
MICHIGAN KID, THE ... Hans J. Salter
MICHURIN ... Dmitri Shostakovitch†
MICKEY ONE ... Eddie Sauter
MICKEY SPILLANE'S MARGIN FOR MURDER (TF) ... Nelson Riddle†
MICKEY SPILLANE'S MIKE HAMMER: MORE THAN MURDER (TF) ... Earle Hagen
MICKEY SPILLANE'S MIKE HAMMER: MURDER ME, MURDER YOU (TF) ... Earle Hagen
MICKEY SPILLANE'S MIKE HAMMER: MURDER TAKES ALL (TF) ... Ron Ramin
MICKI & MAUDE ... Lee Holdridge
MIDAS RUN ... Elmer Bernstein

MIDAS VALLEY (TF) ... Jerrold Immel
MIDDLE AGE CRAZY ... Tony Macauley
MIDDLE AGE CRAZY ... Matthew McCauley
MIDDLE OF THE NIGHT ... George Bassman
MIDNIGHT ... Michael Wetherwax
MIDNIGHT ... Frederick Hollander†
MIDNIGHT CABARET ... Michel Colombier
MIDNIGHT COURT ... David Raksin
MIDNIGHT COWBOY ... John Barry
MIDNIGHT CROSSING ... Steve Tyrell
MIDNIGHT DREAMS ... Carl Dante
MIDNIGHT EXPRESS ... ★★ Giorgio Moroder
MIDNIGHT HOUR, THE (TF) ... Brad Fiedel
MIDNIGHT INTRUDER ... Charles Previn†
MIDNIGHT LACE (TF) ... Stu Phillips
MIDNIGHT MADNESS ... Julius Wechter
MIDNIGHT MAN, THE ... Dave Grusin
MIDNIGHT MARY ... William Axt†
MIDNIGHT OFFERINGS (TF) ... Walter Scharf
MIDNIGHT RUN ... Danny Elfman
MIDNIGHT STORY, THE ... Hans J. Salter
MIDNITE SPARES ... Cameron Allan
MIDSHIPMAN JACK ... Max Steiner†
MIDSUMMER NIGHT'S DREAM, A ... Erich Wolfgang Korngold†
MIDWAY ... John Williams
MIGHT MAKES RIGHT ... Peer Raben
MIGHTY BARNUM, THE ... Alfred Newman†
MIGHTY JOE YOUNG ... Roy Webb†
MIGHTY QUINN, THE ... Anne Dudley
MIGHTY TREVE, THE ... David Raksin
MIGRANTS, THE (TF) ... ☆ Billy Goldenberg
MIJN HACHTEN MET SUSAN OLGA ALBERT ... Elisabeth Luytens†
MIJN VRIENDE ... Georges Delerue
MIKE'S MURDER ... John Barry
MIKE'S MURDER ... Joe Jackson
MIKEY AND NICKY ... John Strauss
MILADY (TF) ... Georges Delerue
MILADY'S REVENGE ... Lalo Schifrin
MILAGRO BEANFIELD WAR, THE ... ★★ Dave Grusin
MILANO CALIBRO 9 ... Luis Bacalov
MILANO ODIA: LA POLIZIA NON PUO SPARARE ... Ennio Morricone
MILANO ROVENTE ... Carlo Rustichelli
MILAREPA ... Daniele Paris
MILDRED PIERCE ... Max Steiner†
MILES FROM HOME ... Robert Folk
MILES TO GO BEFORE I SLEEP (TF) ... Wladimir Selinsky
MILES TO GO... (TF) ... Ken Wannberg
MILKMAN, THE ... Milton Rosen
MILLENNIUM ... Eric N. Robertson
MILLER'S BEAUTIFUL WIFE, THE ... Angelo Francesco Lavagnino†
MILLIE'S DAUGHTER ... Arthur Morton
MILLION DOLLAR BABY ... Frederick Hollander†
MILLION DOLLAR DUCK ... Buddy Baker
MILLION DOLLAR FACE, THE (TF) ... Morton Stevens
MILLION DOLLAR INFIELD (TF) ... Artie Kane
MILLION DOLLAR RIP-OFF, THE (TF) ... Vic Mizzy
MILLION POUND NOTE, THE ... William Alwyn†
MILLIONAIRE FOR CHRISTY, A ... Victor Young†
MILLIONAIRE IN TROUBLE ... Dov Seltzer
MILLIONAIRE, THE (TF) ... Frank De Vol
MILLIONAIRES IN PRISON ... Roy Webb†
MILLIONAIRESS, THE ... Georges Van Parys†
MILLIONS LIKE US ... Hubert Bath†
MIMI ... Riz Ortolani
MIMI METALLURGICO FERITO NELL'ONORE ... Piero Piccioni
MINATOMO YOSHITSUNE ... Toru Takemitsu
MIND BENDERS, THE ... Georges Auric†
MIND OF MR. SOAMES, THE ... Michael Dress
MIND OVER MURDER (TF) ... Paul Chihara
MINDWARP: AN INFINITY OF TERROR ... Barry Schrader
MINE OWN EXECUTIONER ... Benjamin Frankel†
MINER'S DAUGHTER, THE (AS) ... Gail Kubik†
MING, RAGAZZI! ... Carlo Rustichelli
MING, RAGAZZI! ... Carlo Savina
MINI-SKIRT MOB, THE ... Les Baxter
MINISTRY OF FEAR ... Victor Young†
MINISTRY OF VENGEANCE ... Scott Roewe
MINIVER STORY, THE ... Miklos Rozsa
MINOTAUR, THE ... Carlo Rustichelli
MINSTREL MAN ... ★ Leo Erdody†
MINSTREL MAN ... ★ Ferde Grofe†
MINSTREL MAN (TF) ... ☆ Fred Karlin
MINUTE TO PRAY, A SECOND TO DIE, A ... Carlo Rustichelli
MIO CARO ASSASSINO ... Ennio Morricone
MIO DIO, COME SONO CADUTA IN BASSO! ... Fiorenzo Carpi
MIO FIGLIO NERONE ... Angelo Francesco Lavagnino†
MIO FIGLIO PROFESSORE ... Nino Rota†
MIRA ... Georges Delerue
MIRACLE IN HARLEM ... Lud Gluskin†
MIRACLE IN MILAN ... Alessandro Cicognini†
MIRACLE IN THE RAIN ... Franz Waxman†
MIRACLE LANDING (TF) ... Mark Snow
MIRACLE MAN, THE ... W. Franke Harling†
MIRACLE MILE ... Tangerine Dream
MIRACLE OF KATHY MILLER, THE (TF) ... Patrick Williams
MIRACLE OF MORGAN'S CREEK, THE ... Leo Shuken†
MIRACLE OF OUR LADY OF FATIMA, THE ... ★ Max Steiner†
MIRACLE OF THE BELLS, THE ... Leigh Harline†
MIRACLE OF THE HEART: A BOY'S TOWN STORY (TF) ... Lee Holdridge
MIRACLE OF THE HILLS, THE ... Bert A. Shefter
MIRACLE ON 34TH STREET ... Cyril J. Mockridge†
MIRACLE ON MAIN STREET ... Hans J. Salter
MIRACLE WORKER, THE ... Laurence Rosenthal
MIRACLE WORKER, THE (TF) ... Billy Goldenberg
MIRACLE, THE ... Elmer Bernstein
MIRACLES ... Peter Bernstein
MIRACOLO A MILANO ... Alessandro Cicognini†
MIRACULOUS JOURNEY ... Leo Erdody†
MIRROR CRACK'D, THE ... John Cameron
MIRROR, MIRROR (TF) ... Jimmie Haskell
MIRRORS (TF) ... Craig Safan
MIRRORS (TF) ... Craig Safan
MISADVENTURES OF MERLIN JONES, THE ... Buddy Baker
MISADVENTURES OF MR. WILT, THE ... Anne Dudley
MISFITS, THE ... Alex North
MISHIMA: A LIFE IN FOUR CHAPTERS ... Philip Glass
MISS ALL-AMERICAN BEAUTY (TF) ... Paul Chihara
MISS FIRECRACKER ... David Mansfield
MISS GRANT TAKES RICHMOND ... Heinz Roemheld†
MISS LONELYHEARTS ... Leonard Rosenman
MISS O'GYNIE AND THE FLOWER MAN ... Gabriel Yared
MISS POLLY ... Edward Ward†
MISS ROBIN CRUSOE ... Elmer Bernstein
MISS SUSIE SLAGLE'S ... Daniele Amfitheatrof†
MISS TATLOCK'S MILLIONS ... Victor Young†
MISS, THE ... Alfi Kabiljo
MISSING ... Vangelis
MISSING ARE DEADLY, THE (TF) ... Gil Melle
MISSING CHILDREN: A MOTHER'S STORY (TF) ... Fred Karlin
MISSING CORPSE, THE ... Karl Hajos†
MISSING IN ACTION ... Jay Chattaway
MISSING IN ACTION II: THE BEGINNING ... Brian May
MISSING LINK, THE ... Roy Budd
MISSION HILL ... Doug Timm†
MISSION OVER KOREA ... Mischa Bakaleinikoff †
MISSION TO MOSCOW ... Max Steiner†
MISSION, THE ... ★ Ennio Morricone
MISSIONARY, THE ... Mike Moran
MISSIONE PIANETA ERRANTE ... Angelo Francesco Lavagnino†
MISSIONE SPEZIALE LADY CHAPLIN ... Bruno Nicolai
MISSISSIPPI ... Sigmund Krumgold†
MISSISSIPPI BURNING ... Trevor Jones
MISSISSIPPI GAMBLER ... David Broekman†
MISSISSIPPI GAMBLER ... Frank Skinner†
MISSISSIPPI MERMAID ... Antoine Duhamel
MISSOURI BREAKS, THE ... John Williams
MISSOURI TRAVELER, THE ... Jack Marshall
MISTER 880 ... Sol Kaplan
MISTER 880 ... Lionel Newman†
MISTER BUDDWING ... Kenyon Hopkins
MISTER CINDERELL ... T. Marvin Hatley†
MISTER CORY ... Herman Stein
MISTER CORY ... Henry Mancini
MISTER FREEDOM ... Serge Gainsbourg
MISTER KINGSTREET'S WAR ... Harry Sukman†
MISTER MOSES ... John Barry
MISTER ROBERTS ... Franz Waxman†
MISTER SCOUTMASTER ... Cyril J. Mockridge†
MISTER TEN PERCENT ... Ron Goodwin
MISTER V ... John Greenwood†
MISTRAL'S DAUGHTER (MS) ... Vladimir Cosma
MISTRESS (TF) ... Michael Convertino
MISTRESS OF PARADISE (TF) ... John Addison
MISTY ... Paul Sawtell†
MISUNDERSTOOD ... Michael Hoppe
MIX ME A PERSON ... John Barry
MIXED BLOOD ... Andy Hernandez
MIXED COMPANY ... Fred Karlin
MMORTAL BATTALION, THE ... William Alwyn†
MO' BETTER BLUES ... Bill Lee
MOB TOWN ... Hans J. Salter
MOB, THE ... George Duning
MOBILE TWO (TF) ... Nelson Riddle†
MOBY DICK ... Philip Sainton†
MODEL AND THE MARRIAGE BROKER, THE ... Cyril J. Mockridge†
MODEL WIFE ... Hans J. Salter
MODEL WIFE ... Charles Previn†
MODELS, INC. ... Herschel Burke Gilbert
MODERN GIRLS ... Eddie Arkin
MODERN GIRLS ... Jay Levy
MODERN LOVE ... Don Peake
MODERN PROBLEMS ... Dominic Frontiere
MODERN ROMANCE ... Lance Rubin
MODERN TIMES ... Charles Chaplin†
MODERNS, THE ... Mark Isham
MODESTY BLAISE ... John Dankworth
MOGLIAMENTE ... Armando Trovajoli
MOGLIE PER UNA NOTTE ... Alessandro Cicognini†
MOHAMMED, MESSENGER OF GOD ... ★ Maurice Jarre
MOI Y'EN A VOULOIR DES SOUS ... Michel Magne†
MOLE PEOPLE, THE ... Hans J. Salter
MOLE PEOPLE, THE ... Herman Stein
MOLE PEOPLE, THE ... Heinz Roemheld†
MOLEMEN VS. THE SON OF HERCULES ... Armando Trovajoli
MOLLENARD ... Darius Milhaud†
MOLLY ... Nathan Van Cleave†
MOLLY AND ME ... Cyril J. Mockridge†
MOLLY MAGUIRES, THE ... Henry Mancini
MOM, THE WOLFMAN AND ME (TF) ... Fred Karlin
MOMENT BY MOMENT ... Lee Holdridge
MOMENT OF DANGER ... Matyas Seiber
MOMENT OF TRUTH, THE ... Piero Piccioni
MOMENT OF TRUTH, THE ... Paul Misraki†
MOMENT TO MOMENT ... Henry Mancini
MOMENTS ... John Cameron
MOMMIE DEAREST ... Henry Mancini
MON BEAU-FRERE A TUE MA SOEUR ... Philippe Sarde
MON ONCLE ... Alain Romans
MONA LISA ... Michael Kamen
MONA, L'ETOILE SANS NOM ... Georges Delerue
MONDO CANDIDO ... Riz Ortolani
MONDO CANE ... Riz Ortolani
MONDO CANE #2 ... Bruno Nicolai
MONDO NEW YORK ... Johnny Pacheco
MONDO NEW YORK ... Luis Perico Ortiz
MONDO SOMMERSO ... Carlo Rustichelli
MONEY FROM HOME ... Leigh Harline†
MONEY JUNGLE, THE ... Paul Dunlap
MONEY MADNESS ... Leo Erdody†
MONEY MONEY MONEY ... Francis Lai
MONEY ON THE SIDE (TF) ... Richard Bellis
MONEY PIT, THE ... Michel Colombier
MONEY TO BURN ... Christopher L. Stone
MONEY TO BURN (TF) ... Oliver Nelson†
MONEY, POWER, MURDER (TF) ... Miles Goodman
MONEY, WOMEN & GUNS ... Herman Stein
MONGO'S BACK IN TOWN (TF) ... Michael Melvoin
MONIKA ... Les Baxter
MONIKA ... Eric Nordgren
MONITORS, THE ... Fred Kaz
MONK, THE ... Piero Piccioni
MONK, THE (TF) ... Earle Hagen
MONKEY BUSINESS ... Leigh Harline†
MONKEY BUSINESS ... Lionel Newman†
MONKEY MISSION, THE (TF) ... George Romanis
MONKEY ON MY BACK ... Bert A. Shefter
MONKEY SHINES ... David Shire
MONKEY'S PAW, THE ... Max Steiner†
MONKEY'S UNCLE, THE ... Buddy Baker
MONKEYS, GO HOME! ... Robert F. Brunner
MONNAIRE DE SINGE ... Michel Legrand
MONOLITH MONSTER, THE ... Irving Gertz
MONOLITH MONSTERS, THE ... Henry Mancini
MONOLITH MOSTERS, THE ... Herman Stein
MONSEIGNEUR ... Georges Van Parys†
MONSIEUR BEAUCAIRE ... Robert Emmett Dolan†
MONSIEUR LA CAILLE ... Joseph Kosma†
MONSIEUR LUDOVIC ... Joseph Kosma†

MONSIEUR ROBERT HOUDIN (TF) ... Georges Delerue
MONSIEUR VERDOUX ... Charles Chaplin†
MONSIGNOR ... John Williams
MONSOON ... Leo Erdody†
MONSTER CLUB, THE ... Douglas Gamley
MONSTER FROM GREEN HELL ... Albert Glasser
MONSTER ISLAND ... Alfonso Agullo
MONSTER MAKER, THE ... Albert Glasser
MONSTER OF HIGHGATE PONDS, THE ... Francis Chagrin†
MONSTER SQUAD, THE ... Bruce Broughton
MONSTER THAT CHALLENGED THE WORLD, THE ... Heinz Roemheld†
MONSTER ZERO ... Akira Ifukube
MONTA IN SELLA, FIGLIO DI...! ... Luis Bacalov
MONTANA ... David Buttolph†
MONTANA (CTF) ... David McHugh
MONTANA MOON ... Herbert Stothart†
MONTE CARLO ... W. Franke Harling†
MONTE CARLO (TF) ... Stanley Myers
MONTE WALSH ... John Barry
MONTH IN THE COUNTRY, A ... Howard Blake
MONTH OF SUNDAYS, A (CTF) ... Stanley Myers
MONTPARNASSE 19 ... Paul Misraki†
MONTY PYTHON AND THE HOLY GRAIL ... De Wolfe
MONTY PYTHON AND THE HOLY GRAIL ... Neil Innes
MONTY PYTHON AT THE HOLLYWOOD BOWL ... John Du Prez
MONTY PYTHON'S THE MEANING OF LIFE ... John Du Prez
MOON AND SIXPENCE, THE ... ★ Dimitri Tiomkin†
MOON AND THE GUTTER, THE ... Gabriel Yared
MOON IS BLUE, THE ... Herschel Burke Gilbert
MOON IS DOWN, THE ... Alfred Newman†
MOON OF THE WOLF (TF) ... Bernardo Segall
MOON OVER BURMA ... Victor Young†
MOON OVER PARADOR ... Maurice Jarre
MOON PILOT ... Paul J. Smith†
MOON ZERO TWO ... Don Ellis†
MOONCHILD ... Patrick Williams
MOONFLEET ... Miklos Rozsa
MOONLIGHT (TF) ... Patrick Williams
MOONLIGHT IN VERMONT ... Edward Ward†
MOONLIGHT MURDER ... Herbert Stothart†
MOONLIGHT MURDER ... Edward Ward†
MOONLIGHTER, THE ... Heinz Roemheld†
MOONLIGHTING ... Hans Zimmer
MOONLIGHTING ... Stanley Myers
MOONLIGHTING (TF) ... Lee Holdridge
MOONRAKER ... John Barry
MOONRISE ... William Lava†
MOONSHINE COUNTY EXPRESS ... Fred Werner
MOONSPINNERS, THE ... Ron Grainer
MOONSTRUCK ... Dick Hyman
MOONTIDE ... David Buttolph†
MOONTIDE ... Cyril J. Mockridge†
MOONWALKER ... Bruce Broughton
MORDI E FUGGE ... Carlo Rustichelli
MORE THAN FRIENDS (TF) ... Fred Karlin
MORE THE MERRIER, THE ... Leigh Harline†
MORE THINGS CHANGE, THE ... Peter Best
MORE WILD WILD WEST (TF) ... Jeff Alexander†
MORGAN STEWART'S COMING HOME ... Peter Bernstein
MORGAN THE PIRATE ... Franco Mannino
MORGAN! ... John Dankworth
MORIRE A ROMA ... Nicola Piovani
MORITURI ... Jerry Goldsmith
MORNING AFTER , THE(TF) ... Pete Carpenter†
MORNING AFTER, THE ... Paul Chihara
MORNING AFTER, THE (TF) ... Mike Post
MORNING DEPARTURE ... William Alwyn†
MORNING GLORY ... Max Steiner†
MOROCCO ... Karl Hajos†
MORONS FROM OUTER SPACE ... Peter Brewis
MORT, OU EST TA VICTOIRE? ... Maurice Jarre
MORTAL PASSIONS ... Parmer Fuller
MORTE DI UN AMICO ... Mario Nascimbene
MORTE IN VATICANO ... Pino Donaggio
MORTUARY ... John Cacavas
MORTUARY ACADEMY ... David Spear
MOSCA ADDIO ... Ennio Morricone
MOSCOW ON THE HUDSON ... David McHugh
MOSES (MS) ... Dov Seltzer
MOSES (MS) ... Ennio Morricone
MOSQUITO COAST, THE ... Maurice Jarre
MOSQUITO SQUADRON ... Frank Cordell†
MOSS ROSE ... David Buttolph†
MOST DANGEROUS GAME, THE ... Max Steiner†
MOST DANGEROUS MAN IN THE WORLD, THE (TF) ... Stanley Myers
MOST WANTED (TF) ... Patrick Williams
MOST WONDERFUL MOMENT, THE ... Nino Rota†
MOTEL HELL ... Lance Rubin
MOTHER AND DAUGHTER - THE LOVING WAR (TF) ... Lee Holdridge
MOTHER DIDN'T TELL ME ... Cyril J. Mockridge†
MOTHER DIDN'T TELL ME ... Lionel Newman†
MOTHER IS A FRESHMAN ... Alfred Newman†
MOTHER LODE ... Ken Wannberg
MOTHER TERESA (FD) ... Suzanne E. Ciani
MOTHER WORE TIGHTS ... ★★ Alfred Newman†
MOTHER'S COURAGE: THE MARY THOMAS STORY, A (TF) ... Lee Holdridge
MOTHER'S DAY ... Philo Gallo
MOTHER'S DAY ... Clem Vicari
MOTHER'S HEART ... Ennio Morricone
MOTIVE WAS JEALOUSY, THE ... Armando Trovajoli
MOTOR PSYCHO ... Bert A. Shefter
MOTOR PSYCHO, THE ... Paul Sawtell†
MOTORCYCLE GANG ... Albert Glasser
MOTRE-DAME, CATHEDRALE DE PARIS ... Jean Wiener†
MOUCHETTE ... Jean Wiener†
MOULIN ROUGE ... Georges Auric†
MOUNTAIN FAMILY ROBINSON ... Robert O. Ragland
MOUNTAIN JUSTICE ... W. Franke Harling†
MOUNTAIN MEN, THE ... Michel Legrand
MOUNTAIN ROAD, THE ... Jerome Moross†
MOUNTAIN, THE ... Daniele Amfitheatrof†
MOUNTAINS OF THE MOON ... Michael Small
MOUNTBATTEN: THE LAST VICEROY (MS) ... John Scott
MOURIR A MADRID ... Maurice Jarre
MOURNING BECOMES ELECTRA ... Richard Hageman†
MOUSE AND HIS CHILD, THE (AF) ... Roger Kellaway
MOUSE ON THE MOON, THE ... Ron Grainer
MOUSE THAT ROARED, THE ... Edwin Astley
MOUSEY (TF) ... Ron Grainer
MOVE ... Marvin Hamlisch
MOVE OVER, DARLING ... Lionel Newman†
MOVERS & SHAKERS ... Ken Welch
MOVERS & SHAKERS ... Mitzie Welch
MOVIE MOVIE ... Ralph Burns
MOVING ... Howard Shore
MOVING TARGET (TF) ... Fred Karlin
MOVING TARGET (TF) ... Michel Rubini
MOVING VIOLATION ... Don Peake
MOVING VIOLATIONS ... Ralph Burns
MOVIOLA: THE SCARLETT O'HARA WAR (TF) ... Walter Scharf
MOVIOLA: THE SILENT LOVERS (MS) ... ☆ Gerald Fried
MOVIOLA: THIS YEAR'S BLONDE (MS) ... Elmer Bernstein
MR. & MRS. BO JO JONES (TF) ... Fred Karlin
MR. ACE ... Heinz Roemheld†
MR. AND MRS. SMITH ... Edward Ward†
MR. ARKADIN ... Paul Misraki†
MR. BELVEDERE GOES TO COLLEGE ... Alfred Newman†
MR. BELVEDERE RINGS THE BELL ... Cyril J. Mockridge†
MR. BILLION ... Dave Grusin
MR. BLANDINGS BUILDS HIS DREAM HOUSE ... Leigh Harline†
MR. BUG GOES TO TOWN (AF) ... Leigh Harline†
MR. DEEDS GOES TO TOWN ... Dimitri Tiomkin†
MR. DISTRICT ATTORNEY ... Herschel Burke Gilbert
MR. DODD TAKES THEAIR ... Adolph Deutsch†
MR. DOODLE KICKS OFF ... Roy Webb†
MR. DYNAMITE ... Hans J. Salter
MR. FORBUSH AND THE PENGUINS ... John Addison
MR. HERCULES AGAINST KARATE ... Carlo Savina
MR. HERCULES AGAINST KUNG FU ... Carlo Savina
MR. HOBBS TAKES A VACATION ... Henry Mancini
MR. HOBO ... Louis Levy†
MR. HORN (TF) ... Jerry Fielding†
MR. HULOT'S HOLIDAY ... Alain Romans
MR. IMPERIUM ... Bronislau Kaper†
MR. JERICHO (TF) ... Laurie Johnson
MR. KINKY ... Armando Trovajoli
MR. LOVE (TF) ... Willy Russell
MR. LUCKY ... Roy Webb†
MR. MAJESTYK ... Charles Bernstein
MR. MOM ... Lee Holdridge
MR. MOTO'S LAST WARNING ... David Raksin
MR. NORTH ... David McHugh
MR. PATMAN ... Paul Hoffert
MR. PEABODY AND THE MERMAID ... Robert Emmett Dolan†
MR. PERRIN AND MR. TRAILL ... Allan Gray†
MR. QUILP ... Elmer Bernstein
MR. RICCO ... Chico Hamilton
MR. ROBINSON CRUSOE ... Alfred Newman†
MR. SARDONICUS ... Von Dexter
MR. SKEFFINGTON ... Franz Waxman†
MR. SMITH GOES TO WASHINGTON ... ★ Dimitri Tiomkin†
MR. SOFT TOUCH ... Heinz Roemheld†
MR. SYCAMORE ... Maurice Jarre
MR. UNIVERSE ... Dimitri Tiomkin†
MR. WINKLE GOES TO WAR ... Carmen Dragon†
MR. WINKLE GOES TO WAR ... Paul Sawtell†
MRS. BROWN, YOU'VE GOT A LOVELY DAUGHTER ... Ron Goodwin
MRS. DELAFIELD WANTS TO MARRY (TF) ... Peter Matz
MRS. MIKE ... Max Steiner†
MRS. MINIVER ... Herbert Stothart†
MRS. O'MALLEY AND MR. MALONE ... Adolph Deutsch†
MRS. PARKINGTON ... Bronislau Kaper†
MRS. POLIFAX - SPY ... Lalo Schifrin
MRS. R'S DAUGHTER (TF) ... Bob Cobert
MRS. SOFFEL ... Mark Isham
MRS. SUNDANCE (TF) ... Patrick Williams
MRS. WIGGS OF THE CABBAGE PATCH ... Victor Young†
MS. DON JUAN ... Michel Magne†
MUD ... Michael J. Lewis
MUDDY RIVER ... Kuroudo Mori
MUDLARK, THE ... William Alwyn†
MUG TOWN ... Hans J. Salter
MUGGABLE MARY: STREET COP (TF) ... Earle Hagen
MUGGER, THE ... Albert Glasser
MULLIGAN'S STEW (TF) ... George Aliceson Tipton
MUMMY'S BOYS ... Roy Webb†
MUMMY'S CURSE, THE ... Paul Sawtell†
MUMMY'S GHOST, THE ... Hans J. Salter
MUMMY'S GHOST, THE ... Charles Previn†
MUMMY'S GHOST, THE ... Frank Skinner†
MUMMY'S HAND, THE ... Hans J. Salter
MUMMY'S HAND, THE ... Frank Skinner†
MUMMY'S SHROUD, THE ... Don Banks
MUMMY'S TOMB, THE ... Hans J. Salter
MUMMY'S TOMB, THE ... Charles Previn†
MUMMY'S TOMB, THE ... Heinz Roemheld†
MUMMY, THE ... James Dietrich
MUMMY, THE ... Franz Reizenstein†
MUMSY, NANNY, SONNY AND GIRLY ... Bernard Ebbinghouse
MUNCHIES ... Ernest Troost
MUNSTER, GO HOME ... Jack Marshall
MUNSTERS' REVENGE, THE (TF) ... Vic Mizzy
MUPPET MOVIE, THE ... ★ Paul Williams
MUPPETS TAKE MANHATTAN, THE ... Ralph Burns
MURDER 1, DANCER 0 (TF) ... George Romanis
MURDER AHOY! ... Ron Goodwin
MURDER AT THE GALLOP ... Ron Goodwin
MURDER AT THE WORLD SERIES (TF) ... John Cacavas
MURDER BY DEATH ... Dave Grusin
MURDER BY DECREE ... Carl Zittrer
MURDER BY DECREE ... Paul Zaza
MURDER BY MAIL ... Craig Hundley
MURDER BY MOONLIGHT (TF) ... Trevor Jones
MURDER BY NATURAL CAUSES (TF) ... Richard DeBenedictis
MURDER BY NUMBERS ... Bob Summers
MURDER BY PHONE ... John Barry
MURDER BY TELEVISION ... Oliver Wallace†
MURDER BY THE BOOK (TF) ... Mark Snow
MURDER CAN HURT YOU! (TF) ... Artie Kane
MURDER IN COWETA COUNTY (TF) ... Brad Fiedel
MURDER IN MISSISSIPPI (TF) ... Mason Daring
MURDER IN MUSIC CITY (TF) ... Earle Hagen
MURDER IN PARADISE (TF) ... John Cacavas
MURDER IN PEYTON PLACE (TF) ... Laurence Rosenthal
MURDER IN SPACE (CTF ... Arthur B. Rubinstein
MURDER IN TEXAS (TF) ... Leonard Rosenman
MURDER IS A MURDER, A ... Paul Misraki†
MURDER IS EASY (TF) ... Gerald Fried
MURDER IS MY BEAT ... Albert Glasser
MURDER IS MY BUSINESS ... Leo Erdody†
MURDER MAN, THE ... William Axt†
MURDER MOST FOUL ... Ron Goodwin
MURDER OF MARY PHAGAN, THE (MS) ... Maurice Jarre

N

NINE LIVES OF FRITZ THE CAT, THE (AF) ... Tom Scott
NINE MEN ... John Greenwood†
NINE TO FIVE ... Charles Fox
NINI TIRABUSCIO, LA DONNA CHE INVENTO LA MOSSA ... Carlo Rustichelli
NINJA III—THE DOMINATION ... W. Michael Lewis
NINJA III—THE DOMINATION ... Laurin Rinder
NINJA III: THE DOMINATION ... Udi Harpaz
NINJA TURF ... Gary Falcone
NINJA TURF ... Charles Pavlosky
NINJA TURF ... Christopher L. Stone
NINOTCHKA ... Werner R. Heymann†
NINTH CONFIGURATION, THE ... Barry De Vorzon
NINTH HEART, THE ... Petr Hapka
NITCHEVO ... Arthur Honegger†
NITWITS, THE ... Roy Webb†
NO DEPOSIT, NO RETURN ... Buddy Baker
NO DOWN PAYMENT ... Leigh Harline†
NO ESCAPE ... Bert A. Shefter
NO HANDS ON THE CLOCK ... Paul Sawtell†
NO HIGHWAY IN THE SKY ... Malcolm Arnold
NO HOLDS BARRED ... Jim Johnston
NO JOUEZ PAS AVEC LES MARTIENS ... Henri Lanoe
NO LOVE FOR JOHNNIE ... Malcolm Arnold
NO MAN IS AN ISLAND ... Andrea Saparoff
NO MAN OF HER OWN ... Hugo Friedhofer†
NO MAN'S LAND ... Basil Poledouris
NO MAN'S LAND ... Hanns Eisler†
NO MAN'S LAND (TF) ... Mike Post
NO MAN'S LAND (TF) ... Pete Carpenter†
NO MARRIAGE TIES ... Max Steiner†
NO MERCY ... Alan Silvestri
NO MINOR VICES ... Franz Waxman†
NO MORE LADIES ... Edward Ward†
NO NAME ON THE BULLET ... Herman Stein
NO OTHER LOVE (TF) ... Charles Gross
NO OTHER WOMAN ... Max Steiner†
NO PLACE FOR JENNIFER ... Allan Gray†
NO PLACE LIKE HOME (TF) ... Charles Gross
NO PLACE TO HIDE ... Herschel Burke Gilbert
NO PLACE TO HIDE (TF) ... John Cacavas
NO PLACE TO RUN (TF) ... George Aliceson Tipton
NO PROBLEM ... Philippe Sarde
NO QUESTIONS ASKED ... Leith Stevens†
NO RESTING PLACE ... William Alwyn†
NO RETREAT NO SURRENDER ... Paul Gilreath
NO RETREAT, NO SURRENDER ... David Spear
NO RETREAT, NO SURRENDER II ... David Spear
NO ROOM FOR THE GROOM ... Frank Skinner†
NO ROOM TO RUN (TF) ... Brian May
NO SAD SONGS FOR ME ... ★ George Duning
NO SAFE HAVEN ... Joel Goldsmith
NO SMALL AFFAIR ... Rupert Holmes
NO TIME FOR COMEDY ... Heinz Roemheld†
NO TIME FOR FLOWERS ... Herschel Burke Gilbert
NO TIME FOR LOVE ... Victor Young†
NO TIME TO BE YOUNG ... Mischa Bakaleinikoff †
NO TRESPASSING ... Greg Evigan
NO WAY OUT ... Maurice Jarre
NO WAY OUT ... Alfred Newman†
NO WAY TO TREAT A LADY ... Stanley Myers
NO, NO, NANETTE ... Anthony Collins†
NO...SONO VERGINE ... Gianfranco Plenizio
NOAH'S ARK ... Louis Silvers†
NOB HILL ... David Buttolph†
NOB HILL ... Emil Newman†
NOBLE HOUSE (MS) ... Paul Chihara
NOBODY LIVES FOREVER ... Adolph Deutsch†
NOBODY RUNS FOREVER ... Georges Delerue
NOBODY'S BABY ... T. Marvin Hatley†
NOBODY'S CHILD (TF) ... Michael Small
NOBODY'S DARLING ... Walter Scharf
NOBODY'S FOOL ... James Newton Howard
NOBODY'S PERFECT ... Robert Randles
NOBODY'S PERFEKT ... David McHugh
NOCTURNE ... Leigh Harline†
NOI DONNE SIAMO FATTI COSI ... Armando Trovajoli
NOI DUE SOLI ... Nino Rota†
NOMAD RIDERS ... Robert J. Walsh
NOMADS ... Bill Conti
NON SI SCRIVE SUI MURI A MILANO ... Fiorenzo Carpi
NON SIAMO DUE EVASI ... Carlo Rustichelli
NON SON DEGNO DI TE ... Ennio Morricone
NONE BUT THE BRAVE ... John Williams
NONE BUT THE LONELY HEART ... ★ Hanns Eisler†
NONE SHALL ESCAPE ... Ernst Toch†
NOON WINE (TF) ... Paul Chihara
NORA PRENTISS ... Franz Waxman†
NORLISS TAPES, THE (TF) ... Bob Cobert
NORMA RAE ... David Shire
NORMAN ROCKWELL'S BREAKING HOME TIES (TF) ... Jerrold Immel
NORMAN...IS THAT YOU? ... William Goldstein
NORSEMAN, THE ... Jaime Mendoza-Nava
NORTH AND SOUTH (MS) ... ☆ Bill Conti
NORTH AND SOUTH, BOOK II (MS) ... Bill Conti
NORTH AVENUE IRREGULARS, THE ... Robert F. Brunner
NORTH BEACH AND RAWHIDE (TF) ... Earle Hagen
NORTH BY NORTHWEST ... Bernard Herrmann†
NORTH DALLAS FORTY ... John Scott
NORTH SEAS HIJACK ... Michael J. Lewis
NORTH SHORE ... Richard Stone
NORTH STAR, THE ... ★ Aaron Copland
NORTH STAR, THE ... Philippe Sarde
NORTH TO ALASKA ... Lionel Newman†
NORTH TO THE KLONDIKE ... Hans J. Salter
NORTHERN PURSUIT ... Adolph Deutsch†
NORTHSTAR (TF) ... Brad Fiedel
NORTHWEST MOUNTED POLICE ... ★ Victor Young†
NORTHWEST PASSAGE ... Herbert Stothart†
NORTHWEST RANGERS ... Daniele Amfitheatrof†
NOSFERATU THE VAMPIRE ... Hans Erdmann†
NOSFERATU THE VAMPYRE ... Popol Vuh
NOSTALGIE ... Michel Michelet†
NOSTALGIE ROMANE ... Armando Trovajoli
NOT A PENNY MORE, NOT A PENNY LESS (CTF) ... Michel Legrand
NOT AS A STRANGER ... George Antheil†
NOT IN FRONT OF THE CHILDREN (TF) ... Fred Karlin
NOT JUST ANOTHER AFFAIR (TF) ... Arthur B. Rubinstein
NOT MY KID (TF) ... Mark Snow
NOT OF THIS EARTH ... Chuck Cirino
NOT OF THIS EARTH ... Ronald Stein†
NOT QUITE HUMAN (CTF) ... Tom Scott
NOT QUITE JERUSALEM ... Gian Reverberi
NOT QUITE PARADISE ... Gian Reverberi
NOT SINCE CASANOVA ... John Debney
NOT WANTED ... Leith Stevens†
NOT WITH MY WIFE, YOU DON'T! ... John Williams
NOTES FOR AN AFRICAN ORESTES ... Gato Barbieri
NOTHING BUT THE BEST ... Ron Grainer
NOTHING BUT THE NIGHT ... Malcolm Williamson
NOTHING BUT TROUBLE ... Nathaniel Shilkret†
NOTHING BY CHANCE ... Lee Holdridge
NOTHING IN COMMON ... Patrick Leonard
NOTHING LEFT TO LOVE ... Peer Raben
NOTHING SACRED ... Oscar Levant†
NOTORIOUS ... Roy Webb†
NOTORIOUS GENTLEMAN ... William Alwyn†
NOTRE DAME DE PARIS ... Georges Auric†
NOUS IRONS A MONTE-CARLO ... Paul Misraki†
NOUS IRONS A PARIS ... Paul Misraki†
NOUS IRONS TOUS AU PARADIS ... Vladimir Cosma
NOVECENTO ... Ennio Morricone
NOW AND FOREVER ... Bruce Rowland
NOW YOU SEE HIM, NOW YOU DON'T ... Robert F. Brunner
NOW YOU SEE IT, NOW YOU DON'T (TF) ... Lyn Murray†
NOW, VOYAGER ... ★★ Max Steiner†
NOWHERE TO HIDE ... Brad Fiedel
NOWHERE TO HIDE (TF) ... Jerrold Immel
NUDE BOMB, THE ... Lalo Schifrin
NUDE ODYSSEY ... Angelo Francesco Lavagnino†
NUIT D'OR ... Pierre Jansen
NUITS DE FEU ... Jean Wiener†
NUMBER ONE ... Dominic Frontiere
NUMBER ONE WITH A BULLET ... Alf Clausen
NUMBER SEVEN, THE ... Gerard Schurmann
NUN AND THE SERGEANT, THE ... Jerry Fielding†
NUN'S STORY, THE ... ★ Franz Waxman†
NUNCA PASA NADA ... Georges Delerue
NUNS ON THE RUN ... Gerald Gouriet
NUNZIO ... Lalo Schifrin
NUNZIO ... Walter Scharf
NURSE EDITH CAVELL ... ★ Anthony Collins†
NUTCRACKER ... Simon Park
NUTCRACKER: MONEY, MADNESS AND MURDER (MS) ... ☆ Billy Goldenberg
NUTS ... Barbra Streisand
NUTTY PROFESSOR, THE ... Walter Scharf

O

O CANGACEIRO ... Riz Ortolani
O'HARA'S WIFE ... Artie Butler
O'HARA, UNITED STATES TREASURY: OPERATION COBRA (TF) ... William Lava†
O'SHAUGHNESSY'S BOY ... William Axt†
O. HENRY'S FULL HOUSE ... Alfred Newman†
O.K. CONNERY ... Bruno Nicolai
O.K. NERO! ... Mario Nascimbene
O.S.S. ... Daniele Amfitheatrof†
O.S.S. ... Heinz Roemheld†
OASIS ... Paul Misraki†
OASIS, THE ... Christopher Young
OBJECTIF 500 MILLIONS ... Pierre Jansen
OBJECTIVE, BURMA! ... ★ Franz Waxman†
OBLIGING YOUNG LADY ... Roy Webb†
OBLONG BOX, THE ... Harry Robertson
OBSESSED WITH A MARRIED WOMAN (TF) ... Billy Goldenberg
OBSESSED, THE ... Allan Gray†
OBSESSION ... ★ Bernard Herrmann†
OBSESSION ... Paul Misraki†
OBSESSION ... Nino Rota†
OBSESSIVE LOVE (TF) ... Matthew McCauley
OCCHIO ALLA VEDOVA! ... Manuel De Sica
OCCUPATION IN 26 PICTURES ... Alfi Kabiljo
OCEANO ... Ennio Morricone
OCEANS OF FIRE (TF) ... Patrick Williams
OCTAGON, THE ... Dick Halligan
OCTOBER ... Edmund Meisel†
OCTOBER MAN, THE ... William Alwyn†
OCTOPUSSY ... John Barry
ODD COUPLE, THE ... Neal Hefti
ODD JOB, THE ... Howard Blake
ODD JOBS ... Robert Folk
ODD MAN OUT ... William Alwyn†
ODDBALL HALL ... William T. Stromberg
ODE TO BILLY JOE ... Michel Legrand
ODESSA FILE, THE ... Andrew Lloyd Webber
ODETTE ... Anthony Collins†
OF HUMAN BONDAGE ... Ron Goodwin
OF HUMAN BONDAGE ... Erich Wolfgang Korngold†
OF HUMAN BONDAGE ... Max Steiner†
OF HUMAN HEARTS ... Herbert Stothart†
OF JEWELS AND GOLD ... Richard Rodney Bennett
OF LIFE AND LOVE ... Armando Trovajoli
OF LOVE AND DESIRE ... Ronald Stein†
OF MICE AND MEN ... ★ Aaron Copland
OF MICE AND MEN (TF) ... George Romanis
OF PURE BLOOD (TF) ... Brad Fiedel
OF SUCH IS THE KINGDOM ... Milton Rosen
OF UNKNOWN ORIGIN ... Ken Wannberg
OFF BEAT ... James Horner
OFF LIMITS ... James Newton Howard
OFF LIMITS ... Nathan Van Cleave†
OFF THE MARK ... David Frank
OFF THE RECORD ... Adolph Deutsch†
OFF THE WALL ... Dennis McCarthy
OFFICER AND A GENTLEMAN, AN ... ★ Jack Nitzsche
OFFSPRING, THE ... Jim Manzie
OGGI A BERLINO ... Armando Trovajoli
OGGI A ME, DOMANI A TE ... Angelo Francesco Lavagnino†
OGGI, DOMANI E DOPODOMANI ... Nino Rota†
OGGI, DOMANI, DOPODOMANI ... Armando Trovajoli
OGRE, THE ... Les Baxter
OH CALCUTTA! ... Peter Schickele
OH DAD, POOR DAD, MAMA'S HUNG YOU IN THE CLOSET AND I'M FEELIN' SO SAD ... Neal Hefti
OH GOD! BOOK II ... Charles Fox
OH HEAVENLY DOG ... Frank Denson
OH HEAVENLY DOG ... Leon Seith
OH! ALFIE ... Alan Price
OH! THE NOMUGI PASS ... Masaru Sato
OH, GOD! ... Jack Elliott
OH, GOD! YOU DEVIL ... David Shire
OH, LUCKY MAN! ... Alan Price
OH, MEN! OH, WOMEN! ... Cyril J. Mockridge†
OH, MEN! OH, WOMEN! ... Hugo Friedhofer†
OHMS (TF) ... Elizabeth Swados
OKINAWA ... Mischa Bakaleinikoff †
OKINAWAN BOYS ... Shinchiro Ikebe
OKLAHOMA CITY DOLLS, THE (TF) ... Jerrold Immel
OKLAHOMA CRUDE ... Henry Mancini
OKLAHOMA KID, THE ... Max Steiner†
OKLAHOMA TERRITORY ... Albert Glasser

OKLAHOMA TERRITORY .... Albert Glasser
OKLAHOMA WOMAN, THE .... Ronald Stein†
OKLAHOMA! .... ★★ Adolph Deutsch†
OKLAHOMAN, THE .... Hans J. Salter
OKTOBER DAGE .... Carl Davis
OLD ACQUAINTANCE .... Franz Waxman†
OLD BOYFRIENDS .... David Shire
OLD CHISHOLM TRAIL, THE .... Hans J. Salter
OLD DARK HOUSE, THE .... David Broekman†
OLD DARK HOUSE, THE .... Benjamin Frankel†
OLD DRACULA .... David Whitaker
OLD ENOUGH .... Julian Marshall
OLD GRINGO .... Lee Holdridge
OLD HUTCH .... William Axt†
OLD IRONSIDES .... John S. Zamecnik†
OLD LOS ANGELES .... Ernest Gold
OLD MAID, THE .... Max Steiner†
OLD MAN AND THE SEA, THE .... ★★ Dimitri Tiomkin†
OLD MAN RHYTHM .... Roy Webb†
OLD MAN WHO CRIED
WOLF, THE (TF) .... Robert Drasnin
OLD YELLER .... Oliver Wallace†
OLD-FASHIONED GIRL, A .... Herschel Burke Gilbert
OLD-FASHIONED WAY, THE .... Andrea Setaro†
OLIMPIADI DEI MARITI .... Carlo Rustichelli
OLIVE TREES OF JUSTICE, THE .... Maurice Jarre
OLIVER & CO. (AF) .... J.A.C. Redford
OLIVER TWIST .... Sir Arnold Bax†
OLIVER TWIST (TF) .... Nick Bicat
OLIVER! .... ★★ John Green†
OLIVER'S STORY .... Lee Holdridge
OLIVER'S STORY .... Francis Lai
OLLY, OLLY, OXEN FREE .... Robert Alcivar
OLTRE LA NOTTE .... Bruno Nicolai
OLYMPIC ELK, THE .... Paul J. Smith†
OMAR KHAYYAM .... Victor Young†
OMBRE ET LUMIERE .... Joseph Kosma†
OMEGA MAN, THE .... Ron Grainer
OMEGA SYNDROME .... Nicholas Carras
OMEGA SYNDROME .... Jack Cookerly
OMEN, THE .... ★★ Jerry Goldsmith
OMICIDIO PER APPUNTAMENTO .... Armando Trovajoli
OMOO-OMOO, THE SHARK GOD .... Albert Glasser
ON A VOLE LA CRUISSE
DE JUPITER .... George Hatzinassios
ON A VOLE LA JOCONDE .... Carlo Rustichelli
ON AGAIN—OFF AGAIN .... Roy Webb†
ON ANY STREET .... Piero Piccioni
ON ANY SUNDAY .... Dominic Frontiere
ON ANY SUNDAY II (FD) .... Allan Alper
ON AURA TOUT VU .... Philippe Sarde
ON BORROWED TIME .... Franz Waxman†
ON DANGEROUS GROUND .... Bernard Herrmann†
ON FIRE (TF) .... William Goldstein
ON FRIDAY AT ELEVEN .... Claude Bolling
ON GOLDEN POND .... ★ Dave Grusin
ON HER MAJESTY'S SECRET SERVICE .... John Barry
ON MOONLIGHT BAY .... Max Steiner†
ON NE MEURT QUE DEUX FOIS .... Claude Bolling
ON OUR MERRY WAY .... Heinz Roemheld†
ON STAGE EVERYBODY .... Milton Rosen
ON SUCH A NIGHT .... Ernst Toch†
ON THE BEACH .... ★ Ernest Gold
ON THE DOUBLE .... Leith Stevens†
ON THE EDGEHerb .... Philhofer
ON THE GAME .... De Wolfe
ON THE LOOSE .... Leigh Harline†
ON THE NICKEL .... Fred Myrow
ON THE RIGHT TRACK .... Arthur B. Rubinstein
ON THE RIVIERA .... ★ Alfred Newman†
ON THE THRESHHOLD OF SPACE .... Lyn Murray†
ON THE TIP OF THE TONGUE .... Frederic Devreese
ON THE WATERFRONT .... ★ Leonard Bernstein†
ON TRIAL .... Georges Van Parys†
ON VALENTINE'S DAY .... Jonathan Sheffer
ON WINGS OF EAGLES (MS) .... Laurence Rosenthal
ONCE A THIEF .... Lalo Schifrin
ONCE A THIEF .... Michel Michelet†
ONCE AN EAGLE (MS) .... Dana Kaproff
ONCE BITTEN .... John Du Prez
ONCE IN A BLUE MOON .... George Antheil†
ONCE IN PARIS... .... Mitch Leigh
ONCE IS NOT ENOUGH .... Henry Mancini
ONCE UPON A DEAD MAN (TF) .... Jerry Fielding†
ONCE UPON A FAMILY (TF) .... Fred Karlin
ONCE UPON A
HONEYMOON .... Robert Emmett Dolan†
ONCE UPON A SCOUNDREL .... Alex North
ONCE UPON A SPY (TF) .... John Cacavas
ONCE UPON A
TEXAS TRAIN (TF) .... Arthur B. Rubinstein
ONCE UPON A TIME .... Frederick Hollander†
ONCE UPON A TIME (AF) .... Peter Thomas
ONCE UPON A TIME IN AMERICA .... Ennio Morricone
ONCE UPON A TIME IN THE WEST .... Ennio Morricone
ONCE WE WERE DREAMERS .... Misha Segal
ONE AND ONLY, THE .... Patrick Williams
ONE BY ONE .... Stomu Yamashita
ONE COOKS, THE OTHER
DOESN'T (TF) .... Fred Karlin
ONE CRAZY SUMMER .... James Di Pasquale
ONE CRAZY SUMMER .... Cory Lerios
ONE CROWDED NIGHT .... Roy Webb†
ONE DARK NIGHT .... Robert Summers
ONE DEADLY SUMMER .... Georges Delerue
ONE FLEW OVER THE
CUCKOO'S NEST .... ★ Jack Nitzsche
ONE FOOT IN HEAVEN .... Max Steiner†
ONE FOOT IN HELL .... Dominic Frontiere
ONE FROM THE HEART .... Robert Alcivar
ONE FROM THE HEART .... ★ Tom Waits
ONE HOUR WITH YOU .... W. Franke Harling†
ONE HUNDRED AND ONE
DALMATIONS (AF) .... George Bruns
ONE IN A MILLION: THE RON
LeFLORE STORY (TF) .... Peter Matz
ONE IS A LONELY NUMBER .... Michel Legrand
ONE LAST FLING .... David Buttolph†
ONE LITTLE INDIAN .... Jerry Goldsmith
ONE MAGIC CHRISTMAS .... Michael Conway Baker
ONE MAN FORCE .... David Michael Frank
ONE MAN'S JOURNEY .... Max Steiner†
ONE MAN'S WAY .... Richard Markowitz
ONE MILLION B.C. .... ★ Werner R. Heymann†
ONE MILLION YEARS B.C. .... Mario Nascimbene
ONE MINUTE TO ZERO .... Victor Young†
ONE MORE RIVER .... W. Franke Harling†
ONE MORE SATURDAY NIGHT .... David McHugh
ONE MORE TIME .... Les Reed
ONE MORE TRAIN TO ROB .... David Shire
ONE MUST LIVE DANGEROUSLY .... Claude Bolling
ONE NIGHT OF LOVE .... ★ Victor Schertzinger†
ONE NIGHT OF LOVE .... Louis Silvers†
ONE OF OUR DINOSAURS
IS MISSING .... Ron Goodwin
ONE OF OUR OWN (TF) .... Jerry Fielding†
ONE ON ONE .... Charles Fox
ONE POLICE PLAZA (TF) .... Mark Snow
ONE POTATO, TWO POTATO .... Gerald Fried
ONE SHOE MAKES IT
MURDER (TF) .... Bruce Broughton
ONE SPY TOO MANY .... Gerald Fried
ONE SPY TOO MANY .... Nelson Riddle†
ONE SUNDAY AFTERNOON .... David Buttolph†
ONE TERRIFIC GUY (TF) .... Mark Snow
...ONE THIRD OF A NATION .... Nathaniel Shilkret†
ONE TRICK PONY .... Paul Simon
ONE WAY PASSAGE .... W. Franke Harling†
ONE WAY PASSAGE .... Bernhard Kaun†
ONE WAY PENDULUM .... Richard Rodney Bennett
ONE WISH TOO MANY .... Douglas Gamley
ONE WOMAN'S STORY .... Richard Addinsell†
ONE, TWO, THREE .... Andre Previn
ONE-EYED JACKS .... Hugo Friedhofer†
ONE-TENTH OF A NATION (FD) .... Roy Harris†
ONE-WAY STREET .... Frank Skinner†
ONIONHEAD .... David Buttolph†
ONLY ANGELS HAVE WINGS .... Dimitri Tiomkin†
ONLY GAME IN TOWN, THE .... Maurice Jarre
ONLY ONCE IN A LIFETIME .... Robert O. Ragland
ONLY THE FRENCH CAN .... Georges Van Parys†
ONLY THE VALIANT .... Franz Waxman†
ONLY TWO CAN PLAY .... Richard Rodney Bennett
ONLY WAY HOME, THE .... Dan Foliart
ONLY WAY, THE .... Carl Davis
ONLY WHEN I LARF .... Ron Grainer
ONLY WITH MARRIED MEN (TF) .... Jack Elliott
ONLY WITH MARRIED MEN (TF) .... Allyn Ferguson
OPEN ADMISSIONS (TF) .... Charles Gross
OPEN ENDS .... Peer Raben
OPEN SECRET .... Herschel Burke Gilbert
OPENING NIGHT .... Bo Harwood
OPENING TOMORROW .... Christopher Komeda†
OPERATION BIKINI .... Les Baxter
OPERATION CROSSBOW .... Ron Goodwin
OPERATION DAMES .... Richard Markowitz
OPERATION DAYBREAK .... David Hentschel
OPERATION DISASTER .... William Alwyn†
OPERATION KID BROTHER .... Ennio Morricone
OPERATION KID BROTHER .... Bruno Nicolai
OPERATION LIBERTY .... Vyecheslav Ovchinnikov
OPERATION PACIFIC .... Max Steiner†
OPERATION PETTICOAT .... David Rose†
OPERATION PETTICOAT (TF) .... Artie Butler
OPERATION SECRET .... Roy Webb†
OPERATION SNAFU .... Malcolm Arnold
OPERATION SNATCH .... Kenneth V. Jones
OPERATION THUNDERBOLT .... Dov Seltzer
OPERATOR 13 .... William Axt†
OPERAZIONE PARADISO .... Mario Nascimbene
OPERAZIONE PAURA .... Carlo Rustichelli
OPERAZIONE SAN GENNARO .... Armando Trovajoli
OPERAZIONE SAN PIETRO .... Stelvio Cipriani
OPHELIA .... Pierre Jansen
OPIATE '67 .... Armando Trovajoli
OPPENHEIMER (MS) .... Carl Davis
OPPORTUNITY KNOCKS .... Miles Goodman
OPPOSING FORCE .... Marc Donahue
OPPOSITE SEX, THE .... Nicholas Brodzsky†
OPTIMISTS, THE .... George Martin
OPUS 3 .... Hanns Eisler†
ORACLE, THE .... Walter Sear
ORAGE .... Georges Auric†
ORCA .... Ennio Morricone
ORCHESTRA REHEARSAL .... Nino Rota
ORDEAL (TF) .... Patrick Williams
ORDEAL BY INNOCENCE .... Pino Donaggio
ORDEAL OF BILL
CARNEY, THE (TF) .... Billy Goldenberg
ORDEAL OF DR. MUDD, THE (TF) .... Gerald Fried
ORDER OF DEATH .... Ennio Morricone
ORDER OF THE EAGLE .... William T. Stromberg
ORDERS TO KILL .... Benjamin Frankel†
ORDINARY HEROES .... Perry Botkin
ORDINARY PEOPLE .... Marvin Hamlisch
ORDINE FIRMATO IN BIANCO .... Carlo Savina
ORDRES .... Joseph Kosma†
OREGON PASSAGE .... Paul Dunlap
OREGON TRAIL (TF) .... David Shire
OREGON TRAIL, THE .... Paul Dunlap
OREM, THE .... Ennio Morricone
ORGANIZATION, THE .... Gil Melle
ORGANIZER, THE .... Carlo Rustichelli
ORIGINAL SIN (TF) .... Lalo Schifrin
ORPHAN TRAIN (TF) .... Laurence Rosenthal
ORPHANS .... Michael Small
ORPHEE .... Georges Auric†
ORPHEUS .... Georges Auric†
OSA .... Mason Daring
OSCAR .... Georges Delerue
OSCAR WILDE .... Kenneth V. Jones
OSTERMAN WEEKEND, THE .... Lalo Schifrin
OSTIA .... Francesco De Masi
OTHELLO .... Aram Khachaturian†
OTHELLO .... Angelo Francesco Lavagnino†
OTHER LOVE, THE .... Miklos Rozsa
OTHER LOVER, THE (TF) .... Lee Holdridge
OTHER MAN, THE (TF) .... Michel Colombier
OTHER SIDE OF MIDNIGHT, THE .... Michel Legrand
OTHER SIDE OF PARADISE, THE .... Pete Rugolo
OTHER SIDE OF THE
MOUNTAIN - PART 2, THE .... Lee Holdridge
OTHER SIDE OF THE MOUNTAIN, THE .... Charles Fox
OTHER VICTIM, THE (TF) .... Richard Bellis
OTHER WOMAN, THE .... Ernest Gold
OTHER WOMAN, THE (TF) .... Artie Butler
OTHER WORLD OF WINSTON
CHURCHILL, THE .... Carl Davis
OTHER, THE .... Jerry Goldsmith
OTLEY .... Stanley Myers
OTTOKAR, THE WORLD
REFORMER .... Guenther Fischer
OUBLIE-MOI MANDOLINE .... Georges Delerue
OUR BETTERS .... Max Steiner†
OUR BLUSHING BRIDES .... Dimitri Tiomkin†
OUR DAILY BREAD .... Alfred Newman†
OUR DANCING DAUGHTERS .... William Axt†
OUR FAMILY BUSINESS (TF) .... Tom Scott
OUR HEARTS WERE GROWING UP .... Victor Young†
OUR HEARTS WERE YOUNG
AND GAY .... Werner R. Heymann†
OUR MAN FLINT .... Jerry Goldsmith
OUR MAN IN MARRAKESH .... Malcom Lockyer
OUR MISS BROOKS .... Roy Webb†
OUR MODERN MAIDENS .... William Axt†
OUR MOTHER'S HOUSE .... Georges Delerue
OUR NEIGHBORS—THE CARTERS .... Victor Young†
OUR TIME .... Michel Legrand
OUR TOWN .... ★ Aaron Copland
OUR VERY OWN .... Victor Young†
OUR VINES HAVE
TENDER GRAPES .... Bronislau Kaper†
OUR WIFE .... Leo Shuken†

OUR WILLI IS THE BEST ... Peter Thomas
OUR WINNING SEASON ... Charles Fox
OUT COLD ... Michel Colombier
OUT OF AFRICA ... ★★ John Barry
OUT OF BOUNDS ... Stewart Copeland
OUT OF IT ... Michael Small
OUT OF ROSENHEIM ... Bob Telson
OUT OF SEASON ... John Cameron
OUT OF THE BLUE ... Tom Lavin
OUT OF THE BLUE ... Carmen Dragon†
OUT OF THE CLOUDS ... Richard Addinsell†
OUT OF THE DARK ... Paul Antonelli
OUT OF THE DARK ... David Wheatley
OUT OF THE NIGHT ... Leo Erdody†
OUT OF THE PAST ... Roy Webb†
OUT OF TIME ... Alan Parker
OUT OF TIME (TF) ... Andy Summers
OUT ON A LIMB (TF) ... Lalo Schifrin
OUT ON THE EDGE (TF) ... Stanley Clarke
OUTBACK ... John Scott
OUTBACK BOUND (TF) ... Miles Goodman
OUTCAST ... Ernst Toch†
OUTCAST OF THE ISLANDS ... Brian Easdale
OUTCASTS OF POKER FLAT, THE ... Hugo Friedhofer†
OUTCASTS OF POKER FLAT, THE ... Roy Webb†
OUTCASTS OF POKER FLAT, THE ... Lionel Newman†
OUTCASTS OF THE CITY ... Harry Sukman†
OUTFIT, THE ... Jerry Fielding†
OUTING, THE ... Joseph Conlan
OUTING, THE ... Joel Rosenbaum
OUTLAND ... Jerry Goldsmith
OUTLAW BLUES ... Charles Bernstein
OUTLAW BLUES ... Bruce Langhorne
OUTLAW JOSEY WALES, THE ... ★ Jerry Fielding†
OUTLAW'S SON ... Les Baxter
OUTLAW, THE ... Victor Young†
OUTLAWS ... Masaru Sato
OUTLAWS IS COMING!, THE ... Paul Dunlap
OUTLAWS, THE (TF) ... Jerrold Immel
OUTPOST IN MALAYA ... Allan Gray†
OUTPOST IN MOROCCO ... Michel Michelet†
OUTPUT ... Jurgen Knieper
OUTRAGE! (TF) ... Jimmie Haskell
OUTRAGE! (TF) ... Morton Stevens
OUTRAGE, THE ... Alex North
OUTRAGEOUS FORTUNE ... Alan Silvestri
OUTRAGEOUS! ... Paul Hoffert
OUTRIDERS, THE ... Andre Previn
OUTSIDE CHANCE (TF) ... Murphy Dunne
OUTSIDE CHANCE (TF) ... Lou Levy
OUTSIDE IN ... Randy Edelman
OUTSIDE MAN, THE ... Michel Legrand
OUTSIDE THE LAW ... Milton Rosen
OUTSIDE THE LAW ... David Broekman†
OUTSIDER, THE ... John Addison
OUTSIDER, THE ... Leonard Rosenman
OUTSIDER, THE ... Ken Thorne
OUTSIDER, THE ... Ennio Morricone
OUTSIDER, THE (TF) ... Pete Rugolo
OUTSIDERS, THE ... Carmine Coppola
OVER MY DEAD BODY ... Cyril J. Mockridge†
OVER THE BROOKLYN BRIDGE ... Pino Donaggio
OVER THE EDGE ... Sol Kaplan
OVER THE TOP ... Giorgio Moroder
OVER-THE-HILL GANG RIDES AGAIN, THE (TF) ... David Raksin
OVER-THE-HILL GANG, THE (TF) ... Hugo Friedhofer†
OVERBOARD ... Alan Silvestri
OVERBOARD (TF) ... Mark Snow
OVEREXPOSED ... Mark Governor
OVERKILL ... Robert J. Walsh
OVERLANDERS, THE ... John Ireland
OVERLORD ... Paul Glass
OVERNIGHT ... Michael Conway Baker
OVIRI ... Roger Bourland
OVOCE STROMJ RAJSHYCH JIME ... Zdenek Liska
OWEN MARSHALL, COUNSELOR AT LAW (TF) ... Elmer Bernstein
OWL AND THE PUSSYCAT, THE ... Dick Halligan
OWL AND THE PUSSYCAT, THE (FD) ... Matyas Seiber
OX-BOW INCIDENT, THE ... Cyril J. Mockridge†
OXFORD BLUES ... John Du Prez

P

P'TANG YANG, KIPPERBANG ... David Earl
P'TIT CON ... Vladimir Cosma
P.J. ... Neal Hefti
P.K. AND THE KID ... James Horner
P.O.W. THE ESCAPE ... David Storrs
P.T. RAIDERS ... William Alwyn†
PACIFIC 231 ... Arthur Honegger†
PACIFIC CHALLENGE (FD) ... Bill Conti
PACIFIC HEIGHTS ... Hans Zimmer
PACIFIC LINER ... ★ Robert Russell Bennett†
PACK OF LIES (TF) ... Stanley Myers
PACK, THE ... Lee Holdridge
PACKAGE, THE ... James Newton Howard
PACKIN' IT IN (TF) ... Mark Snow
PAD (AND HOW TO USE IT), THE ... Russell Garcia
PADRI E FIGLI ... Carlo Rustichelli
PAID IN FULL ... Victor Young†
PAINT YOUR WAGON ... ★ Nelson Riddle†
PAINTED DESERT ... Roy Webb†
PAINTED HILLS, THE ... Daniele Amfitheatrof†
PAINTED VEIL, THE ... Herbert Stothart†
PAIR OF ACES (TF) ... William Olvis
PAJAMA PARTY ... Les Baxter
PALAIS ROYALE ... Jonathan Goldsmith
PALE FLOWER ... Toru Takemitsu
PALE RIDER ... Lennie Niehaus
PALEFACE, THE ... Victor Young†
PALM BEACH STORY, THE ... Victor Young†
PALS (TF) ... Mark Snow
PAN PROKOUK PRITEL ZVIRATEK (AF) ... Zdenek Liska
PANACHE (TF) ... Frank De Vol
PANAMA HATTIE ... George Bassman
PANAMA LADY ... Roy Webb†
PANCHO BARNES (TF) ... ☆ Allyn Ferguson
PANCHO VILLA ... John Cacavas
PANDEMONIUM ... Dana Kaproff
PANDORA AND THE FLYING DUTCHMAN ... Alan Rawsthorne†
PANE, AMORE E FANTASIA ... Alessandro Cicognini†
PANE, AMORE E GELOSIA ... Alessandro Cicognini†
PANE, AMORE E... ... Alessandro Cicognini†
PANIC ... Jacques Ibert†
PANIC IN ECHO PARK (TF) ... John Spence
PANIC IN THE CITY ... Paul Dunlap
PANIC IN THE STREETS ... Alfred Newman†
PANIC IN THE YEAR ZERO ... Les Baxter
PANIC ON THE 5:22 (TF) ... Richard Markowitz
PANTALASKAS ... Jean Wiener†
PANTHER PANCHALI ... Ravi Shankar
PAOLO E FRANCESCA ... Bruno Nicolai
PAOLO IL CALDO ... Armando Trovajoli
PAPA, MAMA, THE MAID AND I ... Georges Van Parys†
PAPER CHASE, THE ... John Williams
PAPER DOLLS (TF) ... Mark Snow
PAPER LION ... Roger Kellaway
PAPER TIGER ... Roy Budd
PAPERHOUSE ... Hans Zimmer
PAPILLION ... ★ Jerry Goldsmith
PAR LE SANG DES AUTRES ... Francis Lai
PAR OU TES RENTRE...ON TA PAS VU SORTIR ... Alan Silvestri
PAR UN BEAU MATIN D'ETE ... Michel Magne†
PAR-DESSUS LE MUR ... Georges Delerue
PARACHUTE BATTALION ... Roy Webb†
PARADE, THE (TF) ... Arthur B. Rubinstein
PARADES ... Garry Sherman
PARADINE CASE, THE ... Franz Waxman†
PARADISE ... Paul Hoffert
PARADISE (TF) ... Jerrold Immel
PARADISE ALLEY ... Bill Conti
PARADISE CONNECTION (TF) ... Bruce Broughton
PARADISE FOR THREE ... Edward Ward†
PARADISE LAGOON ... Douglas Gamley
PARALLAX VIEW, THE ... Michael Small
PARANOIA ... Teo Usuelli
PARANOIAC ... Elisabeth Luytens†
PARASITE ... Richard H. Band
PARATROOP COMMAND ... Ronald Stein†
PARATROOPS (FD) ... Gail Kubik†
PARDNERS ... Frank De Vol
PARDON MON AFFAIRE ... Vladimir Cosma
PARDON MON AFFAIRE, TOO! ... Vladimir Cosma
PARDON MY PAST ... Dimitri Tiomkin†
PARDON MY RHYTHM ... Hans J. Salter
PARENT TRAP II (TF) ... Charles Fox
PARENTHOOD ... Randy Newman
PARENTS ... Jonathan Elias
PARIGI O CARA ... Fiorenzo Carpi
PARIS ... Jacques Ibert†
PARIS ... Edward Ward†
PARIS AFTER DARK ... Hugo Friedhofer†
PARIS AU MOIS D'AOUT ... Georges Garvarentz
PARIS AU PRINTEMPS ... Georges Van Parys†
PARIS BLUES ... ★ Duke Ellington†
PARIS BY NIGHT ... Georges Delerue
PARIS CALLING ... Richard Hageman†
PARIS DOES STRANGE THINGS ... Joseph Kosma†
PARIS FOLLIES OF 1956 ... Frank De Vol
PARIS HONEYMOON ... Leo Shuken†
PARIS IN SPRING ... Sigmund Krumgold†
PARIS LA NUIT ... Georges Van Parys†
PARIS MODEL ... Albert Glasser
PARIS N'EXISTE PAS ... Serge Gainsbourg
PARIS WHEN IT SIZZLES ... Nelson Riddle†
PARIS, TEXAS ... Ry Cooder
PARIS—UNDERGROUND ... ★ Alexandre Tansman†
PARIS-SECRET ... Alain Gorraguer
PARK IS MINE, THE (CTF) ... Tangerine Dream
PARK ROW ... Paul Dunlap
PARKER ... Richard Hartley
PARKING ... Michel Legrand
PARNELL ... William Axt†
PAROLES ET MUSIQUES ... Michel Legrand
PARRISH ... Max Steiner†
PARSON OF PANAMINT, THE ... John Leipold†
PART 2, SOUNDER ... Taj Mahal
PART 2, WALKING TALL ... Walter Scharf
PARTIR REVENIR ... Michel Legrand
PARTIRONO PRETI, TORNARONO...CURATI ... Luis Bacalov
PARTISANS ... Mikis Theodorakis
PARTNER ... Ennio Morricone
PARTNERS ... Georges Delerue
PARTNERS IN CRIME ... Ron Goodwin
PARTNERS IN CRIME (TF) ... Gil Melle
PARTY GIRL ... Jeff Alexander†
PARTY LINE ... Sam Winans
PARTY, THE ... Henry Mancini
PAS DE PROBLEME ... Philippe Sarde
PAS DE ROSES POUR OSS 117 ... Piero Piccioni
PASCALI'S ISLAND ... Loek Dikker
PASCUAL DUARTE ... Luis De Pablo
PASQUALINO SETTEBELLEZZE ... Enzo Jannacci
PASS THE AMMO ... Carter Burwell
PASSAGE TO INDIA, A ... ★★ Maurice Jarre
PASSAGE TO MARSEILLE ... Max Steiner†
PASSAGE, THE ... Michael J. Lewis
PASSAGE, THE ... Paul Loomis
PASSE MONTAGNE ... Philippe Sarde
PASSENGERS, THE ... Claude Bolling
PASSEPORT POUR RIO ... Paul Misraki†
PASSI DI MORTE PERDUTI NEL BUIO ... Riz Ortolani
PASSING OF THE THIRD FLOOR BACK, THE ... Louis Levy†
PASSION AND PARADISE (TF) ... Hagood Hardy
PASSION FLOWER (TF) ... Miles Goodman
PASSION FLOWER HOTEL ... Francis Lai
PASSION OF JOAN OF ARC, THE ... Victor Allix†
PASSION OF SLOW FIRE, THE ... Georges Delerue
PASSIONATE FRIENDS, THE ... Richard Addinsell†
PASSIONE D'AMORE ... Armando Trovajoli
PASSIONS (TF) ... Bruce Broughton
PASSOVER PLOT, THE ... Alex North
PASSPORT TO CHINA ... Edwin Astley
PASSPORT TO DESTINY ... Roy Webb†
PASSPORT TO PIMLICO ... Georges Auric†
PASTACIATTA NEL DESERTO ... Carlo Rustichelli
PAT AND MIKE ... David Raksin
PAT GARRETT AND BILLY THE KID ... Bob Dylan
PATCH OF BLUE, A ... ★ Jerry Goldsmith
PATERNITY ... David Shire
PATHFINDER, THE ... Mischa Bakaleinikoff †
PATHS OF GLORY ... Gerald Fried
PATRIARCHS OF THE BIBLE, THE ... Teo Usuelli
PATRICK ... Goblin
PATRICK ... Brian May
PATRICK THE GREAT ... Hans J. Salter
PATRIE ... Jean Wiener†
PATRIOT, THE ... Jay Ferguson
PATSY, THE ... David Raksin
PATTI ROCKS ... Doug Maynard
PATTON ... ★ Jerry Goldsmith
PATTY HEARST ... Scott Johnson
PAUL AND MICHELLE ... Michel Colombier
PAULA ... George Duning
PAULINE AT THE BEACH ... Jean-Louis Valero

Q

QUICK, BEFORE IT MELTS ... David Rose†
QUICKER THAN THE EYE ... Georges Garvarentz
QUICKSAND ... Louis Gruenberg†
QUICKSILVER ... Anthony Banks
QUIEN SABE? ... Luis Bacalov
QUIET AMERICAN, THE ... Mario Nascimbene
QUIET COOL ... Jay Ferguson
QUIET DAYS IN CLICKY ... Mathieu Chabrol
QUIET DUEL, THE ... Akira Ifukube
QUIET EARTH, THE ... John Charles
QUIET GUN, THE ... Paul Dunlap
QUIET MAN, THE ... Victor Young†
QUIET PLACE IN THE COUNTRY, A ... Ennio Morricone
QUIGLEY DOWN UNDER ... Basil Poledouris
QUILLER MEMORANDUM, THE ... John Barry
QUINCANNON, FRONTIER SCOUT ... Les Baxter
QUINDICI FORCHE PER UN ASSASSINO ... Francesco De Masi
QUINNS, THE (TF) ... John Scott
QUINTET ... Tom Pierson
QUITE GOOD CHAPS ... Zdenek Liska
QUO VADIS ... ★ Miklos Rozsa

R

R.P.M. ... Perry Botkin
R.S.I.: LA REPUBBLICA DI MUSSOLINI (FD) ... Teo Usuelli
RABBI AND THE SHIKSE, THE ... Dov Seltzer
RABBIT TEST ... Frank Denson
RABBIT TEST ... Mike Post
RABBIT TEST ... Pete Carpenter†
RABBIT TRAP, THE ... Jack Marshall
RACCONTI D'ESTATE ... Piero Piccioni
RACCONTI PROIBITI...DI NIENTE VESTITI ... Stelvio Cipriani
RACE FOR GLORY ... Jay Ferguson
RACE FOR SPACE, THE (FD) ... Elmer Bernstein
RACE FOR YOUR LIFE, CHARLIE BROWN (AF) ... Ed Bogas
RACE STREET ... Roy Webb†
RACE TO THE YANKEE ZEPHYR ... Brian May
RACE WITH THE DEVIL ... Leonard Rosenman
RACERS, THE ... Alex North
RACHEL AND THE STRANGER ... Roy Webb†
RACHEL PAPERS, THE ... Chaz Jankel
RACHEL RACHEL ... Jerome Moross†
RACHEL RIVER ... Arvo Part
RACING LADY ... Roy Webb†
RACING WITH THE MOON ... Dave Grusin
RACING WORLD ... Duke Ellington†
RACK, THE ... Adolph Deutsch†
RACKET BUSTERS ... Adolph Deutsch†
RACKETEERS OF THE RANGE ... Roy Webb†
RACQUET ... Michel Rubini
RAD ... James Di Pasquale
RADAR SECRET SERVICE ... Russell Garcia
RADIO DAYS ... Dick Hyman
RADIOACTIVE DREAMS ... Pete Robinson
RAFFERTY AND THE GOLD DUST TWINS ... Artie Butler
RAFFLES ... Victor Young†
RAFTER ROMANCE ... Max Steiner†
RAGA ... Ravi Shankar
RAGAZZO DI BORGATA ... Nino Rota†
RAGE ... Stelvio Cipriani
RAGE ... Lalo Schifrin
RAGE (TF) ... Laurence Rosenthal
RAGE IN HEAVEN ... Bronislau Kaper†
RAGE OF ANGELS (TF) ... ☆☆ Billy Goldenberg
RAGE OF ANGELS: THE STORY CONTINUES (MS) ... Billy Goldenberg
RAGE OF HONOR ... Stelvio Cipriani
RAGE TO LIVE, A ... Nelson Riddle†
RAGGEDY ANN AND ANDY (AF) ... Joe Raposo†
RAGGEDY MAN ... Jerry Goldsmith
RAGGEDY RAWNEY, THE ... Michael Kamen
RAGING MOON, THE ... Stanley Myers
RAGING TIDE, THE ... Frank Skinner†
RAGTIME ... ★ Randy Newman
RAID ON ENTEBBE (TF) ... ☆ David Shire
RAIDERS OF SAN JOAQUIN ... Hans J. Salter
RAIDERS OF THE DESERT ... Hans J. Salter
RAIDERS OF THE GOLDEN COBRA, THE ... Carlo Savina
RAIDERS OF THE LOST ARK ... ★ John Williams
RAIDERS, THE ... Herman Stein
RAIDERS, THE ... Henry Mancini
RAILS INTO LARAMIE ... Herman Stein
RAIN ... Hanns Eisler†
RAIN ... Alfred Newman†
RAIN MAN ... ★ Hans Zimmer
RAIN PEOPLE, THE ... Ronald Stein†
RAINBOW ... Tangerine Dream
RAINBOW (TF) ... Charles Fox
RAINBOW BOYS, THE ... Howard Blake
RAINBOW BRITE AND THE STAR STEALER (AF) ... Shuki Levy
RAINBOW BRITE AND THE STAR STEALER (AF) ... Haim Saban
RAINBOW ISLAND ... Roy Webb†
RAINBOW, THE ... Carl Davis
RAINMAKER, THE ... ★ Alex North
RAINMAKERS, THE ... Roy Webb†
RAINS CAME, THE ... ★ Alfred Newman†
RAINS OF RANCHIPUR, THE ... Hugo Friedhofer†
RAINTREE COUNTY ... ★ John Green†
RAINY DAY WOMEN (TF) ... Stanley Myers
RAISE THE TITANIC ... John Barry
RAISIN IN THE SUN, A ... Laurence Rosenthal
RAISING ARIZONA ... Carter Burwell
RAISING OF LAZARUS, THE ... Milton Rosen
RAKE'S PROGRESS, THE ... William Alwyn†
RALLY 'ROUND THE FLAG, BOYS! ... Cyril J. Mockridge†
RAMBO III ... Jerry Goldsmith
RAMBO: FIRST BLOOD PART II ... Jerry Goldsmith
RAMONA ... Alfred Newman†
RAMPAGE ... Elmer Bernstein
RAMPAGE ... Ennio Morricone
RAMROD ... Adolph Deutsch†
RAN ... Toru Takemitsu
RANCHO DELUXE ... Jimmy Buffett
RANCHO NOTORIOUS ... Hugo Friedhofer†
RANCHO NOTORIOUS ... Emil Newman†
RANDOM HARVEST ... ★ Herbert Stothart†
RANGE WAR ... Victor Young†
RANGERS OF FORTUNE ... Frederick Hollander†
RANGO ... W. Franke Harling†
RANSOM ... Jerry Goldsmith
RANSOM ... Jeff Alexander†
RANSOM FOR ALICE! (TF) ... David Rose†
RAPE AND MARRIAGE—THE RIDEOUT CASE (TF) ... Gil Melle
RAPE OF INNOCENCE ... Vladimir Cosma
RAPE OF MALAYA ... Matyas Seiber
RAPE OF RICHARD BECK, THE (TF) ... Peter Bernstein
RAPPORTE FULLER BASE STOCCOLMA ... Armando Trovajoli
RAPTURE ... Georges Delerue
RARE BREED, THE ... John Williams
RASCAL DAZZLE ... Ronald Stein†
RASCALS AND ROBBERS—THE SECRET ADVENTURES OF TOM SAWYER AND HUCK FINN (TF) ... James Horner
RASHOMON ... Fumio Hayasaka †
RASPUTIN - THE MAD MONK ... Don Banks
RASPUTIN AND THE EMPRESS ... Herbert Stothart†
RAT DER GOTTER ... Hanns Eisler†
RAT FINK ... Ronald Stein†
RAT RACE, THE ... Elmer Bernstein
RAT, THE ... Anthony Collins†
RATBOY ... Steve Dorff
RATBOY ... Lennie Niehaus
RATINGS GAME, THE (CTF) ... Bruce Kimmel
RATINGS GAME, THE (TF) ... David Spear
RATON PASS ... Max Steiner†
RATS, THE ... Anthony Guefen
RAVAGERS ... Fred Karlin
RAVAGERS ... Fred Karlin
RAVEN, THE ... Les Baxter
RAVEN, THE ... Clifford Vaughan†
RAW DEAL ... Cinemascore
RAW EDGE, THE ... Hans J. Salter
RAW FORCE ... Walter Murphy
RAW WIND IN EDEN ... Hans J. Salter
RAWHEAD REX ... Colin Towns
RAWHIDE ... Sol Kaplan
RAWHIDE YEARS, THE ... Hans J. Salter
RAWHIDE YEARS, THE ... Frank Skinner†
RAYMIE ... Ronald Stein†
RAZOR'S EDGE, THE ... Jack Nitzsche
RAZOR'S EDGE, THE ... Alfred Newman†
REACH FOR THE SKY ... John Addison
REACHING FOR THE MOON ... Alfred Newman†
REACHING FOR THE SUN ... Victor Young†
REAL AMERICAN HERO, A (TF) ... Walter Scharf
REAL GENIUS ... Thomas Newman
REAL GLORY, THE ... Alfred Newman†
REAL LIFE ... Mort Lindsey
REAL LIFE ... David Mindel
REAL MEN ... Miles Goodman
REANIMATOR ... Richard H. Band
REAP THE WILD WIND ... Victor Young†
REAR WINDOW ... Franz Waxman†
REARVIEW MIRROR (TF) ... William Goldstein
REASON TO LIVE, A (TF) ... Miles Goodman
REBECCA ... ★ Franz Waxman†
REBEL ... Bruce Rowland
REBEL ... Chris Neal
REBEL IN TOWN ... Les Baxter
REBEL JESUS ... Alex North
REBEL NUN FLAVIA LA MONACA MUSULMANA, THE ... Nicola Piovani
REBEL SET, THE ... Paul Dunlap
REBEL WITHOUT A CAUSE ... Leonard Rosenman
REBELLION ... Toru Takemitsu
REBELS, THE (MS) ... Gerald Fried
REBETICO ... Stavros Xarchakos
REBUS ... Luis Bacalov
REBUS (TF) ... Bruno Nicolai
RECKLESS ... Thomas Newman
RECKLESS ... Edward Ward†
RECKLESS DISREGARD (CTF) ... Gil Goldstein
RECKLESS MOMENT, THE ... Hans J. Salter
RECKONING, THE ... Malcolm Arnold
RECONTRES SUR LE RHIN ... Georges Van Parys†
RECORD OF A LIVING BEING ... Masaru Sato
RECOURS EN GRACE ... Maurice Jarre
RECRUITS ... Steve Parsons
RECRUITS IN INGOLSTADT ... Peer Raben
RED ALERT (TF) ... George Aliceson Tipton
RED BADGE OF COURAGE, THE ... Bronislau Kaper†
RED BADGE OF COURAGE, THE (TF) ... Jack Elliott
RED BEARD ... Masaru Sato
RED CANYON ... Walter Scharf
RED DANUBE, THE ... Miklos Rozsa
RED DAWN ... Basil Poledouris
RED EARTH, WHITE EARTH (TF) ... Ralph Grierson
RED FLAG: THE ULTIMATE GAME (TF) ... Allyn Ferguson
RED FLAG: THE ULTIMATE GAME, THE (TF) ... Allyn Ferguson
RED HEAT ... James Horner
RED HOUSE, THE ... Miklos Rozsa
RED KING, WHITE KNIGHT (CTF) ... John Scott
RED LANTERNS ... Stavros Xarchakos
RED LIGHT ... Dimitri Tiomkin†
RED LINE 7000 ... Nelson Riddle†
RED LION ... Masaru Sato
RED MANTLE, THE ... Marc Fredericks
RED MOUNTAIN ... Franz Waxman†
RED PONY, THE ... Aaron Copland
RED PONY, THE (TF) ... ☆ Jerry Goldsmith
RED RIVER ... Dimitri Tiomkin†
RED RIVER (TF) ... Ken Wannberg
RED RIVER RANGE ... William Lava†
RED RIVER RIDING HOOD ... Paul Sawtell†
RED ROSE, THE ... Luis Bacalov
RED SCORPION ... Jay Chattaway
RED SHOES, THE ... ★★ Brian Easdale
RED SKIES OF MONTANA ... Sol Kaplan
RED SKIES OF MONTANA ... Lionel Newman†
RED SKY AT MORNING ... Billy Goldenberg
RED SONJA ... Ennio Morricone
RED SPIDER, THE (TF) ... Artie Kane
RED STALLION, THE ... Frederick Hollander†
RED SUN ... Maurice Jarre
RED SUNDOWN ... Hans J. Salter
RED SURF ... Sasha Matson
RED TENT, THE ... Ennio Morricone
RED TOMAHAWK ... Jimmie Haskell
RED WAGON ... W. Franke Harling†
RED ZONE ... Gabriel Yared
RED-LIGHT STING, THE (TF) ... James Di Pasquale
REDEEMER, THE ... David Raksin
REDEEMER...SON OF SATAN!, THE ... Philo Gallo
REDEEMER...SON OF SATAN!, THE ... Clem Vicari
REDHEAD AND THE COWBOY, THE ... David Buttolph†
REDHEAD FROM WYOMING, THE ... Herman Stein
REDNECK ... John Cacavas
REDS ... Dave Grusin
REDS ... Stephen Sondheim
REDSKIN ... John S. Zamecnik†
REFLECTION OF FEAR, A ... Fred Myrow
REFLECTIONS OF MURDER (TF) ... Billy Goldenberg
REFORM SCHOOL GIRL ... Ronald Stein†
REFORM SCHOOL GIRLS ... Tedra Gabriel

REFORMER AND THE REDHEAD, THE ... David Raksin
REGAIN ... Arthur Honegger†
REHEARSAL FOR MURDER (TF) ... Billy Goldenberg
REIGN OF TERROR ... Sol Kaplan
REILLY - ACE OF SPIES (MS) ... Harry Rabinowitz
REINCARNATION OF PETER PROUD, THE ... Jerry Goldsmith
REIVERS, THE ... ★ John Williams
REJUVENATOR, THE ... Larry Juris
RELENTLESS ... Jay Chattaway
RELENTLESS (TF) ... John Cacavas
RELUCTANT ASTRONAUT, THE ... Vic Mizzy
RELUCTANT DRAGON (AF), THE ... Frank Churchill†
RELUCTANT HEROES, THE (TF) ... Frank De Vol
RELUCTANT SAINT, THE ... Nino Rota†
RELUCTANT WIDOW, THE ... Allan Gray†
REMAINS TO BE SEEN ... Jeff Alexander†
REMAKE ... Georges Van Parys†
REMARKABLE ANDREW, THE ... Victor Young†
REMARKABLE MR. KIPPS, THE ... William Alwyn†
REMARKABLE MR. PENNYPACKER, THE ... Leigh Harline†
REMBRANDT: FECIT 1668 ... Laurens Van Rooyen
REMEMBER LAST NIGHT? ... Franz Waxman†
REMEMBER MY NAME ... Alberta Hunter
REMEMBER THE NIGHT ... Frederick Hollander†
REMEMBER WHEN (TF) ... George Aliceson Tipton
REMEMBER? ... Edward Ward†
REMEMBRANCE OF LOVE (TF) ... William Goldstein
REMO WILLIAMS: THE ADVENTURE BEGINS ... Craig Safan
REMOTE CONTROL ... Peter Bernstein
RENATA ... Armando Trovajoli
RENDEZ-VOUS A BRAY ... Frederic Devreese
RENDEZ-VOUS DE JUILLET ... Jean Wiener†
RENDEZVOUS ... Philippe Sarde
RENDEZVOUS ... William Axt†
RENDEZVOUS 24 ... Emil Newman†
RENDEZVOUS HOTEL (TF) ... Jonathan Tunick
RENE LA CANNE ... Ennio Morricone
RENE THE CANE ... Ennio Morricone
RENEGADE RANGER, THE ... Roy Webb†
RENEGADES ... Michael Kamen
RENEGADES OF THE WEST ... Max Steiner†
RENEGADES, THE (TF) ... Joseph Conlan
RENEGADES, THE (TF) ... Barry De Vorzon
RENO ... Roy Webb†
RENT-A-COP ... Jerry Goldsmith
RENTADICK ... Carl Davis
RENTED LIPS ... Van Dyke Parks
REPEAT PERFORMANCE ... George Antheil†
REPENTANCE ... Nana Djanelidz
REPO MAN ... Steven Hufsteter
REPO MAN ... Tito Larriva
REPORT TO THE COMMISSIONER ... Elmer Bernstein
REPTILE, THE ... Don Banks
REPTILICUS ... Les Baxter
REPULSION ... Chico Hamilton
REQUIEM FOR A GUNFIGHTER ... Ronald Stein†
REQUIEM FOR A HEAVYWEIGHT ... Laurence Rosenthal
REQUIEM FOR A VILLAGE (FD) ... David Fanshawe
REQUIEM PER UN GRINGO ... Angelo Francesco Lavagnino†
REQUIESCANT ... Riz Ortolani
RESCUE FROM GILLIGAN'S ISLAND (TF) ... Gerald Fried
RESCUE, THE ... Bruce Broughton
RESCUERS, THE (AF) ... Artie Butler
RESPECTFUL PROSTITUTE, THE ... Georges Auric†
RESTING PLACE (TF) ... Paul Chihara
RESTLESS ... Gil Melle
RESTLESS NATIVES ... Stuart Adamson
RESURRECTION ... Maurice Jarre
RESURRECTION ... Dimitri Tiomkin†
RETENEZ MOIL...OU JE FAIS UN MALHEUR ... Vladimir Cosma
RETOUR A LAUBE ... Paul Misraki†
RETOUR A NEW YORK (FD) ... Michel Legrand
RETREAT, HELL! ... William Lava†
RETRIBUTION ... Alan Howarth
RETURN FROM THE ASHES ... John Dankworth
RETURN FROM THE SEA ... Paul Dunlap
RETURN FROM WITCH MOUNTAIN ... Lalo Schifrin
RETURN OF A MAN CALLED HORSE, THE ... Laurence Rosenthal
RETURN OF CAPTAIN INVINCIBLE, THE ... William Motzig
RETURN OF CASANOVA, THE ... Riz Ortolani
RETURN OF CHARLIE CHAN, THE (TF) ... Robert Prince
RETURN OF COUNT YORGA, THE ... Bill Marx
RETURN OF DESPERADO, THE (TF) ... Michel Colombier
RETURN OF DON CAMILLO, THE ... Alessandro Cicognini†
RETURN OF DR. X, THE ... Bernhard Kaun†
RETURN OF DRACULA, THE ... Gerald Fried
RETURN OF FRANK CANNON, THE (TF) ... Bruce Broughton
RETURN OF FRANK JAMES, THE ... David Buttolph†
RETURN OF GIANT MAJIN ... Akira Ifukube
RETURN OF GILBERT & SULLIVAN, THE ... Lyn Murray†
RETURN OF JACK SLADE, THE ... Paul Dunlap
RETURN OF JESSE JAMES, THE ... Albert Glasser
RETURN OF JOE FORRESTER, THE (TF) ... Richard Markowitz
RETURN OF MARCUS WELBY, M.D., THE (TF) ... Leonard Rosenman
RETURN OF MAXIM GORKY, THE ... Dmitri Shostakovitch†
RETURN OF MICKEY SPILLANE'S MIKE HAMMER, THE (TF) ... Earle Hagen
RETURN OF MONTE CRISTO, THE ... Lucien Moraweck†
RETURN OF MR. MOTO, THE ... Douglas Gamley
RETURN OF OCTOBER, THE ... George Duning
RETURN OF RIN TIN TIN, THE ... Leo Erdody†
RETURN OF SAM McCLOUD, THE (TF) ... Steve Dorff
RETURN OF SHERLOCK HOLMES, THE (TF) ... Ken Thorne
RETURN OF SWAMP THING, THE ... Chuck Cirino
RETURN OF THE BEVERLY HILLBILLIES (TF) ... Billy May
RETURN OF THE FLY ... Bert A. Shefter
RETURN OF THE FLY ... Paul Sawtell†
RETURN OF THE FRONTIERSMAN ... David Buttolph†
RETURN OF THE GUNFIGHTER (TF) ... Hans J. Salter
RETURN OF THE INCREDIBLE HULK, THE (TF) ... Joe Harnell
RETURN OF THE JEDI, THE ... ★ John Williams
RETURN OF THE KING, THE (ATF) ... Maury Laws
RETURN OF THE LIVING DEAD PART II ... J. Peter Robinson
RETURN OF THE LIVING DEAD, THE ... Matt Clifford
RETURN OF THE MAN FROM U.N.C.L.E., THE (TF) ... Gerald Fried
RETURN OF THE MOD SQUAD, THE (TF) ... Shorty Rogers
RETURN OF THE MOD SQUAD, THE (TF) ... Mark Snow
RETURN OF THE MUSKETEERS, THE ... Jean-Claude Petit
RETURN OF THE PINK PANTHER ... Henry Mancini
RETURN OF THE REBELS (TF) ... Michael Melvoin
RETURN OF THE SCARLET PIMPERNEL, THE ... Arthur Benjamin†
RETURN OF THE SECAUCUS SEVEN ... Mason Daring
RETURN OF THE SEVEN ... ★ Elmer Bernstein
RETURN OF THE SHAGGY DOG, THE (TF) ... David Bell
RETURN OF THE SIX MILLION DOLLAR MAN & THE BIONIC WOMAN (TF) ... Marvin Hamlisch
RETURN OF THE SOLDIER ... Richard Rodney Bennett
RETURN OF THE TALL BLONDE MAN WITH ONE BLACK SHOE ... Vladimir Cosma
RETURN OF THE TERROR ... Bernhard Kaun†
RETURN OF THE TEXAN ... Sol Kaplan
RETURN OF THE TEXAN ... Lionel Newman†
RETURN OF THE VAMPIRE, THE ... Mario Castelnuovo-Tedesco†
RETURN OF THE WORLD'S GREATEST DETECTIVE, THE (TF) ... Richard DeBenedictis
RETURN OF WILDFIRE, THE ... Albert Glasser
RETURN TO BOGGY CREEK ... Darrell Deck
RETURN TO EDEN (MS) ... Brian May
RETURN TO GREEN ACRES ... Dan Foliart
RETURN TO HORROR HIGH ... Stacy Widelitz
RETURN TO MACON COUNTY ... Robert O. Ragland
RETURN TO MAYBERRY (TF) ... Earle Hagen
RETURN TO OZ ... David Shire
RETURN TO PARADISE ... Dimitri Tiomkin†
RETURN TO PEYTON PLACE ... Franz Waxman†
RETURN TO SNOWY RIVER ... Bruce Rowland
RETURN TO THE BELOVED ... Antoine Duhamel
RETURN TO TREASURE ISLAND ... Paul Sawtell†
RETURN, THE ... Marc Wilkinson
RETURN, THE ... Dan Wyman
RETURN, THE (TF) ... Donal Lunny
RETURNING HOME (TF) ... Ken Lauber
RETURNING, THE ... Harry Manfredini
REUBEN, REUBEN ... Billy Goldenberg
REUNION ... Philippe Sarde
REUNION ... Emil Newman†
REUNION (TF) ... George Romanis
REUNION AT FAIRBOROUGH (CTF) ... Nigel Hess
REUNION IN FRANCE ... Franz Waxman†
REUNION IN VIENNA ... William Axt†
REVEALING EVIDENCE (TF) ... James Newton Howard
REVENGE ... Jack Nitzsche
REVENGE (TF) ... Dominic Frontiere
REVENGE FOR A RAPE (TF) ... Jerrold Immel
REVENGE OF AL CAPONE, THE (TF) ... Craig Safan
REVENGE OF FRANKENSTEIN, THE ... Leonardo Salzedo
REVENGE OF MECHA-GODZILLA ... Akira Ifukube
REVENGE OF THE CREATURE ... Herman Stein
REVENGE OF THE CREATURE ... William Lava†
REVENGE OF THE MYSTERIONS FROM MARS ... Barry Gray
REVENGE OF THE NERDS ... Thomas Newman
REVENGE OF THE NINJA ... W. Michael Lewis
REVENGE OF THE NINJA ... Laurin Rinder
REVENGE OF THE NINJA ... Robert J. Walsh
REVENGE OF THE PINK PANTHER ... Henry Mancini
REVENGE OF THE PIRATES ... Carlo Rustichelli
REVENGE OF THE SHOGUN WOMEN ... Robert J. Walsh
REVENGE OF THE STEPFORD WIVES (TF) ... Laurence Rosenthal
REVERSAL OF FORTUNE ... Mark Isham
REVOLT AT FORT LARAMIE ... Les Baxter
REVOLT OF GUNNER ASCH, THE ... Rolf Wilhelm
REVOLT OF MAMIE STOVER, THE ... Hugo Friedhofer†
REVOLT OF THE SLAVES, THE ... Angelo Francesco Lavagnino†
REVOLUTION ... John Corigliano
REVOLUTIONARY, THE ... Michael Small
REVOLVER ... Ennio Morricone
REWARD (TF) ... Barry De Vorzon
REWARD, THE ... Elmer Bernstein
REX STOUT'S NERO WOLFE (TF) ... John Addison
RHAPSODY ... Steve Dorff
RHAPSODY ... John Green†
RHAPSODY IN BLUE ... ★ Max Steiner†
RHINEMANN EXCHANGE, THE (MS) ... Michel Colombier
RHINESTONE ... Mike Post
RHINO! ... Lalo Schifrin
RHODES OF AFRICA ... Hubert Bath†
RHOSYN A RHITH ... Michael Storey
RHUBARB ... Nathan Van Cleave†
RICE GIRL ... Angelo Francesco Lavagnino†
RICH AND FAMOUS ... Georges Delerue
RICH ARE ALWAYS WITH US, THE ... W. Franke Harling†
RICH GIRL ... Barry Fasman
RICH GIRL ... Dana Walden
RICH KIDS ... Craig Doerge
RICH MAN, POOR GIRL ... William Axt†
RICH MAN, POOR MAN (MS) ... ☆☆ Alex North
RICH MEN, SINGLE WOMEN (TF) ... Charles Fox
RICH, YOUNG AND PRETTY ... Nicholas Brodzsky†
RICH, YOUNG AND PRETTY ... David Rose†
RICHARD III ... Sir William Walton†
RICHARD PRYOR LIVE ON THE SUNSET STRIP ... Harry Betts
RICHARD'S THINGS ... Georges Delerue
RICHEST CAT IN THE WORLD, THE (TF) ... Peter Bernstein
RICHEST GIRL IN THE WORLD, THE ... Max Steiner†
RICHEST MAN IN THE WORLD: THE ARISTOTLE ONASSIS STORY, THE (TF) ... Billy Goldenberg
RICHIE BROCKELMAN: MISSING 24 HOURS (TF) ... Mike Post
RICHIE BROCKELMAN: MISSING 24 HOURS (TF) ... Pete Carpenter†
RICKY I ... Joel Goldsmith
RIDDLE OF THE SANDS, THE ... Howard Blake
RIDE A WILD PONY ... John Addison
RIDE A WILD PONY ... Ron Goodwin
RIDE BACK, THE ... Frank De Vol
RIDE BEYOND VENGEANCE ... Richard Markowitz
RIDE CLEAR OF DIABLO ... Herman Stein
RIDE IN THE WHIRLWIND ... Robert Drasnin
RIDE LONESOME ... Heinz Roemheld†

RIDE ON, VAQUERO ..... David Raksin
RIDE OUT FOR REVENGE ..... Leith Stevens†
RIDE THE HIGH COUNTRY ..... George Bassman
RIDE THE PINK HORSE ..... Frank Skinner†
RIDE THE WILD SURF ..... Stu Phillips
RIDE 'EM COWBOY ..... Frank Skinner†
RIDE, VAQUERO! ..... Bronislau Kaper†
RIDER IN THE RAIN ..... Francis Lai
RIDERS TO THE STARS ..... Harry Sukman†
RIDING ON AIR ..... Arthur Morton
RIDING SHOTGUN ..... David Buttolph†
RIDING THE EDGE ..... Michael Gibbs
RIEL ..... Matthew McCauley
RIFF RAFF ..... Edward Ward†
RIFFRAFF ..... Roy Webb†
RIFIFI ..... Georges Auric†
RIFIFI IM BEIRUT ..... Ennio Morricone
RIFIFI IN TOKYO ..... Georges Delerue
RIGGED ..... Brian Banks
RIGGED ..... Anthony Marinelli
RIGHT CROSS ..... David Raksin
RIGHT HAND MAN, THE ..... Allan Zavod
RIGHT OF THE PEOPLE, THE (TF) ..... Billy Goldenberg
RIGHT OF WAY (CTF) ..... Brad Fiedel
RIGHT STUFF, THE ..... ★★ Bill Conti
RIGHT TO DIE (TF) ..... Brad Fiedel
RIGHT TO KILL? (TV) ..... Paul Chihara
RIGHT TO LOVE, THE ..... W. Franke Harling†
RIGHT TO ROMANCE, THE ..... Max Steiner†
RIKKY AND PETE ..... Phil Judd
RIKKY AND PETE ..... Eddie Raynor
RING AROUND THE MOON ..... Richard Addinsell†
RING OF BRIGHT WATER ..... Frank Cordell†
RING OF FEAR ..... Emil Newman†
RING OF PASSION (TF) ..... Bill Conti
RING, THE ..... Herschel Burke Gilbert
RINGER, THE ..... Malcolm Arnold
RINGO IL VOLTO DELLA VENDETTA ..... Francesco De Masi
RINGO, DOVE VAI? ..... Bruno Nicolai
RIO ..... Charles Previn†
RIO BRAVO ..... Dimitri Tiomkin†
RIO CONCHOS ..... Jerry Goldsmith
RIO GRANDE ..... Victor Young†
RIO LOBO ..... Jerry Goldsmith
RIO RITA ..... Max Steiner†
RIO RITA ..... Herbert Stothart†
RIOT ..... Christopher Komeda†
RIOT IN CELL BLOCK 11 ..... Herschel Burke Gilbert
RIOT IN JUVENILE PRISON ..... Emil Newman†
RIP-OFF, THE ..... Paolo Vasile
RIPTIDE ..... Herbert Stothart†
RISCATTO ..... Nino Rota†
RISE AND FALL OF LEGS DIAMOND, THE ..... Leonard Rosenman
RISE AND RISE OF MICHAEL RIMMER, THE ..... John Cameron
RISE AND SHINE ..... Emil Newman†
RISING STORM ..... Julian Laxton
RISKY BUSINESS ..... Tangerine Dream
RITA HAYWORTH: THE LOVE GODDESS (TF) ..... Lalo Schifrin
RITA, SUE AND BOB, TOO ..... Michael Kamen
RITZ, THE ..... Ken Thorne
RIUSCIRANNO I NOSTRI EROI A TROVARE L'AMICO MISTERIOSAMENTE SCOMPARSO IN AFRICA? ..... Armando Trovajoli
RIVALS ..... Peter Matz
RIVER BIGER, THE ..... War
RIVER CHANGES, THE ..... Roy Webb†
RIVER GANG, THE ..... Hans J. Salter
RIVER OF GOLD (TF) ..... Fred Steiner
RIVER OF NO RETURN ..... Cyril J. Mockridge†
RIVER RAT, THE ..... Mike Post
RIVER'S EDGE, THE ..... Jurgen Knieper
RIVER, THE ..... ★ John Williams
RIVER, THE (D) ..... Virgil Thomson†
RIVERBEND ..... Paul Loomis
RIVKIN, BOUNTY HUNTER (TF) ..... Arthur B. Rubinstein
ROAD AGENT ..... Hans J. Salter
ROAD BACK, THE ..... Dimitri Tiomkin†
ROAD GAMES ..... Brian May
ROAD HOUSE ..... Cyril J. Mockridge†
ROAD RACERS ..... Richard Markowitz
ROAD RAIDERS, THE (TF) ..... Stu Phillips
ROAD TO GLORY ..... Louis Silvers†
ROAD TO HONG KONG, THE ..... Robert Farnon
ROAD TO RIO, THE ..... ★ Robert Emmett Dolan†
ROAD TO UTOPIA ..... Leigh Harline†
ROAD TO VICTORY ..... Vladimir Horunzhy
ROAD WARRIOR, THE ..... Brian May
ROADHOUSE ..... Michael Kamen
ROADHOUSE 66 ..... Gary Scott
ROADIE ..... Craig Hundley
ROANOAK (TF) ..... Paul Chihara
ROAR ..... Dominic Frontiere
ROAR OF THE DRAGON ..... Max Steiner†
ROARING CITY ..... Bert A. Shefter
ROBBER'S ROOST ..... Paul Dunlap
ROBBERY UNDER ARMS ..... Matyas Seiber
ROBE, THE ..... Alfred Newman†
ROBERT ET ROBERT ..... Francis Lai
ROBERT KENNEDY AND HIS TIMES (TF) ..... Fred Karlin
ROBERTA ..... Max Steiner†
ROBIN AND MARIAN ..... John Barry
ROBIN AND THE SEVEN HOODS ..... ★ Nelson Riddle†
ROBIN HOOD ..... Victor Schertzinger†
ROBIN HOOD (AF) ..... George Bruns
ROBIN HOOD AND THE PIRATES ..... Carlo Rustichelli
ROBIN HOOD OF EL DORADO, THE ..... Herbert Stothart†
ROBIN HOOD, L'INVINCIBILE ARCIERE ..... Bruno Nicolai
ROBINSON CRUSOE (TF) ..... Wilfred Josephs
ROBINSON CRUSOE ON MARS ..... Fred Steiner
ROBINSON CRUSOE ON MARS ..... Nathan Van Cleave†
ROBINSON UND SEINE WILDEN SKLAVINNEN ..... Bruno Nicolai
ROBOCOP ..... Basil Poledouris
ROBOCOP 2 ..... Leonard Rosenman
ROBOT MONSTER ..... Elmer Bernstein
ROBOTJOX ..... Frederic Talgorn
ROCCO AND HIS BROTHERS ..... Nino Rota†
ROCK & RULE (AF) ..... Patricia Cullen
ROCK ALL NIGHT ..... Ronald Stein†
ROCK HUDSON (TF) ..... Paul Chihara
ROCK PRETTY BABY ..... Henry Mancini
ROCK'N'ROLL MOM (TF) ..... Lee Ritenour
ROCK-A-BYE BABY ..... Walter Scharf
ROCKABILLY BABY ..... Paul Dunlap
ROCKABYE ..... Max Steiner†
ROCKABYE (TF) ..... Charles Bernstein
ROCKET GIBRALTAR ..... Andrew Powell
ROCKET MAN, THE ..... Lionel Newman†
ROCKETSHIP X-M ..... Ferde Grofe†
ROCKFORD FILES, THE (TF) ..... Pete Carpenter†
ROCKING HORSE WINNER, THE ..... William Alwyn†
ROCKY ..... Bill Conti
ROCKY HORROR PICTURE SHOW, THE ..... Richard Hartley
ROCKY II ..... Bill Conti
ROCKY III ..... Bill Conti
ROCKY IV ..... Vince DiCola
ROCKY MOUNTAIN ..... Max Steiner†
ROCKY V ..... Bill Conti
RODAN ..... Akira Ifukube
RODEO GIRL (TF) ..... Al DeLory
ROE VS. WADE (TF) W.G. ..... Snuffy Walden
ROGER LA HONTE ..... Antoine Duhamel
ROGER TOUHY, GANGSTER ..... Hugo Friedhofer†
ROGOPAG ..... Carlo Rustichelli
ROGUE COP ..... Jeff Alexander†
ROGUE SONG, THE ..... Herbert Stothart†
ROGUE SONG, THE ..... Dimitri Tiomkin†
ROGUE'S REGIMENT ..... Daniele Amfitheatrof†
ROGUES OF SHERWOOD FOREST ..... Arthur Morton
ROGUES OF SHERWOOD FOREST ..... Heinz Roemheld†
ROLL OF THUNDER, HEAR MY CRY (TF) ..... Fred Karlin
ROLL, FREDDY, ROLL! (TF) ..... Jack Elliott
ROLL, FREDDY, ROLL! (TF) ..... Allyn Ferguson
ROLLER AND THE VIOLIN, THE ..... Vyecheslav Ovchinnikov
ROLLER BOOGIE ..... Bob Esty
ROLLER BOOGIE ..... Craig Safan
ROLLERBALL ..... Andre Previn
ROLLERCOASTER ..... Lalo Schifrin
ROLLING THUNDER ..... Barry De Vorzon
ROLLOVER ..... Michael Small
ROMA BENE ..... Luis Bacalov
ROMA, CITTA LIBERA ..... Nino Rota†
ROMAN HOLIDAY ..... Georges Auric†
ROMAN HOLIDAY (TF) ..... Mark Snow
ROMAN SPRING OF MRS. STONE, THE ..... Richard Addinsell†
ROMANCE IN MANHATTAN ..... Max Steiner†
ROMANCE IN THE RAIN ..... Edward Ward†
ROMANCE OF ROSY RIDGE, THE ..... George Bassman
ROMANCE ON THE ORIENT EXPRESS (TF) ..... Allyn Ferguson
ROMANCING THE STONE ..... Alan Silvestri
ROMANOFF AND JULIET ..... Mario Nascimbene
ROMANTIC AGONY, THE ..... Ennio Morricone
ROMANTIC COMEDY ..... Marvin Hamlisch
ROMANTIC ENGLISHWOMAN, THE ..... Richard Hartley
ROME 11 O'CLOCK ..... Mario Nascimbene
ROME ADVENTURE ..... Max Steiner†
ROME LIKE CHICAGO ..... Ennio Morricone
ROME LIKE CHICAGO ..... Bruno Nicolai
ROME-O AND JULIE 8 IN OUTER SPACE (ATF) ..... Patricia Cullen
ROMEO AND JULIET ..... Bruno Nicolai
ROMEO AND JULIET ..... Nino Rota†
ROMEO AND JULIET ..... Herbert Stothart†
ROMERO ..... Gabriel Yared
ROMULUS AND THE SABINES ..... Carlo Rustichelli
RONA JAFFE'S MAZES AND MONSTERS (TF) ..... Hagood Hardy
ROOF, THE ..... Alessandro Cicognini†
ROOFTOPS ..... Michael Kamen
ROOFTOPS ..... David A. Stewart
ROOGIE'S RUMP ..... Lehman Engel†
ROOKIE COP, THE ..... Roy Webb†
ROOKIE, THE ..... Paul Dunlap
ROOKIES, THE (TF) ..... Elmer Bernstein
ROOM 43 ..... Kenneth V. Jones
ROOM AT THE TOP ..... Mario Nascimbene
ROOM FOR ONE MORE ..... Max Steiner†
ROOM SERVICE ..... Roy Webb†
ROOM UPSTAIRS, THE (TF) ..... Robert Folk
ROOM WITH A VIEW, A ..... Richard Robbins
ROOMMATES ..... Jonathan Hannah
ROOSTER (TF) ..... Stu Phillips
ROOSTER COGBURN ..... Laurence Rosenthal
ROOTS (MS) ..... ☆☆ Gerald Fried
ROOTS (MS) ..... ☆☆ Quincy Jones
ROOTS IN THE EARTH (D) ..... Paul Bowles
ROOTS OF HEAVEN, THE ..... Malcolm Arnold
ROOTS: THE GIFT (TF) ..... Gerald Fried
ROOTS: THE NEXT GENERATION (MS) ..... Gerald Fried
ROOTS: THE NEXT GENERATIONS (MS) ..... Gerald Fried
ROPE ..... David Buttolph†
ROPE OF SAND ..... Franz Waxman†
ROSA LUXEMBOURG ..... Nicolas Economou
ROSALIE ..... Herbert Stothart†
ROSALIE GOES SHOPPING ..... Bob Telson
ROSARY MURDERS, THE ..... Bobby Laurel
ROSARY MURDERS, THE ..... Don Sebesky
ROSE ..... Jean Wiener†
ROSE AND THE JACKAL, THE (CTF) ..... Michael J. Lewis
ROSE GARDEN, THE ..... Egisto Macchi
ROSE MARIE ..... Herbert Stothart†
ROSE TATTOO, THE ..... ★ Alex North
ROSEANNA McCOY ..... David Buttolph†
ROSEANNA McCOY ..... Hugo Friedhofer†
ROSEBUD BEACH HOTEL, THE ..... Jay Chattaway
ROSELAND ..... Michael Gibson
ROSEMARY'S BABY ..... Christopher Komeda†
ROSES ARE FOR THE RICH (TF) ..... Arthur B. Rubinstein
ROSIE! ..... Lyn Murray†
ROSIE: THE ROSEMARY CLOONEY STORY (TF) ..... Frank Ortega
ROSMUNDA E ALBOINO ..... Carlo Rustichelli
ROSOLINO PATERNO, SOLDATO ..... Carlo Rustichelli
ROUGH CUT ..... Nelson Riddle†
ROUGH NIGHT IN JERICHO ..... Don Costa
ROUGHLY SPEAKING ..... Max Steiner†
ROUGHNECKS (TF) ..... Jerrold Immel
ROUGHSHOD ..... Roy Webb†
ROUND MIDNIGHT ..... ★★ Herbie Hancock
ROUNDERS, THE ..... Jeff Alexander†
ROUSTERS, THE (TF) ..... Pete Carpenter†
ROVER, THE ..... Ennio Morricone
ROXANNE ..... Bruce Smeaton
ROXANNE: THE PRIZE PULITZER (TF) ..... Robert Alcivar
ROXIE HART ..... Alfred Newman†
ROYAL AFRICAN RIFLES, THE ..... Paul Dunlap
ROYAL DIVORCE, A ..... Anthony Collins†
ROYAL FLASH ..... Ken Thorne
ROYAL HUNT OF THE SUN, THE ..... Marc Wilkinson
ROYAL REGATTA ..... Vladimir Horunzhy
ROYAL ROMANCE OF CHARLES AND DIANA, THE (TF) ..... David Palmer

S

INDEX OF FILM TITLES

SLAYGROUND ... Colin Towns
SLEEP WELL, MY LOVE ... Alfi Kabiljo
SLEEPER ... Woody Allen
SLEEPING BEAUTY (AF) ... ★ George Bruns
SLEEPING CAR MURDERS, THE ... Michel Magne†
SLEEPING CAR TO TRIESTE ... Benjamin Frankel†
SLEEPING CITY, THE ... Frank Skinner†
SLEEPING TIGER, THE ... Malcolm Arnold
SLEEPY LAGOON ... Walter Scharf
SLENDER THREAD, THE ... Quincy Jones
SLEUTH ... ★ John Addison
SLICE OF LIFE, A ... Brian May
SLIDE, KELLY SLIDE ... William Axt†
SLIGHTLY DANGEROUS ... Bronislau Kaper†
SLIGHTLY FRENCH ... George Duning
SLIGHTLY HONORABLE ... Werner Janssen
SLIGHTLY SCANDALOUS ... Milton Rosen
SLIGHTLY TEMPTED ... Hans J. Salter
SLIM ... Max Steiner†
SLIM CARTER ... Herman Stein
SLIPPER AND THE ROSE: THE STORY
OF CINDERELLA, THE ... ★ Angela Morley
SLIPSTREAM ... Elmer Bernstein
SLIPSTREAM ... Van Morrison
SLITHER ... Tom McIntosh
SLOW BURN (CTF) ... Loek Dikker
SLOW DANCING IN THE BIG CITY ... Bill Conti
SLOW MOTION ... Alfi Kabiljo
SLUGGER'S WIFE, THE ... Patrick Williams
SLUMBER PARTY '57 ... Miles Goodman
SLUMBER PARTY MASSACRE II ... Robert Cox
SLUMBER PARTY MASSACRE, THE ... Ralph Jones
SMALL BACK ROOM, THE ... Brian Easdale
SMALL CIRCLE OF FRIENDS, A ... Jim Steinman
SMALL KILLING, A (TF) ... Fred Werner
SMALL MIRACLE, THE (TF) ... Ernest Gold
SMALL SACRIFICES (TF) ... Peter Manning Robinson
SMALL TOWN GIRL ... Andre Previn
SMALL TOWN GIRL ... Herbert Stothart†
SMALL TOWN GIRL ... Edward Ward†
SMALL TOWN IN TEXAS, A ... Charles Bernstein
SMALLEST SHOW ON EARTH, THE ... William Alwyn†
SMART GIRLS DON'T TALK ... David Buttolph†
SMART WOMAN ... Louis Gruenberg†
SMARTEST GIRL IN TOWN, THE ... Nathaniel Shilkret†
SMASH-UP ON INTERSTATE 5 (TF) ... Bill Conti
SMASH-UP, THE STORY OF
A WOMAN ... Daniele Amfitheatrof†
SMASHING THE CRIME
SYNDICATE ... Nelson Riddle†
SMASHING TIME ... John Addison
SMIC, SMAC, SMOC ... Francis Lai
SMILE ... Daniel Osborn
SMILES OF A SUMMER NIGHT ... Eric Nordgren
SMILEY ... William Alwyn†
SMILEY'S PEOPLE (MS) ... Patrick Gowers
SMILIN' THROUGH ... William Axt†
SMILIN' THROUGH ... Herbert Stothart†
SMILING GHOST, THE ... Bernhard Kaun†
SMILING GHOST, THE ... William Lava†
SMITH! ... Robert F. Brunner
SMOKE IN THE POTATO FIELDS ... Zdenek Liska
SMOKEY & THE BANDIT - PART 3 ... Larry Cansler
SMOKEY AND THE BANDIT ... Bill Justis
SMOKEY AND THE BANDIT ... Jerry Reed
SMOKEY AND THE BANDIT II ... Snuff Garrett
SMOKY ... David Raksin
SMOKY ... Leith Stevens†
SMOKY MOUNTAIN
CHRISTMAS, A (TF) ... Dana Kaproff
SMOOTH AS SILK ... Ernest Gold
SMOOTH TALK ... Russ Kunkel
SMOOTH TALK ... Bill Payne
SMOOTH TALK ... George Massenberg
SMORGASBORD ... Morton Stevens
SMUGGLER'S GOLD ... Mischa Bakaleinikoff †
SMUGGLERS, THE (TF) ... Lyn Murray†
SMURFS AND THE MAGIC
FLUTE, THE (AF) ... Michel Legrand
SNAKE PIT AND THE
PENDULUM, THE ... Peter Thomas
SNAKE PIT, THE ... ★ Alfred Newman†
SNAPSHOT ... Brian May
SNATCHED (TF) ... Randy Edelman
SNIPER'S RIDGE ... Richard LaSalle
SNIPER, THE ... George Antheil†
SNOW DEVILS ... Angelo Francesco Lavagnino†
SNOW GHOST ... Akira Ifukube
SNOW GOOSE, THE (TF) ... ☆ Carl Davis
SNOW KILL (CTF) ... Sylvester Levay
SNOW QUEEN, THE (AF) ... Frank Skinner†

SNOW WHITE AND THE
SEVEN DWARFS (AF) ... ★ Frank Churchill†
SNOW WHITE AND THE
SEVEN DWARFS (AF) ... ★ Leigh Harline†
SNOW WHITE AND THE
SEVEN DWARFS (AF) ... ★ Paul J. Smith†
SNOW WHITE AND THE
THREE STOOGES ... Lyn Murray†
SNOWBALL EXPRESS, THE ... Robert F. Brunner
SNOWBEAST (TF) ... Robert Prince
SNOWFIRE ... Albert Glasser
SNOWS OF KILIMANJARO, THE ... Bernard Herrmann†
SO BIG ... Max Steiner†
SO DARK THE NIGHT ... Hugo Friedhofer†
SO DEAR TO MY HEART ... Paul J. Smith†
SO ENDS OUR NIGHT ... ★ Louis Gruenberg†
SO EVIL MY LOVE ... William Alwyn†
SO EVIL MY LOVE ... Victor Young†
SO FINE ... Ennio Morricone
SO GOES MY LOVE ... Hans J. Salter
SO LONG AT THE FAIR ... Benjamin Frankel†
SO PROUDLY WE HAIL (TF) ... Gil Melle
SO PROUDLY WE HAIL! ... Miklos Rozsa
SO RED THE ROSE ... W. Franke Harling†
SO THIS IS LOVE ... Max Steiner†
SO THIS IS NEW YORK ... Dimitri Tiomkin†
SO THIS IS PARIS ... Herman Stein
SO THIS IS PARIS ... Henry Mancini
SO WELL REMEMBERED ... Hanns Eisler†
SO YOU WON'T TALK ... Leigh Harline†
SOCIETY LAWYER ... Edward Ward†
SOCRATES ... Mario Nascimbene
SODOM AND GOMORRAH ... Miklos Rozsa
SOFT SKIN, THE ... Georges Delerue
SOHO GORILLA ... Peter Thomas
SOIL (FD) ... Hanns Eisler†
SOL MADRID ... Lalo Schifrin
SOLA ... Jorge Calandrelli
SOLAMENTE NERO ... Stelvio Cipriani
SOLANG 'ES HUBSCHE
MADCHEN GIBT ... Allan Gray†
SOLARBABIES ... Maurice Jarre
SOLARIS ... Eduard Artemyev
SOLDIER AND THE LADY, THE ... Nathaniel Shilkret†
SOLDIER BLUE ... Roy Budd
SOLDIER IN THE RAIN ... Henry Mancini
SOLDIER OF FORTUNE ... Hugo Friedhofer†
SOLDIER OF ORANGE ... Rogier Van Otterloo†
SOLDIER'S STORY, A ... Herbie Hancock
SOLDIER'S TALE, A ... John Charles
SOLDIER, THE ... Tangerine Dream
SOLDIERS OF THE SOIL ... W. Franke Harling†
SOLDIERS THREE ... Adolph Deutsch†
SOLE SURVIVOR (TF) ... Paul Glass
SOLEIL DE PIERRE ... Michel Portal
SOLITARY MAN, THE (TF) ... Jack Elliott
SOLO CONTRO ROMA ... Armando Trovajoli
SOLOMON AND SHEBA ... Malcolm Arnold
SOLOMON AND SHEBA ... Mario Nascimbene
SOME CALL IT LOVING ... Richard Hazard
SOME CAME RUNNING ... Elmer Bernstein
SOME GIRLS ... James Newton Howard
SOME KIND OF A NUT ... Johnny Mandel
SOME KIND OF HERO ... Patrick Williams
SOME KIND OF WONDERFUL ... Stephen Hague
SOME KIND OF WONDERFUL ... John Musser
SOME LIKE IT HOT ... Adolph Deutsch†
SOMEBODY KILLED HER HUSBAND ... Alex North
SOMEBODY UP THERE LIKES ME ... Bronislau Kaper†
SOMEONE I TOUCHED (TF) ... Al Kasha
SOMEONE IS WATCHING ME (TF) ... Harry Sukman†
SOMEONE TO REMEMBER ... Walter Scharf
SOMEONE TO WATCH OVER ME ... Michael Kamen
SOMETHING ABOUT AMELIA (TF) ... ☆ Mark Snow
SOMETHING BIG ... Marvin Hamlisch
SOMETHING EVIL (TF) ... Wladimir Selinsky
SOMETHING FOR A
LONELY MAN (TF) ... Jack Marshall
SOMETHING FOR EVERYONE ... John Kander
SOMETHING FOR JOEY (TF) ... David Shire
SOMETHING FOR THE BIRDS ... Sol Kaplan
SOMETHING IN COMMON (TF) ... John Addison
SOMETHING IN THE WIND ... John Green†
SOMETHING IS CREEPING
IN THE DARK ... Angelo Francesco Lavagnino†
SOMETHING IS OUT THERE (TF) ... Sylvester Levay
SOMETHING MONEY CAN'T BUY ... Nino Rota†
SOMETHING OF VALUE ... Miklos Rozsa
SOMETHING SHORT OF PARADISE ... Mark Snow
SOMETHING SO RIGHT (TF) ... Charles Gross
SOMETHING SPECIAL ... David McHugh

SOMETHING TO HIDE ... Roy Budd
SOMETHING TO LIVE FOR ... Victor Young†
SOMETHING TO SHOUT ABOUT ... David Raksin
SOMETHING TO
SING ABOUT ... ★ Victor Schertzinger†
SOMETHING WICKED
THIS WAY COMES ... James Horner
SOMETHING WILD ... Laurie Anderson
SOMETHING WILD ... John Cale
SOMETHING WILD ... Aaron Copland
SOMETIMES A GREAT NOTION ... Henry Mancini
SOMEWHERE I'LL FIND YOU ... Bronislau Kaper†
SOMEWHERE IN THE NIGHT ... David Buttolph†
SOMEWHERE IN TIME ... John Barry
SOMEWHERE, SOMEONE ... Georges Delerue
SOMMARLEK ... Eric Nordgren
SON OF A WITCH ... Wolfgang Zeller†
SON OF ALI BABA ... Milton Rosen
SON OF ALI BABA ... Herman Stein
SON OF BLOB ... Mort Garson
SON OF DR. JEKYLL, THE ... Paul Sawtell†
SON OF DRACULA ... Hans J. Salter
SON OF DRACULA ... Charles Previn†
SON OF DRACULA ... Frank Skinner†
SON OF FLUBBER ... George Bruns
SON OF FRANKENSTEIN ... Frank Skinner†
SON OF FURY ... Alfred Newman†
SON OF GODZILLA ... Masaru Sato
SON OF KONG, THE ... Max Steiner†
SON OF LASSIE ... Herbert Stothart†
SON OF MONTE CRISTO, THE ... Edward Ward†
SON OF PALEFACE ... Lyn Murray†
SON OF ROBIN HOOD, THE ... Leighton Lucas†
SON OF SINBAD ... Victor Young†
SON OF THE BORDER ... Max Steiner†
SON RISE: A MIRACLE OF LOVE (TF) ... Gerald Fried
SON'S PROMISE, A (TF) ... J.A.C. Redford
SON-DAUGHTER, THE ... Herbert Stothart†
SONG ABOUT HEROES, A ... Hanns Eisler†
SONG IS BORN, A ... Hugo Friedhofer†
SONG OF
BERNADETTE, THE ... ★★ Alfred Newman†
SONG OF LOVE ... Bronislau Kaper†
SONG OF RUSSIA ... Herbert Stothart†
SONG OF SCHEHERAZADE ... Miklos Rozsa
SONG OF SURRENDER ... Victor Young†
SONG OF THE CITY ... William Axt†
SONG OF THE FLAME ... Edward Ward†
SONG OF THE OPEN ROAD ... ★ Charles Previn†
SONG OF THE SARONG ... Edward Ward†
SONG OF THE SOUTH ... ★ Daniele Amfitheatrof†
SONG OF THE SOUTH ... ★ Paul J. Smith†
SONG TO REMEMBER, A ... ★ Miklos Rozsa
SONG WITHOUT END ... Harry Sukman†
SONGWRITER ... Larry Cansler
SONNY AND JED ... Ennio Morricone
SONO FOTOGENICO ... Manuel De Sica
SONO STATO IO ... Armando Trovajoli
SONS AND LOVERS ... Mario Nascimbene
SONS OF KATIE ELDER, THE ... Elmer Bernstein
SOONER OR LATER (TF) ... Stephen Lawrence
SOPHIE'S CHOICE ... ★ Marvin Hamlisch
SOPHIE'S PLACE ... John Scott
SOPHISTICATED GENTS, THE (TF) ... Benny Golson
SORCERER ... Keith Jarrett
SORCERER ... Tangerine Dream
SORCERERS, THE ... Paul Ferris
SORCERESS ... Michel Portal
SORORITY GIRL ... Ronald Stein†
SORORITY HOUSE ... Roy Webb†
SORRELL AND SON (TF) ... Patrick Gowers
SORROWFUL JONES ... Robert Emmett Dolan†
SORRY, WRONG NUMBER ... Franz Waxman†
SORRY, WRONG NUMBER (CTF) ... Bruce Broughton
SORTIE DE SECOURS ... Philippe Sarde
SOTTO DIECI BANDIERE ... Nino Rota†
SOTTO IL SOLE DI ROMA ... Nino Rota†
SOTTO...SOTTO ... Paolo Conte
SOUL MAN ... Tom Scott
SOUL OF NIGGER CHARLEY, THE ... Don Costa
SOULS AT SEA ... ★ W. Franke Harling†
SOULS AT SEA ... ★ Milan Roder†
SOULS FOR SALE ... Albert Glasser
SOUND AND THE FURY, THE ... Alex North
SOUND OF ANGER, THE (TF) ... Pete Rugolo
SOUND OF FURY, THE ... Hugo Friedhofer†
SOUND OF MUSIC, THE ... ★★ Irwin Kostal
SOUND OFF ... George Duning
SOUNDER ... Taj Mahal
SOUP FOR ONE ... Bernard Edwards
SOUP FOR ONE ... Nile Rodgers

SOUP FOR ONE ... Johnny Mandel
SOUPCON ... Gerard Anfosso
SOURDOUGH ... Jerrold Immel
SOURSWEET ... Richard Hartley
SOUS LA TERREUR ... Michel Michelet†
SOUS LE CIEL DE PARIS ... Jean Wiener†
SOUS LE CIEL DE PROVENCE ... Paul Misraki†
SOUS LE SIGNE DU TAUREAU ... Jean Prodromides
SOUS LES YEUX D'OCCIDENT ... Georges Auric†
SOUTH BRONX HEROES ... Al Zima
SOUTH OF PAGO PAGO ... Edward Ward†
SOUTH OF RENO ... Nigel Holton
SOUTH OF ST. LOUIS ... Max Steiner†
SOUTH OF SUEZ ... Frederick Hollander†
SOUTH RIDING ... Richard Addinsell†
SOUTH SEA SINNER ... Walter Scharf
SOUTH SEA WOMAN ... David Buttolph†
SOUTH SEAS ADVENTURE ... Alex North
SOUTH TO KARANGA ... Hans J. Salter
SOUTH TO RENO ... Clive Wright
SOUTHERN COMFORT ... Ry Cooder
SOUTHERN STAR, THE ... Georges Garvarentz
SOUTHERNER, THE ... ★ Werner Janssen
SOUTHWEST PASSAGE ... Emil Newman†
SOUVENIRS D'EN FRANCE ... Philippe Sarde
SOUVENIRS PERDUS ... Joseph Kosma†
SOYLENT GREEN ... Gerald Fried
SOYLENT GREEN ... Fred Myrow
SPACE (MS) ... Tony Berg
SPACE (MS) ... Miles Goodman
SPACE CHILDREN, THE ... Nathan Van Cleave†
SPACE MOVIE, THE (FD) ... Mike Oldfield
SPACEBALLS ... John Morris
SPACEBOY ... Bebe Barron
SPACEBOY ... Louis Barron†
SPACECAMP ... John Williams
SPACED INVADERS ... David Russo
SPACEFLIGHT IC-1 ... Elisabeth Luytens†
SPACEHUNTER: ADVENTURES IN THE FORBIDDEN ZONE ... Elmer Bernstein
SPACEMEN AGAINST THE VAMPIRES FROM SPACE ... Chumei Watanabe
SPACESHIP ... David Spear
SPANISH AFFAIR ... Daniele Amfitheatrof†
SPANISH EARTH, THE ... Marc Blitzstein†
SPANISH EARTH, THE (D) ... Virgil Thomson†
SPANISH FLY ... Ron Goodwin
SPANISH MAIN, THE ... Hanns Eisler†
SPARKLE ... Curtis Mayfield
SPARKS: THE PRICE OF PASSION (TF) ... Robert Alcivar
SPARTACUS ... ★ Alex North
SPASMO ... Ennio Morricone
SPASMS ... Eric N. Robertson
SPAWN OF THE NORTH ... Dimitri Tiomkin†
SPEARFIELD'S DAUGHTER (MS) ... Irwin Fisch
SPECIAL DAY, A ... Armando Trovajoli
SPECIAL DELIVERY ... Lalo Schifrin
SPECIAL DELIVERY ... Bernhard Kaun†
SPECIAL DISPATCH ... Richard Addinsell†
SPECIAL EFFECTS ... Michael Minard
SPECIAL FRIENDSHIP, A (TF) ... Teo Macero
SPECIAL INVESTIGATOR ... Roy Webb†
SPECIAL OLYMPICS (TF) ... Peter Matz
SPECIAL PEOPLE (TF) ... Eric N. Robertson
SPECIALISTS, THE (TF) ... Billy May
SPECTER OF THE ROSE ... George Antheil†
SPECTRE (TF) ... John Cameron
SPEED ... Edward Ward†
SPEED CRAZY ... Richard LaSalle
SPEED ZONE ... David Wheatley
SPEEDWAY ... Jeff Alexander†
SPEEDWAY ... William Axt†
SPELL, THE (TF) ... Gerald Fried
SPELLBINDER ... Basil Poledouris
SPELLBOUND ... ★★ Miklos Rozsa
SPELLCASTER ... Nathan Wang
SPENCER'S MOUNTAIN ... Max Steiner†
SPETTERS ... Ton Scherpenzeel
SPHINX ... Michael J. Lewis
SPIDER AND THE FLY, THE ... Georges Auric†
SPIDER BABY ... Ronald Stein†
SPIDER WOMAN STRIKES BACK, THE ... Milton Rosen
SPIDER, THE ... Albert Glasser
SPIDER, THE ... David Buttolph†
SPIDER-MAN (TF) ... Dana Kaproff
SPIES LIKE US ... Elmer Bernstein
SPIES, LIES AND NAKED THIES (TF) ... Jack Elliott
SPIKE OF BENSONHURST ... Coati Mundi
SPIKER ... Jeff Barry
SPIKES GANG, THE ... Fred Karlin
SPIRAL ROAD, THE ... Jerry Goldsmith
SPIRAL STAIRCASE, THE ... David Lindup
SPIRAL STAIRCASE, THE ... Roy Webb†
SPIRAL, THE ... Wojciech Kilar
SPIRIT IS WILLING, THE ... Vic Mizzy
SPIRIT OF ST. LOUIS, THE ... Franz Waxman†
SPIRIT OF THE BEEHIVE, THE ... Luis De Pablo
SPIRIT OF THE EAGLE ... Parmer Fuller
SPIRIT, THE (TF) ... Barry Goldberg
SPIRITS OF THE DEAD ... Jean Prodromides
SPIRITS OF THE DEAD ... Nino Rota†
SPITFIRE ... Max Steiner†
SPITFIRE ... Sir William Walton†
SPLASH ... Lee Holdridge
SPLASH, TOO (TF) ... Joel McNeely
SPLATTER UNIVERSITY ... Chris Burke
SPLENDOR ... Alfred Newman†
SPLENDOR IN THE GRASS ... David Amram
SPLENDOR IN THE GRASS (TF) ... John Morris
SPLIT DECISIONS ... Basil Poledouris
SPLIT IMAGE ... Bill Conti
SPLIT SECOND TO AN EPITAPH (TF) ... Quincy Jones
SPLIT, THE ... Quincy Jones
SPOGLIATI, PROTESTA, UCCIDI ... Ennio Morricone
SPOILED CHILDREN ... Philippe Sarde
SPOILERS, THE ... Hans J. Salter
SPOILERS, THE ... Herman Stein
SPOILERS, THE ... Henry Mancini
SPONTANEOUS COMBUSTION ... Graeme Revell
SPOOK CASTLE IN SPESSART, THE ... Frederick Hollander†
SPOOK WHO SAT BY THE DOOR, THE ... Herbie Hancock
SPOONER (TF) ... Brian Banks
SPOONER (TF) ... Anthony Marinelli
SPORT PARADEF, THE ... Max Steiner†
SPORTING BLOOD ... Franz Waxman†
SPORTING CLUB, THE ... Michael Small
SPRAGGUE (TF) ... Lalo Schifrin
SPRING AND PORT WINE ... Douglas Gamley
SPRING BREAK ... Harry Manfredini
SPRING FEVER ... Fred Mollin
SPRING MADNESS ... William Axt†
SPRING OFFENSIVE ... Brian Easdale
SPRING PARADE ... Hans J. Salter
SPRINGFIELD RIFLE ... Max Steiner†
SPRINGTIME IN ITALY ... Nino Rota†
SPY HUNT ... Walter Scharf
SPY IN BLACK, THE ... Miklos Rozsa
SPY WHO CAME IN FROM THE COLD, THE ... Sol Kaplan
SPY WHO LOVED ME, THE ... ★ Marvin Hamlisch
SPY, THE ... Werner R. Heymann†
SQUARE DANCE ... Bruce Broughton
SQUARE JUNGLE, THE ... Heinz Roemheld†
SQUARE ROOT OF ZERO, THE ... Elliot Kaplan
SQUAW MAN, THE ... Herbert Stothart†
SQUEAKER, THE ... Miklos Rozsa
SQUEEZE, THE ... Miles Goodman
SQUEEZE, THE ... David Hentschel
SQUEEZE, THE ... Paolo Vasile
SQUIRM ... Robert Prince
SSSSSSS ... Patrick Williams
SST - DEATH FLIGHT (TF) ... John Cacavas
ST. ELMO'S FIRE ... David Foster
ST. IVES ... Lalo Schifrin
ST. VALENTINE'S DAY MASSACRE, THE ... Fred Steiner
STABLEMATES ... Edward Ward†
STACKING ... Patrick Gleeson
STAGE DOOR ... Roy Webb†
STAGE FRIGHT ... Leighton Lucas†
STAGE STRUCK ... Alex North
STAGE TO THUNDER ROCK ... Paul Dunlap
STAGECOACH ... Jerry Goldsmith
STAGECOACH ... ★★ Richard Hageman†
STAGECOACH ... ★★ W. Franke Harling†
STAGECOACH ... ★★ John Leipold†
STAGECOACH ... ★★ Leo Shuken†
STAGECOACH (TF) ... David Allan Coe
STAGECOACH (TF) ... Willie Nelson
STAGECOACH BUCKAROO ... Hans J. Salter
STAGECOACH TO FURY ... Paul Dunlap
STAIRCASE ... Dudley Moore
STAIRWAY TO HEAVEN ... Allan Gray†
STAKE-OUT ON DOPE STREET ... Richard Markowitz
STAKEOUT ... Arthur B. Rubinstein
STAKEOUT ... Ronald Stein†
STALAG 17 ... Franz Waxman†
STALK THE WILD CHILD (TF) ... John Rubinstein
STALKER ... Eduard Artemyev
STALKING MOON, THE ... Fred Karlin
STALLION ROAD ... Frederick Hollander†
STAND AND DELIVER ... Craig Safan
STAND BY ME ... Jack Nitzsche
STAND BY YOUR MAN (TF) ... Earle Hagen
STAND UP AND FIGHT ... William Axt†
STAND UP, VIRGIN SOLDIERS ... Ed Welch
STAND-IN ... Heinz Roemheld†
STANDING ROOM ONLY ... Robert Emmett Dolan†
STANDING TALL (TF) ... Richard Markowitz
STANLEY AND IRIS ... John Williams
STANLEY AND LIVINGSTONE ... David Raksin
STANLEY AND LIVINGSTONE ... David Buttolph†
STANZA 17-17: PALAZZO DEL TASSE-UFFICIO DELLA IMPOSTE ... Armando Trovajoli
STAR 80 ... Ralph Burns
STAR CHAMBER, THE ... Michael Small
STAR DUST ... David Buttolph†
STAR IN THE DUST ... Frank Skinner†
STAR IS BORN, A ... Rupert Holmes
STAR IS BORN, A ... Paul Williams
STAR IS BORN, A ... Max Steiner†
STAR MAKER, THE (TF) ... Jimmie Haskell
STAR OF INDIA ... Nino Rota†
STAR OF MIDNIGHT ... Max Steiner†
STAR OF THE SEASON, THE ... Wojciech Kilar
STAR SPANGLED RHYTHM ... ★ Robert Emmett Dolan†
STAR TREK II: THE WRATH OF KHAN ... James Horner
STAR TREK III: THE SEARCH FOR SPOCK ... James Horner
STAR TREK IV: THE VOYAGE HOME ... ★ Leonard Rosenman
STAR TREK V: THE FINAL FRONTIER ... Jerry Goldsmith
STAR TREK: THE MOTION PICTURE ... ★ Jerry Goldsmith
STAR TREK: THE NEXT GENERATION (TF) ... Dennis McCarthy
STAR WARS ... ★★ John Williams
STAR, THE ... Victor Young†
STAR-SPANGLED GIRL ... Charles Fox
STARCHASER: THE LEGEND OF ORIN (AF) ... Andrew Belling
STARCRASH ... John Barry
STARCROSSED (TF) ... Gil Melle
STARFLIGHT: THE PLANE THAT COULDN'T LAND (TF) ... Lalo Schifrin
STARK (TF) ... Peter Myers
STARK: MIRROR IMAGE (TF) ... Peter Myers
STARMAN ... Jack Nitzsche
STARS AND BARS ... Stanley Myers
STARS AND STRIPES FOREVER ... Alfred Newman†
STARS IN MY CROWN ... Adolph Deutsch†
STARS OVER TEXAS ... Karl Hajos†
STARSHIP INVASIONS ... Gil Melle
STARSKY AND HUTCH (TF) ... Lalo Schifrin
START THE REVOLUTION WITHOUT ME ... John Addison
STARTING OVER ... Marvin Hamlisch
STATE FAIR ... ★ Charles Henderson†
STATE FAIR ... ★ Alfred Newman†
STATE OF EMERGENCY, A ... Georges Garvarentz
STATE OF GRACE ... Ennio Morricone
STATE OF SIEGE ... Mikis Theodorakis
STATE OF THE UNION ... Victor Young†
STATE OF THINGS, THE ... Jurgen Knieper
STATE PARK ... Matthew McCauley
STATE REASONS ... Vladimir Cosma
STATE SECRET ... William Alwyn†
STATE'S ATTORNEY ... Max Steiner†
STATION SIX-SAHARA ... Ron Grainer
STATION WEST ... Heinz Roemheld†
STATUE, THE ... Riz Ortolani
STAVISKY ... Stephen Sondheim
STAY AWAY, JOE ... Jack Marshall
STAY HUNGRY ... Bruce Langhorne
STAYIN' ALIVE ... Vince DiCola
STAYING ALIVE ... Johnny Mandel
STAYING TOGETHER ... Miles Goodman
STAZIONE TERMINI ... Alessandro Cicognini†
STEAGLE, THE ... Fred Myrow
STEAL OF THE SKY (CTF) ... Yanni
STEALING HEAVEN ... Nick Bicat
STEALING HOME ... David Foster
STEAMING ... Richard Harvey
STEEL ... Michel Colombier
STEEL BAYONET, THE ... Leonardo Salzedo
STEEL COWBOY (TF) ... Charles Bernstein

SUBTERRANEANS, THE ... Andre Previn
SUBWAY ... Eric Serra
SUBWAY IN THE SKY ... Mario Nascimbene
SUBWAY RIDERS ... John Lurie
SUCCESS ... Maurice Jarre
SUCCESS AT ANY PRICE ... Max Steiner†
SUCCESS IS THE BEST REVENGE ... Hans Zimmer
SUCCESS IS THE BEST REVENGE ... Stanley Myers
SUCH A GORGEOUS KID LIKE ME ... Georges Delerue
SUCH A LOVELY TOWN... ... Paul Misraki†
SUCH GOOD FRIENDS ... Thomas Z. Shepard
SUCKER, THE ... Georges Delerue
SUDAN ... Milton Rosen
SUDARIO DI SABBIA ... Georges Garvarentz
SUDDEN FEAR ... Elmer Bernstein
SUDDEN FURY ... Matthew McCauley
SUDDEN IMPACT ... Lalo Schifrin
SUDDENLY ... David Raksin
SUDDENLY LAST SUMMER ... Malcolm Arnold
SUDDENLY, IT'S SPRING ... Victor Young†
SUDDENLY, LOVE (TF) ... Henry Mancini
SUDDENLY, LOVE (TF) ... David Rose†
SUED FOR LIBEL ... Roy Webb†
SUEZ ... David Raksin
SUEZ ... ★ Louis Silvers†
SUGAR COLT ... Luis Bacalov
SUGARFOOT ... Max Steiner†
SUGERLAND EXPRESS, THE ... John Williams
SUICIDE BATTALION ... Ronald Stein†
SUICIDE SQUADRON ... Richard Addinsell†
SUICIDE'S WIFE, THE (TF) ... David Raksin
SUITE FRANCAISE ... Jean Wiener†
SULLIVAN'S EMPIRE ... Lalo Schifrin
SULLIVAN'S TRAVELS ... Leo Shuken†
SULLIVANS, THE ... Cyril J. Mockridge†
SULTAN A VENDRE (TF) ... Georges Delerue
SULTAN AND THE ROCK STAR (TF) ... Artie Butler
SULTAN'S DAUGHTER, THE ... Karl Hajos†
SUMMER ... Jean-Louis Valero
SUMMER AND SMOKE ... ★ Elmer Bernstein
SUMMER CAMP ... Carl Dante
SUMMER FANTASIES (TF) ... Peter Bernstein
SUMMER GIRL (TF) ... Angela Morley
SUMMER HEAT ... Richard Stone
SUMMER LIGHTNING ... Stanley Myers
SUMMER LOVE ... Hans J. Salter
SUMMER LOVE ... Henry Mancini
SUMMER LOVERS ... Basil Poledouris
SUMMER MADNESS ... Alessandro Cicognini†
SUMMER MAGIC ... Buddy Baker
SUMMER OF MY GERMAN SOLDIER (TF) ... Stanley Myers
SUMMER OF '42 ... ★★ Michel Legrand
SUMMER PLACE, A ... Max Steiner†
SUMMER RENTAL ... Alan Silvestri
SUMMER SCHOOL ... Danny Elfman
SUMMER SEDUCTIONS ... Robert J. Walsh
SUMMER SEDUCTIONS ... Michael Linn
SUMMER SOLDIERS ... Toru Takemitsu
SUMMER STOCK ... John Green†
SUMMER STORM ... ★ Karl Hajos†
SUMMER STORY, A ... Georges Delerue
SUMMER TO REMEMBER,A (TF) ... Charles Fox
SUMMER VACATION: 1999 ... Yuriko Nakamura
SUMMER WISHES, WINTER DREAMS ... Johnny Mandel
SUMMER WITHOUT BOYS, A (TF) ... Andrew Belling
SUMMERFIELD ... Bruce Smeaton
SUMMERTIME ... Alessandro Cicognini†
SUMMERTIME KILLER , THE ... Luis Bacalov
SUMMERTREE ... David Shire
SUMMIT ... Mario Nascimbene
SUN ALSO RISES, THE ... Hugo Friedhofer†
SUN ALSO RISES, THE (TF) ... Billy Goldenberg
SUN COMES UP, THE ... Andre Previn
SUN NEVER SETS, THE ... Frank Skinner†
SUN SETS AT DAWN, THE ... Leith Stevens†
SUN SHINES BRIGHT, THE ... Victor Young†
SUN VALLEY SERENADE ... ★ Emil Newman†
SUNBURN ... John Cameron
SUNDAY DINNER FOR A SOLDIER ... Alfred Newman†
SUNDAY DRIVE (TF) ... Brad Fiedel
SUNDAY IN THE COUNTRY ... Paul Hoffert
SUNDAY IN THE COUNTRY ... Philippe Sarde
SUNDAY LOVERS ... Manuel De Sica
SUNDAY WOMAN ... Ennio Morricone
SUNDAYS AND CYBELE ... ★ Maurice Jarre
SUNDOWN ... ★ Miklos Rozsa
SUNDOWN ... Richard Stone
SUNDOWNERS, THE ... Dimitri Tiomkin†
SUNFLOWER ... ★ Henry Mancini
SUNNY ... ★ Anthony Collins†
SUNRISE AT CAMPOBELLO ... Franz Waxman†
SUNSET ... Henry Mancini
SUNSET BOULEVARD ... ★★ Franz Waxman†
SUNSET LIMOUSINE (TF) ... Frank Denson
SUNSET, SUNRISE ... Nino Rota†
SUNSHINE CHRISTMAS (TF) ... Lee Holdridge
SUPER CHIEF (FD) ... Mark Adler
SUPER COPS, THE ... Jerry Fielding†
SUPER-GIANT 2 ... Chumei Watanabe
SUPERBEAST ... Richard LaSalle
SUPERCARRIER (TF) ... Jack Eskew
SUPERCARRIER (TF) ... Craig Safan
SUPERCHICK ... Allan Alper
SUPERDAD ... Buddy Baker
SUPERDOME (TF) ... John Cacavas
SUPERFANTAGENIO ... Fabio Frizzi
SUPERFLY ... Curtis Mayfield
SUPERGIRL ... Jerry Goldsmith
SUPERGRASS, THE ... Keith Tippet
SUPERMAN ... ★ John Williams
SUPERMAN II ... Ken Thorne
SUPERMAN III ... Ken Thorne
SUPERMAN IV: THE QUEST FOR PEACE ... Alexander Courage
SUPERNATURAL ... Karl Hajos†
SUPERNATURAL ... Milan Roder†
SUPERNATURALS, THE ... Robert O. Ragland
SUPERSTITION ... David Gibney
SUPPORT YOUR LOCAL GUNFIGHTER ... Allyn Ferguson
SUPPORT YOUR LOCAL SHERIFF! ... Jeff Alexander†
SUPPOSE THEY GAVE A WAR AND NOBODY CAME? ... Jerry Fielding†
SUR UN ARBRE PERCHE ... Alain Goraguer
SURE THING, THE ... Tom Scott
SURF AND SEAWEED ... Marc Blitzstein†
SURF II ... Peter Bernstein
SURPRISE PACKAGE ... Benjamin Frankel†
SURPRISE PARTY ... Michel Magne†
SURRENDER ... Michel Colombier
SURVIVAL GAME ... Michael J. Linn
SURVIVAL OF DANA, THE (TF) ... Craig Safan
SURVIVAL RUN ... Gary William Friedman
SURVIVE! ... Gerald Fried
SURVIVING (TF) ... James Horner
SURVIVOR, THE ... Brian May
SURVIVORS, THE ... Paul Chihara
SUSAN AND GOD ... Herbert Stothart†
SUSAN SLADE ... Max Steiner†
SUSAN SLEPT HER ... Leigh Harline†
SUSANNAH OF THE MOUNTIES ... Louis Silvers†
SUSPECT ... Michael Kamen
SUSPECT, THE ... Frank Skinner†
SUSPENSE ... Daniele Amfitheatrof†
SUSPICION ... ★ Franz Waxman†
SUSPICION (TF) ... Larry Grossman
SUSPIRIA ... Goblin
SUTJESKA ... Mikis Theodorakis
SUTTER'S GOLD ... Franz Waxman†
SUZY ... William Axt†
SVEGLIATI E UCCIDI ... Ennio Morricone
SVENGALI ... William Alwyn†
SVENGALI (TF) ... John Barry
SWALLOWS AND AMAZONS ... Wilfred Josephs
SWAMP THING ... Harry Manfredini
SWAMP WATER ... David Buttolph†
SWAN SONG (TF) ... Jonathan Tunick
SWAN, THE ... Bronislau Kaper†
SWANEE RIVER ... ★ Louis Silvers†
SWANN IN LOVE ... Hans Werner Henze
SWARM, THE ... Jerry Goldsmith
SWASHBUCKLER ... John Addison
SWEEPINGS ... Max Steiner†
SWEET BIRD OF YOUTH ... Harold Gelman
SWEET BIRD OF YOUTH (TF) ... Ralph Burns
SWEET BUNCH ... George Hatzinassios
SWEET CHARITY ... ★ Cy Coleman
SWEET COUNTRY ... Stavros Xarchakos
SWEET CREEK COUNTY WAR, THE ... Richard Bowden
SWEET DREAMS ... Charles Gross
SWEET HEART'S DANCE ... Richard Gibbs
SWEET HOSTAGE (TF) ... Luchi DeJesus
SWEET LIBERTY ... Bruce Broughton
SWEET LIES ... Trevor Jones
SWEET LORRAINE ... Richard Robbins
SWEET MONEY ... Emilio Kauderer
SWEET MOVIE ... Manos Hadjidakis
SWEET NOVEMBER ... Michel Legrand
SWEET REVENGE ... Hubert Bougis
SWEET REVENGE ... Paul Chihara
SWEET REVENGE ... Ernest Troost
SWEET REVENGE (CTF) ... Didier Vasseur
SWEET REVENGE (TF) ... Gil Melle
SWEET RIDE, THE ... Pete Rugolo
SWEET SINS ... Stelvio Cipriani
SWEET SIXTEEN ... Tommy Vig
SWEET SMELL OF SUCCESS ... Elmer Bernstein
SWEET SUZY! ... William Loose
SWEETHEARTS ... ★ Herbert Stothart†
SWEETIE ... Martin Armiger
SWELL GUY ... Frank Skinner†
SWEPT AWAY BY AN UNUSUAL DESTINY IN THE BLUE SEA OF AUGUST ... Piero Piccioni
SWIMMER, THE ... Marvin Hamlisch
SWIMMING TO CAMBODIA ... Laurie Anderson
SWIMSUIT (TF) ... John D'Andrea
SWIMSUIT (TF) ... Michael Lloyd
SWINDLE, THE ... Nino Rota†
SWING HIGH, SWING LOW ... Victor Young†
SWING OUT, SISTER ... Milton Rosen
SWING SHIFT ... Patrick Williams
SWING YOUR LADY ... Adolph Deutsch†
SWING, THE ... Peer Raben
SWINGER, THE ... Marty Paich
SWINGIN' MAIDEN, THE ... Eric Rogers†
SWINGING CONFESSORS, THE ... Armando Trovajoli
SWISS FAMILY ROBINSON ... William Alwyn†
SWISS FAMILY ROBINSON ... Anthony Collins†
SWISS FAMILY ROBINSON (TF) ... Richard LaSalle
SWISS MISS ... T. Marvin Hatley†
SWITCH (TF) ... Stu Phillips
SWITCHBLADE SISTERS ... Les Baxter
SWITCHING CHANNELS ... Michel Legrand
SWORD AND THE SORCERER, THE ... David Whitaker
SWORD IN THE DESERT ... Frank Skinner†
SWORD IN THE STONE, THE (AF) ... ★ George Bruns
SWORD OF DOOM, THE ... Masaru Sato
SWORD OF GIDEON (CTF) ... Georges Delerue
SWORD OF HEAVEN ... Christopher L. Stone
SWORD OF LANCELOT ... Ron Goodwin
SWORD OF THE CONQUEROR ... Carlo Rustichelli
SWORD OF THE VALIANT ... Ron Geesin
SWORDKILL ... Richard H. Band
SWORDSMAN OF SIENA, THE ... Mario Nascimbene
SWORDSMAN, THE ... Hugo Friedhofer†
SWORN ENEMY ... Edward Ward†
SWORN TO SILENCE (TF) ... Dennis McCarthy
SYBIL (TF) ... ☆☆ Leonard Rosenman
SYLVESTER ... Lee Holdridge
SYLVIA ... David Raksin
SYLVIA ... Leonard Rosenman
SYLVIA SCARLETT ... Roy Webb†
SYMPHONY FOR A MASSACRE ... Michel Magne†
SYMPHONY OF SIX MILLION ... Max Steiner†
SYMPTOMS ... John Scott
SYNANON ... Neal Hefti
SYNCOPATION ... Leith Stevens†
SYNDICATE SADISTS ... Franco Micalizzi
SYNGENOR ... Tom Chase
SYNGENOR ... Steve Rucker
SYSTEM, THE ... David Buttolph†

T

T.A.G.: THE ASSASSINATION GAME ... Craig Safan
T.A.M.I. SHOW, THE ... Jack Nitzsche
T.R. BASKIN ... Jack Elliott
TABLE FOR FIVE ... Miles Goodman
TABLE FOR FIVE ... John Morris
TAFFIN ... Stanley Myers
TAI-PAN ... Maurice Jarre
TAIL GUNNER JOE (TF) ... Billy May
TAILOR'S MAID, THE ... Carlo Rustichelli
TAILSPIN: BEHIND THE KOREAN AIRLINE TRAGEDY (CTF) ... David Ferguson
TAKE A GIANT STEP ... Jack Marshall
TAKE A HARD RIDE ... Jerry Goldsmith
TAKE A LETTER, DARLING ... ★ Victor Young†
TAKE ALL OF ME ... Stelvio Cipriani
TAKE CARE OF MY LITTLE GIRL ... Alfred Newman†
TAKE DOWN ... Merrill B. Jensen
TAKE HER, SHE'S MINE ... Jerry Goldsmith
TAKE IT EASY ... Andrzej Korzynski
TAKE ME OUT TO THE BALL GAME ... Adolph Deutsch†
TAKE ME TO TOWN ... Herman Stein

TAKE ME TO TOWN ..... Henry Mancini
TAKE MY LIFE ..... William Alwyn†
TAKE ONE FALSE STEP ..... Walter Scharf
TAKE THE HIGH GROUND ..... Dimitri Tiomkin†
TAKE THE MONEY AND RUN ..... Marvin Hamlisch
TAKE YOUR BEST SHOT (TF) ..... Peter Matz
TAKE, THE ..... Fred Karlin
TAKE, THE (CTF) ..... David Beal
TAKE, THE (CTF) ..... Susan Marder
TAKEN AWAY (TF) ..... Rob Mounsey
TAKING OF FLIGHT 847: THE ULI DERICKSON STORY, THE (TF) ..... Gil Melle
TAKING OF PELHAM 1-2-3, THE ..... David Shire
TALE OF TWO CITIES, A ..... Herbert Stothart†
TALE OF TWO CITIES, A ..... Richard Addinsell†
TALE OF TWO CITIES,A (TF) ..... Allyn Ferguson
TALE OF TWO CITIES,A (TF) ..... Serge Franklin
TALENT FOR LOVING, A ..... Ken Thorne
TALES FROM THE CRYPT ..... Douglas Gamley
TALES FROM THE CRYPT (CTF) ..... Ry Cooder
TALES FROM THE CRYPT (CTF) ..... Nicholas Pike
TALES FROM THE CRYPT (CTF) ..... Alan Silvestri
TALES FROM THE CRYPT II ..... Douglas Gamley
TALES FROM THE DARKSIDE: THE MOVIE ..... Chaz Jankel
TALES FROM THE DARKSIDE: THE MOVIE ..... Donald Rubinstein
TALES FROM THE DARKSIDE: THE MOVIE ..... Pat Regan
TALES FROM THE DARKSIDE: THE MOVIE ..... Jim Manzie
TALES OF MANHATTAN ..... Sol Kaplan
TALES OF TERROR ..... Les Baxter
TALES OF THE DARKSIDE: THE MOVIE ..... John Harrison
TALES OF THE GOLD MONKEY (TF) ..... Gary Schyman
TALES OF THE TAIRA CLAN ..... Fumio Hayasaka †
TALES THAT WITNESS MADNESS ..... Bernard Ebbinghouse
TALK ABOUT A STRANGER ..... David Buttolph†
TALK OF THE TOWN ..... ★ Frederick Hollander†
TALK RADIO ..... Stewart Copeland
TALL BLOND MAN WITH ONE BLACK SHOE, THE ..... Vladimir Cosma
TALL GUY, THE ..... Peter Brewis
TALL IN THE SADDLE ..... Roy Webb†
TALL MEN, THE ..... Victor Young†
TALL STORY ..... Cyril J. Mockridge†
TALL STRANGER, THE ..... Hans J. Salter
TALL T, THE ..... Heinz Roemheld†
TALL, DARK AND HANDSOME ..... Emil Newman†
TALVISOTA ..... Juha Tikka
TAMAHINE ..... Malcolm Arnold
TAMANGO ..... Joseph Kosma†
TAMARIND SEED, THE ..... John Barry
TAMING OF THE SHREW, THE ..... Nino Rota†
TAMMY AND THE MILLIONAIRE ..... Jack Marshall
TAMPICO ..... David Raksin
TANGA TIKA ..... Les Baxter
TANGANYIKA ..... Hans J. Salter
TANGANYIKA ..... Herman Stein
TANGANYIKA ..... Henry Mancini
TANGIER ..... Milton Rosen
TANGO & CASH ..... Harold Faltermeyer
TANGO BAR ..... Atilio Stampone
TANK ..... Lalo Schifrin
TANK COMMANDOS ..... Ronald Stein†
TANK FORCE ..... Kenneth V. Jones
TANKS A MILLION ..... ★ Edward Ward†
TANKS ARE COMING, THE ..... William Lava†
TANYA'S ISLAND ..... Jean Musy
TAP ..... James Newton Howard
TAP ROOTS ..... Frank Skinner†
TAPEHEADS ..... Fishbone
TAPS ..... Maurice Jarre
TARANTULA ..... Herman Stein
TARANTULAS: THE DEADLY CARGO (TF) ..... Mundell Lowe
TARAS BULBA ..... ★ Franz Waxman†
TARGET ..... Michael Small
TARGET EARTH! ..... Paul Dunlap
TARGET FOR TONIGHT ..... Leighton Lucas†
TARGET ZERO ..... David Buttolph†
TARGET: HARRY ..... Les Baxter
TARGETS ..... Ronald Stein†
TARNISHED ANGELS, THE ..... Frank Skinner†
TARTARIN DE TARASCON ..... Darius Milhaud†
TARTUFFE ..... Giuseppe Becce†
TARZAN AND THE GREAT RIVER ..... William Loose
TARZAN AND THE JUNGLE BOY ..... William Loose
TARZAN AND THE LEOPARD WOMAN ..... Paul Sawtell†
TARZAN AND THE LOST SAFARI ..... Clifton Parker
TARZAN AND THE MERMAIDS ..... Dimitri Tiomkin†
TARZAN AND THE SHE-DEVIL ..... Paul Sawtell†
TARZAN GOES TO INDIA ..... Kenneth V. Jones
TARZAN IN MANHATTAN (TF) ..... Charles Fox
TARZAN THE APE MAN ..... Perry Botkin
TARZAN THE MAGNIFICENT ..... Kenneth V. Jones
TARZAN'S FIGHT FOR LIFE ..... Ernest Gold
TARZAN'S GREATEST ADVENTURE ..... Douglas Gamley
TARZAN'S PERIL ..... Michel Michelet†
TARZAN'S SAVAGE FURY ..... Paul Sawtell†
TARZAN'S THREE CHALLENGES ..... Joseph Horovitz
TARZAN, THE APE MAN ..... Barry De Vorzon
TASK FORCE ..... Franz Waxman†
TASTE OF BLOOD, A ..... Larry Wellington
TASTE OF EVIL, A (TF) ..... Robert Drasnin
TASTE OF FEAR ..... Clifton Parker
TASTE OF HONEY, A ..... John Addison
TASTE OF SIN, A ..... Joel Goldsmith
TASTE OF THE BLACK EARTH, THE ..... Wojciech Kilar
TASTE THE BLOOD OF DRACULA ..... James Bernard
TATTERED WEB, A (TF) ..... Robert Drasnin
TATTOO ..... Barry De Vorzon
TATTOOED POLICE HORSE, THE ..... William Lava†
TAXI ..... Leigh Harline†
TAXI BLUES ..... Vladimir Chekassine
TAXI DRIVER ..... ★ Bernard Herrmann†
TAXI, MISTER ..... Edward Ward†
TAXING WOMAN, A ..... Toshiyuki Honda
TAZA, SON OF COCHISE ..... Frank Skinner†
TCHAIKOVSKY ..... ★ Dimitri Tiomkin†
TEA AND SYMPATHY ..... Adolph Deutsch†
TEACHER'S PET ..... Roy Webb†
TEACHER, TEACHER ..... Charles Gross
TEACHER, THE ..... Masaru Sato
TEARS ARE FOR TOMORROW ..... Mario Nascimbene
TEARS FOR SIMON ..... Benjamin Frankel†
TEARS OF HAPPINESS ..... Jaime Mendoza-Nava
TED KENNEDY JR. STORY, THE (TF) ..... Teo Macero
TEEN WITCH ..... Richard Elliott
TEEN WOLF ..... Miles Goodman
TEEN WOLF TOO ..... Mark Goldenberg
TEEN-AGE REBEL ..... Leigh Harline†
TEENAGE BAD-GIRL ..... Albert Glasser
TEENAGE CAVEMAN ..... Albert Glasser
TEENAGE MUTANT NINJA TURTLES ..... John Du Prez
TELEFON ..... Lalo Schifrin
TELEFONI BIANCHI ..... Armando Trovajoli
TELEPHONE, THE ..... Christopher Young
TELL IT TO THE JUDGE ..... Werner R. Heymann†
TELL ME A RIDDLE ..... Sheldon Shkolnik
TELL ME MY NAME (TF) ..... Hagood Hardy
TELL ME WHERE IT HURTS (TF) ..... David Shire
TELL ME YOU LOVE ME ..... Claude Bolling
TELL NO TALES ..... William Axt†
TELL THEM WILLIE BOY WAS HERE ..... Dave Grusin
TEMPEST ..... Piero Piccioni
TEMPEST, THE ..... Wavemaker
TEMPEST, THE ..... Stomu Yamashita
TEMPI DURI PER I VAMPIRI ..... Armando Trovajoli
TEMPO DI UCCIDERE ..... Ennio Morricone
TEMPTATION ..... Daniele Amfitheatrof†
TEMPTATIONS IN THE SUMMER WIND ..... Peter Thomas
TEMPTER, THE ..... Ennio Morricone
TEMPTER, THE ..... Bruno Nicolai
TEN COMMANDMENTS, THE ..... Elmer Bernstein
TEN DAYS IN PARIS ..... Miklos Rozsa
TEN DAYS THAT SHOOK THE WORLD ..... Edmund Meisel†
TEN DAYS' WONDER ..... Pierre Jansen
TEN LITTLE INDIANS ..... Malcom Lockyer
TEN LITTLE INDIANS ..... Bruno Nicolai
TEN NORTH FREDERICK ..... Leigh Harline†
TEN SECONDS TO HELL ..... Kenneth V. Jones
TEN TALL MEN ..... David Buttolph†
TEN TO SURVIVE (AF) ..... Luis Bacalov
TEN WHO DARED ..... Oliver Wallace†
TENAFLY (TF) ..... Gil Melle
TENANT, THE ..... Philippe Sarde
TENDER COMRADE ..... Leigh Harline†
TENDER IS THE NIGHT ..... Bernard Herrmann†
TENDER IS THE NIGHT (MS) ..... Richard Rodney Bennett
TENDER MERCIES ..... George Dreyfus
TENDER TRAP, THE ..... Jeff Alexander†
TENDER WARRIOR, THE ..... Ken Wannberg
TENDERNESS OF WOLVES, THE ..... Peer Raben
TENDRE POULET ..... Georges Delerue
TENDRE VOYOU ..... Michel Legrand
TENNESSEE CHAMP ..... Conrad Salinger†
TENNESSEE JOHNSON ..... Herbert Stothart†
TENSION ..... Andre Previn
TENSION AT TABLE ROCK ..... Dimitri Tiomkin†
TENTACLES ..... Stelvio Cipriani
TENTH LEVEL, THE (TF) ..... Charles Gross
TENTH MAN, THE (TF) ..... Lee Holdridge
TENTH MONTH, THE (TF) ..... Peter Matz
TENTH VICTIM, THE ..... Piero Piccioni
TENTING TONIGHT ON THE OLD CAMP GROUND ..... Hans J. Salter
TENUE DE SOIREE ..... Serge Gainsbourg
TEOREMA ..... Ennio Morricone
TEPEPA ..... Ennio Morricone
TEQUILA SUNRISE ..... Dave Grusin
TERESA ..... Vladimir Cosma
TERESA LA LADRA ..... Riz Ortolani
TERMINATOR, THE ..... Brad Fiedel
TERMINUS ..... David Cunningham
TERMS OF ENDEARMENT ..... ★ Michael Gore
TERRACES (TF) ..... Peter Matz
TERRAIN VAGUE ..... Michel Legrand
TERRIBLE JOE MORAN (TF) ..... Charles Gross
TERROR ..... Ivor Slaney
TERROR AMONG US (TF) ..... Allyn Ferguson
TERROR AT ALCATRAZ (TF) ..... Stu Phillips
TERROR BY NIGHT ..... Hans J. Salter
TERROR EYES ..... Brad Fiedel
TERROR HOUSE ..... Bill Marx
TERROR IN A TEXAS TOWN ..... Gerald Fried
TERROR IN THE AISLES ..... John Beal
TERROR IN THE AISLES ..... Richard Johnston
TERROR IN THE AISLES ..... Doug Timm†
TERROR IN THE FOREST ..... Richard Hieronymous
TERROR IN THE FOREST ..... Alan Oldfield
TERROR IN THE JUNGLE ..... Les Baxter
TERROR IN THE SKY (TF) ..... Patrick Williams
TERROR IN THE WAX MUSEUM ..... George Duning
TERROR OF GODZILLA ..... Akira Ifukube
TERROR OF MECHA-GODZILLA ..... Akira Ifukube
TERROR OF SHEBA, THE ..... Paul Ferris
TERROR OF THE STEPPE ..... Carlo Rustichelli
TERROR OF THE TONGS, THE ..... James Bernard
TERROR ON HIGHWAY 91 (TF) ..... Artie Kane
TERROR ON THE 40TH FLOOR (TF) ..... Vic Mizzy
TERROR OUT OF THE SKY (TF) ..... William Goldstein
TERROR SQUAD ..... David C. Williams
TERROR TRAIN ..... John Mills-Cockell
TERROR WITHIN, THE ..... Rick Conrad
TERROR, THE ..... Ronald Stein†
TERRORIST ON TRIAL: THE UNITED STATES VS. SALIM AJAMI (TF) ..... Jimmie Haskell
TERRORISTS, THE ..... Jerry Goldsmith
TERRORNAUTS, THE ..... Elisabeth Luytens†
TERRORVISION ..... Richard H. Band
TERRORVISION ..... Christopher L. Stone
TERRY FOX STORY, THE (CTF) ..... Bill Conti
TESEO CONTRO IL MINOTAURO ..... Carlo Rustichelli
TESS ..... ★ Philippe Sarde
TESS OF THE STORM COUNTRY ..... Bert A. Shefter
TEST PILOT ..... Franz Waxman†
TESTA T'AMMAZZO, CROCE...SEI MORTO... MI CHIAMANO ALLELUJA ..... Stelvio Cipriani
TESTAMENT ..... James Horner
TESTAMENT DES DR. MABUSE, THE ..... Hans Erdmann†
TESTIMONY OF TWO MEN (MS) ..... Gerald Fried
TESTIMONY OF TWO MEN (TF) ..... Michel Colombier
TEX ..... Pino Donaggio
TEXAS ..... Sidney Cutner†
TEXAS ACROSS THE RIVER ..... Frank De Vol
TEXAS CARNIVAL ..... David Rose†
TEXAS CHAINSAW MASSACRE PART 2, THE ..... Tobe Hooper
TEXAS CHAINSAW MASSACRE PART 2, THE ..... Jerry Lambert
TEXAS CHAINSAW MASSACRE, THE ..... Wayne Bell
TEXAS CHAINSAW MASSACRE, THE ..... Tobe Hooper
TEXAS, BROOKLYN AND HEAVEN ..... Emil Newman†
THADDEUS ROSE AND EDDIE (TF) ..... Charles Bernstein
THANK HEAVEN FOR SMALL FAVORS ..... Joseph Kosma†
THANKSGIVING PROMISE, THE (TF) ..... Bruce Broughton
THAT BRENNAN GIRL ..... George Antheil†
THAT CERTAIN WOMAN ..... Max Steiner†
THAT CHAMPIONSHIP SEASON ..... Bill Conti
THAT COLD DAY IN THE PARK ..... Johnny Mandel

THREE STRANGERS .... Adolph Deutsch†
THREE TEXAS STEERS .... William Lava†
THREE TOUGH GUYS .... Isaac Hayes
THREE TREASURES, THE .... Akira Ifukube
THREE VIOLENT PEOPLE .... Walter Scharf
THREE WISE FOOLS .... Bronislau Kaper†
THREE WISE GUYS .... William Axt†
THREE WISHES OF BILLY GRIER, THE (TF) .... Brad Fiedel
THREE WOMEN .... Gerald Busby
THREE WORLDS OF GULLIVER, THE .... Bernard Herrmann†
THREESOME (TF) .... Angela Morley
THRILL OF IT ALL, THE .... Frank De Vol
THRILLING .... Luis Bacalov
THRONE OF BLOOD .... Masaru Sato
THRONE OF FIRE .... Bruno Nicolai
THROUGH NAKED EYES (TF) .... Gil Melle
THROUGH THE LOOKING GLASS .... Arlon Ober
THROUGH THE MAGIC PYRAMID (TF) .... Joe Renzetti
THROW MOMMA FROM THE TRAIN .... David Newman
THRUSTER, THE .... Ennio Morricone
THUMBS UP .... Walter Scharf
THUNDER .... Francesco De Masi
THUNDER .... William Axt†
THUNDER AFLOAT .... Edward Ward†
THUNDER ALLEY .... Robert Folk
THUNDER AND LIGHTNING .... Andrew Stein
THUNDER BAY .... Frank Skinner†
THUNDER BIRDS .... David Buttolph†
THUNDER IN THE CITY .... Miklos Rozsa
THUNDER IN THE EAST .... Hugo Friedhofer†
THUNDER IN THE SUN .... Cyril J. Mockridge†
THUNDER IN THE VALLEY .... Cyril J. Mockridge†
THUNDER ISLAND .... Bert A. Shefter
THUNDER ISLAND .... Paul Sawtell†
THUNDER OF DRUMS, A .... Harry Sukman†
THUNDER ON THE HILL .... Hans J. Salter
THUNDER OVER HAWAII .... Ronald Stein†
THUNDER OVER THE PLAINS .... David Buttolph†
THUNDER RUN .... Jay Levy
THUNDER RUN .... Matthew McCauley
THUNDER WARRIOR .... Francesco De Masi
THUNDERBALL .... John Barry
THUNDERBIRDS .... Victor Young†
THUNDERBIRDS ARE GO .... Barry Gray
THUNDERBIRDS SIX .... Barry Gray
THUNDERBIRDS TO THE RESCUE .... Barry Gray
THUNDERBOLT (FD) .... Gail Kubik†
THUNDERBOLT AND LIGHTFOOT .... Dee Barton
THUNDERHEAD—SON OF FLICKA .... Cyril J. Mockridge†
THURSDAY'S CHILD (TF) .... Lee Holdridge
THX-1138 .... Lalo Schifrin
TI HO SEMPRE AMATO .... Carlo Rustichelli
TI-KOYO E IL SUO PESCECANE ... Francesco De Masi
TICKET TO TOMAHAWK, A .... Cyril J. Mockridge†
TICKLE ME .... Walter Scharf
TIDAL WAVE .... Masaru Sato
TIDY ENDINGS (CTF) .... Stanley Myers
TIE ME UP! TIE ME DOWN! .... Ennio Morricone
TIEFLAND .... Giuseppe Becce†
TIEMPO DE REVANCHA .... Emilio Kauderer
TIFFANY MEMORANDUM .... Riz Ortolani
TIGER MAKES OUT, THE .... Ron Grainer
TIGER TOWN (CTF) .... Eddie Lawrence Manson
TIGER WALKS, A .... Buddy Baker
TIGER WARSAW .... Ernest Troost
TIGER'S TALE, A .... Lee Holdridge
TIGER, THE .... Heinz Roemheld†
TIGERS IN LIPSTICK .... Riz Ortolani
TIGHT LITTLE ISLAND .... Georges Auric†
TIGHT SHOES .... Hans J. Salter
TIGHTROPE .... Lennie Niehaus
TIJUANA STORY, THE .... Mischa Bakaleinikoff †
TILL DIVORCE DO YOU PART .... Carlo Rustichelli
TILL THE END OF TIME .... Leigh Harline†
TILL WE MEET AGAIN .... David Buttolph†
TILL WE MEET AGAIN .... Frederick Hollander†
TILT .... Lee Holdridge
TIMBER .... Hans J. Salter
TIMBER STAMPEDE .... Roy Webb†
TIMBERJACK .... Victor Young†
TIMBUKTU .... Gerald Fried
TIME AFTER TIME .... Jim Parker
TIME AFTER TIME .... Miklos Rozsa
TIME BANDITS .... Mike Moran
TIME BOMB (TF) .... Sylvester Levay
TIME FLIES WHEN YOU'RE ALIVE (CTF) .... Mike Garson
TIME FLYER (TF) .... David Shire
TIME FOR DYING, A .... Harry Betts
TIME FOR KILLING, A .... Van Alexander
TIME FOR MIRACLES, A (TF) .... Fred Karlin
TIME GUARDIAN, THE .... Allan Zavod
TIME LIMIT .... Fred Steiner
TIME LOST AND TIME REMEMBERED .... John Addison
TIME MACHINE, THE .... Russell Garcia
TIME MACHINE, THE (TF) .... John Cacavas
TIME OF DESTINY, A .... Ennio Morricone
TIME OF THEIR LIVES, THE .... Milton Rosen
TIME OF YOUR LIFE, THE .... Carmen Dragon†
TIME OUT OF MIND .... Miklos Rozsa
TIME OUT OF MIND .... Mario Castelnuovo-Tedesco†
TIME SLIP .... Kentaro Haneda
TIME TO DIE, A .... John Cacavas
TIME TO DIE, A .... Robert O. Ragland
TIME TO DIE, A .... Ennio Morricone
TIME TO KILL .... Emil Newman†
TIME TO LIVE, A (TF) .... Georges Delerue
TIME TO LOVE AND A TIME TO DIE, A ... Miklos Rozsa
TIME TO TRIUMPH, A (TF) .... John Cacavas
TIME TRAVELERS, THE .... Richard LaSalle
TIME TRAVELERS, THE (TF) .... Morton Stevens
TIME WALKER .... Richard H. Band
TIME WITHIN MEMORY .... Toru Takemitsu
TIME WITHOUT PITY .... Tristram Cary
TIME, THE PLACE AND THE GIRL, THE .... Frederick Hollander†
TIMERIDER .... Michael Nesmith
TIMES OF HARVEY MILK, THE (FD) .... Mark Isham
TIMES SQUARE LADY .... Edward Ward†
TIMESTALKERS (TF) .... Craig Safan
TIMETABLE .... Walter Scharf
TIMETRACKERS .... Parmer Fuller
TIMIDO Y SALVAJE .... Stelvio Cipriani
TIN DRUM, THE .... Maurice Jarre
TIN MEN .... Andy Cox
TIN MEN .... David Steele
TIN STAR, THE .... Elmer Bernstein
TINGLER, THE .... Von Dexter
TINTIN ET LES ORANGES BLEUES .... Antoine Duhamel
TINTORERA - THE SILENT DEATH .... Basil Poledouris
TIP ON A DEAD JOCKEY .... Miklos Rozsa
TIPS .... Don Preston
TIRO AL PICCIONE .... Carlo Rustichelli
TITAN FIND .... Tom Chase
TITAN FIND .... Steve Rucker
TITFIELD THUNDERBOLT, THE .... Georges Auric†
TITLE SHOT .... Paul Zaza
TO AN UNKNOWN GOD .... Luis De Pablo
TO BE OR NOT TO BE .... John Morris
TO BE OR NOT TO BE .... ★ Werner R. Heymann†
TO CATCH A COP .... Vladimir Cosma
TO CATCH A KING (CTF) .... Nick Bicat
TO CATCH A THIEF .... Lyn Murray†
TO DIE FOR .... Cliff Eidelman
TO DIE IN MADRID (FD) .... Maurice Jarre
TO EACH HIS OWN .... Victor Young†
TO FIND A MAN .... David Shire
TO FIND MY SON (TF) .... Ralph Grierson
TO FORGET PALERMO .... Ennio Morricone
TO HAVE AND HAVE NOT .... Franz Waxman†
TO HEAL A NATION (TF) .... Laurence Rosenthal
TO HELL WITH SCHOOL .... Peter Thomas
TO KILL A COP (TF) .... Lee Holdridge
TO KILL A MOCKINGBIRD .... ★ Elmer Bernstein
TO KILL A PRIEST .... Georges Delerue
TO LIVE AND DIE IN L.A. .... Wang Chung
TO MARY, WITH LOVE .... Louis Silvers†
TO PARIS, WITH LOVE .... Edwin Astley
TO PLEASE A LADY .... Bronislau Kaper†
TO RACE THE WIND (TF) .... John Rubinstein
TO SIR WITH LOVE .... Ron Grainer
TO THE DEVIL A DAUGHTER .... Paul Glass
TO THE ENDS OF THE EARTH .... George Duning
TO THE SHORES OF TRIPOLI .... Alfred Newman†
TO THE VICTOR .... David Buttolph†
TO TRAP A SPY .... Jerry Goldsmith
TO'E MORTA LA NONNA .... Piero Piccioni
TOAST OF NEW ORLEANS, THE .... Nicholas Brodzsky†
TOAST OF NEW YORK, THE .... Nathaniel Shilkret†
TOBACCO ROAD .... David Buttolph†
TOBOR THE GREAT .... William Lava†
TOBRUK .... Bronislau Kaper†
TOCHER (FD), THE .... Benjamin Britten†
TODAY IS FOR THE CHAMPIONSHIP (FD) .... Buddy Collette
TODAY'S F.B.I. (TF) .... Elmer Bernstein
TODAY'S FBI (TF) .... John Cacavas
TODO MODO .... Ennio Morricone
TOGETHER AGAIN .... Werner R. Heymann†
TOGETHER FOR DAYS ..... Coleridge-Taylor Perkinson
TOGETHER? .... Burt Bacharach
TOGNAZZI E LA MINORENNE .... Armando Trovajoli
TOKYO AFTER DARK .... Alexander Courage
TOKYO FILE 212 .... Albert Glasser
TOKYO JOE .... George Antheil†
TOKYO POP .... Alan Brewer
TOM BROWN'S SCHOOLDAYS .... Richard Addinsell†
TOM BROWN'S SCHOOLDAYS .... Anthony Collins†
TOM HORN .... Ernest Gold
TOM JONES .... ★★ John Addison
TOM SAWYER .... ★ John Williams
TOM SAWYER (TF) .... Hal Mooney
tom thumb .... Douglas Gamley
TOM THUMB .... Kenneth V. Jones
TOM THUMB .... Francis Lai
TOM, DICK AND HARRY .... Roy Webb†
TOMA (TF) .... Pete Rugolo
TOMAHAWK .... Hans J. Salter
TOMAHAWK TRAIL .... Les Baxter
TOMB OF LIGEIA, THE .... Kenneth V. Jones
TOMBOY AND THE CHAMP .... Richard Shores
TOMORROW IS ANOTHER DAY .... Daniele Amfitheatrof†
TOMORROW IS FOREVER .... Max Steiner†
TOMORROW NEVER COMES .... Roy Budd
TOMORROW WE LIVE .... Leo Erdody†
TOMORROW'S CHILD (TF) .... Patrick Williams
TON OMBRE EST LA MIENNE .... Maurice Jarre
TONIGHT AT TWELVE .... David Broekman†
TONIGHT FOR SURE .... Carmine Coppola
TONIGHT OR NEVER .... Alfred Newman†
TONIGHT WE RAID CALAIS .... Cyril J. Mockridge†
TONIGHT WE RAID CALAIS .... Emil Newman†
TONIGHT WE SING .... Alfred Newman†
TONIGHT'S THE NIGHT .... Stanley Black
TONIGHT'S THE NIGHT (TF) .... Tangerine Dream
TONKA .... Oliver Wallace†
TONY ROME .... Billy May
TOO FAR TO GO (TF) .... Elizabeth Swados
TOO GOOD TO BE TRUE (TF) .... Michel Rubini
TOO HOT TO HANDLE .... Franz Waxman†
TOO LATE BLUES .... David Raksin
TOO LATE THE HERO .... Gerald Fried
TOO MANY GIRLS .... George Bassman
TOO MANY HUSBANDS .... Frederick Hollander†
TOO MANY PARENTS .... Milan Roder†
TOO MUCH .... George S. Clinton
TOO MUCH TOO SOON .... Ernest Gold
TOO OUTRAGEOUS! .... Russ Little
TOO SCARED TO SCREAM .... Georges Garvarentz
TOO SOON TO DIE .... Ennio Morricone
TOO SOON TO LOVE .... Ronald Stein†
TOO YOUNG FOR LOVE .... Mario Nascimbene
TOO YOUNG THE HERO (TF) .... Steve Dorff
TOO YOUNG TO DIE? (TF) .... Charles Bernstein
TOO YOUNG TO KISS .... John Green†
TOO YOUNG TO KISS .... Bronislau Kaper†
TOO YOUNG TO KNOW .... Heinz Roemheld†
TOOTSIE .... Dave Grusin
TOP BANANA .... Albert Glasser
TOP GUN .... Harold Faltermeyer
TOP HAT .... Max Steiner†
TOP O' THE MORNING .... Robert Emmett Dolan†
TOP OF THE HEAP .... J.J. Johnson
TOP OF THE HILL, THE (TF) .... George Duning
TOP OF THE WORLD .... Albert Glasser
TOP SECRET (TF) .... Stu Gardner
TOP SECRET (TF) .... Teo Macero
TOP SECRET AFFAIR .... Roy Webb†
TOP SECRET! .... Maurice Jarre
TOP SERGEANT .... Hans J. Salter
TOPAZ .... Maurice Jarre
TOPAZE .... Max Steiner†
TOPKAPI .... Manos Hadjidakis
TOPPER .... T. Marvin Hatley†
TOPPER (TF) .... Fred Karlin
TOPPER RETURNS .... Werner R. Heymann†
TOPPER TAKES A TRIP .... Hugo Friedhofer†
TORA! TORA! TORA! .... Jerry Goldsmith
TORCH SONG .... Adolph Deutsch†
TORCH SONG TRILOGY .... Peter Matz
TORCHLIGHT .... Michael Cannon
TORMENT .... Christopher Young
TORMENTED .... Albert Glasser
TORN APART .... Peter Arnow
TORN BETWEEN TWO LOVERS (TF) .... Ian Fraser

TORN CURTAIN ... John Addison
TORRENTS OF SPRING ... Stanley Myers
TORRID ZONE ... Adolph Deutsch†
TORTILLA FLAT ... Franz Waxman†
TORTURE GARDEN ... Don Banks
TORTURE GARDEN ... James Bernard
TORTURE ME, BUT KILL ME WITH KISSES ... Armando Trovajoli
TOTAL RECALL ... Jerry Goldsmith
TOTO CERCA CASA ... Carlo Rustichelli
TOTO CONTRO IL PIRATA NERO ... Carlo Rustichelli
TOTO DE ARABIA ... Angelo Francesco Lavagnino†
TOTO DI NOTTE ... Armando Trovajoli
TOTO E CLEOPATRA ... Carlo Rustichelli
TOTO E IL RE DI ROMA ... Nino Rota†
TOTO E LE DONNE ... Carlo Rustichelli
TOTO E MARCELLINO ... Carlo Rustichelli
TOTO E PEPPINO DIVISI A BERLINO ... Armando Trovajoli
TOTO SEXY ... Armando Trovajoli
TOTO, PEPPINO E LA DOLCE VITA ... Armando Trovajoli
TOUCH & GO ... Sylvester Levay
TOUCH AND GO ... John Addison
TOUCH OF CLASS, A ... ★ John Cameron
TOUCH OF EVIL ... Henry Mancini
TOUCH OF SATAN, THE ... Robert O. Ragland
TOUCH OF SCANDAL, A (TF) ... Sylvester Levay
TOUCHABLES, THE ... Ken Thorne
TOUCHE PAS A LA FEMME BLANCHEI ... Philippe Sarde
TOUCHED ... Shirley Walker
TOUCHED BY LOVE ... John Barry
TOUCHEZ PAS AU GRISBI ... Jean Wiener†
TOUGH AS THEY COME ... Hans J. Salter
TOUGH ASSIGNMENT ... Albert Glasser
TOUGH ENOUGH ... Michael Lloyd
TOUGH ENOUGH ... David Wheatley
TOUGH ENOUGH ... Steve Wax
TOUGH GUY ... William Axt†
TOUGH GUYS ... James Newton Howard
TOUGH GUYS DON'T DANCE ... Angelo Badalamenti
TOUGHEST GUN IN TOMBSTONE ... Paul Dunlap
TOUGHEST MAN IN THE WORLD, THE (TF) ... William Goldstein
TOUGHLOVE (TF) ... Paul Chihara
TOURBILLONS DE PARIS ... Paul Misraki†
TOURIST (TF) ... Jack Smalley
TOURIST TRAP ... Pino Donaggio
TOUS LE CHEMINS MENENT A ROME ... Paul Misraki†
TOUT LE MONDE IL EST BEAU... ... Michel Magne†
TOUT LE MONDE PEUT SE TROMPER ... Vladimir Cosma
TOUT VA TRES BIEN MADAME LA MARQUISE ... Paul Misraki†
TOUTE UNE VIE ... Francis Lai
TOVARICH ... Max Steiner†
TOWARD THE TERRA ... Masaru Sato
TOWER OF HELL ... Kenneth V. Jones
TOWER OF LONDON ... Charles Previn†
TOWER OF LONDON ... Frank Skinner†
TOWERING INFERNO, THE ... ★ John Williams
TOWN BULLY, THE (TF) ... Jorge Calandrelli
TOWN LIKE ALICE, A ... Matyas Seiber
TOWN ON TRIAL ... Tristram Cary
TOWN TAMER ... Jimmie Haskell
TOWN THAT DREADED SUNDOWN, THE ... Jaime Mendoza-Nava
TOWN WITHOUT PITY ... Dimitri Tiomkin†
TOXIC AVENGER, PART II, THE ... Barrie Guard
TOY TIGER, THE ... Herman Stein
TOY TIGER, THE ... Henry Mancini
TOY WIFE, THE ... Edward Ward†
TOY, THE ... Vladimir Cosma
TOY, THE ... Patrick Williams
TRACK 29 ... Stanley Myers
TRACK OF THE CAT ... Roy Webb†
TRACKDOWN ... Charles Bernstein
TRACKDOWN: FINDING THE GOODBAR KILLER (TF) ... Stephen Lawrence
TRACKER, THE (CTF) ... Sylvester Levay
TRACKERS, THE (TF) ... Johnny Mandel
TRADE WINDS ... Alfred Newman†
TRADING HEARTS ... Stanley Myers
TRADING PLACES ... ★ Elmer Bernstein
TRAIL OF THE MOUNTIES, THE ... Albert Glasser
TRAIL OF THE PINK PANTHER ... Henry Mancini
TRAIL OF THE VIGILANTES ... Hans J. Salter
TRAIL OF '98, THE ... William Axt†
TRAILROAD MAN, THE ... Carlo Rustichelli
TRAIN ROBBERS, THE ... Dominic Frontiere
TRAIN TO TOMBSTONE ... Albert Glasser
TRAIN, THE ... Maurice Jarre
TRANSATLANTIC ... R.H. Bassett†
TRANSATLANTIC TUNNEL ... Louis Levy†
TRANSFORMERS - THE MOVIE, THE (AF) ... Vince DiCola
TRANSGRESSION ... Max Steiner†
TRANSPLANT (TF) ... Fred Karlin
TRANSYLVANIA 6-5000 ... Lee Holdridge
TRAP, THE ... Ron Goodwin
TRAPEZE ... Malcolm Arnold
TRAPPED ... Sol Kaplan
TRAPPED (TF) ... Gil Melle
TRAPPED BENEATH THE SEA (TF) ... Joel Hirschhorn
TRAPPED BENEATH THE SEA (TF) ... Al Kasha
TRAPPED IN SILENCE (TF) ... Charles Gross
TRAUMA ... Buddy Collette
TRAUMA CENTER (TF) ... James Di Pasquale
TRAVEL TO THE PLACE OF THE ACCIDENT ... Alfi Kabiljo
TRAVELING EXECUTIONER, THE ... Jerry Goldsmith
TRAVELING HUSBANDS ... Max Steiner†
TRAVELLING MAN, THE (CTF) ... Miles Goodman
TRAVELS WITH ANITA ... Ennio Morricone
TRAVIS LOGAN, D.A. (TF) ... Patrick Williams
TRAVIS McGEE (TF) ... Jerrold Immel
TRAXX ... Jay Gruska
TRE NEL MILLE ... Ennio Morricone
TRE NOTTI D'AMORE ... Carlo Rustichelli
TRE PER UNA GRANDE RAPINA ... Stelvio Cipriani
TRE RAMAZZE IN FUORI GIOCO ... Carlo Rustichelli
TRE SUPERMEN CONTRO LE AMAZZONI ... Franco Micalizzi
TREASURE ISLAND ... Herbert Stothart†
TREASURE OF BIRD ISLAND, THE (AF) ... Zdenek Liska
TREASURE OF JAMAICA REEF, THE ... Christopher L. Stone
TREASURE OF MATECUMBE ... Buddy Baker
TREASURE OF MONTE CRISTO, THE ... Albert Glasser
TREASURE OF PANCHO VILLA, THE ... Leith Stevens†
TREASURE OF SAN GENNARO ... Armando Trovajoli
TREASURE OF THE FOUR CROWNS ... Ennio Morricone
TREASURE OF THE GOLDEN CONDOR ... Sol Kaplan
TREASURE OF THE SIERRA MADRE, THE ... Max Steiner†
TREASURE OF THE YANKEE ZEPHYR ... Brian May
TREAT 'EM ROUGH ... Hans J. Salter
TREE GROWS IN BROOKLYN, A ... Alfred Newman†
TREE GROWS IN BROOKYLN, A (TF) ... Jerry Goldsmith
TREE OF HANDS, THE ... Richard Hartley
TREE, THE ... Kenyon Hopkins
TREMORS ... Ernest Troost
TRENCHCOAT ... Charles Fox
TRENCHCOAT IN PARADISE (TF) ... John Debney
TRENO POPOLARE ... Nino Rota†
TRENT'S LAST CASE ... Anthony Collins†
TRES MUJERES DE NOW ... Stelvio Cipriani
TRESPASSERS, THE ... Bruce Smeaton
TRIAL ... Daniele Amfitheatrof†
TRIAL BY COMBAT ... Frank Cordell†
TRIAL OF BILLY JACK, THE ... Elmer Bernstein
TRIAL OF CHAPLAIN JENSEN, THE (TF) ... Dave Grusin
TRIAL OF JOAN OF ARC, THE ... Francis Seyrig
TRIAL OF LEE HARVEY OSWALD, THE (TF) ... Fred Karlin
TRIAL OF THE INCREDIBLE HULK, THE (TF) ... Lance Rubin
TRIALS OF OSCAR WILDE, THE ... Ron Goodwin
TRIANGLE FACTORY FIRE SCANDAL, THE (TF) ... Walter Scharf
TRIBE, THE (TF) ... David Shire
TRIBE, THE (TF) ... Hal Mooney
TRIBES ... Tangerine Dream
TRIBES (TF) ... Al Capps
TRIBUTE ... Ken Wannberg
TRIBUTE TO A BAD MAN ... Miklos Rozsa
TRICK OR TREAT ... Christopher Young
TRICKS OF THE TRADE (TF) ... Walter Murphy
TRICKY GAME OF LOVE, THE ... Zdenek Liska
TRILOGY OF TERROR (TF) ... Bob Cobert
TRINITA E SARTANA: FIGLI DI... ... Carlo Savina
TRIO ... John Greenwood†
TRIP TO BOUNTIFUL, THE ... J.A.C. Redford
TRIP, THE ... Barry Goldberg
TRIP, THE ... Albert Lloyd Olson
TRIPLECROSS (TF) ... Lalo Schifrin
TRIUMPH OF THE SON OF HERCULES ... Carlo Rustichelli
TRIUMPH OF THE SPIRIT ... Cliff Eidelman
TRIUMPHS OF A MAN CALLED HORSE ... Georges Garvarentz
TROG ... John Scott
TROIS FEMMES ... Georges Van Parys†
TROIS MILLIARDS SANS ASCENSEUR ... Teo Usuelli
TROIS TELEGRAMMES ... Joseph Kosma†
TROJAN WOMEN, THE ... Mikis Theodorakis
TROLL ... Richard H. Band
TROMA'S WAR ... Christopher De Marco
TRON ... Wendy Carlos
TROOP BEVERLY HILLS ... Randy Edelman
TROOPER HOOK ... Gerald Fried
TROP JOLIES POUR ETRE HONNETES ... Serge Gainsbourg
TROPIC OF CANCER ... Stanley Myers
TROTTIE TRUE ... Benjamin Frankel†
TROUBLE ALONG THE WAY ... Max Steiner†
TROUBLE AT 16 ... Van Alexander
TROUBLE COMES TO TOWN (TF) ... Tom Scott
TROUBLE FOR TWO ... Franz Waxman†
TROUBLE IN HIGH TIMBER COUNTRY (TF) ... George Aliceson Tipton
TROUBLE IN MIND ... Mark Isham
TROUBLE IN PARADISE ... W. Franke Harling†
TROUBLE IN PARADISE (TF) ... Chris Neal
TROUBLE IN SUNDOWN ... Roy Webb†
TROUBLE IN THE GLEN ... Victor Young†
TROUBLE WITH ANGELS, THE ... Jerry Goldsmith
TROUBLE WITH DICK, THE ... Roger Bourland
TROUBLE WITH HARRY, THE ... Bernard Herrmann†
TROUBLE WITH SPIES, THE ... Ken Thorne
TROUBLE WITH WOMEN, THE ... Victor Young†
TROUBLE WITH WOMEN, THE ... Robert Emmett Dolan†
TROUBLEMAKER, THE ... Cy Coleman
TROUT, THE ... Richard Hartley
TRUCK TURNER ... Isaac Hayes
TRUE BELIEVER ... Brad Fiedel
TRUE BLOOD ... Scott Roewe
TRUE BLUE (CTF) ... Domenic Troiano
TRUE CONFESSION ... Frederick Hollander†
TRUE CONFESSIONS ... Georges Delerue
TRUE GLORY, THE (FD) ... William Alwyn†
TRUE GRIT ... Elmer Bernstein
TRUE GRIT (A FURTHER ADVENTURE) (TF) ... Earle Hagen
TRUE STORIES ... David Byrne
TRUE STORY OF ESKIMO NELL, THE ... Brian May
TRUE STORY OF JESSE JAMES, THE ... Leigh Harline†
TRUE TO LIFE ... Victor Young†
TRUMAN CAPOTE'S THE GLASS HOUSE (TF) ... Billy Goldenberg
TRUNK TO CAIRO ... Dov Seltzer
TRUTH ABOUT MURDER, THE ... Leigh Harline†
TRUTH ABOUT SPRING, THE ... Robert Farnon
TRYGON FACTOR, THE ... Peter Thomas
TU CHE NE DICI? ... Armando Trovajoli
TUCKER ... Carmine Coppola
TUCKER ... Joe Jackson
TUDOR ROSE ... Hubert Bath†
TUESDAY IN NOVEMBER (D) ... Virgil Thomson†
TUFF TURF ... Jonathan Elias
TUGBOAT ANNIE SAILS AGAIN ... Adolph Deutsch†
TULIPS ... Eddie Karam
TULSA ... Frank Skinner†
TUMBLEDOWN (TF) ... Richard Hartley
TUMBLEWEED ... Herman Stein
TUMBLEWEED ... Henry Mancini
TUMBLEWEED TRAIL ... Karl Hajos†
TUNES OF GLORY ... Malcolm Arnold
TURK 182 ... Paul Zaza
TURKEY SHOOT ... Brian May
TURKISH DELIGHT ... Rogier Van Otterloo†
TURN BACK THE CLOCK ... Herbert Stothart†
TURN BACK THE CLOCK (TF) ... Nan Schwartz
TURN OF THE SCREW (TF) ... Bob Cobert
TURN OF THE TIDE, THE ... Arthur Benjamin†
TURNABOUT ... Arthur Morton
TURNAROUND ... Mark Shreeve
TURNER AND HOOCH ... Charles Gross
TURNING POINT OF JIM MALLOY, THE (TF) ... Johnny Mandel
TURNING POINT, THE ... John Lanchberry
TURNING TABLE, THE (AF) ... Wojciech Kilar

TURNOVER SMITH (TF) ... Bernardo Segall
TURTLE DIARY ... Geoffrey Burgon
TUTTI I COLORI DEL BUIO ... Bruno Nicolai
TUTTI PER UNO, BOTTE PER TUTTI ... Carlo Rustichelli
TUTTLES OF TAHITI, THE ... Roy Webb†
TUTTO A POSTO, NIENTE IN ORDINE ... Piero Piccioni
TUTTO PER TUTTO ... Luis Bacalov
TWELVE ANGRY MEN ... Kenyon Hopkins
TWELVE CHAIRS, THE ... John Morris
TWELVE CROWDED HOURS ... Roy Webb†
TWELVE HOURS TO KILL ... Paul Dunlap
TWELVE O'CLOCK HIGH ... Alfred Newman†
TWENTY PLUS TWO ... Gerald Fried
TWICE DEAD ... David Bergeaud
TWICE IN A LIFETIME ... Pat Metheny
TWICE IN A LIFETIME (TF) ... Al Capps
TWICE-TOLD TALES ... Richard LaSalle
TWILIGHT ... Georges Auric†
TWILIGHT FOR THE GODS ... David Raksin
TWILIGHT OF HONOR ... John Green†
TWILIGHT ON THE PRAIRIE ... Hans J. Salter
TWILIGHT TIME ... Walter Scharf
TWILIGHT WOMEN ... Allan Gray†
TWILIGHT ZONE: THE MOVIE ... Jerry Goldsmith
TWILIGHT'S LAST GLEAMING ... Jerry Goldsmith
TWIN BEDS ... Dimitri Tiomkin†
TWIN DETECTIVES (TF) ... Tom Scott
TWIN PEAKS (TF) ... Angelo Badalamenti
TWIN, THE ... Vladimir Cosma
TWINKLE IN GOD'S EYE, THE ... Van Alexander
TWINKY ... John Scott
TWINS ... Georges Delerue
TWINS ... Randy Edelman
TWINS OF EVIL ... Harry Robertson
TWIRL (TF) ... Jimmie Haskell
TWIST OF FATE ... Malcolm Arnold
TWIST OF FATE (TF) ... Laurence Rosenthal
TWIST OF SAND, A ... Tristram Cary
TWISTED NERVE ... Bernard Herrmann†
TWISTED OBSESSION ... Antoine Duhamel
TWISTER ... Hans Zimmer
TWO ALONE ... Max Steiner†
TWO DOLLAR BETTOR ... Irving Gertz
TWO DOLLAR HAIRCUT, THE ... Antoine Duhamel
TWO ENGLISH GIRLS ... Georges Delerue
TWO FACES OF DR. JEKYLL, THE ... Monty Norman
TWO FATHER'S JUSTICE (TF) ... Jan Hammer
TWO FLAGS WEST ... Hugo Friedhofer†
TWO FOR THE ROAD ... Henry Mancini
TWO FOR THE SEESAW ... Andre Previn
TWO GALS AND A GUY ... Gail Kubik†
TWO GENTLEMEN SHARING ... Stanley Myers
TWO GIRLS ON BROADWAY ... George Bassman
TWO GUYS FROM MILWAUKEE ... Frederick Hollander†
TWO HEARTBEATS ... Misha Segal
TWO IN A CROWD ... Charles Previn†
TWO IN REVOLT ... Max Steiner†
TWO IN THE STARS ... Stelvio Cipriani
TWO JAKES, THE ... Van Dyke Parks
TWO KINDS OF LOVE (TF) ... Mark Snow
TWO LOVES ... Bronislau Kaper†
TWO MARRIAGES (TF) ... Bruce Broughton
TWO MARRIAGES (TF) ... Angela Morley
TWO MOON JUNCTION ... Jonathan Elias
TWO MRS. CARROLLS, THE ... Franz Waxman†
TWO MRS. GRENVILLES, THE (TF) ... Marvin Hamlisch
TWO MULES FOR SISTER SARAH ... Ennio Morricone
TWO NIGHTS WITH CLEOPATRA ... Armando Trovajoli
TWO O'CLOCK COURAGE ... Roy Webb†
TWO OF A KIND ... George Duning
TWO OF A KIND (TF) ... James Di Pasquale
TWO OF US, THE ... Georges Delerue
TWO ON A BENCH (TF) ... Pete Carpenter†
TWO ON A GUILLOTINE ... Max Steiner†
TWO PEOPLE ... David Shire
TWO SECONDS ... W. Franke Harling†
TWO SMART PEOPLE ... George Bassman
TWO SOLITUDES ... Maurice Jarre
TWO THOROUGHBREDS ... Roy Webb†
TWO TICKETS IN LONDON ... Frank Skinner†
TWO TICKETS TO BROADWAY ... Walter Scharf
TWO WEEKS IN ANOTHER TOWN ... David Raksin
TWO WEEKS IN SEPTEMBER ... Michel Magne†
TWO WISE MAIDS ... Karl Hajos†
TWO WOMEN ... Armando Trovajoli
TWO WORLDS OF JENNIE LOGAN, THE (TF) ... Glenn Paxton
TWO YANKS IN TRINIDAD ... John Leipold†
TWO YEARS BEFORE THE MAST ... Victor Young†
TWO-FACED WOMAN ... Bronislau Kaper†
TWO-FIVE, THE (TF) ... Gerald Fried
TWO-HEADED SPY, THE ... Gerard Schurmann
TWO-MAN SUBMARINE ... Mario Castelnuovo-Tedesco†
TWO-MINUTE WARNING ... Charles Fox
TWO-WAY STRETCH ... Kenneth V. Jones
TYCOON ... Leigh Harline†
TYPHOON ... Frederick Hollander†

U

U BOAT 29 ... Miklos Rozsa
U.F.O. BLUE CHRISTMAS ... Masaru Sato
U.H.F. ... John Du Prez
U.M.C. (TF) ... Lalo Schifrin
U.S. MARSHALS: WACO & RHINEHART (TF) ... Tom Bahler
U.S. MARSHALS: WACO & RHINEHART (TF) ... Doug Timm†
UCCELLACI E UCCELLINI ... Ennio Morricone
UCCIDERE IN SILENZIO ... Stelvio Cipriani
UCCIDETE IL VITELLO GRASSO E ARROSTITELO ... Ennio Morricone
UCCIDI E MUORI ... Carlo Rustichelli
UFORIA ... Richard Baskin
UGETSU ... Fumio Hayasaka †
ULTIMATE IMPOSTER, THE (TF) ... Dana Kaproff
ULTIMATE WARRIOR, THE ... Gil Melle
ULTIME GRIDA DALLA SAVANA (FD) ... Carlo Savina
ULTIMOS DIAS DE LA VICTIMA ... Emilio Kauderer
ULYSSES ... Stanley Myers
ULYSSES ... Alessandro Cicognini†
ULYSSES AGAINST THE SONS OF HERCULES ... Angelo Francesco Lavagnino†
ULZANA'S RAID ... Frank De Vol
UMBERTO D. ... Alessandro Cicognini†
UMBRELLAS OF CHERBOURG, THE ... ★ Michel Legrand
UN AMERICANO IN VAZANZA ... Nino Rota†
UN AMI VIENDRA CE SOIR ... Arthur Honegger†
UN AMORE A ROMA ... Carlo Rustichelli
UN AMOUR COMME LE NOTRE ... Armando Trovajoli
UN AMOUR DE GUERRE ... Antoine Duhamel
UN AMOUR DE PLUIE ... Francis Lai
UN AMOUR INTERDIT ... Luis Bacalov
UN ANGE AU PARADIS ... Michel Magne†
UN ANIMAL CHIAMATO UOMO ... Carlo Savina
UN ANNO DI SCUOLA ... Luis Bacalov
UN BEAU MONSTRE ... Georges Garvarentz
UN CAPITAN DE QUINCE ANOS ... Bruno Nicolai
UN CASO DI INCOSCIENZA (TF) ... Luis Bacalov
UN CERTAIN MONSIEUR ... Georges Van Parys†
UN CHAPEAU DE PAILLE D'ITALIE ... Jacques Ibert†
UN CHOIX D'ASSASSINS ... Alain Gorraguer
UN COEUR GROS COMME CA (FD) ... Georges Delerue
UN COEUR GROS COMME CA (FD) ... Michel Legrand
UN COEUR QUI SE BRISE (TF) ... Georges Delerue
UN CUORE SEMPLICE ... Franco Mannino
UN DIVORCE HEUREUX ... Philippe Sarde
UN DOLLARO A TESTA ... Ennio Morricone
UN DRAMMA BORGHESE ... Riz Ortolani
UN DROLE DE DIMANCHE ... Paul Misraki†
UN EROE DEI BOSTRI TEMPI ... Nino Rota†
UN ESTATE IN QUATTRO ... Carlo Rustichelli
UN ETTARO DI CIELO ... Nino Rota†
UN FEMME EN BLANC SE REVOLTE ... Michel Magne†
UN FLIC ... Michel Colombier
UN GENIO, DUE COMPARI, UN POLLO ... Ennio Morricone
UN GIORNO DA LEONI ... Carlo Rustichelli
UN GIORNO IN EUROPA (FD) ... Teo Usuelli
UN GIORNO IN PRETURA ... Armando Trovajoli
UN GRAN PATRON ... Joseph Kosma†
UN HOMME A ABATTRE ... Antoine Duhamel
UN HOMME A MA TAILLE ... Pierre Bachelet
UN HOMME EST MORT ... Michel Legrand
UN HOMME LIBRE ... Francis Lai
UN HOMME QUI ME PLAIT ... Francis Lai
UN JARDIN PUBLIC ... Jean Prodromides
UN LENTESIMO DI SECONDO ... Stelvio Cipriani
UN MALEDETTO IMBROGLIO ... Carlo Rustichelli
UN MAUVAIS GARCON ... Georges Van Parys†
UN MILITARE E MEZZO ... Armando Trovajoli
UN MILLIARD DANS UN BILLARD ... Georges Garvarentz
UN MISSIONNAIRE ... Michel Michelet†
UN MONDE NOUVEAU ... Michel Colombier
UN MONSIEUR DE COMPAGNIE ... Georges Delerue
UN OMBRA NELL'OMBRA ... Stelvio Cipriani
UN OTAGE (TF) ... Georges Delerue
UN PAPILLON SUR L'EPAULE ... Claude Bolling
UN PARTIE DE CAMPAGNE ... Joseph Kosma†
UN POLIZIOTTO SCOMODO ... Stelvio Cipriani
UN POVERE RICCO ... Stelvio Cipriani
UN REVENANT ... Arthur Honegger†
UN ROI SANS DIVERTISSEMENT ... Maurice Jarre
UN SAC DE BILLES ... Philippe Sarde
UN SEUL AMOUR ... Arthur Honegger†
UN SINGE EN HIVER ... Michel Magne†
UN SOIR DE RAFLE ... Georges Van Parys†
UN SOIR UN TRAIN ... Frederic Devreese
UN SOURIRE DANS LA TEMPETE ... Jean Wiener†
UN SUSURRO NEL BUIO ... Pino Donaggio
UN TAXI MAUVE ... Philippe Sarde
UN TAXI POUR TOBROUK ... Georges Garvarentz
UN TENERO TRAMONTO ... Stelvio Cipriani
UN TRENO PER DURANGO ... Carlo Rustichelli
UN UOMO A META ... Ennio Morricone
UN UOMO CHIAMATO APOCALISSE JOE ... Bruno Nicolai
UN UOMO DA RISPETTARE ... Ennio Morricone
UN UOMO FACILE ... Carlo Rustichelli
UN UOMO, UNA CITTA ... Carlo Rustichelli
UN'AVVENTURA DI SALVATORE ROSA ... Alessandro Cicognini†
UNA BREVE STAGIONE ... Ennio Morricone
UNA DOMENICA D'ESTATE ... Armando Trovajoli
UNA GITA SCOLASTICA ... Riz Ortolani
UNA MATTA MATTA CORSA IN RUSSIA ... Carlo Rustichelli
UNA NUVOLA DI POLVERE ... Bruno Nicolai
UNA PISTOLA PER RINGO ... Ennio Morricone
UNA RAGIONE PER VIVERE E UNA PER MORIRE ... Riz Ortolani
UNA ROMANTICA AVVENTURA ... Alessandro Cicognini†
UNA SPADA PER BRANDO ... Carlo Rustichelli
UNA STORIA DI NOTTE ... Armando Trovajoli
UNA STORIA MODERNA - L'APE REGINA ... Teo Usuelli
UNA STRANA PASSIONE ... Luis Bacalov
UNA VERGINE IN FAMIGLIA ... Carlo Savina
UNBELIEVABLE TRUTH, THE ... Jim Coleman
UNBELIEVABLE, THE ... Albert Glasser
UNCANNY, THE ... Wilfred Josephs
UNCERTAIN GLORY ... Adolph Deutsch†
UNCHAINED ... Alex North
UNCLE BUCK ... Ira Newborn
UNCLE JOE SHANNON ... Bill Conti
UNCLE SCAM ... Michael Levanios III
UNCLE TOM'S CABIN ... Peter Thomas
UNCLE TOM'S CABIN (CTF) ... Kennard Ramsey
UNCLE VANYA ... Werner Janssen
UNCLE, THE ... John Addison
UNCOMMON LOVE, AN (TF) ... Miles Goodman
UNCOMMON VALOR ... James Horner
UNCOMMON VALOR (TF) ... Robert Summers
UNCONQUERED ... Victor Young†
UNCONQUERED (TF) ... Arthur B. Rubinstein
UNDEAD, THE ... Ronald Stein†
UNDER CAPRICORN ... Richard Addinsell†
UNDER COVER ... Todd Rundgren
UNDER COVER OF NIGHT ... William Axt†
UNDER FIRE ... Paul Dunlap
UNDER FIRE ... ★ Jerry Goldsmith
UNDER MILK WOOD ... Brian Gascoigne
UNDER MY SKIN ... Daniele Amfitheatrof†
UNDER SIEGE (TF) ... Brad Fiedel
UNDER SUSPICION ... Georges Delerue
UNDER TEN FLAGS ... Nino Rota†
UNDER THE BOARDWALK ... David Kitay
UNDER THE CHERRY MOON ... Clare Fisher
UNDER THE INFLUENCE (TF) ... ☆ Nan Schwartz
UNDER THE PARIS SKY ... Jean Wiener†
UNDER THE RAINBOW ... Joe Renzetti
UNDER THE RED ROBE ... Arthur Benjamin†
UNDER THE VOLCANO ... ★ Alex North
UNDER THE YUM-YUM TREE ... Frank De Vol
UNDER TWO FLAGS ... Louis Silvers†
UNDER WESTERN SKIES ... Frank Skinner†
UNDERACHIEVERS, THE ... Don Preston
UNDERCOVER ... Bruce Smeaton
UNDERCOVER MAN, THE ... George Duning
UNDERCOVER WITH THE KKK (TF) ... Morton Stevens
UNDERCURRENT ... Herbert Stothart†
UNDERGRADS, THE (CTF) ... Matthew McCauley

UNDERGROUND ... Adolph Deutsch†
UNDERGROUND MAN, THE (TF) ... Richard Hazard
UNDERSEA GIRL ... Alexander Courage
UNDERWATER CITY, THE ... Ronald Stein†
UNDERWATER WARRIOR ... Harry Sukman†
UNDERWATER! ... Roy Webb†
UNDERWORLD STORY, THE ... David Rose†
UNDERWORLD, U.S.A. ... Harry Sukman†
UNDYING MONSTER, THE ... David Raksin
UNDYING MONSTER, THE ... Cyril J. Mockridge†
UNE AFFAIRE D'HOMMES ... Vladimir Cosma
UNE AFFAIRE DE FEMMES ... Mathieu Chabrol
UNE ALCHIMIE ... Georges Delerue
UNE AUSSI LONGUE ABSENCE ... Georges Delerue
UNE FEMME A SA FENETRE ... Carlo Rustichelli
UNE FEMME PAR JOUR ... Georges Van Parys†
UNE FILLE COUSUE DE FIL BLANC ... Oliver Dassault
UNE FILLE POUR L'ETE ... Georges Delerue
UNE HISTOIRE D'AMOUR ... Paul Misraki†
UNE JOURNEE BIEN REMPLIE ... Bruno Nicolai
UNE RAVISSANTE IDIOTE ... Michel Legrand
UNEXPECTED RICHES ... Sol Kaplan
UNEXPECTED UNCLE ... Anthony Collins†
UNFAITHFUL, THE ... Max Steiner†
UNFAITHFULLY YOURS ... Bill Conti
UNFINISHED BUSINESS ... Patricia Cullen
UNFINISHED BUSINESS ... Franz Waxman†
UNFINISHED DANCE, THE ... Herbert Stothart†
UNFORGETTABLE YEAR—1919, THE ... Dmitri Shostakovitch†
UNFORGIVEN, THE ... Dimitri Tiomkin†
UNGUARDED HOUR, THE ... William Axt†
UNGUARDED MOMENT, THE ... Herman Stein
UNGUARDED MOMENT, THE ... Henry Mancini
UNHOLY GARDEN, THE ... Alfred Newman†
UNHOLY MATRIMONY (TF) ... Michel Rubini
UNHOLY WIFE, THE ... Daniele Amfitheatrof†
UNHOLY WITCH, THE ... Wolfgang Zeller†
UNHOLY, THE ... Roger Bellon
UNIDENTIFIED FLYING OBJECTS (FD) ... Ernest Gold
UNIDENTIFIED FLYING ODDBALL ... Ron Goodwin
UNINHIBITED, THE ... Georges Delerue
UNINVITED ... Dan Slider
UNINVITED, THE ... Victor Young†
UNION CITY ... Chris Stein
UNION PACIFIC ... John Leipold†
UNION PACIFIC ... Sigmund Krumgold†
UNION STATION ... Leigh Harline†
UNKNOWN GUEST, THE ... Dimitri Tiomkin†
UNKNOWN MAN,THE ... Conrad Salinger†
UNKNOWN TERROR, THE ... Raoul Kraushaar
UNKNOWN WORLD ... Ernest Gold
UNMAN, WITTERING & ZIGO ... Michael J. Lewis
UNMARRIED WOMAN, AN ... Bill Conti
UNNATURAL CAUSES (TF) ... Charles Fox
UNREMARKABLE LIFE, AN ... Avery Sharpe
UNSEEN, THE ... Michael J. Lewis
UNSEEN, THE ... Ernst Toch†
UNSETTLED LAND ... Misha Segal
UNSINKABLE SHECKY, THE ... Scott Smalley
UNSPEAKABLE ACTS (TF) ... Mike Post
UNSUNG SONG ... Vladimir Horunzhy
UNSUSPECTED, THE ... Franz Waxman†
UNTAMED ... Franz Waxman†
UNTAMED ... Victor Young†
UNTAMED BREED, THE ... George Duning
UNTAMED FRONTIER ... Hans J. Salter
UNTAMED WOMEN ... Raoul Kraushaar
UNTAMED WOMEN ... Mort Glickman†
UNTAMED YOUTH ... Les Baxter
UNTEL, PERE ET FILS ... Jean Wiener†
UNTERNEHMEN XARIFA ... Arthur Benjamin†
UNTIL SEPTEMBER ... John Barry
UNTIL THE END OF THE WORLD ... Graeme Revell
UNTIL THEY SAIL ... David Raksin
UNTOUCHABLES, THE ... ★ Ennio Morricone
UNWED FATHER (TF) ... Jerry Fielding†
UNWED MOTHER ... Emil Newman†
UOMINI CONTRO ... Piero Piccioni
UOMINI E LUPI ... Mario Nascimbene
UP FROM THE DEPTHS ... James Horner
UP FROM THE DEPTHS ... Russell O'Malley
UP IN CENTRAL PARK ... John Green†
UP IN MABEL'S ROOM ... Michel Michelet†
UP POMPEII ... Carl Davis
UP THE ACADEMY ... Jody Taylor Worth
UP THE CHASTITY BELT ... Carl Davis
UP THE CREEK ... William Goldstein
UP THE DOWN STAIRCASE ... Fred Karlin
UP THE MACGREGORS ... Ennio Morricone
UP THE SANDBOX ... Billy Goldenberg
UP TO HIS EARS ... Georges Delerue
UPIOR ... Wojciech Kilar
UPS & DOWNS ... Bo Harwood
UPS AND DOWNS ... Patricia Cullen
UPWORLD ... Richard Gibbs
URBAN COWBOY ... Ralph Burns
URSULE ET GRELU ... Alain Gorraguer
URUBU ... Albert Glasser
USED CARS ... Patrick Williams
USERS, THE (TF) ... Maurice Jarre
UTOPIA ... Paul Misraki†

V

V (TF) ... ☆ Joe Harnell
V.I.P.'S, THE ... Miklos Rozsa
V: THE FINAL BATTLE (MS) ... Dennis McCarthy
V: THE FINAL BATTLE (TF) ... Joseph Conlan
V: THE FINAL BATTLE (TF) ... Barry De Vorzon
VA VOIR MAMAN...PAPA TRAVAILLE ... Georges Delerue
VAARWEL ... Ennio Morricone
VACANCES PORTUGAISES ... Georges Delerue
VACANZE A ISCHIA ... Alessandro Cicognini†
VACANZE D'INVERNO ... Armando Trovajoli
VACANZE IN AMERICA ... Manuel De Sica
VACANZE IN VAL TREBBIA ... Nicola Piovani
VACANZE PER UN MASSACRO ... Luis Bacalov
VACATION FROM LOVE ... Edward Ward †
VADO A VIVERE DA SOLO ... Manuel De Sica
VADO, VERO E SPARO ... Carlo Rustichelli
VAGABOND KING, THE ... Victor Young†
VALACHI PAPERS, THE ... Riz Ortolani
VALDEZ IS COMING ... Charles Gross
VALENTINE (TF) ... Lee Holdridge
VALENTINE MAGIC ON LOVE ISLAND (TF) ... Peter Matz
VALENTINO ... Heinz Roemheld†
VALERIE ... Albert Glasser
VALHALLA (AF) ... Ron Goodwin
VALIANT HOMBRE, THE ... Albert Glasser
VALIANT IS THE WORD FOR CARRIE ... Frederick Hollander†
VALLEY OF DECISION, THE ... ★ Herbert Stothart†
VALLEY OF THE BEES, THE ... Zdenek Liska
VALLEY OF THE DOLLS ... ★ John Williams
VALLEY OF THE EAGLES ... Nino Rota†
VALLEY OF THE GIANTS ... Adolph Deutsch†
VALLEY OF THE GIANTS ... Hugo Friedhofer†
VALLEY OF THE GWANGI ... Jerome Moross†
VALLEY OF THE KINGS ... Miklos Rozsa
VALLEY TOWN ... Marc Blitzstein†
VALMONT ... Christopher Palmer
VALUE FOR MONEY ... Malcolm Arnold
VAMOS A MATAR, COMPANEROS ... Ennio Morricone
VAMP ... Jonathan Elias
VAMPIRA ... David Whitaker
VAMPIRE ... Wojciech Kilar
VAMPIRE (TF) ... Fred Karlin
VAMPIRE BEAST CRAVES BLOOD, THE ... Paul Ferris
VAMPIRE CIRCUS ... David Whitaker
VAMPIRE LOVERS, THE ... Harry Robertson
VAMPIRE'S KISS ... Colin Towns
VAMPIRE, THE ... Gerald Fried
VAMPIRES ... Les Baxter
VAMPYR ... Wolfgang Zeller†
VAMPYR OU L'ETRANGE AVENTURE DE DAVID GRAY ... Wolfgang Zeller†
VANESSA, HER LOVE STORY ... Herbert Stothart†
VANISHED (TF) ... Leonard Rosenman
VANISHING ACT (TF) ... Ken Wannberg
VARAN THE UNBELIEVABLE ... Akira Ifukube
VARDO ... Hans Zimmer
VARIETY ... John Lurie
VASECTOMY: A DELICATE MATTER ... Fred Karlin
VATICAN STORY ... Luis Bacalov
VAULT OF HORROR, THE ... Douglas Gamley
VEDO NUDO ... Armando Trovajoli
VEGAS (TF) ... Dominic Frontiere
VEGAS STRIP WARS, THE (TF) ... Jimmie Haskell
VEIL, THE ... Pino Donaggio
VEILS OF BAGDAD, THE ... Herman Stein
VEILS OF BAGDAD, THE ... Henry Mancini
VELVET (TF) ... Dominic Frontiere
VELVET (TF) ... Dominic Frontiere
VELVET TOUCH, THE ... Leigh Harline†
VENDETTA ... David Newman
VENDETTA ... Roy Webb†
VENDETTA EN CAMARGUE ... Joseph Kosma†
VENERE CREOLA ... Carlo Rustichelli
VENETIAN AFFAIR, THE ... Lalo Schifrin
VENETIAN BIRD ... Nino Rota†
VENETIAN BLACK ... Pino Donaggio
VENGEANCE ... Kenneth V. Jones
VENGEANCE IS MINE ... Shinchiro Ikebe
VENGEANCE OF FU-MANCHU, THE ... Malcom Lockyer
VENGEANCE OF SHE, THE ... Mario Nascimbene
VENGEANCE: THE STORY OF TONY CIMO (TF) ... Charles Gross
VENOM ... Michael Kamen
VENUS AND ADONIS ... Paul Bowles
VERA CRUZ ... Hugo Friedhofer†
VERBOTEN! ... Harry Sukman†
VERDICT, THE ... Johnny Mandel
VERDICT, THE ... Frederick Hollander†
VERGOGNA SCHIFOSI ... Ennio Morricone
VERMISAT ... Nicola Piovani
VERONIKA VOSS ... Peer Raben
VERTIGO ... Bernard Herrmann†
VERTIGO EN LA PISTA ... Stelvio Cipriani
VERUSCHKA, POESIA DI UNA DONNA ... Ennio Morricone
VERY BRADY CHRISTMAS, A (TF) ... Laurence Juber
VERY BRITISH COUP, A (TF) ... John Keane
VERY CLOSE QUARTERS ... Jay Chattaway
VERY EDGE OF THE NIGHT, THE ... Bebe Barron
VERY EDGE OF THE NIGHT, THE ... Louis Barron†
VERY HAPPY ALEXANDER ... Vladimir Cosma
VERY MISSING PERSON, A (TF) ... Vic Mizzy
VERY PRIVATE AFFAIR, A ... Fiorenzo Carpi
VERY SPECIAL FAVOR, A ... Vic Mizzy
VERY THOUGHT OF YOU, THE ... Franz Waxman†
VESSEL OF WRATH ... Richard Addinsell†
VESTIRE GLI INUDI ... Franco Mannino
VIA DEGLI SPECCHI ... Pino Donaggio
VIA MARGUTTA ... Piero Piccioni
VIA PADOVA, 46 ... Nino Rota†
VIA RASELLA ... Ennio Morricone
VIBES ... James Horner
VICE RAID ... Bert A. Shefter
VICE SQUAD ... Herschel Burke Gilbert
VICE SQUAD ... Keith Rubinstein
VICE VERSA ... Antony Hopkins
VICE VERSA ... David Shire
VICIOUS BREED, THE ... Les Baxter
VICKI ... Leigh Harline†
VICTIM, THE (TF) ... Gil Melle
VICTIMS (TF) ... Lalo Schifrin
VICTIMS FOR VICTIMS (TF) ... Paul Chihara
VICTOR/VICTORIA ... ★★ Henry Mancini
VICTORIA THE GREAT ... Anthony Collins†
VICTORS, THE ... Sol Kaplan
VICTORY ... Bill Conti
VICTORY ... Frederick Hollander†
VICTORY THROUGH AIR POWER ... ★ Oliver Wallace†
VICTORY MARCH ... Nicola Piovani
VICTORY THROUGH AIR POWER ... Edward Plumb†
VICTORY THROUGH AIR POWER ... ★ Paul J. Smith†
VIDEODROME ... Howard Shore
VIEL LARM UM NICHTS ... Giuseppe Becce†
VIETNAM SCENE DEL DOPOGUERRA ... Fiorenzo Carpi
VIETNAM TEXAS ... Richard Stone
VIETNAM WAR STORIES (CTF) ... Mark Snow
VIETNAM WAR STORY (CTF) ... Jonathan Sheffer
VIEW FROM POMPEY'S HEAD, THE ... Elmer Bernstein
VIEW TO A KILL, A ... John Barry
VIGIL IN THE NIGHT ... Alfred Newman†
VIGILANTE ... Jay Chattaway
VIGILANTE FORCE ... Gerald Fried
VIKINGS, THE ... Mario Nascimbene
VILLA BORGHESE ... Mario Nascimbene
VILLA RIDES! ... Maurice Jarre
VILLAI ... Bert A. Shefter
VILLAGE HARVEST (FD) ... Benjamin Britten†
VILLAGE OF DAUGHTERS ... Ron Goodwin
VILLAGE OF THE DAMNED ... Ron Goodwin
VILLAGE OF THE GIANTS ... Jack Nitzsche
VILLAIN, THE ... Bill Justis
VINCENT, FRANCOIS, PAUL AND THE OTHERS ... Philippe Sarde
VINDICATOR, THE ... Paul Zaza
VINO, WHISKY E ACQUA SALATA ... Luis Bacalov
VINTAGE, THE ... David Raksin
VIOLANTA ... Peer Raben
VIOLATED, THE ... Shirley Walker

VIOLATION OF SARAH McDAVID, THE (TF) ... Robert Prince
VIOLENT ENEMY, THE ... John Scott
VIOLENT EVIL, THE ... Ronald Stein†
VIOLENT FOUR, THE ... Riz Ortolani
VIOLENT MEN, THE ... Max Steiner†
VIOLENT ROAD ... Leith Stevens†
VIOLENT SATURDAY ... Hugo Friedhofer†
VIOLENT SATURDAY ... Lionel Newman†
VIOLETS ARE BLUE ... Patrick Williams
VIOLETTE ET FRANCOIS ... Philippe Sarde
VIOLETTE NOZIERE ... Pierre Jansen
VIPER ... Scott Roewe
VIRGILE ... Georges Van Parys†
VIRGIN AND THE GYPSY, THE ... Patrick Gowers
VIRGIN QUEEN, THE ... Franz Waxman†
VIRGIN SPRING, THE ... Eric Nordgren
VIRGINIA ... Victor Young†
VIRGINIA CITY ... Max Steiner†
VIRGINIAN, THE ... Daniele Amfitheatrof†
VIRTU ... Bruno Nicolai
VIRUS ... Teo Macero
VISA TO CANTON ... Edwin Astley
VISION QUEST ... Tangerine Dream
VISION, THE (TF) ... Bill Connor
VISIONS OF EIGHT ... Henry Mancini
VISIONS... (TF) ... Morton Stevens
VISIT TO A CHIEF'S SON ... Francis Lai
VISIT TO A SMALL PLANET ... Leigh Harline†
VISITING HOURS ... Jonathan Goldsmith
VITA DA CANI ... Nino Rota†
VITA DI MICHELANGELO (TF) ... Bruno Nicolai
VITAL SIGNS ... Miles Goodman
VITAL SIGNS (TF) ... Glenn Paxton
VIULENTEMENTE MIA ... Armando Trovajoli
VIVA ITALIA! ... Armando Trovajoli
VIVA KNIEVEL! ... Charles Bernstein
VIVA MARIA! ... Georges Delerue
VIVA VILLA! ... Herbert Stothart†
VIVA ZAPATA! ... ★ Alex North
VIVACIOUS LADY ... Roy Webb†
VIVE LA SOCIALE! ... Jean-Claude Petit
VIVEMENT DIMANCHE ... Georges Delerue
VIVERE IN PACE ... Nino Rota†
VIVRE LA NUIT ... Claude Bolling
VOGLIAMO I COLONELLI ... Carlo Rustichelli
VOGUES OF 1938 ... Victor Young†
VOICE IN THE MIRROR ... Henry Mancini
VOICE IN THE NIGHT, A ... Nicholas Brodzsky†
VOICE IN THE WIND ... Michel Michelet†
VOICE OF THE HEART (TF) ... Alan Parker
VOICE OF THE HURRICANE ... Paul Dunlap
VOICE OF THE MOON, THE ... Nicola Piovani
VOICE OF THE TURTLE, THE ... Max Steiner†
VOICES ... Richard Rodney Bennett
VOICES ... Jimmy Webb
VOICES WITHIN: THE LIVES OF TRUDDI CHASE (TF) ... Charles Fox
VOICI LE TEMPS DES ASSASSINS ... Jean Wiener†
VOLOCHAYEVSK DAYS ... Dmitri Shostakovitch†
VOLUNTEERS ... James Horner
VON HIMMEL GEFALLEN ... Bernhard Kaun†
VON RICHTOFEN AND BROWN ... Hugo Friedhofer†
VON RYAN'S EXPRESS ... Jerry Goldsmith
VOODOO ISLAND ... Les Baxter
VOODOO TIGER ... Mischa Bakaleinikoff †
VORMITTAGSPUK ... Paul Hindemith†
VOTE FOR HUGGETT ... Antony Hopkins
VOUS N'AVEZ RIEN A DECLARER? ... Maurice Jarre
VOYAGE OF THE DAMNED ... ★ Lalo Schifrin
VOYAGE OF THE YES, THE (TF) ... Richard Markowitz
VOYAGE SURPRISE ... Joseph Kosma†
VOYAGE TO AMERICA (D) ... Virgil Thomson†
VOYAGE TO GRAND TARTARIE ... Gerard Anfosso
VOYAGE TO THE BOTTOM OF THE SEA ... Bert A. Shefter
VOYAGE TO THE BOTTOM OF THE SEA ... Paul Sawtell†
VOYAGE, THE ... Manuel De Sica
VOYEUR ... Brian May
VRAZDA PO CESKY ... Zdenek Liska
VUDU BABY ... Stelvio Cipriani
VYBORG SIDE, THE ... Dmitri Shostakovitch†

W

W ... Johnny Mandel
W.C. FIELDS AND ME ... Henry Mancini
W.W. AND THE DIXIE DANCEKINGS ... Dave Grusin
WACKO ... Arthur Kempel
WACO ... Jimmie Haskell
WACO AND RINEHART (TF) ... Joel Rosenbaum
WAGES OF FEAR, THE ... Georges Auric†
WAGON MASTER ... Richard Hageman†
WAGONS ROLL AT NIGHT, THE ... Heinz Roemheld†
WAIKIKI (TF) ... Stu Phillips
WAIKIKI WEDDING ... Leo Shuken†
WAIT 'TILL THE SUN SHINES, NELLIE ... Alfred Newman†
WAIT TILL YOUR MOTHER GETS HOME (TF) ... Ken Harrison
WAIT UNTIL DARK ... Henry Mancini
WAJAN ... Wolfgang Zeller†
WAKE IN FRIGHT ... John Scott
WAKE ISLAND ... David Buttolph†
WAKE ME WHEN IT'S OVER ... Cyril J. Mockridge†
WAKE ME WHEN THE WAR IS OVER (TF) ... Fred Steiner
WAKE UP AND DREAM ... Cyril J. Mockridge†
WALK IN THE SHADOW ... William Alwyn†
WALK IN THE SPRING RAIN ... Elmer Bernstein
WALK INTO HELL ... Georges Auric†
WALK LIKE A DRAGON ... Paul Dunlap
WALK LIKE A MAN ... Lee Holdridge
WALK ON THE MOON, A ... Paul Chihara
WALK ON THE WILD SIDE ... Elmer Bernstein
WALK PROUD ... Robby Benson
WALK PROUD ... Don Peake
WALK SOFTLY, STRANGER ... Frederick Hollander†
WALK THE ANGRY BEACH ... Bill Marx
WALK THE DARK STREET ... Paul Dunlap
WALK THE PROUD LAND ... Hans J. Salter
WALK THE PROUD LAND ... Herman Stein
WALK WITH LOVE AND DEATH, A ... Georges Delerue
WALK, DON'T RUN ... Quincy Jones
WALKABOUT ... John Barry
WALKER ... Joe Strummer
WALKING DEAD, THE ... Bernhard Kaun†
WALKING HILLS, THE ... Arthur Morton
WALKING MY BABY BACK HOME ... Henry Mancini
WALKING ON AIR ... Nathaniel Shilkret†
WALKING STICK, THE ... Stanley Myers
WALKING TALL ... Walter Scharf
WALKING THE EDGE ... Jay Chattaway
WALKING THROUGH THE FIRE (TF) ... Fred Karlin
WALL OF NOISE ... William Lava†
WALL STREET ... Stewart Copeland
WALL, THE (TF) ... Leonard Rosenman
WALLENBERG: A HERO'S STORY (TF) ... Ernest Gold
WALLFLOWER ... Frederick Hollander†
WALLS OF FIRE ... Jimmie Haskell
WALLS OF JERICHO, THE ... Cyril J. Mockridge†
WALLS OF JERICHO, THE ... Alfred Newman†
WALTZ ACROSS TEXAS ... Steve Dorff
WALTZ OF THE TOREADORS ... Richard Addinsell†
WANDA NEVADA ... Ken Lauber
WANTED: DEAD OR ALIVE ... Joe Renzetti
WANTED: THE SUNDANCE WOMAN (TF) ... Fred Karlin
WAR AND PEACE ... Vyecheslav Ovchinnikov
WAR AND PEACE ... Nino Rota†
WAR AND REMEMBRANCE (MS) ... ☆ Bob Cobert
WAR ARROW ... Herman Stein
WAR BETWEEN MEN AND WOMEN, THE ... Marvin Hamlisch
WAR BETWEEN THE PLANETS ... Angelo Francesco Lavagnino†
WAR BETWEEN THE TATES, THE (TF) ... John Barry
WAR DRUMS ... Les Baxter
WAR GODS OF THE DEEP ... Stanley Black
WAR HERO ... Ronald Stein†
WAR IS HELL ... Hanns Eisler†
WAR IS HELL ... Ronald Stein†
WAR LORD, THE ... Hans J. Salter
WAR LORD, THE ... Jerome Moross†
WAR LOVER, THE ... Richard Addinsell†
WAR OF CHILDREN , A (TF) ... Jerry Fielding†
WAR OF THE COLOSSAL BEAST ... Albert Glasser
WAR OF THE GARGANTUAS ... Akira Ifukube
WAR OF THE ROSES, THE ... David Newman
WAR OF THE WORLDS ... Leith Stevens†
WAR PAINT ... Emil Newman†
WAR PARTY ... Chaz Jankel
WAR PARTY ... Richard LaSalle
WAR WAGON, THE ... Dimitri Tiomkin†
WARGAME ... Arthur B. Rubinstein
WARLOCK ... Jerry Goldsmith
WARLOCK ... Leigh Harline†
WARLORDS OF THE 21ST CENTURY ... Kevin Peak
WARM DECEMBER, A ... Coleridge-Taylor Perkinson
WARM HEARTS, COLD FEET (TF) ... Mark Snow
WARM LIFE, THE ... Carlo Rustichelli
WARM SUMMER RAIN ... Roger Eno
WARNING SHOT ... Jerry Goldsmith
WARNING SIGN ... Craig Safan
WARRIOR EMPRESS, THE ... Angelo Francesco Lavagnino†
WARRIORS FIVE ... Les Baxter
WARRIORS FIVE ... Armando Trovajoli
WARRIORS OF ATLANTIS ... Michael Vickers
WARRIORS, THE ... Barry De Vorzon
WASH, THE ... John Morris
WASHINGTON MASQUERADE ... William Axt†
WASHINGTON STORY ... Conrad Salinger†
WASHINGTON, BEHIND CLOSED DOORS (MS) ... Richard Markowitz
WASHINGTON: BEHIND CLOSED DOORS (TF) ... Dominic Frontiere
WASP WOMAN, THE ... Fred Katz
WATCH ON THE RHINE ... Max Steiner†
WATCHER IN THE WOODS, THE ... Stanley Myers
WATCHERS ... Joel Goldsmith
WATCHERS II ... Rick Conrad
WATER ... Mike Moran
WATER BABIES, THE ... Phil Coulter
WATER BIRDS ... Paul J. Smith†
WATERHOLE #3 ... Dave Grusin
WATERLOO ... Nino Rota†
WATERLOO BRIDGE ... ★ Herbert Stothart†
WATERMELON MAN ... Melvin Van Peebles
WATERS OF TIME ... Alan Rawsthorne†
WATERSHIP DOWN (AF) ... Malcolm Williamson
WATERSHIP DOWN (AF) ... Angela Morley
WATTS MONSTER, THE ... Johnny Pate
WAVELENGTH ... Tangerine Dream
WAXWORK ... Roger Bellon
WAY AHEAD, THE ... William Alwyn†
WAY BACK HOME ... Max Steiner†
WAY DOWN EAST ... Louis Silvers†
WAY DOWN SOUTH ... ★ Victor Young†
WAY OF A GAUCHO ... Sol Kaplan
WAY OF ALL FLESH, THE ... Victor Young†
WAY OUT WEST ... ★ T. Marvin Hatley†
WAY TO THE STARS, THE ... Nicholas Brodzsky†
WAY WE WERE, THE ... ★★ Marvin Hamlisch
WAY WEST, THE ... Bronislau Kaper†
WAY...WAY OUT! ... Lalo Schifrin
WAYWARD ... John Green†
WAYWARD BUS, THE ... Leigh Harline†
WE ALL LOVED EACH OTHER SO MUCH ... Armando Trovajoli
WE ARE NOT ALONE ... Max Steiner†
WE ARE THE CHILDREN (TF) ... Paul Chihara
WE ARE THE LAMBETH BOYS ... John Dankworth
WE ARE YOUNG ... David Amram
WE CHOP THE TEACHERS INTO MINCE MEAT ... Rolf Wilhelm
WE LIVE AGAIN ... Alfred Newman†
WE SAIL AT MIDNIGHT ... Richard Addinsell†
WE STILL KILL THE OLD WAY ... Luis Bacalov
WE THINK THE WORLD OF YOU ... Julian Jacobson
WE WENT TO COLLEGE ... William Axt†
WE WERE DANCING ... Bronislau Kaper†
WE WERE STRANGERS ... George Antheil†
WE WHO ARE YOUNG ... Bronislau Kaper†
WE'LL EAT THE FRUIT OF PARADISE ... Zdenek Liska
WE'RE FIGHTING BACK (TF) ... Fred Karlin
WE'RE NO ANGELS ... George Fenton
WE'RE NO ANGELS ... Frederick Hollander†
WE'RE NOT DRESSING ... Sigmund Krumgold†
WE'RE NOT MARRIED ... Cyril J. Mockridge†
WE'RE NOT MARRIED ... Lionel Newman†
WE'RE ONLY HUMAN ... Roy Webb†
WE'RE RICH AGAIN ... Max Steiner†
WE'VE NEVER BEEN LICKED ... Frank Skinner†
WEAK AND THE WICKED, THE ... Leighton Lucas†
WEATHER IN THE STREETS, THE (TF) ... Carl Davis
WEB OF EVIDENCE ... Douglas Gamley
WEB OF PASSION ... Paul Misraki†
WEB, THE ... Hans J. Salter
WEDDING IN BLOOD ... Pierre Jansen
WEDDING MARCH, THE ... John S. Zamecnik†
WEDDING NIGHT, THE ... Alfred Newman†

WEDDING ON WALTONS MOUNTAIN, A (TF) ... Alexander Courage
WEDDING RINGS ... Edward Ward†
WEDNESDAY'S CHILD ... Max Steiner†
WEE WILLIE WINKIE ... Alfred Newman†
WEEDS ... Angelo Badalamenti
WEEK-END MARRIAGE ... W. Franke Harling†
WEEKEND ... Antoine Duhamel
WEEKEND A ZUYDCOOTE ... Maurice Jarre
WEEKEND AT BERNIE'S ... Andy Summers
WEEKEND AT THE WALDORF ... John Green†
WEEKEND FOR THREE ... Roy Webb†
WEEKEND OF TERROR (TF) ... Richard Markowitz
WEEKEND WAR (TF) ... Brad Fiedel
WEEKEND WARRIORS ... Perry Botkin
WEEKEND WITH FATHER ... Frank Skinner†
WEIRD SCIENCE ... Ira Newborn
WEIRD WOMAN ... Hans J. Salter
WELCOME BACK, ROXY CARMICHAEL ... Thomas Newman
WELCOME HOME ... Henry Mancini
WELCOME HOME, BOBBY (TF) ... David McHugh
WELCOME HOME, JOHNNY BRISTOL (TF) ... Lalo Schifrin
WELCOME HOME, SOLDIER BOYS ... Ken Wannberg
WELCOME STRANGER ... Robert Emmett Dolan†
WELCOME TO 18 ... Tony Berg
WELCOME TO BLOOD CITY ... Roy Budd
WELCOME TO HARD TIMES ... Harry Sukman†
WELCOME TO L.A. ... Richard Baskin
WELCOME TO OBLIVION ... Kevin Klinger
WELCOME TO THE QUEEN (FD) ... Sir Arthur Bliss†
WELL GROOMED BRIDE, THE ... Roy Webb†
WELL, THE ... Dimitri Tiomkin†
WELLS FARGO ... Victor Young†
WELTMELODIE ... Wolfgang Zeller†
WEREWOLF (TF) ... Sylvester Levay
WEREWOLF IN A GIRLS' DORMITORY ... Armando Trovajoli
WEREWOLF OF LONDON ... Karl Hajos†
WEREWOLF, THE ... Mischa Bakaleinikoff †
WEST OF ZANZIBAR ... Alan Rawsthorne†
WEST POINT WIDOW ... Leo Shuken†
WEST SIDE STORY ... ★★ Irwin Kostal
WEST SIDE STORY ... ★ John Green†
WESTBOUND ... David Buttolph†
WESTERN PACIFIC AGENT ... Albert Glasser
WESTERN STORY, THE ... Herman Stein
WESTERN UNION ... David Buttolph†
WESTERNER, THE ... Dimitri Tiomkin†
WESTWARD HO, THE WAGONS ... George Bruns
WESTWARD PASSAGE ... Max Steiner†
WESTWARD THE WOMEN ... Jeff Alexander†
WESTWORLD ... Fred Karlin
WET GOLD (TF) ... Sylvester Levay
WET GOLD (TF) ... John Scott
WET PARADE, THE ... William Axt†
WETBACKS ... Les Baxter
WETHERBY ... Nick Bicat
WHALE FOR THE KILLING, A (TF) ... Basil Poledouris
WHALE GOD, THE ... Akira Ifukube
WHALES OF AUGUST, THE ... Alan Price
WHAT A BLONDE ... Leigh Harline†
WHAT A WAY TO GO! ... Nelson Riddle†
WHAT ARE BEST FRIENDS FOR? (TF) ... Jack Elliott
WHAT ARE BEST FRIENDS FOR? (TF) ... Allyn Ferguson
WHAT ARE THOSE STRANGE DROPS OF BLOOD ON THE BODY OF JENNIFER? ... Bruno Nicolai
WHAT BECAME OF JACK AND JILL? ... Carl Davis
WHAT DID YOU DO IN THE WAR, DADDY? ... Henry Mancini
WHAT EVER HAPPENED TO AUNT ALICE? ... Gerald Fried
WHAT EVERY WOMAN KNOWS ... Herbert Stothart†
WHAT HAPPENED AT CAMPO GRANDE? ... Ron Goodwin
WHAT MAX SAID ... Luis De Pablo
WHAT PRICE GLORY? ... R.H. Bassett†
WHAT PRICE GLORY? ... Alfred Newman†
WHAT PRICE HOLLYWOOD ... Max Steiner†
WHAT PRICE VICTORY (TF) ... Fred Karlin
WHAT WAITS BELOW ... Michel Rubini
WHAT! ... Carlo Rustichelli
WHAT'S A NICE GIRL LIKE YOU...? (TF) ... Robert Prince
WHAT'S NEW PUSSYCAT? ... Burt Bacharach
WHAT'S NEXT? ... Carl Davis
WHAT'S SO BAD ABOUT FEELING GOOD? ... Frank De Vol
WHAT'S THE MATTER WITH HELEN? ... David Raksin
WHAT'S UP, DOC? ... Artie Butler
WHAT? ... Claudio Gizzi
WHATEVER HAPPENED TO BABY JANE? ... Frank De Vol
WHATEVER IT TAKES ... Garry Sherman
WHEELER DEALERS, THE ... Frank De Vol
WHEELS OF FIRE ... Christopher Young
WHEELS OF TERROR (CTF) ... Jay Gruska
WHEN A STRANGER CALLS ... Dana Kaproff
WHEN DINOSAURS RULED THE EARTH ... Mario Nascimbene
WHEN DREAMS COME TRUE (TF) ... Gil Melle
WHEN EIGHT BELLS TOLL ... Angela Morley
WHEN EVERY DAY WAS THE FOURTH OF JULY (TF) ... Walter Scharf
WHEN GANGLAND STRIKES ... Van Alexander
WHEN HARRY MET SALLY ... Marc Shaiman
WHEN HELL BROKE LOOSE ... Albert Glasser
WHEN HELL WAS IN SESSION (TF) ... Jimmie Haskell
WHEN I GROW UP ... Jerome Moross†
WHEN IN ROME ... Carmen Dragon†
WHEN LADIES MEET ... Bronislau Kaper†
WHEN LOVE IS YOUNG ... Charles Previn†
WHEN MICHAEL CALLS (TF) ... Lionel Newman†
WHEN MY BABY SMILES AT ME ... ★ Alfred Newman†
WHEN SHE SAYS NO (TF) ... Brad Fiedel
WHEN STRANGERS MARRY ... Dimitri Tiomkin†
WHEN SVANTE DISAPPEARED ... Benny Andersen
WHEN THE BOUGH BREAKS (TF) ... Paul Chihara
WHEN THE CIRCUS CAME TO TOWN (TF) ... Charles Gross
WHEN THE CLOCK STRIKES ... Richard LaSalle
WHEN THE DALTONS RODE ... Frank Skinner†
WHEN THE LIGHTS GO ON AGAIN ... W. Franke Harling†
WHEN THE TIME COMES (TF) ... Marvin Hamlisch
WHEN THE WHALES CAME ... Christopher Gunning
WHEN THE WHALES CAME ... Ruth Rennie
WHEN TIME RAN OUT ... Lalo Schifrin
WHEN WE WERE YOUNG (TF) ... Peter Matz
WHEN WILLIE COMES MARCHING HOME ... Alfred Newman†
WHEN WOMEN HAD TAILS ... Ennio Morricone
WHEN WOMEN LOST THEIR TAILS ... Ennio Morricone
WHEN WORLDS COLLIDE ... Leith Stevens†
WHEN YOU COMIN' BACK, RED RYDER? ... Jack Nitzsche
WHEN YOUR LOVER LEAVES (TF) ... Randy Edelman
WHERE ANGELS GO...TROUBLE FOLLOWS! ... Lalo Schifrin
WHERE ARE THE CHILDREN? ... Sylvester Levay
WHERE ARE YOU GOING ALL NAKED? ... Armando Trovajoli
WHERE DANGER LIVES ... Roy Webb†
WHERE DID YOU GET THAT GIRL? ... Hans J. Salter
WHERE DO WE GO FROM HERE? ... David Raksin
WHERE EAGLES DARE ... Ron Goodwin
WHERE HAVE ALL THE PEOPLE GONE? (TF) ... Robert Prince
WHERE LOVE HAS GONE ... Walter Scharf
WHERE NO VULTURES FLY ... Alan Rawsthorne†
WHERE PIGEONS GO TO DIE (TF) ... Leonard Rosenman
WHERE SINNERS MEET ... Max Steiner†
WHERE THE BOYS ARE '84 ... Sylvester Levay
WHERE THE BUFFALO ROAM ... Neil Young
WHERE THE DEVIL CANNOT GO ... Zdenek Liska
WHERE THE HELL'S THAT GOLD?!! (TF) ... Arthur B. Rubinstein
WHERE THE LILLIES BLOOM ... Earl Scruggs
WHERE THE NORTH BEGINS ... Albert Glasser
WHERE THE RED FERN GROWS ... Lex De Azevedo
WHERE THE RIVER RUNS BLACK ... James Horner
WHERE THE SIDEWALK ENDS ... Cyril J. Mockridge†
WHERE THE SIDEWALK ENDS ... Lionel Newman†
WHERE THE SPIES ARE ... Mario Nascimbene
WHERE'S JACK? ... Elmer Bernstein
WHERE'S POPPA? ... Jack Elliott
WHEREVER YOU ARE ... Wojciech Kilar
WHICH WAY IS UP? ... Mark Davis
WHICH WAY IS UP? ... Paul Riser
WHIFFS ... John Cameron
WHILE THE CITY SLEEPS ... Herschel Burke Gilbert
WHILE THE SUN SHINES ... Nicholas Brodzsky†
WHIP HAND, THE ... Paul Sawtell†
WHIPLASH ... Franz Waxman†
WHIPPED, THE ... David Rose†
WHIPSAW ... William Axt†
WHIRLPOOL ... Ron Goodwin
WHIRLPOOL ... David Raksin
WHIRLWIND ... Mischa Bakaleinikoff †
WHISKEY GALORE! ... Georges Auric†
WHISPER KILLS, A (TF) ... Charles Bernstein
WHISPERERS, THE ... John Barry
WHISPERING GHOSTS ... David Raksin
WHISPERING GHOSTS ... Leigh Harline†
WHISPERING GHOSTS ... Cyril J. Mockridge†
WHISPERING SMITH ... Adolph Deutsch†
WHISPERS ... Barry Fasman
WHISPERS ... Dana Walden
WHISTLE BLOWER, THE ... John Scott
WHISTLE DOWN THE WIND ... Malcolm Arnold
WHISTLE STOP ... Dimitri Tiomkin†
WHISTLING IN BROOKLYN ... George Bassman
WHISTLING IN THE DARK ... Bronislau Kaper†
WHITE BANNERS ... Max Steiner†
WHITE BONDAGE ... Clifford Vaughan†
WHITE BUFFALO, THE ... John Barry
WHITE CARGO ... Bronislau Kaper†
WHITE CLIFFS OF DOVER, THE ... Herbert Stothart†
WHITE DAWN, THE ... Henry Mancini
WHITE DOG ... Ennio Morricone
WHITE FEATHER ... Hugo Friedhofer†
WHITE FLOOD ... Hanns Eisler†
WHITE GHOST ... Parmer Fuller
WHITE GIRL, THE ... George Porter Martin
WHITE HEAT ... Max Steiner†
WHITE HOT ... Nile Rodgers
WHITE HUNTER, BLACK HEART ... Lennie Niehaus
WHITE LIGHTNING ... Charles Bernstein
WHITE LINE, THE ... Carlo Rustichelli
WHITE LIONS, THE ... William Goldstein
WHITE MAMA (TF) ... Peter Matz
WHITE MISCHIEF ... George Fenton
WHITE NIGHTS ... Michel Colombier
WHITE NIGHTS ... Nino Rota†
WHITE OF THE EYE ... Rick Fenn
WHITE OF THE EYE ... George Fenton
WHITE OF THE EYE ... Nick Mason
WHITE PALACE ... George Fenton
WHITE PHANTOM, THE ... Albert Glasser
WHITE PONGO ... Leo Erdody†
WHITE ROCK (FD) ... Rick Wakeman
WHITE ROSE, THE ... Joseph Carl Briel†
WHITE SAVAGE ... Frank Skinner†
WHITE SHADOWS OF THE SOUTH SEAS ... William Axt†
WHITE SHIEK, THE ... Nino Rota†
WHITE SISTER, THE ... Herbert Stothart†
WHITE SLAVE SHIP ... Les Baxter
WHITE TIE AND TAILS ... Milton Rosen
WHITE TOWER, THE ... Roy Webb†
WHITE WATER REBELS (TF) ... Ken Thorne
WHITE WATER SUMMER ... Michael Boddicker
WHITE WILDERNESS ... ★ Oliver Wallace†
WHITE WITCH DOCTOR ... Bernard Herrmann†
WHITE ZOMBIE ... Xavier Cugat†
WHITY ... Peer Raben
WHO ARE THE DE BOLTS? ...AND WHERE DID THEY GET 19 KIDS? (FD) ... Ed Bogas
WHO DARES WINS ... Roy Budd
WHO DONE IT? ... Hans J. Salter
WHO DONE IT? ... Frank Skinner†
WHO FEARS THE DEVIL ... Roger Kellaway
WHO FRAMED ROGER RABBIT? ... Alan Silvestri
WHO GETS THE FRIENDS? (TF) ... Gary William Friedman
WHO IS HOPE SCHUYLER? ... David Raksin
WHO IS JULIA? (TF) ... Robert Drasnin
WHO IS KILLING THE GREAT CHEFS OF EUROPE? ... Henry Mancini
WHO IS THE BLACK DAHLIA? (TF) ... Dominic Frontiere
WHO KILLED DOC ROBBIN? ... Heinz Roemheld†
WHO KILLED TEDDY BEAR? ... Joel Hirschhorn
WHO KILLED TEDDY BEAR? ... Al Kasha
WHO LEAVES IN THE RAIN ... Zdenek Liska
WHO SLEW AUNTIE ROO? ... Kenneth V. Jones
WHO WAS THAT LADY? ... Andre Previn
WHO WILL LOVE MY CHILDREN? (TF) ... ☆ Laurence Rosenthal
WHO'LL SAVE OUR CHILDREN? (TF) ... Fred Karlin
WHO'LL STOP THE RAIN ... Laurence Rosenthal
WHO'S AFRAID OF VIRGINIA WOOLF? ... ★ Alex North
WHO'S HARRY CRUMB? ... Michel Colombier
WHO'S MINDING THE MINT? ... Lalo Schifrin
WHO? ... John Cameron
WHOLE WORLD IS WATCHING, THE (TF) ... Pete Rugolo

WHOLLY MOSES ... Patrick Williams
WHOM THE GODS WISH TO DESTROY ... Rolf Wilhelm
WHOOPEE BOYS, THE ... Udi Harpaz
WHOOPEE BOYS, THE ... Jack Nitzsche
WHOOPS APOCALYPSE ... Patrick Gowers
WHOSE LIFE IS IT ANYWAY? ... Arthur B. Rubinstein
WHY BOTHER TO KNOCK? ... Elisabeth Luytens†
WHY ME? ... Basil Poledouris
WHY ME? (TF) ... Billy Goldenberg
WHY WOULD I LIE? ... Charles Fox
WICHITA ... Hans J. Salter
WICKED AS THEY COME ... Malcolm Arnold
WICKED DREAMS OF PAULA SCHULTZ, THE ... Jimmie Haskell
WICKED LADY, THE ... Anthony Banks
WICKED STEPMOTHER ... Robert Folk
WICKED WIFE ... John Greenwood†
WICKED WOMAN, A ... William Axt†
WICKER MAN, THE ... Paul Giovanni†
WICKET GATE, THE ... Wojciech Kilar
WIDOWS' NEST ... Francis Lai
WIFE TAKES A FLYER, THE ... Werner R. Heymann†
WIFE VS. SECRETARY ... Herbert Stothart†
WIFE VS. SECRETARY ... Edward Ward†
WIFEMISTRESS ... Armando Trovajoli
WILBY CONSPIRACY, THE ... Stanley Myers
WILD AND THE FREE, THE (TF) ... Gerald Fried
WILD AND THE INNOCENT, THE ... Hans J. Salter
WILD AND WILLING ... Ronald Stein†
WILD AND WONDERFUL ... Morton Stevens
WILD AND WOOLY (TF) ... Charles Bernstein
WILD ANGELS, THE ... Mike Curb
WILD AT HEART ... Angelo Badalamenti
WILD BEDS ... Riz Ortolani
WILD BLUE YONDER, THE ... Victor Young†
WILD BUNCH, THE ... ★ Jerry Fielding†
WILD CHILD, THE ... Antoine Duhamel
WILD COUNTRY, THE ... Robert F. Brunner
WILD DOG IN AMERICA (TD) ... ☆☆ John Scott
WILD DUCK, THE ... Simon Walker
WILD FOR KICKS ... John Barry
WILD FRUIT, THE ... Joseph Kosma†
WILD GEESE II ... Roy Budd
WILD GEESE, THE ... Roy Budd
WILD GOOSE CHASE ... Vladimir Cosma
WILD HARVEST ... Hugo Friedhofer†
WILD HEART, THE ... Brian Easdale
WILD HORSE HANK ... Paul Hoffert
WILD HORSE RUSTLERS ... Leo Erdody†
WILD HORSES ... Dave Fraser
WILD HORSES (TF) ... Hans Zimmer
WILD HORSES (TF) ... Stanley Myers
WILD IN THE COUNTRY ... Kenyon Hopkins
WILD IN THE SKY ... Jerry Styne
WILD IN THE STREETS ... Les Baxter
WILD IS THE WIND ... Dimitri Tiomkin†
WILD LOVE ... Carlo Rustichelli
WILD McCULLOCHS, THE ... Ernest Gold
WILD NORTH, THE ... Bronislau Kaper†
WILD ON THE BEACH ... Jimmie Haskell
WILD ONE, THE ... Leith Stevens†
WILD ORCHID ... Geoff MacCormack
WILD PAIR, THE ... John Debney
WILD PARTY, THE ... Laurence Rosenthal
WILD PONY, THE (TF) ... Hagood Hardy
WILD RIVER ... Kenyon Hopkins
WILD ROVERS ... Jerry Goldsmith
WILD SEED, THE ... Richard Markowitz
WILD SIDE, THE ... Alex Gibson
WILD STRAWBERRIES ... Eric Nordgren
WILD STYLE ... Fred Brathwaite
WILD STYLE ... Chris Stein
WILD THING ... George S. Clinton
WILD TIMES (TF) ... Jerrold Immel
WILD WEST ... Karl Hajos†
WILD WILD PLANET ... Angelo Francesco Lavagnino†
WILD WILD WEST REVISITED, THE (TF) ... Jeff Alexander†
WILD WOMEN OF CHASTITY GULCH, THE (TF) ... Frank De Vol
WILD WOMEN OF CHASTITY GULCH, THE (TF) ... Tom Worrall
WILDCATS ... James Newton Howard
WILDCATS ... Hawk Wolinski
WILDFIRE ... Maurice Jarre
WILL PENNY ... David Raksin
WILL SUCCESS SPOIL ROCK HUNTER? ... Cyril J. Mockridge†
WILL THERE REALLY BE A MORNING? (TF) ... Billy Goldenberg
WILL, G. GORDON LIDDY (TF) ... Mike Post
WILL, G. GORDON LIDDY (TF) ... Pete Carpenter†
WILLA (TF) ... John Barry
WILLARD ... Alex North
WILLIAMSBURG: THE STORY OF A PATRIOT ... Bernard Herrmann†
WILLIE & PHIL ... Claude Bolling
WILLIE DYNAMITE ... J.J. Johnson
WILLIE WONKA AND THE CHOCOLATE FACTORY ... ★ Leslie Bricusse
WILLOW ... James Horner
WILLY MILLY ... David McHugh
WILMA (TF) ... Irwin Bazelon
WILSON ... ★ Alfred Newman†
WINCHESTER '73 (TF) ... Sol Kaplan
WIND AND THE LION, THE ... ★ Jerry Goldsmith
WIND, THE ... Carl Davis
WINDJAMMER ... Morton Gould
WINDMILL OF THE GODS (TF) ... Perry Botkin
WINDOW, THE ... Roy Webb†
WINDOWS ... Ennio Morricone
WINDRIDER ... Kevin Peak
WINDS OF JARRAH, THE ... Bruce Smeaton
WINDS OF KITTY HAWK, THE (TF) ... Charles Bernstein
WINDS OF WAR, THE (MS) ... Bob Cobert
WINDWALKER ... Merrill B. Jensen
WINDY CITY ... Jack Nitzsche
WING AND A PRAYER ... Hugo Friedhofer†
WINGED DEVILS ... Ennio Morricone
WINGED IDOL, THE ... Victor Schertzinger†
WINGED VICTORY ... David Rose†
WINGS ... John S. Zamecnik†
WINGS FOR THE EAGLE ... Frederick Hollander†
WINGS OF DANGER ... Malcolm Arnold
WINGS OF DESIRE ... Jurgen Knieper
WINGS OF EAGLES, THE ... Jeff Alexander†
WINGS OF THE HAWK ... Frank Skinner†
WINGS OF THE MORNING ... Arthur Benjamin†
WINGS OVER HONOLULU ... David Raksin
WINGS OVER HONOLULU ... Charles Previn†
WINK OF AN EYE ... Ernest Gold
WINNER NEVER QUITS, A (TF) ... Dana Kaproff
WINNER TAKE ALL ... W. Franke Harling†
WINNER TAKE ALL (TF) ... David Shire
WINNER TAKE ALL (TF) ... Richard Markowitz
WINNERS TAKE ALL ... Doug Timm†
WINNETOU AND HIS FRIEND, OLD FIREHAND ... Peter Thomas
WINNIE (TF) W.G. ... Snuffy Walden
WINNING ... Dave Grusin
WINNING TEAM, THE ... David Buttolph†
WINSLOW BOY, THE ... William Alwyn†
WINSTON CHURCHILL: THE WILDERNESS YEARS (MS) ... Carl Davis
WINTER A-GO-GO ... Harry Betts
WINTER CARNIVAL ... Werner Janssen
WINTER FLIGHT ... Richard Harvey
WINTER KILL (TF) ... Jerry Goldsmith
WINTER KILLS ... Maurice Jarre
WINTER MEETING ... Max Steiner†
WINTER OF OUR DISCONTENT, THE (TF) ... Mark Snow
WINTER PEOPLE ... John Scott
WINTER RATES ... John Cameron
WINTERHAWK ... Lee Holdridge
WINTERSET ... ★ Nathaniel Shilkret†
WIRED ... Basil Poledouris
WIRED TO KILL ... Russell Ferrante
WIRED TO KILL ... Russell Forante
WISDOM ... Danny Elfman
WISE BLOOD ... Alex North
WISE GUYS ... Ira Newborn
WISEGUY (TF) ... Mike Post
WISER SEX, THE ... John Green†
WISH YOU WERE HERE ... Stanley Myers
WISHING WELL INN ... Edwin Astley
WIT'S END ... Elliot Chiprut
WIT'S END ... Jason Garfield
WITCH, THE ... David Gibney
WITCHBOARD ... Dennis Tenney
WITCHCRAFT ... Randy Miller
WITCHCRAFT PART II: THE TEMPTRESS ... Miriam Cutler
WITCHES OF EASTWICK, THE ... ★ John Williams
WITCHES, THE ... Richard Rodney Bennett
WITCHES, THE ... Piero Piccioni
WITCHES, THE ... Ennio Morricone
WITCHES, THE ... Stanley Myers
WITCHFINDER GENERAL, THE ... Paul Ferris
WITCHING HOUR ... Basil Poledouris
WITCHING HOUR, THE ... Alejandro Masso
WITCHING, THE ... Robert J. Walsh
WITH A SONG IN MY HEART ... ★★ Alfred Newman†
WITH BATED BREATH ... Armando Trovajoli
WITH INTENT TO KILL (TF) ... Paul Chihara
WITH THIS RING (TF) ... Richard Hazard
WITH THIS RING (TF) ... George Aliceson Tipton
WITHIN MEMORY ... Francis Lai
WITHIN THE LAW ... William Axt†
WITHIN THESE WALLS ... David Buttolph†
WITHNAIL AND I ... David Dundas
WITHOUT A CLUE ... Henry Mancini
WITHOUT A TRACE ... Jack Nitzsche
WITHOUT EACH OTHER ... Dimitri Tiomkin†
WITHOUT HER CONSENT (TF) ... Mike Post
WITHOUT HONOR ... Max Steiner†
WITHOUT LOVE ... Bronislau Kaper†
WITHOUT RESERVATIONS ... Roy Webb†
WITHOUT SKIN ... Pino Donaggio
WITHOUT WARNING ... Herschel Burke Gilbert
WITHOUT WARNING ... Dan Wyman
WITNESS ... ★ Maurice Jarre
WITNESS CHAIR, THE ... Roy Webb†
WITNESS FOR THE PROSECUTION (TF) ... John Cameron
WITNESS TO MURDER ... Herschel Burke Gilbert
WITNESS, THE ... Ron Goodwin
WITNESS, THE ... Piero Piccioni
WITNESSES, THE ... Maurice Jarre
WIVES AND LOVERS ... Lyn Murray†
WIZ, THE ... ★ Quincy Jones
WIZARD OF BABYLON, THE (FD) ... Peer Raben
WIZARD OF BAGHDAD, THE ... Irving Gertz
WIZARD OF GORE, THE ... Larry Wellington
WIZARD OF LONELINESS, THE ... Michel Colombier
WIZARD OF OZ, THE ... ★★ Herbert Stothart†
WIZARD, THE ... J. Peter Robinson
WIZARDS (AF) ... Andrew Belling
WIZARDS OF THE LOST KINGDOM ... Christopher Young
WOLF AT THE DOOR, THE ... Roger Bourland
WOLF LAKE ... Ken Thorne
WOLF LARSEN ... Paul Dunlap
WOLF MAN, THE ... Hans J. Salter
WOLF MAN, THE ... Charles Previn†
WOLF MAN, THE ... Frank Skinner†
WOLFEN ... James Horner
WOLVES OF WILLOUGHBY CHASE, THE ... Colin Towns
WOLVES, THE ... Masaru Sato
WOMAN AGAINST WOMAN ... William Axt†
WOMAN ALONE, A ... Louis Levy†
WOMAN CALLED GOLDA, A (TF) ... ☆ Michel Legrand
WOMAN CALLED MOSES, A (TF) ... Coleridge-Taylor Perkinson
WOMAN CHASES MAN ... Alfred Newman†
WOMAN EATER ... Edwin Astley
WOMAN FLAMBEE, A ... Peer Raben
WOMAN FOR JOE, A ... Malcolm Arnold
WOMAN FROM HEADQUARTERS ... Hans J. Salter
WOMAN HE LOVED, THE (TF) ... Allyn Ferguson
WOMAN HUNTER, THE (TF) ... George Duning
WOMAN I LOVE, THE ... Arthur Honegger†
WOMAN IN A DRESSING GOWN ... Louis Levy†
WOMAN IN GREEN, THE ... Hans J. Salter
WOMAN IN HIDING ... Frank Skinner†
WOMAN IN RED, THE ... John Morris
WOMAN IN THE WINDOW, THE ... ★ Hugo Friedhofer†
WOMAN IN WHITE, THE ... Max Steiner†
WOMAN IS A WOMAN, A ... Michel Legrand
WOMAN LAUGHS LAST ... Stelvio Cipriani
WOMAN LIKE EVE, A ... Laurens Van Rooyen
WOMAN LIKE SATAN, A ... Jean Wiener†
WOMAN NEXT DOOR, THE ... Georges Delerue
WOMAN OBSESSED ... Hugo Friedhofer†
WOMAN OF DISTINCTION ... Werner R. Heymann†
WOMAN OF DOLWYN ... John Greenwood†
WOMAN OF MUSAHINO ... Fumio Hayasaka †
WOMAN OF SUBSTANCE, A (MS) ... Nigel Hess
WOMAN OF THE DUNES ... Toru Takemitsu
WOMAN OF THE RIVER, THE ... Armando Trovajoli
WOMAN OF THE RIVER, THE ... Angelo Francesco Lavagnino†
WOMAN OF THE TOWN ... ★ Miklos Rozsa
WOMAN OF THE YEAR ... Franz Waxman†
WOMAN OF THE YEAR (TF) ... Fred Karlin
WOMAN ON PIER 13, THE ... Leigh Harline†
WOMAN ON THE BEACH, THE ... Hanns Eisler†
WOMAN TIMES SEVEN ... Riz Ortolani
WOMAN UNDER THE INFLUENCE, A ... Bo Harwood

X

Y

Z

ZEGEN .... Shinchiro Ikebe
ZELIG .... Dick Hyman
ZELLY AND ME .... Pino Donaggio
ZENABEL .... Bruno Nicolai
ZENOBIA .... T. Marvin Hatley†
ZEPPELIN .... Roy Budd
ZIEGFELD GIRL .... Herbert Stothart†
ZIEGFELD: THE MAN AND HIS WOMEN (TF) .... ☆ Richard DeBenedictis
ZIGZAG .... Oliver Nelson†
ZOLTAN, HOUND OF DRACULA .... Andrew Belling
ZOMBI 2 .... Fabio Frizzi
ZOMBI 2 .... Giorgio Tucci
ZOMBIE FLESH EATERS .... Fabio Frizzi
ZOMBIE FLESH EATERS .... Giorgio Tucc
ZOMBIE HIGH .... Daniel May
ZOMBIES OF MORA-TAU .... Mischa Bakaleinikoff †
ZOMBIES ON BROADWAY .... Roy Webb†
ZONE ROUGE .... Gabriel Yared
ZONE TROOPERS .... Richard H. Band
ZOO GANG, THE .... Patrick Gleeson
ZOO GANG, THE .... Randy Petersen
ZORBA THE GREEK .... Mikis Theodorakis
ZORRO'S FIGHTING LEGION .... William Lava†
ZORRO, MARCHESE DI NAVARRE .... Angelo Francesco Lavagnino†
ZORRO, THE GAY BLADE .... Ian Fraser
ZOTZI .... Bernard Green
ZOYA .... Dmitri Shostakovitch†
ZULU .... John Barry
ZULU DAWN .... Elmer Bernstein
ZUMA BEACH (TF) .... Dick Halligan

★ ★ ★ ★

INDEX OF AGENTS & MANAGERS

A

APRA
P.O. Box 567
Crows Nest, N.S.W. 2065
Australia
Phone: 011-61-2-922-6422
FAX: 011-61-2-925-0314

THE ARTISTS GROUP
1930 Century Park West, Suite 403
Los Angeles, CA 90067
213/552-1100

ASCAP
6430 Sunset Blvd. Suite 1002
Hollywood, CA 90028
213/466-7681

B

BART-MILANDER ASSOCIATES, INC.
4146 Lankershim Boulevard, Suite 300
North Hollywood, CA 91602
818/761-4040
FAX: 818/985-0881

BMI
8730 Sunset Boulevard, Third Floor West
Los Angeles, CA 90069-2211
213/659-9109
FAX: 213/657-6947

NIGEL BRITTON, LEMON UNNA & DURBRIDGE LTD.
24 Pottery Lane
Holland Park, London W11 4LZ
England
Phone: 011-44-1-727-1346

BUMA
Prof. E.M. Meijerslaan 3
1183 AV Amstelveen
Holland
Phone: 011-31-20-540-7911
FAX: 011-31-20-540-7496

C

CREATIVE ARTISTS AGENCY, INC.
9830 Wilshire Boulevard
Beverly Hills, CA 90212-1825
213/288-4545
FAX: 213/288-4800

E

RICHARD LEE EMLER ENTERPRISES
6404 Wilshire Boulevard, Suite 1230
Los Angeles, CA 90048
213/651-0222

F

CAROL FAITH AGENCY
280 South Beverly Drive, Suite 411
Beverly Hills, CA 90212
213/274-0775

G

GEMA
Rosenheimer Str. 11
D-8000 Munchen 80
West Germany
Phone: Munich 011-49-89621400
FAX: 011-49-89-6214620

THE GORFAINE/SCHWARTZ AGENCY, INC.
3815 West Olive Avenue
Suite 201
Burbank, CA 91505
818/954-9500
FAX: 818/955-5836

H

ANDI HOWARD AGENCY
9157 Sunset Blvd., Suite 310
Los Angeles, CA 90069
213/278-6483

I

INTERNATIONAL CREATIVE MANAGEMENT, INC.
8899 Beverly Boulevard
Los Angeles, CA 90048
213/550-4000

J

JASRAC
7-13-1-chome Nishishimbashi
Minato-ku
Tokyo 105
Japan
Phone: 011-81-3-502-6551
FAX: 011-81-3-503-3444

K

KODA
Maltegardsvej 24
DK-2820 Gentofte
Denmark
Phone: 011-45-31-68-38-00
FAX: 011-45-31-68-38-13

L

LH-81 ENTERTAINMENT
8421 Wilshire Blvd., Suite 208
Beverly Hills, CA 90211
213/658-1094

THE ROBERT LIGHT AGENCY
6404 Wilshire Boulevard, Suite 800
Los Angeles, CA 90048
213/651-1777
FAX: 213/651-4933

M

LAWRENCE B. MARKS AGENCY
12239 Eagle Ridge Way
Northridge, CA 91326
818/831-1830
Fax: 818/831-1868

M.C.E.G. MANAGEMENT
2400 Broadway Avenue, Suite 100
Santa Monica, CA 90404
213/315-7800
FAX: 213/315-7850

WILLIAM MORRIS AGENCY
151 S. El Camino Drive
Beverly Hills, CA 90212
213/274-7451

O

OSA
Tr. Cs. Armady 20
160-56 Prague 6-Bubene
Czechoslovakia

P

PRO-CANADA LTD.
41 Valleybrook Drive
Don Mills, Ontario M3B 2S6
Phone: 1-416-445-8700
FAX: 1-416-445-7108

PRS
29/33 Berners Street
London, WIP 4AA, England
Phone: 011-44-1-580-5544
FAX: 011-44-1-631-4138

S

SABAM
Rue d'Arlon 75-77
B-1040
Brussels, Belgium
Phone: 011-32-2-230-2660
FAX: 011-32-2-231-1800

SACEM
225 Avenue Charles de Gaulle
92521 Neuilly sur Seine Cedex
France
Phone: 011-33-14-747-5650
FAX: 011-33-14-745-1294

SACM
San Felipe No. 143
Col, Xoco
03330 Mexico D.F.
Mexico
Phone: 011-525-660-2285
FAX: 011-525-524-0564

SADAIC
Lavalle 1547
Buenos Aires, Argentina
Phone: 011-54-1-35-7132

SGAE
Fernando VI, 4
Madrid 28080
Spain
Phone: 011-34-1-419-2100 or
212/752-7230
FAX: 011-34-1-410-6049

SIAE
Vialle della Letteratura
No. 30 (E.U.R.)
00100 Rome, Italy
Phone: 011-39-6-59-90-1
FAX: 011-39-6-592-3351

STIM
P.O. Box 27327
S-10254 Stockholm
Sweden
Phone: 011-46-8-783-8800
FAX: 011-46-8-626-2175

T

TEOSTO
Lauttasaarentie 1
00200 Helsinki
Finland
Phone: 358-0-692-2511
FAX: 358-0-677-134

TONO
Klingenberggata 5
0161 Oslo 1
Norway
FAX: 011-2-428-789

TRIAD ARTISTS
10100 Santa Monica Blvd., 16th floor
Los Angeles, CA 90067
213/556-2727

U

UBC
Rua Visconde de Inhauma 107
CEP 20091 Rio de Janeiro
Brazil
Phone: 011-55-21-223-3233

V

VAAP
Copywright Agency of the U.S.S.R.
B. Bronnaja 6A
103670 Moscow
U.S.S.R.
Telex: 871-411327

Z

ZAIKS
UL. Hipoteczna 2
00-092 Warsaw
Poland
Phone: 011-48-2-277-577

★ ★ ★ ★

CALLING ALL CREDITS!

The **Second Edition of FILM COMPOSERS GUIDE** is now in preparation. It will be published in early 1992. We update our records continuously. If you are a film composer and you qualify to be listed (please read the Introduction for qualifications), then send us your listing information **ASAP. Photocopy the form on the next page.**

Our editorial deadline is September 1, 1991.

(Please do not wait until then.)

Send all film composers listing information to:

FILM COMPOSERS GUIDE
Second Edition
11940 Weddington Street
North Hollywood, CA 91607
213/471-8066 or 1/800-FILMBKS

If you are a writer (*film or television*), a director (*film or television*), film actor, cinematographer, production designer, costume designer, editor, agent, producer or studio executive, special effects or stunts coordinator and want to find out about getting listed in our other directories, call **213/471-8066** or **1/800-FILMBKS** or write to:

★★★

The
SECOND EDITION
of

FILM COMPOSERS GUIDE

is now in preparation

DON'T BE LEFT OUT!!! Guarantee your *FREE* listing (for qualified composers) by filling out and returning this form to us *IMMEDIATELY.* *(Photocopy as many times as necessary).*

COMPOSER'S INFORMATION

Name

Company

Address

City/State/Zip

Area Code/Phone

Birth Date & Place

Home ❑ Business ❑

PLEASE PRINT OR TYPE

REPRESENTATIVE'S INFORMATION

Agent ❑ Personal Manager ❑ Attorney ❑
Business Manager ❑ Other ❑ AFM ❑

(List as many representatives as you would like. Continue listing on reverse, if necessary.)

Name

Company

Address

City/State/Zip

Area Code/Telephone

PLEASE PRINT OR TYPE

CREDITS

List your credits as follows: Please note alternate (or foreign) titles in parentheses. "French," "British," should be noted for foreign films. Pease note Academy or Emmy nominations/awards for Best Original Score. Also, please note "co-composer(s)" or "adaptation" if applicable. If you need more space, please continue on reverse side.

FEATURES: INTERNAL AFFAIRS co-composer with Brian Banks and Anthony Marinelli, Paramount, 1990
TRADING PLACES ★ adaptation, Paramount, 1983
TELEFEATURES: HOW TO MURDER A MILLIONAIRE (TF) Robert Greenwald Films, 1990

MAIL or FAX form *IMMEDIATELY* to:
FILM COMPOSERS GUIDE
Second Edition
11940 Weddington Street
North Hollywood, CA 91607
213/471-8066 or 213/471-4969 (FAX)

Questions ???
Problems ???
Call 213/471-8066

INDEX OF ADVERTISERS

A special thanks to our advertisers whose support makes it possible to bring you the **FILM COMPOSERS GUIDE.**

ABOUT THE EDITOR

Steven C. Smith is the author of *A Heart at Fire's Center: The Life and Music of Bernard Herrmann* (University of California Press, 1991). He has written about film music for the Los Angeles *Times* and *The Hollywood Reporter*, and has written extensively for television.